THE
GENESIS 6
CONSPIRACY
PART II

HOW UNDERSTANDING PREHISTORY AND GIANTS
HELPS DEFINE END-TIME PROPHECY

By
GARY WAYNE

CONTENTS

PREFACE

I was convinced I would not write a sequel to *The Genesis 6 Conspiracy: How Secret Societies and the Descendants of Giants Plan to Enslave Humankind*. I thought a sequel would be redundant. So, what swayed my mindset? You did—those who read my first book and contacted me with comments, questions, and requests for more information.

What I did not perceive was the level of scriptural angst not appeased by modern clergy, teachers, and leaders in most Christian churches, whether Catholic or Protestant. An uneasy spiritual sense has gripped many Christians—a profound sense that something is incomplete and disconnected within the body of church teaching, something elemental to our raison d'être. Most churches have sanitized scriptural prehistory and prophecy as a sacrificial offering at the altar of secularism and wokeism in exchange for acceptance in the current world order. Some churches avoid teaching prehistory and prophecy altogether. Many churches fear embracing scriptural prehistory. They quiver at the challenge of teaching prophecy. Some Christians are told to stop asking such questions about prehistory and prophecy, and some are even asked to leave their churches.

To help answer many lingering questions many Christians have, and to provide scripturally researched answers and data points for these questions, *The Genesis 6 Conspiracy, Part 2* explores Scripture's accounting of prehistory, history, and its important prophetic connections. This book will avoid repeating what was covered my first book, except as required to connect the new information with the overarching narrative. Although this book was written to be read as a stand-alone enterprise, one may wish to read Part 1 after reading Part 2; both books are designed to help reveal our hidden history and to discern end-time events and chronology.

If indeed we are in the fig tree generation[1] as I suspect, then our church shepherds are inattentive in preparing their flocks for the tribulations that are surely coming, and at a time when Christians will need their shepherds the most. Slipshod Christian shepherds are not nourishing their flocks with the full body of Scripture, which will leave many Christians vulnerable to deception from the "evil beasts,"[2] both visible and invisible, with their corrupted wisdom and world order. Many Christians are awakening to the sad conclusion that they will be required to self-educate, and then teach others about the veracity of our suppressed history and its importance so that they can discern the days of Jesus' visitation.[3]

A growing number of Christians indeed are investigating and teaching prehistory and prophecy outside the mainstream of Christianity. Within these streams of Christian research, prehistory is often understood and taught through the lens and context of the large body of polytheist and/or secular records. I too research polytheist and secular prehistory and find it fascinating. Nevertheless, polytheist prehistory overflows with spurious intrigue. I believe it is important for Christians to understand what polytheists have done with their belief system, what they are currently doing, and what they intend to do "to deceive the very elect."[4] As such, I encourage Christians to be conversant with polytheist prehistory, but to be careful lest they be seduced away from God. Measure all things learned outside of Scripture against what is written in the most preternatural work ever penned in this world, God's Word. The Bible must be your measuring stick.

Meanwhile, Christian eschatology that is interpreted then taught mostly through the lens of a set approach tends to be at odds with the sequential timing of important end-time events once it has been measured against the entire body of end-time prophecy. Set eschatological approaches tend have primary predetermined positions for the timing of Jesus' return, the last week of Daniel's prophetic seventy weeks,[5] or when the millennium occurs, which tend to function as overriding rules for the sequencing of events. All these approaches are biblically based, and thus can be confusing for many just learning about prophecy—since all these approaches cannot be correct.

So that you can better understand what guides my nonbiblical research, my biblical research, and my eschatology research, here are my guidelines. Wherever, or however, polytheist and secular prehistory departs directionally, or runs contrary to Scripture in any way, my approach is to note those diversions, but not to consider them as context or as reliable parallel polytheist pieces of information. My nonbiblical research, whether polytheistic or secular, is always measured against what Scripture says as the arbitrator of truth.

---

[1] Matt 24:32–35; Mark 13:28–31; Luke 21:29–33.
[2] Ezek 34:1–31. Gen 3:1, 15.
[3] Hos 9:7.
[4] Matt 24:24; Mark 13:22.
[5] Dan 9:24–27.

I regard myself as a Christian contrarian, which is an important part of my research, including eschatology; it is an approach akin to the Bereans of Scripture.[6] I tend not to automatically accept what some say, or what someone says is documented, unless I verify it myself. I apply this to all my research. At times my approach reflects the standard definition of a contrarian: one who by their nature opposes or presents an "on the other hand" argument to standard accepted opinion, dogma, theory, or conclusion.[7] However, in most scenarios my contrariness derives from the need to verify things for myself and the conclusions I derive, which tends to place me in the crosshairs of the guardians of the status quo.

My approach to discerning end-time prophecy and its chronology includes comprehending biblical prehistory and history to define prophetic allegory, and the larger context embedded into end-time prophecy. More importantly, my research and eschatological approach recognizes that God and Jesus are the "Alpha and Omega, the beginning and the end, and the first and the last"[8]—who knew all events that would occur, knew all beings that would be created and born from before creation, and knew the choices each would make. It follows that God the Father, His Holy Spirit, and His Word who became flesh knew that the angelic rebellion would occur; that humankind would be deceived by fallen angels and led away from God; that fallen angels would create Nephilim and Rephaim giants to oppress and enslave humankind throughout our history. My approach recognizes that God gifted all sentient beings with free choice. It follows that God has permitted all to continue until all angelic, human, and hybrid beings have an opportunity through free choice to keep their names from being "blotted" out of the Book of Life.[9] This age will continue for all sentient beings, into the millennial reign, where free choice will continue until the last rebellion against God occurs—led by the last rebellious angel, Satan, who will then be sent to the lake of fire.

Angels were created immortal, as spirit beings of heaven, and with intimate knowledge and interaction with God, but many still rebelled. Conversely, Adamites were mortal beings created in the physical world after the angelic rebellion, and who were provided less knowledge and interaction with God. Thus Adamites were created lower than angels, akin to the Word who became flesh in the physical world to become Jesus, and who also was for a short time a little lower than the angels.[10] As such, some of humankind will be raised up to be like angels, adopted as brothers and sisters of the Word who became Jesus,[11] even though we have human fathers.

---

[6] Acts 17:11.

[7] "Contrary, contrariness," *Webster's New Compact Format Dictionary* (New York: Essential Publications, ProSales Inc., 1986), 87.

[8] Rev 1:8, 11; 21:6; 22:13.

[9] Exod 32:33–34; Ps 69.28; Dan 7:10; Rev 3:5; 5:1–14; 17:8; 20:12, 15; 22:19.

[10] Ps 8.5; Heb 2:7.

[11] Matt 22:30; Mark 12:25; Luke 20:3–-36; Heb 7:11.

Adamites were created to be the resolution to the angelic rebellion. It follows that human history, and our future, were and are tied to our free choice, and to the angelic free choice that will come to a climax in the fig tree generation. It further follows that the terrible crimes and events that have marred the Adamite epoch were engineered by the rebellious reign of the fallen angels and their spurious offspring to prevent Adamites from fulfilling our destiny. Contrived crimes and catastrophes by the conspirators will continue through out the end-time, until Jesus returns for Armageddon. All the terrible crimes that have plagued this world through free choice—except for the limited intervention of God to ensure that all those whose names are in the Book of Life would be permitted opportunity to choose—have come about through the choices of rebellion, and the choices of fallen angels to try to stop humans from becoming like angels.

Although employing scriptural prehistory and history to help understand the larger context for end-time events and prophetic allegory is an important part of my approach, it is not the only nor most important piece of my approach. Knowing how I approach my research and eschatology is important to understand my conclusions, whether one fully agrees with my approach and conclusions or not. My approach and conclusions derive from what the research reveals, not what I would like it to reveal. My approach permitted adjustments as I assembled additional scriptural information, because I was not mired with preconceived conclusions.

My first and most important guideline to making chronological sense of end-time prophecy is centered on what Jesus said, as the Word of God who created all things, and taking to heart that the "testimony of Jesus is the spirit of prophecy."[12] As such, I place all prophecy and all Scripture around what Jesus said, not vice versa. I do not apologize for, nor rationalize, what Jesus said. I do not try to redefine or reimagine what Jesus said. My spiritual quest has taught me that when one places all prophecy around what Jesus said, the contradictions disappear. This includes the book of Revelation, which many would describe as obscure. Jesus provided the major signs, events, and sequential template, while His prophets provided additional detail for Jesus' end-time chronology. Jesus and His Word in both testaments is never in contradiction. Scripture's format adds additional details as it unfolds. Knowing this, I prefer to tap Matthew 24 for my end-time framework, then overlay the additional details provided in Mark 13, Luke 17 and 21, and then the details from the prophets, disciples, and apostles.

The second major principle in my eschatological guideline is to include all relevant prophetic end-time passages, sorted into to specific end-time narratives like the abomination, tribulation, second exodus, rapture, the wrath of God, thief in the night, etc., and then overlay them into end-time chronology. I would encourage prophecy students to include all relevant passages, even inconvenient passages that may contradict or blur

---

[12] John 1.1–18; Rev 19:10, 13.

your current position, then rework those passages back in by finding other pieces that those out-of-sort passages fit with, which will then permit one to connect those larger pieces back in to complete the puzzle. Forcing pieces together only distorts the picture, while leaving out pieces leaves glaring holes in the picture. Meeting this challenge may force changes to your current position, but it will deliver clarity. It will take time, and it will help keep you humble. Even though Scripture provides copious quantities of prophecy in both testaments, once one begins to place all prophecy around what Jesus said, all the passages will begin fit together into a consistent event chronology.

Moreover, I accept the literal understanding of Scripture versus the interpretive approach polytheist religions deploy as a core principle within their numinous religions, which is the methodology polytheists employ to reimagine the Bible. In the literal approach, I define biblical allegory from within the Bible, not outside it. This includes defining prophetic allegory from within biblical texts, including the book of Revelation. Adding nonbiblical context is acceptable provided that the additional context is congruent with Scripture in all aspects.

I read the Bible as a linear narrative, beginning in Genesis and ending in Revelation. Where books out of the linear sequential order, such as the books of the prophets and the Psalms, clear markers are included within those books to identify where the book fits in the biblical timeline. As such, I read the Revelation in a similar fashion, noting that the midpoint of the last seven years is marked in Revelation 14:1–7 with the ending of the commission of the 144,000 firstfruits, when the angel preaches the gospel. Revelation 14:8 begins an outline and event sequence for the last three and a half years, detailed through verse 20. The outline's details follow throughout Revelation 15–19. Armageddon is followed by the millennium, the judgment, and then the eternal epoch detailed in Revelation 20–22. The book of Revelation's event chronology overlays perfectly onto Jesus' chronology, noting the last seven years begins in Revelation at the first seal-opening of Revelation, or a few years just before.

My guideline approach does not conflate Old Testament prophecy assigned to Israel with New Testament and new covenant church prophecies. Further, I encourage researchers not to conflate prophecies addressed to Israel with Judah and vice versa. Apply all end-time prophecies addressed to Israel to the exiled, lost northern kingdom of Israel, which will awaken in the last seven years. Apply all end-time prophecy addressed to Judah to the southern kingdom dispersed by the Romans in AD 70. Apply all prophecies addressed to specific tribes of Israel as they are named—Ephraim, Manasseh, Dan, etc.

My guidelines encourage readers to compare several English Bible translations with respect to important passages, in order to analyze the various translations. I have found that doing so can lead one to recognize new avenues of research and understanding. For those who would like to peer more deeply still into discerning end-time prophecy and the Bible in general, I encourage you to take your preferred English translation back to the original Hebrew words and Greek words for the Old Testament and New Testament respectfully. For this tome, I have utilized the

King James Bible, linking it to *Strong's Concordance* that references the original *Strong's Dictionary*. I also utilize *Strong's Cyclopaedia,* penned in part by James Strong, for a more complete definition of each word. The original Hebrew and Greek words hold additional information as understood in those times, which one or two English words are unable to fully communicate.

However, I would encourage Bible students to manage the Hebrew and Greek definition with care. Most Hebrew and Greek words have several meanings; some meanings are similar with nuanced differentiations, but some words have multiple meanings that quite different. Thus, one is required to be careful not to select definitions or meanings that are incongruous or inconsistent with the sentence where that word is found—incongruous with the balance of verse the word is part of, incongruous with the overall chapter or narrative the word is enveloped within, or incongruous with any other directly related passages in the Bible. I encourage Christians to not maneuver Scripture through reimagining the meaning that would place Scripture in conflict in any way. The interpretive approach tends to reimagine Scripture's meaning by redefining words, phrases, and doctrines inspired by a preconceived conclusion, but without regard for how that reimagined metaphorical meaning or substituted definition fits within the balance of the sentence, verse, narrative, chapter, and other directly related Scripture.

Know that I am not a prophet, nor am I prescient in any way. What I have learned and penned comes from Scripture as my guide. What I deduce and what I present for consideration to anticipate is based in what Jesus said, the Bible, and based on the premise of comprehending prehistory to help define prophecy. Know as well that nothing is new under the sun:

> Eccl 1:9 The thing that hath been, it is that which shall be; and that which is done is that which shall be done: and there is no new thing under the sun.
>
> Eccl 1:10 Is there any thing whereof it may be said, See, this is new? it hath been already of old time, which was before us.

And, "Always remember that behind the thick, steel door of superficial history taught by the educated elite sleeps an obscure version that elucidates the enigmatic events of history. Regrettably, there is a shadowy second history hidden from public viewing: a shocking saga of secret societies, lost civilizations, unexplained events, and an unaccounted for hidden hand of history."[13] Our earthly history gyrates around the genesis of the giants, the true house of Dragon which imposed their specious divine right to rule and divine destiny doctrines on humankind; and a terrible history and frightening short-term future begat and continued by the Invisible Ones, the celestial mafia.

---

[13] Gary Wayne, *The Genesis 6 Conspiracy: How Secret Societies and The Descendants of Giants Plan to Enslave Humankind* (Sisters, OR: Trusted Books, an imprint of Deep River Books, 2014), xii.

Section 1:
Angels, Giants, and Demons

Deut 3:13 And the rest of Gilead, and all Bashan, being the kingdom of Og, gave I unto the half tribe of Manasseh; all the region of Argob, with all Bashan, which was called the land of giants.

CHAPTER 1

THE DAYS OF NOAH AND LOT

Gen 9:28 And Noah lived after the flood three hundred and fifty years.

Gen 9:29 And all the days of Noah were nine hundred and fifty years: and he died.

During the past few centuries most churches and clergy began to restrict teaching prehistory and prophecy in a meaningful and interconnected manner with the balance of Scripture. If we are indeed living in the prophetic "fig tree" generation[14] Jesus prophesied, then this abandonment may turn out to be the greatest failing of Catholic and Protestant churches alike.

The prophetic "fig tree" allegory identified a specific generation—one that Jesus stated would endure His sequential accounting of signs, events, and tribulations that would all take place in this generation. Indeed, "Heaven and earth shall pass away, but my words shall not pass away."[15] One would think churches and their clergy would teach the doctrine of the last generation before the millennium in a holistic and in-depth manner, as conveyed by our Redeemer to the disciples; yet most contemporary churches do not.

---

[14] Matt 21:19:46; 24:32–36; Mark 11:13–33; 13:28–37; Luke 21:29–37.
[15] Matt 24:35; Mark 13:31; Luke 21:32.

Included in the end of days signs and events, Jesus, the Word of God "whose testimony is the spirit of prophecy"[16] provided the sign of Noah and Lot, a secondary and overarching indicator of the events and signs that will unfold through out the fig tree generation:

> Matt 24:37 But as the days of Noe were, so shall also the coming of the Son of man be.

> Matt 24:38 For as in the days that were before the flood they were eating and drinking, marrying and giving in marriage, until the day that Noe entered into the ark,

> Matt 24:39 And knew not until the flood came, and took them all away; so shall also the coming of the Son of man be.[17]

Many who study and teach end-time prophecy view "the days of Noah" only as it was described within the text: that people were surprised by the first apocalypse by water; that they did not understand what was going on, and/or did not believe the first apocalypse was close or going to happen at all. Thus, the godless people in the days of Noah before the flood carried on as if they did not know or care about the impending catastrophe about to befall them. And indeed, this will be the case once more in the last three and a half years of the last seven, when Antichrist seizes power by deceiving most all the people that he is the long-awaited messiah.[18] But is this the full understanding of the sign? I submit that the answer no.

The sign of Noah is not included in the chronological event signs Jesus provided prior to the fig tree generation sign. It follows immediately afterward, and encompasses all the previous signs that had been prophesied. The days of Noah sign, like the fig tree generation, is an overarching sign not limited to just the last three and a half years but the entire generation. Limiting the sign of Noah to just the last three and a half years, or even the last seven years, restricts the full understanding of the sign. The sign of Noah certainly incorporates an intense denial of those times and the violence thereof when Antichrist will be crowned in the temple,[19] but more was going on just before the flood catastrophe than simple godlessness and violence.

Knowing that the days of Noah sign comes later in Jesus' end-time oration, as an extension of the overarching sign for a specific generation and after the chronology of events listed in Matthew 24:4–31, makes sense of the disciples' questions to Jesus. The disciples asked: When would the end-time events begin to come to pass?

---

[16] John 1:1, 14; Rev 19:10, 13.
[17] See also Luke 17:26–30.
[18] Dan 7:24–25; 8:9–14,23-25, 9:27, 11:31–39, 12:7–12; Rev 13:1–18.
[19] 2 Thess 2:4.

What would be the signs and events that would mark the end-time? What would be the sign of Jesus' coming? And what would be the sign of the end of this age?

> Matt 24:3 And as he sat upon the mount of Olives, the disciples came unto him privately, saying, Tell us, when shall these things be? and what shall be the sign of thy coming, and of the end of the world?

> Mark 13:4 Tell us, when shall these things be? and what shall be the sign when all these things shall be fulfilled?

> Luke 21:7 And they asked him, saying, Master, but when shall these things be? and what sign will there be when these things shall come to pass?

What I find riveting and eye-opening about the sign of Noah Jesus provided in His end-time prophecy summation is the specificity of the words "the days of Noah," as it was translated from Greek into English. Jesus' choice of words may not have limited the time of Noah to a few short days or years just before the flood when He stated "in the days before the flood." Those days of Noah extend out of and are defined as part of the fig tree generation—which by implication can indicate years. So, the question becomes: Was Jesus indicating literal days, prophetic years, or a prophetic generation? The answer to this question dictates how narrow or how wide our understanding of the scope of the "days of Noah" sign should be.

> Matt 24:38 For as in the days that were before the flood they were eating and drinking, marrying and giving in marriage, until the day that Noe entered into the ark,

> Matt 24:39 And knew not until the flood came, and took them all away; so shall also the coming of the Son of man be.

The Greek word from which "days" is translated from is *haymer'ah*—a word defined as a day, as well as a general period as in the days of a life,[20] and by extension, a generation. Thus, void of further passages to define the application for "days," one is left with a meaning based on one's biases. As a Christian contrarian, I am not comforted by ambiguity. And, as I am riveted by all words Jesus spoke with preternatural specificity while on earth, I conclude that Jesus was encouraging believers to dig deeper into His words, and by extension Scripture, to confirm and discern the larger context of the days of Noah, and how those events connect to end-time prophecy.

---

[20] James Strong, *KJV Bible with Comprehensive Strong's Dictionary* (Best Books Kindle Version, 2015). G2250—*hay-mer'-ah*; day; sunrise to sunset; days; a year; years; a general period; an age; the days of a person's life.

THE GENESIS 6 CONSPIRACY PART II

I believe that if one wishes to fully comprehend end-time prophecy, one is required to understand prehistory documented throughout the Bible. Biblical prehistory and history provide the answers to prophetic allegory and provide the essential context to end-time prophecy, which is the denouement and resolution to the events that took place in prehistory and throughout our history. I think Jesus was encouraging future believers to learn about those murky events Scripture preserved for us, so that we would not be deceived: "For there shall arise false Christs, and false prophets, and shall shew great signs and wonders; insomuch that, if it were possible, they shall deceive the very elect. Behold, I have told you before" (Matthew 24:24–25).

Jesus selected precise wording that would be recognized and understood in the original Hebrew of the Old Testament, words understood clearly by the disciples and people of Judea of that period, and that the sign should be connected to and defined in Genesis 9:29—the verse that introduces this chapter: "And all the days of Noah were nine hundred and fifty years: and he died." "The days of Noah" is a term first used to describe Noah's lifetime—one complete generation that stretched six hundred years before the flood and three hundred fifty years after. Jesus would have known this when He selected His words, and that Genesis 6:3 limited a generation to a maximum of 120 years in the days of Noah.

The Hebrew word *yowm* is translated into the English as "days" and is additionally defined as a day, a year, years, a general period, and as a lifetime (generation).[21] Days, as understood for a lifetime and/or a generation, is further expressed biblically by the phrase "the days of thy life,"[22] and the days of Adam, Seth, Enos, Cainan, Mahalaleel, Jared, Enoch, Methuselah, and Lamech[23] who begat Noah, noting the days of Noah were not listed until Genesis 9:29, and after the flood. However, Genesis 6:9 did say that Noah in his generation(s) was perfect. The New Testament supplied similar examples like "the days of Herod" (Luke 1:5), "the days of Elias" (Luke 4:25), "the days of David" (Acts 7:5), and "the days of Claudius Caesar" (Acts 11:28). Ergo, we ought to be open to the notion that the days of Noah sign was specifically penned to reflect a generation: the fig tree generation that will be akin to "the days of Noah" and its events.

Noah's life was bookended by the Nephilim and flood narratives, spanned into the Babel narrative,[24] and perhaps the Sodom and Gomorrah narrative with its destruction of fire. In typical biblical *modus operandi* of providing additional information in later passages, the book of Luke's account for the sign of Noah drafted the same flood analogy and linked the sign to the time of Sodom's

---

[21] Ibid. H3117—*yowm, yome*: a day; sunrise to sunset; a space of time; an age; days; years; years; a general period; a lifetime.
[22] Gen 3:14.
[23] Gen 5:5–32.
[24] Gen 5:32; 6:1–22; 7:1–24; 8:1–22; 9:1–29; 10:1–32; 11:1–32.

destruction and Lot's escape. Luke's accounting connected the sign analogy to the end-time destruction of fire with Sodom's destruction of fire. The inference, then, is that the events and destruction by water in the time of the Nephilim giants in Genesis 6:1–4, and the destruction of Sodom, provide additional details important to discerning the events that will occur in the fig tree generation. To this end, one deduces that the saints ought to inquire and learn about important events before the flood, at Babel, and the crimes committed at Sodom as part of the days of Noah sign to help comprehend end-time prophecy and its preternatural events.

> Luke 17.26 And as it was in the days of Noe, so shall it be also in the days of the Son of man...
>
> Luke 17:28 Likewise also as it was in the days of Lot; they did eat, they drank, they bought, they sold, they planted, they builded;
>
> Luke 17:29 But the same day that Lot went out of Sodom it rained fire and brimstone from heaven, and destroyed them all.
>
> Luke 17:30 Even thus shall it be in the day when the Son of man is revealed.

Linking the Sodom and Gomorrah destruction—with its violence, corruption, and sexual violations—as a cognate analogy to the sign of Noah indicates that similar Sodom-type sins were ongoing before the flood. It follows that within the usual cognitive dissonance that many Christians experience when they read Genesis 6:1–4 rests additional shocking sexual sins, violence, all forms of abhorrent behavior, and a brutal state-sponsored polytheism that has been purposefully hidden from Christians—important context that relates to the balance of the flood narrative, scriptural history, and to end-time events prophesied by Jesus.

> Gen 6:11 The earth also was corrupt before God, and the earth was filled with violence.
>
> Gen 6:12 And God looked upon the earth, and, behold, it was corrupt; for all flesh had corrupted his way upon the earth.

In fact, I am obligated to point out that the creation of giants documented in Genesis 6:1–4 was sandwiched between the birth of Noah and his sons (Genesis 5:32), the evil and violence that occurred thereafter, and Noah's commission to build the ark (Genesis 6:5–16). The creation of the antediluvian giants by the sons of God, and consequential information, was written purposefully into the introduction to the flood story as important context, to fully understand the flood narrative and end-time events. Similarly, the Rephaim giants documented as roaming the earth shortly after the flood were documented in Genesis 14's "war of giants" and Genesis 15's accounting of the people dwelling in the Covenant Land,[25] just before the destruction of Sodom and Gomorrah. Rephaim giants are the central subject of this tome; we will investigate in the subsequent chapters their connections to the beast empires and to end-time prophecy.

To complete the premise that Jesus indeed was referencing the days of Noah as a generation, and that believers were encouraged to learn about the events and the sins committed in the generation of Noah, one requires additional scriptural support. And in typical scriptural *modus operandi* there is such support. Second Peter 2:4–9 instructs that God did more than just bring about the first apocalypse by water upon the disbelieving and violent ungodly humans: "God spared not the angels that sinned, but cast them down to hell, and delivered them into chains of darkness, to be reserved for judgment" (v. 4). Further 2 Peter 2:4–5 instructs that God did not spare the old world but did save Noah as part of the eight who were righteous, and that God brought the flood on the ungodly,[26] the ungodly humans and the giants.

Second Peter 2 thereafter immediately connected the events in "the days of Noah" and the flood to a postdiluvian event: the destruction by fire and brimstone to Sodom, Gomorrah, and the cities of the plain, where sins akin to what occurred before the flood also occurred. Thus, God made these postdiluvian cities an example to the ungodly, but also delivered the righteous Lot and members of his family as an example for those unjust "unto the day of judgment to be punished"[27] in the wrath of God of the end-time. Just as Jesus in Luke cited the generation of Noah, Jesus connected the period after the flood to postdiluvian events and similar crimes committed at Sodom, and the days of Lot with Sodom's destruction, as the complete overarching sign of the "days of Noah" for the fig tree generation. Accordingly, 2 Peter 2:4–9 expanded the discernment of Jesus' sign of Noah and Lot to include fallen angelic sins by the sons of God, and the sins of their spurious offspring the Nephilim giants, as examples to discern the end-time, and that God will once more save the righteous from the wrath bowls poured out in the last three and a half years.

> 2 Pet 2:4 For if God spared not the angels that sinned, but cast them down to hell, and delivered them into chains of darkness, to be reserved unto judgment;

---

[25] Gen 14:5; 15:20. Strong, James, *KJV Bible With Comprehensive Strong's Dictionary*, H7497— *rapha', raw-faw'*; from 7495 in the sense of invigorating: a giant; giants; Rephaim, an old tribe of giants.
[26] 2 Pet 2:4–5.
[27] 2 Pet 2:6–9.

2 Pet 2:5 And spared not the old world, but saved Noah the eighth person, a preacher of righteousness, bringing in the flood upon the world of the ungodly;

2 Pet 2:6 And turning the cities of Sodom and Gomorrha into ashes condemned them with an overthrow, making them an ensample unto those that after should live ungodly;

2 Pet 2:7 And delivered just Lot, vexed with the filthy conversation of the wicked:

2 Pet 2:8 (For that righteous man dwelling among them, in seeing and hearing, vexed his righteous soul from day to day with their unlawful deeds;)

2 Pet 2:9 The Lord knoweth how to deliver the godly out of temptations, and to reserve the unjust unto the day of judgment to be punished...

Know then that Sodom, Gomorrah, and the cities of the plain were allied cities whose kings led their people in the "war of giants" detailed in Genesis 14[28]—cities later destroyed in God's "anger" and "wrath"[29] as an example, words used throughout Old Testament prophecy for the Lord's year of wrath in the end-time. The five Canaanite cities of prehistory were drafted and deployed as prophetic allegory in both the Old and New Testaments[30] as consequential context for the fig tree generation and specific prophetic destruction thereof. Thus Sodom, Gomorrah, and the other cities of the plain's people were described as exceedingly wicked and sinners before God,[31] just as Jesus warned that the people of the fig tree generation will become increasingly godless akin to the increasing sorrows and birth pangs that will grow stronger throughout the last generation, culminating with God's wrath bowls being poured out.[32] The people of Sodom were exceedingly *m`od,* as in wholly and mightily wicked; *ra`,* as in evil and vicious in their disposition and zealousness as sinners; and *chatta',* meaning a criminal and an offender,[33] like the fallen angels.

---

[28] Gen 14:3, 8, 10, 11, 12, 14, 17, 21, 22.
[29] Deut 29:23.
[30] Isa 13:13–19; Jer 49:18; 50:40; Zep 2:9; Matt 10:15; 2 Pet 2:6; Jude 1:7; Rev 11:7–8.
[31] Gen 13:13.
[32] Matt 24:8; Mark 13:8; 1 Thess 5:3. Strong, *KJV Bible with Comprehensive Strong's Dictionary,* G5604—*o-deen';* akin to 3601: a pang or throe of childbirth; pain; sorrow as in travail; pain of childbirth; birth pangs; intolerable anguish, in reference to the dire calamities precede the advent of the Messiah.
[33] Exceedingly: H3966—*m`od, meh-ode':* vehemently; wholly; speedily; diligently; especially; mightily, mighty; abundance; to a great degree, exceedingly. Wicked: H7451—*ra`:* evil; wickedness; mischief; malignant; worst; unkind; vicious. Sinners: H2400—*chatta', khat-taw':* a criminal, guilty; offender; sinful, sinner.

> 1 Thess 5:3 For when they shall say, Peace and safety; then sudden destruction cometh upon them, as travail upon a woman with child; and they shall not escape.

Further understanding and confirmation for the days of Noah and Lot signs surfaces in the book of Jude. In this passage, believers are taught that the angels who left their first estate habitation [in heaven] were reserved in everlasting chains and darkness until the great day of judgment,[34] inferring that these angels committed crimes—the crimes outlined in Genesis 6:1–4 and 2 Peter 2:4–9, which included angelic crimes in the generation of Lot at Sodom. In fact, the book of Jude connected the crimes of angels to the crimes at Sodom that included fornication with "strange flesh," sins/crimes punishable by the eternal punishment of fire—not the second death of Revelation 20. Sodom serves as an example for those who will suffer the eternal punishment in the lake of fire also reserved for Antichrist, the False Prophet, and all those who take the mark of the beast or worship Satan and Antichrist in the last three and a half years,[35] demons,[36] and fallen angels:

> Matt 13:41 The Son of man shall send forth his angels, and they shall gather out of his kingdom all things that offend, and them which do iniquity;
>
> Matt 13:42 And shall cast them into a furnace of fire: there shall be wailing and gnashing of teeth.

---

[34] Jude 1:6.

[35] Rev 19:20; cf. 13:16–17; 14:9– 11; 16:2; Jude 1:7.

[36] Legion: Mark 5:1–16, whereby evil unclean spirits also called devil and devils in this passage do not wish to be tormented/tortured as in the abyss or lake of fire: 5:7: "I adjure thee by God, that thou torment me not." Devil(s)/demon: G1142—*dah'ee-mown*: a daemon; supernatural spirit of a bad nature; devil; a god or goddess as in an inferior deity; an evil spirit. Transliterated: daimon. Devil/demon: G1140—*dahee-mon'-ee-on*; a derivative of 1142: daemonic being; an inferior deity; devil; evil spirit; ministers of the devil. Possessed by a devil/demon: G1139—*dahee-mon-id'-zom-ahee*; from 1142: to be exercised by a daemon; vexed with or be possessed by a devil(s); to be under the power of a demon and afflicted with severe diseases, either bodily or mentally such as paralysis, blindness, deafness, loss of speech, epilepsy, melancholy, insanity, etc. Devilish: G1141—*dahee-mon-ee-o'-dace*; from 1140 and 1142: daemon-like; devilish; an evil spirit. G1142: devils: Matt 8:31; Mark 5:12; Rev 16:14, 18:2. Devil: Luke 8:29. G1140: devils, Matt 7:22; 9:34; 10:8; 12:24, 27–28; Mark 1:34, 39; 3:15, 22; 6:13; 9:38; 16:9, 17; Luke 4:41; 8:2, 27, 30, 33, 35, 38; 9:1, 49; 10:17; 11:15, 18, 19, 20; 13:32; 1 Cor 10:20, 21; 1 Tim 4:1; Rev 9:19–20. Devil: Matt 9:33; 17:18; Mark 7:26, 29–30; Luke 4:33, 35; 7:33; 9:42; 11:14; John 7:20; 8:48, 49, 52; 10:20, 21. Gods: Acts 17:18. G1141: devilish: Jam 3:15. G1139: possessed: Matt 4:24; 8:16, 28, 33, 9:32; 12:22; Mark 1:32, 5:15, 18; Luke 8:36. Devil: Matt 9:32, 15:22; Mark 5:15, 16, 18; John 10:21. Devils: Matt 4:24; 8:16, 28, 33; Mark 1:32; Luke 8:36. Vexed: Matt 15:22.

> Matt 25:41 Then shall he say also unto them on the left hand, Depart from me, ye cursed, into everlasting fire, prepared for the devil and his angels.

The fallen angels who sinned against the laws of creation in the physical world sinned against the Holy Spirit, and committed crimes against humanity before the flood; and seemingly others who did the same after the flood were sent to the abyss.[37] These are the fallen ones who will be released from the abyss in the last seven years.[38] Fallen angels in the abyss are the spirits who were once commissioned as ministering spirits for humans destined to be heirs of eternity,[39] but rebelled. The fallen ones were the disobedient spirits "in the days of Noah, while the ark was a preparing, wherein few, that is, eight souls were saved by water." Jesus visited these spirits in the angelic prison while still in the grave (1 Peter 3:18–20).

Note the identical language penned in in 1 Peter 3: "the days of Noah" when the ark was being prepared in the days of disobedient spirits. This is the same wording Jesus utilized in the sign of Noah, which by implication connects the crimes of angels recorded in Genesis 6:1–4 as requisite context for the sign of Noah. This period of building the ark was one hundred years, calculated by noting that Noah's sons were begat to him beginning when he was five hundred years old, that Noah entered the ark when he was six hundred years old, and that Shem was documented as one hundred years old and then begat Arphaxad two years after the flood.[40]

Noah's commission was not 120 years, as many suggest, but one hundred years. The 120 years documented in Genesis 6:3 was the length of life permitted going forward by newborns, as supported by the diminishing length of life documented after the flood. Hence the "days of Noah" could date to one hundred years when the ark was being prepared, or a generation of 120 years, or a generation of seventy years,[41] or a generation forty years.[42] Any of these could be the count for the maximum length of years for the fig tree generation guided by what the sign might be that would start the count down.

> Heb 11:7 By faith Noah, being warned of God of things not seen as yet, moved with fear, prepared an ark to the saving of his house; by the which he condemned the world, and became heir of the righteousness which is by faith.

---

[37] 1 Pet 3:18; 2 Pet 2:4 Jude 1:6.
[38] Rev 9:1–11.
[39] Heb 1:7, 14.
[40] Gen 5:32; 6:9; 7:6, 11; 8:6; 11:10.
[41] Ps 90:10.
[42] Num 32:13.

Just as Noah was warned "of things not seen as yet" "and became the heir of righteousness by faith,"[43] Christians, as inheritors of the world to come by faith, were warned of things not yet seen and advised by our Redeemer to consider the trials, tribulations, and events of Noah to help discern and prepare for the terror that is coming. This book will investigate the days of Noah, the Nephilim, and the Rephaim in the spirit of the psalmist:

Ps 77:5 I have considered the days of old, the years of ancient times.

---

[43] Heb 11:7.

GIANTS OF OLD

Gen 6:4 There were giants in the earth in those days; and also after that, when the sons of God came in unto the daughters of men, and they bare children to them, the same became mighty men which were of old, men of renown.

Inexplicably, egregious absolute power the giant ones wielded after the great deluge is one of the most underreported and important facets of prehistory and ancient history.

Giants, as they pertain to humanoid races, are defined as a huge, mythical beings of more or less human form: beings of abnormally great stature that possessed extraordinary powers.[44] History both sacred and secular, as well as myths worldwide, make references to giants. According to the *Encyclopedia Americana*, mythical accounts of giants were rarer than dwarfs and other abnormal creatures, all of which were unusually more sterile than humans.[45]

The word "giant" appears in *Webster's Dictionary* after "ghoul," "ghostly," and "ghost," followed by "giantess" and then and "gibber/gibberish."[46] "Gibber" is defined as uttering senseless and inarticulate sounds, while "gibberish" is defined as rapid unintelligible speech, unknown words, an unknown language, or an esoteric

---

[44] *Webster's Dictionary*, 171: giant.

[45] *Encyclopedia Americana* (Montreal, Toronto, Vancouver, Winnipeg: Americana Corporation of Canada Ltd., 1956), Vol. 12, 637: giants.

[46] *Webster's Dictionary, 171*: giant; *Encyclopedia Americana*, Vol. 12, 637: giants.

language.[47] In times past, gibberish was the term often applied to the speech of demons and ancient giants who spoke quickly and often in unknown languages.

Similarly, Indo-European languages—alternatively known as Aryan, Arya-European, Indo-Celtic, and Indo-Germanic—are terms created by scholars to encapsulate related and mysterious languages descended from a common ancestor-language of an unknown origin.[48] Indo-Europeans arrived in early secular post-diluvian history without adequate explanation, invading the Mediterranean and Middle East regions from before 2000 BC. Indo-European tribes assimilated and/ or destroyed cultures such as the Minoans, Babylonians, Khattites (Hittites, Khassites, Mitanni), and are thought to be the Scythians, Persians, and Aryans, the latter having settled the Indus Valley.[49] Both the mysterious history of languages and the various Indo-European tribes are linked to giants.

Indo-European languages conceal an unexplained historical record well before the flood. What is most interesting is that in polytheist lore, the most ancient of the Scythians predate the antediluvian Sumerians. Moreover, tablets found beneath the village of Tartaria in the famous province of Transylvania evidently predate the first Sumerian texts by as much as a thousand years, according to carbon-14 dating. What is extraordinary about this discovery is that the glyphs/symbols on the tablets were virtually identical with Sumerian glyphs.[50] Early postdiluvian Scythians occupied the Balkans, Transylvania, Carpathia, and the Ukraine,[51] indicating that Scythians somehow inherited the antediluvian Indo-European language.

One cannot clearly comprehend humankind's obscured and often hidden history, religions, and culture unless one adequately accounts for the impact giants and their godfathers imprinted onto the antediluvian and postdiluvian world. Know then, antediluvian giants scripturally described as the mighty ones of old and the Nephilim were spurious children of the divine ones, giants described by some monotheist historians as "the embodiment of absolute power in the ancient world."[52] Their trans-flood and transgenerational legacy imposed a worldwide feudal-like class system, state-sponsored polytheism, and controlled polytheist-inspired education system. Dynastic giant royals—along with their siblings, off-

---

[47] Ibid. *171:* gibber. https://www.etymonline.com/word/gibberish. https://www.merriam-webster.com/dictionary/gibberish.

[48] *Encyclopedia Americana,* Vol. 15, 60: Indo-European Languages; Vol. 24, 471–472: Scythians.

[49] Ibid., Vol. 15, 69: Indo-European Languages.

[50] Laurence Gardner, *Realm of the Ring Lords* (Gloucester, MA: Fair Winds Press, 2003), 66–67, citing Sir C. Leonard Woolley, *The Sumerians,* W.W. Norton, 1965, 20, and Assyriologist Sir Henry Creswicke Rawlinson's address to the Royal Asiatic Society on non-Semitic cuneiform.

[51] Nicholas De Vere, HHRH Prince, Sovereign Grand Master—Imperial and Royal Dragon Court and Order of the Dragon sovereignty, introduction by Tracy Twyman, *The Dragon Legacy: The Secret History of an Ancient Bloodline* (produced in conjunction with Societies Draconis and Ordo Lapsit Exillus, The Book Tree, San Diego, CA, 2004), 63.

[52] J. R. Porter, *The New Illustrated Companion to the Bible* (London: Prospero Books, 2003), 26.

spring, and cousins—conspired through the generations to impose, enforce, and enslave humankind—an ancient world order I coin as the Nephilim World Order (NWO), in the spirit of their "god"-fathers.

Western scientific, historical, archaeological, educational, and Christian hegemony consistently suppress OOPARTS[53] and all inconvenient history not congruent with their dogma. They summarily dismiss the veracity of giants as a collective ancestral figment of the imagination: an unexplained, fantastic mass hallucination experienced on a worldwide scale. Accordingly, many submit that the word "giant," as we understand the meaning today, is a wild exaggeration—that "giant" was understood differently in prehistory, history, and in the Greek language from which the contemporary English word derived. Many in the exaggeration camp assert that "giant" meant "earth-born" in ancient Greek culture, and as such "giant" was a term that applied to renowned but fully human heroes and warriors. Misinformation and disinformation generally contain some truth, but the totality is inaccurate and designed to deceive; such is the case with the exaggeration dogma of the word "giant" and its etymology.

The English word "giant" derives from the Greek *gigas* and Latin *gigant*. *Webster's* etymology looks like this: Middle English *giaunt*, from Anglo-French *geant*, from Latin *gigant* and Greek *gigas*.[54] The word "gigantic," according to *Webster's Dictionary*, derives from Latin: *gigas* and *gigantis* via the Greek word *gigas* (and likely *gigentes*), meaning giant and giants respectfully.[55] Further, the *Jewish Encyclopedia* ascribes "giant" as deriving from *gigas*/γίγας, as it was translated from Hebrew into Greek in the Septuagint and defined as "denoting a man of extraordinary stature; in the English versions the rendering for three Hebrew words: (1) 'Nefilim' (see Fall of Angels), Gen. vl. 4a, an extinct (mythological, only semi human) race, inhabitants of the earth before the flood, the progeny of the Bene Elohim and the daughters of men."[56]

Know then that *gigas*/γίγας and/or *Γίγᾶς/gyyas, (Γίγαες/gyes* plural) are Greek words meaning "giant" and "giants," words originally used to describe the monstrous race of Gigantes in Greek mythology that included Briareus, Centimanes, Cottus, and a Gigantes with the latter spelled both as Gyes and Gyges. The letter "g/γ," pronounced as a hard "gh" sound in Greek and known as the letter gamma, can be pronounced at times with the "y" sound, when the "g" precedes

---

[53] OOPARTS = out-of-place artifacts; coined by Ivan T. Sanderson: "for the various anomalous objects—human, animal, artificial—which have been found throughout the Earth's strata or in geological formations where they should not be located, according to conventional scientific theory." https://hsp.org/blogs/hidden-histories/ooparts-out-of-place-artifacts-in-pennsylvania.

[54] https://www.merriam-webster.com/dictionary/giant.

[55] *Webster's Dictionary*, 172: gigantic.

[56] *The Jewish Encyclopedia, A Descriptive Record of the History, Religion, Literature, and Customs of the Jewish People From the Earliest Times to the Present Day* (New York and London: Funk and Wagnalls, 1903), Vol. 5, 657: giants.

an "e" (epsilon) or an "i" (iota), which explains two transliterated names for one of the Gigantes/*Gigentes*: *Gyges* and *Gyes*. *Gyes* has the "e" (epsilon) following in its variant spelling (Gyges) and thus the "y" sound" for the pronunciation, versus a hard "g" when followed by the "a" (alpha) letter. However, some Greek words with the hard "g" pronunciation utilize the *'Γ'* gamma letter format, and some Greek plural formats replace the a/α in the last suffix with an e/ε, all of which seems to have affected the Greek transliteration and etymology into English.

In Greek, the singular format of "gigantes" was spelled as Γίγᾶντας/*gigantas and* γίγαντας/*gigantas,* while the plural format was spelled as Γίγαντες/*gigantes* and/or γίγεντες/ γίγεντες/*gigentes* for "the gigantic ones." Hence the English transliteration and pronunciation for the singular format could be pronounced giantas/giyantas, and the plural format as giantes/giyantes. The same applies to the various singular spellings of *gigas*/γίγας and/or Γίγᾶς/*giyas* pronounced gigas, **with the plural as** Γίγαες/*gyes* and γίγες/*yiye*s understood as the giant ones. Thus, the name Gyges/Gyes, was a member of the race of gigantic monsters that possessed one hundred hands and fifty heads;[57] giant monsters that were alternatively referred to as γίγαντας/gigantas (singular) and/or plural Γίγαυςες/*giyantes* and γίγεντες/ giyentes. The *Gigentes/Giyentes* were alternatively known as the Hekatoncheires, or Hecatoncheires.[58]

From the various Greek spellings, it would seem to me that the *gygantas* and *gygentes* pronunciation and transliteration for gigantic(s) and/or gigantic, along with *gyas*/*gyes* for giant(s), is the preferred transliteration combination that eventually produced the Latin *gigant,* and English "gigantic" and "giant," with the latter utilizing the y sound for the "g" for the giant ones—thus, the modern English format of giant(s) derived from Middle English that utilized the shortened form of *gygentis* (*gigentes*) to form *giaunt(s)*. The full phonetic etymology from *gigas* to contemporary "giant" looks like this: *gigas* and *giges*/*gyes* begat *gigantas* and *gigentes/giyentes* (plural), which begat the Latin giga and gigant, which begat Anglo/ French *geant* and Middle English *giaunt*. Further, *gigentes/*γίγεντες was the plural Greek word originally utilized by Jewish translators to translate Nephilim (also a plural format) into Greek from Hebrew for the original Septuagint circa 250 BC (and not vice versa as some suggest). The Jewish translators did so to reflect the Nephilim (giant ones) as kin or the same as earth-born Greek titans/*gigentes* who were part men and part gods. Thereafter, the Septuagint translation influenced

---

[57] Hesiod, *Theogony*, verse 150.
[58] Carol Rose, *Giants, Monsters and Dragons: An Encyclopedia of Folklore, Legend, and Myth* (New York: W. W. Norton & Company, 2001), 142. Ignatius Donnelly, *Atlantis: The Antediluvian World* (New York: Dover Publications Inc., 1976), 294–299.

Jerome's application of *gigantas/gygentes* for giant(s) in the Latin Vulgate that influenced the KJV application.[59]

Knowing the etymology of "giant" makes sense of *gigas, gygas,* and *Gyges/Giyes,* the source words for the giant *Giyes/Gyges* in Hesiod's *Theogony.* Both spellings were transliterated into various English translations for a member of the Gigantes/ *Gygentes* monster race that appear many times in Hesiod's works.[60] The size of the Gigantes had to be huge (gigantic) to accommodate all the arms and legs, just as *Webster's Dictionary* defines a giant as huge, a person of abnormally great stature, originating from Greek *gigas* and *gigantos/gigantas.* Note as well that "giantess" is the feminine format of "giant," the adjective format is "gigantic," while "giantism" and "gigantism" are derivatives of "giant." Gigantic is defined as a characteristic of a giant as in huge and derives originally from Greek *gigas.*[61]

Thus, "giant" in Greek derives jointly from *gigas/giges* and *gigantes/gigentes,* noting the latter also were known as *Gegeneis,* with both *gigentes* and *Gegeneis* meaning "earth-born." Giant and Gigantes were earth-born via the gods in the physical world versus the spirit dimension, born of the mother goddess of the earth named as Gaia[62] and Uranus and/or Cronos with their physical world DNA, along with their kin but distinct Cyclops.[63] The original Cyclops—Stereopes, Arges, and Brontes—further produced offspring with human females, producing smaller cyclopean giants that were hairy, savage, and one-eyed, distinct from the giant heroes created by Olympian gods.[64]

The mother earth goddess appellation is the source allegory for "earth-born,"[65] also as it applied to the mighty demigod earth-born giants/heroes that were born of earth-born human females (many who were allegorically raised to mother earth goddess status by their actions) with male gods, as in Hercules son of Zeus and the human female Alcmene; and human males with mother goddesses recorded in *Theogony,* procreating giant(s)/*gigas/giges* renowned as heroe(s). Accordingly, Pausanias documented the giant corpse of Orontes; the Indian (Indo-Aryan) was about eleven cubits (sixteen to nineteen feet) tall, and discovered on the Syrian

---

[59] Daniel E. Woodhead, "The Demonic Interruption of The Messianic Seed Line," in *As the Days of Noah Were, So Also Shall the Coming of the Son of Man Be* (Hart, MI: Scofield Seminary 2014), 4–5; *The Catholic Encyclopedia,* eds. Charles G. Herberman, et al. (New York: Robert Appleton Company, 1907), Vol. 6, 478–479: angels.

[60] Hesiod, *Theogony,* 150, 620–624, 715, 735–740, 820.

[61] *Webster's,* 171: giant; 172: gigantic.

[62] Ibid., 142: Gigantes.

[63] Hesiod, *Theogony,* 132–153. Pausanias, *The Description of Greece,* trans. Arthur Richard Shilleto (London: Chiswick Press, 1886), Vol. 2, 109–110, Book 8:29; Homer, *The Odyssey,* trans. Ian Johnson, rev. ed. (Nanaimo, BC: Vancouver Island University, 2019), Book 7:140 and note 2, 230–250.

[64] Pausanias, *Description of Greece,* 109–110; Johnson, *The Odyssey,* Book 9: 140–566.

[65] Pausanias, *Description of Greece,* 109–110.

Orontes River.[66] Moreover, Gyges/Giyes was a hero (giant) king and dynastic founder in Lydia circa 600 BC, and one of the kings of the Heraclides (descended from Hercules);[67] King Gog was another giant associated with the kings of Lydia. Gog and Magog giants additionally surfaced in early British history, where they were captured, taken to London, and chained. Statues were erected in 1708 after earlier representations burned in the great London fire of 1666. Those latter images were fabricated at fourteen feet tall but were destroyed in Germany's bombing in 1940.[68] Gog and Magog were names recorded in two prophetic Bible wars,[69] and regarded as members of a race of Greek, Gyges giant demigods and their eponymously named descendant kings, warriors, and heroes, whose ancestral branches later reigned in northwest of Assyria.[70]

According to *The Catholic Encyclopedia*, the term "hero" originated with ancient warriors and demigods famous for their bravery and deeds,[71] popularized in Greek mythology. Hesiod, according to Herodotus, was a contemporary of Homer circa 900 BC,[72] and described heroes in "Works and Days" as "men of great renown." Hesiod further wrote in "Goddesses and Heroes" in *Theogony* (generations of the gods) that the gods created a preternatural race through procreating with mortals (humans).[73] The spurious offspring were the demigod giants: "The divine race of Heroes, also called demigods, the race before the present one. They all died fighting in the great wars";[74] and: "Second, Zeus, the father of gods and men, Mightiest of the gods and strongest by far; And then the race of humans and of powerful giants."[75] The *Iliad* also documented several demigod warriors and champions such Acamus, Achilles, Ajax, and Telamon.[76]

Hesiod though, in *Theogony*, seems to refer to two creations of giants in his accounts. The first race of demigods, "the race before the present one" that died in fighting great wars, was likely giant race before the flood created by the parent gods like Cronos, Poseidon, and Iapetus; the latter produced the giants Gog, Magog, and Albion before the flood. The second giant race was created by Zeus and other

[66] Ibid.
[67] Herodotus, *Histories*, Book 1, 6–14.
[68] *Encyclopedia Americana*, Vol. 13, 7: Gog and Magog.
[69] Ezek 38–39; Rev 20:8.
[70] *Encyclopedia Americana*, Vol.13, 7: Gog and Magog.
[71] *Catholic Encyclopedia*, Vol. 6, 292: hero/virtue.
[72] *Encyclopedia Americana*, Vol. 14, 154: Hesiod.
[73] Hesiod, *Theogony*, "Goddesses and Heroes," verses 970–975.
[74] Ibid., *Theogony*, "Works and Days," verse 180.
[75] Ibid., *Theogony*, verse 45-50.
[76] Homer, *The Iliad of Homer*, trans. Alexander Pope, 1899 (Gutenberg EBook, www.gutenberg.org/licensw, 2006), Book 6, 182; Book 7, 97, 216; Book 23, 697, 701.

offspring gods after the flood—giants like Hercules, Theseus, and Perseus.[77] Knowing Josephus equated Nephilim and Rephaim giants with Greek heroes, and just as Sumerian giants like Gilgamesh were described as heroes, one ought to be surprised that a city in the Syrian region of Mount Hermon was named Heroopolis by the Greeks, "the city of heroes."[78]

The parent god regime reigned before the flood, and the offspring gods reigned after the flood, whereby the latter celestial mafia reestablished the Nephilim World Order with their spurious offspring in a Second Incursion, which has continued down through the generations. It follows then that to comprehend how we arrived at our current societal order, and to understand end-time prophecy, one must investigate the foggy events of prehistory and early recorded history, which hold keys to unlocking end-time prophetic allegory.

> Josh 24:15 And if it seem evil unto you to serve the LORD, choose you this day whom ye will serve; whether the gods which your fathers served that were on the other side of the flood, or the gods of the Amorites, in whose land ye dwell.

Scripturally, we are not instructed as to how giants appear after the flood—we only know that they do. Even though one might determine that the flood was intended to rid the earth of all the evil ones who corrupted the earth, this did not expunge the genesis to evil nor the ongoing war against the Adamites. My first book, *The Genesis 6 Conspiracy: How Secret Societies and the Descendants of Giants Plan to Enslave Humankind,* discussed three buckets as to how giants show up after the flood: a) Second Incursion by second group of fallen angels after the flood who were not sent to the abyss for crimes against the laws of creation and against humankind; b) with the aid of fallen angels that either protected giants in the earth, took giants off the earth, or via another ark, as detailed with giants like Utnapishtim in the *Epic of Gilgamesh,* and Deucalion, son of Prometheus in the Greek flood story tradition; c) somehow on the ark with Noah, his three sons, and their unnamed wives.

Knowing Scripture does not furnish a smoking-gun passage as to how giants inexplicably resurface after the flood, I am open to all three options for contemplation. However, I do favor the Second Incursion and a second creation of giants by fallen angels as the best option to explain the renaissance of "absolute power"

[77] Carol Rose, *Giants, Monsters and Dragons: An Encyclopedia of Folklore, Legend, and Myth*, 11, 146, 187, 170, citing Geoffrey of Monmouth (1100–1154), *Historia Regnum Britanniae.*
[78] William Rickets Cooper, *An Archaic Dictionary, Biographical, Historical, and Mythological: From the Egyptian, Assyrian, and Etruscan Monuments and Papyri* (London: Samuel Bagster and Sons, 1876), 228; William Whiston, commentary by Paul L. Maier, *The New Complete Works of Josephus* (Grand Rapids, MI: Kregel Publications, A Division of Kregel, Inc., 1999), Book 2, 7:5.

in the postdiluvian world.[79] A Second Incursion just seems to fit better with the details documented in Scripture both before and after the flood. Scripturally, the totality of how giant creation came about was communicated in the preamble to the flood narrative in Genesis 6:1–4, which detailed the sons of God, a shadowy group within the rebellious angels that sought out and chose daughters of men as their consorts. They did so again after that, whereby human consorts bore giant offspring described as the mighty men of old and the men of renown. Thus, the phrase "after that" in Genesis 6:4 could mean after the first creation of giants but before the flood, or again after, or both.

Although not directly scriptural, the notion that the sons of God were angels, and their offspring giants, was widely held as doctrine in the ancient world, as documented by the Jewish historian Josephus (c. AD 37–100). "Josephus was noble, from the old aristocracy descending from the first twenty-four lines of priests spawned by Aaron and Moses, a descendant from the Maccabees on his mother's side, and a priest of high rank in the Jerusalem temple. He spent three of his most impressionable years among the Essenes and then converted back to the Pharisees' sect, all the while taking time to study the Sadducees'."[80] Josephus was commissioned by the Roman emperor Vespasian to chronicle the history of the Israelites at the time of the Jewish diaspora at the hands of the Roman Empire, so that Israelite history would not be lost to the world.[81] As such, Josephus testified that Genesis 6's giants were akin to a race Greeks also understood as giants, heroes of old like Hercules: "This notion, that the fallen angels were, in some sense, the fathers of the old giants, was the constant opinion of antiquity.. .. For many angels of God accompanied with women, and begat sons that proved unjust, and despisers of all that was good, on account of the confidence they had in their own strength; for the tradition is, that these men did what resembled the acts of those whom the Grecians call giants."[82]

Additionally, the apocryphal book of Enoch (First Enoch) communicates a consistent narrative to that of Genesis 6's account of antediluvian prehistory, giants, Noah, and the flood, all the while serving up bountiful amounts of directionally consistent information and context for consideration. Although we do not have a complete Hebrew Enoch manuscript—only fragments, in which to test the veracity of surviving Greek, Geez, and Aramaic manuscripts—the Bible does reference Enoch as a prophet, indicating the likelihood of a lost hagiographic Hebrew manuscript:

---

[79] J. R. Porter, *The New Illustrated Companion to the Bible*, 26.
[80] Desmond Seward, *Jerusalem's Traitor: Josephus, Masada, and the Fall of Ju*dea (Cambridge, MA: DeCapo Press, 2009), 9–14.
[81] Whiston, *New Complete Works of Josephus*, Introduction, 9; *Encyclopedia Americana*, Vol. 16, 218.
[82] Whiston, *New Complete Works of Josephus*, *Jewish Antiquities*, Book 1 3:1.

Jude 1:14 And Enoch also, the seventh from Adam, prophesied of these, saying, Behold, the Lord cometh with ten thousands of his saints.

Jude 1:15 To execute judgment upon all, and to convince all that are ungodly among them of all their ungodly deeds which they have ungodly committed.

Enoch 36:9 And behold! He cometh with ten thousands of His holy ones To execute judgment upon all, And to destroy all the ungodly.[83]

It follows that most Enochian passages have similar consistencies when compared with Scripture, describing the similar events or prophecies. However, one is obligated to recognize and note where the book of Enoch differs from Scripture, such as angels building the ark[84] versus Noah building it. As such, corruptions have occurred in its translations to other languages that ought to compel the reader and researcher not to rely on those deviations, no matter how interesting those deviations might be; rely on the details in First Enoch that match with Scripture, and only additional details provided that are directionally consistent with Scripture. And in this same spirit, *The Catholic Encyclopedia* noted that evil angels were explained as being sons of God (per Genesis 6:1–4) by the book of Enoch in chapters 6–11.[85] Indeed, First Enoch documented four times that the sons/children of God who created giants were angelic beings:

Enoch 69:4–5 The name of the first Jeqon: that is, the one who led astray all the sons of God, and brought them down to the earth, and led them astray through the daughters of men. And the second was named Asbeel: he imparted to the holy sons of God evil counsel and led them astray so that they defiled their bodies with the daughters of men.

Enoch 71:1 And it came to pass after this that my spirit was translated. And it ascended into the heavens: And I saw the holy sons of God. They were stepping on flames of fire: Their garments were white and their raiment, And their faces shone like snow.

[83] R. H. Charles, trans., *The Book of Enoch, I–V Parable of Enoch on the Future Lot of the Wicked and the Righteous.*
[84] *Book of Enoch:* 67:1–2: "1. And in those days the word of God came unto me, and He said unto me: 'Noah, thy lot has come up before Me, a lot without blame, a lot of love and uprightness. 2. And now the angels are making a wooden building, and when they have completed that task I will place My hand upon it and preserve it, and there shall come forth from it the seed of life, and a change shall set in so that the earth will not remain without inhabitant."
[85] *Catholic Encyclopedia,* Vol. 1, 478–479: angels.

Enoch 6:1 And it came to pass when the children of men had multiplied that in those days were born unto them beautiful and comely daughters. And the angels, the children of the heaven, saw and lusted after them, and said to one another: "Come, let us choose us wives from among the children of men and beget us children."

Enoch 15:2–3 And go, say to the Watchers of heaven, who have sent thee to intercede for them: "You should intercede for men, and not men for you: Wherefore have ye left the high, holy, and eternal heaven, and lain with women, and defiled yourselves with the daughters of men and taken to yourselves wives, and done like the children of earth, and begotten giants as your sons?"

CHAPTER 3

NEPHILIM, GIBBORIM, AND REPHAIM

Gen 14:5 And in the fourteenth year came Chedorlaomer, and the kings that were with him, and smote the Rephaims in Ashteroth Karnaim, and the Zuzims in Ham, and the Emims in Shaveh Kiriathaim.

The word "giant" in Genesis 6:4 derives from the Hebrew word *nphiyl,* meaning bully, tyrant, giant, and giants, as in the latter as *Nphiylim*/Nephilim.[86] The word `*im,* when deployed as a suffix, is generally understood as applied to pluralize the root word, and to convey "to be from" and/or as "in ones"—in this case, giant ones.

In antiquity, `*im* was a suffix to communicate the plural male majesty of angels, gods, and their male progeny.[87] Majesty is defined as the greatness of God, gods, lofty, regal, supreme greatness, supreme authority, the royals (roy-els), and

---

[86] *Comprehensive Strong's Dictionary,* H5303—*nphiyl, nef-eel';* from 5307: a feller; a bully; a giant; giants; the Nephilim. H5974—`*im, eem*; Aramaic corresponding to 5973: by; from; like; with; together with by reason of; for all; like; more than; H5973 ⊠*im eem*: in conjunction with.
[87] Frank L. Benz, *Personal Names in the Phoenician and Punic Inscriptions (Rome:* Bible Institute Press, 1972), 267: *Im.*

the titles of monarchs.[88] The `im is an important suffix with respect to description and definition of Nephilim giants recorded in Genesis 6:4, and other eponymously named tribes giant tribes that will become self-evident as this tome unfolds. Further, Ellicott's *An Old Testament Commentary for English Readers* annotated that Nephilim were deemed by some historians of antiquity as beings akin to hairy beasts of "unique size," as recorded in Assyrian cuneiform texts as the *Naptu*.[89]

Nephilim were described in Genesis 6:4 as mighty men; the Hebrew *gibbowr* transliterated as gibborim, meaning strong, brave, powerful, tyrant, and often used in describing giants. One muses whether *gibbowr* is connected to the word "gibberish." Conversely, gibborim does not always mean giant(s), as with David's mighty men as one example.[90] Further, *gibbowr* is only translated once as "giant" (Job 16:15), indicating gibborim may only be a descriptive title versus a distinct race. Similarly, Nephilim were depicted as "men of renown," deriving equally from two Hebrew words: *shem* meaning famous and/or infamous, as dictated by their deeds of reputation, glory, or evil, and from *Shamayim* (singular *shameh*) meaning lofty, sky, heaven, and heavens.[91] Hence, Nephilim giants were powerful, strong tyrants who acquired reputations for glory, fame, and infamy; and Nephilim were of or from the heavenly ones, the fallen angels.

Linking the meaning of "renowned" to the heavenly ones/*Shamayim* helps confirm *nphiyl's* etymological link to the fallen angels. *Nphiyl* derives from the original Semitic verbal stem *Npl* and *Naphal/Napal* meaning causatively to fall, fall down as in prostrate oneself, as deployed in Satan's fall/*naphal* from heaven

---

[88] *Webster's*, 244: majesty; *dictionary.com*: majestic.

[89] Charles John Ellicott, *An Old Testament Commentary for English Readers* (London, Paris, and New York: Cassell, Petter & Galpin & Co, 1882), Vol. 1, 36, Gen 6:4 note 4 giants citing Lenormant, *Origines de l'Histoire*, 344; J. R. Porter, *The New Illustrated Companion to the Bible* (London: Prospero Books, 2003), 26–27.

[90] *Strong's Dictionary*, H1368—*gibbowr, ghib-bore'*: powerful; by implication, warrior; tyrant; champion, chief; excel, giant; man; mighty; strong; valiant man; 158 occurrences. Mighty, 136: Gen 6:4, 10:8–9; Deut 10:17; Josh 1:14; 8:2, 3; 10:2, 7; Jdg 5:13, 23, 6:12; Ruth 2:1; 1 Sam 2:4, 9:1, 16:18; 2 Sam 1:19, 21–22, 25, 27; 10:7; 16:6; 17:8, 10; 23:7, 8, 9, 16, 17, 22; 1 Kings 1:8, 10; 11:28; 2 Kings 5:1; 15:20; 24:14; 1 Chron 1:10; 5:24; 7:7, 9, 11; 8:40; 11:10, 11; 12:1, 4, 21, 25, 28, 30; 19:8; 26:6, 31; 27:6; 28:1; 29:24; 2 Chron 13:3; 14:8; 17:13, 14, 16, 17; 25:6; 26:12; 28:7; 32:3, 21; Ezra 7:28; Neh 3:16, 9:32, 11:14; Ps 24:8; 33:16; 45:3; 52:1; 78:65; 89:19; 112:2; 127:4; Prov 16:32; 21:22; Song 4:4; Isa 3:2; 5:22; 9:6; 10:21; 13:3; 21:17; 42:13; 49:24–25; Jer 5:16; 9:23; 14:9; 20:11; 26:21, 32:18; 46:5–6, 9, 12; 48:14, 41; 49:22; 50:9, 36; 51:30, 56, 57; Ezek 32:12, 21, 27; 39:18, 20; Dan 11:3; Hos 10:13; Joel 2:7; 3:9, 11; Amos 2:14, 16; Oba 1:9; Nah 2:3; Zeph 1:14; 3:17; Zech 9:13; 10:7. Valiant, 6: 1 Chron 7:2, 5; 11:26; 2 Chron 13:3; Song 3:7. Strong, 5: 1 Sam 14:52; 2 Kings 24:16; Ps 19:5; Eccl 9:11; Joel 3:10. Mighties, 2: 1 Chron 11:12, 24. Champion, 1: 1 Sam 17:51. Chief, 1: 1 Chron 9:26. Excel, 1: Ps 103:20. Giant, 1: Job 16:14. Men, 1: 1 Chron 9:13. Mightiest, 1: 1 Chron 11:19. Strongest, 1: Prov 30:30.

[91] Ibid., H8034—*shem, shame*; compare 8064: name; reputation; fame; glory; H8064—*shamayim, shaw-mah'-yim*: dual of an unused singular shameh: heavens.

in Isaiah 14:12.[92] The New Testament cognate word for *naphal* is *pipto,* meaning the same, as well as fall under judgment, condemnation, and cast down just as Jesus describes Satan's fall/*pipto* from heaven in Luke 10:18.[93] One deduces that Nephilim/*Nopelim*/*Nepelim* giants were spawned by the Naphalim/Napalim, the fallen ones described in Genesis 6:2–4 as the sons of God, the infamous fallen and rebellious angels "cast down to hell, and delivered them into chains of darkness, to be reserved unto judgment" (2 Peter 2:4), and part of the third of angels/stars that will be cast from heaven (Rev 12:4).

Immortal angels are described allegorically in the Bible as stars, host of heaven, children of the Most High, and sons of God, noting that son and children derive from the same Hebrew word, *ben*; god (fallen angel) is translated from *'el* meaning, angel, god, God, and mighty ones. `El is also the singular format of *'Elohiym"* for "the God (Most High)" and small case *'elohiym* for the plural format of gods/angels.[94] When referring to the God Most High, a definite article (*ha*) is generally employed using a specific Hebrew letter to represent "the": ה/*ha,* as in *ha 'Elohiym,*[95] the God Most High. It follows that the sons of God in Genesis 6:2–4 was translated from *ben ha 'Elohym.*

> Job 38:7 When the morning stars sang together, and all the sons of God shouted for joy?
>
> Dan 8:10 And it waxed great, even to the host of heaven; and it cast down some of the host and of the stars to the ground, and stamped upon them.

The Jewish Encyclopedia stated with respect to the sons of God in Genesis 6:1–4: "As there stated, the later Jewish and Christian interpreters endeavored to remove the objectionable implications from the passage by taking the term 'bene ha-Elohim' in the sense of 'sons of judges' or 'sons of magistrates.'. .. In the introduction to the Book of Job (i. 6, ii. 1) the 'bene ha-Elohim' are mentioned as assembling

---

[92] H5307—*naphal, naw-fal':* fall, fell; prostrate oneself; Ps 36:12; Ezek 32:23, 24, 27; Dan 8:10; Luke 10:18. Gary Wayne, *The Genesis 6 Conspiracy,* 75, Chapter 11: "The Great Deluge," citing Joseph Blenkinsopp, *The Pentateuch* (New York: Doubleday, 1992).

[93] G4098—*pip'-to:* fall; fell; fall down as in prostrate oneself, and cast down in judgment and condemnation.

[94] H1121—ben, bane: son, sons, children; H410—*'el, ale':* strength; power; mighty; God, angels; false god; God, god-like one, mighty one; mighty men, men of rank; mighty heroes; angels; H430—*'elohiym, el-o-heem':* gods; specifically used in the plural with the article of the supreme God; magistrates; plural for angels, gods, goddesses, divine ones; great, judges, mighty. Gary Wayne, *The Genesis 6 Conspiracy,* 75, Chapter 11: "The Great Deluge," citing Blenkinsopp, *The Pentateuch,* 76.

[95] Jeff A. Benner, *Learn to Read Hebrew: Volume 2* (College Station, TX: Virtualbookworm.com Publishing Inc., 2011), 15–16; H430—*'elohiym, el-o-heem':* gods in the ordinary sense; but specifically used in the plural thus, especially with the article of the supreme God.

at stated periods, Satan being one of them."[96] The reimagining of the sons of God continues today, within the standard dogma of churches teaching that the sons of God were Sethites or prophetically referencing Christians as sons of God.

Another ancient source documented the "sons of God" appellation from ancient Semitic that has been translated into English as it applied the sons of the Canaanite god El, the *bn il(m)* as recorded in the *Ugaritic Texts*. The sons included Baal and the Baalim gods that created the offspring Rephaim/Rapiu giants, the postdiluvian heroes of old known in the *Ugaritic Texts* and throughout the Middle East as "man/men/kings of healing,"[97] all the while noting that King Og of the Bible was a Rephaim/Rapiu that reigned in Edrei and Ashtaroth of Bashan under Mount Hermon[98]:

> 1.2 Bull EI my father [has tak]en [it] from me: I have no house like [the] gods, no dwelling like [the sons of the Holy] Ones. .. in the midst of the ass[emb]ly of the sons of EI.[99]

> 1.17 Then let Danel, the man of heal]ing, at once let the hero, [the devotee of Hrnm] enrobed, feed the gods, [enrobed), give the holy ones [to drink].

> 1.108 R 1 May Rapiu, King of Eternity, drink [wi]ne, yea, may he drink, the powerful and noble [god]" the god enthroned in Athtarat, the god who rules in Edrei.[100]

The heavenly Naphalim appear to be an ancient patronymic source word identifying Watchers who fornicated with daughters of men to beget the various

---

[96] *The Jewish Encyclopedia*, Vol..6, 15: children of ben ha Elohim.

[97] N. Wyatt, *Religious Texts from Ugarit,* 2nd ed. (New York: Continuum International Publishing Group, 2006),, 250–251: KTU 1, i:1–4 note 5: "Danel carries the double epithet mt rpi and mt hrnmy.. .. The most obvious candidate for the former is Rapiu, the god hymned in KTU 1.108, who appears to be the eponym of the rpum (cf. Heb. rpo'; m) who feature in KTU 1.2–1.22 and KTU 1.161." See Parker (1972), de Moor (1976) and Rouillard (1995). Typical of other translations: Driver (1956: 49): 'Rephaite... hrnmy-man'; Caquot and Sznycer (1974: 419): 'man of healing... man of Hamam' (with explanation: 402, that the latter 'probably reveals the name of his capital'); cf. Jirku (1962: 116); Gibson (1978: 103): 'man of Rapiu. .. man of He- of-Hamam'; de Moor (1987: 225 and nn. 5, 6): 'the Saviour's man. ..the Hama- mite man' (explained n. 5, as Danel being a special protege of Baal"; 393 KTU 1108 R:1.

[98] Deut 1:4; 3; Josh 12:5; 13:31.

[99] Wyatt, *Religious Texts from Ugarit,* 54–55, KTU 1.2, iii:15-20 and note 78: "sons of the Holy One denotes El: bn il(m).. and more generally gods"; 96: KTU 1.4 iii:10-15.

[100] Wyatt, *Religious Texts from Ugarit,* 250–251: KTU 1, i:1–4 note 5: "Danel carries the double epithet mt rpi and mt hrnmy.. .. The most obvious candidate for the former is Rapiu, the god hymned in KTU 1.108, who appears to be the eponym of the rpum (cf. Heb. rpo'im) who feature in KTU 1.21.22 and KTU 1.161."

forms of spurious Naphadim known as Giants, Naphil, and the Eljo (also known as the Elioud) in the book of Jubilees:

> Jub 7:21–23. .. the Watchers against the law of their ordinances went a whoring after the daughters of men and took themselves wives of all which they chose: and they made the beginning of uncleanness. And they begat sons the Naphidim, and they were all unlike, and they devoured one another: and the Giants slew the Naphil, and the Naphil slew the Eljo, and the Eljo mankind, and one man another."[101]

The *Ugaritic Texts* recorded several demigod kings, their dynastic bloodlines, and their eponymously named tribes. These demigod kings were described as hero-like healers and "Saviors", the Rpu/Rephaim like Keret and Ditanu/Dedanu that were closely related to the Rapiu/Rephaim who sat in the august assembly of Ditan. The Ditan/Ditanu/Dedanu, spelled *Ddn* in ancient Semitic, and Keret/*Krt*, were "eponymous ancestors for the Ugaritic royal lines" and "a blessing to come and a future Rapiu."[102]

> KTU 1.15.iii.1 [Be greatly exalted] Keret, among the Saviors] of the underworld. [in the convocation of] the assembly of Ditan.

> KTU 1.124.1 When the lord of the great gods came to Ditan, he asked about the diagnosis of the child.

> KTU 1.15.iii.15 Be greatly exalted among the Saviors of the underwo[rld], in the convocation of the assembly of Dit[a]n. Their last one I will treat as their firstborn. The gods blessed him and went away to their tents, the family of El to their dwellings.[103]

Contrarywise, some western occult organizations note that the Nephilim were the Elvin sons of the Anunnagi/Anunnaki/Watchers and human women, whereby the Nephilim thereafter interbred also with human females that produced the Naphidim. The Naphidim were considered half-breeds, part human and part Nephilim or Rephaim, and lesser beings to the Elvin Nephilim/Rephaim,[104] even though the Nephilim would be and should also be described as hybrid beings produced as spurious offspring of fallen angels and humans. One ponders if the

---

[101] R. H. Charles, The Book of Jubilees, from *Apocrypha and Pseudepigrapha of the Old Testament* (Oxford Press, 1913, Kindle Version), 7:21–23.
[102] Wyatt, *Religious Texts from Ugarit*, 210–212, Keret, notes 153, 156, 423, Ditanu, notes 1, 2, 3, 4, 5, 6; 432–434, KTU 1.61.R.1-R.10 for assembly of Didan and note 12: Ditanu eponymous ancestor, note 19 and 21: rpum; 473 the Ditanu: RS.24.272 and UF 16. 251–255.
[103] Wyatt, *Religious Texts from Ugarit*, 210–212.
[104] De Vere, *The Dragon Legacy*, 101.

occult rendering Naphadim hybrids were named as such to honor their genealogical godfathers via the Nephilim and Rephaim, also known as the Naphadim in the book of Jubilees.

Keeping these terms in mind, know that "giant(s)" only derives from *nphiyl* three times in the Old Testament: Genesis 6:4, and two times in Numbers 13:33. "Giant" derives from *gibbowr* one time in Job 16:14. More importantly, the KJV translates "giant(s)" twenty-five times from *Rapha'*, meaning an invigorating giant, tribe of giants, and the plural format of Rephaim.[105] *Rapha'*, as in an invigorating giant, derives from another word, *rapha'*, defined as to cure, physician, and heal.[106] Invigorating is defined by *Webster's* as: to add vigor as in to animate, to strengthen, to add physical force, and to reenergize, and derives from Latin *vigor,* meaning to be strong.[107] One deduces that the Rephaim possessed powers to heal their bodies, reenergize and reinvigorate themselves, and perhaps heal others as documented in the *Ugaritic Texts.*

In most cases, as Ellicott's *Old Testament Commentary* stated, "the word [Rephaim] is wrongly translated giants, suggesting Rapha or Rephaim, and thus Nephilim ought to have been translated literally. From this wide dispersion of the Rephaim, we may safely conclude that they belonged to the earlier settlers in the land,"[108] before the Canaanites and Amorites. Ellicott suggests *Rapha* and Rephaim ought to have translated directly from Hebrew, as it is spelled in Hebrew, and not as "giant," even though the words are defined as giant(s). According to *The Jewish Encyclopedia* the "'Refa'im' (V.'Rephaim'), [was] a collective appellation for the pre-Canaanite population settled both east and west of the Jordan and described as of immense height (Deut. iii. 11; II Sam. xxi. 16-21); the singular occurs as 'rafah' (with the definite article, 'the giant'; II Sam. xxi. 16, 18, 20, 22) or 'rafa' (I Chron. xx. 4, 6, 8)."[109]

What is fascinating to me about *nphiyl's* two Hebrew applications translated as "giants" in Numbers 13:33 is that the antediluvian Nephilim were known and well understood by the Israelites in the Exodus narrative, well after the flood. Further, the two applications for *nphiyl* in the book of Numbers were included in the evil report portion by the ten terror-stricken scouts of the twelve sent into the Covenant Land. The intent of the evil report was to terrify all Israel to the core and drive fear for their continued earthly existence, all to dissuade Israelites from entering

---

[105] H7497—*rapha', raw-faw'*: an invigorating giant; giants/Rephaim; tribe of giants. Total KJV occurrences: 25: Giants, 10: Deut 2:11, 20; 3:11, 13; Josh 12:4; 13:12; 15:8; 18:15-16. Giant, 7: 2 Sam 21:16, 18, 20; 2 Sam 21:22; 1 Chron 20:4, 6, 8. Rephaim, 6: 2 Sam 5:18, 22; 23:13; 1 Chron 11:15; 14:9; Isa 17:5. Rephaims, 2: Gen 14:5; 15:20.

[106] H7495—*rapha', raw-faw'*: to mend; to cure or heal; physician; repair.

[107] *Webster's*, 217: invigorate; 456: vigor.

[108] Charles Ellicott, *An Old Testament Commentary for English Readers*, Vol. 1, 63–64: Rephaim.

[109] *The Jewish Encyclopedia*, Vol. 5, 656: giants.

the land God promised to them. The terror-stricken scouts wanted Israel to reject the optimistic and accurate report attested by Joshua and Caleb—scouts whose faith was firmly set in God and His promises. The embellished report worked. The terror-stricken scouts funneled fear and foreboding throughout the ranks of Israel, so much so that God opted to divert Israel through the desert for forty years, to forge the faith that would be required to conquer the Covenant Land.

Although the embellishment in the evil report was designed to scare Israel from carrying out God's commands, the evil report did reveal Israel's collective awareness and belief in the veracity of the antediluvian giants documented in Genesis 6:4—their great size and their warrior capabilities as mighty ones of renown. Thus, the terror-stricken scouts referred to the tribes occupying Canaan as "men of great stature." Stature/*middah* means of a great height and/or width, size, or measured proportions,[110] just as *Webster's Dictionary* defines a giant as huge, and a person of abnormally great stature, and anything above the usual size of its kind.[111] By inference and implication, then, we learn that the antediluvian giants were much larger than the postdiluvian giants—so much so that the fear-stricken scouts added that they were as grasshoppers in sight of the alleged Nephilim, embellishments of the size of the postdiluvian Anakim giants cited in the accurate report by Joshua and Caleb. The Anakim in the evil report were stated to be the sons of Nephilim, with the intent to deceive Israel, rather than as sons of the Anakim, a smaller kind of giant that were the Rephaim as stated in the accurate report.

> Num 13:33 And there we saw the giants, the sons of Anak, which come of the giants: and we were in our own sight as grasshoppers, and so we were in their sight.

Conversely, however, one ought not to summarily dismiss the embellishment of the sons of Anak. Joshua and Caleb reported accurately to Moses and Israel, just before the evil report, that indeed they saw the children of Anak (Num 13:28)—not the children of Nephilim, as documented in Numbers 13:22.

> Num 13:28 Nevertheless the people be strong that dwell in the land, and the cities are walled, and very great: and moreover we saw the children of Anak there.

> Num 13:22 And they ascended by the south, and came unto Hebron; where Ahiman, Sheshai, and Talmai, the children of Anak.

---

[110] Num 13:32; H4060—*middah, mid-daw'*: an extension as in height and width: measurement; measured portion; stature; size, garment.

[111] *Webster's*, 171: giant: from Old French *geant* and Greek *gigas*.

The Anak/ʿAnaq, known variantly in Scripture as Anakim/ʿAnaqiy in Deuteronomy 2:10 and 21, is defined as a tribe of giants,[112] but not Nephilim giants. As stated above, the word "giants" in Deuteronomy 2 is translated from Rapha/Rephaim. Anakim were a branch of postdiluvian giants like the Emim and other giant tribes, giants feared throughout the region even though they were not specifically Nephilim.

Hence, Rephaim giants were seemingly smaller than Nephilim based upon the evil report, whereas the Anakim were embellished to Nephilim status to create fear. It follows then that Rephaim were distinct from Nephilim giants. By extension, then, if Nephilim did not survive the flood, and Rephaim were not documented biblically before the flood but populated the earth after the flood, it follows that Rephaim were procreated after the flood by fallen angels in a Second Incursion, by offspring gods of the Baalim. Nephilim were not documented biblically after the flood that tends to indicate from a biblical perspective that the antediluvian giants died in the flood.

> Deut 2:10 The Emims dwelt therein in times past, a people great, and many, and tall, as the Anakims;
>
> Deut 2:11 Which also were accounted giants, as the Anakims; but the Moabites call them Emims.

One would be advised not to dismiss the Anakim as not being giants, even though they were smaller than antediluvian Nephilim. In fact, Josephus classified the people at Hebron were the indeed posterity of giants,[113] and Rephaim by implication. Jewish legends recorded by Louis Ginzberg additionally recorded the Jewish people of old understood the Anakim were giants. In fact, the sight and enormous size of the three Anakim struck terror into the hearts of the scouts, and that Ahiman was the strongest of the three. "Not only were the sons of Anak were of such great strength and size, but his daughters also, whom the spies chanced to see."[114] The Moses in the wilderness legend goes on to note the city of the giants was Kiriatharba, the city of four giants; that the fourth giant was named Arba and the father Ahiman, Sheshai, and Talmai,[115] noting *arba*ʿ is defined as four.[116] The postdiluvian Anakim giants in Jewish legend were believed by Israelites to be offspring of fallen angels (and thus a Second Incursion), half-human and half-angelic whose mortal half, their bodies, withered away with time,[117] but not their spirits.

Forty years later when Israel was about to cross the Jordan River and into the Covenant Land, Moses reminded Israelites that the Anakim lived among the

---

[112] H6060—ʿanaq, aw-nawk'; H6062—ʿAnaqiy, an-aw-kee'.
[113] Whiston, *Josephus, Jewish Antiquities,* Book 3, 14:2.
[114] Louis Ginzberg, *Legends of the Bible,* 430.
[115] Ibid.
[116] H702—'arbaʿ, ar-bah': four; fourteen; forty.
[117] *Catholic Encyclopedia,* Vol. 6, 184: Hebron. Ginzberg, *Legends of the Bible,* 431.

people of Canaan, and yet another people who were also taller than the Israelites but smaller than the Anakim Rephaim. The smaller giants descended from Canaan, people like the Amorites that the Naphadim occult sources accredit for the emergence of human and Rephaim hybrids.

> Deut 1:28 The people is greater and taller than we; the cities are great and walled up to heaven; and moreover we have seen the sons of the Anakims there.

Moses reminded the Israelites that the Anakim were a powerful military nation, with fortress city-states protected with great walls up to heaven. Israelites were reminded that the children of Anak were great, tall, renowned for their warrior prowess, and rhetorically asked, "who can stand before the children of Anak!"[118] Further, Joshua confirmed during the conquest of the Covenant Land that the Anakim dwelled throughout Canaan at the time of the report. Indeed, Joshua fought against these giants in the conquest wars, which we will cover in subsequent chapters.

> Josh 14:12 Now therefore give me this mountain, whereof the LORD spake in that day; for thou heardest in that day how the Anakims were there, and that the cities were great and fenced: if so be the LORD will be with me, then I shall be able to drive them out, as the LORD said.
>
> Josh 14:13 And Joshua blessed him, and gave unto Caleb the son of Jephunneh Hebron for an inheritance.

---

[118] Deut 9:1–2.

CHAPTER 4

DEMONS, DEVILS, AND UNCLEAN SPIRITS

Rev 18:2 And he cried mightily with a strong voice, saying, Babylon the great is fallen, is fallen, and is become the habitation of devils, and the hold of every foul spirit.

The New Testament recorded jarring incidents regarding devils/demons,[119] evil spirits, and foul spirits, including associations between, Babylon, Antichrist, and the False Prophet. Classifying demons as distinct inferior beings from angels, fallen or loyal, but directly connected to fallen angels is important to discern prehistory, ancient history, and what is to come.

Determining where demons derive, and where demons are placed within the fallen angelic hierarchy, is another key for comprehending prehistory and prophecy. As such, Revelation 18:2 is a startling passage, but enlightening with its connection to the demon habitation documented as the hold/*foolakay'*, of unclean spirits, hateful spirits, and birds. *Foolakay'* is defined as a guarding, a watch of

---

[119] Rev 9:21; 16:13–14; 18:2; G1140—*dahee-mon'-ee-on*: devils: 41 times; devil 18 times; god: 1 time.

guards, a prison, and a cage,[120] indicating that the end-time Babylon prophecy has an eery affiliation with demons, with Watcher angels,[121] and specifically with the fallen angels described as the sons of God in Genesis 6:1–4. Revelation's imagery of rebellious angelic beings cohabitating in Babylon at the time of its destruction is reminiscent of the strange end-time beings detailed in the book of Isaiah. Beings like the dancing satyrs, wild doleful creatures, owls, and dragons are described at the time of Babylon's destruction, and again at the time of Armageddon with satyrs, dragons, screech owls, ravens, unicorns, and other wild beasts.[122] One might want to reconcile the Isaiah 13 and 34 passages with the release of fallen angels and demons from the abyss just before the midpoint of the last seven years, followed by the angelic war in heaven in the book of Revelation.[123]

The book of Colossians states that the firstborn of every creation of all creatures,[124] as in sentient beings, possess the image/likeness[125] of the invisible God who is Spirit.[126] Sentient beings of God's creation who possess the likeness of God's Spirit include angels and humans. As such, counterfeited spirits passed on from fallen angels to their spurious offspring, in the firstborn generation of giants both before and after the flood, would not possess an original image of God. Moreover, the original likeness of God's Spirit in the sinful fallen angels manifested corrupted counterfeit spirits, which surfaced in and outside of biblical documentation as disembodied demon spirits of the giants. Accordingly, demons ought to be recognized as part of the categories of beings listed in the book of Colossians, and as part of the fallen angelic hierarchy that reins over this world. Demons ought to be identified as distinct devil-like being within the fallen angelic hierarchy.

> Col 1:15 Who is the image of the invisible God, the firstborn of every creature:
>
> Col 1:16 For by him were all things created, that are in heaven, and that are in earth, visible and invisible, whether they be thrones, or dominions, or principalities, or powers: all things were created by him, and for him.

---

[120] G5438—*foo-lak-ay*: the act of guarding; cage; prison; ward; watch; a watch of guards; keep watch; sentinels; guard(s); transliterated: phulake.
[121] Dan 4:12, 13, 23, 17.
[122] Isa 13:20–22; 34:7–14.
[123] Rev 9:1–9; 12:7–18.
[124] G2937—*ktis'-is*: creation; anything created; created beings; creature; ordinance; building; transliterated: ktisis.
[125] Gen 1:27; G1504—*i-kone'*: a likeness; a profile; a representation; resemblance; an image; transliterated: eikon.
[126] Ps 139:7; John 4:24; 1 Cor 2:12; 2 Cor 3:17.

In Colossians 1:16, principalities were listed after dominions. The principalities/*arkhay*' group of angelic beings holds clues to the distinct demonic spirit, which was embedded into its meaning defined as: in the beginning, leaders, rulers, magistracy, powers, and as the "magistracy of angels and demons."[127] Note how angels are defined as distinct from demons in the definition. Magistracy is understood as a position of dignity, but a lower position in the government or hierarchy.[128] The meaning of "principality," with all its various meanings, opens the door to comprehending demons as distinct beings from angel, a lower branch of terrible creatures who report to specific orders of fallen angels, and a distinct spirit from humans.

The difficulty in discerning who and what demons are in English-speaking nations stems from an ongoing English translation issue. In translating Scripture into English from the original Hebrew and Greek, translators in error—or possibly purposefully—conflated and confused demonic spirits and unclean spirits with other angelic beings, and the devil, Satan, in their translations. Thus, unclean spirits documented in the Old and New Testaments are a good place to begin revealing demons' distinct lower-level and rebellious deity-like entities. The book of Zechariah details an end-time prophecy for Israel and Judah that will occur as the millennial reign of Jesus begins—after second exodus and after Armageddon. This is a prophesied time when idols will be cast out of the Covenant Land, a time when unclean spirits will pass out of the land at God's command.[129] "Spirit" in the Old Testament derives from *ruwach*, a word that also has many applications: the Spirit of God; the spirit of humans; the spirit of animals; the spirit of angels; the spirit of a disembodied beings; breath, wind, mind.[130] Note the disembodied beings as a definition.

The question then becomes: Is the book of Zechariah referring to a fallen angel spirit when it cites an unclean spirit? A fallen angel or a demon qualifies as an unclean/*tum'a* spirit, noting that unclean is defined as impure, polluted, corrupted, defiled sexually, defiled ritually defiled, and defiled in a moral sense.[131]

---

[127] G746—*ar-khay*': a commencement; a chief; beginning; corner; from the first estate as in Jude 1:6; magistrate; power; principality; principle; rule; and "magistracy of angels and demons"; transliterated: arche.

[128] *Webster's*, 243: magisterial.

[129] Zech 13:2–3.

[130] H7307—*ruwach, roo'-akh*: wind; air; breath; mind; life; spirit of the living; breath in man and animals; a gift preserved by God as in God's spirit; disembodied being; the Spirit of God, the Holy Spirit.

[131] Unclean: H2932—*tum'a; toom-aw'*: religious impurity; filthiness; uncleanness as in sexually, ethically, ritually, and religiously; H2930—*tame', taw-may'*: to be foul in a ceremonial or moral sense; contaminate; defiling of oneself by idolatry; ceremonially; sexually; religiously; to profane God or His name.

Unclean spirit beings are evil spirits, and part of the fallen hierarchy of which both fallen angels and demons are part of.

> Zech 13:2 In that day, saith the Lord of hosts, that I will cut off the names of the idols out of the land, and they shall no more be remembered: and also I will cause the prophets and the unclean spirit to pass out of the land.

Similarly in the New Testament, spirit/*pnyoo'mah* is cognate to *ruwach* but adds daemon/demon and ghost as part of the kinds of spirits.[132] Hence, the four kinds of sentient spirit of beings outside of the Triune Beings include a demon/daemon, a disembodied spirit that is distinct from fallen angels and reports up to angels in the hierarchy. It follows that if demons are distinct spirits from angels, then one deduces Scripture would supply the source for when and how demon spirits were created, just as Scripture supplies passages detailing angelic creation by God.[133]

An unclean/*tum'a/tame'* spirit is an important description to discern the source of demons. The unclean spirits described in the Zechariah 13 passage appear to be akin to disembodied spirits no longer able to fashion physical bodies, unlike angels who can still take a physical form. Many believe demons are the disembodied Nephilim or Rephaim spirits, and the best fit for the evil spirits not permitted to sleep or enter heaven, recorded in the book of Enoch.[134] Additionally, "passengers," "passing," and "'pass" "through the land" recorded in Ezekiel 39's Gog war were translated from `*abar,* a word associated with death for "passengers" who pass between the underworld/*sheowl* and earth,[135] and who are often associated with Rephaim.

Keeping the above in mind, the scriptural accounting for demon spirits begins in the Nephilim creation narrative of Genesis 6:1–4. The origination of the counterfeit demon spirit is the corrupted spirit of fallen angels who passed on a counterfeit spirit into the physical world via physical copulation with human females to produce spurious offspring. This illegal union of heavenly immortal spirit with a mortal physical human and their spirit is part of the immoral and sexually impure spirit definition of unclean and unclean spirits. Impure, unclean, counterfeit

---

[132] G4151—*pnyoo'-mah*: a current of air; breath; a breeze or wind; a spirit as in human; an angel; a daemon; a ghost; life; mind; God as Spirit; Christ's Spirit; the Holy Spirit.

[133] Ps 104:4; 148:1–5; Col 1:15–17.

[134] Enoch 15:6-12.

[135] Job 34:20–22; Ezek 39:11, 14, 15; H5674—`*abar, aw-bar*`: to cross over; to cover in copulation; alienate, alter; bring over, through; carry over; come over; convey over; deliver; do away; enter; escape; get over; pass over; pass on; to pass away; to dedicate; to devote; pass over; pass away; to emigrate; to leave one's place.

spirits seem to be the spirits created not of God, but of fallen angels that became corrupted through rebellion and sexual sins. This distinction is this: some angels became corrupted, as opposed to counterfeit spirits that were created unclean like the Nephilim and Rephaim spirits.

God's reaction to His Spirit being illegally reproduced in the physical world to produce demigod physical beings—angelic-human hybrids, whose creation transformed mortal flesh into a kind of immortal body and soul that could hold the counterfeit immortal spirit—was dealt with swiftly by the God Most High. Within the four-verse Nephilim creation narrative, God limited the life span of all flesh beginning in verse 3, and immediately after the sons of God in verse 3 had taken as many human wives as they had chosen in verse 2:

> Gen 6:3 And the LORD said, My spirit shall not always strive with man, for that he also is flesh: yet his days shall be an hundred and twenty years.

Josephus concurred, and penned in his tome on Israel's history that the lifespan of the giants was reduced to 120 years, and understood as such in Judaic society, just as Genesis 6:3 states. Josephus indicated the shortened lifespans affected the giants after the flood (whether they survived or were recreated). He cited additional sources from the book of Enoch, *Authentic Writings,* to support this doctrine and asserted the Genesis 6:3 edict took several generations to come into full effect through postdiluvian giants. Josephus indicated that the lifespan reduction affected Noah's descendants after the flood as well, and in a similar manner, whereby subsequent lifespans reduced until the generation of Moses.[136] One can follow the declining age of Noah's descendants through the Shemites and Abraham's descendants. One muses whether Josephus had access to a Hebrew manuscript for the book of Enoch earlier in his life, because his reference does not appear in surviving Enoch translations. From whichever language the book of Enoch was written in that Josephus read and referenced, he testified to the creation

---

[136] Josephus, *Ant.*, book 1, 3:1, note 12, citing the fragment of Enoch, sect. 10, citing *Authentic Records.* Part I, 268: "Josephus here supposes that the life of these giants, for of them only do I understand him, was now reduced to 120 years; which is confirmed by the fragment of Enoch, sect. 10, in Authent. Rec. Part I. p. 268. For as to the rest of mankind, Josephus himself confesses their lives were much longer than 120 years, for many generations after the flood, as we shall see presently; and he says they were gradually shortened till the days of Moses, and then fixed [for some time] at 120, ch. 6. sect. 5. Nor indeed need we suppose that either Enoch or Josephus meant to interpret these 120 years for the life of men before the flood, to be different from the 120 years of God's patience [perhaps while the ark was preparing] till the deluge; which I take to be the meaning of God when he threatened this wicked world, that if they so long continued impenitent, their days should be no more than 120 years]."

of giants, the evil and unclean acts of the giants, and reduction of their life span to 120 years as such:

1. ... For many angels of God accompanied with women, and begat sons that proved unjust, and despisers of all that was good, on account of the confidence they had in their own strength; for the tradition is, that these men did what resembled the acts of those whom the Grecians call giants. But Noah was very uneasy at what they did; and being displeased at their conduct, persuaded them to change their dispositions and their acts for the better: but seeing they did not yield to him, but were slaves to their wicked pleasures, he was afraid they would kill him, together with his wife and children, and those they had married; so he departed out of that land.

2. Now God loved this man for his righteousness: yet he not only condemned those other men for their wickedness, but determined to destroy the whole race of mankind, and to make another race that should be pure from wickedness; and cutting short their lives, and making their years not so many as they formerly lived, but one hundred and twenty only.[137]

Genesis 6:5–7 describes a manifest of consequences that followed the creation of Nephilim, followed thereafter by the flood as a reprieve and restart to ensure all names written in the Book of Life from before creation[138] would have an opportunity to choose God. Hence, Noah and his sons were reintroduced as part of the flood narrative previously recorded in the genealogies of Genesis 5:32, and again after Genesis 6:4. Noah found grace from God because of his righteousness and purity. One deduces that Noah and his sons selected wives accordingly to repopulate the earth.

With all this in mind, a study of Genesis 6:3's Hebrew accounting verifies Josephus' assertion. First, God said/*'amar* (avowed, appointed, commanded)[139] His Spirit/*Ruwach* would not always/*'owlam* (forever, eternity, everlasting)[140]

---

[137] Josephus, *Ant.*, book 1, 3:1–2.

[138] Dan 12:1; Rev 3:5, 13:8; 17:8; 20:12, 15; 21:27; 22:19.

[139] H559–*'amar, aw-mar'*: to say; answer; appoint; avouch; bid; boast self; call; certify; challenge; charge; command; declare; demand; desire; determine; expressly; promise; publish; report; speak.

[140] H5769–*'owlam, o-lawm'*: the vanishing point; time out of mind, eternity; always: ancient time; anymore; eternal; everlasting; long time; of old time; perpetual; at any time; beginning of the; world without end.

strive (contend, govern, or judge)[141] with man/adam[142] for he is flesh (jointly from basar *and shagag:* body, mankind, skin; and sinful, go astray, and deceived),[143] and that his days will be 120 years. I would submit that nowhere does this passage in Hebrew or English infer Noah's commission was 120 years, as some assert. I further submit that Genesis 6:2 is evidently God's response to the violations and consequences to angels taking human wives that produced human/angelic hybrids described in 6:4; that God avowed and then commanded that His eternal Spirit would not contend within human or human hybrid bodies forever, because both were flesh in the physical world. Ergo, the counterfeit spirit in Nephilim was unclean in its creation, and that spirit was further corrupted by the flesh and soul by the corrupted world governed by fallen angels. Thus, the days/*yowm* (a space of time, years, lifetime) were 120 years.

> Gen 6:3 And the LORD said, My spirit shall not always strive with man, for that he also is flesh: yet his days shall be an hundred and twenty years.

Pertinent to discerning the distinction between demonic spirits and human spirits, the Bible states more than a hundred times that humans sleep when they die, while our spirits return to heaven.[144] "Sleep" is a term often utilized in the coming of Jesus for rapture and the resurrections in the end-time prophecies.[145] On the other hand, the counterfeit spirit of Nephilim and Rephaim does not sleep when their body/flesh dies, and as per God's edict the counterfeit spirit was then released from its former body, but was not permitted to go to heaven. Only Satan of the corrupted spirits, angelic or demonic, is permitted access to heaven to present himself and accuse Adamites[146] for a short while longer. Counterfeit unclean spirits are permitted for a time to pass over/ `abar into the underworld, roam the earth, and usurp vulnerable humans by possession.

Unclean counterfeit spirits are the same evil spirits who—except when they come face to face with Jesus—deny Jesus as the Christ, deny Him as the One

---

[141] H1777—*duwn*, doon: a straight course; judge; plead the cause; contend; govern; strive.

[142] H120—*'adam, aw-dawm'*; from 119: ruddy; red; a human being; an individual; the species, mankind; low man; a low degree person; city in Jordan valley H119—*'adam, aw-dam'*: to show blood in the face; flush or turn rosy; red as in ruddy; to glare; to look red.

[143] H1320–*basar, baw-sawr'*: flesh; body; person; mankind; skin; H7683—*shagag, shaw-gag'*: to stray; sin; deceived; err; go astray; sin ignorantly.

[144] Exod 12:7.

[145] Examples: Deut 31:16; 2 Sam 7:12; 1 Kings 11:43; 14:20; 16:6; 22:50; 2 Kings 2:10; 15:7; Job 7:21; 14:10–12; Ps 13:3; Dan 12:2; Matt 9:24, Mark 5:39; Luke 8:52; John 11:11-14; 1 Cor 15:6, 18; 1 Thess 4:13–16.

[146] Job 1:6–7; 2:1–2.

who came in the flesh, and deny Him as the One who came from God. These evil spirits are antichrist-like spirit(s) that have haunted the world, endeavoring to bring about the Antichrist via the beast empires. Antichrist spirits are not angelic but demonic. Counterfeit spirits did not come directly "of God" and were not created in the likeness of or by God. Demon spirits were created in the image and likeness of self-corrupted fallen angels, who manipulate their demonic offspring (and humans) to slander God. Knowing this makes sense of Michael, the righteous archangel who fights against the beast empires not from rising and reigning, but to ensure that the antichrist spirit does not come to power through the beast empires until the ordained time—the midpoint of the last seven years. Thereafter Michael fights against Satan and Antichrist in the war in heaven.[147]

> 1 John 2:18 Little children, it is the last time: and as ye have heard that antichrist shall come, even now are there many antichrists; whereby we know that it is the last time.

> 1 John 4:2 Every spirit that confesseth that Jesus Christ is come in the flesh is of God:

> 1 John 4:3 And every spirit that confesseth not that Jesus Christ is come in the flesh is not of God: and this is that spirit of antichrist, whereof ye have heard that it should come; and even now already is it in the world.

Unclean spirit(s) in the New Testament are often translated as "devil(s)." These devils ought to be translated as "demons" to ensure they are not confused with Satan or Satans. "Unclean devil(s)" is translated from a series of four related words rooted in *dah'eemown*,[148] defined as a daemon [demon], a supernatural spirit of a bad nature, an inferior deity [demigod], and an evil spirit.[149]

---

[147] Dan 8:10, 11, 13, 20, 21; 12:1; Rev 12:7–9. See also: 1 John 2:22: "Who is a liar but he that denieth that Jesus is the Christ? He is antichrist, that denieth the Father and the Son"; 2 John 1:7: "For many deceivers are entered into the world, who confess not that Jesus Christ is come in the flesh. This is a deceiver and an antichrist."

[148] G1139—*daheemonid'-zom-ahee*. Devil: Matt 9:32; 15:22; Mark 5:15, 16, 18; John 10:21. Devils: Matt 4:24; 8:16, 28, 33; Mark 1:32; Luke 8:36. Vexed: Matt 15:22; G1140—*daheemon'eeon*. Devils: Matt 7:22; 9:34; 10:8; 12:24, 27, 28; Mark 1:34, 39; 3:15, 22; 6:13; 9:38; 16:9, 17; Luke 4:41; 8:2, 27, 30, 33, 35, 38; 9:1, 49; 10:17; 11:15, 18, 19, 20; 13:32; 1 Cor 10:20, 21; 1 Tim 4:1; Rev 9:19, 20. Devil: Matt 9:33; 17:18; Mark 7:26, 29, 30; Luke 4:33, 35; 7:33; 9:42; 11:14; John 7:20; 8:48, 49, 52; 10:20, 21. Gods: Acts 17:18; G1141—*daheemoneeo'-dace*. Devilish, James 3:15; G1142—*dah'eemown*. Devils: Matt 8:31; Mark 5:12; Rev 16:14; 18:2. Devil: Luke 8:29.

[149] G1142—*dah'ee-mown*; a daemon; supernatural spirit of a bad nature: devil; an inferior god or goddess; and an evil spirit; transliterated: daimon.

The translation of "devil" versus "demon" many times in the KJV is confusing and misleading because this spirit/devil/demon is an inferior deity that ought not to be conflated with the devil, Satan. Devil/*deeab'olos* is defined as Satan the false accuser, devil, author of evil, *ha Satan* in Hebrew, and the prince of demons who commands them to afflict humans with diseases and to possess humans.[150] Satan is the ultimate leader over demons, but demons are not angelic beings. Understanding the devil in the KJV New Testament requires knowing which Greek word "devil" is translated from. For example, "devil" in Matthew 4 and Ephesians 6 derives from *deeab'olos*.

> Matt 4:1 Then was Jesus led up of the Spirit into the wilderness to be tempted of the devil.

> Eph 6:11 Put on the whole armor of God, that ye may be able to stand against the wiles of the devil.

Additionally, demon/*daheemonid'* is another Greek source word for devil(s)[151] and a word that is translated into English for possessed and vexed.[152] As such, demons are disembodied spirits of giants like Legion, devils/*dah'eemown*, who possess and afflict humans.[153] It follows that possessing devil-demons are alternatively described as unclean spirits in Matthew 10, Mark 3, and elsewhere in the New Testament,[154] and that Jesus and the disciples cast demons out of humans. As such, "unclean spirits" and "devils" are interchangeable terms. "Unclean" in the New Testament derives from *akath'artos* meaning impure, foul, and demonic;[155] as in disembodied giant spirits commanded by Satan to afflict and destroy Adamites.

> Matt 4:24 And his fame went throughout all Syria: and they brought unto him all sick people that were taken with divers

---

[150] G1228—*dee-ab'-ol-os*: a traducer: Satan as in Hebrew; H7854—*Satan*: false accuser; devil; slanderer; Satan the prince of the demons; author of evil; transliterated: diabolos: the author of evil, afflicting them with diseases by means of demons who take possession of their bodies at his bidding. Matt 4:1, 5, 8, 11; 13:39; 25:41; Luke 4:2–3, 5–6, 13; 8:12; John 6:70; 8:44; 13:2; Acts 10:38; 13:10; Eph 4:27; 6:11; 1 Tim 3:6–7; 2 Tim 2:26; Heb 2:14; James 4:7; 1 John 3:8, 10; Rev 2:9-10; 12:9, 12; 20:2, 10.

[151] Matt 9:32; 15:22; Mark 5:15, 16, 18; John 10:21; Devils: Matt 4:24; 8:16, 28, 33; Mark 1:32; Luke 8:36.

[152] Matt 4:24; 8:16, 28, 33; 9:32; 12:22; Mark 1:32; 5:15, 16, 18. Vexed: Matt 15:22.

[153] Mat 8:29–30; Mark 5:9, 15; Luke 8:30.

[154] See also Matt 10:1; 12:43; Mark 5:2, 8, 13; 6:7. 7:25; Luke 4:36; 6:18; 8:29; 9:42; 11:24; Acts 5:16; 8:7; Rev 16:13; 18:2.

[155] G169—*ak-ath'-ar-tos*: cleansed; impure; daemonic; foul; ceremonial unclean; transliterated: akathartos.

diseases and torments, and those which were possessed with devils, and those which were lunatick, and those that had the palsy; and he healed them.

Matt 10:1 He gave them power against unclean spirits, to cast them out.

Mark 3:11 And unclean spirits, when they saw him, fell down before him, and cried, saying, Thou art the Son of God.

Devil/*dah'eemown* was directly connected to unclean/*akath'artos* spirits in several passages[156] including Luke 9:42: "And as he was yet a coming, the devil threw him down, and tare him. And Jesus rebuked the unclean spirit, and healed the child, and delivered him again to his father." Other passages in the New Testament connect devils/*daheemonid'* that possessed humans to spirits that make people sick;[157] devils/*dah'eemown* with evil spirits;[158] devils/*dah'eemown* with unclean spirits.[159] And in the book of 1 Timothy, seducing/*plan'os* spirits and devils/*dah'eemown* were connected as working together and prophesying to deceive humankind. Seducing/*plan'os* is defined as roving deceiving and impostor spirits,[160] spirits of fallen angels posing as gods.

1 Tim 4:1 Now the Spirit speaketh expressly, that in the latter times some shall depart from the faith, giving heed to seducing spirits, and doctrines of devils.

The same kind and cognate demon/devil spirit appeared in the Old Testament with the evil/*ra`*[161] spirit/*ruwach* that troubled King Saul,[162] an evil spirit that David later removed for Saul with the use of a harp. This evil spirit was not a fallen angel, but distinct evil spirit akin to familiar spirits discussed elsewhere in the Old Testament. Familiar spirits/*'owb*, meaning ghost, spirit of the dead, and mumbler was also discussed in the Old Testament in conjunction with necromancers, wizards, and charmers, who worshipped and contacted these deceiving spirits.[163] One

---

[156] See also Rev 18:2: *foul/akath'artos* used with devils.

[157] Matt 8:16.

[158] Luke 8:2.

[159] Luke 4:33, 36.

[160] G4108—*plan'-os*: roving; an impostor; misleader; deceive; seducer; transliterated: planos.

[161] H7451—*ra`, rah*: bad or evil; adversity, affliction; malignant; wicked; calamity; 1 Sam 16:14–16, 23.

[162] H1204—*ba`ath, baw-ath'*: to fear; frighten; terrify; troubled; a terror; transliterated: ba`ath.

[163] H178—*'owb, obe*: a mumble from its hollow sound; a necromancer; ventriloquist as from a jar or bottle; a familiar spirit; one who evokes the dead; ghost; spirit of a dead one. Familiar Spirit: Lev 19:31; 20:6; Deut 18:11; 1 Sam 28:3, 9; 2 Kings 21:6; 23:24; Isa 8:19; 19:3. Spirit: Lev 20:27; 1 Sam 28:7, 8; 1 Chron 10:13; 2 Chron 33:6; Isa 29:4.

once more ponders the connection between mumbling spirits and unknown languages, gibber, and the Indo-Aryan languages of the gibborim/mighty Nephilim and Rephaim.

> Lev 20:27 A man also or woman that hath a familiar spirit, or that is a wizard, shall surely be put to death: they shall stone them with stones: their blood shall be upon them.

> Isa 8:19 And when they shall say unto you, Seek unto them that have familiar spirits, and unto wizards that peep, and that mutter: should not a people seek unto their God? for the living to the dead?

These verses make sense of what Jesus stated about unclean spirit-demons that always look to possess bodies. They roam the earth in dry places thirsting for places of rest, but can only find rest in humans, and can only interact physically with the physical world when they usurp a soul and body, a dwelling place to house their wandering spirit.

> Matt 12:43 When the unclean spirit is gone out of a man, he walketh through dry places, seeking rest, and findeth none.....

> Mat 12:45 Then goeth he, and taketh with himself seven other spirits more wicked than himself, and they enter in and dwell there: and the last state of that man is worse than the first.

Rephaim/*Rapha'*, meaning an invigorating giant and a tribe of giants, derived from *rapha'*, meaning healer and physician. Similarly, another *rapha'* word directly linked to and part of the Rephaim understanding derives from the same Hebrew source word for giant/*rapha'*, a word defined as spirits of the dead, ghosts, shades, and depicted as "dead" Rephaim kings imprisoned in the sides of the pit prison in hell/*Sh'eowl* in Isaiah 14 and Ezekiel 32.[164] Further, evil/*shed/shedim* devils were documented in Psalm 106:37 and Deuteronomy 32:17: *doemons* to which some Israelites worshipped and sacrificed their sons and daughters.[165]

As anecdotal support, the book of Enoch distinguished the immortal angelic spirits of heaven from of the disembodied spirits of giants by distinguishing them as evil spirits who afflict and oppress humankind, just as Jesus described them:

---

[164] Dead: Isa 14:9, 14–16; Job 25:5; Ps 88:10; Prov 9:18; Eze 32:1–32. H7496—*rapha', raw-faw'*; from 7495: a ghost; the dead; deceased; shades, spirits; H7495—*rapha'*; H7497—*rapha'*.
[165] H7700—*shed, shade*: a doemon as in malignant; devil; demon.

Enoch 15:3–11 Wherefore have ye left the high, holy, and eternal heaven, and lain with women, and defiled yourselves with the daughters of men and taken to yourselves wives, and done like the children of earth, and begotten giants as your sons? And though ye were holy, spiritual, living the eternal life, you have defiled yourselves with the blood of women, and have begotten children with the blood of flesh, and, as the children of men, have lusted after flesh and blood as those also do who die and perish. Therefore have I given them wives also that they might impregnate them, and beget children by them, that thus nothing might be wanting to them on earth. But you were formerly spiritual, living the eternal life, and immortal for all generations of the world. And therefore I have not appointed wives for you; for as for the spiritual ones of the heaven, in heaven is their dwelling. And now, the giants, who are produced from the spirits and flesh, shall be called evil spirits upon the earth, and on the earth shall be their dwelling. Evil spirits have proceeded from their bodies; because they are born from men, and from the holy Watchers is their beginning and primal origin; [they shall be evil spirits on earth, and evil spirits shall they be called]. As for the spirits of heaven, in heaven shall be their dwelling, but as for the spirits of the earth which were born upon the earth, on the earth shall be their dwelling. And the spirits of the giants afflict, oppress, destroy, attack, do battle, and work destruction on the earth, and cause trouble: they take no food, but nevertheless hunger and thirst, and cause offenses. And these spirits shall rise up against the children of men and against the women, because they have proceeded from them.

Knowing who the counterfeit spirits are helps us make sense of their mention in Revelation passages. They are the same demons, devils, and unclean spirits who are destroyers of Adamites, who will be charged with parading what is left of humankind into utter destruction at Armageddon.

Rev 16:13 And I saw three unclean spirits like frogs come out of the mouth of the dragon, and out of the mouth of the beast, and out of the mouth of the false prophet.

Rev 16:14 For they are the spirits of devils, working miracles, which go forth unto the kings of the earth and of the whole world, to gather them to the battle of that great day of God Almighty.

CHAPTER 5

THE SERPENT'S ROOT

Isa 14:29 Rejoice not thou, whole Palestina, because the rod of him that smote thee is broken: for out of the serpent's root shall come forth a cockatrice, and his fruit shall be a fiery flying serpent.

If one acknowledges that the events of the days of Noah will be akin the end-time fig tree generation, then one is led to scrutinize closely what happened shortly before and after the flood. It follows that the events in the days of Noah are connected to the "beginning of sorrows" catastrophes[166] that increase in intensity through out the fig tree generation and last seven years.

If one accepts Jesus as the Word of God, the Spirit and testimony of prophecy, and that the Bible is the Word of and from God, then Jesus' reference to the days of old and Noah, by implication, would be defined and understood within Scripture. Accordingly, Scripture provides the fundamental information and events that occurred before and during Noah's lifetime. Moreover, the book of Ecclesiastes instructs the saints why it is important to understand ancient archetypical events, and how that knowledge ought to guide our discernment of end-time prophecy.

> Eccl 1:9 The thing that hath been, it is that which shall be; and that which is done is that which shall be done: and there is no new thing under the sun.

---

[166] Matt 24:8.

> Eccl 1:10 Is there any thing whereof it may be said, See, this is new? it hath been already of old time, which was before us.

> Eccl 1:11 There is no remembrance of former things; neither shall there be any remembrance of things that are to come with those that shall come after.

As indecipherable, preternatural, and seemingly inconceivable as so many end-time events recorded in the book of Revelation appear to be, Scripture does provide keys to unlocking those cryptic prophecies and the chronology of events, if we let Scripture do so. What will take place in the fig tree generation and the last seven years has all occurred in similar ways in prehistory and through out history many times; events recorded in Scripture. What will be unique about the end-time and the millennium events is that these will be the ordained times reserved by God for the denouement to the angelic rebellion.

In that spirit, Revelation 9 and 12 are the most vivid and striking connections back to days of Noah, when fallen angels walked among humankind, committed crimes against creation and humanity, and sentenced to the abyss to be held until the release in the end times of those impassioned angels, to try once more to storm heaven and win a realm of their own. The demons imprisoned in the sides of the abyss, the slain Terrible Ones, will also be released; those who once reigned with terror on earth over humans.[167] The releasing of the impassioned angels and demons in the end times is a direct consequence of the days of Noah and events that occurred after angels rebelled. Hence, the cryptic angel who will lead those who ascend out of the smoke of the abyss is Abaddon/Apollyon, a destroyer angel who will once more vex the people of the earth for a short time. The end-time release event of imprisoned angels and demons is renowned in prophecy as the first of the three terrifying woes.

> Rev 9:1 And the fifth angel sounded, and I saw a star fall from heaven unto the earth: and to him was given the key of the bottomless pit.. ..

> Rev 9:11 And they had a king over them, which is the angel of the bottomless pit, whose name in the Hebrew tongue is Abaddon, but in the Greek tongue hath his name Apollyon.

> Rev 9:12 One woe is past; and, behold, there come two woes more hereafter.

As part of the end times, one might anticipate that somehow the Nephilim and/or the Rephaim will impact the end times through their recreation, reappearance, incarnation as demon spirits by possessing humans or other kinds of hosts

---

[167] Ezek 32:21–32.

created for them, or through their bloodline descendants from the beast empires of prophecy described in Daniel 2, 7, and 8, and Revelation 12, 13, 16, 17, and 19. Some or all the above influences will be in play.

From before the days of Noah, in the time of Satan's first revenge[168] that caused the fall of Adam and Eve in Eden, God forewarned believers regarding two competing seed lines: the seed of Adam and Eve and the seed of the serpent—the offspring of the serpentine sons of God, the Seraphim Dragon Watchers. The serpent seed is the infamous original house of Dragon, a notorious rival seed line to Adamites illicitly inserted both before and after the flood, which has plagued the epoch of Adamites. The serpent seed line continues and is active to this very day, beast bloodlines that will once more usurp absolute power through the end-time beast kingdoms.

> Gen 3:15 And I will put enmity between the serpent and the woman, and between thy seed and her seed; it shall bruise thy head, and thou shalt bruise his heel.

Seraphim/*seraph* angels are fiery, six-winged Watchers that perform specific duties before throne of God and for the governance of the earth, angels with serpentine faces.[169] Dragons/*tanniyn* are defined in the physical realm as serpent monsters, dragon monsters, and sea monsters.[170] Six-winged Seraphim are heavenly dragons, rebellious or otherwise. Hence, the fiery flying serpent—the serpent's root in the Isaiah 14 passage introducing this chapter—is a Seraphim with serpent translated from *seraph*. Isaiah 14 is the same chapter that documented an angel's fall from heaven in disgrace, the angelic leader of rebellious angels recorded in Revelation 12:9 as "the great dragon," "that old serpent, called the devil and Satan."

The serpent seed prophesied in Genesis 3:15 and fulfilled in Genesis 6 with the creation of numerous houses of Dragon, the giants/Nephilim, whose godfathers were numerous fallen Watcher Seraphim. If giants were indeed recreated after the flood, they too were produced by another group of rebellious Seraphim as the postdiluvian serpent seed for the Rephaim giants and house of Dragon. Either way, celestial godfathers were the angelic serpent's root both before and after the flood.

Adding to the body of scriptural evidence testifying to the serpent seed line is found the book of Psalms. Psalms 21 warns believers about a spurious offspring that has maintained their tyrannical grip through out the generations; humankind's nemesis seed line that perpetually plots evil against Adamites. The spurious serpent seed will do so until their seed is permanently removed from among men/*'adam* in

---

[168] Gary Wayne, *The Genesis 6 Conspiracy*, 94–103.

[169] Isa 6:1–6; Dan 4:8–27; H8314—*saraph, saw-rawf'*: figuratively poisonous serpent; specifically, a seraph; plural seraphim; copper colored as in fiery serpent; angels with six wings, human hands, and in attending God.

[170] H8577—*tanniyn; tan-neen'*: a marine or land monster; sea-serpent or jackal; dragon; sea-monster; serpent; whale.

the fiery anger of God's wrath/`aph. Men/'adam is defined as red, ruddy, a human, and humankind,[171] Adamites. Psalm 41:2 distinguishes the seed lines as the low race, dually translated from ben (son) and 'adam for the poor/`ebyown also meaning oppressed and needing deliverance. The high race is dually translated from ben and `iysh meaning man, a great man, a champion, and a mighty man that is rich/`ashiyr as well as noble—thus, the lowly sons of Adam and the sons the nobility/royals of the mighty men.[172]

> Ps 21:8 Thine hand shall find out all thine enemies: thy right hand shall find out those that hate thee.
>
> Ps 21:9 Thou shalt make them as a fiery oven in the time of thine anger: the LORD shall swallow them up in his wrath, and the fire shall devour them.
>
> Ps 21:10 Their fruit shalt thou destroy from the earth, and their seed from among the children of men.

As such, the spurious serpent seed was documented in Isaiah 25 and other Old Testament passages as the branch of Terrible Ones who will be destroyed upon the mountain towering over the end-time Armageddon battle. The Terrible Ones' transgenerational seed led by Antichrist will likely be destroyed around the slopes of Mount Hermon. The Terrible Ones, the `Ariyts or Arytim meaning powerful, tyrannical, strong, violent, oppressors, and greedy ones[173] were/are the "strong people." Strong/`az means fierce, greedy, mighty, and strong, derives from `azaz, defined as stout [wide] as in strong, hardened, and impudent,[174] all the while noting both words are inexplicably connected to an infamous angel, Azazel,[175] the leader of the Watchers sent to the abyss in the book of Enoch.[176] People/`am as in

---

[171] H120—'adam, aw-dawm': ruddy; red; a human being; an individual or the species, mankind; low, man; a low degree person; city in Jordan valley H119—'adam, aw-dam': to show blood in the face; flush or turn rosy; red as in ruddy; to glare; to look red.

[172] H1121—ben: son; children; family name or house; H376—'iysh, eesh: a man; a male person; husband; champion; great man; H6223—`ashiyr, aw-sheer': rich; wealthy; noble; H34—'ebyown, eb-yone': poor man; lowest class; oppressed; needing deliverance.

[173] Isa 13:11; 25:3–5; 49:25; Ezek 28:7; 32:11–12. H6184—`ariyts, aw-reets': fearful; powerful; tyrannical; mighty; oppressor; in great power, strong, terrible, violent; greedy; awesome as in terrifying; terror-striking; ruthless; awe-inspiring; childless; bare of children.

[174] H5794—`az, az; from 5810: strong; vehement; harsh; fierce; greedy; mighty; power; roughly; strong; H5810—`azaz, aw-zaz'; a primitive root: to be stout as in strong; hardened; impudent; prevail; strong.

[175] Lev 16:8, 10, 26: scapegoat. H5799–`aza'zel; az-aw-zale' from 5795: goat of departure; scapegoat; H5795—`ez; aze: she-goat; plural format is masculine; strong.

[176] R. H. Charles, The Book of Enoch, 54:5, 8:1, 10:8.

the "strong people" is defined as a tribe, troops, nation and kindred,[177] indicating a distinct tribe or race of strong ones and terrible tyrants.

> Isa 25:3 Therefore shall the strong people glorify thee, the city of the terrible nations shall fear thee.. ..

> Isa 25:5 Thou shalt bring down the noise of strangers, as the heat in a dry place; even the heat with the shadow of a cloud: the branch of the terrible ones shall be brought low.

> Isa 25:6 And in this mountain shall the LORD of hosts make unto all people a feast of fat things, a feast of wines on the lees, of fat things full of marrow, of wines on the lees well refined.

> Isa 25:7 And he will destroy in this mountain the face of the covering cast over all people, and the vail that is spread over all nations.

The book of Daniel prophesied regarding the metallic empires: Babylon, Persia/Medes, Greece, Rome, and the future end-time empire. In Daniel 2, Babylonian King Nebuchadnezzar received a prophetic dream, whereby he was identified as the leader of the first metallic empire of gold.[178] The metallic empires prophecy is connected to the Isaiah 25's "strong people," "terrible," and men/'adam as part of its prophetic allegory, with some additional eye-popping use of language. The metallic empire prophecy describes the end-time empire of ten empires led by ten kings, an alliance empire that rises out of the ashes of fourth empire of iron (Rome)—an empire Antichrist will usurp. These ten end-time kings are the same beast kings and empires described in Daniel 7–8 and Revelation 13, 16, 17, and 19. Antichrist, too is described as a beast king who establishes the eighth beast empire at the mid point of the last seven years.

> Dan 2:31 Thou, O king, sawest, and behold a great image. This great image, whose brightness was excellent, stood before thee; and the form thereof was terrible.

The seventh empire of the end times, noting Egypt and Assyria came before Babylon, is the fifth empire as described in Daniel 2 as ten toes on the two giant feet of the great metallic statue of empires. "Great image" is translated twice to describe the great statue of great empires.[179] The first great/*saggiy'* means exceedingly large in size and numbers, while the second great/*rab* is defined as chief, lord, great, and

---

[177] People: H5971—'am: a people; a congregated unit; specifically, a tribe; a troops; folk, a nation; a people; compatriots; country-men; kinsman; kindred.
[178] Dan 2:37–38.
[179] Dan 2:31.

stout.[180] Additionally, the metallic statue was described in its form as terrible/*dchal* meaning dreadful, to make one afraid as in the fear of serpents.[181] Hence, the image is giant-sized and terrifying in the sense of a serpent somehow. Accordingly, The Access Bible annotated that colossal giant statues of kings and gods were common in ancient times.[182] The giant statue emoted a sense of terror, due to the long-standing reign of terror by giant kings with their serpentine nature. This terror was reflected in prophecies like Genesis 3, Psalm 21, Isaiah 13, 14, and 25, and Daniel, 7, 8, and 11 is jarring when first discerned, but also eye-opening.

And yet, the jarring associations do not stop there. The metallic statue of the giant of empires described in Daniel 2:31 is eerily reminiscent of the branch of the Terrible Ones, the strong ones of Isaiah 25. In fact, the *NIV Study Bible* connects Isaiah 25:3–5 as a reference for a clearer understanding for "great" and "terrible" giant statue detailed in Daniel 2:31.[183] Further, *The Access Bible* annotated that the decreasing value of the metals (gold, silver, bronze, and then iron) symbolized a steady decline of the kingly majesty and their empires of some kind.[184] I would assert the prophetic allegory indicates a steady decline in purity to the serpent seed blood-lines of the royals that included the nobility, priest, and elite classes, who controlled and essentially enslaved the working class along with the slave class—Adamites.

Discerning the prophetic allegory makes sense of the prophetic the end-time empire of ten toes/kings that extend out of the iron Roman legs: a future world empire described as even less majestic than the iron empire. The ten-king empire will be composed partly of iron and partly of clay, reflecting the declining metal value, and figuratively a diluted royal seed line. The end-time world empire will be divided into to two groups of five at odds with each other, adding to the partly strong yet partly divided/broken understanding.[185] The prophetic allegory indicates a degree of autonomy among the ten kings and their empires. Hence, the ten kings and their empires will be partly divided because of the makeup of potter's clay (wet and malleable by inference) and thus a low-grade alloyed iron. One deduces that the prophetic allegory indicates two races: one a stronger part from the race from the metallic empires, and secondly a clay race that has a close kinship in prophetic

---

[180] H7690—*saggiy', sag-ghee'*: large as in size, quantity, or number; exceedingly great; H7229—*rab, rab*: captain; chief; great; lord; master; stout.

[181] Dan 2:31. Terrible: H1763—*dchal, deh-khal'*; Aramaic corresponding to 2119: to slink; to fear, to be formidable; make afraid; dreadful; fear; terrible; H2119—*zachal, zaw-khal'*: to crawl as in to fear; be afraid: serpent; worm.

[182] *The Access Bible, New Revised Standard Version with the Apocrypha* (New York: Oxford University Press, 1999), Dan 2:31: notes.

[183] Kenneth Barker, gen. ed., *The NIV Study Bible New International Version* (Grand Rapids, MI: Zondervan, 1985), Dan 2:31 note m.

[184] *The Access Bible,* Dan 2:31: notes.

[185] H8406—*tbar, teb-ar'*: to be fragile figuratively; broken; broken in pieces; Clay: H2635—*chacaph, khas-af'*: a clod; clay; potsherd.

allegory for humans, as in Adam. The prophetic allegory indicates a shared empire made of bloodline royals and non royal kings, or something even stranger.

> Dan 2:41 And whereas thou sawest the feet and toes, part of potters' clay, and part of iron, the kingdom shall be divided; but there shall be in it of the strength of the iron, forasmuch as thou sawest the iron mixed with miry clay.

> Dan 2:42 And as the toes of the feet were part of iron, and part of clay, so the kingdom shall be partly strong, and partly broken.

The ten kings/toes prophecy goes on to describe the clay as miry/*tiyn* clay/*chacaph*. Miry/*tiyn* is interchangeable with *tiyt* meaning sticky, clay, mud, and calamity. *Tiyn* derives from *tuw'* meaning to sweep away.[186] *Tiyn* in the book of Psalms is the word translated as "miry 'clay'," noting the application includes the "horrible" pit/*bowr* defined as a hole, cistern, and prison; a term used through out the Old Testament for the abyss prison in the underworld for fallen angels and the spirits of the demons, the Terrible Ones.[187] Secondly, the definition from *tiyt* included the cryptic explanation: "rath. Perb. A demon. From 2894, through the idea of dirt to be swept away." So, we have a definition leading the reader to inquire as to the meaning of sweeping away, while noting *tiyn* is translated as dirt as in Psalm 18:42 and Isa 57:20. Scripture does provide a passage whereby Jesus connected demons and possession to dirt and "swept" or sweeping away, indicating that the ten end-time kings are associated with demon spirits and the abyss prison.

> Matt 12:43 When the unclean spirit is gone out of a man, he walketh through dry places, seeking rest, and findeth none.

> Matt 12:44 Then he saith, I will return into my house from whence I came out; and when he is come, he findeth it empty, swept, and garnished.

> Matt 12:45 Then goeth he, and taketh with himself seven other spirits more wicked than himself, and they enter in and dwell there: and the last state of that man is worse than the first.

---

[186] H2917—*tiyn, teen*; Aramaic; by interchange corresponding to 2916; clay; miry; H2916—*tiyt, teet*; from 2894 as in to sweep or swept away: from an unused root meaning to be sticky; "rath. Perb.Aa demon;" from 2894 as in sweeping; mud or clay; figuratively calamity; dirt, mire; H2894—*tuw', too*; a primitive root; to sweep away; sweep.

[187] Ps 40:2. H953—*bowr, bore*; from 952: a pit hole; a cistern or a prison; dungeon; fountain; pit; well. Ps 28:1; 30:3; 40:2; 88:4; 143:6, 7; Isa 14:15, 19; 24:22; 38:18; Ezek 26:20; 31:14, 16; 32:18, 23, 25, 29,30.

One should not be surprised that Jesus encouraged believers to search out Daniel's prophecies regarding the abomination, and by implication the beast and metallic empire prophecies to discern His end-time prophecies. One deduces Jesus would have included the understanding of the metallic and beast empire prophecies for further context to the abomination event.[188]

The scriptural links made in this chapter explicate a passage in Daniel 2 which declares that just as iron mixed with clay, that they (the iron ones) will mingle themselves with the seed of men (the clay ones). Whatever race or species makes up the iron kings of the end-time empire, Daniel 2:43 is clearly depicting that they are different from the seed of men:

> Dan 2:43 And whereas thou sawest iron mixed with miry clay, they shall mingle themselves with the seed of men: but they shall not cleave one to another, even as iron is not mixed with clay.

Men/'enash in Daniel 2:43 is defined as a mortal man, humans, or people, "differing from the more dignified 120 adam, 'adam,"[189] perhaps inferring hybrid royal bloodlines. Mingle/`arab is defined as commingle, mingle oneself, or mix.[190] However one wants to reconcile Daniel 2:43, one ends up with a jarring understanding in conflict with both standard church theology and secular theology of history. One is left with the notion that either a distinct race, or less pure hybrid race, of the ancient serpent seed bloodlines will mix or commingle with the seed men: posterity, children, descendants, offspring and/or semen.[191] Moreover, a curious passage foretelling end-time signs in 2 Esdras states, "wild animals shall roam beyond their haunts, and menstruous women shall bring forth monsters."[192] The wild animals are reminiscent of those mentioned in the seals in Revelation 6:8, when the ten kings rise.

Even though seeds commingle, they will not cleave one to another, even as iron does not mix with clay. This part of Daniel 2:43 perhaps suggests that something more than just flesh and blood and seed tries to commingle. Cleave/dbaq is defined as to stick with, to impinge [as in encroach on someone's rights], to

---

[188] Matt 24:15; Mark 13:14; Luke 21:20.
[189] H606—'enash, en-awsh'; Aramaic or enash, Aramaic en-ash'; cognate with 582: a man; human being; mankind. H582—'enowsh, en-oshe'; H605—'anash, aw-nash': to be frail; feeble; incurable; sick; woeful. H120—'adam, aw-dawm'; from 119: ruddy; red; a human being; mankind; low, man; a low degree person; H119—'adam, aw-dam': to show blood in the face; flush; rosy; red as in ruddy; to glare; to look red.
[190] H6151—`arab, ar-ab': to commingle; mingle self, mix.
[191] H2234—zra`, zer-ah'; Aramaic corresponding to 2233; posterity; seed; offspring; H2233—zera`, zeh'-rah: seed: seed of fruit, plant, sowing-time; posterity; child; fruitful; semen; virile; offspring; children.
[192] Access Bible, 2 Esdras 5:8.

catch by pursuit, to overtake; to take, and/or to be joined together.[193] The Daniel 2 prophecy seems to be indicating the ten kings and/or five of the clay/human kings and nobility will be forcibly possessed, or seduced into sharing their soul and body with dominant demon spirits in the end-time, a union that will not continue for long in the suppressed host. The passage might be indicating that the spirit mingling will occur in exchange for helping the kings come to power, or shortly thereafter. This interpretation of demon possession by Rephaim/Nephilim demon spirits is akin to a curious passage in the book of Revelation just before Armageddon, noting Antichrist is the king of the eighth empire who receives power and strength from the ten kings.[194]

> Rev 16:13 And I saw three unclean spirits like frogs come out of the mouth of the dragon, and out of the mouth of the beast, and out of the mouth of the false prophet.

> Rev 16:14 For they are the spirits of devils, working miracles, which go forth unto the kings of the earth and of the whole world, to gather them.

---

[193] H1693—*dbaq, deb-ak*; Aramaic corresponding to 1692; to stick to; cleave; cling; H1692—*dabaq, daw-bak*: to impinge; cling; adhere; catch by pursuit; abide fast; cleave; joined together; keep; overtake; pursue hard; stick; take.
[194] Rev 17:13, 17.

CHAPTER 6

SECOND INCURSION

Gen 15:20 And the Hittites, and the Perizzites, and the Rephaims,

Gen 15:21 And the Amorites, and the Canaanites, and the Gir-gashites, and the Jebusites.

Rephaim, Zuzim, and Emim inexplicably surface as mystery races in the underexplained war of giants recorded in Genesis 14, tribes unaccounted for in the table of nations.[195] Moreover, *Rapha'l Rephaim* surfaces twenty-five times in the Old Testament Hebrew to describe a tribe of giants, an individual giant, and places named after these giants of old.[196]

Rephaim and their associated tribes were enigmatically recorded in the Old Testament from the time of Abraham until the time of kings David and Solomon. Rephaim tribes impacted the early postdiluvian world in ways akin to the Nephilim before the flood. Scripture does not provide a clear, smoking-gun verse as to how giants appear after the flood, only narratives that clearly demonstrate that they did. Scripture does not directly explain whether Rephaim giants were created before the flood like Nephilim and somehow survived, or were created

---

[195] The seventy patriarchs of nations descended from the offspring of Noah in Genesis 10 and 1 Chronicles. See also Deuteronomy 32.

[196] H7497 occurrences: 25 times. Giants: 10: Deut 2:11, 20; 3:11, 13; Josh 12:4; 13:12; 15:8; 18:15–16. Giant: 2 Sam 21:16, 18, 20, 22; 1 Chron 20:4, 6, 8. Rephaim: 2 Sam 5:18, 22; 23:13; 1 Chron 11:15; 14:9; Isa 17:5. Rephaims: Gen 14:5; 15:20.

after the flood but were somehow distinct from the Nephilim. Scripture does, though, make obscure references to a Second Incursion after the flood through the otherwise baffling details in those narratives—narratives like the war of giants in Genesis 14, and the accounting of the lands God promised to Abraham's descendants in the Genesis 15 passage above. As such, and as the "days of Noah and Lot" end-time sign encourages believers to inquire about Noah's life both before and after the flood, one is enticed to investigate the "days of Lot," Rephaim, and the pentapolis city-states of the plain centered at Sodom that were destroyed. The five-city alliance was listed in Genesis 14:2 and 8 as Sodom, Gomorrah, Admah, Zeboiim, and Bela/Zoar in the war of giants.

Keeping with the adages of days of Noah and the idea that nothing is new under the sun at top of mind, consider that Genesis 6:4 mysteriously recorded that Nephilim were on the earth in "those days,"—the days of violence described before the flood, followed by the restating of the birth of Noah's sons. Genesis 6:4 goes on to note that giants were on the earth in those days and also after that when angels bore children with human females, possibly indicating other incursions took place before the flood, after, and/or both, but restricted to within the 600 years before the flood, and 350 years after the flood.[197] Accordingly, a Second Incursion by the celestial mafia with Noah's posterity after the flood would have created more giants and more days of violence.

The Nephilim creation narrative was positioned in the preamble of the flood narrative as essential context, which identified Nephilim as root cause for the extraordinary violence and the cause for the flood. Nephilim were the proverbial serpent's root created by fallen Seraphim angels to perpetuate evil and violence through out the earth before the flood, and perhaps after that: at Sodom, and perhaps again in the end times. Accordingly, the original Hebrew words in the text adds clarity to message of the narrative. In those days/*yowm*, defined as a day(s), year, generation, lifetime, and/or a period,[198] both before and after the flood seems to underscore the context for "and after that." Further, in "after that," that/*ken* is defined in this application as in like manner, straightaway, and afterward,[199] and a word deriving from *kuwn*: set up, establish, re-establish, and restored.[200] After/*'Achar* means again, once more, afterward, and hereafter.[201] "After that" is

---

[197] Gen 9:28–29.

[198] H3117—*yowm, yome*: to be hot; a day (sunrise to sunset); a space of time defined by an associated term; an age; days; a year(s); a general period; a lifetime.

[199] Gen 9:29; Matt 24:36; Luke 17:26; 1 Pet 3:20. H3651—*ken, kane*: set upright: hence just and rightly or so; after that; following; howbeit; in the like manner; straightway; therefore, this being so; afterward.

[200] H3559—*kuwn, koon*: to be erect; stand; perpendicular: causatively to set up; be established; be fixed, secure; enduring; steadfast; to constitute, to direct, re-established; restored.

[201] H310—*'achar, akh-ar'*: the hind part: after that; again; at, away from; back; beside; follow; from; hereafter.

communicating violations both before and after the flood, but within Noah's lifespan. The text corroborates angels created giants again in like manner in Noah's lifetime; by inference, likely again before the flood, and seemingly again after the flood to restore the Nephilim World Order, just as the Bible makes known the presence of giants after the flood.

> Gen 6:4. .. giants in the earth in those days; and also after that, when the sons of God came in unto the daughters of men. .. .

The Rephaim and their kin tribes appeared as the newly reestablished branches of giants begat in a like manner by fallen angels and humans. Sodom and the cities of the plain were located in Canaan, where Canaan, Heth, and Sidon dwelled after Babel and interbred with Rephaim, forming diluted hybrid Rephaim nations like the Amorites——the taller peoples.[202] Some of these hybrid races were recorded in the scout report by Joshua and Caleb: Hittites, Jebusites, Amorites, and Canaanites, as well as the Amalekites that were distinct from the Anakim/Rephaim.[203] Nine Canaanite tribes documented in the table of nations[204] are patriarch-less, indicating to me that that the nine were eponymously named after a Rephaim patriarch.

> Gen 10:19 And the border of the Canaanites was from Sidon, as thou comest to Gerar, unto Gaza; as thou goest, unto Sodom, and Gomorrah, and Admah, and Zeboim, even unto Lasha.

Abraham and Lot also settled in Canaan, in the Kiriatharba region,[205] the city of Arba later named Hebron, and home city of the Anakim where Hittites and Perizzites dwelled. Arba was the patriarch of the Anakim,[206] but was not listed in the table of nations. Kiriatharba was located close to Sodom and the cities of the plain that were also infested with Rephaim, as witnessed by the five governing Rephaim kings listed in the war of giants[207] we will detail in a subsequent chapter. Along with Sodom's infamy and destruction, Sodom, Gomorrah, and the cities of the plain are the most likely suspects as the epicenter of the postdiluvian Second Incursion. This deduction explains God's dismay from the cry

---

[202] Deut 1:27.
[203] Num 13:28–29; Deut 1:19, 20, 27.
[204] Gen 10:15–17; 1 Chron 1:13–16.
[205] Gen 13:3–18; 23:2, 19.
[206] Jos 14:14; 15:1.
[207] Gen 14:1, 2, 4, 8–10.

of sin that arose out of the cities of the plain; so much so that God went down to inspect the sins and crimes committed against God, humanity, and creation.[208]

Sodom surfaces first biblically in the table of nations among the cities marking the further regions where Canaanites dwelled, cities that by inference were established by the Aboriginal Rephaim tribes before Babel.[209] Sodom surfaced again when Lot settled in there in Genesis 13, and then again in Genesis 14 with the war of giants, and thereafter in Genesis 18 and 19 that detailed the destruction of the cities of plain. Sodom was wicked, evil, immoral, and wretched[210] from before the time Lot or the Canaanites settled there.

> Gen 13:12 Abram dwelled in the land of Canaan, and Lot dwelled in the cities of the plain, and pitched his tent toward Sodom.
>
> Gen 13:13 But the men of Sodom were wicked and sinners before the LORD exceedingly.

The evil and violence of Sodom and the cities of the plain began with its post-diluvian Aboriginal Rephaim inhabitants.[211] Scripturally, Canaanites migrated to the Covenant Land after Babel 101 years after the flood, utilizing Peleg's genealogy as third generation, as was Nimrod who was accredited with building Babel. Nonbiblical sources similarly date the building of Babel Tower.[212]

The book of Ezekiel described the sins committed at Sodom as abominable, haughty, iniquitous, and selfish—a city allegorically born out of a mixed marriage from a Hittite and an Amorite.[213] Sodom's descriptions are classic descriptions regarding the giants. "Iniquitous" is defined as perverse, depraved, immoral, and evil;[214] haughty: lofty, arrogant, and proud;[215] abominable: abhorrent, idolatrous, and ritually unclean in terms of food, use of idols, and mixed marriages.[216] More was going on in Sodom than mere human-to-human abominations. The abomi-

---

[208] Gen 18:20–21.

[209] Gen 10:19.

[210] H7451—*ra` rah*: evil; bad; calamity; distress; evil; wretchedness; wrong; good for nothing; immoral.

[211] John D. D. M'Clintock and James Strong, *Cyclopaedia of Biblical, Theological, and Ecclesiastical Literature* (New Ork: Harper & Brothers, 1867), Vol. 8, 1043: Rephaim; Merrill F. Unger and R. K. Harrison, *The New Unger's Bible Dictionary* (Chicago: The Moody Bible Institute, 1988), 1073–1074: Rephaim.

[212] Gen 10:11, 29; 11:10–12. Arphaxad was born two years after the flood, Shelah thirty-five years later, Eber thirty years after that, and Peleg thirty-four years after Eber: 101 years. Albert Mackey, *The History of Freemasonry* (New York: Gramercy Books, 1996) 58, The Tower of Babel.

[213] Ezek 16:1–50.

[214] H5771—*`avon, aw-vone`*: perversity; evil; iniquity; mischief; depraved.

[215] H1361—*gabahh, gaw-bah`*: soar as in be lofty; haughty; proud; arrogant; raise to a great height.

[216] H8441—*tow` ebah, to-ay-baw`*: something disgusting morally; abhorrent; idolatrous; ritually unclean food, idols, and mixed marriages.

nable mixed marriages refer to same-sex marriages, as well as marriages between angels and humans that produced spurious offspring in the days of Noah, and later mixed marriages between fertility-challenged Rephaim and the fertile human Canaanites. The books of Wisdom and Baruch state Nephilim were born with "great in stature," were arrogant, and were experts in war, but perished in the flood because they lacked wisdom. It follows that if Rephaim were created after the flood, as in "after that," they would follow in the same abhorrent behavior as the Nephilim, and in the same like manner described at Sodom.

> Wis 14:6 For even in the beginning, when arrogant giants were perishing, the hope of the world took refuge on a raft.

> Bar 3:28 The giants were born there who were famous of old, great in stature, expert in war. God did not choose them, or give them the way to knowledge; so they perished because they had no wisdom.

"Great in stature" is same terminology employed to describe the people and races the terrified Israelite scouts saw in the land of Canaan, and then tried to convince the Israelite people that the Covenant Land was filled with Anakim that the scouts called giants/*nephiyl,* versus Rephaim and their hybrid human Rephaim giants. However, the language in the embellished evil report indeed testified to the veracity of the original antediluvian giants and their great size/stature,[217] and thus were somewhat larger than the Rephaim and their spawned human hybrids.

The book of Deuteronomy connected serpent/dragon imagery to Sodom's abominations and to the restoration of a postdiluvian serpent's root of serpentine offspring from Seraphim Watchers. The fruitful vines of grapes of Sodom and Gomorrah were described as the "grapes of gall," and the wine "the poison of dragons and the cruel venom of asps" (snakes).[218] Gall/*ro'sh* is a poison extracted from plants like hemlock, poppies, and/or venom from a snake, which are poisonous to humans and snakes.[219] The wine thereof is the poison of dragons from the genealogical vine and branches of Sodom and Gomorrah who rule this world, the postdiluvian house of Dragon that imposes their ritual abominations and religions as the daughters of Babylon religion. Accordingly, Sodom's poisonous serpent/dragon roots vines, and seeds, along with its fiery destruction is an example for Babylon's end-time destruction and its spurious seed.[220]

The house of Dragon was planted by fallen Seraphim via the evils of angelic worship at Sodom, which became poison for all who consumed Sodom's produce.

---

[217] Num 13:33.
[218] Detu 32:32–33.
[219] H7219—*ro'sh, roshe*; or rowsh: a head; a poisonous plant; likely the poppy with its conspicuous head; a poison; hemlock; venom.
[220] Deut 29:23; Isa 13:19; Jer 50:52; Zeph 2:9; Rev 18:1–24.

As such, the cities of the plain were populated with the spurious offspring of the celestial mafia and Rephaim/human hybrids: Hittites, Amorites, and Canaanites.

In the days of Moses, more than four hundred years after Sodom's destruction, southern Amorites, Hittites, Jebusites, and Canaanites were still reigned over by Anakim kings like Sheshai, Ahiman, and Talmai.[221] Amorites in the north were reigned over by Rephaim kings like Og, Sihon, and Jabin. The kings of Canaan were listed among the mighty kings like Og and Sihon in the book of Psalms.[222] One deduces that the kings of Canaanite pentapolis at the time of the war of giants were Rephaim or a branch of Rephaim: "Birsha king of Gomorrah, Shinab king of Admah, and Shemeber king of Zeboiim, and the king of Bela, which is Zoar."[223]

> Ps 135:10 Who smote great nations, and slew mighty kings;
>
> Ps 135:11 Sihon king of the Amorites, and Og king of Bashan, and all the kingdoms of Canaan: Ps 135:12 And gave their land for an heritage, an heritage unto Israel his people.

Further, Josephus linked the kings of the Sodom alliance as allies and the offspring of giants in the war of giants, indicating that the ruling class were the pure blood or mixed hybrid human offspring of giants:

> At this time, when the Assyrians had the dominion over Asia, the people of Sodom were in a flourishing condition, both as to riches and the number of their youth. There were five kings that managed the affairs of this county: Ballas, Barsas, Senabar, and Sumobor, with the king of Bela; and each king led on his own troops: and the Assyrians made war upon them; and, dividing their army into four parts, fought against them…. These kings [of Assyria] had laid waste all Syria and overthrown the offspring of the giants. And when they were come over against Sodom, they pitched their camp at the vale called the Slime Pits.[224]

Although I disagree with biblical historian Julian Morgenstern's timing of his supposition for two angelic incursions, I certainly agree with his statements stating that in the second temple era the Jewish people believed there were two occasions when the sons of God created giants with human females,[225] a belief which is con-

---

[221] Num 13:22, 29.

[222] Num 21:21, 29, 35; 32:33; Deut 3:8–9; Josh 11:1; Judg 11:19; Ps 135:11; 136:19.

[223] Gen 14:2, 8.

[224] Josephus, *Ant*, Book 1:9:1.

[225] Julian Morgenstern, *Mythical Background of Psalm 82*, The Hebrew Union College, 1939, Vol. 14, VII, 105–106: notes 134, 135, 135a.

sistent with Josephus' testimony. Thus, the First Incursion manifested from their rebellion from God, whereas the Second Incursion was brought about by spite toward Noahites; as such, there were two separate groups of angels who at separate times sinned against God.[226]

Ergo, the presence of Rephaim kings and their offspring at Sodom and the cities of the plain, its fiery destruction, and New Testament passages linking fallen angels, Sodom, and the flood to the crimes of creating of giants is all context for why Jesus connected the days of Lot to the days of Noah to end-time destruction by fire. The evidence indicates that Sodom, Gomorrah, Admah, Zeboiim, and Bela/Zoar were the epicenter and womb for Rephaim creation after the flood. Accordingly, the book of Isaiah referenced the evil rulers/princes of the Sodom pentapolis, their vile rituals, their abominable sacrifices, and their oppression of God's children.[227] The descendants of the Aboriginal rulers of Sodom, the Rephaim, are the *kine*/bulls of Bashan that God will overthrow, and then will destroy their seed from the earth in the end times.[228]

---

[226] Morgenstern, *Mythical Background of Psalm 82,* VII, 98; VII, 107.
[227] Isa 1:9–12; 3:8–9.
[228] Ps 21:9–11; Amos 4:1–11.

CHAPTER 7

THE HABITATION OF ANGELS, HUMANS, AND DEMONS

Jude 1:6 And the angels which kept not their first estate, but left their own habitation, he hath reserved in everlasting chains under darkness unto the judgment of the great day.

Jude 1:7 Even as Sodom and Gomorrha, and the cities about them in like manner, giving themselves over to fornication, and going after strange flesh, are set forth for an example, suffering the vengeance of eternal fire.

Canaanite nations were well acquainted with the gods who created Rephaim after the flood, the infamous offspring gods biblically authenticated as the Baalim led by Baal, son of El. Like the Rephaim, Canaanites worshipped the Baalim gods of Mount Hermon. Knowing this provides context for many of the details documented in Sodom and Gomorrah narrative.

Lot greeted and bowed before two angels/*mal'ak*[229] who went to Sodom. Lot recognized them as angels, noting that two angels accompanied the "Lord"

---

[229] H4397—*mal'ak, mal-awk'*: to despatch as a deputy; a messenger of God; an angel; ambassador; king; messenger.

in Genesis 18 in bodily form when Abraham was informed that Sodom and its four sister cities were about to be destroyed—angels described as men/ *'enowsh*[230] who ate and interacted with Abraham and Sarah. The two angels in human bodily form thereafter went to Sodom to inspect their crimes, and to search for any innocent people.[231] The two angels sent to Sodom that Lot bowed to in Genesis 19 were described as men—physical men, not spirit. Even so, both Lot and the Sodomites still recognized them as angelic beings in human form.[232] In fact, Sodomites understood the two men/angels came from God to judge/*shaphat*: condemn, punish,[233] and to execute judgment upon the inhabitants of Sodom. Moreover, the Sodomites understood the two as angelic spirits dwelling in human bodies. Yet the Sodomites still wished to "know them"—to have sex with the angels—and in the same manner Lot offered his daughters to the Sodomites in the angel's stead—daughters who had yet to know a man. [234]

Questions arise from the Sodomite demands. Did the Sodomites wish to have sex with the angels in a homosexual way, or did they understand angels could take a physical form of their choosing that included gender? Genesis 19:4 notes both the men, and all the people young and old, came to Lot's house. Did the Sodomites want the angels to take a female form to create more pure-bred Rephaim? Or did the Sodomites intend for the angels to create Rephaim with the daughters of Sodom? Sodomites were aware through their mystical religion and their reigning Rephaim kings how the first postdiluvian generation of giants that included King Og and Sihon were created—perhaps at Sodom and Gomorrah. At top of mind for the Sodomites might well have been the fertility issue with the original Rephaim demigod kings.

> Gen 19:9. .. This one fellow came in to sojourn, and he will needs be a judge: now will we deal worse with thee, than with them.

Contrary to standard dogma, the book of Jude perhaps captured in the angelic encounter at Sodom, the spirit of sexual violations against the laws of creation after the flood, a doctrine that by inference was well known at Sodom. The book of Jude's account connected pre-flood sexual crimes committed by fallen angels and the daughters of men, to the sexual intentions that occurred at Sodom with angels, who appeared in male physical forms. The implication in the Jude text is that the residents of Sodom and Gomorrah gave themselves over to

---

[230] H582—*'enowsh, en-oshe'*: a mortal; a man; men; mankind; people; person, husband; servant.
[231] Gen 18:1, 2, 16; 19:1, 15.
[232] Gen 19:5, 10, 12, 16.
[233] H8199—*shaphat, shaw-fat'*: to judge; pronounce sentence against; punish; condemn; be a judge; rule; govern.
[234] Gen 19:5, 8.

sexual sins and "in like manner" (Jude 1:7) as to what occurred before the flood. The cognate "in like manner" understanding was communicated in Genesis 6:4 as "after that when the sons of God came unto the daughters of men, and they bare children to them," noting that/ *ken* means in like manner. Accordingly, the book of Jude indicates that Sodom and the sister cities were the locations for the Second Incursion after the flood. The book of Jude testifies the Sodomites possessed knowledge regarding fallen angelic changeling, sexual, and reproductive capabilities. Hence, the question remains open to me whether the Sodomites intended to solicit explicitly homosexual or simply reproductive relations with the changeling angels.

Canaanite knowledge of how giants were created after the flood and their intimate association with the Rephaim indicates Sodomites and their sister cities held this knowledge before the days of Lot in Sodom. As such, Canaanites gave up their daughters to fornication in a "like manner" with fallen angels before Babel City and perhaps again in the Sodom plain—angels who thereafter were bound in chains to await judgment in the abyss in like manner to the parent gods. Accordingly, the Jude text goes on to state that Canaanites fornicated with "strange flesh," seemingly the strange flesh of angels. Strange/ *Het'eros* is understood as different, altered, and not of the same nature, class, or kind, as in a species or race.[235] Additionally, the fornication "in like manner" with strange flesh by Sodomites was set forth as an example for all generations that this violation against creation was and is punishable by suffering the eternal punishment in the lake of fire reserved for fallen angels, versus the second death of most sinful humans. The book of Jude seems to identify the Second Incursion taking place at Sodom and Gomorrah, as well as many other abominations. Knowing this puts this at the time before the Genesis 14 war of giants, when the men/ *'enowsh*/people "of Sodom were wicked and sinners, before the LORD exceedingly" (Gen 13:13),[236] whereby sins by their nature had already reached into heaven—sins that had previously brought about the flood, sins grievous enough for *Yhovah* to inspect.

> Gen 18:20 And the LORD said, Because the cry of Sodom and Gomorrah is great, and because their sin is very grievous;
>
> Gen 18:21 I will go down now, and see whether they have done altogether according to the cry of it, which is come unto me; and if not, I will know.

---

[235] G2087— *het'-er-os*; of uncertain affinity; different; altered; strange; other thing; not of the same nature or form, class, kind; kind: H4327— *miyn, meen*: a sort, as in species. Gen 1:21, 25; 6:20.
[236] H582— *'enowsh, en-oshe'*.

Further, the 2 Peter 2:4–7 narrative linked angelic sexual crimes and punishment before the flood to angelic sexual sins at Sodom with the same "filthy conversation" Sodomites had with the angels in Genesis 19. The "filthy conversation" is an ensample/example of those who lived ungodly at Sodom. Filthy/*aselg'ia* meaning unbridled sex; wantonness, lasciviousness, and licentiousness,[237] as in sexually outrageous, unrestrained, and immoral beyond the proper limits or law. Ergo, the 2 Peter and Jude narratives both link the outrageous sexual sins of angels to Sodom and Gomorrah and to the antediluvian angelic sexual violations. This does not mean that other sexual sins were not rampant in Sodom and the cities of the plain, but those sins were not marked for, or required, everlasting punishment.

> 2 Pet 2:4 For if God spared not the angels that sinned, but cast them down to hell, and delivered them into chains of darkness, to be reserved unto judgment;
>
> 2 Pet 2:5 And spared not the old world, but saved Noah the eighth person, a preacher of righteousness, bringing in the flood upon the world of the ungodly
>
> 2 Pe 2:6 And turning the cities of Sodom and Gomorrah into ashes condemned them with an overthrow, making them an ensample unto those that after should live ungodly
>
> 2 Pet 2:7 And delivered just Lot, vexed with the filthy conversation of the wicked.

Many Christians who oppose the notion that angels procreated human-angelic hybrids assert as one of their arguments that angelic spiritual beings, as such, are not capable of physical sex and reproduction in the physical world. The biblical anti-giant line of thought typically then cites support from Matthew 22:30 and Mark 12:2, where it states that humans after the resurrection (when we are adopted as sons of God even though we have human fathers) will be like angels in heaven and not given in marriage—thus, no marriage and no sex in heaven is permitted for spiritual beings. However, the passages do not state that procreation by angels in the physical world is not possible by taking physical forms. Moreover, we know that angels can take physical form in the physical world, as witnessed with the two angels who appeared as men in the Sodom narrative and other passages.[238]

---

[237] G766—*as-elg'-i-a*: licentiousness; filthy; lasciviousness; wantonness; unbridled lust; outrageous; shameless; transliterated: aselgeia.

[238] Zech 2:1; Mark 16:2-5; Luke 24:4; John 20:11–14; Acts 1:9–11.

Heb 13:2 Be not forgetful to entertain strangers: for thereby some have entertained angels unawares.

Typically, Luke 20, which also addresses the same line of prophetic doctrine, is overlooked in the anti-giant camp's arguments. Luke provides additional context. Humans of this world require marriage to reproduce because at this stage we are mortal. However, at the resurrection we will be adopted as sons of God, becoming equal to immortal angels in heaven who have no need to procreate to maintain the numbers of their race. What is overlooked in the anti-giant argument is that both Matthew and Luke's passages only discuss heaven, the home of the spirit beings, but does not discuss the physical world where giants were created by angels, even though this act also violated the laws of physical creation. One deduces that humans resurrected into eternity will be forbidden from procreation in the physical world thereafter as well.

Luke 20:34 And Jesus answering said unto them, The children of this world marry, and are given in marriage:

Luke 20:35 But they which shall be accounted worthy to obtain that world, and the resurrection from the dead, neither marry, nor are given in marriage:

Luke 20:36 Neither can they die any more: for they are equal unto the angels; and are the children of God, being the children of the resurrection.

Knowing the spiritual nature of angels makes sense of the odd language in Jude 1:6, whereby angels "kept not their first estate, but left their own habitation." Heaven was/is the angelic first estate: their place and base of dwelling and assigned authority from the beginning of creation.[239]

Thus, the fallen angels departed both their dwelling place and assigned commission when they departed heaven; their "habitation." Habitation/*oykaytayreeon* transliterated is defined as a residence as in a house to dwell in, and a dwelling place for the spirit.[240] *Oykaytayreeon* surfaces just one other time in the New Testament: 2 Corinthians 5:2 for "house" in heaven—the heavenly dwelling place for spirits in heaven.

---

[239] G746—*ar-khay*: a commencement; beginning; the first estate; first place; chief in order, time, place, or rank; magistrate; power; principality; principle; rule; transliterated: arche.
[240] G3613—*oy-kay-tay'-ree-on:* a residence habitation; house; dwelling place; the body as the dwelling place for the spirit; transliterated: oiketerion.

> Jude 1:6 And the angels which kept not their first estate, but left their own habitation, he hath reserved in everlasting chains under darkness unto the judgment of the great day.

> 2 Cor 5:2 For in this we groan, earnestly desiring to be clothed upon with our house which is from heaven.

The dwelling place/*oykaytayreeon* is the place a spirit resides in the heavenly spiritual realm. Another dwelling place/habitation for the spirit is required in the physical world for a human, angel, or demon to interact physically. Humans are made up of three parts: the soul and the body of the physical world, and the spirit we receive from God in heaven.[241] Know as well that *oykaytayreeon* is a part of and related to a set of Greek words utilized in 2 Corinthians 5:1–2. This passage begins by stating that there is also an earthly house/*oykee'ah:* an earthly residence, abode, and dwelling space;[242] and that if dissolved/destroyed we have a building/*oykodomay'* of God,[243] a house/*oykee'ah* in heaven that is eternal and reserved for us. The earthly habitation is where human's heavenly spirit resides on earth to interact with the physical world. This is the same concept/house angels utilize for their spirits to dwell in, a body and a soul, when they take a physical form in the physical world, to interact in a physically way in the physical world. Angels, like demons, can exist in the physical world as spirit but require an *oykaytayreeon* to interact with the physical world, just as the two angels did in the Sodom narrative and just as angels did to create Nephilim and Rephaim. To this end, 2 Corinthians 5:1–2 completed the doctrine discussed at the end of 2 Corinthians 4, whereby we are instructed that things we see are temporal, but the things we do not see are eternal—our spirit and our heavenly tabernacle.

> 2 Cor 4:18 While we look not at the things which are seen, but at the things which are not seen: for the things which are seen are temporal; but the things which are not seen are eternal.. ..

> 2 Cor 5:1 For we know that if our earthly house of this tabernacle were dissolved, we have a building of God, an house not made with hands, eternal in the heavens.

Now, the buildings in 2 Corinthians 5:1 are the literal and figurative basis for verse 2's house/*oykaytayreeon* from heaven, the dwelling place/habitation for the

---

[241] 1 Thess 5:23.

[242] G3614—*oy-kee'-ah*; a residence; an abode; home; household; house; an inhabited edifice, a dwelling; house; transliterated: oikia.

[243] G3619—*oy-kod-om-ay'*: architecture as in a structure; a building; act of building; promoting spiritual growth; transliterated: oikodome.

angelic spirits and our spirit in heaven, and why humans groan to be clothed in our future house/*oykaytayreeon* in heaven:

> 2 Cor 5:2 For in this we groan, earnestly desiring to be clothed upon with our house which is from heaven.

Accordingly, our spirits groan from within our earthly house, "tabernacle/*skay'nos*: a hut, a temporary residence, and figuratively the human body where the soul dwells [co-mingling with the spirit]";[244] which groans for our house prepared in heaven. Tabernacle/*skay'nos* is cognate to Old Testament tabernacle/*mishkan*, meaning hut, residence, tent, dwelling place, temple, and the tent where God dwelled among Israel.[245] Similarly, the tabernacle was the dwelling place for the Holy of Holies, "the most holy house" and "the most holy place" in the temple, a dwelling place for God to dwell among His people in the physical world.[246]

> 2 Cor 5:4 For we that are in this tabernacle do groan, being burdened: not for that we would be unclothed, but clothed upon, that mortality might be swallowed up of life.

> 2 Cor 5:5 Now he that hath wrought us for the selfsame thing is God, who also hath given unto us he earnest of the Spirit.

> 2 Cor 5:6 Therefore we are always confident, knowing that, whilst we are at home in the body, we are absent from the Lord.

Accordingly, spirit angels left their habitation/dwelling space, their heavenly house/*oykaytayreeon* as recorded in Jude 1:6, whereby they manifested bodies and souls to hold their spirits. Some fallen angels procreated Nephilim in Genesis 6:4 and Rephaim after the flood, whereby they passed on their DNA and immortal spirit on to their spurious offspring.

If one rolls the above concepts forward to the end times, we might anticipate fallen angels not sent to the abyss once more taking bodily form to walk again among humans, and to guide their loyal followers to parade the world into

---

[244] G4636—*skay'-nos*: a hut; temporary residence; figuratively the human body as the abode where the spirit dwells; tabernacle; tent; transliterated: skeno; G4637—*skay-no'-o*; from 4636: to tent; encamp; to occupy as a mansion; reside in as God did in the Tabernacle; a symbol of protection; dwell in; transliterated: skenoo; G4638—*skay'-no-mah*; from 4637; an encampment; figuratively the temple as God's residence; the body as a place for the soul, a tabernacle; the human body as the dwelling place for the soul; transliterated: skenoma.

[245] H4908—*mishkan, mish-kawn'*: a residence; a shepherd's hut; lair of animals, figuratively the grave; the temple; specifically, the tabernacle: dwelleth; dwelling place; habitation; tent; transliterated: mishkan. Exod 33:3, 7, 9, 10, 11; 39:32–43; Lev 1:1; Num 1:1.

[246] 1 Kings 6:16–17; 7:50; 8:4, 6, 8, 10; 1 Chron 29:3; 2 Chron 3:8, 10; 4:22; 5:7; 8:11; 29:7; 30:27.

destruction. Angels not sent to the abyss may create more spurious offspring again to help in their schema. We may wish to further anticipate the angels, when released from the abyss as recorded in Revelation 9 in the first three and a half years of the last seven, will also take bodily form. Fallen angels will be present and likely in bodily form after the war in heaven in Revelation 12 at the midpoint of the last seven years.

One might anticipate demons from the abyss and those not in the prison possessing human hosts, or having humans create other kinds of *oykaytayreeon*s for demon spirits, as we close in on the last seven years. One might anticipate various kinds of cloned human bodies, chimera-like bodies, or some form of trans-human bodies provided for disembodied spirits of giants. All will be interacting with humankind in the end times, just as they had in the days of Lot and Noah.

Section II:
Hierarchy of the Naphalim

Ps 104:3 Who layeth the beams of his chambers in the waters: who maketh the clouds his chariot: who walketh upon the wings of the wind:

Ps 104:4 Who maketh his angels spirits; his ministers a flaming fire.

Ps 104:5 Who laid the foundations of the earth, that it should not be removed for ever.

CHAPTER 8

THE SEVENTY NATIONS AND THE ASSEMBLY OF GODS

Eph 6:12 For we wrestle not against flesh and blood, but against principalities, against powers, against the rulers of the darkness of this world, against spiritual wickedness in high places.

Many are aware of the notion of seventy original nations, but most are not fully briefed as to how that number was arrived at, or the overarching implications past, present, and future.

Genesis 10 and 1 Chronicles 1 lists Noah's seventy descendants: Shem: 26; Japheth 14; Ham: 30. All were dispersed to the four winds of migration after the confounding of languages at Babel.[247] These seventy patriarchs comprise the postdiluvian table of nations that helps to comprehend early postdiluvian history and is important to help discern the information documented in Deuteronomy 32:7–9. The seventy patriarchs and nations of Noah comprise a consistent number directly related to the seventy sons of Jacob/Israel, and the seventy gods who govern the

---

[247] Gen 11:7–8.

THE GENESIS 6 CONSPIRACY PART II

earth under Satan's oversight and direction. Discerning Deuteronomy 32 in its full context provides valuable information explicating why God required Israel to take the Covenant Land by force, as well as comprehending the full visible Nephilim World Order directed by the (now invisible) Naphalim World Order, both before and after the flood.

The book of Deuteronomy recorded events regarding Israel when they were still forging their faith, and before they crossed the Jordan River to seize the Covenant Land—land God previously reserved for Himself and His chosen people of destiny from the beginning for His divine purposes. Deuteronomy 32:7–9 was provided in part for context and justification for Israel, just before Joshua led Israel's invasion of the Covenant Land. From the beginning, God apportioned land He would later bequeath to Israel to dwell in after the flood. God then bound Israel's promised inheritance into His Holy Covenant with them during the Exodus period,[248] as part of His grander plan to save humankind from rebellious angels and their spurious offspring. I summarized this notion in *The Genesis 6 Conspiracy: How Secret Societies and the Descendants of Giants Plan to Enslave Humankind:*

> As you will recall in Deuteronomy 32:8, God divided the nations in the beginning according to the number of the sons of God. One concludes from Scripture that God kept the Promised Land for Himself, for His specific intentions, because God clearly bequeathed the land to the descendants of Abraham, the future nation of Israel (Genesis 12:7, 13:14–15, 17:8–9, 18:17–21, 48:5–6, Acts 7:5–6), and clearly stated the land was His (Leviticus 25:23). God then gave the land to Israel (Joshua 24:11–13, Deuteronomy 1:21, 3:27, 32:38, Numbers 27:12, 34:1–29) as their inheritance. The posterity of the Nephilim surely would have remembered this. The remnant of the Nephilim then settled knowingly in the Land of the Covenant after the deluge, in full support of their ancestors and progenitors. It was in the Promised Land that the postdiluvian Nephilim nation chose to make its stand against God and the future, infant nation of hope, endeavoring to thwart God's plan of salvation for humankind when Israel was at their weakest point.[249]

In the same way that God established the seventy nations after the flood, Deuteronomy 32 instructs the reader that God had previously divided the earth among the nations in the days of old, in the days of and according to Adam's sons,

---

[248] Exod 24:1–18.
[249] Wayne, *The Genesis 6 Conspiracy*, 174.

and according to the same number of Israel's sons born in Egypt—seventy,[250] and just as Noah's seventy descendants/patriarchs were listed in the table of nations.

> Deut 32:7 Remember the days of old, consider the years of many generations: ask thy father, and he will shew thee; thy elders, and they will tell thee.

> Deut 32:8 When the most High divided to the nations their inheritance, when he separated the sons of Adam, he set the bounds of the people according to the number of the children of Israel.

Many readers note that Deuteronomy 32:7–8's accounting of events appears out of sorts at first glance, because Israel was not a nation before the flood, nor a nation at the time of the table of nations' accounting of Genesis 10 (and later, 1 Chronicles 1). Israel's appearance in Deuteronomy is out of sorts chronologically—until one asserts that Israel's insertion was prophetic. As such, God's original prophetic edict ordained that there would be a constant number of seventy nations beginning with Adam, and then Noah and Jacob/Israel. Thus, the original division of nations numbered by Adam's sons was the constant for the entire epoch of Adam by the Alpha and Omega.[251] It follows that Israel was accounted for in the postdiluvian seventy nations through Jacob, via Arphaxad son of Shem.[252] Hence, the wording "according to the number of the children of Israel" was the fulfillment of God's ancient prophetic edict from the beginning for the antediluvian and postdiluvian epoch. As such, Jacob's name was changed to Israel before he bore his sons in Egypt[253]—as an inheritance title, and to fulfill all aspects of God's edict. Jacob was prophetically accounted for as Israel in verse 8 and apportioned their inheritance lot that God had reserved and bequeathed to them in verse 9: "For the LORD's portion is his people; Jacob is the lot of his inheritance." Israel's inheritance lot extended from the Nile River to the Euphrates,[254] including land illegally squatted on by Rephaim and then the Canaanites of the Ham branch after Babel.

The Hebrew word translated "Israel" in the KJV, specifically as it surfaces in Deuteronomy 32:8, has a dual purpose and larger meaning which holds the key to understanding why this verse is translated so differently in other English translations, the Septuagint, and Dead Sea Scroll manuscripts. Know that the "sons of Israel" was translated from Hebrew to English from the Masoretic Text, manuscripts copied and recopied down the generations by rabbis that became the source for most of the 1610–11 KJV Old Testament translations. On the other hand,

---

[250] Gen 46:27; Exod 1:5.
[251] Rev 1:8.
[252] Gen 10:21-32; 1 Chron 1:12–34, 2:1–2.
[253] Gen 32:22–32.
[254] Gen 11:22–29; 15:18–21.

older Dead Sea Scroll Hebrew and Aramaic manuscripts, dated earlier than the copies of the Masoretic Text received from the rabbis, were discovered well after the KJV publication, which translated the sons of Israel as "sons of God" in those later published English translations. Moreover, the Greek Septuagint translated the passage as "Angels of God." Note: the bracketed texts below are my insertions with the Hebrew words from the Masoretic Text:

> *DSC* Deut 32:8 When Elyown [Elyon as in most High] gave the nations as an inheritance, when he separated the sons of man [Adam], he set the boundaries of the peoples according to the number of the sons [ben] of [ha] God [El/Elohiym].[255]

> *LXX* Deut 32:8 When the most High divided the nations, when he separated the sons of Adam, he set the bounds of the nations according to the number of the angels of God.

The Dead Sea Scrolls and Septuagint are not wrong in their translations from Hebrew, Aramaic, and Greek respectfully, nor do we have a contradiction in Scripture. Rather, both translations do not carry forward the full meaning of the text in their translations, as understood by the Israelites, just as the KJV translation also falls short of the fuller translation to the word Israel/*Yisra'el*.

Yisra'el in Deuteronomy 32:8 is the originating compounded Hebrew word understood originally differently than the singular word/title Israel to which God changed Jacob's name, a new name based in the original edict and prophecy of God. In the original understanding the compound word *Yisra'el* describes supernatural beings before the flood. These supernatural beings were directly connected to ruling over the seventy antediluvian nations. Israel, in its singular meaning as the nation of Jacob, is never scripturally applied to the descendants of Adam's complete progeny, so one deduces that the compound word and its meaning references the ruling council of fallen angels/gods.

Accordingly, *Yisra'el* derives jointly from *sarah,* meaning to prevail, have power as in a prince, and to contend with as in persevere. *Yisra'el* is jointly derived from *El,* defined as mighty, angel, god and/or God Most High. The correct meaning and translation for the ancient application would derive from the meaning of both words. Typically, the compounded meaning for *Yisra'el* is understood as rule/reign as God,[256] and translated together with the sons: "according to the sons ruling as or with God, sons ruling as a gods/angels, or ruling sons [angels] of the reigning God," all the while noting that sons of God are described as an order of

---

[255] Dead Sea Scrolls, 4QDeutJ, 4QDeutQ.

[256] H3478 —*Yisra'el, yis-raw-ale';* from 8280 and 410: he will rule as God; Jisrael; a symbolical name of Jacob; of his posterity; H8280—sarah, saw-raw': to prevail; have power as a prince. H410—'*el, ale*; god, god-like one, mighty one men angels, false god, and God.

angels in Genesis 6:4 and Job 1:6, 2:1, and 38:4–7. Details defining angels, all their obscure orders, and their hierarchy are slowly revealed throughout Scripture as to their roles, interaction, and importance to humanity. We learn more and more about those roles in the later books of each testament.

The children/son(s)[257] of Israel/*Yisra'el* translates as powerful gods/angels who reigned over the seventy nations counted by the sons of Adam before the flood, the descendants of Noah after the flood, and a prophetic allegory and double entendre for the nation of destiny[258] that I refer to the latter as a dual prophecy. A dual prophecy holds significance to the time shortly after the prophecy is made, has ramifications for the end times, and where the context is defined by the valuable prehistory information provided within the prophecy. All was recorded for context and in preparation for the millennium prophecies when Israel will inherit the full lot.

Although similar sons of God terms were applied to Israel after the flood, these applications were prophetic allegory that requires contextual recognition for discernment. For example, Exodus 4:22 references Israel allegorically as sons of God, not literal sons of God as angels were. Israelites were humans begat by humans, set aside for a specific commission as a nation of priests,[259] to bring about the Messiah and their eventual redemption[260] as dictated in the Holy Covenant's blessings and curses. In the end times, all Israel will be adopted as sons of God, to be like angels, along with the church after the resurrection(s), and after Israel accepts Jesus as their Messiah.[261] The resurrection promises were entrenched at Pentecost, even though Israel and Christians have human fathers.[262] *Nelson's Illustrated Bible Dictionary* concurs with this conclusion regarding the New Testament sons of God, who then became sons of God in a covenant relationship, adopted and grafted into the covenant. *Nelson's* further stated that the sons of God were part of the covenant relationship recorded in Isaiah, noting this phrase does not appear with this meaning in the Old Testament, but the idea is implied in Isaiah 45:6, 45:11, and Hosea 1:10:[263]

> Hos 1:10. .. and it shall come to pass, that in the place where it was said unto them, Ye are not my people, there it shall be said unto them, Ye are the sons of the living God.

---

[257] H1121—*ben, bane*; from 1129; a son; a builder of the family name; grandson, figuratively a subject or nation.

[258] Dual Prophecy examples: Isa 13–14; 25, Ezek 28, 29, 31, 32; Jer 51.

[259] Exod 19:6; Deut 14:1–2; Rev 1:6.

[260] Ezek 37:1-48; Dan 12:2; Mic 2:12–13; 4:5–8; 5:5–15.

[261] Zec 9:14; 12:10; Matt 24:27, 30, 31; Mark 13:26–27; Luke 20:34–36; John 19:37.

[262] John 1:12–13; Acts 2:1–38; Rom 8:13–17; Phil 2:15; Gal 4:5–7; Heb 1:14; 12:7–9; 1 Peter 3:18–19.

[263] R. F. Youngblood, F. F. Bruce, and R. K. Harrison, *Nelson's New Illustrated Bible Dictionary* (Oxford: Nelson Publishers, 1995), 1194: sons of God.

Knowing *Yisra'el*, governing gods of the nations, did so both before and after the flood makes sense of the mysterious congregation/assembly of gods detailed in Psalm 82:1-8—princes who will eventually die like men. "Prince" is reminiscent of the variant meanings of *sarah* in *sarah- el(s)/Yisarel*, of Deuteronomy 32:8, rebellious angels who will be sent to the lake of fire in the end-time.[264] Princes/*sar* includes as part of its many meanings, angel, prince, principal, ruler, and Ruler of rulers, as in God.[265] Similarly, the word Israel/*Israhale'* in the New Testament is additionally defined as a prince of God.[266]

The gods/princes in the council of gods are described as the children/*ben* of the most High/*Elyown*,[267] which not coincidentally is remarkably similar language to Deuteronomy 32:8: children/*ben Yisra'el*, and the sons/*ben* of God/*Elohiym* in Genesis 6:4. Gods/*Elohiym* is defined as rulers, angels, gods, and God as in the plural, capitalized superlative of god/*el* with the latter.[268] The assembly of ruling sons of God is named the congregation of the mighty/*el* and the singular version of *elohiym* for gods and angels,[269] the congregation of the gods.

> Ps 82:1 God standeth in the congregation of the mighty; he judgeth among the gods.. ..

> Ps 82:6 I have said, Ye are gods; and all of you are children of the most High.

Psalm 82's evil council of gods, the sons of the God Most High, are the sons of God described in Deuteronomy 32:7–9 who reigned over the seventy nations. Thus, the Deuteronomy sons of God are the gods/princes that God Most High will judge in the end times for the angelic rebellion and crimes against creation and humanity.[270] The end-time judgment will include the sons of God's spurious offspring, the Nephilim and Rephaim demigods. Jesus confirmed Psalm 82's veracity

---

[264] Matt 25:41.

[265] H8269—*sar, sar*; from 8323: a head person: principal; ruler; chief; head; overseer of other official classes; princes of religious office; elders of representative leaders of people; merchant-princes of rank and dignity; patron-angel; Ruler of rulers (of God).

[266] G2474—*is-rah-ale'; Yisra'el*: a prince of God; Israel; Jacob's adopted name including his descendants; transliterated: Israel.

[267] Ps 82:6. H5945—*'elyown, el-yone'*; from 5927: Highest, Most High; name of God; rulers; monarchs; angel-princes; H5927—'*alah, aw-law'*: to ascend; intransitively to be high.

[268] H430—*'elohiym, el-o-heem'*; plural of 433: rulers; judges; divine ones; angels; gods; and God; H433—*'elowahh, el-o'-ah*; rarely *eloahh, eloahh el-o'-ah* from 410: a deity; H410—*'el, ale*; god; god-like one; mighty one; mighty men; men of rank; mighty heroes; angels; false god; demon; God; the one true God; Jehovah; strength; mighty; and power.

[269] H410—*'el, ale*.

[270] Ps 82:8; Matt 25:41; Deut 32:9.

in the book of John when He stated that the council of gods, sons of the most High was an accurate accounting; that Scripture cannot be broken; and that He was the Son of God[271] come to save humankind from the oppression of the ruling gods and their offspring led by Satan.[272]

In the Greek Atlantean tradition, Poseidon and/or Iapetus was the angel/son of God, a Watcher/Ruler/Archon to whom the continent of Atlantis was portioned out to, while the balance of the earth was allotted to the other gods.[273] Apportioning out the lands to the gods of the ruling pantheon and council was a common doctrine in most all the polytheist religions and history as in Grand Assembly of the Anunnaki at Nippur.[274]

God too has a counsel of angels called the Counsel of the Lord, a holy congregation where His throne sits before all the high-ranking angels and host of heaven.[275] The assembly of the gods in Psalm 82 is a counterfeit counsel/congregation of God established by Satan, and populated by Satan's high-ranking rebellious angels, to reign over the earth and perhaps the physical universe. Thus, Satan, the fallen angel called Lucifer in the KJV, Hebrew *Heylel*,[276] was identified by the Word/Jesus as the angel and leader of rebellious angels who fell in disgrace from heaven to the earth.[277] The angel *Heylel* wanted to raise his throne to heaven to be like God, to sit on God's throne, and to reign from the "mount of the congregation."[278] Thus, the assembly of the gods is chaired by Satan located on a high mountain assembly. And, knowing this makes sense of Satan being described in the New Testament as the god and prince of this world, noting world/*aheeohn'* transliterated as *aion* is defined as the perpetuity of time, an age, the worlds, and the universe[279]—the physical universe until the completion of the end times documented in the book of Revelation.

> 2 Cor 4:4 In whom the god of this world hath blinded the minds of them which believe not.

---

[271] John 10:34–38.

[272] Rev 12:7, 9.

[273] Charles Berlitz, *The Mystery of Atlantis* (New York: Norton Publications Inc., 1969), 37; Ignatius Donnelly, *Atlantis: The Antediluvian World*, 12.

[274] Gardner, *Realm of the Ring Lords*, 3.

[275] 1 Kings 22:19; Ps 22:25; 33:11; 49:9–10; 149:1; Isa 14:13; Jer 23:18.

[276] H1966—*heylel, hay-lale'*: shining one; morning star; light bearer; Lucifer; figurative for the King of Babylon Helel.

[277] Luke 10:18: "And he said unto them, I beheld Satan as lightning fall from heaven."

[278] Isa 14:13.

[279] G165—*ahee-ohn'*; from the same as 104: for ever; an unbroken age; perpetuity of time; eternity; the worlds; the universe; period of time; age; transliterated: aion.

CHAPTER 9

SATAN, HEYLEL, AND LUCIFER

Isa 14:12 How art thou fallen from heaven, O Lucifer, son of the morning! how art thou cut down to the ground, which didst weaken the nations!

Isa 14:13 For thou hast said in thine heart, I will ascend into heaven, I will exalt my throne above the stars of God: I will sit also upon the mount of the congregation, in the sides of the north:

Isa 14:14 I will ascend above the heights of the clouds; I will be like the most High.

Oddly, the KJV names the temporary god of this world as Lucifer. Lucifer is an Italian word inserted by translators for the Hebrew word *Heylel*, which appears to be one of Satan's names. *Heylel* is defined in *Strong's Dictionary* as morning star, shining one, light-bearer, and oddly Lucifer.[280] Typically the "el" suffix indicates an angelic name as in Michael or Gabriel.

Heylel in part derives from *Halal* meaning to shine, boast, be praiseworthy, and to act like a madman.[281] Understanding the meaning of *Halal* helps to explain

---

[280] H1966—*heylel, hay-lale'*; from 1984: shining one; morning star; light bearer; Lucifer; figurative for the King of Babylon Helel.
[281] H1984—*halal, haw-lal'*: to be clear; to shine; to make a show; to be praiseworthy; boast; foolish; rave; celebrate; to act like a madman.

the actions of the rebellious Satan when he bragged that he would raise his throne above the stars of God to be like God, just as the Babel/Babylon incarnations of beast empires did and will do in the end times with Antichrist.[282]

Heylel, after his fall from grace and heaven, and after his failed angelic rebellion was degraded by God to Satan status: an accuser, adversary, attacker, and archenemy of good, God,[283] and humans as depicted in the book of Job and throughout the Old and New Testament.[284] Isaiah 14:15 seems to indicate *Heylel* was degraded to Satan status at the time of his prehistoric fall and edict for his fate. It follows then that the Word who became Jesus stated, "He beheld Satan as lightening fall from heaven,"[285] identifying *Heylel's* newly degraded Satan status, whereby his realm of rule was thereafter restricted to the earth to and to the underworld.[286]

Heylel's fate was set as the chief satan, a role Satan was sentenced to play out for a specific period known only by God. After *ha Satan's* reign of terror over the earth as chief accuser and deceiver of humankind, *ha Satan* will be sent to the abyss at the end of this age for a thousand years—[287] the same place the impassioned and most evil of the Naphalim were sent.

Isa 14:15 Yet thou shalt be brought down to hell, to the sides of the pit.

In addition to being the god and prince of this world, Satan[288] was/is the chief god/*el* of *heyl* alternatively known as the underworld where the bottomless pit prison, the abyss is located, and where Satan will be imprisoned at the end of this age. *Heyl/Hel* was seemingly transliterated as "hell" by KJV translators. "Hell" is cognate to a hale: a cavern, a hollow, and/or a dark hidden place.[289]

Conversely, in polytheist understanding, heaven is not above as in the stars, but in the Otherworld/Underworld, a place in another dimension adjacent to our dimension,[290] and seemingly a counterfeit heaven. Occult religions refer to hell as the

---

[282] Isa 14:12; Jer 51:53; Dan 8:10; Rev 13:1–18, 18:5–7.

[283] H7854—*satan, saw-tawn*'; from 7853: an opponent; especially with the article "ha" prefixed with Satan; the archenemy of good; adversary; withstand; superhuman adversary; H7853—*satan, saw-tan*': to attack; accuse; to be an adversary; oppose.

[284] 1 Chron 21:1; Job 1:6–9, 12; 2:1–4, 6–7; Ps 109:6; Zech 3:1–2; Matt 4:10; 12:26; 16:23; Mark 1:13; 3:23, 26; 4:15; 8:33; Luke 4:8; 11:18; 13:16; 22:3, 31; John 13:27; Acts 5:3; 26:18; Rom 16:20; 1 Cor 7:5; 2 Cor 2:11; 11:14; 12:7; 1 Thess 2:18; 2 Thess 2:9; 1 Tim 1:20; 5:15; Rev 2:9, 13, 24; 12:9; 20:2, 7.

[285] Luke 10:18.

[286] Job 1:6; 2:1.

[287] Rev 20:2, 7.

[288] Matt 4:8–9; Luke 4:5–6; John 12:31; 14:30; 16:11; Eph 2:2; 2 Cor 4:4; 1 John 5:18–19; Rev 12:9.

[289] *Catholic Encyclopedia*, Vol. 6, 207: hell.

[290] De Vere, *The Dragon Legacy: The Secret History of an Ancient Bloodline*, 66.

"Mirror World" as recorded in the *Mabinogion*, where the previous gods, the Portal Guardians could enter and leave freely, and the home of the transcended ones—the ancestral royals. Elphame, Hades, Caer Glas, Tir Na N'og,[291] Valhalla, and Swarga Loka are some of the many other names, all the while noting that magic mirrors are often depicted as windows and portals into another dimension in fairy tale literature.

Hell as a concept is thought by many scholars to have derived from Germanic and Norse sources, *hel* as it relates to the goddess of the underworld.[292] and/or the Saxon word *helan/halan* meaning an invisible place for the spirits who have left this world.[293] *Heyl/hel* surfaced in Old English as *hell/helle*, where it evolved to hell in the new (Baconian) English and took on a wider scope in its meaning.[294] Thus, Satan is the god of hell as one of his names/titles indicate: *Heyl-el*. *Heylel* is also the source word for *Helel*, one of the antichrist archetypes in prophetic allegory known as the king of Babylon cognate with the Assyrian in many dual prophecies that include Isaiah 13 and 14, and Ezekiel 31 and 32, among others. Within segments of polytheism, the god of hell is the god of the Freemasons whom they called the Great Architect of the Universe and Lucifer, and which further raises eyebrows as to how an Italian word replaced the Hebrew *Heylel* in an English translation.

Heylel derives from *halal* defined as to shine, to boast, to rave, act like a madman and other superlative descriptions[295] both good and evil, all of which describe Satan before and after sin was found in him.[296] *Heylel* is additionally rooted in *yalal*: to howl; howling; wailing.[297] Many times, "al" shows up biblically as a transliteration of "el," as in the Baal god and Baalim gods worshipped by the Rephaim and the twelve Canaanite tribes. If the transliteration is applied to Satan, then *Halal* would translate as the proud shining god and *Yalal*, the howling god. If so, one ponders whether both these attributes of Satan were part of his unique being and titles. *Yalal* has occult connotations depicting shapeshifting gods like Zeus who took a form of a wolf at times and howling jackal gods like Anubis. Howling gods are reminiscent of the doleful creatures/ *'oach* that howl like jackals[298] recorded Isaiah 13 and 34 who dwell among satyrs, owls, dragons, unicorns, vultures, and other wild beasts all reminiscent of the rebellious angelic realm.

---

[291] Ibid., 66.
[292] *Catholic Encyclopedia*, Vol. 6, 207: hell; Rebecca Parks, ed, *Encyclopedia of World Mythology* (Farmington Hills, MI: Gale, 2009), 502: hell.
[293] M'Clintock, *Cyclopaedia of Biblical, Theological, and Ecclesiastical Literature*, Vol. 4, 165: hell.
[294] Ibid.
[295] H1984—*halal, haw-lal'*.
[296] Ezek 28:15: "Thou wast perfect in thy ways from the day that thou wast created, till iniquity was found in thee."
[297] H3213—*yalal, yaw-lal'*: to howl with a wailing tone; yell with a boisterous voice; howl; be howling; Isa 14.12: "How art thou fallen from heaven, O Lucifer [3213], son of the morning!"
[298] H255—*'oach, o'-akh*: a howler or lonesome wild animal; doleful creature; jackal; hyena; Isa 13:21–22, 34

Howl/*yalal* surfaces again in Isaiah 14:31 following the serpent's root and the "fiery serpent" passage of verse 29, which I believe is not coincidental. Howl/*yalal* imagery runs throughout the unique dual prophecy that is Isaiah 14 and is connected to the serpentine imagery as well through Satan. Thus, serpentine imagery of the fiery serpent-faced seraphim, an angelic dragon, is directly connected in the above said passages to the serpent's root of Genesis 3:15, Genesis 6:4 offspring of Seraphim Watchers, the serpentine imagery connected to Satan in Luke 10:18–19, the serpentine and dragon imagery of Satan in Revelation 12:9, and the end-time prophetic allegory for the Assyrian and the King of Babylon/*Helel* Antichrist who will serve Satan.

> Isa 14:25 That I will break the Assyrian in my land, and upon my mountains tread him under foot.. ..
>
> Isa 14:29 Rejoice not thou, whole Palestina, because the rod of him that smote thee is broken: for out of the serpent's root shall come forth a cockatrice, and his fruit shall be a fiery flying serpent.. ..
>
> Isa 14:31 Howl, O gate; cry, O city; thou, whole Palestina, art dissolved: for there shall come from the north a smoke, and none shall be alone in his appointed times.

Heylel is the light-bearer, shining one, and metaphorically a morning star,[299] whereby *Heylel's* "heart was lifted up by thy beauty, thou hast corrupted thy wisdom by reason of thy brightness,"[300] all the while noting brightness/*yiph`ah* means splendor, beauty, shining and brightness.[301] Knowing this makes sense that Satan still likes to transform himself or show himself as a beautiful angel of light to deceive the descendants of human/angelic hybrids and their human followers as long as Satan is permitted to do so. It follows then that Satan's earthly followers are similar deceitful workers and false prophets transforming themselves into apostles of Christ,[302] just as initiates of secret societies and mystical religions refer to themselves as children of light, and Lucifer as good god of light and knowledge. Below is an excerpt from my first book that sums what had been written in the first seventy chapters on secret societies, Satan and the mystical polytheist religions:

> The initiates of high degrees are maintained in the purity of Luciferian doctrine. Albert Pike wrote to the Supreme Councils that they were to know Lucifer was indeed the secret god of the Masons. Pike further wrote that the (glorious) "light" that all Masons seek is the knowledge of who god is, for they believe Lucifer is the real god of the universe.

---

[299] H1966—*heylel.*
[300] Eze 28:17.
[301] H3314—*yiph`ah, yif-aw':* splendor; figuratively; beauty; brightness; shining.
[302] 1 Cor 11:13.

In this book, I have danced all around the Satan scenario while dropping many hints and subtle conclusions. It is now time to nail down this notion. The Freemasons and all their genitive and associated organizations believe the real god of the universe is Lucifer. Freemasonry and all their associate organizations are ultimately preparing to bring about the New World Order under the New Babel that worships Lucifer.

The teachings of all the diverse forms of mysticism preach the same doctrine, all declaring Lucifer to be the fallen seraphim angel. This is certainly witnessed by the Freemasons; the New Age movement; and particularly, the reticent organization at the centre of the Freemasonry, the Illuminati. They all are on record as worshipping the fallen angel of mysticism, which views Lucifer as a good god to whom a great wrong has been done. Lucifer, as this deluded idea goes, is the good god, while the true God of the universe is evil, and the devil.

Lucifer masquerades as an angel of light. Light is the masonic symbol for intelligence, information, knowledge, and truth; darkness is ignorance and evil and the followers of Adonai: Jews, Muslims, and Christians. Lucifer is the god of light and the god of good—the god who struggles against darkness and evil for humankind.[303]

One should anticipate diabolical deceptions designed by polytheist forces to transform Satan back into an angel of light, deceptions that craftily prepare many Christians to fall away in the end times. Venus is perhaps a good starting point to unravel polytheists' clever allegories and diabolical double entendres. Venus is renowned worldwide as the morning star, but less famously as the twilight star for half the year. The morning star allegory sets the tempo for transforming Satan back to a god/angel of light, and is used dually as a slur against Jesus, as we will cover shortly.

Polytheists tend to worship Satan in his original creation as brightness, defined in Hebrew as shining, splendor, and beauty,[304] and as described in Ezekiel 28:17, but leaving out Satan's fall from heaven and into disgrace and his degraded Satan status. Leaving out, dismissing, and reimagining inconvenient passages in Scripture are part of the interpretive and mystical approach and tactics employed by polytheists and their moles inside Christianity, as they continue their preparation for the end times.

---

[303] Wayne, *The Genesis 6 Conspiracy*, 499–500, citing Demond Wilson, *The New Age Millennium*, 155–156, quoting from Morals and Dogma of the Ancient And Accepted Scottish Rite of Freemasonry/Pamphlets and 137, 159, 170; and citing Ralph A. Epperson, *Masonry: Conspiracy against Christianity* (Tucson, AZ: Publius Press, 1997), 112.
[304] H3314—*yiph`ah.*

Ezek 28:17 Thine heart was lifted up because of thy beauty, thou hast corrupted thy wisdom by reason of thy brightness: I will cast thee to the ground, I will lay thee before kings, that they may behold thee.

Ergo, discerning the distinct differences between *Heylel* and Lucifer, the son of the morning, and day star (as some English translate Isaiah 14:12) is essential to comprehend the Isaiah 13–14 dual prophecy, and the usurping of Jesus' title, the Morning Star to begin Satan's transformation into the counterfeit morning star, allegorically called Venus and Lucifer in mysticism.

In a cognate kind of word insertion, the pre-Christian Septuagint Greek translation for some reason substituted *heosphoros/ἑωσφόρος* for *Heylel* rather than Lucifer, as done in the KJV. *Heosphoros* is used seven times in the Septuagint, of which *Heosphoros* was substituted two times for different Hebrew words, all dealing with the dawn or morning.[305] The Septuagint has many corruptions as compared to the Masoretic Hebrew texts, including an inclination to substitute Greek names and belief biases Greek translators thought to be the Greek equivalent. *Heosphorus* appears to be one of those substitutions based on Greek history, religion, and mythology that Gnostics seized upon for their agenda to slur Jesus and honor Satan.

A god named Hesperus/Ἕσπερος in Greek mythology was personified in the planetary realm as the evening star, Venus. Hesperus/*Heosphorus* was a god who was sometimes later conflated with his half brother Eosphorus, alternatively called Phosophorus. Both were sons of Eos the Dawn. They were half brothers via their mother, Eos. Eosphorus's/ἑωσφόρος personification in the planetary realm was the "Dawnstar" morning star, Venus.[306] Eosphorus/ἑωσφόρος is generally defined as the bearer or bringer/*phorus* of the dawn/*eos* and is the ancient Greek word substituted for *Heylel*. Both Greek gods were personified in a conflated and similar way to *Heylel* son of the morning, but neither Hesperus nor Eosphorus were high-level gods in the hierarchy of gods/angels, whereas Satan is the leader of the gods.

Sept Isa 14:12 πῶς ἐξέπεσεν ἐκ τοῦ οὐρανοῦ ὁ ἑωσφόρος ὁ πρωῒ ἀνατέλλων; συνετρίβη.

Sept Isa 14:12 How has Lucifer, that rose in the morning fallen from heaven.[307]

Heosphoros is not found in the Greek language of the New Testament, nor in early Christian writings. However, a related word, φωσφόρος,/*focefor'os,* transliterated

---

[305] Job 11:17; 38:12.
[306] Hesiod, *Theogony*, verses 370-380, Eosphorus/Dawn-star, son of Eos and Astraios; note 22.
[307] Septuagint, Complete Greek and English Edition (Ancient Classic Series, 2016 Kindle Version), Isa 14:12.

as "phosphorus," does appear. Phosphorus means light-bringer or bearer, phosphorus, morning star, day star, Venus, and also a metaphor for Christ,[308] as it is employed in 1 Peter 1:19 for day star and morning star in some English translations. Phosphorus, meaning day star and morning star, then opens the door to confusion and deceptions about Jesus. "Day star" and/or "morning star" in 2 Peter 1:19 should not be understood as Venus, *Heylel*, or Lucifer, morning star or day star of Isaiah 14:12, but prophetic for Jesus and His authentic title of the true morning star, recorded in Revelation 2:28.

> *KJV* 2 Peter 1:19 We have also a more sure word of prophecy; whereunto ye do well that ye take heed, as unto a light that shineth in a dark place, until the day dawn, and the day star arise in your hearts:

> *NIV* 2 Peter 1:19 We also have the prophetic message as something completely reliable, and you will do well to pay attention to it, as to a light shining in a dark place, until the day dawns and the morning star rises in your hearts.

The Latin word for Venus is *Lucifer*, which corresponds to Greek phosphorus/φωσφόρος, the word used in 2 Peter 3;19. For some odd reason, Jerome translated *Heylel ben shachar* in Isaiah 14:12 into the Latin Vulgate Bible as "Lucifer son of the morning," perhaps utilizing 2 Peter 2:19 as the basis for his translation, because he had difficulty understanding and then correctly translating *Heylel* into Latin using other words. What is also noteworthy is that Jerome did not use ἑωσφόρος/heosphoros as used in the Septuagint in Isaiah 14:12 Thus, "Lucifer" first appeared in the Vulgate Bible and was later adopted into the KJV and English translations of the Septuagint.

Lucifer, then, ought not to have appeared into the English language and English translation but for the inexplicable choices of the KJV and Septuagint translators to insert a Latin word cognate with a Greek into English, a word used by Gnostics for Satan. *Heylel*, son of the morning or dawn, is a more logical Christian translation, just as Michael's (one who is like God[309]) and Gabriel's (warrior of God[310]) names were translated directly rather than as the meanings of their names. Or if translators insisted on using the meaning of *Heylel*, the translation in my opinion ought to have read "light-bringer," "son of the morning," or "dawn."

Utilizing the meaning of the name *Heylel* versus directly translating the name is a clever deception by Gnostic moles. Ergo, this brings into focus why KJV translators annotated a preface on the margin for Isaiah 14:12. In short, the KJV

---

[308] G5459—φωσφόρος, *foce-for'-os*: light-bearing; light bringing; phosphorus; the morning-star; figurative day star; metaphor for Christ; the planet Venus.

[309] H4310—*Miyka'el*: one who is like God: an archangel.

[310] G1043—*gab-ree-ale'* of Hebrew origin 1403: man of God; an archangel; H1403—*Gabriy'el, gab-ree-ale'*: man of God; warrior of God; an archangel: Gabriel.

translators would not denounce those who depart from the KJV text "Lucifer" to adopt the KJV margin translation as "daystar," "morning star," and thus *Heylel*.

> The Translators to the Readers: Now in such a case doth not a margin do well to admonish the reader to seek further, and not to conclude or dogmatize upon this or that peremptorily? For as it is a fault of incredulity to doubt of those things that are evident, so to determine of such things as the Spirit of God hath left (even in the judgment of the judicious) questionable, can be no less than presumption.. .. They that are wise had rather have their judgments at liberty in differences of readings, than to be captivated to one when it may be the other [tenth unnumbered page of this preface].

Should *Heylel* in Isaiah 14:12 really be defined or translated as day star or morning star, as that title applies to Jesus in 2 Peter 1:19 as many polytheists propose? Likely not. The meaning to *Heylel* should not be substituted for the name. I believe the verse should read: "*Heylel* son of the morning/dawn." One should anticipate Gnostics will enlist the Bible utilizing the interpretive approach, cleverly manipulated passages, and perhaps dubious or diabolical translations for selective words, as part of their end-time brainwashing and preparation to bring about Babylon and the Antichrist and his religion.

Lucifer is not directly associated with *Heylel*, but Lucifer is fondly referred to as Venus in Gnostic religions and secret societies. Figuratively then, Satan is Venus the morning star in occult religions. Gnostics reimagine "son of the morning" *ben shachar* [311] into morning star, but son of the dawn or morning is not "the Morning or Day Star" as Jesus is referred to. *Heylel* is merely the son of the morning, as one of the angelic sons of God orders. Conversely, Jesus is never referred to as "son of the morning/dawn" even though Jesus is referred to as "Day Star" in 2 Peter 1, the Star in Numbers 24:17, and the morning star in Revelation 22 in the latter in clear reference to future end-time events in Revelation prophecy. Revelation records Jesus will give those who overcome this world the "morning star" when He comes in the end-time as Jesus, Day Star, Morning Star "arise[s] in their heart[s]."

> Rev 2:28 And I will give him the morning star.

> Rev 22:16 I Jesus have sent mine angel to testify unto you these things in the churches. I am the root and the offspring of David, and the bright and morning star.

The morning star order of angels were noted singing together in the book of Job at the time of creation, where this order of angels was grouped among the sons

---

[311] H7837—*shachar, shakh'-ar*: dawn; daybreak; early; light; morning.

of God who shouted for joy.[312] The morning star order of angels indicate *Heylel* was not unique as one of the sons/stars of the morning and sons/stars of the dawn, but this was one of likely many titles Satan jointly held before his fall. Morning derives from *boqer*, meaning dawn,[313] which derives from `ereb, and `arab, both that mean dusk or sundown.[314] Both dusk and dawn have a twilight period when many stars can appear. It follows then that the Greek gods Eosphorus and Heosphorus were the polytheist personification or part of the rebellious gods/stars of the sunset and sunrise, the gods of twilight. The Eosphorus and Heosphorus myth appears to have been conflated and overlayed onto Lucifer's mythos by Gnostics and their affinity to Greek gods and history.

The morning star angelic order of dusk and dawn was captured in Job 3:8–9 where the stars of the twilight/*nesheph*, meaning the dark of the dawn or dusk,[315] are discussed in a cryptic narrative about those who curse the day, "who are ready raise their mourning." What is fascinating to me about this passage is the word "mourning" employed by the KJV translators, which at a first glance seems noteworthy. Upon closer scrutiny, though, one learns "mourning" derives from *livyathan*, transliterated as "leviathan": a serpent, dragon, sea monster[316] associated with the angelic realm, and possibly another allegory for Satan and/or the end-time hydra dragon of the beast empires that rises out of the sea in Revelation 13 that Satan sponsors. Leviathan and Satan are judged in the Revelation prophecy at the end times and then millennium respectively.[317] Further, "dawning of the day" in Job 3:9 derives from *shachar*, or as it is understood in Isaiah 14:12 *Heylel ben shachar.*

> *KJV* Job 3:8 Let them curse it that curse the day, who are ready to raise up their mourning.
>
> Job 3:9 Let the stars of the twilight thereof be dark; let it look for light, but have none; neither let it see the dawning of the day.
>
> *NIV* Job 3:8 May those who curse days curse that day, those who are ready to rouse Leviathan.
>
> Job 3:9 May its morning stars become dark; may it wait for daylight in vain and not see the first rays of dawn.

[312] Job 38:7: ". . . when the morning stars sang together, and all the sons of God shouted for joy?"
[313] H1242—*boqer, bo'-ker*: dawn; daybreak; sunrise; morning; day; early; morrow.
[314] H6153—`ereb, eh'-reb; from 6150: dusk: day; evening; sunset; night; H6150–`arab, aw-rab': to grow dusky at sundown; twilight; be darkened; toward evening.
[315] H5399—*nesheph, neh'-shef*: a breeze as in the evening breeze; dark; dawn; morning; night; twilight.
[316] H3882—*livyathan, liv-yaw-thawn'*: a wreathed animal; a serpent; crocodile; a large seamonster; figuratively the constellation of the dragon; a dragon; mourning.
[317] Ps 74; Isa 27:1; Rev 20:10, 13:1–2, 19:19–21.

Lucifer is personified as Venus as the former light-bringer, the son of the dawn, drafted to usurp the morning star title to speciously transform Satan into an angel of light by his earthly followers, just as the New Testament states Satan does in 2 Corinthians 11:14. Venus's orbit, when placed against the backdrop of the zodiac, forms a five-pointed star (the pentagram). Venus traces a pentagram/star across the sky every eight years. The five-pointed star overlays the dog rose with a bright light (representing the sun, Venus, and or illicit knowledge), which adorns most ceilings in masonic temples. In freemasonry, the mystical five-petal dog rose is intimately related to the five-pointed star of the Venus orbit, for the points of the star fall between the petals.[318] The five-pointed star in freemasonry and Rosicrucianism personifies their god, the also called the Grand Geometrician/Architect of the Universe. The pentagram is associated with most all satanic cults, a symbol that Robert Moray associated with secrecy, invisibility, and true worth.[319] Moray was considered one of the Royal Society's Foundation Fellows, a Rosicrucian, and a Freemason.[320]

Further, one wants to discern the distinctions between *Heylel*/Satan and *Helel* the king of Babel/Babylon penned in prophetic allegory in dual prophecies.[321] *Helel* is an archetypical antichrist figure for the postdiluvian epoch. The end-time Antichrist will be the king who rises in the years of Babylon's reign before turning on Babylon to destroy her and replace her.[322] Antichrist is the eighth empire that extends from the seven previous world beast empires, with the seventh empire's ten kings subservient to Babylon, the woman who rides the beast of empires.[323] Antichrist is the one who negotiates the establishment of this seventh empire for Babylon beginning his ascent to power,[324] and is the end-time fulfillment of the King of Babylon who will try to raise his throne to heaven as Satan once did.[325] It follows then that *Helel* derives from *Heylel* etymologically and only in the definition for *Heylel* that includes *Helel* as a figurative term for the King of Babylon. The King of Babylon who surfaces in Isaiah 14 is the figurative *Helel*; note that *Helel* is not a Hebrew word used in the Old Testament.

> Isa 14:4 That thou shalt take up this proverb against the king of Babylon, and say, How hath the oppressor ceased! the golden city ceased!

---

[318] Christopher Knight and Robert Lomas, *Uriel's Machine: The Ancient Origins of Science* (London: Arrow Books Ltd., 2000), 108–110.

[319] Robert Lomas, *The Invisible College* (London: Headline Book Publishing, 2002), 220–222.

[320] Laurence Gardner, *The Shadow of Solomon* (London: Harper Element, 2005), 35.

[321] H1966—*heylel, hay-lale'*; transliterated: *heylel*; pronounced: *hay-lale'*: shining one; morning star; light bearer; Lucifer; figurative for the King of Babylon: Helel.

[322] Rev 17:10–18.

[323] Rev 17:1–8.

[324] Dan 9:27.

[325] Isa 14:13–22; Dan 8:9–12.

SATAN, HEYLEL, AND LUCIFER

Isaiah then prophesied a destruction for the Assyrian king and his army in
Isaiah 14:25, a king who became known as Sennacherib,[326] and a dual prophecy
that is applicable in the end times. Hence, Isaiah 14's King of Babylon/*Helel* is
prophetic allegory for antichrist-like kings like Sennacherib, and later Nebuchadnezzar of Babylon, as well as the kings of the beast empires of prophecy past and
future, the Terrible Ones.

Babylon/Babel derives from Babel city with Nimrod located in Shinar/Sumer
and includes Babylonia and the Babylonian empire in its definition.[327] To this
end Nebuchadnezzar, first king of the beast Babylon empire, is named as one of
the branches of Terrible Ones: the terrible of the nations.[328] Nebuchadnezzar perhaps exhibited the most antichrist traits since Babel and Nimrod. Nebuchadnezzar
commanded a large image of himself to be built, that all were to bow down and
worship or be cast into a fiery furnace. Nebuchadnezzar additionally surrounded
Jerusalem, overran Jerusalem, and desecrated the temple and the Holy of Holies—
all similar acts that Antichrist will do in the end times.[329] In my first book, I wrote
this about some infamous antichrist figures past:

> The future Führer will be a great war leader in the spirit of Napoleon
> and Hitler at the start of their reigns; the Antichrist will be unstoppable,
> even though he will ascend to power on a pastoral platform of peace.
> In the same way that Nimrod, Alexander, Napoleon, and Hitler bent
> the world to their will for a short time, so will the future Antichrist.
> Once this Antichrist has seized absolute power, he will transform into
> a warrior in the same scurrilous spirit as the Nephilim, Nimrod, Nebu-
> chadnezzar, Alexander, Caesar, Napoleon, and Hitler.. ..[330]

> Becoming a deity is a prerequisite for the Antichrist, just as Nebu-
> chadnezzar, Alexander, and Julius Caesar endeavored to bring about.
> We know that Hitler and Mussolini had already considered them-
> selves in messianic terms. In fact, Hitler considered himself second in
> his Aryan pantheon, behind only Nazism's perverted characterization
> of Jesus as a Nordic, Aryan leader. Hitler had already portrayed him-
> self as a prophet of his new doctrines pertaining to his New Testament.
> Hitler, according to Peter Godman, declared himself to be the Messiah

---

[326] 2 Kings 19:1–37.
[327] H894—*Babel, baw-bel'*: confusion; Babel as in Babylon including Babylonia and the
Babylonian empire. Gen 10:10.
[328] Isa 25:4–5; Ezek 30:10–11.
[329] 2 Kings 25:1–30; Ezek 26:7; Dan 2:37; 3:1–11.
[330] Wayne, *The Genesis 6 Conspiracy*, 362–363.

of his political religion and heroized himself as a savior and redeemer of Aryan blood, a Christlike figure."

In Alexander birth legends, his bloodlines were traced back through his mother, Olympias, and through unexplained Egyptian bloodlines to a divine lineage of pharaohs, which is why Alexander eventually had himself crowned pharaoh in Thebes, home to Amun. Darius III previously claimed the crown of Egypt that was a vassal province to Persia. Alexander was the rightful successor to the Egyptian throne after defeating Darius three times in battle.[331]

Antichrist too may very well claim his pedigree in a similar manner as Alexander and other beast kings like Darius, through their genealogies as successors of the beast kings and empires that came before.

> Dan 8:21 And the rough goat is the king of Grecia: and the great horn that is between his eyes is the first king.
>
> Dan 8:22 Now that being broken, whereas four stood up for it, four kingdoms shall stand up out of the nation, but not in his power.
>
> Dan 8:23 And in the latter time of their kingdom, when the transgressors are come to the full, a king of fierce countenance, and understanding dark sentences, shall stand up.
>
> Dan 8:24 And his power shall be mighty, but not by his own power: and he shall destroy wonderfully, and shall prosper, and practice, and shall destroy the mighty and the holy people.

Accordingly, Isaiah 14:16 transitions away from Satan and into prophetic allegory, to the king of Babylon, described as the "man that made the earth to tremble" both in his time, and as antichrist will do in the end-time. The end-time Antichrist will make the world a wilderness, destroy the cities, and refuse to let awakened lost Israel go from the prisons the Babel religion locked them into.[332] We know the dual prophecy transitions from Satan in Isaiah 14 because Satan is not a man, and the king of Babylon did not ascend to heaven; nor did Tyrus walk among the fiery stones of heaven, as and Tyrus and *Helel* were not cherubim.[333] However, Tyrus, the Assyrian, and the king of Babylon were Terrible Ones descended from the terrible branches as beast kings.

---

[331] Ibid., citing Peter Godman, *Hitler and the Vatican* (New York: Free Press, 2004), 4, 49, 64, note 10; Graham Hancock and Robert Bauval, *Talisman: Sacred Cities, Sacred Faith* (Toronto, ON: Doubleday Canada, 2004), 190–198, note 11; *History of the World*, 596, note 12.

[332] Isa 14:16–17; 61:1–11; Luke 4:19.

[333] Isa 14:12; Ezek 28:13–14.

CHAPTER 10

HEYLEL: GOD OF HELL

Isa 14:15 Yet thou shalt be brought down to hell, to the sides of the pit.

Even though Heylel is the likely etymologically root for "hell," Isaiah 14:15's "hell" is not translated from *Heyl-el*, or a variant thereof in Hebrew, but oddly from the Hebrew word Sheowl/*Sh'owl*. The KJV translators conflated, as did later translators, four distinct and places and or concepts—Sheol, Hades, Gehenna, and the lake of fire—into the umbrella term "hell" in English. One suspects the dastardly deed to conflate these four concepts was designed for specious, double entendre, end-time deployment aligned to the Gnostic interpretive approach of Scripture.

It follows then that to fully discern much of prehistory and its related context to define prophetic allegory, one must audit the original Hebrew and Greek meanings for selected words that unwind the nuances between the various words or terms like the abyss, underworld, and lake of fire represented in the umbrella term "hell." As such, Jesus grouped hell/hades and death/*than'atos* when discussing the first death versus the second death through the lake of fire.[334]

> Rev 1:18 I am he that liveth, and was dead; and, behold, I am alive for evermore, Amen; and have the keys of hell and of death.

---

[334] Rev 20:11–15; 21:8. G2288—*than'-at-os*: death; deadly; separation of the soul from the body by which life on earth ends; transliterated: Thanatos.

Sheowl/*Sh'owl* is the cognate Hebrew word in the Old Testament for Greek Hades in the New Testament. Sheowl in Hebrew was understood as the home of the dead, the underworld, and a place of exile and punishment.[335] Hades/*Hah'dace* in the New Testament is defined as a place of disembodied spirits, departed souls, the wicked, and a grave. Because the human spirit sleeps when the first death occurs, Hades/Sheowl is the abode of fallen angels, the abyss prison, the occult heaven, and a place of disembodiment Nephilim and Rephaim spirits.

Hades is translated ten times as "hell" and one time as "grave."[336] "Hell" in 2 Peter 2, though, derives from *tartaroo*/tartarus: the subterranean region that includes the deepest abyss (prison) of Hades and abode of the most wicked; a doleful place of darkness holding captives;[337] a place reserved for angels that sinned.

> 2 Peter 2:4 For if God spared not the angels that sinned, but cast them down to hell, and delivered them into chains of darkness, to be reserved unto judgment.

Building on the underworld descriptions of Tartarus and Hades, Jude 1:6 describes the abode of convicted fallen angels as a place containing everlasting chains to hold the convicts (as in a prison), and a place of darkness/*dzof'os*: gloom and the darkness of the netherworld. *Dzof'os*/darkness is the same word used in 2 Peter 2, the definition of which describes Tartarus as a place in Sheowl/Hades and a place of "chains and darkness."[338] First Peter 3 describes the place where Jesus, while His body was in the grave so to speak, spoke to those disobedient spirits/angels from the days of Noah at the prison that held the fallen angels. Prison/*fulakay* in this application is defined as a cage, imprisonment, a concrete guard, and a watch (over).[339]

The underworld prison described above is the bottomless pit described in Revelation 9—the place the Naphalim angels will be released from in the last seven years and in the days of the trumpet blasts. Bottomless/*abussos* is defined as depthless, the abyss, the deepest chasm in the earth/underworld.[340] Pit/*freh'ar*, as in the

---

[335] H7585—*sh'owl, sheh-ole'*: Hades; the world of the dead; a subterranean retreat, including its accessories and inmates; underworld; pit; grave; place of exile and punishment.

[336] G86—*hah'-dace*: Hades; place of departed souls; grave; hell; place of disembodied spirits; place of the wicked; transliterated: hades. Hell: Matt 11:23; 16:18; Luke 10:15; 16:23; Acts 2:27, 31; Rev 1:18; 6:8; 20:13–14. Grave: 1 Cor 15:55.

[337] 1 Peter 3:18–20. G5020—*tar-tar-o'-o*: the deepest abyss of Hades; a place of eternal torment; a subterranean region; doleful, dark place; regarded by ancient Greeks as the abode of the wicked; a place of punishment for evil deeds; equivalent of Gehenna of the Jews; to hold captive in Tartarus; transliterated: tartaroo. 2 Peter 2:4: hell.

[338] G2217—*dzof'-os*: shrouding like a cloud; blackness; darkness; darkness of the netherworld. Darkness: 2 Peter 2:4; Jude 1:6. Blackness: Jude 1:13. Mist (of darkness): 2 Peter 2:17.

[339] G5438—*foo-lak-ay'*: to guard; cage; hold imprisonment; a ward; a watch; transliterated: phulake. 1 Peter 3:19–20.

[340] G12—*ab'-us-sos*: depthless; infernal abyss; deep, bottomless pit; deepest chasm in lowest parts of the earth; receptacle of the dead; abode of demons. Rev 9:1, 2; 9:11; 11:7; 17:7–8, 20:1, 3.

bottomless pit, means a hole in the earth, a cistern, well, the pit of the abyss prison which has narrow orifice,[341] and which seems to be in another dimension occupying the same space as the underworld. The bottomless pit prison in Hades leads one back to Isaiah 14:15's pit that Satan will be sent to after the end of this age. Pit/*bowr* means dungeon, prison, cistern, shaft, or well.[342] The pit/*bowr* of the Old Testament is the abyss prison and/or bottomless pit of the New Testament and the abode of the worst of the demons[343] the pit/*bowr* prison in hell/*Sh'owl* for the Terrible Ones slain in Ezekiel 32:20–25.

Tartarus is additionally defined in *Strong's Concordance Dictionary* as the equivalent to "*geheena* of the Jews,"[344] which is a little odd because we are not provided a passage for the original word for *gheh'ennah* in the Old Testament. Geheena/*Gheh'ennah*, transliterated into English as geena, derives from Hebrew *gay'* meaning a steep valley, and *Hinnom* meaning a Jebusite named Hinnom, lamentation, and a valley southwest of Jerusalem and north of the "hill of evil counsel," "plain of Rephaim" to the south, and a place defined in the New Testament as a valley named after Hinnom's son, a place of everlasting judgment, and hellfire.[345] Geheena/geena is translated in the New Testament as "hell" twelve times and three times as "hell fire."[346]

But how does a valley become equivalent with hellfire? *Geheena/Gay'hinnom* was figuratively understood in Israel of old as a place of eternal fire, beginning in Deuteronomy 32 where fire was grouped with God's anger that would burn unto the lowest *Sh'owl*/hell.

> Mark 9:47.. . it is better for thee to enter into the kingdom of God with one eye, than having two eyes to be cast into hell fire.

> Deut 32:22 For a fire is kindled in mine anger, and shall burn unto the lowest hell, and shall consume the earth with her increase, and set on fire the foundations of the mountains.

---

[341] G5421—*freh'-ar*: a hole in the ground; a pit; a cistern; well; an abyss prison; pit of the abyss with narrow orifice; transliterated: phrear.

[342] H953—*bowr*: a pit hole especially one used as a cistern or a prison; cistern, dungeon; fountain; well; shaft.

[343] G12—*ab'-us-sos*.

[344] G5020—*tar-tar-o'-o*.

[345] G1067—*gheh'-en-nah*; of Hebrew origin Hebrew 1516 *gay'* and Hebrew 2011 Hinnom: valley of the son of Hinnom; gehenna or Ge-Hinnom; a valley of Jerusalem; a name for the place of everlasting punishment; hell, or Gehenna of fire; transliterated: geenna; H1516—*gay', gah'-ee*: a steep narrow gorge from its lofty sides; valley; H2011—*Hinnom, hin-nome'*: a Jebusite; lamentation; "a valley southwest of Jerusalem separating Mount Zion to the north from the hill of "evil counsel." and the rocky plateau of the "plain of Rephaim" to the south." Josh 15:8; 18:16; 2 Chron 33:38; Neh 11:32; Jer 32:8; 19:16; 32:35.

[346] G1067—*gheh'-en-nah*. Hell: Matt 5:22, 29, 30; 10:28; 18:9; 23:15; 25:33; Mark 9:43, 45, 47; James 3:5, 6. Hell fire: Matt 5:22, 18:9; Mark 9:48.

Further, the valley of the son of Hinnom was a place where the high places of Baal were erected, where some Israelites sacrificed their sons and daughters to Molech by passing them through the fire (Jer 32:35). "Pass through" in Jeremiah 32:35 derives from *abar* meaning to pass over, cross over, or pass away, in this application[347] and as supported in other Old Testament passages,[348] a Hebrew word associated with death and the passengers that pass between the underworld/Sheowl and earth,[349] and as a valley that will become a valley of slaughter in the end times, likely by fire.

> Jer 32:35 And they built the high places of Baal, which are in the valley of the son of Hinnom, to cause their sons and their daughters to pass through the fire unto Molech; which I commanded them not, neither came it into my mind, that they should do this abomination.

The future valley of slaughter, likely by fire, may very well be the end-time Gog war of Ezekiel 38–39 that is fought just after the abyss is opened in Revelation 9. It follows then that the two hundred-million-man army of Revelation 9 belongs to the Gog war, and is an extension of the first woe, which will be the counterfeit Armageddon Antichrist will take credit for winning. The Gog and Revelation 9 war is the same war described in Joel 1–2; Joel 3 is the Armageddon war. We will cover these subjects later. What boggles the mind with intrigue and connections, though, is that the valley of Hinnom is located adjacent to the valley of the giants,[350] indicating that this Armageddon-like war may be influenced by giants in some way.

Thus, geheena/*gheh'ennah* translated as "hell" fire in the New Testament perhaps ought to translated as *gehenna* fire because it not literally the underworld or the abyss prison in the Sheowl/Hades or the lake of fire. And, the hell/geheena fire is not the lake of fire reserved for the fallen angels, demons, the worst of humankind, and those who accept the mark of the beast, worship Satan, and/or worship and Antichrist in the last three and a half years.[351] One wants to be careful, and to take time to discern which hell is being discussed in English translations: the underworld, the abyss prison, the lake of fire, or the valley adjacent to the valley of giants, ritual fire sacrifices, or the fire destruction and location of an end-time war.

---

[347] H5674—' *abar, aw-bar*': to cross over; to cover in copulation; alienate, alter; bring over, through; carry over; come on over; convey over; deliver; do away; enter; escape; get over; pass over; to pass on; to pass away; to dedicate; to devote; to cause to pass over; to cause to pass away; to emigrate; to leave one's place, etc.

[348] 2 Chron 33:6; Jer 7:31, 33; 19:6.

[349] Ezek 39:11, 14, 15; Job 34:20–22.

[350] Josh 15:8; 18:16.

[351] Matt 25:41, 46; 10:28; 13:50; 2 Peter 2:4; Jude 1:6; Rev 14:11; 19:20; 20:10, 14, 15.

CHAPTER 11

REALM OF
THE NAPHALIM

*Job 38:7 When the morning stars sang together, and all the sons of
God shouted for joy?*

Fallen angels, the Naphalim, intimately knew God and His omnipotent power. The rebellious angels knew from the outset of their schema that they could not defeat God. Therefore, the rebellious angelic plan from the outset, according to Isaiah 14, was to establish a counterfeit realm away from the reach of God and independent of His laws and oversight.

Satan was created by the Eternal God Most High, just as all the host of angels were created immortal,[352] and created with free choice to follow God and His ways, or not. Many chose not—seemingly one-third of the angels.[353] The number of rebellious angels is a large number. God's loyal angels are described as innumerable,[354] while the book of Revelation numbers them at one hundred million.[355] The number of loyal angels counted as "ten thousand times ten thousand" and "thousands of thousands" could also be understood as innumerable versus the literal one hundred million. And in this spirit First Enoch tallied the number

---

[352] Ps 33:6; 146:8; Neh 9:6; Luke 20:36; Col 1:16.
[353] Rev 12:4.
[354] Luke 2:13: "multitude of the heavenly host"; Heb 12:22: "innumerable company of angels."
[355] Dan 7:10; Rev 5:11.

of angels as "a thousand thousands and ten thousand times ten thousand."[356] The Naphalim number is at least thirty-three million to fifty million, depending how one wants to calculate one-third.

Angels, sons of God, were required to report to God at their appointed times, as documented in Job 1:6 and 2:1. Angels, as intelligent, powerful, and immortal beings, clearly understood what they were contemplating, the risks involved, and potential consequences when they did not report to God at their appointed time in First Enoch, which may have been the official start to the larger rebellion:

> Enoch 18:15. And the stars which roll over the fire are they which have transgressed the commandment of the Lord in the beginning of their rising, because they did not come forth at their appointed times.

Accordingly, the no-show sons of God in the book of Enoch were part of the same sons of God recorded of Genesis 6:1–4 who created giants with human females, and part of the same sons of God recorded in the book of Job. The sons of God order was depicted with the morning star angel order that sang together, and "all the sons of God shouted with joy" at the time of the creation of the physical universe.[357] Knowing loyal angels must present themselves to God begins to make sense of Satan accompanying the sons of God on two occasions recorded in the book of Job. Satan seemingly decided to tag along to God in his degraded Satan status after the failed uprising, and after many of the Naphalim were sent to the abyss prison. Satan agreed to perform as an accuser to help sift the tares from the wheat until the end times, before being sent to the abyss.

The book of Enoch went on to indicate that even though the rebellious Watchers in heaven were intimate with God, and learned many things, God did not reveal to the Watchers all the mysteries.[358] And ultimately, as powerful as the Naphalim are, they are no match for the Alpha Omega, Omnipotent, and All-Knowing true God of the Bible. As such the "princes" of the world, Greek *ar'khone*/archon, angelic leaders of the assembly of the gods,[359] are the beings referenced in 1 Corinthians 2:7–8: "But we speak the wisdom of God in a mystery, even hidden wisdom, which God ordained before the world unto our glory: Which none of the princes of this world knew: for had they known it, they would not have crucified the Lord of glory."

After the angels' original sedition, the rebels implemented their universal view to justify their sedition and to oppose God's grand plan. The Naphalim schema

---

[356] Enoch 60:1.
[357] Job 38:4–7.
[358] Enoch 16:2.
[359] Ps 82:1-8. G758—*ar'-khone*; a first in rank or power; chief; ruler; magistrate; prince, ruler.

included diabolical ways to destroy humankind, but not directly by their hands.[360] The rebellious angels organized in a similar manner to the perfection of God's organization; as Isaiah 14:13–14 notes, Satan wanted to raise his throne up to heaven and to "be like the most High." Ultimately though, Satan's plan was to accept ruling in a separate realm from God—not to defeat our powerful God Most High. What Satan achieved for a short time is a realm ruled by his fellow Naphalim on the earth, and perhaps restricted to within the firmament, where Satan's angelic army was bound thereafter by certain restrictions. Satan established his counterfeit council of gods, implemented their universal view based opposition to God, separation from God, and their genocidal schemas against humankind. Restrictions imposed by God upon the Naphalim included no direct destruction of humankind by angels, no reproducing with humans or animals of the earth in any way or manner, sharing of forbidden knowledge from heaven, and perhaps other restrictions that would ensure all names written in the book of life from before creation would be given opportunity to be to keep their name in the book.

"Angel" is an umbrella term, as are other angelic appellations and metaphors like stars and the host of heaven, which envelops several distinct orders including the sons of God, Watchers, Morning stars,[361] and other orders. The various kinds and ranks of angels are part of a larger organization called the "host of heaven" in the Bible.[362] Angels are called sons of God and the children of God,[363] as stars,[364] and as part of the host of heaven. Host/*tsaba'* is defined as soldiers or angels of an army.[365]

Heavens/*Shamayim*, as you will recall is defined in part as the lofty ones and the heavenly ones.

Thus, angels are renowned as the host of the heaven just as the stars, moon, sun, and planets are understood as host of the heavens as used in Genesis 2:1. Understanding the narrative is the key to the application as to whether heavenly beings are being depicted or actual planets and stars are being described. Knowing angels are figuratively called stars and the hosts of heaven, and that other celestial luminaries are called the hosts of heaven makes sense of Psalm 148:

Ps 148:2 Praise ye him, all his angels: praise ye him, all his hosts.

Ps 148:3 Praise ye him, sun and moon: praise him, all ye stars of light.

---

[360] Wayne, *The Genesis 6 Conspiracy*, 138–149.
[361] Gen 6:4; Job 1:6, 2:1; 3:8–9; 34:7; Dan 4:12, 13, 17, 23.
[362] Gen 32:2; Josh 5:14; 1 Chron 12:22; Ps 33:6; 103:21; Luke 2:1.
[363] Gen 6:4; Job 1:6; 2:1; 38:7; Ps 82:6.
[364] Deut 4:19; Job 38:7; Isa 14:13; Dan 8:10; Amos 5:26; Matt 24:29; Mark 13:25; Rev 1:20; 12:4.
[365] H6635—*tsaba', tsaw-baw'*: to be in service; a mass of persons; an organized army; host or army of angels; celestial bodies as in the sun, moon, and stars.

> Ps 148:4 Praise him, ye heavens of heavens...
>
> Ps 148:5 Let them praise the name of the LORD: for he commanded, and they were created.
>
> Ps 148:6 He hath also established them for ever and ever.

The host of heaven is a hierarchal organization of angels analogous to an army with ranks and orders, distinct designations, and specific responsibilities who report to God at the holy mount of the congregation/*mow`ed* in heaven.[366] Satan counterfeited this rebellious host of angels complete with a hierarchy that reports to their sacred counterfeit congregation of seventy gods who reign over the seventy nations of humankind, both before and after the flood.

God's authentic solemn and holy congregation/*mow`ed* was described in First Enoch where all the host of the heavens were summoned,[367] and Job 1:6 and 2:1. What is fascinating and illuminating in First Enoch's accounting is that the host of the heavens included the cherubim, seraphim, ophannim, and the angels of power (likely archangels like Michael and Gabriel), angels of principalities, the Elect One (the Word), and the angels of the powers of the earth and waters.

> Enoch 60:1–2. I saw how a mighty quaking made the heaven of heavens to quake, and the host of the most High, and the angels, a thousand thousands and ten thousand times ten thousand, were disquieted with a great disquiet. And the Head of Days sat on the throne of His glory, and the angels and the righteous stood around Him.. ..
>
> Enoch 60:10 And He will summon all the host of the heavens, and all the holy ones above, and the host of God, the Cherubic, Seraphin and Ophannin, and all the angels of power, and all the angels of principalities, and the Elect One, and the other powers on the earth (and) over the water.

Conversely, congregation/*`edah* in Psalm 82 for Satan's congregation/council of the gods is defined as a congregation, concourse, assembly, or gathering;[368] similar but distinct from God's *mow`ed*. Satan's *`edah* lacked the solemnity and aspect of God's holy congregation in heaven—the dignified, formal, and ceremonious character.[369] Satan's assembly of gods is a counterfeit reigning from a holy moun-

---

[366] Isa 14:12–14. H4150—*mow`ed, mo-ade*: an appointment; a fixed time or season; specifically, a festival; a year; an assembly; congregation; place of meeting; solemn assembly.

[367] Enoch 61:10.

[368] H4150—*mow`ed*. H5712—*`edah, ay-daw*: specifically, a concourse; a family or crowd; assembly, congregation, gathering; multitude; swarm.

[369] Webster's, 384: solemn.

tain on earth versus heaven. As such, the Bible does reference Satan's throne on earth as recorded in Revelation 2:13. Satan's seat/*thron'os* of kingly earthly power counterfeits God's holy throne/*kicce'* in heaven at His holy mountain.[370]

> Rev 2:13 I know thy works, and where thou dwellest, even where Satan's seat is.

The ruling council of the gods reigning in the physical realm are the rebellious host of heaven located at Mount Hermon, represented in the postdiluvian epoch by Baal and the Baalim.[371] The Naphalim both before and after the flood are the "host of the high ones" described in Isaiah 24. Note the kings (Nephilim and Rephaim) of the earth in Isaiah 24 report to and receive their divine right to rule from the assembly of the gods. The rebellious host of heaven and their spurious hybrid offspring of the past and present have been reserved a rendezvous with destiny where they will not escape their punishment.[372] Scripturally, we are warned about and instructed not to worship gods like Baal, Asherah, and Milcom[373] associated with the planets and or wandering stars within the firmament, all of whom are stated to be part of the host of heaven.

> Ps 82:1 God standeth in the congregation of the mighty; he judgeth among the gods.

> Ps 82:2 How long will ye judge unjustly, and accept the persons of the wicked?

The Baalim council of gods at Mount Hermon was recorded in the *Ugaritic Texts* with surprising consistency with Scripture, and stunning clarity:

> 1.2.i.10. .. set your [faces] toward the convocation of the Council, to [wards the mountain]. [At the feet of El] you shall fall; you shall honor the convocation of the [Council]!

> 1.2. i. 15 Bull El my father [has tak]en [it] from me: I have no house like [the] gods, no dwelling like [the sons of the Holy] Ones". .. in the midst of the ass[emb]ly of the sons of El.[374]

---

[370] G2362—*thron'-os*; from: to sit; a stately seat; a throne; a power or a potentate; a seat of kingly power or royalty; allegorically for God of the world, and to Christ; H3678—*kicce', kis-say'*: properly, a throne as canopied; a seat of honour, royal dignity, authority, and power.
[371] Judg 2:12; 8:33; 10:6; 1 Kings 18:18; Isa 12:11; Hos 11:2.
[372] 2 Kings 17:16; Ps 82:1–8; Isa 24:21–23.
[373] Deut 4:19; 17:3; 2 Kings 21:35; 23:4–5; 2 Chron 33:3–5; Jer 19:13; Zeph 1:5.
[374] Wyatt, *Religious Texts from Ugarit*, 52, 58, 59: KTU 1.2, iii:15–20 and note 78: "sons of the Holy One denotes El: bn il(m). .. and more generally gods": The Baal Cycle of Myths; 96: KTU 1.4 iii:10–15.

1.2.i Yam sends messengers to the divine assembly to demand Baal's surrender. Baal reacts violently and is restrained.[375]

According to First Enoch, Azazel was the leader of the rebellious angels, as one of the violent Satans of sorcery—those who accuse like Satan but were no longer permitted to accuse in heaven as Satan was permitted, because the lower Satans went to the abyss.[376] The antediluvian Satans and demigod god-kings on earth were and are answerable to the chief serpent, of violence, Satan.[377] The Satans in Enoch were likely the wandering stars before the flood, replaced by so-called offspring gods after the flood, after the parent gods were sent to the abyss. The Satans appear to be the "seven stars burning like seven great mountains" (they reigned from), who were sent to the "prison for the stars and the host of heaven."[378] One deduces postdiluvian gods like Baal and Mot were also be considered Satans and were sent to the abyss for similar crimes.

Enoch 40:7 And I heard the fourth voice fending off the Satans and forbidding them to come before the Lord of Spirits to accuse them who dwell on the earth.

The seven Satans/gods were generally represented as Saturn, Venus, Jupiter, Mars, Mercury, the sun, and the moon in the various pantheons around the world—the wandering stars. Wandering stars were recorded in the book of Jude as those "to whom is reserved the blackness and darkness for ever."[379] Wandering/*planay'tace* is defined as a roving planet, figurative for an erratic teacher, and is derived from *plan'os* for an impostor, deceiver, corrupter, and a seducer.[380] Wandering stars act in the same kind of spirit as the great seducer Satan, who masquerades as an angel of light[381] providing knowledge, and as an impostor of the God Most High.

Satan was not sent to the abyss with the impassioned parent gods/angels who reigned before the flood. One ponders then if Satan's consort goddess was sent to the abyss or was slain and sent to the lake of fire. As such, one notes God that slew one Leviathan in prehistory (female) and will slay Satan (male) in the end times;[382] Satan will go first to the abyss and then to the lake of fire. Polytheism

---

[375] Ibid., 37 1.2.i: The Baal Cycle of Myths.
[376] Enoch 40:7; 55:3; 65:6; 69:1–4.
[377] Enoch 53:4; 54:6.
[378] Enoch 18:13–14.
[379] Jude 1:13.
[380] G4107—*plan-ay'-tace*; from 4108: a rover planet, figurative for an erratic teacher; a wanderer: wandering stars; G4108—*plan'-os*: roving; an impostor; misleader; deceiver; seducing; leading into error; a corrupter.
[381] 2 Cor 11:14.
[382] Ps 74:14; Isa 27:1.

worldwide records accounts of powerful female goddesses like Tiamat, Lotan, and Verita being slain by offspring gods like Baal, Marduk, and Indra.[383]

In western Gnostic polytheism and their branch secret societies like Freemasons and Rosicrucianism, postdiluvian sun gods like Osiris were an allegory for Lucifer/Satan.[384] Antediluvian fertility and moon goddesses were typically partners/wives of the chief male deity of a pantheon. Thus, the favored allegory of gods representing the three great lights of Freemasons are the Sun/Osiris, the Moon/Isis, and Mercury/Horus[385] (postdiluvian offspring gods). "Freemasons teach Osiris is the god who is Lucifer, just as they teach that the All-Seeing Eye is also god, or Lucifer, and just as both these symbols represent the Great Architect of the Universe."[386] "As the initiate ascends the ziggurat of enlightenment, he is introduced first to the Osiris allegories, defining him as the sun god, and then the initiate is introduced to the concept of the Great Architect of the Universe."[387] One deduces adepts are revealed in the hidden mother goddess allegory of the Moon reflected in Isis, for Satan's consort, the female Leviathan/Tiamat/Sophia renowned as the occult Queen of Heaven.

One might anticipate then that the fully revealed Satanic world order of the last three and a half years would reflect Satan as the chief ruling god above the standard pantheons, with Antichrist as some form of incarnated son of Satan or Azazel.[388] One ponders if the consort of Leviathan will be the goddess that Antichrist will worship in secret. In Daniel 11:36–38 god/*'elowahh* is the feminine format of *el* and *elohyim*, noting god in verse 36 derives from *el*, and god in verse 37 derives from *elohyim*.[389] On the other hand, the god of forces may indicate that Antichrist will worship Azazel, noting forces/*ma`owz* derives from *`azaz*.[390]

The rebellious upper counterfeit triune requires a counterfeit Holy Spirit, the original polytheist Queen of Heaven[391] also allegorically represented as Ashtaroth,

---

[383] Wayne, *The Genesis 6 Conspiracy*, 579–584.

[384] Demond Wilson, *The New Age Millennium: An Expose of Symbols, Slogans and Hidden Agendas* (Forestville, MD: Demond Wilson Enterprises Inc./CSE Books, 1998), 157, 161, 186, citing Albert Pike, *Morals and Dogma of the Ancient and Accepted Scottish Rite of Freemasonry/Pamphlets,* (Whitefish, MT: Kessinger Pub. Co., 1992); Albert G. Mackey, *An Encyclopedia of Freemasonry* (New York: The Masonic History Company, 1873); Manly P. Hall, *The Secret Teachings of All Ages* (Los Angeles, The Philosophical Research Society Inc, 1984).

[385] Ibid., 173.

[386] Wayne, *The Genesis 6 Conspiracy,* 499, citing Ralph A. Epperson, *Masonry Conspiracy against Christianity,* 117.

[387] Ibid., 499, citing Alan F. Alford, *When the Gods Came Down* (London: Hodder and Stoughton, 2000), 57.

[388] Rev 13:1–8, 14-18; 14:9–11; 16:2; 19:20.

[389] H433—*'elowahh, el-o'-ah*; from 410: god or God; false god.

[390] H4581—*ma`owz, maw-oze'*: from 5810 `azaz; a fortified place; a defence; force; fortress; strength; stronghold.

[391] Jer 7:18; 44:19, 25.

Inanna, and Gaia parent goddesses, and Isis, Hera, and Juno offspring goddesses. Ashtaroth, known otherwise as Astarte, was a two-horned mother goddess associated with the Phoenician goddess Venus worshipped by the Rephaim, who dwelled in the city of King Og.[392] The goddess of Venus may also allegorically reflect Satan's consort, noting Satan is also associated with the planet Venus. The female goddess was an archetypical pillar to hierarchal structure of dualistic pantheons around the world. The Queen of Heaven was represented as the equal to the male god, and thus one might anticipate will be an essential component reflected in the coming end-time Babylon religion, and Antichrist's religion of the last three and a half years. One might further anticipate the coming world religion will prepare its followers to be the counterfeit bride to be wedded to Antichrist, complete with marriage and loyalty vows sworn to the counterfeit messiah and sealed with the mark of his number recorded in Revelation 13. The hidden female goddess of polytheism is reflected in the woman depicted riding the beast of empires, controlling the subservient end-time ten kings,[393] the ancient religion of Nimrod's Babel, and its daughter religion of Nebuchadnezzar's Babylon.[394]

The celestial mafia of council godfathers is capped by a counterfeit triune throne/seat, above seven Satans and seventy gods of the nations. The word "hierarchy" derives from Greek *hierarkhia* and *hierarkhes*, meaning a ruler of sacred matters and a "collective body of angels grouped in three divisions and nine orders." "Hierarchy" derives from *hieros*, meaning sacred, and archein meaning to rule.[395] In the New Testament "ruler" is translated from *ar'khone* (archon), defined as the first rank; chief, prince, ruler, and magistrate.[396] Archon is employed to describe rulers of the heavenly realm and as well as the reign of terror imposed upon earth by rebellious angels like Satan. Archon is the past participle of *ar'kho,* meaning to be first in rank or power and forms the first word in the compound word, archangel.[397] *Strong's Dictionary* states Zoroastrianism recognized seven Amshaspands as the highest spirits of their religion,[398] atop the congregation of gods who also reported to a Satan-like angel.

---

[392] Ellicott, *Old Testament Commentary*, Vol. 1, 64: Genesis 14 Ashteroth Karnaim. Deut 1:4.
[393] Rev 17 and 18.
[394] Isa 47:1; Jer 51:33; Zech 2:7.
[395] *Webster's*, 190: hierarch, hierarchy.
[396] G758—*ar'-khone*; transliterated: archon. Rulers: Luke 23:13, 35; 24:20; John 7:26, 48; 12:42; Acts 3:17; 4:5, 8; 13:26–27; 14:5; 16:19; Rom 13:3. Prince: Matt 9:34; 12:24; Mark 3:22; John 12:31; 14:30; 16:11; Eph 2:2; Rev 1:5. Ruler: Matt 9:18; Luke 8:41; 18:18; John 3:1; Acts 7:27, 35; 23:5. Chief: Luke 11:15; 14:1; John 12:42. Princes: Matt 20:25; 1 Cor 2:6, 8. Magistrate: Luke 12:58. Rulers: Matt 9:23.
[397] G757—*ar'-kho*: first in political rank or power; to reign; to rule over; transliterated: archo.
[398] G743—*ar-khang'-el-os*; from 757 and 32; an archangel; a chief angel. The Jewish people after the exile distinguished several orders of angels; transliterated as archaggelos. Archangel: 1 Thess 4:16; Jude 1:9.

CHAPTER 12

FIRST ANGELIC HIERARCHY: WATCHERS

Matt 26:53 Thinkest thou that I cannot now pray to my Father, and he shall presently give me more than twelve legions of angels?

If one wants to bring into focus the obscure events recorded in prehistory and foretold in prophecy, one is led to scrutinize the angelic beings and their rebellious counterparts, the gods.

Only seven books in the Bible of sixty-six books of the standard Bible used today do not make mention of angels: Ruth, Nehemiah, Esther, the three epistles of John, and James.[399] Scripture documents the host of heaven as intelligences [spirit beings] who inhabit another state of being (or dimension), and beings constituting a family or hierarchy over which God presides.[400] "The Bible does not, however, treat of this matter professedly and as a doctrine of religion, but merely adverts to it incidentally as a fact, without furnishing any details to gratify curiosity."[401] *Strong's Cyclopaedia* notes that the apostles documented the angelic orders occupying the

---

[399] *Unger's Dictionary*, 61, angel.
[400] M'Clintock and Strong, *Cyclopaedia of Biblical, Theological and Ecclesiastical Literature*, Vol. 1, 226: angel.
[401] Ibid.

highest ranking within the hierarchy (Greek *hierarkhia*), angels that included the thrones, dominions, principalities, and powers.[402] First Enoch provided a sweeping reference to angelic orders but did not provide the rankings in the hierarchy, nor a complete accounting:

> Enoch 61:10 And He will summon all the host of the heavens, and all the holy ones above, and the host of God, the Cherubic, Seraphim and Ophannin, and all the angels of power, and all the angels of principalities, and the Elect One, and the other powers on the earth and over the water.

The Encyclopedia Americana noted nine angelical orders arranged in an ascending hierarchy: "Angels, Archangels, Principalities, Dominations, Virtues, Powers, Thrones, Cherubim, and Seraphim atop the hierarchy."[403] Scripture is also clear that there is a host and a hierarchy in the armies of angels led by Satan on the rebellious side and Michael for the loyal angels to God:

> Matt 25:41. .. Depart from me, ye cursed, into everlasting fire, prepared for the devil and his angels.
>
> Rev 12:7 And there was war in heaven: Michael and his angels fought against the dragon; and the dragon fought and his angels.

The Encyclopedia Americana, in its secular tally of angels, appears to have based their hierarchy upon the research of a Catholic church father, Dionysius the Areopagite (c. fifth/sixth century AD). Dionysius, sometimes referred to as Pseudo-Dionysius, penned a book named *On the Heavenly Hierarchy.* Many early church fathers and theologians from the nascence of the Roman church concurred directionally with Dionysius' hierarchy calling:

> [A]ll the Heavenly Beings together 'Angels;' but when they come to a more accurate description of the super mundane orders, they name exclusively as the 'angelic rank,' that which completes the full tale of the Divine and Heavenly Hosts. Before this, however, they range pre-eminently, the Orders of Archangels, and the Principalities, the Authorities, and Powers, and as many beings as the revealing traditions of the Oracles recognize as superior to them. Now, we affirm that throughout every sacred ordinance the superior ranks possess the illuminations and powers of their subordinates, but the lowest have not the same powers as those who are above them. The theologians

---

[402] Ibid., Vol. 1, 367: archangel, citing Eph 3:2; Col 1:16; 1 Peter 3:22.
[403] *Encyclopedia Americana*, Vol. 1, 681: angel; *Webster's*, 190: hierarch, hierarchy.

also call the most holy ranks of the highest beings 'Angels,' for they "also make known the supremely Divine illumination." But there is no reason to call the lowest rank of the celestial Minds, Principalities, or Thrones, or Seraphim. For it does not possess the highest powers, but, as it conducts our inspired Hierarchs to the splendors of the Godhead known to it; so also, the saintly powers of the beings above it are conductors, toward the Divine Being, of that Order which completes the Angelic Hierarchies.[404]

Determining the hierarchy, though, can be pieced together to a large degree through Scripture. Jesus referenced the hierarchal nature to the angelic organizational structure, stating that if He asked, God would send more than twelve legions of angels to his aid, as noted in the biblical verse introducing this chapter—legions being part of the host or army of heaven. Jesus often utilized understood concepts to express doctrine, parables, and teachings—in this case, the Roman army.

The book of Hebrews described the host of heaven as an "innumerable company of angels."[405] It follows that an army of angels with ranks and orders would have a hierarchy dwelling within the collective body of angelic society, where members had separate and unequal power and excellence, a hierarchy with chiefs, rulers and messengers:[406] chief/*ri'shown*, meaning first in rank, those from the beginning of creation, and the eldest; along with prince/*sar* meaning a ruler, head person of any rank or class, a general, prince; and patron angel,[407] reflects the hierarchal and militaristic structure to the army of heaven. Chief prince titles were conflated into archangel/*arkhang'elos* in the New Testament, for Michael's title and his accompanying order. "Archangel" is a word meaning chief angel(s), and one of seven angelic orders as speculated by the Jewish people.[408]

---

[404] Dionysius the Areopagite, trans. John Parker, *The Works of Dionysius the Areopagite* (Grand Rapids, MI: Christian Classics Ethereal Library, 2004), ccel.org/ccel/dionysius/works.html.), 120: Caput V, *On The Heavenly Hierarchy.*

[405] Heb 12:22.

[406] *Strong's Cyclopaedia*, Vol. 1, 226: angel.

[407] Chief: H7223—*ri'shown, ree-shone'*: first in place, time, or rank; ancestor, those who were before time; beginning; eldest; fore father; former as in of old time; Prince: H8269—*sar, sar*: a head person of any rank or class; captain that ruled; chief; general; governor; keeper; lord; ruler, steward; noble; prince; patron-angel; rulers of God.

[408] 1 Thess 4:16; Jude 1:9. G743—*ar-khang'-el-os*: a chief angel as in archangel; chief of the angels; transliterated: archaggelos. The people of Judah, "after the exile, distinguished several orders of angels; some reckoned four angels (according to the four sides of God's throne) of the highest rank; but the majority reckoned seven (after the pattern of the seven Amshaspands, the highest spirits of the religion of Zoroaster)."

> Dan 10:13. .. but, lo, Michael, one of the chief princes, came to help
> me; and I remained there with the kings of Persia.

Dionysius divided the host of heaven into nine distinct kinds of angels with three divisions, orders or columns. He listed in order and rank within the groupings: 1) Seraphim, Cherubim, and Thrones; 2) Dominions/Lordships, Virtues/ Powers, and Powers/Authorities;[409] 3) Principalities, Archangels, and Angels.[410] The first hierarchy of beings encircle God's throne. The first hierarchy were theorized to be the orders of the heavenly Mind of God streaming out His lawful knowledge and wisdom down through the other ranks and orders,[411] and as it pertained to the authority and role of the lower orders. The Second Hierarchy in this theory administers the Power and Authority of God as the Divine Lordships, and as guided by the first hierarchy and the Mind of God.[412] The Third Hierarchy, according to Dionysius, carry out the edicts of the higher orders. Dionysius noted that the archangels occupied the middle position in the third ranking and are equal in rank to principalities of the same hierarchy but are higher than the angels of the same hierarchy.[413]

On the other hand, the status quo dogma set forth by Dionysius and generally accepted throughout the church age does not appear to logically explain the reporting functions set out in Colossians 1:16. Further, the standard dogma does not seem to logically explain how the lower orders report up the hierarchy ranks, nor does the standard dogma logically explain the divisions of government, religion, and military, and the administering thereof throughout the lower orders led by the first hierarchy of the seraphim, cherubim, and thrones. Colossians 1:16 lists thrones, dominions, principalities, and powers—four orders, not three. One might argue though that the thrones are the chief angels from the order they are listed, with the subsequent three reporting to the thrones. However, using the listing order to establish the rank in Colossians 1:16 places principalities higher than powers and conflicts with Dionysius' hierarchy, and oddly does not include the balance of the archangels and messenger-class angels of third hierarchy of angels. Further, the status quo dogma does not adequately explain who the throne angels are that were documented in Colossians 1:16, and then mysteriously and without explanation grouped in Dionysius' hierarchy with the seraphim and cherubim, angels clearly accounted for in Scripture.

---

[409] Depending on the translation, the second tier is named as Dominions or Lordships, and Virtues or Powers, and Powers or Authorities. The Bible does not record Virtues or Lordships as a rank of angel.

[410] *The Works of Dionysius the Areopagite,* 121: Caput VI, *On the Heavenly Hierarchy.*

[411] Ibid., 123–124: Caput VII.

[412] Ibid., 124–125: Caput VIII.

[413] Ibid., 126: Caput IX.

Col 1:16 For by him were all things created, that are in heaven, and that are in earth, visible and invisible, whether they be thrones, or dominions, or principalities, or powers: all things were created by him, and for him.

Ephesians 1:21 also lists principalities before powers, the mighty (angels) who are not part of the status quo hierarchy as well, and the dominions. Perhaps then, there is another way of viewing the angelic hierarchy, chain of command, and divisions of responsibility that is more congruent to the functions ascribed to them in Scripture. I think the discerning begins with the definitional meaning to the various orders and titles provided in the original Hebrew and Greek, which has not been fully transmitted into the English translations.

Eph 1:21 Far above all principality, and power, and might, and dominion, and every name that is named, not only in this world, but also in that which is to come.

Discerning the obscured angelic hierarchy begins with investigating the throne angels. In the first hierarchy seraphim, fiery six-winged serpent-faced angels,[414] and four-faced cherubim (man, lion, ox/bull, and eagle)[415] are generally thought to be part of the Watcher orders encircling God's throne. Most, however, are not familiar with Dionysius' third order in the first hierarchy—the thrones identified seemingly only once in Scripture (Col 1:16). *Strong's Dictionary* does not assign the word "throne" to a specific order of angels even though Colossians 1:16 indicates there indeed is an order of high-ranking throne angels. Throne/ *thron'os* is defined as a stately seat of power, a governor, king, a potentate, and metaphorically God and Jesus' rule.[416] So who or what are obscure throne order of tier one?

Know that *thron'os* is also used to describe throne of God in Revelation 7:15, and the seat/throne of Satan in Revelation 2:13. Satan's earthly throne is a counterfeit of God throne, which presupposes rebellious seraphim, cherubim, and throne angels encircle Satan's earthly throne atop the counterfeit congregation

---

[414] H8314—*saraph, saw-rawf*: poisonous serpent; specifically, a saraph; from their copper color a fiery serpent; plural seraphim; angels with 6 wings and human hands. Num 21:8; Isa 6:2, 6, 29; 30:6.
[415] H3742—*kruwb, ker-oob*: plural cherubims; an angel; guardians of Eden; angels flanking God's throne; angels hovering over the ark of the covenant; part of the chariot of Jehovah. Cherubim: Gen 3:24; Exod 25:18, 19, 20, 22; 26:1, 31; 36:8, 35; 37:7, 8, 9; Num 7:89; 1 Sam 4:4; 2 Sam 6:2; 1 Kings 6:23, 25, 27, 28, 29; 6:32, 35; 7:29, 36; 8:6, 7; 2 Kings 19:15; 1 Chron 13:6; 28:18; 2 Chron 3:7, 10, 11, 13, 14; 5:7, 8; Ps 99:1; Isa 37:16; Ezek 10:1, 2, 3, 6, 7, 8, 9, 15–16, 18, 19, 20; 11:22; 41:18, 20; 41:25. Cherub: Exod 25:19; 37:8; 2 Sam 22:11; 1 Kings 6:24, 25, 26, 27; 2 Chron 3:11, 12; Ps 18:10; Ezek 9:3; 10:2, 7, 9; 28:14, 16; 41:18; cherubims: Ezek 10:5.
[416] G2362—*thron'-os*.

of the gods. One deduces that throne angels embody some special and important connection to God's holy throne and Satan's counterfeit throne. Knowing the throne of God and of Satan connections to throne angels starts to make sense of Daniel 7:9, where thrones will be cast down in the end-time, and when 100 million plus host of heaven stand before God. One notes in Revelation 5:11 a scene with 100 million plus angels and additionally four living beasts encircling God's throne. Daniel 7 seems to be indicating Satan and his throne, thrones of Satan's seven assisting Satans, Antichrist, and all other rebellious thrones along with the accompanying rebellious throne angels, cherubim, and seraphim will be overturned and given to the saints led by Jesus, and loyal to God.

> Dan 7:9 I beheld till the thrones were cast down, and the Ancient of days did sit whose garment was white as snow, and the hair of his head like the pure wool: his throne was like the fiery flame, his throne was like the fiery flame, and his wheels as burning fire.. :.

> Dan 7:26 But the judgment shall sit, and they shall take away his dominion, to consume and to destroy it unto the end.

Daniel 7 further reveals, as it relates to the first hierarchy, that God's throne area is like a fiery flame, while noting that seraphim ministered among the fiery stones in the altar around God's throne[417] as well as that the throne wheels contained fire.[418] "Wheel" in Hebrew derives from *gilgal*, which also produces the name of three places named as Gilgal in the Bible and in the Covenant Land. Gilgal Rephaim, the famous Wheel of the Giants (demigods) megalith site, was one of the most important polytheist religious sites of the Middle East region and located at the foot of Mount Hermon, home of the Baalim and his ruling council. Gilgal/*galgal* is additionally the root Hebrew word used to translate the wheel of a chariot,[419] and is likely one of the sources to the popular ancient alien mythos idiom and a popular book, *Chariots of the Gods*.

Know then that wheel/*galgal*, a word deriving from *gilgal*[420] and a word used in association with the wheels of God's throne, is related to angelic beings surrounding God (Ezek 1 and 10).[421] However, *galgal* is not the only word utilized in Hebrew for wheel(s) in Ezekiel 1, 3 and 10 when employed to describe Ezekiel's vision of God's throne:

[417] Isa 6:6.
[418] Ezek 1:4, 13; 10:2, 6, 7.
[419] Isa 5:28; Jer 47:3; Ezek 23:24; 26:10.
[420] H1537—*Gilgal, ghil-gawl'*; cognate with 1536; Gilgal, the name of three places in Palestine; a wheel, rolling; H1536—*gilgal, ghil-gawl'*; a variation of 1534: wheel; H1534—*galgal, gal-gal'*; a wheel; a whirlwind; dust as whirled; a rolling thing; wheel; H1535—*galgal, gal-gal'*; Aramaic corresponding to 1534; a wheel.
[421] Ezek 10:2, 6, 13.

Ezek 10:2 And he spake unto the man clothed with linen, and said, Go in between the wheels, even under the cherub, and fill thine hand with coals of fire from between the cherubims, and scatter them over the city.

Ezek 10:6 And it came to pass, that when he had commanded the man clothed with linen, saying, Take fire from between the wheels, from between the cherubims; then he went in, and stood beside the wheels.

Wheel and wheels, in a few limited passages, are translated from *'owphan* and transliterated as *ophan,* meaning wheel.[422] `*Owphan* is the dominant word used in the Ezekiel's throne visions to describe the wheels within wheels[423] of God's throne.[424] In the midst of the wheels were four living creatures with four faces. The four living creatures dwelling in the wheels are cherubim-like angels but distinct. The wheel angels are the throne angels, the ophannim.

Ezek 1:5 Also out of the midst thereof came the likeness of four living creatures.. ..

Ezek 1:15 Now as I beheld the living creatures, behold one wheel upon the earth by the living creatures, with his four faces.

Ezek 1:16 The appearance of the wheels. .. and they four had one likeness: and their appearance and their work was as it were a wheel in the middle of a wheel.

Ezekiel stated the ophannim angels were positioned between and under the cherubim, and as such distinct from the cherubim. The wheel angel's four faces were recorded in Ezekiel 10:14 as a cherub, a man, a lion, and an eagle, whereas cherubim had faces of an ox/bull, man, lion and eagle in Ezekiel 1:10. Ophannim were similar to the cherubim but different according to their location around the throne, one of their faces, and because ophannim dwelled among the fire within the wheels. Ophannim then have some kind of kinship to seraphim that dwelled among the fiery stones of the altar before the throne. The ophannim were the living creatures described in Ezekiel 1:19–20 whose spirit "was in the wheels" of God's throne—likely the throne angels of Colossians 1:16. Ophannim seem to be the Dionysius' throne angels in the first hierarchy.

---

[422] H212—*'owphan, o-fawn'*; or *ophan*: a wheel; wheels; a chariot; wheels in Ezekiel's visions; wheels underneath basins in Solomon's temple.

[423] H212—*'owphan*. Wheels: Exod 14:25, 1 Kings 7:30, 32, 33; Ezek 1:16, 19, 20, 21; 3:13; 10:6, 9, 12, 13, 16, 19; 11:22; Nah 3:2. Wheel: 1 Kings 7:32, 33; Isa 28:26, 27; Ezek 1:15, 16; 10:9–10. Verses used for non-throne applications: Exod 14:25; Isa 28:26–27; Nah 32: chariot and cartwheels.

[424] Ezek 1:16.

Ezek 10:2. .. Go in between the wheels, even under the cherub, and fill thine hand with coals of fire from between the cherubims.. ..

Ezek 10:6. .. Take fire from between the wheels, from between the cherubims; then he went in, and stood beside the wheels.. ..

Ezek 10:13 As for the wheels, it was cried unto them in my hearing, O wheel.

Ezek 10:14 And every one had four faces: the first face was the face of a cherub, and the second face was the face of a man, and the third the face of a lion, and the fourth the face of an eagle.

One wonders if the four-faced ophannim and cherubim living beings merged into a mosaic or blended form displaying one face when they manifested in the physical world. And if so, what did the face look like? Certainly, cherubim/ophannim-like images like the sphinx or kerubs tended to take the face of a lion, human, ox/bull, or eagle/falcon/owl face on ancient statues throughout the Middle East. Whatever the single face of a cherub was as one of the four faces of the ophannim, Ezekiel did not describe it, so it remains a secret. Even the cherubim that decorated the ark of the covenant were always covered in public.[425] One wonders though if the cherubim, or some cherubim, took the eagle/falcon face in their bipedal form, carrying some form of a purse in the physical world, because some scholars include the Anunnaki form as cherubim.[426] The eagle representing a cherub is commonly portrayed on royal coat of arms as a taciturn representation for the originating bloodline.

Cherubim/*Kruwb* and Greek *Kheroobeem'* are also four living creatures described in Ezekiel 1:4–14, who accompanied God's throne which *Strong's Dictionary* described as a chariot in the Hebrew definition.[427] The cherubim were positioned at the sides of God's throne, covering the throne with their wings, just as they were depicted on the ark of the covenant. Satan too was described as a covering cherub, but a special cherub who walked among the fiery stones of the altar as did seraphim.[428] Perhaps Satan also contained traits of the ophannim. Such was Satan before his fall as seraphim, cherubim, perhaps ophannim, and more, set above all angels.

The cherub name is believed by some theologians to have originated from root Semitic words for "abundance of knowledge,"[429] perhaps reflecting their mindset of God as members of the First Hierarchy. Although cherubim are associated with

---

[425] Num 4:5, 6.

[426] *Strong's Cyclopaedia,* Vol, 2, 234 figure C-3: cherubim.

[427] H3742—*kruwb*; G5502—*kher-oo-beem'*; plural of Hebrew origin 3742 *kruwb*: plural cherubim; transliterated: cheroubim.

H5894—` *iyr, eer*: a watcher as in an angel; a guardian; a watcher angel; waking; watchful; wakeful.

[428] Isa 6:1–6; Ezek 28:14, 16.

[429] *Strong's Cyclopaedia,* Vol.2, 232: cherubim.

knowledge and covering the throne of God, they are also renowned as protectors wielding a flaming sword. Cherubim were also commissioned to guard the gates into Eden with a flaming sword(s), to ensure no human or human/angelic hybrid could access the tree of life.[430]

Cherubim were known throughout a variety of ancient Middle East cultures, and variantly portrayed and displayed as winged sphinxes and kerubs flanking the entrances to palaces and temples throughout the Middle East and Semitic peoples. Cherubim were portrayed with a lion's body, a human face, and conspicuous wings. Semitic peoples often employed winged creatures to guard temples and palaces[431] just as Watchers encircled God's throne.

"All nations of antiquity seem to have those monstrous beings [sphinxes] of various shapes and forms as objects of awe, compelling adoration and worship."[432] According to *Nelson's Bible Dictionary*, cherubim were akin with the ancient Assyrians portrayal of the karibu as winged creatures, with the face of a man or a lion, while the body was that of a sphinx.[433] Assyrians portrayed the sphinx/kerub as a human-headed lion or bull, eagle-headed with a human's body, and human-headed with an eagle's body.[434] The latter two seem to be identified with the Anunnaki. If cherubim spawned offspring from one of their singular-headed physical forms, those demigods would have included darked-haired human heads, lion-headed, eagle-headed and bull-headed giant offspring.

Assyrian griffins with heads of eagles and the with chimera-like forms that included wings, a lion's body, and a serpent's tail were also kin to the cherubs.[435] Griffins in Greek mythology sometimes pulled the chariots of Zeus and Apollo.[436] Sphinxes in Egypt were typically portrayed with the body of a lion, head of a human, wings of a bird, and tail of a serpent.[437] However, Egyptians additionally portrayed sphinxes as: Androsphinx: a human-headed lion symbolizing wisdom and intelligence; Criosphinx: a ram-headed lion; and Hierachosphinx: a hawk-headed lion.[438]

The Catholic Encyclopedia notes that "cherub" derived from an ancient Semitic word *kerub* that means "to ride." Thus, through a linguistic process known as metathesis, the transposition of letters or syllables, cherub is thought to have derived from Hebrew *rakab* meaning to ride, by repositioning the "r" and "k" to derive *karab* or *karub*, and also in the same linguistic process from

---

[430] Ibid. Gen 3:25.
[431] *Unger's Dictionary*, 222: Cherub.
[432] *Encyclopedia Americana*, Vol. 25, 403: sphinx.
[433] *Nelson's Dictionary*, 257: Cherub.
[434] *Encyclopedia Americana*, Vol. 25, 403: sphinx.
[435] *Encyclopedia of World Mythology*, 464–465: griffin.
[436] Ibid., 465: griffin
[437] *Encyclopedia Americana*, Vol. 25, 403: sphinx.
[438] Ibid.

merkab meaning chariot, noting *merkab* derives from *rakab*.[439] In this line of etymological investigation, know that God is described in Scripture that which dwelleth/*yashab* among or between the cherubim;[440] *yashab* also is defined as: to sit down in a seat as a judge, and a seat.[441] It follows that another Hebrew word, *kruwb*, pronounced kerub, and defined as the same as *kruwb*/cherub is the name of a place Scripture places in Babylonia,[442] and one of the likely originations to the word cherub/Kerub.

Ergo, Psalms 18:10 states "God rode [*rakab*] upon a cherub and did fly," noting the ophannim were the chariot/throne portion of God's movable throne. Knowing this makes sense of Ezekiel's mind-blowing vision of the supernatural cherubim and ophannim that God rode, whereby Ezekiel had to communicate what he did not understand in human terms—as a chariot powered by ophannim and led by cherubim:

> Ezek 10:16 And when the cherubims went, the wheels went by them: and when the cherubims lifted up their wings to mount up from the earth, the same wheels also turned not from beside them.

Cherubim/griffins, then, would be accurately depicted as pulling or leading the chariot or throne of God, where the distinct ophannim dwell within and power the wheels. The distinct ophannim had numerous eyes[443] that cherubim did not. Cherubim had four wings while ophannim were not described as having four wings, but rather four wheels.[444] The four wheels included one large wheel, and wheels within wheels is further described in Solomon's temple as a chariotlike wheel, and wheels, noting wheel(s) derives from *'owphan*.[445]

Surprisingly, John's vision of God's throne in the book of Revelation does not depict seraphim, cherubim, and ophannim as separate and distinct beings. The throne setting depicts twenty-four humans (likely firstfruits of the resurrection sequence[446]) with their seats/thrones each sporting golden crowns, seven angels (likely archangels), and four living beasts versus creatures in

---

[439] *The Catholic Encyclopedia*, Vol. 3, 646–648: Cherub; H7392—*rakab, raw-kab*: to ride on an animal or in a vehicle; to despatch; bring on horseback; carry; get oneself up on horse- back; to mount and ride; to ride in or on a chariot; H4817—*merkab, mer-kawb*; from 7392: a chariot; a seat in a vehicle; saddle; a place to sit and ride; H4818—*merkabah, mer-kaw-baw*; feminine of 4817: a chariot.

[440] 1 Sam 4:4; 2 Sam 6:2; 2 Kings 19:15.

[441] H3427—*yashab, yaw-shab*: sit down and judge; seat; set down; dwell; remain; settle; marry; inhabitant; abide.

[442] H3743—*Kruwb, ker-oob*: a place in Babylonia; a blessing. Cherub as a place: Ezra 2:59; Neh 7:61.

[443] Eze 1:18; 10:12.

[444] Ezek 1:6; 10:21; Rev 4:6,

[445] 1 Kings 7:29–34; Ezek 1:15–16.

[446] 1 Cor 15:23.

Ezekiel, and that have six wings saying "holy, holy, holy" before God like the six-winged seraphim saying the same, as well as full of eyes within like ophannim. Note as well each of the four separate beasts in the book of Revelation had one of the faces of a cherub: lion, calf/ox, man, and eagle.[447] At the time of the end of this age, either the three Watcher orders of the First Hierarchy are removed from the Watcher ranks and replaced by a mosaic of angelic beings of the three; or, John's vision blends the three orders as prophetic allegory whereby all three angels act in perfect harmony after the example of God, the Word, and the Spirit.

> Rev 4:6 And before the throne there was a sea of glass like unto crystal: and in the midst of the throne, and round about the throne, were four beasts full of eyes before and behind.
>
> Rev 4:7 And the first beast was like a lion, and the second beast like a calf, and the third beast had a face as a man, and the fourth beast was like a flying eagle.
>
> Rev 4:8 And the four beasts had each of them six wings about him; and they were full of eyes within: and they rest not day and night, saying, Holy, holy, holy. ... .

The counterfeit throne created by Satan as documented In the gnostic gospel *On the Origin of the World*, Saboath was a dwelling place for Satan in the polytheist eighth heaven complete with a "great throne on a four-faced chariot called 'cherubim.'. .. And seven Archangels stand before him. He is the eighth having authority.. .. For from this chariot the seventy-two gods receive a pattern; and they receive a pattern so they might rule over the seventy languages of the nations.. .. And he created some other dragon-shaped angels called 'seraphin.' Who glorify him continually."[448] One ponders who the additional two gods in Satan's order were and perhaps accompanying languages. One deduces Satan and his consort are the two other gods.

Ialdabaoth/Ialtbaoth/Altabaoth in gnosticism is the first and chief ruler whose names include Saklas and Samael.[449] Lilith was Samael's consort with the latter

---

[447] Isa 6:1–3; Ezek 1:10, 18; 10:12; Rev 4: lion; calf; man; eagle. Cherub: lion, ox, man; eagle. Ophan: lion; cherub; man; eagle.

[448] Willis Barnstone, *The Other Bible* (New York: HarperCollins, 1984), 65–67.

[449] Bentley Layton, *The Gnostic Scriptures: Ancient Wisdom for the New Age* (New York: Doubleday, 1995), 25; *The Secret Book according to John*: The Rulers II; 36, Its Creation Of Other Rulers 10:15–16; Barnstone, *The Other Bible*, 36; James M. Robinson, *The Nag Hammadi Library*, (New York: HarperCollins Publishers, 1990), 162: Introduction to the *Hypostasis of the Archons*, and 167–168: *Hypostasis of the Archons* 94:25; 95:5–25.

alternatively known as Enki in Sumerian legend.[450] Louis Ginzberg cites Samael in biblical legends as the angel of death, and even as Satan in his seraphic form. In this mystical Jewish line of thinking, Satan took on his seraphic form as Enki and/or Samael as the one who assaulted Eve, impregnating her with the radiant child that became Cain.[451] Satan was similarly recorded in the Talmud as riding a serpent when he deceived Eve in Eden. Additionally, the Talmud named Samael, meaning "venom of [a] god" (venom now that is carried in snakes) as the angel who is Satan.[452]

Ialdabaoth, the first ruler is said to have created/established seven other androgynous beings: Athoth who had the face of a sheep, Iao a seven-headed serpent, Sabaoth with the face of a serpent or dragon, Adonin with the face of an ape, Eloaios who had the face of a donkey, Astaphaios who had the face of a hyena, and Sabbede who had the face of a glowing fire.[453] Ialdabaoth is said to have twelve different outward physical appearances and to have dwelled in the midst of seraphim. Ialdabaoth then assigned a power and realm to each of his seven angels along with a heaven within the firmament named after them.[454] Gnostics equate God with Ialdbaoth, otherwise known as the "Demiurge Ialdabaoth."[455] The title Demiurge is a derogatory Greek phrase that translates as "a lowly public craftsman," and is intended to slander God as a lowly deity that created an imperfect world for His personal turf, all to force humans to worship Him.[456] However, Ialdabaoth more accurately fits Satan, the occult Great Architect of the Universe.

One also might want to anticipate that polytheists will classify Sabaoth as God, or the Word of God/Jesus, or perhaps Michael in the end-time utilizing dubious and disappointing KJV translations, all to degrade God to just another angel and/or an angel no more powerful than Satan/*Heylel*. Sabaoth is Ialdabaoth's offspring god, the authority and lord over the forces of chaos, while noting the Word/Jesus created all the angelic host at the command of God.[457] Anticipate then than Romans 9:29 and James 5:4 will be drafted in the end times as part of the deceptions and delusions to bring about the universal religion and world

---

[450] Laurence Gardner, *Genesis of the Grail Kings* (London: Bantam Press, 2000), 138–139.

[451] Louis Ginzberg, *Legends of the Bible*, The Ten Generations, 54.

[452] J. F. Bierlein, *Parallel Myths* (Toronto, ON: Ballantine Publishing Group, 1994), 77–78; Rosemary Ellen Guiley, *The Encyclopedia of Demons and Demonology*, 221: Samael.

[453] Barnstone, *The Other Bible*, 37, The Secret Book according to John; Its Creation of Other Rulers 10:26–33.

[454] Ibid., 37, The Secret Book according to John; Its Creation of Other Rulers 10:35; 11:2–3, 15–23, 25–33.

[455] Ibid., 63: The Creation of the World and the Demiurge.

[456] Graham Hancock and Robert Bauval, *Talisman: Sacred Cities, Sacred Faith*, 91, citing Charles S. Clifton, ed., *Encyclopaedia of Heresies and Heretics* (Santa Barbara, CA: ABC-Clio, 1992), 50.

[457] Col 1:16. Robinson, *The Nag Hammadi Library*, 175: On the Origin of the World, 104.

government whereby the "lord of Sabaoth" will be presented as God and/or the Word Jesus. Sabaoth/*Sabahowth'* was directly translated from Greek into the KJV in Romans 9:29 to say "the Lord of Sabaoth," a passage that references Isaiah for its premise, conversely translated from Hebrew as "the Lᴏʀᴅ of hosts": *Yehhovaw' tsaba',* and noting the KJV translators did not take *tsaba'* directly from Hebrew, preferring "hosts."[458] *Sabahowth'* in the New Testament, like *tsaba'* in the Old Testament, is defined as armies, the military epithet for God, and the armies of Israel. *Sabahowth'* derives from the Hebrew word *tsaba';*[459] not the Greek god Sabaoth as it was translated in Romans 9:29 and James 5:4; both ought to have been translated as the Lord of Hosts not the Lord of Sabaoth.

The gnostic accounts of Ialdabaoth's seven angels sound eerily like the seven Satans reporting to Satan in the book of Enoch, and the seven wandering stars/planets reporting to Satan in the book of Jude. To this end, know that Ialdabaoth was "cast down into the Tartaros below the abyss" by Sophia,[460] just as Azazel was leader of the rebellious host in First Enoch, whom Scripture titled Abaddon in Hebrew and Apollyon in Greek.[461] Polytheist Scripture is not always consistent in distinguishing the roles between Satan, Azazel, and the offspring gods in their counterfeit hierarchy. Such is the case with Sabaoth Gnostics called the God of the Jews.[462] Thus, Sabaoth, an offspring god like Baal and Zeus established a throne in the eighth heaven for Ialdabaoth to counterfeit God's holy throne. It follows that the seven Satans also established thrones, as did their offspring gods after the flood; thrones with similar accompaniments to Satan's throne populated with rebellious cherubim, seraphim, ophannim, and archangels.

Seraphim too are ranked as the first order of angels in Dionysius's First Hierarchy; angels with six wings that continually praise God saying "holy, holy, holy." They work before God's altar in the fiery stones acting as ministers, just as one seraphim took away Isaiah's sins with a coal from the altar. Seraphim were described as human-like except for their faces. They possessed six wings, a human form, feet, hands, serpent faces, and were fiery, copper-colored,[463] thought to be chief among the Watchers by virtue of their ranking in the First Hierarchy. The six wings of the seraphim match with the merged image of the six-winged living creatures in

---

458 Isa 1:9; Rom 9:29.

459 G4519—*sab-ah-owth';* of Hebrew origin 6635 *tsaba':* armies; sabaoth as in tsebaoth; a military epithet of God; Lord of the armies of Israel; those under the leadership and protection of Jehovah; transliterated: sabaoth.

460 Robinson, *The Nag Hammadi Library,* 168: *Hypostasis of the Archons* 95:10.

461 Enoch 54:5; Rev 9:11.

462 Bentley Layton, *The Gnostic Scriptures: Ancient Wisdom for the New Age,* 167: *Satorinos according to St. Irenaeus* Introduction and 1.24.1–2.

463 Isa 6:1–7. *Strong's Cyclopaedia,* Vol. 9, 568 describing Seraphim as angels and ministers; H8314—*saraph.*

Revelation 4–5. First Enoch provided a partial description to the seraphim angels and described them as the "holy sons of God":

> Enoch 71:1–2. .. And I saw the holy sons of God. They were stepping on flames of fire: Their garments were white [and their raiment], And their faces shone like snow. And I saw two streams of fire, and the light of that fire shone like hyacinth.

The seraphim are likely Watchers from the throne of God in Daniel 4:12, 13, 17, and 23, and the sons of God in Genesis 6:2 and 4.

CHAPTER 13

FIRST ANGELIC HIERARCHY: ARCHANGELS

1 Thess 4:16 For the Lord himself shall descend from heaven with a shout, with the voice of the archangel, and with the trump of God: and the dead in Christ shall rise first.

Seraphim, according to *Unger's Bible Dictionary*, were an order of angels who performed as intermediators between heaven and earth[464] as to the governance of the earth. The book of Job underscored that the sons of God regularly reported or presented themselves to God, whereupon Satan did so also, as well as those who shouted for joy at creation.[465]

First Enoch ranked seraphim first in listing and rank of those who encircle God's throne: those who do not sleep and by inference to watch, as in Watchers that included the cherubim and ophannim orders:

> Enoch 71: 1, 6–7 And it came to pass after this that my spirit was translated, And it ascended into the heavens: And I saw the holy sons of God.. .. And my spirit saw the girdle which girt that house of fire,

---

[464] *Unger's Dictionary*, 1160: Seraphim, citing Isa 6:3.
[465] Job 1:6; 2:1; 34:7.

> And on its four sides were streams full of living fire, And they girt that house. And round about were Seraphin, Cherubic, and Ophannin: And these are they who sleep not and guard the throne of His glory.

The sons of God, Watchers, were the same sons of God orders who procreated with human females to create the Nephilim in Genesis 6:4. The sleepless Watchers were the same "sons of God" who "defiled their bodies with the daughters of men."[466] First Enoch refers to the First Hierarchy as Watchers multiple times: as those who were governing the earth, those responsible for humankind, and those who created giants through the daughters of men and taught them illicit knowledge from heaven.[467] It follows that the Watchers were the sons of God described in Genesis 6:1–4, Job 1:6, and Job 2:1. The seraphim sons of God were trusted with mediation and communication between heaven and earth for government and religion[468] as angelic administrators working before God's altar. It seems likely then the seraphim, from a scriptural perspective, were the Watchers/sons of God who first procreated Nephilim, but as we will learn in subsequent chapters there were other incursions by other Watchers, and perhaps other angelic orders.

> Enoch 15: 1–3 And He answered and said to me, and I heard His voice: 'Fear not, Enoch, thou righteous man and scribe of righteousness: approach hither and hear my voice. And go, say to [the Watchers of heaven], who have sent thee to intercede [for them: "You should intercede"] for men, and not men for you: Wherefore have ye left the high, holy, and eternal heaven, and lain with women, and defiled yourselves with the daughters of men and taken to yourselves wives, and done like the children of earth, and begotten giants (as your) sons?

For those looking for scriptural links between the sons of God, seraphim and the Watchers, know that the title Watcher(s) does appear in Scripture four times, all in the book of Daniel chapter 4.[469] Watcher/`Iyr is defined by *Strong's Dictionary* as awake, watchful, and Watcher angel; a word rooted in `uwr meaning wake, awaken, etc.[470] Words and phrases like, sons of God, Watchers, and ophannim recorded in First Enoch demonstrates this book's ancient roots as deriving from Hebrew, even though corruptions occurred through the generations as it was translated into other languages.

---

[466] Enoch 69:4.
[467] Enoch 10:7, 9, 16; 12:2, 3, 4; 13:10; 14:1, 3; 15:2, 9; 16:1, 2; 36:5; 56:4.
[468] Dan 4:1–27.
[469] Watcher: Dan 4:12, 13, 23. Watchers: Dan 4:17.
[470] H5894—` *iyr, eer;* Aramaic corresponding to 5782: a watcher angel: guardian; wakeful; wakeful one; watchful; H5782—`*uwr, oor.* to wake; lift up; raise up; rouse; master.

Watchers from the First Hierarchy, seraphim, not only rebelled, but some created offspring violating the laws of creation. Seraphim Watchers provided illicit knowledge from heaven to both human and human/angelic hybrids that was the source knowledge to create a counterfeit religion to worship fallen angels, an earthly government to carry out their edicts of rebellion, and the seven sacred sciences to develop the wisdom of the corrupted Naphalim world,[471] to corrupt the earth in all kinds of ways by their followers, and to lead people away from God.

The Daniel 4 Watchers delivered messages from God with respect to governance, just as Watchers in First Enoch governed the antediluvian world and then the early postdiluvian world without restrictions as the celestial mafia, as well as establishing their polytheist knowledge cult, Enochian Mysticism developed by Enoch son of Cain to house the seven sacred sciences.[472] One deduces then, the Watchers of Daniel 4 were the seraphim sons of God, and that the seraphim established rule and religion on earth after their own serpentine likeness. This then explains why so many of the ancient gods were depicted as serpents and dragons, as were the early kings created in the image of their godfathers, and why serpentine imagery dominated the earthly religions, monarchs, and thrones. Dragons, serpents, and cherubic imagery commonly populate royal coat of arms reflecting a taciturn genealogy for the royal house.

We should anticipate our government, religious, scientific, and learning centers mask a secret and hidden hierarchy on earth established from Watcher angels that is reflected in their imagery and names. This hidden hierarchy will become more visible as the end times approach and the last seven years of this age begin.

Dan 4:17 This matter is by the decree of the watchers, and the demand by the word of the holy ones: to the intent that the living may know that the most High ruleth in the kingdom of men, and giveth it to whomsoever he will, and setteth up over it the basest of men.

Based on Dionysius' principle that those in the First Hierarchy are represented in God's throne room, one deduces that another angelic order encircling God's throne ought to be included in the First Hierarchy. Following this line of thinking, *Strong's Cyclopaedia* noted the apostles included archangels in the First Hierarchy, not in the Third Hierarchy as Dionysius and standard Christian dogma places them.[473] If true, then including archangels in the First Hierarchy begins to reshape Dionysius's tripartite First Hierarchy into a quadripartite First Hierarchy of Watchers encircling God's throne but does not necessarily change the concept of tripartite rails of authority, which we will cover in the next chapter. Recognizing

---

[471] 1 Cor 1:19–20; 2:6; 3:19; Col 2:8; 1 Tim 6:20–21; Jam 3:15.

[472] Wayne, *The Genesis 6 Conspiracy*, 61–80, 92–111.

[473] *Strong's Cyclopaedia*, Vol. 1, 367: archangel.

archangels as part the First Hierarchy overturns Dionysius's model, but is logical based on scriptural accounts pertaining to archangels.

Archangel/*arkhang'elos* is defined as a chief angel and chief of angels,[474] indicating a very high rank and part of the First Hierarchy. Further, Michael's name is defined as one who is like God and the archangel who stands against the beast empires in defense and support of Israel's destiny.[475] The archangel Michael stands against Antichrist from taking power before the ordained time, the chief angel/prince who will lead loyal angels to fight Satan and his angels in the end times, and the angel sent to protect Moses' body from Satan,[476] which indicates that archangels may be a higher rank than seraphim.

Indeed, Scripture documented another First Hierarchy angel defined as an archangel in *Strong's Dictionary,*[477] the angel who stated: "I am Gabriel, that stand in the presence of God"[478] as First Hierarchy Watchers do. Gabriel went to Daniel to explain the vision of beast empires in Daniel 8, and thus likely the archangel among others that "stood by"[479] in the vision in Daniel 7 to interpret that vision. Gabriel was sent to Zacharias to announce the coming of John the Baptist.[480] Yet another archangel blasts his trumpet at the time of the rapture, during the last trumpet of Revelation.[481] An order of angels represented in the Bible by Gabriel, Michael, and other biblically anonymous archangels stand among the other Watchers encircling God's throne.

Archangels are intimately involved with the fulfillment of prophecy. Scripture indicates seven seemingly archangels are positioned in the presence of God. The seven archangels appear to be the seven angels that stand before God in the book of Revelation as Gabriel does. Archangels will be provided the trumpets to begin the trumpet catastrophes (Rev 8:2), just as an archangel blows the last trumpet at the time of rapture, in the time when Michael rises at the midpoint of the last seven years. The seven archangels are likely the seven stars/angels of the churches recorded in Revelation 1,[482] seemingly in the same spirit of Michael being the

---

[474] G743—*ar-khang'-el-os*: a chief angel; chief of the angels; transliterated: archaggelos.

[475] H4317—*Miyka'el, me-kaw-ale'*: who is like God; name of an archangel; the first archangel described as the one who stands in time of conflict for Israel.

[476] Dan 10:13, 21; 12:1; Jude 1:9; Rev 12:7.

[477] H1403—*Gabriy'el, gab-ree-ale'*; man of God; warrior of God; an archangel; the angel God used to send messages of great importance to man and as sent to Daniel, to Zacharias, and to Mary; G1043—*gab-ree-ale'*; of Hebrew origin 1403 *Gabriy'el*: an archangel; one of the angel princes or chiefs of the angels.

[478] Dan 7:16; 8:16, 9:21; Luke 1:19, 26.

[479] H6966—*quwm, koom*: appoint, establish; raise up; arise; to stand; set up.

[480] Dan 7:16; 8:21; Luke 1:14–17.

[481] Matt 24:31; Mark 13:21; 1 Thess 4:16; 1 Cor 15:52; Rev 11:15.

[482] Matt 24:31; 1 Cor 15:52; 1 Thess 4:16; Rev 1:16, 20; 2:1; 3:1.

protector of Israel and Judah. The seven wandering stars of polytheism seem to be the counterfeit seven archangels and known in Enochian books as the seven Satans.

> Zech 4:2. .. and behold a candlestick all of gold, with a bowl upon the top of it, and his seven lamps thereon, and seven pipes to the seven lamps.

> Rev 1:20 The mystery of the seven stars which thou sawest in my right hand, and the seven golden candlesticks. The seven stars are the angels of the seven churches: and the seven candlesticks which thou sawest are the seven churches.

> Rev 8:2 And I saw the seven angels which stood before God; and to them were given seven trumpets.

The Apocrypha books that were originally included in the KJV make mention of Raphael and Uriel as two additional archangels.[483] First Enoch lists these two archangels, Michael, Gabriel, plus Raguel, Saraqael, and Remiel as those who watch and by inference part of the First Hierarchy of Watchers. Additionally, the archangels of First Enoch sent the fallen angels to the abyss for their antediluvian crimes against creation and humanity. In this enlightening passage, Gabriel is stated to be is higher than cherubim, and Michael is affirmed as the archangel set over the best of humankind:[484] Israel, Judah, and the Christian church.

> Enoch 20:1–8 Name and Functions of the Seven Archangels. And these are the names of the holy angels who watch. Uriel, one of the holy angels, who is over the world and over Tartarus. Raphael, one of the holy angels, who is over the spirits of men. Raguel, one of the holy angels who takes vengeance on the world of the luminaries. Michael, one of the holy angels, to wit, he that is set over the best part of mankind [and] over chaos. Saraqael, one of the holy angels, who is set over the spirits, who sin in the spirit. Gabriel, one of the holy angels, who is over Paradise and the serpents and the Cherubim. Remiel, one of the holy angels, whom God set over those who rise.

First Enoch further described four archangels: Michael, Gabriel, Raphael, and Phanuel,[485] who were distinct from within the angels who do not sleep, Watchers, and who carried out special functions. Phanuel was not listed among the seven in Enoch 20:1–8, indicating a corruption to the manuscript, or that Phanuel is

---

[483] Tobit 3:17; 5:4; Uriel: 2 Esdras 4:34.
[484] Enoch 88:1–3.
[485] Enoch 40:1–9; 53:6; 71:8, 9, 12.

another name for one of the other five, or more likely their order is populated by more than seven. *Smith's Bible Dictionary* states the four (arch)angels before God and lists Uriel as the fourth, citing Jewish tradition.[486]

> Enoch 40:2 And on the four sides of the Lord of Spirits I saw four presences, different from those that sleep not, and I learned their names: for the angel that went with me made known to me their names and showed me all the hidden things.

The book of Enoch states that the four archangels are part of the seven arch-angels before God, but oddly are distinguished as being like "white men." The four are the same four who took the fallen angels to the abyss,[487] and in like manner as the angel who takes Satan to the abyss in the end times.[488] What is fascinating is that the four archangels include Gabriel and Michael among the four described as "presences," "voices," as well as archangels.[489] One contemplates the language of "voices" as it might pertain to Jesus' return with the "shout, voice of an archangel" and the trump of God."[490]

One wonders if the term "presence" was originally translated from *ruwach*, meaning a spirit.[491] And if so, is First Enoch referencing the four winds and spirits of prophecy recorded in several books of the prophets and Revelation 6? Knowing that angels are spirits in their own habitation[492] forms a strong connection between the four spirits, angels, winds, and presences that stand before God as archangels. The word "presence," as it is translated from *paniym* in the KJV, is understood as before, and face, meaning before, face, faces, and presence as in "Gabriel stand in the presence of God," Jonah "fled from the presence of the Lord,"[493] and "Satan went forth from the presence of the Lord." Presence in the angelic context could be understood as standing before God or as a presence/spirit before God, or both.

Following a similar line of inquiry, "four spirits" go forth from standing before God or standing in the presence of God in the book of Zechariah. The four spirits are the four chariots, their horses, and the riders of the chariots.[494] The book

---

[486] "Ra'phael (the divine healer). According to Jewish tradition, Raphael was one of the four angels which stood round the throne of God-Michael, Uriel, Gabriel, Raphael."

[487] Enoch 87:2, 3; 88:1, 3; 89:1.

[488] Rev 20.1.

[489] Enoch 20:2, 3, 9.

[490] Mat 24:30; 1 Cor 15:52; 1 Thess 4:16.

[491] H7307—*ruwach*.

[492] Ps 104:4; Heb 1:7; Jude 1:6.

[493] Gen 4:16; Job 2:7; Jer 4:26; Jon 1:3, 10; Nah 1:5; Zeph 1:7; Luke 1:19; H6440—*paniym, paw-neem*; plural of *paneh, paw-neh*: face; favour; forefront; presence.

[494] Zech 6:1–8.

of Zechariah is a book of prophecy that connects to and supports many details documented in the book of Revelation, including details regarding the throne area of God. In this example, the book of Zechariah describes the four spirits riding four chariots led by horses that emerge from standing before God, just as the four archangels did.

> Zech 6:5 And the angel answered and said unto me, These are the four spirits of the heavens, which go forth from standing before the Lord of all the earth.

What is fascinating to me is the imagery of the chariot, noting this is a similar description for God's throne, Zeus's throne, and Satan's throne powered by the ophannim (wheels) and pulled by horses/unicorns/cherubim. One ponders if the horses are prophetic allegory for cherubim. The four spirits in the book of Zechariah do not represent thrones on the earth as the occult thrones do. Rather, the four spirits riding in the chariot led by horses in Zechariah's vision represent the power of the omnipotent God, and perhaps as four faces/*paniym* of God, sent as the four winds of prophecy and as it pertains to the beast empires. The four spirits go throughout the earth in the Zechariah vision while Judah is still exiled in Babylon, in which the prophecy continues with the building of the Second Temple, then coming of the Branch/Jesus and His return in the time of the seventh and eighth beast empires during the last seven years.[495]

> Zech 6:11 Then take silver and gold, and make crowns, and set them upon the head of Joshua the son of Josedech, the high priest;
>
> Zech 6:12 And speak unto him, saying, Thus speaketh the LORD of hosts, saying, Behold the man whose name is the BRANCH; and he shall grow up outof his place, and he shall build the temple of the LORD.

Consistent language and prophetic allegory are markers and keys to help unlock prophetic allegory and prophetic chronology, if we heed those markers. The four winds of prophecy and empires are first documented in the book of Jeremiah, describing the disbursement of the people of Elam by the four winds in the book of Jeremiah as part of a series of prophecies detailing the rise of Nebuchadnezzar, the first of Daniel's vision of five beast empires, with Babylon being the third beast empire of seven recorded in the book of Revelation.[496] In perfect prophetic symmetry Daniel 7 prophesied four winds stirring up the four beast empires from

---

[495] Zech 6:10–15.
[496] Jer 49:36; Dan 7:1–28; Rev 17:7–11.

the sea, whereby Antichrist's empire will rise out of Daniel's fourth beast empire, and seventh of Revelation 17. Antichrist's empire will rise out of the sea as part of a seven-headed hydra dragon holding the traits of the four beast empires described in Daniel 7.[497]

The four winds are further present in the rough/shaggy goat beast empire, Greece, from whom Antichrist also rises out of Daniel 8 and 11[498]; rough/*sa`iyr* can be hairy, he-goat, and a devil goat god.[499] The beast empire of Daniel 8, Alexander's Greece, was split after his death into four succeeding empires that included Rome. Rome rose from the four-part remnant of Alexander's empire to become the fourth beast empire of Daniel 7 and is a parallel prophecy to Daniel 2 and 7, which are all used to define the seven empires seven empires of Revelation 17, from which the eighth empire of Antichrist rises from.

The four spirit/winds fit as part of four of the seven archangels and the other chief angels that stand in the presence of God as the First Hierarchy: the ophannim, cherubim, and seraphim. Discerning the thrones as the ophannim and archangels as the fourth order of the first tier make sense and brings order to the top of hierarchy, if one discerns each First Hierarchy order has specific functions supported by specific lower ranks of angels in the Second and Third Hierarchies. However, the archangels may be in the presence of God, but perhaps not regarded as one of the three Watchers around the throne who never sleep. I further think the First Hierarchy might have an appointed chief angel, an archangel that oversees all four First Hierarchy orders. As such, Michael would lead the archangels, and as the book of Enoch indicates, if accurate, Gabriel oversees the cherubim, paradise (likely Eden), and the serpents, likely the *nachash,* the Hebrew for the serpent in Eden and elsewhere in the Bible. It follows that two other archangels, perhaps Uriel and Raphael, are the chief angels for the seraphim and ophannim.

Just as Michael fights against the beast empires from bringing about Antichrist until the ordained time, and just as Michael will lead his angels in battle against Satan and his angels at the midpoint of the last seven years, archangels head the military and warrior orders of angels. Michael is the great prince/*sar*, meaning chief, chief captain, general, commander of military, ruler, and ruler of rulers, rulers of God.[500] One deduces then that four representative archangel leaders head the four First Hierarchy angelic orders that populate the throne room of God on four sides. Throne scenes in the books of Daniel and Revelation depict the ten thousand times ten thousand loyal angels assembled on the sides of the First Hierarchy that leads their lower orders.

---

[497] Dan 7:2; Rev 13:1–2.

[498] Dan 8:8–21; 11:2–5.

[499] H8163—*sa`iyr, saw-eer':* shaggy; a he-goat; a faun as in devil, goat god, and satyr. Lev 17:7; 2 Chron 11:15; Isa 13:21; 34:14.

[500] H8269—sar, sar. Dan 12:1.

One might further deduce that Satan's counterfeit seat/throne on earth includes a similar First Hierarchy of those who rebelled, just as the gnostics and other polytheist cultures have documented in their religions and mythologies. Each counterfeit Naphalim order reigns atop a hierarchy of lower ranks and orders of fallen angels that report up to them. One might further deduce that the seven wandering star angels would have additional counterfeit thrones and throne rooms, as well as the fallen angels leading the seventy nations, complete with chief male and female deities for their dualist knowledge religion. It follows then that the Naphalim's spurious offspring, the royals, would govern with the authority from invisible ones on earth, with the divine right to rule, and from similar kinds of throne rooms, just as dynastic royals have done with their kings and queens throughout our history both before and after the flood.

CHAPTER 14

SECOND AND THIRD HIERARCHIES OF ANGELS

Eph 1:21 Far above all principality, and power, and might, and dominion, and every name that is named, not only in this world, but also in that which is to come...

Dionysius' Second Hierarchy angels included the Dominions, Virtues, and Powers. Dominions leading Dionysius' first order in the Second Hierarchy were recorded in Colossians 1:16 and Ephesians 1:20, and were grouped last among principalities, powers, and might(s).

Typically, when the Bible lists sons, the first son is named first with subsequent sons listed in the order of their birth, as in the table of nations. Nations listed together, as in the four Mesopotamian kings in the war of giants in Genesis 14, are done in order of the leadership or power. Both seem to be the basis for Dionysius' model for the hierarchy of angels with the higher ranked order listed first in each hierarchy. However, Dionysius' ranking seems in conflict with New Testament order of angelic accounting of Ephesians 1:21. Dionysius identified the Second Hierarchy as: dominions/lordships, virtues/powers, and powers/authorities; and the Third Hierarchy as: principalities, archangels, and angels,[501] noting that powers were ranked lower than dominions/lordships. Dionysius further listed principalities in the Third Order, and might(s) were not listed in Dionysius' hierarchy of angels. In Colossians 1:16, dominions were listed right after thrones and before principalities and powers.

> Col 1:16 For by him were all things created, that are in heaven, and that are in earth, visible and invisible, whether they be thrones, or dominions, or principalities, or powers.

Hence, we can not use the groupings of angels as they were translated in into English in the New Testament to establish the hierarchy, but perhaps we can from the original Greek. One can note the various orders of angels as they were recorded in Greek, the meanings, and descriptions of those orders, and then connect them to other passages to establish their rankings within the hierarchy and to whom these orders report to.

Such is the case for dominion/lordships that derives from Greek *kooreeot'ace* meaning rulers, government, a sovereign, and one who possesses dominion, which in turn derives from *koo'reeos* meaning supreme in authority.[502] Seemingly, dominions command nations or lands; angels who report up the hierarchy to one of the orders in the First Hierarchy. *Kooreeot'ace* is only translated as dominion(s) and government.[503] According to Dionysius, dominions are lords aspiring to true lordship.[504] Lordships/*katakooreeyoo'o* does surface in the Bible, meaning lords and exercising lordships and dominion over,[505] and perhaps where Dionysius pulled his alternative name for dominions. One deduces the dominions/lordships are involved with the thrones and government on earth with the angelic offspring. As used in the book of Daniel, a dominion is a realm or empire in heaven and on earth as with King Nebuchadnezzar's beast empire.[506]

---

[501] *The Works of Dionysius the Areopagite,* 121: Caput VI, On The Heavenly Hierarchy. Depending on the translation, the second tier is named as Dominions or Lordships, and Virtues or Powers, and Powers or Authorities.

[502] G2963—*Koo-ree-ot'-ace*; from 2962: rulers; government; power; lordship; one who possesses dominion; transliterated: kuriotes; G2962—*koo'-ree-os*; supremacy; supreme in authority; title for God and the Messiah; Lord; master; sovereign; prince; chief; transliterated: kurios.

[503] Dominion(s): Eph 1:21; Jude 1:8. Government: 1 Peter 2:10.

[504] *The Works of Dionysius,* 124: Caput VIII, *On the Heavenly Hierarchy.*

[505] G2634—*kat-ak-oo-ree-yoo'-o*: to lord against; control; subjugate; exercise dominion; be lord over; overcome; transliterated: katakurieuo. Exercise dominion over: Matt 20:25. Exercise lordships: Mark 10:42. Lords: 1 Peter 5:3; Rev 17:14. Overcame: Act 19:16.

[506] H7985—*sholtan, shol-tawn'*: empire; dominion; sovereignty; realm.

Dan 4:3 How great are his signs! and how mighty are his wonders! his kingdom is an everlasting kingdom, and his dominion is from generation to generation.. ..

Dan 4:22 It is thou, O king, that art grown and become strong: for thy greatness is grown, and reacheth unto heaven, and thy dominion to the end of the earth.

In New Testament passages, *kooreeot'ace* is used in a narrative with those who defile the flesh and are also those who despise the (holy) dominions, the government of God in heaven, and speak evil toward God ways and heaven, as brute beasts.[507] The passage in the book of Jude is a reference to angelic offspring and many humans whose spirits are like brute beasts and devilish/*daheemoneeo'* as in demon-like (James 3:14–15).[508] The beast like and demon-like spirits include the royal dynasties, their beast empires, Antichrist, polytheistic religions on earth, and those who will take the mark of the beast; all who slander God for fallen angels, even though angels are careful not do so.[509] The vile beast nature of the beast kings toward God and heaven, as well as their empires sponsored by the fallen angels, is demonstrated in Daniel 7 with the prophecy of the beast empires. Included in the beast empires is Antichrist:

Dan 7:11 I beheld then because of the voice of the great words which the horn spake. ..

Dan 7:12 As concerning the rest of the beasts, they had their dominion taken away: yet their lives were prolonged for a season and time.. ..

Dan 7:25 And he shall speak great words against the most High, and shall wear out the saints of the most High, and think to change times and laws: and they shall be given into his hand until a time and times and the dividing of time.

Dan 7:26 But the judgment shall sit, and they shall take away his dominion.

Authorities were listed in 1 Peter 3:22 along with angels and powers. "Authorities" in 1 Peter 3:22 derives from Greek *exoosee'ah*, which is a distinct angelic order. "Powers" in 1 Peter 3:22 derives from *doo'namis*, which very well may not be the powers order, and is often confused with *exoosee'ah* orders in English translations. Dionysius' hierarchy, as it was translated into English,

---

[507] 1 Pet 2:10; Jude 1:8.
[508] G1141—*dahee-mon-ee-o'-dace*: demon-like; devilish.
[509] Ps 73:22; Dan 7:11, 20; 1 John 2:22; 4:2–3; Jude 1:8–10; Rev 13:1, 5, 6, 16:9, 11, 21; 17:5.

classified both virtues and authorities as powers adding to the confusion. To sort out the English translation inconsistencies and to piece together the hierarchy as it is documented in the Bible, we will return to Ephesians 1:21 with an often-overlooked angelic order, the mighties or mighty angels, which will begin to light the way through haze.

In Ephesians 1:21, might/*doo'namis* is listed after powers but before dominions. The English translation in my reckoning likely should have read mighty, Mighties, or Mighty Ones versus might in this application. Perhaps the *doo'namis* are the mysterious virtues/power order of Dionysius's Second Hierarchy along with dominions/lordships and powers/authorities. One should note though that virtues does not show up as an order of angels in the Bible but are recognized as such in today's English lexicon as great heroes, mighty ones.[510] *Doo'namis* can mean force, miraculous power, power, strength, mighty deed, and mighty.[511]

However, *doo'namis* in Ephesians 1:21 is translated from Greek into English as powers in 1 Peter 3:22. "Power" in Ephesians 1:21 derives from *exoosee'ah*, not *doo'namis* as in in 1 Peter 3:22, which underlines some of the confused Greek to English translations. *Doo'namis* in the Bible is oddly translated into English in its angelic application as powers, in Jesus' end-time chronology and prophecy: "and the stars shall fall from heaven, and the powers of the heavens shall be shaken"[512]— an event that occurs at the midpoint of the last seven years, and which corresponds to the Revelation 12 prophecy and timing for the war in heaven where mighty angelic ones would be expected to fight. *Doo'namis* is further translated as powers in its angelic sense in Romans 8, where powers is grouped among angels and principalities of Dionysius's Third Hierarchy. *Doo'namis* is translated into English as "virtue" three times; not as an angel but as an ethical principle,[513] and is the likely the source for virtue as a name for the *doo'namis* angels.

> Rom 8:38 For I am persuaded, that neither death, nor life, nor angels, nor principalities, nor powers, nor things present, nor things to come. ..

Thus, the 1 Peter 3:22 English translation of powers/*doo'namis* is more of a description of their strength/power than position, in the same way authorities in 1 Peter 3:22 derives from *exoosee'ah* and translated for "powers" in Ephesian 1:21. Perhaps the translation for 1 Peter 3:22 should have said angels, powers/*exoosee'ah*

---

[510] Dictionary.com: virtue. *Webster's*, 457, virtues.

[511] G1411—*doo'-nam-is*: force; miraculous power; a miracle; abundance, might; mightily; mighty; mighty deed; power; strength; violence; power consisting in or resting upon armies, forces, or hosts.

[512] Matt 24:29–30; Mark 13:25; Luke 21:26.

[513] Mark 5:30, Luke 6:19; 8:46.

(versus authorities), and mighty ones or virtues/*doo'namis* (versus powers) to keep the KJV translation consistent.

> 1 Peter 3:22 Who is gone into heaven, and is on the right hand of God; angels and authorities and powers being made subject unto him.

Virtues/Mighties, according to Dionysius, are generally thought of in terms of mighty strongholds from within—strong and powerful centered in their virtue from within.[514] The angelic "mighty ones," then, appear to be the same angels recorded in Isaiah 13:3—part of the host of heaven who fight in the end times for God (likely led by Michael). The mighty ones of Isaiah 13 are the loyal counterparts to the rebellious mighty/*el* of Psalms 82. *El* can also be translated as "mighty." Hence, The mighty/*el* in the assembly of the gods of Psalm 82 describes gods of power that include fallen mighty ones.[515] I find it fascinating as well that the Nephilim demigods were called the mighty ones/gibborim of old, and men of renown *Shem*/*Shemayim*: infamous heavenly ones.

> Isa 13:3 I have commanded my sanctified ones, I have also called my mighty ones for mine anger, even them that rejoice in my highness.
>
> Isa 13:4 The noise of a multitude in the mountains, like as of a great people; a tumultuous noise of the kingdoms of nations gathered together: the LORD of hosts mustereth the host of the battle.

The mighty ones/*el*, the angelic virtues of Isaiah 13:3 are the angels that excel/*gibbowr* in strength as part of God's dominion/*memshalah* meaning government realm, rule (Ps 103:20–22),[516] and consistent with New Testament application for dominion/*kooreeot'ace*. Further, the mighty ones/virtues appear to be the strong/mighty/*iskhooros'* angels of Revelation 5:2, 10:1 and 18:21, who do mighty deeds.[517] Mighties/Virtues are a powerful class of angelic beings—army super angels but are not the powers/*exoosee'ah* in the Second Hierarchy.

Powers in Ephesians and Colossians[518] derives from *exoosee'ah* meaning force, authority, power; superhuman; potentate; jurisdiction, magistrate, and power

---

514 *The Works of Dionysius*, 124–125: Caput VIII, *On the Heavenly Hierarchy.*

515 H410—*'el, ale*; strength; mighty; mighty one; the Almighty but used also of any deity; mighty men; men of rank; mighty heroes; angels; gods, false god(s); God mighty things in nature; power.

516 H4475—*memshalah, mem-shaw-law'*: rule; a realm; a ruler; dominion; government; power.

517 G2478—*is-khoo-ros'*: forcible; boisterous; mighty; mightier; powerful; strong; valiant; strong in body or mind; internal strength; transliterated: ischuros.

518 Eph 1:21; 3:10; 6:12; Col 1:16.

over government, as in governing humankind.[519] The powers/authorities ensure order, implement regulations, and adjudicate authority of all the divine receptions, including the intellectual authority.[520]

> Eph 6:12 For we wrestle not against flesh and blood, but against principalities, against powers, against the rulers of the darkness of this world, against spiritual wickedness in high places.

Thus, Dionysus' third angelic order of the Second Hierarchy is translated into English as both powers and authorities, just as 1 Peter 3:22 lists authorities that derives from *exoosee'ah*, underscoring powers/*exoosee'ah* have authority over humankind and its sponsored kings, governments, and magistrates. Similarly, power/*exoosee'ah* of the "prince of power of the air" is the "spirit that now worketh in the children of disobedience" that now govern the course of this world (Ephesians 2:2). The Second Hierarchy understood in Greek from Greek are the *kooreeot'ace*/dominions sometimes called lordships. The *doo'namis*/mighty ones sometimes called virtues. The *exoosee'ah*/powers sometimes translated as "authority," as in 1 Corinthians 15:24 with the latter. First Corinthians 15:24 translated "rule" from a*rkhay'*, "authority" from *exoosee'ah*, and "powers" from *doo'namis*. The verse might have been better translated as ruler/*arkhay'* (or principality/*arkhay'* as in Romans 8:38), with "authority" translated as power/*exoosee'ah*, and "power" as mighty one/virtues/*doo'namis*, just as Romans 8:38 ought to have translated power/*doo'namis* as mighty ones or virtues.

> 1 Cor 15:24 Then cometh the end, when he shall have delivered up the kingdom to God, even the Father; when he shall have put down all rule and all authority and power.

> Rom 8:38 For I am persuaded, that neither death, nor life, nor angels, nor principalities, nor powers, nor things present, nor things to come.

We must always be mindful that we still wrestle with forces that are both visible and invisible, forces that are not flesh and blood—that we wrestle with rebellious spirit beings of heaven and their unseen hierarchy, who enforce the Satan's World Order through their spurious offspring. Understanding this makes sense that powers, rulers, authorities, etc., can refer to both angelic beings, and their will as in actions to carry out as in rule, power, and authority levied in the earthly

---

[519] G1849—*ex-oo-see'-ah*: force, capacity; mastery; magistrate; superhuman; potentate; authority; jurisdiction; power; strength; the power of authority; right privilege; the power of rule or government; authority over mankind; the sign of regal authority, a crown.
[520] *The Works of Dionysius,* 125: Caput VIII, *On the Heavenly Hierarchy.*

dominions carried out by the spurious offspring of the celestial mafia. Hence one does need to discern between Scripture detailing angelic beings and Scripture detailing the actions and implementation of their commands being carried out in the earthly institutions, because the same Greek word is used for both. The earthly implementation of the Naphalim/Nephilim World Order derive from the rebellious orders' names.

> Col 1:16 For by him were all things created, that are in heaven, and that are in earth, visible and invisible, whether they be thrones, or dominions, or principalities, or powers: all things were created by him, and for him.

> Rom 8:38 For I am persuaded, that neither death, nor life, nor angels, nor principalities, nor powers, nor things present, nor things to come.. ..

Included in the invisible spirit forces we battle is Dionysius's Third Hierarchy, where Dionysius positioned the principalities, archangels, and angels. Principalities/rulers/*arkhay'* is defined as first, chief, principality, rule, power, and magistracy of angels and demons,[521] and is the first word of the compounded word for archangel. *Arkhay'* are the chief magistrates for the rule of fallen angels and demons. Magistrates tend to be positioned further down in the governmental hierarchal structure with a more limited purview. Magistrates fit in the hierarchal governship roles as implementors of laws and decrees, versus the religious or military structures and their hierarchal orders. Even so, principalities according to Paul were indeed invested with powers and rendered as rulers.[522]

Titus 3:1 translated principalities/*arkhay'* and power/*exoosee'ah* in a passage reminding Christians to be mindful and subject to them and to obey magistrates, although "magistrate" does not derive from *arkhay'*. Further, "obey" was inserted by translators. Magistrate/*pitharkheh'o* is defined as to be persuaded or have confidence in;[523] it is a word compounded from *pi'tho* meaning to convince by argument or persuade, and *ar'kho* meaning first in political rank, power, and/ or chief.[524] Seemingly, the original Greek in Titus 3:1 endeavored to make a distinction between the magistrates/*arkhay'* and the magistrates/*pitharkheh'o* of the

---

[521] G746—*ar-khay'*.

[522] *Unger's*, 1038: principalities. Rom 8:38; 1 Cor 15:24.

[523] G3980—*pi-tharkh-eh'-o*: to be persuaded by a ruler; submit to authority; conform to advice; hearken; obey; transliterated: peitharcheo. Obey: Acts 5:29, 32. Hearkened: Acts 27:21. Magistrates: 1 Titus 3:1.

[524] G3982—*pi'-tho*: convince by argument; persuade; pacify; conciliate fair means; assent to evidence or authority; believe; trust in; transliterated: peitho; G757 —*ar'-kho*; to be first in political rank or power; reign or rule over; chief; transliterated: archo.

earth, but the KJV translators seemingly wanted to link *pitharkheh'o* as earthly magistrates/*arkhay'*. Hence, the Titus 3:1 passage perhaps ought to have been translated as: put them in mind to be subject to principalities and powers and to be obedient (or persuaded) to be ready to every good work.

> Titus 3:1 Put them in mind to be subject to principalities and powers, to obey magistrates, to be ready to every good work.

Arkhay', as noted above, can also be translated as "beginning" or "first," and is the Greek word used in "first estate" in Jude 1:6, referencing to those angels who left their heavenly habitation and are kept in chains for judgment (in the abyss, for the violations against creation and humanity). One should not be surprised then that *arkhay'*/principalities surfaces in Colossians 2 where Paul discussed how Jesus' crucifixion nailed the consequences of legalism to the cross, and in doing so disarmed the principalities/*arkhay'* and powers/*exoosee'ah* and "triumphing over them in it."[525] The passage in Colossians then warns Christians to not let anyone who delights in false humility and the worship of angels beguile you away from God, Jesus, the Holy Spirit, and your salvation.[526] The Colossians verse has eery parallels the serpent and Eve in Genesis 3.

> Col 2:15 And having spoiled principalities and powers, he made a shew of them openly, triumphing over them in it.. ..
>
> Col 2:18 Let no man beguile you of your reward in a voluntary humility and worshipping of angels.

Angels are generally regarded in the Bible as the lowest-ranking order in the hierarchies. Angels are defined in both Hebrew/*mal'ak* and Greek/*ang'elos*; as messengers, envoys, ambassadors of God, and as theophanic angels,[527] as in a manifestation or the appearance of God, but more likely the reflection of God within them, the Word of God. Angels, in a general sense, were beings created to execute God's purposes[528] identified as host of angels of God in the Bible, versus the Third Hierarchy's singular order of angels. Conversely, Naphalim angels devoted themselves to executing Satan's purposes.

---

[525] Col 2:13–15.

[526] Col 2:18.

[527] H4397—*mal'ak, mal-awk'*: a messenger; specifically, a messenger from God as in an angel a prophet, priest, or teacher, or a king; an angel; the theophanic angel; G32—*ang'-el-os*: a messenger; especially an angel; envoy; a messenger from God; transliterated: aggelos. *Strong's Cyclopaedia*, Vol. 1, 225: angel.

[528] *Strong's Cyclopaedia*, Vol. 1, 225: angel.

The angels of the Third Hierarchy are further defined as, and referred to in the New Testament as, "ministering spirits sent forth to minister for them who shall be heirs of salvation."[529] Knowing this explains why the celestial mafia vowed to create the Nephilim: to usurp lordship over humankind, exert the physical manifestation of the celestial mafia's will on earth, to lead humankind away from God, and to work relentlessly to ensure humankind did not fulfill their destiny—to ultimately obliterate humankind from eternity, all the while using humankind to justify their rebellion via human collaborators.

Envoys/ministering angels seemingly are the most numerous. The singular angel order could alternately be well described as the foot soldiers among both the heavenly host and the army of the Naphalim rebels, which included their roles as envoys/ambassadors for the government, religious, and military columns that descend from the First Hierarchy through the Third Hierarchy.

Perhaps then the angelic hierarchy would be better understood as four orders in the First Hierarchy whereby archangels are placed in the First Hierarchy as an order versus Dionysius' hierarchy that positioned archangels in the Third Hierarchy. Hence, four orders present before God sit atop their hierarchal columns of lower orders as defined by their roles within the angelic hierarchy, and as it is manifested on earth: 1) seraphim: government and religion; 2) archangels: military/army; 3) cherubim and ophannim: thrones.

Thus, seraphim perform as priest-angels working in and around the fiery stones of God's altar, carry out God's desires as to governance extending out of religious worship: a theocracy. It follows then that powers/authorities/*exoosee'ah* of the Second Hierarchy have authority over humankind and its sponsored governments and religious institutions that are overseen by dynastic kings and queens. Thus, ancient polytheist government and religion was dominated by serpentine gods, serpentine kings, queens, priests, and priestesses, and otherwise unexplained serpentine imagery in their religion and government.

Principalities/rulers/*arkhay'* of Dionysius's Third Hierarchy implement authority of religious institutions and through their magistracy and hierarchy of courts within each branch. So-called secular courts in contemporary times, from within their polytheist architectural temples and magistracy today, implement their polytheist objectives of their related organizations: to lead people away from God, to degrade God, to not give God credit for anything, and to honor their pantheon of gods. Secular courts bind their authority through oaths. Religious institutions act as counterfeit ministers of the those within the true Christian organizational structure represented in the Jerusalem church of the disciples and apostles. Angels of the Third Hierarchy would act as ministering angels, envoys, ambassadors, and messengers in the first rail of the host of heaven.

---

[529] Heb 1:14. See also Heb 1:7.

Because the cherubim and ophannim are so intimately connected in their accounts in Scripture to the throne of God, it follows that they too are included within the Naphalim hierarchy, but who jointly lead the second rail of authority. Cherubim and ophannim represent the thrones in the global pantheons that begins with Satan's throne, synagogue, and assembly,[530] and which extends to the thrones of the seven Satan's (known perhaps as the leaders of "chiefs of tens"[531]), and to the thrones of the gods of the seventy nations of the council of gods.[532] As witnessed by the numerous serpentine gods around the world, seraphim populated the thrones with their gods and goddesses, just as Satan is classified in part as a seraphim/serpent/dragon. Additionally, the Watchers who governed the antediluvian world in First Enoch were seraphim documented in polytheism as gods like El, Anu, Tiamat, Cronos etc., and just as Zeus, Osiris, Bel/Baal, and Enki among others were classified as serpentine gods after the flood.[533]

Satan's seat/*thron'os* in the book of Revelation after the flood was allegorized in polytheism as Zeus's altar that was located at Peramos/Pergamum in Asia Minor. Pergamenians believed they were descendants of Arcadians who migrated to the birthplace of Zeus in legend.[534] Eumenes II (c. 197–159 BC) was a great patron of the arts and sciences (seven sacred sciences linked back to Enoch, son of Cain), and built a great library rivaling Alexandria to archive this knowledge. Eumenes II also renovated the existing throne and altar of Zeus that his father had built.[535] Pergamum's throne was modeled after Zeus's throne and altar, which Zeus inherited/usurped from his parent god, Cronos/Uranus, at Mount Olympus. Pergamum's throne and altar was transferred to Berlin at the close of the 1800s[536] whereby the second museum to house the altar was completed in 1930, which displayed the classic triptych architecture just in time for the rise an antichrist figure, Adolf Hitler. Following occult dogma, the triptych arches adopted by masonic secret societies may well have represented the portal to Zeus's throne located on Mount Olympus but in another dimension.

> Rev 2:12 And to the angel of the church in Pergamos write; These things saith he which hath the sharp sword with two edges;
>
> Rev 2:13 I know thy works, and where thou dwellest, even where Satan's seat is.

---

[530] Psa 82:1–8; Rev 2:13, 8; 3:9.

[531] Enoch 6:8.

[532] Deut 32:7–9; Ps 82:1–8.

[533] Rose, *Giants, Monsters and Dragons*, 136. 44; Joseph, *Destruction of Atlantis*, 148; Gardner, *Grail Kings;* Gardner, *Realm of the Ring Lords*, 324–326.

[534] *Strong's Cyclopaedia*, Vol. 7, 946 Peramos.

[535] Ibid.

[536] *Unger's*, 986, Pergamum.

Knowing the Naphalim established many thrones of governance over the earthly seventy nations makes sense of Zeus's chariot throne, led by unicorns/cherubim pulling the chariot/throne in which the ophannim dwelled within the wheels. The rebellious angelic thrones were then manifested on the earth through their spurious dynastic offspring, the Nephilim and Rephaim, led by a king and queen representing the father god and mother goddess of heaven—in the Greek case Uranus/Gaea and/ or Cronos/Rhea before the flood and then Zeus/Hera after the flood. All the earthly religious, lower-level governments, and military institutions, then, report to the god's divine royal representatives, the kings and queens representing the mother goddess and father god of the throne each of the seventy nations.

With each of the seventy postdiluvian nations, as the peoples migrated to the four corners of the earth, new dynasties spawned from within or through a grafting of a male scion with a pure-blood female of another dynasty/nation. New dynasties for newly created countries reported back to their founding dynasty from the seventy nations. In polytheist tradition, the word "king" derived from a Gothic word, *kuningzam,* meaning "wise one" and "knowing one," who was a scion in the "Noble Race," all the while noting Gothic/*Guth* held the power over the fates and destiny of humankind.[537] It follows then that the coat of arms belonging to royal families encode their genealogies with imagery back to their godfathers, and thus will change at times from generation to generation as other ennobled bloodlines are grafted in.

The dominions/*kooreeot'ace* of the Second Hierarchy would fall below the ophannim and cherubim column as the thrones overseeing the realms, nations, and empires. Dominions then would establish and support the throne angels for each of the seventy nations that answer in the angelic realm to the two throne angelic orders to the thrones of the seven Satans, and then to Satan's throne. One deduces cherubim and ophannim are assigned to each of additional thrones of angels governing the seventy nations, and perhaps to the offspring dynasties spawned from the original seventy nations. One further deduces rebellious angels from Dionysius's Third Hierarchy act as messengers and ambassadors in this second rail of angelic authority.

Hence, dominion/lordships derives from Greek *kooreeot'ace* meaning rulers, a sovereign, and one who possesses dominion, which in turn derives from *koo'reeos:* supreme in authority.[538] Seemingly dominions support the thrones of nations and their lands and report up the hierarchy to cherubim and ophannim in First Hierarchy. *Kooreeot'ace* is only translated as "dominion(s)" and "government."[539] Dominions are lords aspiring to true lordship, according to Dionysius.[540] Thus lordships/ *katakooreeyoo'o* surface in the Bible, meaning lords and exercising lordships over

---

[537] Nicholas De Vere, *The Dragon Legacy,* 42, 200, 201.
[538] G2963—*koo-ree-ot'-ace*; G2962—*koo'-ree-os.*
[539] Dominion(s): Eph 1:21; Jude 1:8. Government: 1 Peter 2:10.
[540] *The Works of Dionysius,* 124: Caput VIII, *On the Heavenly Hierarchy.*

their dominion.[541] One deduces the dominions/lordships are intimately involved with the thrones and government on earth with the spurious offspring. As used in the book of Daniel, a dominion is a realm or empire in heaven and/or on earth, as with King Nebuchadnezzar's Babylonian beast empire.[542]

Ergo, I think the four orders of the First Hierarchy might be led by an archangel, the four presences, that forms columns throughout the Second and Third Hierarchies:

Gabriel	Seraphim	Governments:	Powers	Angels
		Religions:	Principalities	Angels
Michael	Archangel	Army:	Mighties	Angels
Uriel/Raphael	Cherubim/Ophannim	Thrones:	Dominions	Angels

One might further visualize the fallen hierarchy in the imagery of a chess game that has been replicated on earth. The chess board has black and white opposing sides representing their dualistic doctrine, good versus evil, in perpetual conflict both in the physical and spiritual realms. Imagine the back rows of each player as the throne room represented by the ophannim. The king is the father god and the queen is the mother goddess with each having a throne. The king and queen have a bishop/seraph, a knight/chariot/cherub, and a rook/mighty fortress/archangel representing leadership over their columns of orders. The pawns represent the myriad of angels before the throne. In the polytheist physical realm, with the chess pieces represent the reigning demigod dynasties, some use their knowledge and power for good and some for evil, as in the white magic and black magic of the magi. The chess board, pieces, and two opposing players represent the polytheist doctrine: as above, so below. The board represents the earth. The dynastic ancient king and queen represents the father god and mother goddess on earth, archangels. Their throne represents the ophannim that carry out the will of the player, god/goddess of that nation. The bishop represents the polytheist theocracy government of the king and queen. The knight represents the chariot and cavalry of the army, reflecting the cherub. The rook represents the mighty high-walled castles/fortresses and the ancient mighty ones, the warriors of renown in the army. The pawns represent the human foot soldiers used to lead the assault and readily sacrificed that reflect the angel order. Further, occult imagery often depicts Satan playing a perpetual game of chess against his nemesis, the God of the Bible, in the preternatural game and doctrine of good versus evil.

---

[541] G2634—*kat-ak-oo-ree-yoo'-o.*
[542] H7985—sholtan, shol-tawn'; Aramaic from 7981: empire; dominion; sovereignty; realm.

CHAPTER 15

THE ANGEL OF THE LORD

Zech 3:1 And he shewed me Joshua the high priest standing before the angel of the LORD, and Satan standing at his right hand to resist him.

The Angel of the Lord recorded in the Old Testament is a spirit being. The Angel of the Lord title and role is indispensable to fully understanding the resolution to the ancient angelic rebellion.

What we know is that the Angel of the Lord is alternatively named the Angel of God in Scripture.[543] So, who is the Angel of the Lord and how does this Angel fit into the angelic hierarchy?

In the New Testament we know Gabriel is one of the angels that stands in the presence of God was sent by God to Zacharias, and likely the same angel described as "an angel of the Lord" in the books of Matthew, Luke, and Acts.[544] Conversely, the New Testament seemingly equated the "angel of God" with "Jesus Christ" in Galatians 4:14. In Acts 27:23, Paul seems to imply that the Angel of God is the "I am" whom Paul serves: "For there stood by me this night the angel of God, whose I am, and whom I serve."

---

[543] Exod 14:19; Judg 13:6; 1 Sam 29:9; 2 Sam 14:17, 20; 19:27.
[544] Luke 1:19; Angel of the Lord NT: Matt 1:20, 24; 2:13, 19; 28:2; Luke 1:11; 2:9; 8:26; Acts 5:19, 8:26; 12:7, 23.

Further, the Angel of the Lord is described in the book of Isaiah as the "angel of his presence" who "carried them all the days of old."[545] The Angel of the Lord is the One who comes in the year of the Lord's wrath to tread the wine press of wrath bowls for Armageddon, and the wars leading up to Armageddon; the One who has his robes stained by winepress, the Savior who delivered Israel in the time of Exodus and divided the Red Sea for Israel and Judah in the days of old, and whom Israel and Judah violated their covenant with.[546] And this is the Angel of the Lord whose name is the Word of God who created all things at the command of God.[547]

> Rev 19:13 And he was clothed with a vesture dipped in blood: and his name is called The Word of God.

One might be a little surprised to learn that the Word of God is referred to as an angel, but remember that all beings in heaven are spirit, as was the Word before He became flesh as Jesus and returned to sit at God's right hand after His resurrection. In fact, the book of Proverbs instructs the reader that God brought the Word forth as the first of His works—before His deeds of old, appointed for eternity from the beginning that was before the creation of the heavens, earth, and angels. The Word was at God's side always as His Architect, Craftsman, and or Artificer. Those who find Him find life and favor from God; those who hate Him love death.[548]

The Angel of the Lord is depicted in the Old Testament as a manifestation of God, the Word, or both, who possessed and displayed the powers and characteristics only attributed to God, such as forgiving sins or not, for lack of faith in Him or rebellion against Him.[549] The similarities between the Angel of the Lord and the Word who became Jesus indicates to me that the Angel of the Lord was the Word of God manifested in angel-like form on earth before He became flesh.[550]

> Respectfully put, I believe God speaks through His Word/Jesus just as this conclusion is reflected Genesis 1:1–31: "And God said [Word/Jesus], Let there be. .." and all things were then created. I conclude Jesus is God's Word and thus God speaks to us through the Word/Jesus, just as God created all things through His Word/Jesus: "But in the last days he has spoken to us by his Son, whom he appointed heir of all things, and through whom he made the universe" (Hebrews 1:2). Thus God and Jesus are the Creator in perfect union and yet the Word Jesus is

---

[545] Isa 63:9.

[546] Isa 63:1–19; Rev 14:19–20; 16:14–16; 19:13–17.

[547] John 1:1, 2, 3, 14.

[548] Prov 8:22–36; 8:30 brought up: H525—*'amown, aw-mone'*: in the sense of training; skilled; an architect; artificer; master workman; skilled workman.

[549] *Nelson's*, 56: angel. *Strong's Cyclopaedia*, Vol. 1, 226: angel.

[550] John 1:1, 14.

somehow distinct from God that I will endeavor to explain. Ergo, the Word/Jesus and the Holy Spirit appear to us as God's greatest beings that operate in unison but separate from God; doing God's greatest beckoning. In this sense, Jesus' imagery as the Branch of God would be precision accuracy. The Son is the radiance of God's glory and the exact representation of his being, sustaining all things by his powerful word. After he had provided purification for sins, he sat down at the right side of the Majesty in heaven" (Hebrews 1:3). "He [Jesus] is the image of the invisible God, the first born over all creation" (Colossians 1:15).[551]

Adamites via Noah, Abraham, Isaac, Jacob/Israel, and Judah are how the Word chose to become flesh, to become Jesus, and to ensure the names written in the book of life from the beginning were preserved and not blotted out, all through their free choice.[552] With the crucifixion and subsequent resurrection of Jesus, the resolution to the angelic rebellion will be completed in the end times, and in the same period and era the resurrection sequence will begin: the firstfruits martyred for the testimony of Jesus, those who died in Jesus, those who are still alive, Israel and Judah's resurrection and judgment at the time of the Second Exodus, the resurrection of those who refuse the mark of the beast or to worship Satan, and then the resurrection of the dead at the end of Jesus' millennial reign. The Angel of the Lord protected Israel and Judah from their beginning, with Abraham, and will be with them again for ultimate salvation in the end times.

The Angel/*Mal'ak* of the Lord/*Yhovah* first manifested as such biblically, to Hagar, Abraham's consort, to bless and protect Ishmael, and again later appearing as the Angel of God/*'Elohiym*.[553] The words "of the" and "of" part the two titles were inserted by translators, indicating *Yhovah* appeared angel-like to Hagar as well as angel-like of *ha 'Elohiym* as in the Triune God.

I find the ways God and Lord God appear to Abraham fascinating. The Lord/ *Yhovah* first spoke to Abraham while Abraham was still in Mesopotamia and then again in Canaan.[554] The Word of the Lord/*Yhovah* first came to Abraham when Abraham was fretting over an heir.[555] One might argue that the Angel of the Lord/ *Yhovah* first appeared to Abraham to bless Sarah to become pregnant with Isaac, as *Yhovah* appeared in the form of a man along with two other men that were angels, the two angels thereafter went to Sodom. One deduces the Sodom narrative is the first time *Yhovah* appeared in a physical man-like to Abraham,[556] after Melchizedek blessed Abraham.

---

[551] Wayne, *The Genesis 6 Conspiracy*, 334. Isa 11:1; Jer 23:5; 33:14; Zech 3:8; 6:12.

[552] Exod 32:33–34; Deut 9:13–14; Ps 69:28; Dan 7:10; Rev 3:5; 13:9; 17:8; 20:12, 15; 22:19.

[553] Gen 16:1–16; 21:17.

[554] Gen 12:1–20.

[555] Gen 15:1–4.

[556] Gen 18:1–15.

God/ *'Elohiym* is the title or name we are provided to represent the tripartite nature of God the Father, the Word, and the Holy Spirit throughout Genesis 1. God/ *'Elohiym* is the continued expression of choice in first few verses of Genesis 2. Lord God/ *Yhovah 'Elohiym* is introduced beginning in Genesis 2:4 when Adam was about to be created: "the LORD God made the earth and the heavens," which is a cognate verse to John 1:2 that states regarding the Word: "All things were made by him, and without him not any thing was made that was made" when God spoke as the Word. Both Genesis 2:4 and John 1:2 are consistent with Colossians 1:14–16: "In whom we have redemption through his blood, even the forgiveness of sins: Who is the image of the invisible God, the firstborn of every creature: For by him were all things created, that are in heaven, and that are in earth, visible and invisible, whether they be thrones, or dominions, or principalities, or powers: all things were created by him, and for him." It further follows that in Genesis 3:1, 3 and 5 that God/ *'Elohiym* set down the only law of Eden, which prohibited eating from the fruit of the tree of the knowledge of both good and evil, but *Yhovah 'Elohiym,* Lord God is the language used in Genesis 3:1 as the One who created the serpent. *Yhovah* is the Lord of hosts referenced two hundred and forty-four times and is the Word of God who is the central theme and principle that dominate the Old Testament narratives.[557] Ergo, the Word Jesus was the firstborn of all creation as the Branch of God, the Beginning, Origin, and/or Ruler of the creation of God,[558] who created all the orders of angels with whom He sits above with God and the Holy Spirit:

> Col 1:17 And he is before all things, and by him all things consist.

> Col 1:18 And he is the head of the body, the church: who is the beginning, the firstborn from the dead; that in all things he might have the preeminence.

The engagement between Adam and Eve after Genesis 3:5 was with *Yhovah 'Elohiym.* It follows then that Word of God is the New Testament title for *Yhovah* of *'Elohiym* of the Old Testament. It seems to me that Old Testament language distinguishes between the plural, superlative tripartite nature of *ha 'Elohiym,* and the singular-like interventions of *ha Yhovah* of the *'Elohiym* in a similar manner as the singular intervention of the Word/*Log'os* of God/*Theh'os* who became flesh as Jesus. The *Log'os* Spirit, then, is the New Testament equivalent the Lord/*Yhovah* Spirit. Knowing this makes sense that *Yhovah 'Elohiym's* singular intervention began with Adam's creation to begin the resolution to the angelic rebellion. I would additionally advise that one note the interaction between God/ *'Elohiym's* with Noah in the flood narratives that outnumbers *Yhovah's* interaction and

---

[557] Isa 31:3–6.
[558] Rev 3:14. Beginning: G746—*ar-khay'.*

interpret those versus with the same distinctions, and as a renewal of Genesis 1 from with Noah. Thus, the Lord/*Yhovah* begins His intercessions again at Babel, when *Yhovah* "came down to see the city" (Gen 11:5).

The Babel dispersement is another intervention of the Lord/*Yhovah*, the Word/ *Log'os*, to ensure humankind will be made available for the Word made flesh plan, after the Noahites were converted to the antediluvian Enochian mysticism under the Naphalim World Order by Nimrod. After Babel, Abraham was selected in Mesopotamia by *Yhovah* to be the patriarch for the revival of postdiluvian monotheism and faith.[559] The Angel of the Lord then blessed Sarah, promising that Abraham would become great and the patriarch for many nations.[560] The Angel of the Lord later led and protected Israel from the Rephaim-led nations during the Exodus and conquest of the Covenant Land, as well as protection from the beast empires like Egypt and Assyria providing Israel and Judah held up the Holy Covenant.[561]

Knowing this then makes sense of the book of Acts stating the Angel of the Lord was Jesus, as the One in the burning bush who spoke to Moses in the book of Exodus. Acts 7 notes the voice/*fonay'* (Word) "of the Lord" came upon Moses as the "Angel of the Lord in a flame of fire in a bush,"[562] the Angel and Word of the Great "I Am" recorded in the book of Exodus:

> Exod 3:2 And the angel of the LORD appeared unto him in a flame of fire out of the midst of a bush: and he looked, and, behold, the bush burned with fire.. ..

> Exod 3:4 And when the LORD saw that he turned aside to see, God called unto him out of the midst of the bush.. ..

> Exod 3:6. .. I am the God of thy father, the God of Abraham, the God of Isaac, and the God of Jacob. And Moses hid his face; for he was afraid to look upon God.. ..

> Exod 3:14 And God said unto Moses, I AM THAT I AM: and he said, Thus shalt thou say unto the children of Israel, I AM hath sent me unto you.

The Angel of the Lord appeared among God's throne in the book of Zechariah. In this vision, the high priest, Joshua, stands before the Angel of the Lord. Satan stands on Joshua's right side to accuse Joshua.[563] Joshua/*Yhowshuwa`* is a compound word meaning Jehovah/*Yhovah* is salvation. The Greek *Eeaysooce'/Iesous*

---

[559] Gen 12:1.
[560] Gen 16:1–16; 22:11–15.
[561] Exod 3:2; Num 22:23–35; 14:19; Judg 2:1; 6:11–22; 13:3–21; 2 Kings 19:35–37; Isa 31:3–6.
[562] Exod 3:14; Acts 7:30–38. G5456—*fo-nay'*: sound; a tone; voice; word; words; speech.
[563] Zech 3:1, 3.

is the English transliterated Jesus that also means "Jehovah/ *Yhovah* is salvation."[564] Joshua, the high priest in Zechariah's prophetic vision, foretold the Angel/Spirit of the Lord, the Word of God would become flesh by dwelling in the soul and body of Jesus. Joshua/Jesus, in this prophecy, by following and upholding the ways of God would thereafter be awarded the clothes of the high priest, "protested" as in testified or bore witness to by the Angel of the Lord,[565] the precognate Jesus. Joshua too in Zechariah's vision is the precognate Jesus who would come forward as the God's Servant and Branch to take away the iniquity/sins of the world in a single day—crucifixion day,[566] and/or the day of the Lord and wrath at Armageddon, when the Angel of the Lord will destroy all those who come against Jerusalem.[567]

The book of Zechariah's visions of the Angel of the Lord that bore witness to the precognitive Joshua/Jesus, the Word of God/Angel of the Lord would be made flesh and would become the High Priest, overflows with important information regarding Satan. The mystery to Satan falsely accusing the future High Priest will be resolved in the end times, along with the mystery to the Word/Jesus becoming the High Priest void of sin.[568]

> Heb 8:1 Now of the things which we have spoken this is the sum: We have such an high priest, who is set on the right hand of the throne of the Majesty in the heavens;
>
> Heb 8:2 A minister of the sanctuary, and of the true tabernacle, which the Lord pitched, and not man.

The Word was created perfect. As flesh, He overcame the world He created, free from sin, in a world that was corrupted by rebellious angels. Jesus was sacrificed without cause and sinless to atone for the sins of the world begat by Satan. Jesus thereafter was resurrected to be High Priest of God in the "order of Melchisedec,"[569] among many of His exalted titles including "the Author of Eternal Salvation."[570] Jesus is now the immortal High Priest of the Melchizedek Order: the guarantor of God's Holy Covenant Jesus grafted Christians into, The One who intercedes for His brethren, and backed by God's oath whereby humankind will be

---

[564] H3091—*Yhowshuwa`, yeh-ho-shoo'-ah*; or *Yhowshua, yeh-ho-shoo'-ah*: Jehovah-saved; Jehovah is salvation; Greek 2424 *Ihsouv* and 919 *barihsouv*; G2424—*ee-ay-sooce'*: of Hebrew origin 3091 *Yehowshuwa`*; Jesus as in Jehoshua or Joshua; Jehovah is salvation; Saviour of humankind; the name of our Lord; transliterated: Iesous.

[565] Zech 3:4–8. H5749—`*uwd, ood*; a primitive root: to duplicate or repeat: to protest; testify; bear witness to; restore.

[566] Zech 3:8–9.

[567] Zech 12:8.

[568] Heb 4:14.

[569] Heb 5:5–6.

[570] Heb 5:8–10; 6:20.

joint heirs of eternity.[571] Melchizedek [572] was a very important figure to note. Genesis notes he was king and priest of Salem, priest of the most High God,[573] after the account of the Mesopotamian alliance in Genesis 14's war of giants.

> Heb 7:1 For this Melchisedec, king of Salem, priest of the most High God, who met Abraham returning from the slaughter of the kings, and blessed him.. ..

> Heb 7:2 To whom also Abraham gave a tenth part of all; first being by interpretation king of righteousness, and after that also King of Salem, which is, king of peace.

Other than the above information, we are starved of any further details about Melchizedek or his genealogy. In my view, it is unlikely Melchizedek was a Jebusite, Amorite, or Hittite associated with Jerusalem at that time or a king of these Canaanite clans.[574] Hebrews states Melchizedek was the "king of peace,"[575] a term one would attribute to Jesus (Isa 9:6; Eph 2:13). Melchizedek was further defined as a figure in both Greek and Hebrew as a "king of righteousness,"[576] which is yet another title attributed to Jesus.[577] Further, Melchizedek in Hebrews 7:2 is stated to be "a being by interpretation" the king of righteousness—Jesus. Hence, I do not believe that Melchizedek's titles are coincidentally part of Jesus' titles, nor that our Redeemer would be part of a human priestly order, nor a successor to a human priestly order.

The book of Hebrews noted there was a need to replace the human Aaronite priesthood with another; the order of Melchizedek was based not on tribal affiliation with the Levites, but in the power of eternal life through the resurrected Word/Jesus as High Priest,[578] to fulfill a void. As such, there is an underexplained connection between the Word/Jesus to the human Aaronite priestly order and Melchizedek and his order. Melchizedek blessed Abraham, the patriarch of Israel, who in turn produced the Aaronite order of Levi, and the tribe of Judah that made the way for the Word to become flesh. Jesus replaced the human Aaronite priesthood of Levi as an immortal and the order that has roots in the underex-

---

[571] Ps 110:4; Heb 7:17–21. Joint heirs: Matt 25:34; Acts 20:32; Rom 8:16–17; 11:1-36; Gal 3:29; 4:7; Titus 3:7; Heb 1:2, 14; 5:6; James 2:5; 1 Peter 1:3–5.
[572] Gen 14:18; Ps 110:4; Heb 5:6, 10; 6:20; 7:1, 10, 11, 15, 17, 21.
[573] Gen 14:18–20.
[574] Josh 15:8; Eze 16:3.
[575] Isa 9:6; Eph 2:13–14; Col 3:15.
[576] H4428—*melek, meh'-lek*: a king; a royal; H6664—*tsedeq, tseh'-dek*: righteous; justice; G3198—*mel-khis-ed-ek'; Malkiy-Tsedeq*: a patriarch, Melchisedec; king of righteousness; king of Salem; priest of God the Most High; transliterated: Melchisedek.
[577] Isa 9:7; 11:5; 32:1; 52:7; Jer 23:5–6; 33:15–16; Heb 1:8; 7:2; Rev 19:11–12.
[578] Heb 7:11–15.

plained order led by Melchizedek. Perhaps then, the Melchizedek Order is not a human order. The book of Hebrews tells us Melchizedek was recorded without a father, without a mother, without a descent, and without record of genealogy;[579] Melchizedek did not have a beginning of days nor an end of life, yet was one who remains a priest forever made like the Son of God, to whom Abraham tithed.[580]

> Heb 7:3 Without father, without mother, without descent, having neither beginning of days, nor end of life; but made like unto the Son of God; abideth a priest continually.

The book of Hebrews seemingly submits that Melchizedek was not human, but preternatural. Because Melchizedek did not have a beginning nor end, he is Alpha/Omega. Melchizedek could only be God, or the Word/Jesus.[581] Hebrews 7:3 further stated Melchizedek was "made like unto the Son of God," as in and the Angel of God, who "abideth as a priest continually,"[582] or forever, like Jesus. Thus, Melchizedek was "made like unto" the Son of God, meaning a model, image, copy, facsimile, etc.[583] The mystery revealed within the language of the text describing Melchizedek is that he indeed was the manifestation in a physical form as a man of Yehovah/Log'os, akin to or identical the Man/Angel that visited Abraham in the Sodom narrative.

The book of Hebrews goes onto support my supposition, stating, "for that after the similitude of Melchisedec there ariseth another priest,"[584] Jesus. Similitude/homoyot'ace is defined as likeness or resemblance.[585] The Word Jesus would not be in the likeness of a human; the only likeness to Jesus would be God, in my opinion. Thus, after the likeness of the Angel of the Lord, the Word of God arises another priest who became Jesus and was raised up to God forever in the order of Melchizedek. Ariseth/anis'taymee is defined as stand up, raise up, rise again, raised from the dead, and to be born,[586] all of which applies to the Word made flesh.

> Ps 110:4 The LORD hath sworn, and will not repent, Thou art a priest for ever after the order of Melchizedek.

---

[579]G35—ag-en-eh-al-og'-ay-tos: an unregistered as to birth: without descent; without genealogy; transliterated: agenealogetos.
[580] Heb 7:4.
[581] Prov 8:22–35; John 1:1–3, 14; Rev 1:8; 21:6; 22:13.
[582] G1336—dee-ay-nek-es': carried through perpetually; continually; forever; transliterated: dienekes.
[583] Heb 7:3, "make like unto." G871—af-om-oy-o'-o: to assimilate closely; make like; a model, image, or shape like it; a copy; a produced facsimile; transliterated aphomoioo.
[584] Heb 7:15.
[585] G3665—hom-oy-ot'-ace: resemblance; like as; similitude; transliterated: homoiotes.
[586] Heb 7:3, 14c17. G450—an-is'-tay-mee: stand up; arise; lift-up; raise up again; rise again, raise up from laying down; raise up from the dead; cause to be born; transliterated: anistemi.

Ps 110:5 The Lord at thy right hand shall strike through kings in the day of his wrath.

One might want to anticipate Antichrist, after his counterfeit resurrection,[587] will claim his position as the counterfeit high priest Melchizedek Order through the spurious Canaanite Order of Melchizedek celebrated by secret societies, gnostics, and the Essenes and their gnostic gospels of Melchizedek.[588] Anticipate Antichrist will usurp his counterfeit title of "King of Jerusalem" through claiming to be a Melchizedek-like priest, and through counterfeit bloodlines traced back to King David, Saul, and Jesus.[589] Anticipate that Antichrist will do this after taking credit for winning the counterfeit Armageddon war;[590] then surrounds Jerusalem with his army;[591] and then proceeds to declare himself in the Jerusalem temple to be God whom all must worship[592] in an event infamously renowned as the abomination that causes desolation.[593]

[587] Rev 13:3, 14, 15; 14:9–11; 16:2; 19:20; 20:4.
[588] Wayne, *The Genesis 6 Conspiracy*, 585–590.
[589] Ibid., 415–422, 441–448: 461–468, 478–483, 564–569, 585–590.
[590] Ezek 38–39; Joel 1–2; Rev 9:14–20.
[591] Dan 11:30–31; Luke 21:20–21.
[592] Dan 8:25; 11:36–38; 2 Thess 2:4; Rev 13:5, 8.
[593] Dan 9:27; 11:31; 12:11; Matt 24:15–20; Mark 13:14; Luke 21:22.

CHAPTER 16

SATAN: THE ANOINTED OF ANGELS

Ezek 28:14 Thou art the anointed cherub that covereth; and I have set thee so: thou wast upon the holy mountain of God; thou hast walked up and down in the midst of the stones of fire.

Ezek 28:15 Thou wast perfect in thy ways from the day that thou wast created, till iniquity was found in thee.

Viewing Satan as just a powerful fallen angel does not adequately describe who he was before his fall, or how far *Heylel* fell from his former position. Even after Satan's fall, he has continued to reign, enthroned above the fallen congregation of gods depicted in Psalm 82 as the god of this world, counterfeiting God's heavenly assembly.

Scripture does not provide a complete tally of titles and/or names Satan once held, but Scripture does detail several of *Heylel's* traits, titles, and positions before he was degraded to Satan status. One of Satan's former positions completes the mystery to why Jesus became the High Priest of the Melchizedek Order before God. The key to unlocking the answer to the priestly Melchizedek mystery begins with discerning that one of Satan's former positions included the angelic high priest serving at God's heavenly altar atop the Seraphim angelic order. The High Priest position in heaven was not filled after Satan's fall. It follows that Jesus became flesh to fill the void of Satan's former high priest position. The basis for the above Satan discernment can be found within the seemingly disparate details describing the devil distributed throughout the Bible.

Satan was perfect from creation but did not remain loyal and obedient to God. Iniquity took root in him and infected his perfection and his extraordinary high designation before God. Iniquity led Satan to rebel against God and inspired his failed coup d'état.[594] Iniquity perpetuated Satan's continued rebellion that manifested in his wrath and revenge directed at humankind, all to justify his poorly conceived uprising[595] and to endeavor to prevent humankind from becoming heirs to eternity.[596]

Before Satan's fall, he was distinguished in the book of Ezekiel as the "anointed cherub" who walked among the fiery stones on the holy mountain as a "covering cherub" like those that adorn the ark of the covenant.[597] The cherubic and anointed cherub walked among the fiery stones like the seraphim, but unlike the cherubim Watchers that cover the throne with their wings. Satan/*Heylel* was also the cherubim permitted to enter in Eden.[598] Thus, covering is defined as: to cover, entwine as a screen, shade, and figuratively protect or defend.[599] It follows that Satan was in part a powerful, cherub Watcher, yet unique, for he walked among the fiery stones.

Satan's cherubic title included being the anointed/*mimshack'*, defined in the sense of anointed with outstretched wings or expansion, and a Hebrew word that derives *from mimshakh'*: to consecrate, anoint, anoint (generally) with oil.[600] Satan's former anointing indicates an expanded, more prestigious, and honored position and role as compared to other cherubim and other angels. In fact, anointing indicates *Heylel* was bestowed with a ceremonial or holy office akin to monarchs and priests. Similarly, Jesus too was anointed to speak to the meek, as recorded in Isaiah and Luke in the "Year of the Lord's Favor" end-time prophecy.[601] Anointed in Isaiah 61:1 applied to the future Messiah, also derives from *mimshakh'*. Anointed in Luke 4:18 derives from *khree'o*, also meaning consecrated to a religious service or office.

Satan's former anointing as the high priest makes sense that he would have "walked up and down in the midst of the stones of fire," and of "O covering

---

[594] Isa 14:12–15; Ezek 28:15–18; Matt 25:41; Luke 10:8; John 8:44; Rev 12:9; 20:2.

[595] Matt 4:10; 25:41; Rev 12:9; 20:2–3.

[596] Matt 5:5; 25:34; Rom 8:17; Titus 3:7; Heb 1:14; 6:17; Jam 2:5; Rev 21:7.

[597] Exod 25:18, 19, 20, 22; 26:31; 36:8, 25; 37:7, 8, 9; Num 7:89; Ezek 28:14, 16.

[598] Ezek 28:13.

[599] H5526—*cakak, saw-kak'*: entwine as a screen; fence in; cover over; protect; defence; defend; join; set; shut up.

[600] H4473—*mimshach, mim-shakh'*; from 4886: the sense of expansion; outspread; outstretched wings; anointed; H4886—*mashach, mim-shakh'*: rub with oil; anoint; consecrate; smear/paint.

[601] Ps 45:7; Isa 61:1; Luke 4:18; Acts 4:27; Heb 1:9.

cherub, from the midst of the stones of fire."[602] Fiery stones/ '*eben*[603] are akin to the fiery coals of God's altar, documented in the book of Isaiah where the seraphim served like priests and flew above the throne.[604] Coal/*ritspah* is a glowing stone or piece of coal, and red-hot coal or stones.[605] Satan by implication was in part the anointed cherubim and anointed seraphim, the high priest, and "perfect in his ways"[606] before God, and one who walked upon God's holy mountain and who was in Eden.[607] It follows that Satan was adorned with nine precious stones representing his priestly status, just as Levite priests wore vests with twelve precious stones representing their priestly status. The twelve Levite stones represented by their number and likely application, a future higher order of priests than that of Satan, one begat by the Word/Melchizedek with Abraham.

> Exod 28:21 And the stones shall be with the names of the children of Israel, twelve, according to their names, like the engravings of a signet; every one with his name.

> Ezek 28:13. .. every precious stone was thy covering, the sardius, topaz, and the diamond, the beryl, the onyx, and the jasper, the sapphire, the emerald, and the carbuncle, and gold.

Seraphim angels were fiery-like from working within the coals of God's altar, and were serpent-faced angels with six wings,[608] just as Satan and his sponsored beast empires were allegorically the "red dragon"[609]—a serpent with wings. Red/ *poorhros'* means the color of fire and fire-like,[610] which is rooted in *poor* that is the primary word for fire and figurative for lightening.[611] The red/*poorhros'* dragon allegory works in perfection with Luke 10:18 where Jesus said: "I beheld Satan as lightning fall from heaven." And so, Satan is additionally described as "the great dragon was cast out, that old serpent, called the Devil, and Satan, which deceiveth the whole world."[612] One wonders then if Samael is indeed Satan's seraphim

---

[602] Ezek 28:14, 16.

[603] H68—'*eben, eh'-ben*: to build; a stone; a weight.

[604] Isa 6:1–6.

[605] H7531—*ritspah, rits-paw'*; feminine of 7529: a hot stone; a mosaic pattern pavement; live coal; glowing stone; coal; H7529—*retseph, reh'-tsef*: a red-hot stone for baking; glowing stone; coal; flame; firebolt.

[606] Ezek 28:12, 15.

[607] Isa 14:13; Ezek 28:13, 14.

[608] H8314—*saraph, saw-rawf'*.

[609] Rev 12:3–4.

[610] G4450—*poor-hros'*: fire-like; flame-coloured; red; transliterated: purrhos.

[611] G4442—*poor*: a primary word for fire; figurative for lightning; fiery; transliterated: pur.

[612] Rev 12:9.

appellation and/or name, just as *Heylel* represents Satan's former shining or morning star status.

In the same line of thought, note that First Enoch recorded *Gadreel* as the Jeqon who led Eve astray in Eden, while noting Satan was recorded biblically as the cherubim in Eden.[613] In Hebrew, *gader* means an enclosure, wall, fence, or hedge. *Gader* derives from the Hebrew word *gadar*, meaning to wall around, fence up hedge, enclose, repairer, and (seemingly) mason.[614] Combined with *el* as in *Gadreel*, one arrives with the meaning: wall or enclosure of God, or God's wall, which by implication might have been Satan's cherubic name or his cherubic title. What I find is an extraordinary choice of translation is that *gadar* was translated two times in the KJV as "masons," which by inference one might translate *Gadreel* in the book of Enoch as the mason god, or god of the masons.

> 2 Kings 12:12 And to masons, and hewers of stone, and to buy timber and hewed stone to repair the breaches of the house of the LORD, and for all that was laid out for the house to repair it.[615]

Satan's formers titles and traits continue into the New Testament with the title of prince, and a hagiographic title for archangels: "Now shall the prince of this world be cast out."[616] "Prince" derives from *ar'khone*/archon, meaning first in rank, power, a chief ruler, and is the present participle of *ar'kho* meaning first in rank, chief, reign over.[617] Archangel/*arkhang'elos* is a compounded Greek word first from *ar'kho*/chief, *ar'khone*/prince[618] and then angel/*ang'elos*, a messenger/envoy from God;[619] titles held biblically by Michael and Gabriel as archangels who worked in the presence of God. Satan, by the New Testament application and implication as "prince of this world,"[620] once held the title archangel, archon, and chief of all angels. *Heylel* was only lower in rank to the Word who created all the angels including Satan at God's command, and the Holy Spirit.[621] As archon, archangel, cherubim, seraphim, and high priest, Satan was also a Watcher by implication, but likely in an elevated hierarchal position as a presence.

---

[613] Enoch 59:6; Ezek 28:13.

[614] H1447—*gader, gaw-dare'*; from 1443: an enclosure; fence; hedge; wall; H1443—*gadar, gaw-dar'*: to wall in or around; close; fence up; hedge; enclose; make up a wall; mason; repairer.

[615] See also 2 Kings 22:6 for *gadar* translated as "mason."

[616] John 12:31; 16:11.

[617] G757—*ar'-kho;* G758—*ar'-khone;* present participle of 757. Prince/*ar'-khone*: Matt 9:34; 12:24; Mark 3:22; John 12:31; 14:30; 16:11; Eph 2:2; Rev 1:5.

[618] G743—*ar-khang'-el-os.*

[619] G32—*ang'-el-os.*

[620] John 12:31.

[621] Col 1:15–16.

John 14:30 Hereafter I will not talk much with you: for the prince of this world cometh, and hath nothing in me.

Eph 2:2 Wherein in time past ye walked according to the course of this world, according to the prince of the power of the air, the spirit that now worketh in the children of disobedience.

One concludes Satan was demoted in rank from chief archangel and power/ *exoosee'ah* when he was cast down from standing in the presence of God in Isaiah 14:12–16. One deduces that four to seven archangels were promoted in rank in God's army *tsaba'*, with more power than Satan, or that Satan's power was reduced. The world will witness the power of the loyal archangels, in the end-time with the war in heaven led by Michael against Satan, and three and a half years later when Satan is sent to the abyss.[622] One deduces the angel who sends Satan to the abyss and later to the lake of fire would be a powerful archangel, even though the text in the book of Revelation says "angel."

The book of Enoch noted that archangel Uriel was in charge of Tartarus[623] defined biblically as hell/*tartaro'o*, the pit prison where fallen angels are restrained by "chains and darkness, to be reserved unto judgment" from the days Noah; a place understood by the Greeks as place to hold those to suffer punishment for their evil deeds, and the place of imprisoned angels where Jesus went to speak to while still in the grave.[624] Additionally, the book of Enoch noted the archangels Michael, Gabriel, Raphael, and Phanuel cast unrighteous angels subject to Satan into the abyss in the days of Noah.[625]

Rev 20:1 I saw an angel come down from heaven, having the key of the bottomless pit and a great chain in his hand.

Rev 20:2 And he laid hold on the dragon, that old serpent, which is the Devil, and Satan, and bound him a thousand years.

From anointed cherubim, seraphim, archangel, archon, and high priest serving God in the heavenly temple, Satan seemingly plea-bargained his crimes after his rebellion, to delay his imprisonment in the abyss, in exchange for Satan status: an accuser, slanderer, sifter, and tester of humankind.[626] Satan acquiesced to the

---

[622] Rev 12:7–9; 20:1,10.

[623] Enoch 20:1; 21:1–10; 88:1–2.

[624] G5020—*tar-tar-o'-o*: the deepest abyss of Hades; incarcerate in eternal torment; regarded by Greeks as the abode of the wicked dead, where they suffer punishment for their evil deeds; Gehenna of the Jews; a place to hold captives; transliterated: tartaroo. Hell: 1 Peter 3:19–20; 2 Peter 2:4.

[625] Enoch 54:5–6.

[626] Job 1:6; 2:1; Zech 3:1–2; Eph 6:11–12; Rev 12:10.

omnipotent power of God to delay, and perhaps prevent his fate of going to the abyss and then the lake of fire. Satan likely thought he could delegitimize and destroy humankind thereby just justifying his rebellion, but Satan and his fallen princes/*ar'khone* did not know about the resurrection.[627]

Remember though, Satan is still the god of this world, for a short time longer, reigning from his throne atop the rebellious angelic hierarchy, even though he lost his heavenly titles and positions. All this is important context given how John and Paul describe Satan: as the prince/*ar'khone* and the power/*exoosee'ah* of the air in this world: "the spirit that works in children of disobedience."[628]

> 2 Cor 4:4 In whom the god of this world hath blinded the minds of them which believe not, lest the light of the glorious gospel of Christ, who is the image of God, should shine unto them.

Satan is defined from Hebrew as a superhuman adversary of God,[629] but is not God's nemesis. Satan and his celestial mafia are the archenemies of humankind. Satan derives another word *satan* meaning to oppose, resist, attack and accuse as an adversary,[630] and which in turn is a derivative of *sitnah* meaning accuser, opposition, and enmity.[631] Satan in Greek, *sat-an'*, derives from the Hebraic *satan*, defined as the adversary name given to the prince of spirits and leader of demons.[632] Satan in Greek is associated with *Satanas'* of Chaldean origin for the devil, prince of spirits and demons.[633] Devil/*deeab'olos* means accuser, slanderer, prince of demons and author of evil who entices humans to sin against God, and leads humans away from God.[634] Devious, Latin *devius*, meaning out of the way, remote, trickery, and dishonest, follows "devil" in *Webster's Dictionary;* and diabolical, Greek *diobolikos* and *diabolos* is assigned to the devil as in devilish. [635]

One further notes that Satan was entitled after his fall as the ancient devil, the dragon, the serpent who leads the world astray,[636] and as the prince of this world

---

[627] 1 Cor 2:7–9.
[628] Joh 12:31; Eph 2:2.
[629] H7854—*satan, saw-tawn'*: opponent; especially with the article [*ha*] prefixed to Satan; archenemy of good; adversary; superhuman adversary; transliterated: sitnah.
[630] H7853—*satan, saw-tan'*: to attack figuratively accuse; an adversary; resist; oppose.
[631] H7855—*sitnah, sit-naw'*: opposition; accusation; enmity.
[632] G4566—*sat-an'*: the devil; prince of evil spirits; adversary of God and Christ and humans who incites apostasy from God and to sin.
[633] G4567—*sat-an-as'*: the accuser; the devil: Satan; prince of evil spirits; the one who incites beings to apostasy; transliterated: Satanas.
[634] G1228—*dee-ab'-ol-os*: a traducer: Satan; false accuser, devil, slanderer; prince of demons; author of evil; transliterated: diabolos; https://www.etymonline.com/word/devil Greek diaballein: to slander or attack.
[635] *Webster's*, 110: devious; 111: diabolical.
[636] Rev 12:9.

and archon of mysticism and secret societies. One should not confuse or conflate the KJV's translation of devil/*deeab'olos* with devil/*daheemon'eon*, a demonic being, an evil spirit, and a messenger of the Devil/Satan.[637] Demons are the disembodied spirits of the Nephilim and Rephaim, of which the worst ones, the "Terrible Ones," were locked in cells along the sides of the abyss; evil spirits that will also be released in the end-time along with the fallen angels locked in the abyss.[638] It follows that Satan, the prince of demons was entitled Belial and Beelzebub, prince of the devils/*daheemon'eons*. Beelzebub is of Chaldean and Aramaic origin and was an epithet for Satan deriving from *Ba`al Zebuwb*, meaning lord of the house.[639]

> Matt 12:24 But when the Pharisees heard it, they said, This fellow doth not cast out devil, but by Beelzebub the prince of the devils.

Baal is the offspring god of Mount Hermon, son of El. Baal is not Satan but an allegory for Satan, just as Osiris, another offspring god, is an allegory for Satan in freemasonry.[640] In masonic tradition, Satan dwells in the house of judgment of the Archeion, allegorically Baal's house. As such, one suspects *ar'kho* would be a word well represented to glorify and worship Satan in the Naphalim World Order, nations they reign over, and the languages spoken to honor the Naphalim hierarchy. *Ar'kho* has many derivatives built into our Baconian English.

Generally "architecture," a word born from antediluvian building knowledge, was first employed to describe the ruling, knowledge, and religious centers. Ancient polytheist-inspired buildings were built with encoded sacred geometry, aligned with celestial alignments, built on important occult locations, adorned

---

[637] G1140—*dahee-mon'-ee-on*; a daemonic being; an inferior deity; devil; a [demi]god; a spirit; messengers of the devil. Transliterated: daimonion; https://www.etymonline.com/word/demon, Latin Daemon and Greek daimon for a spirit and a lesser deity.
ᴰevils: Matt 7:22; 9:34; 10:8; 12:24, 27, 28; Mark 1:34, 39; 3:15, 22; 6:13; 9:38; 16:9, 17; Luke 4:41; 8:2, 27, 30, 33, 35, 38; 9:1, 49; 10:17; 11:15, 18, 19, 20; 13:32; 1 Cor 10:20, 21; 1 Tim 4:1; Rev 9:20. Devil: Matt 9:33; 17:18; Mark 7:26, 29, 30; Luke 4:33, 35; 7:33; 9:42; 11:14; John 7:20; 8:48, 49, 52; 10:20, 21. Gods, Acts 17:18.
[638] Eze 32: 22-32; Rev 9:1-21.
[639] G955—*bel-ee'-al*; of Hebrew origin 1100: worthlessness; wickedness; an epithet of Satan; transliterated: Belial; H1100—*bliya`al, bel-e-yah'-al*: without profit; worthlessness; destruction; wickedness; evil; ungodly; 2 Cor 6:15; G954—*beh-el-zeb-ool'*: of Chaldean and Aramaic origin by parody upon Hebrew *Ba`al Zebuwb*: lord of the house; a name of Satan; prince of evil spirits. Matt 10:25, 12:24, 27; Mark 3:22; Luke 11:15, 18, 19.
[640] Demond Wilson, *The New Age Millennium*, 157, 161, 186, citing Albert Pike, *Morals and Dogma of the Ancient and Accepted Scottish Rite of Freemasonry/Pamphlets* (Whitefish, MT: Kessinger Pub. Co., 1992); Albert G. Mackey, *An Encyclopedia of Freemasonry* (New York: The Masonic History Company, 1873); Manly P. Hall, *The Secret Reachings of All Ages* (Los Angeles The Philosophical Research Society Inc, 1984).

with sculptures and reliefs displaying their gods, history, genealogies, and religion if one takes the time to notice. Architecture is the science or art of building structures with a distinctive style, deriving from the Greek *archetekton* from *archi* meaning chief and *tekton* meaning builder,[641] all of which is eerily and not coincidentally honoring Satan the so-called Great Architect of the Universe. Within the masonic craft, buildings transform architecture when structures rise above their intended use to satisfy the eye through its visual form, which then "contents the spirit of man" and are "incarnations of the time spirit."[642] The fifth of the seven sacred sciences from the time of Cain's rebellion against God was employed to honor the Naphalim World Order and to lead people away from God.

"According to the Anderson Legend, Cain took to the sacred knowledge, practicing the disciplines with uncommon vigor. From this knowledge, and particularly the fifth science, geometry or masonry, Cain built a city named Hanoch (Enoch), after his first born son, and of course, Cain built sixty-five other cities after Hanoch. The Anderson Legend also recorded that the employment of masonry was practiced vigorously up until the deluge, noting many a curious work was built, likely alluding to such projects as the Great Pyramid," which the masonic adept Manley P. Hall described as a "sermon in stone" and "supreme among the temples of the Mysteries."[643]

As god of this world, Satan ensured that a specious archive of archetypal words survived their way into the occult lexicon and western languages to honor Satan and the Naphalim in plain sight. The earthly physical government representing Satan and his celestial mafia is populated by the descendants of their spurious offspring controlling government, the military, religion, the courts, education, science, media, entertainment, secret societies and much more. The names of these organizations, the titles within, and their Satan/Baal inspired buildings overflow with polytheist imagery and language. Even though knowledge, science, language and most all things can be used for good or evil in their applications, one ought to be very wary and critically analyze the actions and spirit of any earthly organization inundated with words and titles deriving from the Greek word *ar'kho*, Latin *arca*, and their derivative or associated words like the word ark for a chest. However, ark in the Old Testament derives from *tebah* as in ark of the covenant/testament, and in the New Testament *kibotos*; not *ar'kho*.

Genitive words springing from *arca*, and Latin *arcus*, meaning a bow, are words such as arch also meaning a bow or a chest,[644] which spawned other interesting

---

[641] *Webster's,* 20: architect; *Encyclopedia Americana,* Vol. 1, 169: architecture.

[642] *Encyclopedia Americana,* Vol. 1, 169–170: architecture.

[643] Wayne, *The Genesis 6 Conspiracy,* 11, citing Albert Mackey, *The History of Freemasonry,* 146, and Gen 4:17; Manly P. Hall, *The Secret Teachings of All Ages* (New York: Jeremy P. Tarcher, 2003; original publication, 1928), 41, 44, 64.

[644] *Webster's,* 20: arch.

words, such as archaic, architecture, and archon, all of which contain provocative links to Freemasons, the Templars, mysticism, and the hierarchy of angels both loyal and fallen. An archon was the chief magistrate [principality] in Athens who possessed all the power, dignity, and privileges of a king, and who derived from a specific race/bloodline, the Codrus,[645] a spurious descendant from Poseidon.

An archive (Greek *arkhe/arkheia* and Latin *archiva*) is a collection of government, public and/or historical documents—a library of knowledge or records.[646] Arcane (Greek *arkos* and Latin *arcanus*) is defined as secret, mysterious, obscure, and known by a few, and is a cornerstone doctrine for mystery religions with their arcane oaths, rituals, and secret knowledge.[647] This spurious spirit of the lost/hidden knowledge is embedded into the word, archaic, meaning ancient and prehistoric,[648] as in archives of secret knowledge provided from fallen archons in archaic times. Laurence Gardner wrote that an "'ark, according to the Oxford Word Library is an obsolete form of the modern word arc, equivalent to the Latin *arca*, and thus 'arcane' derives from the Latin *arca*, meaning 'a box or a chest, as ark, or Ark of the Covenant.'" Gardner further noted that something hidden in a box, chest, or ark is additionally called arcane and that other genitive words of *arca*, such as archive, suggests mysterious, hidden treasures, knowledge, and records as the Chamber of the Archives and the Archives of the Masons. Archive/*arkhe/arkheia* derived from *archeion* where those records were stored.[649]

Other derivative words, such as "archaeology," is the science of ancient things and the critical evaluation of ancient records. "Archaeology" derives from *arche*: the beginning, and *logos*: disclosure or word,[650] meaning knowledge disclosed by Satan and fallen angels from the beginning of the Adamite epoch and perhaps before. It follows then that the great archon of mysticism, the "Great Architect of the Universe," dwells in a "House of Judgment" called the "Archeion."[651] Thus, "archetype" means first, ancient first model, as in religion, government, society, education, science, and buildings[652] on earth.

Further, the arch, as in a curved structure for an entrance or a gate to a building, was re-introduced and popularized by Romans from the ancient Assyrians and Egyptians.[653] An arch in the occult is a common allegory and artistic depiction for a portal along with the occult triptych architecture popular in Gothic and masonic

---

645 *Encyclopedia Americana,* Vol. 1, 186: archon.
646 Dictionary.com: archive; *Webster's,* 20: archives.
647 *Webster's,* 20: arcane; Dictionary.com: arcane.
648 Dictionary.com: archaic; *Webster's,* 20: archaic.
649 *Encyclopedia Americana,* Vol. 1, 186: archive; *Webster's,* 20: archive.
650 *Unger's,* 93: archaeology; John 1.1: Word, G3056—*log'-os.*
651 Wayne, *The Genesis 6 Conspiracy,* 537, citing Gardner, *Lost Secrets,* 60, 94 notes 45, 47.
652 Dictionary.com: archetype; Webster's, 20 archetypes.
653 *Encyclopedia Americana,* Vol. 1, 149: arch.

architecture. An arcade was the archaic word for a structure containing a series of arches and columns, which was rooted in the Latin word *arcus*.[654]

It follows then that an architect is one who has knowledge of building, a chief/ *ar'kho/arkhi* builder/*tekton* of curved or domed buildings in the ancient world. Western government buildings, universities, libraries, and courts are populated with ancient Greek, Roman, Mesopotamian, and Egyptian architecture from beast empires, reflecting polytheist history and their gods. In government the term "archon" was the title for the highest magistrate in ancient Greece who adjudicated in the highest/supreme court known as the "archcourt." In Greek antiquity, an archeion was the official residence of an archon, chief magistrate, the College of Magistrates, and a chamber for public archives.

---

[654] *Websters*, 48: bow; 20: arcade.

CHAPTER 17

THE BAALIM ASSEMBLY OF MOUNT HERMON

John 12:31 Now is the judgment of this world: now shall the prince of this world be cast out...

Eph 2:2 Wherein in time past ye walked according to the course of this world, according to the prince of the power of the air, the spirit that now worketh in the children of disobedience...

Satan is the god of this world, prince of this world, and the prince of the power of the air; power/*exoosee'ah* is understood as universal authority over humankind[655] for a time. Prince(s)/*ar'khone/archon*, meaning chief ruler and magistrate,[656] is a word typically applied to powerful ruling archangels, indicating a governing assembly of gods.

Adding further testimony for the assembly of gods reigning over this world is the phrase "princes of the world,"[657] whereby world/*aion* means an age, perpetuity of

---

[655] G1849—*ex-oo-see'-ah*: the power of authority, power of rule or government universally, authority over mankind.
[656] G758—*ar'-khone*: present participle of 757.
[657] 1 Cor 2:8.

time, the worlds, and universes.[658] It follows that Scripture repeatedly warns about invisible rebellious forces we must battle; evil forces that are not flesh and blood: rulers of darkness, principalities, thrones, dominions, powers, mighties, authorities, and angels, as well as Watchers: archangels, seraphim, cherubim, and ophannim.[659]

The apostle Paul stated that the ruling assembly of rebellious princes/gods of this world did not anticipate the resurrection, otherwise they would not have had Jesus crucified without cause—hidden wisdom of the Alpha and Omega kept from the "princes of this world," wisdom that was ordained from before the creation of the world. Paul's testimony indicates that the celestial mafia assembly was the muscle behind the conspiracy to crucify Jesus but did not directly bloody their hands. The Naphalim employed their controlled visible forces, humans, spurious offspring, and the Roman beast empire to ensure Jesus was slain. One of the key invisible ones was Satan who entered Judas to ensure that Judas betrayed Jesus.[660]

1 Cor 2:7 But we speak the wisdom of God in a mystery, even the hidden wisdom, which God ordained before the world unto our glory:

1 Cor 2:8 Which none of the princes of this world knew: for had they known it, they would not have crucified the Lord of glory.

The celestial mafia, the rebellious host of heaven, were depicted throughout history as the sun, moon, stars, and planets, to whom God divided and allotted the nations to before the flood, as described in Deuteronomy 32, and overseen by the assembly of gods in Psalm 82. Typically, polytheism names seven of these luminaries after the seven major gods leading their pantheon: Sun, Moon, Mercury, Venus, Mars, Jupiter, and Saturn.

Deut 4:19 And lest thou lift up thine eyes unto heaven, and when thou seest the sun, and the moon, and the stars, even all the host of heaven, shouldest be driven to worship them, and serve them, which the Lord thy God hath divided unto all nations under the whole heaven.

Deut 29:26 For they went and served other gods, and worshipped them.

---

[658] G165—*ahee-ohn*; Transliterated: aion: an age; perpetuity of the world; for ever; an unbroken age; perpetuity of time; eternity; the worlds; universe; period.
[659] Col 1:16: Principalities, Thrones, Dominions, and Powers. Eph 6:12: Principalities, Powers, Rulers of darkness in this world. Eph 3:10: Principalities, Powers. Eph 1:21: Principalities, Mighties, Dominions, Powers. 1 Peter 3:22: Angels, Powers, and Authorities. 1 Cor 15:2: Rulers, Principalities, Powers, Authorities, Mighties. Rom 8:38: Angels, Principalities, and Powers. Isa 6:1–6; Ezek 1 and 10; Dan 4:12–13, 17, 23; Rev 4:6–9; 5:6–14 and 1 Enoch 61:10; 71:7: Watchers: Seraphim, Cherubim, and Ophanim. 1 Thess 4:16; Jude 1:9; Rev 8:2: Archangels and 7 angels before God.
[660] Luke 22:3; John 13:27.

The gods of the assembly are part of the hierarchal order of the host led by Satan and the Seven Jeqons (Satans) who taught the mystical religion of idolatry, illicit knowledge of heaven, sorcery, witchcraft, the corrupted wisdom of this world, and violence to the people of the earth both before and after the flood, to the nobility and priest class to impose on humankind.[661] The Seven Jeqons may head groups of ten[662] that include each of the seven totaling seventy that make up the nations of the earth both before and after the flood.

Stars, angels, sons of God, and host of heaven are all terms describing the angelic order, loyal or rebellious, with gods yet another term for the celestial mafia. As such, Deuteronomy 4:19–20 grouped the stars, host of heaven and gods together as the same. In the same way, Job 38:7 grouped the morning stars and sons of God together as angelic beings at the time of creation. Angels were classified as part of the host of heaven in Psalm 148:1–6. Sons of God presented themselves to God in heaven in Job 1:6 and 2:1 as did Satan, an angel; the Septuagint and several English translations substitutes angels, heavenly beings, and/or divine beings for "sons of God" in the Job passages.[663] Some of the loyal host of heaven are prophesied as the starry host trampled in the end times by Antichrist in Daniel 8:10, just as all the rebellious angels led by Satan are cast to the earth in Revelation 12:7. Scriptural intermixed references to sons of God, angels, stars, and the host of heaven circularly support each other as the same host of beings with gods denoting the rebellious angels.

Host/*tsaba'* is defined as something that goes forth as in an army, host of angels, and host celestial bodies like stars,[664] underscoring that army infers rank and hierarchy. Heaven/*shameh* means lofty, sky, heaven, abode of celestial, bodies, atmosphere, and the home of God and angels. The Hebrew plural format for heaven is *shamayim*.[665] In the host/*tsaba* of heaven/*shameh* application, angelic-like beings are the *Shamayim*. Many *Naphalim* (fallen ones) of the heavenly ones/*Shamayin* were sent to the abyss; they were among those to whom Jesus spoke while in the grave.[666]

Polytheist recollections in most cultures account for parent gods like Cronos and Gaea of the Greek pantheon, Anu and Ki/Ninkhursag of the Sumerian pantheon, El and Asherah/Athirat of the Canaan pantheon, and Ra and Nut in the Egyptian pantheon, alongside the other parent gods who reigned with them in their world order. Parent gods were overthrown in polytheist history, and seemingly

---

[661] Enoch 65:6; 69:1–3.

[662] Enoch 6:7

[663] Lancelot C. L Brenton, trans., *The English Translation of the Septuagint Bible*, Kindle Version, Job 1:6,2:1: Angels. Angels: NIV, CEV, WEB. Heavenly beings: GNT, NLT, ISV, NSRV.

[664] H6635—*tsaba'*.

[665] H8064—*shamayim, shaw-mah'-yim*; dual of an unused singular *shameh, shaw-meh'*: to be lofty: the sky; abode of the stars; the visible universe; atmosphere; abode of God.

[666] 1 Peter 3:19; 2 Peter 2:4; Jude 1:6.

slain by offspring gods like Zeus, Baal, Enki, and Osiris. Polytheist accountings of the missing parent gods seem a little out of sorts to me, from the perspective that preternatural gods by definition cannot die. What seems more likely to me is that the original antediluvian assembly of parent gods, and all gods who committed crimes against humanity and creation, were sent to the abyss at the time of the flood. Thereafter, the offspring gods moved up in rank to replace the exiled parent gods, as would happen in an army to replace lost leadership positions. It follows that gods like Baal, Zeus and Osiris reigned from the assembly after the flood.

Gods like Baal and his ruling Baalim were sent to the abyss after the flood as well for creating the postdiluvian Rephaim giants, which were thereafter accounted also as dead. The gods' physical world bodies/*oiketerions* may have died, but their immortal spirits continued. This makes sense of the Baalim gods documented in *The Baal Cycle of Myths* of the *Ugaritic Texts*:

> 1.5 vi 1 [They rolled back the tent of El]and came [to the pavilion of the King, the Father of] the Bright One. [They lifted up their voices and cri]ed: "We traveled to [the ends of the earth]". ..
>
> 1.5 vi 5 to the edge of the abyss; we came to 'Paradise' the land of pasture, to 'Delight,' the steppe by the shore of death. We came upon Baal fallen to the earth: dead was Valiant Baal. ..
>
> 1.5 vi 10 perished was the Prince, Lord of the earth!"[667]

Scripturally, people worshipped and served Baal, and the reigning Baalim, as the host of heaven in the Covenant Land region after the flood.[668] Mount Baalhermon, meaning lord of destruction or lord/master of (Mount) Hermon,[669] was located in the Bashan region and part of the three peaks of Mount Hermon known as the Hermonites.[670] Baalim is the plural for Baal and a term used to identify the many gods of Baal's assembly[671] in Baal's house/*Ba`al Zebuwb* associated with Ashteroth, and other places like Baalberyith god of Shechemites and Philistines, and Baalzebub god of Ekronites—"the lord of the fly."[672] Baal/Bael/Bel/Baell is known in occult religions

---

[667] N. Wyatt, *Religious Texts from Ugarit*, 126: KTU 1.5–10, *The Baal Cycle of Myths*.

[668] Ibid. 2 Kings 21; 2 Chron 33:3; Jer 18:13; Zeph 1:5: "and he reared up altars for Baalim, and made groves, and worshipped all the host of heaven, and served them" (2 Chron 33:3).

[669] Judg 3:3; 1 Chron 5:23. H1179—*Ba`al Chermown; bah'-al kher-mone'*: lord of destruction; city of Mount Hermon. *Unger's*, 132: Baalhermon.

[670] Psa 42:6. H2769—*Chermowniym, kher-mo-neem'*: the name for the three summits of Mount Hermon located on the border of Palestine and Lebanon.

[671] Baalim: Judg 2:11; 3:7; 8:33; 10:6, 10; 1 Sam 7:4; 12:10; 1 Kings 18:18; 2 Chron 17:3; 24:7; 34:2–4; Jer 2:23; 9:14; Hos 2:13, 17; 11:2.

[672] H1170—*Ba`al Briyth, bah'-al ber-eeth'*: lord of the covenant; deity of the Shechemites and Philistines; H1176—*Ba`al Zbuwb, bah'-al zeb-oob'*: Baal of the Fly; Baal-Zebub; Philistine deity

as a triple-headed fallen angel, the greatest of the Baels, son of El, and said to be an equal rank of Raphael in the loyal hierarchy of angels.[673] It follows that Baal may have had several titles and names, one that may have been similarly spelled as Raphael and the patronymic name of Rapa, for the eponymously named Rephaim tribes.

The *Ugaritic Texts* tallied a host of seven reigning Baals/Adads like Baal of Saphon among six others named only as numerically numbered Baals/Baalim:

> Sacrifices of Saphon. .. Baal of Saphon an ox and a ram; Baal (II) an ox and a ram; [Baal (III) an ox and a ram; Baal (IV) an ox and a ram]; Baal (V) an ox and a ram; Baal (VI) an o[x] and a ram; Baal (VII) an ox and] a ram.[674]

Mount Saphon was the name for the divine mountain of inheritance and sanctuary for El and then Baal[675] in the *Ugaritic Texts*. Mount Saphon, is the mountain Israelites called Mount Hermon, by the Sidonians as Sirion, Amorites as Shenir/Senir, Mount Sion by others, as well as Khursag of Nippur.[676] Mount Hermon was the home of the assembly of the gods both before and after the flood, and one of the most revered sites in polytheism.

> 2 Kings 21.3 and he reared up altars for Baal, and made a grove, as did Ahab king of Israel; and worshipped all the host of heaven, and served them.

> 1 Chron 5:23 And the children of the half tribe of Manasseh dwelt in the land: they increased from Bashan unto Baalhermon and Senir, and unto Mount Hermon.

The Semitic root word for Hermon, *H-R-M,* was recorded in the *Ugaritic Texts* (KLU 1.13) and means devotion (or consecration, dedicate, doom[677]); its meaning is associated with the oath fallen angels swore at Mount Hermon to create

---

of the Ekronites: Baal-zebub "lord of the fly"; H1187—*Ba`al P`owr; bah'-al peh-ore*: lord of the gap, deity of Moab.

[673] Rosemary Ellen Guiley, *The Encyclopedia of Demons and Demonology* (New York, Facts on File, 2009), 22: Baal.

[674] Wyatt, *Religious Texts from Ugarit*, 361: host of the seven Baals that includes Baal of Saphon from KTU 1.47 5–11, 142: Note 3 Baals including the god Saphon; 427: from KTU 1.48 R: 1–4; 361–363: pantheon lists and the gods of Saphon that include the seven Baals and in Akkadian the seven Adads from KTU 1.118 and 1.47.

[675] Ibid., 76: KTU1.3 iii:25–30.

[676] Deut 3:9; 4:48; 1 Chron 5:23. Andrew Collins, *From the Ashes of Angels*, (Toronto, ON: Penguin Books Canada Ltd., 1997), 215–16, quoting Christian O'Brian, *The Genius of the Few, The Story of Those Who Found the Garden in Eden* (Wellingborough: Turnstone Press, 1985), 120.

[677] *Webster's*, 111: devote.

antediluvian Nephilim.[678] H-R-M appears within a postdiluvian fertility incantation for Anat (goddess) to create another Ba-al son, A Rapiu/Rephaim. Wyatt notes for the below verse that "may the Dam(sel)" (woman) is translated by others as "from the womb,"[679] but either way the ritual is plotting another creation of giants. This hymnic text according to Wyatt is thought of in terms of the destructive birth process[680] of birthing more Rephaim/Rapiu giants. The passage seems to reflect an infertility issue between Rephaim that required them to intermarry with human females to create hybrid humans; I will explore this in subsequent chapters.

[r]hm. tld ['ibr. lbcl.]:	may the Dam(sel) bear (a bull to Baal)
hrm. in. ym m.:	Devote to destruction in two days,
S[kl. tit] ymm. Ik.:	Annihilate in (three) days. Go,
hrg,'ar[bc] ymm. bsr:	Kill in fo(ur) days.[681]

Wyatt, in his page notes, indicates that "healer" is the translation for the *Rapiu* king, noble and/or god who was enthroned at Ashteroth and reigned from Edrei. Hebrew Rapha(im) can be also translated as healer, ghost, or giant(s) depending on its numeric designation for the Rapha. The *Ugaritic Texts* translate R-P-M, opting for healer as their preferred bias to define *Rapha*,[682] perhaps reflecting the occult alternative name to Baal as Raphael meaning healer of god or god heals. The *Ugaritic Texts* further stated regarding Rapiu kings: "My Rapiu king, of eternity, drink [wi]ne, yea may he drink, the powerful noble, god enthroned at Athtarat, the god who rules in Edriei."[683] Og was Rephaim and king of Bashan, dwelling at Ashtaroth and reigning at Edrei;[684] giants were regarded as demigods.

From whichever root the Semitic word *Rapiu* is based, we must also be open to the notion that Rapiuel, Rapiel, or a Raphiel may have been a god/fallen angel within the Baalim, and that all the Hebrew words that extend out of *Rapiu* are very much related. It follows then that whether a god or giant and likely both, the *Ugaritic Texts* documented *Rapiu* as the eponymous name taken by the Rephaim, of which Og was the last of the original generation.

[678] Enoch 6:6.
[679] Philip D. Stern, *The Biblical Herem: A Window into Israel's Religious Experience* (Providence, RI: Brown Judaic Studies, 1991), 5–6, citing J. C. de Moor, *An Incantation*, 306, KLU 1.13 r:1–5. Wyatt, *Religious Texts from Ugarit*, 169.
[680] Wyatt, N., *Religious Texts from Ugarit*, 169.
[681] Stern, *The Biblical Harem*, 6 KLU 1.13 r:1–5, citing de Moor.
[682] Wyatt, *Religious Texts from Ugarit*, 395, note 2; *Strong's Dictionary*, Rapha: H7495, H7496, and H7497.
[683] Ibid., 395, KTU 108 R:1.
[684] Deut 1:4; Josh 12:4; 13:12, 31.

MOUNT HERMON

Josh 12:4 And the coast of Og king of Bashan, which was of the remnant of the giants, that dwelt at Ashtaroth and at Edrei,

Josh 12:5 And reigned in Mount Hermon, and in Salcah, and in all Bashan, unto the border of the Geshurites and the Maachathites, and half Gilead, the border of Sihon king of Heshbon.

Mount Hermon was connected to giant creation in nonaccepted canon accounts before and after the flood. One ponders if biblical canon supporting those claims have been suppressed. Scripture's accounting of King Og and Sihon certainly seem to support the noncanonical accounts for giant creation after the flood.

King Og, without further explanation, is described as the remnant/*yether* of giants/*rapha* as in Rephaim, after the flood.[685] Remnant as in residue or remainder[686] indicates by the original Hebrew text Og was last of first generation of Rephaim post diluvian giants, versus antediluvian Nephilim created by fallen angels before the flood. King Og made his home in Bashan of Mount Hermon. Both Og's description as a *rapha* king and his choice to reign from Mount Hermon are underexplained biblical details connecting Og to a Second Incursion of angelic giant creation that was also connected to Mount Hermon.

---

[685] Deut 3:11; Josh 12:4; 13:11–13.
[686] H499—*yether, yeh'-ther*: overhanging; excess, superiority; remainder; residue; remnant; rope hanging free.

Discerning the events surrounding Mount Hermon both before and after the flood provides proper context to the subversive and preplanned events lapping over this generation, contrived by the spurious offspring of fallen angels. Grasping the free choice decisions made on Mount Hermon, the consequences thereof, and the implication for this generation is vital to awakening and preparing Christians for what must take place and will take place. With this mind, many conclude an angelic pact and sworn oaths were consummated upon Mount Hermon; a pact that seemingly was recorded in First Enoch that begat and memorialized the place of their crimes. Not only did the fallen angels memorialize this day of infamy through the mystery religions, but First Enoch states the impassioned rebellious angels renamed the summit (by inference) to Mount Hermon after the oath sworn there indicating that before the oath sworn, Mount Hermon was known by another name—Saphon, Senir, Sirion, Sion, or another name.

> Enoch 6:3–4 And Semjaza, who was their leader, said. .. "I fear ye will not indeed agree to do this deed, and I alone shall have to pay the penalty of a great sin." And they all answered him and said: "Let us all swear an oath, and all bind ourselves by mutual imprecations not to abandon this plan but to do this thing.". .. .

> Enoch 6:6 And they were in all two hundred; who descended [in the days] of Jared on the summit of Mount Hermon, and they called it Mount Hermon, because they had sworn and bound themselves by mutual imprecations upon it.

One would suspect then that such deeds of infamy were embedded into the etymological source meaning the Mount of Hermon, and indeed it is. Certainly, in the fertility incantation to create another son from Baal covered in chapter 17 (*Ugaritic Texts* KLU 1.13), the Semitic word *H-R-M* was translated by J. C. de Moor as "devoted" (dedicated and consecrated), and others as associated with destruction.[687] Both translations seem related to the oaths sworn on the Mount of Hermon. However, one should keep in mind that the tri-consonant *H-R-M* *is* an ancient Semitic root word for several words with several derivative meanings in several Semitic languages, including Hebrew. Hence, Mount Hermon's name derives from the Semitic root *H-R-M* meaning "taboo" or "consecrated" or perhaps both, just as *H-R-M* is the root word for Arabic "al-haram" meaning "sacred enclosure."[688] *H-R-M* is also the Semitic source word for several words in

[687] Stern, *The Biblical Herem: A Window into Israel's Religious Experience*, 5–6, citing J. C. de Moor, *An Incantation*, 306, KLU 1.13 r:1–5; Wyatt, *Religious Texts from Ugarit*, 169.
[688] E. A. Myers, *The Ituraeans and the Roman Near East: Reassessing the Sources* (Cambridge: Cambridge University Press, 2010), 65.

Hebrew, and the Semitic source word that *Chermown*/Hermon is transliterated from. *Chermown* is defined as a sanctuary,[689] akin to "al-haram."

Unger's Dictionary defines Mount Hermon as meaning "sacred mountain."[690] But a sacred mountain to who? One deduces Hermon was a sanctuary where gods/fallen angels devoted/consecrated themselves to an oath before the flood, and again after the flood as the *Ugaritic Texts* indicate,[691] oaths consecrated in spite by the Naphalim to lead humankind into oblivion first through the Nephilim and then through Rephaim races and their mystical religions. For fallen angels, humankind destruction was an existential a holy war to ensure humankind will not be raised up to be like angels, and then to judge the rebellious angels[692] for those crimes.

Hermon/*Chermown* derives from *charam* meaning to consecrate, to devote or dedicate to destruction, mutilate, divide, and to make accursed.[693] It follows then that Mount Hermon in part also carries the *charam* meaning as in a sanctuary of dedication and consecration, as in accursed and for destruction. According to *The Catholic Encyclopedia*, Mount Hermon is defined as the "sacred mountain," and the home of the "Temple of Baal of old."[694]

Chermown and *charam* is reminiscent of First Enoch's accounting of the oath fallen angels devoted themselves to do a great sin (destroy humanity).[695] Following this line of thinking, *charam* is also the Hebrew source word for *cherem*, which is translated three times as "accursed," and one time translated as "curse" in Joshua 6:17–18, as the discussion pertained to the destruction of Jericho. *Charam* is additionally used in Joshua 6:18 for "lest you make yourselves accursed"; in the same kind of spirit the fallen angels made themselves accursed with their crimes against creation and humanity. Additionally, the use of *charam* and *charem* in the same narrative testifies to the translation as "curse" and "accursed" as being contextually accurate.

> Josh 6:17 And the city shall be accursed, even it, and all that are therein, to the LORD: only Rahab the harlot shall live, she and all that are with her in the house, because she hid the messengers that we sent.

---

[689] H2768—*Chermown, kher-mone*: sanctuary; a mountain overlooking the border city of Dan.

[690] *Unger's*, 554–555: Hermon.

[691] Collins, *Ashes of Angels*, 6, 9, citing Julian Morgenstern, who suggested in *The Hebrew Union College Annual of 1939* that there were two separate occasions when angels fell from heaven: the first from lust and the second from pride, meaning the second procreation of Nephilim was performed deliberately to spite God.

[692] Matt 22:30; Luke 20:36; 1 Cor 6:3.

[693] H2763—*charam, khaw-ram*: to seclude by a ban; devote to religious uses, especially destruction; make accursed; consecrate; or destroy; devote; forfeit; dedicate for destruction; exterminate; completely destroy; split; slit; mutilate a part of the body.

[694] *Catholic Encyclopedia*, Vol. 6, 288–289: Hermon.

[695] Enoch 6:3–4.

Josh 6:18 And ye, in any wise keep yourselves from the accursed thing, lest ye make yourselves accursed, when ye take of the accursed thing, and make the camp of Israel a curse.

Another word deriving from *charam* is *cherem*, defined as shutting in a net, something banned, devoted, dedicated doomed, extermination, appointed to utter destruction,[696] usually through a curse. Other words deriving from *charam* are *Chorem*/Horem, meaning devoted and sacred; *charim*/harim, defined as dedicated; and *Chormah*/Hormah, meaning devoted.[697] The various Hebrew words extending out from *charam* carry within them the history of their ancient etymology of diabolical deeds devoted to destroying humanity by the Devil and the impassioned rebellious angels dedicated the accursed cause.

Ergo, the infamous two hundred in Jewish tradition swore an accursed oath to mate with humans under the penalty of "Harem-Anathema," to carry it through to the end,[698] the cursed oath of Harem, or Hermon, noting *(c)harem*/*(c)haram* in Hebrew is often transliterated into English as Hermon. Anathema is defined as "a solemn ecclesiastical curse of denunciation,"[699] that they would be pronounced accursed to carry it through to the end.[700] The oath to create giant demigods from procreating with humankind set in motion the schema to destroy the purity of the Adamite line from the face of the earth, and to ultimately to have the giants lead humankind away from God, humankind's destiny, and to have humankind destroyed into spiritual extinction.

Ancient Jewish tradition dictated that when the excommunicated persisted in impenitence, they were charged with *shamata*/imprecation: cursed onto final judgment,[701] as in the lake of fire for the second death, or for eternal punishment for fallen angels, Antichrist, False Prophet, and those who accept the mark of the beast or worship antichrist and Satan in the end times.[702] *Strong and M'Clintock's Cyclopaedia* noted that anathema, in the ecclesiastical sense, is the process of cutting one off from the church and from salvation.[703] Watchers in First Enoch swore their accursed oath on Mount Hermon, bound by mutual imprecation,

---

[696] H2764—*cherem, khay'-rem*: a doomed object; extermination; dedicated thing; things which should be "utterly destroyed"; appointed to utter destruction; a devoted thing; ban.

[697] H2765—*Chorem, khor-ame'*: sacred; devoted; fortified town in Naphtali; H2766—*Charim, khaw-reem'*: dedicated; snub-nosed; H2767—*Chormah, khor-maw'*: devotion; devoted; a Canaanite town conquered by Joshua.

[698] Ginzberg, *Legends of the Bible*, 63.

[699] *Webster's*, 39: anathema.

[700] Knight and Lomas, *Uriel's Machine: The Ancient Origins of Science*, 95.

[701] *Strong's Cyclopaedia*, Vol. 1, 217–219: anathema.

[702] Mat 13:42; 25:41; Rev 14:9–11, 19:20; 20:10, 15.

[703] *Strong's Cyclopaedia*, Vol. 1, 217–219: anathema.

Harem-Anathema, knowing the consequences that could follow. Such was and is their commitment and hate of humankind.

Oaths sworn in the mystery religions and in their genitive secret societies, and legal, medical, educational systems, and any sworn oath of allegiance stems from the accursed oath at Mount Hermon. Oaths honor the rebellious angels in a form of ritual religious idolatry to the gods of this world. A devoted, legal, ritual-based, and oath-based system was imposed upon humanity by angelic offspring, the royals, and their nobility kin who all swore oaths via the mystical religions to lead humanity away from God through servitude, enslavement, worship, and into ultimate spiritual destruction. One ponders if the accursed oath of harem-anathema of angels was the event that led to God instructing humanity not to take oaths of any kind.

> Matt 5:34. ... Swear not at all; neither by heaven; for it is God's throne:

> Matt 5:35 Nor by the earth; for it is his footstool: neither by Jerusalem; for it is the city of the great King.

> Matt 5:36 Neither shalt thou swear by thy head, because thou canst not make one hair white or black.

> Matt 5:37 But let your communication be, Yea, yea; Nay, nay: for whatsoever is more than these cometh of evil.

Noting *cherem* is translated as "accursed" and additionally translated as "curse" in Joshua 6:18, Isaiah 34:5, and Micah 4:6, and "cursed" in Deuteronomy 7:26 and 13:17, further underscore the words link back to Mount Hermon, the accursed fallen angels and their Hermon sanctuary, their accursed oath, and their accursed deeds of their offspring. The angelic oath of Harem-Anathema was a solemn ecclesiastical curse of denunciation,[704] with those pronounced accursed for not carrying out the plan to create Nephilim, and then Rephaim after the flood. Accursed, according to Strong and M'Clintock's *Cyclopaedia*, is a term used in two senses: for an oath and to curse, while anathema were irrevocable vows carried out with consequences of death,[705] which is consistent with First Enoch's angelic accounting.

> Enoch 6:5–7 Then sware they all together and bound themselves by mutual imprecations upon it. And they were in all two hundred; who descended [in the days] of Jared on the summit of Mount Hermon, and they called it Mount Hermon, because they had sworn and bound

---

[704] *Webster's*, 39: anathema.
[705] *Strong's Cyclopaedia*, Vol. 1, 54: accursed.

themselves by mutual imprecations upon it. And these are the names of their leaders: Semeazaz, their leader, Arakiba, Rameel, Kokabiel, Tamiel, Ramiel, Danel, Ezeqeel, Baraqijal, Asael, Armaros, Bataral, Ananal, Zaqiel, Samsapeel, Satarel, Turel, Jomjael, Sariel.

Thus, First Enoch's language in 6:1–2 regarding the creation of the giants that precedes the verses describing the angelic accursed oath is strikingly similar to Genesis 6:1–2, suggesting First Enoch's lost original uncorrupted Hebrew manuscript likely came from Moses. However, Enoch 6:6 added the location where a forbidden oath for giant creation sworn took place.

Gen 6:1 And it came to pass, when men began to multiply on the face of the earth, and daughters were born unto them,

Gen 6:2 That the sons of God saw the daughters of men that they were fair; and they took them wives of all which they chose.

Enoch 6:1–2 And it came to pass when the children of men had multiplied that in those days were born unto them beautiful and comely daughters. And the angels, the children of the heaven, saw and lusted after them, and said to one another: "Come, let us choose us wives from among the children of men and beget us children.". ...

Enoch 6:6 And they were in all two hundred; who descended in the days of Jared on the summit of Mount Hermon, and they called it Mount Hermon, because they had sworn and bound themselves by mutual imprecations upon it.

Oddly, no location for the oath taken for giant creation was recorded in the Genesis 6:1–4 account, or for "after that." In fact, Mount Hermon's first biblical reference surfaces in Deuteronomy 3:9–10, at the time of the Covenant Land conquest when Moses and Joshua battled the Rephaim kings Sihon and Og, east of the Jordan in the eastern campaign. In that passage, we learn Mount Hermon's name was alternatively known as Shenir by the Amorites and Sirion by the Sidonians—humans who held with close relationships with Mount Hermon,[706] and by inference the Rephaim.

Shenir/*Shniyr* derives from an unused root word meaning pointed, peak, and snow mountain. What is intriguing, and from my perspective not coincidental, *Shniyr* is book-ended in *Strong's Concordance* by *Shniynah* meaning something pointed or a taunt, which in turn derives from *Shanan* meaning to point, pierce, teach, and to inculcate that generally means to do repeatedly. One ponders if

---

[706] *Catholic Encyclopedia*, Vol. 6, 288: Hermon.

Shenir refers to multiple violations against creation law, and the Second Incursion at Mount *Shniyr*.[707] Additionally, the `*iyr* suffix in *Shniyr*, the Hebrew word for Watcher is recorded in Daniel 4 four times,[708] and perhaps represents the mountain of Watchers.

Sidonians named Mount Hermon Sirion/*Shiryown* metaphorically because of snow and iced-blanketed peaks. Sirion is additionally defined as breastplate deriving from *shiryown*, meaning body armor or a weapon like a lance.[709] *Shiryown* in turn derives from *sharah* meaning to direct, free, or let loose and is part of a series of primitive words including *sarah* meaning to prevail, exert oneself; have power, and a prince.[710] *The Catholic Encyclopedia* noted Hermon's many names all signified in their meaning: a coat of armor.[711] Conversely, "breastplate" is the English translation for vests worn by Levite priests, whereby the embedded urim/`*urwriym*, precious jewels, were employed to determined God's decisions.[712] The thummim/*tummiym*, precious stones, determine a sacred lot conducted in some of God's decisions.[713] However, the Levite breastplate derives from *choshen*, meaning the sanctuary for God to dwell in,[714] versus *shiryown*, a breastplate of war as translated as "habergeons" in 2 Chronicles 26:14. The military breastplate conjures up images of escaping gods/angels in Revelation 9:9–10.

The temples and/or priories constructed at Mount Hermon honor and memorialize the gods of Mount Hermon, their ancient oath sworn there, and their destructive actions against humanity thereafter. At the base of Mount Hermon is the location for the Pan Temple positioned at the Rock of the Gods. In the center, there is a huge cave called the Gates of Hades, because it is the gate that Baal would use to enter and leave the underworld. Overseeing the Rock of Gods, the Pan Temple, and the cave of the Gates of Hades was the location where many

---

[707] H8149—*Shniyr, shen-eer*`; or *Sniyr, sen-eer*`: a peak; a summit of Lebanon; snow mountain; the Amorite name for Mount Hermon; H8148—*shniynah, shen-ee-naw*`; from 8150: something pointed; a taunt; H8150—*shanan, shaw-nan*`: to pierce; to prick, sharp; teach diligently.

[708] H5894—`*iyr, eer*: a watcher angel; waking, watchful, wakeful one, watcher, angel. Dan 4:12–13, 17, 23: watcher(s).

[709] H8303– *shiryown, shir-yone*`; and Siryon; same as 8302: sheeted snow; breast place; a name of Mount Hermon used by Sidonians; H8302–*shiryown, shir-yone*`: a twisted corslet breastplate; coat of mail; habergeon; harness; body armour; a weapon like a lance or javelin.

[710] H8281– *sharah, shaw-raw*`: set free, let loose; direct; H8280– *sarah, saw-raw*`: to prevail, persist, exert; a prince.

[711] *Catholic Encyclopedia*, Vol. 6, 288: Hermon.

[712] H224—`*Uwriym, oo-reem*`: lights; oracular brilliancy of stones kept in a pouch on the high-priest's breastplate that were used to determine God's decisions in certain questions and issues.

[713] H8550—*Tummiym, toom-meem*`: perfection; technology; one of the epithets of stones in the high priest's breastplate as an emblem of truth; stones used in a sacred lot with the Urim whereby God's the will was revealed.

[714] H2833—*choshen, kho'-shen*: to contain; sparkle; breastplate; breast-piece; a pocket holding the Urim and Thummim. Exod 25:7–8.

conclude the accursed oath by fallen Watchers was consummated, and by First Enoch's accounting, where the Naphalim memorialized the place of their infamy by changing the mountain's name to Mount Hermon.[715]

Scripture does provide details buttressing the supposition Mount Hermon was so named because of the ancient infamy and legacy begat there, titillating details like the Hermonites/*Chermowniym* people. *Chermowniym* is typically understood in the standard Christian dogma as the name for the three summits of Mount Hermon.[716] The only scriptural appearance of Hermonites surfaces in Psalm 42:6. However, the text is not as clear as theologians and some translators tend to infer. "The land of Jordan, and of the Hermonites, from the hill of Mizar" does not appear to be speaking to the three sister summits of Mount Hermon, but to a people from the hill of Mizar, the *Chermowniym*/Hermonim. Further, the hill of Mizar is not Mount Hermon. Hill/*har* also means hills or mountain(s).[717] The words preceding the Hermonites, "and of the," were inserted by translators. As such, one can interpret the verse by stating the Hermonites were from the hill or small mountain of Mizar located in in Lebanon near Mount Hermon.[718] The Hermonim might very well be David's oppressors and enemies described in Psalm 42:9–10. If so, who were the Hermonim/Chermowniym?

> Ps 42:6 O my God, my soul is cast down within me: therefore will I remember thee from the land of Jordan, and of the Hermonites, from the hill Mizar.

The Chermowniym people were seemingly connected to the *Chorim* people; David fought the Horim in Edom and Syria.[719] As such, Chermowniym people were likely grouped among the Horim/*Choriy*/*Chorim*, the giants who also migrated to Mount Seir of Edom.[720] Horim were recorded as tribe of Rephaim in Deuteronomy 2, a nation listed in the war of giants, and were the mysterious dukes of Edom,[721] all of which we will investigate thoroughly in subsequent chapters.

What one cannot readily dismiss are the phonetic and etymological connections between *Choriym* and *Chermoniym*, *charam*, and *cherem*. Horim are connected to Harem/Hermon through Horem/*Chorem*, one of the ancient high-walled

---

[715] Enoch 6:6.
[716] H2769—*Chermowniym, kher-mo-neem*; Hermon; Hermonites; Mount Hermon's three summits.
[717] H2022—*har, har*: a mountain, or range of hills; hill country, mount; hill.
[718] H4706—*Mits`ar, mits-awr*; the same as 4705: a peak of Lebanon; a mountain near Mount Hermon; H4705—*mits`ar, mits-awr*: petty in size or number; a short time; little one; small.
[719] Gen 36:35; 2 Sam 8:13; 1 Chron 1:46; 18:12; Ps 60:1.
[720] H2752—*Choriy, kho-ree*: cave-dweller; troglodyte; aboriginal Idumaean; inhabitants of Mount Seir and of Edom; H2753—*Choriy, kho-ree*; or *Chowriy, kho-ree*; same as 2752; cave dweller; son of Lotan son of Seir.
[721] Gen 14:6; 36:20, 29–39; Deut 2:12, 22.

city-state fortresses of the Rephaim in Naphtali's territory, positioned between Sidon on the Mediterranean coast and Mount Hermon. Horem was founded by and patrial-named by the Horim before sojourning to southern Canaan. Horem/ *Charem* is defined as sacred and devoted deriving from *charam*.[722] As such, a fortress city built to worship gods, and consecrated to the destruction of Israelites and humankind in general.

Yet another link in the series of related words connected to angelic infamy at *Har Chermown* is the word Hormah translated from *Chormah*, a word defined as devoted and rooted in *charam*, and several patrial-named city fortresses of giants conquered by Joshua. The "ah" suffix of *chormah* is a feminine format possibly indicating power, might, mighty, and forces related to Horim/*Choriym*, and akin to `elowahh and *gbuwrah*. [723] Certainly, the Hormah were located in the regions where Horim dwelled. Hormah immediately precedes Hermon in *Strong's Dictionary*.[724] Horim/*Chroiym* is part the same series of words as Hermon/*Chermown* and Harem/*Charem*.

[722] H2765—*Chorem, khor-ame*; devoted; sacred; fortified town in Naphtali. Josh 19:38. *Strong's Cyclopaedia*, Vol. 4, 338: Horem.

[723] H433—`elowahh. God of forces: Ps 114:7; Is 44:8; Dan 11:37, 38, 39; Hab 3:3; H1369— *gbuwrah*: might; strength; valour; mighty deeds of God.

[724] H2767—*Chormah, khor-maw*; devoted; devotion; a town of the Canaanites, conquered by Joshua, allotted to Judah, and located in the south of Judah. Num 14:45; 21:3; Deut 1:44; Josh 12:14; 15:30; 19:4; Judg 1:17; 1 Chron 4:30. *Strong's Cyclopaedia*, Vol. 4, 338: Horem.

CHAPTER 19

THE HERMONIM OF MOUNT HERMON, UGARIT, AND SUMER

Deut 3:8 And we took at that time out of the hand of the two kings of the Amorites the land that was on this side Jordan, from the river of Arnon unto Mount Hermon;

Deut 3:9 (Which Hermon the Sidonians call Sirion; and the Amorites call it Shenir;)

One might anticipate Mount Hermon, its priories, and its gods will become important and newsworthy as we approach the last seven years. "Is there any thing whereof it may be said, See, this is new? it hath been already of old time, which was before us."[725]

What is not coincidental, in my view, with Mount Hermon's biblical introduction in Deuteronomy 3:8–9 is that Hermon's introduction occurs as part of the details that documented King Og as the remnant of the giants. Scripture underlined Og was the last of the giants three times, naming him the king of Bashan who reigned from Ashtaroth and Edrei in the Mount Hermon region.[726]

---

[725] Eccl 1:10.
[726] Deut 3:11; Josh 12:4–5; 13:12.

The Rephaim tribe was located at Ashteroth Karanaim in Bashan of Mount Hermon in the war of giants.[727] Mount Hermon was the epicenter for giants and the feudal Naphalim World Order system enslaving humans, both before and after the flood. The Rephaim as well as the Horim are part of the Hermonim.

Additionally, the Golan Heights below Mount Hermon hosts the famous worship site, Gilgal Rephaim. Gilgal Rephaim translates "Wheel of The Giants" from *gilgal*/wheel[728] and *rapha'*/giant. The ancient Gilgal Rephaim site is shaped like wheels within wheels, akin to depictions of Atlantis. The Gilgal Rephaim megalith is otherwise renowned as the Wheel of the Spirits, Wheel of the Ghosts, as well as Rujim el-Hiri, and Rogem Hiri meaning "heap of the wild cat."[729] *Rapha'* in Hebrew as you will recall has three distinct but related variations—one that is defined as spirits, ghosts, and shades/sidhe. Archaeologists dated the villages around Gilgal Rephaim from 4500–3300 BC[730] and Gilgal Rephaim to circa 3500–2700 BC, depending on the archaeologist—thus antediluvian and to the time of the First Incursion and the oath sworn upon Mount Hermon. The region experienced a significant decline toward the end of the third century BC.[731]

Gilgal Rephaim is positioned without coincidence on a plateau at the foot of Mount Hermon and located close to Caesarea Philippi within Og's empire, centered in Ashtaroth of Bashan. This mysterious megalithic monument contains about 42,000 basalt stones, with the central monument marked with oval stone heap five meters high and twenty-five meters in diameter, surrounded by concentric circles of stone. Some believe the tomb in the central cairn is the earliest element of the megalith that at one time housed the remains of an ancestor so revered that he eventually acquired mythical status:[732] perhaps the burial site for King Og. Archaeologists theorize this megalith was constructed to align with sacred astronomical alignments such as solstices, a solar calendar, for polytheist rituals, and/or a burial site for Rephaim kings. Around 3000 BC the sun's rays shone through the northeastern gate on the summer solstice.[733] The Gilgal Rephaim worship site is inundated with hundreds of dolmens, with thousands more throughout the Golan

---

[727] Gen 14: H6255—*Ashtroth Qarnayim, ash-ter-oth' kar-nah'yim*; Ashtaroth of the double horns or peaks; symbol of the deity; a city in Bashan east of the Jordan.
[728] H1536—*gilgal, ghil-gawl'*: wheel; rolling; Israelite basecamp west of the Jordan, east of Jericho.
[729] Jerome Murphy-O'Connor, *The Holy Land: An Oxford Archaeological Guide from Earliest Times to 1700* (New York: Oxford University Press Inc, 2008, Kindle edition), 457.
[730] Ibid., 294.
[731] Ibid.
[732] Ibid., 457.
[733] Ibid.

region,[734] which adds mercurial ambience to it. Dolmens are thought to be mini-megalith structures; the word means portal or portal tomb.[735]

According to researcher and author Yoel Elitzer: "All scholarly literature speaks in a single voice: *gilgal* is a mound of stones or stone or a circle of stone pillars used for a cultic purpose."[736] Jack Sasson wrote in his commentary regarding the Gilgal quarry in Judges 3:19: "In Hebrew the name is always preceded by and article (the [*ha*] Gilgal), implying it was descriptive, having to do with something rounded or in a circle. .. the name Gilgal might refer to its shrine, with round of stones or images. It might also allude to its topography, because it reminded a skull (*gulgolet*) or columns (*gelilot*)."[737] *Gulgoleth* is the Hebrew word for Greek *golgoya*, transliterated into English as Golgotha where Jesus was crucified, a place that also resembled a skull.[738] One ponders as to the connection of the large skull like shape to *ha Gilgal*/*Gulgoleth* and the elongated skulls of the Rephaim and Nephilim. One's curiosity is raised as to the Chaldean origination to Golgotha/*Gulgoleth* with Gilgamesh.

> Matt 27:33 And when they were come unto a place called Golgotha, that is to say, a place of a skull.

One contemplates the spelling similarity between Gilgamesh and Gilgal Rephaim, and that Gilgamesh was a giant eleven cubits high (16'6"–19'3") and four cubits wide (6'–7') in the Sumerian Epic of Gilgamesh.[739] Gilgamesh was further recorded as a great hero giant in the *Ugaritc Texts* discovered in 1996 at Ras Sharmra in a "scriptorium library of the house of Urtenu" and the house of

---

[734] Ibid., 294; Avraham Negev and Shimon Gibson, eds. *Archaeological Encyclopedia of the Holy Land* (London: Continuum International Publishing Group, 2005), 207, 443, 518.

[735] Murphy-O'Connor, *The Holy Land*, 295, 457; Dictionary.com: dolmen.

[736] Yoel Elitzur, "The Meaning of Gilgal," *Revue Biblique*, 126, Issue 3, 2019, DOI:10.2143/RBI. 126.3.3286845), 33, citing numerous sources.

[737] Ibid., 332 citing Jack M. Sasson. Judges 1-12, *The Anchor Yale Bible* (New Haven, CT/London: Yale University Press, 2013), 179.

[738] H1538—*gulgoleth, gul-go'-leth*; reduplication of 1556; a skull as round; a head; Greek 1115 golgoya; G1115—*gol-goth-ah*; of Chaldee origin; cognate of H1538 gulgoleth: the skull; a knoll near Jerusalem; the place outside Jerusalem where Jesus was crucified that resembled a skull; transliterated: Golgotha. Matt 27:33; Mark 15:22; Luke 23:33; John 19:17.

[739] Tablets 1 and 11 Epic of Gilgamesh, lines 34–36, Of the Ugarit Gilgamesh as 11 cubits high and 4 cubits wide; Andrew R. George, *The Gilgames Epic at Ugarit* (*Aula Orientalis*, journal Article 25, 2, London 2007). https://eprints.soas.ac.uk/5654/, 242, lines 34–35. Alexander Heidel, *The Gilgamesh Epic and Old Testament Parallels* (Chicago: University Chicago of Press, 1949; e-book edition by Misty and Lewis Gruber), 17, lines 8–9.

Rap'anu.[740] Gilgamesh was granted heroism from the god Adad/Baal,[741] the god(s) of Mesopotamia, Ugarit, Canaan, Mount Hermon and of the Hermonim.

From a Semitic perspective, *gilgal* is sometimes transliterated as *gilga,*[742] the first syllable or word of Gilgames, as Gilgamesh is sometimes transliterated. The Sumerian goddess Inanna stole the divine *me-s* stones of power and knowledge of the gods possessed by Enki at Eridu and moved the *me-s* stones to Uruk[743] the city-state Gilgamesh later became its king. One ponders if there is a connection between the divine *me-s* stones and the last syllable or suffix in the compounded word and name for Gilgames/Gilgamesh with the wheel of stones at Gilgal Rephaim, and other cultic Gilgal stone sites of worship. *Mes* is further defined as black, a hero, or both as in black hero, which may reflect Gilgamesh's skin, hair or both.[744] A combined Hebrew and Sumerian meaning for Gilgames/Gilgamesh would be "hero of the stones" or "hero of the wheel stones," as one connects Gilgamesh back to Ugarit, the Rephaim, and to Gilgal Rephaim.

From a Sumerian and Akkadian linguistic perspective, one can rebuild the meaning of Gilgamesh/Gilgames with intriguing connections. Both the Sumerian *Bil.ga.mes* and Akkadian *Gil.ga.mes*[745] translations were connected to Lilith of Bilgames of the Underworld,[746] and Sumerian *Bil* meaning burn or roast.[747] In the Sumerian language, the letter "g" was spelled with a "b." Knowing this makes sense of M. Daniel Arnaud's translation of the Ugaritic Texts on Gilgamesh, with his otherwise odd transliteration of Gilgames as *Gis.bil-ga-mes,* which then was not a repetition error (dittography) of the copyist or translator.[748] Seemingly, Arnaud added important information to help decipher Gilgamesh's name, and perhaps helps to explain the various translations for Gilgamesh.

---

[740] George, *The Gilgames Epic at Ugarit,* 238, and note 2 on 238.

[741] Heidel, *The Gilgamesh Epic and Old Testament Parallels,* 17, line 6.

[742] H1536—*gilga*: wheel, Isa 28:28. H1537—gilga; total KJV occurrences: 41; gilgal, Deut 11:30; Josh 4:19–20 (2); 5:9–10 (2); 10:6–7 (3), 9, 15, 43; 12:23; 15:6–7 (2); Judg 2:1; 3:19; 1 Sam 7:16; 10:8; 11:14–15 (3); 13:4, 13:7–8 (2), 12, 15; 15:12, 21, 33; 2 Sam 19:15, 40; 2 Kings 2:1; 4:38; Neh 12:29; Hos 9:15 (2); 12:11; Mic 6:4–5 (4).

[743] George, *The Gilgames Epic at Ugarit:* Hymn to Enki for Isme-Dagan: 8–10; Enki and the World Order: Lines 1–16, 221–237; Inanna and Enki: Section C 27–30; Sect. D 1–27; Sect. E 1–36; Sect. F 1–34; Sect. H 1–178.

[744] Ed Peter and Tara Hogan, *Sumerian Cuneiform English Dictionary,* Mug Sar Dictionary e-book, https://ia800903.us.archive.org/25/items/SumerianCuneiformEnglishDictionary 12013CT26i14PDF/Sumerian%20Cuneiform%20English%20Dictionary%2012013CT%20 26i14%20PDF.pdf#, 28, 51, 52, 54, 54, 57: 12229 mes: black hero.

[745] Ibid., 8, 53, 57, Bil: 1224b, burnt, black; Ga: 120B5, young bull; Mes: 12229, hero and black.

[746] Ibid., 47.

[747] Ibid., 56, 124B: burn/burnt; *Sumerian Dictionary,* e-book, 23, bil: roast, https://www. magicgatebg.com/Books/INDEXII/Sumerian_Dictionary.pdf.

[748] George, *The Gilgames Epic at Ugari*t, 243, note 18: Gis.bil-ga-mes.

The postdiluvian Sumerian empire Gilgamesh reigned over was eventually over-run by the Akkadian empire by Sargon the Great, whose mother was a change-ling[749] (fallen angel). Sargon's reign began circa 2300 BC.[750] Sargon's Akkadians were Semitic-speaking Anunnaki tribes from the mountains toward the north who defeated Lugalzaggesi of Uruk. The Akkadians thereafter took the title King of Kish.[751] Sargon's originating capitol was Agade/Akkad in the mountains,[752] one of the cities previously founded or renovated by Nimrod, known biblically as Accad, just as Nimrod renovated Erech/Uruk in the land of Sumer/Shinar.[753] The Semitic-speaking Akkadians led by Sargon, a Rephaim or Anunnaki, overthrew the Enmera-kar/Nimrod-founded Sumerian dynasty, which was later inherited by Gilgamesh.

Nimrod, after Babel, seemingly intermarried with Aryan-Elamites that over-ran Sumer circa 2450–2400 BC. Aryan-Elamites thereafter reigned over descen-dants of Shem and his people, the Elam(ites),[754] after leaving Babel. The Aboriginal Aryan-Elamites were regarded by historians like George Smith as a different race from the Shemite Elamites,[755] which indicates that the Shemites accepted the name for their people from the Aryans, or that the Aryan name was assigned to the Shemite branch by Hebrew scribes to reflect their intermarriage with the giants. One deduces the merged Elamites were a hybrid human/Anunnaki tribe.

Gen 10:10 And the beginning of his [Nimrod] kingdom was Babel, and Erech, and Accad, and Calneh, in the land of Shinar.

Recognizing the Akkadian spelling and meaning of Gilgamesh is equally important to the Sumerian spelling and meaning, to understand Gilgamesh's place in history and legend. Sumerians were the *Ki.en.gi. Ki* was defined earth and/or underworld; *en* meant lord/rulers; and *gi* was the word for reed, permanent, the earth, and the underworld; *ki* was alternatively spelled as *gi* or *kia*.[756] *Gilim,* and/or

---

[749] Bauer, *History of the World,* 95, citing James P. Pritchard, ed., *The Ancient Near East: An Anthology of Texts and Pictures,* 1958, 85–86, 94; Rohl, *Lost Testament,* 41: Anunnaki.

[750] Bauer, *History of the World,* 96, 99, citing Kramer, *The Sumerians,* 324: Akkadians were Sumerian Anunnaki.

[751] Ibid., 97–98, citing *The Sargon Legend,* Segment B in Electronic Text corpus of Sumerian Literature, and Kramer, *The Sumerians,* 324; Rohl, *Lost Testament,* 41.

[752] Rohl, *Lost Testament,* 41, 66; Bauer, *History of the World,* 96–99.

[753] Gen 10:8–12.

[754] George Smith, *The Chaldean Account of Genesis* (New York: Scribner, Armstrong & Co, 1876; Global Grey ebooks, 2018): *The Legends of Izdubar,* 146–147.

[755] Ibid., 144, 251.

[756] Rohl, *Lost Testament,* 36, 46; Peter and Hogan, *Sumerian Cuneiform English Dictionary,* Ki 120A0; 31, en12097: lord, masters, and rulers of Sumer; 36, gi 12100: reed as gig en permanent. *Sumerian Dictionary,* 13, earth: ki, gi, or kia; Smith, *Chaldean Account of Genesis: The Legends of Izdubar,* 38.

singular *gi*, is defined as entwined, as in a reed rope or ropes (perhaps as symbol for DNA of gods), which is associated with *ge* meaning bad and evil. The *gi*/*ge* portion in Gilgames/Bilgames name perhaps reflects his tyrant credential.[757]

One's curiosity is activated with respect to *gi*/*gilim's* connection to the Sumerian Igigi/Anunnaki gods of heaven that included En-ki, lord of the earth and/or underworld. Igigi was rooted in *igi* meaning eye and to watch; Shinar/Sumer was the land of Igigi/Watchers of heaven, the Anunnaki, and the land of earthborn Anunnaki giants. Hence, *gil*/*gi* in the Akkadian spelling of Gilgames could represent earth or underworld,[758] the heavenly realm of the Naphalim. Further, *ga* was defined in Sumerian as a young bull,[759] just as Gilgamesh was described as a wild bull and tyrant. Ergo, the Akkadian north Sumerian meaning defined Gilgames as the black or black-haired hero/king (*mes*) and young bull (*ga*) of the earth or underworld of the Igigi (*gi*/*ki*).

The Sumerian *Bilgames* includes *bil*, meaning roast or burn[760] indicating a blackened or black-haired hero/king and young bull of the divine stones (*me-s*). It follows that Bilgames was described as the "young lord of Kallab,"[761] and that Gilgames/Bilgames was described as a wild ox/bull: "Renowned for bodily stature, hero born in Uruk, butting wild bull."[762] Gilgames/Bilgames was further described as having dark lapis hair (black or a deep navy blue); hair thick like wool (likely curly) with a long thick beard to match.[763] The archetypical Gilgamesh depiction was the same as other Sumerian kings, as well as Hittite and Syrian Hermonim kings, and Anunnaki/Igigi gods. Thus, Sumerians were renowned as black heads[764] whether human or Anunnaki giants. The demigod kings of Ugarit and Mount Hermon held close relations with Sumerian gods and giants.

In the *Ugaritic Texts,* gods like Baal, Mot, and El traveled to and from the underworld. Baal spoke from the underworld when he threatened to slay Yam,[765] a serpent monster cognate to Leviathan of the Bible and Tiamat of Sumer.[766]

---

[757] Peter and Hogan, *Sumerian Cuneiform English Dictionary,* 36, 12103: gilim; 12100: gi/ge and gel; 115, gil-gi: entwined,

[758] *Sumerian Dictionary,* 2, 4, Igigi: those who watch or observe; 4, Sumer/Shin Ar: the land of Watchers; Peter and Hogan, *Sumerian Cuneiform English Dictionary,* 34, 37, 41, 117, 12146 igi: eye, vision watch.

[759] Ibid., 32, 120B5: young suckling cow or bull.

[760] *Sumerian Dictionary,* 23, roast; Peter and Hogan, *Sumerian Cuneiform English Dictionary,* 8, 53, 56, 57 1224b: burn, burnt.

[761] George, *The Gilgames Epic at Ugarit,* 248, fragment RS 94.2191.

[762] Heidel, *The Gilgamesh Epic and Old Testament Parallels,* 18, line 20; George, *The Gilgames Epic at Ugarit,* 241, lines 13, 17, 18.

[763] George, *The Gilgames Epic at Ugarit,* 242.

[764] Alan F. Alford, *When the Gods Came Down,* 31; Thomas Cahill, *The Gifts of the Jews* (Toronto, ON: Anchor Books, 1999), 19.

[765] Wyatt, *Religious Texts from Ugarit,* 64: KTU 1.2 iv 5: The Baal Cycle of Myths and note 127.

[766] Wayne, *The Genesis 6 Conspiracy,* 738–735.

Demigod Rephaim kings of Ugarit too "traveled" back and forth between earth and the underworld through portals both before and after death.

> 1.161 R 20 After your lords, from the throne, after your lords into the underworld go down:
>
> Into the underworld go down, and into the dust. .. down to the anci[ent] saviors.. ..
>
> 1.161 R 25 down to Ammithtamru the king and also down to Niqmad the king.. ..
>
> 1.161 V 30. .. five-and make an offering.. .. Peace on Ammurapi, and peace on his son(s); peace on his kinsmen.

The lords in the above passage were the kings/bulls of Ugarit, Rapiu/Rephaim kings whose spirits were not permitted to sleep; demons commanded to accompany the recently deceased king Nimqad to the underworld, mirroring the ritual past events for the descent of parent god El and Baal to the underworld,[767] the abyss prison. *Ugaritic Texts* documented several kings patronymically named Nimqad and Ammithmru/Ammith-Amru in a similar manner as the last king of Ugarit was named Ammurapi/Ammurabi, as we will detail later.[768] This Ammurapi, according to researchers, was the last Rephaim king of Ugarit,[769] but his Hermonim sons and bloodline continued.

Now, the Rpum/Rapiu of Ugarit were demigod kings connected to underworld ghosts and shades/sidhe when they died. Rapiu/Rpum is thought by historians to be the source for *rapha* for healer[770] as well as ghost, spirit, shade and giant. The *Ugaritic Texts* recorded Rapum/Rapiu as kings: "My Rapiu king enthroned at Ashteroth" (KTU1.108),[771] the city of the Rephaim King Og. As such, one ponders if Ugarit was the patrial-named city for Og before he moved to Mount Hermon. Ug-arit/ might very well be formed from Og: *Owg* and *uwg*, as well as from `*ariyts*/terrible one,[772] that would form the city of Og the Terrible One.

In another of the *Ugaritic Texts,* The Story of King Keret, Keret's death mirror's Baal's death.[773] A search is carried out in the text by Rapiu kings that includes traveling to the ends of the earth that inferred the underworld of the earth as

---

[767] Wyatt, *Religious Texts from Ugarit*, 438–39, note 38: KTU 1.161: A Royal Funeral Liturgy.
[768] Ibid., 399–403, likely previous kings, KTU 1.113–15: A Royal Liturgy. and the Ugaritic King-List.
[769] Ibid, 440 note 49: KTU 1.161: A Royal Funeral Liturgy.
[770] Ibid., 395: KTU 1.108 R 1 Miscellaneous Texts.
[771] Ibid.
[772] H5747—`*Owg* from 5746 – `uwg; H6184—`*ariyts*.
[773] Ibid., 231 note 248.

well,[774] where the abyss prison is also located. It is not clear to me if the searching travelers were kings, priests, or both, but all were of the demigod royal bloodlines. Travelers through the portals included the living demigods, and/or were used for demigod funeral rituals. Some disembodied spirits of deceased Rephaim were permitted to travel between the underworld and the face of the earth—at least the demigod spirits not already sentenced to the abyss, those designated the Terrible Ones in Ezekiel 32.

> 1.16 III And he said: "Explore earth and heaven; travel to the ends of the earth, to the edge of the abyss."

Rephaim "Travelers" appear to be the "Passengers" documented in the aftermath of the end-time Gog war in Ezekiel 39:11 and 14. Passenger/`Abar is defined by multiple meanings and variations of which the ones of import to this book's line of investigation are: to cross over, pass over, travel across, pass away, emigrate, leave one's place.[775] Some English Bibles utilize "travel" and "travelers" in their translations of *abar*,[776] while others utilize variations of "passengers." Germane to the `abar meaning and the Ezekiel passage, Gog and Magog were giant sons of the Greek god Iapetus in Greek history.

> Ezek 39:11. .. I will give unto Gog a place there of graves in Israel, the valley of the passengers on the east of the sea: and it shall stop the noses of the passengers: and there shall they bury Gog and all his multitude: and they shall call it The valley of Hamongog.
>
> *NIV* Ezek 39:11. .. I will give Gog a burial place in Israel, in the valley of those who travel east of the Sea. It will block the way of travelers, because Gog and all his hordes will be buried there. So it will be called the Valley of Hamon Gog.

In Job 34:20–22 *abar* was the Hebrew word employed to describe the mighty who pass away and are taken away. "Mighty" derives from `abbiyr, a word meaning stout, mighty, strong, valiant often used for angels, princes, Nephilim, and Rephaim.[777] `Abbiyr's meaning is reminiscent of *gibbowr* used in the same way for the same beings, as well as the Terrible Ones who were stout as in wide and strong. In fact, the Semitic word *gbr* meaning warrior was the source word for *gibbowr*

---

[774] Ibid.

[775] H5674—`abar.

[776] Ezek 39:11, 14—Travellers: NIV, ESV, Berean, NJKV, CSB, CEV; JNT; Travel: NLT; HCSB; Access Bible.

[777] H47—`abbiyr, ab-beer': angel; bull; mighty one; stout, strong one; valiant; princes of angels, princes; mighty ones.

and was utilized to describe the Rapiu rulers/king of the *Ugaritic Texts*, as well as their tribes, and spawned human hybrid nations like the Hurrians, Hittites, and Cypriots.[778]

> Job 34:20 In a moment shall they die, and the people shall be troubled at midnight, and pass away: and the mighty shall be taken away without hand.

Following this line of thought, application, and scriptural consistencies, Ezekiel 39:18 references the princes of the end-time war as mighty/*gibbowr*,[779] the same word used to describe Nephilim in Genesis 6:4 as mighty men. The mighty ones of Ezekiel 39 are the slain princes of the earth (bloodline descendants of Rephaim), ancient offspring the fallen ones,[780] and thus descendants the postdiluvian Hermonim. The fallen princes are described as "fatlings of Bashan," the kingdom of the Rephaim kings Og and Sihon.[781] The end-time will be a time of reckoning for fallen angels and all their spurious offspring and descendants.

> Ezek 39:14 And they shall sever out men of continual employment, passing through the land to bury with the passengers those that remain upon the face of the earth, to cleanse it.. ..
>
> Ezek 39:18 Ye shall eat the flesh of the mighty, and drink the blood of the princes of the earth, of rams. .. of bullocks, all of them fatlings of Bashan.

In ancient Sumerian, *Nibiru* means crossing and the planet, or place of crossing, while *Nibruki* is the earth place/location for *Nibiru*,[782] indicating *Nibiru* is in another dimension. Anu, the Heavenly One (*Shemayim*) was *Nibiru's* ruler, and the first of several princes of heaven/*an*.[783] Typically the Sumerian underworld/netherworld is understood as *Kurnugi* and associated with *Kur* and *Kurgal*, the house of the great mountain,[784] all of which is akin to Mount Hermon's cave/gate to Hades and Pan's Temple.

What further links the Ugarit "traveler" references together with the end times, and likely the UN UNDOF mission, is that Gog's alliance of kings and their armies will likely be destroyed by God (Ezek 39) in Og's kingdom of Bashan

---

778 Wyatt, *Religious Texts from Ugarit*, 154, notes 8–9; 345–347: KTU 1.40.25–42.

779 H1368—*gibbowr.*

780 Eze 39:5: fall: H5307—*naphal.*

781 Num 32:33; Deut 1:4; 3:1–2; 29:7.

782 *Sumerian Dictionary*, 11: crossing, 21: Place.

783 Ibid., 3–4, Anu, Anshargal, and An.

784 Ibid., 20: netherworld; 4: Ekurm Kur, Kurgal.

on the Golan Heights,[785] where the largest manned UN base is located. The Golan Heights of Mount Hermon, home of Gilgal Rephaim, is the all-important high ground for military dominance in the Covenant Land. Golan was a haven city for fleeing murderers in the time of Israel, and is defined as captivity, and as their rejoicing.[786]

The Gog war after the opening of the abyss will be the counterfeit Armageddon war and destruction that Antichrist rides to power upon, leading to the abomination.[787] The Gog war of the passengers/travelers leads to the promise of peace and safety by Antichrist that ultimately leads to the mark of the beast.[788] The mark of loyalty, the worship of Antichrist and Satan, will be the reincarnated spirit of the oath of Hermon sworn by angels to destroy God's people, and an oath sworn by giants to wipe Israel from the face of the earth. The mark of the beast will be in part the accursed oath of Hermon, Harem-Anathema, to carry out to the end the destruction of all those who follow Jesus and the Holy Spirit and worship God, and to take their stand against the God Most High.[789]

> Rev 12:17 And the dragon was wroth with the woman, and went to make war with the remnant of her seed, which keep the commandments of God, and have the testimony of Jesus Christ.

---

[785] Deut 4:43; Josh 20:8; 21:27; 1 Chron 6:71.
[786] H1474—*Gowlan, go-lawn'*: captive; captivity; their rejoicing; a place and a town in the heights of Bashan east of the Jordan; a city of refuge.
[787] Dan 11:21–34; Luke 21:19–22.
[788] Dan 11:24; 1 Thess 5:3; Rev 13:16–18.
[789] Dan 11:31–45; Rev 19:19–21.

MOUNT SION AND HAR MEGIDDOWN

CHAPTER 20

Lev 5:4 Or if a soul swear, pronouncing with his lips to do evil, or to do good, whatsoever it be that a man shall pronounce with an oath, and it be hid from him; when he knoweth of it, then he shall be guilty in one of these.

The Naphalim World Order on earth was born out of their oath-based conspiracy to create an angelic hybrid race to lead humankind away from God, into rebellion and into utter destruction.

The reincarnated Naphalim World Order reigned after the flood through their dynastic empires, which produced the six beast empires past, and will produce the seventh end-time beast empire.

Such was the world of Israel dominated by the Hermonim/Rephaim, a world populated with secret societies, mystical religions, military organizations, and kingly coronations complete with oaths for loyalty that have continued ever since. Such will be the end-time NWO of the ten beast kings of the seventh beast empire, and then Antichrist's eighth beast empire—both of which will overflow with oaths, mystical rituals, obscure symbolism, embedded allegories, double entendres, sacred geometry, numerology, hidden history, and endless genealogies hidden in plain sight. Antichrist's empire will be distinguished with the mark of the beast and its accompanying oath of Harem-Anathema. One should not be surprised to learn then that Mount Hermon's hidden history is actively being employed in preparing for the rise of the seventh beast empire.

Mount Hermon's latitude is set at thirty-three degrees, a sacred prime number in the geomancy of Freemasons, Rosicrucianism, Templarism, and occult religions. Mount Hermon was alternatively named Mount Sion in the Bible. Sion is a term polytheist organizations have seized upon to utilize in their allegories and double entendres. Sion/*Siyon* is defined as the summit of Mount Hermon, peak, and lofty;[790] *Shamayim*, the heavenly ones, are also defined in part as lofty.

> Deut 4:48 From Aroer, which is by the bank of the river Arnon, even unto Mount Sion, which is Hermon.

One might anticipate that a rising end-time Babylon religion will utilize Mount Sion as part of the overall strategy of misdirection and misinformation to persuade the people of the world that monotheism rose as a rogue cult after Moses; that Moses was taught and initiated into polytheism at Heliopolis as a royal; that Moses was not monotheistic. The end-time universal religion will de-deify Jesus and endeavor to bring all monotheism home to the religion of Mount Hermon/Sion,[791] not Mount Zion of Jerusalem and monotheism.

Genesis 6's "men of renown" appellation for the Nephilim derives from the Hebrew *shem* meaning fame, infamy, reputation, etc.[792] *Shem* is sourced equally from *shamayim* meaning heaven(s), and from its singular root word *shameh* meaning to be lofty. Sion, the variant name for Hermon, also means lofty.[793] The Heavenly Ones, the *Shamayim* that fell in rebellion, are the Naphalim. By inference, the Hermonim/giants were the inferior demigod copies of fallen lofty ones, heavenly ones. It follows that the Nephilim and Rephaim held similar reputation and infamy—as tyrants.

Mount Sion/*Siy'on* of Bashan should not be confused or conflated with Zion/*Tsiyown*, the mountain of Jerusalem city.[794] These are two distinct Hebrew words: one to describe the home of lofty fallen angels, and one to describe the mountain of the God Most High and His city. *Tsiyown* is used 154 times in the Old Testament to describe to a mountain in Jerusalem, the city taken by David (2 Sam 5:7), but never for Mount Hermon. Sion, as it was translated in the KJV in Deuteronomy 4:48, likely ought to have been translated into English as it was spelled in Hebrew *Siyon* and not Sion, which appears to be a translator masonic marker.

---

[790] H7865—*Siy'on, see-ohn'*: the summit of Mt. Hermon; lofty; peak; another name for Mount Hermon.

[791] Wayne, *The Genesis 6 Conspiracy*, 339–349, 384–389, 602–609.

[792] H8034—*shem, shame*; an appellation, as a mark or memorial of individuality; honour; authority; reputation; fame; infamous; renown.

[793] H7865 —*Siy'on*.

[794] H6726—*Tsiyown, tsee-yone'*: a parched place; a mountain of Jerusalem; another name for Jerusalem.

> 2 Sam 5:7. .. David took the strong hold of Zion: the same is the city of David.

> 1 Kings 8:1 Then Solomon assembled the elders of Israel… unto king Solomon in Jerusalem, that they might bring up the ark of the covenant of the LORD out of the city of David, which is Zion.

One might overlook Deuteronomy 4's translation corruption if it was nor for Romans 11 where "Sion" is translated from Greek *Seeown*, which derived from Hebrew *Tsiyown*/Zion.[795] The New Testament translation corruption in favor of Sion over Zion was made six more times.[796]

> Rom 11:26 And so all Israel shall be saved: as it is written, There shall come out of Sion the Deliverer, and shall turn away ungodliness from Jacob.

One might anticipate Antichrist, and perhaps end-time Babylon will exploit the Sion/Zion conflation and diabolical double entendre as one and the same, when they convert many Christians to polytheism. One would further expect that Mount Sion/Hermon will hold a very special place in Antichrist's hardened heart and hubris, so much so that one might further anticipate Antichrist will fight his final battle at Mount Hermon. Armageddon's actual location is a riddle the prophet John embedded into Revelation 16. The Armageddon location mystery was not created to hide or deceive, but rather created out of necessity, including enough breadcrumbs in the text for Christians to solve it. Christians need to know the resolution to the riddle, lest they be deceived by a counterfeit Armageddon that Antichrist will ride to power on as the dragon messiah.

> Rev 16:14 For they are the spirits of devils, working miracles, which go forth unto the kings of the earth and of the whole world, to gather them to the battle of that great day of God Almighty.. ..

> Rev 16:16 And he gathered them together into a place called in the Hebrew tongue Armageddon.

The mystery derives from the fact that Megiddo, from which the English "Armageddon" word is in part derived, does not have a mountain directly associated with it. Megiddo is a valley or a plain, described as such in Zechariah 12:11. The Megiddo location has a city, but no mountain or large hill(s) associated with it. Armageddon then is presented by many to be a symbolic name for the actual

---

[795] G4622—*see-own*'; a parched place; a hill of Jerusalem; figuratively Jerusalem.
[796] Matt 21:5; John 12:15; Rom 9:33; Heb 12:22; 1 Peter 2:6; Rev 14:1.

location of the great end-time battle between the good forces of God and Jesus and the evil forces of Satan, fallen angels, and Antichrist, a place of the great slaughter akin to the two battles fought long ago at Megiddo/Megiddon.[797] However, a deeper dive into John's Revelation 16:16 mystery reveals the actual location.

Armageddon/*Armageddohn* derives from Hebrew *har*, meaning a mount, mountain(s), or hill(s); and *Megiddown/Megiddo* is defined as a rendezvous place of crowds and meetings close to Mount Carmel and Jerusalem.[798] According to Wilhelm Gesenius, a Hebrew lexicography pioneer, Har Megiddo is a place of troops.[799] Additionally, Armageddon is often connected to the valley of Megiddo in Zechariah's prophecy about the gathering of the nations to Jerusalem, whereby God will protect and save Judah.[800] On the other hand, the Bible is not inaccurate; biblical writings would not conflate a valley or plain with a mountain. Further, the Bible does not present prophetic allegory unless Scripture provides the meaning and additional details to explain the verse in question. As such, the Armageddon narrative contains details to discern the Revelation mystery.

To discern how and why the prophet John communicated the location for Armageddon the way he did requires one to understand a little about Hebrew letters and the history of linguistic Hebrew. Some Hebrews letters tend to be enunciated slightly differently than English letters can fully communicate. The silent א, *aleph,* for example, is used to indicate the "vowel pointing," but in some applications indicates a syllable break represented by an apostrophe.[801] Similarly, the `*ayin* ע vowel sound is silent or pronounced as an "ah" and/or "h" sound.[802]

There is a long-standing tradition in Semitic philology to render the `*ayin* like that of the "Greek breathing marks" above the letter, and thus as an "ah" sound for the rough breathing mark, and silent for the smooth breathing mark. In Hebrew, this concept is marked by a backward apostrophe that is transliterated into English as with `*Amorah* for Gomorrah.[803] `*Amorah* derives from *'amar*[804] meaning to boast,

---

[797] G717—*ar-mag-ed-dohn*`: Armageddon or Har-Megiddon: a symbolical name; the hill/mountain of Megiddo; a place where two famous battles were fought and won by Barak over the Canaanites and Gideon over the Midianites; a place of slaughter for the wicked.

[798] H4023—*Mgiddown, meg-id-done*`: rendezvous; a place of crowds; an ancient Canaanite city; place close to Mount Carmel, Nazareth, and Jerusalem. Megiddo מְגִדּוֹן:; H2022—*har*; a mountain or range of hills; hill country; mount or mountain.

[799] *Strong's Cyclopaedia,* Vol. 6, 44.

[800] Zech 12:1–11.

[801] Jeff A. Benner, *Learn to Read Hebrew,* Vol. 2, 9, notes 1–3.

[802] Ibid., Vol 2, 11, note 4.

[803] *The Hebrew Hebrew-Greek-& English Bible: The Holy Scripture of the Old & New Testaments in the Original Languages with English Translation* (Westminster Leningrad Codex Hebrew, Tischendorf 8th Edition Greek, 1917, Jewish Publication Society OT, Lexham English Bible English NT. Kindle Version, 2014). Gen 14:2: Gomorrah הֲרֹמֲע.

[804] H6017—*`Amorah, am-o-raw*`; from 6014: a ruined heap; Gomorrah; submersion; G1116—*gom'-or-hrhah*; of Hebrew origin H6017 `*Amorah*: submersion; Gomorrha as in Amorah;

or to act proudly, and generally pronounced with the "ah" sound as aw-mar.[805] `Amorah, however, is enunciated with a sound similar with but a distinctive "g" like sound at the end because of the `ayin. The English enunciation for of `Amorah is with a hard "g" sound (G`Amorah) in part derived from the Greek version of the New Testament translation,[806] and perhaps the Greek Septuagint, as both translated `Amorah in Greek as Γόμορρα with the hard "g" (gamma) as in Gomorrha, and then into English, is related to the pronunciation of Armageddon from Greek.

> *Sep Greek* Gen 14:2 ἐποίησαν πόλεμον μετὰ Βαλλα βασιλέως Σοδομων καὶ μετὰ Βαρσα βασιλέως <u>Γομορρας</u> καὶ Σεννααρ βασιλέως Αδαμα καὶ Συμοβορ βασιλέως Σεβωιμ καὶ βασιλέως Βαλακ [αὕτη ἐστὶν Σηγωρ].

> *Sep* Gen 14:2 made war with Balla king of Sodom, and with Barsa king of Gomorrha, and with Sennaar, king of Adama, and with Symobor king of Seboim and the king of Balac, this is Segor.[807]

The consonantal sound of the Hebrew `ayin is made beginning in the throat, but less deep than the *aleph* according to medieval grammarians,[808] Thus the `ayin is enunciated with a rough and slightly rolling sound, articulated more like a consonant than a vowel akin to "a-g-h," and although like a hard "g," the `ayin sound is slightly longer and distinct.

Adding in a little important history into the `ayin mystery, *Standard Tiberian Hebrew Text's*[809] and most Non-Standard Tiberian manuscripts' `ayin application was void of a stronger dagesh mark, a dot within the letter to indicate whether the pronunciation was the original "hard plosive" or the "soft fricative." The dagesh dot prevented the consonant-like `ayin sound from being pronounced with pressure.[810] Some Non-Standard Tiberian-age texts though, did continue to mark the `ayin with the dagesh dot to seemingly protect the ancient consonantal pronunciation of `ayin utilizing a *raphel rafe* sign (a bar over top).[811] Seemingly, though, the softer fricative `ayin was selected that included a silent version, over the consonant-like

---

transliterated: Gomorrha; H6014—`amar, aw-mar`; to heap; to gather grain; manipulate; act as a tyrant; to enslave; chastise.

[805] H559 —'amar, aw-mar`: to say; speak; answer; utter appoint, boast; act proudly; challenge.

[806] G1116—*gom'-or-hrhah.*

[807] Septuagint, Complete Greek and English Edition (Delphi Classics: Ancient Classic Series, 2016 Kindle Version), Gen 14:2.

[808] Geoffrey Khan, *The Tiberian Pronunciation of Biblical Hebrew* (Cambridge: Open Book Publishers, 2020), Vol. 1, 194, 209.

[809] The Tiberian Text was the canonical pronunciation of the Old Testament as used by the Masoretic scholars of the Jewish community and thus the Masoretic Text.

[810] Khan, *The Tiberian Pronunciation of Biblical Hebrew,* 209–210.

[811] Ibid., 305, notes 78, 210, 211.

`ayin at the time of the introduction of Tiberian Hebrew, or just before. Knowing the `ayin transition from hard to soft/silent makes sense of the Dead Sea Scrolls, where the `ayin was weakened or replaced with an aleph or "he" in its application, beginning sometime in the Second Temple period, as compared to the *Standard Tiberian Text*.[812] In fact, medieval readers of the Masoretic Text were required to make a special effort to not weaken the `ayin in the transmission and communication of specific words of the Masoretic Text.[813]

Adding to this linguistic minutiae and intrigue is that English and Greek do not have a letter that directly equates to or produces the exact the phonetic sound of a hard or strong `ayin. English, though, is reliant on Greek translations that provides a hard "g" for the comparatively lighter-sounding `ayin. The phonetic sound of the consonantal Hebrew `ayin was like the hard "g," gamma ג in Greek, but still distinct and not captured fully in any of the English or Greek letters. Thus, the ancient "a-h-g" consonantal of `ayin versus the silent "h," or "ah" vowel-like sound was captured in the closest sounding Greek letter for both. The hard "g" gimmel ג was selected when translating from Hebrew to Greek, and then Hebrew to English. Further, others have a view that the lost `ayin consonantal sound that some refer to as *ghayn* was absorbed into the silent or "h" or "ah" `ayin sometime after the Old Testament was transcribed into the Greek Septuagint.

Hence, the same phonetic scenario surfaces scripturally with Gaza/`Azzah (a city of the Anakim in the Philistine empire[814]) that followed a similar kind of phonetic evolution into English as Gomorrah/`Amorah, but with an important twist helpful to substantiate the lost consonantal application for `ayin. The KJV translators without explanation translated `Azzah as Gaza eighteen times, and three times directly from Hebrew as Azzah. *Strong's Concordance* and the *Catholic Encyclopedia* note Azzah is an alternative name for Gaza. [815] Hence we can see, through the translation of `Azzah from Hebrew to English in the KJV, the Greek influence with both the hard and soft/silent application and pronunciation of `ayin, and/or a Hebrew gimmel/Greek gamma substitution.

Another illuminating passage in Genesis 10:19 paired Gerar and Gaza together, as well as including Gomorrah, which provides the modern Hebrew `ayin backward apostrophe on `Azzah indicating a lost distinct consonantal pronunciation with the harder "ahg," and noting we pronounce `Azzah as Gaza today, whereas Gerar is spelled with the Hebrew *gimel* for "g." The same goes for Gomorrah/`Amorah

---

[812] Ibid., 211.

[813] Ibid., 212.

[814] Josh 11:22.

[815] H5804—`*Azzah, az-zaw*': strong; a place in Palestine; another name for Gaza a city of the Philistines. Gaza: Gen 10:19; Josh 10:41; 11:22; 15:47; Judg 1:18; 6:4; 16:1, 21; 1 Sam 6:17; 2 Kings 18:8; 1 Chron 7:28; Jer 47:1; Amos 1:5, 6, 7; Zech 9:4, 5. Àzzah: Deut 2:23; 1 Kings 4:24; Jer 25:20. *Catholic Encyclopedia*, Vol. 6, 399: Gaza.

and its `ayin in its proper form has distinct consonantal sound beginning in the throat—ahg[816] versus the hard "g" sound of gimel and Greek gamma.

> Gen 10:19 And the border of the Canaanites was from Sidon, as thou comest to Gerar, unto Gaza; as thou goest, unto Sodom, and Gomorrah, and Admah, and Zeboim, even unto Lasha.

As noted, the *ayin* consonantal sound was absorbed into the silent application after the Second Temple period for reasons that are seemingly unknown today, but oddly kept alive today with a hard "g" in some words. Knowing this presupposes other words were once enunciated in the same way Gomorrah and Gaza were enunciated in the past, and may have been absorbed into the silent format of `ayin or transliterated with a hard "g'" sound—all of which reveals the mystery of Armageddon and its connection to Mount Hermon.

In standard church dogma, Armageddon/*Armageddohn* is thought of as a symbolic name for the place of the great slaughter of the wicked at the mountain or hill of Megiddo/Megiddon.[817] However, the connection to Meggidon in Zechariah 12 does seem to be connected to the Armageddon time frame, but to an earlier end-time event when God will save Jerusalem and Judah, and the time when Judah will mourn for the one they pierced, Jesus, with such wailing that it will be like the mourning as with Hadadrimmon[818] in the valley of Megiddo, as Judah wailed for the death of King Josiah. The timing of the mourning at Megiddo will be the time of Jesus' sign in Matthew 24:30 that will occur after the Gog war of Ezekiel 38–39, Joel 1–2, and Revelation 9:14–21. Antichrist will utilize this counterfeit Armageddon, and then move his armies into Jerusalem to bring about the abomination. Judah then accepts Jesus as their Messiah, the One they pierced, and then flees Jerusalem for three and a half years under God's protection.[819] Ergo the mourning of Judah occurs about three and a half years before the battle of Armageddon. The Megiddo location for Armageddon based on Zechariah 12 does seem to fit as the defining essence and timing.

Further, John placed the most important clue within the passage itself: "a place called in the Hebrew tongue Armageddon"[820]—not as understood in the Greek tongue Revelation was copied down. John's words guide the reader to learn about the Hebrew language at that time and before, to grasp his meaning. Greek was not able to capture accurate and Hebrew meaning.

---

[816] עַזָּה/Gaza; גְּרָר/Gerar; עֲמֹרָה/Gomorrah. *The Hebrew Hebrew-Greek-& English Bible: The Holy Scripture of the Old & New Testaments in the Original Languages with English Translation*. Gen 10:19.
[817] G717—*ar-mag-ed-dohn'*: Megiddown.
[818] Zech 12:10–14. H191—*Hadadrimmown, had-ad-rim-mone'*: rendezvous; a place of crowds; a place in the valley of Megiddo in Palestine where a national lamentation was held for the death of King Josiah; named after two Syrian gods. Megiddo: Josh 12:21; 17:11; Judg 1:27; 5:19; 1 Kings 4:12; 9:15; 2 Kings 9:27; 23:29–30; 1 Chron 7:29; 2 Chron 35:22. Megiddon: Zech 12:11.
[819] Dan 11:21–35; Matt 24:15–31; Luke 21:20–28.
[820] Rev 16:16.

Knowing this brings in the *gimel* ג versus `*ayin* ע mystery of linguistic transition during John's lifetime, and to understand the Greek word as it would be understood in Hebrew. As noted above, the transition of the `*aiyn's* consonantal sound was not fully completed in John's time, even though Tiberian Hebrew had made the transition to an absorbed and silent sounding `*ayin*, but many Non-Standard Hebrew manuscripts had not yet made that transition. Knowing this brings up the question: Did the Hebrew word John documented not have an adequate letter in Greek for the spelling he was looking to communicate—and thus, John's curious instructions?

Megiddo does fit with John's curious instructions, noting Megiddo in Hebrew is spelled with the hard-sounding *gimel*,[821] and would be pronounced and translated accordingly into Greek. Megiddo holds the allegorical meaning John was communicating, though, in conjunction with Hadadrimmon, as both are defined as meeting places and assemblies. Megiddon derives from *gadad*, meaning assembling troops, crowds, to attack, and invade.[822] Hadadrimmon was named after two Syrian Baalim gods: Hadad, the Mesopotamian name for Baal; and the god Rimmom.[823] John may have been communicating in Greek in part and allegorically through Zechariah's passage that the end-time battle will be fought at the foot of the mountain of Baal's assembly.

> Zech 12:11 In that day shall there be a great mourning in Jerusalem, as the mourning of Hadadrimmon in the valley of Megiddon.

Adding to this line of thinking, Hebrew derived from the original Semitic language did not use vowels, and as such ancient Hebrew did not include vowels in its writings, which again is part of the Armageddon riddle. Mount Megiddo would have been transliterated in English without vowels as: *HRMGD*. Now if the "g" in Armageddon was an `*ayin* but replaced with a *gimel* because that was the closest letter in Greek alphabet available, John's instructions begin to make sense. The dual prophecy of Isaiah 14 instructs the reader that Satan not only stated he would ascend to heaven to be like God, but amazingly, as it is pertinent to this narrative, to sit enthroned on the "mount of the congregation." God's holy mount of the congregation is in heaven unlike Satan's assembly of the gods, located on the earth and on a

---

[821] *The Hebrew Hebrew-Greek-& English Bible: The Holy Scripture of the Old & New Testaments in the Original Languages with English Translation.* Zech 12:11: Megido: מְגִדּֽוֹן.

[822] H1413—*gadad, gaw-dad'*: to crowd; to gash by pressing into; assemble; gather crowds or troops; cut oneself; attack; invade.

[823] H191—*Hadadrimmown, had-ad-rim-mone'*: rendezvous; a place of crowds; a place in the valley of Megiddo in Palestine where a national lamentation was held for the death of King Josiah; named after two Syrian gods. Josh 12:21; 17:11; Judg 1:27; 5:19; 1 Kings 4:12; 9:15; 2 Kings 9:27; 23:29–30; 1 Chron 7:29; 2 Chron 35:22; H7417—*Rimmown, rim-mone'*; Rimmon, rimmone': pomegranate; Syrian storm deity; also of five places in Palestine.

mountain (Ps 82), and the mountain where Antichrist will make his last stand. One deduces this assembly is located at Mount Hermon, the home of the Baalim gods led by Baal after the flood, and El and his assembly of parent gods before the flood.

"Congregation" in Isaiah 14:13 is translated from the Hebrew word *mow`ed* and is defined as a solemn and appointed assembly, congregation or feast.[824] *Mow`ed* contains the mystery letter `*ayin*.[825] *Mow`ed's* `*ayin* consonantal sound would seem to be a linguistic victim silenced in the time of the Second Temple, The Tiberian Hebrew Text, and in the prophet John's time. Knowing this makes perfect sense of John's instruction to interpret the Greek spelling in the Hebrew tongue before the silencing of `*ayin* and pronounced in the consonantal sound of some Non-Standard Hebrew texts of his time. It seems to me then that *mow`ed* was once enunciated with the distinct consonantal "ahg" from the throat, and not silent as it is today. Further, the translation and transliteration into English from Hebrew in Isaiah 14:13 ought to have been akin to Gomorrah and Gaza with the *gimel* letter and the hard "g," as Mount *Mowged,* and the same as same manner as Armageddon was translated into Greek and English. Megiddo did not suffer the silencing of the *ayin* letter because its "g" was the *gimmel* letter.

> Isa 14:13 For thou hast said in thine heart, I will ascend into heaven, I will exalt my throne above the stars of God: I will sit also upon the mount of the congregation, in the sides of the north.

Har Megiddown/Megido was translated into Greek with the gamma letter utilizing the Hebrew gimel letter cognate, because the "ahg" consonantal sound of the `*ayin* had been silenced, as in *mow`ed.* Accordingly, the Armageddon "g" translation, as in *mow`ed* was silenced and would have been *har me`do* or *har mehgido* with the "ahg" consonantal sound for the assembly place of end-time armies, just as `*Amorah*/Gomorrah should be pronounced with the `*ayin,* as Aghmorah versus the "g" sound of the gimmel and gamma. Moreover, *HRM* is the Semitic root word for [Mount] Hermon, Satan's mountain of mountains on earth. As such, Mount Sion is the earthly counterfeit of God's *Har Mow`ed/Mowged* in heaven, *Hr Mgd/M`d* in the voweless English transliteration of old Semitic and Hebrew. Mount Hermon of the accursed oaths appears to be the location for Antichrist's last battle versus Megiddo, and what John was communicating.

Antichrist will deploy numerous counterfeit deceptions during his reign including convincing the world Mount Sion/Hermon is the true Mount Zion. Sion in Deuteronomy 4 and its New Testament translations appear to be masonic

---

[824] H4150—*mow`ed, mo-ade*; or *moled, mo-ade*: an appointment; a fixed time or season; specifically, a festival; conventionally a year; an assembly convened for a definite purpose; congregation; place of meeting; a signal or appointed sign; place of solemn assembly; tent of meeting.
[825] H4150—*mow`ed*: מוֹעֵד.

markers carefully embedded into the KJV translation for end-time deception by Babylon, and then by Antichrist. Know then that secret societies believe and state they have proof that the official KJV translation committee completed their work in 1610, whereby the manuscript was forwarded to King James I. King James, in turn, mysteriously sent the manuscript to Sir Francis Bacon until 1611 for final editing, and thereafter it was published:

> The first edition of the King James Bible, which was edited by Francis Bacon and prepared under masonic supervision, bears more Mason's marks than the Cathedral of Strasburg.[826]

We will likely confirm before the end times if indeed the Rosicrucian Bacon made any changes, or know how many changes, he might have made during the review period before publication. But we do need to be on guard against their stated seditions. Inexplicable translations like Sion for *Tsiyown* and unicorn for *r'em* (wild bull) indicate that marker translations for the end-time deceptions were seemingly made. Sion was transliterated into French from Latin, Zion, and Hebrew, Zion. Thus, the mercurial Priory of Sion was a French Royal Masonic secret society of adepts that founded the Knights Templar Order, established to protect endless Nephilim "scioned/grafted" royal bloodlines, Rex Deus,[827] they believe are bloodlines of the house of Dragon and their Dragon Messiah. Note, the "al" suffix on "royal," along with il, ilu, allah, and other variants that are transliterations of Hebrew *el* for a god, an angel, mighty ones, mighty heroes, and men of rank.[828] Royals believe they are the kings of God/Rex Deus.

Most do not make the Knights Templar connection, the duplicitous gnostic order that burrowed their way into the Roman church who were otherwise known as The Order of Sion.[829] Thus, the figurative definition of Greek *Seeown* is the "church militant or triumphant,"[830] from which the founding Templar military order speciously portrayed as their mission. Sion was a gnostic double entendre used to deceive Christians and provide camoflage for their hidden agenda. Templars were a royal masonic organization founded in a small priory on Mount Zion in Jerusalem (c. 1099–1118) named Abbey Notre Dame du Mont Sion, where their headquarters was located until the fall of Jerusalem in 1187.[831]

---

[826] Manley P. Hall, *Rosicrucian and Masonic Origins* (Los Angeles: The Hall Publishing Company, 1929), 14.

[827] Wayne, *The Genesis 6 Conspiracy,* 398, 401–402, 422, 462.

[828] H410—'*el.*

[829] Wayne, *The Genesis 6 Conspiracy,* 521–533, 549–561.

[830] G4622—*see-own':* figuratively, the church (militant or triumphant); transliterated: Sion.

[831] Mackey, *The History of Freemasonry,* 219–228.

CHAPTER 21

UNICORNS OF MOUNT HERMON

Ps 29:5 The voice of the LORD breaketh the cedars; yea, the LORD breaketh the cedars of Lebanon.

Ps 29:6 He maketh them also to skip like a calf; Lebanon and Sirion like a young unicorn.

Mount Sirion—and by implication Mount Sion, Shenir, and Hermon[832] in Psalm 29:6—is without explanation connected to the occult word "unicorn," a word oddly inserted into the KJV. "Unicorn" was translated into the KJV from *r'em*: a wild bull;[833] and is not the innocent fun-loving antediluvian casualty or the heraldic one-horned white horse in the Stuart coat of arms.

The Latin Vulgate translated *r'em* as *rinocerotis*, for rhinoceros, but English translations of the Vulgate used unicorn. Roman historian Pliny the Elder utilized *unicornis* both as an adjective to describe one-horned oxen and asses (his page note links them to the rhinoceros), and to a *monkeros*, a fabled postdiluvian chimera-like animal with the head of a stag, body of a horse, tail of a boar, and feet of an elephant.[834]

---

[832] Deut 3:9; 4:48.

[833] H7214—*r'em, reh-ame'*: a wild bull; unicorn; probably the great aurochs or wild bulls that are now extinct.

[834] Pliny The Elder, *Natural Histories* (77 AD), Book VIII 31:72 & 76: unicornis oxen, Book XI:255: unicornis asses, and Book VIII 31:76: Monkeros for Rhinoceros.

Vulg Latin Ps 29:6 Et despergit quasi vitulis Lebani et Sarion quasi filius rinocerotis.

Vulg Ps 29:6 And shall reduce them to pieces, as a calf of Libanus, and the beloved son of unicorns.

Akin to Pliny, and in the spirit of the Latin Vulgate translation, Greeks translated *r'em* into the Septuagint as *monokeros*, meaning one-horned, followed by English Septuagint translations that in turn, and after the KJV publication, began to translate *monkeros* as unicorn after the mythical horse beast in the same stratagem as the KJV.

NIV Ps 29:6 He makes Lebanon leap like a calf, Sirion like a young wild ox.

KJV Ps 29:6 He maketh them also to skip like a calf; Lebanon and Sirion like a young unicorn.

Sep Ps 29:6 And he will beat them small, even Libanus itself, like a calf; and the beloved one is as a young unicorn.

Pliny, Jerome, and the Septuagint were historical seeds to the modern occult unicorn mythos that was planted as an occult stratagem into the KJV to reimagine the meaning of *r'em* from a wild bull or oxen into a one-horned fairy tale horse and allegory for a beast recorded in occult history and legend. "Unicorn" was substituted for a wild bull six times in the KJV[835] as hubris and a ploy to enhance the mythos of specific pure-blood royals.

Further, Lebanon/*Lbanown,* as it is connected in Psalm 29:5–6 as a mountain(s) with cedars associated with Sirion/Hermon, is defined as whiteness, and as the name of a specific mountain or range of mountains in northern Canaan. In Phoenician mythology, the Lebanon mountain and mountain range were named after Libanus, an Aboriginal Lebanon giant whose skin was pale-white,[836] a Rephaim. The text in Psalm 29:6 connects specific pale-white giants as source names for the white-capped mountains, like Hermon, and that unicorn bloodlines, the Albi-gens of those Aboriginal giants to gods, also figuratively represented unicorns.

Royal houses like the Hanover dynasty of Germany, the Stuart dynasty of Scotland and England, and the Windsor dynasty of England display with pride

---

[835] Unicorn: Num 23:22; Job 39:8–10; Ps 29:6; 92:10. Unicorns: Deut 33:17; Ps 22:21; Isa 34:7.

[836] H3844—*Lbanown, leb-aw-nohn'*; from 3835: the white mountain from its snow: whiteness; a heavily forested mountain range on Israel's northern border; H3835—*laban, law-ban'*; become white: be white; make white; purify; make bricks. William Rickets Cooper, *An Archaic Dictionary, Biographical, Historical, and Mythological: From the Egyptian, Assyrian, and Etruscan Monuments and Papyri,* 303: Libanus.

and hubris their coats of arms that boast unicorns. Coats of arms are taciturn stories hidden in plain sight, communicating their occult history and genealogies through allegorical imagery to mystical adepts and members of royal families. The coat of arms evolves with additional imagery when a family scion intermarries with a partner of importance from another royal bloodline, or when a new dynasty is begat from two powerful bloodlines.

The unicorn horse is one of many occult heraldic symbols displayed in the coat of arms for King James Stuart I of England (James VI of Scotland), which depicted a white single-horned stallion of (Nephilim) kings. Typically, the unicorn appears with the lion in the Stuart coat of arms, noting King James was coronated in 1601, and that the Bible bearing his name was published in 1611. One ought not to be too surprised to learn that just a few years after the publication of the KJV, both the lion and a snow-white unicorn were paired together in the 1619 English publication of the occult book, *The Chymical Wedding of Christian Rosenkreutz*:

> .. . there came forth a beautiful snow-white unicorn with a golden collar (having on it certain letters) about his neck...he bowed himself down upon both his forefeet, as if hereby he had shown honor to the lion.... The lion immediately took the naked sword which he had in his paw, and broke it in two.. .. And so the unicorn returned to his place.[837]

Johann Andrea became the Grandmaster for the Priory of Sion from 1637–1654.[838] Rosenkreutz was the occult fairy tale founder of modern Rosicrucianism according to freemasonry.[839] Rosenkreutz was fabled to have established Rosicrucianism in 1378 to illuminate humankind; the objective was to spread gnosis to all humankind.[840] Rosenkreutz is accredited within occult organizations to have written *Fama Fraternities* and *Discovery of the Fraternity of the Most Noble Order of the Rosy Cross*, which were published posthumously in 1619, and which are renowned as the Rosicrucian manifestos.[841] Rosicrucianism was originally a Royal Masonic Order of Adepts that split away from Knights Templars before the fall of the Templars in AD 1307.

---

[837] Originally published in German in 1616, this edition derives from an English translation published in 1690. Johann Valentin Andrea, *The Chymical Wedding of Christian Rosenkreutz* (Adobe Acrobat edition prepared by Benjamin Rowe, October 2000), 34.

[838] Wayne, *The Genesis 6 Conspiracy*, 535.

[839] Mackey, *History of Freemasonry*, 331.

[840] Peter Marshall, *The Philosopher's Stone: A Quest for the Secrets of Alchemy* (London: Pan Books, An Imprint of Pan Macmillan Ltd., 2002), 362–363.

[841] Graham Hancock and Robert Bauval, *Talisman: Sacred Cities, Sacred Faith*, 258–261.

One should not be surprised that King James—the Royal Mason initiated into the mysteries from childhood as all pure-blood royals are—publicly promoted his heraldic history within his coat of arms, and within the KJV. Just as disturbing, King James authored a book, *Daemonologie: In Forme of a Dialogue* in 1599 (reprinted in 1603), which was an occult apologetics dissertation on necromancy and the historical relationships and methodology of divination and black magic, which included studies on demonology and sorcery.

Origins to royal and religious heraldry is "shrouded in mystery," but the visual presentation provided and proclaimed their prestigious identities of the family, house, or organization, and was proudly displayed on seals, shields, surcoats, and coats of arms.[842] Heraldry is the science of proclaiming genealogies in taciturn imagery and expression.[843] Heraldry dates back to ancient times; to the (beast) empires like Persia, Medes, Greece, Rome, and to the ancient priesthoods.[844]

Unicorn horses, understood in their ancient mythos, were depicted as fierce fighters[845] perfect for battle—regal steeds ridden by warrior giant kings of renown before the flood. The occult unicorn steed mythos was inserted into Deuteronomy 33:17, and other passages, to flatter King James who believed he was bestowed with the divine right to rule from Mount Sion, as a Rephaim and scioned royal bloodline, and the rightful inheritor of the Davidic crown. King James believed he was de facto authorized with a kind of manifest destiny to establish a worldwide empire, which became the British Commonwealth Empire where the sun never set.

> Deut 33:17 His glory is like the firstling of his bullock, and his horns are like the horns of unicorns: with them he shall push the people together to the ends of the earth: and they are the ten thousands of Ephraim, and they are the thousands of Manasseh.

A horned helmet (generally) capped beautiful white or black steeds ridden by Rephaim kings after the flood, which was well represented in John Duncan's masterpiece painting *The Riders of the Sidhe* (1911), capturing a Tuatha De Danann king with his (snow-white) fairy queen and entourage riding white stallions. This Tuatha De Danann Dragon king rides a white steed, sporting a golden face mask with a protruding horn, reflecting their history and imagery of antediluvian giant kings. The Tuatha De Danann were giant offspring both before and after the flood.[846] King/Kuningzam of "the legendary Tuadha D'Anu (tribe of Anu by a traditional, widely known derivation: 'people of the stars') or *daouine sidhe*

---

[842] *Catholic Encyclopedia*, Vol. 6, 243: heraldry.
[843] *Webster's*, 189: herald.
[844] *Encyclopedia Americana*, Vol. 14, 111: heraldry.
[845] Rebecca Parks, *U.X.L. Encyclopedia of World Mythology*, 1028: unicorn.
[846] Wayne, *The Genesis 6 Conspiracy*, 708–725, 842–857.

(meaning 'people of the powers')" was the source word for Arya-Sidhe. Dragon kings and queens were renowned as ancient Overlords and Elvin goddess-queens and god-kings.[847]

Aryans of the Media Magna empire, which preceded the beast Persian empire recorded in the book of Daniel, reared Nisaean white stallions which Herodotus stated were very large, swift, and renowned for their "pure whiteness," horses that surpassed those reared in India,[848] which was also populated by Aryans. Herodotus noted that Xerxes waged war accompanied by a riderless chariot named Jupiter/Zeus no mortal was permitted to ride in, which was pulled by eight Nisaean white horses of "unusual size." Xerxes followed in his chariot, also pulled by Nisaean horses.[849] Alexander's horse, Bucephalus, was black with a star representing his sponsoring god,[850] while Julius Caesar rode white and black horses. In Greek mythology the unicorn was a symbol of purity associated with the goddess Artemis, who rode a chariot drawn by eight unicorns.[851]

The western unicorn mythos further derives from several Greek historians who quoted Ctesias' fourth-century BC *Indica,* which described this mythical creature that thereafter surfaced in the English translation of the Greek Septuagint. *Indica* only survives today in fragments written down by Photios, a patriarch of Constantinople (AD 813–893); the tome documents India's recollections of unicorns: "Their head is of a dark red color, their eyes blue, and the rest of their body white. They have a horn on their forehead, a cubit in length. This horn for about two palm breadths upward from the base is of the purest white, where it tapers to a sharp point of a flaming crimson, and, in the middle, is black."[852]

The unicorn was the perfect Nephilim warrior steed: a DNA-altered antediluvian chimera beast, designed large enough to support its rider, and for battle. One deduces Nisaean horses were an early postdiluvian re-created counterpart. In medieval mythology, the unicorn was described in *Le Beastiare Divin de Guillaume Clerc de Normandie* as a large beast designed for battle: "The unicorn has but one horn in the middle of its forehead. It is the only animal that ventures to attack the

[847] De Vere, *The Dragon Legacy: The Secret History of an Ancient Bloodline,* 42.

[848] Talboys J Wheeler, *The Geography of Herodotus* (London: Longman, Brown, Green, and Longmans, 1854), 286, 288, citing Herodotus, *The Histories,* 7:40.

[849] Herodotus. *The Histories,* trans. George Rawlinson (Moscow, ID: Romans Road Media, 2013), 446, Book 7:40.

[850] Jude 1:13.

[851] Parks, *Encyclopedia of World Mythology,* 1028: unicorn.

[852] J.W. McCrindle, *Ancient India as Described by Ktesias the Knidian: A Translation Of His* "Indika," reprint (Calcutta: Thacker Spink & Co., 1881), 26.

elephant; and so sharp is the nail of its foot, that with one blow it can rip the belly out of that beast."[853]

Nisaean horses in the Middle Ages were popularized as the "great mare" by an unknown author in *The Grand and Priceless Chronicles of the Great and Enormous Giant Gargantua* (circa AD 1532). Seemingly, Francois Rabelais was inspired by *The Priceless Chronicles* and drafted or reimagined the Great Mare into his writings *Gargantua and Pantagruel: Five Books of the Lives, Heroic Deeds and Sayings of Gargantua And His Son Pantagruel* (c. 1537). Rabelais described Gargantua riding a hideous giant white horse whose "feet were cloven into fingers like of Julius Caesar's horse," and known as the "great mare" sent to Grangousier, Gargantua's giant father, from the African king of Numidia. The chimera beast possessed "slouching-hanging ears, like the goats of Languedoc, and a little horn." The horse had a light reddish-brown color with a mix of dappled gray spots, a terrifying tail that was long, heavy, and akin to a Scythian ram.[854]

If unicorns did exist before the flood, the beasts were not the cuddly, friendly animals of today's mystical fairy tale literature or the New Age reimagining of unicorns. Mystical Jewish legends indicate the unicorn was so large it was too big to go on the ark.[855] Unicorns were allegorized into magical beings in fairy tales who missed their opportunity to escape onto the ark because they were playing or otherwise disposed. If unicorns did exist, and certainly polytheism has kept the mythos alive for a purpose, then the chimera-like beast was not called to the ark because it was part of the violations against the laws of creation akin to the violations of giant creation. Just as the favored *nachash*/serpent of the seraphim were utilized by fallen angels, one deduces the unicorn, if it existed was a DNA designed or altered animal by Naphalim technology.

Unicorns were creations ridden by Nephilim demigod kings and by the goddess Artemis. As per New Age author and spiritualist Diana Cooper, unicorns lived before the flood in the "Golden Age" where the people created "Heaven on Earth."[856] The Golden Age is a reference to Atlantis, which was the antediluvian inspiration for Francis Bacon's end-time New Atlantis, and the New Age millennium. According to Cooper, "It [unicorn] told me that they were etheric beings, seventh-dimensional ascended horses, fully of the angelic realms. It said they had been present in Atlantis during the Golden Times.. .. But when the civilization of

---

[853] *The American Universal Encyclopedia: A Complete Library of Knowledge*, reprint (New York: S.W. Green's Sons Publishing, 1882), Vol. 2 491: bestiares.

[854] Francois Rabelais, *Gargantua And Pantagruel: Five Books Of The Lives, Heroic Deeds and Sayings Of Gargantua And His Son Pantagruel*, trans. Sir Thomas Urquhart and Peter Anthony Martteux (Derby, UK: Moray Press, 1894; Project Gutenberg e-book #1200, 2004, Kindle Edition), Book 1: XVIII, XXXIV, XXXVI.

[855] Diana Cooper, *The Wonder of Unicorns: Ascending with the Higher Angelic Realms* (Rochester, VT: Find Horse, a Division of Inner Traditions International Press, 2008; Kindle Edition, 2019), 208.

[856] Cooper, *The Wonders of Unicorns*, 163, 240.

Atlantis declined, the unicorns had to withdraw as they could not reach down to such a low level of frequency."[857]

What we do know scripturally is that God called all the (pure) animals[858] not corrupted by DNA manipulation or other creation violations by Nephilim and fallen angels. Note that at the time of the flood, the whole earth had become corrupt/*shachath,* meaning causatively to ruin, spoil, pervert, etc.[859] The corruption by inference included altered DNA of humans, animals, and the plant genomes. Conversely, the eight of Noah's family were pure in spirit and DNA, and the animals called to the ark to represent their kind/species had uncorrupted DNA.

The unicorn was remembered in many early postdiluvian civilizations before Europe such as Mesopotamia, India, China, Japan, and remembered as *qilin* and *kirin* in China and Japan respectively. The Chinese unicorn represented the death and birth of a great person, and was included among four magical and spiritual beings equivalent to the dragon, phoenix, and tortoise.[860] The Chinese unicorn was a "royal beast" associated with gods and kings.[861]

In the Middle Ages the unicorn evolved into the symbol of Christ,[862] but likely a polytheist or Aryan Christ, the dragon messiah. Further, the Christ consciousness concept surfaced in the west via Middle Ages gnostic moles within Christianity, and through royal masonic societies. The lion too is a heraldic symbol for the king of kings[863] in Gnosticism and of the royals, all the while noting gnostics believe "the unicorn represents Jesus Christ, who took on Him our nature in the virgin's womb was betrayed to the Jews and delivered into the hands of Pontius Pilate. Its one horn signifies the Gospel of Truth."[864] Thus the single horn is an allegory for Jesus in Gnosticism, mysticism, and Antichrist that employs an interpretive allegorical approach to reimagine the Bible and truth. In the words of author Diana Cooper: "In the West, our psychics and mystics have always seen unicorns as pure white ascended horses of light. Early Christian mystics understood that they embody the Christ consciousness or pure unconditional love and

---

[857] Cooper, *The Wonders of Unicorns,* 15.

[858] Gen 7:14–16.

[859] H7843—*shachath, shaw-khath':* to decay; causatively ruin; corrupt; spoiled; marred; perverted; rotted; decay; destroyed. Note in Gen 7:16: "him" does not have a corresponding Hebrew word. It is inserted two times, changing the meaning to Noah commanded the animals versus God. Gen 7:15: "And they went in unto Noah into the ark, two and two of all flesh, wherein is the breath of life. Gen 7:16: And they that went in, went in male and female of all flesh, as God had commanded [him]: and the LORD shut him in."

[860] Stephen Friar, *A New Dictionary of Heraldry* (New York: Harmony Books, 1987), 354; unicorn; Parks, *Encyclopedia of World Mythology,* 1027–28: unicorn.

[861] Ibid., 354: unicorn.

[862] Ibid., 353–54: unicorn.

[863] Ibid., 218; lion.

[864] *The American Universal Encyclopedia: A Complete Library of Knowledge,* Vol. 2 491: bestiares.

this became folklore. Unicorns form part of Christian mythology."[865] This is antichrist doctrine.

Polytheists believe some unicorns come from the angelic realm dwelling in the seventh dimension, the seventh heaven. Gnostics believe unicorns are aspects of the divine, in the same way angels are.[866] Unicorns in polytheist angelic dogma are heavenly beings, *Shamayim*. Cooper notes that unicorns receive instructions from seraphim and are the same rank in the angelic hierarchy as archangels,[867] and thus are Watchers. As such, the heavenly unicorn horn is an allegory of light representing the third eye, the chakra for enlightenment and wisdom in polytheism.[868] The occult unicorn is an allegory for the rebellious cherubim Watchers, who channel their enlightenment and wisdom through the third eye, the allegorical horn.

Cooper's fascination with the fallen *Shamayim* is reflective of Isaiah 34 where unicorns are grouped with fallen princes in the end times along with dragons (seraphim), owls (lilith), and satyrs (goat gods like Pan):

> Isa 34:7 And the unicorns shall come down with them, and the bullocks with the bulls; and their land shall be soaked with blood, and their dust made fat with fatness.

> Isa 34:8 For it is the day of the LORD's vengeance, and the year of recompences for the controversy of Zion.. ..

> Isa 34:12 They shall call the nobles thereof to the kingdom, but none shall be there, and all her princes shall be nothing.

> Isa 34:13 And thorns shall come up in her palaces, nettles and brambles in the fortresses thereof: and it shall be an habitation of dragons, and a court for owls.

> Isa 34:14 The wild beasts of the desert shall also meet with the wild beasts of the island, and the satyr shall cry to his fellow; the screech owl also shall rest there.

Biblically, unicorns did not ascend whether they were chimera-like creations, or if they were indeed offspring of angels, just as Nephilim and Rephaim demon spirits did not ascend. Unicorn spirits, if counterfeited from fallen cherubim, would merely roam as dispossessed demon spirts not permitted into heaven and not permitted to sleep. In my way of reckoning, the polytheist dogma of unicorns

---

[865] Cooper, *The Wonders of Unicorns, 107.*
[866] Ibid., 19.
[867] Ibid., 45.
[868] Ibid., 20, 55, 57, 61, 64, 87, 101, 118.

reflects the chimera-unicorn horses were created after the image or ideology of high-ranking cherubim associated with the counterfeit throne of Satan. Imagery of the unicorn drawn chariot of Artemis mirrors immortal horses, the four *Hippoi Athantoi* (likely unicorns) that drew the chariot of Zeus, and the immortal horses that drew the chariots of Helios, Poseidon, Ares, etc. Typically, the four horses of Zeus were wind gods disguised as horses, and thus some form of angel/god. Moreover, physical unicorn chimeras would have been highly prized among the Nephilim, Rephaim, and/or royals to pull their earthly chariots/thrones.

From a New Age perspective, Cooper described a similar accounting of unicorns as it related to eastern mysticism and the Lords of Karma, she equates with the powers: "One of the most wondrous sights is to see the Lords of Karma, who are of the angelic rank of Powers, cross the heavens as they perform their duties, surrounded by hundreds of unicorns. Powers vibrate at a frequency far beyond the archangels and are mighty lights."[869]

The four unicorns/horses powering Zeus's and Artemis's chariots are contrived counterfeits of God's throne depicted in Ezekiel's vision. The comparative of the four unicorn/horses in Greek mythology becomes clear when we understand that the four spirits contained power wheels/ *'owphan[nim]* filled with eyes[870] in Ezekiel 1 and 10 defined as wheel and or chariot,[871] and that Elijah witnessed horses and chariots of fire from heaven when he prayed to open the eyes of a young man.[872] Cherubim were renowned as protectors wielding a flaming sword commissioned to guard the gates into Eden.[873] Additionally, Ezekiel in his vision described four cherubim that pulled the chariot/throne.[874]

The cherub's name originated from Semitic words for "abundance of knowledge,"[875] reflecting their mindset of God as members of the First Hierarchy. Thus, in Buddhism, Hinduism, and Taoism, the unicorn's horn is the third eye of one of the seven chakras located in the spot of the horn that functions as allegorical antenna receiving information and instructions from the All-Seeing Eye or eyes of Satan's throne. Seemingly, all the details about the ophannim and cherubim of God's throne seen in Ezekiel's vision were counterfeited into polytheism and the thrones/chariots of the various gods pulled by unicorns/cherubs, as well as embedded into royal coats of arms. The lion, dragon, jackal, eagle, and unicorn represent the godfathers for Nephilim creatures, noting cherubim had

---

[869] Ibid., 20.
[870] Ezek 1:18; 10:12; Rev 4:6, 8.
[871] Ezek 10:9, 10. H212—*'owphan, o-fawn'*; or shortened *ophan, o-fawn'*: a wheel; chariot wheel.
[872] 2 Kings 6:17.
[873] Gen 3:25.
[874] Ps 18:10; Ezek 1:5.
[875] *Strong's Cyclopaedia*, Vol.2, 232: cherubim.

the face of a lion, an eagle, an ox/bull, and a man, while seraphim had the face of a serpent/dragon.

Knowing the unicorn connection to Nephilim and Rephaim horses, and to cherubim, makes sense as to why masonic editor Francis Bacon and masonic translators connected lions in Song 4:8 to the inserted unicorn for "wild ox" in Psalm 29:6 and 22:21 to capture the two most prominent heraldic imagery on the Stuart coat of arms, and their bloodline connections to Mount Sion/Hermon and Lebanus giants. It follows that the trilogy author of *Daemonologie* was acclaimed as the "Mighty Prince James," a king who asserted the "Divine Right to Rule" authorized from Mount Hermon/Sion.

> Son 4:8 Come with me from Lebanon, my spouse, with me from Lebanon: look from the top of Amana, from the top of Shenir and Hermon, from the lions 'dens, from the mountains of the leopards.
>
> Psa 29:6 He maketh them also to skip like a calf; Lebanon and Sirion like a young unicorn.
>
> Psa 22:21 Save me from the lion's mouth: for thou hast heard me from the horns of the unicorns.

The KJV has been used to swear oaths upon for testimony in courts, secret societies, governments, and coronation rituals for English kings and queens ever since. Queen Elizabeth, at her 1953 coronation, kissed the KJV Bible, swore an oath, and signed documents to govern the empire according to the law, uphold law and justice in her judgments, while preserving the "true profession of the Gospels" and the laws of God.[876] These are the ongoing Harem-Anathema oaths undertaken on earth led by the bloodline offspring of Rephaim, and sworn to fallen angels of Mount Hermon and Satan, not to God who warns against oaths.

Anticipate that unicorn markers embedded in the KJV will be part of the Antichrist pedigree and mythos as he ascends to power. One might further anticipate the mark of the beast will come with the Harem-Anathema of mutual imprecations, to carry it out even onto judgment from God. Anticipate that Antichrist will kidnap Palms 92:10 as part of his false messianic claim:

> Ps 92:10 But my horn shalt thou exalt like the horn of an unicorn: I shall be anointed with fresh oil.

Bashan and Mount Hermon will play prominently in the end-time universal religion, and with Antichrist who will negotiate the end-time covenant (Dan 9:27)

---

[876] https://www.royal.uk/coronation-oath-2-june-1953.

for the universal religion, which brings about the ten-king/horned empire and then Antichrist, the little horn.[877] Antichrist is the single-horned king who rises to power out of the ten-horned beast empire at the midpoint of last seven years. Unicorn will be another allegory for Antichrist and his bloodlines.

> Dan 7:8 I considered the horns, and, behold, there came up among them another little horn, before whom there were three of the first horns plucked up by the roots: and, behold, in this horn were eyes like the eyes of man, and a mouth
>
> Dan 7:21. .. and the same horn made war with the saints.. ..
>
> Dan 8:5. .. an he-goat came from the west on the face of the whole earth, and touched not the ground: and the goat had a notable horn between his eyes.. ..
>
> Dan 8:9 And out of one of them came forth a little horn, which waxed exceeding great, toward the south, and toward the east, and toward the pleasant land.

Horn/*Qeren* is defined as a horn of a beast, horn of an animal, and a musical instrument. *Qeren* in turn derives from another Hebrew word of the same spelling, defined as the same, and additionally as power, a peak of a mountain, or a captured hill thought to be Bashan as it translates into English in Isaiah 5:1.[878] Antichrist is prophesied to be the little horn, the unicorn from Mount Hermon, who will be given power by Satan the dragon.[879]

In polytheist traditions, the unicorn represents or is the Christ-consciousness.[880] Cooper juxtaposes this unicorn doctrine in her New Age interpretation of unicorn in the KJV:

> BIBLE: But my horn shalt thou exalt like the horn of a unicorn: I shall be anointed with fresh oil. Psalms xcii.10. MY TRANSLATION: You will exalt in the Enlightenment of Christ consciousness. Everything will appear fresh and new.
>
> BIBLE: His glory is like the firstling of his bullock, and his horns are like the horns of unicorns; with them he shall push the people together

---

[877] Rev 13:5.

[878] H7162—*qeren, keh'-ren*; Aramaic corresponding to 7161: a horn of an animal; a horn for sound as in trumpet or cornet; H7161—*qeren, keh'-ren*: a horn as projecting; by implication a flask for oil; a musical instrument; an elephant's tooth; ivory; a corner of the altar; peak of a mountain; figuratively, power; a hill; a place conquered by Israel in Bashan.

[879] Rev 13:2, 4.

[880] Cooper, *The Wonders of Unicorns*, 192, 199, 208.

to the ends of the earth; and they are the ten thousands of Ephraim, and they are the thousands of Manasseh. Deuteronomy xxxiii.17. MY TRANSLATION: His glory is like the new and innocent masculine force, with the Enlightenment of Christ consciousness and he shall gather people throughout the world.[881]

One should expect many rival and scioned unicorn bloodlines worldwide to position to become Antichrist, including those who claim to possess the King of Jerusalem title. Chinese legend recorded Genghis Khan received a unicorn vision before invading India—a vision that included the unicorn having his father's eyes.[882]

---

[881] Ibid., 199–201.
[882] Ibid., 196.

Section III:
The Hybrid Human Canaanite Confederacy

Gen 15:18 In the same day the LORD made a covenant with Abram, saying, Unto thy seed have I given this land, from the river of Egypt unto the great river, the river Euphrates:

Gen 15:19 The Kenites, and the Kenizzites, and the Kadmonites,

Gen 15:20 And the Hittites, and the Perizzites, and the Rephaims,

Gen 15:21 And the Amorites, and the Canaanites, and the Girgashites, and the Jebusites.

CHAPTER 22

NIMROD AND BABEL CITY

Gen 11:4 And they said, Go to, let us build us a city and a tower, whose top may reach unto heaven; and let us make us a name, lest we be scattered abroad upon the face of the whole earth.

The events recorded in Genesis 10–11 serve up a treasure trove of tidbits that expounds upon the early presence of postdiluvian giants, giants linked to the mercurial Nimrod and Babel city.

Babel city and Babel tower were constructed shortly after the flood to make "a name" for Noah's posterity, and to protect them from being scattered across the world.

Genesis 11:4 above is an odd text. Standard Christian dogma dictates that only Noah's posterity dwelled on the earth at that time. In the ancient world a city was constructed for protection; they were generally described as city-state fortresses with very large walls. "Built" in Genesis 11:4 is defined in Hebrew as to build or rebuild,[883] indicating Babel city was either built anew at that time or renovated from an antediluvian city to enclose and safeguard the tower project. City/`iyr* is defined as anguish, terror, and place guarded by a waking watch. `Iyr derives from `*uwr*, meaning to wake, watch, and incite—the same word Watcher/`*Iyr,* derives

---

[883] H1129—*banah, baw-naw*: to build; begin to build; obtain children; make; repair; set up.

from.[884] One muses whether fortress city-states originated with the fallen Watchers and/or Azazel before the flood as part of the arts of war taught to Nephilim.[885]

The Noahite actions directly contradicted God's command for Noah and his sons to multiply and replenish the earth, and seemingly an antichrist doctrine to remain gathered. Moreover, "make us a name" is translated from *shem* meaning a mark, memorial, name, and reputation,[886] just as "renown" in the men of renown, Nephilim in Genesis 6:4, derives equally from *shem* and *shamayim*.[887] The Noahites collectively decided to build Babel city and tower so as not to be scattered. The inference is that the Noahites decided to huddle together behind walls for protection and because of fear.

> Gen 9:1 And God blessed Noah and his sons, and said unto them, Be fruitful, and multiply, and replenish the earth.

The original Hebrew text's details indicate that the city-state fortress was a defensive maneuver. So, who were the Noahites so afraid of? To whom was the message of "make us a name" addressed to? One suspects Nephilim and/or Rephaim were the motivation. Scripture does not directly indicate giant involvement, but one might deduce giants were the source to the terror driven decision provided for building Babel city.

Scripture indicates Nimrod, son of Cush, was the warrior leader of the Noahites who built or renovated Babel city. He was a described as a mighty hunter who began to be a "mighty one" in the earth. "Mighty" is used four times to describe Nimrod to underscore his possible size, his strength, his warrior prowess, his political power, and his political agenda. Mighty/*gibbowr* is defined as powerful, strong, warrior, tyrant, chief, and sometimes a giant, just as "giant" is translated from *gibbowr* in Job 16:14 and noting Genesis 6:4 described Nephilim as gibborim.

> Gen 10:8 And Cush begat Nimrod: he began to be a mighty one in the earth.

> Gen 10:9 He was a mighty hunter before the LORD: wherefore it is said, Even as Nimrod the mighty hunter before the LORD.

---

[884] H5892—`*iyr, eer*; from 5782: anguish; of terror; city; town; a place of waking or guarded; H5894—`*iyr, eer*; from 5782; a watcher angel; waking; watchful; wakeful one; H5782—`*uwr, oor*: to wake; awaken; raise up; stir up; incite.

[885] Enoch 8:1.

[886] H8034—*shem*.

[887] H8064—*shamayim, shaw-mah'-yim*.

The Nephilim were understood to be demigods, defined as children of the angels, and as progeny of gods in polytheism, the great heroes.[888] "Spurious" is defined as illegitimate, bastard, not genuine, forged, counterfeit, and essentially different.[889] Hebraic thought contends that the human and the divine ought not to be confused; otherwise, the entire structure of the physical world is violated.[890] *Unger's Bible Dictionary* described this violation: "Nephilim are considered by many to be giant demigods, the unnatural offspring of 'daughters of men' in cohabitation with the 'sons of God' (angels). This utterly unnatural union violating God's creative order of being, was of such shocking abnormality as to necessitate the worldwide judgment of the flood."[891] Accordingly, First Enoch documented that fallen angels transgressed God's Word, the law of heaven, when they copulated with mortal women:

> Enoch 107:13–14, 17, 15. .. some of the angels of heaven transgressed the word of the Lord. And behold they commit sin and transgress the law and have united themselves with women and commit sin with them, and have married some of them, and have begot children by them. (17) And they shall produce on the earth giants not according to the spirit, but according to the flesh, and there shall be a great punishment on the earth, and the earth shall be cleansed from all impurity. (15) Yea, there shall come a great destruction over the whole earth, and there shall be a deluge and a great destruction for one year.

On the other hand, Cush was the father for Nimrod, thereby disqualifying Nimrod as Nephilim in the traditional sense, but this does not necessarily disqualify Nimrod as gibborim. The distinction is simply this: Nephilim can be accurately called gibborim, and gibborim can be Nephilim, Rephaim, angels, and humans, but humans cannot be accurately defined as Nephilim and Rephaim. One deduces then that Nimrod behaved very much like a giant with his physical talents, and in his reign of terror. As such, Scripture did not state Nimrod was Nephilim or Rephaim, but gibborim, because he was the human son of Cush. As such, Nimrod "began" to be a mighty one—yet another obscure statement in the manner it was translated from Hebrew. Began/*chalal* means to break your word or vow, dissolve, open a wedge, pollute, violate, defile ritually, and defile sexually.[892] It follows that Nimrod broke a vow dissolving his leadership covenant with God,

---

[888] *Unger's*, 106: demigod.
[889] *Webster's*, 392: spurious.
[890] Porter, *The New Illustrated Companion to the Bible*, 2003, 26.
[891] *Unger's*, 916: Nephilim.
[892] H2490—*chalal, khaw-lal'*: to dissolve; break one 's word or vow; to profane; defile; pollute; violate; dishonour ritually and sexually; to begin to wound or pierce; play a flute.

whereby Nimrod somehow began/became a "mighty one." *Chalal* derives from *chalah*, meaning to become weak, sick, afflicted or to fall.[893] The inference intended with "began" seems to indicate something changed spiritually and/or physically with Nimrod. Something led him away from following God, likely through his imposed Babel religion and the oaths he swore thereof. Nimrod fell from grace akin to the Naphalim and the Nephilim of renown/infamy.

Nimrod's name as the first king at Babel, pronounced Nim-a-rode, was of foreign origin, and thought to mean rebellion or valiant.[894] Nimrod may be more of a title than a name. Rebel and rebellion in Hebrew derive from the word *marah*[895]; the "ah" suffix is the female plural expressing the application of Nimrod's strength, akin to gibborah the female format of gibborim.[896] Accordingly, some historians conclude Nimrod's name derived from Ninmarradah, Lord of Marad of Kish in antediluvian Sumer/Shinar. Chaldean emperors adopted the Ninmarradah title meaning "Kings of the World" from their antediluvian counterparts.[897] Tell Nimrud near Bagdad is thought to bear witness to the veracity of Nimrod as a historical figure.

Josephus' recollection of Nimrod, like Scripture, did not reflect Nimrod was Nephilim or Rephaim. Josephus' writings reflected the ancient Jewish perspective that Noahites migrated from Mount Ararat to Shinar, where Nimrod usurped control as king. Nimrod provoked Noahites to defy God's commandments to build colonies abroad for fear of being easily oppressed after they divided.[898] Josephus' accounting clearly indicates Noahites were anguished with fear and terror by unnamed oppressors, when there ought not to have been an enemy.

> He [Nimrod] was the grandson of Ham, the son of Noah, a bold man, and of great strength of hand. He persuaded them not to ascribe it to God, as if it was through his means they were happy, but to believe that it was their own courage which procured that happiness. He also gradually changed the government into tyranny, seeing no other way of turning men from the fear of God, but to bring them into a constant dependence on his power.[899]

Nimrod, from the Jewish perspective, was gibborim but not Nephilim or Rephaim. As king, Nimrod dictated that following God was cowardice. According

---

[893] H2470—*chalah, khaw-law'*: become weak; sick; afflicted; fall; wounded.
[894] H5248—*Nimrowd, nim-rode'*: of foreign origin; pronounced: nimarode', meaning rebellion or valiant.
[895] H4784—*marah, maw-raw'*: to rebel; make bitter; be disobedient; to provoke.
[896] H1369—*gbuwrah, gheb-oo-raw'*.
[897] *Unger's,* 924, quoting W. F. Albright in *O.T. Commentary,* 1948, 138.
[898] Whiston and Maier, *Antiquities,* Book 1 4:1–2.
[899] Ibid., Book 1:4:2.

to Josephus, Nimrod commanded a tower be built to represent their rebellion from God,[900] a tower protected within a city-state fortress to signal to the unnamed oppressors their allegiance to a pantheon of gods. The fortress city further signaled to the oppressors that Noahites were a united people determined to fight against their oppressors. Nimrod thereafter established his reputation as a mighty warrior and mighty one before God, fighting the oppressors. The oppressors seem to have been the notorious race of Rephaim, whom *Unger's* accounted as an old and Aboriginal [postdiluvian] race of giants.[901]

The Septuagint supports the supposition that Nimrod/Nebrod established his reputation battling giants. The Septuagint, by inference, established giants roamed the earth before Babel, and thus within a hundred years after the flood.[902] It follows that Noahites submitted to Nimrod's tyranny and polytheist religion in exchange for protection from an unnamed race that struck terror into their hearts, the roving Aboriginal Rephaim tribes. Building the fortress of Babel sent a message to the giants that Nimrod was in charge and would protect the Noahites. Building Babel tower sent a message to God that Nimrod would protect the Noahites, not God, and that Noahites would thereafter worship the pantheon of gods that produced the Rephaim. One deduces the Rephaim terrified the Noahites in the same manner as the giants terrified Israelites after escaping Egypt.[903]

Orientalist writers, Armenian legends, and other mythology recorded Nimrod as a giant, ten to twelve cubits high[904] (15–18' and 19–21' tall[905]), but masonic critics labeled this an exaggeration, concluding Nimrod was of great physical stature but was not Nephilim.[906] Similarly, Hebrew legends noted Nimrod boasted unconquerable strength; that Nimrod was the greatest of hunters; that he set himself up as God on a throne[907] in typical antichrist fashion. Nimrod's naturally born human dimensions could not have been the dimensions noted in legends. If Nimrod was born a hybrid human via a Rephaim mother, he would have been seven to nine feet tall akin to the *Shasu* hybrids documented by Egyptians.[908] Scripture

---

[900] Ibid., Book 1:4:3.

[901] *Unger's*, 1074: Rephaim.

[902] Septuagint, Gen 10:8–9.

[903] Num 13:31–33; 14:1–10.

[904] Collins, *From the Ashes of Angels*, 206, quoting from *The History of the Armenians*.

[905] Ginzberg, *Legends of the Bible*, 83–85. A common cubit was 18" while a royal cubit was 21"; Nimrod was a king and would have been measured with a royal cubit. Josephus, *Ant.*, Book 1, 3:2: "That he should make an ark of four stories high, three hundred cubits." Note 13: "A cubit is about 21 English inches."

[906] Mackey, *The History of Freemasonry*, 64, *The Legend of Nimrod*; 54, *The Tower of Babel*.

[907] Ginzberg, *Legends of the Bible*, 83–85.

[908] William Rickets Cooper, *An Archaic Dictionary, Biographical, Historical, and Mythological: From the Egyptian, Assyrian, and Etruscan Monuments and Papyri*, 517.

does not support Nimrod's mother being Rephaim or angelic; nor were Rephaim or angels documented dwelling among the Noahites before Babel.

Masonic historical accounts derive from their sacred oral history, renowned in the Craft as the Polychronicon,[909] which teems with Nimrod anecdotes. *The Cook Poem* and *The Tower of Babel* recorded Nimrod as a mighty man, strong like a giant.[910] *The Legend of Nimrod* and *The Legend of the Craft* recorded Nimrod as a mighty leader.[911] *The History of Freemasonry* further noted that a nineteenth-century "learned scholar," George Smith, identified Nimrod with a Babylonian king "to whom he gave the provisional name of Izdubar" from fragments of twelve cuneiform tablets he discovered. The inscriptions thereof presented Izdubar as a "mighty leader," a man of great prowess in war and hunting, and who by his ability and valor united minor kingdoms throughout the Euphrates valley.[912] Izdubar was depicted in the identical manner as Gilgamesh: a giant with long, black curly hair, a thick black beard, clutching a snake in his right hand, and strangling a lion under his arm while grasping its paw, on the Khorsabad Sculpture.[913]

Izdubar was described as a "the mighty giant" who was "like a bull tower over the chiefs." In the twelve tablets of *The Legends of Izdubar*, [914] whom George Smith and A. H. Sayce stated Izdubar was strong, a giant, a hunter, and a warrior king who established the first empire of ancient Babylonia.[915] Izdubar's empire was centered in Erech/Uruk, an empire that stretched from the Persian Gulf to Armenia. Although both Smith and Sayce identified Izdubar as the biblical Nimrod,[916] the dating of the Babylonian/Akkadian tablets indicates 2000 BC or just before, using secular dating,[917] and which is more akin to the dating of The *Epic of Gilgamesh* and its twelve tablets. Gilgamesh was sixth generation in secular dynastic chronology, versus Nimrod ruling in the third generation. Izdubar was Gilgamesh, not Nimrod, even though Nimrod did gain his reputation fighting Elamite/Aryan giants just as Izdubar/Gilgamesh did three generations later with Elamite giant kings[918] like Humbaba/Habada. Further, Smith noted Izdubar was always represented with thick black curly hair and a matching beard, and was distinct from the

[909] Mackey, *The History of Freemasonry*, 64, *The Legend of Nimrod*.

[910] Ibid., 53–62, *Tower of Babel*.

[911] Ibid., 63–66, *Legend of Nimrod;* 18–24, *Legend of the Craft*.

[912] Ibid., 63–66, *Legend of Nimrod,* citing Smith, *Chaldean Account of Genesis,* 174.

[913] Smith, George, *The Chaldean Account of Genesis* (New York: Charles Scribner's Sons; e-book Edition by Project Gutenberg, 2019), Introduction, v.

[914] Ibid., *The Legends of Izdubar,* 133, 158, 160: Tablet 3, Col. IV, lines 37, 38, 44, 45. Smi, *Chaldean Account of Genesis,* rev. ed. by A. H. Sayce, 12:212: Tablet 3, Vol. IV lines 37, 38, 44, 45.

[915] Smith, *Chaldean Account of Genesis,* 131, 160; Smith, *Chaldean Account of Genesis,* rev. ed., 12:214.

[916] Smith, *Chaldean Account of Genesis,* 136, 137, 141, 142, 147, 160; Smith, *Chaldean Account of Genesis,* rev. ed., 2:22,11:176, 190.

[917] Smith, *Chaldean Account of Genesis,* 19; Smith, *Chaldean Account of Genesis,* rev. ed., 2:22.

[918] Smith, *Chaldean Account of Genesis,* 251.

typical Babylonian depictions,[919] but identical to Gilgamesh's depictions that seem to have been conflated with Nimrod in the secular mythos.

Izdubar reigned in Uruk/Erech as did Gilgamesh, but neither were accredited with founding Uruk as Nimrod was accredited, which further dates both Gilgamesh and Izdubar to about three generations later. In fact, *The Legends of Izdubar* recorded identical narratives and heroes recorded in *The Epic of Gilgamesh* that included the flood, the searching out of the Mesopotamian Noah, Xishthus/Ziusudra (Utnapishtim in *The Epic of Gilgamesh*), and King Humbaba of the Cedar Forest.[920] *The Larsa List* of Sumerian kings "listed Ziusudra as the last of those kings that reigned before the flood."[921] Knowing this makes sense of later Semitic-speaking Akkadians led by Sargon, a Rephaim, who eventually overthrew the Enmerakar/Nimrod-founded Sumerian dynasty at Uruk that Gilgamesh/Izdubar reigned over afterward.

Secular historians like Smith and Sayce were likely influenced by the Septuagint's translation of *gibbowr* into Greek as giant/γίγας,[922] when they conflated Nimrod with Izdubar and Gilgamesh. Likewise the Septuagint translators were biased in their interpretive translation of Nimrod, equating him with the giant heroes of Greek history.

> *Sept* Gen 10:8–9 And Chus begot Nebrod: He was a giant hunter before the Lord God; therefore they say, As Nebrod the giant hunter before the Lord.

Just as masonic history intersects with Scripture regarding Nimrod, so does Peleg, son of Eber of the Shem lineage. Peleg was born 101 years after the flood.[923] *Unger's Bible Dictionary* defined Peleg as division, thus Peleg likely marks the generation when Noah's posterity was scattered from Babel city.[924] *Strong's Dictionary* states Peleg's name means "earthquake" and "division." Both definitions fit with Babel's destruction.[925] Josephus documented that Phaleg/Peleg was born at the time Noahites were scattered into their countries, noting "Phaleg among the Hebrews signifies division."[926] Masonic records concur that the Peleg generation begat Babel city and tower construction, stating that building began 101 years after

---

[919] Ibid., 149.

[920] Ibid, 13, 14, 251.

[921] Wayne, *The Genesis 6 Conspiracy*, 150, citing Knight and Lomas, *The Hiram Key*, 114–115.

[922] Lancelot C. L. Brenton, *Delphi Septuagint*, Complete Greek and English Edition, Gen 10:8–9.

[923] Gen 11:10–12: Arphaxad was born two years after the flood, Shelah thirty-five years later, Eber thirty years after that, and Peleg thirty-four years after Eber: 101 years.

[924] *Unger's*, 982: Peleg; H6389—*Peleg, peh'-leg*.

[925] H6389—*Peleg, peh'-leg*.

[926] Whiston and Mair, *Josephus*, Ant. 1:6:4.

the flood, and continued for fifty-three years before the project was stopped. Babel was the origin to postdiluvian masonry, led by Nimrod as its first Grand Master.[927]

> ... he [Nimrod/Nembrothe or Cam/Cham/Ham] he gan the towre of babilon, and he taught to his werkemen the craft of mesurie [geometry/masonry], and he had with him mony masonys mo than XL. thousand and he louyd [loved] and chereshed them well, and hit is wryten in the Polyconicon and the master of stories. [928]

Scripture does not furnish the source to where or how Nimrod discovered the knowledge to build Babel city and tower. That kind of knowledge was not stated to be on the ark, nor would Noah have any part in teaching Nimrod knowledge or skills to beget rebellion against God. Noah lived for 350 years after the flood,[929] so one deduces Noah was present at the rebellion. One muses if the antediluvian knowledge caused Nimrod's falling away from God, or abetted Nimrod's enhanced strength and size that would explain how Nimrod began to be *gibbowr*.

One deduces Nimrod violated (*chalal*) his leadership covenant to impose polytheist Enochian mysticism upon the people of Babel, and later partook in intermarriage and sexual rituals (*chalal*) with the Rephaim that produced Mesopotamian hybrid human dynasties allied with fertility challenged Rephaim dynasties. The Rephaim/Anunnaki whom Nimrod intermarried with were the Elamites, accredited with overrunning Sumer/Shinar/Chaldea shortly after 2450 BC.[930] The hybrid dynasties, like that of Nimrod's Erech/Uruk, and succeeded by Sargon, Lugalbanda, and Gilgamesh, kept a genealogical mythos that in part linked them back to Enmerakar/Nimrod. As such, Scripture did not document Nimrod's progeny in the table of nations, or elsewhere.

The *Legend of the Craft* recounts Hermaynes/Hermes found the two Pillars of Lamech from the antediluvian Cain lineage, which led to the storehouse of nine vaults of knowledge written by Enoch, son of Cain. The vaults contained the fully developed antediluvian Seven Sacred Sciences that merged with the forbidden knowledge provided by the Naphalim. The vaults further contained Enoch's mystical angelic worshipping religion. Both the knowledge and religion were imposed upon Noahites to build Babel city and tower,[931] and again at Erech/Uruk,[932] Accad, and Calneh in Shinar/Sumer, and Babel (Gen 10:10).

---

[927] Mackey, *History of Freemasonry,* The Tower of Babel, 54–62.

[928] Ibid., 54–62: quoting the Cooke Manuscript (1490 AD) and quoting the *Polychronicon,* meaning "Universal History," notes 2, 3 & 4.

[929] Gen 9:28.

[930] Smith, *The Chaldean Account of Genesis,* 146-147.

[931] Mackey, *History of Freemasonry,* 20, *Legend of the Craft*; 398, *The Legend of Enoch.*

[932] *Unger's,* 371; *Nelson's,* 412, Erech.

In *The Genesis 6 Conspiracy*, I revealed Nimrod's hybrid royal bloodlines and their importance.[933] Nimrod spawned the first postdiluvian pharaonic dynasty of Egypt[934] after uprooting and replacing the existing Hamite king with Nimrod's son or grandson, depending on the account one references. This fantastic claim was supported by the *Targum*, a collection of the Old Testament translations into Aramaic which added commentary and details by Rabbis, to aid in interpreting and understanding key texts. The *Targum-Jonathan* stated Nimrod was the father of a pharaoh, even though no name was provided.[935] David Rohl named this pharaoh as Aha who is associated with Menes,[936] the founder of the Egyptian pharaonic title of kingship after the deluge. Aha is known as "Hor-Aha" and Manetho's "Athothis," the successor of Narmer or Menes.[937] Another Ethiopian text on the Old Testament named this pharaoh son of Nimrod as Yanuf, known elsewhere as Anedjib.[938] Further, Gardner alternatively suggested Raneb as this pharaoh of the Second Dynasty.[939] Gods and kings of prehistory held many names and titles in the nations they governed, and as they were documented in surrounding nations, which mars the accuracy of secular chronology through double accountings of the same kings or dynastic reigns.

The zodiacal sign of the goat was first introduced to the postdiluvian Egyptians by Nimrod's grandson Pharaoh Raneb, circa 2800 BC utilizing secular dating, in the ancient city of Mendes. Egypt was the land of Ham/*Chem*,[940] known in Coptic as *Chame* and *Chemi* meaning "black" and transliterated as Kem and Khem.[941] Egypt was the second pillar of postdiluvian mysticism after Babel. "Azazel is the Khem of Mendes in Alchemy and Rosicrucianism. Khem, like Azazel, was the source of illicit knowledge. Azazel is the Goat of Mendes, in the same spirit as Ham, where the Goat of Mendes was upheld as the symbolic representation of Ham's title 'The Archon of the Tenth Age of Capricorn.'" All this directly relates back to Satan, who owns the zodiacal image of Capricornus, the leaping goat, and whose attribute is liberty (from God). The goat, according to Gerald Massey, author of *Ancient Egypt and the Light of the World*, is renowned as the zodiacal sign of Mendes in the Egyptian zodiac.[942]

---

[933] Wayne, The *Genesis 6 Conspiracy*, 623–628.

[934] Gardner, *Genesis of the Grail Kings*, 213.

[935] Ibid., 216, citing Genesis in the *Targum-Jonathan* section 16: "Gen 16:5: 'so that we will not need the children of Hagar, the daughter of Pharaoh, the son of Nimrod who threw you into the furnace of fire.'"

[936] Rohl, *The Lost Testament*, 102.

[937] Susan Wise Bauer, *The History of the Ancient World from the Earliest Accounts to the Fall of Rome* (New York: W. W. Norton & Company, Inc., 2007), 61, 62, notes.

[938] Gardner, *Genesis of the Grail Kings*, 216–217.

[939] Gardner, *Realm of the Ring Lords*, 242.

[940] Ps 105:23, 27.

[941] *Strong's Cyclopaedia*, Vol. 3, 75: Egypt.

[942] Wayne, *The Genesis 6 Conspiracy*, 685, citing Blake and Blezard, The *Arcadian Cypher*, 61.

CHAPTER 23

THE ANAKIM AND PATRIARCH- LESS NATIONS

Gen 10:20 These are the sons of Ham, after their families, after their tongues, in their countries, and in their nations.

At the time of Babel and confusion of languages,[943] the seventy eponymously named Noahite nations were established, along with their patriarchs, as documented in the table of nations.[944] Standard Christian dogma asserts Canaan, Heth, and Sidon were the patriarchs for the other nine Canaanite nations, but the Bible does not state this in the table of nations or elsewhere.

The accounting of the seventy eponymic nations entrenched [945] in the table of nations (Gen 10; 1 Chron 1) did not include Nephilim or Rephaim nations; nor did the table of nations name Rephaim patriarchs for hybrid human nations. Knowing this begins to explain the nine patriarch-less Canaanite clans documented as such in the table of nations.

---

[943] Gen 11:1–9.
[944] Gen 10:1–32; 1 Chron 1–54.
[945] Deut 32:7–9.

Accordingly, Rephaim patriarchs like Rapha were not listed in the table of nations, but without explanation appear in Scripture. Goliath, for example was included among five giants of Gath: Ishbibenob, Saph/Sippai, Lahmi, and an unnamed six-fingered and six-toed giant of great stature.[946] All five giants were sons of one giant in Gath, while underscoring giant in these passages were translated from from *rapha'* meaning tall, giant, and the same as *rapha'*, meaning to heal as in an invigorating giant.[947] The text in the KJV is not clear as to whether one should read *rapha'* as generic for a giant or that this *rapha* was a patronymically classified from one of his ancestors beginning with the first Rapha patriarch of the Rephaim, or both. Scholars split on whether Rapha was the name of Goliath's father, whether Rapha was the Rephaim patriarch, or whether *rapha'* was generic for giant(s).

Nevertheless, the Ishbibenob narrative indicates Rapha, at a minimum, was a giant name passed down patronymically through the generations. In many English translations Ishbibenob, Saph, Lahmi, and the six-digited giant were stated to be "one of the descendants of the Rapha" or "among the descendants of the giant." The KJV translated these passages as "one of the children/descendants the giant(s)," "of the sons of the giant," or "born to the giant."[948] *Strong's Dictionary* accounts Ishbibenob as: a son of Rapha, and one of the Philistine giants in the time of David.[949] Thus, one can view Ishbibenob, Goliath, and the other three giants as descendants of the patriarch Rapha of the Rephaim, the son of a giant patronymically named Rapha, or both.

Some scholars conclude Rapha was one of the gods of the underworld,[950] and perhaps the angelic patronymic name for Rapha. In cabalistic astrology Raphael was the angel of the sun,[951] and seemingly distinct from Raphael in Enochian apocrypha and the apocrypha of the original KJV. Raphael is additionally thought to derive from a Chaldean tradition,[952] seemingly adopted into cabalistic traditions during the Judean exile in Babylon. The cabalistic Raphael mythos indicates he was a (counterfeit) "healer of the earth" equivalent to Asclepius, the Greek god

---

[946] 2 Sam 21:16–22; 1 Chron 20:4– 8.

[947] H7498—*Rapha', raw-faw'*; or *Raphah, raw-faw'*; Rapha; giant: tall.

[948] 2 Sam 21:15–16. H7497—*rapha'*. English translations of 2 Sam 21:16's "of the sons of the giant" as "descendants pf Rapha": NIV, BSB, NB, NHEB; as "descendants/children of the giants": NLT, ESV, NASB, CSB, HCSB, ISV, YLT.

[949] H3430—*Yishbow b-Nob, yish-bo'beh-nobe*: his dwelling is in Nob; son of Rapha, one of the Philistine giants.

[950] Theresa Bane, *The Encyclopedia of Giants and Humanoids in Myth, Legend, and Folklore* (Jefferson, NC: McFarland and Company, 2016), 140: Rapha, citing Mandel, *Who's Who in the Jewish Bible*, 331; Ward, *Homiletic Review*, Vol. 26, 559.

[951] Cooper, *An Archaic Dictionary*, 462: Raphael.

[952] Gustav Davidson, *A Dictionary of Angels, including the Fallen Angels* (New York: The Free Press, 1967), 240: Raphael.

of healing, medicine, science, and knowledge. According to the fifteenth-century occultist Trithemius of Sphaneim, the occult Raphael will be involved in the end times. It follows that the occult Raphael—the underworld guide, and likely Rapiuel, Rapiel, or Raphiel (names for Baal)—was the Ugarit godfather of the Rapiu. Raphael/Rapiuel was depicted on an Ophite diagram as a beast like daemon, but this is likely his offspring Rapha also defined as daemon.[953]

Moreover, Josephus identified Ishbibenob as "Achmon, the son of Araph," as "one of the sons of the giants."[954] `Araph` in Hebrew means to destroy, neck, and to cut off the neck as in behead. Both the Rephaim king Og and the Anak branch of Rephaim are connected to neck and long neck in their respective meanings.[955] `Araph`, by virtue of its last syllable, is seemingly connected patronymically to Rapha, the likely patriarch for Rephaim nation. One further ponders `araph`'s decapitation connection that was the ancient standard to ensure proof of death for giants. The Sumerian *Stela of Eannatum* (2450 BC, using secular chronology) portrayed a defeated army whose heads were severed to ensure they no longer posed a threat,[956] that they were indeed dead and could not self-heal as Rephaim were thought to do. As such, the Assyrian king Ashurnasirpal II proudly boasted, "I felled 800 of their combat troops with the sword (and) cut off their heads."

In ancient Egypt, the most abhorrent fate that could befall an Egyptian royal was decapitation, because it abnormally affected the promises of afterlife as documented in their ancient texts. Decapitation of royals represented something akin to the second death that terminated their aspirations in the afterlife, and which condemned the slain to some form of oblivion; perhaps the abyss prison. Beheading was so "grisly and ideologically reprehensible" to royals that it was reserved for only the king's enemies, rebels, and foreigners.[957]

Biblically, we learn of beheading in the time of Joseph at Pharaoh's court, indicating this was a well-established practice by that time, from ancient times.[958] Beheading was an accepted way to kill warriors, Nephilim and Rephaim, just as in David decapitated Goliath.[959] The Hebrew source word for giant and demon spirit is *rapha'* meaning healer, which was demonstrated with all three applications with

[953] Ibid.
[954] Whiston, *Josephus*, Ant. 7:12:1.
[955] H6202—`araph, aw-raf`: to break the neck; to destroy; beheaded; break down; break; cut off; strike off the neck; H6061—`Anaq: neck; H5747—*Owg*: long-necked.
[956] Joel M. LeMon, "Beheading in the Ancient World," Bible Odyssey 2021, https://www.bibleodyssey.org/passages/related-articles/beheading-in-the-ancient-world.
[957] Nicholas S. Picardo, "'Semantic Homicide' and the So-called Reserve Heads: The Theme of Decapitation in Egyptian Funerary Religion and Some Implications for the Old Kingdom," *Journal of the American Research Center in Egypt*, 2007, Vol. 43, 221–226. https://www.jstor.org/stable/pdf/27801614?refreqid=fastly-default%3Ac1da51261ce769fa5b075877de83df56.
[958] Gen 40:19–20. *Unger's*, 1053: punishment.
[959] 1 Sam 15:33; 17:51; 31:9.

the Rapiu of the *Ugaritic Texts*. Royals in pre-Christian history were renowned for their healing capabilities, titled "Repha'im or Rapha'Elohim."[960]

Following a similar kind of scriptural genealogical eponymous pattern, Arba, the patriarch for the Anakim and a kin to Rapha, was not listed in the table of nations. The patrial named city of Arba, Kiriatharba, later changed to Hebron, was home to three Anakim kings: Sheshai, Ahiman, and Talmai—the children of Anak.[961] The patriarch Arba is defined as fourth.[962] One deduces from Arba's definition he was perhaps fourth among the Anakim dwelling at Kiriatharba, meaning the city of Arba or the city of four.[963] One could further define Arba as fourth among a number of originating Rephaim created after the flood that included Rapha. Or perhaps Arba was Rapha's fourth son. Often overlooked historical records detailing patrial named cities and places may contain additional Rephaim names.

> Josh 14:15 And the name of Hebron before was Kirjatharba; which Arba was a great man among the Anakims.
>
> Josh 15:13. .. even the city of Arba the father of Anak, which city is Hebron.

Anakim were not Canaanites. Anakim were described by *Strong's Dictionary* as long-necked giants dwelling in Canaan.[964] Other sources describe Anakim as a "species of giants": "These fierce wild beings were prone to acts of violence and considered war and warfare to be a normal way of life. When there was no enemy to fight, they would wage war on one another. The Anakim were described as have being pale skinned, having golden hair, lightly bearded, wore striped cloaks, upon their necks wore toques."[965] Knowing this, it makes sense that Talmai, a son of Anak, was depicted on a wall in the tomb of Pharaoh Oimenepthah I as tall and fair-skinned.[966]

---

[960] De Vere, *The Dragon Legacy*, 42.

[961] Gen 23:2; 35:27; Josh 14:15; 15:13–14, 54, 20:7; 21:11; Judg 1:10, Neh 11:25.

[962] H704—*'Arba`, ar-bah'*; Arba, one of the Anakim; fourth.

[963] H7151—*qiryah, kir-yaw'*: a city: —city; building a city; town.

[964] H6061—*`Anaq*: long-necked; progenitor of a family; tribe of the giant people in Canaan; H6062—*`Anaqiy*; patronymically from 6061: long-necked; an Anakite; descendant of Anak; a tribe of giants.

[965] Bane, *Encyclopedia of Giants and Humanoids in Myth, Legend, and Folklore*, 28: Anakim, citing Deloach, *Giants*, 47, 57; Henstenberg, *Dissertations on the Genuineness of the Pentateuch*, Vol. 2, 153, 195; Taylor, *Calmets Great Dictionary of the Holy Bible:* Anakim.

[966] Ibid., 154: Talmai, citing Deloach, *Giants*, 278; Taylor, *Calmets Great Dictionary of the Holy Bible:* Talmai.

Sheshai was stated by some to be six cubits tall (9'–10'6," likely the latter as Sheshai was a king measured with a royal of twenty-one inches).[967] Moreover, Josephus' description of the Anakim of Kiriatharba leaves no doubt to their angelic human hybrid nature as understood by Judeans: "For which reason they removed their camp to Hebron; and when they had taken it, they slew all the inhabitants. There were till then left the race of giants, who had bodies so large, and countenances so entirely different from other men, that they were surprising to the sight, and terrible to the hearing. The bones of these men are still shown to this very day, unlike to any credible relations of other men."[968]

Accordingly, the "sons/children of 'Anak'" phrase[969] has a larger meaning than just the three kings listed in Numbers 13:28. The three or four Anakim kings were not the remnant of the Anakim, but part of a larger Anakim tribe spread across a wide slice of Middle East. Anak is defined as a progenitor/patriarch of a family or tribe of Anakim giants in Canaan—a fierce people great and tall, renowned for their warriorcraft.[970] Joshua described Anakim cities as great high-walled fortress city-states. Fenced/*batsar* in this application means fortified with high strong walls,[971] the great walled cities described Numbers 13:28 by Moses's scouts.

> Josh 14:12 Now therefore give me this mountain, whereof the LORD spake in that day; for thou heardest in that day how the Anakims were there, and that the cities were great and fenced.

Polytheist sources believe the Anakim alternatively spelled Anukim were children of Anu, the Sumerian parent god. Anukim were the "people of the stars," the Tuatha D'Anu[972] (tribe of the Anu god) and more populously known as the Tuatha De Danann. The people of the stars are understood as the children of the gods, the heavenly ones, the Naphalim of the Shamayim. Polytheist sources further believe the Anukim/Anakim were a race of ancestral kings that originated in Scythia,[973] where polytheist sources place the origin to the various Tuatha De Danann tribes. The tribe of Anu were the Mesopotamian tribe named by Akkadians as the Ditanu, Didanu, Datnu, and or Tidanu meaning "warlike." The Ditanu tribes are the same race that produced an Ugaritic tribe and royal bloodline of dynastic Rephaim kings. The Ditanu tribe and their patronymic name surfaced as names

---

[967] Ibid., 149: Sheshai, citing Deloach, *Giants*, 260; Taylor, *Calmets Great Dictionary of the Holy Bible: Sheshai*.
[968] Josephus, *Ant.*, Book 5, 2:3.
[969] Deut 1:28; 9:2.
[970] H6060—'*Anaq*; H6061—'*Anaq*; H6062—'*Anaqiy*. Deut 9:2.
[971] H1219—*batsar, baw-tsar'*: to clip off as in gather grapes; to be isolated; inaccessible by height or fortification; fenced; fortify; mighty things; strong; wall up.
[972] De Vere, *The Dragon Legacy*, 216.
[973] Ibid., 42, 216.

among two kings of first dynasty of Babylon: Ammiditana and Samsuditana.[974] The Ditanu/Dedanu might be linked to Dedan/Dedanites, known in Hebrew as *Ddan, Dedaneh, Ddaniym*, and the *Dedanim* of the low country.[975] One deduces Dedanites of Cush may have intermarried with the Ditanu and or Anakim to produce hybrid humans who accepted the eponymous name from Ditanu.

Egyptian Execration Texts dated to 1850 BC placed Anakim tribes throughout Canaan and Palestine and documented them as distinct from Canaanites and Amorites. Ancient Egyptians, in surviving molded clay models, depicted their enemies with hands bound behind their backs on clay jars, with the names of those leaders, and then baked them into pottery. This common Egyptian practice often included smashing their baked enemies into pieces in a creepy, torturous, voodoo-like occult ritual of cursing their most dreaded enemies.[976] Egyptians were so terrified of the Anakim that they mentioned them four times in the Execration Text curses,[977] which tallied the *Iy'anaq* among the feared giant nations generically classified as Asiatics.

The Asiatic classification may indicate Anakim roamed east of the Jordan River in Moab and Ammon as the Tidanu, as well as dwelling through out southern Canaan.[978] The Anakim of the Egyptian Execration Texts were recorded as both the *Iy-nq and Iy-Anaq*.[979] The Egyptian transliteration seemingly inserted the "im/iy" plural suffix (*Anaqiy*) as the prefix "Iy." As such, John A. Wilson identified the *Iy'anaq* as *Shutu* rulers of Moab in the Execration Texts, as recorded in James Pritchard's *The Ancient Near East: An Anthology of Texts and Picture*,[980] which placed Anakim and their many kings dwelling in Moab and Ammon adjacent to the Rephaim of Mount Hermon, as well as placing Anakim in southern Canaan, consistent with biblical accounts.

> ... the Ruler of Shutu, Ayyabum and all the retainers who are with
> him; the Ruler of Shutu, Kushar, and all the retainers who are with
> him; the Ruler of Shutu, Zabulanu, and all of the retainers who are
> with him; the Ruler of Asqanu, Khalu-kim, and all of the retainers

---

[974] Kspronk.files.wordpress.com/2020/07/spronk-dedan-ddd.pdf, 232: Dedan.

[975] H1719—*Ddan, ded-awn*; Dedaneh of Ezekiel 25:13: Dedan; name of two Cushites and of their territory; "low country"; the son of Raamah and grandson of Cush; H1720—*Ddaniym, ded-aw-neem*; plural of 1719 as patrial; Dedanites; descendants or inhabitants of Dedan; Dedanim; "low country."

[976] Clyde E. Billington, "Goliath and the Exodus Giants: How Tall Were They?", Journal *of the Evangelical Society*, JSTOR 50.3 (2007), 500.

[977] Ibid., 500, quoting J. B. Pritchard, *The Ancient Near East: An Anthology of Texts and Picture* (*ANET*), 225, 328.

[978] Ibid., 501, 506, citing J. B. Pritchard, *ANET*, 225.

[979] E. Mills Watson and Roger Aubrey Bullard, *Mercer Dictionary of the Bible* (Macon, GA: Mercer University Press, 1990), 329: giant. Execration Texts, *ANET*, 225, 328.

[980] Billington, "Goliath and the Exodus Giants," 501, 506, citing J. B. Pritchard, *ANET*, 225: nn. 3, 6.

who are with him; the Ruler of Jerusalem, Yaqar-'Ammu and all of the retainers who are with him; the ruler of Jerusalem, Setj-'Anu, and all of the retainers who are with him.. ... All the rulers of Iysipi and all the retainers who are with them; all the Asiatic of Byblos, of Ullaza, of Iy'anaq, of Shutu, of Iymu'aru, of Qehermu, of Iyamut, of Rehob, Yarimuta, of Inhia, of Aqhi, of 'Arqata of Yarimuta, of Isinu, of Asqanu, of Demitiu, of Mut-ilu, of Jerusalem of Akhmut, of Ianhenu, and Iysipi;"[981]

Three other possible ancestors or related kings to the Anakim kings of Numbers 13:22 were recorded in the Execration Texts circa 1850 BC: "The Ruler of Iy'anaq, Erum, and all the retainers who are with him; the Ruler of Iy'anaq, Abi-Yamimu and all the retainers who are with him; the Ruler of Iy'anaq 'Akirum and the retainers who are with him."[982] What is intriguing about King Abi-Yamimu is that his name also has Amoritic links, and Akirum has Phoenician connections, both which were likely patronymically passed down titles. Additionally, one notes the Shutu of Iymu'aru as possibly Amorites, noting Amorite hybrids were described with similar descriptions of skin, hair, eye color, and lived with the Anakim.

Anakim remained in Gaza after Israel's Covenant Land conquest that was yet another epicenter for giant sedition we will cover in subsequent chapters. According to the book of Joshua, Anakim remained in Gath and Ashod after the time of the conquest (circa 1400 BC)[983] along with other giants. Gath was the city of Goliath.[984] The Execration Texts placed the Anakim in Gaza,[985] before Israel's conquest of the Covenant Land, and before the Philistines expropriated Gaza from the Avvim, and seemingly the Anakim (circa 1550–1500 BC).[986] Knowing this makes sense of "the Ruler of Asqanu, Khalu-kim" was the ruler of Ashkelon who could have been Avvim or Anakim.

Excluding Arba and Rapha from the table of nations is consistent with Nimrod's posterity excluded, likely for intermarrying with female giants, even though Nimrod was king over nations and cities he founded after Babel. Even Assyria, the land of Nimrod (Mic 5:6) was not documented as Nimrod's posterity in the table of nations. Many Shemites were reigned over by Nimrod's dynastic

---

[981] Ibid., 501, 506, citing J. B. Pritchard, *ANET*, 225–226.

[982] Ibid.

[983] Josh 11:22.

[984] 2 Sam 21:20; 1 Chron 20:6.

[985] Billington, "Goliath and the Exodus Giants," 501, citing *ANET* 225, nn. 3, 6.

[986] Deut 2:23. Bauer, *History of the World*, 285–286, 314–319.

hybrid posterity, and giants. Shem's second son Asshur begat Assyria.[987] Asshurites dwelled in Nineveh, one of Nimrod's cities.[988] Shem's firstborn, Elam, and his posterity merged with another (biblically unnamed) people/giants that begat the Persians.[989] Shem's third son, Arphaxad begat the Chaldeans.[990] Shem's fifth son Aram begat the Syrians.[991]

Another important group of giant-like nations were the *Shasu*. The *Shasu* were documented in the Egyptian text *The Craft and the Scribe* from the Papyrus Anastasi I in the reign of Rameses II, son of Seti I. The texts indicate that *Shasu* dwelled in southern Canaan at the same time as the Anakim.[992] The *Shasu/Shashous* Canaanites were enemies of Egypt.[993] Seti I of Egypt defended the fortress of Kanana in Hebron against the Shasu, noting Hebron was the home of the Anakim kings Sheshai, Talmai, and Ahiman. One deduces the *Shasu* were present among the Anakim at the time of the Israelite conquest as well.[994] The *Shasu* were blond-haired, blue-eyed, and possessed "dolichocephalic heads" (elongated skulls); they were connected to or were the blond-haired Amorites.[995] The *Shasu* additionally dwelled in Edom.[996] Egyptian texts further placed the giant *Shasu* among the Apiru (Israel), Amorites, Amalekites, Moabites, Ammonites, Kenites, Edomites, Midianites, Aramaeans, and Canaan, as well as west of the Jordan River.[997] Egyptian records noted the *Shasu* sometimes warred with other Shasu. During Israel's judges

[987] H804—'*Ashshuwr*: second son of Shem; Asshur's descendants and the country occupied by them was Assyria—Asshur, Assur, Assyria, Assyrians.

[988] Gen 10:11; Whiston, *Josephus*, Ant. 1:6:4.

[989] H5867—'*Eylam, ay-lawm*'; or Owlam: Ezra 10:2; Jeremiah 49:36; *o-lawm*': a province east of Babylon and northeast of the lower Tigris. Whiston, *Josephus*, Ant. 1:6:4.

[990] H775—'*Arpakshad, ar-pak-shad*': a son of Shem and region settled by him. Whiston, *Josephus*, Ant. 1:6:4. H3778—*Kasdiy, kas-dee*'; *Kasdiymah*: toward the Kasdites; Chaldea; patronymically from 3777; a descendant of Kesed; H3777—*Kesed, keh'-sed*: a nephew of Abraham; fourth son of Nahor.

[991] H758 —'*Aram, arawm*': the highland; Aram or Syria, and its inhabitants; the name of the son of Shem, a grandson of Nahor; Aram; Mesopotamia; Syria; Syrians. Whiston and Mair *Josephus*, Ant. 1:6:4.

[992] Billington, "Goliath and the Exodus Giants," 505–506.

[993] Cooper, *An Archaic Dictionary*, 517: Shasu.

[994] Archibald Henry Sayce, *The Races of the Old Testament*, second edition (Oxford: The Religious Tract Society, 1893), 106–107, 117.

[995] Sayce, *Races of the Old Testament*, 114, 115, 117.

[996] Billington, "Goliath and the Exodus Giants," 502, citing S. Herrmann, *Israel in Egypt* (Naperville, IL: Alex R. Allenson, 1973), 25: "Another communication to my [lord], to wit: We have finished letting the Shasu tribes of Edom pass the Fortress [of] Mer-ne-ptah Hotep-hir-Maat—life, pros- perity, health!—which is [in] TKW, to the pools of Per-Atum [of] Mer-[ne]-ptah Hotep-hir-Maat, which are [in] Twk, to keep them alive and to keep their cattle alive, through the great Ka of Pharaoh."

[997] Ibid., 504–505, citing K. R. Cooper, *The Shasu of Palestine in the Egyptian Texts*, Artifax 21/4, 2006, 22–25.

period, Israelites fought against Ammonites, Moabites, Midianites, and Amorites—the *Shasu*.[998]

Some scholars conclude the *Shasu* were Anakim, but this does not seem to be accurate. Egyptian records like the Execration Texts classified Anakim as distinct from the *Shasu*. Further, the *Shasu* seem to be more a generic term for a similar kind of people—perhaps hybrid human Rephaim. *The Egyptian Craft of the Scribe* documented the *Shasu* ranged in height from four to five cubits from the foot to the nose. The Egyptian royal cubit was 20.65"; this establishes the height of the Shasu as ranging at 6'9"–7'3" to 9'0," if one includes about six inches for the balance of the head and foot: "The face of the pass is dangerous with Shasu, hidden under the bushes. Some of them are 4 or 5 cubits, nose to foot, with wild faces."[999] *Shasu* were smaller than the Rephaim; Goliath was six cubits and a span: 11'2" by royal cubit of 21" as asserted by Josephus. King Og was taller still: 13–15' based on his bed size.[1000] *Shasu* seemingly was the catch-all phrase for hybrid Rephaim people like the Amalekites in the south; Hittites, Jebusites, and Amorites of the mountains; the Canaanites listed in Numbers 13:29; as well as Sidonians and the balance of the patriarch-less Canaanite tribe.

---

[998] Ibid., 505.

[999] Ibid., 505, citing W. W. Hallo, ed., *The Context of Scripture*, 3 vols. (Leiden: Brill, 2003), 3.9.

[1000] Deut 3:11; 1 Sam 17:4.

CHAPTER 24

THE JEBUSITES OF THE MIGHTY SEVEN NATIONS

Exod 3:8 And I am come down to deliver them out of the hand of the Egyptians, and to bring them up out of that land unto a good land and a large, unto a land flowing with milk and honey; unto the place of the Canaanites, and the Hittites, and the Amorites, and the Perizzites, and the Hivites, and the Jebusites.

Knowing the biblical historical, genealogical, eponymous, and patrial patterns are the keys to unlock precious informational nuggets embedded in important and often overlooked passages.

The eponymous and patrial keys reveal much about the Jebusites, the Mighty Seven nations, the balance of patriarch-less Canaanite families, and biblical nations not listed in the table of nations.

Many believe the twelve Canaanite tribes were giant tribes, but there is not a biblical smoking gun verse stating this as so. What the Bible does indicate is that Canaanite tribes dwelled among the Rephaim, Anakim and other giant tribes in and around the Covenant Land. Thus, discerning whether Canaanite clans were giants, humans, or human/Rephaim hybrids is one of the historical keys to unlocking the hidden history of the early postdiluvian epoch in the Middle East.

Knowing Rephaim patriarchs were not documented in the table of nations helps makes sense of the nine patriarch-less Canaanite families in Genesis

10:16-18,[1001] which indicates by implication, nine of the twelve Canaanite families were hybrid Rephaim/humans begat by Rephaim patriarchs. Remember, Rephaim unlike their antediluvian Nephilim counterparts were plagued with infertility issues, as reflected in their overlooked appellation, the Terrible Ones, the Arytim.[1002] Infertility forced Rephaim to marry human females that created Rephaim/human hybrids to prevent the extinction of the roy-el race. Accordingly, Rephaim females like Timna, daughter of Seir married Eliphaz that begat the hybrid human Amalekite race and the dynastic Agag kings.[1003]

Know then that families/mishpachah penned to represent Canaanite patriarch-less tribes is explained in *Strong's Dictionary* as a class of people, species, of a kind, aristocrats, or family.[1004] The application of "families" in Genesis 10:18 indicates that unnamed Rephaim patriarchs, royals, and/or aristocrats of another species interbred with Canaanite females to create eponymously and patronymically named hybrid tribes or families, which were originally distinct from Canaan, Sidon, and Heth. It follows that the patriarch-less Canaanite clans, important in Israel's history, were included in the table of nations descending from Noah's posterity via Canaan, Sidon, and Heth, but through some of their daughters that married Rephaim. For this reason, the Rephaim patriarch's names were purposefully excluded from the genealogical record.

> Gen 10:18. .. and afterward were the families of the Canaanites spread abroad.

Josephus wrote that a few (patriarch-less) Canaanite clans indeed left an imprint in the surviving historical record, but knowledge was lost for six other of the (patriarch-less) Canaanite clans because their cities were overthrown and utterly destroyed by conquering Israelites.[1005] On the other hand, most nations' names were embedded into the eponymous name of his nation, partially in his royal city, and as patronymic king's names and dynastic titles, as with Elamites from Elam in Persia. Some names further connect to a godfather as well.

[1001] Also, 1 Chron 1:13–16.

[1002] Isa 13:11; 29:1–5, 20; 49:25; Jer 15:21. H6184—`ariyts, aw-reets`; from 6206: fearful; powerful; tyrannical; mighty; oppressor; great power, strong, terrible, violent; terrifying; terror-striking; ruthless; childless; bare of children.

[1003] Gen 36:12, 23; 1 Chron 1:37, 40.

[1004] H4940—*mishpachah, mish-paw-khaw*': a family; circle of relatives; class of people; a species; tribe; people; kind; aristocrat.

[1005] Whiston, *Josephus*, Ant 1:6:2: "The sons of Canaan were these: Sidonius, who also built a city of the same name; it is called by the Greeks Sidon Amathus inhabited in Amathine, which is even now called Amathe by the inhabitants, although the Macedonians named it Epiphania, from one of his posterity: Arudeus possessed the island Aradus: Arucas possessed Arce, which is in Libanus."

Tracking unnamed patriarchs can sometimes be done through sources recorded in more than one language, because the transliterations into other languages often hold overlooked clues. The English KJV transliteration for the Canaanite clans, their original Hebrew names, and variant Greek transliterations translated into to English in the Septuagint, and Latin to English from either Greek or Hebrew by Josephus is also helpful as comparatives.

Bible	Hebrew	Septuagint	Josephus
Canaan	Kn'an	Chanaan	Canaan
Sidon/Zidon	Tsiydown	Sidon	Sidonius/Sidon
Heth	Cheth	Chettite	Chetteus
Jebusite	Yebuwciy	Jebusite	Jebuseus
Amorite	'Emoriy	Amorite	Amorreus
Girgasite	Girgashiy	Girgashite/Gergesite	Gergesus
Hivite	Chivviy	Evite	Eudeus
Arkite	`Arqiy	Arukite	Arucas
Sinite	Ciynay	Asennite	Sineus
Arvadite	'Arvadiy	Aradian	Arudeus
Zemarite	Tsmariy	Samarean	Samereus
Hamathite	Chamathiy	Amathite	Amathe/Amathine

The notion that one can trace unnamed Rephaim patriarchs through eponymous, patrial, and patronymic ways is hinted at in an allegorical passage in Ezekiel 16. Jerusalem's postdiluvian renaissance came about through its Amorite/*'Emoriy* father and Hittite/*Cheth* mother; the passage states Sodom and Samaria were Jerusalem's sisters.[1006] Heth was the son of Canaan, not a daughter of Canaan, while the Amorites were a patriarch-less Canaanite clan. The language of the mother being a Hittite then seems to indicate a daughter of the Hittites married an Amorite hybrid, or more likely an Anakim patriarch associated with the Amorites to found postdiluvian Jerusalem and its inhabitants. What we know biblically about the Jebusites is that they were the first inhabitants of Jerusalem,[1007] and a clan grouped in the table of nations immediately after Heth, followed by the Amorites, as the firstborn of the patriarch-less clans. The grouping pattern indicates a relationship by implication between the Jebusites, Heth/Hittites, and Amorites, as inferred in Ezekiel 16. One also notes a kinship with the Canaanite cities Samaria and Sodom.

[1006] Ezek 16:3, 45, 46.
[1007] Josh 15:63.

The region immediately surrounding Jerusalem included Jebusite, Amorite, and Hittite settlements, as well as Amalekites and Anakim.[1008] Jebus was the postdiluvian Aboriginal name for Jerusalem,[1009] occupied by Jebusites from before 2000 BC.[1010] Jebusites were not driven out of Jerusalem[1011] until David conquered Jerusalem a thousand years later. King Abdi-Hiba of Jerusalem petitioned Pharaoh in the *Armana Letters* about the power of Habiru/Apiru/Israelite renegades overrunning Abdi-Hiba's villages and towns.[1012] Jerusalem endured Jebusite occupation in Abraham's time and the war of giants, whereby Melchizedek king of Salem/Jerusalem blessed Abraham.[1013]

Just as Kiriatharba was patrial—named after the Anakim patriarch, Arba, as the city's founder—it was a common custom for a giant to have his royal city named after him. Thus was the case for the royal Jebusite city of Jebus. Jebus/Jebusi then appears to be the name for the Jebusite Rephaim patriarch. Accordingly, Jebusites/*Yebuwciy* is defined as patrial from Jebus/*Ybuwc,* and as inhabitants of Jebus city.[1014] In fact, *Strong's Cyclopaedia* indicates that Jebus city was most likely named after the progenitor of the powerfully warlike and eponymously named Jebusite tribe,[1015] who dominated large portions of the mountain region.[1016] However, either Jebus city's name changed to Salem sometime before the war of giants, or Hebrew scribes utilized the antediluvian name.[1017]

In the Egyptian Execration Texts, dated prior to Israel's Covenant Land conquest, two kings of Jerusalem were listed: Yaqar-`Ammu and Setj-Anu.[1018] *Yaqar* in

---

[1008] Sayce, *Races of the Old Testament*, 111, 131. Gen 23:19–20; Num 13:22, 28, 29; Josh 10:5.

[1009] Josh 18:28. H2982—*Ybuwc, yeb-oos'*: trodden; threshing-place; aboriginal name of Jerusalem. Josephus, *Ant.*, Book 7:3:2 note 5: "Some copies of Josephus have here Solyma, or Salem; and others Hierosolyma, or Jerusalem. The latter best agree to what Josephus says elsewhere [*Of the War*, B. VI. ch. 10], that this city was called Solyma, or Salem, before the days of Melchisedec, but was by him called Hierosolyma, or Jerusalem. I rather suppose it to have been so called after Abraham had received that oracle Jehovah Jireh, 'The Lord will see, or provide,' Genesis 22:14. The latter word, Jireh, with a little alteration, prefixed to the old name Salem, Peace, will be Jerusalem; and since that expression, 'God will see,' or rather, 'God will provide himself a lamb for a burnt-offering,' ver. 8, 14, is there said to have been proverbial till the days of Moses, this seems to me the most probable derivation of that name, which will then denote that God would provide peace by that 'Lamb of God which was to take away the sins of the world.'"

[1010] *Unger's*, 655: Jebusite.

[1011] Josh 15:63.

[1012] Mills and Aubrey, *Mercer Dictionary of the Bible*, 430: Jebusites; William L. Moran, trans., *The Armana Letters*, (Baltimore: Johns Hopkins University Press, 1992; originally published as *Les Lettres D'el-Marna*, Les Editions du Cerf, 1987), 317–325: EA 271–284; Wayne, *The Genesis 6 Conspiracy*, 258, citing Silberman and Finkelstein, *David and Solomon*, 44, 51, and Karen Armstrong, *A History of God*, 11.

[1013] Gen 14:18–20. H8004—*Shalem, shaw-lame'*: peaceful; peace; an early name of Jerusalem; the place where Melchizedek was king; Jewish commentators affirm as Jerusalem.

[1014] H2983—*Yebuwciy yeb-oo-see'*: patrial from 2982: a Jebusite or inhabitant of Jebus; H2982—*Ybuwc*.

[1015] Strong's *Cyclopaedia*, Vol. 4, 795: Jebusite.

[1016] Josh 11:3.

[1017] Gen 14:18; 33:18.

[1018] Billington, "Goliath and the Exodus Giants," 500–501, citing Pritchard, *ANET*, 225–226.

Hebrew is defined as precious, valuable, shining, and of reputation, while `Ammu is a transliteration of Amorite/Amuru/Ammuru and the Amuru god, son of Anu in Mesopotamia.[1019] Both Yaqar-`Ammu and Setj-Anu were listed among the the Anakim/Iy'anaq and the Amorites/Iymu'aru as allies, and as strong men who were associated with the obscure Mentu of Asia. The Mentu, likely the Menti of Sati was the Egyptian name for the hordes led by Hyksos kings from Sinai, Syria, and Asia Minor.[1020] The "Mentu in Asia," according to translator John Wilson, was an ancient designation for Egypt's immediate neighbors to the northeast.[1021] The Jebusites, by implication, held a close relationship with the Amorites and Anakim led by Anakim kings. Another king who reigned in Jerusalem was named Mut-ilu.

> ... . the Ruler of Jerusalem, Yaqar-'Ammu and all of the retainers who are with him; the ruler of Jerusalem, Setj-'Anu, and all of the retainers who are with him. .. of Iy'anaq, of Shutu, of Iymu'aru, of Qehermu, of Iyamut, of Rehob, Yarimuta, of Inhia, of Aqhi, of 'Arqata of Yari-muta, of Isinu, of Asqanu, of Demitiu, of Mut-ilu, of Jerusalem, and Iysipi; their strongmen, their swift runners, their allies, their associ-ates, and the Mentu in Asia.[1022]

Jebusites were further listed by Moses' scouts as dwelling among the Anakim, and described as strong, mighty, greater, and taller than the Israelites.[1023] In fact, Jebusites were listed among the infamous Mighty Seven (nations) described as greater and mightier than Israel.[1024] The Jebusites indeed were a powerful, perpetu-ally warlike and giant-like people, but distinct from the larger Anakim who reigned over Jebusites from inside mighty fortress with "walls up to heaven."[1025]

> Deut 7:1 When the LORD thy God shall bring thee into the land whither thou goest to possess it, and hath cast out many nations before thee, the Hittites, and the Girgashites, and the Amorites, and the Canaanites, and the Perizzites, and the Hivites, and the Jebusites, seven nations greater and mightier than thou.

[1019] H3368—*yaqar, yaw-kawr'*: valuable; brightness; precious; reputation. Bauer, *History of the Ancient World*, 139; Rohl, *The Lost Testament*, 112.
[1020] Sayce, *The Races of the Old Testament*, 109–110.
[1021] Billington, "Goliath and the Exodus Giants," 500–501, citing Pritchard, *ANET*, 328, note 14.
[1022] Ibid., 501, 506, Pritchard, *ANET*, 225–226.
[1023] Num 13:29; Deut 1:28.
[1024] Exod 13:5; Deut 7:1; Josh 3:10.
[1025] Num 13:28, 29; Deut 1:28.

The word "greater" applied in Deuteronomy 7:1, describing the mighty seven nations who occupied the Covenant Land, derives from *rab* meaning many.[1026] Mightier/ˋ*atsuwm* also means vast, numerous, countless, as well as strong. The text is not being redundant here but directs the meaning of many/*rab* that are stronger. ˋ*Atsuwm* is a participle of ˋ*atsam*, meaning powerful as with a paw in the denominative sense from ˋ*etsem*, as in "to crunch bones or break the bones,"[1027] and as it was applied in Jeremiah 50:17.[1028] Both the giants and the hybrid human giants held the denominative reputation as the "Bone Crunchers" who crunch bones with their beastly paws/hands.

All this diverse information makes sense as to why Josephus described Jebusites as a nation extracted from the Canaanites (by a Rephaim patriarch), and by inference likely countless other intermarriages thereafter between Canaanite daughters and Jebus' brethren Rephaim: "Now the Jebusites, who were the inhabitants of Jerusalem, and were by extraction Canaanites, shut their gates, and placed the blind, and the lame, and all their maimed persons, upon the wall, in way of derision of the king."[1029] Extraction can mean a lineage/descent extracted from and or foreign from[1030] the "Canaanites." Similarly, some scholars believe Jebusites were somehow connected to the Hurrians: biblically, Horim and/or Hivvim (Rephaim), as well as the Hittites, but still a Canaanite nation. As this line of thinking goes, Jebusites replaced the Amorites in Jerusalem circa 1950–1550 BC,[1031] even though other sources dates Jebusites in Jerusalem prior to 2000 B.C.

The book of Joshua that noted the mighty seven nations[1032] were so numerous, so militarily powerful, so tall, so strong, so giant-like, that Israel would come to know that the living God Almighty was among them when they drove out the mighty seven. Israel had no chance to win a single battle or skirmish on their own, let alone a transgenerational war that followed, except through faith in God and His assistance.

> Josh 3:10 And Joshua said, Hereby ye shall know that the living God is among you, and that he will without fail drive out from before you the Canaanites, and the Hittites, and the Hivites, and the Perizzites, and the Girgashites, and the Amorites, and the Jebusites.

[1026] H7227—*rab*: much, many, great.
[1027] H6099—ˋ*atsuwm, aw-tsoom*ˋ: mighty; vast; numerous; countless; strong as a passive participle of 6105; powerful, specifically a paw; H6105—ˋ*atsam, aw-tsam*ˋ: powerful; numerous; "denominatively" from 6106 to crunch the bones; break bones; H6106—ˋ*etsem, eh'tsem*; from 6105: a bone as in strong; by extension the body.
[1028] Jer 50:17: "Israel is a scattered sheep; the lions have driven him away: first the king of Assyria hath devoured him; and last this Nebuchadnezzar king of Babylon hath broken his bones."
[1029] Whiston, *Josephus*, Ant., 7:31.
[1030] Webster's, 194: extract/extraction; Dictionary.com: extraction.
[1031] Mills and Aubrey, *Mercer Dictionary of the Bible*, 430–31: Jebusite.
[1032] Deut 7:1; 24:11: Mighty Seven Nations.

CHAPTER 25

THE AMORITES

Amos 2:9 Yet destroyed I the Amorite before them, whose height was like the height of the cedars, and he was strong as the oaks; yet I destroyed his fruit from above, and his roots from beneath.

Some believe Amorites were Nephilim or Rephaim, based on Amos 2:9. However, the passage does not directly state that Amorites were Rephaim or Nephilim. Rather, it compared the height of Amorites to cedar trees and the Amorite strength to oak trees.

Cedar and oak trees were common in the forests of Bashan[1033] of Mount Hermon. Cedar trees were the giant trees of the Middle East, growing to a girth of forty to fifty feet, a height of one hundred feet, [1034] and a two-to-one height-to-width ratio, like giants. Cedar trees of "high stature" grew in Eden.[1035] Cedar was a prized wood for architectural applications such as beams, pillars, and carvings. Cedars forests of Lebanon and Mount Hermon produced wood used in the grandest of temples and palaces throughout the known world: the temple of Artemis (Diana) at Ephesus, the temple of Apollo at Utica, Persian kings at Susa, etc.,[1036] and prized wood used in the construction of Solomon's Jerusalem temple.[1037] Cedars of Senir and Mount Hermon[1038] were additionally valued for shipbuilding and specifically

---

[1033] Isa 2:13.
[1034] *Nelson's,* 1002–1003: plants of the Bible.
[1035] Eze 31:8, 9, 16, 18.
[1036] *Unger's,* 1329: vegetable kingdom. Ezek 17:22, 31:3, 27:5; Acts 19:27, 28, 34, 35, 37.
[1037] Cedars: 1 Kings 6:9–10; 7:11; 10:27; 1 Chron 17:1, 6; 2 Chron 2:3. Cedars: 1 Kings 6:15, 16, 18, 20, 36; 7:2, 3, 7, 12; 9:11; 2 Kings 14:9; 19:23; 1 Chron 22:4; 2 Chron 1:15; 2:8; 9:27.
[1038] Deut 3:9: "Which Hermon the Sidonians call Sirion; and the Amorites call it Shenir".

tall masts (Ezek 27:5). Cedars of Bashan and Hermon comprised the famous cedar forest reigned over by King Humbaba in The *Epic of Gilgamesh*.

The oak tree of Bashan was also a giant-like tree growing a massive trunk.[1039] The oak tree was prized in the ancient world for its strength, and used to manufacture oars for ships and for idols, as were cedar and ash trees.[1040] The "Great Oak Tree, Bile" was venerated by the Tuatha De Danann, tribe of D'Anu, the Ditanu, and the giant tribes of Diana/Dianu/Danu and/or Anu: Scythians, Aryans, and Irish lore.[1041]

Mount Hermon and the Baalim were constitutive cultural and religious pillars for the Amorites, who venerated the mountain of infamy as Shenir.[1042] As noted above, though, Amos 2:9 does not state that Amorites were offspring of fallen angels, but rather allegorically compares Amorite size and strength for visual and hyperbole impact within a grammatical simile "like": "whose height was like the height cedars" associated with Mount Hermon and giant creation. Amorites in Amos 2:14–16 were connected to the mighty/*gibbowr*, but not directly to the Nephilim or Rephaim.[1043] All we can deduce from Amos 2 is that Amorites were giant-like compared to Israelites, but not necessarily Rephaim or Nephilim, and certainly not one hundred feet tall or forty feet wide.

Amorites are regarded as an Aboriginal tribe of Canaan dated by the *Shar-Kali-sharri* records to dwelling at Jebel Bisri, Syria, to circa 2250 BC.[1044] Amorites were recorded in Accad and Sumer annals as barbarians who dwelled of the mountains just beyond Sumer.[1045]

Amorites are generally regarded as somewhat interchangeable with Canaanites.[1046] The *Mercer Bible Dictionary* oddly stated that Amorites and Canaanites ought not to be regarded as distinct peoples, even though both names were used for peoples in separate geographic regions, and the adoption of one name did not eliminate the other from use.[1047] Conversely, I think historian Archibald Sayce was directionally correct when he stated, "the tribes and cities of which Canaan is said to have been the father were related to one another only geographically. The blond Amorite and the yellow-skinned Hittite of the north had nothing in common from a racial point of view either with one another or with the Semitic tribes of Canaan. Geography and not ethnology has caused them to be grouped

---

[1039] *Nelson's*, 1007: plants of the Bible. Deut 4:47; Josh 12; 1 Chron 5:23.
[1040] Isa 44:14; Ezek 27:5.
[1041] Wayne, *The Genesis 6 Conspiracy*, 123; 664, 668, citing Peter Beresford Ellis, *The Celts*, (London: Robinson, 2003), 162, and Gardner, *Realm of the Ring Lords*, 31–32.
[1042] Deut 3:9.
[1043] Amos 2:14, 16.
[1044] *Mercer Dictionary of the Bible*, 25: Amorites.
[1045] Bauer, *History of the Ancient World*, 131, 139.
[1046] *Mercer Dictionary of the Bible*, 24: Amorites.
[1047] Ibid., 25.

together."[1048] The eponymous and racial feature conundrum is resolved when one entertains the notion that Canaanite daughters intermarried with different kinds of Aboriginal Rephaim patriarchs.

Canaanites and Amorites were listed as distinct nations among the mighty seven nations and as seemingly the most dominant branches of the early Canaanite clans. The Amorites' powerful presence was imposed upon the Mount Hermon region, throughout the Covenant Land and beyond. Thus, the Amorites were generally regarded by historians as the most powerful Canaanite clan,[1049] but not Rephaim. Josephus regarded the Canaanite clans of Syria and Canaan as the offspring of giants, versus fallen angelic offspring,[1050] when Josephus described the war of giants, also documented in Genesis 14 that included Amorites.[1051] Josephus' accounting synchro-meshes with Joshua and Caleb's scouting report to Moses that identified Anakim in the Covenant Land, as well as other giant-like tribes taller than Israelites that included Amorites. Moreover, the *Shasu* of southern Canaan were represented by Egyptians as belonging to the same blond type as the Amorites; both dwelled among the blond-haired Anakim, and both were considered humans of a larger physical stature,[1052] but not Rephaim or Anakim. *Shasu*, as you recall, ranged from seven to nine feet tall, as included among the stronger tribes listed in Numbers 13:28–29: Amalekites, Hittites, Jebusites, Canaanites, and Amorites. Sayce described the physical attributes of the Amorites:

> What the Amorite was like we know from the portraits of him which have been left to us by the artists of Egypt. His features were handsome and regular, his nose straight and somewhat pointed, his lips and nostrils thin, his cheek-bones high, his jaws orthognathous [straight], and his eyebrows well defined. His skull is apparently dolichocephalic [elongated], he possessed a good forehead, and a fair amount of whisker which ended in a pointed beard.. .. [I]t is plain that the Amorite belonged to the blond race. His blue eyes and light hair prove this incontestably. So also does the color of his skin, when compared with that of other races depicted by the Egyptian artists. At Medinet Habu, for example, where the skin of the Amorite is a pale pink.[1053]

The fair-skinned, light-haired, blue-eyed, aquiline/hooked-nosed, pointy-bearded Amorites[1054] were akin to descriptions of some Aryans, Tuatha De Danann,

---

[1048] Sayce, *Races of the Old Testament*, 59.

[1049] *Strong's Cyclopaedia*, Vol. 1, 203.

[1050] Whiston, *Josephus*, Ant 1:91.

[1051] Gen 14:7.

[1052] Sayce, *Races of the Old Testament*, 114–115.

[1053] Ibid., 112–113.

[1054] Kemal Yildirim, *The Ancient Amorites (Amurro) of Mesopotamia* (Saarbrucken: Lambert Academic Publishing, 2017), 12, 83.

and antediluvian Atlanteans.[1055] Amorites were ostensibly diluted giant-hybrids, much taller than Israelites but smaller than Rephaim or Nephilim. Amorite clans settled vast and diverse tracts of the Covenant Land dwelling among the Anakim, Rephaim, and Zamzummim.[1056] One deduces Amorites were hybrid human off-spring of Anakim/Ditanu. The supposition becomes more evident when one considers other Amorite references. *Unger's* submits Amorites were renowned as "the tall ones,"[1057] but not giants. *Strong's Cyclopaedia* submitted Amorite derives from an obsolete Hebrew word meaning height and/or warlike mountaineer.[1058]

Strong's Dictionary defines Amorites/*'Emoriy* as patronymic in part from an unused name for a Canaanite tribe, meaning a mountaineer and a "sayer," and from `amar.[1059] It follows that if Amorite *'Emoriy* derives from an unused source name, parts of that source name would remain within *'Emoriy* and from `amar meaning to speak, boast, and act proudly[1060]—traits of Nephilim and Rephaim. The *'Emoriy* were the transliterated *Iymu'aru* of the Execration Texts who dwelled among the Anakim/*Anaqiy*, the *Iy'anaq* in the texts.[1061] As such, Amorites became a catch-all phrase in antiquity for giant-like peoples and nations, not only because of their larger size, but because of their close affinity with the Rephaim, Anakim, Zamzummim and other giant tribes throughout Canaan and beyond, and because of their dominance. The Amorite catch-all phrase became commonplace for Canaanites tribes[1062] as witnessed at times in the Old Testament.[1063] The catch-all Amorite phrase for Canaanites utilized by Assyrians and Babylonians came about with the Amorite takeover of the Babylonian and Assyrian empires as rulers.

> Josh 24:15 And if it seem evil unto you to serve the LORD, choose you this day whom ye will serve; whether the gods which your fathers served that were on the other side of the flood, or the gods of the Amorites, in whose land ye dwell.

The dominance Amorites exercised over the Covenant Land region was reflected in the Egyptian *Armana Letters* where *Amauri* was recorded as the name

[1055] Frank Joseph, *The Destruction of Atlantis* (Rochester, VT: Bear and Co., 2002), 219–221, 225; Bauer, *History of the World,* 470; John Greer, *The Element Encyclopedia of Secret Societies,* (London: Harper Element, 2006), 499.
[1056] Yildirim, *The Ancient Amorites (Amurro) Of Mesopotamia,* 128.
[1057] *Unger's,* 54: Amorites.
[1058] *Strong's Cyclopaedia,* Vol. 1, 203: Amorites citing Gesenius and Simonis.
[1059] H567—*'Emoriy, em-o-ree'*: patronymic from an unused name derived from 559 amar: a mountaineer; a sayer.
[1060] H559—*'amar, aw-mar'*: to say; speak; to boast, to act proudly.
[1061] Billington, "Goliath and the Exodus Giants," 501, 506, citing Pritchard, *ANET,* 225–226.
[1062] *Strong's Cyclopaedia,* Vol. 1, 203: Amorites.
[1063] Josh 10:5: the five kings of the Amorites of Jerusalem and Hebron that would have also included Canaanites, Jebusites, and perhaps Hivites. See also Gen 15:16; 48:22; Deut 1:27–28.

of Palestine and Phoenicia. Other sources note Egyptians identified Amorites as Amar; while Akkadians named them Amarrum,[1064] and/or Amurru.[1065] Sumerians knew Amorites as the Martu and Amerru, noting the land of Palestine and Syria was recognized as the land of the Amorites in the third millennium BC.[1066] The Martu were included in the *Chaldean Work on Astrology* and the *Exploits of Lubara* with Akkad, Sumer, Elam, Goim, Gutim, Kassi, Kassati, Subartu, Assan, Nituk, Asmin, Yamutbal, Assyria, Suti, and Lullubu.[1067]

Amurru was a Sumerian deity, son of Anu, a god seemingly added to the pantheon later, likely after the flood and perhaps with Amorites succeeding to Mesopotamian thrones, whereby the appearance of variants for the Amurru name coincide. The people of Amurru in the east were thought by many to be Martu people,[1068] who also worshipped the gods Martu and Adad/Hadad, chief god of the Arameans,[1069] with the latter a variant name for Baal, god of Ugarit, Mount Hermon, Rephaim, and Canaan.

The Amurru god was likely one of the postdiluvian Baalim reigning from Mount Hermon. Baal son of El was equivalent with Enki the son of Anu. Accordingly, the *Ugaritic Texts* indicated Amurr/Amurru was a distinct god from Baal/Hadad/Adad. The *Ugaritic Texts* align with Scripture to verify that Amorites worshipped Baal as the chief god and his pantheon of offspring gods, and the Baalim assembly of gods Amurr was part of. Postdiluvian Ugaritic gods reigned in their various nations across the Middle East in places like Egypt, Crete, and Mesopotamia. One deduces Amorites imposed Amurr/Amurro upon the Mesopotamians to replace antediluvian gods like Anu and in honor of the godfather of their Rephaim patriarch, or imposed the demigod worship of the Amorite patriarch. Amurr was discussed several times independently of Baal in the *Ugaritic Texts*, along with Qadesh, another god connected to giants where all three are discussed:

> Bull [El] [and the Great Lady]- who-trample[s Yam replied]: '[Listen, O Qadesh and Amu[rr].. .. Prepare the harnes of [my] she-ass!' Qadwsh-and-Amur[r] obeyed.. ... Qadesh-and-Amurr clasped: he set Athirat on the back of the ass… Qadesh took hold of a torch; Amurr was like a star in front. Virgin Anat followed behind. And Baal departed for the heights of Saphon.[1070]

[1064] Yildirim, *The Ancient Amorites (Amurro) of Mesopotamia*, 7, 183; Sayce, *Races of the Old Testament*, 110.

[1065] *Mercer Bible Dictionary*, 24, Amorite; Sayce, *Races of the Old Testament*, 102.

[1066] *Unger's*, 54: Amorite. Gen 15:16. Bauer, *History of the Ancient World*, 139.

[1067] Smith, *The Chaldean Genesis*, 19, 20, 101, Exploits of Lubara Tablet 1, Col. 4, lines 9–24.

[1068] Bauer, *History of the Ancient World*, 139; Rohl, *The Lost Testament*, 112.

[1069] Benz, *Personal Names in the Phoenician and Punic Inscriptions*, 302, HDD citing UT Gordon, CH, Ugaritic Text Book, 750: ancient Semitic HDD akin to Baal and Zeus.

[1070] Wyatt, *Religious Texts from Ugarit*, 98–99; 89: KTU 1.3 vi:10; 92, 1.4 i:40.

Baal's parent god El was a lustful, morbid, tyrant god, a father of gods and of Nephilim before the flood.[1071] El reigned from Mount Hermon before he was locked in the abyss for sexual crimes. Baal succeeded El along with his Baalim gods who also reigned from Mount Saphon/Hermon and the assembly of gods recorded in the *Ugaritic Texts*, the biblical Baalim gods[1072] that reigned over much of the ancient world:[1073]

> .. . you shall honor the convocation of the [Council]! [Standing upright you shall then spe]ak, declaring your message. And you shall say to Bull [your] father [El], [declare to the convocation of] the Council.. .. The divine assistants depart; they do not delay. T[hen]they set their [faces] toward the divine mountain, toward the convocation of the Council. Now the gods were sitting to ea[t], the sons of the Holy One to dine. Baal.. .. The gods lowered their heads onto their knees, and onto the thrones of their princeships. Baal rebuked them: 'Why, O gods, have you lowered your heads onto your knees, and onto the thrones of your princeships?. .. Lift up, O gods, your heads from on your knees, from the thrones of your princeships.. .. The gods raise their heads from on their knees, from the thrones of their princeships. When the messengers of Yam arrived. .. they did indeed honor the convocation of the Council.[1074]

An Amorite splinter group honored Amurru from the Baalim as their god when they migrated to Mesopotamia, and then inserted Amurru into the Mesopotamian pantheon. In this line of thinking, the Amorites were connected to an unnamed mountain (Deut 1:7), and to Mount Shenir (Deut 3:8), the mountain of Watchers known otherwise known as Mount Hermon.[1075] Mount Shenir was the land where Rephaim kings Og and Sihon reigned over the Amorites circa 1450 BC (Deut 31:4), and well before. Og and likely Sihon by implication were the last of the first-generation Rephaim giants,[1076] who had succeeded as kings of the Amorites from the originating eponymous founder for hybrid Amorites, and the kin of Arba of the Anakim and Rapha of the Rephaim. Og and Sihon likely succeeded as kings of migrated Amorites to Bashan after Genesis 14's war of giants, where the four giant kings of Mesopotamia defeated the Rephaims of Ashteroth Karnaim, whereby the

---

[1071] *Unger's*, 341: El.

[1072] H1172—*ba`alah, bah-al-aw*; feminine of 1167; H1167—*ba`al, bah'-al*: a mistress in Nahum 3:4: "Because of the multitude of the whoredoms of the well-favoured harlot, the mistress of witchcrafts."

[1073] Judg 2:11; 3:7; 8:33; 10:6, 10; 1 Sam 7:4; 12:10; 1 Kings 18:18; 2 Chron 17:3; 24:7; 34:2–4; Jer 2:23; 9:14; Hos 2:13, 17; 11:2.

[1074] Wyatt, *Religious Texts from Ugarit*, 59–60, KTU 1.2 i:15–20.

[1075] Deut 3:9: "Which Hermon the Sidonians call Sirion; and the Amorites call it Shenir"; Deut 31:4: "Sihon and to Og, kings of the Amorites."

[1076] Deut 3:11; Josh 12:4; 13:11–13.

kings and numerous Rephaim were slain.[1077] The war of giants that Amorites were part of may have been the motivation for Amorites to overthrow the Mesopotamian dynasties.[1078] This supposition: that Og and Sihon succeeded as Rephaim kings over Amorites was captured in the apocryphal book of Jubilees, where it states Amorites replaced the Rephaim of Mount Hermon, Karnaim, Ashtaroth, and Edrei after God had them destroyed the Terrible Ones for their evil deeds:

> ... for it was the land of the Rephaim, and the Rephaim were born (there), giants.... And their habitation was from the land of the children of Ammon to Mount Hermon, and the seats of their kingdom were Karnaim and Ashtaroth, and Edrei, and Misur, and Beon. And the Lord destroyed them because of the evil of their deeds; for they were very malignant, and the Amorites dwelled in their stead, wicked and sinful, and there is no people to-day which has wrought to the full all their sins, and they have no longer length of life on the earth.[1079]

Ergo, Hammurabi was an Amorite king of Babylonians (c. 1981–1950 BC), according to secular historians, and 1992–1950 BC for biblical chronology based on the events and biblical timing of Genesis 14's war of giants.[1080] King Hammurabi, an antichrist archetype, was self-titled "King of Righteousness" after writing his famous code, in typical Rephaim narcissism. Hammurabi was alternatively spelled Hammurapi;[1081] both variations contain the Ham/Cham patronymic name in the first syllable, which is defined as also as a patronymic title for Ham's descendants,[1082] and in this case from Ham through Canaan, and a Rephaim patriarch who bred with a daughter of Canaan. One deduces, then, that Hammurabi was of Amorite descent, in a similar manner perhaps of Amraphel/Amarapi of Shinar (Gen 14:1). (H)ammurapi was a patronymic dynastic kingship title like Pharaoh and Agag, as witnessed by the last Rapiu/Rephaim King Ammurapi of Ugarit circa 1250–1180 BC.[1083] Further, Assyrian King Sennacherib (circa

---

[1077] Gen 14:4. H6255—'*Ashtroth Qarnayim, ash-ter-oth' kar-nah'yim*: Ashtaroth of the double-horned or peaks symbol of a deity; city in Bashan east of the Jordan.

[1078] Gen 14:1–7.

[1079] Charles, *Book of Jubilees,* 29:9–12.

[1080] *Encyclopedia Americana,* Vol. 13, 666–668; Bauer, *History of the Ancient World,* 161, 163, 177. Flood 2348 BC, or fifty years earlier if setting the flood at 2400 BC. Abram was born 292 years after the flood, migrating to Canaan at age seventy-five. Genesis 14 happens shortly thereafter, c. 1981–1950 BC; https://www.britannica.com/biography/Hammurabi.

[1081] *Encyclopedia Americana,* Vol. 13, 666–668.

[1082] H2526—*Cham, khawm*: hot; son of Noah; patronymic for his descendants and country.

[1083] Wyatt, *Religious Texts from Ugarit,* 401–402: KTU 113 vv. 9–11, 20; Jean Nougayroll, Emmanuel Laroche, and Charles Virollaud, *Ugaritica V: New Texts of the Accadians, Horites, and Ugarites from the Archives Ugarit's Private Library* (Stony Brook, NY: Stony Brook University Press, 1968), 87–90, quoting Letter RS 18.147 Ugaritica Vol. 24.

700 BC) referred the kings of Phoenicia, Philistia, Ammon, Moab, and Edom as Amurro kings,[1084] dynastic bloodlines that seemingly continued and scioned into other Rephaim dynastic bloodlines.

Hebrew `am, which may also be inferred in part of the root syllable in Hammurabi/Hammurapi, means male, people, tribe or nation;[1085] *ammu* means paternal kinsmen in Akkadian.[1086] Additionally, the suffix ending Hammurabi/Hammurapi: "rapi/rabi" means "healer" in Akkadian; *rapha'* means "healer" in Hebrew,[1087] and is the root word for *rapha'*, meaning an invigorating giant or tribe of giants.[1088] Further, one might infer "abi" in the last syllable as meaning "father" in Hebrew, as in father of a bloodline or father of a people.[1089] The meaning of Hammurapi's kingship title communicates a self-healing giant man-king, or a healing giant man-king of a paternal nation, and or both. The Rephaim Ditan/Didan/Dedan/Tuatha De Danann eponymous ancestor, Ditanu/Didanu of Ugarit was an ancestor of Hammurapi/Hammurapi,[1090] based on the kingship title of each dynasty. One further notes the similarity in spelling, pronunciation, and suffix to prefix inversion of *Iy'anak/Anaqiy* King *Abi-yamimu* (Yamimu-Abi)[1091] from the Execration Texts, as compared to Hammurabi.

Thus, the etymological and historical record affirms the name of the Amorite/Amurru/*'Emoriy* hybrid people, derived eponymously and patronymically from an unused name for a Rephaim giant akin to Hebrew `Amar, and/or `Emor as in Hamor/*Chamowr*, a Hivite prince of Shechem known in the New Testament as Emmor/*Emmor'*.[1092] One deduces that Emmor, Emoriy, and Amar are transliterations for the Amorite Rephaim patriarch created by the god Ammur.

[1084] *Mercer Bible Dictionary,* 25: Amorite.

[1085] H5971—`am, am; from 6004: people, nation, kinsmen, and men/Ammi as in male(s)/sons used four times as in Ezek 46:18 where people are referred to as sons; H1121—*ben, bane*; a son as a builder of the family name as in people in Ezek 46:18: "Moreover the prince shall not take of the people's inheritance by oppression, to thrust them out of their possession; but he shall give his sons inheritance"; as Ammi in Hos 2:1: "Say ye unto your brethren, Ammi; and to your sisters, Ruhamah"; as in men in Num 31:32: "And the booty, being the rest of the prey which the men of war had caught"; as folk in Gen 33:15.

[1086] Yildirim, *Ancient Amorites (Amurro) of Mesopotamia,* 32.

[1087] H7495—*rapha'.*

[1088] H7497—*rapha'.*

[1089] H1—*'ab awb*: father; patrimony; principal; father of a people or a family line; compare names in "Abi-."

[1090] Wyatt, *Religious Texts from Ugarit,* 433, notes 1, 2, citing Finkelstein (1994, 72–82). Kspronk. files.wordpress.com/2020/07/spronk-dedan-ddd.pdf, 232: Dedan, quoting Finkelstein (1966), 98, and Schidt (1994), 75–78.

[1091] Billington, "Goliath and the Exodus Giants," 501, 506, citing Pritchard, *ANET,* 225.

[1092] H2544—*Chamowr, kham-ore'*: male donkey; Hivite prince of Shechem; Greek 1697 Emmor. Acts 7:16. G1697—*em-mor'*; of Hebrew origin 2544 *Chamowr*: an ass; the father of Sychem. Gen 33:17; 34:30; Josh 9:17; Acts 7:16.

CHAPTER 26

THE GIRGASHITES AND HIVITES

Gen 15:19 The Kenites, and the Kenizzites, and the Kadmonites,

Gen 15:20 And the Hittites, and the Perizzites, and the Rephaims,

Gen 15:21 And the Amorites, and the Canaanites, and the Girgashites, and the Jebusites.

The Girgashites and Hivites were part of the mighty seven,[1093] but only the Girgashites were listed among the mighty ten nations. Scripturally very little is known about the Girgashites, or where they lived. Girgashite/*Girgashiy* was "patrial" from an unused name, of uncertain derivation,[1094] and perhaps eponymous.

According to Jewish legend, the Girgashites were the only nation among the mighty seven to depart the Covenant Land after Israel's wars of conquest.[1095] Author Yoel Elitzur noted that Jewish scholar "R. Shmuel b. Nahman" stated, "Joshua sent three proclamations to [the Canaanites in] the Land of Israel prior to the [Israelites'] entry into the land: 'Whoever wishes to emigrate should emigrate; [whoever wishes] to make peace should make peace; [and whoever wishes] to wage war should do so.' The Girgashites emigrated, for they believed in the Holy One,

---

[1093] Gen 15; 21; Josh 24:10–11.

[1094] H1622—*Girgashiy, ghir-gaw-shee'*: patrial from an unused name of uncertain derivation; a Girgashite; one of the native tribes of Canaan; a dweller on "clayey soil."

[1095] Ginzberg, *Legends of the Bible*, 511.

blessed be He, and they went to Afrike."[1096] Eliztur noted that at the time of the Exodus, North Africa was understood to be "Afrike."[1097]

The transplanted North African Girgashite settlement, as this line of investigation goes, became famous with the addition of Phoenician migration to the city known as Carthage. Carthage was known to the Greeks as *Qart-hadast*, as *Karkhedon* to Greeks and Romans, and to the Phoenicians as *Kart-Hadasht*; Kart/Qart meant "city."[1098] According to a Greek myth of Carthaginian origin, *Karkhedon* was founded by Queen Dido of Tyre.[1099] As such, and during Alexander the Great's reign, the people of "Afrike" brought a claim against the Judean nation, arguing Canaan belonged to them. Moreover, another peculiar historical annotation arose in the Greek work *History of the Wars,* by Procopius of Caesarea, in the sixth century AD. Procopius astonishingly dropped a comment stating Moors of North Africa were descended from the Girgashites and the Jebusites who fled from Joshua—that they were not permitted to settle in Egypt, and so continued onward to Libya.[1100] In the Procopius account, Girgashites established cities throughout Libya as far as the Straits of Gibraltar, where they erected two columns made of white stone near a spring with inscribed writings in the Phoenician language that said: "We are they who fled from before the face of Joshua, the robber, the son of Nun!"[1101]

Egyptians additionally knew Girgashites as the *Kirkash/Qarqish* of Carchemish/Karkemish city in region of Turkey, and on the west bank of the Euphrates River. Scripture references Carchemish/*Karkmysh* in a war campaign waged by Pharaoh Necho in the fourth year of the Judean king Jehoiakim son of Josiah.[1102] Carchemish was additionally mentioned in the book of Isaiah along with Hamath and Arpad of Syria, at the time of the Assyrian prophecy that foretold the northern kingdom of Israel's destruction.[1103] Carchemish was transliterated as Kar-kem-ish and was defined as the "fortress of Chemosh," a god of the Moabites, Ammonites, and one of the Baalim associated with Mars.[1104] The foreign word *Karkmiysh* recorded in the Hebrew lexicon appears to be a compounded and conflated word of *Kark* and their

---

[1096] Yoel Elitzur, *Places in the Parasha: Biblical Geography and Its Meaning*, trans. Daniel Landam (New Milford, CT: Maggid Books, 2020), 1.

[1097] Ibid., 10.

[1098] Ibid., 257; *Encyclopedia Americana, Vol. 5,* 681: Carthage.

[1099] Ibid., 257.

[1100] Ibid, 257–258.

[1101] Ibid., 258.

[1102] *Encyclopedia Americana,* Vol. 5, 597: Carchemish; Elitzur, *Places in the Parasha,* 258. 2 Chron 35:20; Jer 46:2.

[1103] Isa 10:9.

[1104] H3751—*Karkmiysh, kar-kem-eesh'*: a city-state fortress in Syria along the Euphrates River; fortress of Chemosh; Hittite capital on the Euphrates River captured by Pharaoh Necho and then from him by Nebuchadnezzar; H3645—*Kmowsh, kem-oshe'*; or Jeremiah 48:7 *Kmiysh, kem-eesh'*: to subdue; god of the Moabites; the subduer; a god of the Ammonites identified with Baal-peor, Baal-zebub, Mars and Saturn.

god (Kemish) perhaps identifying *Kark* as the people (of champions/*'iysh*)[1105] worshipping Chemosh versus fortress/city of Chemosh, or both.

I submit that the *Kark* perhaps represents a people because the Rameses II records stated Hittites were allied with a people written in Egyptian as *Krks* as it connects to *Kirkash*. The earliest known reference surfaces in the capture of Carchemish circa 1479 BC by Egyptian Pharaoh Thutmosis III. Later-dated Rameses II inscriptions recorded the Kadesh/Qadesh campaign circa 1288 BC,[1106] indicates most Girgashites, by their absence, likely departed Canaan during the Exodus (c. 1450–1400 BC), and after Abraham's account in Genesis 15:21. However, some Girgashites remained in the Covenant Land, as recorded in the books of Deuteronomy and Joshua.[1107] The lack of a notable Girgashite presence in the Old Testament indicates most Girgashites fled before the Covenant Land conquest, because they were no longer a significant force amongst the Canaanite nations. Accordingly, Girgashites were intermittently included among the mighty seven.[1108]

Scripturally, what is revealed about the Girgashites is that they dwelled west of the Jordan River. *Strong's Dictionary* indicates Girgashites dwelled east and north of the Galilee Sea, on the edge of the Bashan and Mount Hermon region of the Rephaim kings Og and Sihon.[1109] Girgashites first appear between the Amorite and Hivite clans in the table of nations, indicating they dwelled in northern Canaan, where the Hivites' larger population dwelled,[1110] and near the Hittites. Patriarchless Girgashites suggest they were hybrids akin to the Jebusites and Amorites.

In search of the Girgashite patriarch, know that the Girgashite Semitic source word *Gsr* means "strong," and that Akkadian *Gasru* and *Gargamis* are also connected to Geshur/*Gshuwr* (2 Sam 3:3), and toponymic for the Gesuri/*Gshuwriy*.[1111] In Sumerian, *gal* communicated great or big, as in *lugal* for great man or king, and was cognate to Sumerian *rugal*, transliterated into Latin as *regalis* and English as "regal."[1112] Similarly, *Gur* was the Sumerian alternative word for "big,"[1113] but

[1105] H376 'Iysh: champion; men; man; great men or man; husband; servant. H377 'Iysh: man; champion; great man.

[1106] *Encyclopedia Americana*, Vol. 5, 597: Carchemish; Elitzer, *Places in the Parasha*, 258.

[1107] Deut 7:1; Josh 24:10–11.

[1108] Judg 3:5, 1 Kings 9:20; 2 Chron 8:7; Ezra 9:1; Neh 9:8.

[1109] H1622—*Girgashiy*.

[1110] Gen 10:16.

[1111] Frank L. Benz, *Personal Names in the Phoenician and Punic Inscriptions* (Rome: Biblical Institute Press, 1972), 300, citing F. Grondahl, *Die Personennamen der Texte aus Ugarit: PTU* 131. H01650—*Gshuwr: geshur*, 2 Sam 3:3; 13:37–38; 14:23, 32; 15:8; 1 Chron 2:23; 3:2; H01651—*Gshuwriy*: Geshurites: Josh 12:5; 13:11, 13; 1 Sam 27:8; Geshuri: Deut 3:14; Jos 13:2.

[1112] Peter and Hogan, *Sumerian Cuneiform English Dictionary.* Mug Sar Dictionary: Ebook pdf, 38: 12121; Lugal, 51: from 121FD Lu man: or ruler, and 120F2 Gal: big man and king and interchangeable with rugal that is equivalent to Latin regalis and English regal. *Mercer Dictionary of the Bible*, 975: Lugal.

[1113] *Sumerian Dictionary*, 9, big: gur.

disassociated from royal bloodlines. *Gur* fits phonetically with the first syllable of "Girgashites." Further, the Semitic source word *Gsr* is part of a series of words that includes *Gr*, as in gir/ger/gar/gur meaning dweller, and possibly a source for Hebrew *gur* meaning "dweller and dwelling place as in Gurbaal" (dwelling place of Baal). *Grg* is included in this Semitic series of related words, as in *Bn Grg*, the root for Girgasi and Girgisi and Girgisu,[1114] which indicates a link between the Geshurim and the Girgashites. Moreover, Hebrew *ger*, means stranger, foreigner, sojourner, and is rooted in *guwr*, defined as to gather for hostility, dwell, gather, fear, dread, and stranger.[1115]

Some scholars theorize Semitic *Gsr*, meaning "strong" from the *Ugaritic Texts*, is the source word for Akkaddian *Gasru*, and Hebrew, Geshur/*Gshuwr*.[1116] Scholars further connect Semitic *Gr* for Hebrew *Ger*, meaning foreigner and sojourner, as a possible combination root for the compounded, Girgashites/*Girgashiy*.[1117] Ergo, etymological connections related to Girgashite seem to indicate the *Bn Grg* were the offspring of a big and strong stranger, a Rephaim named *Grg* who was part of a band of giant foreign warriors and wanderers.

In the *Ugaritic Texts, Grg* was recorded as a personal name, a place, and as the *Bn Grg* people.[1118] *Bn Grg*, meaning son(s)/*bene* of *Grg* in Hebrew, were transliterated as girgisi, girgisu, and girgasi.[1119] The Semitic *Bn Grg* appear to the source words for English, Hebrew, Greek, Latin, and Akkadian transliterations: Girgasite, Girgashiy, Girgashite, Gergesite, Gergeseus, and Gargamis. Aside from the *Ugaritic Text* examples of *Grgs* and *Bn Grgs*, the greatest concentration of names of this kind surfaces in Carthaginian inscriptions from Qart-hadast (Tunis) in the language of "Hazal Afrike."[1120] "Dedication inscriptions for pagan temples in the city feature the names of donors to the temple, including Blytn Bn Grgs, Grgs Bn and Mtn Bn Grgsm. Considering these findings, Professor Nahum Slouschz

---

[1114] Benz, *Personal Names,* 298, 299, citing *Ugaritic Texts* KTU 145:15, 113:9, 328:14 referencing PRUV Ch. Vorolleaud, *Le Palais Royal d'Ugarit V Textes en Cuniforms Alpabetique des Archives Sud, Sud Ouest et Petit Palais;* UTGL Gordon, CH, *Ugaritic Text Book* and J. Nougarol, *Le Palais Royal d'Ugarit III: Textes Accadiens des Archives, Sud,* 18:02:14: I:20, 18:20:V:12. H1485 — *Guwr-Ba`al, goor-bah'-a*: dwelling of Baal; a place in Arabia. 2 Chron 26:7: "And God helped him against the Philistines, and against the Arabians that dwelt in Gurbaal, and the Mehunims."
[1115] H1616—*ger, gare; or geyr*; from 1481: a guest: foreigner; alien; sojourner; stranger; H1481—*guwr, goor*: sojourn as a guest; to shrink; fear; dread; gather for hostility as afraid; be afraid; dwell; gather; stand in awe; stranger.
[1116] Benz, *Personal Names,* 300.
[1117] H1616—*gêr gare.*
[1118] Benz, *Personal Names,* 299, citing *Ugaritic Texts* KTU 145:15, 113:9, 328:14 referencing PRUV Ch. Vorolleaud, *Le Palais Royal d'Ugarit V Textes en Cuniforms Alpabetique des Archives Sud, Sud Ouest et Petit Palais;* UTGL Gordon, CH, *Ugaritic Text Book,* and J. Nougarol, *Le Palais Royal d'Ugarit III: Textes Accadiens des Archives, Sud,* 18:02:14: I:20, 18:20: V:12.
[1119] Ibid.
[1120] Elitzur, *Places in the Parasha: Biblical Geography and Its Meaning,* 258–259.

speculated: 'In the Talmud it is told that the Girgashites went to Africa. .. and perhaps the donator is of Girgashite descent.'"[1121]

Assembling *gur* and *gerg* with Geshuri forms Ger-Geshurite/ *Ger-Gshuwriy*.[1122] Geshurites were a people that did not connect back to the table of nations—rather, they were a giant tribe that seemingly produced hybrid Canaanites known as the Girgashites begat by a giant named *Grg*, and or the ancient Egyptian transliteration *Krk;* the "k" and "g" letters were sometimes transliterated as the same.

Adding to this line of investigation, Assyrian inscriptions noted Damascus was located a district called *Gar-Emeris*. *Gar-Emeris* was a Hittite appellation meaning the "Place of the Amorites," noting the Hittite capital of Carchemish was written as *Gar-Gamis* in Assyrian texts. It follows that Girgashite in some Assyrian circles may have been transliterated as Gar-Gis, just as it was recorded in cuneiform texts found along the shores of the Gulf of Antioch.[1123] Knowing this seems to make sense of the Septuagint recording the Gergesi as the KJV Geshurites in Joshua 12:5, noting they lived next to King Og of Bashan and King Sion. *Grg* and/or Gergesi seems to be the likely name for the Rephaim patriarch of the Girgashites and Geshurites. Gergesi and *Grg* then, perhaps explains why Josephus named Gergesus for the Girgashites reflecting the patriarch's original name for the *Girgashiy* and the *Bn Grgs*. [1124]

> *Sept* Josh 12:4–5 And Og king of Basan, who dwelt in Astaroth and in Edrain, was left of the giants ruling from mount Aermon and from Secchai, and over all the land of Basan to the borders of Gergesi, and Machi, and the half of Galaad of the borders of Seon king of Esebon.

What is interesting about the Girgashites and their inclusion in the mighty seven nations is that the book of Exodus lists only six mighty nations illegally occupying the Covenant Land in three passages, whereby Girgashites were excluded.[1125] The exclusion of the Girgashites in the three Exodus verses indicates that only pockets of Girgashites dwelled in the land promised to Joshua and Moses at that time. Thus, and as noted before, smaller numbers of Girgashites dwelled in northern Canaan, along the seacoast, and at Ugarit where they dwelled among the famous Ugaritic Rapiu/Rephaim kings. Joshua fought Girgashites in the northern

---

[1121] Ibid., 259.

[1122] Benz, *Personal Names*, 300, citing F. Grohahl, *Die Personenennamen der Texte aus Ugarit*, 131. H1651—*Gshuwriy, ghe-shoo-ree';* patrial from 1650: a Geshurite; inhabitants of Geshur; Geshuri; H1650—*Gshuwr, ghesh-oor';* Geshur or Geshurites: proud beholder. Deut 3:14; Josh 13:12: Geshuri.

[1123] Sayce, *Races of the Old Testament*, 122.

[1124] *Josephus*, Ant 1:6:2.

[1125] Exod 3:8, 17; 23:23.

campaign who were part of the northern alliance. Girgashites held pockets of satellite settlements there.

Similarly, the book of Nehemiah (c. 440 BC) listed only six of the seven mighty nations as well, when Judah returned from Babylon exile a thousand years later.[1126] In this passage, though, Girgashites were included as dwelling in the land, but not the Hivites; some Girgashites returned to the Covenant Land after Assyria dispersed Israel (c. 721 BC). Further, the book of Ezra, of similar dating as the book of Nehemiah, excluded both the Hivites and Girgashites[1127] indicating the number of Girgashites must have been small. Before Judah's exile in Babylon, five hybrid nations dwelled in the Covenant Land in Solomon's time, whereby King Solomon made them vassal kings and nations, imposing tributes on them[1128] (c. 900 BC), but Girgashites were not listed at that time. Again, this indicates Girgashites migrated back after the northern kingdom of Israel had been exiled by Assyria circa 721 BC.

Hivites were listed immediately after the Girgashites in the table of nations. Hivites too were another of the mighty seven nations. Hivites were yet another Canaanite clan that provides additional evidence about hybrid human/Rephaim races with unexpected twists. Hivites dwelled near Sidon and Tyre in the mountains of Lebanon, near Mount Hermon, in the central region of the Covenant Land, and in Gibeon just north of Jerusalem.[1129] Hivite/*Chivviy*, as with all the patriarch-less Canaanite clans, is documented as singular in Hebrew, suggesting a patronymic link even though English translators utilize Hivite and Hivites.

Hivite/*Chivviy* is defined as a villager and one of the Aboriginal tribes of Palestine.[1130] Aboriginal people means first, native, original and from the beginning;[1131] Canaan and his families were born in Shinar before migrating to the Promised Land. Rephaim Aboriginals at the time of Babel roamed the lands outside the city walls and in the Covenant Land.[1132] This then indicates Hivite Canaanites were not the Covenant Land's Aboriginal people. *Nelson's Bible Dictionary*, though, notes some scholars believe Hivites were a branch of Horites/Horim, a Rephaim tribe.[1133] *Strong's Cyclopaedia* submits the Hebrew word *Chirri* for the spelling of Hivite, and that "the name is in the original, uniformly found in the singular form, and never in the plural format (*Cherrim* in this case), which indicates Hivites were *Ben Cherrim*—sons/children a patriarch *Cherri*."[1134] *Chirri*, however, does not

---

[1126] Neh 9:8.

[1127] Ezra 9:1.

[1128] 1 Kings 9:20–21; 2 Chron 8:7–8.

[1129] Gen 34:2; Josh 9:7; 11:3, 19; Judg 3:3–5; 2 Sam 24:7.

[1130] H2340—*Chivviy, khiv-vee*'; a villager; a Chivvite; aboriginal tribes of Palestine.

[1131] *Webster's*, 2: aboriginal.

[1132] *Unger's*, 1074: Rephaim. H7497—*rapha', raw-faw*': giants, old tribe of giants.

[1133] Gen 14:6; Deut 2:12, 22.

[1134] *Strong's Cyclopaedia*, Vol. 4, 281.

appear in the Hebrew lexicon though, making it unclear as to how *Strong's Cyclo-paedia* arrived at its source word for Hivite. Foreign, patronymic names though do extend from *Chirri*: Hiram and Huram/*Chiyram*, and Huri/*Chuwriy* of Sidon and Tyre.[1135] Knowing this meshes with *Nelson's* reference to Hivites (at least in part) as a branch of Horites/Horim, because Horim are understood in secular historical records as Hurrians.[1136]

Unger's and *Nelson's* note that the Horim/Hurrians migrated to the Middle East after 2400 BC, as determined from Mari Archaeology on the Euphrates, where the Mitanni dynasty was established.[1137] Hurrians were non-Semitics who welcomed a splinter group of Aryans, the Maryannu, into their tribes, and who thereafter bullied their way into the ruling class.[1138] Hence, *Nelson's* connection that Hivites were a kin branch of Horim[1139] may derive from Zibeon, the son of Seir the Horim (Gen 36:20) who was called a Hivite (Gen 36:2). Knowing that both the Horim and Hivvim were biblically Rephaim tribes that produced hybrid humans helps to resolve the confusion and conundrums. Hurrian and Horim were eponymous names from *Chirri*/*Cherrim*/*Chuwriy* and *Chori* respectfully, linked both etymologically and historically as the kin branches indicating Rephaim patriarchs like Huri or Hori, versus sons of Hivi/*Chivviy* of the Hivvim who begat hybrid Hivites. *Chori* and *Chuwriy* likely begat hybrids as well.

Even though standard dogma states that there is no record existing outside the Bible for the hybrid Hivite tribe,[1140] the Luwian/Luvian people mentioned in the *Hattusa Tablets* is thought by some to be a reference to the Hivites.[1141] Luwians first appear as a people and a language from 2000 BC or before, as a nation with a close language and geographical proximity to Hittites, but distinct. Luvian religion and gods include a strong Indo-European/Aryan influence, which was stronger than the same Indo-Aryan influence on the Hittite religion.[1142]

The Bible mentions two cities named Luz/*Luwz* located in proximity to various Hittite settlements. One was the original name for Bethel located twelve miles north of Jerusalem. The second city was located close to Arkites, Sidonians, and

---

[1135] H2438—*Chiyram khee-rawm'* or *Chiyrowm khee-rome'*: Chiram or Chirom; the name of two Tyrians: Hiram, and Huram; H2359—*Chuwriy khoo-ree'*: Churi: an Israelite: Huri.

[1136] *Nelson's*, 577: Horites.

[1137] *Nelson's*, 577: Horites; *Unger's*, 587: Horites.

[1138] *Nelson's*, 577: Horites; *Unger's*, 587: Horites; Bauer, *History of the World*, 470.

[1139] *Nelson's*, 571: Hivites.

[1140] Ibid.

[1141] *Hattusa Tablets*, CTH 291–292 Hittite Laws: law number 21 of the *Code of the Nesilim*: "If anyone steal a slave of a Luwian from the land of Luwia, and lead him here to the land of Hatti, and his master discover him, he shall take his slave only."

[1142] Manfred Hutter, The *Luwians: Handbook of Oriental Studies: Section One The Near Middle East*, ed. H. Craig Melchert (Leiden: Konninklyke Brill LV, 2003), Vol. 1, 68, Chapter 6: *Aspects in Luwian Religion*, 215.

was built in Hittite land.[1143] According to Patrick Skipworth of Leidon University, author of a paper on Luwian language: "it is clear that the texts demonstrate a unique Luwian religious system of magic and festival rituals, although from an early date Hattian and Hurrian elements can also be detected penetrating into Luwian religion."[1144] Hittites were recorded in cuneiform records as the Hatti.[1145]

The Luwian language was a member of the Anatolian family of languages originating with or influenced by Indo-European languages. The Luwian language, along with Anatolian siblings like the Hittite language, formed a language group distinct from the other members of the Indo-European family.[1146] The Hittite language Nesili, in early cuneiform writings, maintained a significant Luwian influence that reflected its royal dynastic origins, which included Indo-European and Hurrian roots.[1147] One muses if the Hebrew word for Luz, *Luwz*, was a name reflecting the people who begat cuneiform writing on tablets in Canaan and Anatolia—the Hurrians and Luwians. Biblically, Luz is part of an unexplained series of words connected to *luwach*, meaning polished stone tablet, which Israelites later adopted in the time of Exodus.[1148]

Understanding Hivites are linked to Luwians, know that Hivites were also linked to Gibeonite Rephaim in central Canaan,[1149] a detail many overlook. Accordingly, the Hivites/Luwians hybrid tribes inherited their language and culture from their Hivvim/Gibeonim giant patriarchs.

Scripture further noted Hivites dwelled in the Mount Lebanon region, from Baalhermon to Hamath, and were not conquered. They remained to test future Israelites' faith against the Baalim-led nations, and Israelite commitments to the skills of war along with the Sidonians, Philistines, Hittites, Amorites, Perizzites, and Hivites.[1150] Hence, Hivites survived as a nation dwelling close to Tyre until the monarchy period of Israel, beginning with David and beyond.[1151] In fact, at the time of Judah's return from exile circa 440 BC, descendants of the hybrid Canaanite clans of the mighty seven intermarried with Judeans of the southern kingdom, so much so that Scripture recorded, "so that the holy seed mingled themselves with the peoples of those lands."[1152]

[1143] H3869—*luwz, looz*; of foreign origin: nut-tree, perhaps the almond or hazel; H3870—*Luwz, looz*; from 3869: growing there: the early name of Bethel; the name of the town close the altar and pillar of Jacob; a Hittite town. Gen 28:19; Josh 16:2; 18:13; Judg 1:26.

[1144] Patrick Skipworth, *An Investigation of the Hieroglyphic Luwian Sign <SA5>* (Leiden: Leiden University, 2016), 8: citing Hutter, *The Lewians*, 215, in support of his argument.

[1145] *Catholic Encyclopedia*, Vol. 6, 305: Hittites.

[1146] Patrick Skipworth, *An Investigation of the Hieroglyphic Luwian Sign*, Introduction, 5.

[1147] Ibid., 6.

[1148] Ibid. H3871—*luwach, loo'-akh*; or luach, loo'-akh: listen: a polished tablet of stone, wood or metal; a board; plate; table. Exod 24:12; 31:18; 32:15, 16, 19; 34:1, 4, 28, 29; Deut 4:13; 5:22, 9:9, 10, 11, 15, 17; 10:1–5; 1 Kings 8:9; 2 Chron 5:10; Hab 2:2.

[1149] Josh 8:1–7; 11:19.

[1150] Judg 3:2–6.

[1151] 2Sa 24:7; 1Ki 9:20, 2Ch 8:7.

[1152] Ezr 9:1-2.

CHAPTER 27

ARKITES, SINITES, ARVADITES, ZEMARITES, AND HAMATHITES

Gen 10:17. .. and the Arkite, and the Sinite,

Gen 10:18 And the Arvadite, and the Zemarite, and the Hama-thite: and afterward were the families of the Canaanites spread abroad.

Phoenician mythology recounts a Lebanon mountain; the mountain range it is part of was patrial named after Libanus, an Aboriginal Lebanon giant whose skin was pale white.[1153]

Regarding many Canaanite families Josephus said: "we have nothing in the sacred books but their names, for the Hebrews overthrew their cities."[1154] The

---

[1153] H3844—*Lbanown, leb-aw-nohn'*; from 3835: the white mountain from its snow: whiteness; a heavily forested mountain range on Israel's northern border; H3835—*laban, law-ban'*; white: to be white; to make white; purify. Cooper, *An Archaic Dictionary*, 303: Libanus.
[1154] *Josephus*, Ant 1:6:2.

Canaanite families associated with the Phoenician stock were known as ruddy, white-skinned people, versus the more olive-colored stock of most Semitic peoples,[1155] including the Hittites. The Canaanite families listed in Genesis 10:17–18 were northern tribes closely affiliated with the Sidonians and Phoenicians[1156] geographically, culturally, politically, and religiously.

Arkites were commonly understood by historians as a people of Lebanon.[1157] According to Josephus, the Arkites/Arucas were a nation that occupied Arce city in the *Libanus*/Lebanon region.[1158] Arkites were known as the *Arkantu* in Egypt during Thutmose III's reign (c. 1479–1425 BC), and later as *Irkata* in the *Armana Letters*.[1159] Some historians believe Arkites belong within Sidon's lineage[1160] (likely via daughter intermarriage) because Arkites dwelled alongside Sidonians and Tyrians. Josephus confirmed Arkites were closely aligned with the Sidonians, as were the Amathites and Aradians: "But the parts about Sidon, as also those that belonged to the Arkites, and the Amathites, and the Aradians, were not yet regularly disposed of."[1161]

Scripturally, Arkite/`Arqiy* in its Hebrew singular patronymic format is defined as patrial from an unused name, and unexpectedly as an inhabitant of Erech in Shinar.[1162] One deduces the Arkite patriarch was similarly named to `Arqiy* or `Erek*. Similarly, *'Arkevay* is translated as Archevites in Ezra: 4:9, which is also patrial of *Erek* meaning a native of Erech/Uruk, just as *'Arkiy* is also translated as Archi and Archite meaning the same.[1163]

Erech/*Erek* was a city Nimrod restored after Babel; Uruk city was later reigned over by giant kings Lugalbanda and Gilgamesh.[1164] Gilgamesh had ties to Ugarit city, which connects `Arqiy* to giants by patrial and perhaps patronymic implications. Additionally, *The Uruki Epic Cycle* was an epic literary work set in Uruk city and centered around three Uruki kings: Enmerukar, Lugalbanda, and Gilgamesh, all giants. *Uruki* is Sumerian for the giants of Uruk/Erech that is the patrial root for *Arqiy/'Arkiy* and patronymic, reflecting the Arkite's patriarch. From a Sumerian perspective, one might define Uruk as the giant city. To this

---

[1155] Ellicott, *Old Testament Commentary*, Vol. 1, 51, Gen 10: note 11.

[1156] Ibid., 51, Gen 10: notes 7, 8, 9, 10.

[1157] Ibid., Vol. 1, 51, Gen 10: note 7.

[1158] *Josephus*, Ant 1:6:2.

[1159] *Unger's*, 103: Arkite.

[1160] *Strong's Cyclopaedia*, Vol. 1, 404.

[1161] *Josephus*, Ant 4:1:23.

[1162] H6208—`Arqiy, ar-kee`; patrial from an unused name meaning a tush; inhabitant of Erek—Arkite.

[1163] H756—'Arkəvay ar-kev-ah'ee; Aramaic patrial from 751; native of Erek: Archevite; H751— 'Erek, eh'-rek: length; a place in Babylon; H757—'Arkiy ar-kee'; patrial from a place in Palestine; native of Erek; Archi, Archite: 2 Sam 15:32; 16:16; 17:5, 14; 1 Chron 27:33. Archi: Josh 16:2.

[1164] Cahill, *Gifts of the Jews*, 20; *Encyclopedia Americana*, Vol. 12, 653–654.

end, Arkam was the (patronymic) king's title of the (eponymous) Arkam people, a people otherwise known as the Amalekites of the east.[1165] Arkam may have been an Amaleqim giant noting Amaleqim were listed in the war of giants.[1166] Thus the Arkite patriarch was likely named `Arkiy, Archi, and/or Arkam.

Very little is known about Sinites/ *Cynay*,[1167] a people that appear only two times in the Bible, and only in the table of nations. Biblical scholars believe Sinites were few and small in geographical size, and closely tied to a neighboring nation, the Arkites.[1168] Sinites were not listed as a people Israel fought in the conquest of the Covenant Land. Sinites are thought to have first settled in close proximity to Arkites and Sidonians, and in the area where Greek historian Strabo mentioned a mountain fortress called Sinna.[1169] Church father Jerome mentioned Sinu/Sinum/Sin ruins in his time, sites thought to be connected to Sinites.[1170] Syn was mentioned as a village by the Arca River near Tripolis in North Africa by Gesenius.[1171] Sin/ *Cyn* was further recorded in eastern Egypt,[1172] in the time of Nebuchadnezzar. One deduces some Sinites migrated to North Africa with the Phoenicians.

Sinite/ *Ciynay* is the singular form of Sinim/ *Ciyniym*, the land of the Sinim, a land from afar (Isa 49:12), whom many equate with the Chinese.[1173] What is fascinating is that "Sino" is a cognate name for Chinese. The etymology for Sino derives from the Ptolemaic Greek *Sinai* from Arabic *Sin,* from Sanskrit *Cyn/ Cyna*, of which the source is Indo-Aryan.*[1174]* One contemplates whether the Sinites/ *Ciyniym* may play a roll as part of the kings of the east of Armageddon.[1175] One further contemplates Sinite/ *Ciynay's* possible connection to Mount Sinai/ *Ciynay's* name that has an unknown derivation, and a name transliterated in English in the New Testament as Sina from Greek *Seenah'*.[1176] Mount Sinai/Sina/ *Ciynay* and *Cyn* mean thorn or thorny; Sinim/ *Ciyniym* also means thorns.

[1165] Cooper, *An Archaic Dictionary*, 81: Arkam.

[1166] Gen 14:7.

[1167] H5513—*Ciynay, see-nee'*; "from an otherwise unknown name of a man": a Sinite, or descendant.

[1168] Ellicott, *Old Testament Commentary*, Vol. 1, 51, Gen 10: note 8.

[1169] *Unger's*, 1201: Sinite; *Strong's Cyclopaedia*, Vol. 9, 777: Sinite, quoting Strabo, xvi, 755, and Jerome, *Hebrew Questions on Genesis, Locations and Cities.*

[1170] Ibid.

[1171] *Strong's Cyclopaedia* Vol. 9, 777: Sinite, quoting Gensenius Thesaurus, 948.

[1172] Ezek 30:15–16. H5512—*Ciyn*, seen; of uncertain derivation: Sin; thorn or clay; a town in eastern Egypt.

[1173] *Strong's Cyclopaedia*, Vol. 9, 777: Sinim. H5515—*Ciyniym, see-neem'*; Sinim; plural of an otherwise unknown name: a distant Oriental region likely southern China; thorns.

[1174] https://www.etymonline.com/word/sino; https://www.merriam-webster.com/dictionary/Sino.

[1175] Gen 16:12.

[1176] H5514—*Ciynay*; G4614—*see-nah'*; of Hebrew origin 5514; thorny; transliterated: Sina. Acts 7:31.

What surfaces from the limited information on the Sinites is a source name of Sin/*Cyn* for the unknown eponymously named tribe of the Sinim/*Ciyniym*. *Cyn* is very close to the name of a biblically recorded Rephaim king named Sihon/*Ciychown* and from the same series of words as *Cyn*, meaning thorns.[1177] One wonders whether Sihon/*Ciychown* was a patronymic king title of the *Ciyniym* becoming king over the Amorites,[1178] after the Senites/Sinim fled the Covenant Land to the far east. *Ciychown* and *Cyn* appear immediately before the seemingly source words for *Ciynay* and *Cyn*. On the other hand, Hebrew legends recount Sihon's original name as Arad.[1179]

The Arvadites/*'Arvadiy* is defined as descendants and patrial of Arvad City near Sidon.[1180] Arvadites were also thought to be inhabitants of the island of Aradus, the Greek transliteration for Arvad;[1181] noting *'Arvad* is an island city near Sidon.[1182] In Scripture, the *Arvad* (Arvadites) were dependent on and connected to Sidon and Tyre[1183] as wise men, mariners, and warriors;[1184] Tyrus was king of Tyre, a Rephaim depicted in prophetic allegory as Satan-like and antichrist-like.[1185] Tyrus was included among Zidon/Sidon and the kings of the north, those who caused terror in the land of the living.[1186]

The *Arvad* were a warrior people depicted in the book of Ezekiel as fighting in organized units on and around the walls of Tyre.[1187] The *'Arvadiy* fought for the Phoenicians as their mighty warriors[1188] along with the enigmatic Gammadim who fought from the towers. The Gammadim were brave, valorous men of war, a word rooted in *gomed* meaning a cubit, half a cubit, and span of nine inches,[1189] suggesting the Gammadim were little people of war—less than two feet tall.

[1177] H5512—*Ciyn*.

[1178] H5511—*Ciychown, see-khone*; or *Ciychon*: tempestuous; warrior; an Amoritish king.

[1179] Ginzberg, *Legends of the Bible*, 461.

[1180] H721—*'Arvadiy, ar-vaw-dee*; patrial from 719: an Arvadite or citizen of Arvad; I shall break loose; descendants of Arvad; a son of Canaan; H719—*'Arvad, ar-vad'*: I shall break loose; a city-island near Sidon.

[1181] Ellicott, *Old Testament Commentary for English Readers*, Vol. 1, 51, Gen 10: note 9; Vol 5, 280, Ezek 27:8, 11: note 8; *Strong's Cyclopaedia*, Vol. 1, 449–450: Arvad and Arvaties.

[1182] H719—*'Arvad*.

[1183] *Strong's Cyclopaedia*, Vol. 1, 449–450: Arvad and Arvadites.

[1184] Ezek 27:8, 11.

[1185] Ezek 28:2, 12.

[1186] Ezek 32:30.

[1187] Ezek 27:11. H5439—*cabiyb, saw-beeb'*: a circle; neighbor; around; round about; circuit; compass; on every side; in a circuit.

[1188] Ezek 27:11. H719—*'Arvad*.

[1189] H1574—*gomed, go'-med*: a span or and/or cubit: half-cubit-the measure is a span of nine inches; H1575—*gammad, gam-mawd'*; from and same as 1574: a warrior as in grasping weapons: brave men; valorous men.

> Ezek 27:11 The men of Arvad with thine army were upon thy walls round about, and the Gammadims were in thy towers: they hanged their shields upon thy walls round about; they have made thy beauty perfect.

Arvadites were renowned for their architectural flare, artistic techniques, naval expertise, and warriorcraft. They aligned strategically with Tyre and Sidon in maritime trade, from their island two miles off the Syrian coast, where the "family of Arvadites" settled.[1190] Greeks named this island Arad, Arud, and Arudus,[1191] which explains the Septuagint referencing Arvadites as Aradian, and Josephus referencing them as Arudeus as well as Aradians closely associated with Sidon: "Arudeus possessed the island Aradus."[1192] Aradus/Arudus formed a confederacy with Sidon and Tyre known to historians as the "Triopolies" that boasted of a ruling council of three kings and their accompanying senators that numbered three hundred.[1193]

What is fascinating about the Arad connection is that Israel battled the Canaanite king Arad, from Arad city, one of the Canaanite royal cities at the beginning to the Covenant Land conquest. Arad means "fugitive";[1194] it appears to be a patronymic name and dynastic Rephaim kingship title and eponymous for a Canaanite hybrid nation, and the likely patriarchal candidate for the Arvadites/Aradites and/or Arvad/Arudus. What we do know is that a Arod/'Arowd, son of Gad, was orthographically a variation of 'Arvad/Aradus; 'Arvad also means: I shall roam or subdue, perhaps like a fugitive, as connected to ruwd meaning wanderer and rule.[1195]

Zemarites/Tsmariy is a patrial from an unused name or place in Palestine, Tsmarayim/Zemaraim: a city in Benjamin and a mountain in Ephraim,[1196] which possibly indicates migrations.[1197] Zemarites are thought to have first settled in the area of Sumra on the Mediterranean coast between Arvad and the Tripolis city-states.[1198] Zemar and Arvad were the first nations documented on Egyptian monu-

---

[1190] *Nelson's*, 124; *Unger's*, 110: Arvad and Arvadite.
[1191] *Strongs's Cyclopaedia*, Vol. 1, 449–450: Arvad and Arvadite.
[1192] *Josephus*, Ant 1:6:2, 4:1:23.
[1193] Willis Boughton, *History of Ancient Peoples* (New York: Knickerbocker Press, 1897), 329.
[1194] H6166—'Arad, ar-awd': to sequester; a fugitive; a wild ass; a Canaanite royal city. Num 21:1; 33:40; Josh 12:14.
[1195] Gen 46:16; Num 26:17. H720—'Arowd, ar-ode'; an orthographical variation of 719; fugitive; Arod; I shall subdue; I shall roam; H7300—ruwd, rood: to tramp about, ramble free; roam; wander; have the dominion; be lord; rule; H719—'Arvad, ar-vad': a refuge of roving.
[1196] H6786—Tsmariy, tsem-aw-ree'; patrial from an unused name of a place in Palestine: Zemarite; Zemaraim double woolens; H6787—Tsmarayim, tsem-aw-rah'-yim: Zemaraim; double fleece of wool; a city in northern Benjamin.
[1197] *Unger's*, 1384: Zemarite and Zemaraim.
[1198] *Nelson's*, 1336–1337: Zemarite and Zemaraim.

ments when Tyre and Sidon were still regarded as city-states.[1199] Zemar/Zumar/
Sumru was recorded in the *Armana Letters* as one of the most important cities of
Phoenicia before its destruction.[1200] The pentapolis city-states of the later Phoeni-
cian empire were Sidon, Tyre, Arvad/Aradus, Arka, and Zemar.[1201] One deduces
Zem, Zemar or Sum was the Zemarite patriarch.

Hamathite/*Chamathiy* is patrial from a city of the Bashan region and was the
capital of northern Syria, situated on the Orontes River. The Macedonians/Greeks
referred to Hamath as Epiphaneia.[1202] Hamath/*Chamath* means "fortress." Hamath
of Bashan was the city the Baalim god Ashima dwelled in.[1203] Ashima is source
word for the name of the licentious fallen seraphim angel Asmodeus, portrayed in
the occult in his degraded form with three heads: an ogre, a ram, and a bull, along
with bird feet and serpentine tail; Asmodeus rides a fire-breathing dragon.[1204]

The Rephaim of Bashan held close ties religiously with the Sidonians, worshipping Baal and Ashtaroth, as did the Rephaim of Ugarit. It follows that Hamath/
Chamath is patrial through *Chammath* in Canaan as it relates to Canaanite Hamathites, a city fortress of the northern alliance in the Rephaim wars in the Covenant
Land conquest.[1205] Fenced/*mibstar* (cities) is defined as a castle as in fortification,
fortress, and stronghold.[1206]

Chamath is singular, once more indicating it is eponymous from an ancestor
connected to the Baalim god Ashima. One wonders whether *Chamesh/Chemisyshi*,
both meaning ordinal from five, might be the patriarch for the Hamathites,[1207] just
as Arba (four) was the patriarch for the Anakim. A Septuagint variant accounting in Genesis 10 transliterates "Hamathites" as "Amathites." Josephus added
that Sidon city was referred to by the Greeks as "Sidon Amathus inhabited in
Amathine, which is even now called Amathe."[1208] Hence the Rephaim patriarch for
the Hamathites may have been transliterated Amathiy or Amath from *Chamath*.

[1199] Boughton, *History of Ancient Peoples,* 305–306.

[1200] *Armana Letters,* Aziru to Pharaoh, EA 161, Clay Tablet BM 29818 at the British Museum,
Paragraph V, 35–40: "The king, my lord, has spoken about the building of Sumer [Zemar]."

[1201] Matthew George Easton, *Easton's Dictionary and World English Bible* (Norway: TruthBeTold
Ministry, 2017), Phoenicia, 1013; *Encyclopedia Americana,* Vol. 21, 786.

[1202] Ellicott, *Old Testament Commentary,* Vol. 1, 51, Gen 10: note 11.

[1203] 2 Kings 17:30. H807—'*Ashiyma*', *ash-ee-maw*'; of foreign origin: a deity of Hamath; H2577—
Chamathiy, kham-aw-thee'; patrial from 2574: a Chamathite; native of Chamath; Hamathite;
Hamath; H2574—*Chamath, kham-awth*'; walled; a place in Syria; fortress.

[1204] Guiley, *Encyclopedia of Demons and Demonology,* 18: Asmodeus.

[1205] Josh 19:35. H2577—*Chamathiy, kham-aw-thee*'; patrial from 2574; H2574—*Chamath,
kham-awth*'; H2575—*Chammath, klam-math*': hot springs; hot spring, fortified city of Naphtali.

[1206] H4013—*mibtsar, mib-tsawr*': castle; fortification; fortress; fortified city; stronghold.

[1207] H2549—*chamiyshiy, kham-ee-shee*'; ordinal from 2568: ordinal number, 5th; H2568—
chamesh, khaw-maysh'; masculine *chamishshah*; a primitive numeral; five, fifteen, fifth, five.

[1208] *Josephus,* Ant., 1:6:2.

THE CANAANITES

CHAPTER 28

Gen 10:6 And the sons of Ham; Cush, and Mizraim, and Phut, and Canaan.

Gen 9:25 And he said, Cursed be Canaan; a servant of servants shall he be unto his brethren.

Of the Canaanite patriarchs, only Heth and Sidon were sons of Canaan, the son of Ham. All three were accredited with begetting eponymously named tribes in the table of nations. The three Canaanite patriarchs are regarded by some as giant nations, even though each had a human father. Like Nimrod, though, all three began to behave as giant-like nations—gibborim.

Canaan/*Kna`an* is regarded as the grand patriarch of all the Canaanite twelve clans that occupied Canaan, biblically mapped as: "from Sidon, as thou comest to Gerar, unto Gaza; as thou goest, unto Sodom, and Gomorrah, and Admah, and Zeboim, even unto Lasha."[1209] Canaan's name derives from *kana`*, meaning to humiliate, humble, and subjugate,[1210] which is odd because Canaanites and all the clans were thought of as powerful giant-like nations—part of the mighty seven, and seemingly not slaves. We learn from the Egyptian *Khu-n-Aten Tablets* the origination of the geographical term known as *Kinakhkhi* (Greek *Khna*), which signified the region beginning just north of Beirut and Lebanon, and inland east

---

[1209] Gen 10:19. H3667—*Kna`an, ken-ah'-an*: humiliated; merchant; a son a Ham; country inhabited by Canaan; progenitor of the Phoenicians and of the various nations of Canaan.
[1210] H3665—*kana`, kaw-nah'*: to bend the knee; to humiliate, vanquish, bring into subjection, humble, subdue.

and south to the mountains of Jerusalem, whereby Egyptians classified Canaanites as the southern Phoenicians.[1211]

Canaan's name derives from an obscure incident shortly after the ark came to rest on Mount Ararat, from Noah's obscure curse cast upon Ham for his crime against Noah. Curse/'*Arar* is defined as to execrate as in bitterly curse, denounce, and abhor,[1212] in the biblical and religious sense to ecclesiastically censure as anathema and/or abomination. Curse/'*Arar* immediately precedes '*Ararat* in *Strong's Dictionary* and is directly linked to '*Ararat* meaning Armenia, the precipitation or a reversal of a curse, the mountain the ark landed after the flood,[1213] and the place where Noah levied his curse upon Ham.

> Gen 8:4 And the ark rested in the seventh month, on the seventeenth day of the month, upon the mountains of Ararat.

When "cursed" with God's authority, as Noah cursed Canaan, the maledictions are not merely impotent whims or wishes but impart those intended miseries and effects as prophesied in the denunciation.[1214] One deduces that Ham violated Noah so grievously that Noah regarded the violation as an abomination and then issued a curse within a prophecy embedded with allegory against a portion of Ham's seemingly unborn son and posterity (Gen 9:25). Ham "uncovered" Noah when Noah was in his tent, intoxicated, and unconscious[1215]—a sexual crime.[1216]

One contemplates if Ham decided to name his youngest son Canaan to bear the burden of the curse versus all of Ham's sons, or his firstborn Cush, who begat Nimrod. One might muse whether Canaan later followed in Nimrod's rebellious footsteps by intermarrying with giants, and then spitefully settled in the land reserved for Shemites and Israelite posterity, akin to Nimrod settling in the land of the Euphrates versus Africa. Certainly, Canaanites, after Babel, settled the Covenant Land populated by Aboriginal Rephaim, whom many scholars conclude Rephaim were begat as offspring of Watchers and Canaanite daughters.[1217] If so, this indicates fallen angels procreated with Canaanites before the confusion of languages, and perhaps before Nimrod built the walls of Babel city, and shortly after the Ararat incident. *The Jewish Encyclopedia* noted pre-Canaanite Rephaim were

---

[1211] Sayce, *Races of the Old Testament*, 101–102.

[1212] H779—'*arar, aw-rar*': bitterly curse; curse; cursed.

[1213] H780—'*Ararat, ar-aw-rat*'; Ararat or Armenia: a curse reversed or started; a mountainous region of eastern Armenia; mountain where Noah's ark came to rest.

[1214] *Strong's Cyclopaedia*, Vol. 2, 610.

[1215] Gen: 9:21–26.

[1216] Lev 18:1–30; 20:10–27.

[1217] Bane, *Encyclopedia of Giants and Humanoids in Myth*, 141: Rephaim, citing Aichele, *Violence, Utopia, and the Kingdom of God*, 52, and Garnia, *Worship of the Dead*, 93–94; *The Jewish Encyclopedia*, Vol. 5, 657: giants.

absorbed later into Canaanite nations that included the Amorites via intermarriage citing Genesis 10:15–20,[1218] Canaan's patriarch-less nations.

Ham's name means "hot," as in tropical habitat. His allotment was apportioned in Africa, and is understood as patronymic for his posterity, country, and a collective name for Egyptians.[1219] Cush settled in Ethiopia and southern Africa.[1220] Mizraim settled in Upper and Lower Egypt with Ham,[1221] which may account for the unified two kingdoms explicating how Egypt rose to power quickly after the flood. Phut settled in North Africa west of Egypt.[1222] Canaan, by inference, did not receive an allotment of land in Africa as did his siblings, perhaps as part of the consequences of the curse. Canaan seemingly rejected their fate to be subservient, choosing instead to settle the Covenant Land with Rephaim, land God reserved for Himself and Israel. Canaan and his two sons, Heth and Sidon, then conspired to create offspring hybrid giant/human nations via Rephaim. Knowing this may explain why Canaanite Phoenicians expropriated Carthage[1223] circa 814 BC, motivated in part by what they considered their rightful inheritance.

Canaan's gambit to align and intermix with Rephaim was the Canaanite retort to the servitude curse—a strategy to steal God's reserved land and defend their ill-begotten plunder as a giant-like race reinforced with Rephaim warriors, led initially by Rephaim kings. Canaanite clans were insulated by the Rephaim, Emim, and Zamzummim east of the Jordan River, and in the south protected by Horim, Amaleqim, and Anakim.[1224] Knowing this makes sense of the dynastic Mesopotamian kings struck first at the Rephaim nations protecting the rebellious Canaanite pentapolis.[1225] In describing the war of giants, Josephus described the five kings of Sodom as offspring of giants: "There were five kings that managed the affairs of this county: Ballas, Barsas, Senabar, and Sumobor, with the king of Bela; and each king led on his own troops; and the Assyrians made war upon them; and, dividing their army into four parts, fought against them.. .. These kings had laid waste all Syria, and overthrown the offspring of the giants."[1226]

Josephus underscored that Canaanites were hybrid offspring of giant patriarchs, not fallen angels. Canaanite hybrid clans burgeoned forth throughout the

---

[1218] *The Jewish Encyclopedia*, Vol. 5, 657: giants.
[1219] H2526—*Cham, khawm*: hot from a tropical habitat; a son of Noah; as a patronymic for his descendants or their country; collective name for Egyptians.
[1220] H3568—*Kuwsh, koosh*; of foreign origin; Ethiopia; a son of Ham and his territory; a synonym for black.
[1221] H4714—*Mitsrayim, mits-rah'-yim*: Upper and Lower Egypt; land of the Copts; Egyptians.
[1222] H6316—*Puwt, poot*; of foreign origin: a son of Ham, name of his descendants or their region; nation and people of northern Africa; Libyans.
[1223] *Strong's Cyclopaedia*, Vol. 2, 133.
[1224] Gen 14:5–7; Deut 2:10–21.
[1225] Gen 14:8–11.
[1226] Josephus, *Ant.*, Book 1 9:1.

Covenant Land. As such, Scripture documents the "daughters of Canaanites" and the daughters of Canaan" in the context of wives for patriarchs. Abraham and Isaac went to great lengths to ensure their sons did not marry from the daughters of Canaanites, even though Esau did with Adah, the daughter of a Hittite, as well as Aholibamah, daughter of Anah, who was daughter of Zibeon the Hivvim.[1227] The "daughters of Canaan" phraseology is akin to the "daughter of men" phraseology with the creation of Nephilim in Genesis 6:2 and 4. It follows that if Canaanite daughters procreated with fallen angels to create Rephaim, then other daughters did so with Rephaim to create the patriarch-less clans.

One ponders if Canaan and his two sons interbred with female Rephaim to produce their hybrid human Rephaim nations, as Eliphaz did with the Horim Timna.[1228] An interesting annotation regarding Pharaoh Amenhotep II documented his capture of 640 Canaanites along with the Maryannu[1229] giants. As such, this fits with Canaan, Sidon and Heth listed first as Canaanite patriarchs in the table of nations, followed by their kin nine patriarch-less clans.[1230]

The new-man strategy and Rephaim alliances met with limited success. The Canaanite pentapolis of the Dead Sea region somehow fell under the dominance of Mesopotamian kings as vassal states, first with the Ur III Dynasty led by King Amraphel, and enforced by King Chedorlaomer of Elam, Amraphel's tax collector.[1231] After the fall of the Ur III Dynasty (c. 1950 BC), and after the utter destruction of Sodom Gomorrah and the cities of the plain, Canaanite clans fell under the dominance of the Babylonian empires, and then Egyptian dynasties as vassal states. In fact, the Egyptian dispatches between Egyptian governors and vassal Canaanite kings indicate the chief centers Egyptians established to dispense their authority were Gebal/Byblos of Zemar in Phoenicia, Megiddo in the central region, and Gaza city in the south where Egyptian governors were stationed. Elsewhere, native kings were commissioned to exercise Pharaoh's authority backed by Egyptian garrisons.[1232]

The greater Canaanite clan military defense strategy evolved after the war of giants, likely in the era of the Hyksos kings in Egypt, whereby the Canaanite pentapolis fortress city-states were reinforced with walls up to the sky,[1233] with networks of village defense fortifications working together. Knowing this makes sense that Canaanite hybrid clans were reported among the mighty seven nations as nations stronger, taller, mightier, and greater than Israelites, and that giant-

---

[1227] Gen 28:1,6, 8; 24:3; 36:2.
[1228] Gen 36:12, 20–22; 1 Chron 1:39.
[1229] *Mercer's*, 129.
[1230] Gen 10:15–18.
[1231] Gen 14:1–5.
[1232] Sayce, *Races of the Old Testament*, 101.
[1233] Num 13:28–30; Deut 1:27–28.

like Canaanite clans dwelled in mighty fortresses and among the Anakim and kings, [1234] and alongside Ugarit city. It follows that Canaanite religion and culture would reflect Rephaim religion and culture, and it did. The Canaanite pantheon was centered around El as the parent god, succeeded by his offspring, Baal and his wife Ashteroth, the Queen of heaven, Great Mother of Fertility, and the Great Mother,[1235] as described in the *Ugaritic Texts*. Ashteroth, the partner goddess of El and then Baal, was classified as a fallen seraphim angel in the occult on par with Beelzebub and Lucifer.[1236] Further, archaeological evidence indicates Rephaim were visibly present in Canaanite civilizations. Rephaim images captured in Canaanite art vividly portrays serpentine beings with long, serpentine necks, heads like cobras, small mouths, and coffee-bean eyes.[1237] Rephaim crop up often in Canaanite texts, where the appellation translates as "divine beings,"[1238] demigod kings of the House of Dragon.

Canaanites were referenced in the *Ugaritic Texts* as a group with merchant peoples that indicated Canaanites were a distinct people from the Rephaim Ugarit civilization.[1239] Although the Canaanite and Ugarit civilizations were distinct, the Ugarit culture overflowed into Canaanite culture and religion in their gods like El and Baal,[1240] along with many of their dynastic kings. The Ugaritic culture was in full bloom in the late Bronze Age, which many historians date from 1550 to 1200 BC using secular dating.[1241] Biblical dating then would place Ugarit's demise well before the conquest of the Covenant Land circa 1400 BC, and well before 1550 BC.

Rephaim is a word found in many ancient Canaanite texts, referring to them as divine kings like Og of Mount Hermon and Bashan.[1242] Canaanite kings considered themselves to be living gods, descended from the demigod offspring of El and Baal, as witnessed by the famous Phoenician King Hiram who abetted Solomon in building the Jerusalem temple. Phoenician tomb inscriptions describe a dynastic lineage of kings who represented themselves as the earthly representatives of gods.[1243] Rephaim initially begat the dynastic royal bloodlines of the Canaanites clans that was succeeded by hybrid bloodline Canaanite/Rephaim kings due to Rephaim infertility issues. Thus, "Canaanite" became a catch-all name for hybrid

---

[1234] Num 13:29; Deut 1:28.

[1235] Knight, *Uriel's Machine*, 371.

[1236] Guiley, *Encyclopedia of Demons and Demonology*, 19: Asteroth/Ashteroth.

[1237] Lorraine Evans, *Kingdom of the Ark* (London: Simon and Schuster UK Ltd., 2000), 268–269.

[1238] Porter, *The New Illustrated Companion to the Bible*, 62.

[1239] *Mercer's*, 129: Canaan; *Ugaritic Texts* UT 311.1, 1089.7, 10.

[1240] Ibid., 129.

[1241] Wyatt, *Religious Texts from Ugarit*, 13, Introduction.

[1242] Porter, *The New Illustrated Companion to the Bible*, 62.

[1243] Christopher Knight and Richard Lomas, *The Book of Hiram* (London: Century, 2003), 93, 98.

human/Rephaim offspring as the patronymic founder to the larger hybrid Canaanite clans.

The Canaanite clans scattered throughout the Levant and surrounding region, claiming the lands from Sidon toward Gerar as far as Gaza, and then toward Sodom and Gomorrah, Admah, and Zeboiim, as far as Lasha,[1244] land that all Canaanite clans would defile with the sins of Ham that created Canaan's curse. Later, Israel was forbidden to follow the abominations of Egypt (Ham) or the abominations of Canaanites (and Rephaim) in the Covenant Land, lest Israel be spewed out like Israel was about to do to Canaanite nations and Rephaim nations.[1245]

> Lev 18:3 After the doings of the land of Egypt, wherein ye dwelt, shall ye not do: and after the doings of the land of Canaan, whither I bring you, shall ye not do: neither shall ye walk in their ordinances.. ..

> Lev 18:27 (For all these abominations have the men of the land done, which were before you, and the land is defiled;).

Ham's crime that brought about the anathema/abomination curse/`arar was much more than just taking Noah's clothes off while Noah was intoxicated, even though the passage's obscure language states Ham uncovered Noah to see his nakedness.[1246] In Leviticus 18:6–30 Israel was instructed not to approach any kin to "uncover their nakedness" and then continues with all the variations and consequences thereof. Verses 18:7–8 begin with instructing: do not uncover the nakedness of one's father, mother, sister, and expands the perimeter from there. Nakedness/`ervah is defined as nudity, naked, exposing the genitals, and figuratively as disgrace, blemish, shame, unclean and improper behavior.[1247] As such, uncovering nakedness indicated biblically that an improper sexual connotation was in play. Further, "uncover" translated from *galah* meaning to denude, and especially in a disgraceful sense, captives that were stripped, exile, reveal, remove, discover, etc.[1248] As such, Noah's "nakedness" and "uncovering" requires further investigation to discern how seeing Noah naked was raised to an abomination that begat a curse.

Leviticus 20 explains that within the sexual violation laws against close kin as: if a man takes his sister and sees her nakedness this is a wicked thing and he will bear that iniquity, and that if someone takes a wife and her mother it is wickedness

---

[1244] Gen 10:19.

[1245] Lev 18:28–30.

[1246] Gen 9:21–22.

[1247] H6172—`ervah, er-vaw`: nudity, especially the genitals; disgrace; exposed; blemish; nakedness; shame; unclean; indecency; improper behavior.

[1248] H1540—*galah, gaw-law`*: to denude in a disgraceful sense; to exile captives being stripped; uncover nakedness, to be uncovered, to be disclosed.

because he has uncovered their nakedness.[1249] Hence, "uncovering" when used with "nakedness" is more than seeing someone's nakedness or denuding them. Further, "taking" has sexual implications and is the same language used for fallen angels who "took any women they chose" to produce Nephilim.[1250]

Leviticus 18:24–26 raised some forms uncovering and nakedness transgressions to forbidden sexual sins status as defiling and abominations—abominations Canaanites previously defiled the land with. The same language was penned for illicit sexual sins against a neighbor's wife and daughter-in-law surfaces in Ezekiel 22 with discovering, defiling, and nakedness, causing humbling, pollution, and abomination.[1251]

> Lev 18:24 Defile not ye yourselves in any of these things: for in all these the nations are defiled which I cast out before you:
>
> Lev 18:25 And the land is defiled: therefore I do visit the iniquity thereof upon it, and the land itself vomiteth out her inhabitants.
>
> Lev 18:26 Ye shall therefore keep my statutes and my judgments, and shall not commit any of these abominations; neither any of your own nation, nor any stranger.

Discovered/*Galah* in Ezekiel 22:10 is used in conjunction with nakedness, just as uncovered/*galah* and nakedness are used together in Leviticus 18 and 20's sexual laws.[1252] Discover/*galah* surfaces again in Deuteronomy 22 with "lie and lay with her," and with "discover his father's skirt." "Skirt" can also be an allegory for nakedness, and combined with discovered/*galah* is another allegory for sex.[1253] The phraseology for sexual allegory of discovered/uncovered comes together in Deuteronomy 27:20 with "lieth with his father's wife" and "uncovereth his father's skirt." Ergo, Leviticus 18:20 and 20:11, 12, 18 are defining verses for the discovered and uncovered allegories as laws of forbidden sex, stating: if one lies with near kin, this is uncovering their nakedness.

Now, Leviticus 20:11 and 18:7–8 notes that if a "man lieth with his father's wife, he has uncovered his father's nakedness," as in illicit sex and the shame thereof. But note in these examples that the mother is named in the act, as in Deuteronomy 27:20, which is very important. The shame of the person who was sexually violated continues to the spouse also as uncovering the nakedness, even though the latter was not violated and did not have their nakedness uncovered physically

[1249] Lev 20:14–18.
[1250] Gen 6:2, 4.
[1251] Ezek 22:10–11.
[1252] Ezek 22:10–11.
[1253] Deut 22:28.

or sexually. Both are shamed, but differently. Further, in Leviticus 18:7, 11, 20:17, and elsewhere, we are instructed that when a female kin's nakedness is uncovered, her nakedness indicates she uncovered sexually. Typically, the person is identified in the physical sexual crime as the one uncovered, just as Leviticus 18:7 says not to uncover the nakedness of the father or the mother, even though the shame passes on to the parent or the spouse.

Knowing the importance of the language in the sexual laws then makes sense of Genesis 9:29. Noah drank wine. Noah became drunken. Ham uncovered Noah's nakedness. Noah awoke and knew what Ham did to him. Hence, Noah was identified as being drunken, sexually violated by Ham, and left naked, not Noah's wife. As such, and as outlined in the Leviticus law examples, Noah was violated. Ham's brothers then took a blanket to cover Noah, not their mother.

> Gen 9:21 And he drank of the wine, and was drunken; and he was uncovered within his tent.
>
> Gen 9:22 And Ham, the father of Canaan, saw the nakedness of his father.. ..
>
> Gen 9:23 And Shem and Japheth took a garment, and laid it upon both their shoulders, and went backward, and covered the nakedness of their father; and their faces were backward, and they saw not their father's nakedness.
>
> Gen 9:24 And Noah awoke from his wine, and knew what his younger son had done unto him.

Leviticus 20:13 defined Ham's crime: a man who lies with a man as with a woman (uncovering the other's nakedness) is an abomination, and thus worthy of a curse. These were same sexual sins and abominations that Rephaim and Canaanites did to defile the Covenant Land.

> Lev 20:13 If a man also lie with mankind, as he lieth with a woman, both of them have committed an abomination.
>
> Lev 18:3. .. and after the doings of the land of Canaan, whither I bring you, shall ye not do: neither shall ye walk in their ordinances.
>
> Lev 18:27 (For all these abominations have the men of the land done, which were before you, and the land is defiled;).

Ham's defiling of Noah was the way of the antediluvian Nephilim docu-mented in Enochian books,[1254] and the abominable ways of the postdiluvian Rephaim: sodomy and other sexual crimes common in Sodom, Gomorrah, Admah, Zeboiim, Bela/Zoar,[1255] the crimes of fornication and going after strange flesh recorded there in Jude 1:7. The apocryphal Manichaean *Book of Lamech of Cain,* thought to be originally part of the *Enoch Book of Giants,* supports that many of the sexual laws forbidden in Leviticus 18 and 20 were committed by Nephilim in the city of Enoch before the flood, and seemingly carried on after the flood by Rephaim at Sodom, Gomorrah, the cities of the plain, and elsewhere:

> 8.5 And the [sons of God] in the midst of the city of Enoch were [mighty]. 8.6 They had power and authority, and they had their way with anyone they laid their hands upon. 8.7 And the [sons of God] showed man how to mix the blood and [other] abominations in the city of Enoch. 8.8 The [sons of God] were [extravagant] and ruled over the city of Enoch with [misery] and there was no rest in their hatred. 8.9 With this [misery] they mocked men with songs, for the destruction of the wicked is singing. 8:10 And there was violence on the Earth and violence in all things. 8.11 For there were less women, and the men continually sought strange flesh for gratification.
>
> 8:14 Men then uncovered the nakedness of their fathers and their mothers. 8.15 They uncovered the nakedness of their brothers and sisters and the nakedness of their own children. 8.16 And men approached their blood relatives to uncover their nakedness. 8.17 Sharing all that was carnal within their family. 8.17 And the prize was to uncover a woman's nakedness during her menstrual impurity.[1256]

Canaanites were not completely driven from driven from the land during the conquest, nor were their ongoing sins. Polytheist beliefs, practices, and sins

---

[1254] Joseph Lumpkin, *The Book of Giants: The Watchers, Nephilim, and The Book of Enoch* (self-published, 2014), Introduction, 14, citing 1 Enoch 7:2–6, 25:11; Enoch Book of Giants 1Q23 Frag. 9 + 14 + 15: "[. ..] they knew the secrets of [. ..]. .. sin was great in the earth [. ..] [. ..] and they killed many [. .] [. ..] they begat giants [. ..], 1Q23 Frag. 1 + 6 [. ..] two hundred donkeys, two hundred asses, two hundred. .. rams of the flock, two hundred goats, two hundred. .. beast of the field from every animal, from every bird [...] [. ..] for miscegenation (inbreeding of people considered to be of different races) [. ..], 4Q531 Frag. 3 [. ..] everything that the earth produced [. ..] [. ..] the great fish [. ..] [. ..] the sky with all that grew [. ..] [. ..] fruit of the earth and all kinds of grain and all the trees [. ..] [. ..] beasts and reptiles. .. all creeping things of the earth and they observed all [. ..] [. ..] every harsh deed and [. ..] utterance [. ..] [. ..] male and female, and among humans [. ..]."
[1255] Gen 14:8; 19:1.
[1256] Ichabod Sergent Demmon, trans., *Book of Lamech of Cain and Leviathan* (Hammersmith, London: Independently Published, Kindle Version, 2019), 20, 22.

continued to plague Israel throughout the epoch of the judges and monarchy. Some Israelites intermarried with Canaanites and five other nations of the mighty seven, serving their gods of Mount Hermon, the Baalim.[1257] However, Israel did subjugate the Canaanites throughout the Covenant Land, binding them in ongoing tribute.[1258]

[1257] Judg 3:5–6.
[1258] Judg 1:8–10, 28–30

THE SIDONIANS

CHAPTER 29

1 Chron 1:8 The sons of Ham; Cush, and Mizraim, Put, and Canaan

1 Chron 1:13 And Canaan begat Zidon his firstborn, and Heth.

Gen 10:15 And Canaan begat Sidon his firstborn, and Heth.

Sidon was Canaan's firstborn from a human mother—sisters of Sidon and Heth, the "daughters of Canaan,"[1259] procreated with fallen angels to produce the postdiluvian Rephaim.

One deduces that Canaan and his sons, at some time after the birth of Canaan's sons, married an unnamed Rephaim female(s) to produce Canaanite giant-like hybrids. If Canaan bred giant-like hybrids from a Rephaim female, those offspring kept their eponymous and patronymic status from Canaan. One further deduces, based in historical sources we will cover, that Sidon followed in Canaan and Nimrod's rebellious footsteps, and that Sidon intermarried with Rephaim females that produced giant-like hybrid humans but kept his patriarchal position in the table of nations as did Canaan, Heth, Nimrod, and Eliphaz.

Even though Sidon is mentioned in the book of Joshua, Israel did not engage Sidon in an all-out war in the Covenant Land conquest. However, there may have been some Sidonian cities and towns in the northern regions Israel captured

---

[1259] Gen 24:3; 28:1,6, 8.

because God did say He would drive out some Sidonians as part of the lots assigned to the twelve tribes.[1260]

Sidon city was the oldest city and capitol of the Phoenicians, a city built on a promontory connected to the mainland and several other islands by bridges, located twenty miles north of Tyre.[1261] Sidon/Zidon was the "the town of the fishermen." Ancient tradition recounted that Sidon had journeyed from the Babylonian and/or the Persian Gulf region, as indicated from the Phoenician Semitic language,[1262] but likely Sidonians discarded their Hamitic language and adopted a Semitic language.

Sidon became a powerful military, seafaring, trading city-state long before Tyre, and is regarded as the mother city for Tyre. As the leading Phoenician city-state, Tyre succeeded as the trading and military force some time before the prophet Isaiah (c. 700–800 BC).[1263] Sidon was often grouped among, but still distinct from, the seacoast-based Philistine city-state pentapolis not completely captured or driven in the Covenant Land conquest, along with the Hivites, Canaanites, Jebusites, and Amorites—nations left to test Israel's faith so that Israel would not dull their edge for battle.[1264] The pentapolis cities of Phoenicia were Sidon, Tyre, Arvad/ Arados, Gebal/Byblos, and Zemar.[1265]

Sidonians and Phoenicians have historically unexplained similarities and connections to the Hyksos kings of Egypt, northern Canaan, and Syria of the greater Mount Hermon region. The northern "Greater Hyksos" were Indo-Aryans that were also part of the ancient nobility of the Mitanni whom the Hyksos kings were allied with. The Mitanni reigned over, or with, indigenous Hurrians (Horim)[1266] that the Hittites intermarried with. The Hyksos were also part of the seafaring nations of the Mediterranean. The powerful Hyksos military makeup included a fleet of ships manned by Aegean Sea warriors (Minoans) as well as a powerful Hurrian (Horim) cavalry (and/or chariots).[1267] Thus, Phoenician kings were depicted in a similar manner to the Hyksos, Hittites, Syrian, and Sumerian kings: with thick black hair and black, curly beards.

Egyptian Hyksos kings worshipped Baal/Hadad as depicted on scarabs at Tell el-Dab'a and elsewhere. Sidonians, Canaanites, and Rephaim of Ugarit also

[1260] Josh 11:8; 13:6.
[1261] *Unger's*, 1193; Nelson's, 1176: Sidon.
[1262] Sayce, *Races of the Old Testament,* 102, citing Strabo i. 2, 35; xvi. 3, 4; 4, 27; Justin xviii. 3, 2; Pliny, N. H. iv. 36; Herodotus i. 1; vii. 89; Scholiast on Homer, Od. iv. 84. According to the legend, the cause of the migration was an earthquake in the vicinity of the "Assyrian" or "Syrian Lake"; this refers to the Persian Gulf, not the Dead Sea.
[1263] *Strong's Cyclopaedia,* Vol. 10, 1093: Zidon; *Easton's Bible Dictionary,* 1324: Zidon.
[1264] Judg 1:21–31; 2:3; 3:1–4.
[1265] *Easton's,* 1013: Phenicia, 515: Gebal; *Encyclopedia Americana,* Vol. 21, 786: Phoenicia.
[1266] Rohl, *Lost Testament,* 276.
[1267] Ibid., 289.

worshipped Baal, Ashtoreth, and other Baalim gods.[1268] In AD 1855, a third-century BC sarcophagus for Sidon's King Eshmanezar was discovered with an inscription that communicated his mother was a priestess of Ashtoreth and Baal was the chief god of the Sidonians.[1269] The Sidonian and Phoenician city-states all worshipped the trinity of gods El, Baal, and Baalat more commonly known as Asherah, Ashtoreth, and Astarte of Ugarit:

> They ca[me] to the sanctuary of Athirat of Tyre and to the goddess of Sidon. There Keret the votary vowed a gift: O Athirat of Tyre, and goddess of Sidon.[1270]

Sidonians were among the first Israelite oppressors after the conquest sputtered to a halt at Joshua's death.[1271] One presumes Sidon sought revenge for their brethren Canaanite clans pummeled by Israel in the conquest of Canaan. Not only was Sidon a perfect foe for Israel to test their military prowess in the age of judges, but Sidon was also a well-suited tempter to continue to test Israel's faith in God and devotion to their holy covenant. In fact, the infamous Jezebel of Sidon encapsulates the Second Incursion within the meaning of her name Jezebel: Baal exalts and/or Baal is husband. Jezebel/ *Iyzebel* was the Sidonian daughter of King Ethbaal of Sidon.[1272]

So great was Sidon that the book of Joshua entitled Sidon as the "Great Zidon."[1273] Sidon's daughter city was Tyre in Joshua's time, not yet the lead city of the Sidon pentapolis but a powerful military city-state described as the "strong city Tyre," along with Zidon and Hamath.[1274] Strong/*mibtsar* means a castle, fortress, stronghold, and fenced city,[1275] and is the same word that described the stronghold cities with walls up to the sky in the reconnaissance report by the Israelite scouts into Canaan.[1276] Fenced cities of the Old Testament were built on hills with "solid masonry," watchtowers at regular intervals, parapets, and an almost impregnable acropolis in the city center.[1277] Tyre may have been greater than the fortress

---

[1268] *Unger's*, 1193: Sidon.
[1269] *Easton's*, 1324: Zidon.
[1270] Wyatt, *Religious Texts from Ugarit*, 200-201, KTU 145 iv: 35–40.
[1271] Judg 10:12.
[1272] 1 Kings 16:31. H348—*Iyzebel, ee-zeh'-bel*; Izebel, the wife of king Ahab; Jezebel: Baal exalts, or Baal is husband to; H856—*'Ethba`al, eth-bah'-al*: with Baal; Phoenician king Ethbaal.
[1273] Jos 11:8; 19:28.
[1274] Josh 19:29; 2 Sam 24:7; Zech 9:2–3.
[1275] H4013—*mibtsar, mib-tsawr'*.
[1276] Num 13:19. *Mibstar*; Num 13:28: walled and very great; Deut 1:28: walls up to heaven.
[1277] *Encyclopedia Americana*, Vol. 11, 113: Fenced Cities.

city-states conquered in the northern campaign by Joshua—city-states with fences/ *mibstar* such as Hamath, Hazor, and Chinnereth with their villages.[1278]

Phoenician tomb inscriptions describe a lineage of kings who represented themselves as the earthly representatives of gods—demigod kings like Huram/ Hiram of Tyre, Abibaal, Shiptiball, and Elibaal of Gebal/Byblos,[1279] and of course the infamous prince of Tyre, Tyrus (Ezek 28). Some conclude *Iy'anaq*/Anakim King Akirum of the Egyptian Execration Texts was an archaic form of the Phoenician name Ahiram or Hiram. Further, the reference in the Execration Texts to "Asiatics of Byblos" addressed the Phoenician empire as reigned by *Iy'anaq*/ Anakim kings, which included Akirum and King Abi-yamimu.[1280] Josephus listed Hiram's father as Abibalus (Abibaal),[1281] indicating another Rephaim patronymic king title nexus. *Strong's Cyclopaedia* listed kings of Tyre who reigned before the Exodus as those "whose very names mostly prove them to be mere types of deities, or special tribes": Aegenor, Phoenix, Phallis, Tetramnestus, and Tennes, Strato, and Abd-alonim.[1282]

Understanding Tyre's Rephaim history makes sense of the dual prophecy in Ezekiel 32 where King Tyrus was portrayed as an archetypical antichrist figure like Nimrod, the Assyrian, and the king of Babylon/Babel in prophetic allegory—a dual prophecy for Ezekiel's time and for the end-time antichrist, which is wrapped within important prehistory information regarding Satan the anointed cherubim and the angelic rebellion. Thus King Tyrus, a demigod Rephaim with the divine right to rule granted by the Baalim godfathers of Mount Hermon's celestial mafia, in typical antichrist narcissism, declared himself to be God reigning from the seat of God in Ezekiel 28, just as Satan/*Heylel* was recorded as doing in Isaiah 14:12–14. Thus, Tyrus the prince/*nagiyd*, meaning commander of civil, military, and/or religious institutions as prince,[1283] was listed among the infamous, renowned Terrible Ones of the nations,[1284] a demigod mighty/gibborim.[1285] Rephaim were referenced as kings in Ezekiel 32, and by implication Ezekiel 26 and 28, and Isaiah 13–14.

> Ezek 28:2 Son of man, say unto the prince of Tyrus, Thus saith the Lord GOD; Because thine heart is lifted up, and thou hast said, I am a God, I sit in the seat of God, in the midst of the seas; yet thou art a man, and not God, though thou set thine heart as the heart of God.

[1278] Josh 19:35–38.

[1279] Knight and Lomas, *The Book of Hiram*, 93, 98.

[1280] Billington, "Goliath and the Exodus Giants," 500, quoting Pritchard, *ANET*, 225, 328.

[1281] Josephus, *Ant.*, Book 7, 5:3, quoting historians Menander and Dius.

[1282] *Strong's Cyclopaedia*, Vol. 10, 614.

[1283] H5057—*nagiyd, naw-gheed'*: a commander civil military or religious; captain; chief; excellent thing; chief governor; leader; noble; prince; chief ruler.

[1284] Ezek 28:7–9.

[1285] Ezek 32:12, 21, 27.

The slain Terrible Ones communicating with Pharaoh in Ezekiel 32 include the "princes of the north, all of them, and all the Zidonians" whose graves are in the sides of the abyss—those who created terror among the living.[1286] Rephaim kings after the flood spawned the beast and metallic empires of the books of Daniel and Revelation that will lead to the end-time ten-king beast empire to deliver their power to the eighth beast empire and king, the antichrist.[1287] Nothing is new under the sun. God was against the Sidonians and Tyrus in Ezekiel's time. God stirred up the terrible of nations King Nebuchadnezzar of the Babylonian/*Babel* beast empire against another Terrible One, Tyrus of Sidon.[1288] We will see this once more in the end times when antichrist destroys Babylon.[1289]

Tyre is one of the allegories from history and prehistory that helps define end-time Babylon city, along with Nineveh, Babel/Babylon, and antediluvian Atlantis. End-time Babylon will be a worldwide trading empire like Tyre, a universal religion, a powerful political organization controlling the ten kings, and a city.[1290] Ezekiel 26 is another a dual prophecy working in harmony with Ezekiel 28, 31, 32 and other dual prophecies prophesying Tyre/Tyrus's destruction by Nebuchadnezzar in Ezekiel's time,[1291] and prophesying the end-time alliance of nations, the ten beast kings, and antichrist.[1292] The daughters/branches of Babel/Babylon will rise in a renowned end-time city to cause terror.[1293] The ten kings of Atlantis, Babel/Babylon, Nineveh, and Tyre are the prophetic allegory to discern the coming end-time Babylon.[1294]

Isaiah 23, another dual prophecy describes the destruction of Tyre, the daughter of Zidon by a Rephaim descended Assyrian Tartan (perhaps Scythian) king[1295] (c. 722–705 BC), an Assyrian king who also destroyed and exiled the northern kingdom of Israel.[1296] The Assyrian is prophetic allegory for the founding king of the Chaldeans, Babylon, noting that Nimrod built Babel (Gen 10:10–12), and that out of that land came Asshur/*Ashshuwr*[1297] who built Nineveh the Assyrian royal city. Thus, the Babylon beast empire of the Rephaim descended from Nebuchadnezzar was begat by the Assyrian and king of Babylon, Nimrod. The Assyrian

---

[1286] Ezek 32:23, 26, 32.

[1287] Rev 17:11–13.

[1288] Ezek 28:21–23.

[1289] Rev 17:16–17.

[1290] Wayne, *Genesis 6 Conspiracy*, 314–320. City: Rev 14:8; 17:18; 18:10 (2), 16, 18, 19, 21.

[1291] Ezek 26:1–7.

[1292] Rev 17:15–18; 18:1–24.

[1293] Isa 23:15, 17; Ezek 26:3, 6, 8, 16, 20, 21.

[1294] Wayne, *Genesis 6 Conspiracy*, 126–138.

[1295] H8661—*Tartan, tar-tawn*'; of foreign derivation: an Assyrian; Tartan-field marshal; general; commander; a title used by the Assyrian military.

[1296] Isa 23:11–13. Sargon: Isaiah 20:1, the Tartan Assyrian; *Encyclopedia Americana*, Vol. 24, 304: Sargon; Vol. 2, 431: Assyria.

[1297] H804—*'Ashshuwr, ash-shoor*'; Shem;'s second son; eponymous ancestor of Assyrians; Assyria land of Asshur.

is prophetic allegory applied to antichrist, who will be slain on the mountains of Israel in the end times, as recorded in Isaiah 14:25.

With all this in mind, Tyre's destruction detailed in Isaiah 23 is baffling, unless understood from a dual prophecy perspective and principles. Tyre's Isaiah 23's destruction comes from the forces of nature, by the roar and strength of the sea and by God's outstretched hand over the sea that shook/quaked the kingdoms to destroy the strongholds of Tyre,[1298] not at the hands of the Assyrians, or Babylonians in the time of Isaiah and Ezekiel, or by Jesus with the Assyrian antichrist of the end times. Tyre's Isaiah 23's destruction echoes the destruction of antediluvian Atlantis and the great flood, although Tyre was not an island but a coastal city.

Within Isaiah 23's cryptic passage are significant, enigmatic Atlantean and antediluvian markers that one should not dismiss, particularly when considering other cryptic flood-like passages from Job, Amos, and the Psalms in context with Nephilim creation in the preface to the flood narrative in Genesis 6.[1299] Tyre is cited as the bestower of crowns and merchant kings,[1300] which stirs up curious echoes of the Ring Lords of Nippur, the place where heaven met earth, and where the grand assembly of gods appointed and anointed antediluvian Nephilim kings with the divine right to rule[1301]—the council/assembly of the gods of Psalm 82. Thus, God brought low the pride and glory of all the renowned of the earth (Isa 23:9), the antediluvian kings through a watery, global catastrophe,[1302] just as Genesis 6:4 described the evil Nephilim potentates as the men of renown. The "joyous city whose antiquity is of ancient days" is yet another primeval marker.[1303] Berosus, the Chaldean historian priest of the temple of Belus who had access to antediluvian tablets of Sippar preserved at the temple, wrote that Babylon was utilized allegorically by the Chaldean priests as an antediluvian city, the "first city" of cities, which could only have been Atlantis;[1304] both are end-time allegories helping to define Babylon of Revelation 17.

[1298] Isa 23:4. H3220—*yam, yawm*: to roar; a sea as breaking in noisy surf; large body of water; specifically, the Mediterranean Sea. Isa 23:11, shake: H7264—*ragaz, raw-gaz'*: quiver with any violent emotion as in anger or fear; be afraid; stand in awe; disquiet; fall out; fret; move; provoke; quake; rage; shake; tremble; trouble; be wroth.

[1299] Gen 6:1–4; Job 9:9; 38:31; Ps 18:7–16; Amos 5:8–9.

[1300] Isa 23:8.

[1301] Gardner, *Realm of the Ring Lords*, 52.

[1302] The Access Bible, Wisdom 14:6–16.

[1303] Isa 23:7. H6927—*qadmah, kad-maw'*: antiquity; former state or estate or situation; before; origin; beginning; H6924 —*qedem, keh'-dem*; or *qedmah, kayd'-maw*: east; antiquity; that which is before; aforetime; ancient time; aforetime; ancient; from of old; earliest time; anciently of old. Deut 33:15; Ps 77:5; Prov 22:28; Eccl 1:10; Isa 19:11; Jer 5:15; Dan 7:9; 1 Peter 3:15; 2 Peter 2:5; The Access Bible: Sirach 17:7; Baruch 3:26; Wisdom 14.

[1304] *Encyclopedia Americana*, Vol. 3., 577; Zecharia Sitchin, *The Lost Book of Enki* (Rochester, VT: Bear and Company, 2004), Introduction, 4; Joseph, *Destruction of Atlantis*, 122, 125.

CHAPTER 30

THE HITTITES

Gen 23:10 And Ephron dwelt among the children of Heth: and Ephron the Hittite answered Abraham in the audience of the children of Heth, even of all that went in at the gate of his city.

Heth, second son of Canaan, was the patriarch for the Hittites otherwise referenced in Scripture as the sons of Heth; some who dwelled in Hebron, where Abraham settled.[1305] The Hittite/*Chittiy* name derives patronymically from Heth/*Cheth*, the son of Canaan, son of Ham; a people famous for their Anatolian empire of Asia Minor and north Lebanon.[1306]

Heth/*Cheth* is defined as an Aboriginal Canaanite meaning terror, whereas Hittite/*Chittiy* is defined as a patronymically from *Cheth*, a descendant of *Cheth*, and a nation descended from *Cheth*.[1307] Oddly though, Josephus listed Sidon as the only named son of Canaan, and then grouped Heth/Chetteus among the families of the patriarch-less Canaanites families, where as Scripture clearly indicates Heth was the second-named son of Canaan.

Heth was grouped with Canaan and Sidon, immediately following Sidon as throughout the table of nations, with named sons in order of their birth. The patriarch-less tribes listed after Canaan, Sidon, and Heth were also tallied in groups of

---

[1305] *Ungers*, 566: Heth. Sons of Heth: Gen 23:3, 5, 7, 10, 16, 18, 20; 25:10; 49:32; Deut 7:1; Josh 1:4. H2845—*Cheth, khayth*: terror; an aboriginal Canaanite; son of Canaan; progenitor of the Hittites.

[1306] H2850—*Chittiy, khit-tee'*: a Chittite; descendant of Cheth/Heth; the nation descended from Heth; Canaan's second son; inhabitants of central Anatolia (modern Turkey) and north Lebanon.

[1307] H2845—*Cheth, khayth*: an aboriginal Canaanite; terror; H2850—*Chittiy, khit-tee'*; patronymically from 2845.

three. Those who assert Sidon was the singular son of Canaan rely on the biblical text "and Heth" in Genesis 10's accounting, suggesting the "and" indicates Heth was a family of Canaan as in "and the Jebusite," versus "son." However, in the table of nations the first son is always listed first, with "and" utilized after to denote sons born thereafter.[1308] Further, the distinction in the Canaanite accounting is this: Heth is a named as Canaan's son, whereas "Jebusite" is designated a patriarch-less family eponymously named from the Rephaim, Jebus, through a daughter of Canaan, Sidon, or Heth. Moreover, the Josephus account tallied Heth with the patriarch-less tribes because at that time no records existed for them as Canaanites.

> Gen 10:2 The sons of Japheth; Gomer, and Magog, and Madai, and Javan, and Tubal, and Meshech, and Tiras.. ..

> Gen 10:15 And Canaan begat Sidon his firstborn, and Heth, and the Jebusite.

Josephus' accounting also stated both Arudeus/Arvadites and Arucas/Arkites were the posterity of Sidon indicating his daughters married Rephaim patriarchs of similar names:

> The sons of Canaan were these: Sidonius, who also built a city of the same name; it is called by the Greeks Sidon Amathus inhabited in Amathine, which is even now called Amathe by the inhabitants, although the Macedonians named it Epiphania, from one of his posterities: Arudeus possessed the island Aradus: Arucas possessed Arce, which is in Libanus. But for the seven others, [Eueus,] Chetteus, Jebuseus, Amorreus, Gergesus, Eudeus, Sineus, Samareus, we have nothing in the sacred books but their names, for the Hebrews overthrew their cities; and their calamities came upon them on the occasion following.[1309]

Strong's Cyclopaedia described Hittites as Hamites who were "neither of the country nor the kindred of Abraham and Isaac,"[1310] even though pockets of Hittites dwelled in Hebron and elsewhere. The Hittites were a warlike people that reigned at various times from the Euphrates river to Asia Minor, which included Carchemish, Damascus in Syria, Hebron in Canaan, Kades and Orontes just inland and parallel with the Mediterranean coast, north Asia Minor with the latter Hittite empirical center at Anatolia, and the Mediterranean coast region that enveloped Ugarit of the Rephaim.[1311] It follows that Hittites surfaced in Akaddian, Egyptian,

---

[1308] Gen 10:2, 3, 4, 6, 7, 14, 14, 22, 23.
[1309] Josephus, *Ant* 1:6:2.
[1310] *Strong's Cyclopaedia*, Vol. 4, 223: Heth.
[1311] *Easton's*, 626: Hittite. *Nelson's*, 563: Heth. Gen 13:18; 23:2, 19.

and Ugarit records as seemingly four distinct sects, ethnic groups, or settlements of Hittites in the ancient Near East.[1312] Egyptians recorded the Hittites as the Khiti and Khita on their monuments.[1313] Carchemish and Kadesh were regarded as southern capital cities for the Hittite empire.[1314] Knowing this then makes sense that the Bible stated Hittites had many kings reigning at one time:

> 2 Kings 7:6 For the LORD had made the host of the Syrians to hear a noise of chariots, and a noise of horses, even the noise of a great host: and they said one to another, Lo, the king of Israel hath hired against us the kings of the Hittites.

Hittites were mentioned in the *Ugaritic Texts in* KTU 140 with the Hurrians, Cypriots, and the *Gbr* (Semitic root word for gibborim):

> .. . or by the accusation of the Hurrians, or by the accusation of the Hittites, or by the accusation of the Cypriots, or by the accusation of the *gbr*, or by the accusation of your oppressed ones.[1315]

Hittites, otherwise known as Hattians, dwelled in the central Anatolian plateau from before 2000 BC.[1316] *Chat*, pronounced Hat, was the name recorded for a people in Palestine on ancient Egyptian monuments.[1317] At the Hittite capital city Hattushash/Hattusa, ancient Hurrian literature was also discovered,[1318] supporting *Ugarit Text* links between Hittites and Hurrians. These *Boghaz-keui Tablets* recorded Akkadian narratives received from the Hurrians.[1319]

The Hittites' rise to power coincided with an immigration of Indo-Aryans from the north, a sect of Indo-Europeans that spoke a non-Semitic language called Nasili. The migrants first settled in a city named Nesha, and a people who thereafter assimilated with the Hattians.[1320] Hittites are conceded by some historians

---

[1312] *Mercer's*, 382: Hittites.

[1313] *Catholic Encyclopedia*, Vol. 6, 305: Hittites.

[1314] Boughton, *History of Ancient Peoples,* 104.

[1315] Wyatt, *Religious Texts from Ugarit,* 346–347, KTU 140 r:30–40, 140, note 9: gbr: warrior: H1368—*gibbowr, ghib-bore'*; or *gibbor, ghibbore'*; the same as 1397: powerful; warrior; tyrant; champion; chief; excel; giant; mighty man; strong man; valiant man; *gibbor* from 1396; H1397—*geber, gheh'-ber*; from 1396: valiant man or warrior; a person; everyone; man; mighty; from 1396; H1396—*gabar, gaw-bar'*; a primitive root: to be strong; by to prevail; act insolently; exceed; confirm; be great; be mighty; strengthen; stronger; valiant; H1399—*gbar, gheb-ar'*; from 1396: the same as 1397; a person, a man.

[1316] *Mercer's*, 382: Hittites.

[1317] *Strong's Cyclopaedia*, Vol. 4, 223: Heth.

[1318] *Unger's*, 587: Horites; *Mercer's Dictionary of the Bible*, 382: Hittites.

[1319] *Unger's*, 579: Hittites.

[1320] *Mercer's*, 382: Hittites.

(who ignore what the Bible contributes about Hittite history) as purely northern Indo-Europeans who sojourned down through Asia Minor and into the Middle East before 2300 BC, as Aryans whose black-haired kin branches migrated east to India[1321] and Persia. "Aryan Hittites" were one of numerous Scythian and Aryan settlements in and adjacent to Israel and Judah. Syrians called Scythopolis city in Galilee Beth-Shean, the "House of Power" and the "House of Sidhe."[1322] Beth-Shean was alternatively known biblically as Bethshan and was an interchangeable name with Scythopolis up to the time of the Hasmonian dynasty, according to the books of Judith and 1 and 2 Maccabees.[1323]

Scythians were part of the Indo-Aryan ancestors of the latter Tartans and akin to the Tartan warriors of Sargon of Assyria, seemingly connected to the Avvim god Tartak,[1324] and dynastic kings like the Hyksos. Polytheist history noted that early on, "Aryan royal families didn't intermarry with other tribes or castes, but despite this with the development by many of their clans of settled city-states, they became urban multi-racial and appreciated cultural diversity."[1325]

Aryans were a loose knit set of tribes from southern Russia (Black Sea region of Scythia), whose common Indo-European language formed the basis for many Asiatic and European languages.[1326] Aryan traditions were elemental for Hinduism, establishing powerful priests from among the royal bloodlines of the aristocracy; priests were only those born into their own clan, an order renowned as Brahman.[1327] Scythians were renowned in polytheist circles as a "sept of the Aryans," "the noble tribe," or the "Royal Scythians." A "sept" is otherwise understood as a clan, and was a symbol of royal bloodline descent reflected in the above titles. [1328]

Indo-Europeans were regarded by historians as a kin race to Hittites, Mycenaeans, Celts and various Aryans[1329] that included the Medes and Persians,[1330] and were regarded in other circles of investigation as giants or giant-like. According to historian Susan Wise Bauer, the similarity of languages between the four Indo-European peoples indicates a common root people who settled in four separate

---

[1321] Bauer, *History of the World*, 174, 199, 470.

[1322] BethShean: Josh 17:11, 16; Judg 1:27; 1 Kings 4:12; 1 Chron 7:29. BethShan: 1 Sam 31:10, 12; 2 Sam 21:12. *Strong's Cyclopaedia*, Vol. 9, 490: Scythopolis; Gardner, *Realm of the Ring Lords*, 68; Josephus, *Ant.*, book 5, 1:22; book 6, 14:8, book 12, 8:5.

[1323] Access Bible, Judith 3:10; 1 Maccabees 5:52; 2 Maccabees 12:29.

[1324] 2 Kings 17:31; 18:17; Isa 20:1. *Strong's Cyclopaedia*, Vol. 9, 489: Scythian.

[1325] De Vere, *The Dragon Legacy*, 62.

[1326] Karen Armstrong, *The Great Transformation: The Beginning of Our Religious Traditions* (Toronto, ON: Vintage Canada, 2006), 3, 59.

[1327] Bauer, *History of the World*, 483.

[1328] De Vere, Nicholas, *The Dragon Legacy*, 2, 60, 63, 75.

[1329] Bauer, *History of the World*, 470.

[1330] Sayce, *The Races Of The Old Testament*, 46.

regions.[1331] *Unger's Dictionary* suggests then that Hittites were non-Semitic and perhaps Aryan or at least in part Aryan via Indo-Europeans who brought their "harbinger Sanskrit language and religion with them."[1332]

From a biblical perspective though, Hittites likely intermarried with the Aryans/Arya and the Hurrians/Horim. Biblically, Hittites were originally Hamites, not Aryans. Hittites were eponymously named after Heth/*Cheth* the son of Canaan as testified to in Genesis 23, where Hittites of Hebron were called the sons of Heth, whom Abraham dwelled among.[1333] Heth and his sons and daughters intermarried with Rephaim, as did Canaan, Sidon, Esau, Eliphaz, and Nimrod, who produced Aryan-like or giant-like hybrids.

Aryan Indo-European drifted into two distinct languages, the Avestan dialect and the early form of Sanskrit. The Avestan language begat the Old Iranian language of the Medes and Old Persian.[1334] The Aryan pantheon spilled over into both Indian and Mediterranean cultures. Avestan Aryans named their gods Daevas, meaning "Shining Ones," while in Sanskrit their gods were Devas and Amrita.[1335] Arya/Aryans who settled in the Indus valley carried their religion and language with them, which is important for understanding historical cross-references and connections. As such, an ancient treaty signed between the Mitanni and Hittite empire drafted the gods of India: Indra, Veruna, and Mitra as witnesses into their treaty, indicating that both Hittites and Aryans recognized those gods as part of ancient kinship.[1336]

Horim too were non-Semites closely associated with the Hurrians, and date back to shortly after the flood, circa 2400 BC. Both Horim and Hurrian etymology and definition connects back to early cave-dwellers. Moreover, Hurrian/Horim tablets discovered in Nuzi and Mari linked the Horim/Hurrian nation to the kingdom of Mittanni:[1337] "The Hur syllable in Hurrian has been asserted by scholars, including George Contenau (*La Civilisation des Hittites et des Hurrites de Mitanni*) to be Har or Ar, indicating the Hurrians like the Scythians were Aryans, that venerated 'an Aryan Vedic royal-sacral family of gods. They bestowed these upon the Hittites whose culture they dominated.'"[1338] The light-haired Horim branch was part of the ancient people that became known to historical records as the Hurrians, who entered Mesopotamia from the Zagros mountains before

---

[1331] Bauer, *History of the World*, 470.

[1332] *Unger's*, 580: Hittites.

[1333] Gen 23:3,4, 7, 10, 11, 19; 49:33.

[1334] Kent, Roland G, *Old Persian: Grammer, Text, Lexicon*, (American Oriental Society, New Haven, CT, 1950), 6: point 3. Armstrong, Karen, *The Great Transformation: The Beginning of Our Religious Traditions*, 3.

[1335] Armstrong, *The Great Transformation*, 3-4.

[1336] Bauer, *History of the World*, 264-265.

[1337] *Unger's*, 586-87: Horites.

[1338] De Vere, *The Dragon Legacy*, 62.

2000 BC.[1339] Hurrians had previously welcomed a splinter group of kin Aryans, the Maryannu, into their tribes, who then muscled their way into the ruling class, later forming the upper and lower strata to the famous Mittanni of Mesopotamia. Hurrians later became the lower part, after the demise of the Mittanni empire.[1340]

Hittites, then, early on intermarried with Hurrians/Horim and Aryans, whereby they continued to consolidate their power and empire through much of their history via treaties and alliances with the Indo-European, Hurrian, and Mitanni dynasties from upper Mesopotamia and Syria.[1341] Hittites at their peak rivaled the Egyptians and Assyrians.[1342] Hittites conquered Aleppo and Babylon (c. 1595 BC) bringing down the Hammurapi/Hammurabi dynasty.[1343]

Knowing the early postdiluvian history of Hittites, and their relationship with Aryans and Horim, explicates why Hittites were listed among the mighty seven nations of Canaan, and among the nations occupying Canaan in Numbers 13 and Deuteronomy 1 as a people who were taller, stronger, and greater than Israelites, and a people who dwelled with the Anakim in the south. And knowing Hittites, Canaanites, and Sidonians intermarried with Rephaim shortly after the flood makes sense of Hittites, Canaanites, Amorites, Girgashsites, and Jebusites being listed among the mighty seven that included the Rephaim and mysterious Perzzim, shortly after Abraham fled to Hebron for Ur:

> Gen 15:20 And the Hittites, and the Perizzites, and the Rephaims,
>
> Gen 15:21 And the Amorites, and the Canaanites, and the Girgashites, and the Jebusites.

[1339] Unger's, 586–77; Nelson's, 577: Horites.

[1340] Nelson's, 577: Horites.

[1341] Mercer's, 382: Hittites.

[1342] Easton's, 626: Hittites; Unger's, 576: Hittites.

[1343] Mercer's, 382; Unger's, 580: Hittites.

Section IV:
The Postdiluvian Rephaim World Order

Deut 2:20 (That also was accounted a land of giants: giants dwelt therein in old time; and the Ammonites call them Zamzummims;

Deut 2:21 A people great, and many, and tall, as the Anakims; but the LORD destroyed them before them; and they succeeded them, and dwelt in their stead:

Deut 2:22 As he did to the children of Esau, which dwelt in Seir, when he destroyed the Horims from before them; and they succeeded them, and dwelt in their stead even unto this day:

Deut 2:23 And the Avims which dwelt in Hazerim, even unto Azzah, the Caphtorims, which came forth out of Caphtor, destroyed them, and dwelt in their stead.)

CHAPTER 31

THE HIVVIM

Gen 36:2 Esau took his wives of the daughters of Canaan; Adah the daughter of Elon the Hittite, and Aholibamah the daughter of Anah the daughter of Zibeon the Hivite...

The Rephaim reigned over the nations of the Covenant Land region as dynastic kingships, which evolved into militaristic networks comprised of pentapolis city-states supported by satellite villages. First-generation Rephaim, like Kings Sihon and Og, later came to reign over Amorites of Mount Hermon, while other Rephaim dynastic offspring led Canaanite nations past the time of Exodus.

Rephaim dynasties were the reincarnated Nephilim World Order that has reigned ever since the flood with their bloodline royals and empires that will reassert their visual dominance in the end times. Genesis 14's war was fought between giant kings from Mesopotamia connected to Nimrod and black-haired Aryans, and the Rephaim and Rephaim led hybrid human nations surrounding the Covenant Land. Genesis 14 is a stunning documentation of the physical Naphilim World Order manifested on earth with rival offspring perpetually dueling for dominance.

The Naphilim World Order of Nephilim dynastic kings was born in the oath-based conspiracy sworn upon Mount Hermon to lead Adamites away from God, into rebellion, and to the second death.[1344] The Rephaim World Order was the reincarnated postdiluvian order Israel squared off against in the Exodus. Hivvim were part of this Rephaim World Order that also included Anakim.

[1344] Rev 20:15; 21:8.

Num 13:22 And they ascended by the south, and came unto Hebron; where Ahiman, Sheshai, and Talmai, the children of Anak.

Nelson's assertion that Hivites were a kin branch of Horim/Hurrian[1345] likely derives from Zibeon, the son of Seir the Horim Genesis in 36:20. Zibeon was also classified as Hivite/*Chivviy* in 36:2. Horim and Hivvim were Rephaim tribes that produced hybrid humans, the Hivites and Horites. (In this book I reference Rephaim tribes with the same *im* Hebrew suffix as Rephaim, Nephilim, and Gibborim, as seraphim and perhaps cherubim offspring, but for biblically named hybrid Rephaim/human nations and human nations I utilize the "-ite(s)" suffix.) It follows that the eponymous Hivite name was received from the singular *Chivvy*, a Rephaim patriarch and tribe, and somewhat distinct from Chori/Horim and *Chirriy/Chuwriy*/Hurrian.

Hivvim, according to *Unger's Bible Dictionary*, was identified or conflated with the Avvim by church father Jerome, who concluded that the city of Ha-Avvim (the Avvim) in the north[1346] was the Hivite city populated by Canaanite Hivites.[1347] The Septuagint translation seems to conclude that Avvim were Hivvim or Hivites, translating `Avviym/Avvim[1348] as Evites, just as the Septuagint translates Hivites as "Evites" in Genesis 10's Canaanite clans.[1349] Hivvim/*Chivviy* were indeed related to Horim and Avvim, but because Hivvim/*Chivviy* is a distinct Hebrew word from Horim/*Choriy* and distinct Avvim/`Avviym, and because the Hivvim dwelled both with and in separate areas from Horim and Avvim, it follows that the Hivvim were a distinct Rephaim tribe. Further, the Hivvim do not appear to be the Ivvim recorded in Jewish legends.[1350] The Ivvim seem more likely to be the Avvim that is patrial of Ivvah/Ava, a city that was in Assyria.[1351]

As noted previously, *Nelson's Dictionary* states that Hivites (at least in part) were akin to or a branch of Horites/Horim, the ancient people secular history records as the Hurrians.[1352] The Hurrians dwelled mostly in Mesopotamia, in the Mari region along the Euphrates River, established the Mitanni dynasty, and were a kin branch of Horim.[1353] Horim dwelled mostly in Edom, but some dwelled

---

[1345] *Nelson's*, 571; *Unger's*, 580: Hivites.
[1346] Josh 18:22–23.
[1347] *Unger's*, 127: Avvim.
[1348] H5761—`Avviym, av-veem`; plural of 5757: Avvim as inhabited by Avvites; a place in Palestine; ruins; H5757—`Avviy, av-vee`; an Avvite or native of Avvah; Avims, Avites.
[1349] *Septuagint* Gen 10:18; Deut 2:23; Jos 13:3.
[1350] Ginzberg, *Legends of the Bible,* 70: Noah.
[1351] H5755—`Ivvah, iv-vaw`; or Avvae, (2 Kings 17:24) *avvaw*`; Ivvah or Avva: a region of Assyria: ruin; a city conquered by the Assyrians; H5757—`Avviy, av-vee`; patrial from 5755; an Avvite, native of Avvah; Avims, Avites.
[1352] *Nelson's*, 577: Horites.
[1353] Ibid.; *Unger's*, 587: Horites.

in Syria, while Hivvim dwelled in the Mount Hermon region in Syria, central Canaan, and elsewhere. Horim royal cities alternated between Edom and Syria throughout the reign of the dukes of Edom[1354] and remained allied into the age of King David and his Edomite and Syrian wars. What seems likely to me is that three distinct branches of Horim existed: one branch from *Chori*/Horim, one from Chuwriy/Huri, and one from *Chivviy*/Hivi.

Hivvim were part of the Rephaim tribes, who created at least one family of Canaanites. This is an important discernment to define Genesis 10's families of Canaan, and the nations tallied in the mighty seven.[1355] Hivites/Hivvim recorded in the mountains of Lebanon from Baalhermon to Hamath likely account for the Hivites recorded in 2 Samuel.[1356] Of the five regions Hivites were documented dwelling in, one region stands out. Hivites were recorded in Mizpeh "under Mount Hermon," the home of Rephaim and "the land of giants."[1357] The inclusion of Hivites dwelling in the land of Rephaim, Emim, and Zanzummim indicates that these Hivites were Hivvim.

Further, when one compares Genesis 15's original rendition of the mighty seven in Abraham's time, neither Hivite hybrids nor Hivvim were listed. However, Rephaim were listed among the mighty seven nations. Later, the Hivvim appear to be the Rephaim tribe of the Mount Hermon region who replaced the Rephaim root nation after the war of giants, and who replaced the Rephaim in the mighty seven listed in the time of Moses and Joshua. Hivvim replacing the Rephaim in the mighty seven makes sense when one considers Og, and perhaps Sihon, were the last of the original Rephaim tribe in the time of Exodus.

> Josh 11:3 And to the Canaanite on the east and on the west, and to the Amorite, and the Hittite, and the Perizzite, and the Jebusite in the mountains, and to the Hivite under Hermon in the land of Mizpeh.
>
> Gen 15:20 And the Hittites, and the Perizzites, and the Rephaims,
>
> Gen 15:21 And the Amorites, and the Canaanites, and the Girgashites, and the Jebusites.

Zibeon's classification as both Horim and Hivvim in Genesis 36 is not a scribal error, nor a contradiction;[1358] the Bible does contradict itself. Zibeon's accounting helps define Hivvim as one of three Horim tribes or branches. Genesis's 36's accounting describes the close relationship between Hivvim, Horim, and Avvim.

[1354] Gen 36:30–43; 1 Chron 1:43–54.
[1355] Deut 7:1; Jos 3:10; 24:11.
[1356] Judg 3:3; 2 Sam 24:7.
[1357] Gen 14:5; 15:20; Deut 2:20; 3:15; Josh 11:3.
[1358] Gen 36:2, 14, 20, 24, 29; 1 Chron 1:38, 40.

Hivvim were part of a military alliance where intermarriage was common among the Avvim, Horim, Amaleqim, Anakim, and Hivvim giants that made up the early post-diluvium southern federation of Rephaim pentapolis city-states in Gaza and Seir, all of whom intermarried with Canaanites to create subservient hybrid human nations.

Geography dictated and Scripture documented a close Hivvim and Hivite relationship with the Avvim, Horim, Amaleqim, and Anakim federation in Gaza, in the central and southern Covenant Land. It follows that Hivite hybrids in the north would have held similar subservient relationships to Rephaim alliances as they did in the central region, which we will cover in subsequent chapters. The southern Avvim, Horim, Hivvim, Amaleqim, and Anakim federation was reshaped later by the Philistine, Capthorim, and Cherethim invasion.[1359]

Hivvim were also directly related to the Gibeonites in central Canaan. "Gibeonite" is a patrial name for Gibeon, one of the cities Gibeonites dwelled in. *Gibown* is defined as hilly and hill city. "Giebonite" derives from *Giboniy*: plural *Giboniyim*.[1360] "A city on a hill" is a popular expression for Nephilim/Rephaim cities of light like Sodom, Gomorrah, Camelot, etc. Scriptural information points toward Hivvim having been Rephaim, and also states that Joshua recognized the Gibeonites as Hivvim and interchanged the names for one another.[1361]

Gibeon/*Giboniy* may have been the Hivvim patriarch for hybrid Gibeon-ites. *Gibown* is eerily close to *gibbowr*, for mighty man/tyrant, used to describe Nephilim in Genesis 6:4, and for Rephaim descendants.[1362] *Gbr*, meaning warrior in the *Ugaritic Texts*, was the source word for *gibbowr* and was utilized to describe the Rapiu rulers/king of the *Ugaritic Texts*, their tribes, their spawned human hybrid nations, and perhaps a specific giant and/or tribe of giants.[1363] One should not be surprised to learn that the book of Joshua revealed Gibeon as one of the great cities, the "royal [Hivvim] city" whose men were mighty/gibborim:

> Josh 10:1. .. and how the inhabitants of Gibeon had made peace with Israel, and were among them;

> Josh 10:2 That they feared greatly, because Gibeon was a great city, as one of the royal cities, and because it was greater than Ai, and all the men thereof were mighty.

[1359] Deut 2:23; Josh 18:23.
[1360] H1391—*Gib' own, ghib-ohn'*: a place in Palestine; hilly; a hill city five miles (8 km) from Jerusalem; H1393—*Gib'oniy, ghib-o-nee'*; patrial from 1391: a Gibonite; inhabitant of Gibon: little hill; hilly; Gibeon inhabitant.
[1361] Jos 8:1–7; 11:19.
[1362] H1368—*gibbowr, ghib-bore'; gibbor, ghibbore'*: powerful; warrior; tyrant; champion; chief; excel; giant; mighty one; strong; valiant man.
[1363] Wyatt, *Religious Texts from Ugarit*, 154, notes 8–9; 345–347: KTU 1.40.25–42.

Gibeon was the royal city of the Hivvim pentapolis network of city-state fortresses, with great, mighty, and high walls reaching into the heavens, fortresses described by Moses' scouts.[1364] The four other Hivvim/Gibonim city-state strongholds of central Canaan included Chephirah/Kephirah, Beeroth, Kirjathearim, and of course Shechem,[1365] which most do not connect to the Hivvim pentapolis network. Hamor/*Chamowr* of Shechem was a prince/*nasiy' of* the country, an exalted one as in a king, sheik, or chief.[1366] Knowing Gibeonites were at least in part Hivvim clarifies the important role the Hivvim played in the geopolitical alliances in Canaan's central region. John A. Wilson, translator of the Egyptian Execration Texts, included Shechem as a royal city of the Shutu and Iy'anak/Anakim rulers,[1367] supporting a Hivvim and Anakim relationship.

Biblically, "royal" and "seed royal" translates from *mamlakah*: a king or queen's reign and a kingdom, which derives from the root word *melak*, meaning king.[1368] It follows that royal Rephaim cities were the location for the thrones of divine kings appointed by the assembly of gods with the divine right rule on their behalf. Knowing this makes sense of the English word "royal" derived from secular and polytheist history and etymology, essentially from roy-el; *al* is a transliteration of *el,*[1369] which was attached to the word king/roy. Royal, pronounced roi'al, is the adjective for a king or a queen, meaning kingly magnificent, founded, chartered, patronized as in a palace, and descended from or related to a king or line of kings as in a royal prince.[1370] A member of a royal family is a roy-al who descends from Nephilim/Rephaim demigods and gods, otherwise renowned as kings of god, Latin *Rex Deus*. Royal's etymology descended into English from Latin *regalis* of a king as in regal, and Old French *roial*.[1371] Latin *regalis* derives from *rex* and its genitive *regis* for King, noting *roi* is French for king.[1372] Further, Latin *reg*/king is rooted in the Proto-Indo-European (Aryan) word meaning draw a line, and to lead or rule.[1373] *Reg* also forms, or is part of, such words as German *reich*, and the

---

[1364] Num 13:9, 28; Deut 1:28.

[1365] Gen 33:17, 34:30; Josh 9:17.

[1366] H2544—*Chamowr, kham-ore'*: donkey; Chamor/Hamor, Hivite prince of the city of Shechem when Jacob entered Palestine; H5387—*nasiy', naw-see'*; or *nasi, naw-see'*: an exalted one; a king; sheik, chief; ruler; prince; a rising mist.

[1367] Billington, "Goliath and the Exodus Giants," 501, 506, citing Pritchard, *ANET*, 225, notes 3, 6.

[1368] H4467—*mamlakah, mam-law-kaw'*; from 4427: kingdom; dominion; reign; sovereignty; H4427—*malak, maw-lak'*: a primitive root to reign, ascend the throne; induct into royalty; king or queen. Royal City: 1 Sam 21:6; 2 Sam 12:7. Seed Royal: 2 Kings 11:1; 25:25; 2 Chron 22:10.

[1369] H410—*'el, ale*: god; god-like one; mighty one; mighty men; men of rank; mighty heroes; angel; false god; demons, God; the one true God; mighty things in nature; strength; and power.

[1370] *Webster's*, 352; Dictionary.com: royal.

[1371] https://www.etymonline.com/word/royal.

[1372] https://www.etymonline.com/word/royal.

[1373] https://www.etymonline.com/word/*reg-?ref=etymonline_crossreference.

English rex, rich, regent, regime, regiment, region, regulate, reign, viceroy, realm, reckless, arrogant, and Alaric.[1374]

This divine royal line of thinking makes sense of the Hivvim Prince Hamor of Shechem narrative with Jacob's sons' reaction to Hamor and his royal family. Simeon and Levi slaughtered all the *Chivviy* males because King Hamor's dynastic son, Shechem, slept with and defiled Dinah. Levi and Simeon did this after Hamor communed for peace, offering to have Shechem and Dinah marry after the incident. All the Hivvim and Hivite males had been weakened by circumcision, which had been part of the agreement.[1375] Simeon and Levi ensured a Rephaim Israelite hybrid nation was not going be created in the same manner as daughters from Canaan, Sidon, and Heth had created the nine patriarch-less hybrid human Canaanite clans.

In summation, Genesis 15 noted "Rephaims," multiple tribes of Rephaim nations, were originally part of the mighty nations that populated the Covenant Land bequeathed to Abraham's posterity. Hivvim were included in the larger accounting of "Rephaims" tribes. The mighty seven of Abraham's period were made up of Rephaims, hybrid/Rephaim Canaanites, Amorites, Girgashites, Jebusites, and another mysterious tribe, the Perizzites.

> Gen 15:20 And the Hittites, and the Perizzites, and the Rephaims,
>
> Gen 15:21 And the Amorites, and the Canaanites, and the Girgashites, and the Jebusites.
>
> Deut 7:1 When the LORD thy God shall bring thee into the land whither thou goest to possess it, and hath cast out many nations before thee, the Hittites, and the Girgashites, and the Amorites, and the Canaanites, and the Perizzites, and the Hivites, and the Jebusites, seven nations greater and mightier than thou.

[1374] https://www.etymonline.com/word/*reg-?ref=etymonline_crossreference.
[1375] Gen 36:1–26.

THE PERIZZIM

Gen 13:7 And there was a strife between the herdmen of Abram's cattle and the herdmen of Lot's cattle: and the Canaanite and the Perizzite dwelled then in the land.

Perizites were generally classified as a Canaanite clan by biblical scholars, but Perizzites were not accounted for in Genesis 10 with the nine other Canaanite patriarch-less clans. Like the Rephaim and Anakim, Avvim, and various Horim tribes, Perizzites were not accounted for with a patriarch in the table of nations tally. By implication, Perizzites were a Rephaim tribe.

Even though Perizzim dwelled among the Canaanites, Amorites, and Jebusites, they were always scripturally distinguished from Canaanites[1376] and Canaanite tribes, indicating that Perzzim were a distinct tribe. *Strong's Cyclopaedia* describes the Perizzim enigma as the same kind of mystery that envelops the Avvim and Gerizzites, whose "origin remain in Scriptural obscurity,"[1377] as were other nations that will be explored. *Strong's Cyclopaedia* notes that Perizzim were referenced with a "greater distinctness" that was equal to the collective Canaanite and patriarch-less clans, as in "Canaanites and Perizzites," [1378] when Perizzim were mentioned outside the mighty seven nations. In Genesis 13:7 and 34:30 Perizzim possessed the numbers and power to destroy Jacob and his sons, despite that Jacob and his sons had easily handled Hamor and his Hivvim of Shechem.[1379]

[1376] Sayce, *Races of the Old Testament*, 120.
[1377] *Strong's Cyclopaedia*, Vol. 7, 951: Perizzites. Gen 13:7; 34:30; Exod 23:23; Judg 1:4, 5.
[1378] Ibid.
[1379] Ibid.

> Gen 34:30 And Jacob said to Simeon and Levi, Ye have troubled me to make me to stink among the inhabitants of the land, among the Canaanites and the Perizzites: and I being few in number, they shall gather themselves together against me, and slay me; and I shall be destroyed, I and my house.

Perizzim are first mentioned in Genesis 13, when Abraham returned from Egypt and Lot settled in the Sodom and Gomorrah region where Canaanites and Perizzites dwelled. At that time a dispute with Abraham and Lot erupted with Canaanites and Perizzim over cattle herding in the Sodom and Gomorrah region.[1380] Perizzim were unaccounted-for Aboriginals of Canaan known for their agricultural prowess, and renowned as the "cultivators of the plain."[1381] As such, Canaanites, and seemingly the Canaanite confederacy of clans, were grouped with the Perizzim as distinct and with equal power, indicating that Perizzim were Aboriginal Rephaim. The Perizzim anecdote dropped in Genesis 13 is not coincidental or incidental, but an elemental detail purposefully positioned at the nascence of the Sodom and Gommorah narrative (chapters 13–19), which included the war of giants, but oddly Perizzim were not mentioned in that war. Nor were Perizzim mentioned in the destruction by God of Sodom, Gomorrah, and the cities of the plain, but they were included in the mighty ten of Genesis 15, and later the mighty seven nations. Perizzim seem to have melded into the Canaanite civilization yet remained distinct, a people renowned for their power. Canaanites, and by implication then Perizzim, were flagrant practitioners of Nephilim, Rephaim, and Hamite sexual sins and idolatry, which utterly defiled the entire Covenant Land.

One deduces Perizzim were included among the Rephaim tribes that provided impassioned patriarchs for the daughters of Canaan, Sidon, and Heth to create the nine Canaanite families—and by implication, Rephaim daughters for Canaan, Sidon, and Heth to intermarry for the creation of their eponymously named hybrid nations. Further, one deduces the Canaanite pentapolis of city-state fortresses[1382] were led by Rephaim kings, and likely Perizzim kings by virtue of the Perizzim's close relationship with Canaanites both before and after the war of giants. One ponders if this is why the Perizzim in Genesis 15, after the war of giants, were listed apart from the "Rephaims" for the above reasons as important context. It follows that Gomorah/`Amorah was a patrial named city deriving from

---

[1380] Gen 13:7.
[1381] Sayce, *Races of the Old Testament*, 120; *Strong's Cyclopaedia*, Vol. 7, 951: Perizzites.
[1382] Gen 14:8: Sodom, Gomorrah, Admah, Zeboiim, and Bela/Zoar.

`Amar,[1383] the root word for "Amorite" and their Rephaim patriarch Amar, Emor, or Amerru.

Second Esdras, in the apocrypha of the original KJV, additionally identified the Perizzim as a distinct nation from the Canaanites but included them among the Canaanites and the Philistines;[1384] the latter also dwelled among many giant tribes. Perizzim/*Prizziy* in Hebrew is the singular format, again indicating Perizi or a variant was the patriarch for the Perizzim. Knowing Perizzim were giants makes sense of the under explained connections between the Perizzim/*Prizziy* with King Og and with the Avvim and Anakim of Philistia. At the time of the Exodus and the Covenant Land conquest, Perizzim were documented as dwelling in the land of giants assigned to the tribes Ephraim and Manasseh to conquer thereafter.[1385]

> Josh 17:15 And Joshua answered them, If thou be a great people, then get thee up to the wood country, and cut down for thyself there in the land of the Perizzites and of the giants.. ..

The Perizzim were understood as village dwellers; *praziy* means village, and unwalled rural dwellers.[1386] The Bashan, the twelve-pentapolis city-state empire King Og of Mount Hermon reigned over, included unwalled villages/*praziy,* the source word for Perazzim.[1387] Unwalled villages are reminiscent of the Hazerim/*Chatersiym,* of the Avvim in Philistia; Hazerim means villages and likely a city of the same name. Avvim dwelled from Hazerim to Azzah/Gaza, and were a giant race later replaced in part by Caphtorim, and Philistines.[1388] This is yet another connection indicating that southern Perizzim were Rephaim, akin to, and aligned with, Avvim and likely the Anakim.

The Septuagint, without explanation, translates the "unwalled towns" of Deuteronomy 3:4 that supported Og's twelve-pentapolis city-state network as cities (villages) of the Pherezites/Perizzim, once more indicating Perizzim were part of the tribal umbrella under the catch-all term Rephaim, along with the Hivvim. In fact, the Perizzim were listed alongside the "Rephaims" in the original mighty

---

[1383] H6017—`*Amorah, am-o-raw*'; from 6014: a ruined heap; Amorah, a place in Palestine: Gomorrah also meaning submersion; H6014—`*amar, aw-mar*': a primitive root to heap; figuratively to chastise as if piling blows; binding sheaves as in gathering or to manipulate or deal tyrannically with.

[1384] The Access Bible, 2 Esdras 1:21.

[1385] Josh 17:14–18.

[1386] H6522—*Prizziy, per-iz-zee*'; for 6521: belonging to a village; inhabitant of the open country of southern Canaan; a Perizzi; H6521—*praziy, per-aw-zee*': a rustic village; unwalled.

[1387] Deut 3:5. H6521—*praziy, per-aw-zee*'; H2699—*Chatseriym, khats-ay-reem*': yard; a place in Palestine called Hazerim, and villages.

[1388] Deut 2:23. H5804—`*Azzah, az-zaw*'; strong; a place in Palestine: Gaza meaning the strong.

seven (Gen 15:20), indicating a close geographical and racial connections with King Og.

> *Sept* Deut 3:4 And we mastered all his cities at that time; there was not a city which we took not from them; sixty cities, all the country round about Argob, belonging to king Og in Basan:

> *Sept* Deut 3:5 all strong cities, lofty walls, gates and bars; besides the very many cities of the Pherezites.

> *KJV* Deut 3:4 And we took all his cities at that time, there was not a city which we took not from them, threescore cities, all the region of Argob, the kingdom of Og in Bashan.

> Deu 3:5 All these cities were fenced with high walls, gates, and bars; beside unwalled towns a great many.

One further contemplates, with respect to the Greek spelling Pherezite, whether there might be some form of etymological, phonetic, or transliterated link to the Egyptian kingship title of pharaoh/*Par`oh*. *Prazzi* is the source word for *Prizziy*, which in turn stems from *prazah*, also meaning unwalled village, which in turn originates in *paraz* meaning separate, decide, chieftain, and warrior. *Prazown*, immediately preceding *prazzi* in *Strong's Dictionary,* is defined as magistracy, leadership, and chieftains of people dwelling in unwalled villages.[1389]

Adding to the stack of biblical documentation that continually connects Perizzim to giants is the beguiling narrative of the "toe collector" king of Bezek. The Perizzim were once more included among Canaanites in southern Canaan in this narrative, when Judah attacked the infamous Rephaim King Adonibezek of Bezek city, who collected forty-six sets of thumb and toe trophies from (Rephaim) kings he slew.[1390] *Nelson's* concludes that Bezek was the stronghold city of the Perizzim,[1391] the Perizzim royal Rephaim city of the south. Adonibezek is defined as lord from adoni/*'adown* meaning lord, king, and master, and Bezek/*bezeq* meaning lightning-forming lord or king of Bezek and/or lord/king of lightning.[1392] Adonibezek was king of the Perizzim and the Canaanites in this battle, supporting

---

[1389] H6519—*prazah, per-aw-zaw'*: from the same as 6518; open country; unwalled town or village; H6518—*paraz, paw-rawz'*: from an unused root meaning to separate; decide; a chieftain; leader; warrior; village; H6520—*prazown, per-aw-zone'*; from the same as 6518: magistracy; leadership; chieftains; village; rural population; rustics; rural people; people of unwalled villages.
[1390] Judg 1:4–7.
[1391] *Nelson's*, 968: Perizzites.
[1392] H137—*'Adoniy-Bezeq, ad-o"-nee-beh'-zek*; from 113 and 966: lord of Bezek; a Canaanitish king; my lord is Besek; king of the Canaanite city of Bezek, killed by Israelites; H966—*Bezeq, beh'-zak*; from 965: lightning; Bezek, a city in Palestine; lightning; H113—*'adown, aw-done'; adon, aw-done'*; from an unused root meaning to rule: sovereign, controller; lord; master; owner.

the notion that the Perizzim were kings of the Canaanites in the Sodom pentapolis, and supported that pentapolis with their village network.

The Israelites did subdue the various Perizzim factions roaming through out Canaan but did not eliminate them. Perizzim survived into the days of King Solomon, likely as hybrids, who forced them into bondservice and tribute[1393] but kept their eponymous name from a specific Rephaim, *Perizziy*. Perizzim were part of the polytheist contaminates that plagued Israel through the age of the judges and monarchy, and until the time of Judah's return from Babylonian exile in the time of Ezra.

> Ezra 9:1 Now when these things were done, the princes came to me, saying, The people of Israel, and the priests, and the Levites, have not separated themselves from the people of the lands, doing according to their abominations, even of the Canaanites, the Hittites, the Perizzites, the Jebusites, the Ammonites, the Moabites, the Egyptians, and the Amorites.

> Ezra 9:2 For they have taken of their daughters for themselves, and for their sons: so that the holy seed have mingled themselves with the people of those lands: yea, the hand of the princes and rulers hath been chief in this trespass.

[1393] Josh 11:3; 17:15; Judg 1:4, 5; 3:5; 2 Chron 8:7; 1 Kings 9:20; Ezra 9:1; Neh 9:8.

CHAPTER 33

THE HORIM ELVIN BLOODLINE

*Deut 2:12 The Horims also dwelt in Seir beforetime; but the chil-
dren of Esau succeeded them, when they had destroyed them from
before them, and dwelt in their stead.*

Horim/*Choriy*, like Anakim,[1394] have the *im* suffix identifying them as Rephaim.
The KJV also translates *Choriy* as Horite(s)indicating spawned hybrid human
nations in some cases. Unfortunately, the KJV often conflates the two related tribes,
which obstructs the understanding of the Horim narrative and the larger biblical
narrative of giants. As such, this confusion opens the door for some to assert that
Hori of the tribe of Simeon as the Horite/Horim patriarch,[1395] even though Horite
and Horim accounts predate Hori's birth,[1396] as in the war of giants.[1397]

Others point to Hori son of Lotan, son of Seir, as the patriarch of the Horites.
However, Seir is Hori's grandfather, and while Seir and his sons were identified as a
Horites;[1398] all were predated by the Horites/Horim in Genesis 14 in the war of
giants. The Horites represented in the war of giants were assigned to the Mount

---

[1394] Horims: Deut 2:12, 22. Anakim: Deut 1:28; 2:10, 11, 21; 9:2; Josh 11:21, 22; 14:12, 15.
[1395] Num 13:5.
[1396] Horites: Gen 14:6; 36:21, 29. Horite: Gen 36:20. Horims: Deut 2:12, 22; Hori: Gen 36:22, 30, 1 Chron 1:39.
[1397] Gen 14:6.
[1398] Gen 36:20–22; 1 Chron 1:38–39.

Seir region, indicating Seir and his branch of Horim migrated there well before the war. Likewise, the Horim were confirmed to have reigned in the Mount Seir region well before Esau, grandson of Abraham, settled there. It follows that the "Horim" in Deuteronomy 2 were replaced by the children of Esau in the Seir region who dwelled there since the flood as the Aboriginal people.[1399] Seir was not eponymously named for the Horim tribe, nor was Seir eponymous for the Horim, indicating an older patriarch whom Seir's grandson, Hori, was patronymically named after. Seir led a Horim branch to the region of his name, and perhaps was a son of *Choriy*.

> Deut 2:12 The Horims also dwelt in Seir beforetime; but the children of Esau succeeded them, when they had destroyed them from before them, and dwelt in their stead.

In fact, Horim/*Choriy* means troglodyte, cave-dweller, and Aboriginal Idumeans of Mount Seir and Edom, and derives equally from Hori/*Choriy*, penned for the son of Lotan, meaning cave-dweller.[1400] The *Choriy* further includes later inhabitants of Edom, referring to the hybrid human branch that remained until the time of David, and that Horim and hybrid Horites received their nationhood names eponymously, the latter perhaps from Seir's grandson.

Horim/*Choriy* is also regarded by *Strong's Dictionary* as the same as *Chowr* meaning a cave, hole den, and cavity, and that *Chowr* is the same as *Chuwr* meaning a serpent's den, cell of a prison, and a hole.[1401] *Chuwr*, the serpent's den, appears to be the source word for *Chuwriy*/Huri of the Mesopotamian branch. However, another Hebrew candidate word, *chuwr*, is delineated as white linen and white, deriving from *chavar* meaning to wax pale, to be white, and to grow white; another Hebrew word, *Chori*, immediately precedes Hori/*Choriy* in *Strong's Dictionary* and means Horite, Hori, and white bread.[1402] Accordingly, the Horim, Hurrian, and Hivvim, the "Horims" of Deuteronomy 2:12 were pale, white-skinned, red-haired, and dwelled in caves or underground cities like snakes. Nephilim and Rephaim possessed pale white skin, long serpentine necks, and with serpent-like faces and elongated skulls after the image of their seraphim godfathers.

[1399] Gen 36:31; Deut 2:12, 22.

[1400] H2752—*Choriy, kho-ree'*: cave-dweller; troglodyte; aboriginal Idumaean and of Mount Seir; later inhabitants of Edom; H2753—*Choriy, kho-ree'*; or Chowriy, kho-ree'; the same as 2752; grandson of Seir.

[1401] H2356—*chowr, khore*; the same as 2352: a cavity; socket; den; cave; hole; H2352—*chuwr, khoor*: to bore; crevice of a serpent; cell of a prison; hole.

[1402] H2353—*chuwr, khoor*; from 2357: white linen; white; H2357—*chavar, khaw-var'*: to blanch as with shame; wax pale; to be white; grow white; H2753—*choriy, kho-ree'*; from the same as 2353: white bread; white cake; white; Horite; Hori.

Seir, the patriarchal Horim of Edom and patrial for Mount Seir, derives from *se`iyr* meaning rough, hairy, and shaggy,[1403] yet another trait of Nephilim and Rephaim. Seir in turn stems from *sa`iyr* meaning a shaggy/hairy male goat, a faun, and a devil goat god, transliterated as satyr.[1404] Satyrs are degraded rebellious seraphim angels portrayed in the end-time prophecies of Isaiah 13:21 and 34:14 with other kinds of fallen angels, foretelling the destruction of Babylon at the midpoint of the last seven years, and Isaiah 34 foretelling the day/year of the Lord's wrath. Further, *se`iyr* is a compound word with the first shortened word *se* from *she/sah* an denoting shaggy, rough, hairy, and goat. The second word `*iyr* means Watcher. The compound word forms in its meaning a degraded hairy Watcher, likely seraphim degraded to an impassioned hairy goat-like god[1405] like Pan and Azazel. In Daniel 8, rough/*sa`iyr* provides important context in "the rough goat" for king Alexander, his royal seed, and the coming end-time beast king, antichrist.

> Dan 8:21 And the rough goat is the king of Grecia: and the great horn that is between his eyes is the first king.

Atlantean giants possessed ruddy, white skin, with blond and red hair, and glowing eyes.[1406] Postdiluvian Scythians, Tuatha De Danann/Ditanu, and Celts were the fair-skinned, blue and green-eyed, blond and red-haired Aryans, whom polytheists believe survived the flood. Indo-Europeans in polytheist reckoning were the surviving Aryan fifth race.[1407] Sumerian kings too were generally recorded as white with hairy, rough and/or ruddy skin, as was Enkidu of the *Epic of Gilgamesh*.[1408] Enkidu was described in the *Epic of Gilgamesh* as having hair covering his body,[1409] noting that Gilgamesh was very much similar to Enkidu with very long hair.[1410] Similarly, Esau was born hairy, ruddy, and with reddish hair.[1411] Esau, although smaller than Horim or Horites, seems to have found com-

---

[1403] H8165—*Se`iyr, say-eer':* rough; a mountain of Idumaea and its aboriginal occupants; hairy; shaggy; patriarch of Horites; inhabitants of Edom before Esau; land of Edom south of the Dead Sea; mountain range in Edom.

[1404] H8163—*sa`iyr, saw-eer';* or *sabir, saw-eer':* shaggy; a he-goat; by analogy a faun as in devil; goat god; satyr. Lev 17:7, 2 Chron 11:15; Isa 13:21; 34:14.

[1405] H5894—`*iyr, eer:* a watcher; an angel as in guardian; waking; watchful; wakeful one; watcher, angel; H7716—*seh, seh;* or *sey, say;* pushing out to graze; a sheep or goat; H8181—*se`ar, say-awr';* or *saar* in Isaiah 7:20: hair; hairy; hair of animals or man; garment made of hair.

[1406] Joseph, *Destruction of Atlantis,* 218–219.

[1407] Greer, *The Element Encyclopedia of Secret Societies,* 499.

[1408] Gardner, *Grail Kings,* 233–234.

[1409] Heidel, *The Gilgamesh Epic and Old Testament Parallels,* 19: Table 1, lines 36–37; 29: Tablet line 23; 90: Tablet 11 lines 237, 240, 248.

[1410] Ibid., 31: Tablet 2, lines 15, 49; Tablet 6: lines 1–2, notes 93 and 94; 64: Tablet 8, Col 4, line 7.

[1411] Gen 25:25. Red: H132—*'admoniy, ad-mo-nee':* reddish hair or complexion; red; ruddy; H6215—`*Esau, ay-sawv':* of handling; rough; hairy.

fort, commonality, and common cause with the hairy, pale-skinned, red-haired Horim and their hatred of Israel. Edomites coveted Israel's blessings, birthright, messianic promise, and destiny. Knowing this makes sense of Esau and his posterity intermarrying with Horim, as with Eliphaz who married Timna.

> Gen 25:25 And the first came out red, all over like an hairy garment; and they called his name Esau.

Duke Seir produced male progeny: Lotan, Shobal, Zibeon, and Anah, as well as one daughter named Timna.[1412] Aholibamah was the daughter of Anah, who married Esau to produce Jeush, Jaalam, and Korah.[1413] Although few in numbers, Rephaim produced daughters who married Canaan, Sidon, Heth, Nimrod, Eliphaz, Amalek, and one presumes others from Noah's posterity.

"Duke" in the KJV derives from Hebrew, *'alluwph,* and by extension the *Alluphim* of Edom as the *Catholic Encyclopedia* transliterates them. *'Alluwph* means chief in the Genesis 36 applications and is rooted in *'alph* meaning to teach or learn[1414] as in knowledge or gnosis. The dynastic dukes of Edom included Seir's posterity as well as the succeeding Esau and Eliphaz posterity. The etymology source of "duke" in English is Latin *dux,* Italian *duca,* and French *duc,* made popular in the reign of Emperor Constantine for hereditary military leaders and chiefs of the nobility, and then adopted into the nobility class of European nations.[1415] Dukes, as generally understood in contemporary peerage systems, hold the highest hereditary rank outside the royal family and among the nobility class, below the title of prince but above marquis. However, a "royal duke," as with the English royal family, is entitled to the Prince and Royal Highness titles as a prince of the "blood royal" who also possess dukedoms as part of that exclusive royal distinction.[1416]

Duke Eliphaz's name holds special significance among polytheists because they draft Eliphaz into their mythos via his marriage to (Duchess) Timna, the Horim princess. Eliphaz was the son of Esau and the Hittite hybrid Adah. Eliphaz/*Eliyphaz,* meaning gold of God, derives from *el* meaning god, God, or a mighty one, and from *paz* meaning pure gold,[1417] all which reflected Eliphaz's newly acquired status as a prince of the blood royal. "Eliph" in Eliphaz was

---

[1412] Gen 36:20, 22.
[1413] Gen 36:25.
[1414] H441—*'alluwph, al-loof'*; or shortened *alluph, al-loof'*; from 502: a familiar; a friend; gentle; tame; docile; intimate; chief; H502—*'alph, aw-lof'*: to learn; to teach; utter; *Catholic Encyclopedia,* Vol. 7, 638: Idumea.
[1415] *Encyclopedia Americana,* Vol. 9, 390–391: Duke.
[1416] Ibid., Vol. 9, 390–391: Duke; Vol. 21, 469–470: Peerage.
[1417] H464—*'Eliyphaz, el-ee-faz'*: God of gold.

drafted into a craft deployed by adepts, wordsmithing to pen occult allegory and legominism, alternatively known as the green language. "Eliph" of Eliphaz and *alluwph* and its Hebrew source word *alph* were penned into the fairy and dragon bloodline mythos to distinguish and track their royal bloodline dynasties, and the new dynasty spawned with Amalek.

> Gen 36:15 These were dukes of the sons of Esau: the sons of Eliphaz the firstborn son of Esau; duke Teman, duke Omar, duke Zepho, duke Kenaz,

> Gen 36:16 Duke Korah, duke Gatam, and duke Amalek: these are the dukes that came of Eliphaz in the land of Edom; these were the sons of Adah.

According to Laurence Gardner, an adept and famous royal bloodline genealogist,[1418] the fairy precept was born directly from Dragon/Ring/Grail culture. Gardner added that fairies were the Shining Ones of the kingly, Cathar Elven race, the Albi-Gens descended from the Tuatha De Danann, *Tuadhe d'Anu*—the tribe of Anu, parent god of the Anunnaki.[1419] De Vere documented that the Aryans and Scythians were the Taudhe d' Anu, the Daouine Sidhe, the tribe of Anu, the Fairies, Dragons, Elves, "Kings above kings," the Shining Ones, and the star children of the heavenly Anunnaki Watchers.[1420] By implication, the Ditanu of Ugarit and the Rephaim were titled the Shining Ones, the Nogahim[1421] kings of *Heylel/*Satan and fallen opalescent angels.

Gardner noted that Edomite marriages into the dukes of Edom was the nascence for the Tuatha D'Anu fairy kings (at least in part). The Lords of Anu were in this scenario were the lords of Edom.[1422] Gardner stated: "It is within their [Edomite] history that we find another root of the Elf distinction, for the members

---

[1418] Wayne, *Genesis 6 Conspiracy*, Introduction, xiv, citing Gardner, *Realm of the Ring Lords,* notes about the author: "Gardner was the past Master Mason of the United Grand Lodge of England for twenty years. He also held a plethora of other distinguished positions and titles. He was a noted prior of the Celtic church's Sacred Kindred of St. Columbia, Prior of the Knights Templar of St. Anthony, and internationally recognized as a sovereign and chivalric genealogist. Gardner was distinguished as the Chevalier Labhran de Saint Germain and was the Presidential Attaché to the European Council of Princes, all while being formally acknowledged as being attached to the Noble Household Guard of the Royal House of Stewart founded at St. Germain. Gardener was appointed Jacobite Historiographer Royal, a Fellow of the Society of Antiquities of Scotland, and a Professional Member of the Institute of Nana Technology. In addition to all this, Gardner was an attaché to the Grande Protectorate of the Imperial Dragon Court."

[1419] Gardner, *Realm of the Ring Lords,* 30–31.

[1420] De Vere, *The Dragon Legacy,* 32, 114.

[1421] H5051—nogahh, no'-gah; brilliancy: brightness; light; shining.

[1422] Gardner, *Realm of the Ring Lords,* 63, 226.

of this influential king-tribe were described in old biblical Hebrew as Elefs"—the Noble Elven Race.[1423] And: "The noble princes were the very race from whom the Tuadhe d'Anu fairy kings emerged."[1424] The Tuatha De Danann are renowned in the fairy mythos as the world's most noble race, alongside dynastic Egyptian kings. Gardner's archives of royal genealogies indicated to him that the word "fairy" is in part rooted in the word *phare*, or *pharo*, meaning pharaohs, of the House of Dragon: kings of fate, or fairy kings.[1425] Pharaoh was the ancient Egyptian king-ship title meaning "great house," alternatively transliterated as *Par`oh* in Hebrew, and spelled in ancient texts as Per'o, P-ra, and Ph-ra, signifying the sun and the god Ra.[1426] Further, *phare* and its plural format *phares* are source words for the French word for lighthouse, deriving from Latin *pharus* and Greek *pharos*, and of course the famous Alexandria Lighthouse, Pharos. Pares and Pharos are phoneti-cally reminiscent of the Greek version of Perizzim: Pherez-ite, noting Perizzim is rooted in *prazzi*: magistracy; leadership, chieftains.

Egyptian conquests of Canaan and Syria after the fall of the Ur III dynasty brought them into contact with the kingdom of Nahrina otherwise known as Mitanni, Aram Naharaim of the Old Testament.[1427] Pharaohs thereafter regularly married into the royal Mitanni.[1428] Three important dragon bloodlines were grafted together through marriages from Mesopotamia, Egypt, and Edom to establish the Dragon House of Scythian Ring Lords, [1429] but likely vice versa. Scythian giants, the race Japhethites previously married into,[1430] accepted or changed their names after giants such as Magog. Gog, Magog, and Albion were identified as Greek giants by historian Geoffrey Monmouth and as sons of the parent god Iapetus.[1431] Gog, Magog, and Gyges were common names for kings in northwest Assyria and the Black Sea region of the Trojans.[1432]

The Scythian Ring Lord dynasty split into three dynastic bloodlines sometime before 1100 BC, forming the Fir Bolg, Milesians, and of course, the Tuatha De Danann. Royal Scythians were otherwise unaccountably chronicled as the Lords of Anu, just as Tuatha De Danann were the tribe of Anu.[1433] The three great Dragon

---

[1423] Gardner, *Realm of the Ring Lords,* 103–115 and 64, citing Robert Alter, trans., *Genesis* (New York: W. W. Norton, 1996), 204, and 1 Chron (likely referencing 1 Chron 1:51–54).

[1424] Ibid., 226.

[1425] Ibid., 33, 108.

[1426] H6547—*Par`oh, par-o';* of Egyptian derivation; Paroh, title of Egyptian kings; great house; *Encyclopedia Americana,* Vol. 21, 707: Pharaoh.

[1427] Ps 60:10.

[1428] Sayce, *Races of the Old Testament,* 100.

[1429] Gardner, *Realm of the Ring Lords, 58.*

[1430] Gen 10:1–5.

[1431] Rose, *Giants, Monsters and Dragons,* 11, 146, 187, citing Geoffrey of Monmouth (1100–1154), *Historia Regnum Britanniae.*

[1432] *Encyclopedia Americana,* Vol. 13, 7: Gog.

[1433] Gardner, *Realm, 58.*

dynastic lines carried significant Grail/Ring bloodlines from Esau that also held three Rephaim tribal bloodlines: Horim, Hivvim, and Amaleqim. The Amalek dynasty created the most venerable family of that period, which later remarried into the Scythian and Tuatha De Danann of Ireland, creating the renowned and elitist Albi-Gens/Elven race.[1434]

Tuatha De Danann, according to the *Dictionary of Celtic Mythology,* were a tribe of gods, offspring of Danann, D' Ana (Anu), and/or a seed tribe from three gods, *tri' dee dana* and/or the *fir TrinDea*: men of three gods. Tuatha De Danann were the "Ever-Living Ones called the people of the *Sidhe/Sidh*."[1435] The Tuatha De Danann were indistinguishable from the fairy people or the *Sidhe,* a tribe led by the king of the fairies, Finnbheara first king of Tuatha De Danann.[1436] The main gods of the Tuatha De Danann were Dian Cecht (Diana), Lir (Poseidon/Iapetus), and D'Ana (Anu), while Dagda was a demigod king who specialized in Druidic magic.[1437]

The Albigensian religion, a sister religion of the Cathars, derived from Albi-Gens, the Elven bloodline.[1438] By extension, Albi-gensian means the "bloodline of fate/fairies." Both gnostic religions recognized the (alleged) messianic succession of Mary Magdalene, the Sangreal that was grafted into the Albi-Gens bloodline[1439] of the coming (dragon) messiah. In the Celtic culture, specific royal families carried the elite fairy blood, the fate of the Grail bloodline denoted with Dragon, Owl, and Fairy titles whereby Grail princesses were titled Elf-Maidens.[1440] The ancient bloodline includes the "Shining Elven Messianic" bloodline of Nephilim, Cathars, gnostics, Templars, Merovingians, Arthur, Rollo, Tuatha De Danann, Aryans, Horim, and the Albigensians: the Noble White Elves neatly woven into Tolkien's Lord Of The Rings trilogy.[1441]

Typically, Albi represents the patriarchal bloodline of the Dragon or Raven, while Elf/*Elbe* represents the matriarchal bloodline: fairy or owl bloodlines[1442] for the future antichrist. *Albi/Albus* in Latin means white, bleached, pale, fair skin, bright, and hoary.[1443] Hoar means gray, white, white frost, as well as ancient, and venerable,[1444] an apropos metaphor for the Tuatha D'Anu and Horim pale

[1434] Gardner, *Realm,* 64–75.
[1435] James Mackillop, *Dictionary of Celtic Mythology* (New York: Oxford University Press, 1998), 366–67: Tuatha De Danann.
[1436] Ibid., 367: Tuatha De Danann.
[1437] Ibid.
[1438] Gardner, *Grail Kings,* 315.
[1439] Laurence Gardner, *Lost Secrets of the Sacred Ark* (London: Harper Element, 2003), 229.
[1440] Gardner, *Grail Kings,* 315.
[1441] Ibid.
[1442] Ibid.
[1443] https://www.etymonline.com/search?q=albi; https://etymologeek.com/ron/albi/90876344.
[1444] *Websters*: Hoar; Dictionary.com: hoary.

skin. *Gens* in Latin means race, tribe, or bloodline of a common patriarch. *Albi* in French Norman means bright nobility, Shining Ones, and is the source for the name Albert. Legend indicates Albion derived from the Dover white/*albus* cliffs, and "from the common tradition that earth was inhabited by giants, 'that there were giants in those days.'"[1445]

Alba was the Scottish Gaelic name and Modern Irish name for Scotland, while *Albu* was the Old Irish name for Great Britain, likewise known as Albion, but later changed to represent just Scotland with the arrival of the *Dal Riada* kings to Scotland, the *Fir Alban*.[1446] In other traditions, Albina was the matriarch for the Albi-Gens bloodline and foundress of Albion, ancient Britain. Albina was the eldest (Titanides) daughter of a Greek demigod giant king. She and her sisters were exiled for treason, where she took possession of the land naming the island Albion. Albina and her two sisters were mated with Incubi changelings that produced giants. The three sisters then later mated with their giant offspring that produced the fairy race, which conquered ancient England. Generations later, Gogmagog led the fairy race in a war against Brutus.[1447]

Albi in Celtic Norman lore was Albion the giant, who along with Gog and Magog were protectors of London. Their father Iapetus/Japetus was the name Japheth, seemingly adopted, just as one of Japheth's sons accepted Magog's name.[1448] Magog is defined as a barbarous northern region in the land of Gog. Gog is a prophesied end-time antichrist-like figure in Ezekiel 38–39.[1449] Moreover, Albion derives from a Celtic word, *alp*/*alb*, meaning both high and white.[1450] Alp/Alb in German lore was a shapeshifting, vampiric, ghost demon akin to succubus and incubus, who sucked blood and life breath from its victims[1451]—all reminiscent traits of Nephilim, Rephaim, and demon spirits, as Hebrew *Rapha* words translate as ghosts, shades, and spirits.[1452]

Now, the Horim documented in the war of giants dwelled from Mount Seir to Elparan "from before time," along with Amaleqim in Kadesh in the extreme south of Judah in the desert.[1453] It follows that Gardner chronicled fairy kingdoms from the dukes/`alluwphs* of Edom, continued beyond the early postdiluvian

---

[1445] Richard Barber, *Myths and Legends of the British Isles* (New York: The Boydell Press, 2004), 1.
[1446] Mackillop, *Dictionary of Celtic Mythology*, 11: Alba and Albu, citing T. H. O'Rahilly, *Early Irish History and Mythology* (Dublin: Dublin Institute for Advanced Studies, 1946), 385–87.
[1447] Barber, *Myths and Legends of the British Isles*, 3–7.
[1448] Gardner, *Grail Kings*, 225, 268. Gen 10:2: Magog son of Japheth.
[1449] H4031—*Magowg, maw-gogue*; from 1463: son of Japheth; a barbarous northern region; land of Gog; H1463—*Gowg, gohg*: of uncertain derivation: a northern nation; mountain; prophetic prince of Rosh: Meshech and Tubal, and Magog.
[1450] *Encyclopedia Americana*, Vol. 1, 338: Albion.
[1451] Guiley, *The Encyclopedia of Demons and Demonology*, 7: Alp.
[1452] H7496—*rapha*: ghosts of the dead; shades; spirits.
[1453] Gen 14:6–7; Deut 2:12.

period and into the age of Saul and David, as verified by the Bible. The kings of the Horim/Edomite royal bloodline carried patronymic names/titles that begat with originating Horim kings like Hadad, meaning mighty and fierce.[1454] Hadad is the variant name for Baal and Adad in Mesopotamia[1455] worshipped by the Hurrians; Adad/Hadad was the chief god of the Arameans.[1456] Aramaeans, the exalted ones, dwelled in Syria,[1457] the region of Mount Hermon, with Baalim, Rephaim, and King Og and Sihon confirming an ancient connection between the Horim, Rephaim, and Aramaeans. Details documented in Genesis 36 and 1 Chronicles recorded Horim bloodlines from Seir, through various duke branches advertising their Horim, Edomite, and Aramaean patronymic kingship titles. Thus, the dissonant genealogies of the kings of Edom and Horim that intermarried with Esau and his sons was an addition to the table of nations genealogies, and a shocking testimonial to Horim dwelling there since the flood.

Following the above genealogical patronymic ideology, Balaam, son of Beor the Horim, a patronymically descendant of Beor of Edom, was the evil priest hired by King Balak of Moab to curse Israel. Balaam was an Aramaean soothsayer from Pethor located on a mountain river in the land of his people, Aram/Syria.[1458] Beor and his son of Bela were Horim kings who reigned in Dinhabah city in Edom, before Edomites settled there.[1459] After Bela, the royal city of the Horim transferred to Bozrah, another city in Edom,[1460] with Jobab succeeding as chief prince of the Horim people, followed by Husham in Temani in east Edom.[1461] The royal seat and royal city of the Horim moved in accordance to the city of succeeding chief princes and outside of Edom at times, as with Duke Hadad who smote the Midianites in the land of Moabites.[1462]

[1454] Gen 36:35, 36; 1 Kings 11:14, 17, 21, 25; 1 Chron 1:30, 46, 47, 50–51. H1908—*Hadad, had-ad*; of foreign origin; compare 111: mighty, name of an idol; several kings of Edom; H111— *'Adad, ad-ad*; Adad or Hadad, an Edomite: Hadad. H2301—Chadad, khad-ad'; from 2300 fierce: mighty.

[1455] Bauer, *History of the World*, 139; Rohl, *Lost Testament*, 112.

[1456] Benz, *Personal Names,* 302: HDD, citing UT Gordon, CH, *Ugaritic Text Book,* 750: ancient Semitic HDD akin to Baal and Zeus.

[1457] H758—*'Aram, arawm*': highland; exalted; Aram or Syria and its inhabitants; son of Shem; grandson of Nahor; H761—*'Arammiy, ar-am-mee*'; patrial from 758; an Aramite or Aramaean; Syrian; H762—*'Aramiyth, ar-aw-meeth*'; feminine of 761: Aramean; Syrian language; language of Aram, Aramaic.

[1458] H6604—*Pthowr, peth-ore*': a place in Mesopotamia; home of Balaam; Pethor means soothsayer. Gen 36:32; Num 22:5; 24:3, 15; 31:8; Deut 23:4; Josh 13:22; 24:9; 1 Chron 1:43; Mic 6:5.

[1459] Gen 14:6; 36:31, 32; Deut 2:12; 1 Chron 1:43.

[1460] Gen 36:33; 1 Chron 1:44. H1224—*Botsrah, bots-raw*'; town in Edom; town in Moab.

[1461] Gen 36:34; 1 Chron 1:45. H8489—*Teymaniy, tay-maw-nee*': a Temanite; inhabitant of Teman located east of Idumea.

[1462] Gen 36:35; 1 Chron 1:46.

Midianites dwelled east of the Jordan River and to the north, a long way from the Horim of Edom. Midianites, and their five dukes of their pentapolis, were aligned with King Og and Sihon in the time of the Exodus.[1463] Hadad was the renowned patronymic name of kings within the Horim and hybrid Edomite bloodline, as with Hadad kings of Edom along with Ben-Hadad, son of one of the dynastic Hadad kings of Damascus and Syria/Aramaea.[1464] Knowing this makes sense of Hadad, the son of Bedad successor of Husham, whose royal city was in Avith, a lost city typically understood as an Edomite city in Palestine; but scriptural details indicate otherwise, as underscored with Hadad's war with the Midianites. *Strong's Cyclopaedia* suggest Avith's location was north and east of Mount Seir.[1465] Avith/`Aviyth, meaning ruins, is derived from `avvah meaning ruin, distort, make crooked, pervert, commit iniquity, and do evil.[1466] Avith is also the plural of `Ay, a city located near Jericho known in Joshua's time as Ai, also meaning a heap of ruins, as well as a city connected to Sihon's Heshbon city.[1467] Avith was likely a branch of Sihon's empire and his royal city Heshbon in the time of the Exodus.

Further, `Avah, the source word for `Aviyth, is part of a series of related Hebrew words that include `Ivvah/`Avah, a region of Assyria and an Avvim or Hivvim city conquered by Assyrians in Syria.[1468] Ergo, Hadad's reign in Avith establishes the conception for Edom/Horim kingship sharing with Aram from before Hadad, via the Horim royal cities the kings reigned from. The Edomite/Aramaean transgenerational military alliance included the Aramaean kingship dynasties of the Hivvim. After Hadad, Samlah of Masrekah city reigned in Edom,[1469] followed by Shaul/Saul of Rehoboth city by the river.[1470] The river/*nahar*, as used in this kind of application, typically refers to the Nile or Euphrates,[1471] and based on the narrative is the Euphrates River, indicating the Horim king Saul reigned in the Syria region as did Hadad. Rehoboth/*Rchobowth* has several locations named, including Nim-

---

[1463] Num 31:7–8; Josh 13:21.

[1464] Hadad Edom: 1 Kings 11:14, 17, 19, 21, 25. Edom Hadar/Hadad: Gen 36:39; 1 Chron 1:50. Benhadad Syria and Damascus: 1 Kings 15:18; 20:1, 5, 9, 10, 16, 17, 20, 26, 30, 32, 34; 2 Chron 16:2, 4; Jer 49:27; Amos 1:4–5. Syria: 2 Kings 6:24; 8:7; 13:3, 24, 25.

[1465] *Strong's Cyclopaedia*, Vol. 1, 570.

[1466] Ai: Josh 7:2–5; 8:1–29; 9:3; 10:1–2; 12:9. H5762—`Aviyth, av-veeth'; or Ayowth, ah-yoth'; from 5753: ruin; a place in Palestine; city of Hadad Ben-Bedad a king of Edom; H5753—`avah, aw-vaw': to crook; do amiss, bow down; make crooked; commit iniquity; pervert; trouble; do wickedly; do wrong; distort; ruin.

[1467] H5857—`Ay, ah'ee; or feminine Aya (Neh 11:31) ah-yaw'; or Ayath/aiath (Isa 10:28) ah-yawth': Ai, Aja or Ajath, a place in Palestine: heap of ruins; a city lying east of Bethel and beside Bethaven near Jericho; the second city taken on the invasion of Canaan; an Ammonite city east of the Jordan connected to Heshbon.

[1468] H5755—`Ivvah, iv-vaw'; or Avvae (2 Kings 17:24): Ivvah or Avva, a region of Assyria; ruin; a city.

[1469] H4957—*Masreqah, mas-ray-kaw':* vineyard; a place in Idumaea. Gen 36:36; 1 Chron 1:47.

[1470] Gen 36:37; 1 Chron 1:48.

[1471] H5104—*nahar, naw-hawr':* a stream; a river; the Euphrates or Nile, as used in the river.

rod's city in Genesis 10:11.[1472] Rehoboth is the plural format *rchob* and is rooted in *Rchob*/Rehob, the city in Syria/Aram and/or the House of Rehob, Bethrehob in David's time (2 Sam 10:6). The royal city of Horim kings shifted between Syria and Edom until to David's time, which explains why Edomites marched in support of Hadadezer to Salt Valley to battle King David. Baalhanan, son of Achbor, succeeded Saul, but no city was named, so one presumes Baalhanan reigned from Rehoboth in Syria below Mount Hermon where the Baalim reigned.[1473] Hadad/Hadar succeeded Baalhanan, reigning from Pau and or Pai City in Seir.[1474]

Gardner adds that Edomite kings descending from Esau not only inherited Edom, but thereafter became the kings of Assyria circa 1710 BC, and the Lords of Babylonia, as part of the twelve Elef kingdoms that derived from the Horim genealogies listed in Genesis 36 and 1 Chronicles. Gardner regarded the Edomite and Kassite kingdoms as cousins, which suggests the Kassite kings also descended from Horim or Hurian and/or perhaps Esau as well.[1475] The Kassite Lords of Babylon ruled after the fall of Amorite Babylon to the Hittites circa 1595 BC.[1476] Gardner seems to be referring to the hybrid Elef kings of Esau that number eleven in Genesis 36 and 1 Chronicles. The prime number eleven may be part of the occult allegories and double-entendres for the originating Elven/Eleven bloodline of Edom.

One surmises Gardner added Amalek son of Eliphaz and Timna to arrive at the twelve tribes from Esau, to match the twelve tribes of Jacob. The Elven bloodline of Edom and Horim later produced King Herod, the infamous Edomite king of Israel who endeavored to murder the baby Messiah Jesus to prevent the salvation of humankind.

[1472] H7344—*Rchobowth, rekh-o-both*: wide places or streets; a place in Assyria; a place in Palestine; the third of a series of wells dug by Isaac in Philistia; one of four cities built by Asshur or Nimrod in Asshur close to Nineveh; a city of Saul, one of the early Edomite kings.

[1473] Gen 36:38; 1 Chron 1:49.

[1474] H6464—*Pa` uw, paw-oo*; or *Pamiy, paw-ee*: a place in Edom; bleating; capital of king Hadar of Edom: site uncertain. Gen 36:39; 1 Chron 1:40.

[1475] Gardner, *Realm of the Ring Lords,* 63–67; *Encyclopedia Americana*, Vol. 16, 313.

[1476] Bauer, *History of the Ancient World*, 174, 199, 200, 273.

CHAPTER 34

THE AMALEQIM AND AGAGITE BLOODLINE

*Gen 27:41 And Esau hated Jacob because of the blessing where-
with his father blessed him: and Esau said in his heart, The days
of mourning for my father are at hand; then will I slay my brother
Jacob.*

Amalek's mother was Timna, Eliphaz's concubine, daughter of Seir, and sister of Lotan. Timna was one of a few female Horim,[1477] perhaps identifying the source to the Rephaim infertility crisis. As such, Timna was of pure and precious matriarchal royal stock via her Horim parents. Eliphaz descended from Abrahamic stock via Isaac and Esau, and royal Hittite stock via Adah.[1478]

Daughters of Dragon kings with pure matriarchal dragon blood in antiquity were wedded to kings to propagate new fairy dynasties.[1479] A new fairy house/dynasty of hybrid begat via Esau's marriage to Ohilibamah, the daughter of Anah, daughter of Zibeon the Hivvim.[1480] Thus, another fairy dynasty was created via Eliphaz through

---

[1477] Gen 36:20, 22; 1 Chron 1:38, 39.
[1478] Gen 36:2–4.
[1479] Gardner, *Lost Secrets of the Sacred Ark,* 49.
[1480] Gen 36:2, 5.

Timna. Amalek was not listed among Gardner's Elvin dukes of Edom,[1481] but according to *Strong's Cyclopaedia* Amalek was provided equal status among the Edomite hybrid Edomite dukes.[1482] As such, the addition of Amalek seems to be how Gardner arrived at twelve duke/elef dynasties of Edom designed to emulate the twelve tribes of Esau's brother, Jacob/Israel. Counterfeiting twelve Abrahamic kingdoms of in the form of dragon kingdoms was the first step toward usurping the Covenant blessings, birthright, and messianic promise both in ancient times and the end times.

> Gen 36:12 And Timna was concubine to Eliphaz Esau's son; and she bare to Eliphaz Amalek.

The unnerving Amalekite accounting first bubbles up in Genesis 14's war of giants, where the Amaleqim surface as a powerful nation of giants at Kadesh, generations before Amalek was born in Genesis 36. The Amalekites, according to Christian scholars, dwelled around Kadesh in the extreme south of Judah, the Negev/*Negeb*.[1483] As such, Josephus placed Amalekites at Petra and Gobolitis.[1484] One muses if Petra was the city of Amalek King Saul laid siege to.[1485]

Conversely, Kadesh has fascinating connections to eastern giants, as in Kadmonites. The eastern connection may be why Arabian historians assert Amaleqim giants originally dwelled along the shores of the Persian Gulf before migrating to southern Edom.[1486] Amalekites and/or Amaleqim did not all migrate to Edom and Mount Seir because some were identified with Midianites and peoples of the east/*qedem* in the epoch of judges,[1487] which included giants. Note as well that *qedem* means ancient time, from old, antiquity, and from immediately after or before the flood.

An anecdote dropped in 1 Samuel 27:8, some eight hundred years after the earliest accounts of Amaleqim in Genesis 14, adds to *qedem* understanding: "And David and his men went up, and invaded the Geshurites, and the Gezrites, and the Amalekites: for those nations were of old the inhabitants of the land, as thou goest to Shur, even unto the land of Egypt." Geshurites, Gezrites, and Amalekites were part of the nations of old/*owlam*, meaning antiquity, ancient time, time of

---

[1481] Gen 36:40.

[1482] *Strong's Cyclopaedia*, Vol. 1, 186: Amalek.

[1483] *Mercer's*, 21: Amalek/Amalekite. H5045—*negeb, neh'-gheb*; from an unused root: to be parched; the south; region of southern Judah.

[1484] Josephus, *Ant.*, Book 3 2:1.

[1485] 1 Sam 15:5.

[1486] *Strong's Cyclopaedia*, Vol. 1, 186: Amalekite.

[1487] Judg 6:3, 33, 10:12, 12:15. H6924—*qedem, keh'-dem*, or *qedmah*: east; antiquity; front, that which is before, aforetime; ancient time; ancient; from of old, earliest time.

old, or old time,[1488] much like the mysterious Kadmonites of the east whose name is connected to *qedem*, and akin to the Elam giants whose name is alternatively enunciated as Owlam.[1489]

Owlam/old was the same Hebrew word penned in some notable passages like Genesis 6:4's Nephilim creation: "mighty men, which were of old"; Joshua 24:2: "Your fathers dwelt on the other side of the flood in old time"; and Deuteronomy 32:7–8: "Remember the days of old, consider the years of many generations: ask thy father, and he will shew thee; thy elders, and they will tell thee. When the most High divided to the nations their inheritance, when he separated the sons of Adam," among many others.

First Samuel 27:8 confirms that the original Amaleqim predated Amalek son of Eliphaz and Timna of Genesis 36. Amaleqim were giants created either before the flood or immediately after the flood, as an Aboriginal race from the east. Amaleqim then migrated to Kadesh in Edom either shortly after the flood, or from Kadesh of the east after the war of giants; their remnant later merged with the posterity of Amalek and Timna to form what *Unger's* calls the "Great Amalekite race that was closely associated with the Horim and Edomites."[1490]

> Gen 14:6 And the Horites in their mount Seir, unto Elparan, which is by the wilderness.

> Gen 14:7 And they returned, and came to Enmishpat, which is Kadesh, and smote all the country of the Amalekites, and also the Amorites, that dwelt in Hazezontamar.

Numbers 24:20 described Amalekites as the first among nations, inferring that they did survive the flood or were part of the first Rephaim nation(s) after the flood. Consequently, the dissonant Amalekites accounting indicates two races of the same name. The Amaleqim were a true Aboriginal giant nation, which makes sense of the "mount of the Amalekites" located in the land of Ephraim in the north.[1491] Further, first/*re'shiyth* is defined as the first in place, first order, a firstfruit, beginning, principal thing, chief, or choice part.[1492] The Amaleqim, according to Numbers 24, were the first among nations after the flood, likely as

---

[1488] H5769—*'owlam, o-lawm'*; or *olam, o-lawm'*; long duration; antiquity; futurity; forever; everlasting; evermore; eternity; perpetual; old; ancient; ancient time; long time of past. Gen 6:4; Deut 32:7; Josh 24:2; 1 Sam 27:8; Job 22:15; Ps 25:6; 119:52; Eccl 1:10; Isa 51:9, 58:11–12; 61:4; 63:9, 11; Jer 2:20; 6:16; 28:8; Lam 3:6; Ezek 25:15; 26:20; Amos 9:11; Mic 7:14; Mal 3:4.
[1489] H5867—*'Eylam, ay-lawm'*; or *Owlam*.
[1490] *Unger's*, 49–50: Amalekites.
[1491] Judg 12:15.
[1492] H7225—*re'shiyth, ray-sheeth'*: the first in place, time, order, or rank; specifically, a firstfruit; beginning, chief; principal thing; choice part.

in chief of nations with dominant military power. Knowing this gives one pause for thought about the obscure passage in Numbers 13 that infers Amalekites were either descendants of Anak, synonymous or equal to the Anakim, and/or closely associated with the Anakim as hybrids. So, questions arise like: Were the Amalekites of Numbers 13 the remnant from the war of giants? Were they hybrids spawned by the Amaleqim? Or were they hybrids of Hivvim or Horim in Edom?

> Num 13:28 Nevertheless the people be strong that dwell in the land, and the cities are walled, and very great: and moreover we saw the children of Anak there.

> Num 13:29 The Amalekites dwell in the land of the south: and the Hittites, and the Jebusites, and the Amorites, dwell in the mountains: and the Canaanites dwell by the sea.

I find it noteworthy that Amalekites were tallied in the Numbers 13 accounting as immediately following the Anakim and before the hybrid Canaanite, Hittite, Jebusite, and Amorite families. The order indicates that Amalekites were more powerful than the other hybrid nations or were Amaleqim closely related to the Anakim. In the scouts' report, Amalekites dwelled south of Hebron, in the Negev and thus in the Edom/Horim region.

Nelson's Dictionary authenticated that Amalek's name was patronymic from the Amaleqim, that Amalekites were the eponymously named posterity,[1493] as were the original Amaleqim by implication. It follows that Amalek's patronymic name came about by some form of close association with the Amaleqim. *Unger's Dictionary* concurs, suggesting Amalekites merged with the original inhabitants of Seir,[1494] the Amaleqim by implication, versus Horim. Hence the Amalekites documented in Numbers 13 were likely the remnant of Amaleqim that included hybrids.

Josephus commented on the descendants of Amalek and Timna, stating: "Amalek was not legitimate, but by a concubine, whose name was Thamna. These dwelled in that part of Idumea which is called Gebalitis, and that denominated from Amalek, Amalekitis; for Idumea was a large country, and did then preserve the name of the whole, while in its several parts it kept the names of its peculiar inhabitants."[1495] *Strong's Dictionary* concurred with Josephus, stating that `*Amaleqiy* derived "patronymically from" `*Amaleq*, a name of foreign origination meaning a valley dweller, an eponymous and patrial name of their people and country respectively.[1496] Scripturally, Gebal was an Idumean mountain located toward the

---

[1493] *Nelson's*, 44–45: Amalek.

[1494] *Unger's*, 49: Amalekites.

[1495] *Josephus*, Ant. Book 2 1:2.

[1496] H6003—`*Amaleqiy, am-aw-lay-kee*`; patronymically from 6002: descendants of Amalek; "people of lapping"; H6002—`*Amaleq, am-aw-lake*`: a descendant of Esau; his posterity and their country; dweller in a valley.

Dead Sea, a word meaning "a boundary," and the name of a people listed in the conspiracy to wipe Israel from the face of the earth.[1497] A remnant group of Gebal were described later dwelling in Sidon as the "ancients of Gebal" and "wise men" and "calkers" (Ezek 27:9). The Gebalim ancients/*zaqen* were wise/*chakam* meaning intelligent, skillful, artful, and cunning, and calkers/*chaqaz* meaning strong, courageous, and stout,[1498] akin to how the Rephaim and Terrible Ones were described. The Gebalim were a patrial and anonymous branch of the Aboriginal Amaleqim.

Now `*Anammelek*, a name phonetically close to Amalek, was an Assyrian god whose name meant "image of the king" according to *Strong's Dictionary,* and according to *Unger's,* "Anu is king."[1499] Amalek was a foreign word likely shortened in its transliteration into Hebrew. One might conclude, in its original Assyrian or Sumerian meaning, that Amalek bore the image of the king/*melek* (fallen) angel/*mal'ak*[1500] Anu, the image of heaven/An, or the image Anu king of heaven. However, `*Anammelek* was the goddess while Adrammelech/`*Adrammelek* was the god.[1501] "Adra" of *Adrammelek* is thought to be Adar, a transliteration of Adad/Hadad/Baal and similar to the Horim Duke of Edom, Hadar/Hadad of the Horim.[1502] Adar-amalek incorporates Amalek and forms, by extension, Baal's dwellers of the valley when combined with the definition of `*Amaleq* in *Strong's Dictionary,*[1503] and perhaps the image of Baal, godfather of the Rephaim. Either way, the Amaleqim name likely derived from their originating gods in Assyria and Persia.

The notion that Timna and Eliphaz dwelled among Amaleqim giants is consistent with Scripture and was likely the inspiration for naming their son patronymically after `*Amaleq,* the likely patriarch for the Amaleqim. However, the patronymic king title for the royal hybrid house was memorialized in the name Agag, not Amalek, for the new fairy dynasty. Thus, Duke Amalek was the twelfth and uniquely ennobled Elef/Elvin king of Edom Gardner was alluding to, versus Esau as the twelfth, because Esau the patriarch was of pure human stock as son of Isaac and Rebekah.[1504] Accordingly, Amalek was included among Gardner's twelve "names of the dukes that came of Esau, according to their families,"[1505] with fam-

---

[1497] Ps 83:7. H1381—*Gbal, gheb-awl'*: a mountain region in Edom; a boundary.

[1498] H2205—*zaqen, zaw-kane'*: old; ancient man, eldest; old man, men; senator; H2450—*chakam, khaw-kawm'*: wise; intelligent; skilful; or artful; cunning; H2388—*chazaq, khaw-zak'*: to seize; be strong; strengthen; stout; courageous.

[1499] H6048—`*Anammelek, an-am-meh'-lek*; of foreign origin: an Assyrian deity; image of the king; *Unger's,* 483: gods, false. 2 Kings 17:31.

[1500] H4428—*melek, meh'-lek*: a king; royal; H4397—*mal'ak, mal-awk'*: a messenger of God; an angel.

[1501] 2 Kings 17:31; 19:37; Isa 37:38. *Easton's,* 97: Anammelech; 59: Adrammelech.

[1502] *Easton's,* 59: Adrammelek; *Unger's,* 483, gods, false. Hadad: Gen 36:35; Hadar: 1 Chron 1:39. H152—*'Adrammelek, ad-ram-meh'-lek*: splendor/honour of the king; the name of an Assyrian idol of the Sepharvites; a son of Sennacherib; "Adar is prince or Adar is Counsellor or Decider."

[1503] Num 14:25. H6002—`*Amaleq.*

[1504] Gen 25:19–27.

[1505] Gen 36:40.

ilies implying a different species or kind of people akin the nine patriarch-less families/*mishpachah* of Canaan. One deduces the royal houses of Horim, Horites, Edomites, Amaleqim, and Amalekites interbred with each other and perhaps other dynasties like the Egyptians, Mitanni, and Kassites.

Amalek was used to seemingly distinguish the hybrid nation of Amalekites from the Amaleqim at the battle of Rephidim three months into the Exodus,[1506] although one suspects Amaleqim and Horim likely bolstered their ranks. Oddly, Amalekites were never included among the mighty seven, even though they were "the most warlike of all the [hybrid] nations that lived thereabout; and whose kings exhorted one another, and their neighbors, to go to this war against the Hebrews."[1507] The hybrid Amalekite dynasty distinguished their kings with a hereditary Agagite title of Agag accompanying the royal house.[1508] An Agagite is a descendant of Agag and either patrial or patronymic thereof.[1509] King Agag in the time of the Covenant Land conquest was identified after the battle of Rephidim in Balaam's oracles:

> Num 24:7 He shall pour the water out of his buckets, and his seed shall be in many waters, and his king shall be higher than Agag, and his kingdom shall be exalted.

King Agag, in Balaam's oracle, was described as a great and powerful king and kingdom drafted as an antichrist comparative to the coming Messiah Jesus, whose kingdom will be exalted higher than Agag. Agag and his Amalekites conspired with other nations like Edom, Horim, and Gebal to form a confederate "to cut them off as a nation; that the name of Israel may be no more in remembrance."[1510] The confederate conspiracy was to displace Israel from the Abrahamic covenants; prevent the coming of the Messiah; and replace Jesus with their dragon messiah from the Agagite and Hadad royal houses. Thus came the battle of Rephidim. One might anticipate a similar set of circumstances with the end-time antichrist who will try to destroy Israel and Judah.[1511]

The heraldic reverence accredited to the Agagite royal bloodlines was underscored during the reign of King Ahasuerus of Persia, who established Haman the Agagite above all other princes of Ahasuerus' court of vassal kings.[1512] Josephus

---

[1506] Exod 17:8, 9, 10, 11, 13, 14, 16.
[1507] Josephus, *Ant.* Book 3 2:1.
[1508] Agag: Num 24:7; 1 Sam 15:8–9, 20, 32, 33. Agagite: Esth 3:1, 10; 8:3, 5; 9:24. *Strong's Cyclopaedia*, Vol. 1, 186–87.
[1509] H91—*'Agagiy, ag-aw-ghee'*: descendant or subject of Agag; "I will overtop"; Haman the Agagite.
[1510] Ps 83:3–6.
[1511] Rev 12:12 –17.
[1512] Esth 3:1.

stated that Haman the Agagite of the book of Esther was from the posterity of Agag of the "old kings of the Amalekites."[1513] Moreover, Agag, pronounced Ag-awg,[1514] is eerily close to King Og in Agag's last syllable, and/or phonetically close to Gog if one silences the "a" in the first syllable of Agag. Although the giant Gog does not show up in the table of nations as Magog (m-agog) does, he surfaces in an Ezekiel end-time prophecy where Gog is described as being from the land of Magog, and is the chief prince of Mechech and Tubal.[1515] Gog's name appears in the Septuagint's translation of Amos 7:1 where he is named as the leader of the locust army, which seems to reflect the locust army of Joel 1–2, Revelation 9, and Ezekiel 38–39. Goyim/*Gowyim*, Hebrew for the non-Israelite nations, is also used metaphorically for a troop of animals and a swarm of locusts.[1516]

> *Sept* Amos 7:1 Thus has the Lord God shewed me; and, behold, a swarm of locusts coming from the east; and, behold, one caterpillar, king Gog.

The Septuagint's translation for Numbers 24:7's exalted Agag, translated Agag as the kingdom of Gog, likely reflects Greek cultural biases and understanding of Gog as a giant and a synonym for giant in their history, and that Amalekite kings derived from giant bloodlines. Further, the Septuagint regarded Gog and Agag as synonymous. Gog/*Gogue* in the New Testament Greek is identified as a symbolic name for some future antichrist,[1517] just as Numbers prophesies about Agag. However, the Septuagint's grammatical structure in Numbers 24 seems to state that Gog's seed will come from Israel and his kingdom shall be exalted.

> *Sept* Num 24:5 How goodly are thy habitations, Jacob, and thy tents, Israel!
>
> 24:6 as shady groves, and as gardens by a river, and as tents which God pitched, and as cedars by the waters.
>
> 24:7 There shall come a man out of his seed, and he shall rule over many nations; and the kingdom of Gog shall be exalted, and his kingdom shall be increased.

[1513] Josephus, *Ant.*, Book 6, 7:1, note 15.

[1514] H90—*'Agag, ag-ag'*; or *Agag, Ag-awg'*: flame; a title of Amalekitish kings.

[1515] Gen 10:2; Ezek 38:2–3; 39:1.

[1516] H1471—*gowy, go'-ee; goy, go'-ee*: nations; a foreign nation; a Gentile; figuratively a troop of animals, or a flight of locusts; heathen; people.

[1517] G1136—*gogue*; of Hebrew origin Hebrew 1463 Gowg: a symblical name for a future Antichrist; mountain; king of the land of Magog of the north. Transliterated: Gog; H1463—*Gowg, gohg*; of uncertain derivation: the name of an Israelite; a northern nation; mountain; the prophetic prince of Rosh, Meshech and Tubal, and Magog.

Understanding the transgenerational blood oath held by the royal houses of Amalek and Edom to wipe Israel from the face of the earth explains Haman the Agagite's plot to gain authority over the Jews. Haman sought to usurp the Abrahamic birthright inheritance, blessings, and messianic bloodline away from Judah and Israel, and to avenge his ancestors. Hence, Haman was called the Jewish enemy.

> Esth 9:24 Because Haman the son of Hammedatha, the Agagite, the enemy of all the Jews, had devised against the Jews to destroy them, and had cast Pur, that is, the lot, to consume them, and to destroy them.

The Amalekite and Edomite blood oath makes sense of the Edomite King Herod's attempt to murder the baby Jesus[1518] before He could complete His holy commission. The Herodian king title derives from *Herodes*, meaning hero/heroic[1519] as in the "mighty men of old" of Genesis 6:4, the heroes of old, and heroes of Greece, Mesopotamia, and the Tuatha De Danann. Herod the Great's name was renowned before it was recorded in the New Testament,[1520] a patronymic name that reflected his genealogy back to the dukes of Edom.

Julius Caesar appointed Antipater II procurator/tetrarch of Judea circa 37 BC after a series of promotions from other Romans.[1521] Herod the Great married into the Hasmonean dynasty through Miriam, daughter of Alexander Maccabeus and Alexandra, one of his five marriages. *Strong's Dictionary* stated Herod was son of Antipater of Idumea/Edom.[1522] Herod's mother Cypros was Idumean,[1523]

[1518] Matt 2:1–13.
[1519] G2264—*Herodes, hay-ro'-dace*: compound of hero and heroic.
[1520] *Catholic Encyclopedia*, Vol. 6, 289: Herod.
[1521] *Encyclopedia Americana*, Vol. 14, 136: Herod. "When after this Antony came into Syria, Cleopatra met him in Cilicia, and brought him to fall in love with her. And there came now also a hundred of the most potent of the Jews to accuse Herod and those about him and set the men of the greatest eloquence among them to speak. But Messala contradicted them, on behalf of the young men, and all this in the presence of Hyrcanus, who was Herod's father-in-law 24 already. When Antony had heard both sides at Daphne, he asked Hyrcanus who they were that governed the nation best. He replied, Herod and his friends. Hereupon Antony, by reason of the old hospitable friendship he had made with his father [Antipater], at that time when he was with Gabinius, he made both Herod and Phasaelus tetrarchs, and committed the public affairs of the Jews to them and wrote letters to that purpose." *Josephus*, Ant 14:13:1. Luke 3:1.
[1522] G2264—*hay-ro'-dace*: a hero; heroic as in Herodes; name of four Jewish kings: "Herod Antipas, Herod the Great, Herod Agrippa I, Herod Agrippa II name of a royal family among the Jews in the times of Christ; Herod the Great was the son of Antipater of Idumea appointed king of Judaea B.C. 40 by the Roman Senate at Antony's the suggestion and consent of Octavian. Herod destroyed the entire royal family of Hasmonaeans and proceeded to kill his wife Mariamne of the Hasmonaean line." *Catholic Encyclopedia*, Vol. 6, 289: Herod.
[1523] Josephus, *Ant.*, Book 15:7:3.

a princess from an eminent royal family and king of the Arabians,[1524] the Nabateans that reigned from Petra after driving out Idumeans.[1525] Nabateans were part of the twelve sons of Ishmael that Josephus recognized as the Nabatene, likely eponymously named after Ishmael's firstborn son Nabaoith/Nebajoth. Ishmael produced another son named Idumas/Dumah,[1526] and one of the root words for Idumean along with Edom. Josephus recorded that Idumeans were descendants of Esau.[1527] Assyrian inscriptions recorded Edom as *Udumi/Udumu*; Egyptians: *Aduma*; Greeks: *Idumea*.[1528]

Petra, before the Nabateans, was the ancient stronghold of Mount Seir of the Amalekites and then of the Edomites, a place David Rohl accounts as Mosera, the Rose-Red City,[1529] and the former home of the Amalekites/Amaleqim according to Josephus.[1530] Arabian writers attached great importance to the primeval Amaleqim people of Petra, a nation they say once ruled Egypt,[1531] perhaps connected to the Hyksos. Greeks called Petra the most esteemed Arabian metropolis of the time. It was originally named Acre/Arecem after the founder of the city, King Arecem. Josephus says the name of Petra's builder was a name also held by one duke of the Midian pentapolis allied to Rephaim King Sihon: Rekem.[1532] John Wilson, translator of the Egyptian Execration Texts, included Acre among the royal cities reigned over by Iy'anak/Anakim and Shutu.[1533] Arecem was likely an Aboriginal postdiluvian Rephaim, Amaleqim, Anakim, or Horim. The Horim/Hivvim Hadad kingship bloodline, derived from Baal's offspring, continued in the Edomite and the Agag bloodlines of Seir, Petra, and Idumea.

[1524] Josephus, *Jewish Wars*, Book 1, 8:9; *Ant.*, Book 14 7:3. Herod was the son of Antipater of Idumaea. *Catholic Encyclopedia*, Vol. 6, 289: Herod.

[1525] *Unger's*, 606, Idumea.

[1526] Josephus, *Ant.*, Book 1, 12:3–4. Gen 25:13—15.

[1527] "So he fell upon the Idumeans, the posterity of Esau, at Acrabattene," *Josephus*, Ant., 12:8:1.

[1528] *Mercer's*, 232: Edom; *Catholic Encyclopedia*, Vol. 7, 638: Idumea, citing Burkhardt, *Travels in Syria and the Holy Land*, London, 1822; Robinson, *Biblical Researches in Palestine II* London, 1856; Palmer, *The Desert of the Exodus*, Cambridge, 1871; Hull, *Mount Seir*, London, 1889; Idem., *Memoir on the Geology and Geography of Arabia Petra, Palestine and adjoining districts*, London, 1889; Musil, *Arabia Petra, II Edom* Topographischer Reisebericht, Vienna, 1907; Buhl, Geschichte der Edomiter, Leipzig, 1893; Lagrange, *L'Itinéraire des Israélites du Pays de Gessen aux bords du Jourdain. De Cadès à 'Asion-Gaber in Revue Biblique* , 1900, 280; Jaussen, Saviignac, and Vincent, *'Abdeh in Revue Biblique*, 1904, 403; 1905, 74, 235.

[1529] Rohl, *Legends*, 225, citing Deut 10:6.

[1530] Josephus, *Ant.*, Book 3 2:1.

[1531] *Jewish Encyclopedia*, Vol. 1, 483–84: Amalek/Amalekites.

[1532] Josephus, *Ant.*, Book 4, 4:7; 7:1. Num 31:8; Jos 13:21; 18:27.

[1533] Billington, "Goliath and the Exodus Giants," 501, 506, citing Pritchard, *ANET*, 225, notes 3, 6.

The Baalim Molech/*Molek* god is synonymous with *melek* for king and malak for angel.[1534] Molech worship was wider spread in Israel and the surrounding area than appears at first glance, hidden in the Old Testament in verses like Isaiah 30:33 and Amos 7:13.[1535] Molech is the same god as Moloch,[1536] Malcham, Milcom,[1537] Malcam, and Micom,[1538] and was transliterated by Phoenicians as Malcander, Milichus, and Milicia.[1539] Molech was documented as Baalim in the *Ugartic Texts*, recorded as Maliku, Malik, Milk, and his host, the Maliku,[1540] was otherwise known as Ba'almaluku and 'BMLK.[1541] As such, Molech was the fire god of Ammon, Chemosh of the Moabites, and is comparable to or cognate with the Adrammelech, the fire god of Sepharvim[1542] and the god connected to the Amaleqim. In this line of thought, `am in Hebrew means male, people, tribe or nation.[1543] It follows then that the Amaleqim (Am-malek or Am-molech) were the Aboriginal people of Molech, otherwise known as Adrammelek/Adarmelek/ Hadadmelek, and Baa'almaluku.

[1534] H4432—*Molek, mo'-lek*: king, chief Ammonite deity; H4397—*mal'ak, mal-awk'*: to despatch as a deputy or messenger of God, angel, prophet, priest, or teacher; ambassador; H4428—*melek, meh'-lek*: king; a royal.

[1535] *Strong's Cyclopaedia*, Vol. 6, 437: Molech.

[1536] H4432—*Molek, mo'-lek*: the chief Ammonite deity. Molech: Lev 18:21; 20:2–5; 1 Kings 11:7; 2 Kings 23:10; Jer 32:35. Moloch: Amos 5:26. G3434—Moloch: Acts 7:43.

[1537] H4445—*Malkam, mal-kawm'*; or *Milkowm, milkome'*. Milcom: 1 Kings 11:5, 33; 2 Kings 23:13. Malcham: 1 Chron 8:9; Zeph 1:5.

[1538] *Strong's Cyclopaedia*, Vol. 6, 437: Molech.

[1539] Ibid.

[1540] Wyatt, *Religious Texts from Ugarit*, 381, note 22: Malik(u) is related to Molek and Milkom on KTU 1.100 B: IX; 354, note 50; 417, note 5 on dynastic gods of Malik from KTU 147.33; 421, note 34, on MLKM: Milkom and dynastic gods from KTU 1.119 V:25; and 361, Pantheon Lists KTU 1.118 and 1.47.33.

[1541] Benz, *Personal Names*, 344: MLK.

[1542] *Strong's Cyclopaedia*, Vol. 6, 437: Molech. H3645—*Kmowsh, kem-oshe'*: subdue; powerful; Moabite god. Num 21:29; Judg 11:24; 1 Kings 11:7, 33; 2 Kings 23:13; Jer 48:7, 13, 46.

[1543] H5971—`am: people, nation, kinsmen, and men/ammi as in male(s)/sons used four times as in Ezek 46:18 where people are referred to as sons; H1121—*ben, bane*: a son as a builder of the family name; as in people in Ezek 46:18: "Moreover the prince shall not take of the people's inheritance by oppression, to thrust them out of their possession; but he shall give his sons inheritance"; as Ammi in Hos 2:1: "Say ye unto your brethren, Ammi; and to your sisters, Ruhamah"; as in men in Num 31:32: "And the booty, being the rest of the prey which the men of war had caught"; as folk in Gen 33:15.

CHAPTER 35

THE ZUZIM, ZAMZUMMIM, AND EMIM

Gen 14:5 And in the fourteenth year came Chedorlaomer, and the kings that were with him, and smote the Rephaims in Ashteroth Karnaim, and the Zuzims in Ham, and the Emims in Shaveh Kiriathaim.

Genesis 14:5 purposefully grouped the Rephaim, Zuzim, and Emim nations together in the war of giants as giant nation empires east of the Jordan River. The Mesopotamian alliance attacked Rephaim nations protecting Canaanites, en route to reimposing the Mesopotamian tribute on the upstart vassal Canaanite city-states.[1544]

The Rephaim, Zuzim, and Emim nations were the Eastern alliance of the early postdiluvian period, and part of the "Rephaims" listed in Genesis 15:20. The Eastern alliance supported and protected the Canaanite hybrid nations who supplied willing female surrogates to subsidize increasingly infertile female giants. The Horim, Amaleqim, Avvim, and Anakim of the Southern alliance offered protection for Canaanite hybrids from the Egyptian empire.

[1544] Gen 14:4.

The Mesopotamian alliance attacked the Rephaim in the Mount Hermon region of the north first, then marched south to Ammon to wage war on the Zuzim. The campaign continued in a southerly direction to wage war on the Emim of Moab, then southwest to war with the Horim of Seir, then returned or turned back to battle the Amaleqim at Kadesh, likely in the south but perhaps in the east. The Mesopotamians then marched to attack the Amorites at Hazezontamar in the desert of Judah. The Mesopotamian alliance finally marched to the south Dead Sea region to reinstate their tribute upon the Canaanite pentapolis, which begat the great war.[1545]

The Zuzim giants surface only once in Scripture, in the war of giants, and only with its *im* suffix applied to Nephilim, Rephaim, Gibborim, and angels like seraphim and cherubim. Oddly, Zuzim is a plural male noun translated into English in a double plural format, as "Zuzims" in Genesis 14, as were the "Rephaims" and "Emims," suggesting there were multiple tribes of these giants. Just as strange, *Strong's Dictionary* defined Zuzim/*Zuwziym* as Zuzites even though KJV translators inked them as Zuzims. Contrarywise, *Strong's* further noted that the Zuzim were an Aboriginal tribe of Palestine, even though Scripture states they were from the land of Ham[1546] (Egypt), as does *Unger's*.[1547] Hamites, as you will recall, inherited Africa for their eponymously named tribes, but Nimrod and Canaan opted to stay to annex parts of the greater Covenant Land.

The Zuzim were a branch or kin of the greater Rephaims, and a giant nation whose "great ethnical body was called by the Egyptians, Sati," and speculated as being from Semitic origin.[1548] Sati in Egyptian tradition was a seventy-cubit-long (105 feet) serpent mentioned in the *Ritual of the Dead,* as well as the goddess of the sunbeam wearing a white crown and horns.[1549] One infers from the Sati association that the Zuzim were giant serpent-like giants and spurious offspring of the gods, fallen seraphim. *Ellicott's Commentary on the Old Testament* described the Zuzim as an inferior branch of the Rephaim, and that their eastern capital was identified with Hameitat, east of the lower part of the Dead Sea,[1550] which was south of Ammon and Moab, indicating Zuzim maintained multiple settlements. Knowing this indicates some Zuzim may have had an influence and/or settlements just south of Mount Hermon and perhaps in Ammon. As such, many scholars conclude Zuzim were part of the Zamzummim of Ammon.[1551] Zamzummim giants were

---

[1545] Gen 14:4–11. H2688—*Chatstsown Tamar, khats-ets-one' taw-mawr'*; or *Chatsatson Tamar*: division of the date-palm; Amorite city in the desert of Judah.
[1546] H2104—*Zuwziym, zoo-zeem'*: aboriginal tribe of Palestine of uncertain origin; male patrial of an unknown place; roving creatures. Gen 14:5.
[1547] *Unger's*, 1392: Zuzim.
[1548] Cooper, *An Archaic Dictionary,* 636: Zuzim.
[1549] Ibid., 492: Sati.
[1550] Ellicott, *Old Testament Commentary,* Vol. 1, 64, Genesis 14: Zuzim.
[1551] Deut 2:20–21.

defined as part of the Rephaim nations, a numerous nation of giants and plotters of evil. Zamzummim/*Zamzom* means planners and plotters of evil.[1552] "Zamzummims," as they were translated into English, might also refer to multiple tribes that included the Zuzim.

> Deut 2:20 (That also was accounted a land of giants: giants dwelt therein in old time; and the Ammonites call them Zamzummims;
>
> Deut 2:21 A people great, and many, and tall, as the Anakim. ..).

Oddly though, Zamzummim is not shown in *Strong's Dictionary* as having an etymological link to the Zuzim, even though the word Zuzim is essentially enveloped within the word Zamzumin. Further, *Strong's Cyclopaedia* states that nothing is known of the "etymology or signification" for Zuzim.[1553] Based on the Scripture provided, though, and again noting we do not have other Scripture placing Zuzim in the Covenant Land, the "Zuzims of Ham" were likely centered in Africa with kin Zamzummim satellite settlements in Ammon and the south Dead Sea region. It follows that some conclude Zamzummim derives from Ham-Zuzims: Zuzim from Ham or dwelling in Ham,[1554] Africa.

The Zuzim were further defined by *Strong's Dictionary* as of unknown origin, patrial of an unknown place, and roving creatures, stemming from the word *ziyz*, meaning conspicuous, fullness of the breast (as in large-chested or stout), a roving creature, and a wild beast as in wild boar of the mountains.[1555] *Ziyz* is the root word for *Ziyza*, meaning prominence and shining;[1556] Nephilim and Rephaim creatures/beasts were likewise known in Sumer, Ireland and elsewhere as the Shining Ones and stout ones. Knowing this makes sense that Zuzim were known outside the Bible as the offspring of the Watchers' and Canaanite women—beings of great stature and strength.[1557] Although the latter is not biblical, the source does indicate a Second Incursion of fallen angels with rebellious and bitter Canaanites who readily provided daughters to create the Rephaim nations, and by inference, daughters to create hybrid human/Rephaim giants, as testified by the patriarch-less families in the table of nations.

[1552] H2157—*Zamzom, zam-zome*; from 2161: intriguing; plotters; Ammonite name for Rephaim; a numerous nation of giants perhaps the same as 'Zuzim; native tribe of Palestine; H2161—*zamam, zaw-mam*: to plan or plot in a bad sense; evil. *Unger's,* Zamzumin: noisemakers; mumble; possibly the same people as the Zuzim.

[1553] *Strong's Cyclopaedia,* Vol. 10, 1111: Zuzim.

[1554] *Mercer's,* 1309: Zamzummim.

[1555] Psa 80:13; 50:11.

[1556] H2123—ziyz, zeez: conspicous; fulness of the breast; a moving creature; wild beast; and abundance. H2124– Ziyza', zee-zaw'; from/same as 2123; prominence; shining.

[1557] Bane, *Encyclopedia of Giants and Humanoids,* 174: Zuzim, citing Garnier, *Worship of the Dead,* 93–94.

The Zuzim were not named with the Septuagint's accounting of Genesis 14:5, but were seemingly included among the giants/Rephaim of Mount Hermon, as the "strong nations" with them, and thus were thought of as giants/Rephaim as translated in Deuteronomy 2, although other Rephaim tribes like the Emim/Ommaens were listed by name.

> *Sept* Gen 14:5 And in the fourteenth year came Chodollogomor, and the kings with him, and cut to pieces the giants in Astaroth, and Carnain, and strong nations with them, and the Ommaeans in the city Save.

The Septuagint, then, translated Zuzim as more of an appellative than a name, and in the same way the *Targum of Onkelos* and the *Samaritan Targum* translated Zuzim as the "strong people," perhaps relying on a compounded Hebrew word to support their translation [*ha*] *az-zuzim* that *Unger's* set forth.[1558] `Az is defined as strong, mighty, and fierce, which derives from `*azaz* meaning stout (as in fullness of breast or wide: *ziyz*), strong, strengthen, and prevail.[1559] `Az is the word translated as strong in the "strong people" of the Terrible Ones in Isaiah 25:3 and seemingly the source for the "strong nations" substituted for Zuzim in the Septuagint. *The Jewish Encyclopedia* alternatively submitted the appellation preferred by translations, discarding Zuzim may have relied on the Hebrew words `*ezuwz*, meaning might and strength, and/or `*izzuwz* defined as strong, mighty, and collectively as an army, of which both are source words *Azaz* and *Az*.[1560] All the above words were related, and each in part were the source words for Zuzim as words inked in Israelite prehistory to describe giants.

In this same line of thinking, the book of Jubilees referenced the land of Rephaim, where the Rephaim were born, as the land from Ammon to Mount Hermon. Jubilees stated that the Rephaim reigned from Karnaim, Ashteroth, Edrei, and Beon, which was inclusive of the land of Zuzim, Zamzuzim, and Rephaim. Jubilees tallied that the height of the Terrible Ones ranged from 10'6"–12'3" to 15'–17'6":[1561] Karanim Ashteroth and Edrei were the twin cities of worship and rule for the Rephaim and King Og.[1562] Biblically, Beon was a city east of the Jordan River listed as part of Heshbon[1563] of Sihon's empire.

[1558] *Unger's*, 1392: Zuzim.

[1559] H5794—`*az, az*; from 5810; strong; vehement; harsh; fierce; greedy; mighty; power; roughly; strong; H5810—`*azaz, awzaz*: to be stout; harden; prevail; strengthen; strong; and impudent.

[1560] H5807—`*ezuwz, ez-ooz*': forcibleness; might; strength; fierceness; H5808—`*izzuwz, iz-ooz*': forcible; a powerful army; strong; mighty; *Jewish Encyclopedia*, Vol. 12, 706: Zuzim.

[1561] Jubilees 29:10.

[1562] Gen 14:4; Deut 1:4; Josh 14:12.

[1563] Num 32. H1194—*B'on, beh-ohn*': Beon, a city east of the Jordan; in the dwelling.

Jubilees 29:9–11 But before they used to call the land of Gilead the land of the Rephaim; for it was the land of the Rephaim, and the Rephaim were born (there), giants whose height was ten, nine, eight down to seven cubits. And their habitation was from the land of the children of Ammon to Mount Hermon, and the seats of their kingdom were Karnaim and Ashtaroth, and Edrei, and Misur, and Beon. And the Lord destroyed them because of the evil of their deeds.

The Emim were grouped with the Rephaim, and the Zuzim in Genesis 14's war of giants as part of the Eastern alliance. The Emim dwelled in Moab just south of the Zuzim. Emim were rendered as great, many, tall, and like the Anakim.[1564] "Emims," as the KJV translates Emim, indicates multiple tribes, likely being communicated in part with many/*rab*.[1565] As such, some historians believe the Emim were documented as the Imu in Egyptian texts, and part of the Syrian peoples conquered by Tutmosis III, sometime before the Exodus.[1566]

The Septuagint transliterated Emim as the Ommaeans in Genesis 14:5 and as the Ommin in Deuteronomy 2:11. The Emim were accounted as a warlike tribe of gigantic stature,[1567] and as Aboriginals[1568] akin to the Anakim, Rephaim, and Amaleqim, but located in Moab. Emim were defined as terrors,[1569] as part of the notorious Terrible Ones, the Ariytim. In fact, *Strong's Cyclopaedia* states that the Emim were part of the same stock of fierce and warlike giants as the Zuzim, Zamzumim, Rephaim, Anakim, and Horim—the "Terrible Men."[1570]

Deut 2:10 The Emims dwelt therein in times past, a people great, and many, and tall, as the Anakims;

Deut 2:11 Which also were accounted giants, as the Anakims; but the Moabites call them Emim.

Such was the destruction levied by the Mesopotamian alliance of giant empires that weakened the Covenant Land giants to point where the sons of Lot, Moab and Ammon, later drove the various giant nations from their portion of the Covenant Land, as did some sons of Esau to drive out giants from their land—those

---

[1564] Gen 14:5; Deut 2:10–11, 20–23.
[1565] Gen 14:6, Deut 2:10, 12. H7227—*rab*.
[1566] Cooper, *An Archaic Dictionary*, 250: Imu.
[1567] *Strong's Cyclopaedia*, Vol. 3, 178: Emim.
[1568] *Unger's*, 361: Emim.
[1569] H368—*'Eymiym, ay-meem'*; plural of 367: terrors; an early Moab tribe; H367—*'eymah, ay-maw'*; same as 366: fright; terror; dread; horror; H366—*'ayom, aw-yome*: to frighten; terrible; dreadful.
[1570] *Strong's Cyclopaedia*, Vol. 3, 178; Mercer's, 426: Emim.

to the east who did not intermarry with the Amaleqim and Horim. These were the Edomites God commanded Israel not to war with, which extended to the Ammonites and the Moabites,[1571] when Israel marched to battle Sihon and Og of the Rephaim.

[1571] Gen 19:36–38; Deut 2:8, 9, 19.

GESHURIM, GIRZIM, AND MAACHATHIM

1 Sam 27:8 And David and his men went up, and invaded the Geshurites, and the Gezrites, and the Amalekites: for those nations were of old the inhabitants of the land, as thou goest to Shur, even unto the land of Egypt.

The Geshurites and the Gezrites were not documented in the table of nations. The Geshurites and Gezrites are part of the same mystery of the Amaleqim and other Rephaim nations. First Samuel 27 included Geshurites/Geshurim and Gezrites/Gizrim as the nations of old, Aboriginals dwelling in Shur to Egypt in southwest Palestine adjacent to the Philistines.[1572]

The Geshurim and the Gizrim were part of the powerful military network of giant nations that produced dynastic kings and royal bloodlines. Geshurim not only dwelled in the southwest of the Covenant Land region but additionally inhabited parts of Syria/Aram,[1573] in the northern part of Bashan, a land not taken by Joshua;[1574] the region of Rephaim and King Og;[1575] and near the

---

[1572] *Strong's Cyclopaedia*, Vol. 3, 840: Geshuri. Josh 13:2.
[1573] 2 Sam 15:8; 1 Chron 2:23.
[1574] *Jewish Encyclopedia*, Vol. 4, 646: Geshur. Deut 3:14; Josh 13:13.
[1575] Deut 3:14; Josh 12:5; 13:11, 12. H1651—*Gshuwriy, ghe-shoo-ree';* patrial from 1650: inhabitants of Geshur: Geshuri, Geshurites; H1650—*Gshuwr, ghesh-oor':* join; proud beholder; bridge; Syrian district.

Hivvim. Geshurim, like the Zuzim, Horim, Hivvim, Amaleqim, and Anakim maintained branch factions in the Covenant Land.

The Gezrites/Gizrim are mentioned only once in the Bible (1 Sam 27:8), dwelling among the Amaleqim and the Geshurim in the southwest. Gizrim are sometimes referred to as Girzites, Gerizzites, and/or Gizrites, all who hold phonetic and etymological links to Gezer and Mount Gerizim.[1576] The singular *Gizriy* translated as Gezrite is defined as inhabitants of Gezer, cutters-off, and inhabitants of Mount Gerizim.[1577] *Gizriy* is patrial from *Gezer,* a city on the border of Ephraim in the north. *Griziym/*Gerizim is defined as a mountain in northern Israel in Ephraim,[1578] as well as a city in the central region of the Hivites,[1579] and/or Hivvim. Mount Gerizim was the mountain Moses proclaimed the blessing from the Holy Covenant, while the curses of the Holy Covenant were announced from Mount Ebal.[1580] Mount Gerizim was home to a large altar built before 1600 BC[1581] to worship the Baalim. Gezer was an ancient city rebuilt after the flood, and dates to 3100 BC.[1582] Gerazim/*Griziym* and Gezer/*Gizriy* indicate a Rephaim patriarch of a similar name.

King Horam of Gezer was destroyed by Joshua, leaving none of Horam's people alive, which accounts for 1 Samuel 27:8 only recording Gizrim of that time in Shur. Horam is defined as exalted, towering up, and high. King Horam was a giant king[1583] of the Gizrim. Although Horam does not have etymological, patronymic, or patrial links to Hori or Horim denoted in *Strong's Dictionary,* the phonetic and Rephaim links are too much of a coincidence to ignore. *Hor* is defined as a mountain derived from *har* meaning mountain or hill and is a mountain in Edom on the eastern side of Petra, and Syria.[1584] Horam could be defined as the people/*am* of the mountain, and/or the people of King Hor the giant, from which King Horam received or provided his name.

The above connections placed the Gizrim in the southwest of Palestine and in Syria, just as the Geshurim dwelled in Syria and southwest Palestine. In fact, the *Gshuwri* of the south were listed among the Philistines and other nations Joshua did not conquer in the south.[1585] The singular *Gshuwri* also indicates an eponymous

---

[1576] *Strong's Cyclopaedia,* Vol. 3, 843: Gezrites.

[1577] H1511—*Gizriy, ghiz-ree';* patrial from 1507: inhabitants of Gezer; a piece; a portion cut off; cutters off; inhabitants of Mt Gerizim.

[1578] H1507—*Gezer, gheh'-zer,* the same as 1506: portion; a city on Ephraim's border; H1506—*gezer, gheh'-zer.* something cut off; a portion, part; piece; H1630—*Griziym, gher-ee-zeem':* cut up as in rocky; a mountain near Shechem. Deut 11:29; 27:12; Josh 8:33; Judg 9:7.

[1579] Josh 10:33; 12:12.

[1580] Deut 11:29; 27:12; Josh 8:33.

[1581] *Mercer's,* 326: Mount Gerizim.

[1582] *Mercer's,* 328: Gezer; *Unger's,* 470: Gezer.

[1583] H2036—*Horam, ho-rawm':* exalted; to tower up; high; a Canaanite king Horam of the conquest. Josh 10:33.

[1584] H2023—*Hor, hore;* another form of 2022: mountain; a peak in Idumaea on the eastern side of Petra, and Syria; H2022—*har, har.* a mountain; hill; range of hills; mount. Num 20:22-23, 25, 27, 21:4, 33:37, 39, 39, 33:41, 34:7, 8; Deut 32:50.

[1585] Josh 13:2.

name from a patriarch. *Mercer's Dictionary* placed the Geshurim in the Negev, home of King Arad, the Amaleqim, and the Anakim.[1586] In the north, the Geshurim were conquered, but not exorcised from the land that came back to haunt David.

Moreover, and as discussed previously, Akkaddian *Gasru* is close to the Semitic source for the Hebrew transliteration Geshur/Gshuwr,[1587] which indicates that the Geshurim were connected to Mesopotamian giants. The Semitic *GSR*, meaning "strong," has toponymic connections to Geshur/*Gshuwr* and eponymously to Gesuri/*Gshuwriy*,[1588] as inhabitants of Geshur meaning proud beholder.[1589] It follows that the northern Geshurim dwelled alongside other Rephaim in the land of giants:[1590]

> Josh 13:11 And Gilead, and the border of the Geshurites and Maachathites, and all mount Hermon, and all Bashan unto Salcah. ..

> Josh 13:12 All the kingdom of Og in Bashan, which reigned in Ashtaroth and in Edrei, who remained of the remnant of the giants: for these did Moses smite, and cast them out.

> Josh 13:13 Nevertheless the children of Israel expelled not the Geshurites, nor the Maachathites: but the Geshurites and the Maachathites dwell among the Israelites until this day.

Some believe the Geshurim of Syria broke away from Israelite dominance sometime before the monarchy.[1591] Geshur in the time of King David was reigned over by King Talmai, a patronymically named king seemingly descended from the Anakim King Talmai of Kiriatharba. The dynastic Talmai's name binds the Geshurim to the southern Anakim, and to the Horim, Hivvim, and Hurrim of Syria because Talmai was a Hurrian/Horim name. Talmai's father was Amihud/'*Ammiychuwr* remembered as from people of nobility and majesty. '*Ammiyhuwd* is defined as a people of splendor and kinsman of majesty,[1592] which resonates connections to *im,* the suffix to underline the male plural for ones of

---

[1586] *Mercer's,* 327: Geshur.

[1587] Benz, *Personal Names,* 300.

[1588] Ibid., 300, citing F. Grondahl, *Die Personennamen der Texte aus Ugarit:* PTU 131. H1650—*Gshuwr: geshur,* 2 Sam 3:3; 13:37–38; 14:23, 32; 15:8; 1 Chron 2:23; 3:2; H1651—*Gshuwri:* Geshurites: Josh 12:5; 13:11, 13; 1 Sam 27:8. Geshuri: Deut 3:14; Josh 13:2.

[1589] Ibid., 300 citing F. Grohahl, *Die Personennamen der Texte aus Ugarit,* 131. H1651—*Gshuwriy, ghe-shoo-ree';* patrial from 1650: inhabitants of Geshur; H1650—*Gshuwr, ghesh-oor':* Geshur or Geshurites : proud beholder. Deut 3:14; Josh 13:12.

[1590] Also: Josh 12:4–5: Og's land as the remnant of the giants/Rephaim was in Bashan and Saclah to the border of the Geshurites and Maachathites. Deut 3:14.

[1591] *Mercer's,* 327: Geshur.

[1592] H5991—'*Ammiychuwr, am-mee-khoor':* people of nobility; a people of majesty; a Syrian prince or ruler; H5989—'*Ammiyhuwd, am-mee-hood':* a people of splendor; my kinsman is majesty. 2 Sam 13:37.

majesty, as in angels, gods and their male progeny.[1593] Majesty is defined as the greatness of God, gods, lofty, regal, title of monarchs, and the royals.[1594]

North Geshur was allied with the powerful military network of Sihon and Og of Bashan before the Israelite conquest. Later the Geshurim were an ally with the Maachathim on Geshur's northwest border as part of the Syrian peoples in David's era.[1595] Maachah was situated on Bashan's west side,[1596] likewise known as Syriamaachah/*Aramma`akah*,[1597] located just north of King Hadadezer's Aramaean/Edomite empire.[1598] It follows that the Geshurim King Talmai fathered a daughter named Maachah who married King David, which produced Absalom.[1599] Israelites, though, were instructed not to intermarry with them.[1600]

Maacha was an eponymous name for the Maachathites, patronymic for several kings, patrial for the Maachah city, and matronymic for queens.[1601] For examples, Maachah was the name of the giant king of Gath, the father of King Achish, a king of Syria in David's time; Maachah was the mother of King Abijam and Asa of Judah, and Maacha was the daughter of Absalom and the wife and of King Rehoboam.[1602]

The Maachathim/*Ma`akathiy* were a warrior-like Syrian/Aramean kingdom centered in Maachah city at the foot of Mount Hermon, bordering Geshur.[1603] Royal Rephaim cities were often patrial, named from obscure Rephaim; note that *Ma`akathiy* is the singular format. The Maachathim and their royal city reflect their patriarch Maachah/*Ma`akathiy*,[1604] a Rephaim from Bashan and Syria. A Maachathim was among the warriors of in David's mighty men.[1605]

The Maachathim were not listed in the table of nations, further indicting them as a Rephaim nation. The Maacha name surfaces first in Genesis 22:24 as a daughter

---

[1593] Benz, *Personal Names*, 267: Im.

[1594] *Websters's*, 244: majesty. *Dictionary.com:* majestic.

[1595] Josh 12:5; 13:13; 2 Sam 10:6; 1 Chron 19:6.

[1596] *Nelson's*, 783: Maacha.

[1597] *Strong's Cyclopaedia*, Vol. 5, 592: Maacah. 1 Chron 19:6. H758—'*Aram, arawm*'; H4601— *Ma`akah; mah-ak-aw'*. *Nelson's*, 783: Maacha.

[1598] 2 Sam 8:3, 5, 7–10, 12; 1 Kings 11:23.

[1599] 1 Chron 3:2; 1 Sam 3:3.

[1600] Deut 7:2-4.

[1601] H4601—*Ma`akah, mah-ak-aw'*: depression; Maakah or Maakath: she has pressed; oppression; city in Syria; a Mesopotamian; three Israelites; four female Israelites; one Syrian woman; father of King Achish of Gath in Solomon's reign; daughter of king Talmai of Geshur: wife or David and mother of Absalom; daughter of Absalom the wife of king Rehoboam of Judah and mother of king Abijam of Judah; a mercenary people hired to fight David. Maacha: Gen 22:24; 1 Kings 2:39; 15:2, 10, 13; 1 Chron 2:48; 3:2; 7:15–16; 8:29; 9:35; 11:43; 19:7; 27:16; 2 Chron 11:20– 22; 15:16. Maacah: 2 Sam 3:3; 10:6, 8.

[1602] 2 Sam 10:6, 10, 13; 2 Kings 15:1–2; 1 Chron 19:7; 2 Chron 11:20–21.

[1603] *Strong's Cyclopaedia*, Vol. 5, 592: Maacah; Nelson's, 783: Macchathites

[1604] H4602—*Ma`akathiy, mah-ak-aw-thee'*: inhabitant of Maakah; pressure; she has pressed; one of David's mighty warriors; descendants of Maachah; *Nelson's*, 783: Maachathites.

[1605] 2 Sam 23:34.

of Nahor, after the documentation of the table of nations in Genesis 10, demonstrating the ancient name was already in popular use at that time. Maachathim kings and queens carried the patriarchal and matriarchal royal bloodlines of Horim, Anakim, and likely Rephaim and Amaleqim, whose scioned royal bloodlines produced dynastic names for queens and kings. Bethmaacha, the house of Maacha, was a place or city[1606] named after the patriarch Rephaim Maacha and his royal dynasty, as was Maacah city.

Israelites were instructed to destroy the giants and giant-like nations.[1607] David did not destroy north Geshur, even though he destroyed their southern kingdom.[1608] Thus, when David opted to war with Ammon, the king of Ammon sent money to the king of Maacha to hire their skilled Maachathim and hybrid warriors to war against King David and Israel. Even so, the Maachathim fled before Israel on the battlefield, as did the Ammonites. The Maacathim then called upon their allies, the Syrians and King Hadarezer, but David defeated the Bashan alliance. The alliance negotiated a surrender of vassalage with David to pay ongoing tribute.[1609] The peace treaty likely was the reason David accepted Maacha, daughter of King Talmai, as a wife, even though David's treaty and marriage may have conflicted with the war edicts.[1610] David may have determined that Geshur, Maacha, and Syria were outside of the Covenant Land, and thus subject to Deuteronomy 20's provisions that permitted treaties with tributes from nations conquered outside the Covenant Land, which permitted marrying their women.[1611] Whatever David's reasoning was, his marriage to the Maachathim princess testified to the nobleness of house of Maachah and their ancient scioned royal bloodlines of Rephaim. Later, King Rehoboam of Judah took Maacah, daughter of Absalom (David's third son, whose mother was Maacha) as one of his favorite wives. Maachah and Rehoboam produced Abijam, the next king of Judah,[1612] further testifying to the ennobled matriarchal Maachah bloodline.

David's decision to marry Maachah/Maacah created a snare that catapulted Israel into a civil war, with an attempted coup d'état to usurp the Israelite throne and messianic bloodline, birthright, and blessings, in the spirit the Amaleqim blood oath. Absalom's spliced bloodlines from Maachah brought in outside influences dedicated to replacing the intended Messiah with a Dragon messiah; an ennobled House of Dragon determined rule the world. Extraordinarily ennobled fairy/owl princesses (like Maachah and Timna) were required to begin a new dragon/fairy dynasty. One contemplates if Absalom's wife also held dubious

---

[1606] 2 Sam 20:15. H1038—*Beyth Ma`akah, bayth mah-ak-aw'*: house of Maakah; a place in the northern kingdom of Israel; house of pressure.

[1607] Deut 7:2-6, 17:14-20, 20:10-16; Num 33:56; 1Sa 15:3.

[1608] 1Sa 27:8-9.

[1609] 2 Sam 10:1–19; 1 Chron 19:6–20.

[1610] Gen 24:4; Exod 34:15–16; Num 32:56; Deut 7:2–6; 17:14–20; 20:10–16; Josh 23:12; 1 Sam 15:3; 1 Kings 11:2.

[1611] Deut 20:11–14.

[1612] 2 Chron 11:20–21; 1 Kings 15:1–2.

bloodlines because her name is not provided. Absalom fathered three sons and two daughters: one named Tamar,[1613] and the other Maachah.[1614] Absalom's sons died sometime before Absalom created a memorial for himself: "a pillar after his own name" because he had no son to keep his name.[1615]

Absalom was born in Hebron.[1616] No-one was praised more in Israel than Absalom; his beauty/*yapheh* was unmatched in the land and he was adorned with flowing long hair. He was a royal son without blemish, from his foot to his crown.[1617] Beauty/*yapheh* means handsome, fair, and fairest.[1618] One wonders if the word *yapheh* was referencing the fair white skin of the Horim and Rephaim and/or his hair, inherited from his fairy queen mother.

Absalom fled Israel after slaying his half brother Amnon, for his forced sex with Tamar,[1619] escaping to Geshur and the protection of his grandfather King Talmai.[1620] Absalom was exiled in Geshur for three years, under the seditious influence of Talmai. While Absalom plotted, David mourned the separation of perhaps his most favored son.[1621] Absalom returned to overthrow David, where he established his home city at Hebron/Kiriatharba, where Talmai of the Anakim once reigned.[1622] Absalom's rebellion forced David to vacate Jerusalem, but David and his mighty men rallied, returning to Israel to soundly defeat Absalom's army at the forest of Ephraim. Absalom was killed shortly thereafter.[1623]

[1613] 2 Sam 14:27.
[1614] 1 Ki 8–10, 13; 2 Chron 11:20, 21, 22.
[1615] 2 Sam 18:18.
[1616] 2 Sam 3:2–5; 1 Chron 3:1–4.
[1617] 2 Sam 14:25–26.
[1618] H3303—*yapheh, yaw-feh*; from 3302: beautiful; beauty, fairest, fair; pretty. H3302—*yaphah, yaw-faw*; beautiful; bright; handsome; to be fair.
[1619] 2 Sam 13:5–39.
[1620] 2 Sam 13:37.
[1621] 2 Sam 13:37, 18:33.
[1622] 1 Sam 15:6–9.
[1623] 2 Sam 18:6–14.

THE AVVIM

Josh 13:2 This is the land that yet remaineth: all the borders of the Philistines, and all Geshuri,

Josh 13:3 From Sihor, which is before Egypt, even unto the borders of Ekron northward, which is counted to the Canaanite: five lords of the Philistines; the Gazathites, and the Ashdothites, the Eshkalonites, the Gittites, and the Ekronites; also the Avites.

Secular records do not directly indicate that the Avvites/Avvim existed; the only known accounts derive from Scripture. Yet, assembling the biblical Avvim narrative reveals an inflection point that leads to other kinds of giants overlooked or dismissed by standard modern theological and secular dogma.

The obscure Avites/Avvim of Gaza were an important partner in the early postdiluvian Southern alliance of giant nations. The Avvim tribe is also associated with the ancient Benjamite city of Avim located in the vicinity the Valley of Rephaim,[1624] the Valley of Giants.[1625] The central Canaan Avvim dwelled among the Jebusite, Hivite, and Amorite hybrids, as well as among the central Hivvim.[1626] Church father Jerome linked the Avvim with the city of "Ha-Avvim (AV Avvim)" located in the district of the Hivites of Gibeon. Ha-Avvim/AV Avvim is derived

---

[1624] Valley of Rephaim: Berean, Amplified, ESV, NIV, NLT, NASB, CSB, ASB, CEB, GNT. Jos 15:8 18: 16, 23, 2 Sam 5:18, 22; 1 Chron 11:15; 14:8; Isa 17:5.

[1625] KJV, Aramaic: Valley of Giants: Josh 15:8; 18:16, 23, 2 Sam 5:18, 22; 1 Chron 11:15; 14:8; Isa 17:5.

[1626] *Strong's Cyclopaedia*, Vol. 4, 282: Hivites. Josh 9:3–7; 18:11-28.

from inserting the definite article the/*ha*/ה, that forms "the Avvim."[1627] Additionally, both Jerome and the Septuagint reckoned Avvim as Hivites/Evites.[1628]

> *Sept* Deut 2:23 And the Evites who dwell in Asedoth to Gaza, and the Cappadocians who came out of Cappadocia, destroyed them, and dwelt in their room.

On the other hand, *Strong's Cyclopaedia* wrote that both Jerome and the Septuagint translations "were not careful exacting on names"—that the Avvim disappear from Scripture before the (hybrid) Hivites, and that the Avvim were accounted as Rephaim in Deuteronomy 2:23,[1629] not as Hivvims or Hivites. What seems likely is that the Avvim were a distinct but kin branch of Hivvim, just as Hivvim were a kin branch of Horim; that Avvim dwelled in central Canaan with both Hivites and Hivvim and southwest alongside Horim, Amaleqim, Geshurim, and Gizrim.

Accordingly, Avvim is connected to Avith city of south Canaan. Avith, defined as ruins, was the capital city for the southern Horim and Duke Ben-Badad in Edom—one of the Elven/fairy kings. Avith city has visible phonetic and etymological connections to Avvim/Avite.[1630] The nexus with `*Avvim*/Ha-Avvim becomes clear when one learns `*Avvim* is also defined as ruins, and that `*Avvim* is transliterated as Avith.[1631]

> Gen 36:35 And Husham died, and Hadad the son of Bedad, who smote Midian in the field of Moab, reigned in his stead: and the name of his city was Avith.[1632]

Avith city indicates that Avvim Aboriginals were the founders for the Ben-Bedaad's inherited Horim capital city, and that Avvim arrived before or at the same time as the Horim. It follows that Avvim were a kin branch with the Horim and Hivvim giants, and part of the larger Southern alliance of Rephaim and hybrid Rephaim nations of Palestine, Seir, and Edom. Knowing this explicates why the

---

[1627] Benner, *Learn to Read Hebrew*, Volume 2, 15–16: article ה: ha. H5761—`*Avviym, av-veem*`; Avvim city inhabited by aboriginal Avvites, a place in Palestine with the article prefix AV Avim; ruins.

[1628] *Unger's*, 127: Avvim; *Strong's Cyclopaedia*, Vol. 4, 282: Hivites.

[1629] *Strong's Cyclopaedia*, Vol. 4, 282: Hivites.

[1630] H5762—`*Aviyth, av-veeth*`; or *Ayowth, ah-yoth*`: ruins; city of Hadad Ben-Bedad, one of the kings of Edom.

[1631] 1 Chron 1:47. H5761—`*Avviym, av-veem*`; Avvim as inhabited by Avvites: ruins; a place in Palestine (with the article prefix [ha]) Avim; transliterated: Aviyth.

[1632] Also see 1 Chron 1:36.

Mesopotamian alliance in the war of giants felt it necessary to attack the Amaleqim, Horim, and Amorites, whom Avvim also dwelled among—an alliance that also supported the Rephaim led Canaanite hybrids of Sodom, Gomorrah, and the cities of the plain. As such, Joshua concisely detailed the land toward the south that were still unconquered.[1633] The southern lands included the borders of the Philistines, the Geshurim from Sihor along the Egyptian border, and lands north to Ekron that was still accounted as a Canaanite city, which were governed by the five Philistine lords. The lands included the mysterious Avites/Avvim dwelling there, and the giants of Gizrim and the Amaleqim, who dwelled with the Geshurim.[1634] We must further add the Anakim to this tally of giants and hybrid giants, because Anakim still dwelled in Gaza, Gath and Ashod cities during and after the conquest of the Covenant Land:

> Josh 11:22 There was none of the Anakims left in the land of the children of Israel: only in Gaza, in Gath, and in Ashdod, there remained.

The *Catholic Encyclopedia* notes that Anakim and Rephaim remained in Gaza,[1635] dwelling among the Philistines, occupying and ruling the cities of Gath and Ashdod. The Philistine empire included Canaanite hybrids of Ekron ruled by Anakim, Avvim, or hybrid Philistines and Ashkelon. The Philistine pentapolis city-states were reigned over by a mysterious council of kings, the lords of the Philistines, which we will detail in a subsequent chapter. The above list of giant nations and hybrid human giants of the Philistine confederacy were part of the larger Southern alliance that emerged after the war of giants and with the Philistine invasion, which continued into the epoch of Israel's monarchy as testified to Goliath, a Gittite Rephaim.[1636] It follows that *Unger's* and *Nelson's* defined Avites/Avvim as indigenous giants who dwelled among the diverse clans of Canaanites in southwest Palestine on the plains of Gaza, and a people who may have migrated northward from the southern desert[1637] after the Philistines invaded Avith/`*Avviym* City.[1638]

It follows that the "Avvims" in Deuteronomy 2:23 indicate multiple tribes and locations, encapsulated by parentheses from verses 20–23 as part of the giant nation nomenclature known comprehensively as Rephaim. Deuteronomy 2 instructed that the Avvim dwelled in Hazerim and in Azzah. `*Azzah*, meaning "the strong," is the feminine format of `*az* and *azaz* also meaning strong and stout,

---

[1633] Josh 13:2–3.
[1634] 1 Sam 27:8.
[1635] *Catholic Encyclopedia*, Vol. 6, 399: Gaza.
[1636] 2 Sam 21:16–22. Giant: H7497—*Rapha*.
[1637] *Unger's*, 127; *Nelson's*, 141: Avvim.
[1638] *Unger's*, 127. H5761—`*Avviym, av-veem*`; *Strong's Cyclopaedia*, Vol. 1, 569: Avites. Josh 18:23.

which produced the name Azazel. `*Azzah* city is believed to be one of the oldest cities in the world.[1639] The Avvim of Gaza were the transliterated in the KJV as Gazathites/*ha`Azzathiy* (Josh 13:3) meaning "the strong ones,"[1640] and/or the strong and stout ones, the Azzazim/Azazim connected to the Hazerim also documented in Deuteronomy 2. Hazerim/*Chatseriym* was a place and/or village(s), yard(s), or court(s) surrounded by walls.[1641]

> Deut 2:23 And the Avims which dwelt in Hazerim, even unto Azzah, the Caphtorims, which came forth out of Caphtor, destroyed them, and dwelt in their stead).

What is mesmerizing about Azzah city is its overlooked connection with the Gazathites in Joshua 13:3. Gazathites/`*Azzathiy* is defined as an inhabitant of the city of Azzah, just as it was translated as such in in Deuteronomy 2, and that `*Azzathiy* was their patrial name from Azzah.[1642] What we learn from Deuteronomy 2:23, supported in Joshua 13:3, is that the Avvim were in part supplanted by the Philistine invasion, but some Avvim remained at Azzah/Gaza city, where thereafter Avvim merged with the mercurial lords of the Philistines within the infamous Philistine pentapolis,[1643] which included the Anakim.[1644]

> 1 Sam 6:17 And these are the golden emerods which the Philistines returned for a trespass offering unto the LORD; for Ashdod one, for Gaza one, for Askelon one, for Gath one, for Ekron one.

Avviym/Avvim, the strong ones, and the male plural format of *Avviy,* was transliterated as `*Ivyah,* meaning inhabitant of `*Avvah* that is patrial from `*Ivvah/ Avvae,* a region of Assyria documented in 2 Kings 17:24 which also means ruin or

---

[1639] H5804—`*Azzah, az-zaw*`: the strong; a place in the extreme southwest of Palestine close to the Mediterranean, Gaza; Gaza city; *Catholic Encyclopedia,* Vol. 6, 299: Gaza.
[1640] H5841—`*Azzathiy, az-zaw-thee*`: the strong; an Azzathite or inhabitant of Azzah; Gazathites or Gazites; an inhabitant of the city of Gaza. Gazathites: Josh 13:3. Gazites: Judg 16:2. *Catholic Encyclopedia,* Vol. 6, 399: Gaza.
[1641] H2699—*Chatseriym, khats-ay-reem*`; plural masculine of 2691: yards; villages; a place in Palestine; H2691—*chatser, khaw-tsare*`: a yard as enclosed by a fence; a hamlet surrounded with walls; court; tower; village.
[1642] H5841—`*Azzathiy.* Judg 16:2.
[1643] *Strong's Cyclopaedia,* Vol. 1, 569: Avites.
[1644] Deut 2:10, 11, 21, 23.

overthrown.[1645] One deduces `Ivvah/`Avvah was named after the Rephaim patriarch of his eponymous tribe.

As previously noted, some believe Avvim fled northward into central Canaan (Josh 18:23: Avim) and toward Assyria (2 Kings 17:24, 31: Ava), from the invading hordes of Philistines, Caphtorites, and Cherthites[1646] sometime before the Exodus circa 1400–1450 BC. This assertion is possible, but one ought to note as well that the Avvim were an Aboriginal nation of southwestern Palestine, and that they migrated down from the northern mountains where they established satellite states in Assyria, Edom, Gaza, Benjamin, and perhaps elsewhere.

> 2 Kings 17:24 And the king of Assyria brought men from Babylon, and from Cuthah, and from Ava, and from Hamath, and from Sepharvaim, and placed them in the cities of Samaria instead of the children of Israel: and they possessed Samaria, and dwelt in the cities thereof.

The Ava region of Assyria was one of the regions where the Assyrian king later imported people to replace the Israelites of the northern kingdom after their exile (c. 721 BC). *Ivvah/Avvae* was the city where Avvim worshipped the god, Nibhaz. Nibhaz/*Nibchaz*, meaning to bark like a dog, was of foreign origin; his idolatrous image exhibited a man's body with a dog or jackal's head.[1647] The worship of a god with a human body and animal head was common in the Assyrian beast empires.[1648] Nibhaz dog-like depictions conjures up images of gods like Anubis of Egypt. In Sabian texts, Nibhaz was evil, a god who sat on a throne upon the earth, while his feet rested upon Tartarus (Abyss),[1649] which invokes images of fallen angels, the assembly and thrones of the gods, and impassioned Naphalim sent to the abyss for creating spurious Nephilim, Rephaim, and other kinds of giants that looked just like the fathers. The Avvim Nibhaz god was grouped scripturally with the child-sacrificing worship of the Amaleqim gods of the east: Adrammelech and

---

[1645] H5757—`*Avviy, av-vee*`; patrial from 5755: native of Avvah: Avims, Avites; perverters; transliterated as ivya and inhabitants of Iva; H5755—`*Ivvah, iv-vaw*`; or *Avvae* (2 Kings 17:24) *avvaw*: a region of Assyria; ruin; H5754—`*avvah, av-vaw*`: overthrow; overturn; distortion, ruin.

[1646] *Strong's Cyclopaedia*, Vol. 1, 569: Avites.

[1647] H5026—*Nibchaz, nib-khaz*`; of foreign origin: Avite god; the barker; idol of a dog worshipped; H5024—*nabach, naw-bakh*`: bark as a dog; H5025—*Nobach, no'-bach*; from 5024: bark.

[1648] *Strong's Cyclopaedia*, Vol. 7, 44: Nibhaz, citing Rawlinson, *Anc. Monarchies*, i, 294.

[1649] Ibid., Vol. 7, 44: Nibhaz, citing Gesen. *Thesaur.*, 842; Iken, *deIdola Nibchuz*, in his Dissertations, i, 15G sq; Norberg, Ono, mast. Cod. Nasar, 99; Beyer, Add. to Selden's Dii Syr., 321.

Anammelech; Molech was a god associated both with the Amaleqim and the Baalim gods who demanded child sacrifice.[1650]

The Avvim worshipped another bizarre god named Tartak/ *Tartaq*, which was also a god of foreign derivation, whose name meant prince of darkness. Tartak was worshipped in the form of an ass, or perhaps a horse or unicorn.[1651] Tartak is thought by some of Persian origination, a god of war, prince of the underworld, and a hero of darkness/underworld.[1652]

> 2 Kings 17:31 And the Avites made Nibhaz and Tartak, and the Sepharvites burnt their children in fire to Adrammelech and Anammelech, the gods of Sepharvaim.[1653]

The Avvim had curious associations and settlements in the proximity to the Mesopotamian Aryans, and thus connections to the peoples of the east/*qedem* recorded in the book of Judges.[1654] The people of the east included giants; *qedem* means ancient time, from old, antiquity, from immediately after the flood or even before. Similarly, the Geshurim, Gezirim, and Amaleqim were giants of old/ *owlam*, antiquity, ancient and times.[1655] So too were the Kadmonites, Kenizzites, and Kenites ancient people connected to *qedem*/east and listed in the mighty ten of Genesis 15.

[1650] *Unger's*, 488: Molech.

[1651] H8662—*Tartaq, tar-tawk'*: Avvite deity; prince of darkness; Tartaq was worshipped in the form of an ass.

[1652] *Strong's Cyclopaedia*, Vol. 10, 222, citing Gesenius, *Thesaur.* s. v.; Furst, *Handub.* s. v.

[1653] Also: Isa 37:13: "Where is the king of Hamath, and the king of Arphad, and the king of the city of Sepharvaim, Hena, and Ivah?"; 2 Kings 18:34: "Where are the gods of Hamath, and of Arpad? where are the gods of Sepharvaim, Hena, and Ivah? have they delivered Samaria out of mine hand?"

[1654] Judg 6:3, 33; 10:12; 12:15. H6924—*qedem, keh'-dem* or *qedmah*: east; antiquity; front, that which is before, aforetime; ancient time; ancient; from of old, earliest time.

[1655] H5769—'*owlam, o-lawm'*; long duration; antiquity; futurity; forever; everlasting; evermore; eternity; perpetual; old; ancient; ancient time; long time of past. Gen 6:4; Deut 32:7; Josh 24:2; 1 Sam 27:8; Job 22:15; Ps 25:6; 119:52; Eccl 1:10; Isa 51:9; 58:11–12; 61:4; 63:9, 11; Jer 2:20; 6:16; 28:8; Lam 3:6; Ezek 25:15; 26:20; Amos 9:11; Mic 7:14; Mal 3:4.

CHAPTER 38

THE KENIZZIM AND KENIM

Gen 15:19 The Kenites, and the Kenizzites, and the Kadmonites,

Gen 15:20 And the Hittites, and the Perizzites, and the Rephaims,

Gen 15:21 And the Amorites, and the Canaanites, and the Girgashites, and the Jebusites.

Genesis 15 is an often overlooked chapter with respect to the documentation of giants and the geopolitical map of the early postdiluvian epoch—a chapter that follows the war of giants.

Although there is limited biblical explanation, the Kenites, Kenizzites, and Kadmonites were connected to the mighty seven nations that occupied the Covenant Land from before Abraham's time. The mighty seven in Abraham's period included the "Rephaims" that were later replaced by the Hivvim by the time of the Exodus and Israel's Covenant Land conquest. Genesis 15's larger accounting of the mighty ten included God's blessings to make Abraham's seed like the stars of the heavens, in striking and noteworthy contrast.[1656] Abraham's Jacobian posterity was raised into adulthood while in bondage within a strange nation (Egypt) for some 400–480 years, until the prophesied iniquity of the Amorites came to fruition.[1657] Further, Abraham was promised lands bound into a covenant—lands that

---

[1656] Gen 15:5.
[1657] Gen 15:16.

included the Nile to the Euphrates occupied by those mighty ten.[1658] The original mighty ten is an odd accounting, unless the passage was designed to encourage one to glean intelligence regarding Israel's relationship with prophetic beast empires.

The mighty ten included the "ancient KKK": the Kenites, Kenizzites, and Kadmonites. Kenizzite/*Qnizziy,* derives from and is defined as descendants of Kenaz/*Qnaz,* a patronymic name meaning "hunter" and the name of one of the sons of Eliphaz. *Qnz* is an unexplained Semitic name theorized to link back to the *bn Qnd* in the *Ugaritic Texts* for the *Qnz/Qnaz* and the tribal affiliation thereof, the *Qnzm/Qenizzi.* [1659] The *bn Qnd* has a closer phonetic and vowelless spelling association with the Kadmonites than the *Qnz,* so one concludes the Kenizzites and Kadmonites were closely associated as well.

Biblically though, Kenaz and Eliphaz were classified as among the dukes/`alluwphs* of Edom. Kenaz/Kenizzites were hybrid Horim/humans via intermarriage[1660] that later begat the Aryan hybrid Kassite dynasties of Babylon.[1661] Scripturally, Kenaz's wife was not listed, so one deduces with the Kassite connection that Kenaz's mother may have been Horim, Hivvim, or Hurrian. As interesting as Kenaz's connections are to Horim/Edomite dukes, to Amalek, and to Kenaz's patronymic name/title like Amalek in Genesis 36, the larger mystery is that Kenaz, son of Eliphaz, cannot be the patriarch for Kenizzites of Genesis 15. The Genesis 15 Kenizzites predate Isaac's promised birth in Genesis 17; Kenaz was born five generations later.[1662] *Strong's Cyclopaedia* concurs, stating that the enigmatic Kenizzim could not be descendants of Kenaz, born a century and half after Genesis 15's Kenizzim accounting.[1663]

The most famous of biblical Kennizites likely descended from Kenaz was Caleb,[1664] and Caleb's younger brother Kenaz, who was the father of Othaniel.[1665] Caleb fought alongside Israel in the Promised Land conquest, and inherited Hebron/Kiriatharba controlled by Anakim.[1666] What is not clear with Caleb, though, is whether he was a descendant of Kenaz or Kenizzim Rephaim, and we

---

[1658] Gen 15:13–16, 18; see Gen 6:3 for a generation of 120 years.

[1659] Benz, *Personal Names,* 405: QNZ, citing F. Grondahl, *Die Personennamen der Texte aus Ugarit:* PTU 176.

[1660] H7074—*Qnizziy, ken-iz-zee*; patronymic from 7073: descendant of Kenaz; H7073—*Qnaz, ken-az*: to hunt; hunter; an Edomite duke and son of Eliphaz and grandson of Esau; a brother of Caleb and father of Othniel. Gen 36:11, 15, 42; 1 Chron 1:35, 53.

[1661] Gardner, *Ring Lords,* 63–67; *Encyclopedia Americana,* Vol. 16, 313.

[1662] Gen 17:19; 36:11, 15, 42; 1 Chron 1:36, 53.

[1663] *Strong's Cyclopaedia,* Vol. 5, 40: Kenizzites.

[1664] Num 32:12; Josh 14:6, 14.

[1665] Josh 14:6–16; Judg 1:13; 3:9, 11; 1 Chron 4:13.

[1666] Kiriatharba: Gen 23:2; 35:28; Josh 14:15; 15:54; 20:7; Judg 1:10; Neh 11:25. Arba: Josh 14:15; 15:13–14; 21:11. Arbah: Gen 35:27. Talmi, Ahiman, and Sheshai: Num 13:22; Deut 1:28; Josh 15:14; Judg 1:10.

do not know who Kenaz's mother was. Caleb was likely an Edomite, based on the fact that Caleb's brother was patronymically named Kenaz.

Very little is known about the Kenizzim in or outside the Bible. *Strong's Cyclopaedia* suggests the Kenizzim were a nomadic tribe that dwelled beyond the land Israel.[1667] Kenizzim likely were eastern giants based on the geography presented in the land awarded to Abraham's descendants, from the Nile to the Euphrates. Not only were the *bn Qdm* listed as a people of the east, but *qdm* was also translated as "ancient" in the *Ugartic Texts*.[1668] There are no Egyptian records recording Kenizzim, but *Knz* does surface as a personal Berber name,[1669] indicating an ancient patronymic tradition by that name. The Kenizzim were not listed in the Bible among any of the nations in the time of the conquest of the Covenant Land, nor was their patriarch tallied in the table of nations, with the latter indicating Kenizzim were Rephaim.

Kenizzites, according to *Nelson's* and *Unger's* dictionaries, were very skilled in the arts of metalworking, like Cain and Tubal-Cain, and were closely related to Kenites.[1670] One deduces the metalworking crafts were devoted mostly to weapons of war, yet another characteristic of Rephaim nations. The close Kenizzim kinship with the Kenim shines light on the obscure Kennizzim and the peoples of the east and the west. Duke Kenaz/Qnaz, son of Eliphaz of Edom,[1671] seems to have been named in the same tradition as Amalek, to honor a giant race, as the patriarch for the hybrid Kenizzites/*Qnizziy* of the Edom region. Kenaz may have been the patriarch for the Balaam-cursed Kenite hybrids who dwelled among the Amalekites/Amaleqim of the same region.[1672] *Qeyniy* were smiths from the tribe Kajin/*Qayin*, of whom Moses' father-in-law Jethro was a Kenite priest practicing among western Midianitess.[1673] Thus, Kenites are thought by some to have been an elder branch of the Midianites.[1674] Jethro, by virtue of geography, was a member of the eponymously named Kenite tribe of Edom and named in the same way as the western hybrid Kenizzites to whom Caleb belonged.

[1667] *Strong's Cyclopaedia*, Vol. 5, 40: Kenizzites.
[1668] Benz, *Personal Names*, 405: QNZ, citing F. Grondahl, *Die Personennamen der Texte aus Ugarit*: PTU 176. Wyatt, *Religious Texts from the Ugarit*, 109, KTU 1.4 vii 30, and note 154: Ug. Qdmym "peoples of the east," 384–385 KTU 1.100 V 60a, note 33: nuances of qdm, eastern city.
[1669] Benz, *Personal Names*, 405: QNZ, citing J. B. Chabot, *Recueil des Inscriptions Libiques*, RIL, 125, 361.
[1670] *Nelson's*, 724–725; *Unger's*, 734.
[1671] Gen 36:11, 16, 42; 1 Chron 1:36, 53. H7073—*Qnaz*. H7074—*Qnizziy*.
[1672] Num 24:20–22.
[1673] H7017—*Qeyniy, kay-nee'*; or *Qiyniy, kee-nee'*; a Kenite is a member of the tribe of Kajin; smiths; the tribe that lived in the area between southern Palestine and the mountains of Sinai. Exod 3:1; 18:1; Judg 1:16, 4:11.
[1674] Ellicott, *Old Testament Commentary*, Vol. 2, 174: Judg 1, note 16: Kenites.

Qeyniy's source word is Cain/Kajin/*Qayin*, meaning smith, possession, and an oriental tribe, and in turn derives from *Qayin*, meaning spear and to strike fast.[1675] Semitic *Qn* and *Qny* also surface in the *Ugaritic Texts*, meaning property, possession, acquire and create.[1676] Biblically, "oriental" is understood as Mesopotamia, home of the Babylonian "wise ones" and sorcerers that derive from *mag'os*, Greek for a magi, magician, magus, and oriental scientist from Babylon, Persia, or Media.[1677] What makes the oriental tribe designation of Mesopotamia significant is the Euphrates River connection in the geography provided in Genesis 15. Kenites/ *Qeyniy* of the east were giants, Kenim.

The patronymic root to the eastern Kenim Rephaim tribe was from Cain son of Adam, versus one of the Kenaz tribes of Edom that Kenim predated. It follows that Kenim of Genesis 15 have no patriarch attributed to them in the table of nations. The Kenim deliberatively named their tribe in honor of the antediluvian Cain, his craft, his crimes, and his rebellion against God. One concludes that either hybrid Nephilim Cainites survived the flood, or more likely that Rephaim created in the Second Incursion adopted the patronymic name.

Ergo, two divergent Kenite nations existed: one in the east, and an Edomite related nation of Mount Seir that chose to live alongside Amalekites to the south and west.[1678] Kenites that dwelled with the Amalekites were more likely to have been Horim human hybrids from Kenaz of Edom versus a son of Judah[1679] or an eastern hybrid branch from the Genesis 15's Kenim. However, the passage detailing Kenites becoming scribes is less clear in determining as to which branch these Kenites derived from:

> 1 Chron 2:55 And the families of the scribes which dwelt at Jabez; the Tirathite, the Shimeathite, and Suchathites. These are the Kenites that came of Hemath, the father of the house of Rechab.

The Kenite scribe families only appear in 1 Chronicles 2:55. The Kenite families were part of the house of Rechab, and from a specific patriarch, Hemath. Hemath/*Chamath*, meaning fortress, was a fortress city in Mount Hermon of

---

[1675] H7014—*Qayin, kah'-yin*; Cain/Kajin, the name of the first child; a place in Palestine; an Oriental tribe; Kenite: smiths; possession; transliterated: Qayin; G2535—*Kain*; Cain; H7013— *qayin, kah'-yin*: a lance as in striking fast.
[1676] Benz, *Personal Names*, 404: QN and QNY, citing F. Grondahl, *Die Personennamen der Texte aus Ugarit*: PTU, 39.
[1677] G3097—*mag'-os*: a Magian, Oriental scientist; sorcerer, wise man, and/or a priest so-called by Babylonians, Medes, and Persians' transliterated: magos. Wise: Matt 2:1, 7, 16. Sorcerer: Acts 13:6, 8.
[1678] Num 20:14–25; Deut 2:12, 22.
[1679] Gen 36:12, 20, 32; 1 Chron 1:36, 53; 4:13,16.

THE KENIZZIM AND KENIM

Syria,[1680] likely patrial from Hemath. Rechab and the house of Rechab/*Rekab* was used interchangeably in meaning with *Rekah,* translated as Recabites and their home.[1681] The Syrian city was recorded from the time of the Exodus and conquest of the Promised Land.[1682] The families of Kenite scribes were from a branch of Kenites in the north from before the Exodus, according to the book of Judges. At this time, the house of Heber the Kenite was at peace with the patronymic king Jabin of Hazor, indicating that the Kenite house of Heber was an influential family.[1683] Knowing this indicates that the northern Kenites, and the Kenite scribes, were Rephaim from Genesis 15 or hybrids thereof.

Further, Balaam the sorcerer from Pethor, Mesopotamia[1684] prophesied that Kenite punishment would be administered by Asshur/Assyria,[1685] the beast empire that would exile the Kenite nation. In that prophetic campaign fulfilled by Tiglath-pileser, Hazor, Kadesh, and Abelbethmaachah of the Kenites were taken. Abelbethmaachah, meaning "a meadow of the house of Maachah," was located near Beth Maachah.[1686] What is eye-opening is that the men of *Rekah*/Rechah of Hemath included a patriarch named Bethrapha living among Israelites in the book of 1 Chronicles. The descendants/men of Bethrapha/*Beyth Rapha* is translated as the house of giants or house of the giant,[1687] and a branch of the Aboriginal Rephaim, given the patronymic name for the Rephaim tribe. Some of the "Rechah" Kenim of the "Rephaims" became scribe-servants akin to the Gibeonite/Hivvim temple slaves.

> 1 Chron 4:12 And Eshton begat Bethrapha, and Paseah, and Tehinnah the father of Irnahash. These are the men of Rechah.

Moreover, Rechab/*Rekab* derives from *rakab,*[1688] as does *rekeb* and *rakkab* as part of an intriguing series of words meaning rider; chariot, wagon, charioteer, and

---

[1680] H7394—*Rekab, ray-kawb'*: rider; Rechabites; H2574—*Chamath, kham-awth'*: walled; fortress; the principal city in Syria; father of the house of Rechab: Hamath 34 times, Hemath 3 times.
[1681] H7397—*Rekah, ray-kaw'*: softness: a place in Palestine: Rechah, the Rechabites; uttermost part. Rechabites, Jer 35:2, 3, 5, 18. Rechah: 1 Chron 4:12. H7394—*Rekab*: Rechab 2 Sam 4:2, 5, 6, 9; 2 Kings 10:15, 23; 1 Chron 2:55; Neh 3:14; Jer 35:6, 8, 14, 16, 19.
[1682] Num 13:21; 34:8; Josh 13:5.
[1683] Judg 4:17; 5:24.
[1684] Num 22:5, Deut 23:4.
[1685] H804—*'Ashshuwr.*
[1686] 2 Kings 15:29; 1 Chron 5:23, 26; 18:11. H62—*'Abel Beyth-Ma `akah, aw-bale' bayth ma-akaw'*; meadow of Beth-Maakah; Abel of Beth-maakah; "meadow of the house of Maachah"; northern city near Beth Maachah.
[1687] H1051—*Beyth Rapha', bayth raw-faw'*; house of (the) giant(s).
[1688] H7394—*Rekab, ray-kawb'*: rider.

horseman.[1689] The house of Rechab of the Kenim were one of mighty ten nations of Genesis 15, boasting a legacy of chariot-centered warfare as did the Indo-Aryans. The Persian beast empire was also famous for chariot weaponry in their armies, and were linked to the Indo-Aryans.

[1689] H7392—*rakab, raw-kab*: to ride an animal, chariot, or cart; to despatch on horseback; get up on a horse; H7393—*rekeb, reh'-keb*; from 7392: a vehicle; by implication a team; a cavalry; a rider of a chariot; multitude; wagon; chariotry; troop of riders; horsemen; pair of horsemen; camel-riders; H7395—*rakkab, rak-kawb'*; from 7392: a charioteer; chariot driver; horseman.

CHAPTER 39

THE KADMONIM AND ARYANS OF PERSIA

Judg 6:3 And so it was, when Israel had sown, that the Midianites came up, and the Amalekites, and the children of the east, even they came up against them.

Just as Kenim and Kenizzim were classified as oriental nations, so were other Rephaim and Rephaim hybrid peoples that begat the Mesopotamian beast empires. Darius and Xerxes asserted they were dynastic Achaemenian kings,[1690] a Persian bloodline of Indo-Aryans; in fact, the Old Persian name for Darius, *Daryus/Darayavaus,*[1691] enveloped Ari-an/Arya-n.

Just as Assyria held curious relationships and inter-marital bloodlines begat by Nimrod with Mesopotamian Rephaim, so did the succeeding Babylonian and Mede/Persian kings and empires.

[1690] Bauer, *History of the World,* 506.

[1691] Roland G. Ķent, *Old Persian: Grammer, Text, Lexicon* (New Haven, CT: American Oriental Society, 1950), 135: Dpa, DPb, DPc, DPd; 141: DSa, DSb, DSc, DSd; 157: SDa. https://en.wiktionary.org/wiki/Darius.

Achmetha/Ecbatana was the Medes' royal city, which Cyrus captured circa 550 BC.[1692] Ecbatana was originally commissioned to be built by King Deioces. The city-state fortress, in the tradition of the Rephaim royal city-state with high-walled fortresses, boasted seven ascending walls in height, some thirty feet high or higher, and was set upon a mountain side, one hundred fifty feet above the plain. Each wall was of a different color, representing seven orbiting planets and gods (the biblical wandering stars). The first and smallest exterior wall was white; the second wall black; the third purple; the fourth blue; the fifth red; the sixth silver; and the seventh gold.[1693]

Deioces had united six Median tribes under his leadership. All originally called themselves Aryans: the Busae, the Perataceni, the Struchates, the Arizanti, the Budii, and the Magi.[1694] Persian Achaemenian rulers spoke their Aboriginal tribal language of Old Persian, a language belonging to the "Indo-Iranian or Aryan group of languages which is one of the main divisions of the Indo-European family of languages."[1695] The Medes too spoke Old Iranian that was an earlier form of Old Persian.[1696]

Herodotus, in *The Histories,* wrote: "The Medes had the same equipment as the Persians; and indeed, the dress common to both is not so much Persian as Median. They had for commander Tigranes, of the race of the Achaemenids. These Medes were called anciently by all people Arians; but when Media, the Colchian, came to them from Athens, they changed their name. Such is the account which they themselves give."[1697] The Medes were the ruling race that later produced Cyrus of the Persians because of the sonless Mede King Astyages, who sent his daughter to marry the vassal king of Persia, Cambyses.[1698] It follows then that the Persian empire emulated and modeled the Median rulers and empire, as did other empires that followed.[1699]

The Achaemenid Arians/Persians were in ancient times called the Cephenes by Greeks, a name derived from Perseus, son of Danae and Zeus, who wedded Andromeda, daughter of Cephenes. Andromeda's son was named Perses, from whom the Persians accepted their eponymous name. Cephenes did not produce a male son, which led to Perses succeeding to the throne.[1700] Thus, Herodotus

---

[1692] Ezra 6:1–3. H307—'*Achmtha*', *akh-me-thaw*'; of Persian derivation; Achmetha or Ecbatana; capital of Media, captured by Cyrus in 550 BC and then summer residence of Persian kings.

[1693] J. Talboys Wheeler, *The Geography of Herodotus: Illustrated from Modern Researches and Discoveries* (Charleston, NC: Nabu Press, 2010), 288–89.

[1694] Ibid., 289, 291, citing Herodotus 7:62.

[1695] Kent, *Old Persian*, 6: points 1, 2.

[1696] Ibid., 6: point 3.

[1697] Herodotus, *The Histories,* trans. George Rawlinson, 455, Book 7:62.

[1698] Bauer, *History of the World,* 456–457; Herodotus, *The Histories,* 429–30, Book 7:8.

[1699] *Encyclopedia Americana,* Vol. 1, 86: Achaemenids.

[1700] *Herodotus,* 455, Book 7:61.

linked the Meses/Aryans, the Achaemenids, to Perseus, the demigod giant son of Zeus. Greek history further indicated a connection between Aryans and tribes in Scythia, as well as connections to Greek islands like Crete and Cyprus, whose people included Aryan Minoans, Hyksos, and the Tuatha De Danann Scythians. Ancient Egyptians understood that Arya of Bactria in west Asia was the sacred home of the various Aryan races.[1701]

The Achaemenids title derived in part from Greek Achaea of southern Thessaly, and its Achaean league of twelve city-states making up its confederacy.[1702] Further, historian Susan Wise Bauer suggests that the classical Greek/Mycenaen civilization was populated by people Homer identified as the Achaeans, known elsewhere as Dananns, and the earliest of the Greek heroes (Nephilim and/or Rephaim).[1703] Achaia was the appellation Hittites and Egyptians assigned to the southern Greeks that dwelled in in the Bronze Age, but Greek poet-historians often assigned the name to the entirety of ancient Greece and its formed league of related states.[1704]

The Sumerian Ari were a deified race of kings renowned as the "Shining Ones," depicted as a race of great stature/height on seals.[1705] The Sumerian Ari were the Ariazantus, "Men of the Aryan Race," celebrated as the second great caste of the Medes, also known to the Greeks as the Arizante.[1706] Achaemenids were a distinct dark-haired race with dynastic patronymically named kings, Aryans, who led the "sons/children of the east." Persia/*Parac* is defined biblically as pure, splendid, and a people of the east.[1707] King Ahasuerus' empire stretched from India to Ethiopia:

> Esth 1:1. .. in the days of Ahasuerus, (this is Ahasuerus which reigned, from India even unto Ethiopia, over an hundred and seven and twenty provinces:).

Ahasuerus' name, *'Achashverows*,[1708] descends from Achaemenes, the patronymic title for Achaemenid/Persian royals,[1709] and the legendary patriarch of the

---

[1701] Cooper, *An Archaic Dictionary*, 79: Ari.

[1702] *Encyclopedia Americana*, Vol. 1, 85: Achaea.

[1703] Bauer, *History of the World*, 224, citing William Taylour, *Mycenaeans*; 254, citing Homer naming King Agamemnon the high king of the Achaeans.

[1704] *Mercer's*, 8: Achaia; *Strong's Cyclopaedia*, Vol. 1, 50: Achaia.

[1705] Bane, *Encyclopedia of Giants*, 33: Ari, citing De Lafayette, *Sumerian-English Dictionary*, 176.

[1706] Cooper, *An Archaic Dictionary*, 79: Ariazantus.

[1707] H6539—*Parac, paw-ras'*: Paras Persia; an Eastern country: Persian empire from India to Egypt and Ethiopia, and all western Asia including the Black Sea region, the Caucasus, the Caspian and the Jaxartes to the north; pure; splendor; pronounced: paw-ras'.

[1708] H325—*'Achashverowsh, akh-ash-vay-rosh'*; or *'Achashrosh akh-ash-rosh'* (Esth 10:1): of Persian origin; Achashverosh as in Ahasuerus or Artaxerxes, but in this case Xerxes; the title of a Persian king: Ahasuerus.

[1709] Bauer, *History of the World*, 413, circa 675.

Persian dynasty. Herodotus accounted Achaemenes as the father of Teispes, father of Cambyses, father of Cyrus.[1710] *'Achashdarpan* was translated as "princes" in the *KJV;* "satrap," in other translations, was another royal title assigned in the empire to provincial vassal kings, princes, and governors.[1711]

> Dan 6:1 It pleased Darius to set over the kingdom and hundred and twenty princes, which should be over the whole kingdom.

Just as Kenim were categorized as an oriental tribe, the Kadmonites/*Qadmoniy* of Genesis 15's mighty ten were defined as easterners, oriental, Aboriginals, ancients, and from old in the east. The singular *Qadmowniy* also means they that went before in the east, and ancient(s) in the east.[1712] Similarly, Kamiel/*Qadmiy'el,* the name of three Israelites, is defined as before, or in the presence of God, and God is the ancient One.[1713] *Qadmown* means east,[1714] and appears to be the source word *Qadnowniy; Qadmown* derives from *Qadam,* meaning to be in front, before, and confront.[1715] The term "oriental" and the "people of the east" was a collective phrase to describe peoples dwelling east of the Jordan River and east of the Euphrates River, and which signified ancient and/or races of the earliest origin after the flood,[1716] giants Nimrod battled.[1717] Ergo, the Kadmonim were an ancient tribe/clan of eastern giants from the Euphrates River and beyond, part of the original mighty ten, and likely Persian/*Parac* Aryans.

Unger's and *Easton's* Bible dictionaries concluded Kadmonites were the unnamed "sons/children of the east," the *ben-Qedam* recorded in the book of Judges;[1718] a people allied with Midianites and Amalekites east of the Jordan River who fought to destroy Israel. The "children of the east" were the biblical accounting for Persians and Rephaim.

[1710] Herodotus, *Histories,* 434, Book 7:11.

[1711] H324– *'achashdarpan, akh-ash-dar-pan';* from 323: prince; satrap as in a governor of a Persian province; H323—*'achashdarpan, akh-ash-dar-pan';* of Persian derivation; a satrap or governor of a province of Persia; lieutenant. Dan 6:1 Satrap: NIV, ESV, Berean, NASB New KJV, CSB, Access etc.

[1712] H6935—*Qadmoniy, kad-mo-nee';* the same as 6931: easterners; ancient; aboriginal; a tribe in Palestine: H6931—*qadmowniy, kad-mo-nee';* or *qadmoniy, kad-mo-nee';* ancient and oriental; they that went before in the east of old; former; things of old.

[1713] H6934—*Qadmiy'el, kad-mee-ale';* before or in the presence of God; God is the ancient one; *Strong's Cyclopaedia,* Vol. 5, 4: Kamiel.

[1714] H6930—*qadmown, kad-mone';* from 6923: eastern; east; H6923—*qadam, kaw-dam';* a primitive root: to project oneself; precede; before; to anticipate.

[1715] H6923—*qadam, kaw-dam':* to project oneself; precede; before; to anticipate; hasten; go; flee; prevent.

[1716] *Strong's Cyclopaedia,* Vol. 5, 4: Kadmonites.

[1717] Brenton, *Septuagint,* Gen 10:8–9; 15:20: The Septuagint recorded Kadmonites as the Kedmoneans.

[1718] *Unger's,* 732, *Easton's,* 755: Kadmonites. Judg 6:3, 33; 7:12; 8:12.

Some theological historians submit that Cadmus, the legendary hero and dragon slayer, was the son of a Phoenician king, and sister to Europa; that Cadmus founded of Thebes in Egypt and was the Kadmonim patriarch. Thus, Cadmus built the Cadmea Citadel of Thebes of Boetotia. Cadmus' wife Hermione originated from Mount Hermon,[1719] one of the Hermonim, or a goddess. Cadmus' name (*Qdm*) was preserved through the Nusariyeh people north of Tripoli in Libya, who maintained the tradition that their people originated from a race expelled by Joshua during the Covenant Land conquest.[1720]

The high-walled city-state fortress of Kedesh/*Qedesh* located in the Mount Hermon region was biblically listed among Og's cities that included Ashtaroth, which has intriguing connections to *Qdm of* Ugarit City, city of Og the Terrible One. Kedesh, meaning a holy place, was the name of four cities in the Covenant Land.[1721] Qadesh was named as both a god and a Rephaim in the *Ugaritic Texts* and was closely associated with the goddess Athirat/Ashtaroth, and with Baal. Qadash appeared as a god of the east alongside Amurr, and as servants of gods,[1722] implying there was also patronymically named demigod offspring. Further, the *Ugaritic Texts* indicate that the *bn Qdm*, the *rpim-qdmym*, were the ancient saviors, and that the *bn Qdm*/Qdmym were qualified as *Rpim*/Rephaim and the "*Ug* Qdmym," as members of the *Rpum*/Rephaim royal ancestors of Ugarit,[1723] and connected to Og/*Owg*/*Uwg*. Kadesh city was a place where Ashtaroth was worshipped, a patrial name after the Qadesh of the *bn Qdm*, with the latter eponymous for the Kadmonin. The ancient/*qdmym* and "the peoples of the east" in the *Ugaritic Texts* is the Semitic root for *Qadmoniy* and its plural *Qadmoniym*,[1724] and is congruent with *Strong's Dictionary*.

Josh 13.12 All the kingdom of Og in Bashan, which reigned in Ashtaroth and in Edrei, who remained of the remnant of the giants.

[1719] *Strong's Cyclopaedia*, Vol. 5, 4: Kadmonites, citing Boaeotia (*Canaan* I, 19); *Encyclopedia Americana*, Vol. 5, 135: Cadmus.

[1720] *Strong's Cyclopaedia*, Vol. 5, 4: Kadmonites, citing Thompson, *Land and Book*, I, 242.

[1721] Josh 19:37. H6943—*Qedesh, keh'-desh*; a sanctum; a holy place; a city in south Judah; a city of Issachar; a fortified Canaanite city allotted to Naphtali; a city of refuge in Naphtali.

[1722] Wyatt, *Religious Texts from the Ugarit*, 40, KTU1.1. ii 15, note 10: servants, citing 1.4.iv and messengers citing 1.1.iii.4; 89, KTU 1.3 vi 10; 98, 99 1.4 iv 1, 10.

[1723] Ibid., 433–434, KTU 1.161 R 5 ancient saviors, notes 17, 19, 21. "Ug. qdmym. The term evokes primordiality, and thus authority and prestige. Presumably these members of the rpum are to be included among the list of legendary royal ancestors of the Ugaritic dynasty, though they were perhaps earlier than the kings whose names appear in KTU l."

[1724] Ibid., 109, 1.4 vii 30: "ancient," note 154, citing "Ug. qdmym. Gibson (1978: 65): 'the peoples of the east.' Virolleaud (1949: 94–95) followed by Caquot and Sznycer take this to mean 'before Yam.' Del Olmo (1981: 209): 'the [shores] along the sea.'" 384–385, 1.100 V 60: C1: "eastern city" note 33: Or "primaeval": Caquot (1989: 90, n. 278, 'antique')."

According to Herodotus, Cadmus was the patriarch of the Phoenician Cadmeian dynasty, which introduced the Greeks to a variety of arts that included writing;[1725] underscoring that Athirat was the goddess of Tyre. Cadmus/Cadmos was a Greek hero/giant who provided a daughter to Zeus to produce yet another demigod: "And Cadmos' daughter Semele bore to Zeus a splendid son after they mingled in love, laughing Dionysos, a mortal woman giving birth to a god. But they are both divine now."[1726] Cadmeians is eerily too close to Kadmoneans, recorded in the Septuagint for the Kadmonites, to be coincidental.[1727] Herodotus placed the life of Cadmus to circa 2000 BC, before the birth of Hercules whom Cadmus was equated with.[1728] The Cadmeian/Phoenician priestly class of Gephyrae were prominent in early Egypt, Athens, and Sparta, making those cities their permanent home. The Gephyrae built great Achaean temples to Demeter that Greeks were not permitted to enter. Cadmeians, beginning in Cadmus' time, governed Thebes.[1729] And, from Hesiod's *Theogony*: "To live off the land, juster and nobler, the divine race of heroes, also called Demigods, the race before the present one. They all died fighting in the great wars, Some at seven-gated Thebes, Cadmos' land."[1730]

Cadmus appears to be the transliterated *Qdm* Rephaim of the *Ugaritic Texts* who played an important role in the royal class throughout the Middle East shortly after the flood. Kadmonim were in part the seed for the Egyptian beast empire (via Thebes) along with the Zuzim, Ham's descendants including his son Mizraim. Kadmonim were in part ancestors for the Assyrian and Babylonian bloodlines and subsequent beast empires with the Aryans and descendants of Nimrod. Kadmonim and Aryans were further part of the seed of the Greek beast empire begat in Athens and Sparta, and the Persian beast empire begat by the Medes.

One further contemplates whether the kings of the east in the end-time beast empire of ten global empires (Rev 16) are bloodlines of the Kadmonim. Are these end-time kings descended from the Aryan/Persian bloodlines of Rephaim who migrated to the far reaches of India, China, Japan, and Southeast Asia that created heraldic dragon dynasties? "East" in Revelation 16 derives dually from *hay'leeos/*helios, the sun, and by implication east, and *anatolay'* meaning rising of light, dawn, and east[1731] of the Euphrates River.

One further ponders if Kenim, Kenizzim, and Kadmonim were the underlying allegories for contemporary Aryan KKK white supremacists. Ku Klux Klan

[1725] Herodotus, *Histories*, 241, Book 5, 57, 58.
[1726] Hesiod, *Theogony*, verses 945–949.
[1727] Brenton, Septuagint, 15:20: Kedmoneans.
[1728] Herodotus, *Histories*, 159, Book 2:142.
[1729] Wheeler, *The Geography of Herodotus*, 53, 63, 64, 67.
[1730] Hesiod, *Theogony*, verses 180–184.
[1731] G2246—*hay'-lee-os*: the sun; sun light; east; transliterated: helios; G395—*an-at-ol-ay'*: a rising of light; dawn; the east; east rising. Transliterated: anatole.

derives from Greek *kyklos*, meaning circle, clan, a tribe.[1732] A circle/ring of clans and kings is eerily like the Ring Lord kingships of Sumer, Lord of The Rings imagery, and with King Arthur's incarnated Knights/Kings of the Round Table alliance, which were based in the antediluvian Atlantean alliance of ten Aryan kings. "The earthly Anunnaki were the Ring Lords of Nippur. The obligation of the lugal/king, meaning "big man" (giant), was to govern and provide security for the land, while the Cainites/Enochians/Sumerians/Black Heads (of a specific clan or Snake Order) were to be the spiritual leaders, communicating with the gods. Earthborn Anunnaki were regarded as archons and rulers, but not full-fledged gods, i.e., immortal Nephilim. Even though they were initially regarded as leaders, the Anunnaki eventually assumed the role of (earthly) gods. The earthly Anunnaki were the despotic potentates of Genesis, who imposed Enochian mysticism upon humankind through tyranny."[1733]

Albert Pike was a Masonic adept and senior member of the Aryan KKK, a hateful organization founded by freemasons and originally led by Nathan Bedford Forrest.[1734] The KKK was closely related to freemasonry as a branch initiatory organization. "K" is the eleventh letter of the alphabet. Hence, three Ks represent 3 X 11 = 33 Scottish Rite degrees required for adept-hood. The Scottish Rite was founded in 1802 by American freemasons claiming lineage from bloodline Knights Templar Adepts and/or Jacobite Masonry, later raised to prominence by Pike.[1735]

The KKK overflows with Atlantean/Aryan and fallen angel imagery, representing an invisible empire centered in Atlanta (Atlantis), led by the Imperial Wizard and his fifteen Genii (Jinn), whereby each state is a realm under the authority of a Grand Dragon and eight Hydras. Each district is a dominion under a Grand Titan and six Furies, each province under a Grand Giant and four Goblins, and each town under a Grand Cyclops with two nighthawks. KKK members view themselves as heroic figures.[1736]

The Atlantean empire was governed by an alliance of ten kings and nation empires,[1737] just as there were ten mighty Rephaim and Rephaim/human hybrid clans listed in Genesis 15. Ten is the number of the biblical end-time kings and their global empire. The Templar agenda imagined a New Atlantis, and that a golden age had once existed in the ancient past and will rise once more in the New

[1732] Greer, *Element Encyclopedia of Secret Societies*, 281: Klu Klux Klan.
[1733] Wayne, *The Genesis 6 Conspiracy, 117,* Chapter 15: Isis Ishtar, Gaea, and Ninkhursag, citing Rohl, *Lost Testament*, 42; Gardner, *Grail Kings*; Sitchin, *The Lost Book of Enki*, 6, 108. 19, 325–327.
[1734] Greer, *Element Encyclopedia of Secret Societies*, 393–94.
[1735] Ibid., 30–31: Ancient and Accepted Rite [AAR].
[1736] Ibid., 281–82: Ku Klux Klan.
[1737] Donnelly, *Atlantis: The Antediluvian World*, 11–13, citing Plato's accounts in *Timaeus* and *Critias*: Atlas and Gadeirus, Ampheres and Evaemon, Mneseus and Autochhthon, Elassippus and Mesior, and Azaes and Diaprepes.

Age of light,[1738] Francis Bacon's New Atlantis.[1739] One muses whether the ancient KKK clans of Genesis 15 are not lost, and whether their bloodlines will play an important role in the end-time beast empire, just as they did with the ancient beast empires.

[1738] Knight and Lomas, *The Hiram Key*, 21.
[1739] Mackey, *History of Freemasonry*, 310.

CHAPTER 40

THE HYKSOS, AAMU, AND SHEMAU

Exod 12:40 Now the sojourning of the children of Israel, who dwelt in Egypt, was four hundred and thirty years.

After the war of giants, and after the fall of the Ur III dynasty circa 1950 BC, the Eastern alliance and Southern alliance of giants surged back to power. In the years following the war of giants, Jacob and Esau were born. Some time later Esau and his posterity began to intermarry into the hegemony of Horim and other giant royal houses.

Jacob and his sons fled to Egypt circa 1880–1830 BC; Israel escaped Egypt during the Exodus circa 1450–1400 BC.[1740] Although not biblically identified, the dawn of the Hyksos Egyptian dynasty was likely the catalyst for the abrupt change in Egyptian attitude and policy toward the Israelites, from welcomed guests to despised slaves. Further, grasping the Hyksos relationships with the Southern alliance, the Eastern alliance, and the Indo-Aryan giants reveals who the obscure Hyksos kings and people were, and their hidden impact on history.

[1740] Depending on the flood date of 2350 or 2400 BC. Biblically the flood could be as far back 2450. With the flood at 2348 BC: Abram born 292 years after the flood; goes to Canaan at age 75; Genesis 14 happens shortly after circa 1981–1950 BC. Using 1980 BC and 210 years when Jacob went to Egypt places the entry date to 1720–1820 BC.

The Hyksos dynasty reigned circa 1720–1550 BC, or 1762–1630 depending on the historian. The Hyksos first conquered Memphis and then rendered the Theban dynasties and the whole of Egypt to pay tribute as vassals. Thereafter the Hyksos revolutionized Egypt's military capability and weaponry. The Hyksos introduced the iron-fitted chariot, iron swords, composite bows, and accompanying military tactics in their stunning defeat of Egypt.[1741] Large earthen enclosures housed Hyksos horses as corroborated by Egyptian construction of these enclosures at its military outposts at Jericho, Shechem, Lachish, and Tell-el-Ajjul.[1742] The Hyksos empire stretched north to Canaan and Phoenicia, east and north to Carchemish, and enveloped the mountain region source for the Euphrates and Tigris rivers.[1743]

Indo-European Scythians and Aryans were expert horsemen and a kin branch of the Kassites who first exploited the horse with the revolutionary chariot war weapon,[1744] technology the Hyksos inherited and improved. As the most fearsome warriors of their age, Aryans revolutionized warfare. Manetho, a historian who translated Egyptian history into Greek, rendered the Hyksos as invaders from the east that subdued Egypt without war.[1745] Such was the Hyksos power and intimidation that their military technologies wielded.

With their terrifying weaponry, Aryans launched lightning campaigns against neighboring nations. Aryans believed they were "heroes" who begat a renaissance heroic age who fought wars with the assistance of their gods.[1746] Aryans emulated their god Indra, the great dragon slayer who "rode in a chariot above the heavens."[1747] Scythians and Aryans were renowned as the "horse lords," the overlords and masters of horsemanship and chariot technology, whose Mesopotamian-spawned nations included the Akkadians, Mitanni, Hurrians,[1748] and Kassites. The Kassites invaded northern Mesopotamia via the Persian Zagros mountains after inheriting and improving the Scythian horse-drawn chariots circa 1750 BC, and likely before, because Kassites were included as a branch of dukes of Edom.[1749] Pre-

---

[1741] Bauer, *History of the World*, 179; *Unger's*, 598: Hyksos; J. M. Roberts, *History of the World* (New York: Oxford University Press, 1993), 65.

[1742] *Unger's*, 598: Hyksos.

[1743] Ibid., 598: Hyksos.

[1744] *Encyclopedia Americana*, Vol. 24, 421–422: Scythians; Roberts, *History of the World*, 72.

[1745] *Josephus, Against Apion*, Book 1:14.

[1746] Karen Armstrong, *The Great Transformation: The Beginning of Our Religious Traditions* (New York: Random House, 2006), 8, citing Mircea Eliade, *Patterns in Comparative Religion*, trans. Rosemary Sheed (London: Sheed & Ward, 1958), 7, 8, 10.

[1747] Ibid., 188–89; Norman Cohn, *Cosmos, Chaos and the World to Come: The Ancient Roots of Apocalyptic Faith* (New Haven, CT/London: Yale University Press, 1993), 94–95.

[1748] De Vere, *The Dragon Legacy*, 62, 73.

[1749] Gardner, *Realm of the Ring Lords*, 64; Bauer, *History of the World*, 176. Gen 36:20–31; 1 Chron 1:52–54.

vious chapters noted Hurrians/Horim and Aryans migrated down from the Zagros mountains, indicating a direct link between the three groups of peoples, and to the Hyksos by implication.

Kassite kings interbred with the Elef Edomite/Horim hybrid dukes who later succeeded as the Lords of Babylon after the fall of Amorite Babylon circa 1595 BC,[1750] and were kin to the Mitanni dynasts. Ancient Horim/Hurrians entered Mesopotamia and the Covenant Land well before 2000 BC[1751] as Aboriginal Aryan splinter branches, who in part also established the Mitanni dynasty.[1752] Indo-European groups assimilated, replaced, and then established the Minoan, Babylonian, Hittite, Khassite, and Mitanni dynasties. Indo-Europeans included Scythians, Persians, and Aryans that settled the Indus valley, Persia, southern Greece and its islands,[1753] and the giants of the Covenant Land.

One should not be shocked to learn that the Hyksos were described with colossal-sized heads whose faces exhibited thick beards; curly black hair with prominent pigtails dangling behind the head; wide, aquiline noses; high cheek-bones, square foreheads, and prominent lips.[1754] The Asiatic Hyksos were classified as a differentiated and/or peculiar Semitic stock to that of Semitics who dwelled in Canaan.[1755] The Hyksos black curly hair and beards stood out in contrast to blond and red hair that were common physical traits of Nephilim, Rephaim, Anakim, and Horim, underscoring that postdiluvian giants had two distinct strains. The Hyksos' dark curly hair traits were common among the inhabitants of Syria/Aram and the district where the Mitanni and Hittites dwelled,[1756] which were akin to depictions of Gilgamesh, Nimrod, and Persians.

Hyksos depictions are reminiscent of the long black-haired and bearded Merovingian kings that secreted within their heraldry, a bloodline ancestry from a Quinataur: "legomin language" that concealed their true bloodlines traced back to the Aryans. Merovingians held numinous Fisher/Shepherd King appellations inherited through the dark-haired Alain of Scythia, whose royal bloodlines also produced Hyksos kings.[1757] Merovingians were priest-kings, dukes/*alluwphim* of the Cathar and Albigensian religions, and the "Shining Elvin Ones" of the dragon messianic bloodline. The Merovingian dynasty, via Dagobert, passed on their ennobled bloodlines to the de Payen, de Bouillon, and Anjou families,[1758] founders

---

[1750] Bauer, *History of the World*, 174, 199, 200, 273.

[1751] *Unger's*, 586–77; *Nelson's*, 577: Horites.

[1752] *Nelson's*, 577: Horites.

[1753] *Encyclopedia Americana*, Vol. 15, 69; Cooper, *An Archaic Dictionary*, 79: Ari.

[1754] Sayce, *Races of the Old Testament*, 95–97.

[1755] Boughton, *History of Ancient Peoples*, 202–204.

[1756] Sayce, *Races of the Old Testament*, 95–97; Boughton, *History of Ancient Peoples*, 202–204.

[1757] Wayne, *Genesis 6 Conspiracy*, 462–464.

[1758] Ibid., 464–465; *Catholic Encyclopedia*, Vol. 7, 638: Idumea.

of the Knights Templar, keepers of the bloodline,[1759] and the genesis of modern secret societies as we know them today.

One of Manetho's eye-opening Egypt historical accounts stated: "Hyk (`uk) in the word Hyksos was the Rephaite name for King," and that "it has been inferred that Og [`Owg/`Uwg] was an attempt to represent the same in Hebrew letters."[1760] Manetho added that the Greek suffix *sos* to *hyk*, a word connected to Egyptian *su* or *sau* meaning sheep, shepherd, watcher, and/or guardian[1761] formed the Shepherd King title,[1762] dually from *hykau-khasut*. Others state *khasut* means mountains (perhaps the Kassite source word), and when combined with *hyk* translates as "king of the mountains," noting Egypt does not have mountains.[1763]

Josephus, citing Manetho, provided a similar translation to Hyksos: "This whole nation was styled Hycsos, that is, Shepherd kings: for the first syllable— 'hyc' according to the sacred dialect denotes as a king, and the second syllable, sos as a shepherd. .. but some say that these people were Arabians," and "for that Hyc, with the aspiration, in the Egyptian tongue again denotes shepherds." Manetho also stated: "These people, whom we have before named kings, and called shepherds also."[1764] The Egyptians understood Hyksos as *hyk*/ruler and *shasu*/shepherds, the terrible Syrian (Mount Hermon Rephaite/Rephaim) invaders of a mixed race,[1765] or species, and as part of the black-haired Aryan Terrible Ones. Hyksos were likewise known as the terrible *Shasu* of the Execration Texts. Hyksos hordes blew into Egypt like a cyclone, razing temples and monuments to the ground.[1766]

The seat of the Hyksos rule was established at a "desert mansion,"[1767] where they built large, strong walls around Avaris[1768] in the tradition of the mighty walled fortress city-states of Canaan. Avaris was the home for the Aboriginal Aamu people, whom most associate with the Hyksos. Aamau was homophonic for "shepherd," and another source for the Shepherd King title.[1769] Avaris was cognate with "a citizen of Avaris" or "an Asiatic."[1770]

The name of Pharaoh Khyan, the third Hyksos king, was inscribed on an alabaster jar at Knossos of Crete, discovered on Theran/Santorini by Sir Arthur Evans

---

[1759] Wayne, *Genesis 6 Conspiracy*, 402, citing Gardner, *Bloodlines*, 109; Wallace-Murphy, Hopkins, and Simmons, *Rex Deus*, 146–147.
[1760] *Strong's Cyclopaedia*, Vol. 7, 317: Og, citing "Jour. Sac. Lit. Jan. 1852, p. 363."
[1761] Ralph Ellis, *Tempest & Exodus* (Cheshire, UK: Edfu Books, 2000), 283.
[1762] *Encyclopedia Americana*, Vol. 14, 594: Hyksos; Bauer, *History of the World*, 179.
[1763] Ellis, *Tempest & Exodus*, 282.
[1764] Josephus, *Against Apion*, Book 1:14.
[1765] Cooper, *An Archaic Dictionary*, 244: Hyksos.
[1766] Boughton, *History of Ancient Peoples*, 206–207.
[1767] *Encyclopedia Americana*, Vol. 14, 594: Hyksos; Bauer, *History of the World, 180.*
[1768] Josephus, *Against Apion*, Book 1:14.
[1769] Ellis, *Tempest & Exodus*, 283.
[1770] Ibid., 284, 289, 290.

and dated to 1660–1550 BC. Khyan was a patronymic dynastic title for Minoan kings like King Minos, home of the Minotaur. Avaris' palace walls were decorated in a Minoan style.[1771] The Hyksos further acknowledged ties to the dark-haired Minoan Indo-Aryans via patronymic titles for their kings.

The first Hyksos king was named Sheshi, a foreigner Manetho stated belonged to a notorious race called the "Desert Princes," the *Hikau-khoswet* transliterated as the Hyksos.[1772] One cogitates at the phonetic connection between Sheshi and Sheshai, the Anakim king of Kiriatharba in southern Canaan's desert region. Sheshai is pronounced shay-shaw-ee and means "noble."[1773] Further, the Hyksos, at least in part, were viewed as a western Semitic-speaking race,[1774] which links them to the Anakim. Biblical historian David Rohl identified the Hyksos as Asiatic Indo-Europeans closely connected to Amalekites, among whom the three famous Anakim kings resided: Sheshai, Ahiman, and Talmi/Talmai. Sheshai was the most powerful of the three,[1775] and perhaps also patronymic from the Hyksos King Sheshi. Knowing the Hyksos reigned over the growing nation of Israel in Egypt, and were associated with the Anakim and Amalekite hybrids, perhaps shines additional light on the Amalekite oath to wipe Israel from the face of the earth. Rohl's Anakim and Sheshai connection provides contextual concerns regarding the Amalekites and their unprovoked attack at the battle of Rephidim.[1776]

Knowing the Hyksos usurped the Egyptian empire, and their pharaonic dynasty, may help to explain some of the odd language in the Bible that documented how Israel was relegated from guest to slave. Exodus 1 states a new pharaoh came to power whom Joseph did not know, which is odd because Joseph was promoted to ruler of all Egypt, traveled throughout the empire, and was second only to Pharaoh.[1777] Joseph would have known all the possible bloodline successors or contenders, but not an outside invader. Moreover, the Exodus 1:8 text did not state a bloodline relative succeeded the throne. Second, the words "now there arose" were inserted by translators to better define the word "up," from the Hebrew word *quwm*, defined as: arise, arise as in a hostile sense, to become powerful, come onto the scene, be established, and impose.[1778] The new/*chadash*,

---

[1771] Bauer, *History of the World*, 186; Mechthild J. Mellink, *Egypt and the Levant: New Perspectives and Initiatives in the Hyksos Period* (Vienna: Austrian Academy of Sciences Press, 1995), Vol. 5, 85–89: citing Arthur Evans, *The Palace of Minos at Knossos*, I (London: Macmillan, 1921), 419–20; Ellis, *Tempest & Exodus*, 308.

[1772] Bauer, *History of the World*, 179.

[1773] H8344—*Sheshay, shay-shah'-ee*: noble; son of Anak; one of the giants in the land of Canaan.

[1774] Bauer, *History of the World*, 235.

[1775] Rohl, *The Lost Testament*, 250–251.

[1776] Exod 17:1–16.

[1777] Gen 41:40–43.

[1778] H6965—*quwm, koom*: to rise; arise in a hostile sense; to arise to become powerful; come on the scene; to stand; be established; be confirmed; impose; raise up; raise oneself; build.

as in "a new king," means new, fresh, a new thing.[1779] Third, the new leader was first described as a king/*melek* versus Pharaoh/*Par`oh,* meaning great house.[1780]

> Exod 1:8 Now there arose up a new king over Egypt, which knew not Joseph.
>
> Exod 1:9 And he said unto his people, Behold, the people of the children of Israel are more and mightier than we.

The original Hebrew language indicates that a new royal dynasty outside the great house of Pharaoh usurped power in a hostile way and established a new line of Egyptian kings. This new royal from another Rephaim bloodline usurped, or was then given from the former dynasts, the title of pharaoh, because the new king is later called Pharaoh two times in Exodus 1.[1781] The reign of terror by foreign kings left a lasting imprint on the Egyptian house of Pharaoh regarding foreigners, for generations after the Hyksos were driven out, a hatred and fear that was then levied against Israel:

> Exod 1:10 Come on, let us deal wisely with them; lest they multiply, and it come to pass, that, when there falleth out any war, they join also unto our enemies, and fight against us, and so get them up out of the land.
>
> Exod 1:11 Therefore they did set over them taskmasters to afflict them with their burdens. And they built for Pharaoh treasure cities, Pithom and Raamses.

Rohl's research confirmed that King Sheshi was the "leader of the Nile delta [Hyksos] Asiatic invaders and the usurper of the Red Crown of Lower Egypt." Accordingly, Sheshi was given pharaonic titles and the coronation name of Maibre."[1782] Rohl further wrote, "The Anakin pharaonic dynasty were referred to by the native Egyptians as the *hekau-khasut* ('rulers of the hill country'), because they hailed from the hill country of Canaan."[1783] Previous to this, the Mentu/Menti whom Egyptians named for invading hordes of giants reigned over by Hyksos kings in Sinai, Syria, and Asia Minor.[1784] The "Mentu in Asia" was a com-

---

[1779] H2319—*chadash, khaw-dawsh':* new; fresh, new thing.
[1780] H4428—*melek, meh'-lek:* a king; royal; H6547—*Par`oh, par-o';* of Egyptian derivation: great house; a title of Egyptian kings.
[1781] Exod 1:11, 19.
[1782] Rohl, *The Lost Testament,* 251.
[1783] Ibid.
[1784] Sayce, *Races of the Old Testament,* 109–110; Billington, "Goliath and the Exodus Giants," 500–501, citing Pritchard, *ANET,* 328, note 14.

mon glyph used for Egypt's immediate neighbors to the northeast.[1785] Manetho described the Hyksos as the ancients, the Aboriginal Phoenicians before Israel,[1786] and by implication Rephaim and/or Indo-Aryans. Knowing this makes sense of historical accounts that when Egyptians forced the hated Hyksos out of Egypt (c. 1570 BC), part of the refugee Hyksos fled to their strongholds, high-walled fortresses in south Canaan. The Egyptians, who by this time possessed the weapon technology of the Hyksos, hunted them into Palestine, seized their territories, and then continued their campaign to Syria,[1787] to subdue kin Hyksos branches.

The Hyksos were alternatively called the Aamu, renowned as the "Lesser Hyksos," a distinct but modified genealogical descent of kings, which may be why Josephus described them as "ignobled."[1788] The Egyptians named the people of west Asia the Aamu, a people who dwelled in both Palestine and Syria.[1789] The Aamu were depicted as giants in the tomb of Khnumhotep II circa 1900 BC or before. At that time the Aamu was led by King Abisha. A Theban pharaoh, Sinhue, additionally documented that the Aamu king of Avaris warred with the Asiatics to attack the "Rulers of the Hill Countries" of Canaan circa 1900 BC: "When the Asiatics conspired to attack the Rulers of the Hill Countries, I opposed their movements."[1790]

What is curious about the above excerpt from the *Story of Sinhue* is that the writings predate the Hyksos' takeover of Avaris by more than one hundred years. One deduces the Aamu giants occupied Avaris well before the Hyksos' new war technology-driven invasion, and that the Hyksos used Avaris as their military home base to take Egypt by force. One further ponders if the *Story of Sinhue* excerpt might indicate that the Aamu of Avaris were Anakim or Zuzim of Ham referenced in the war of giants, whose kin branch were Zamzummim of the Ammon region.[1791]

After usurping power in Egypt, the Hyksos Pharaonic appellation passed on to a kin branch from the northeast, the Shemau, renowned as "The Greater Hyksos." The first of the northern Hyksos kings of Egypt was Shalek, whom Manetho called Salatis.[1792] The Shemau held a similar titular epithet to the Aamu, the *heka-khasut*. The female pharaoh, Hatshepsut, recorded these eastern pharaoh lords: "the Asiatics were in the midst of Avaris of the Northland and the Shemau were in the midst of them, overthrowing that which had been made. They ruled without the consent of Re.. .".[1793] The northern "Greater Hyksos" were also part of the nobility of the Mitanni who the

---

[1785] Billington, "Goliath and the Exodus Giants," 500–501, citing Pritchard, *ANET*, 328, note 14.

[1786] *Strong's Cyclopaedia*, Vol. 4, 429: Hyksos.

[1787] Roberts, *History of the World*, 65.

[1788] Rohl, *Lost Testament*, 251, 289; Josephus, *Against Apion*, Book 1:14.

[1789] Ellis, *Tempest & Exodus*, 283, citing *Oxford History of Ancient Egypt*, 187.

[1790] Ibid., 332–333, quoting Pritchard, *Story of Sinuhe, ANET*.

[1791] Gen 14:5; Deut 2:20.

[1792] Rohl, *Lost Testament*, 289; *Josephus, Against Apion*, Book 1:14.

[1793] Rohl, *Lost Testament*, 289, quoting the *Speos Artemidos Inscription*.

Hyksos were allies with, and who reigned with indigenous Hurrians.[1794] It follows that the Hyksos military makeup included a fleet of ships manned by Aegean Sea-warriors (Minoans) and Hurrian cavalry[1795] and/or chariots.

According to Manetho, Pharaoh Amenophis pursued the fleeing Hyksos from Egypt to Syria: "Amenophis, some time afterward, came upon them, and conquered them in battle, and slew his enemies, and drove them before him as far as Syria."[1796] Manetho further recorded that the Hyksos leadership and nobility class settled in Jerusalem: "they went away with their whole families and effects, not fewer in number than two hundred and forty thousand, and took their journey from Egypt, through the wilderness, for Syria; but that as they were in fear of the Assyrians, who had then the dominion over Asia, they built a city in that country which is now called Judea, and that large enough to contain this great number of men, and called it Jerusalem."[1797]

What is very important about Manetho's account is that Jerusalem was resettled and rebuilt by the Hyksos/Aamau/Shemau/Anakim (c. 1550 BC) well before they were driven from Egypt. By implication, Jerusalem the city of the scripturally patriarch-less Jebusites seemingly had a kin relationship with the Anakim/Aamu/Hyksos, indicating Jebus may have been the Anakim patriarch. As such, one ponders then if the king of Jerusalem recorded in the Execration Texts was reflecting his patronymic connections to the Aamau/Anakim: "the Ruler of Jerusalem, Yaqar-'Ammu and all of the retainers who are with him."[1798] Yaqar-Ammu was listed among the Anakim/*Iy'anaq* and the Amorites/*Iymu'aru* as allies and strong men, who were associated with the Mentu of Asia.[1799]

The Hyksos regularly traded with and exported Egyptian produce to their Indo-European kin in the Aegean islands of Crete and Cyprus, with the Ugarit city, and with cities along the coast of Syria.[1800] When the Hyksos were driven from Egypt, some also traveled by ship to settle in the Aegean islands and on the mainland of Greece. Crete and Cyprus were islands where some Shemau (perhaps Anakim) of southern Canaan, including a King Khamudy, settled and merged with the Pelast Aryan nobility of Crete.[1801] Hyksos were part of the same Aryan mosaic as the Pelastoi of Gaza.[1802]

The Hyksos connections to the Jebusites and the Anakim of central Canaan and Gaza, combined with the Hyksos' underexplained connections to the Minoans of Crete and Cyprus, provides important context to the reformatted Southern alliance with the Philistine second invasion of Gaza.

[1794] Ibid., 276.

[1795] Ibid., 289.

[1796] Josephus, *Against Apion*, Book 1:27.29.

[1797] Ibid., Book 1:14, 26, 28.

[1798] Billington, "Goliath and the Exodus Giants," 501, citing Pritchard, *ANET*, 225–226.

[1799] Ibid.

[1800] Rohl, *Lost Testament*, 289; Ellis, *Tempest & Exodus*, 179, 278, 322.

[1801] Rohl, *Lost Testament*, 275.

[1802] Rohl, *Lost Testament*, 276.

CHAPTER 41

THE PHILISTINES, CHERETHIM, CAPHTORIM, AND CALUSHIM

Gen 10:14 And Pathrusim, and Casluhim, (out of whom came Philistim,) and Caphtorim.. ..)

Knowing the Hyksos/Aamu role in the ancient Southern alliance, and their Minoan relationship, is contextually important to appreciate the geopolitical landscape in the time of the Exodus. Understanding the Hyksos relationship with the Minoans helps to clarify the complex Philistine confederacy that Israel faced through the epoch of the judges and the reigns of Saul and David.

The Amaleqim, Horim, Anakim, Avvim and the southern Amorites, Canaanites, and Hittites of the original Southern alliance reigned until Genesis 14's war of giants. Thereafter, the Southern alliance required military support from the Aamu, who settled in Avaris well before 1900 BC[1803] to ward off the Mesopotamians of the Ur III dynasty, and then the upstart Amorite Babylonian empire. Military support continued from the Egyptian Hyksos/Aamu dynasty after their annexation

---

[1803] Ellis, *Tempest & Exodus*, 332–333, quoting Pritchard, *Story of Sinuhe, ANET.*

of the Egyptian empire circa 1762–1720 BC. From the time of the war of giants until the fall of the Hyksos Egyptian dynasty circa 1550 BC, Egyptian incursions into the Covenant Land appear to have been part of the Hyksos Southern alliance obligations. The obligations included sharing the new war technologies the Hyksos inherited from their northern Kassite brethren. It follows that Aamu and Hyksos support included building large military outposts at Jericho, Shechem, Lachish, and Tell-el-Ajjul[1804] just south of Gaza city. The Hyksos empire stretched to Canaan and Phoenicia in the north, and east to Carchemish and the mountain regions of Assyria.[1805] The collapse of the Hyksos Egyptian empire before the Exodus was a key historical turning point, which likely led to building of high-walled fortresses in the traditions of Avaris, not documented biblically in numbers in Canaan until the Exodus. The repercussions set the geopolitical landscape Israel faced in the Covenant Land conquest more than a century later.

The Hyksos royal bloodline, along with their familial nobility, fled by ship to settle in the Aegean islands and in Jerusalem. The Shemau/Anakim nobility of southern Canaan included a King Khamudy, last of the Hyksos Egyptian kings who had previously merged with the Pelast nobility of Crete.[1806] This begins to make sense when one understands the Hyksos were part of the same people as the Pelastoi of Gaza,[1807] commonly known as the Philistines.

Among the Assyrians, the Philistine Sea Peoples were referred to as the Philisti, or the Palastu; Pelishti was the base word for Palestine.[1808] Palestine derived from the Greek transliteration Palastinoi for Philistine descendants.[1809] Palestina/Palestine is translated from Hebrew *Plesheth* four times in the KJV, and three times as Philistia.[1810]

> Exod 15:14 The people shall hear, and be afraid: sorrow shall take hold on the inhabitants of Palestina.

The Philistines were a powerful sea people who carved out a coastal strip of land in southwest Canaan, from Joppa to Gaza along the Mediterranean seacoast,[1811] whereby they rejoined their Hyksos kin. The Philistines were recorded as migrating from the country/island of Caphtor:

[1804] *Unger's*, 598: Hyksos.
[1805] Ibid., 598: Hyksos.
[1806] Rohl, *Lost Testament*, 275.
[1807] Ibid., 276.
[1808] *Nelson's*, 986: Philistines.
[1809] *Mercer's*, 685: Philistines.
[1810] H6429—*Plesheth, pel-eh'-sheth*: a land of sojourners; rolling; migratory; region of Canaan; Palestina, Palestine, Philistia, and Philistines. Palestina: Exod 15:14; Isa 14:29, 31; Philistia: Ps 60:8; 87:4; 108:9; Palestine: Joel 3:4.
[1811] *Unger's*, 1003: Philistines.

Jer 47:4 Because of the day that cometh to spoil all the Philistines, and to cut off from Tyrus and Zidon every helper that remaineth: for the LORD will spoil the Philistines, the remnant of the country of Caphtor.[1812]

Caphtor was the island of Crete,[1813] and part of the Minoan empire. Philistine, according to *Unger's*, derives from the Egyptian word *Prst*, or *Plst* for early settlers of the Egyptian delta region who later migrated to southern Canaan, and who also settled in the Aegean region among the Minoans of Crete.[1814] According to the *Ugaritic Texts*, Crete and Egypt, places Ammur and Qadesh traveled to by ship, were reigned over by Baal; some scholars assert *Kptr* refers to Kaphtor.[1815] What is additionally noteworthy in the following Ugaritic passage is that Baal's inheritance included Crete and parts of Egypt, reminiscent of Ezekiel 32:8: "When the most High divided to the nations their inheritance," and Psalm 82's council of the gods.

1.13 vi 10 Set off, O fisherman of Athirat, go forth, O Qadesh-and-Amurr! Then indeed set your face <toward Kothar-and-Hasis, toward Egypt, of all of which he is go. ..

1.13 vi 15 Crete the seat of his dwelling, Egypt the land of his inheritance.Over a thousand miles, ten thousand leagues."[1816]

Egyptians reckoned Philistines as the sea people of Caphtor.[1817] Later Egyptian inscriptions recorded the Philistines as the Pulista, while Assyrian inscriptions documented Philistines as the Piliste and Palastu whom Assyrians considered as Phoenicians that originated from Caphtor.[1818] Others connected Philistines with the Pelgasi of Krete/Crete.[1819] The ancient Philistine race was described as

---

[1812] Amos 9:7: "Are ye not as children of the Ethiopians unto me, O children of Israel? saith the LORD. Have not I brought up Israel out of the land of Egypt? and the Philistines from Caphtor, and the Syrians from Kir?"

[1813] *Unger's*, 1003: Philistines.

[1814] Ibid., 1003: Philistines.

[1815] Wyatt, *Religious Texts from the Ugarit*, 89, 1.13 vi 10–15, note 83: "In view of this passage, we might expect kptr also to refer to Egypt, but no plausible explanation has been offered. The usual explanation (Crete, cf. Heb. Kaptor, Eg. Keftill) is quite plausible in view of the close economic ties between Minoan Crete and Egypt, now revealed by the discoveries at Tell ed Daba. See now Morgan (1995). Political symbolism has perhaps preempted geographical realism. Kothar is of course Ptah, the artificer god of Memphis (above at KTU 1.1 iii *I). Cf. also n. 36 to KTU 1.1 iii 20–21."

[1816] Ibid., 89, 1.13 vi 10–15.

[1817] *Nelson's*, 986: Philistines.

[1818] Sayce, *Races of the Old Testament*, 126.

[1819] Ibid., 127.

non-Semitic, from an Indo-European group that later became a "semitized" peo-ple, but depicted as tall and Hellenic-looking, at the Medinet temple of Rameses III.[1820]

According to *Mercer's Dictionary* though, many scholars believe the Philistine name is anachronistic because it does not appear in nonscriptural sources before 1200 BC.[1821] On the other hand, scholars note the numerous details embedded into Genesis' narratives documenting the Israelite patriarchs accurately reflect the biblical dating of those accounts to 1450 BC and before.[1822] A deep dive is required to make sense of the ethnological history to the Indo-Aryan Sea Peoples that seem-ingly adopted migrating Philistines from Egypt.

Ancient Philistines were a non-Semitic race of Aryans, according to *Unger's*.[1823] Aryans were giants, which suggests then that Philistines became hybrid Rephaim akin to Amorites. The table of nations documented the Philistines descended from Casluhim, son of Mizraim, son of Ham.[1824] Philistines likely became a hybrid race, intermarrying with Indo-Aryan Minoans who settled Crete and Cyprus. Thus, Philistines were taller than Israelites and other humans, but were not giants.

Philistines were akin to the *Shasu*, and to the Amorites, Canaanites, Amale-kites, and Jebusites described in Numbers 13 and Deuteronomy 1, who were taller than the Israelites but not giants. It follows that Philistines were depicted in reliefs as tall with long legs and torsos, and long straight noses, void of the depression between the nose and forehead, without facial hair, small chins, high cheek bones, and large wrap-around eyes, sporting helmets and tunics akin to other Sea Peoples like the Cretans, and similar to the Rameses III Medinet Habu reliefs.[1825] Of inter-est as well is that the Philistines of Ashkelon in Gaza reflected more of the typical and bearded Hittite appearance,[1826] or Hyksos appearance. The different depic-tions seem to support two branches and migrations of Philistines into Canaan in a similar way Hyksos were of two branches: the Shemau and Aamu.

After migrating to Crete, most scholars agree the Philistines migrated to southern Canaan from the Aegean basin of the Mediterranean,[1827] likely motivated by a natural disaster. *Plishtiy*/Philistine/Philistim is defined as immigrants, and descendants of Mizraim/Egypt from Caphtor/Crete, which is rooted in *Plesheth*/

[1820] *Unger's*, 1004: Philistines; *Encyclopedia Americana*, Vol. 21, 761: Philistines.

[1821] *Mercer's*, 685: Philistines.

[1822] Israel Finkelstein, *Journals for the Study of the Old Testament* (London: Continuum, 2002), Vol. 27.2, 153.

[1823] *Unger's*, 1004: Philistines.

[1824] Gen 10:12–13; 1 Chron 1:11-12.

[1825] *Mercer's*, 685; *Nelson's* 987: Philistines; *Unger's*, 1003–1004: Philistines.

[1826] Sayce, *Races of the Old Testament*, 127.

[1827] *Mercer's*, 685: Philistines.

Phisitia/Palestina/Palestine, meaning migratory and a land of sojourners.[1828] The Philistines/*Plst* migrated to Egypt with Mizraim, then to Caphtor/Crete, and then to southwest Canaan. Even though the Philistines descended from Mizraim's son Casluhim, and from Caphtor, Casluhim was not the patriarch for the Philistines: "Casluhim, (out of whom came Philistim,) and Caphtorim."[1829]

Kachluchiym/Casluhim were a little-known people of foreign derivation meaning fortified, a people cognate to Egyptians and only mentioned in the table of nations.[1830] Scholars assert the Casluhim followed the Pathrusim people that settled between Upper and Lower Egypt.[1831] The Septuagint names the lost Casluhim people as the *Chasmoniim*, while Josephus references them as the *Chesloim,* whose cities and peoples were wiped out in the Egyptian/Ethiopic wars led by Moses in his early life.[1832] The Septuagint scribes may have taken their lead from the Hebrew word *Chashman*/princes of Ethiopia, used in Psalm 68.[1833]

Sept Gen 10:13 And Mesrain begot the Ludiim, and the Nephthalim, and the Enemetiim, and the Labiim,

10:14 and the Patrosoniim, and the Chasmoniim (whence came forth Phylistiim) and the Gaphthoriim.

Ps 68:31 Princes shall come out of Egypt; Ethiopia shall soon stretch out her hands unto God.

The *Plst* of Egypt were a migratory branch of Casluhim daughters and an unknown giant patriarch, which intermarried with Indo-Aryans of Caphtor/Crete, at which point the patriarch's name was lost to history or was a derivative of *Plst.* The Caphtorim may very well be the Hebrew name for the giant Aboriginal

---

[1828] H6430—*Plishtiy, pel-ish-tee';* patrial from 6429; immigrants; inhabitant of Philistia, Pelesheth, or Philistine; descendants of Mizraim from Caphtor (Crete); H6429—*Plesheth, pel-eh'-sheth:* land of sojourners; rolling; migratory; a region of Canaan Palestina, Palestine, Philistia, and/or Philistines.

[1829] Gen 10:12–13; 1 Chron 1:11–12.

[1830] H3695—*Kacluchiym, kas-loo'-kheem;* a plural format of foreign origin: fortified; a people cognate to the Egyptians; progenitors of the Philistines and Caphtorim. Casluhim: Gen 10:14; 1 Chron 1:12.

[1831] *Strong's Cyclopaedia,* Vol. 2, 138: Casluhim.

[1832] Josephus, *Ant.,* Book 1, 6:2, note 17: "[One observation ought not here to be neglected, with regard to that Ethiopic war which Moses, as general of the Egyptians, put an end to, Antiq. B. II. ch. 10., and about which our late writers seem very much unconcerned; viz. that it was a war of that consequence, as to occasion the removal or destruction of six or seven nations of the posterity of Mitzraim, with their cities; which Josephus would not have said, if he had not had ancient records to justify those his assertions, though those records be now all lost.]"

[1833] H2831—*chashman, khash-man':* ample in resources; wealthy; ambassadors; *Catholic Encyclopedia,* Vol. 6, 400: Gaza.

inhabitants of the patrial named Caphtor/Crete, Indo-Aryans whom the Philistines in part derived from. Both the Philistines and Caphtorim later migrated to Gaza, where they uprooted many Avvim and settled in their place.[1834]

> Jer 47:4 Because of the day that cometh to spoil all the Philistines, and to cut off from Tyrus and Zidon every helper that remaineth: for the LORD will spoil the Philistines, the remnant of the country of Caphtor.

The *Ugaritic Texts* classified Crete, Semitic *Kptr*, as the source word for Hebrew Kaphtor, Egyptian Keftiu,[1835] and English Caphtor. The *Ugaritic Texts* also classified the god of Crete/Kaphtor and Egypt as a son of El, Kothar-Hasis, whose throne was in Crete but dwelled in Egypt.[1836] Ugaritic Kaphtor[1837] is the same spelling as in Hebrew *Kaphtor,* defined as the wreath-shaped island of Crete, home of the Philistines, and the patrial source word for *Kaphtoriy*/Caphtorim meaning crown, Cretans, and distinct from the Philistines[1838]—Indo-Aryans. Minoans/Cretans were one of four Indo-Aryan branches that migrated from Asia Minor, or perhaps even a fifth branch.[1839]

> 1 Chron 1:12 And Pathrusim, and Casluhim, (of whom came the Philistines,) and Caphthorim.

The *Ugaritic Texts* documented a dynastic Cretan king Keret, a king classified as one of the heroes, and the king who begat the eponym of the Cretans. Cretans are equated with the Cherethites/*Keretim* of the Bible who also dwelled among the Philistines.[1840] Keret was a Rephaim in the assembly of the Ditanu, and one of the "exalted" saviors of the underworld.[1841] Keret was a *bn il*, son of a god, and one

---

[1834] Deut 2:23.

[1835] Wyatt, *Religious Texts from Ugarit,* The Baal Cycle of Myth, *89,* KTU 1.3.vi.15, note 83; 45, KTU 1.1.iii.15, note 34.

[1836] Wyatt, *Religious Texts from Ugarit,* 34, KTU 1.1.iii; 45, KTU 1.1 iii; 15, note 34; 383, KTU 1.100.v.45 [BX]; 43–45, KTU 1.1 iii.1:15 and note 24.

[1837] Wyatt, *Religious Texts from Ugarit,* 45, KTU 1.1.iii.15, note 34.

[1838] H3732—*Kaphtoriy, kaf-to-ree*; patrial from 3731; a crown; Caphtorite; Caphtorim; native of Caphtor; Cretans as inhabitants of Caphtor distinct from the Philistines. H3731—*Kaphtor, kaf-tore*; Kaphtowr; a crown; a wreath-shaped island; original home or staging land of the Philistines on the island of Crete; the island of Crete.

[1839] Bauer, *History of the World,* 196–197, footnote.

[1840] H3774—*Krethiy, ker-ay-thee*; executioner; life-guardsman; Cretans; proto-Philistines.

[1841] Wyatt, *Religious Texts from Ugarit,* 179–180, The Story of King Keret, KTU 1.14 iii.1–10, notes 5, 6; 210–212, KTU 1.15.iii.1–15 and note 156.

of the "divine assistants" who served the "convocation of the Council, toward the divine mountain" "the Great Assembly"[1842] of Mount Hermon.

Philistines migrated to Gaza during the Neo-palatial period, circa 1550–1400 BC.[1843] Their pottery was distinctly Mycenaean.[1844] We know the Hyksos dynasty fell circa 1630–1550 BC or shortly before,[1845] whereby some fled from Egypt to Crete to settle with their kin the Minoans, and some fled to Canaan and Jerusalem to settle with kin there, and that before the Philistines fled Crete Hyksos were regarded as the same people as the Pelastoi of Gaza.[1846] One should not be surprised to learn then that Minoan/Cretan Philistine hybrids and their Indo-Aryan allies chose to invade southwestern Canaan to reunite with their kin branches likely after a catastrophe, the Santorini/Thera volcanic eruption circa 1628–1530 BC.[1847] The Thera eruption set in motion a series of cataclysmic events like tsunamis[1848] and suffocating volcanic ash clouds that spread to nearby islands like Crete.[1849] This disaster was so comprehensive that refugees fled en masse from Thera and the Minoan empire in Crete.[1850] The *Tempest Stele* of Pharaoh Ahmose I, circa 1550 BC, seemingly recorded the fallout of Thera:

> ... . the gods declared their discontent. The gods [caused] the sky to come in a tempest of r[ain], with darkness in the western region and the sky being unleashed without [cessation, louder than)] the cries of the masses, more powerful than. .. [while the rain raged] on the mountains louder than the noise of the cataract which is at Elephantine. Every house, every quarter that they reached. .. floating on the water like skiffs of papyrus opposite the royal residence for a period of. .. days, while a torch could not be lit in the Two Lands [of Egypt]. Then His Majesty said: "How much greater this is than the wrath of the great god, than the plans of the gods!"[1851]

[1842] Ibid., 58, KTU 1.2.i.10 and notes 99, 100.

[1843] Bauer, *History of the World*, 184, 285, 286, 314–318.

[1844] Ibid., 314.

[1845] Ibid., 179; *Unger's*, 598: Hyksos.

[1846] Rohl, *Lost Testament*, 275, 276.

[1847] Bauer, *History of the World*, 184, 188, 189: footnotes; Ellis, *Tempest & Exodus*, 72, citing Michael 1978, Meuengracht 198; John Michael Greer, *Atlantis: Ancient Legacy, Hidden Prophecy* (Woodbury, MN: Llewellyn Publications, 2007), 106–110.

[1848] Ellis, *Tempest & Exodus*, 82, note 83: "In fact, whether the sea retreats first or not is a function of the geological event. If the sea floor rises, the first event witnessed will be the tsunami. If the sea floor lowers, the sea will retreat first before the tsunami rushes in. As it happens, the Thera wave event was caused by the collapse of the island into the present-day caldera, and so the sea would indeed have initially retreated."

[1849] Bauer, *History of the World*, 190.

[1850] Ellis, *Tempest & Exodus*, 322–323.

[1851] Ibid., 72, quoting *Une Tempete sous le regne d'Ahmosis, Revue d'Egyptologie*, 1967, 19.

The Cherethim were closely associated with the Philistines on Crete, and accordingly settled together with them in southern Philistia.[1852] Cherethim were described biblically as a nation within the greater Philistine nation.[1853] The Cherethim/*Krethiy*, defined as executioners, were foreign mercenaries, Cretans and proto-Philistines.[1854] Cherethim were Aboriginal Indo-Aryans of Crete and sons of the god Keret. *Nelson's Dictionary* states that the Cherethim were a distinct nation from Cretans, while the *Catholic Encyclopedia* notes that the Cherethim were a distinct tribe from the Philistines from Crete.[1855] The Septuagint translated "Cherethim" as "Cretans."[1856] Egyptian monuments from the time of Rameses III described the *Shayretana*, a people of the sea who were cognate to the Philistines. The first letters of *Shayretana*, the "sh," are pronounced "kh," as in the Cherethim/*Krethiy*, a people who supplied mercenaries to Egyptian pharaohs.[1857]

Some Cherethim were hired as mercenaries by King David, along with Pelethites and Gittites;[1858] Gath was an Anakim city. The Pelethim and Cherethim were mighty men, Gibborim.[1859] Pelethim were posterity of yet another unknown patriarch.[1860] The Pelethites/*Plethiy* are thought in most scholarly circles to be both Philistine mercenaries[1861] as well a distinct nation included among the various Sea Peoples,[1862] and in like manner as the Cherethim. In this line of research, the Pelethim name is derived from the Greek word *pelte* meaning light shield, for a Cretan nation of warrior mercenaries—a people and a name closely associated with the late Bronze Age and rise of the early Iron Age (sometimes called Iron I).[1863] Crete had a long and renowned history for supplying mercenaries. To this end, another related source word for the Pelethim name is suggested by some to be the Peletasts, meaning "medium-armed warriors"[1864]; Peletasts could easily be a transliteration of the *Plethiy* in Hebrew or *Pelte* in Greek.

The Philistines/*Plesheth/Plishtiy* were also identified with a group of peoples called the Peleset, renowned as part of the Aegean Indo-Europeans.[1865] Note as

---

[1852] 1 Sam 30:14. *Strong's Cyclopaedia,* Vol. 2, 231: Cherethim.

[1853] Ezek 25:16; Zeph 2:5.

[1854] H3774—*Krethiy, ker-ay-thee'.*

[1855] *Nelson's,* 257: Cherethites; *Catholic Encyclopedia,* Vol. 6, 400: Gaza.

[1856] Septuagint, Ezek 25:16; Zeph 2:5.

[1857] *Strong's Cyclopaedia,* Vol. 7, 877: Pelethites.

[1858] 2 Sam 15:18; 20:23; 1 Kings 1:38

[1859] 2 Sam 20:7, 1 Chron 18:17. Mighty ones: 2 Sam 20:23. H1368—*gibbowr.*

[1860] H6432—*Plethiy, pel-ay-thee':* courier; official messenger; name for the guardsmen of David; descendants of an unknown person; Philistine mercenaries.

[1861] Ibid.

[1862] Finkelstein, *Journals for the Study of the Old Testament,* Vol. 27.2, 149; *Strong's Cyclopaedia,* Vol. 7, 877: Pelethites.

[1863] Ibid., Vol. 27.2, 149.

[1864] Ibid., Vol. 27.2, 150.

[1865] Rohl, *Lost Testament,* 266.

well, the lords of the Philistines were the Shemau/Palast nobility, and longtime allies with the northern Hurrians and the Mitanni.[1866] One deduces Philistines were close allies with the Horim in Edom as well. All the various names applied to the Philistines link them with the Aboriginal giants of Crete and the Aegean basin, as well as with the Aboriginal giants of southern Canaan like the Aamu, Anakim, Horim, Amaleqim, and Avvim, just as the Hyksos were. Philistines seemingly accepted their eponymous name from a giant of Crete and perhaps *Plst* of the Pelethim.

Disparate documentation of the Philistines indicated at the minimum, a double migration from Crete:[1867] one before the time of Abraham and another just before the Exodus. Discerning this makes sense of Scripture recording King Abimelech and Philistines in Canaan in the time of Abraham and Isaac, which predates the Philistine migration (c. 1550–1500 BC) by several hundred years.

> Gen 21:32 Thus they made a covenant at Beersheba: Abimelech rose up, and Phichol the chief captain of his host, and they returned into the land of the Philistines.
>
> Gen 21:33 And Abraham planted a grove in Beersheba, and called there on the name of the LORD, the everlasting God.
>
> Gen 21:34 And Abraham sojourned in the Philistines' land many days.

Understood from the clear perspective of Abraham, and as understood by Moses and the Israelites at the time of recording the Torah, the kings of the Philistine confederacy were recognized as the same people as the migratory Hyksos/Aamu, versus an anachronistic style of writing claimed by some scholars.[1868] Two Philistine migrations to Canaan was seemingly a well understood premise in ancient times, as documented by nations like Egypt.

According to *Strong's Cyclopaedia*, Philistines comprised of at least two significant branches, and the Philistine ruling class was a distinct and proper branch and stock akin to the Hyksos kings. Herodotus, too, noted the Philistines were led by infamous and disgraceful shepherd kings of Philition or Philitis, and recorded as such likely because of the expropriation of large parts of the coastal regions of Canaan after the expulsion of the Hyksos from Egypt, and after the patriarchal age begat with Abraham, but before the Exodus.[1869]

[1866] Ibid., 276, 289.
[1867] *Strong's Cyclopaedia*, Vol. 8, 104: Philistines, citing Herodotus ii, 128, and Knobel.
[1868] Bauer, *History of the World*, 134.
[1869] *Strong's Cyclopaedia*, Vol. 8, 104: Philistines, citing Herodotus ii, 128, and Knobel.

Section V:
The Covenant Land Rephaim Wars

Exod 23:28 And I will send hornets before thee, which shall drive out the Hivite, the Canaanite, and the Hittite, from before thee.

Exod 23:29 I will not drive them out from before thee in one year; lest the land become desolate, and the beast of the field multiply against thee.

Exod 23:30 By little and little I will drive them out from before thee, until thou be increased, and inherit the land.

THE PHILISTINE
MILITARY COMPLEX

CHAPTER 42

*Judg 3:1 Now these are the nations which the L*ORD *left, to prove Israel by them, even as many of Israel as had not known all the wars of Canaan.. ..*

Judg 3:3 Namely, five lords of the Philistines, and all the Canaanites, and the Sidonians, and the Hivites that dwelt in mount Lebanon, from mount Baalhermon unto the entering in of Hamath.

The second Philistine/Caphtorim migration to the Covenant Land, after the Hyksos collapse in Egypt, expropriated most of Gaza from the Anakim, Avvim, and the Canaanite people.[1870] The Philistines restructured the Southern alliance, adding a complex military network of walled satellite villages to pentapolis city-state fortresses.

According to the *Americana Encyclopedia*, Philistines built a diverse confederation of cities, towns, peoples, and a robust military poised for perpetual war, both offensive and defensive.[1871] Philistines in the first migration to Canaan in the time of Abraham intermarried with the Anakim, Avvim, Amaleqim, Geshurim, and Horim, just as the second migration of Indo-Aryan Philistines did. Knowing this

---

[1870] Deut 2:23.
[1871] *Encyclopedia Americana*, Vol. 21, 761: Philistines.

begins to explicate the obscure title "lords of the Philistines,"[1872] as it related to the Philistine king Abimelech of Gerar in the time of Abraham.

Gerar was situated eight miles south of Gaza,[1873] one of the Avvim cities.[1874] Abimelech's name is understood as: my father is king, or Melech is my father.[1875] Abimelech was a Rephaim kingship title and was heraldic and patronymic like Agag or Hadad.[1876] As such, Abimelech surfaces again in Isaac's time, which likely indicates a different king, or perhaps Abimelech's son; and again in the epoch of the judges as a king of Shechem,[1877] the royal city of Hivvim.[1878] Abimelech in Abraham's generation was a powerful warrior king. Phichol, meaning strong, was Abimelech's captain of his host/army,[1879] in the tradition of Rephaim warriors. King Abimelech of Abraham's period was one of the originating lords of the Philistines.

Gerar was an ancient city-state fortress that controlled an important trade route, positioned just south of Hebron and toward the Mediterranean Sea;[1880] it was an important city in Israel's patriarchal period.[1881] The Hyksos built military bases at Jericho, Shechem, and Lachish, as well as Tell-el-Ajjul,[1882] with the latter located just south of Gaza city. Tell-el-Ajjul is likely Gerar or associated with Gerar. The Hyksos maintained relations with Amorites and Jebusites of Jericho and Jerusalem, the Hivvim of Shechem, and the Amorites of Lachish.[1883] Throughout the postdiluvian world and until the period of King Saul and David, the Southern alliance cooperated with their kin Philistine giants and hybrids of both migrations.

> Gen 10:19 And the border of the Canaanites was from Sidon, as thou comest to Gerar, unto Gaza; as thou goest unto Sodom, and Gomorrah, and Admah, and Zeboim even unto Lasha.

One notes the prefix syllable of Abimelech with kingly names documented in the *Execration Texts* and elsewhere, names like King *Abi-yamimu*[1884] and Abibaal

---

[1872] Josh 13:3.

[1873] *Unger's*, 467: Gerar; *Strong's Cyclopaedia*, Vol. 3, 814–815: Gerar. Gen 10:19; 20:2.

[1874] Josh 11:22.

[1875] *Unger's*, 7: Abimelech. H40—*'Abiymelek, ab-ee-mel'-ek*: father of the king; Melek is father; my father is king.

[1876] *Ibid.*, 7: Abimelech.

[1877] *Ibid.*, 7: Abimelech. Gen 26:1–31, Judg 9:1–5.

[1878] H2544—*Chamowr, kham-ore'*: donkey; Hivite prince of Shechem city of Shechem. Gen 34:2.

[1879] H6369—*Piykol, pee-kole'*: strong; Philistine King Abimelech's chief captain of the army in Gerar. Gen 21:32.

[1880] *Nelson's*, 488: Gerar; Bauer, *History of the World*, 132, 134.

[1881] Finkelstein, *Journals for the Study of the Old Testament*, Vol. 27.2, 153.

[1882] *Unger's*, 598: Hyksos.

[1883] Josh 10:5.

[1884] Billington, "Goliath and the Exodus Giants," 501, 506, citing Pritchard, *ANET*, 225.

of Tyre. The patronymic similarities in the kingship bloodline titles demonstrate a close relationship between various giant nations and hybrid Rephaim/human nations like the Amorites, Sidonians, and Phoenicians, further indicating that Rephaim held most kingships as strong, big, princes—Lugal.[1885]

> The Ruler of Iy'anaq, Erum, and all the retainers who are with him; the Ruler of Iy'anaq, Abi-yamimu and all the retainers who are with him; the Ruler of Iy'anaq 'Akirum and the retainers who are with him.[1886]

The Philistine lords, including early Philistine kings like Abimelech held close bloodline ties to the southern Hyksos Aamu and the Greater/northern Hyksos Shemau and their spawned the Indo-Aryan settlements of Caphtor, Caphtorim, and Kefitiu, with the latter being the Caphtorim transliteration in the *Egyptian New Kingdom Records*.[1887] Understanding this is the key to revealing the identity of the enigmatic "lords of the Philistines," and how some of their pentapolis city-states became controlled by Avvim and Anakim within the Philistine confederacy.

> Josh 13:2 This is the land that yet remaineth: all the borders of the Philistines, and all Geshuri, Josh 13:3 From Sihor, which is before Egypt, even unto the borders of Ekron northward, which is counted to the Canaanite: five lords of the Philistines; the Gazathites, and the Ashdothites, the Eshkalonites, the Gittites, and the Ekronites; also the Avites.

Anakim in the time of the Covenant Land conquest controlled Gath and Ashod, and perhaps other parts of Gaza,[1888] while the Avvim controlled Gaza/Azzah city as the Gazathites/*ha`Azzathiy*.[1889] Hence, the Philistines replaced much Avvim and Anakim, but Philistines permitted Anakim and Avvim to control three of the five pentapolis city-states, and to dwell among Philistines, Caphtorim, Cherethim, and Pelethim, as opposed to driving the Anakim and Avvim completely out. Philistines were centered at Eshkalon and Ekron. The Avvim dwelled from Sihor to Egypt (Josh 13:3), and from Hazerim to Azzah (Deut 2:23) before they were absorbed into the "Canaanite five lords of the Philistines" hegemony.

The Philistine confederacy was a military superpower of warrior giants and hybrid humans before and after the Covenant Land conquest, a networked nation of city-state fortresses designed for perpetual war. The Avvim's Hazerim/*Chatseriym*

[1885] *Mercer's*, 975: Lugal.

[1886] Billington, "Goliath and the Exodus Giants," 500, citing Pritchard, *ANET*, 225, 328.

[1887] Rohl, *Lost Testament*, 267 citing Gen 10:13–14.

[1888] Josh 11:22.

[1889] H5804—`*Azzah*; H5841—`*Azzathiy*. Gazathites: Josh 13:3; Gazites: Judg 16:2.

walled towns and villages[1890] were incorporated into the Hyksos inspired city-state military complex. Hazerim's singular format, *Chatsowr* from *Chatser,* means towns and cities protected by walls.[1891] The Philistine innovation spread to the Eastern and Northern alliances of giants. King Jabin's pentapolis that Joshua battled in the northern campaign included his royal city of Hazor/*Chatsowr* that derives from *Chatser.*[1892] The twelve pentapolis city-state fortresses of King Og's empire included unwalled villages as part of their defensive military strategies, the *praziy* of the Perizzim.[1893]

The Philistine pentapolis cities housed the "five Lords" detailed in 1 Samuel 6 as a complex network of "fenced cities" and villages, with the latter as an inherited network of fortified villages and towns of the Avvim, which were allies within the greater Southern alliance of Amalekites, Edomites, and Horim. The military network was described as both "fenced" cities and country villages, where fenced/*mibstar* is defined as a walled castle, fortress, fortified city, stronghold, and a defended town or village,[1894] which were accounted allegorically as mice in 1 Samuel's accounting of the Philistines returning the ark of the covenant to Israel:

> 1 Sam 6:18. .. the golden mice, according to number of all the cities
> of the Philistine belonging to the five lords, both of fenced cities, and
> of country villages…

The ark of the covenant, previously taken without God's permission by Philistines, was returned in an extraordinary narrative, where offerings were made to God and Israel by the Philistines in the form of images of five golden emerods that represented tumors from the disease afflicted upon the Philistines.[1895] The atonement offering included five golden mice according to number of the lords of the Philistines, the mice leaders of the five pentapolis city-states. The mice further represented the leaders of the villages, who marred the land.[1896]

> 1 Sam 6:11 And they laid the ark of the LORD upon the cart, and the
> coffer with the mice of gold and the images of their emerods.

[1890] H2674—*chatsowr, khaw-tsore*; village; castle; royal city of northern Palestine; city of Judah in the south; town north of Jerusalem; a site in Arabia.

[1891] H2691—*chatser.*

[1892] Josh 19:35.

[1893] Deut 3:5. H6521—*praziy, per-aw-zee*: a rustic village; unwalled; H2699—*Chatseriym.*

[1894] H4013—*mibtsar, mib-tsawr'.*

[1895] H2914—*tchor, tekh-ore*: burn; a boil or ulcer from the inflammation; piles; hemorrhoids.

[1896] 1 Sam 6:17–18, combined with 1 Sam 6:4–5.

Golden mice/`akbar is defined as attacking and as mouse nibbling.[1897] The allegory implied is that all the Philistines within their confederacy are no more than mice nibbling at the Covenant Land before God, with an added double-entendre dose of "attacking" that represented the vast Philistine military network of city-states, towns, and villages that marred the land. Mice/`akbar derives `akk-abiysh defined as a spider's web and a weaved network.[1898] It follows that `akbar represented the mice lords of the Philistine and the military network of walled cities, and villages. What I do not find to be coincidental is that Akbowr was the Hebrew name for Duke Akbor, a Horim king of Pau city in Seir, and a word derived from akbar meaning mouse or attacking.[1899] Akbowr/Akbar reflected the patronymic allegory for Rephaim warrior kings.

> 1 Sam 6:4. .. What shall be the trespass offering which we shall return to him? They answered, Five golden emerods, and five golden mice, according to the number of the lords of the Philistines: for one plague was on you all, and on your lords.
>
> 1 Sam 6:5 Wherefore ye shall make images of your emerods, and images of your mice that mar the land.

The military fortress networks were not mentioned in the war of giants likely because they did not yet exist. One cogitates whether the new military mice strategy was inspired or pioneered by Duke Akbor. Certainly, the Hebrew words are grouped together as though they were directly related in *Strong's Dictionary*: H5907 *Akbowr* as the source word, followed by H5908 *akkabiysh* and H5909 *akbar*.

The Philistine lords deployed their powerful pentapolis fortress and strategic mice network of villages and towns after carving out Gaza as their new home before the Exodus, which threatened and oppressed Israel for more than four hundred years thereafter. The Philistine Cretan superpower was readily accepted into the greater Southern alliance likely because of the revolutionary military technology they brought with them from Crete. Scripturally we understand the Philistines were skilled in the secrets of smelting iron from before 1400 BC. Judah could not annex Gaza because of the Philistine iron chariots and weapons, which perhaps explains why Israel did not take on the Philistine confederacy at the beginning of the conquest or after.[1900] Moreover, before Joshua died he added lands to Ephraim's allotment, the lands of Mount Hermon where the Rephaim, the Perizzim, and some northern Canaanites dwelled, peoples described as a formidable military force. Peoples that possessed the period's superweapon, the iron-enhanced

---

[1897] H5909—`akbar, ak-bawr`: same as 5908; in the sense of attacking: a mouse as nibbling.
[1898] H5908—` akkabiysh, ak-kaw-beesh`: entangling; a spider weaving a network or a web.
[1899] Gen 36:39. H5907—` Akbowr, ak-bore`: mouse; an Edomite duke, father of Duke Baal-hanan.
[1900] Judg 1:19.

chariot.[1901] One deduces the Southern alliance shared that iron technology with Rephaim tribes of the north, sold them the weaponry, or the northern giants already held the same Indo-Aryan technology via the Hyksos.

Further, the Ephraim narrative of iron weapons in Joshua 17 mentioned the city of Bethshean and her towns through out the valley by Jezreel.[1902] Bethshean was a city fortress with towns akin to the military network of the Philistines. Towns/*bath* also is translated as "daughters," just as the Philistine towns and villages were called daughters.[1903] Syrians called Bethshean in the Galilee the "House of Power," the "House of Sidhe," and Scythopolis, the city of the Scythians.[1904]

Philistines and their Hyksos Indo-Aryan allies controlled the early iron trade of the ancient world.[1905] Although iron is generally accepted in secular history as being discovered and popularized into military weaponry sometime after 1200 BC, scriptural accounts testify that the Philistines possessed mastery over the iron smelting technology well before then, which provided them a fierce advantage in war.[1906] Knowing this helps account for how the Philistines easily overran Gaza and other parts of the Covenant Land region after migrating from Crete. It follows that the Philistine iron smelting technology and supply came with them from Crete to reestablish Hyksos and Philistine dominance in the land of Abimelech.

Crete and Santorini were home to the Philistines and Minoans, both of whom fled the Santorini/Thera volcanic eruption circa 1628–1530 BC.[1907] Minoans were renowned for their skillful art of smelting bronze and other metals, as well as being famous for being the home of the legendary labyrinth, minotaur, and King Minos.[1908] One deduces the Philistines and Minoans learned to smelt iron before they fled. Anthropologists assert that ironworking technology spread from Mycenae along the sea trade routes, noting the latter Philistine nation originated from within the Mycenaean culture.[1909] Knowing this explicates the otherwise unaccounted-for iron bed of King Og biblically recorded in the Israelite eastern cam-

---

[1901] Josh 17:14–18.

[1902] Josh 14:16. H1052—*Beyth Sh'an, bayth she-awn'*; or *Beyth Shan, bayth shawn'*: house of ease; a place in Manasseh, west of the Jordan.

[1903] H1323—*bath, bath*: a daughter; granddaughter; daughter-in-law; sister; cousin, female child; town; village. Towns: Josh 15:45, 47; 17:11, 16; Judg 1:27; 11:26; 1 Chron 5:16; 7:28; 8:12; 18:1; 2 Chron 13:9. Villages: Num 21:25, 32; 32:42; 2 Chron 28:18; Neh 11:25, 27, 28, 30–31.

[1904] Wayne, *The Genesis 6 Conspiracy*, citing Gardner, *Realm*, 68; The Access Bible, Judith 3:10; 2 Maccabees 12:29; 1 Maccabees 5:52. *Josephus*, Ant., Book 4, 1:22; Book 12, 8:20, note 20.

[1905] Bauer, *History of the World*, 318–319.

[1906] *Unger's*, 1004: Philistines.

[1907] Bauer, *History of the World*, 184, 188, 189: notes; Ellis, *Tempest & Exodus*, 72, citing Michael 1978, Meuengracht 1981. Greer, *Atlantis*, 107–108.

[1908] Greer, *Atlantis*, 109–110; *Encyclopedia Americana*, Vol. 19, 211: Minoans.

[1909] Bauer, *History of the World*, 319: notes.

paign of the Rephaim Wars circa 1400 BC, a bed or technology passed onto the greater house of the Hyksos of Syria, the Shemau who abided among the Rephaim and their Amorite hybrids in the Mount Hermon region, and the Shemau nobility that merged with the Pelast nobility of Crete.[1910] As Manetho's history noted, "Hyk (`uk) was the Rephaite name for King," and "it has been inferred that Og [`Owg/`Uwg] was an attempt to represent the same in Hebrew letters."[1911]

> Deut 3:11 For only Og king of Bashan remained of the remnant of giants; behold, his bedstead was a bedstead of iron; is it not in Rabbath of the children of Ammon? nine cubits was the length thereof, and four cubits the breadth of it, after the cubit of a man.

The Philistine oppression of the Israelites throughout the generations of the judges featured an iron embargo against Israel. The Philistines prevented Israel from training blacksmiths from manufacturing their farm implements, for fear the Israelites would smelt iron for the use in weapons of war.[1912] Such was the respect and fear Philistines held for Israel's capability to wage war with inferior weaponry, let alone what Israel might do with iron. Iron smelting technology, combined with the Hyksos chariot technology, were the secrets to the hybrid Philistine pentapolis power, along with their military mice network.

Knowing the Philistine/Hyksos/Minoan/Crete and Indo-European relationships to the Sea Peoples, and to the Anakim and Avvim, makes sense of historians identifying the ancient god of Gaza, Marnas with "Zeus Kretagenes" (Gaia hid the infant offspring god Zeus in a cave from Cronus on the island of Crete/Kreta).[1913] Kretagenes means Crete-born but could also translate as gene of K'ret/Keret. What is most noteworthy in the Crete-Gaza god connection to Zeus is that Deuteronomy 2:23 clearly connected the Caphtorim to have settled in Azzah/Gaza. Further, Stephanus of Byzantium, a sixth-century AD author who published a geographical dictionary titled *Ethnica*, partially preserved in the *Epitome by Hermolaus*, noted that Gaza was once named Minoia after Minos of Minoa,[1914] for his patronymic ancestors.

[1910] Rohl, *Lost Testament*, 275.

[1911] *Strong's Cyclopaedia*, Vol. 7, 317: Og, citing "Jour. Sac. Lit. Jan. 1852, p. 363."

[1912] 1 Sam 13:19–22.

[1913] Finkelstein, *Journals for the Study of the Old Testament*, Vol. 27.2, 151, citing "Macalister 1965: 108–109; see also M.A. Meyer 1966: 119–21."

[1914] Ibid., Vol. 27.2, 151, citing "Meyer 1966: 6, 14, 119; de Vaux 1978: 505; Delcor 1978: 415–16."

CHAPTER 43

THE SERANIM AND SARIM

Judg 16.23 Then the lords of the Philistines gathered them together for to offer a great sacrifice unto Dagon their god, and to rejoice: for they said, Our god hath delivered Samson our enemy into our hand.

The "lords" of the Philistines were documented twenty-two times in the Bible to describe the underexplained Philistine kings.[1915] Oddly, "lord," in the case of the lords of the Philistines, does derive not from *'adonay*, meaning my lord, nor from *Yhovah* that is perplexingly translated as Lord or Lord's 6,530 times in the KJV.[1916]

"Lord," in the Philistine applications, is translated from *ceren*, meaning lord, ruler, tyrant, or plate, and pronounced *seh'ren*, cryptically deriving from an "unused root of an uncertain meaning."[1917] Historian Israel Finkelstein, identified the five rulers of the Philistine pentapolis as the Seranim,[1918] but in other biblical passages the Seranim are numbered as greater than five—yet another important clue to the composition of the Philistine hegemony.

[1915] Lords of Philistines: Josh 13:3, Judg 3:3; 16:5, 8, 18, 23, 27, 30; 1 Sam 5:8, 11; 6:4, 12, 16, 18; 7:7; 29:2, 6, 7; 1 Chron 12:19.
[1916] H136—*'Adonay, ad-o-noy'*: the Lord used as a proper name of God only; my Lord. H3068—*Yhovah, yeh -ho-vaw'*: the self-Existent or Eternal; Jehovah; the Existing One; name of the one true God; translated as Lord 6,412 times, Lord's 108, God 4, Jehovah 4.
[1917] H5633 —*ceren, seh'-ren*: a peer; lord; plate. Lord 21 times, plate 1 time.
[1918] Josh 13:3. Finkelstein, *Journals for the Study of the Old Testament*, Vol. 27.2, 136.

Ceren's transliterate plural format is Seranim, a mysterious word/title under-stood by scholars to be an adopted non-Semitic word into the Hebrew language.[1919] The Philistine Indo-Aryan branch language largely went extinct; only a few words survived. *Ceren* is thought then to be one of those surviving Philistine words. *Cereniym*/Seranim's etymology derives from and is cognate with Greek *tyrannos*/tyrant. Gyges, a king of Lydia in Asia Minor, was the first documented *tyrannos*.[1920] Earthborn Greek Titans were called Gyges, from the source word *gygas* for giant and gigantic,[1921] and from Greek *gigantes/gigentes,* from which King Gyges took his heraldic name.[1922] *Tyrannos* was introduced into the Greek language as the translit-erated equivalent of the Luwian word *tarwanas,* a title assigned to their rulers.[1923]

Luwian was a member of the Anatolian family of languages originated from or influenced by Indo-European languages, and a sibling language of the Hittites.[1924] Early Luwian cuneiform writings reflected their dynastic and dialectal origins from Indo-European and Hurrian.[1925] As such, scholars conclude the Caphtorim, Cher-ethim, Pelethim, and the Sea Peoples originated from Aboriginal Anatolian settle-ments.[1926] The Aegean Sea Basin settlers were part of the four or five branches of Aboriginal Indo-European nations.

The Indo-European kingship title, *Ceren*/Seran was accepted by Avvim, Phi-listine, and Anakim rulers that perhaps was re-introduced by the Cretan invaders. Seran is thought to have represented a political system governing over a league of cities.[1927] According to *Strong's Cyclopaedia*, Seran was a title awarded to many of the pentapolis kings,[1928] but not all, indicating a higher council of Seranim the kings of Philistine answered to.

Further, the Avvim Gaza city is believed to have held hegemony over the other city-states because Gaza was listed first in Joshua 11:22, 13:3, and Amos 1:7–8. When Gaza was not listed as the first city of the confederacy, another city was listed to express its specific prominence and context for that narrative, as in Ashdod in 1 Samuel 6:17, whereby Ashdod received the ark of the covenant first.[1929] Fur-thermore, there was a hegemonic pattern demonstrated in the pentapolis account-

[1919] Neil Asher Silberman and Israel Finkelstein, *David and Solomon* (New York: Free Press, 2006), 289–90; Finkelstein, *Journals for the Study of the Old Testament*, Vol 27.2, 136.
[1920] Silberman and Finkelstein, *David and Solomon,* 289–90; *Encyclopedia Americana*, Vol. 13, 587: gyges.
[1921] Donnelly, *Atlantis The Antediluvian World*, 294, 299; *Encyclopedia Americana*, Vol. 13, 587: gyges.
[1922] *Encyclopedia Americana*, Vol. 12, 637: giants; Rose, *Giants, Monsters and,* 132: gigantes.
[1923] Finkelstein, *Journals for the Study of the Old Testament,* Vol. 27.2, 136–137.
[1924] Ibid., Introduction, 5.
[1925] Ibid., 6.
[1926] Ibid, Vol. 27.2, 151.
[1927] Ibid., Vol. 27.2, 156.
[1928] *Strong's Cyclopaedia*, Vol. 8, 107: Philistines.
[1929] 1 Sam 5:6.

ings, and in the governing of lords and kings. Each city-state had its own territory and mice network/daughter of towns and villages,[1930] and within the confederacy of the other four cities and their mice networks.

The five Seranim dynasties continued until King Saul and David's period.[1931] Each were represented at the famous Shocoh dual between Goliath and David. David selected five smooth stones from a brook that day for his sling,[1932] not because he was fearful of missing; David was prepared to slay all five Seranim that day if required. Goliath was a giant Gittite from Gath, and seemingly the king of Gath,[1933] who was succeeded by Achish. Gath was one of the two cities of the Philistine pentapolis that Anakim still reigned from,[1934] and Achish was Gath's king when David sought refuge in Gath from King Saul.[1935] Achish was the son of Maacha, a prominent patronymic, matronymic, and heraldic name among the Maachathim Rephaim of Syria and Mount Hermon, for the posterity of the giant Maacha.[1936] Achish's Anakim father seems to have been given a patronymic name in honor of the Maacha dynasty or was a grafted Maachathim and Anakim bloodline via intermarriage. Further, the Achaean bloodline from Greece may have been embedded into Achish's patronymic name akin to Philistine royal titles like Abimelech.[1937] Achish/'Akiysh is defined as: I will blacken or terrify, but the last part of the compounded word, "ish," likely is the Hebrew word 'iysh meaning a champion, and/or a great man[1938] in this case. Hence Ach-ish likely means a great/champion/man descended Achaia/Greece, as in Crete and akin to Achilles' name.

Knowing Anakim, Avvim, Caphtorim, Cherethim and Pelethim dwelled among the Philistine hybrids begins to sort out the titles Seranim/Lords and Princes of the Philistines. In one of the Philistine wars against King Saul, David was still employed as a mercenary for Achish that provoked a controversy among the princes of the Philistines, whom Achish was answerable to. The princes were angry with Achish for bringing David to fight alongside the Philistines:

[1930] *Strong's Cyclopaedia*, Vol. 8, 107: Philistines. Josh 15:45, 47; 1 Chron 18:1; 2 Chron 26:6; 1 Sam 5:6; 2 Sam 1:20 (daughters); Ezek 16:27, 57.

[1931] 1 Sam 5:8, 11; 6:4, 12, 16, 18; 7:7; 1 Sam 29:2, 6, 7; 1 Chron 12:19.

[1932] 1 Sam 17:40.

[1933] 2 Sam 21:19; 1 Chron 20:6.

[1934] Josh 11:22.

[1935] 1 Sam 21:10.

[1936] H4602—*Ma`akathiy, mah-ak-aw-thee'*: a people dwelling in Transjordan, descendants of Maachah; *Nelson's*, 783: Maachathites.

[1937] *Unger's*, 21: Achish.

[1938] H397—*'Akiysh, aw-keesh'*: I will blacken or terrify; only a man; Philistine king of Gath; H376—*'iys, eesh*: a man; male person; husband; human being; a person in contrast to God; servant; mankind; champion; great man.

1 Sam 29:2 And the lords of the Philistines passed on by hundreds, and by thousands: but David and his men passed on in the rereward with Achish.

1 Sam 29:3 Then said the princes of the Philistines, What do these Hebrews here? And Achish said unto the princes of the Philistines, Is not this David, the servant of Saul the king of Israel, which hath been with me these days, or these years, and I have found no fault in him since he fell unto me unto this day?

1 Sam 29:4 And the princes of the Philistines were wroth with him; and the princes of the Philistines said unto him, Make this fellow return, that he may go again to his place which thou hast appointed him.

The lords were a part of a senior governing council of royals who appointed the pentapolis kings such as Achish that reported up to the senior council.[1939] Accordingly, Achish was summoned with other giant lords for the battle against Saul, where the senior princes objected to David. These princes were alternatively referred to as the Lords/Seranim in the same narrative, the ruling council of Seranim,[1940] governing the junior Seranim. Achish was ordered by the senior council to ensure David departed, whereby Achish advised David that he should not displease the "lords of the Philistines."[1941]

Achish was called king/*Melek* of Gath, not a lord or a prince, and Achish's other name/title was Abimelech.[1942] *Melek* was the usual Hebrew word for a king, versus Lord/Ceren; or Princes/*Sar*, in the "princes of the Philistines," defined as chief, general, prince, ruler, elder, a patron angel, and ruler for God,[1943] or gods. The male plural format was *Sarim*, for the elder/senior princes of the confederacy. As such, some scholars assert Achish's king title was a deliberate distinction indicating the military promise and influence, or distinct royal patronymic title of a different bloodline.[1944] Whatever the distinction intended, Achish was subservient to the to the shadowy lords/princes. The Sarim senior council governed the Philistine alliance of peoples[1945] and the kings, because of their ennobled Rephaim bloodlines of old.

[1939] 1 Sam 21:10.

[1940] 1 Sam 21:7, 9.

[1941] 1 Sam 29:7.

[1942] Ps 34:1.

[1943] H8269—*sar, sar*; from 8323; a prince; ruler; steward; a head person that had rule; chief; captain; general; governor; keeper; lord; patron-angel; Ruler of rulers (of God). 1 Sam 18:30; 29:3, 4, 9.

[1944] Finkelstein, *Journals for the Study of the Old Testament,* Vol. 27.2, 138. note 9; *Strong's Dictionary,* Vol. 1, 52: Achish.

[1945] https://www.britannica.com/topic/Philistine-people.

Although *Sar*/Sarim/Prince is not connected by *Strong's Dictionary* to another Hebrew word *s'ar*—meaning "hair" as used in Daniel 4:32–33 to describe Nebuchadnezzar's long hair when he was punished by God[1946]—there are obvious phonetic connections, and perhaps intriguing connections. Philistines and giants were renowned for their hair. *S'ar* derives from *se'ar* meaning hairy as in disarranged, untidy, rough and wild-like hairy,[1947] which in turn is derived from *sa'ar* meaning to storm, come like a whirlwind, to fear, and to be horribly afraid.[1948] *Sa'r, se'ar,* and *sa'ar* are connected in meaning to something sinister. What is noteworthy about *sa'ar,* translated as "afraid," is that this translation is used in association with the fear of devils/*shed* (pronounced shade), meaning a shade/sidhe spirit just one of the translations for *rapha* means spirit, shade, or ghost.[1949] One further ponders possible connections to the Terrible Ones.

Another word rooted in *sa'ar* is *sa'iyr,* a word translated as "satyr," meaning a shaggy/hairy he-goat, rough, a faun; devil, goat; possessed goat, and goat god[1950] like Azazel. *Sa'iyr* is a compound word with the *'iyr* for Watcher angel.[1951] The first of the compound word forming sa'iyr/satyr is *sa',* a contracted word from *sa'arah* meaning hairiness and hair, *se'ar* meaning hairy, as well as *s'arah* meaning a storm, hurricane, and or tempest, as does *sa'ar.*[1952] One suspects that *sar* for prince and chief derived this series of words. Further, one contemplates the etymological or orthographical connection between seraphim/*saraph*,[1953] and *sa'iyr* a degraded hairy-goat Watcher. And one ponders as to the connection between "raphim" in "seraphim" to the postdiluvian Rephaim and the Semitic source, *rpm.* The devil gods Israel were instructed not to worship, recorded in Leviticus 17:7 and 2 Chronicles 11:15, is translated from *sa'iyr*/satyr.

Sa'ar is translated as "afraid" in Ezekiel 32:10, and *s'arah* for "horribly," to form "horribly afraid" in a passage about the Terrible Ones, Rephaim kings, sent to the abyss. In Deuteronomy 32:1 and 7, *sa'ar* is the word translated as "feared" in conjunction with devils/*shedim*[1954] and gods. Additionally, Duke Seir of the

---

[1946] H8177—*s'ar, seh-ar'*; Aramaic corresponding to 8181: hair. Dan 3:27; 4:33; 7:9.

[1947] H8181—*se'ar, say-awr'*; from 8175: dishevelling; hair tossed or bristling; hairy as in rough; hair of an animal or man; garment made of hair.

[1948] H8175—*sa'ar, saw-ar'*: to storm and by implication to shiver, fear; be horribly afraid; dread; be tempestuous; come like a whirlwind.

[1949] H7700—*shed, shade*; a daemon; malignant devil; H7496—*rapha'*: ghosts; dead; shades; spirits.

[1950] H8163—*sa'iyr, saw-eer'*; shaggy; a he-goat; a faun: devil, goat; hairy; rough; satyr, a demon-possessed goat.

[1951] H5894—*'iyr, eer*: a watcher as in an angel; waking; watchful; wakeful one; watcher.

[1952] H8185—*sa'arah, sah-ar-aw'*; feminine of 8181; hairiness; hair; H8183—*s'arah, seh-aw-raw'*: a hurricane; storm, tempest; H8181—*se'ar, say-awr'*; or *saar* in Isaiah 7: 20: rough hair; disheveling; hairy: hair; garment made of hair.

[1953] H8314—*saraph.*

[1954] *Jewish Encyclopedia,* Vol. 11, 74: Satyr; Vol. 4, 514–521: Demonology.

Mount Seir derives from *Se`iyr*, meaning rough, hairy, and shaggy,[1955] deriving from *sa`iyr*.[1956] It follows that *se`iyr* is often transliterated as Se`irim,[1957] the hairy goat ones, and likely is linked to the Philistine Sarim/Princes.

From a prophetic perspective, *se`iyr/sa`iyr* is important because Alexander the Great's royal seed will produce the coming Antichrist beast king, described as a rough goat in Daniel 8:21. "Rough" is translated from *sa`iyr*, while "goat" is translated from *tsaphiyr*;[1958] Antichrist derives out of Greece that was divided into four empires.[1959] The same prophetic allegory surfaces with Antichrist in Daniel 11:40 when Antichrist rises to power wielding his military to strike "like a whirlwind," sa'ar, and *sa`arah*. Moreover, *sar*/prince[1960] is the same Hebrew word penned when Antichrist will magnify himself to be like the "prince of the host" at the time of the abomination. *Sar* is the same word used for the prince of Persia and Greece, beast empires.[1961]

> Dan 11:40 And at the time of the end shall the king of the south push at him: and the king of the north shall come against him like a whirlwind, with chariots, and with horsemen, and with many ships; and he shall enter into the countries, and shall overflow and pass over.

[1955] H8165—*Se`iyr, say-eer*: rough; an Idumaean mountain and its aboriginal occupants; hairy; shaggy; patriarch of Horites.

[1956] h8163—*sa`iyr*. Lev 17:7; 2 Chron 11:15; Isa 13:21; 34:14.

[1957] *Jewish Encyclopedia*, Vol. 11, 74: Satyr; Vol. 4, 514–521: Demonology.

[1958] H6842—*tsaphiyr, tsaw-feer*: a male goat prancing. Dan 8:5, 21: goat; 8:21: he (goat/`ez).

[1959] Dan 7:24–26; 8:23–27.

[1960] H8269–*sar*.

[1961] Dan 8:11, 25; 10:20, 21.

CHAPTER 44

THE WAR OF GIANTS

Gen 14:1 And it came to pass in the days of Amraphel king of Shinar, Arioch king of Ellasar, Chedorlaomer king of Elam, and Tidal king of nations;

Gen 14:2 That these made war with Bera king of Sodom, and with Birsha king of Gomorrah, Shinab king of Admah, and Shemeber king of Zeboiim, and the king of Bela, which is Zoar.

Most churches, ministers, or priests do not provide proper context for Genesis 14's war of four kings against five, as some name the war, or provide details about those kings and nations. Nor do churches teach in context the Rephaim Wars that followed some four hundred years later, in the Covenant Land conquest in the days of the Exodus.

The eastern Rephaim World Order, post-Babel, encompassed the giant Shinar/Sumer kings in the land of Nimrod, where the biblical king began to be a mighty one.[1962] Abraham left Ur, the land of Aryan giants and Nimrodian royal bloodlines, to settle in the land of Rephaim kings and Canaanite hybrids of the western order.

Nimrod remained in Sumer, the land of the "people of the east" that included the Kadmonim, Kenim, Kenizzim, Elamites, and Aryans. Nimrod intermarried with the giants of Elam to produce his dynasty of Shamau-like kings and bloodlines

---

[1962] Gen 10:8–9.

that in turn produced the beast kings and empires of Assyria, Babylon, and the Medes/Persia, and the Ur III dynasty of Uruk. Nimrod established his post-Babel empire in cities like Erech/Uruk, Accad, and Calneh from which Asshur, patriarch of the Assyrians, later built Nineveh, the Assyrian royal city.[1963] Shinar was the land between two rivers[1964] (Euphrates and Tigris) where Erech/Uruk was located (Gen 10:1). Uruk was Gilgamesh's city.[1965]

A relationship existed between Rephaim kings from Egypt, Greece, Canaan, and Mesopotamia. Knowing this makes sense that the Ugarit civilization maintained a version of the *Epic of Gilgamesh,* the hero king of Uruk. Gilgamesh and Utnapishtim were two-thirds god and one-third human. Gilgamesh was eleven cubits tall and four cubits wide: 19¼' tall and 7' wide using a royal cubit,[1966] and thus at least four feet taller than Og and one or two feet wider.

The founder of the Ur III dynasty, King Ur-Nammu (2113–2095 BC), and his successor son Shulgi (2095–2048) were bestowed with the hero title of "Lugal" (large man) and were kings of Ur city. Each claimed, in their royal mythos, genealogies from Uruk as brothers/family of Gilgamesh. Ur was the sister city to Uruk.[1967] As such, Ur-Nammu and Shulgi were giants. Shulgi was "the mighty man, King of Ur."[1968] Shulgi's royal accounting included the title of "The Avenger," some form of a miraculous birth, sexual ties to the goddess Inanna the Queen of Heaven, and support from other gods to ensure Shulgi ascended to King of Ur.

Secular researchers dismiss Ur-Nammu and Shulgi's claim, placing Gilgamesh as king of Uruk circa 2600–2700 BC based on dating the flood to circa 2950–3000.[1969] On the other hand, the Ur-Namu and Shulgi dating does fit with the biblical chronology that dates the flood to 2400–2450 BC, whereby Ur-Nammu and Shulgi reigned just after or at the time Gilgamesh of Ur's sister city of Uruk. Ur-Nammu and Shulgi's claims fit the fourth and fifth kings of Ur after Utnapish-

---

[1963] Gen 10:11.

[1964] *Unger's,* 371: Erech; 1185: Shinar. H8152—*Shin`ar, shin-awr'*; of foreign derivation: a plain in Babylonia country between two rivers; the ancient name for Babylonia or Chaldea.

[1965] *Encyclopedia Americana,* Vol. 12, 653. H751—*'Erek, eh'-rek*: length; long; a city in Babylon northwest of Ur on the Euphrates River.

[1966] Andrew R. George, *The Gilgames Epic at Ugarit,* 242, lines 34–35. Tablets 1 and 11; *Epic of Gilgamesh,* lines 34–36 of the Ugarit Gilgamesh. Both state eleven cubits high and four cubits wide.

[1967] John Miles Foley, ed., *A Companion to Ancient Epic* (Malden, MA: Blackwell Publishing, 2005), 236; John B. Nogel, "Mesopotamian Epic," *Gilgamesh Epic Traditions,* citing Jacob Klein, *Sulgi and Gilgamesh* (Las Cruces, NM: Two Brothers Press, 1976), 271–292; Marek Stepien, *From the History of State System in Mesopotamia—The Kingdom of the Third Dynasty of Ur* (Warsaw: Rektora Uniwersytetu Warszawskiego I Dyrecje Insytutu Historycznego, Akme, Strudia Historica, 2009), 10, 11, 16.

[1968] Marek, *From the History of State System in Mesopotamia—The Kingdom of the Third Dynasty of Ur,* 17, 18: "mu sul-gi nita kala-ga lugal uri".

[1969] Foley, *Companion to Ancient Epic,* 236; Stepien, *From the History of State System in Mesopotamia,* 10–11.

tim of the Sumerian flood story, as Enmurakar, son of Meskiagkasher, was third generation from Upnapishtim.[1970] Enmerukar is the biblical equivalent of Nimrod, third generation after Noah. The giant kings of Ur and Uruk set the context for the four Mesopotamian kings of Genesis 14.

King Amraphel in Genesis 14:9 was a Shinar king. Amraphel, according to *Ellicott's Commentary,* was an Akkadian name recorded on Babylonian cylinders that meant "the circle of the year."[1971] Amraphel's likely father, Amar-Sin, was the successor son of Shulgi and third ruler of the Ur III dynasty[1972] circa 2048–2000 BC. King Amraphel of the Bible reigned circa 2000–1975 BC. Amar-Sin and Amraphel, then, held genealogical ties to Gilgamesh, and to Nimrod, who reestablished the Shinar kingdom after Babel about 250 years previous to Amraphel.

Amraphel's name is thought to be of foreign derivation, but biblically defined as "sayer of darkness."[1973] In Sanskrit, Amarapala means "keeper of the gods."[1974] Amraphel is translated into English from Greek in the Septuagint as Amarphal.[1975] *'Amar* is a Hebrew word meaning to speak, boast, and to act proudly,[1976] as would a demigod. Amar-Sin was asserted as being Amraphel by Rohl, whereby Rohl noted Sin was a moon god/el with the same translated meaning as Amraphel. Conversely, Amraphel could be translated as *Amr*/Amurru is god. Historical dating of Amar-Sin and Amraphel also suggest a patronymic title passed from father to son.

Further, *'Amraphel* contains even more Hebrew etymological connections and meanings. *'Amar* is the source word for Amorite/*'Emoriy,* a people who later succeeded to the thrones of Babylon, and a word meaning mountaineer and a proud sayer.[1977] Amraphel might also be translated from a Hebrew understanding as broken into three separate words: Am-raph-el. The Hebrew meaning would be translated as: *'am* a people, tribe, nation, or men;[1978] of *rapha'*: a giant(s);[1979] of *'el*: a god, demigods, or mighty ones.[1980] As such, Amraphel was a Rephaim king of Shinar connected to the royal bloodline of Gilgamesh, Aryans, and perhaps a Kadmonim.

[1970] Rohl, *Lost Testament,* 58.
[1971] Ellicott, *Old Testament Commentary,* Vol. 1, 63.
[1972] Rohl, *Lost Testament,* 118–119.
[1973] H569—*'Amraphel, am-raw-fel':* a king of Shinar; sayer of darkness; fall of the sayer"; the king of Shinar (Babylon).
[1974] *Strong's Cyclopaedia,* Vol. 1, 207: Amraphel.
[1975] *Septuagint,* Gen 14: 1, 9.
[1976] H559 —*'amar, aw-mar'.*
[1977] H567—*'Emoriy, em-o-ree'.*
[1978] H5971—*'am.*
[1979] H7497 —*rapha'.*
[1980] H410—*'el.*

The second king of Mesopotamia listed in Genesis 14 was Arioch/*'Aryowk* king of Ellasar of Elam. Ellasar was the city of Asshur.[1981] Chaldean tablets indicate Arioch was Eri-Aku (servant of the moon god), the king of of Larsa/Al Larsa and son of the Elamite king, Kudar-Mabug.[1982] In Sanskrit, Arioch is known as Arjaka, meaning venerable.[1983] Rohl suggests Arioch was identified with Zariku, a ruler in Asshur during the reign of Amar/Sin, whereby Rohl suggests the "z" in Zariku is dropped (or silent) in pronunciation.[1984] Arioch was also listed as king of Sellasar in the book of Jubilees,[1985] with the "s" being silent akin to Zariku.

Ellasar city was just east of Ur, closely connected to the Ur III dynasty;[1986] it is thought to be the Babylonian transliteration of Larsa located halfway between Ur and Uruk.[1987] Ellasar was conquered by Eri-Aku's father Kudar-Mabug, who placed his son at Ellasar to rule, circa 2000 BC.[1988] Eri-Aku's name was inscribed as Uru-aku, in what is known as the "cone of Arioch" found hidden in a wall: "I am Uru-aku, the favorite prince of Nippur, the restorer of the city of Ur, the governor of the cities Girsu and Shirpnrla, who is revered in the temple Ebabbar. (I am) king of Larsa; King of Sumer and Akkad. .. the warrior who turns the enemy back."[1989] Some traditions transliterated Arioch's name as Urukh. Arioch was a non-Semitic name;[1990] perhaps Aryan with Ari in the first syllable. Arioch was further named in the *Targum of Palestine*, known also as *The Targum of Jonathan Ben Uzziel on the book of Genesis*, as the "Giant King Arioch" of Ellasar, and surprisingly as "tall among giants."[1991]

'Aryowk in Hebrew means lion-like.[1992] Arioch's name encapsulates images of the lion-like men/*'ariy'el* of Moab[1993] because *'ariy'el* is defined as: lion of God, heroic, lion-like, and sons of Ariel.[1994] "Heroic" brings to mind imagery

---

[1981] Cooper, *An Archaic Dictionary*, 188: Ellasar.

[1982] Ellicott, *Old Testament Commentary*, 63, Genesis 14: Arioch; Cooper, *An Archaic Dictionary*, 79: Arioch.

[1983] *Strong's Cyclopaedia*, Vol. 1, 395: Arioch.

[1984] Rohl, *Lost Testament*, 133,

[1985] Jubilees 13:22.

[1986] H495 —*'Ellacar, el-law-sawr'*: God is chastener; a town in Babylonia twenty-eight miles east of Ur.

[1987] *Strong's Cyclopaedia*, Vol. 3, 166; *Unger's* 360: Ellasar.

[1988] *Unger's* 360: Ellasar, excavations by the Louvre's Andre Parrot, 1932–33.

[1989] Edgar J. Banks, "Who Was the Biblical Arioch of the Days of Abraham?," *The Open Court*, Vol. 28 (1914), Issue 9, 557–559.

[1990] Cooper, *An Archaic Dictionary*, 79: Arioch.

[1991] Bane, *Encyclopedia of Giants*, 149: Sheshai, citing Boulay, *Flying Serpents and Dragons*, 198, 199; Deloach, *Giants*, 19; Taylor, *Ultimate Who's Who in the Bible*, 62.

[1992] H746—*'Aryowk, ar-yoke'*: lion-like; the ancient king of Ellasar, ally of Chedorlaomer; the chief of the executioners for Nebuchadnezzar.

[1993] 2 Sam 23:20; 1 Chron 11:22.

[1994] H739—*'ariy'el, ar-ee-ale'*; lion of God; heroic; lionlike men; two sons of Ariel of Moab.

of Greek heroes who were sons of gods, as well as "men of renown" in Genesis 6:4. Ariel may be a name of a fallen angel who produced lion-like Nephilim or Rephaim warriors and heroes of old. Ari-el moreover conjures images of Arian/ Aryans and the dynastic kings of Mede and Persian beast empires like Darius. Further, Elamites of Susa and Awan intermixed with wandering Aryans from the Indus valley, who intermixed with Amorites and were grouped biblically with the Medes and Persians.[1995]

The lion-like men/ *'ariy'el* used in 1 Chronicles 11:22 and 2 Samuel 23:20 is a related but distinct word from lion/*ariy* that was slain in a pit, and which does not have the el suffix,[1996] indicating the Moabite warriors were akin to lions but distinct. The lion-like men were valiant men/`*iysh*, as in champions.[1997] Some Gadite warriors also featured faces of lions/*ariy*. These lion-faced, lion-like warriors were swift men fit for battle. They were men of might and wilderness men, the latter word deriving from *gibbowr*.[1998] Hence the lion-like giant king Arioch/ Ari-Aku appears to be ancestral stock for the lion-like heroes of Moab and the *gibborim* Gadites with faces of lions. Arioch was either their postdiluvian lionmen patriarch, or a direct descendant of the giant patriarch, perhaps named Ariy.

Ariel/ *'Ari'el* surfaces six times in the Old Testament, meaning lioness of God, an allegorical name for Jerusalem, and for the altar in the temple. *'Ari'el* is classified the same as *'ariy'el*.[1999] Ariel could be a similar name of a fallen angelic and patriarch to Aryan giants, or a branch of the Aryans connected to the Persians and Medes. In fact, Ariel, meaning lion of God, appears in many apocryphal, gnostic, Coptic, and occult writings; and Aariel, the lioness of God, was inscribed on the Ophite (gnostic) Amulet along with Ialdbaoth.[2000]

The Renaissance-period occultist Agrippa referred to Ariel as a demon angel.[2001] In Kabbalism, Ariel is classified as a (fallen) virtue angel in the hierarchy (mighties/*doo'namis*); occult religions describe Ariel as a lion-headed angel[2002] akin to Nergal in Mesopotamia. Ariel is mentioned seven times in the gnostic gospel *Pistis Sophia*: "Then it is brought below into Amenti unto Ariel, that it may be

---

[1995] Bauer, *History of the World*, 88, 89, 104. Isa 21:22; Jer 25:25; Dan 8:2.

[1996] H738—*'ariy, ar-ee*'; violence: a lion.

[1997] H376—`*iysh: man*; husband; champion; great man.

[1998] 1 Chron 12:8.

[1999] H740—*'Ari'el, ar-ee-ale*'; same as 739: lioness of God; a symbolical name for Jerusalem. Ezra 8:16; Isa 29:1, 2, 7. H741—*'ari'eyl, ar-ee-ale*'; orthographical for 739; the altar of the temple; altar; hearth. H739—*'ariy'el*.

[2000] Guiley, *Encyclopedia of Angels*, 52: Ariel; Gustav Davison, *A Dictionary of Angels including Fallen Angels* (New York: Free Press, 1967), 1: Aariel.

[2001] Guiley, *Encyclopedia of Angels*, 52: Ariel.

[2002] Ibid.

chastised in his torments for twenty months. After that, it is brought into the chaos of Yaldabaoth and his nine and forty daemons."[2003]

In Sumer, Babylon, and Persia Nergal (Sumerian Enirigal)[2004] was a war god represented by the planet Mars in the seven wandering stars,[2005] just as was Aries was the god of war in Greek mythology. Nergal, son of Enlil and Ninlil, was a Chaldean, Assyrian, and Babylonian god worshipped as a man-lion idol at Cuth.[2006] Nergal/Nirgal/Nirgali/Irragal[2007] was a planetary ruler among the Babylonians and a protecting Genni (Jinn). To the Akkadians Nergal was a lion-headed god; to the Chaldeans he answered to Baal as a deity of Hades.[2008] Nergal was renowned as a great Watcher of the Anunnaki in the land of Sumer/*Shin'ar*, "the Land of Watchers," as one who observes like Enki.[2009] In Gnosticism, Nergal is the king of Hades, the chief archon in the nether regions, the god of war. In the *Collection de Clercq, Catalog, Vol. 3: Les Bronzes,* Nergal was depicted with a bronze lion head, winged, with clawed feet.[2010]

Evidently, Nergal was a popular deity before Ur-Nammu founded the Ur III dynasty, as well as during the Ur III dynasty, including Arioch's generation. Nergal was a powerful god mentioned many times in the *Epic of Gilgamesh* circa 2100 BC, and was described as a war-like hero, the offspring of Belit-ile/Ningal, and the god who opened a hole in the underworld for Enkidu's spirit to visit with Gilgamesh:[2011] "When I lifted up mine eyes, war-like Nergal sat on (his) royal throne, he wore his royal tiara, in his two hands he held two terrifying [missing]. .. weapons each having two heads [missing]. .. from his two arms issued lightening; the Anunnaki, the great gods, stood bowed at (his) right hand."[2012]

The Babylonian city Kutu/Cuth was the sacred city of Nergal known in Sumerian as Uragal, the great city.[2013] Nergal's titles were "King of Battle" and "Champion of the Gods."[2014] Tigaba was another sacred city of Nergal worship, which in

---

[2003] John M. Watkins, *Pistis Sophia* (London, 1896; electronic version, Leeds: Celephais Press, 2007), 319, 384.
[2004] https://www.encyclopedia.com/environment/encyclopedias-almanacs-transcripts-and-maps/nergal.
[2005] *Sumerian Dictionary*, 2, Mars: Nergal.
[2006] *Strong's Cyclopaedia*, Vol. 6, 950: Nergal.
[2007] Heidl, *The Gilgamesh Epic and the Old Testament Parallels*, 84–85, Tablet XI, note 185; 245: Irragal, another name for Nergal.
[2008] Davison, *Dictionary of Angels including Fallen Angels*, 206: Nergal, citing R. J. Forlong, *Encyclopedia of Religions.*
[2009] *Sumerian Dictionary*, 2: Sphere of the Zodiac: Enki (Igigi), Sphere of Mars: Nergal; 4, Igigi: those who see and observe; 5, Nergal: Great Watcher; 28: Watcher: Nergal the great watcher; Heidl, *The Gilgamesh Epic and the Old Testament Parallels*, 245, 84, Tablet XI, lines 101–106.
[2010] Davison, *Dictionary of Angels including Fallen Angels*, 206: Nergal.
[2011] Heidl, *The Gilgamesh Epic and the Old Testament Parallels*, 84–85, *The Gilgamesh Epic*, 99-100, Tablet 12, lines 73-99; note 238: the Sumerian version Nergal is the son of Ningal.
[2012] Ibid., 133–134, *The Gilgamesh Epic*, Related Material: Nergal and Ereshkigal, lines 11–12.
[2013] Ibid., 171.
[2014] *Strong's Cyclopaedia*, Vol. 6, 950: Nergal.

Arabian tradition that was a special city of Nimrod.[2015] Nergalsharezar of Babylon, meaning Nergal the prince of fire, was a prince in Jeremiah's time, demonstrating the importance of the Nergal god and his offspring kings.[2016]

> 2 Kings 17:30 And the men of Babylon made Succothbenoth, and the men of Cuth made Nergal, and the men of Hamath made Ashima.

Nergal was also a great hero and great king in Babylonian mythology,[2017] and a king and hero of Sumer akin to the earthborn Anunnaki giants like Gilgamesh and Sargon. Thus, Nergal produced postdiluvian offspring, and a patronymically named giant in his likeness, a war-like and lion-like giant king. Thus, Nergal's son was known as the "great man and great hero."[2018] The Shemite name for Cuth's Nergal god was Aria, signifying lion in Hebrew and Syriac,[2019] the war god of Medes-Persia[2020] Ur, Uruk, and Larsa/Ellasar,[2021] the latter being Arioch's city. It follows that Arioch was the offspring or descendant of Nergal/Ares/Aria/Ariel.

One muses whether there is an etymological connection of `Ariyts/Arytim, the Terrible Ones with Aryans and Arioch. Ariytim were an arrogant and evil seed line distinct from humankind.[2022] Aryan etymology originates with Old Persian "Ariya" meaning noble, family, and of a kind,[2023] and Iran's etymological root. Arian/lion-like bloodline kings like Arioch of Ellasar in Persia[2024] held an otherwise unaccountable place within the ancient world, as did Arisai, son of Haman the Agagite, who held a seat above all the vassal princes at Ahasuerus' court.[2025] Arisai/`Ariycay was patronymic from the Aryan bloodline; `Ariycay means "lion of my banners," a name of Persian origin.[2026] The Agagite Amaleliqim bloodline intermarried with Persian/Aryan bloodlines. Ahasuerus/`Achashverowsh was a title for a Persian king; likely Xerxes.[2027] `Achashverowsh's title was patronymically

---

[2015] Ibid.

[2016] Jer 39:3, 13. H5371—*Nergal Shar'etser*, from 5370 and 8272: prince of fire; a chief soothsayer; a ruler in the army of Nebuchadnezzar; H8272—*Shar'etser, shar-eh'-tser*: son of king Sennacherib of Assyria.

[2017] Davison, *Dictionary of Angels including Fallen Angels,* 206: Nergal.

[2018] *Strong's Cyclopaedia,* Vol. 6, 950: Nergal.

[2019] Ibid.

[2020] *Nelson's,* 507: gods, pagan.

[2021] "Nergal," *Ancient Gods and Goddesses,* http://oracc.museum.upenn.edu/amgg/listofdeities/nergal.

[2022] Gen 3:15; Ps 21:9–11; Isa 13:11; 25:5.

[2023] https://www.etymonline.com/word/aryan.

[2024] *Strong's Cyclopaedia,* Vol. 3, 172: Ellasar.

[2025] Ezra 3:1; 9:7–10. H91—*'Agagiy*: descendant of Agag.

[2026] H747—*'Ariycay, ar-ee-sah'-ee*; of Persian origin: a son of Haman; lion of my banners.

[2027] H325—*'Achashverowsh, akh-ash-vay-rosh'*; of Persian origin: Ahasuerus or Artaxerxes, but in this case Xerxes; two hor the title rather than name of a Persian king.

derived from Achaemenes, the Persian dynastic patriarch. Ahasuerus reigned from Shusham/Susa,[2028] a city connected to King Chedorlaomer of Genesis 14.

Knowing the Elamite connection to the Terrible Ones/Ariytim brings clarity to Enkidu and Gilgamesh's trek to Mount Hermon and the Cedar Forest to slay the giant King Humbaba, the appointed sevenfold terror, warrior, and the Terrible One that "Enlil appointed. .. as a terror to mortals."[2029] King Humbaba of the Cedar Forest was additionally documented in the twelve tablets of *The Legends of Izdubar* that detailed the slaying of the "tyrant Khumbaba" and destruction of Humbaba/Khumbaba's city and "at the hands of Izdubar,"[2030] whereas the *Epic of Gilgamesh* recorded Enkidu slew Humbaba and was alternatively named Hea-bani.[2031] Hababa/Humbaba/Khumbaba/Hea-bani's name derived in part from the Elamite god *Humba* and from *ba*, from which ban, bana, and bani were contractions of the latter communicating: the god "Humba has made me."[2032] Other compounded forms of Humba's name surfaced in ancient inscriptions for Elamite leaders: Humba-sadir, Humba-nigas (the king who opposed Sargon), and Humbaudasa the general that opposed Sennacherib.[2033]

The third king in Genesis 14's Mesopotamian alliance, Tidal, possessed the title "King of Nations," which holds clues to his generally underexplored importance to Amraphel and Arioch. Hebrew *Tid'al* means great son and chief of nations[2034] and fear, renown, and first in Semitic.[2035] The aggregate meaning suggests a great, fearful, and renowned son of a god with the transliterated last syllable *al/el*. Tidal was further recorded as Tudkhula on Arioch's brick,[2036] and as Thargal in the Septuagint.[2037] Tidal's empire of nations was not in Mesopotamia proper but was of close enough proximity to be an important ally or a vassal king. Rohl's research suggests Tidal was King Tishdal of the Hurrians during the Ur III dynasty.[2038] The Tishdal transliteration is consistent with *Strong's Dictionary's* accounting, whereby

---

[2028] Esth 1:1–2. H7800—*Shuwshan, shoo-shan'*: Susa; lily; winter residence of Persian kings; the river Ulai or Choaspes.
[2029] Heidl, *The Gilgamesh Epic and the Old Testament Parallels*, 84–85, *The Gilgamesh Epic*, 6, 11, 35, Tablet 2 line 5, Tablet 3, lines 96, 131-137; 6, Huwawa was the Baylonian name for Humbaba the terrible one: Tablet 3, lines 96, 109, 110, 150.
[2030] Smith, *Chaldean Account of Genesis*, 164, 168, 169, 188, 196, 251, Tablet 4, Col. 2, lines 10–17; Tablet 5, Col. 1, lines 1–45.
[2031] Smith, *Chaldean Account of Genesis*, 152–167: Tablet 2, Col. 4, lines 10–18; Tablet 3, Col. 2, lines 12–34; Tablet 4, Col. 4, lines 33–45; Col. 2, lines 12–14; Col. 4, lines 1–10.
[2032] Ibid., 144.
[2033] Ibid.
[2034] H8413—*Tid`al, tid-awl'*: fearfulness; great son; chief of nomadic tribes; ally of Chedorlaomer.
[2035] *Strong's Cyclopaedia*, Vol. 10, 401: Tidal.
[2036] *Easton's*, 1245–1246, Tidal.
[2037] Septuagint, Gen 14:1, 9.
[2038] Rohl, *Lost Testament*, 133.

Tidal derived from *dchal* meaning to fear, make afraid, and terrible.[2039] Horim/ Hurrim migrated from the mountains after 2400 BC, and accepted into their mix a splinter group of Aryans, the Maryannu,[2040] the Persians/Aryans. As such, mighty kings of Gentile nations, gowy/*goyim*,[2041] were the Terrible Ones. Tidal was king of many giant tribes from the Tigris River to the eastern borders of Media, which included the land that later became known as Assyria.[2042]

The fourth king in Genesis 14's Mesopotamian Alliance was Chedorlaomer/ *Kdorla`omer*. He was a Persian king of Elam meaning handful of sheaves.[2043] Arioch was also the son of Elamite king Kudar-Mabug/Mabuk circa 2100 BC,[2044] and possessed a similar title expressed in the first word of Chedorlamer's compound name. In Babylon, a King Kuder-mapula was recorded on bricks as the "Ravager of the West";[2045] some equate him with *Kdorla`omer,* which indicates Kdor, Kudar, or Kadar meaning king and/or son of Laomar. Some scholars believe Laomer is the transliteration of the Elamite god Lagamar.[2046] Kudur-Mabuk/Mabug further claimed the title of Adda Martu, the lord of Phoenicia, showing that he too, like Chedorlaomer, must have conquered Syria.[2047]

The Annals of Assurbanipal, king of Assyria (c. 645 BC) recorded his conquering of Elam and Susa. At that time Ashurbanipal reclaimed an image of Nana, which Kudur N Akhunte/Kudor-nanhundi had removed from Uruk earlier (c. 2280 BC). Kudor-nanhundi's Elamite dynasty later ended with Humbaba/Haba-ba.[2048] Elam city was populated by a distinct race that reigned from the southern shores of the Caspian Sea to the Persian Gulf.[2049] La`omar/Lagomar was an Elamite god of which Chedorlaomer/*Kdorla`omer* was a servant, son, or king of the local god. Other sources noted Chedor-la(g)omer of Elam was otherwise known as king Kutir-Lagamar of Susa, the loyal vassal king and tax collector for Amraphel, of the

---

[2039] H1763—*dchal, deh-khal'*: to slink; to fear; make afraid; dreadful; terrible.

[2040] *Nelson's,* 577; *Unger's,* 587: Horites; Bauer, *History of the World,* 470.

[2041] H1471—*gowy, go'-ee; goy, go'-ee*; massing; a foreign nation; a Gentile or non-Hebrew people; figuratively a troop of animals, or swarm of locusts; heathen, a people.

[2042] Ellicott, *Old Testament Commentary,* Vol. 1, 63, note 1: Tidal, Genesis 14.

[2043] H3540—*Kdorla`omer, ked-or-law-o'-mer*; of foreign origin: an early Persian king of Elam; handful of sheaves quoting Gesenius Thes. Heb p, 650b.

[2044] Ellicott, *Old Testament Commentary,* Vol. 1, 180, Excursus E: Upon Elam and the Conquests and Route of Chedlaomer, Genesis 14, citing Rawlinson, Sayce, and Tomkins.

[2045] *Strong's Cyclopaedia,* Vol. 2, 227: Chedorlaomer.

[2046] *Nelson's,* 256: Chedorlaomer; Ellicott, *Old Testament Commentary,* 180, Excursus E, Genesis 14.

[2047] Ellicott, *Old Testament Commentary,* 180, Excursus E, Genesis 14, citing Rawlinson, Sayce, and Tomkins; Cooper, *An Archaic Dictionary,* 294, Kudat-Lagamar.

[2048] Ellicott, *Old Testament Commentary,* 180, Excursus E, Genesis 14, citing Rawlinson, Sayce, and Tomkins; Cooper, *An Archaic Dictionary, Biographical,* 294, Kudat-Lagamar; Smith, *Chaldean Account of Genesis,* 147.

[2049] Ellicott, *Old Testament Commentary,* 52, Gen 10: Elam.

Ur III dynasty.[2050] Elamites occupied the cities of Susa and Awan from before 2700 BC in secular chronology (c. 2200 BC using biblical chronology); these people intermixed with wandering Aryans from the Indus valley, and with Amorites.[2051]

Chedorlaomer subjugated the five Canaanite cities of the plain for twelve years, requiring tribute. The Canaanite kings rebelled in the thirteenth year. Chedorlaomer then called in support from Amraphel's Ur III dynasty and his Rephaim-led allies. The alliance invaded west in the fourteenth year.[2052] The five miscreant Canaanite cities threatened the stability of the Ur III empire for quite some time, and the Canaanite refusal to pay tribute became the final insult.[2053] Moreover, the Ur III dynasty was continually threatened by Canaanite allies, roving Amorite tribes along the western border.[2054] Knowing this explicates and aligns Genesis 14:1's dating: "in the days of Amraphel" versus Chedorlaomer, which utilized the well-known reign of the Ur III dynasty to date the invasion.

The war of giants was the largest military campaign since before the flood, and perhaps for millennia thereafter with the Assyrian campaign circa 721 BC. The powerful four-king alliance marched west to war with the loose alliance of the Rephaim and hybrid human nations of Canaan. The Mesopotamians marched first to the Mount Hermon region, where they smote the Rephaim of Ashteroth Karnaim, the Zuzim, and Emim giants. From Syria, the locust-like army marched south to Mount Seir in Edom to smite the Horim, Amaleqim, and Amorites. After taking out the Eastern and Southern alliances of giant-like nations, the Mesopotamians then marched to the plain of Sodom to defeat the five Rephaim kings and their hybrid Canaanites.[2055] The Mesopotamian romp through the Covenant Land did not war against Hittites, Avvim, and Anakim for some reason, perhaps because the Mesopotamian alliance had no quarrel with them or because there were links between them. Perhaps the Mesopotamians feared the Avvim and Anakim, or were too weak by that point to engage them. One can only speculate.

The Sodom confederacy was a pentapolis city-state alliance, perhaps the forerunner to the enhanced Philistine pentapolis of Gaza.[2056] Little is known about the rulers/*qatsiyn* and princes/*sar* who governed the confederacy of the plain, but what is known revealed that those tyrants opposed God and oppressed those they considered mundane, humans loyal to God.[2057] As such, their names/titles of the kings provide a glimpse into their true nature. Sodom's *Bera`* was defined the "son

---

[2050] Rohl, *Lost Testament*, 118–119.

[2051] Bauer, *History of the World*, 88, 89, 104.

[2052] Gen 14:4–5. Rohl, *Lost Testament*, 118–119.

[2053] Ginzberg, *Legends of the Bible*, 104–105.

[2054] Bauer, *History of the World*, 139.

[2055] Gen 14:8–16, 14, 24.

[2056] Ellicott, *Old Testament Commentary*, 52, Gen 14: note 3.

[2057] Isa 1:9–10, 3:9–15. H710—*qatsiyn, kaw-tseen*': a captain; prince; ruler; chief; dictator. H8269—*sar*.

of evil"[2058] and likely a name from the Rephaim nomenclature. Gomorrah's *Birsha*' was defined as wickedness and iniquity; Admah's *Shin'ab* meant "splendor of the father" (brightness) and to alter or change; Zeboim's *Shem'eber* meant long wings like an eagle, lofty, figuratively a Babylonian king.[2059] The king of Bela/Zoar was unnamed.

After the Mesopotamian alliance crushed the Sodom confederacy, Lot was captured by the victors. Against the most powerful alliance of the early postdiluvian period, Abraham formed a posse of commandos led by Mamre the hybrid Amorite, a brother of Eshkol and Aner,[2060] whereby they somehow defeated the great Mesopotamian alliance of giants to free Lot. Mamre/*Mamre'* was a chief in Hebron/Kiriatharba whose name means vigor, lusty, and strength.[2061] The brother of Mamre was Eshcol/*'Eshkol* whose name meant cluster, which derives from *'eshkowl* meaning the cluster of grapes,[2062] from the region of the Anakim described in the scout's report from the Covenant Land in the time of the Exodus.[2063] Further, *Ellicott's Commentary* states Abraham dwelled in Hebron at the consent of the lords of that region, which included a league of mutual defense.[2064] Mamre was the place Abraham purchased a plot of land from the sons of Heth to bury his wife Sarah.[2065] Hebron was the city of Arba, the father of the Anakim, a region later ruled by Sheshai, Ahiman, and Talmai at the time of the Covenant Land conquest.[2066] One deduces the Abrahamic league may have included Anakim warriors among the Amorites hybrids of Hebron, which made the posse more lethal than is commonly taught.

The war of giants and its fallout set the geopolitical stage for the Nephilim World Order for centuries to follow. The destruction created the void for the beast

---

[2058] H1298—*Bera*', *beh'-rah*; of uncertain origin; a Sodomite king; son of evil.

[2059] H1306—*Birsha*', *beer-shah*'; from 7562; wickedness; iniquity; H7562—*resha*', *reh'-shah*: iniquity, wickedness; H8134—*Shin'ab, shin-awb*'; from 8132: splendor of the father; H8132—*shana, shaw-naw*'; to alter; change; to be changed; H8038—*Shem'eber, shem-ay'-ber*, from 8034 and 83: name of pinion as illustrious; lofty; H8034—*shem*, an appellation for a mark or memorial of individuality; honor; authority; character; renown; reputation; fame; glory; H83—*'eber, ay-ber*'; from 82: a pinion as in long-winged; wings like a dove or eagle; figurative a Babylonian king; H82—*'abar, aw-bar*': to soar; fly; to move wings.

[2060] Gen 14:11–13.

[2061] Gen 14:13. H4471—*Mamre', mam-ray*'; vigor; lusty; an Amorite ally of Abraham; strength or fatness; an oak grove on Mamre's land where Abraham dwelt; a place near Abraham's burial place in Hebron. Chief: *Strong's Cyclopaedia*, Vol 5., 687: Mamre.

[2062] H812—*'Eshkol, esh-kole*'; the same as 811: an Amorite brother to Mamre; cluster; an area of Hebron, the valley of Eshcol; H811—*'eshkowl, esh-kole*'; or *meshkol, esh-kole*': a bunch of grapes or other fruit; cluster of grapes or flowers. Num 13:22–24; Deut 1:24–25.

[2063] Num 13:23.

[2064] Ellicott, *Old Testament Commentary*, 52: Gen 14, note 13.

[2065] Gen 13:18; 23:16–19.

[2066] Gen 23:2; 35:27; Josh 14:15; 15:13–14; 21:11.

Egyptian empire to fill, and then to house the infant nation of Israel to grow into early adulthood as a stiff-necked young nation. The three kings of the Mesopotamian alliance—Amraphel, Arioch, and Chedorlaomer—was largely an Akkadian/ Elamite empire that spawned the rise of the Assyrian, Babylonian, and Mede/ Persia Beast empires. Tidal, the king of nations from the north, held ties to the Scythians and Aryans of Greece and Rome.

The fallout from the war of giants also permitted the Hyksos to rise to power, which in turn provided the opportunity for the Philistines to migrate from Crete to expropriate Gaza, establishing their pentapolis city-state nation after the Santorini catastrophes. Further, the destruction levied against the Covenant Land nations in the war of giants brought about a change in military strategy by the defeated nations. The Rephaim-led Canaanite nations begat more formalized alliances backed by evolving pentapolis city-states with giant and mighty walls. The new fortress city-state strategy was further backed by iron-enhanced chariots and iron. The Central, Northern, Southern, and Eastern alliances comprised the geopolitical world Israel entered into after fleeing the first of the beast empires, Egypt.

CHAPTER 45

THE BATTLE OF REPHIDIM

Exod 19:6 And ye shall be unto me a kingdom of priests, and an holy nation. These are the words which thou shalt speak unto the children of Israel.

Exod 19:7 And Moses came and called for the elders of the people, and laid before their faces all these words which the LORD commanded him.

Exod 19:8 And all the people answered together, and said, All that the LORD hath spoken we will do.

Israel proliferated into a nation of slaves during their four hundred years of servitude in the Egyptian beast empire, hardships that began with the Hyksos king "which knew not Joseph."[2067] Throughout Israel's Egyptian period, the sons of Lot—Moab, Ammon, and their posterity—drove out the Emim and Zamzummim.[2068]

Likewise, the Southern alliance was overrun by the Philistine confederacy that included giant nations from Crete like the Caphtorim, Cherethim, and Pelethim (c. 1550 BC), who expropriated the Gaza region.[2069] Anakim and Avvim

---

[2067] Gen 15:13, 16; Exod 1:8–9.
[2068] Deut 2:10, 11, 20.
[2069] Deut 2:30.

remained active within the Philistine confederacy in the cities of Gath, Ashod, the Hazerim, and Gaza city. Further, hybrid humans taller than humans but smaller than Rephaim dwelled among the various giants throughout the Covenant Land. All were dumbfounded as to what had just happened to the Egyptian empire. They sent ambassadors with frenetic messages among each other, discussing plots to destroy the Israelites.[2070] The demagogue who stirred the nations was the Amalekite Agag king:

> Those that induced the rest to do so, were such as inhabited Gobolitis and Petra. They were called Amalekites, and were the most warlike of the nations that lived thereabout; and whose kings exhorted one another, and their neighbors, to go to this war against the Hebrews; telling them that an army of strangers, and such a one as had run away from slavery under the Egyptians, lay in wait to ruin them; which army they were not, in common prudence and regard to their own safety, to overlook, but to crush them before they gather strength, and come to be in prosperity: and perhaps attack them first in a hostile manner.[2071]

The Amalekite/Edomite blood oath to wipe Israel from the face of the earth evolved into a transgenerational harem anathema, to carry the oath out to the end no matter the consequences. This blood oath was underlined by Josephus, who cited numerous biblical passages supporting his conclusion.[2072] Accordingly, Edomites, during Assyrian and Babylonian wars of destruction and exile against Israel and then Judah, reactivated the blood oath, attacking Israel and then Judah when they were most vulnerable.[2073] The blood oath will bubble to the surface once more when the end-time demagogue, Antichrist, endeavors to wipe Israel, Judah, and Christians from the face of the earth so that they will be remembered no more.[2074] This ancient conspiracy to wipe Israel from the face of the earth, to be remembered nor more, was dutifully recorded in the Psalms as "taken crafty counsel against thy people" by Edom, Amalek, Ishmaelites, Hagarenes, Moabites, Ammonites, and Midianites. All were nations that had claims to the blessings,

---

[2070] Josephus, *Ant.*, Book 3, 2:1.

[2071] Ibid.

[2072] Josephus, *Ant.*, Book 6, 7:1, note 15: "[The reason of this severity is distinctly given, 1 Samuel 15:18, 'Go and utterly destroy the sinners the Amalekites:' nor indeed do we ever meet with these Amalekites but as very cruel and bloody people, and particularly seeking to injure and utterly to destroy the nation of Israel," citing Exod 17:8–16; Num 14:45; Deut 25:17–19; Judg 6:3, 6; 1 Sam 15:33; Ps 83:7; Esth 3:1–15.

[2073] Amos 1:11; Ezek 25:12–15.

[2074] Rev 12:13–17.

birthright, and messianic promise beginning with Abraham[2075] if Israel was no more. Conspiracy/*Qesher* is defined by *Strong's Dictionary* as the unlawful alliance or confederacy, and as treason.[2076]

Accordingly, Israel's first battle was waged against the Amalekites before Israel sent scouts into the Covenant Land,[2077] when Israel was still a ragtag group of refugee slaves untrained in war. Israel did not have access to sufficient materials or manufacturing facilities to properly arm themselves and did not have adequate time to train their people for war. Throughout the Covenant Land conquest, Israel marched to battle nations stronger, greater in numbers, larger in physical size, and armed with superior iron-reinforced weaponry including the chariot.

The chronology of Exodus and Numbers placed the Amalekite war in the third month after leaving Egypt,[2078] and as recorded throughout Exodus 17. After departing from Elim, Israel made camp in the wilderness of Sin between Elim and Sinai on the fifteenth day, in the second month after departing from Egypt. From the wilderness of Sin, Israel marched to Rephidim, where Israelites murmured again because there was no water. God then provided Israel water from the rock.[2079]

> Num 33:14 And they removed from Alush, and encamped at Rephidim, where was no water for the people to drink.

Then came Amalek to Rephidim to wipe Israel from the face of the earth. Before the battle, Amalek tracked Israel in their desert movements for a period, where they harassed Israel and slew stragglers. Amalek came forward with their full army when they knew Israel was faint and weak from their journey:

> 1 Sam 15:2 Thus saith the LORD of hosts, I remember that which Amalek did to Israel, how he laid wait for him in the way, when he came up from Egypt.

> Deut 25:18 How he met thee by the way, and smote the hindmost of thee, even all that were feeble behind thee, when thou wast faint and weary; and he feared not God.

[2075] Ps 83:3–9; Isa 8:7–12.

[2076] H7195—*qesher, keh'-sher*; an unlawful alliance; confederacy; conspiracy; treason. Conspiracy: 2 Sam 15:12; 2 Kings 12:20; 14:19; 15:15, 30; 17:4; 2 Chron 25:27; Jer 11:9; Ezek 22:25. Treason: 1 Kings 16:20; 2 Kings 11:14; 2 Chron 23:13. Confederacy: Isa 8:12.

[2077] Num 13:1–33.

[2078] Exod 19:1–2.

[2079] Exod 17:1–7; Num 33:10–14.

The Amalekites and Amaleqim lived adjacent to the Seir region, south of the Covenant Land by the wilderness,[2080] and near to where Israel was wandering about. The Amalekite hybrids descended from Timna, and Amalek was led then by King Agag.[2081] The Amalekites were described as "old" inhabitants of Shur, a desert south of Palestine Israel marched through after crossing the Red Sea,[2082] and east of the Seir region of Horim and Edomites. Amalekites also dwelled with Geshurim and Gezrim by the Egypt border. Knowing this makes sense that giants reinforced the Amalekite army and that "Amalek was the first of nations."[2083]

The Amalekite intent was to dispossess Israel from their blessings, birthrights, and messianic promise by wiping Israel from the face of the earth. By doing so the Amalekites—via their genealogy through Esau, Eliphaz, and Amalek—thought to usurp Esau's lost and due inheritance as the firstborn of Isaac, the inheritance they believed stolen by Jacob.[2084] Amalekites plotted to replace Israel in God's Holy Covenant, to insert their dynastic Agagite kingship born in part from Elvin/Alluphim bloodlines from Seir, the Horim, and later Amaleqim bloodlines, to bring about their dragon messiah.

"Then came Amalek, and fought with Israel at Rephidim."[2085] Moses commanded Joshua to select and prepare his Israelite warriors for the battle to follow the next day. Moses instructed Joshua that he would stand atop a hill to oversee the battle while holding the rod from God in his hand, and that he would be accompanied by Aaron and Hur.[2086] During the battle, Moses stood atop the hill where he raised his rod from God with both hands above his head while the battle raged. When Moses' arms were raised, Israel prevailed, but when his arms tired and slumped downward the Amalekites began to prevail. Aaron and Hur assisted Moses through the battle to help keep Moses' arms raised until the sun went down. Thus was the determined strength of the Amalekite army that they would wage battle against Israel even though God was with Israel. Such was the faith and commitment to God by Israel, Moses, Aaron, and Hur throughout the day.[2087] The power of God was displayed before all Israel in a manner to assure Israel that if they had faith, were loyal, and lived in the ways of the Holy Covenant, even a nation untrained in war could and would defeat the giants and hybrid armies. The demonstration and lesson further communicated that if Israel did not do as they

[2080] Gen 14:6–7.
[2081] Num 24:7.
[2082] H7792—*Shuwr, shoor*: a wall; a desert region on the eastern border or within the border of Egypt.
[2083] Num 24:20.
[2084] Gen 25:26–34; 27:1–46.
[2085] Exod 17:8.
[2086] Exod 17:8–10.
[2087] Exod 17:10–13. H2522—*chalash, khaw-lash*: to prostrate; to overthrow, decay; waste away; weaken; disable.

later swore to in the Holy Covenant oath, the giant-dominated nations would easily destroy Israel.

By sundown, Joshua and his army "discomfited Amalek," as in wasted, overthrew, disabled, and severely weakened them.[2088] By day's end Israel had routed the Amalekite army. Amalek was defeated in this battle, but remained a very strong force in their eastern and southern locations, conspiring thereafter in tandem with other nations and alliances throughout the conquest of the Covenant Land, the epoch of the judges, and into the nascence of the monarchy with Saul and David. Nonetheless Israel, with God's help, had just defeated the most warlike nation of the Covenant Land region.

To memorialize this astounding victory, God decreed that the battle was to be venerated and written into a book, complete with the tally of atrocities and cowardice committed by the Amalekites—that their treachery and genocidal war was to be remembered from generation to generation until a time when God would command Israel to blot out the name of Amalek from under heaven,[2089] for their crimes committed against God and Israel. The unforgivable crime was not just the war Amalek fought against Israel but the plot to usurp the birthrights, blessings, and messianic promise bound into Israel's Holy Covenant with God.

One deduces that if all the miracles God had performed in Egypt for Israel and for the destruction of the Egyptian army in the Red Sea was not enough to bring about Israel's complete devotion and loyalty, God's patient and omnipotent power demonstrated at Rephidim against the Agagite-led hybrid Amalekites and giants[2090] should have. God demanded and often tested Israel's faith in exchange for His support against the spurious visible forces and invisible forces of this world, before delivering the Messiah via the curses of the covenant versus the blessings. The covenant was first sworn to after the battle of Rephidim, and as testified to in the passage introducing this chapter from Exodus 19.[2091] Israel achieved a special place in the history and future of humankind, in much more difficult manner than what could have been through the blessings of the covenant. Israel's commitment to the Holy Covenant decided whether Israel's future would be dominated and fulfilled through the blessings or curses of the covenant they swore to with God:

> Deut 28:1 And it shall come to pass, if thou shalt hearken diligently unto the voice of the LORD thy God, to observe and to do all his commandments which I command thee this day, that the LORD thy God will set thee on high above all nations of the earth:

[2088] Exod 17:13.
[2089] Exod 17:14–15.
[2090] Num 24:7.
[2091] Exod 19:1-25; 24:1–18.

Deut 28:2 And all these blessings shall come on thee, and overtake thee, if thou shalt hearken unto the voice of the LORD thy God.. ..

Deut 28:14 And thou shalt not go aside from any of the words which I command thee this day, to the right hand, or to the left, to go after other gods to serve them.

Deut 28:15 But it shall come to pass, if thou wilt not hearken unto the voice of the LORD thy God, to observe to do all his commandments and his statutes which I command thee this day; that all these curses shall come upon thee, and overtake thee.

The core principles of loyalty, following God's laws, His instructions, and His covenant was center stage in the long and arduous process of forging faith into the nation of hope, a nation of choice and destiny that ebbed and flowed with curses and blessings through their history.

After the battle of Rephidim in the third month of the Exodus, Israel departed Rephidim, pitching their tents at Kibrothhattaava in the wilderness by Sinai, until the first month of the second year. There, the people then began again to murmur against God, that they were led into the wilderness only to die from starvation.[2092] God then began providing manna and quail to Israel.[2093] The location was named Kibrothhattaavah, after the names of the people buried for their lusting after meat.[2094] Faith was not yet fully forged within Israel to fulfill their covenant obligations.

In the second month of the second year, after the manna and quail events unfolded, Israel journeyed out of the wilderness of Sinai to the wilderness of Paran.[2095] There, they camped until after the tabernacle was reared up, and after appointing the Passover Sabbath.[2096] Israel then marched to Hazeroth to make their new encampment.[2097] Thereafter Israel pitched their tents at Ritmah in the wilderness of Paran, just before Moses commissioned the scouts to explore the Promised Land,[2098] where the ragtag nation of slaves had their faith in God tested again.

For important context, one should consider all the miracles God had already performed for Israel before the scouts' report regarding the Promised Land documented in the Numbers 13 narrative. God further promised Israel after Rephidim that He would be an enemy to Israel's enemies; that God would send the Angel of the Lord before Israel to destroy the Amorites, Hittites, Perizzim, Canaanites, Hivvim, and

---

[2092] Num 11:34, 35; 33:16, 17; Deut 9:22.

[2093] Exod 16:1–35; Num 11:1–13; 33:11–14.

[2094] Num 11:34–35.

[2095] Exod 16:1–36; Num 10:11; 11:1–36.

[2096] Exod 19:1–2; 40:17; Num 1:1; 9:1–2; 10:11; 11:35–36; 33:25–26.

[2097] Num 11:36; 33:17.

[2098] Num 12:16; 33:18. H7575—*Rithmah, rith-maw*: a place in the desert northeast of Hazeroth; heat.

Jebusites.[2099] Additionally, God promised to send out hornets to terrify, confuse, and serve up the dazed enemy to Israel for slaughter.[2100] God guaranteed Israel's success in all things if they upheld the Holy Covenant and did as God commanded—promises that included giving Israel the Promised Land of milk and honey, good things for Israel, and use of the superweapon: the ark of the covenant.[2101] And God, at the time of the scouts' report, once more promised to drive out the illegal occupants of the Covenant Land if Israel did as God commanded.[2102]

Considering the Exodus miracles and guarantees God made before the scouts were sent into Canaan helps explain what the twelve scouts encountered in the Promised Land and reported back to the Israelites. Joshua reported that the land was flowing with milk and honey and provided some of the fruits of the land to the Israelites, and accurately detailed the mighty nations and Anakim that dwelled there.[2103] However, the terror-stricken and disloyal ten scouts stated "the land eats up the inhabitants thereof," and then inaccurately stated that the land contained giants/Nephilim (versus the Anakim/Rephaim, which were smaller by implication), and reported that (hybrid) men were also of great stature. The disloyal scouts exaggerated the Canaanite races as larger than the Amalekites and Amaleqim Israel had just defeated.[2104] King Sheshai of the Anakim was documented to be six cubits tall, 10'6" as measured by a royal cubit, so certainly a giant but smaller than King Og, let alone antediluvian giants.[2105]

> Num 13:32 And they brought up an evil report of the land which they had searched unto the children of Israel, saying, The land, through which we have gone to search it, is a land that eateth up the inhabitants thereof; and all the people that we saw in it are men of a great stature.
>
> Num 13:33 And there we saw the giants, the sons of Anak, which come of the giants: and we were in our own sight as grasshoppers, and so we were in their sight.

After all that was done for and performed by God before Israel, they believed the "evil report" by the frightened and disloyal scouts. The evil report terrified the Israelites, so much so that they rebelled against God, rejected God's promises of

---

[2099] Exod 23:22–23, 27; 34:1, 2, 11, 24; 40:38.
[2100] Exod 23:22–28.
[2101] Exod 33:1–3; Num 10:29, 32, 35.
[2102] Exod 3:8, 10, 17, 18; 13:5; 33:3; Lev 20:24; Num 13:27.
[2103] Num 13:26–27.
[2104] Num 13:29.
[2105] Bane, *Encyclopedia of Giants*, 149: Sheshai, citing Deloach, *Giants*, 260; Taylor, *Calmet's Great Dictionary of the Holy Bible:* Sheshai.

protection, dismissed what God had already done for them, and rejected the fruits of the land of milk and honey.[2106] One deduces the sheer numbers of giants, the many hybrid nations, the mighty fortress city-states, and their weaponry as an aggregate must have dwarfed the Israelite Egyptian and Amalekite experiences by comparison, to stir up such fear to oppose God's instructions.

But for the intercession of Moses on Israel's behalf, God would have destroyed Israel and started anew with Moses to produce a new Abrahamic nation spiritually stronger than this nation. God relented for the sake of Moses, Moses' faith in God, and Moses' belief in the Israelite nation. God forgave the Israelites for tempting Him "ten times, and have not hearkened to my voice," but also decreed that the generation of stiff-necked people would be relegated to a forty-year period to forge their faith, and a new generation raised in the faith would take hold of Israel's destiny—a duration long enough so that all who rebelled would die for their sins and not partake in the conquest.[2107] God then instructed Israel to turn away from the Amalekites in the valley, and the Canaanites in the mountains who dwelled southern Canaan, and to retreat toward the wilderness along the Red Sea.[2108]

> Num 14:11 And the LORD said unto Moses, How long will this people provoke me? and how long will it be ere they believe me, for all the signs which I have shewed among them?
>
> Num 14:12 I will smite them with the pestilence, and disinherit them, and will make of thee a greater nation and mightier than they.

God destroyed the disloyal scouts but spared Joshua and Caleb for their faith, loyalty, and for accurately reporting what they saw.[2109] In response to all that had just occurred, and guilt for their previous sins, many Israelites chose poorly to try to enter the land by going to war with the Amalekites and Canaanites. Moses warned Israel not to do so, because God instructed otherwise. God would not be with them and they would surely die, for their opportunity had passed in God's eyes. But some Israelites persisted in direct opposition to what God had instructed them to do: retreat to the wilderness.[2110] Israel once more defied God's instructions. They marched out to meet the Canaanites and Amalekites without Moses, the ark, and God—and were routed and chased all the way back to Hormah:

[2106] Num 14: 1–4, 8–10.
[2107] Num 14:10–24, 27–35.
[2108] Num 14:25.
[2109] Num 14:36–38.
[2110] Num 14:40–43.

Num 14:44 But they presumed to go up unto the hill top: nevertheless the ark of the covenant of the LORD, and Moses, departed not out of the camp.

Num 14:45 Then the Amalekites came down, and the Canaanites which dwelt in that hill, and smote them, and discomfited them, even unto Hormah.

Once more, many failed the test. This time they failed to follow God's instructions. In so doing, Israel had unwittingly gifted courage and optimism to their nemesis nations in the Covenant Land, that those nations could stand with their gods and defeat Israel. Thus, the conquest forty years later would come with hardened resistance and preparation from Israel's enemies.

God did support Israel in the conquest forty years later, but Israel was required to do battle for a generation, and in a similar way as they had previously defeated the Amalekites at Rephidim. Israel could only win with God's support. Conquest success would come to Israel, with many ups and downs akin to Moses' arms at Rephidim, an ebb and flow of success and defeat based on Israel's actions—a saga that continued throughout the epoch of judges, the monarchy, and the second temple, through the curses of the covenant versus the blessings of the covenant.

CHAPTER 46

THE BATTLE OF ATHARIYM

Deut 2:7 For the LORD thy God hath blessed thee in all the works of thy hand: he knoweth thy walking through this great wilderness: these forty years the LORD thy God hath been with thee; thou hast lacked nothing.

Israel received forty years of faith-forging to produce a battle-ready people prepared to war against giant-infested nations, a forging that was tested at the battle at Athariym and then Oboth.

The time had arrived for Israel to seize their destiny, to march into the dragon's den of fortresses occupied by the mighty seven nations, and to repossess of the Covenant Land.

Israel departed Kadesh to camp again at Mount Hor, where Aaron died. This march on the first day of the fifth month of the fortieth year after exiting Egypt marked an eminent turning point in world history, whereby Israel relaunched their commission to remove the Rephaim and hybrid humans from the Covenant Land.[2111]

Israel originally planned to depart Kadesh by marching along the seacoast (likely the Dead Sea) of Edom, then north. Accordingly, Moses sent messengers to Edom petitioning for safe passage. Moses sought permission to march through Edom, Ammon, and Moab to war with the giants east of the Jordan, to battle

---

[2111] Num 20: 11–13; 33:37–39.

against the infamous Rephaim kings of Mount Hermon, Og and Sihon. Parts of Edom, specifically along the route Moses marched through, were free from giants. Horim still lived in Seir, but some Edomites east of Seir drove out the Horim with God's assistance, as did Ammon and Moab.[2112] Moses dispatched his messenger to the king of Edom to gain permission to march directly through eastern Edom, but the king refused, threatening war if Israel entered his territory.[2113] Moses respected the decision by the Edomite king, and directed Israel to march back to Mount Hor.

God had previously proclaimed Aaron would die before entering the Covenant Land because of his insubordination at Meribah. Moses appointed Aaron's son, Eleazar, to succeed the priesthood leadership. Aaron died at Mount Hor, and Israel mourned his death for thirty days before leaving.[2114] From Mount Hor, Israel marched to the region where Moses had sent scouts to explore the Covenant Land forty years previous, which begat the infamous and embellished evil report. Israel marched to the place they knew as "the way of the spies," the road of 'Athariym, to address the failure of the previous generation, to test their faith in God before moving on. At 'Athariym, Israel was intercepted by Canaanite hybrids reigned over by King Arad.[2115] King Arad marched out his powerful hybrid army to destroy Israel.

Arad, according to *Unger's Dictionary*, was a southern Canaanite city in the Negev, positioned seventeen miles south of Hebron, the royal city of Arad. The Negev region was called the "south" country of Canaan, as recorded in Genesis 20, and was located between Kadesh and Shur.[2116] "South" derives from *negeb* from which Negev is transliterated from and understood as the southern desert district of what became Judah's land.[2117] The Negev was the region Abram made his home, a region that included Shur, the home of western Amalekites. Arad city was a mighty walled fortress originally built before the flood (c. 2700–2900 BC) that the postdiluvian Rephaim inherited and renovated, on the road from Petra (city of Amaleqim) to Kiriatharba (city of Anakim). Arad is defined as a fugitive, wild ass, a royal Canaanite city, and a Canaanite king.[2118] Arad, as a royal city, was part of the

---

[2112] Deut 2:10-12, 18–22.

[2113] Num 20:14–21.

[2114] Num 20:23–29.

[2115] Num 21:1; 33:40; Judg 1:16. H1870—*derek, deh'-rek*: a road; along; away; journey; passenger; through; toward; direction; "way of the searchers"; Ellicott, *Old Testament Commentary*, Vol. 1, 538: Num 21:1, note 1; H871—'*Athariym, ath-aw-reem*': places; Atharim; a place near Palestine; of the spies.

[2116] Gen 20:1; Num 13:17, 22, 29; 21:1; 33:40; as it applies to the conquest narrative.

[2117] H5045—*negeb, neh'-gheb*: parched: the south from its drought; specifically, the Negeb or southern district of Judah; occasionally, Egypt as on south to Palestine; south country; region of southern Judah.

[2118] *Unger's*, 91: Arad; *Strong's Cylcopaedia*, Vol. 1, 352: Arad. H6166—'*Arad, ar-awd*': fugitive; a wild ass; a Canaanite king; a royal city of the Canaanite.

greater Canaanite alliance, which was related to the pentapolis city-state alliance of Sodom on the Dead Sea plain.

As you will recall, Arad and Aradus/Arudeus were the Greek transliterations of Arvad(ite) in the Septuagint and according to Josephus. However, the Septuagint named the king in Numbers 21:1 as Arad.[2119] Josephus wrote, regarding Joshua's conquest wars, that Arvadites of the Sidon region were named Aradians: "But the parts about Sidon, as also those that belonged to the Arkites, and the Amathites, and the Aradians, were not yet regularly disposed of."[2120] As such, Arad was an important patronymic name of Rephaim kings, patrial for cities and places named after the originating patriarch, and a leading candidate for the patriarch of the Arvadites. Egyptian records as late as 920 BC, recorded in Pharaoh Sheshonq/Shishak's accounting of conquered cities, cited a king renowned as "Arad the Great" and "Arad of Yrhm."[2121] The King Arad at the time of the battle of *Athariym* was descendant of the first Arad, a Horim, Anakim, or Amaleqim, and a dynastic king.

Arad city was positioned seventeen miles south of Kiriatharba,[2122] the city of Arba of the Anakim reigned over by Anakin kings: Ahiman, Sheshai, and Talmai at that time.[2123] Biblically, Kiriatharba dates to 1800 BC and before, built before Zoan/Tanis in Egypt. Josephus noted that Hebron was 2,300 years old in his time (first century AD),[2124] suggesting by the odd way of dating in Numbers 13 that perhaps there were long-existing cultural ties between the two cities.[2125] Zoan was located in the eastern bank of the Nile delta, and defined as the "place of departure," the capital for the "Shepherd dynasty" (Hyksos), and the residence of the Pharaoh at the time of the Exodus.[2126] The Egyptian name for Zoan was *Ilaaicar* and/or *Panwar*, but the Semitic name was Avaris.[2127] Avaris was the city the Hyksos retreated to before being forced to depart from Egypt.[2128]

[2119] Josephus, *Ant.*, Book 1, 6:3. *Septuagint* Gen 36:39: Hadar is named as Arad.

[2120] Josephus, *Ant.*, Book v, 1:23.

[2121] *Mercer's*, 52: Arad: `Rd Yrhm, recorded in records of Pharaoh Shishak. Num 14:44; Deut 1:44.

[2122] *Unger's*, 91: Arad.

[2123] Num 13:22.

[2124] *Catholic Encyclopedia*, Vol. 6, 184: Hebron.

[2125] *Mercer's*, 367: Hebron. Num 13:22. *Catholic Encyclopedia*, Vol. 6, 184: Hebron.

[2126] H6814—*Tso`an, tso'-an*; of Egyptian derivation: an Egyptian city; Greek knew as Tanis; a city bank of the Tanitic branch of the Nile; the capital of the Shepherd dynasty; built; place of departure.

[2127] *Strong's Cyclopaedia*, Vol. 10, 1104: Zoan. Isa 19:11, 13; 30:4.

[2128] Ibid., Vol. 10, 1104: Zoan, citing Manetho.

> Num 13:22 And they ascended by the south, and came unto Hebron; where Ahiman, Sheshai, and Talmai, the children of Anak, were. (Now Hebron was built seven years before Zoan in Egypt.)

Arad was a royal city and, one deduces, the center for a pentapolis of allied cities as was the norm for Rephaim-governed city-states. Arad was recorded to be part of several cities of Canaanites destroyed at the time of the *Athariym* battle.[2129] The Arad Canaanite pentapolis would have been part of the greater Southern alliance. King Arad and the Canaanites got the upper hand against Israel in the first battle, taking many prisoners.

> Num 21:1 And when king Arad the Canaanite, which dwelt in the south, heard tell that Israel came by the way of the spies; then he fought against Israel, and took some of them prisoners.

The battles with Arad were a needed reminder that Israel could not defeat the giants and giant hybrids in a battle without the help of God—let alone perpetual war for a generation to push the spurious offspring out of the Covenant Land. God instructed Israel not to go up and fight with King Arad's army, but Israel persisted, against God's warnings. God was not with Israel in the first battle because Israel once more did not follow God's instructions. Thus, in the first skirmish Israel was roughed up by the Rephaim-led hybrid Canaanites and Amorites. They chased down Israelites like a swarm of "bees" from Seir to Hormah.[2130]

After the first battle, Israel did not cower away as the previous generation would have. This new generation of Israelites understood clearly after this battle that they would require the support of the God Most High to overcome the warrior nations, who wished to wipe Israel from the face of the earth. Thereafter Israel doubled down and vowed to God that if He delivered King Arad and his army into their hands, Israel would "utterly destroy" Arad's people and cities.[2131]

God delivered up the Canaanite hybrids and their kings for slaughter. Israel utterly destroyed them and their cities, naming the place of the battle Hormah. Hormah/*Chormah* means "devotion," as in devotion to God.[2132] Destroyed/*charam* is defined as consecrated, devoted, and as in this application to completely destroy, to devote to a religious destruction, to make accursed, and to exterminate.[2133] The term "utterly destroy" was the level of devotion Israel required to continue to

---

[2129] Num 21:3.

[2130] Deut 1:42–44.

[2131] Num 21:2.

[2132] H2767—*Chormah, khor-maw*; from 2763.

[2133] H2763—*charam, khaw-ram*: to devote to religious uses, especially destruction; make accursed; utterly destroy; devote or dedicate to destruction; forfeit, exterminate; completely destroy.

receive God's support, and to cleanse the Covenant Land of the spurious offspring, just as fallen angels had sworn to do against the Adamites at Mount Hermon.

> Num 21:3 And the LORD hearkened to the voice of Israel, and delivered up the Canaanites; and they utterly destroyed them and their cities: and he called the name of the place Hormah.

Israel's faith in God still was not yet fully forged. God knew this. Thus, God directed Israel to depart Mount Hor, travel south and then east around Edom, and then north through Moab and Ammon. God's decision flushed out many whose faith was still weak and still wished to question God's decisions; it was yet another test. Discouragement soon set in that led to murmuring against God, that God had led them to the desert without food to die. Then came the famous fiery serpent incident at Oboth.[2134] God sent poisonous "fiery serpents" among Israel, snakes with bites that burned like fire from their venom. The Israelites confessed they had sinned again against God, whereby Moses prayed to God that He might lift the scourge from them. God relented, instructing Moses to make a pole and crown it with a "fiery serpent" for the afflicted Israelites to look upon to remedy their affliction.

The fallout from the *Athariym* battle that was sorted out at Oboth, and the miraculous cure sent, rippled downstream into future generations. During the reign of Hezekiah of Judah (c. 715–686 BC), the king ordered the removal of all idols Israelites were worshipping at that time, which included the "brazen" (bronze) serpent.[2135] This brazen serpent was the cherished religious and historical artifact, the serpent image protected from the time of Moses and Oboth. Brazen/ *nchosheth* in this narrative means copper, brass, or bronze, just as the serpent was made of brass/*nchosheth* in Numbers 21. The serpent image was named Nehushtan, meaning something made from copper, to which Israelites burned incense before and worshipped; the name derives from *nchosheth*.[2136] The Nehushtan serpent was made of copper and was worshipped as a god, important details to discern the serpents described in the incident at Oboth.

"Fiery" was translated into English as an adjective for serpent, from *saraph* meaning burning— figuratively, the poisonous serpent from the burning sensation of the poison, and fiery six-winged copper-colored angels who minister before God

[2134] Num 21:4–10.
[2135] 2 Kings 18:4.
[2136] H5180—*Nchushtan, nekh-oosh-tawn*; from 5178: made of copper; the copper serpent of the desert; a thing of brass; name of brazen serpent made by Moses in the wilderness that was worshipped in the time of king Hezekiah; H5178—*nchosheth, nekh-o'-sheth*: copper; made of copper: brazen; brass; bronze; chain; filthiness; lust; harlotry.

in heaven: seraphim.[2137] Serpent/*Nachash* is defined as a snake.[2138] *Nachash* was the being in Eden that deceived Eve, and Satan is described as a serpent (*ophis* in Greek) in Revelation 12:9 and 20.:2. "Fiery serpent," *saraph nachash*, is used twice in the narrative and serpent/*nachash* is used singularly four times in the narrative.[2139] So the questions are: Were the Israelites attacked by fiery, copper-colored, serpentine angels, or were the Israelites attacked by poisonous copper-colored snakes?

One deduces the fiery serpents biting and killing Israelites were indeed snakes versus angels, and thus the translation ought to have been the "copper-colored poisonous serpent" definition of *saraph,* which better fits the narrative, versus "fiery serpents" as the KJV translated. Further, the "serpent" part of the "poisonous serpent" was not included to avoid the obvious redundancy of stating "serpent" twice, as in "poisonous/fiery serpent serpent." One further deduces the poisonous snake was the copper-colored *Echis coloratus* found in the Covenant Land region, Sinai, the Arabian Peninsula, Saudi Arabia, Yemen, and Eastern Egypt, or another copper-colored variety.[2140]

> Num 21:6 And the LORD sent fiery serpents among the people, and they bit the people; and much people of Israel died.

Echis coloratus was a snake Israelites were likely familiar with from Egypt, and often encountered in Sinai. The local copper-colored *Echis coloratus* was indigenous within Canaanite society as a serpent that populated copper mines in the Arabah and Sinai regions, as well as a renowned Canaanite idol representing their gods, akin to the flying serpent gods and goddesses depicted in Egypt, the Uraeus gods.[2141] Nissim Amzallag's research noted, "The account of the mass attack by burning serpents in Num 21:6–9 indicates that this species is abundantly encountered in the region between Mount Hor and the Red Sea (Num 21:4), corresponding to the Arabah Valley and its surrounding mountains. The most common venomous serpent in this area is a species of viper, Echis coloratus. As shown in Fig. 1, two subspecies of Echis coloratus coexist in Canaan. One, Echis coloratus terraesanctae, inhabits the Negev and the mountainous areas around the Jordan Valley and the Dead Sea. The other, Echis coloratus is a reddish morph encountered only in the Arabah Valley and its surrounding mountains, as well as in southern Sinai."[2142]

[2137] H8314—*saraph.*

[2138] H5175—*nachash, naw-khawsh'*: a snake from its hiss: serpent; snake; image of serpent; a fleeing serpent.

[2139] Fiery Serpent(s): Num 21:6, 8. Serpent(s): Num 21:7, 9.

[2140] Nissim Amzallag, "The Origin and Evolution of the Seraph Symbol," *Antiguo Oriente,* Volume 13 (Buenos Aires: Libreria Elcosteño, 2015), 99.

[2141] Ibid.

[2142] Ibid., 106.

Amzallag also noted that *Echis coloratis'* poison was deadly and produced an intense burning sensation.[2143]

Accordingly, the Bible provided another passage during the Exodus that states Israel was aware of these copper-colored poisonous (fiery) *saraph* serpents/*nachash* that dwelled in the wilderness desert with scorpions.

> Deut 8:15 Who led thee through that great and terrible wilderness, wherein were fiery serpents, and scorpions, and drought, where there was no water; who brought thee forth water out of the rock of flint.

Conversely, Moses's "fiery serpent," mounted atop a pole, cured anyone bitten who looked upon the mounted image (Num 21:8), and perhaps forgiveness for their murmuring sins against God. The translation from Hebrew to English by translators is equally as perplexing in this part of the narrative as it was in verse 6. In verse 8, "fiery" does not have a word assigned to it in the original Hebrew manuscripts but was added by translators. Further, "serpent" does not derive from *nachash* in this sentence, but from *saraph*, as in seraphim angels that minister in the fiery stones before God's altar. One of the seraphim took a fiery stone from the altar to remove Isaiah's sin.[2144] The Hebrew in Numbers 21:8 indicates the translation ought to have been "seraph," to indicate the Moses-made image representing a shining, fiery Watcher angel with a serpent's face with wings.[2145] The image atop the pole acted like a seraphim angel, and as a conduit for God's power. The seraphim translation for Numbers 21:8 explicates why Israelites worshipped the seraphim Nehushtan idol as a god of healing: a Raphael-like angel or an Uraeus god.

> Num 21:7 Therefore the people came to Moses, and said, We have sinned, for we have spoken against the LORD, and against thee; pray unto the LORD, that he take away the serpents from us. And Moses prayed for the people.
>
> Num 21:8 And the LORD said unto Moses, Make thee a fiery serpent, and set it upon a pole: and it shall come to pass, that every one that is bitten, when he looketh upon it, shall live.

[2143] Ibid., 109: "Burning effect: Two main types of serpent venom coexist in the wild: neurotoxic and hemotoxic. Neurotoxic venoms produce muscle paralysis accompanied by a cold and heavy sensation that spreads gradually from the bite wound. Hemotoxic venoms cause internal bleeding and rapid cell necrosis, stimulating a general inflammatory reaction due to the massive release in blood of cellular components. They provoke a sensation of intense burning that rapidly diffuses from the bite wound.. .. The venom of Echis coloratus also falls into the hemotoxic category; it stimulates an intense sensation of burning that rapidly diffuses from the bite wound."

[2144] Isa 6:1–7.

[2145] Dan 4:12, 13, 17, 23.

Seraphim idol worship is thought to have been introduced to the greater Canaanite culture by the Hyksos:[2146] "Furthermore, the serpent iconography in LBA [Late Bronze Age] and Iron Age Canaan displays strong Egyptian influence especially characterized by an abundance of uraeus representations. This uraeus symbol and the seraph have much in common: both are burning and flying creatures that are acknowledged for their protective functions, and both are similarly associated with divine powers and kingship authority."[2147]

The serpent/*nacash* made of brass cured only when Israelites looked upon it. *Nacash* was utilized singularly, and three times in Numbers 21:9 as such. The inference is that the image, only when looked upon, performed as a seraphim when God's power flowed through.

> Num 21:9 And Moses made a serpent of brass, and put it upon a pole, and it came to pass, that if a serpent had bitten any man, when he beheld the serpent of brass, he lived.

Thus, the image Moses made from brass represented the seraph(im) angel and not just a snake, but was not a live seraph based on the narrative. God then, through His omnipotent power, either sent a seraphim Watcher to work through the image to cure the Israelites, or did it directly. What does seem to be clear in the messaging, though, is that God was declaring He was more powerful than all the fallen seraphim gods idolized as Uraeus gods by the Egyptians, Canaanites, Sumerians, and cultures around the world.

One might anticipate seraphim imagery will return in the end times when Antichrist's House of Dragon begins to rise. Anticipate Babylon and Antichrist will declare God was just another Watcher equal to other seraphim archons, and that Jesus was a follower of the dragon angel, Satan, but was not the Messiah. The argument is and will be targeted to weaken Christians' faith. This polytheist argument is already in play, speciously drafting John 3:14 out of context and reimagined. As such, one must look at the context of the narrative and how the word serpent/*ophis* is applied. The passage does not say God or Jesus was a seraphim angel or a snake, only that Jesus would be lifted up on a pole/cross in a similar manner the serpent was in the time of the Exodus, as a sign and a prophecy for that generation of Judeans, for future generations of Christians and monotheists testifying to the validity of Jesus' credentials, and to the other nations that God

---

[2146] Nissim, "Origin and Evolution of the Seraph Symbol," 101: note 8: "Mettinger (1999: 743) assumes that the Hyksos introduced the Egyptian uraeus in Canaan and naturalized it into a seraph. Even the name saraph is interpreted by Morenz and Schorch (1997: 376–367, 372– 379) and by Wildberger (1991: 264) as a borrowing from two Egyptian terms: srf, denoting the act of burning, evoking the Egyptian griffin."

[2147] Ibid., 101, notes 6—10.

was with Israel even though Israel was stiff-necked—and that like the healing seraphim but not as a seraphim, all who look upon Jesus as the Word made flesh, and the One crucified to atoned for our sins will be cured, saved.

> John 3:14 And as Moses lifted up the serpent in the wilderness, even so must the Son of man be lifted up:
>
> John 3:15 That whosoever believeth in him should not perish, but have eternal life.
>
> John 3:16 For God so loved the world, that he gave his only begotten Son, that whosoever believeth in him should not perish, but have everlasting life.

Expect polytheists to imply Jesus was impaled on a pole versus staked to a cross. "Crucify" derives from the Greek *stowro'o*, meaning to impale on a post or on a cross with stakes, and derives in turn from *stowros',*[2148] defined as stakes or posts set upright in a cross formation. "Crucify" and "cross" could be translated as either a single stake or cross depending on the narrative and other related passages. In Numbers 21, pole/*nec* as it applies to this application, is defined as a flag, flagstaff, a pole, and a sign.[2149] Anticipate Antichrist will present counterfeit signs, based on John 3:14–16.

After the fiery serpent incident, Israel marched from Oboth to Ijeabarim in the wilderness before Moab, en route to battle King Sihon of the Amorites.[2150] Israel then marched to the valley of Zared, and then camped on the other side of Arnon in the wilderness at the border of the northeastern Amorites and Moab. Israel crossed the brook of Zered and to Kadesh/Kadesbarnea, which marked the thirty-eighth year of the Exodus. Israel encamped there until all the generation for the time of scouts exploring the Covenant Land died out.[2151]

[2148] Crucify: G4717—*stow-ro'-o*; from 4716: to impale on the cross with stakes as in crucify; to stake; drive down stakes; to fortify with driven stakes; to crucify; Cross: G4716—*stow-ros*: "a stake or post set upright or cross as an instrument of capital punishment"; by implication the atonement of Christ; a cross.

[2149] H5251—*nec, nace*: a flag; a sail; a flagstaff; a signal; sign; banner; pole; ensign; standard; something lifted up.

[2150] Num 21:11.

[2151] Num 21:12; Deut 1:46; 2:13–15.

CHAPTER 47

THE EASTERN CAMPAIGN

Ps 136:17 To him which smote great kings: for his mercy endureth for ever:

Ps 136:18 And slew famous kings: for his mercy endureth for ever:

Ps 136:19 Sihon king of the Amorites: for his mercy endureth for ever:

Ps 136:20 And Og the king of Bashan…

God commissioned Israel to war against giants and hybrids east of the Jordan, but not to war with Lot and Abraham's posterity who drove out giants.[2152] Moses summarized the eastern campaign in the book of Numbers after the campaign, providing additional details to the eastern wars in Deuteronomy 1:6–46 and 2:1—9.

The first king and empire engaged in the eastern campaign was King Sihon of Heshbon. Sihon was cataloged as a king of the Amorites.[2153] He dwelled in Heshbon but reigned from Aroer positioned across the Arnon River, which was regarded

---

[2152] Num 20:14; Deut 2:1–23.
[2153] Num 3:2; 4:46; 21:21, 26, 34; 31:4; 32:33; Deut 1:4; 2:24; Josh 9:10; 12:2; 13:10, 21; Judg 11:19; 1 Kings 4:19; Ps 135:11; 136:19.

as an outer boundary to the Bashan region.[2154] Aroer was Sihon's royal city where Israel camped opposite thereof, when they requested safe passage through Sihon's empire, but Sihon refused.[2155] As with Sihon, God ensured that the Rephaim kings would be foolish and try to wipe Israel from the face of the earth: "For it was of the LORD to harden their hearts, that they should come against Israel in battle, that he might destroy them utterly, and that they might have no favor, but that he might destroy them, as the LORD commanded Moses."[2156] The notorious Sihon and his empire were sentenced to be utterly destroyed/*charam*, by their refusal to let Israel pass.

Sihon and Og headlined the lists of infamous conquered kings that Psalm 136 proclaimed for following generations to contemplate. Once more the English translation does not fully convey from Hebrew the larger context to the passage. Great/*gadowl* is defined as older, haughty, proud, large in magnitude, and mighty, deriving from *gadal* meaning made large as in a body, proud, one who does great things, and powerful.[2157] Famous/*'addiyr* is defined as wide and generally large, powerful, glorious, a mighty one, a noble and a majestic one.[2158] Both Hebrew words describe giants akin to the Terrible Ones who were ruthless, strong, large and stout and used language akin to the Nephilim mighty ones and men of infamy in Genesis 6:4. Yet the language drafted in Psalm 136 was targeted at postdiluvian giants, to ensure they were not confused or conflated with their antediluvian predecessors.

Sihon and Og stood above other kings of the Amorites and Canaanites. Og and Sihon were singled out for their infamy, more so than Arad, Sheshai, Ahiman, or Talmai. Sihon and Og were so notorious that they were named in the Psalms instead of the Canaanite kings, even though the Canaanite kings were accredited as "mighty" kings who governed "great nations" in Psalm 135, similar to descriptions penned in Deuteronomy 7:1 for the mighty seven nations. Great/*rab* means many, great, and chief,[2159] while mightier/*'atsuwm* is defined as vast, numerous, countless, and strong. *'Atsuwm* is a participle of *'atsam*, meaning powerful as in a paw, and denominative from *'etsem* meaning "to crunch bones" and break the

---

[2154] Aroer: Josh 12:2. Heshbon: Num 21:26, 34; Deut 1:4; 2:24, 36; 3:2; 4:46, 47, 49; Josh 12:2, 4; 13:21.

[2155] Num 21:23.

[2156] Josh 11:20.

[2157] H1419—*gadowl, gaw-dole*; from 1431: great in any sense; older; insolent; haughty; elder; high; mighty, large in magnitude; more; noble; large in number. H1431—*gadal, gaw-dal*: to be made large as in body, mind, estate, honour; pride; boast; excellent; lift up; magnify oneself; do great things; make powerful.

[2158] H117—*'addiyr, ad-deer*; from 142; wide; large; powerful; famous; gallant; glorious; lordly; mighty one; noble; great one; majestic one. H142—*'adar, aw-dar*: great; magnificent; become glorious; majestic; wide; noble.

[2159] H7227—*rab*: much; many; great; chief.

bones,[2160] as recorded in Jeremiah 50:17.[2161] Mighty/ `atsam` was drafted to describe just how strong the giants were.

> Ps 135:10 Who smote great nations, and slew mighty kings;
>
> Ps 135:11 Sihon king of the Amorites, and Og king of Bashan, and all the kingdoms of Canaan.

Both were giant kings that reigned from Arnon to Mount Hermon over powerful empires in the "land of giants."[2162] Sihon's empire was separate from King Og's empire, as were the northern Geshurim and Maachathim empires, but all were understood as the land of giants in Bashan:

> Josh 12:4 And the coast of Og king of Bashan, which was of the remnant of the giants, that dwelt at Ashtaroth and at Edrei,
>
> Josh 12:5 And reigned in Mount Hermon, and in Salcah, and in all Bashan, unto the border of the Geshurites and the Maachathites, and half Gilead, the border of Sihon king of Heshbon.

Sihon's empire comprised at least thirty cities,[2163] at least six pentapolis city-state networks bound in a military alliance for defense and offense. This powerful confederacy of giants and hybrids included, among the biblically identified twenty-five cities, Ay city, along with many unnamed cities located west of the Jordan in the Chinneroth/Chinneroth sea region. Additional "cities of the plain" in Sihon's empire were unnumbered and unnamed.[2164] Chinneroth was documented in the book of Joshua as one of the "fenced cities," city-states west of the Jordan River that were a northern pentapolis that included Ziddim, Zer, Hammath, and Rakkath.[2165]

[2160] H6099—`atsuwm`; passive participle of 6105; H6105—`atsem`; from 6106; H6106—`etsem`; from 6105.

[2161] Jer 50:17: "the king of Assyria hath devoured him; and last this Nebuchadnezzar king of Babylon hath broken his bones."

[2162] Deut 2:20; 3:8, 11, 14.

[2163] Josh 13:16–21: Aroer, an unnamed city in the river, Dibon, Bamothbaal, Bethbaalmeon, Jahazah, Kedemoth, Mephaath, Kirjathaim, and Sibmah, Zarethshahar, Bethpeor, Ashdothpisgah, and Bethjeshimoth. Josh 13:25–27: Rabbaah, Heshbon unto Ramathmizpeh, Betonim; from Mahanaim unto the border of Debir and in the valley, Betharam, Bethnimrah, and Succoth, and Zaphon, Jordan. H5857—`Ay: Ammonite city east of the Jordan connected to Heshbon.

[2164] Josh 13:21, 27.

[2165] Josh 19:35. H3672—*Kinnrowth, kin-ner-oth'*; or Kinnereth, kinneh'-reth: Kinneroth or Kinnereth, Chinnereth, Chinneroth, and Cinneroth; G1082—*Gennhsaret*: the early name of the Sea of Galilee; a city near the Galilee Sea.

Heshbon city surfaces as an end-time reference for the destruction of Moab in the books of Isaiah and Jeremiah.[2166] Isaiah 15 extends out of chapters 13 and 14, with its prophecy of the Assyrian destruction by Jesus on the mountains of Israel, Mount Hermon/Sion,[2167] where the assembly of the gods is located. Moab's destruction will occur just before Armageddon.[2168] Heshbon, Moab, and Ammon will be destroyed like Sodom and Gomorrah in the day/year of the Lord's anger, a time like the days of Noah.[2169] Moab and Heshbon's end-time destruction was decreed by our King Jesus, whose name is the Lord/*Yhovah* of hosts/*tsaba'*, God's angelic army. The destruction will include slaying the mighty/*gibbowr* and strong men of war.

Jer 48:14 How say ye, We are mighty and strong men for the war?

Jer 48:15 Moab is spoiled, and gone up out of her cities, and his chosen young men are gone down to the slaughter, saith the King, whose name is the LORD of hosts.

Sihon was an audacious tyrannous whose infamy was legendary through out Israel's subsequent generations; a king documented thirty-seven times in the Old Testament.[2170] Sihon, before the Israelite battle warred with an unnamed Moabite King whereby Sihon viciously expropriated Moabite territory as far south as the Arnon River and Heshbon. Sihon ravaged Moab's royal city of Ar, the heights of Chemosh worship, and captured daughters of Moab for himself.[2171]

In Jewish legend, Sihon and Og were brothers—sons of Ahiah, son of a fallen angel named Shemhazai[2172] (Semyaza/Shemyaza/Azazel). Many linguistic experts contend Azazel and Semyaza were derived from the same Hebrew source word, but were spirited into two separate angels sometime before their introduction in the book of Enoch.[2173] Keeping Hebrew words in mind, Shamayazazel might be the preferred spelling and title that presents a true meaning to the fallen Azazel as the strong, harsh, mighty impudent (*az/azaz*) angel (*el*) of the heavenly ones

---

[2166] Isa 15:4; Jer 48:2, 34, 45; 49:3.

[2167] Deut 4:46–49; Isa 14:25–27, 15:1–9.

[2168] Dan 9:27; 11:31, 36–45; 12:11; Zeph 2:9; Matt 24:15–20.

[2169] Zeph 2:1–11; Luke 17:26–29.

[2170] Num 21:21, 23, 26, 27, 28, 29, 34; 32:33; Deut 1:4; 2:24, 26, 30, 31, 32; 3:2, 6; 4:46; 29:7; 31:4; Josh 9:10; 12:1, 2, 5; 13:10, 21, 27; Judg 11:19, 20, 21; 1 Kings 4:19; Neh 9:22; Ps 135:11; 136:19; Jer 48:45.

[2171] Num 21:26–30.

[2172] Ginzberg, *Legends of the Bible*, 460–461; Bane, *Encyclopedia of Giants*, 130: Og.

[2173] Collins, *Ashes of Angels*, 25, 26, 118. Davison, *Dictionary of Angels including the Fallen Angels*, 265: Semjaza, citing Allegro, *Vocabulaire de l'Anghlologie*, identifies Semyaza with Azazel.

of infamy (*Shamayim/Shemeh/Shem*).[2174] In Byron's version or recreation of the book of Enoch called *Heaven and Earth, a Mystery*, Semyaza was transliterated into Azazel,[2175] or vice versa.

Shemhazai, recorded in Jewish legend by its inference, appears to be a post-diluvian god of the Baalim, godfather of Ahiah, and thus Ahiah was likely a brother to Sihon and Og, as Og was the last of the original Rephaim. Josephus recorded that Sihon was Og's best friend,[2176] and scripturally Sihon was an equal to Og. Ahiah in some circles is regarded as a transliteration of Hiyya/Hahya, an antediluvian giant and brother of Ohya, the sons of Semyaza/Azazel.[2177] Naming postdiluvian giants after antediluvian giants was common, as was the case with King Gilgamesh of Uruk, who seemingly was named after the giant recorded in the Enochian *Book of Giants*.[2178] Ahiah has `ach as its first syllable that means brother.[2179] Ahi/`ach appears in proper names and is reflected in the Ahiah's name that derives '*Achiyah* meaning brother or worshipper of God, as understood by Israelites as in Ahijah/'*Achiyah*.[2180] It follows that the legendary giant, Ahiah, if he existed, was a brother of Og and Sihon and of the same tribe from Rapha. Moreover, ahi/'*ach* is the first word of the compounded name Ahiman/'*Achiyman*, meaning my brother is a gift or a portion.[2181] Ahiah likely was the patronymic source for Ahiman/'*Achiyman*, son of Anak.

As such, Sihon was described as of enormous stature, a giant in legend who was fleet of foot: "Sihon, 'foal,' to indicate the celerity with which he moved."[2182] Sihon/*Ciychown* is defined in Hebrew as "warrior,"[2183] but according to legend Sihon's original name was Arad, for whom the king of Arad of the battle of *Athariym* was seemingly patronymically named. Perhaps the original spelling was `*Irad*, the name

[2174] H8064—*shamayim*; H5794—`az; H5810—`azaz; H8034—*shem*. Semjaza: Enoch 6:3; 8:2; 9:7; 10:11. Semiazaz: 6:7; Samjaza: 69:2, along with Azazel two times in the famous twenty-two. In 8:1–2 and 10:8–11 Azazel and Semjaza appear together but seemingly are the same angel.

[2175] Davison, *Dictionary of Angels including Fallen Angels*, 265: Semjaza.

[2176] Josephus, *Ant.*, Book 4, 5:3.

[2177] Davison, *Dictionary of Angels including Fallen Angels*, 12: Ahiah; Lumpkin, *The Book of Giants, The Watchers, Nephilim, and The Book of Enoch*, 4Q530, fragment 4, 7.

[2178] Lumpkin, *The Book of Giants, The Watchers, Nephilim, and The Book of Enoch*, 4Q531, fragment 1; 4Q530, Col. 2.

[2179] H251—'*ach, awkh*: a brother; kindred; in proper names as a prefix, "ah" or "ahi."

[2180] H281—'*Achiyah, akh-ee-yaw*; or '*Achiyahuw*: brother or worshipper of Jah as in Achijah; Ahiah, Ahijah; brother of Jehovah Yahu; one of David's mighty men.

[2181] H289—'*Achiyman, akh-ee-man*'; or '*Achiyman akh-ee-mawn*'; from 251 and 4480: brother of a portion or a gift; my brother is a gift; name of an Anakite; a son of Anak; name of a Levite; H251—'*ach, awkh*: a brother; kindred; like; half-brother; kinship; same tribe; same resemblance.

[2182] Ginzberg, *Legends of the Bible*, 460–461.

[2183] H5511—*Ciychown, see-khone*'; or *Ciychon, see-khone*': tempestuous; an Amoritish king of the Transjordan; warrior; king of the Amorites at the time of the conquest.

of "an antediluvian" meaning "fugitive" and "fleet" and cognate with Arad.[2184] *Strong's Cyclopaedia* stated regarding Sihon's biblical accounting: "the name of Sihon fixed itself in the national mind, and the space which his image occupies in the official records and in the later poetry of Israel, that he was a truly a formidable chieftain."[2185]

After receiving Israel's request to pass through, Sihon impulsively commanded his empire to gather in preparation for total war against Israel. Even though Sihon possessed numerous and seemingly impregnable fortresses, Sihon's hubris and with his hardened heart assembled his armies to battle in open warfare against Israel. Sihon recklessly marched his multitude to Jahaz to war with Israel,[2186] to swarm them like bees and wipe them from the face of the earth. However, Israel easily defeated Sihon's massive army of giants, hybrid Amorites, and all their state-of-the-art weaponry, likely because God sent the hornets He had promised, to confuse and deliver up the powerful armies Israel would encounter.[2187] Josephus described Sihon's enormous army as not able to stand against the Israelite army, that Sihon's army turned from confidence to "timorous," whereby the multitude fled in panic.[2188] Sihon's disoriented army fled toward their fortified cities in such a discombobulated state that the Israelites chased, caught, and slew the giants with ease from beneath their light armor, utilizing spears, arrows, and slings.[2189] Israel then conquered all of Sihon's great cities, took all the villages, and expropriated all of Sihon's land from "Arnon unto Jabbok." Israel plundered the spoils of the cities, plundered the cattle, smote the people, and slew Sihon and his sons.[2190] The battle of Jehaz marked in earnest the beginning of the Covenant Land conquest.[2191] The battle success at Jehaz marked the start of a new promise God made just before the battle: that He would place dread, fear, and anguish in the minds of all the nations under heaven from reports they would hear of the slaughter of one of greatest warrior kings and armies of that time.[2192]

After the battle of Jahaz, Israel marched on Jaazer/Jazer, taking all the villages of the Amorites.[2193] I find it interesting that Scripture noted the taking of the Amorites, their villages, and cities as a separate account, indicating the northern

---

[2184] H589 —'*Iyrad, ee-rawd'*; fugitive; Irad, an antediluvian; "fleet."

[2185] *Strong's Cyclopaedia*, Vol. 9, 737: Sihon.

[2186] Num 21:23; Deut 2:32; Judg 11:20.

[2187] Exod 23:28, Deut 7:20; Josh 24:12.

[2188] Josephus, *Ant.*, Book 4, 5:2.

[2189] Ibid.

[2190] Num 21:24–25, 35; Deut 2:33–37.

[2191] Num 21:31; Deut 2:31.

[2192] Deut 2:25.

[2193] Num 21:31–32. Jazer: Num 32:1, 3; Josh 13:25; 21:39; 2 Sam 24:5; 1 Chron 6:81; 26:31, Isa 16:8, 9; Jer 48:32. Jaazer: Num 21:32; 32:35.

Amorites maintained a separate pentapolis within the Sihon or Og empire, but were vassal kings and cities thereof.

Israel then marched toward Bashan, where Og and his Amorite/Rephaim army met Israel for the battle at Edrei.[2194] Og's name surfaces twenty-three times in Scripture, less than Sihon.[2195] Nonetheless Og was a renowned and notorious ancient king. Og/`Owg's name means long-necked and round, indicating he was serpent-like from the neck up and was stout.[2196] Anak and Anakim also were defined as long-necked, indicating a relationship between Og and Arba and Anakim. Rephaim's serpent-like necks may have been long and wide, cobra-like, akin to pharaonic headdress—strong necks that supported suture-less elongated skulls, and serpentine faces crowning muscularly stout and tall frames.

Og, and by inference Sihon, "remained as the the remnant of the giants," which is odd language because Anakim and other tribes tallied in Deuteronomy 2 were also Rephaim, giants like Talmai and Ahiman who dwelled among the Canaanites after Sihon and Og died. Remained/*sha'ar* means, in this application, left, remnant, or survivor, while remnant/*yether* means remainder or residue.[2197] The language indicates Og was the last of the first generation of postdiluvian giants, the last of the first generation Rephaim branch documented in Genesis 14 and 15.

King Og's iron bed was nine cubits long and four cubits wide—15'9" long and 7' wide measured with Josephus's royal cubit of twenty-one inches.[2198] Og's bed signifies he was twelve to fourteen feet tall and five to six feet wide. Understanding this makes sense that Og's bed was preserved in Rabbath as a testimonial to Og's "huge stature."[2199] Jewish thought on memorializing Og's bed into the Torah and kept on display served to underscore for future generations that Og was not an Amorite, even though he reigned over the Amorites,[2200] that Og's species was altogether different and larger. Josephus described Og "in the largeness of his body, or handsomeness of his appearance. He was also a man of great activity in the use of his hands, so that his actions were not unequal to the vast largeness and handsome appearance of his body. And men could easily guess at his strength and magnitude when they took his bed at Rabbath, the royal city of the Ammonites; its

[2194] Num 21:33; Deut 3:1.
[2195] Num 21:33; 32:33; Deut 1:4; 3:1, 3, 10, 11, 13; 4:47; 29:7; 31:4; Josh 9:10; 12:4; 13:12, 30, 31; 1 Kings 4:19; Neh 9:22; Ps 135:11; 136:20.
[2196] H5747—`Owg, ogue: a king of Bashan; long-necked; last representative of the giants of Rephaim; H3499—yether, yeh'-ther: an overhanging; an excess; superiority; remainder; a small rope/cord/string hanging free; remnant; residue.
[2197] Deut 3:11; Josh 12:4; 13:12. H7604—sha'ar, shaw-ar': to swell up as in make redundant: leave; be left; remnant; reserve, the rest; left over; left behind; be left alive; survive; remainder; H3499—yether.
[2198] Deut 3:11. Josephus, Ant., Book 1, 3:3, note 13.
[2199] Strong's Cyclopaedia, Vol. 7, 317: Og. Deut 3:11.
[2200] Elitzer, Places in the Parasha, 571.

structure was of iron, its breadth four cubits, and its length a cubit more than double thereto."[2201] Jewish legend recorded that Og sat upon iron chairs and slept in iron beds because wooden ones collapsed from his great weight, that Og's gigantic proportions were tallied with his width as half the proportion of his height, and that Og was proportioned like his bed.[2202]

Nonbiblical sources connect Og to Sahm of *The Manichaean Book of Giants,* sometimes called the *Ogias Book of Giants.* Ogias in the *Babylonian Talmud* was stated to be Og's father, an antediluvian giant who slew a dragon.[2203] In *The Manichaean Book of Giants,* Ogias/Ohyah/Sahm's brother was Ahyah/Hahyah.[2204] In another book thought to be closely associated with the *Enoch Book of Giants* and *The Manichaean Book of Giants, The Lost Book of King Og,* Ogias is named as Og's son;[2205] biblically, Og's son(s) were not named and were slain with Og.[2206] Ogias/Ohyah would appear to be patronymic names from Greek sources.

Another name seemingly related to Og surfaces in Josephus' account of Abraham in the war of giants: "Now Abram dwelt near the oak called Ogyges—the place belongs to Canaan, not far from the city of Hebron."[2207] The Greek historian Pausanias (c. AD 110–180) wrote that Ogyges/Ogygus/Ogygos was a son of Poseidon, an Aboriginal from Ectene, married to Thebe; and the first king of Thebes. Ogyges' name derived an epithet for Thebes—an Ogygian. The Ectenes died off from pestilence and were replaced by local races including the Boetians, conquered later by Cadmus and his Phoenician army[2208] (c. 2000), which establishes Ogyges' reign beginning shortly after the flood. As you will recall, Cadmus's wife was from Mount Hermon, where Og succeeded as king after the defeat of the Rephaim in the war of giants. One contemplates the connections between Og, Ogyges, and the giant oak tree. Further, "Ogygian" derived the Latin *ogygius,* from the Greek word ogygios/ogygos/ogyges that was understood in ancient history as primeval, from earliest ages, and gigantic as it related to Ogyges, king of Boeotia and his Aboriginal race.[2209] Thus, the second "g" in the Greek variant Ogyges is enunciated as a "y," producing Ogias; gyges/gigas was the root word for "gigantic" and "giant(s)."

Additionally, Manetho wrote that "Hyk (`uk) in the word Hyksos is the Rephaite name for King" and that "it has been inferred that Og/`Owg is but an

[2201] Josephus, *Ant.,* Book 4, 5:3.

[2202] Ginzberg, *Legends of the Bible,* 462.

[2203] Bane, *Encyclopedia of Giants,* 130: Ogias, citing Nidah, chapter 9.

[2204] Lumpkin, *The Book of Giants, The Watchers, Nephilim, and The Book of Enoch,* 24, 25, 31.

[2205] Demmon, *The Lost Book of King Og,* 14.

[2206] Num 21:35.

[2207] Josephus, *Ant.,* Book 4, 10:4.

[2208] Pausanias, trans. M. A. Arthur Richard Shilleto, *The Description of Greece,* Vol. 2, 157, Book 9, 5:1–2.

[2209] https://www.merriam-webster.com/dictionary/Ogygian.

attempt to represent the same in Hebrew letters."[2210] The "k" in Mesopotamia was often transliterated as a "g" as in Uruk transliterated as Unug. If Manetho was correct, Og could have been Og's title of king, and therefore his name is unknown. Perhaps then, Og-gyges was the epithet "king of the giants," just as Gyges was a patronymically named giant king who founded a new Lydian dynasty circa 600 BC, which ended the Heraclides dynasty of kings descended from Hercules.[2211] Jewish legends assert Og and Sihon were giant kings ruling the Amorites, who fully integrated with the giants[2212] to become hybrids.

Og, like Sihon, was named in Psalms 135 and 136 for his infamy as a mighty king of great nations.[2213] It follows that Og's realm in Bashan was appropriately called "land of giants,"[2214] the land of Mount Hermon where the Perizzim dwelled among Og's unwalled villages.[2215] Og reigned over sixty city-states, twelve pentapolis royal fortresses; cities with high and mighty walls, gates, and bars.

> *Sept* Deut 3:4 And we mastered all his cities at that time; there was not a city which we took not from them; sixty cities, all the country round about Argob, belonging to king Og in Basan:
>
> Deut 3:5 all strong cities, lofty walls, gates and bars; besides the very many cities of the Pherezites.

Og reigned over his empire from the cities of Ashteroth and Edrei near Mount Hermon,[2216] with the former in the Golan Heights whose ruins are known today as Tell Ashtara,[2217] where Enoch states sons of God swore their oath to create giants before the flood.[2218] Ashtaroth, as it is sometimes spelled, is the plural feminine format of Ashteroth.[2219] Ashteroth was the city for the temple of Ashtereth, home of the gods of Sidon, and the home of the Baalim and Ashtereth.[2220] The Baalim and Ashtereth were worshipped by the Rephaim at Ugarit and throughout

---

[2210] *Strong's Cyclopaedia,* Vol. 7, 317: Og, citing "Jour. Sac. Lit. Jan. 1852, 363."

[2211] Herodotus, *Histories,* Book 1:9–14.

[2212] Ginzberg, *Legends of the Bible,* 463.

[2213] Ps 135:10–12; 136:18–20.

[2214] Gen 14:5; 15:20; Deut 3:13.

[2215] H6522—*Prizziy;* H6521—*praziy.*

[2216] Deut 1:4; Josh 9:10; 12:4; 13:12, 31.

[2217] Elitzur, *Places in the Parasha,* 565.

[2218] Enoch 6:4–7; 7:1–4; 41:5.

[2219] Ellicott, *Old Testament Commentary,* Vol. 2. 181, Judg 2: note 13: Baal and Ashtaroth.

[2220] Ashtoreth goddess and Baal god: Judg 3:11; 6:30–32; 10:10–12; Num 22:31; 1 Kings 11:5, 33; 2 Kings 23:13. H6252—ʿAshtarowth, ash-taw-roth'; or Ashtaroth, ash-taw-roth': a Sidonian deity; a city in Bashan; star; false goddesses of a fertility cult; H6253—ʿAshtoreth, ash-to'reth: the Phoenician goddess of love; star; the principal female deity of the Phoenicians worshipped in war and fertility; Ishtar of Assyria; Astarte by Greeks and Romans.

Canaan. Ashteroth Karnaim was the Rephaim capital city of in the war of giants. Ergo, Og governed from Ashteroth, city of the Rephaim of Genesis 14:5, the city of the fertility goddess of the Baalim of Mount Hermon, the Rephaim Aboriginal home.

Ashteroth, alternatively called Baalti, was associated with both the moon and Venus and held the "Queen of Heaven" title recorded in the book of Jeremiah.[2221] The Queen of Heaven is the mother goddess in polytheism, and prophetic allegory for the woman who rides the beast of empires in the end times. Branches of polytheism are allegorically named the daughters of Babylon descended from the mother polytheist religion at Nimrod's Babel.[2222] The mystical religion was an equal partner in the Rephaim beast empires' hegemony. Ashteroth Karnaim was the double-horned city and religious center for Bashan;[2223] the dualistic bull cult was represented with the two horns through Baal and Ashtoreth, the parent god and mother goddess of the Sidonian, Canaanite, and Rephaim pantheons. Karanim/*qeren* means horn, a mountain peak, power, and strength,[2224] prophetic allegory for the end-time "bulls of Bashan" princes.[2225]

Antichrist is described scripturally as the single horn (unicorn) of the goat empire Greece, of which Alexander was the first king/horn whose empire was divided among the four notable ones, from which Antichrist will derive.[2226] The second horn will be the end-time Queen of Heaven Babylon religion, which Antichrist's religion replaces Babylon. One deduces by the prophetic allegory that Antichrist will have bloodline connections back to the Rephaim, fallen angels of Mount Hermon, and Nimrod, just as end-time Babylon descends from the Babel religion whose daughter was centered at Ashtoreth Karnaim. One might anticipate Antichrist will draft the unicorn mistranslations and pertinent horn passages, referencing Jesus to make his counterfeited claim as the long-awaited messiah.[2227]

Og's heart was hardened like Sihon, and perhaps with even more hubris. Og believed he could easily avenge his brethren. As such, Og marched out to swarm Israel in open battle, rather than remain within their mighty walled fortresses. Og too was delivered up for slaughter by God, along with all Og's army before Israel

---

[2221] Ellicott, *Old Testament Commentary*, Vol. 2, 181, note 13: Baal and Ashtaroth. Jer 7:10–17; 44:17, 18.

[2222] Rev 17:1–18. Daughter of Babylon: Ps 137:8; Isa 47:1; Jer 51:33; Zech 2:7. Daughter Chaldeans/Babylon: Isa 47:1, 5. Daughters of nations: Ezek 32:16, 18.

[2223] H6255—`*Ashtroth Qarnayim, ash-ter-oth' kar-nah'yim*: Ashtaroth of the double horns; symbol of the deity; a city East of the Jordan in Bashan; "Ashtoreth of the two horns or peaks."

[2224] H7161—*qeren, keh'-ren*: a horn; a flask or cornet; an elephant's tooth; a corner of the altar, a mountain peak; a ray of light; power; strength.

[2225] Ps 22:12; Ezek 29:18.

[2226] Dan 7:8, 11, 20, 21; 8:5, 8–14, 21.

[2227] Deut 3:9; 33:17; Num 23:21-23; Ps 22:21; 29:6; 92:10; Isa 34:7–8; Luke 1:68–80.

at the battle of Edrei, just as God had promised Israel.[2228] Israel battled Og, his sons, and all his people "until there was none left him alive"—utterly destroying/ *charam* them.[2229] Israel destroyed all of Og's great cities and towns, as Israel had done to Sihon and his empire.[2230] Israel's rout of Sihon and Og's hybrid armies and utter destruction of their empires sent fear rippling through out the Rephaim-led Canaanite nations.

Nonetheless, Israel was not yet finished with the eastern campaign. Moses was instructed to wage one more battle before he died east of the Jordan—unfinished business with the Midianites for the offenses they committed against Israel.[2231] The charges levied against the Midianites involved the sorcerer Balaam hired by the king Balak of Moab, who conspired with the elders of Midian to curse Israel after learning about the destruction of the Amorites and their Rephaim kings.[2232] Balaam further instructed the Moabites and Midianites to lure weak-in-faith Israelites back into idolatry. Moabite women were led by Cozbi, a daughter of the Midianite prince Zur, who vexed Israel via cunning and deceits.[2233] Seemingly Ammonites followed Balaam's instruction to vex the Israelites, for they too were not permitted thereafter in God's congregations.[2234] However, the Midianites were held to a higher standard of accountability and punishment by war.

The crimes of the Midianites, and to a lesser extent the crimes of the Ammonites, are crimes that surface in Revelation 2 as the cursing of Israel, eating things sacrificed unto idols, and worshipping/fornicating with the end-time Babylon religion.[2235] End-time Babylon, followed by Antichrist, will once more endeavor to wipe out all those who follow God and His Holy Covenant from the face of the earth. Both will reign in a dystopian age of false prophets, idolatry, mystical rituals, sacrifices, and in the ways of Cain and Balaam. The ways of Cain and Balaam were recorded as the ways of fallen angels and Sodom in the book of Jude. [2236]

Midianites of the eastern campaign dwelled north and east of the Jordan River and away from the southern Midianites. Five Midianite dukes of the north and their pentapolis city-state fortresses were part of the Eastern Alliance and titled the "dukes of Sihon."[2237] Midianites were descendants of Abraham and Keturah.[2238] As such, Midianites, like the Amalekites, were in the succession line to receive the

---

[2228] Num 21:33–35; Deut 3:1–11.
[2229] Num 21:35; Deut 3:6.
[2230] Deut 3:5–7.
[2231] Num 31:2.
[2232] Num 22:1–8.
[2233] Num 25:1–3, 14–18; 2 Peter 2:14–15.
[2234] Num 31:16; Deut 23:3–4; Neh 13:1.
[2235] Rev 2:14.
[2236] Jude 1:6–11.
[2237] Num 31:7–8; Josh 13:21.
[2238] Gen 25:1–2.

blessings, birthright, and messianic promise.[2239] Midianite crimes were motivated by their greed and their Eastern alliance obligations. It follows that Midianites east of the Jordan, after the Covenant Land conquest, forged an alliance with the Amalekites and the peoples of the east, the *qedem*/Kadmonim, where they continued their blood oath against Israel.[2240] Midianites before and after the conquest conspired to "take to ourselves the houses of God in possession" with Edom, Amalek, Ishmaelites, Hagarenes, Moabites, Ammonites, and Midianites.[2241]

The five Midian dukes of Sihon were likely Rephaim kings who likely provided troops in the Sihon and Og battles. Duke Zur, father of the Midianite princess, Cozbi[2242] was a the dynastic "head over a people and from a chief house in Midian."[2243] Duke Eviy/ *'Eviy's* name derives from *'avah*, suggesting a link to the city of the Avvim in Assyria: Avith, Avvah, Ava, and/or Ivah: *'avah*/ *'avvah*.[2244] Duke Rekem was defined as "variegation," meaning of different colors or diversified, perhaps indicating a different skin color, physical features, or race.[2245] Josephus' account states Rekem's name was patronymic from the builder of Petra (home of the Amaleqim, who also took titles as dukes). Duke Hur/*Chuwr* is defined as a hole, from *chuwr* meaning a serpent's crevice, and from *chuwr* and *chavar* meaning white, white stuff, and to wax pale and grow white.[2246] Accordingly, *Chuwr* is part of the series of words including Horim/*Choriy* that intersects through *chuwr*, meaning a prison cell.[2247] Horim were white-skinned and part of the Hurrians/

[2239] Gen 25:1–2.

[2240] Judg 6:1–40; 7:1–25; 8:1–35; Ps 86:3–9. People of the east: Judg 6:3, 33; 10:12; 12:15. H6924—*qedem*.

[2241] Ps 83:3–12.

[2242] Num 31:8.

[2243] Num 25:15.

[2244] H189—*'Eviy, ev-ee'*; from 183: desirous; a Midianitish chief; my desire; one of five chiefs of Midian; H183—*'avah, aw-vaw'*: covet; greatly desire; long for; lust after; be greedy; crave after; H5754—*'avvah*; from 5753: ruin; H5753—*'avah*: make crooked; bow down; commit iniquity; pervert; do wickedly; H5755—*'Ivvah, iv-vaw'*; or *Avvae*; H5757—*'Avviy, av-vee'*: patrial from 5755; perverters; an Avvite or native of Avvah.

[2245] H7552—*Reqem, reh'-kem*: a city in Palestine; a Midianite king; variegation. *Websters*, 452: variegate.

[2246] H2354—*Chuwr, khoor*; the same as 2353 or 2352; name of four Israelites, and one Midianite King; hole; H2352—*chuwr, khoor*, or *chur, khoor*: to bore; the crevice of a serpent; the cell of a prison; hole; H2353—*chuwr, khoor*; from 2357; H2357—*chavar, khaw-var'*: to blanch; figuratively to shame: wax pale; to be white; grow white.

[2247] H2354—*Chuwr*; the same as 2353 or 2352; H2352—*chuwr*; H2353—*chuwr, khoor*; from 2357: white linen; white; H2357—*chavar*; H2752—*Choriy*; from 2356; H2356—*chowr*; same as 2352; H2352—*chuwr*; H2753—*Choriy*; same as 2752; H2353—*chuwr*; from 2357; H2753—*choriy*; same as 2353; H2359—*Chuwriy*: Huri.

Chuwri. Duke Reba's name meant four or the fourth part.[2248] One wonders if Reba was heraldic of Arba or if he too was the fourth of four other Rephaim sons.

> Josh 13:21 And all the cities of the plain, and all the kingdom of Sihon king of the Amorites, which reigned in Heshbon, whom Moses smote with the princes of Midian, Evi, and Rekem, and Zur, and Hur, and Reba, which were dukes of Sihon, dwelling in the country.

Israel's army led by Phinehas, son of Eleazar the priest, brought with them the "holy instruments."[2249] Jewish legend indicates the "holy instruments" was the ark of the covenant,[2250] which led all God-authorized campaigns. The Midianites, though, anticipated the Israelite attack. They dispatched their troops to the entrances of their territory and awaited the Israelite onslaught.[2251] Even so, the Midian dukes were defeated. After the battle all males were slain, the five dukes were slain, and Balaam was slain.[2252] Israel captured women, children, cattle, flocks, and goods as their own, then burned all the Midianite cities and castles. The capturing of the spoils infuriated Moses because it was a violation of their instructions to utterly destroy the Midianites, a sin that then required a special cleansing.[2253] As such, some Midianites escaped.

The end of the eastern campaign marked the end of Moses' leadership. Moses was not permitted to enter the Promised Land for his actions at Kadesh and the waters of Meribah. Moses did not speak to the rock in God's name as God instructed; rather, Moses struck the rock with his rod. For this reason, God told Moses he would not enter the Promised Land.[2254] Moses died in the land of Moab, according to God's Word, at the age of one hundred and twenty years.[2255] Israel was camped on the plains of Moab by Jordan near Jericho[2256] when Joshua succeeded Moses. Moses laid his hands upon Joshua who became full of the spirit of wisdom—the Holy Spirit.[2257]

[2248] H7254—*Reba`, reh'-bah*; same as 7253: a Midianite king; four; H7253—*reba`*, reh'-bah; a fourth part or side.

[2249] Num 31:1–6.

[2250] Ginzberg, *Legends of the Bible*, 472.

[2251] Josephus, *Ant.*, Book 4, 4:7.

[2252] Num 31:7–8.

[2253] Num 31:8–54.

[2254] Num 20:1–14.

[2255] Deut 34:5–7.

[2256] Num 36:13.

[2257] Deut 34:9.

BASECAMP GILGAL

CHAPTER 48

Josh 1:2 Moses my servant is dead; now therefore arise, go over this Jordan, thou, and all this people, unto the land which I do give to them, even to the children of Israel.

Israel made preparations to cross the Jordan River without Moses—into the dragon realms of the mighty seven, even though they could have settled in Sihon and Og's conquered lands.

Joshua sent two scouts across the Jordan to do reconnaissance on their enemies in the Covenant Lan, which included Jericho.[2258]

Joshua marched Israel to Shittim after the scouts returned, and they encamped alongside the Jordan River.[2259] Joshua then addressed all Israel,[2260] to remind them that across the river awaited a hostile land of vicious, battle-ready giants and their vassal hybrids bound in an axis of evil, bent on wiping Israel from the face of the earth. Joshua understood that Israel needed to strike first before the numerous houses of Dragon gathered like bees to swarm Israel. Joshua warned the Israelites that they were entering into a generational war, but reassured them that God and the ark of the covenant would be with them to drive their foes out, provided Israel kept the Holy Covenant and hearkened to God's commands.[2261]

[2258] Josh 2:1.
[2259] Josh 3:1.
[2260] Josh 3:2–8.
[2261] Josh 3:9.

Just before Passover, Israel traversed the Jordan River on dry land, with the ark of the covenant at the forefront. God dried up the river for Israel as a sign and a message to all the miscreant trespassers of Canaan that God came with Israel to repossess the Covenant Land.[2262] Israel camped at a location close to the city of palms in the valley, Jericho.[2263] Israel named their basecamp Gilgal (wheel), because God had "rolled away" the shame of Egypt off Israel.[2264]

When Gilgal was preceded by the definite article *ha Gilgal*, it referred to a worship place encircled by stones. Each Israelite tribe selected a large stone from the riverbed as they crossed the Jordan River, to represent the twelve tribes at their new basecamp. The stones were circularly erected to memorialize the miracle crossings at the Jordan River and the Red Sea.[2265] The campsite was named Gilgal, as yet another message to the Rephaim kingdoms. *Ha Gilgal* became an important Israelite worship site, a home for prophets,[2266] the place Saul was crowned king, a place where Samuel slew Agag, and the place Elijah was taken to heaven.[2267]

> Josh 5:10 And the children of Israel encamped in Gilgal, and kept the passover on the fourteenth day of the month at even in the plains of Jericho.

I do not conclude that the basecamp's name was coincidental. Israel selected a specific location to send a clear message to the Canaanite-led Rephaim nations. Rephaim and Canaanite worship included aligned circles of worship sites that included the Golan Heights below Mount Hermon. Gilgal Rephaim was a renowned mound of stones and a circle of stone pillars used for polytheist worship, pilgrimages, and rituals.[2268] Gilgal was also a city of the north conquered by Joshua in the Northern Campaign, the home city of the "king of nations,"[2269] a patronymic title connecting back to Tidal in the war of giants. The West Bank was an excellent source for hewing rock slabs from the land that sustained numerous quarries for use in religious sites. Israel's Gilgal basecamp in the West Bank was

---

[2262] Josh 3:10–17; 4:1–24; 5:1.

[2263] Deut 34:3.

[2264] Josh 5:10. H1556—*galal, gaw-lal'*: to roll; commit; remove; roll away; H1537—*Gilgal, ghil-gawl'*; with the article *ha*; rolling; the first site of an Israelite camp west of the Jordan, east of Jericho; where Samuel was judge; where Saul was made king; dwelling place of prophets. Josh 4:19; 5:9; 1 Sam 15:22–35; 2 Kings 2:1–22.

[2265] Judg 4:5–20.

[2266] Yoel Elitzur, "The Meaning of Gilgal," *Revue Biblique* 126 (2019), 332, citing Jack M. Sasson: Judges 1–12, The Anchor Yale Bible, 179. H1537—*Gilgal, ghil-gawl'*.

[2267] 1 Sam 11:15; 15:33; 2 Kings 2:1.

[2268] Elitzur, "The Meaning of Gilgal," 330–333.

[2269] Josh 12:23.

located by a rock quarry,[2270] thus indicating the site and quarry was utilized in the construction of the Gilgal circuits of polytheist worship—which, with Israel's presence, came to an abrupt halt.

Geliloth is thought to be a variant name for Israel's Gilgal basecamp and memorial site[2271] that may reflect the polytheist basecamp once located there. Geliloth/*Gliyowth* means circuit/circuits. Before the age of electricity, "circuit(s)" were understood as "circuit rider(s)," preacher(s) traveling to towns without a church, or as the round made by judges on their travels in their jurisdictions.[2272] The circuit term for judges and priests originates in prehistory from pilgrimage circuits/*cabab*, understood in the time of Samuel as going around in a regular tour:[2273]

> 1 Sam 7:16 And he went from year to year in circuit to Bethel, and Gilgal, and Mizpeh, and judged Israel in all those places.

Gelioth/Gilgal was Israel's basecamp for the Covenant Land campaign. They returned to Gilgal after traveling through the Valley of the Giants/Rephaim to the Stone of Bohan, a marker used later to divide the territories of Judah and Benjamin.[2274] Gelioth is the plural format of *gilgal*/wheel, which summons imageries of multiple wheel sites. In the same line of thinking, *gal* is *gilgal's* second syllable, meaning heap of stones and derives from *galal*, meaning to roll away.[2275] Gilgal's orthographical and etymological connections indicates Israel's chosen name for their basecamp was not just a memorial. The erected twelve stones were arranged in a wheel or circular pattern to communicate a warning to the Canaanites that their religious sites and their cities were about to be overturned into ruinous heaps of stones, in the same way Og and Sihon's empires were utterly destroyed/*charam*.

As difficult as the four previous campaigns were, the Covenant Land nations, fortified behind their numerous high-walled city-states, would prove more formidable by virtue of the sheer number of their empires and aggregate multitude, bolstered by the bone-crushing superwarrior Rephaim. Knowing this explains Joshua's encouraging words before crossing the Jordan River: that God would

---

[2270] Judg 3:19.

[2271] *Unger's*, 462: Geliloth; 477: Gilgal; *Strong's Cyclopaedia*, Vol. 3, 766: Gelioth.

[2272] *Webster's*, 70: circuit; *Encyclopedia Americana*, Vol. 6, 693: circuit; 694: circuit rider.

[2273] H5437—*cabab, saw-bab'*: surround border: bring; cast; walk, round about; be about on every side; go about or around; encircle; march around; go partly around; circle about; make a round; make a circuit.

[2274] Josh 18:16–17. H932—*Bohan, bo'han*: thumb: a boundary stone between Judah and Benjamin.

[2275] 1530—*gal*; something rolled as in a heap of stone or dung: a billow; stones placed over a dead body; spring; wave.

be with Israel when they entered the dragon's lair to battle the seven Rephaim-infested Canaanite empires.

> Josh 3:10 And Joshua said, hereby ye shall know that the living God
> is among you, and that he will without fail drive out from before you
> the Canaanites, and the Hittites, and the Hivites, and the Perizzites,
> and the Girgashites, and the Amorites, and the Jebusites.

God previously promised He would be with Joshua as He had been with Moses. No one and no fortress would successfully stand in opposition before Joshua all the days of his life.[2276] The takeaway for Christians is that Joshua was to wage a holy battle against the Rephaim and their vassal hybrids to utterly destroy them from the land, just as Jesus will do in the end times with His sword to remove their fruit and destroy them "and their seed from among the children of men."[2277] Even though Israel encroached upon the Gilgal Rephaim worship site with their basecamp and memorial, they were not attacked.[2278] Israel's foes cowered behind their mighty walled city-state fortresses. The people of Jericho and its neighboring allies understood the mistakes and destruction thereof that befell Sihon and Og in open battle against the Israelites. They were not going to make the same mistake, thinking their castles were impregnable.

Before Israel engaged in the first battle, God required all the males be circumcised to bring all Israel back into full compliance with the Holy Covenant. None born in the wilderness in the forty years were circumcised, as part of the penance passed on from the generation who rebelled against God.[2279] The circumcision ceremony, followed by the Passover ceremonial requirements, marked the end to the daily supply of manna by God for food. Israel thereafter would live off the bounties of the land of milk and honey, "the fruit of the land of Canaan," just as God had promised.[2280]

At the time of the Passover, Joshua saw a man approach with his sword drawn—the captain/sar of the host of the Lord.[2281] One concludes this man was either Michael or the Angel of the Lord, the Word. Michael is the great prince/sar who battles against the beast empires, and who stands up in the end times to protect Israel from Antichrist and Satan;[2282] but the text does not seem to refer to Michael. The text refers to the Word because Joshua fell to the ground to worship

---

[2276] Josh 1:5.
[2277] Rev 19:15; Psa 21:10.
[2278] Josephus, *Ant.*, Book 5, 1:5.
[2279] Josh 5:5–8.
[2280] Josh 5:12–13.
[2281] H8269—*sar*.
[2282] Dan 10:13; 12:1; Rev 12:7.

this "Man." If this Man was an just angel, the angel would have instructed Joshua not to worship, as only God is to be worshipped.[2283] The Man did not instruct Joshua to stand up, but instructed Joshua to take off his shoes, because Joshua was standing on holy ground.[2284] The same instructions were provided to Moses when the Angel of the Lord appeared before Moses.[2285] The Angel of the Lord was the Word who accompanied Israel during the Exodus.

One ponders at the possible prophetic connection between Joshua's meeting with the Angel of the Lord, the preexistent Jesus, on the eve of warring with the Rephaim beast-like kingdoms. Michael battled the beast empires to prevent Antichrist's crowning before his ordained time, while Jesus' ultimate destruction of the beast empires occurs when He comes at Armageddon. One further ponders the possible prophetic allegory between Joshua's name and the name for the Word when He became flesh. Jesus/*Eeaysooce'* (Greek transliterated *Iesus*) was a cognate format of Joshua that derived from Yehowshuwa,[2286] and just as *Eeaysooce'* was translated as "Jesus" in the book of Acts that referenced Joshua in the KJV.[2287]

Acts 7:44 Our fathers had the tabernacle of witness in the wilderness, as he had appointed, speaking unto Moses, that he should make it according to the fashion that he had seen.

Acts 7:45 Which also our fathers that came after brought in with Jesus into the possession of the Gentiles, whom God drave out before the face of our fathers, unto the days of David.

In the same prophetic allegory and spirit, the high priest Joshua is presented in the book of Zechariah as representative of the High Priest to come of the Melchizedek order, standing before the preexistent Jesus/Joshua, the Angel of the Lord. Joshua in this prophecy is accused by Satan before God, because Joshua will become the Word made flesh, God's Servant, and God's Branch who will remove iniquity in the day when He comes: first to atone for sins, and then in the end times to remove the fallen angels and beast empires who enslave humankind in this world.[2288]

Jericho was already an ancient city at the time of the Exodus, a city renowned as a strong city for its size, and as a royal city of the Rephaim.[2289] Jericho was per-

---

[2283] Dan 8:15–18; Matt 24:9–10; Col 2:18; Rev 22:8–9.
[2284] Josh 5:15.
[2285] Exod 3:2–6.
[2286] G2424—*ee-ay-sooce'*: Jesus as in Jehoshua; Jehovah is salvation; Jesus, the Son of God; the Saviour of mankind; God incarnate.
[2287] Acts 7:45; Heb 4:8: other translations use Joshua: NKJV, NIV, NLT, ESV, NASB, Berean, etc.
[2288] Zech 3:1–10.
[2289] Josh 1-:1–2.

haps the most important city in Canaan at the time of the Exodus, referenced as a notable landmark throughout the march and wars.[2290] Jericho, the moon city, was located five miles west of the Jordan River and seven miles north of the Dead Sea.[2291]

Ergo, Israel celebrated the Passover at Gilgal and ate unleavened bread, and again on the next day with the Feast of Unleavened Bread.[2292] Immediately thereafter, Israel marched to Jericho.[2293] The Feast of Unleavened Bread was celebrated for a week.[2294] On preparation day all leavened bread was removed because yeast represented sin from pride, as in puffing oneself up. The Israelites were about to remove the prideful giants from the land. Joshua then led a battle-hardened forty-thousand-man army into war, beginning at Jericho.[2295]

[2290] *Strong's Cyclopaedia*, Vol. 4, 825: Jericho. Num 22:1; 26:3, 63; 31:12; 33:48, 50; 34:15; 35:1; Deut 32:49; 34:1, 3; Josh 13:2; 16:1, 7; 18:12, 21; 20:8; 24:11.

[2291] H3405—*Yriychow, yer-ee-kho*: its moon; a city five miles west of the Jordan and seven miles north of the Dead Sea.

[2292] Josh 5:10.

[2293] Josh 6:1.

[2294] Exod 12:18, 19, 20; 13:6, 7; 23:15–20, 39; Lev 23:6, 8; Num 28:17, 19–24; Deut 16:3, 4.

[2295] Josh 4:13–19.

CHAPTER 49

THE CENTRAL CAMPAIGN

Josh 6:1 Now Jericho was straitly shut up because of the children of Israel: none went out, and none came in.

The central campaign began with Jericho, famous in that time for its remarkable history, its abundant agriculture, its legendary high and mighty walls, and their mighty men/*gibbowriym*. Jericho was selected to convey another specific warning to all those who defiantly inhabited God's chosen land: leave or suffer a similar utter destruction as Jericho.

Jericho was a former fortress of the Hyksos Egyptian empire and a city allied with the former Rephaim/Amorite Syrian empire led by Sihon. The powerful Rephaim and hybrid Amorites of Jericho cowered within their mighty walls, afraid to war with Israel. The leaders of Jericho city would have received reports that God dried up the Jordan River for Israel to cross. As an ally of Sihon, the Jericho leaders were up to date on other discombobulating reports regarding Israel's shocking victories over Og and Sihon's armies in the open field. Thus, people of Jericho and other city-states did not attack Israel at Gilgal.[2296]

Jericho was confirmed as populated by Amorites[2297] in the report by Israelite scouts Joshua sent in advance of the battle,[2298] the same Amorites described in a

---

[2296] Josh 5:1.
[2297] Josh 5:1; 7:7; 12:8–9; 24:11.
[2298] Num 13:28–29; Deut 1:19, 20, 27, 28, 44.

hyperbolic simile in the book of Amos: "the Amorite before them, whose height was like the height of the cedars, and he was strong as the oaks."[2299] The Amorites were not forty to one hundred feet tall like the cedars of Lebanon, but were certainly giant-like hybrids. Accordingly, the king of Jericho and his warriors were described as mighty ones/gibborim.[2300]

The mighty Amorites of Jericho and their neighboring city-states felt safe behind the high walls of their mighty fortresses. Jericho was selected first for annihilation because of its renowned power reputation; it was an antediluvian city of gods and giants, a city (according to archaeologists) that protected its inhabitants with thick walls stretching sixteen feet high and enhanced by a deep ditch gouged out of hard bedrock, which encircled the great walls.[2301] The walls were so thick that Rahab, whom the two Israelite scouts dispatched by Joshua received intelligence from, built her house upon the wall.[2302]

The battle of Jericho commenced after the Feasts and Sabbaths of Unleavened Bread, which began the first day after the Passover with a special Sabbath and ended with a special Sabbath. Preparation Day began the day before Passover, a day reserved to remove all leavened bread and all yeast from every home and dwelling among the Israelites.[2303] The puffing action of the yeast on the bread was symbolic of pride, haughtiness, and sin.[2304] The Jericho battle indeed was a special religious ritual of curse and destruction/*charam* to "utterly destroy" and to exterminate.[2305] The battle began with blowing trumpets and marching around Jericho city to announce the renewal of the land, the firstfruits of the harvest, and the removal of the proud puffed-up giants from the Covenant Land. The Covenant Land conquest was to be an absolute cleansing of and removal of Rephaim and their hybrid human offspring who defiled God's reserved territory physically and spiritually.

Jericho being selected specifically for religious destruction explains the peculiar preparatory and ritualistic ceremonies performed before Jericho throughout the seven-day Feast of Unleavened Bread to the Lord. All the feasts of God[2306] have prophetic implications, embedded as reminders to Israel and Christians that there is indeed an ordained timetable where all things that must take place will take place. The Feast of Trumpets announced the harvest in the seventh month

---

[2299] Amos 2:9.

[2300] Josh 6:2.

[2301] Barry Cunelife, *The Holy Land: An Oxford Archaeological Guide from Earliest Times to 1700*, fifth edition (New York: Oxford University Press, 2008), 199, 327; Collins, *Ashes of Angels*, 310–311.

[2302] Josh 2:1, 15.

[2303] Exod 12:15–20; 34:18; Num 28:16–25; Deut 16:1–8.

[2304] Job 41:34; Prov 21:4; Hab 2:4; Matt 16:5–12; Mark 8:15–21; 1 Cor 5:6–8.

[2305] H2763—*charam*.

[2306] Passover, Unleavened Bread, First Fruits, Weeks, Trumpets, Day of Atonement, and Tabernacles.

was about to take place,[2307] just as the seven trumpets of Revelation occur before the harvest of the last three and a half years, which included the removal of the tares.[2308] It follows that the Jericho battle was preceded with blowing trumpets and marching around Jericho city for seven days to announce the harvest, and then the renewal of the land—that Jericho was the firstfruits of the conquest harvest, the removal of the tares from the Covenant Land.

> Matt 13:38 The field is the world; the good seed are the children of the kingdom; but the tares are the children of the wicked one;
>
> Matt 13:39 The enemy that sowed them is the devil; the harvest is the end of the world; and the reapers are the angels.

On the seventh day, seven priests with seven trumpets marched with the army seven times around Jericho led by the ark of the covenant. After the seventh circle had been marched around Jericho, the trumpets were blown, all the people shouted, and the mighty walls of Jericho came tumbling down.[2309] Jericho's king and mighty men of valor were served up for sacrifice and slaughter as an "accursed city."[2310] "Israel utterly destroyed all that was in the city, man, woman, young old, ox, sheep, and ass with the edge of the sword."[2311] The power of the giants, their gods, or their walls could not stop the supernaturally strengthened Israel as long as they obeyed God. Jericho's destruction reverberated more fear and increased Joshua's fame throughout Canaan.[2312]

Some in Israel, though, did not obey God. They trespassed the "accursed" designation and instructions assigned to Jericho, and kept the spoils of Jericho. God consequently delivered many of Israel into the hands of the people in the first battle of Ai.[2313] Afterward, God forgave Israel for the "accursed" transgression, whereby Joshua led Israel in battle to utterly destroy to Ai city, in the same way Israel destroyed Jericho, but this time God permitted Israel to keep the plunder.

Archaeological excavations of a city with mighty fortifications of walls and gates burned by fire and left in ruins, believed by some archaeologists to be Ai city, were dated to circa 2000 BC or before.[2314] Ai/`Ay city is defined as a "heap of

---

[2307] Exod 23:16; Lev 23:24–25; Num 21:1–5.
[2308] Matt 13:15–27, 37–45; Rev 14:14–20.
[2309] Josh 6:3–20.
[2310] Josh 6:17–18. H2764—*cherem, khay'-rem*: shutting in a net; a doomed object; sentenced to extermination; dedicated things which should be utterly destroyed; appointed to utter destruction.
[2311] Josh 6:21.
[2312] Josh 6:27.
[2313] Josh 7:1–5.
[2314] Elitzer, *Places in the Parasha*, 41–42.

ruins,"[2315] which indicated it was either re-named posthumously after its destruction or was rebuilt after a previous destruction of the mighty city. Scripturally we know Ai was a city close to where Abraham camped, Bethel and Hai. Ai was the royal city of the Rephaim and Canaanites, but not as great as Gibeon city of the Gibeonim/Hivvim.[2316] Some theologians assert Avvim and Gaza/`Azzah were variants of `Ay[2317] indicating that Ai may have been an Avvim royal city. Avith is the plural of `Ay/Aya. Moreover, both Ai and Avith's names mean "heap of ruins," and both were in Jericho's vicinity.[2318] Ai was rebuilt after Joshua's destruction, based on references to Ai that come later in the Bible.[2319]

Details captured in Israel's siege strategy for Ai's destruction presents an example for Christians to take heed when identifying gibborim as only giants. Joshua selected thirty thousand of his mighty/*gibbowr men*/'*iysh,* whereby these "mighty men of valor," were sent at night to take their position for the battle to follow.[2320] Israel's men/champions/'*iysh* were not Nephilim, Rephaim, or hybrid humans, nor were David's "mighty men" whose description derives from the same words recorded in Joshua 8:3. However, this does not preclude that God preternaturally strengthened Joshua's men of valor and David's mighty men to defeat giant armies.

Joshua conceived a brilliant plan to conceal seventy-five percent of his army in tactically advantageous positions around Ai city. Joshua then presented the balance of his army and himself before Ai the next morning. The visible Israelite army then fled before the people of Ai in a staged panic, to lure out Ai's army to pursue the panic-stricken Israelites. Israel's shrewd tactics drew Ai's army out of the city. The hidden Israelites then encircled Ai's army, slew the army, then slaughtered Ai's inhabitants, burned the city to the ground, and hung the king of Ai from a tree. Ai was left a great heap/*gal* of stones and a desolation.[2321]

After the utter destruction of the royal Rephaim/Amorite cities of Jericho and Ai, the balance of the Central Canaanite city-state nations recommitted themselves to fight Israel. They activated the central alliance that aligned themselves "with one accord" (one hive mind), with the Northern and Southern alliances committed to wipe Israel from the face of the earth. The central Canaanite empires understood they could not fight alone, that to do so would bring to them the utter destruction

---

[2315] H5857—`Ay, ah'ee; or feminine Aya, Neh 11:31 ah-yaw'; or Ayath Isa 10:28 ah-yawth': "heap of ruins"; Ai, Aja, and Ajath; a city east of Bethel and beside Bethaven near Jericho connected to Heshbon.
[2316] Gen 12:8; 13:3; Josh 10:1–2; 12:9. *Strong's Cyclopaedia,* Vol. 1, 123: Ai.
[2317] *Strong's Cyclopaedia,* Vol. 1, 123–124: Ai, citing Josh 18:23; 1 Chron 7:28.
[2318] H5857—`Ay, ah'ee.
[2319] Ezra 2:28; Neh 7:32; 11:31; Isa 10:28; Jer 49:3.
[2320] Josh 8:2–3; 2 Sam 23:8. Men: H376—'*iysh, eesh*: a man or a male person; husband; human being; servant; mankind; champion; great man.
[2321] Josh 8:4–22. H1530—*gal.*

that befell their brethren. The greater alliance further realized with Jericho and Ai's destruction that hiding within their fortresses made them vulnerable to be crushed by those walls and was far worse than meeting Israel in open battle, where they could at lease wage battle.

> Josh 9:1 And it came to pass, when all the kings which were on this side Jordan, in the hills, and in the valleys, and in all the coasts of the great sea over against Lebanon, the Hittite, and the Amorite, the Canaanite, the Perizzite, the Hivite, and the Jebusite, heard thereof;
>
> Josh 9:2 That they gathered themselves together, to fight with Joshua and with Israel, with one accord.

The subsequent battles reflected the unification of the various city-state pentapolis empires and their alliances. Yet one Rephaim pentapolis centered at the Gibeon city chose another path.[2322] The inhabitants of Gibeon sought to make peace with Israel, albeit through duplicity. Gibeonites feared what Israel did to Jericho and Ai and sent ambassadors to Joshua at Gilgal, seeking a peace treaty in the guise of a foreign people.[2323]

Gibeonite is patrial named from Gibeon and one of several cities Gibeonites inhabited, translated from *Giboniy* and its plural *Giboniyim*.[2324] Gibeon/*Gibown* is defined as hilly and as a hill city. "A city on a hill" is a popular expression for a Nephilim/Rephaim city of light like Sodom, Gomorrah, and Camelot: shining cities on a hill. Contemporary shining cities on a hill are important globalist cities in the west, whose influence is dedicated to bringing about world government. Scripture states Joshua was dismayed when he realized the Gibonim were residents of Canaan and a branch of the Hivvim.[2325] Gibeon was one of the great cities among the Canaanite and Amorite empires, a royal city whose men were mighty/*gibborim,* Hivvim giants:

> Josh 10:1. .. and how the inhabitants of Gibeon had made peace with Israel, and were among them;
>
> Josh 10:2 That they feared greatly, because Gibeon was a great city, as one of the royal cities, and because it was greater than Ai, and all the men thereof were mighty.

[2322] Josh 10:1–2.
[2323] Josh 9:3–16.
[2324] H1391—*Gib`own, ghib-ohn*: hilly; hill city five miles from Jerusalem; H1393—*Gib`oniy, ghib-o-nee*: inhabitant of Gibeon; a little hill, hilly.
[2325] Josh 9:1–7; 11:19.

Gibeon city was the royal city of the Hivvim pentapolis network, boasting great, mighty, and high walls reaching into the heavens, as described by Moses's scouts.[2326] The four other Hivvim/Gibonim city-state strongholds of the central Canaanite pentapolis were Chephirah/Kephirah, Beeroth, Kirjathearim, and Shechem;[2327] Shechem had close ties with Anakim rulers.[2328] Not all Gibonim made peace with Israel, only those from Gibeon city. Joshua equated the Gibonim as Hivvim; the Hivvim were closely connected to the southern Horim via Anah.[2329] One might further deduce Gibonim were a branch of Hivvim eponymously named after a giant named *Gibown*. Some Gibeonites, outside of the Gibeonite temple servants within Israel, survived into the age of King Saul and the prophet Nehemiah.[2330] These Gibeonites appear to be hybrids and were considered Amorites, a catch-all term for hybrids.[2331]

One can appreciate the blow that was struck against the greater giant alliance with the Gibonim treachery, and the rage that must have manifested when one of the strongest of the royal city-states defected: "they feared greatly, because Gibeon was a great city, as one of the royal cities, and because it was greater than Ai, and all the men thereof were mighty."[2332] Indeed, the Gibeon fallout provoked King Adonizedek of Jebusite Jerusalem to invoke the renewed Rephaim pact and alliance against Gibeon before battling Israel.[2333] Adonizedek's Canaanitish name reflected his status as a royal of the Baalim, meaning the "lord of justice/righteousness" and/or "lord Baal/Adoni is righteous." [2334]

Adonizedek understood the danger the Gibonim turncoats brought, and that betrayal could spread. Adonizedek summoned four kings of southern Canaan from the immediate region of Jerusalem, who were likely part of his pentapolis or royal cities of other pentapolis confederacies. Hoham (his god(s) impels) was the Canaanitish king of Hebron/Kiriatharba, where the Anakim kings Talmai, Sheshai, and Ahiman dwelled at or in the vicinity. Piram (a wild ass or beast) was an Amorite (or Amoritish) king of Jarmuth located between Hebron and Lachish. Japhia (bright/shining) was a Canaanitish king of Lachish, a king in the tradition of the shining ones of the Rephaim. Debir (sanctuary for the oracle) was the Amoritish king of Eglon located just west of Hebron in the mountains.[2335] All appear to have been Hivvim, Avvim, and/or

---

[2326] Num 13:9, 28; Deut 1:28.
[2327] Gen 33:17; 34:30; Josh 9:17.
[2328] Billington, "Goliath and the Exodus Giants," 501, 506, citing Pritchard, *ANET*, 225, notes 3, 6.
[2329] Gen 36:2, 20; Josh 9:1–4, 7; 11:19.
[2330] 2 Sam 21:2.
[2331] 2 Sam 21:1–4, 19; 1 Chron 12:4; Neh 3:7. *Strong's Cyclopaedia*, Vol. 1, 203: Amorites.
[2332] Josh 10:2.
[2333] Josh 10:1–5.
[2334] H139—'*Adoniy-Tsedeq, ad-o"-nee-tseh'-dek*: lord of justice or my lord is righteous: a Canaanitish king of Jerusalem; H1168—*Ba`al, bah'-al*: lord; master.
[2335] H1944—*Howham, ho-hawm'*: a Canaanitish king of Hebron; god impels/drives; H6502—*Pir'am, pir-awm'*: Amorite king of Jarmuth; a wild ass; H3412—*Yarmuwth, yar-mooth'*: heights; a Canaanitish city between Hebron and Lachish; H3309—*Yaphiya`, yaw-fee'-ah*: shining; Canaanitish

Anakim. Thus, the five Amoritish/Canaanitish kings marched to Gibeon, encamped there, and prepared to battle Gibeon and perhaps the Hivvim pentapolis.[2336]

Gibeon then appealed to Joshua for protection from Adonizedek's army, demonstrating the earned respect Israel held in Canaan by inference, and the fear of God's power that strengthened Israel. Gibeon feared Israel more than Adonizedek's alliance of Rephaim and hybrids and the sum of all Canaanitish empires. Joshua honored his treaty with the Gibonim and marched his army to Gibeon city, where Israel demolished Adonizedek's alliance, and then hunted the fleeing remnant armies to Azekah and Makkedah.[2337]

As the panic-stricken Canaanitish multitude fled the battlefield, God "cast down great stones from heaven" upon the army all the way to Azekah. Those not slain by the great stones were slain by hailstones, and those who escaped the hailstones were slain by Israel. Gibeon was the prodigious battle where God constrained the sun, forcing it to stand still at Gibeon, and then the moon in the valley of Ajalon, so Israel could complete their vengeance against their sworn enemies—a day not seen before where God "hearkened onto the voice of a man," Joshua.[2338] One can only imagine the panicked thoughts dashing through the hive minds of the giants that day.

The five giant kings split from their discombobulated army in favor of self-preservation, opting to hide in a cave at Makkedah. Meanwhile, Joshua's main army returned to Gilgal, but some remained to hunt the missing kings. The five terror-stricken kings were discovered recoiling like serpents in their cave. Joshua decreed the five to be executed and then hung them on five trees. Joshua turned his attention to Makkedah city and its king. Makkedah was "utterly destroyed"; none were left alive, including the king, in like manner as Jericho.[2339]

Makkedah was near Libnah city.[2340] Israel assaulted Libnah, another fortress city-state with suburbs close to Hebron and another royal city, grouped with Adullam, Ether and Ashan.[2341] One deduces Makkedah was part of Libnah's pentapolis. Libnah and its king were dealt with in the same way as was Jericho, utterly destroyed.[2342] Joshua then marched to Lachish city in the Hebron region where king Japhia reigned. Joshua destroyed Lachish city in the same manner as Libnah.[2343]

---

king of Lachish; H3923—*Lachiysh, law-keesh*: invincible; a city south of Jerusalem of the Amorites; H1688—*Dbiyr, deb-eer*; or *Dbir*. Amoritish king of Eglon; sanctuary; a town in the mountains west of Hebron; H1687—*dbiyr, deb-eer*; or *dbir: deb-eer*: innermost part of the sanctuary as in the oracle; H5700—`*Eglown, eg-lawn*: vituline; calf-like; a royal city in Canaan; king of Moab.
[2336] Josh 10:5.
[2337] Josh 10:5–10.
[2338] Josh 10:11–14.
[2339] Josh 10:15–28.
[2340] H4719—*Maqqedah, mak-kay-daw*: a place of shepherds; near Bethhoron and Libnah.
[2341] Josh 12:15; 15:42; 21:13. H3841—*Libnah, lib-naw*: pavement; a southwest Canaanite royal city; site unknown.
[2342] Josh 10:29–30.
[2343] Josh 10:31–32.

King Horam of Gezer marched to Lachish in support, but was also defeated by Joshua. Gezer, in the central region,[2344] dated back to 3100 BC;[2345] it was a Nephilim city seemingly refurbished after the flood. Horam was a Rephaim king of the Girzim,[2346] whose name is defined as exalted, towering up, and high.[2347]

After the battles at Lachish, Joshua marched to Eglon in the mountains west of Hebron, the city of King Debir. Joshua captured the city in the same day. Joshua thereafter marched directly to Hebron city, destroying it as well as other cities and kings in the Hebron region.[2348] From Hebron Joshua marched to Debir, captured that city, killed its king, and defeated all the cities associated with Debir.[2349] Debir was an important Anakim city, which we will detail further in the mountain campaign, a city named after a former Anakim. It follows that the defeated King Debir's name (of Eglon) was patrial and patronymic of the former Anakim. One deduces Debir and Hebron controlled other cities in the pentapolis style of alliances and military defensive strategy.

> Josh 10:38 And Joshua returned, and all Israel with him, to Debir; and fought against it: Josh 10:39 And he took it, and the king thereof, and all the cities thereof; and they smote them with the edge of the sword. All the cities thereof; and they smote them with the edge of the sword, and utterly destroyed all the souls that were therein; he left none remaining: as he had done to Hebron, so he did to Debir, and to the king thereof; as he had done also to Libnah, and to her king.

Israel's central campaign conquered the Hivvim, Avvim, and Anakim of the central region and then extended into the south to war against empires that supported the central region empires.[2350] The lowlands of central Canaan were secured, but Israel did not eliminate the Anakim, Amaleqim, and their hybrids in the south; many fled to safety in the mountains. After defeating the major city-states of the central and south, their kings, and their armies, Joshua returned to basecamp Gilgal to prepare for the northern campaign.[2351]

[2344] Josh 10:33; 12:12.
[2345] *Mercer's*, 328: Gezer; *Unger's*, 470: Gezer.
[2346] H1507—*Gezer*; the same as 1506; H1506—*gezer*; H1630—*Griziym*.
[2347] H2036—*Horam, ho-rawm'*: exalted; tower up; high; Canaanite king Horam. Josh 10:33.
[2348] Josh 10:34–37.
[2349] Josh 10:38–39.
[2350] Josh 10:40–42.
[2351] Josh 10:43.

CHAPTER 50

THE NORTHERN CAMPAIGN

Josh 24:11 And ye went over Jordan, and came unto Jericho: and the men of Jericho fought against you, the Amorites, and the Perizzites, and the Canaanites, and the Hittites, and the Girgashites, the Hivites, and the Jebusites; and I delivered them into your hand.

The northern campaign began when King Jabin of Hazor received reports of Israel's shocking rampage throughout the central and southern regions of Canaan. Jabin sent urgent messages to the Rephaim-infested and Canaanite hybrid nations of the north to gather and to march south:[2352] to destroy the Israelite nation from the face of the earth.

The Northern alliance tallied six of the mighty seven nations.[2353] The Northern alliance was not included in the war of giants of Genesis 14 but they too were a powerful Rephaim-dominated alliance. Jabin of Hazor was the pendragon of the Northern alliance. The alliance boasted king Jobab of Madon, the unnamed and unnumbered kings of the northern mountains, and the cities of Shimron, Achshaph, Chinneroth, and Dor.[2354]

Jobab's name means desert and derives from a word meaning "howler," as in in to "cry shrilly."[2355] Jobab of Madon was seemingly connected patronymically by his

---

[2352] Josh 11:1.
[2353] Josh 11:3.
[2354] Josh 11:2.
[2355] H3103—*Yowbab, yo-bawb'*; from 2980, howler: a desert; a king of Madon; a king of Edom; a son of Peleg; H2980—*yabab, yaw-bab*: to bawl; cry out.; cry shrilly.

name or title with Jobab, the Horim duke of Seir in Edom.[2356] One further specu-
lates whether Jobab's name reflected a Horim, Hivvim, or Hurrian presence in the
northern campaign or just a kingly presence; Horim, Hivvim, and Hurrian kings
had a presence in Syria up to the time of King David, and Avith and Rehoboth were
royal cities of the Horim/Hivvim Dukes in Syria.[2357] Moreover, Hivite hybrids and/
or perhaps Hivvim were included among the six mighty nations of the alliance.

King Jabin's name means one whom a god observes and derives from a word
meaning intelligent and one who discerns.[2358] Jabin was classified as a Canaanitish
king akin to the description of the central and southern Rephaim kings. Jabin's
name is generally concluded to be a dynastic title in the tradition of Agag[2359] and
perhaps Jobab. Jabin was the patronymic name/title for another "Jabin of Hazor
and the house of Heber the Kenite" and a "king of Canaan" in the book of Judges.[2360] Jabin was a Rephaim perhaps of the Kenim variety.

What is telling about Jabin's pendragon credentials though was the illustrious
title he possessed as king of Hazor: "for Hazor before time was the head of all those
kingdoms," and the same kingdoms Jabin organized for battle against Joshua.[2361]
"Beforetime" is both curious and tantalizing language in this application that is often
overlooked. Beforetime/*paniym* means in this application a former time, a time of
old, and before them,[2362] from since the time of the flood or before. The phrase
"beforetime" that the KJV translators chose here holds the same connotation as "in
times past," "old time," and "before them," all translated from *paniym* in Deuteronomy 2:10, 12, 20, and 22 respectfully, which accounted for the Aboriginal inhabitants of the Covenant Land: Emim, Anakim, Zamzummim, Avvim, and Horim
giants. Likewise, *paniym* was translated as "before" in the accounting for the Aboriginal the Horim dukes of Edom, where the first Jobab was introduced.

> Gen 36:31 And these are the kings that reigned in the land of Edom,
> before there reigned any king over the children of Israel.
>
> Gen 36:32 And Bela the son of Beor reigned in Edom: and the name
> of his city was Dinhabah. Gen 36:33 And Bela died, and Jobab the
> son of Zerah of Bozrah reigned in his stead.

Prophetically, "beforetime" was also translated from *paniym* in the book of
Isaiah's foretelling of Jesus coming from the north in the end times—the One who

---

[2356] Gen 36:33–34; 1 Chron 1:44–45.
[2357] Avith: Gen 36:35, 1 Chron 1:46. Rehoboth: Gen 36:38; 1 Chron 1:48.
[2358] H2985—*Yabiyn, yaw-bene'*: discern; intelligent: one whom a god observes; two Canaanitish
kings.
[2359] *Strong's Cyclopaedia*, Vol. 4, 723: Jabin.
[2360] Judg 4:2, 7, 17, 23, 24; Ps 83:9.
[2361] Josh 11:10.
[2362] H6440—*paniym*.

comes that was there from "beforetime" as in "the beginning." When Jesus comes from the north, the tiding will cause such concern with Antichrist that it will drive him to destroy many and to prepare for his stand at Mount Hermon.[2363]

With Jabin, "beforetime" indicates a dynastic bloodline of Hazor(im) Kings, Rephaim kings, and pendragons led from Hazor city and the northern Canaanite empires east of Sidon, since shortly after the flood and before the Canaanite migration from Babel. Knowing this makes sense that hazor/*chatsowr* was the Hebrew word for castle, high-walled fortress, and a northern royal Canaanite city[2364] established in the "before time" by Rephaim. The Hazor(im) were city-states of the north, and the same kind of high-walled fortresses and royal cities built by Anakim in the south, and by Hivvim/Gibonim across in the central region. Hazor, Madon, and all the other cities listed in Joshua 11 were the cities of the kings, royal cities/*iyr*: cities always on watch, guarded,[2365] cities of the Watchers and perhaps antediluvian cities originally built by Watchers.

Hazor, too, held heraldic significance that formed compounded words for the names of several cities in in the south toward Edom: Hazzargaddah, Hazarshual, Enhazor, Hezron/Hazor and Baalhazor.[2366] Similarly named southern cities indicates a closer kinship between northern and southern Rephaim than is generally accepted, and specifically with the Horim and Avvim.

Hazer perhaps represented the Avvim and their Hazerim.[2367] The plural format of Hazer, Hazerim/*Chatseriym*, means towns and villages enclosed by walls[2368] of the Avvim. Hazerim derives from the same source word, *chatser*, meaning enclosed by walls, as did Jabin's Hazor/*Chatsowr* city;[2369] and Hazerim/*Chatseriyim* is plural for Hazor/Hazer/*Chatser* establishing Jabin's Hazor as part of or related to the Hazerim of the Avvim in the south, and the various city-state fortress of the south like Baalhazor. One muses if *Chatser* was a Rephaim that many cities were patrial named after.

Deut 2:23. .. the Avims which dwelt in Hazerim, even unto Azzah, the Caphtorims, which came forth out of Caphtor, destroyed them, and dwelt in their stead.

The shock of Joshua's victories in the central and southern regions gripped the northern Rephaim-infested nations with trepidation. Jabin assembled a mighty

---

[2363] Isa 41:25–26; Dan 11:44–45.
[2364] H2674 —*Chatsowr, khaw-tsore*: castle; a royal city of northern Palestine; a city of Judah; a Benjamite town north of Jerusalem. *Strong's Cyclopaedia*, Vol. 4, 723: Jabin.
[2365] H5892—`*iyr*.
[2366] Josh 15:23–27.
[2367] Deut 2:23.
[2368] H2699—*Chatseriym, khats-ay-reem*; plural of 2691: villages; H2691—*chatser, khaw-tsare*: a yard as enclosed by a fence; hamlet enclosed with walls; court; enclosed tower.
[2369] H2691—*chatser, khaw-tsare*: a yard as enclosed by a fence; a hamlet enclosed with walls; court; enclosed tower.

alliance of empires created to reap destruction upon the upstart Israelite nation, calling first on a set of murky unnamed kings and little-known city-states where Jabin was overlord, archduke, and pendragon.[2370] Madon/*Madown*—meaning strife, height and stature of the walls and its mighty men—was a city reigned over by the Horim or Hivvim King Jobab.[2371] Shimron/*Shimrown* was defined as guardian city, watcher city, a city of height, and was a Canaanite royal city.[2372] Achsaph/*'Akshaph* meant "I will be bewitched," from its source word *kashaph* meaning sorcery/witchcraft.[2373] All four northern city-state fortresses were all important Rephaim royal cities leading a pentapolis. Jabin sent additional dispatches to the kings further north in the mountains, to kings of the plain south of Chinneroth, and to the border of Dor to the west.[2374] These likely Rephaim kings ruled Canaanite nations toward the east and west: the Amorites, Hittites, and Jebusites in the mountains, and the Hivvim and Perizzim of Mount Hermon, six of the mighty seven.

> Ps 135:10 Who smote great nations, and slew mighty kings;
>
> Ps 135:11 Sihon king of the Amorites, and Og king of Bashan, and all the kingdoms of Canaan.

Only the Girgashites were not listed, indicating many Girgashites had fled the Covenant Land. Some Girgashites were tallied in Joshua 24:11 as people delivered up to the Israelites. Girgashites were only referenced among the Northern alliance.[2375] Girgashites dwelled in pockets alongside and among various nations listed in Joshua 11:1–4. The *Bn Grg's* settlements were in the northern mountains and among Hittites,[2376] and were also associated with the Rephaim of Ugarit city, which some scholars believe was the *Bn Grg's* royal city.[2377] Additionally, Girgashites dwelled west of the Jordan River and north of the Galilee Sea,[2378] the home of Gergesenes.[2379]

[2370] Josh 11:1; 12:19–20.

[2371] H4068—*Madown, maw-dohn'*: strife; one of the principal Canaanite cities; H4067—*madown, maw-dohn'*: extensiveness as in stature and height; large.

[2372] H8110—*Shimrown, shim-rone'*: guardianship: watch; height; a Canaanite royal city.

[2373] H407—*'Akshaph, ak-shawf'*; from 3784: I shall be bewitched; city in north Canaan at the foot of Mt Carmel; H3784—*kashaph, kaw-shaf'*: whisper a spell; to enchant; practise magic; sorcery; witchcraft.

[2374] Josh 11:2.

[2375] Josh 12:7.

[2376] *Encyclopedia Americana, Vol. 5,* 597: Carchemish; Elitzur, *Places in the Parasha,* 258.

[2377] Wyatt, *Religious Texts from Ugarit,* 306, note 247, citing Margalit (1976); 173–175 (1989a); 233–234; 310, KTU 1.19 iv:40 note 265: Kinneret. Chinneroth/Kennereth of the Aqhat Epic: Corpus Tablettes Alphabétiques [CTA] 17–19; Ugarit was the Girgashite royal city.

[2378] H1622—*Girgashiy, ghir-gaw-shee'*; patrial from an unused name: tribe of Canaan dwelling east of the Galilee Sea.

[2379] Matt 8:28.

Chinneroth was a city located on the Sea of Galilee and was the ancient name for the sea. Chinneroth was known in the New Testament time as Gennesaret,[2380] the land of the Gergesenes. Chinneroth is further thought by some scholars to be recorded in *Ugaritic Texts: Epic of Aqhat* as *Knrt,* meaning "the sea." It follows that the people of Chinneroth/*Kennereth* were Girgashites and the *Bn Grg* of the *Ugaritic Texts.*[2381] Girgashites/*Girgashiy* later became known as the Gergesenes/ *Gergesenos* in the New Testament, a name sourced from *Girgashiy* for early settlers along on the eastern coast of Gennesaret toward Bashan. Lake Gennesaret became the transliterated name over time of Chinneroth/*Kinnereth.*[2382] The Gergesenes were alternatively recognized as the Gadarenes of Lake Gennesaret.[2383] Gadara of Gadarene, where Jesus encountered Legion, was located on the north edge of Galilee and eastward. As such, Israel did not live among Girgashites after the Covenant Land conquest[2384] as they did with other Canaanites, because Girgashites had migrated outside of the Covenant Land by that time. Knowing this explicates why Girgashites were not acknowledged in Deuteronomy 20:17 and elsewhere, even though some Girgashites fought alongside Jabin's alliance in support.

Many of the cities of the Northern alliance like Chinneroth, Hammath, and Hazer were accounted in Joshua 19 as fenced cities/*mibstar*, meaning fortress, walled city, and castle,[2385] as does Hazor/*Chatsowr.* Jabin dictated that all the kings and their armies were to depart their fortresses, to assemble at Merom to form their multitude in preparation for war against Israel.[2386] Jabin's swarm was likely the largest army assembled since the flood. The swarm was figuratively described "as the sands that is upon the seashore in multitude, with horses, and chariots."[2387]

Biblically, "as sand" is a phrase often drafted to describe incredible numbers of Israel's descendants, and for their gathering in the end-time Second Exodus.[2388] The sand simile was additionally drafted to describe extraordinarily large locust armies Israel later warred against in the age of the judges against the Amalekites, Midianites, and children of the east, as well as the Philistine alliance in the genera-

---

[2380] Matt 14:34; Mark 6:53, Luke 5:1. G1082—*ghen-nay-sar-et*; a harp; sea of Galilee; sea of Tiberias.
[2381] Wyatt, *Religious Texts from Ugarit*, 306, note 247. Bn Grg: Benz, *Personal Names in the Phoenician and Punic Inscriptions,* 299, citing Ugaritic Texts KTU 145:15, 1.113:9, 328:14, referencing PRUV Ch. Vorolleaud, *Le Palais Royal d'Ugarit V Textes en Cuniforms Alphabetique des Archives Sud, Sud Ouest et Petit Palais;* UTGL Gordon, CH, *Ugaritic Text Book,* and J. Nougarol, *Le Palais Royal d'Ugarit III: Textes Accadiens des Archives, Sud,* 18:02:14: I:20, 18:20: V:12.
[2382] G1086—*gher-ghes-ay-nos*; of Hebrew origin H1622 Girgashiy; G1046—*gad-ar-ay-nos*: a town east of the Jordan; in habitant of Gadara; a Gergesene. Matt 5:1; 8:28; Luke 8:26, 27.
[2383] Ibid.
[2384] Judg 3:5.
[2385] H4013—*mibtsar.*
[2386] Josh 11:4.
[2387] Josh 11:5.
[2388] Gen 22:17; 32:12; 2 Sam 17:11; 1 Kings 4:20; Isa 10:22; 48:19; Hos 1:10; Hab 1:9; Rom 9:29; Heb 11:12.

tion of King Saul.[2389] Such was the army gathered at Merom to destroy the nation of hope from the face of the earth, but God was with Israel. God reassured Joshua not to be afraid, for God would deliver the Northern alliances' army up before Israel to slay them, hamstring their horses, and burn their chariots.[2390]

Joshua marched his army northward through mountain roads to engage Jabin's army encamped alongside the waters of Merom. Israel struck Jabin's army suddenly and by surprise. Jabin did not anticipate the speed that Joshua would march his army through the mountains.[2391] Josephus noted that Joshua marched his army through the mountains in five days to Merom from Gilgal.[2392] Israel routed the Northern alliance army while they were still in their camp. Israel then slaughtered the swarm as they fled in panic and terror. Israel pursued the discombobulated warriors, first to Sidon, north of Tyre, which indicates Sidonian Canaanites supported the Northern alliance whether they supplied troops or not. Israel smote the refugees in "great Zidon" until none remained, including any of the Sidonians who helped by implication. After Sidon, Israel tracked others who fled eastward to Mizpeh, home of more Rephaim and Hivvim under Mount Hermon, slaying all they caught and destroying their chariots.[2393]

Joshua then pivoted his army to advance south and west, back to Hazor to capture Jabin's city-state fortress, the royal city of the Northern alliance from beforetime. There, Jabin and his army was slain, and Hazor city was burned and utterly destroyed in like manner as other kings and royal cities of the south. The same destruction was accorded to the other kings and royal cities of the alliance; Israel did not burn the vassal cities under Jabin authority that opted to remain neutral in the war.[2394] After the major battles in the north, Joshua oversaw many clean-up operations that included Baalgad in the valley of Lebanon and to Mount Herman, where Israel hunted down the balance of the kings and their forces, slaying them all. Joshua's clean-up campaign seemingly included pockets of resistance in the south and central regions like Seir, Goshen, and the mountains of Israel, making war with those kings for many years.[2395] Joshua's astonishing victory over Jabin's northern army is likely the greatest military victory in humankind's history.

[2389] Judg 7:12; 1 Sam 13:5; 2 Sam 17:11.
[2390] Josh 11:6.
[2391] Josh 11:7. Ellicott, *Old Testament Commentary,* Vol. 2, 130, note 7: suddenly.
[2392] Josephus, *Ant.,* Book 5, 1:18.
[2393] Josh 11:7–9; 13:6.
[2394] Josh 11:10–14.
[2395] Josh 11:16–18.

CHAPTER 51

THE MOUNTAIN AND SOUTHERN CAMPAIGN

Josh 11:18 Joshua made war a long time with all those kings.

God did not promise a quick campaign for Israel. The land would have become desolate from the destruction and overrun by beasts if taken in a year. God promised the Covenant Land little by little, to permit Israel's numbers to increase, in what may have seemed like endless war against giants. But, this was the covenant Israel swore to.[2396]

In the heady days of Joshua's southern and northern campaigns, God hardened Rephaim hearts to war with Israel, delivered up their enemies' heads up for decapitation, and empowered Israel to "destroy them utterly" and without "favor."[2397] The wars in the open field took time, but the tracking down of the remnant took much longer, as witnessed in the northern campaign. Some of the remnant scurried back their high-walled fortress. Josephus noted that long sieges were required because of the mighty walls, "and the confidence the inhabitants had

---

[2396] Exod 23:29–30.
[2397] Josh 11:20.

in them."[2398] Such was the case in the mountain regions, which led to the mountain and southern campaign.

Scripture does not record how many years Joshua waged war in his campaigns, but we do know that "it came to pass a long time after that the LORD had given rest given rest from their enemies, round about, that Joshua waxed old and stricken with age."[2399] We further know Joshua died at the age of 110,[2400] after the mountain and southern campaign when "the land rested from war,"[2401] although the southern campaign continued with Caleb thereafter. We know Caleb was forty years old when he scouted Canaan with Joshua, and that forty-five years had passed in the campaigns since that time.[2402] We know that from the time of Israel's scouts to Israel's encampment at the brook of Zered just before the start of the eastern campaign was thirty-eight years.[2403] We know Israel ate manna for forty years, beginning in the first year of the second month after leaving Egypt.[2404] Israel consumed manna until they crossed into Canaan and established basecamp Gilgal, where they began to eat from the bounty of the land there.[2405] We also know that Israel sent the scouts into Canaan at the beginning of the second year and after Passover.[2406]

Thirty-nine years had passed since Israel left Egypt to the time of the Zered encampment, just before the start of the eastern campaign. At the end of the southern campaign Caleb was eighty-five, indicating Moses died five years earlier, immediately before Israel had crossed the Jordan. One deduces then that the eastern campaign lasted about one year, with the three Covenant Land campaigns lasting five years, before Caleb continued with the southern campaign some time later.

Josephus stated that Joshua spent forty years with Moses and led Israel for twenty-five years.[2407] The math indicates as well that the central, northern, and mountain/southern campaigns lasted five years before Israel rested, indicating that twenty years of mostly peace transpired after Joshua brought all but Judah and Caleb to rest; all this lines up with the biblical chronology. Hence the giant wars lasted six years, plus a year or so that account for the battles at *Atharym* with King Arad and the march to Zered. Knowing this seemingly accounts for Jewish legend that stated Joshua rested Israel after seven years of war.[2408]

[2398] Josephus, *Ant.*, Book 5, 1:20.

[2399] Josh 23:1.

[2400] Josh 24:29.

[2401] Josh 11:23; 14:5.

[2402] Josh 14:7, 10–11.

[2403] Deut 2:14.

[2404] Exod 16:1–16, 35; Num 13:33, 34; Deut 2:7; 8:4; 29:5.

[2405] Josh 5:12.

[2406] Num 1:1; 9:1.

[2407] Josephus, *Ant.*, Book 5:1:29

[2408] Ginzberg, *Legends of the Bible*, 511: Joshua.

Understanding the timelines provided for Israel's various campaigns helps to understand many events and details documented in the Bible. Israel was bound by their sworn oath in acceptance of the Holy Covenant, requiring Israel to utterly/*charam* destroy/*shamad* their enemies: annihilate, exterminate, overthrow in an accursed dedication to God,[2409] without favor/*tchinnah*: without forgiveness.[2410] Israel's utter destruction of the giants and Canaanite nations stemmed from the abominations they purposefully committed in the Covenant Land and their oath against Israel and the Holy Covenant, which is akin to the abominations of Antichrist in the end times. His "heart shall be against the holy covenant. .. he shall be grieved, and return, and have indignation against the holy covenant: so shall he do; he shall even return, and have intelligence with them that forsake the holy covenant."[2411] Antichrist will commit abominations that lead to desolation, God's wrath, and utter destruction of those who oppose God, the Word, and the Holy Spirit at Armageddon.[2412]

Joshua's striking victories were spectacular and sweeping in the south, central, northern, and Bashan regions, but the wars were not over. More war and more sacrifice and commitment were required. Joshua marched Israel once more to war against the Anakim and their loyal hybrids. In previous campaigns, refugee Anakim fled to mountain regions for protection in the south, hoping to avoid annihilation, and to regroup for future wars. The mountain and southern campaign would be waged in two parts: first with Joshua and later, when Joshua died, by Caleb.

Joshua maneuvered his forces to flush out the refugees burrowed into the mountains. Joshua deployed his forces "to cut off the Anakim dwelling in the mountains, from Hebron, from Debir, from Anab."[2413] "Cut off/*karath* is defined as to destroy, consume, cut down, and make a covenant with."[2414] Joshua did not march into the dangerous mountain regions to negotiate a treaty or an alliance, but to utterly destroy the remnant of the Anakim giants and their forces, where they still flourished. Joshua then "destroyed them utterly with their cities."[2415] Very little was recorded on this campaign, but we can extract important information and context from the cities that were named: Hebron, Debir, and Anab.

The Anakim had returned to Hebron/Kiriatharba, the city of the Anakim patriarch,[2416] likely after regrouping in the mountains and due to the lack of Isra-

---

[2409] Josh 11:20. H2763—*charam*; H8045—*shamad, shaw-mad'*: to desolate, destroy, bring to nought, overthrow: to destroy, exterminate; annihilate; devastate.
[2410] H8467—*tchinnah, tekh-in-naw'*; graciousness; grace; supplication for favor.
[2411] Dan 11:28, 30.
[2412] Dan 11:31, 32–45; Rev 12:13–17; 16:12–16; 19:14–21.
[2413] Josh 11:21.
[2414] H3772—*karath, kaw-rath'*: to cut off; cut down; to destroy; to covenant as in make an alliance or bargain.
[2415] Josh 11:21.
[2416] Josh 14:14–15, 15:13.

elite presence with Joshua's multi-year preoccupation in the northern campaign. One further deduces from passages documented later in Scripture that the Anakim for a time, persistently and resiliently, returned to the Hebron region. At the end of Joshua's life and after the conquest ended, Joshua awarded Caleb the Hebron region, but Caleb still had to drive out Anakim in that region, which he did. The Anakim included the three kings first mentioned by Moses' scouts so many years before: Ahiman, Sheshai, and Talmai.[2417] Caleb drove out the Anakim and the three Anakim kings, but did not slay them at that time.

> Josh 15.14 And Caleb drove thence the three sons of Anak, Sheshai, and Ahiman, and Talmai, the children of Anak.

The three Anakim kings returned once more after Joshua died and early in the age of the judges. At that time Hebron was once more an ally of the Jebusites of Jerusalem. The tribe of Judah finally slew Ahiman, Sheshai, and Talmai in that campaign.[2418] One deduces from Scripture that the Anakim did not return to Kiriatharba thereafter but folded into the Philistine pentapolis. The various battles at Kiriatharba testifies to the devotion the Anakim had in maintaining control of the city of their patriarch.

Debir city was built in the mountains near Hebron. Debir means "sanctuary," likely because it became a city of refuge for Levite priests, and a city of refuge for the Anakim. Debir was also the name of a "Amoritish king."[2419] Debir city was formerly named Kiriathsepher.[2420] The city/Kiriath of Sepher was the ancient "city of records," books, learning, and arts for the Anakim.[2421] Kiriathsepher was deemed noteworthy for its destruction because of its importance to the Anakim. One contemplates what history, and details regarding the Anakim, Canaanites, and other Rephaim were destroyed in the destruction. Records akin to the *Ugaritic Texts* were kept in the city of records, which would have provided genealogies and names of the dynastic kings.

Anab/`Anab city was a name cognate with `enab, Hebrew for grapes and/or fruit; it was an Anakim city in the mountains eighteen miles southwest of Hebron. Anab was renowned as the city of grapes and grouped with Debir/Kiriathsepher,

---

[2417] Josh 14:14–15; 15:13-14.

[2418] Judg 1:1–13.

[2419] H1688 —*Dbiyr, deb-eer*; or *Dbir* Josh 13:26: an Amoritish king; sanctuary; a city of refuge west of Hebron.

[2420] Josh 15:15, 19.

[2421] H7158—*Qiryath Cannah, keer-yath' san-naw*; or *Qiryath Cepher, keer-yath' say-fer*: the city of branches; city of the book; a town in the mountains west of Hebron. Kirjathsepher: Josh 15:15, 16; Judg 1:11, 12. Kirjathsannah: Josh 15:49.

also known as Kiriathsannah.[2422] Anab induces images of the grape vines Moses' scouts brought back from the brook of Eshcol in the Hebron region, as a testimony to the fruits of the Promised Land.[2423] Eshcol/ *Eshkol* too is defined as cluster of grapes deriving from *'eshkol* meaning a cluster of grapes, flowers, or a cluster in general. Additionally, Eschol was an Amorite chieftain, the brother of Mamre;[2424] the chieftains allied with Abraham in the raid against the Mesopotamian alliance in the war of giants.[2425] Eschol and Mamre of Hebron were Anakim hybrids from the Anab region.

Israel conquered a large portion of the land bequeathed to them in Joshua's generation, but not all the bequeathed land occupied by the mighty ten.[2426] Joshua had grown old by the end of the mountain and southern campaign.[2427] Israel did conquer enough to begin rest from total war, even though transgenerational war would continue throughout the ages of the judges and the monarchy. At the end of the mountain and southern campaign, and just before Joshua died, the promised inheritance was divided among the tribes. Thereafter Israel rested from total war.

The tally of kings conquered in the Israelite conquest renders one speechless: the kings of Jericho, Ai, Jerusalem, Hebron, Jarmuth, Lachish, Eglon, Gezer, Debir, Geder, Hormah, Arad, Libnah, Adullam, Makkedah, Bethel, Tappuah, Hepher, Aphek, Lasharon, Madon, Hazor, Shimeron Meron, Acshaph, Taanach, Megido, Jokneam, Naphoth Dor, Gigal, and Tirzah. In all, Joshua defeated thirty-one (Rephaim) kings.[2428] Each of the thirty-one kings had an army Israel battled with that were "utterly destroyed."[2429] Let us not forget Israel's victories over the king of Arad, the five kings of Midia, Sihon, Og, Agag of the Amalekites, and Pharaoh of the Egyptians.

The nations and lands not captured by Israel remained to ensure that Israel would not forget the skills of war to defend themselves, and that they required God's support to maintain their independence from Gentile nations.[2430] God did promise to help drive out the balance of Rephaim-led nations for Israel's posterity, but with the provision that Israel upheld God's Holy Covenant—an oath Israel

---

[2422] H6024—`Anab, an-awb`; from the same as 6025; fruit: fruit and or grapes; a city in the mountains eighteen miles southwest of Hebron; H6025—`enab, ay-nawb`: bear fruit as in grapes; wine. Josh 11:21; 15:50.
[2423] Num 13:22–23.
[2424] H812—`Eshkol, esh-kole`; the same as 811: an Amorite, brother of Mamre; a valley in the Hebron region; cluster; H811—`eshkowl, esh-kole`: a bunch of grapes or other fruit: cluster of grapes; cluster of flowers; cluster in general. Gen 14:13, 24; Num 13:23–24; 32:9, Deut 1:24.
[2425] Gen 14:13.
[2426] Gen 15:18–21; Josh 11:23.
[2427] Josh 13:1.
[2428] Josh 12:9–24.
[2429] Josephus, *Ant.* Book 5, 1:20
[2430] Judg 3:1–2.

renewed when Joshua died, and memorialized in its entry into the book of the Law, and a great stone erected under an oak tree.[2431]

Lands Israel did not conquer during Joshua's reign included the crown jewel, Jerusalem, which remained under Jebusite control.[2432] Other lands included the territory from Sihor to Egypt, and to Ekron in the north where the five Canaanite "lords of the Philistines" reigned[2433] with Anakim and Avvim.[2434] Other lands not conquered were: southern Canaanites, Sidonians in north Canaan, some mountain regions, Byblos and Tyre, unspecified regions of the Amorites, and land of the Hivites/Hivvim of Mount Hermon from Baal Hermon to Lebo and Hamath.[2435]

Accordingly, Israelites dwelled and married among Canaanites, Hittites, Amorites, Jebusites, Perizzim, and Hivites/Hivvim, which opened the door for a repeating pattern of covenant apostasy and worshipping of Baalim gods.[2436] Apostate recidivism and then repentance continued throughout the ages of the judges and the monarchy. As such, the curses versus the blessings of the Holy Covenant were deployed to resolve the angelic rebellion. The curses of the Holy Covenant will continue until Jesus returns in his "days of visitation," to bring lost Israel and visible Judah back into the Holy Covenant as their Redeemer, and in time for the supper of the Lamb.[2437]

After Joshua died, the various giant tribes and hybrid humans seized the opportunity to capture lands Joshua previously conquered. The Canaanites were in a "flourishing condition" as Josephus described them, appointing government and kingship to Adonibezek[2438] as overlord, pendragon, and/or archduke of the disoriented southern Canaanite tribes. Hence, the southern campaign continued a little longer. The tribe of Judah led by Caleb[2439] "went up" to battle the southern Canaanites at Bezek near Hebron, in the mountains by inference as the word up/`alah means to ascend.[2440] The Perizzim bolstered the Canaanites in this battle.[2441] The Canaanites were led by King Adonibezek, a Canaanitish king whose name meant "lord of Bezek" or "my lord is Bezek."[2442] Another translation for

---

[2431] Josh 13:6; 24:17–29.

[2432] Josh 15:63; Judg 1:8.

[2433] Deut 2:23; Josh 13:2–6; Judg 3:3.

[2434] Josh 11:22.

[2435] Josh 13:4–6; Judg 3:4.

[2436] Judg 3:5–8

[2437] Days of visitation: Hos 9:7; Micah 7:4; Days of the son of Man: Luke 17:22, 26. Supper of the Lamb: Rev 19:7–10. Second Exodus led by Jesus: Mic 2:9–10.

[2438] Josephus, *Ant.*, Book 5, 2:1.

[2439] Judg 1:12.

[2440] Judg 1:4. H5927—`alah, aw-law`: to ascend as in be high: to go up. *Strong's Cyclopaedia*, Vol. 1, 796: Bezek.

[2441] Judg 1:1–4.

[2442] H137—'*Adoniy-Bezeq, ad-o"-nee-beh'-zek*; lord of Bezek; my lord is Bezek; a Canaanitish king; of Bezek.

Adonibezek is "lord of lightning" from Bezek meaning lightning; Adoni is also defined as a demigod[2443] and is another title for Baal the storm god.[2444] "Lord of lightning" was the title associated with the ninth of the twenty fallen Watcher leaders, Baraq'el/Virogdad, in the Enoch *Book of Giants*.[2445]

The Canaanitish Adonibezek seemingly was Perizzim or perhaps an Anakim refugee, but a Rephaim of some sort. He was a mighty toe collector, who severed thumbs and toes as trophies from seventy kings he slew.[2446] The warrior king, though, fled in terror after his Perizzim and Canaanite army was destroyed at Bezek. Judah's army hunted the scurrying king, caught him, cut off his thumbs and toes, and took Adonibezek to Jerusalem where he was killed.[2447]

Adonibezek's giant thumbs and big toes hold some deeper meanings, as the digits relate to giants. Thumb/*bohen* derives from two Hebrew words. The first can mean thumb or the great toe and is defined as thick. Second, thumb/*bohen* derives from *yad* for hand and an open hand, meaning power and strength. Toe/*regel* is defined as toes, feet, and for the great feet or legs of seraphim, cherubim, and animals.[2448] When combined with the bone-crunching strength of mighty/`atsuwm` Rephaim hands, and the strong/`az/`azaz Terrible Ones meaning stout or thick, one begins to fully understand how large and powerful the hands, feet, and digits of the Rephaim demigods were. Adonibezek displayed his trophy toes and thumbs under his table as a testimony to his warrior status.

Judah transported Adonibezek as their prisoner to Jerusalem[2449] before executing him, likely to intimidate the Jebusites and convince them to surrender or suffer utter destruction as well. Judah at Jerusalem battled the Jebusites, defeated them, and then burned the city.[2450] The Jebusites refused to surrender, placing their confidence in the mighty walls and fortifications of their city-fortress. The lower city fell reasonably quickly, but the upper city was much more difficult because of its walls and elevated nature, "the nature of its place," so much so that Israel moved their basecamp for this campaign to Hebron after failing to take the upper city.[2451]

[2443] H113—*'adown, aw-done*; *adon*: to rule, a sovereign neither human or divine: lord; master; owner; used as a reference to God; H966—*Bezeq, beh'-zak*; lightning: a city in Palestine; home of Adonibezek.

[2444] Knight and Lomas, *Book of Hiram*, 89–95; Porter, *New Illustrated Comanion to the Bible*, 16.

[2445] Lumpkin, *The Book of Giants, The Watchers, Nephilim, and The Book of Enoch*, Aramaic Book of Giants Synopsis on 4Q530, Col. 2.

[2446] Judg 1:7.

[2447] Judg 1:4–7.

[2448] Thumbs: H931—*bohen, bo'-hen*: thick; the thumb of the hand or great toe of the foot; H3027—*yad, yawd*: a hand as the open one indicating power; strength. Great toe: H7272—*regel, reh'-gel*: a foot; feet; leg; feet or legs of Seraphim, Cherubim, and animals used in idolatry.

[2449] Josephus, *Ant.*, Book 5, 2:2.

[2450] Judg 1:8.

[2451] Josephus, *Ant.*, Book 5, 2:2.

THE GENESIS 6 CONSPIRACY PART II

Judah thereafter marched on other Canaanites in the mountains, in the south, in the valley, and then in Hebron once more, where Ahiman, Sheshai, and Talmai were finally slain,[2452] versus just "expelling. .. the three sons of Anak" as Caleb had before.[2453] From Hebron, Caleb marched back to reconquer Debir/Kiriathsepher, previously conquered by Joshua.[2454]

Josephus chose this juncture in his recounting of Israelite history to describe the giants Israel fought against in the Covenant Land conquest: "There were till then left the race of giants, who had bodies so large, and countenances so entirely different from other men, that they were surprising to the sight, and terrible to the hearing. The bones of these men are still shown to this very day, unlike to any credible relations of other men."[2455]

The tribes of Judah and Simeon then took Zephath, occupied by Canaanites, and marched on the Philistines of Gaza along the coast and the mountain regions, but did not defeat the Philistines in the valleys because of their great number of iron chariots that "sorely galled" the Israelites.[2456] The southern campaign after Joshua's death stalled at this point against the Philistines, and the tribe of Benjamin was charged with not keeping Jerusalem from the Jebusites.[2457] In the northerly regions, Manasseh did not drive the Canaanites out from Bethshean/Scythopolis, Dor, Megiddo, Tannaach, or Ibleam in the central mountains. Ephraim did not drive out the Canaanites of Gezer; nor did Zebulon drive out the Kirton and Nahaal Canaanites. Asher did not drive out the Canaanites of Accho, Zidon, Ahlab, Achzib, Helbah, Aphik, and Rehob. Naphtali did not drive out the Canaanites of Bethshemesh and Bethanath. The Danites did not drive out the Amorites who remained at Mount Heres in Aijalon.[2458]

The failures of completing the conquest set the table for covenant backsliding,[2459] and the giant wars that raged throughout the epoch of the judges and into the reigns of kings Saul and David.

> Judg 2:20 And the anger of the LORD was hot against Israel; and he said, Because that this people hath transgressed my covenant which I commanded their fathers, and have not hearkened unto my voice;
>
> Judg 2:21 I also will not henceforth drive out any from before them of the nations which Joshua left when he died.

[2452] Judg 1:9–10.
[2453] Judg 1:20.
[2454] Josh 11:23; 15:16; Judg 1:11–12.
[2455] Josephus, *Ant.*, Book 5, 3:2.
[2456] Judg 1:18–19. Josephus, *Ant.*, Book 5, 2:3.
[2457] Josh 1:21.
[2458] Judg 1:27–36.
[2459] Judg 2:11–23.

CHAPTER 52

GIANT WARS OF THE JUDGES

Judg 2.18 And when the LORD raised them up judges, then the LORD was with the judge, and delivered them out of the hand of their enemies all the days of the judge...

During the epoch of the judges, Israel fought battles against Ammonites, Moabites, Midianites, Philistines, and Amorites, whom Egyptians noted the *Shasu* dwelled among.[2460] God left the Philistines, Canaanites, Hivites, Amorites, Jebusites, and Perizzim for Israel to contend with; to experience and test Israelites in warcraft.

Israel's success or failure depended on their devotion to God, His ways, and the Holy Covenant. Unfortunately, Israel often backslid into serving the Baalim and were subsequently oppressed by fierce enemies. To this end, early into the epoch of judges, King Chushanrishathaim of Assyria forced Israel into servitude for eight years. Chushan, as Josephus named him, besieged Israel, killing many. Israel submitted to Chushan as a vassal state and paid an oppressive tribute.[2461]

Chushanrishathaim was a title of hatred, likely assigned by the Israelites.[2462] Chushanrishathaim's name means "twice-wicked Cushan." One deduces he was a dynastic giant king, from the additional meanings to the compound words in

---

[2460] Billington, "Goliath and the Exodus Giants," 505.
[2461] Josephus, *Ant.*, Book 5, 3:2.
[2462] Ellicott, *Old Testament Commentary*, Vol. 2, 63 note 8.

his title. Chushan is defined as "their blackness," describing an unknown people of Arabia and Mesopotamia descended from Cush, father of Nimrod, and patriarch of the Ethiopians; Cush additionally means "black." Rishathaim means "wickedness."[2463] One deduces the double portions of wickedness derives from his ancestor Nimrod and the terrible actions of Chushanrishathaim.

Israel, after eight years of oppression and servitude, cried out to God for deliverance. God raised up Othniel, son of Kenaz, brother of Caleb, to judge over and to save Israel. Othniel organized willing Israelites to raid the Assyrian garrison Chushan had set over them. Othniel successfully captured the garrison, which begat an outpouring of Israelite support to join him in battle against the Assyrians.[2464] Othniel prevailed. Israel was freed from Chushanrishathaim's tyranny.[2465] Othniel's leadership provided forty years of peace.

The Amalekites, Ammonites, and Moabites, led by Moabite King Eglon, attacked, defeated, and imposed servitude on Israel for eighteen years as a vassal nation. The alliance captured the city of palms/*iyr hattmariym*, another name for Jericho. Eglon, the Moabitish, king built a royal palace for his summer days at Jericho.[2466] Ammon and Moab had previously driven out the Emim and Zamzummim giants from their lands, so one would think the Moabite war was not against giants. Even so, Ammon and Moab were in league with the eastern Amalekites, which opens the door to giants and Amalekite hybrids giants bolstering the Ammonite and Moabite armies. The eastern Amaleqim/Amalekites kept close military ties with the Kadmonim and other peoples east of the Jordan like the Midianites. The eastern Amaleqim tribe was the elder branch to the western branch. Amaleqim originally dwelled along the shores of the Persian Gulf before migrating to southern Edom.[2467] Both branches and the Amalekites were perpetual foes to Israel, all bound to the blood oath to wipe Israel from the face of the earth.

King Eglon was a dynastic Rephaim king or hybrid. His name was patrial from a royal Canaanite city reigned over by the Anakim King Debir that Joshua conquered, and a city allied with kings of Jerusalem and Hebron in the central

---

[2463] H3573—*Kuwshan Rish `athayim*; from 3572 and the dual of 7564: double wicked; twice-wicked Cushan; a king of Mesopotamia; H3572—*koo-shawn'*; from 3568; Cushan: a region of Mesopotamia site unknown: their blackness; H3568—*Kuwsh, koosh*: black; Cush; Ethiopia; a son of Ham; H7564—*rish ` ah, rish-aw'*: wrong or especially moral: fault; wickedness.

[2464] Josephus, *Ant.*, Book 5, 2:3.

[2465] Judg 3:9–11.

[2466] Judg 3:13–14, 20. H5899—*Iyr hat-Tmariym, eer hat-tem-aw-reem'*; from 5892 and 8558: city of the palm trees; another name for Jericho. Ellicott, *Old Testament Commentary*, Vol. 2, 185, Judges, note 13: city of palm trees.

[2467] *Strong's Cyclopaedia*, Vol. 1, 186: Amalekite, Gen 14:7; Ellicott, *Old Testament Commentary*, Vol. 2, 185, Judg 3, note 13: Amalek.

campaign.[2468] Eglon is defined as a calf-like,[2469] a reference to the bull cult, the bulls of Bashan of Mount Hermon, and the Ugarit Rephaim who were referenced as strong bulls. Eglon's rule levied tribute and servitude upon Israel that reduced them to poverty. "God strengthened Eglon,"[2470] as in hardened his heart to provide courage to punish Israel.

Strengthen can also mean to grow stout,[2471] which is interesting because Eglon was described as a "very fat man." Very/*m`od* can alternatively be translated as mighty, mightily, and force, while fat/*bariy'* can be translated as firm, with the latter connected to strength in Psalm 73:4: "but their strength is firm"; "firm" is translated from *bariy'*.[2472] One could translate "a very fat man" as "a mighty firm/stout man" of strength. Non-Israelite nations favored dynastic giant kings or giant-like kings. Eglon was either a giant-like king, a very fat king, or perhaps both.

According to Jewish tradition, Rephaim mingled among the Moabites in the time of Ruth and Eglon. Orpah, a daughter of King Eglon, married a Rephaim named Araph, whereby at least five giants were born that included Goliath.[2473] Goliath was six cubits and a span tall: 11'3" using a royal cubit as Josephus defined it.[2474] Orpah, according to the Dead Sea *Scroll of Orpah*, was the daughter of the king of Moab, Eglon.[2475] One deduces Eglon was a patronymically named Rephaim, as perhaps so was his wife. Goliath and other Rephaim were documented as sons of the giant/*rapha* of Gath,[2476] an Anakim city of the Philistine pentapolis. Araph, as Josephus named the giant father of Goliath,[2477] was the very tall Philistine warrior who passed through Moab in Jewish legend, a descendant of the prehistoric giants: "Orpah saw this glorious man and joined herself to him immediately; she then followed him back to Gath."[2478]

God raised up Ehud as a "deliverer" to save Israel from Moab after Israel cried for deliverance.[2479] Ehud was a strong man who worked among the Gilgal quarries

---

[2468] Josh 10:3, 5, 23, 34, 36, 37; 12:1; 15:39.

[2469] H5700—'*Eglown, eg-lawn*': a Moabitish king; calf-like; Canaanite royal city. *Strong's Cyclopaedia*, Vol. 3, 75: Eglon.

[2470] Judg 3:12, 20, 23, 24. Josephus, *Ant.*, Book 5, 4:1–2.

[2471] Judg 3:12; 1 Sam 12:9–10. Strengthen: H2388—*chazaq, khaw-zak'*: to seize; be strong; courageous; strengthen; cure; to grow stout; grow rigid; grow hard.

[2472] Very: H3966—*m`od, meh-ode'*: exceeding; exceedingly; might; mightily; force; abundance; magnitude; H1277—*bariy', baw-ree'*: fatted; plump; rank; fat; fat-fleshed; plenteous; firm.

[2473] Josephus, *Ant.*, Book 7, 12:1; Ginzberg, *Legends of the Bible*, 518.

[2474] 1 Sam 17:4.

[2475] Wayne, *The Genesis 6 Conspiracy*, 265, citing: Robert Pinsky, *The Life of David* (New York: Schocken Books, 2005), 15–17.

[2476] 1 Sam 21:22.

[2477] Josephus, *Ant.*, Book VII, 12:1.

[2478] Wayne, *The Genesis 6 Conspiracy*, 265, citing: Pinsky, *The Life of David*, 15–17.

[2479] Judg 3:15.

near Jericho.[2480] Ehud crafted a large double-edged dagger eighteen inches long to assassinate Ehud.[2481] One deduces the assassination occurred at Jericho, Eglon's summer palace, and that Ehud had some form of a special relationship with Eglon from his access to the king. Josephus noted that Ehud found favor among Eglon and those around him,[2482] perhaps because of the supply of building blocks for the reconstruction of Jericho and its palace.[2483] When the opportunity arose, Ehud said he wanted to convey a special message to Eglon. Instead, Ehud thrusted his dagger into Eglon's belly; "fat closed upon the blade" that did not permit Eglon to pull it out, likely muscle versus fat.[2484]

Thereafter, Ehud led Israel into battle where they defeated Moab's army, slaying ten thousand men, "all lusty, and men of valor."[2485] Lusty/*shamen* can be translated as plenteous, robust, and stout, and derives from a word that means oily and to become fat. Valor/*chayil* can be translated as force, mighty, and strength.[2486] The "men of valor" were certainly not fat or fatty, but plenteous in height and stout in width, mighty men/gibborim, as was Eglon. One deduces the Moabite army included Amaleqim, Amalekite hybrids, and perhaps other mercenary hybrid warriors. The land had peace for eighty years.[2487]

War broke out after Ehud's reign with the Philistines, whereby Shamgar was raised up by God. He led Israel for one year.[2488] The Philistines were the most lethal and enduring nemesis for Israel. Shamgar delivered Israel from the Philistine oppression when he slew six hundred Philistine hybrids and associated giants with an ox goad, a pointed wooden stick or spear used to prod cattle along. Judges 3:31 is the only verse Scripture provides on Shamgar's amazing exploit.

Sometime after Shamgar's death, when Canaanites of a resurgent Northern alliance led by King Jabin of Hazor rose up.[2489] Jabin's alliance included Hivvim and Amorites of Mount Hermon.[2490] Josephus identified Hazor city as positioned over the Semechonitis, known today as the Hula/Huleh Valley in the hills of Bashan between the Golan Heights and the Naphtali Mountains.[2491] Jabin was

[2480] Josephus, *Ant.*, Book 5, 4:2.
[2481] Judg 3:16.
[2482] Josephus, *Ant.*, Book 5, 4:2. Judg 3:20.
[2483] Judg 3:17–20.
[2484] Judg 3:16–24.
[2485] Judg 3:29.
[2486] H8082—*shamen, shaw-mane'*; from 8080: plenteous; stout; robust of men; H8080—*shaman, shaw-man'*: oily; gross; fat; rich; H2428—*chayil, khah'-yil*: a force of men; an army; wealth; valor; strength; might.
[2487] Judg 3:30.
[2488] Josephus, *Ant.*, Book 5, 4:3.
[2489] Judg 4:2.
[2490] Judg 3:3.
[2491] Barry, *The Holy Land, 325,* 327, 428, 500; Elitzer, *Places in the Parasha,* 196.

either a dynastic descendant of the former Jabin of Hazor in Joshua's northern campaign, or (was a Rephaim who) accepted the dynastic title of Jabin, in the same tradition as "Abimelech, Melchizedek, Pharaoh, Hadad, and Agag."[2492] The latter Jabin's army comprised nine hundred iron chariots and ten thousand horsemen.[2493] The captain of Jabin's army, Sisera, was depicted as a "Canaanitish king" whose name meant "battle array."[2494]

As terrible as both Jabins are remembered in Jewish tradition, Sisera was recounted as more notorious: as "one of the greatest heroes known to history." Sisera was accounted as (king) of Harosheth of the Gentiles/*gowyim* in a similar way to that of Tidal the king of nations/*gowyim* in the war of giants, thus another "king of nations." However, Sisera chose to reign from Gigal.[2495] He was remembered as enormous in size, a giant with a bellowing voice, a great warrior, a great conqueror, and a tyrant.[2496] Sisera was also the name of a Hivvim who surfaced with the Gibeonite/Nethinim/Hivvim temple servants in the time of Ezra and Nehemiah.[2497]

Jabin "mightily oppressed" Israel for twenty years. God raised up Deborah the prophetess to save Israel after they once more repented.[2498] Deborah commissioned Barak to assemble an Israelite army of ten thousand men to war with Jabin's mighty/*gibbowr* army.[2499] Barak marched his army to Kadesh and to Mount Tabor. Sisera assembled his troops and nine hundred iron-reinforced chariots to the Kishon River. Deborah encouraged Barak that God would be with him if he battled Sisera's army. Barak marched his army to Mount Tabor to engage Sisera and his army. God vexed and confused Sisera's swarm into a noisy state of panic-stricken terror. Israel easily put the sword to the discomfited Canaanite army. The Canaanite distress was so extensive that Sisera dismounted his chariot to flee the battlefield on foot.[2500]

Israel trounced the Canaanites as they fled to Harosheth, but Sisera scurried in a different direction for safe shelter, to the house of Heber the Kenite whom was at peace with King Jabin at that time. Sisera was greeted by Heber's wife, Jael, who permitted him refuge in a tent and covered him with a rug. When Sisera fell asleep, Jael collected a hammer and a large spike. She pounded the nail through Sisera's temple, fastening Sisera's head to the ground to ensure Sisera's death,[2501]

[2492] Ellicott, *Old Testament Commentary*, Vol. 2, 189:2.

[2493] Judg 4:3. Josephus, *Ant.*, Book 5, 5:1.

[2494] Judg 4:3. H5516—*Ciycra'; see-ser-aw'*: a Canaanitish king; a Nethinim; battle array; the conquering. Josephus, *Ant.*, Book 5, 5:1; Ginzberg, *Legends*, 520.

[2495] Gen 14:1, 9; Josh 12:23. H1471—*gowy, go'-ee*.

[2496] Ginzberg, *Legends*, 520; *Strong's Cyclopaedia*, Vol. 9, 783: Sisera.

[2497] Ezra 2:53; Neh 7:55.

[2498] Judg 4:3–4.

[2499] Judg 4:5–11; 5:13.

[2500] Judg 4:7–15. Discomfit: H2000—*hamam, haw-mam'*: to disturb; drive; destroy; trouble; vex; move noisily; make noise; confuse; break; consume.

[2501] Judg 4:16–21.

a sudden and devastating death blow akin to a decapitation strike required to kill giants. Israel humbled Jabin and his army that day, a day that included the destroying/*karath* of King Jabin, the cutting-off or hewing-off of his head.[2502] Thereafter Israel maintained dominion over those princes and the mighty/*gibbowr*, whereby the land rested from war for forty years.[2503]

Then came the Midianite oppression for seven years after Israel backslid into apostasy. The Midianites oppressed Israel from their dens, caves, and mountain strongholds from where they rained down terror unto Israel. The Midianites then warred against Israel bolstered by their allies, the notorious Amalekites and the abstruse "children of the east." The alliance annihilated Israel's crops, leaving Israel without "sustenance" for their domesticated animals, or for themselves.[2504] The Eastern alliance came with a great multitude, like uncountable locusts, goyim nations to occupy, to destroy the land,[2505] and to destroy Israel. After enduring cries from the oppressed Israelites, God sent the Angel of the Lord to raise yet another judge to save Israel. Gideon was selected; he ripped down Baalim worship sites.[2506]

The Midianites, Amalekites, and the children of the east, the *bn qedem,* gathered their locust army to the valley of Jezreel. One deduces the *bn qedem* because *qedem* also means ancient time, from old, and antiquity that perhaps included the Sinim,[2507] Kenim, Kadmonim and/or Aryans of Persia. The ancient people of the east appear to be the ancestors for the nations referred to in the end times as the "kings of the East" in the book of Revelation who will march to Armageddon.[2508] As you will recall, Achaemenids were Aryan kings, the "sons of the east." The Kadmonim were Aboriginal tribes of the east/*qadmown/qadam,*[2509] and thus the *ben-Qedem* in the book of Judges,[2510] who partnered with Midianites and Amalekites east of the Jordan.

God sent the Holy Spirit to Gideon to strengthen him for his charge. Gideon blew the trumpet for war, then dispatched messengers throughout Israel to assemble an army to battle the goyim locust army of Midianites, hybrids, and giants.[2511]

[2502] Judg 4:24; 5:25. H3772—*karath, kaw-rath*: cut off, cut down; to destroy; behead; cut off a body part; cut out; kill. Cut off head: 1 Sam 17:51 (Goliath); 31:9; 2 Sam 20:22.

[2503] Judg 5:12–13, 23, 31.

[2504] Judg 6:1–4.

[2505] H1471—*gowy, go'-ee; goy, go'-ee*: massing: nations; a foreign nation; a Gentile; a troop of animals; flight of locusts; heathen; people.

[2506] Judg 6:11–32.

[2507] Judg 6:3, 33, 10:12, 12:15; H6924—*qedem*; Sinim Isa 49:12: people of the east; H5515—*Ciyniym, see-neem*: a distant Oriental region, Sinim; thorns; the inhabitants of southern China; H5511—*Ciychown*; Sihon.

[2508] Rev 16:12.

[2509] H6539—*Parac, paw-ras*; Persia. Esth 1:1; H6935—*Qadmoniy*; H6931—qadmowniy, ka; H6930—*qadmown*; H6923—*qadam*.

[2510] *Unger's,* 732; *Easton's,* 755: Kadmonites. Judg 6:3, 33; 7:12; 8:12.

[2511] Judg 6:34–40.

Gideon gathered Israel's army at the well of Harod. The Midianite army was encamped on the north side of the valley by the hill of Moreh. However, so many Israelites gathered that God decided Gibeon should sift the army down to three hundred with a test, keeping only those who lapped water like dogs when asked to drink. All those who drank water prostrated on their knees to drink, as they would do in Baal worship rituals, were sent away. God did not want Israelites to think they had won the battle by their numbers and strength as Baal worshippers.[2512] God wanted to demonstrate to the faithful that He would fight for Israel and triumph, no matter what number their foe—that only with God's help could Israel defeat their enemies. The battle in the valley by Moreh was like the overwhelming odds Moses and Joshua faced in the Exodus and conquest campaigns, and why God sent the Angel of the Lord.

That night *Yhovah* awakened Gideon and his three hundred to descend to the valley because *Yhovah* had prepared the locust army to be delivered up for slaughter. Gideon's raiders were strengthened by God in preparation for the gargantuan task of attacking the resting army that were like "grasshoppers for multitude; and their camels were without number, as the sand by the seaside for multitude."[2513] Gideon and the three hundred packed trumpets and empty jars. When Gideon sounded his trumpet so did the three hundred, using their right hand with a lamp in the left, shouting "The sword of the LORD, and of Gideon." As at Jericho, the trumpets set in motion invisible forces. The empty pitchers shattered, and the battle began.[2514] The entire Midianite host sang a cacophony of fear and terror in response and then fled the camp in horror, so much so that the locust army set their swords to one another as they fled "to Bethshittah in Zererath, and to the border of Abelmeholah, unto Tabbath."[2515] Gideon then sent word to the Israelite encampment to pursue and to utterly destroy the locust army from the Covenant Land.

Two Midianite kings were captured: Oreb and Zeeb/*Ze'eb*, meaning wolf.[2516] What is fascinating about the Midianite King Zeeb's name is that an Avvim god of the east, Nibhaz, was idolized as a barking god.[2517] One wonders if Zeeb was an Avvim king reigning over some of the Midianites, and or if the five kings of Midia allied with Sihon were Avvim. The other Midianite king Oreb/`*Oreb*'s name meant raven,[2518] which elicits images of falcon gods like Horus and the Anunnaki gods of

---

[2512] Judg 7:1–8.

[2513] Judg 7:9–12.

[2514] Judg 7:13–19.

[2515] Judg 7:20–23.

[2516] H2062—*Ze'eb, zeh-abe'*; the same as 2061: wolf; prince of Midian; H2061—*z'eb, zeh-abe'*: to be yellow: a wolf. 2 Kings 17:31.

[2517] H5026—*Nibchaz, nib-khaz'*: the barker; the Avites' deity whose idol was the figure of a dog.

[2518] H6159—`*Oreb, o-rabe'* or *Owreb, o-rabe'*; the same as 6158: raven; chieftains of the Midianite army defeated by Gideon; H6158—`*oreb, o-rabe'*; or *owreb, o-rabe'*; from 6150: a raven. Isa 34:11.

the east, just as ravens were depicted among the dancing dragons, owls, and satyr gods in the end-time.[2519] Oreb in Hebrew and Aramaic derives from `arab, meaning to grow dusky (as in daylight mixing with darkness);[2520] Tartak was a god of the east and of the Avvim, meaning the "prince of darkness."[2521] Oreb and Zeeb's names indicate patronymic connections to those gods.

> 2 Kings 17.31 And the Avites made Nibhaz and Tartak, and the Sepharvites burned their children in fire to Adrammelech and Anammelech, the gods of Sepharvaim.

Oreb, Zeeb, Jabin, and Sisera were grouped together in the book of Psalms for their infamy as part of the many confederacies of nations and kings who conspired to "cut off" Israel as a nation, and then to possess the habitation of God as their own.[2522] Accordingly, they were referred to as nobles/nadiyb: grandiose princes and tyrants.[2523] Moreover, Oreb and Zeeb were decapitated in like manner as Jabin and Sisera, indicating they were all giants. Oreb and Zeeb's heads were delivered to Gideon.[2524]

Two other participating Midianite kings in the Midianite war were named in the book of Psalms: Zebah and Zalmunna,[2525] kings that fled. Gideon pursued them across the Jordan River, flanked by his chosen three hundred. Gideon found Zebah and Zalmunna at Karkor, protected by fifteen thousand men, the remnant of the locust army.[2526] Gideon and the three hundred slew the host/army in their tents, because they were also discomfited. Gideon captured Zebah and Zalmunna, executing them at Succoth;[2527] the account does not state whether Gibeon cut off the heads of Zebah and Zalmunna. The land enjoyed peace for another forty years.[2528]

Jerubbaal/Gideon begat seventy sons, from many wives and concubines. His concubine in Shechem bore a son, Abimelech, which was the name of two

---

[2519] Isa 34:11–15.

[2520] H6150—`arab, aw-rab`: covering with a texture; to grow dusky at sundown; be darkened toward evening; grow dark; H6151—`arab, ar-ab`: to commingle; mingle self; mix; join.

[2521] H8662—Tartaq, tar-tawk`: prince of darkness; deity of Avites, whose idol was a form of a donkey or mule.

[2522] Ps 83:3–11.

[2523] Ps 83:11. H5081—nadiyb, naw-deeb`: magnanimous; a grandee; tyrant; a noble; princely in rank.

[2524] Judg 7:25.

[2525] Ps 83:11.

[2526] Judg 8:1–10.

[2527] Judg 8:11–21.

[2528] Judg 8:28.

Philistine kings.[2529] When Gideon died, Israelites returned to Baalim worship, selecting Baalberith, a Philistine and Shechemite deity whose name means Baal/lord of the covenant.[2530] With this in mind, Abimelech, son of Gideon, journeyed to Shechem and to his mother's kin, where Abimelech convinced the people of Shechem to follow him with the full support of the house of Baalberith. Abimelech then marched his army to Orphah, Gideon's city, where he slew all Gideon's sons save Jotham who hid himself, who then cursed Abimelech. Then the men of Shechem declared Abimelech king without God's blessing. After three years, God sent an evil spirit to turn Shechemites and Gaal, son of Ebed, against Abimelech. Each gathered their armies for war, but Gaal and Abimelech opted to duel one-on-one at Shechem gate before both armies. Gaal fled the duel, but Abimelech gave chase, resulting in Abimelech and his army pushing back Gaal's army. The next day civil war broke out within Shechem, but Abimelech overcame that revolt.[2531] Abimelech then marched to Thebez with different results. He took the city, but not the fortified tower within the city. Abimelech assaulted the tower and set it afire, but a woman in the tower cast down a rock that crushed much of Abimelech's skull. Abimelech commanded a young soldier to slay him so that he would not be remembered as being killed by a woman. The young man thrusted Abimelech through with Abimelech's sword, fulfilling Jotham's curse.[2532]

Sometime later Tola was raised up as judge for twenty-three years. After Tola came Jair, who judged for twenty-two years.[2533] No wars were recorded during this time, but one expects a judge was required to end or prevent oppressions. Some time after Jair, Israel reverted to worshipping the Baal and Ashtaroth gods of Syria, Sidon, Moab, Ammon, and Philistia. Consequently, Israel was forced into servitude to the Philistines, Ammonites, and Amorites for fourteen years, whereby God raised up Jephthah to oppose the Ammonites who had just invaded.[2534] Jephthah led Israel to victory, sweeping over twenty-two cities of Ammon and recapturing the land of Ephraim. Jephthah judged for six years.[2535]

Ibzan judged for seven years, Elon for ten years, and Abdon for eight years. Thereafter Israel backslid again into polytheism, and was oppressed by the Philistines for forty years.[2536] The Philistine subjugation begat the coming of Samson. The Angel of the Lord/*Yhovah* prophesied that Samson would come as a Nazarite

---

[2529] Judg 8:29–32. H40—*'Abiymelek, ab-ee-mel'-ek*: father of the king; Melek is father; my father is king; two Philistine kings.
[2530] Gen 21:22–34; 26:1–18; Judg 8:33. H1170—*Ba`al Briyth, bah'-al ber-eeth*; Baal of the covenant: lord of the covenant; a Shechemite and Philistine deity.
[2531] Judg 9:1–40.
[2532] Judg 9:1–57.
[2533] Judg 10:1–5.
[2534] Judg 10:6–18; 11:1–11.
[2535] Judg 11:33; 12:1–7.
[2536] Judg 12:8–15; 13:1.

to free Israel from the Philistine confederacy.[2537] Samson judged for twenty years, opposing Philistia through his enormous strength supplied by the Spirit/*Ruwach* of *Yhovah*. Indeed, Samson slew one thousand Philistine hybrids and Rephaim in one encounter, sporting only a jawbone for a weapon. So powerful was Samson in the Spirit that he completely intimidated all of Philistia. As such, the Philistines deviously plotted Samson's downfall through Delilah's seduction. She cut Samson's hair and thus, the covenant source for his Nazarite strength. Subsequently, a captive and blinded Samson slew more Philistines at his death than he did in his reign as judge; the Spirit of *Yhovah* restored Samson's strength so that he could die a warrior.[2538]

> Judg 16:5 And the lords of the Philistines came up unto her, and said unto her, Entice him, and see wherein his great strength lieth, and by what means we may prevail against him, that we may bind him to afflict him.

[2537] Judg 13:2–25.
[2538] Judg 14:1–20; 15:1–20; 16:1–31.

CHAPTER 53

SAUL'S PHILISTINE WARS

1 Sam 6:17 And these are the golden emerods which the Philistines returned for a trespass offering unto the LORD; for Ashdod one, for Gaza one, for Askelon one, for Gath one, for Ekron one;

1 Sam 6:18 And the golden mice, according to the number of all the cities of the Philistines belonging to the five lords, both of fenced cities, and of country villages.

The five Philistine lords' powerful pentapolis and strategic village network threatened or oppressed Israel throughout the four hundred years of the judges. The Philistine network of walled cities/*mibstar* and country villages were cryptically linked to mice when Philistines foolishly possessed the ark of the covenant for seven perilous months.[2539]

The Philistines returned the ark of the covenant with five golden emerods, reflecting the painful anus tumors the Philistines were inflicted with for keeping the ark of the covenant without God's permission.[2540] The five golden mice that represented the five kings and city-states of Philistia were a trespass offering to God: "Five golden emerods, and five golden mice, according to the number of the lords of the Philistines: for one plague was on you all, and on your lords. Where-

---

[2539] 1 Sam 5:1-12, 6:1. H4013—*mibtsar, mib-tsawr'*.
[2540] H2914—*tchor, tekh-ore'*; a boil; ulcer; tumor; hemorrhoids; piles; affliction of the anus.

fore ye shall make images of your emerods, and images of your mice that mar the land."[2541]

Mice were a symbol in antiquity for pestilence according to Herodotus,[2542] which makes sense of the Philistine offering of mice and emerods from the tumor perspective. The five golden mice also represented the kings and the five cities, which is mysterious. One might view at the hubris of the Philistine Seranim stand against God was rodent-like, and that Philistine incursions were infestations of the Covenant Land. The offering did include the humbling of the Seranim, but this is only part of the overall meaning. The golden mice/*akbar* is defined as a mouse biting in the sense of attacking,[2543] allegoric language for the Philistines' military network. `Akbar's source word, `akkabiysh, is a spider's web: a woven network,[2544] walled country villages centered by city-state fortresses that marred the Gaza region.[2545]

The Philistine mice network was bolstered by the Avvim, Anakim, Perizzim, Cherethim, Caphtorim, and Pelethim giants with their village fortress networks, the Hazerim/*Chatseriym* akin to Jabin's Hazor/*Chatsowr* fortresses, and Duke Akbor/`Akbowr's Pau fortress city-states of the Horim, Amalekim, and Edomite alliance.[2546] Scripture indicates a close geopolitical association between the Horim, Amalaqim, and Edomite alliance with the Philistine confederacy.

The remnant royal bloodlines of the Avvim, Anakim, and perhaps Hivvim and Havvim were invited into the internal ruling council, the lords of the Philistines that selected the kings who reigned over the pentapolis royal cities. Both the term "lords" and "princes" are used to describe the Philistine hierarchal ruling structure. Princes appear to be the kings appointed to rule the pentapolis cities, while lords appear to be elder council of royals representing branches of giant nations in the Philistine confederacy, a secret council that exercised authority over the kings.[2547]

The Anakim kept Gath and Ashod, while the Avvim kept Gaza[2548] as their portion within the alliance, grafting their royal scion bloodlines with the Cretan Aryans. The Philistines' ancestors, as you will recall, dwelled among the Rephaim nations of southern Canaan in Abraham's time.[2549] Hence, a Philistine remnant familial within the southern Rephaim royal bloodline likely remained in conjunc-

[2541] 1 Sam 6:4–5.
[2542] Ellicott, *Old Testament Commentary*, Vol. 2, 312, note 6, 2 Sam 5.
[2543] H5909—`akbar, ak-bawr`: attacking; mouse nibbling; mouse.
[2544] H5908—`akkabiysh, ak-kaw-beesh`: entangling; a spider as in weaving a network like a spider; web; house(s) of spiders.
[2545] 1 Sam 6:4–5, 18.
[2546] Deut 2:23. H2699—*Chatseriym;* H2674 —*Chatsowr;* H2691—*chatser.* Gen 36:39; 1 Chron 1:49. H5907—`Akbowr.
[2547] Ellicott, *Old Testament Commentary*, Vol. 2, 420, note 2, 1 Sam 29.
[2548] Deut 2:23; Josh 11:22.
[2549] Gen 21:22–34; 26:1–18.

tion with the Hyksos that were receptive to the invading Cretan confederacy. Sometime after Joshua's conquest wars, the Philistine confederacy was accepted into an association with the Southern alliance of Horim, Amaleqim, Hivvim, and Edomites, underlining that both were outside of the lands Israel was able to maintain authority over.

The Cherethim were the military glue that kept the greater Southern/Philistine alliance bound together. Cherethim/*Krethiy* were proto-Philistines, and Cretans, an extraordinary race of warriors and executioners[2550] deployed to enforce an imposed confederacy. *Karath* is the source word for *krethiy*, meaning a covenant bound with a cut of the skin, to cut off, and to destroy was the word translated as "'are,' confederate" (*briyth*) for nations who swore their oath to destroy Israel from the face of the earth.[2551] Moreover, the Philistine confederacy controlled the iron trade along with the remnant Hyksos, and their northern Aryan allies in Canaan. Philistines maintained iron-reinforced chariots and iron weapons throughout their reign.[2552] This was the formidable Philistine confederation and military network Israel faced in era of judges, a Cretan superpower backed by the Southern alliance.

In time of the judge Eli, Israel marched out to battle the Philistines at Aphek. The Philistines routed the Israelites, slaying four thousand men. Israelite leaders then sent for the ark of the covenant to be brought up from Shiloh to do battle against the Philistines. God did not sanction this war, nor was God with Israel in this war. The Philistines slaughtered the Israelite army, killing thirty thousand men, then captured the ark of the covenant. Eli had led Israel for forty years.[2553]

The ark was kept thereafter at Kirjathjearim for twenty years until Israel once more repented—hence, twenty more years of Philistine oppression.[2554] Israel cried out for God for deliverance again, which led to Samuel's rise to prominence. Samuel gathered all Israel to Mizpeh to confess their sins to God. The Philistine lords received word that Israel had gathered, and marched their army to Mizpeh to plant a mortal blow against Israel, thinking Israel was now vulnerable. Fear grew as the Philistine military machine approached, but God interceded for Israel that day. He "thundered with a great thunder" in a loud noise or voice that completely discombobulated the Philistine army, so that they could be "smitten before Israel." Israel seized the moment. They hunted the discomfited Philistines all the way to Bethcar.

[2550] H3774—*Krethiy.* Cherethites: 1 Sam 30:14; 2 Sam 15:18; 20:7, 23; 1 Kings 1:44; 1 Chron 18:17; Zeph 2:5. Cherethims: Ezek 25:16.

[2551] Ps 83:3–7. H3772—*karath, kaw-rath';* to cut off; to destroy; consume; specifically, to covenant as make an alliance or bargain by cutting flesh and passing between to be chewed; be confederate.

[2552] Judg 1:19; 1 Sam 17:7.

[2553] 1 Sam 4:1–20.

[2554] 1 Sam 6:21; 7:1–2.

Samuel's crushing victory over the massive Philistine army dispirited them from encroaching on Israel's borders throughout Samuel's stewardship.[2555]

Toward the end of Samuel's life he appointed his sons as judges, but they reigned poorly. The Israelites subsequently demanded a king to lead them, as was the tradition in other nations. They desired to be like the other nations with a king who would always be there to protect them, versus the intermittent reigns of judges. As per Ellicott's *Commentary on the Old Testament*, "There is something strangely painful in these terms with which the elders urged their request—the wish 'to be like other nations' seems to have been very strong with them."[2556] After fighting Rephaim-led hybrid human nations for more than four hundred years, Israel desired dynastic hero-like kings to lead them.

> 1 Sam 8.19 Nevertheless the people refused to obey the voice of Samuel; and they said, Nay; but we will have a king over us;
>
> 1 Sam 8:20 That we also may be like all the nations; and that our king may judge us, and go out before us, and fight our battles.

Saul, the first monarch of Israel, was the son of Kish, from a very respected Benjamite bloodline.[2557] He was a mighty/*gibbowr* man of power/*chayil*, with the latter meaning wealth, might, strength, and valor.[2558] The biblical text indicated Kish was a man of influence and standing within the Israelite ruling class, a strong warrior, and a larger than the average Israelite. However, Kish was not a Rephaim nor of Rephaim blood.

Saul was described a "choice young man, and a goodly," and "from his shoulders and upward he was higher than any of the people."[2559] Saul was regarded as of "great stature" comparatively to his compatriots, a warrior in his prime renowned for his "manly beauty."[2560] "Goodly" and "goodlier" described Saul's wealth, position in Israelite society, and physically pleasant appearance.[2561] "Higher," from *gaboahh* meaning powerful, lofty, proud, high, and tall,[2562] is part of a series of words that precedes *gibbowr,* with like meanings in *Strong's Dictionary.* Moreover,

---

[2555] 1 Sam 7:3–14. Thundered: H7481—*ra` am, raw-am*: to thunder; to make the sound of thunder; to rage; cause to tremble. Thunder: H6963—*qowl, kole*; or *qol, kole*: to call aloud: voice; sound; noise. Smitten: H5062—*nagaph, naw-gaf*: hurt; slain; struck; stumble; beat.

[2556] Ellicott, *Old Testament Commentary*, Vol. 2, 323, note 20, 1 Sam 9.

[2557] 1 Sam 9:1; 1 Chron 8:30, 33; 9:39.

[2558] H2428—*chayil, khah'-yil*: army; man of valour; wealth; might; strong; strength; force.

[2559] 1 Sam 9:2.

[2560] Ellicott, *Old Testament Commentary*, Vol. 2, 334 note 23, 2 Sam 10.

[2561] Goodly and goodlier: H2896—*towb, tobe*: good in the widest sense: pleasant; agreeable to the senses; good, excellent of its kind; rich; prosperous. Higher: H1364—*gaboahh, gaw-bo'-ah*; or *gabowah, gawbo'-ah*: elevated; powerful; arrogant; haughty; height; highest; lofty; proud; tall.

[2562] 1 Sam 9:2. Higher: H1364—*gaboahh*.

"the one gift Saul undoubtably, in an extraordinary degree, possessed—the one gift by which, in that primitive time, a man seemed to be worthy of rule. .. from his shoulders and upward he towered above all the people.. .. That there is no one like him among his people."[2563]

God did permit Israel to have a giant-like king from the Israelite ruling class to lead them into battle like Gentile nations, but Saul was not Rephaim. On the other hand, Saul/*Sha'uwl* was not a king God wanted for Israel, but the kind of king for which Israelites desired/asked/*sha'uwl*.[2564] God viewed Israel's demand for a king as a rejection of Him,[2565] yet graciously permitted the monarchy to go forward. Accordingly, Saul was likely not his name, but a title applied reflecting Israel's demand to be led by a king—and a name of a Horim duke.[2566] Saul's coronation begat the age of the monarchy and the next stage to the transgenerational giant wars. Saul was anointed king by Samuel at Gilgal.[2567] The people shouted "God save the king"[2568] at Saul's selection, an adopted phrase of heraldic royal bloodlines who claim an ennobled bloodline that includes Saul and David, like the Merovingians, and the English dynasties that memorialized the phrase in the English national anthem.

The *Armana Letters* acknowledged a chief of Shechem named Lebaya/Lab'ayu who united the Habiru/Apiru southern tribes with their kin northern tribes, when the Habiru routed the Philistines at Michmash, and a Jebusite king recorded Labaya captured Shechem city.[2569] These historical references indicate Labaya was Saul's original transliterated name before becoming king. Labaya was the transliterated compound format for *labiy'*, meaning a great or stout lion, and *Yahh* the contraction format of *Yhovah*.[2570] The name meant "lion of God," or lion of *Yhovah*.

In the second year of Saul's reign, conflict erupted with the Philistines. Saul selected two thousand men to join Jonathan's one thousand men from Benjamin of the south, and they assaulted a Philistine garrison in Geba. Saul commanded the trumpet be sounded throughout Israel, announcing Saul had sacked the Philistine

---

[2563] Ellicott, *Old Testament Commentary*, Vol. 2, 334 note 23, 2 Sam 10.

[2564] H7586—*Sha'uwl, shaw-ool'*; passive participle of 7592: asked; desired; an Edomite Duke and two Israelites; H7592—*sha'al, shaw-al'*; or *shael, shaw-ale'*: to inquire; to request; demand; ask for.

[2565] 1 Sam 10:19.

[2566] Gen 36:37, 38.

[2567] 1 Sam 11:14–15.

[2568] 1 Sam 10:24.

[2569] *El-Armana Letters*, Tablet EA 252–254 and 288–289; Rohl, *Lost Testament*, 304–305; Wayne, *Genesis 6 Conspiracy*, 257–259.

[2570] H3833—*labiy', law-bee'*; or Ezek 19:2 *lbiyao, lebee-yaw'*; masculine plural *lbaiym, leb-aw-eem'*: to roar as in a lion or a lioness; great; old, or stout lion; lioness; young lion; H3050—*Yahh; Yaw*: contraction for *Yhovah*; Jah, the sacred name of the Lord; compounded into names using "-iah," "- jah."

garrison, as well to warn the Israelites that he and they now had become an "abomination" to the Philistines for this unprovoked attack. Israel's army was summoned to gather at Gilgal to prepare for the inevitable war against the Philistines.[2571] The Philistines assembled their massive army and marched them to Michmash, where they made camp. The Philistine war machine came with thirty thousand iron chariots, six thousand cavalry, and foot soldiers that were numbered as sand on a beach—a locust army. Once more Israel was at a considerable military and numerical disadvantage.[2572]

When the Israelite soldiers gathered at Gilgal, they perceived the catastrophe they were about to participate in. Israelite soldiers trembled with fear and began to desert. Some hid in caves and thickets; some fled across the Jordan to Gad. Saul remained in Gilgal with the remnant of his fear-stricken army. Samuel then arrived with instructions to rebuke Saul for not seeking God's support. If Saul had done so, God would have established his kingdom for all time; instead, God had already chosen another man after His own heart and had already anointed him as future king. Saul and his six hundred men hid in Gibeah in Benjamin, while Philistine raiding parties sent from Michmash foisted a weaponry manufacturing ban upon Israel. Only Saul and Jonathan were equipped with a sword or a spear on the day of battle,[2573] thus Israelites resorted to converting agriculture tools into weapons.

The Philistine war machine came with three units of "the spoilers," yet another word translated from *schachath* meaning to destroy, a destroyer, and or mar[2574] as in the mice network that marred the land. *Schachath* is the same Hebrew word utilized for "destroyer of the Gentiles," the prophesied antichrist-like figure, Nebuchadnezzar and his beast empire in the generation of Jeremiah.[2575] Likewise the Antichrist destroyer prophesied by Jeremiah will "destroyest the earth" in the last three and a half years of this age: the "destroying wind/spirit/*ruwach*" and the destroyer/*abad* who comes up out of the abyss, Abaddon/Apollyon meaning destroyer.[2576] One deduces the "spoilers" were a special forces unit of Anakim, Avvim, Caphtorim, and Casluhim, or perhaps Cherethim who were destroyers/spoilers/corrupters of land and of men; Philistines had three of these units. The

---

[2571] 1 Sam 13:1–4.

[2572] 1 Sam 13:5, 19–22.

[2573] 1 Sam 13:6–22.

[2574] 1 Sam 13:17; 14:15. H7843—*shachath, shaw-khath*: decay; ruin; destroy; a destroyer; corrupt; mar; perish; a spoiler; spoil; pervert.

[2575] Jer 4:7; 22:7.

[2576] Jer 51:1, 11, 25, 55; Rev 9:11; 17:8, 11. H11—*'abaddown, ab-ad-done'*; from G6: perishing; Hades; destruction; place of destruction; ruin; H6—*'abad, aw-bad'*; wander away; lose oneself as in to perish or destroy; exterminate; fail; be void; vanish; lost; G3—*ab-ad-dohn'*; of Hebrew origin H11: a destroying angel; destruction; ruin; G623—*ap-ol-loo'-ohn*: angel of the bottomless pit; the Destroyer; transliterated: Apolluon.

spoiler companies were charged with enforcing the weapons ban, while one of the units was sent to occupy the pass at Michmash.

Jonathan, accompanied by a young armor-bearer, went to the pass to engage with the Philistines encamped at the garrison. Jonathan slew twenty of the Philistine "spoilers" that day.[2577] Fear and foreboding gripped the Philistines at the Michmash garrison, and throughout the entire Philistine army. Then God caused the earth to tremble under the feet of the Philistine soldiers, which discomfited them even more. Saul's watchmen reported the mass panic and desertions back to Saul. The tumult in the Philistine camps grew in intensity, so much so that the Philistines turned their swords against one another. Saul called upon his men to attack the discomfited Philistines. The Israelites found their foe in a state of utter confusion, and slew them and the spoilers where they stood, and they fled from Michmash to Aijalon.[2578]

The victory at Michmash solidified Saul's position as king of Israel and caught the attention of the Egyptians as a rising power. Saul fought many wars after Michmash against Moab, Ammon, Edom, the kings of Zobah/Syria, the Amalekites, and more Philistine wars as the transgenerational wars continued. "And there was sore war against the Philistines all the days of Saul."[2579] Perpetual war persuaded Saul to enlist all the strong/gibborim and valiant men he saw. We do not know if this included Rephaim or hybrid human mercenaries, but the text's detail underlines the perpetual war state of mind that vexed Saul.[2580]

Subsequently, the Philistines once again gathered for war against Israel between Shochoh and Azekah. Israel mustered their army by the valley of Elah. Israel's host encamped on one mountain and the Philistines on another mountain, with the valley set between them.[2581] Each occupied high ground. Neither wanted to lose the high ground by attacking the other. Saul had lost his invincibility protection from God by this point, for not carrying out God's instructions against in the Amalekites, which we will cover in the next chapter.[2582] A classic standoff arose, with both parties wary and respectful of each other. Neither side wished to give the other the advantage, prompting a forty-day stalemate, and the opportunity for the king of Gath, Goliath, to step forward.

The Goliath narrative at the battle of Shochah is charged with details affirming the veracity of postdiluvian giants, the Rephaim. Goliath/*Golyath's* name, meaning "splendor" and exile/*galah*, is delineated by *Strong's Concordance* as a Philistine

---

[2577] 1 Sam 14:1–14.
[2578] 1 Sam 14:15–31.
[2579] 1 Sam 14:52.
[2580] 1 Sam 14:47–52.
[2581] 1 Sam 17:1–3.
[2582] 1 Sam 15:9–23.

giant.[2583] Arabic sources contend Goliath/*Gialout* was the dynastic name or title for Philistine chiefs/lords.[2584] Other scholars conclude Goliath's name was a derivative of an Arabic word meaning "stout."[2585] Goliath, in Jewish tradition, was one of the sons of a beautiful/fair Rephaim who traveled to Moab where he married a Moabite princess, Orpah. Josephus identified this Rephaim as "Araph, he was one of the of the giants." Goliath was the strongest of Araph's five sons. Josephus identified another son as Achmon, the original name for the biblically recorded Ishibenob giant,[2586] noting Achmon was of Aryan origin.

Because Goliath was "a man of war from his youth," Saul offered his armor to David, but David refused.[2587] Goliath was six cubits and a span tall, 11'3" using a royal cubit as Josephus defined it.[2588] Josephus stated Goliath was of vast bulk, describing his width as "stout" to signify his muscled strength.[2589] Goliath was a great and mighty man, and a champion/*benayim* who paraded between two armies.[2590] In antiquity, two champions often dueled instead of engaging armies in battle. Goliath fought under scaled armor weighing 125 pounds, and wielded a spear with an iron point weighing fifteen pounds.[2591] Goliath was a Gittite, the king of Gath.[2592] He was a giant/Rephaim, an Avvim or perhaps Anakim, as who controlled Gath in the Philistine confederacy. Goliath "belonged to a race or family of giants, the remnant of the sons of Anak (see Josh. xi 22) who still dwelled in Gath and Gaza and Ashod."[2593]

The battle at Shochah was the nascence for David's time. David was not a large man but was pure of heart for God. The Holy Spirit had previously departed from Saul and thereafter dwelled within David, while Saul was sent an evil spirit to trouble him.[2594] Knowing God was with David that day, not with Saul, explains why Saul did not go out to meet Goliath in mortal one-on-one combat, nor did he send out one of his own men of valor against the giant from Gath. Knowing God was with David further explains how David slew Goliath

---

[2583] H1555—*Golyath, gol-yath'*; perhaps from 1540 for an exile: splendor, the Philistine giant of Gath slain by David's sling; H1540—*galah*.

[2584] *Strong's Cyclopaedia*, Vol. 3, 919: Goliath, citing Ahmed al-Fassi D'Herbelot, Bibl, s. v. Gialout.

[2585] Ibid., Goliath, citing Somonis (Onom. s. v.).

[2586] 1 Sam 17:4. Josephus, *Ant.*, Book 7, 12:1; Ginzberg, *Legends of the Bible*, 518, 536.

[2587] 1 Sam 17:33–39.

[2588] 1 Sam 17:4.

[2589] Josephus, *Ant.*, Book 6, 9:1.

[2590] H376—*'iysh, eesh*: a champion; consent, a great man; a mighty man; a husband, mankind, a man; H1143—*benayim, bay-nah'-yim*: a double interval; the space between two armies.

[2591] NIV 1 Sam 17:5, note 2; 17:7, note 3.

[2592] 1 Sam 17:4; 2 Sam 21:19; 1 Chron 20:5.

[2593] Ellicott, *Old Testament Commentary*, Vol. 2, 363, note 4, 1 Sam 17.

[2594] 1 Sam 16:7–13.

that day, and why Saul acquiesced to David's request to duel with Goliath to decide Israel's future.[2595]

Goliath opportunistically seized the stalemate at Shochah to humiliate the Israelites. Every morning and evening for forty days Goliath suited up with his armor to challenge Israel to send their bravest warrior to do mortal combat with him, with the victor winning the subjugation of the loser's people. Israelites were discouraged by the challenge; they were mortified by the sight of Goliath parading his hubris before them every morning and every evening.[2596]

One ought not to be surprised that a giant champion from the Cretan Philistine confederacy demanded a duel between renowned chieftains or champions. This sort of prideful performance was common in Greek/Aryan conflicts: "in colloquies before the deadly duel—words not unlike the haughty, boastful challenge of the giant Philistine. See for instances, the speeches of Glaucus Diomede in Book VI. Of the *Iliad*: 'Come hither,' says Glaucus, 'that you may quickly reach the goal of death.'"[2597] Mortal combat was common in ancient times to avoid the gruesome bloodletting of a battle. Similar battles were recorded in the *Iliad*, as with the heroes Menelaus versus Paris, and Hector and versus Ajax in the Trojan War.[2598] Homer described the duel of champions as an oath and sacrifice to settle border disputes or subjugation intents.[2599] Ajax and Menelaus were from the proud Achaean/Aryan Cretan race:

> The king ask'd (as yet the camp view'd)
> "What chief is that, with giant strength endued,
> Whose brawny shoulders, and whose swelling chest.
> And lofty stature, far exceed the rest?"
> "Ajax the great (the beauteous queen replied,)
> Himself a host: the Grecian strength and pride.
> See! Bold Idomenous superior towers
> Amid yon circle of his Cretan Powers.". ..
> And next his bulk gigantic Ajax appear'd. ..
> "Now Ajax braced his dazzling armor in;
> Sheathed in bright steel the giant-warrior shone:
> He moves to combat with majestic pace."[2600]

[2595] 1 Sam 17:37.

[2596] 1 Sam 17:11–16.

[2597] Ellicott, *Old Testament Commentary*, Vol. 2, 363, note 9, 1 Sam 17.

[2598] Cahill, *Gifts of the Jews*, 178–179; Homer, *The Iliad of Homer*, 31, 93–102, 217–220, 296, 297.

[2599] Homer, *The Iliad of Homer*, 85.

[2600] Ibid, 96, 216, 218.

As David sauntered down to battle Goliath, he sifted through pebbles until he found five, selected for smoothness to use as projectiles for his sling.[2601] "Why choose five smooth stones? At first read, this may appear to be innocent, normal, and nominal if one assumes David decided to pack extra projectiles just in case he should miss. This natural conclusion, however, does not stand the test of scrutiny. If David was under the protection of the Almighty, and he was, one stone would be ample, and God would have seen to it that it was, just as the epic described. So why did David select five stones?. .. David was prepared to do combat with all five kings from the Philistine pentapolis, should the events require it,"[2602] or Goliath's four giant siblings.

The one-on-one battle to the death was an anticlimactic spectacle. David simply selected one of the smooth stones and slung it toward Goliath. It sank into Goliath's forehead, dropping him like a giant cedar or oak. Once Goliath was felled, David advanced toward the giant, then beheaded Goliath with Goliath's own sword. David raised Goliath's decapitated head in the air for all to see. The Israelites clamored with excitement, but the Philistines trembled with foreboding as to what would follow (1 Sam 17:49–51).

The terror-stricken Philistines fled at the sight of their vanquished hero. The Israelites surged forward to overtake the fleeing Philistines. The Israelites hunted the Philistines and their spoilers all the way to Shaarim (village fortress), Gath, and Ekron.[2603] The Philistines suffered one of their greatest military defeats of all time that day, leaving thousands of their dead strewn from Sochah to Gath and Ekron.[2604] David kept Goliath's armor, and then took Goliath's head to Jerusalem,[2605] likely as a warning that David would come for Jerusalem in the future. One muses if the Jebusites kept Goliath's head or buried it at Jerusalem on Golgotha Hill, where Jesus was later crucified. Golgatha Hill was named as such because it resembled a skull. Golgatha/*gulgoleth*, of Chaldean origin and Greek format *golgoya*,[2606] might be a transliteration and patrial of the Greek originated name *Golyath*[2607] because the "i" sound of the "y" in *Golyath* may have originally been the letter "g" and pronounced as a "gh" sound because of the "a" that followed in the Greek/Cretan language. Further, the `*ayin* in Hebrew may have silenced the original "g" into an "ah" akin to Gaza/`*Azzah*. If so, Goliath would be pronounced Golgath(ah).

[2601] 1 Sam 17:40.
[2602] Wayne, *Genesis 6 Conspiracy*, 273.
[2603] 1 Sam 17:51–52.
[2604] 1 Sam 17:52.
[2605] 1 Sam 17:54.
[2606] G1115—*gol-goth-ah*; of Chaldee origin; compare Hebrew 1538 *gulgoleth*: the skull; Golgotha, a knoll near Jerusalem the name of a place outside Jerusalem where Jesus was crucified; so-called, apparently because its form resembled a skull; H1538—*gulgoleth, gul-go'-leth*; a skull as round: skull; a head: a census poll; Greek *golgoya*.
[2607] H1555—Golyath, gol-yath'.

Matt 27:33. .. they were come unto a place called Golgotha, that is to say, a place of a skull.

As rivalry grew between Saul and David, Saul sought to trick David by demanding a dowry for marrying Saul's daughter Michal: one hundred Philistine foreskins. Saul hoped the Philistines would kill David, but David did not die. Saul then became more afraid of David, and sought more ways to slay David.[2608] David opted to leave Israel.

Considering David's history with the Philistines, it is surprising that David sought refuge in Gath from King Achish, yet another king with a Cretan/Aryan name akin to the Achaemenids. Achish was alternatively known by the patronymic title Abimelech in the book of Psalms. Achish drove David away because he thought David was insane. David fled to Adullam, where four hundred warriors gathered to him in support.[2609] When word came to David that the Philistines were attacking Keilah, David marched his fighting men to battle and defeated the Philistines at Keilah. When Saul received intelligence that David was at Keilah, Saul sent his army after David, chasing him to the wilderness. Saul's army did not have time to catch David because Saul received word the Philistines had invaded Israel once more, causing Saul to divert his army to battle the Philistines.[2610]

After Samuel's death David again decided to seek refuge at Gath with King Abimelech/Achish where David and his six hundred mighty men earned the trust of Achish, because David had found favor as Saul's enemy. David and his mighty men were then deployed as a mercenary force.[2611] Achish was the son of Maoch/Maacha, not Goliath;[2612] Achish's father's name was patronymic from the Rephaim house of Maccha in Syria. It follows that Achish was appointed king of Gath after David slew Goliath, and Achish's name may infer he was another great champion appointed king by the council of the reigning lords of the Philistines for Gath city. David encountered Achish two times in the Bible,[2613] which may indicate Achish lived to a long age, or that another king was appointed and patronymically named after the first Achish died. Either way, David became a mercenary vassal of Achish in the second encounter.[2614]

At David's request, Achish granted David the city of Ziklag, where David lived for sixteen months.[2615] David did not fight against Israel as he told Achish

---

[2608] 1 Sam 18:17–30; 19:1–24; 20:1–42.
[2609] 1 Sam 21:10–15; 22:1–2; Ps 34:1.
[2610] 1 Sam 22:1–29.
[2611] 1 Sam 27:1–5. H2580—*chen, khane*: favor; precious; well-favored; elegance; acceptance.
[2612] 1 Sam 27:2; 1 Kings 2:39.
[2613] 1 Sam 21:10–15; 27:5–12.
[2614] *Mercer's*, 9; *Unger's*, 21: Achish.
[2615] 1 Sam 17:5–7.

but against the allies within the Southern alliance: Geshurim, Gezrim, and the Amalekites. Achish believed David's deception and believed Israel abhorred David, and considered David his servant forever.[2616]

At this time the Philistines once more gathered their armies to Shunem to war with Saul and Israel. Saul assembled his Israelite army at Gilboa, where he scouted the Philistine army. Meanwhile, Achish summoned David and his mighty men to battle with the Philistines under Achish's command.[2617] The Philistines then marched their large army to Aphek to war against Israel. As the Philistine units presented themselves at Aphek, David and his mighty men marched at the rear of the procession. The princes of the Philistines who saw David and his mighty men were furious with Achish, fearing David would turn on them during battle to regain favor with Saul. The Philistine lords ordered Achish to send David and his unit away. Achish obeyed, telling David: "go in peace, that thou displease not the lords of the Philistines," which demonstrated Achish's subservient position to the Seranim ruling council. The next morning David departed Aphek, and the great Philistine army marched to Jezreel.[2618]

Saul, according to Rohl, had incorporated Amalekites into his army after defeating the Amalekites six months before; the vassal Amalekite army protected Saul's rear flank. The Amalekites deserted the night before the battle, exposing Israel to a surprise rear assault.[2619] The Philistines attacked Israel on the exposed flank on the mountain of Gilboa. The surprised and shocked Israelites were slain as they fled, along with Saul and his sons. The Philistines found Saul's body the next day, decapitated the body, stripped the body armor, and sent the body parts to the house of Ashtaroth, where Saul's body and his sons' bodies were fastened to the fortress walls at Bethshan/Bethshean/Scythopolis.[2620]

An Armana letter between the king Abdi-Heba and Pharoah captured Laba-yu's death: "Moreover, I urged my brothers, 'if the god of the king, our lord, brings it about that we overcome Lab'ayu, then we must bring him alive to the king of our Lord.' My mare, however having been put out of action I rode with Yashdata. But before my arrival they had struck him down."[2621] "Moreover, Lab'ayu who used to take our towns is dead, but [an]other Lab'ayu is and he seizes our towns."[2622]

Israel's kingship transferred to David, and the transgenerational wars against the Philistines and other nations of the Southern alliance continued throughout David's reign.

[2616] 1 Sam 17:8—12.
[2617] 1 Sam 28:1–6. Rohl, *Lost Testament*, 311–313.
[2618] 1 Sam 29:2–11. Rohl, *Lost Testament*, 311–313.
[2619] Rohl, *Lost Testament*, 311–312.
[2620] 1 Sam 31:1–10.
[2621] *Armana Letters*, EA 245, lines 1–14 from King Biridiya of Megiddo to Pharaoh of Egypt.
[2622] *Armana Letters*, 321, EA 280, lines 30–35.

CHAPTER 54

DAVID'S PHILISTINE WARS

1 Sam 16:6. .. Surely the LORD's anointed is before him.

1 Sam 16:7 But the LORD said unto Samuel, Look not on his countenance, or on the height of his stature; because I have refused him: for the LORD seeth not as man seeth; for man looketh on the outward appearance, but the LORD looketh on the heart.

David learned about Saul's death, and of Israel's shocking defeat at Gilboa mountain after David returned to Ziklag, and after he routed the remnant Amalekites in the southern region.[2623] David was not a large man as Saul was, but he was chosen by God to be king over all Israel because of what God saw in David's heart. Nevertheless, David was indeed a warrior king.

David departed Ziklag for Hebron, accompanied by his mighty men. There David was met by men from Judah who crowned him king of Judah; David was king of Judah thereafter about eight years before he became king of Israel as well.[2624] The northern tribes anointed Ishbosheth, a surviving son of Saul, king. Seven years of bitter civil war followed before Ishbosheth was assassinated, which then led to unification monarchy under David.[2625]

[2623] 2 Sam 1:1–4.
[2624] 2 Sam 2:1–5, 11; 5:5.
[2625] 2 Sam 2:10, 12–32; 3:1–39; 4:1–12.

The elders of Israel trekked to Hebron/Kiriatharba to reestablish the Israelite tribes under one king, whereby David reigned for another forty years.[2626] David was again anointed as king of Israel at Hebron, the infamous Anakim royal city, as a sign of God's blessing upon David and as notice to the giant hegemony that David would complete the covenant obligations. Men from all Israel streamed to Hebron to join with David until a "great host like the host of God" was assembled.[2627] David's famous mighty men were his phalanx that led the great army in the giant wars that followed.

Although mighty/gibborim is the same word utilized to describe the Nephilim and Nimrod,[2628] the phrase does not apply to most David's mighty men in that sense; most were Israelites. Nevertheless, Uriah was a Hittite and a hybrid Rephaim human. Ismaiah was a Gibeonite, Hivite hybrid, or Hivvim. Eliphelet was a Maachathim from the Mount Hermon region. And of course, there were the famous wilderness men/gibborim who were swift as gazelles and possessed faces of lions. Gadites could be understood as Israelites from Gad or as a kind of Rephaim: as invaders, and a troop of foreign mercenaries who could successfully take on one hundred men at a time, and the greatest of them a thousand men.[2629] David hired and attracted dissident mercenaries as part of his mighty men. Hiring mercenaries was part of David's military tactics. David further established his sons as chiefs. In addition, Benaiah commanded the Cherethim and Pelethim mercenaries, and Joab commanded David's mighty men after David established himself as king over all Israel.[2630] These Cherethim, Cretan Aryans were executioners, bodyguards, and mercenaries, while the Pelethim were Philistine mercenaries and bodyguards.[2631]

During David's reign and while Absalom was still alive, David was protected by the Cherethim, the Pelethim, and six hundred Gittites from Gath.[2632] One deduces the mercenary Gittites included hybrid Philistines and perhaps Anakim or Avvim. The Cherethim and Pelethim traveled with and fought for Joab and David's mighty men. Philistine mercenaries were still employed when Solomon became king.[2633] David's Cherethim and Pelethim were mercenary orders

---

[2626] 2 Sam 5:3–5; 1 Chron 11:3.

[2627] 1 Chron 12:22–38.

[2628] Gen 6:4; 10:8–9.

[2629] Uriah the Hittite: 2 Sam 23:39. Ismaiah the Gibeonite: 1 Chron 12:4. Eliphelet the Maachathite: 2 Sam 23:34. H4602—*Ma`akathiy.* 1 Chron 12:8–14. H1425—*Gadiy:* an invader; a troop of fortune.

[2630] 2 Sam 8:15–18, 20:23; 1 Chron 18:17.

[2631] H3774—*Krethiy:* executioner: a bodyguard; H6432—*Plethiy:* Philistine mercenaries. 2 Sam 15:18; 20:7, 23; 1 Kings 1:38, 44; 1 Chron 18:17.

[2632] 2 Sam 15:17–22.

[2633] 2 Sam 20:7; 1 Kings 1:38, 44.

employed outside Philistia,[2634] and perhaps were spoilers. The Chaldeans and Syrians understood Cherethim and Pelethim as appellatives for executioners, hired captains for eastern armies.[2635]

Israelites permitting Rephaim or hybrid human mercenaries or servants to dwell among them dated back to the Covenant Land conquest when Joshua forged a peace treaty with the Gibonim who became temple servants, later known as the Nethinim temple servants.[2636]

> 1 Chron 9:2 Now the first inhabitants that dwelt in their possessions in their cities were, the Israelites, the priests, Levites, and the Nethinims.

Scripture provides a partial genealogy for temple slaves beginning with Solomon, but not a direct accounting as to who the Nethinim were. Nethinim genealogy descends back to Ziha that included Ami of Solomon's 292 temple servants. Ami/ *amiy* is defined as bondservant.[2637] Curiously, *'ammiyts* means strong, mighty, and courageous, immediately follows *'amiy* in *Strong's Dictionary*, and as such is related to *'amiy* by implication.[2638] Moreover, there is Scripture indicating Nethinim were Gibonim. Joshua, after agreeing to the peace treaty, institutionalized Gibonim, a branch of the Hivvim sworn by oath by the "princes of the congregation," to be "wood hewers," "water drawers," and "servants to work for Levite priests in the congregation and altar of God." Gibonim were not free because of their deception but cursed to be bondsmen "even unto this day."[2639]

Israel's irregular accommodation within the temple religious institutions included protection for the Gibonim, just as Israel protected them against the five Rephaim kings who viewed Gibeon's treaty as utter betrayal.[2640] The protections guaranteed in Joshua's treaty resurfaced in King Saul's reign when famine occurred. Saul endeavored to destroy all Gibeonites because they were the descendants/remnant of the Amorites,[2641] but a remnant survived. A famine then struck Israel because of Saul's violation to the Joshua treaty established by oath with

---

[2634] Ellicott, *Old Testament Commentary*, Vol. 2, 407, note 18: The Cherethites and Pelethites, 2 Sam 9.

[2635] Ibid., Vol. 2, 407, note 18: The Cherethites and Pelethites, 2 Sam 9.

[2636] H5411—*Nathiyn, naw-theen'*: Temple-servants. 1 Chron 9:2; Ezra 2:43; 58, 70; 7:7; 8:17, 20; Neh 3:26, 31; 7:46, 60, 73; 10:28; 11:3, 21.

[2637] Ezra 2:43, 57; Neh 7:46. H532—*'Amiy, aw-mee'* Ami, an Israelite: bondservant.

[2638] H533—*'ammiyts, am-meets'*; or *ammits, am-meets'*: strong one: mighty; courageous; strong.

[2639] Josh 9:1–27.

[2640] Josh 10:1–12.

[2641] 2 Sam 21:2.

THE GENESIS 6 CONSPIRACY PART II

God. David later made reconciliation with the remnant Gibeonites for Saul's violation.[2642]

Thus, Gibeonite hybrids, the remnant of Amorites,[2643] continued as the Nethinim temple bondmen/`ebed,[2644] and perhaps other positions of servitude. Knowing this explains how Ismaiah the Gibeonite became a "mighty man" among David's mighty men. One Nethinim was named patronymically from Sisera, the Hivvim King of Harosheth, the commander of Jabin's Canaanite army. Harosheth was a land of woodlands and woodcutters, the Hivvim from Hermon's cedar and oak forests;[2645] recall that the Gibonim/Hivvim temple servants were employed as wood hewers.[2646]

The Philistines mobilized their forces to seek and destroy David and his army when they learned that David had united Israel under his leadership.[2647] The Philistines understood how fearsome a foe David the giant slayer was from his exploits as Achish's mercenary, and the indignation David levied on the Philistines in the foreskin affair. The Philistine blood oath to destroy Israel once more boiled, which begat a series of obsessive, suicidal Philistine battles to destroy Israel at all costs.

The war began with the battle at Baalperazim. The Seranim amassed their forces augmented with their "spoiler" regiments throughout the Valley of the Giants/Rephaim south and west of Jerusalem.[2648] David prayed to God for guidance. God instructed David to engage the Philistine hordes; that God would deliver the locust army into David's hands.[2649] David's army planted a punishing blow against the Philistines that day. "David smote them there, and said, The LORD hath broken forth upon mine enemies before me, as the breach of waters". Therefore, he called the name of that place Baalperazim. Baalperazim means "the Lord breaks," figuratively "outburst of God's wrath,"[2650] or perhaps "Baal(s) were broken" because David had destroyed the Philistine idols throughout the Valley of Giants.[2651] Shortly thereafter the Philistines regrouped for war once more in

---

[2642] 2 Sam 1:1–14.

[2643] 2 Sam 21:2.

[2644] H5650—`ebed, eh'-bed: a servant in bondage; bondman; slave; servant; manservant; worshippers of God; servant in special sense as prophets, Levites.

[2645] Judg 4:2, 21; 1 Sam 12:9; Ezra 2:53; Neh 7:55. Ginzberg, *Legends of the Bible*, 520; *Strong's Cyclopaedia*, Vol. 9, 783: Sisera; Ellicott, *Old Testament Commentary*, Vol. 2, 190, note 2, Judg 4. H2800—*Charosheth, khar-o'-sheth*: woodland; a city in northern Canaan.

[2646] Josh 9:27.

[2647] 2 Sam 14:8; 1 Chron 14:9.

[2648] 2 Sam 5:1–20; 1 Chron 14:8–9. Ellicott, *Old Testament Commentary*, Vol. 2, 457, note 18, 2 Sam 5.

[2649] 2 Sam 5:19–22; 1 Chron 14:10.

[2650] 2 Sam 5:20–21; 1 Chron 14:11–12. H1188—*Ba`al P`ratsiym, bah'-al per-aw-tseem*; from 1167 and the plural of 6556: possessor of breaches; lord of the breaks; a great destruction of idols; also called Mount Perazim; H6556—*perets, peh'-rets*: a break; breaking forth; breach; bursting forth, outburst; outburst of God's wrath.

[2651] 2 Sam 5:21.

the Valley of Giants. This time God went before Israel to confound the Philistines and prepare them for slaughter. Then Israel emerged from the mulberry trees they had hidden among to wait for God to deliver the discomfited army.[2652] The Valley of the Rephaim battles were examples of God's wrath against the giants and hybrids, and a foreshadowing for the Armageddon battle that will be waged at the base of Mount Hermon.

David then established a new home for the ark of the covenant in the city of David, Jerusalem, which he had previously conquered for Israel and this purpose.[2653] Jerusalem, the city from "old time,"[2654] with its capture became central for prophetic events of the monarchy, a requisite sign and marker for the end times, and for the fig tree generation Jesus spoke to.[2655] One ponders if the ark of the covenant will be reestablished in Jerusalem after Armageddon when Jesus establishes His millennium-centered reign in Jerusalem.

Old/`alam is understood in this application as from remote, an indefinite time, eternity, and perpetuity past and future.[2656] Jerusalem—the city of God, David, and Jesus—was a city built before the flood perhaps occupied by Nephilim, rebuilt after the flood and occupied by Rephaim and their hybrids, a city destroyed by the beast empires of Babylon and Rome, and a city of the end times, millennium, and the city of the new heavens and earth.[2657] Jerusalem will become the city of Antichrist, with the abomination at the midpoint of the last seven years, figuratively called the (new) Sodom,[2658] as the polytheist shining city on a hill for their promised new age. One might anticipate Antichrist will make claims to Jerusalem through his alleged dynastic right of inheritance from Nephilim, Rephaim, and Israelite kings.

David continued to war against the Philistine nemesis in several more battles, eventually subduing them. In this final campaign against the Philistines to rid the giants from Gaza, David conquered Methegammah/*Metheg ha'Ammah*, an "ephitet of Gath" meaning the metropolis mother city of authority of the Philistines.[2659] Gath was the military city of the authority for the Philistine empire, the city of the Anakim, and the city of Goliath and Achish.

[2652] 2 Sam 5:22–25; 1 Chron 14:13–17.

[2653] 2 Sam 6:1–12.

[2654] Ezra 4:15.

[2655] Matt 24:32; Mark 13:28; Luke 21:29.

[2656] H5957—`alam, aw-lam`; corresponding to 5769: remote time in the future or past; indefinitely; forever; perpetuity; antiquity; H5769—`owlam: eternity past or future: ancient; futurity; perpetual; eternity; H5957: Ever and ever: Dan 2:4, 44; 3:9; 4:34; 5:10; 6:6, 21, 26; 7:18. Everlasting: Dan 4:3, 34; 7:14, 27. Old: Ezra 4:15, 19.

[2657] Rev 21:2, 10.

[2658] Rev 11:8.

[2659] 2 Sam 8:1. H4965—*Metheg ha-'Ammah, meh'-theg haw-am-maw*: the metropolis; an epithet of Gath; mother city; mother city of authority.

In the battles leading up to capturing Gath city, the exploits of David's most famous of mighty men were memorialized in Scripture. In one of these exploits, Ishbibenob the giant/*rapha* endeavored to slay David as he tired.[2660] In many English translations Ishbibenob, "one of the sons of the giant," is translated as "one of the children/descendants the giant(s)" or as "one of the sons of Rapha."[2661] *Strong's Dictionary* defines Ishbibenob as "his dwelling is in Nob" city near Jerusalem, son of Rapha, and one of the Philistine giants.[2662] Ishbibenob was either a descendant of the patriarch Rapha or the son of a giant patronymically named Rapha that Josephus named as Araph, or both. Ellicott's *Commentary* noted the term children/*yaliyd* of the giant that accounted for the giant Sippai referenced a collective "tribal designation of the gigantic Rephaim (Gen. xiv. 5)." As such, Ellicott's *Commentary* also stated the phrase "son of a giant. .. was born to the Rephaite: i.e., the clan so named,"[2663] indicating Ishbibenob was both son of Rapha and of the Raphaim tribe. Abishai, David's kinsman,[2664] saved David from Ishbibenob and slew this Rephaim. Ishbibenob's spearhead weighed three and a half kilograms.[2665] David's men thereafter persuaded David not to enter battle lest "thou quench the light of Israel."[2666]

Another Philistine battle broke out at Gezer and nearby Gob.[2667] At the Gezer/Gob battle, Sibbechai the Hittite slew Sippai and/or Saph,[2668] including many "who bragged they were of the posterity of the giants and vaunted themselves highly on that account."[2669] Sippai and Saph were sons of the giant(s). *Strong's Cyclopaedia* similarly noted to *Ellicott's Commentary* that this could refer to one specific giant or the race of Rapha.[2670] Sippai was slain at Gezer, and Saph was slain at Gob, by the two accounts in Scripture. Sippai/*Cippay*'s name meant a vestibule or basin-like, while Saph/*Caph*'s name meant tall. Both names derive from *Caph*

[2660] 2 Sam 21:16. H7498—*Rapha', raw-faw'*; or *Raphah, raw-faw'*: giant; tall.

[2661] 2 Sam 21:15–16. H7497—*rapha'*. Bibles translating the KJV 2 Sam 21:16's "of the sons of the giant" as "descendants of Rapha": NIV, BSB, NB, NHEB; as "descendants/children of the giants": NLT, ESV, NASB, CSB, HCSB, ISV, YLT.

[2662] H3430—*Yishbow b-Nob, yish-bo'beh-nobe*: his dwelling is in Nob near Jerusalem; son of Rapha, one of the Philistine giants slain by Abishai.

[2663] Ellicott, *Old Testament Commentary*, Vol. 3, 299, note 4, 6, 8. 1 Chron 20. H3211—*yaliyd, yaw-leed'*; born as in child or son: born; children; sons.

[2664] H52—*'Abiyshay, ab-ee-shah'ee; Abshay abshah'ee*: father of a gift; my father is Jesse; my father is a gift.

[2665] *NIV* 2 Sam 21:16, note 2.

[2666] 2 Sam 21:17.

[2667] 2 Sam 21:18; 1 Chron 20:4. H1359—*Gob, gobe*; or *Gowb, gobe'*: pit; cistern.

[2668] 2 Sam 21:18; 1 Chron 20:4.

[2669] Josephus, *Ant.*, Book 7, 12:2.

[2670] *Strong's Cyclopaedia*, Vol. 9, 350: Saph; 780: Sippai.

meaning threshold, doorkeeper, and goblet.[2671] One can view that Sibbechai slew two giants: one at the cistern/Gob and one at Gezer, or that Sibbechai slew one giant known by two different names or titles. Both were documented as "one of the sons of the giant" (2 Sam 21:18) and "that was of the children of the giant" (1 Chron 20:4).[2672] Likewise, the giant Lahmi was accounted for at Gob where Elhanan slew Goliath's brother Lahmi,[2673] who was a son of the same giant, Rapha, which by implication confirmed Goliath was a Rephaim and son of Rapha/Araph.

In a subsequent battle waged at the royal city of Gath/Methegammah, the Israelites encountered a giant of great stature.[2674] Considering Goliath was 11'3" tall, one deduces by acknowledgment of this giant's great stature that this giant was perhaps in the height range of Goliath. "Man of great stature" further communicated that this warrior was of a different form to other men.[2675] Accordingly, Josephus wrote this Gittite giant was six cubits tall,[2676] like Goliath's stature. Moreover, this Gittite giant possessed six fingers on each hand and six toes on each foot. The Gittite giant seems to be of a different variety of giant, giants often associated with a second row of teeth. However, the Gittite giant was also accounted as a son born to Rapha.[2677] One deduces that perhaps there was another giant bloodline scioned into the father that produced the six-digit anomaly. This unnamed giant was slain by Jonathan.[2678] It follows that Gath was the city of the four giants listed in the book of 2 Samuel: Ishbibenob, Saph, the brother of Goliath (Lahmi) and the unnamed six-digited giant. Goliath, Lahmi's brother, tallies five giants born from Rapha, and perhaps six giants if Saph and Sippai were distinct giants.

> 2 Sam 21:22 These four were born to the giant in Gath, and fell by the hand of David, and by the hand of his servants.

Another giant, one from Egypt, was slain by Benaiah. This giant, perhaps a Zuzim, was described as a "goodly man" as in a vision of beauty or a phenomenon.

[2671] H5598—*Cippay, sip-pah'-ee*; from 5592 basin-like: son of the Philistine giant; H5593—*Caph, saf*; the same as 5592: tall; son of the Philistine giant; H5592—caph, saf: a basin, bowls; goblet; threshold, doorkeeper.

[2672] H7498—*Rapha', raw-faw'*; or *Raphah, raw-faw'*; giant: tall.

[2673] 2 Sam 21:19; 1 Chron 20:5.

[2674] H4067—*madown, maw-dohn'*; extensiveness as in height: stature; size; H4055—*mad, mad*; or *med, made*; height and stature, and a measure, armor, clothes, garment: measure; stature; cloth garment; carpet.

[2675] Ellicott, *Old Testament Commentary*, Vol. 3, 299, note 6, 1 Chron 20.

[2676] Josephus, *Ant.*, Book 7, 12:2.

[2677] 2 Sam 21:22. Josephus, *Ant.*, Book 7, 12:2.

[2678] 2 Sam 21:20; 1 Chron 20:6.

He was five cubits tall (8'9").[2679] Josephus wrote that the Egyptian giant was of great bulk like Goliath, stout or very wide.[2680] Further, Josephus noted Nephan, a kinsman to David, fought the stoutest giant of the Philistines and put the rest to flight,[2681] indicating there were many giants there.

David defeated the mighty Philistine alliance, and captured the Philistine city of Gath and its surrounding network of mice villages.[2682] David brought this transgenerational war to a close. However, King David had other nations to quell. David led a life of perpetual war.

[2679] 2 Sam 23:21; 2 Chron 11:22–23. H4758—*mar'eh, mar-eh'*; an appearance or shape displaying comeliness, beauty, and or handsomeness: a vision; a sight; a phenomenon; a spectacle.
[2680] Josephus, *Ant.*, Book 7, 12:4.
[2681] Ibid., Book 7, 12:2.
[2682] 2 Sam 8:11; 1 Chron 18:1.

CHAPTER 55

THE AMALEKITE WARS

Exod 17.14. ... Write this for a memorial in a book, and rehearse it in the ears of Joshua: for I will utterly put out the remembrance of Amalek from under heaven.

Amaleqim were documented as giants in the *war of giants*, which predated Amalek's birth from Eliphaz and Timna in Genesis 36:12.[2683] Amalekites were documented as part of the hybrid humans dwelling among Anakim giants in Joshua and Caleb's accurate report to Moses.[2684]

The Amalekites and Amaleqim warred with Israel several times during the epoch of the judges. Amalek was the first nation after Egypt that attacked Israel at Rephidim, when Israel was most vulnerable.[2685] God did not look kindly upon the dastardly deeds of the Amalekites. God reserved a future time for Amalek to address their judgment, a period when God would deliver rest to Israel within the Covenant Land, when Israel would be commanded to "blot out the remembrance of Amalek from under heaven" for their crimes against Israel.[2686]

Amalek's time of judgment arrived when Samuel anointed King Saul. Saul was decreed to utterly destroy/*charam* the hybrid Amalekite nation in the same

---

[2683] Gen 14:7; 36:12.
[2684] Num 13:28–29.
[2685] Exod 17:1–14.
[2686] Deut 25:19.

way and manner as Moses and Joshua destroyed many of the Rephaim and hybrid Canaanites. Amalekites were marked as accursed and criminals to be consumed, to come to an end, vanish, and to be destroyed.[2687] The Amalekites and their Rephaim kings were identified as wicked, Sodom-like, reserved for divine judgment.[2688]

Saul's Amalekite war occurred before the Philistine battle at Shochoh, which provides context for why Saul refused to duel with Goliath, because Saul lost his favor with God during the Amalekite war. After the Amalekite war, Samuel no longer went to see Saul. God sighed in compassion, disappointment, and grief,[2689] because Saul failed to follow God's edicts. God viewed Saul's rejection of God's word as rebellion cognate to the sin of witchcraft, and as stubbornness, arrogance, and insolence.[2690]

> 1 Sam 15:23 For rebellion is as the sin of witchcraft, and stubbornness is as iniquity and idolatry. Because thou hast rejected the word of the LORD, he hath also rejected thee from being king.

Saul marshaled his army for the Amalekite war at Telaim, a site unknown today in Judah[2691] but thought by scholars to be Telem in the Negeb, close to Amalekite territory and the royal city.[2692] Saul then marched his army to Petra, the "city of Amalek and laid wait in the valley."[2693] Petra was the ancient stronghold of Mount Seir of the Edomites and Horim, a place David Rohl accounted as Mosera, the Rose-Red City.[2694] Petra, according to Josephus, was the former home of Amaleqim giants.[2695] Petra/Acre/Arecem was the perpetual capital city of sedition, home of the Amalekite blood oath, and a royal city reigned over by Iy'anak/Anakim rulers.[2696] After Petra, Saul pursued the remnant from Havilah to Shur and attacked other cities and villages there, from Petra to the Egyptian border and to the region known today as Yemen.[2697]

[2687] 1 Sam 15:2–3. H2400—*chatta', khat-taw'*: a criminal; offender; sinful; sinner; condemnation; reckoned; H3615—*kalah, kaw-law'*: end, be finished; perish from the earth: destroy; vanish.

[2688] Gen 13:13.

[2689] H5162—*nacham, naw-kham'*; to sigh, be sorry; pity; rue: have compassion; suffer; grief; repent; comfort.

[2690] 1 Sam 15:23–24. H6484—*patsar, paw-tsar'*; dull; stubbornness; insolent; arrogance; presumption.

[2691] H2923—*Tla'iym, tel-aw-eem'*: an unknown site in southern Judah; lambs; H2928—*Telem, teh'-lem*: to break up or treat violently; oppression; a place in Idumaea; one of the cities in the Negeb.

[2692] Josh 24:4; 1 Sam 15:4–5. Ellicott, *Old Testament Commentary*, Vol. 2, 354, note 4, 1 Sam 15:4.

[2693] 1 Sam 15:5.

[2694] Rohl, *Legends*, 225, citing Deut 10:6

[2695] Josephus, *Ant.*, Book 3, 2:1.

[2696] Billington, "Goliath and the Exodus Giants," 501, 506 citing Pritchard, *ANET*, 225, notes 3, 6.

[2697] H7793—*Shuwr, shoor*: a region of the desert on the border of Egypt: wall; H2341—*Chaviylah, khav-ee-law'*: circle; a part of Eden the Pison River flowed through; northeast corner of Asia Minor; district of Kualan in Yemen.

Sadly, Saul did not utterly destroy all the Amalekites, which violated God's instructions.[2698] Regrettably, Saul chose to spare some Amalekites, King Agag, and the prized animals. Saul spared Agag because Saul admired the tall and handsome king. Saul was a very large warrior himself, yet Saul found Agag comparatively taller still. One ponders just how large Agag was, noting his title was patronymic after the Amaleqim Agag in the time of the Exodus, a dynastic bloodline from the time of the flood, which undoubtedly suggests Rephaim blood flowed through the veins of Amalekite kings from the Amaleqim of Genesis 14:7. Timna and Eliphaz named their son Amalek after the Amaleqim patriarch, which then became the eponymous name for the Amalekite hybrids, who dwelled with the Amaleqim.

Samuel stated that just as Agag's sword had put (Israelite) women to the sword, Samuel would subject Agag to the sword at Gilgal. Samuel did not just kill Agag with a single strike of the sword, but hewed Agag into pieces, in a "peculiar kind" of slaying akin to quartering,[2699] and a death that included decapitation by inference, and as Rephaim were beheaded. Further, hacking Agag into pieces inferred that Agag was viewed as accursed for his crimes.[2700] Ellicott's *Old Testament Commentary* described Agag's condemnation as "even among a wicked race, to have been pre-eminent in wickedness."[2701]

Consequently, Samuel denounced Saul for his defiance of God's edict, and then proclaimed the everlasting kingdom of God would not continue through Saul's descendants as kings. God removed the right of succession for Saul's sons to the throne of Israel, and therefore the lineage of the Messiah, as proper punishment for his failure. The messianic bloodline and the everlasting throne were transplanted to the tribe of Judah, just as it had been prophesied in Genesis.[2702]

> 1 Chron 10:13 So Saul died for his transgression which he committed against the LORD, even against the word of the LORD, which he kept not, and also for asking counsel of one that had a familiar spirit, to enquire of it;
>
> 1 Chron 10:14 And enquired not of the LORD: therefore he slew him, and turned the kingdom unto David the son of Jesse.

Ironically, it was Saul's empathy for the Agag that killed him, for it was Saul's vassal army of Amalekites, according to Rohl, which had been hired to protect the back of Saul's army during the Gilboa battle against the Philistines. The Amalekites

---

[2698] 1 Sam 15:7–9.
[2699] Ellicott, *Old Testament Commentary*, Vol. 3, 358 note 33, 1 Sam 15.
[2700] 1 Sam 15:53. *Strong's Cyclopaedia*, Vol. 1, 98–99: Agag.
[2701] Ellicott, *Old Testament Commentary*, Vol. 3, 358 note 32, 1 Sam 15.
[2702] 1 Sam 15:23–26, 16:1–2. Ginzberg, *Legends of the Bible*, 528.

THE GENESIS 6 CONSPIRACY PART II

betrayed Saul, which permitted the Philistines to encircle the Israelites,[2703] whereby Israel fled before the Philistines.

At this time, David departed from the Philistine army at Aphek. On the third day after David left for Ziklag, the Amalekites burned Ziklag and took two of David's wives as prisoners.[2704] The timing of the Amalekite invasion was not coincidental. The Amalekites were part of the greater Southern alliance and part of the larger Philistine campaign, which lends support to Rohl's assertion that the Amalekites betrayed Saul at Mount Gilboa. The burning of Ziklag "in the south that is the Negeb"[2705] was part of the larger Philistine strategy plotted by the Philistine lords to take out Saul, his sons, and David in one campaign. The Amalekites had been motivated by the destruction Saul had previously reaped upon the Amalekite nation, and for David's previous raids into Amalekite country.[2706] Thus, Ziklag was smitten, as in punished and sent judgment:[2707] "This was as an act of vengeance, Ziklag being the city of the famous Israelite chieftain David, who had done so much damage to Amalek, and who had treated the captives with such cruelty. While other parts of the south were simply plundered, Ziklag was marked for destruction—was sacked and burned."[2708]

Knowing the larger Philistine schema explicates the true reason the Philistine lords were wrought with anger at Achish, and forced Achish to send David back to Ziklag[2709] to be destroyed by the Amalekites. However, David had yet to reach Ziklag when the attack occurred. David seized the terrible sacking of Ziklag as justification to destroy the remnant Amalekite settlements not previously destroyed by Saul. David and four hundred of his men chased after the Amalekites. With the help of an Egyptian slave of the Amalekites who had been abandoned, David located the Amalekite army and slaughtered them.[2710] The Amalekites of the south were essentially destroyed.

After the northern tribes anointed David king over all Israel at Hebron, David, in his first directive over a united Israel, marched on Jerusalem and the Jebusites.[2711] Jerusalem, the holy and eternal city of God, had been apportioned to the tribe of Benjamin in the time of Joshua,[2712] yet the Benjamite King Saul inexplicably did not attempt to conquer it. Conversely David, with his heart devoted, to God did conquer Jerusalem, cementing David's kingship legitimacy. Thereafter

---

[2703] Rohl, *Lost Testament*, 312–313. 1 Sam 21:12–13; 31:1–7; 1 Chron 10:1–6.
[2704] 1 Sam 27:6 30:1–7.
[2705] Ellicott, *Old Testament Commentary*, Vol. 3, 421, note 1, 1 Sam 30:1.
[2706] 1 Sam 27:8. Ellicott, *Old Testament Commentary*, Vol. 3, 421, note 1, 1 Sam 30:1.
[2707] H5221—*nakah, naw-kaw'*: to strike; murder; punish; slaughter; smite; scourge; destroy; ravage; send judgment.
[2708] Ellicott, *Old Testament Commentary*, Vol. 3, 421 note 1, 1 Sam 30:1-3.
[2709] 1 Sam 29:7.
[2710] 1 Sam 30:9–20.
[2711] Josh 15:63; Judg 1:21; 2 Sam 5:6–10.
[2712] Judg 18:28.

David reigned from God's Holy City, in God's holy land, just as our Messiah will do. Knowing this explains David's motivation for taking Jerusalem, an act that made him beloved throughout Israel.

> 1 Chron 11:5 And the inhabitants of Jebus said to David, Thou shalt not come hither. Nevertheless, David took the castle of Zion, which is the city of David. (see also 2 Sam 5:6–7).

Letters from Abdi-Heba to Pharoah recorded the Habiru/Apiru as treasonous cutthroats operating outside Egyptian authority, and as notorious enemies of King Abdi Heda.[2713] A Habiru/Apiru strongman emerged from Hebron to capture Jerusalem, from the sons of Lab'ya/Saul of the Apiru after Saul had died.[2714] This exchange in the *Armana Letters* is the secular and polytheist accounting of David's rise to power and his taking of Jerusalem.

Samuel anointed David after Saul's disobedience in the Amalekite war, when David was still a boy. The Holy Spirit departed Saul that day to rest in David,[2715] who would finish the transgenerational giant wars to fulfill God's will, and to be the seed for the future Messiah.[2716] David's name is defined as "beloved," as in the beloved of God. Some biblical scholars suggest David/*Dawveed'*[2717] was not his original name, but a title to raise the persona of David and his dynastic kingship—that David was an adopted Hurrian title given to him,[2718] or a word derived from the Hurrian language. We do not have Scripture for either Saul or David changing their names, but *Unger's* notes that David/*Dawveed'* possibly did derive from the Hurrian/Horim word *dawidum*, meaning chieftain or leader, as documented on the *Mari Tablets* from the Euphrates region.[2719] *Dawveed'* and *dawidum* are phonetically close from a transliteration perspective, as is *Daoud* in Arabic.[2720] Unger's seemingly referenced *dowdow/dowdavahuw* meaning his beloved, and/or *Dowdavahuw* meaning beloved of Yah, both rooted in *dowd* as is David. [2721]

[2713] Silberman and Finkelstein. *David and Solomon*, 44, 46, 48, citing M. Greenberg, 1955, The Hab/piru (New Haven, CT: American Oriental Society, 1955) and N. Na'aman, "Habiru and Hebrews: The Transfer of a Social Term to the Literary Sphere," *Journal For Eastern Studies* 45 (1986): 271–288. Tablets EA 271, 287, 288, 289, 299.

[2714] *Armana Letters*, 327, EA 286, lines 1–43; 328, EA 287, lines 19–33.

[2715] 1 Sam 16:12–14.

[2716] Acts 13:22–23.

[2717] H1732—*David, daw-veed'; Daviyd, dawveed'*; same as 1730: loving; beloved; H1730—*dowd, dode*; or *dod, dode*: to boil; figuratively to love; a love token; beloved; lover; friend; specifically, an uncle.

[2718] Rohl, *Lost Testament*, 306, 311; Gardner, *Lost Secrets*, 137, 212.

[2719] *Unger's*, 280: David. H1732—*daw-veed'; Daviyd, dawveed'*.

[2720] *Strong's Cyclopaedia*, Vol 2, 685: David.

[2721] H1734—*Dowdow, do-do'*; from 1730; H1735—*Dowdavahuw, do-daw-vaw'-hoo*; from 1730 and 3050: love of Jah; H1732—*David, daw-veed'*; same as 1730; H1730—*dowd, dode*.

Moreover, Jewish tradition and some Jewish scholars suggest that Elhanan was David's original name.[2722] Rohl suggests David/Dadua was the title first given to him by Achish of Gath and his Hurrian bodyguard, and then by David's mighty men and the people of Judah when David was crowned at Hebron.[2723] The Hurrian format was Tadua, the beloved of a deity, that was transliterated into Hebrew as Dadua and David. Tadua was recorded in the *Armana Letters* at the time of the Lab'yu/Saul's death and the taking of Jerusalem.[2724]

Whether the battle of Ziklag was the last Amalekite war or not, Scripture does not say, but we note that four hundred Amalekite young men escaped Ziklag.[2725] Major Amalekite battles were not recorded thereafter, so perhaps David waged mop-up operations in the south and east. Jewish tradition, though, indicates Joab, David's chief general, was remembered for his remarkable achievement of capturing the Amalekite capital.[2726] Saul had already captured the Amalekite capital, so this Jewish tradition appears to be an accounting for the capitol city east of the Jordan River. According to Jewish tradition, Joab laid siege to the Amalekite city for six months without success. Joab then accessed the city by disguising himself as an Amalekite escapee, whereby he slew Amalekite warriors over several weeks. After forty days, the Israelite army attacked, slaying all the inhabitants, and brought the Amalekite king to David[2727] for execution.

Scripture documents that David dedicated to God all the silver and gold from nations he subdued, which included the Amalekites.[2728] This is the only other scriptural reference to a war David waged against the Amalekites after being crowned king. Saul defeated the Amalekites, but the Amalekites were a nation of many tribes and locations.[2729] It follows that David waged war with the remnant tribes of the east. Further, Psalms documented that David "destroyed the wicked" and "put out their name for ever and ever,"[2730] language likely referring to Amalekites.

A remnant of the Amalekites did survive likely from Eastern Amalekites[2731] out of the reach of Israel, or refugees from the four hundred young men from the southern Amalekites, remnants that surface later in the time of King Hezekiah and again in the time of Esther,[2732] but the Amalekites did not rise as a nation of distinction again and were lost into history.

[2722] Finkelstein and Silberman, *David and Solomon,* 196, 199.

[2723] Rohl, *Lost Testament,* 324–325.

[2724] *Armana Letters,* 308–309: EA 255, 256. Rohl, *Lost Testament,* 311, 322, 324, 325, 330, citing EA 256 for Tadua.

[2725] 1 Sam 30:17.

[2726] 1 Chron 1:11:6, 20; 27:34; Ps 60:1. Ginzberg, *Legends of the Bible,* 542–543.

[2727] Ginzberg, *Legends of The Bible,* 543–545.

[2728] 2 Sam 8:11; 1 Chron 18:11.

[2729] Ellicott, *Old Testament Commentary,* Vol. 2, 466 note 12: Amalek, 2 Sam 8.

[2730] Ps 9:5–6.

[2731] Judg 6:33.

[2732] 1 Chron 4:41; Esth 3:1.

CHAPTER 56

DAVID'S EDOMITE WARS

*2 Sam 8:11 Which also king David did dedicate unto the L*ORD*, with the silver and gold that he had dedicated of all nations which he subdued;*

2 Sam 8:12 Of Syria, and of Moab, and of the children of Ammon, and of the Philistines, and of Amalek, and of the spoil of Hadadezer, son of Rehob, king of Zobah.

After David subdued the Philistine confederacy that included the expropriation of Gath and her mice network, David pivoted to war against the Moabites, making them a vassal state.[2733]

Moab and Ammon had cleansed the land of the Emim and Zamzummim previously, but Rephaim or human hybrid giants still reigned over the Moabites in the epochs of judges and the monarchy. Moab and Ammon fell under the influence of Sihon and Og's great empires before the Covenant Land conquest. It follows that both nations continued their ties to the military muscle of the Mount Hermon nations not captured by Israel. One should not be surprised that the Moabite king Eglon's name was patrial and/or patronymic from a city

---

[2733] 2 Sam 8:1; 1 Chron 18:1–2. Ellicott, *Old Testament Commentary*, Vol. 3, 292, note 1, 1 Chron 18; Josephus, *Ant.*, Book 7, 5:1.

in Hebron and a previous Rephaim king of Moab.[2734] Eglon, his dynastic sons, and his daughters intermarried with Rephaim, as witnessed by Orpah marrying Araph/Rapha of Philistia.

Moabites and Ammonites of this period worked closely with each under the protection of the Syrians, the senior partners in this resurgent Eastern alliance. As such, David conquered King Hadarezer of Zobah, the son of Rehob, east of the Euphrates River, immediately after conquering Moab. David's empire then extended to the western shores of the Euphrates River.[2735] Hadarezer is a variant spelling of Hadadezer, underscoring that Hadad was the Mesopotamian name for Baal.[2736] Zobah was a kingdom in Syria in the Mount Hermon region that had formed before Saul's reign in Israel, and which Saul also waged battle with. Aramzobah was connected to Aramnaharaim in Joab's defeat over the Edomites in the Salt Valley, referenced in the book of Psalms.[2737] Similarly, Hadadezer was patronymically tied to the Horim. Hadad, Hadadu, and Adad Syrian storm god names for Baal and Rammon of the Hittites.[2738]

> Judg 10:6 And the children of Israel did evil again in the sight of the LORD, and served Baalim, and Ashtaroth, and the gods of Syria, and the gods of Zidon, and the gods of Moab, and the gods of the children of Ammon, and the gods of the Philistines…

David captured from Hadarezer a thousand chariots, destroying all but one hundred, seven thousand horsemen, and twenty thousand men. Other Syrians from Damascus marched out in support of Zobah, but David defeated the Damascus Syrians as well. Josephus added that the title of this king was Hadad,[2739] and part of the royal seed line of the Syrian confederacy. The Hadad of Damascus was described by Josephus as "excellent of all their kings in strength and manhood," and the warrior-like Syrian king who fought for fortune in many wars. His posterity succeeded his throne in a dynasty of ten generations with his title.[2740]

[2734] Judg 3:12-17. H5700—' Eglown, eg-lawn': a royal city in Canaan; king of Moab killed by the judge Ehud.
[2735] 1 Sam 14:47; 2 Sam 8:3, 12; 1 Chron 18:3, 5, 9; 19:6. Josephus, *Ant.*, Book 7, 5:1 and note 10.
[2736] H1928—*Hadar ` ezer: Hadar* as in Hadad: a Syrian king defeated by David. Ellicott, *Old Testament Commentary*, Vol. 2, 465, note 3: Hadadezer/Hadadezer.
[2737] 1 Sam 14:47; Ps 60:1. H6678—*Tsowba', tso-baw'*: a station; a portion of Syria which formed a separate kingdom in the times of Saul, David northeast of Damascus.
[2738] *Encyclopedia Americana*, Vol 13, 608: Hadad; Ellicott, *An Old Testament Commentary*, Vol. 2, 465 note Hadadezer, 2 Sam 8.
[2739] 1 Chron 18:3–6. Josephus, *Ant.*, Book 7, 5:2.
[2740] Josephus, *Ant.*, Book 7, 5:2.

King Tou/Toi was the Hadadezer of Hamath located on the Orontes River. He sent his son Hadoram/Joram to David to congratulate David with gifts of gold for his victory over Tou/Toi's adversary, Hadarezer of Zohab, whom he too had warred with.[2741] Tou/Toi sought and achieved an alliance with David against Tou's rival Syrian kings.[2742] David then established garrisons in Syria/Aram and rendered the Syrians as vassals, as he had with Moab.[2743]

After King Nahash of Ammon died, his son Hunan succeeded to the throne. Nahash/*Nachash* means serpent and is the same word utilized for the serpent that deceived Eve in Eden.[2744] Saul had defeated the first Nahash of Ammon, which led to Saul's crowning at Gilgal.[2745] Hanun[2746] disgraced David's representatives sent to honor the former Nahash, and to comfort and honor Hanun as the new king.[2747] Hanun hired mercenaries to defend Ammon from Mesopotamia, Syria-maacha, Zoba/Bethrob and Ishtob. Mesopotamia/`AramNaharayim* was an Aramaean empire between the Tigris and Euphrates rivers. King Maacha was from Maacha/Syriamaacha (AramMaacha: the dominions of Maacha). Ishtob was located between Syria and Ammon. The book of 2 Samuel listed Bethrehob for the Syrians of Zoba listed in 1 Chronicles 19.[2748] Syria/*'Aram*/*'Arammiy* means exalted,[2749] from *'armown*, meaning castle and fortress,[2750] and akin to the city-state fortresses of the Southern alliance that included the Horim.

Knowing the backdrop to the Syrian confederacy reveals the context as to why Hanun hired Syrian muscle. Zoba/Zobah was a region in Syria that included Bethrehob, which formed a separate kingdom in the time of Saul, David, and Solomon.[2751] Bethrehob was a city-state in Syria on the road to Hamath previously called Laish. Rehob/*Rehob* was a city documented by Moses' scouts close

[2741] 2 Sam 8:9; 1 Chron 18:9–10. Ellicott, *Old Testament Commentary*, Vol. 3, 294, note 10: 1 Chron 18; Vol. 2, 465, note 9: Toi King of Hamath, 2 Sam 8:9–10.

[2742] Josephus, *Ant.*, Book 7, 5:3.

[2743] 2 Sam 8:14; 1 Chron 18:6.

[2744] 1 Chron 19:1–2. H5176—*Nachash, naw-khawsh'*: a serpent.

[2745] 1 Sam 11:1–2, 11–15; 12:12.

[2746] 1 Chron 19:3, 7. H2586—*Chanuwn, khaw-noon'*; from 2603: gracious; son of Nahash; king of Ammon; H2603—*chanan, khaw-nan'*: stoop in kindness to an inferior; show favor; gracious; pitied; loathsome.

[2747] 2 Sam 10:2–5; 1 Chron 19:4–5.

[2748] Gen 36:37; 2 Sam 10:6–8; 1 Chron 19:6. *NIV* 1 Chron 19:6 the "Mercenaries of Mesopotamia" is translated as Aram Naharaim. Ellicott, *Old Testament Commentary*, Vol. 3, 296, note 6 for Aram-Naharaim referencing Judg 3:8, King Cushanrishathaim of Mesopotamia, and Aram-Maacha, 1 Chron 19; 469, note 6: Bethrrehob, 2 Sam 10; and note 7, Ish-tob, 2 Sam 10.

[2749] H761—*'Arammiy, ar-am-mee'*; patrial from 758: exalted; Aramaean; Syrian. H758—*'Aram, arawm'*: the highland; exalted; Syria, and its inhabitants. Josephus, *Ant.*, Book 7, 6:1.

[2750] H759 —*'armown, ar-mone'*: to be elevated as in a citadel from its height; castle; palace.

[2751] 2 Sam 14:47. H6678—*Tsowba', tso-baw'*: a station; a region of Syria: Zoba or Zobah that formed a separate kingdom in the era of Saul, David, and Solomon.

to Hebron, and a city Israel did not drive the inhabitants from in the conquest of the Covenant Land.[2752] However, the city of Bethrehob in the Davidic wars was another city-state along the Euphrates: Rehoboth city of the Horim that Duke Saul had reigned from by the river,[2753] which is important context to understand this Syrian/Edomite war. Bethrehob/*Beythrechowb* translates as "house of the street," with rehob/*rchob* meaning a wide like a street or plaza, and a royal house connected to and appears immediately before Bethrapha in *Strong's Dictionary*. *Rchob* derives from *rachab*, meaning to make wide, grow wide and grow large reflecting the attributes of tall and stout giants. Further, Rehob/*Rchob* was the father of Hadarezer, of Zobah/Zoba[2754] indicating both Rehob and Hadarezer were Rephaim or hybrid kings. Rehob cities were patrial named after Rephaim, and patronymic for their kings, as in Hadarezer's father. One deduces the various Rehob cities were Edomite or Horim/Hivvim/Hurrian cities.

King Maacha of Syriamaacha was connected to the Rephaim of the Mount Hermon region. North Geshur was an ally of Sihon and Og of Bashan before the conquest. Syriamaacha was an ally with the Maachathim on Geshur's northwest border as part of the greater Syrian peoples in King David's era.[2755] Maacha was situated on Bashan's west side,[2756] known at that time as Syriamaacha/*Aramma`akah*[2757] and located north of King Hadadezer's Syrian/Edomite empire.[2758] The Geshurim king Talmai's daughter, Maachah, married King David, which produced the rebellious son Absalom.[2759] Maacha was an eponymous name of a Rephaim tribe/house, a matronymic name for princesses, patronymic kings, and patrial for the city of Maacah.[2760] The Maachathim were a warrior Syrian/Aramean kingdom named after the Rephaim Maacha, which centered in the royal Maacha city located at the

---

[2752] Num 13:21; Josh 19:28; Judg 1:31.

[2753] Gen 36:37; Judg 18:28–31; 2 Sam 10:6, 8; 1 Chron 1:48. H1050—*Beyth Rchowb, bayth re-khobe*; house of the street.

[2754] 2 Sam 8:3, 12. H1050—*Beyth Rchowb, bayth re-khobe*; from 1004 and 7339; H1052—*Beyth Rapha*; H7339—*rchob, rekh-obe*; from 7337: a width; an avenue; broad place; street; plaza; H7340—*Rchob, rekh-obe*: same as 7339: a broad place; a city-state in Syria and Judah; father of Hadadezer the king of Zobah killed by David; H7337—*rachab, raw-khab*: make large; make room; make wide; grow wide; be or grow large.

[2755] Josh 12:5; 13:13; 2 Sam 10:6; 1 Chron 19:6.

[2756] *Nelson's*, 783: Maacha.

[2757] *Strong's Cyclopaedia*, Vol. 5, 592: Maacah. 1 Chron 19:6. H758–'*Aram*; H4601–*Ma`akah. Nelson's*, 783: Maacha.

[2758] 2 Sam 8:3, 5, 7–10, 12; 1 Kings 11:23.

[2759] 1 Sam 3:3; 1 Chron 3:2.

[2760] H4601—*Ma`akah*: depression; she has pressed; a place in Syria; a Mesopotamian.

foot of Mount Hermon not far from Geshur.[2761] It follows then that Bethmaacha represented the Rephaim house of Maacha.[2762]

The Syrian mercenary army hired by Hanun consisted of thirty-two thousand chariots and charioteers. David responded by commissioning Joab and all David's mighty men to march against Ammon. Joab led the best Israelite warriors against the Syrian giants and hybrids, while Abishai led the balance of warriors against the Ammonites. The Syrians fled before Joab's warriors. When the Ammonites saw this, they too fled the field to their city, likely Rabbah city where Og's bed was on display. Joab then returned to Jerusalem to report to David.[2763]

The Syrians, though, sent messengers to their ally's army staged east of the Euphrates River/*Nahar*, to the Aram Naharaim [2764] led by Shopach/Shobach the captain of Hadarezer's army. One deduces this was son or kin of the former Hadarezer. David organized Israel's army to counter the new threat. They marched through the Trans-Jordan region to battle the Syrians at Helam. Israel slew seven thousand charioteers and forty thousand footsoldiers from beyond the Euphrates River, which included Shobach/Shopach whose name meant a "spiller of blood."[2765] In Jewish legend, the Aramaean Shobach was renowned for his gigantic size, height, and strength whose presence struck terror into the heart of the beholder.[2766] Thereafter, Syrians sued for peace and became vassals of David and did not assist the Ammonites in war again against Israel.[2767] With the Syrian threat eliminated, Joab marched his army against Ammon in the springtime. Rabbah, Ammon's capital city, was destroyed.[2768]

After the battle in Syria, and perhaps before the assault on Ammon, David sent Abishai, son of Zeruiah, to the Valley of Salt, where he slew eighteen thousand Syrians. Subsequently David, seemingly incongruently with the narrative, established Israelite garrisons throughout Edom, forcing the Edomites into a vassal kingdom.[2769] The parallel accounting in the book of 1 Chronicles identified

---

[2761] *Strong's Cyclopaedia*, Vol. 5, 592: Maacah; Nelson's, 783: Macchathites. H4602—*Ma`akathiy*.
[2762] 2 Sam 20:14, 15. H1038—*Beyth Ma`aka*h; from 1004 and 4601: house of Maakah; a place in the northern kingdom of Israel; house of pressure.
[2763] 2 Sam 10:7–14; 1 Chron 19:7–8.
[2764] H5104—*nahar, naw-hawr'*: stream; sea; the Nile and Euphrates rivers; flood; Aramnaharaim. *NIV* 1 Chron 19:6, the "Mercenaries of Mesopotamia" is translated as Aram Naharaim; H2431— *Cheylam, khay-lawm'*: a fortress; stronghold; a place west of the Euphrates.
[2765] 2 Sam 10:18; 1 Chron 19:16. H7780—*Showphak, sho-fawk'*; from 8210: poured out; expansion; a Syrian general of Hadarezer; H8210—*shaphak, shaw-fak'*: to spill forth blood; a libation; gush out; expand; pour out; spill. Ellicott, *Old Testament Commentary*, Vol. 3, 297, note 16: beyond the river, 1 Chron 19.
[2766] Ginzberg, *Legends*, 540.
[2767] 2 Sam 10:16–19; 1 Chron 19:9–19.
[2768] Deut 3:11; 2 Sam 12:26–31; 1 Chron 20:1–3. H7237—*Rabbah*: great; capital city of the Ammonites.
[2769] 2 Sam 8:13–14.

the eighteen thousand slain in the Salt Valley as Edomites rather than Syrians. Josephus too documented that the battle was waged against the Idumeans.[2770]

The book of 2 Samuel is not in error. The Salt Valley battle was part of the Syrian campaign, just as the kings of Zobah of Syria were listed immediately following the Edomites in the war King Saul previously fought.[2771] The Salt Valley battle was waged just south of the Dead Sea on the border of Edom and Judah, but generally stated to be in Edom and Seir.[2772] Knowing this helps to makes sense as to why David established garrisons throughout all Edom as he did in Syria. Just as Hadarezer's forces from the east came in support of the Syrians, so did their southern Edomite brethren, invading Judah by the Dead Sea. Psalms 60:1–9 connected the Syrian campaign of Aramzobah and Aramnaharaim with the Salt Valley battle in Edom as the same campaign, noting Zobah was the city of Hadarezer and Aramanaharaim between the two rivers, Tigris and Euphrates.[2773] Knowing this explicates why 2 Samuel documented that David dedicated the silver and gold to God from all the nations he subdued, which included Syria, but the parallel account in the book 1 Chronicles included Edom but not Syria.[2774] The Syrian campaign narrative confirmed the twin Edomite/Horim empire of Edom and Syria begat with the dukes of Edom and continued into David's era. Accordingly, some scholars assert the Syrians who supported the Ammonites and Moabites were the northern branch of the Horim/*Choriym*.[2775]

> Ps 60:1 To the chief Musician upon Shushaneduth, Michtam of David, to teach; when he strove with Aramnaharaim and with Aramzobah, when Joab returned, and smote of Edom in the Valley of Salt twelve thousand.

The Edomite/Horim bloodline of Aram led by the Hadad/Hadar dynasty indicates an intimate relationship with their Rephaim neighbors, as underscored with Betharam. The house of Aram/*Beyth ha-Ram* was listed among the kingdom of Sihon and his numerous pentapolis city-states in the book of Joshua.[2776] Aram in Betharam does not derive from Aram/*Arawm*, but from ha-Rawm/Ram and its source word *ruwm*, both which mean exalted, haughty, and lofty[2777]—Rephaim

---

[2770] 1 Chron 18:12-13. Josephus, *Ant.*, Book 7, 5:4.

[2771] 1 Sam 14:47.

[2772] *Unger's*, 1114: Salt, Valley of. 2 Kings 14:7; 2 Chron 25:11; Ps 60:1.

[2773] H760—'*Aram Tsobah, ar-am' tso-baw'*: Aram of Tsoba or Coele-Syria: the exalted station; exalted conflict; the land northeast of Damascus.

[2774] 2 Sam 8:12; 1 Chron 18:11.

[2775] Stern, *The Biblical Herem*, 5–6, citing J. C. de Moor, *An Incantation*, 306, KLU 1.13 r:1–5.

[2776] Josh 13:27.

[2777] H1027—*Beyth ha-Ram, bayth haw-rawm'*; from 1004 and 7311: house of the height; a place East of the Jordan; H7311—*ruwm, room*: to be high; to rise or raise; bring up; exalt; go up; haughty; lift up; proud; tall; lofty; exalted.

descriptions. The house of the Ram/*Rawm* was yet another Rephaim tribe and a branch of the Horim of Edom.

Following this northern Edomite/Horim line of thought, the sorcerer Balaam was an Aramaean son or descendant of Beor. Balaam originated from Pethor, meaning soothsayer,[2778] located in Mesopotamia along the Nahar/Euphrates, Aram-naharaim.[2779] Beor was a Horim duke of Dinhabah city in Edom.[2780] Knowing this elucidates the Hadad-son-of-Bedad narrative, where he smote the Midianites in Moab. The patronymically named Hadad's royal city, Avith, was located close to Assyria and Syria, a city of the Avvim, Hivvim, or both that was connected to Sihon's Heshbon city; Duke Zibeon was documented as a Hivvim and Horim.[2781] Ergo, Hadad's reign in Avith came after the reign of Duke Bela of Bozrah[2782] that began the Syrian Hivvim kingship and empire from the time of the Aboriginal Rephaim and Horim settlers.

After Hadad, Samlah of Masrekah city reigned in Edom,[2783] followed by Shaul/Saul of Rehoboth city by the river/nahar, the Euphrates River,[2784] indicating the Horim King Saul reigned in the Syria region as did Hadad. Baalhanan, son of Achbor, succeeded Saul, but no city was named, so one presumes Baalhanan reigned by implication from Rehoboth in Syria.[2785] Hadad/Hadar succeeded Baalhanan reigning from Pau and or Pai city in Seir.[2786] The capital city of the Horim empire seemingly shifted between Syria and Seir until the time of King David, revealing why the Edomites came to the support of the Syrian king Hadadezer at the Salt Valley battle.

[2778] Num 22:5; 23:7; 24:3, 15; 31:8; Deut 23:4; Josh 13:22; 24:9, Mic 6:5. H6604—*Pthowr*: a soothsayer; a town in Mesopotamia; home of Balaam; located on a river; H5104—*nahar, naw-hawr'*.

[2779] Ps 60:1.

[2780] Gen 36:31–32; Deut 2:12; 1 Chron 1:43.

[2781] H5755—'*Ivvah*. Gen 36:2, 20; 1 Chron 1:38, 41. H5857—'*Ay*: Ammonite city east of the Jordan connected to Heshbon.

[2782] Gen 36:33; 1 Chron 1:44.

[2783] H4957—*Masreqah, mas-ray-kaw'*: vineyard; a place in Idumaea. Gen 36:36; 1 Chron 1:47.

[2784] Gen 36:37; 1 Chron 1:48. H5104—*nahar*.

[2785] Gen 36:38; 1 Chron 1:49.

[2786] H6464—*Pa`uw, paw-oo'*: bleating; capital of king Hadar of Edom: site uncertain. Gen 36:39; Hadad: 1 Chron 1:50.

CHAPTER 57

KING HIRAM AND SOLOMON'S WARS

1 Kings 11:1 But king Solomon loved many strange women, together with the daughter of Pharaoh, women of the Moabites, Ammonites, Edomites, Zidonians, and Hittites;

1 Kings 11:2 Of the nations concerning which the LORD said unto the children of Israel, Ye shall not go in to them, neither shall they come in unto you: for surely they will turn away your heart after their gods: Solomon clave unto these in love.

David secured the borders of Israel. He elevated Israel's eminence to a new status: an influential nation among international world order of that era. When Solomon began his reign, Israel was no longer preoccupied with their nemesis nations, the Philistines and Amalekites, but Edom remained a determined foe.

Solomon increased Israel's wealth, prestige, and respect among the neighboring nations, which included close ties with the Phoenician king of Tyre. After twenty years of Solomon's reign, construction of the first temple and royal palace of Jerusalem were completed. King Huram of Tyre supplied building materials, gold, and architectural expertise in exchange for twenty towns in the Galilee region.[2787] Solomon ordered the construction of a new fortress wall surrounding Jerusalem. He oversaw the rebuilding of strategically important fortresses at Hazor,

---

[2787] 1 Kings 9:10–14.

Megiddo, and Gezer. Egypt, some time before Solomon rebuilt Gezer, had sacked and captured it as an outpost. Pharaoh gifted Gezer to his daughter, and thus Israel, after she married Solomon.[2788]

Each of the cities Solomon restored were of strategically blocked avenues of invasion. Hazor was Jabin's former fortress in the north at the foot of the Galilee Mountains by the Hula Valley and Lake Merom that controlled the "Way of the Sea," an important trade route that connected Egypt with Asia Minor, Syria, and Mesopotamia.[2789] Megiddo, located on the northern plain of Jezreel, controlled the passes from the north to the hill country and was also located on the "Way of the Sea." Gezer was at one time a Philistine city and then a Canaanite city, which protected a pass from the coastland of the Philistines and was on the "Way of the Sea" trade route.[2790] Solomon further overhauled Bethhoron, the house of the caves located near Gezer that protected a mountain pass coming from the coastland. Solomon also restored both Baalath, which protected another pass from the coastland of the Philistines; and Tadmor, located in the desert of Syria, which was a day's march from the Euphrates River.[2791] Solomon built designated storehouse cities, chariot cities, and horsemen cities from Jerusalem to Lebanon, from the Euphrates River to Gaza, and to the Egyptian border. All nations that dwelled therein paid tribute to Solomon.[2792] Solomon further commissioned the building of four thousand stalls for chariot horses, and stalls for twelve thousand horses in the designated cities. He addressed the Rephaim hybrid remnant that still dwelled within Israel's borders: the Amorites, Hittites, Perizzites, Hivites, and Jebusites. Solomon conscripted them into forced labor for his building projects.[2793] In so doing, Solomon continued Joshua's tradition which began with the Gibonim/Nethanim temple servants.[2794]

To build the temple and royal palace, Solomon engaged in ongoing relations with Tyre's king Huram/Hiram, which began while David was king, to acquire Tyre's architectural knowledge and building supplies.[2795] David's capture of Jerusalem, Solomon's building the first temple, and the introduction of the king of Tyre

---

[2788] 1 Kings 9:14–18. Josephus, *Ant.*, Book 8, 6:1.

[2789] Josh 11:1, 13; Isa 9:1. *Strong's Cyclopaedia*, Vol. 4, 108–109: Hazor. Cunelife, *The Holy Land*, 194: Ashqelon; 306: Hazor.

[2790] Ellicott, *Old Testament Commentary*, Vol. 3, 45, note 15: Megiddo and Gezer, 1 Kings 9. *Strong's Cyclopaedia*, Vol. 7, 44: Megiddo; Vol. 3, 842: Gezer. Josephus, *Ant.*, Book 8, 6:1. Cunelife, *The Holy Land*, 194: Ashqelon; 290: Gezer; 386: Megiddo.

[2791] 1 Kings 9:19. Ellicott, *Old Testament Commentary*, Vol. 3, 46, note 17: BethHoron; note 18: Baalath, and Tadmor, 1 Kings 9; Josephus, *Ant.*, Book 8, 6:1.

[2792] 1 Kings 4:20–21, 24; 9:19. Josephus, *Ant.*, Book 8, 2:4.

[2793] 1 Kings 19:20–23; 2 Chron 8:1-9.

[2794] Josh 9:21–27; Judg 1:28, 30, 33, 35; 1 Kings 9:20–21. Ellicott, *Old Testament Commentary*, Vol. 3, 46, note 20, 1 Kings 9.

[2795] 2 Sam 5:11; 1 Kings 5:1–18; 2 Chron 2:1–8. Josephus, *Ant.*, Book 8, 2:5–7.

were important historical events to help discern prophetic events. Jerusalem was the epicenter for Holy Covenant prophetic events and is and an essential sign to mark the prophetic fig tree generation. Further, Tyre and their king were drafted into prophecies for the age of the covenant prophets, with important prophetic allegories for the end times.

"Tyre" and "Tyrus" derive from the same word, *Tsor*, defined as rock and the Phoenician city.[2796] It follows that Tyre and Tyrus are cognate in prophecies regarding the king of Tyre. In prophetic allegory, Tyre appears first in the Isaiah 23 dual prophecy, where Tyre is described as an island of merchants versus a coastal city with a man-made peninsula. In this prophecy, Tyre was destroyed by the sea, not by the Assyrians as it was in Isaiah's time, nor was Tyre destroyed by the sea in Jeremiah's time but sacked by Babylonians; both beast empires were referenced in Isaiah 23.[2797] Tyre rose back to its trading prominence after its sacking by Shalmaneser of Assyria and Nebuchadnezzar of Babylon, and with the blessing of Cyrus of Persia. Tyre was captured but not destroyed by Alexander's beast empire and then Rome's beast empire in the second temple period, whereby it once more flourished in its commercial enterprises.[2798] Tyre was not a beast empire in the same manner of Egypt, Assyria, Babylon, Persia, Greece, and Rome, but it was an economic and trading beast empire for the six empires past, and will be again allegorically for the seventh empire of the end times.

Within the Isaiah 23 dual prophecy are significant, enigmatic, antediluvian and Atlantean-like markers, when one considers Genesis 6, Deuteronomy 32, and Psalm 82 with respect to the nations divided among the sons of the God Most High both before and after the flood. Consider that Tyre was cited as the bestower of crowns[2799] to kings, which stirs up curious echoes of Poseidon's ten Atlantean kings, and Sumer's Nippur (Mount Hermon) where antediluvian Nephilim kings were anointed with the divine right to rule. Isaiah's dual prophecy pressed on to declare that God brought low the pride and glory of all the renowned of the earth through a watery, global catastrophe. This island city was destroyed by the sea and trembling of the earth, echoing the conflagration of deluge disasters that included earthquakes, volcanoes, and flood. Tyre was the allegorical "joyous city" (exultant and proud), whose "antiquity [*qadmah*] was of ancient [*qedem*] days"—phrases in Scripture often used to denote the epoch before the flood.[2800]

[2796] H685—*Tsor; tsore; Tsowr*: a rock; Tyrus or Tyrus; a Phoenician city on the Mediterranean coast.

[2797] Isa 23:2, 6, 12, 13.

[2798] *Encyclopedia Americana*, Vol. 27, 245: Tyre.

[2799] Isa 23:8, 9, 10, 11.

[2800] Isa 23:7. *Access Bible*: Sirach 17:7; Baruch 3:26; Wisdom 14; *KJV*: Deut 33:15; Ps 77:5; Prov 22:28; Eccl 1:10; Isa 19:11; Jer 5:15; Dan 7:9; 1 Pet 3:15; 2 Pet 2:5. Joyous: H5947—`*alliyz, al-leez*: exultant; jubilant.

Berosus penned three books that were professed as founded upon the ancient archives from the temple of Belus. Berosus wrote that Babylon was utilized allegorically by the Chaldean priests for an antediluvian city, the "first city" of cities, Atlantis. In fact, some secular scholars believe that Tyre and Babylon in these passages described the prosperity and destruction of Atlantis, the seaborn, antediluvian empire.[2801] Thus, in Plato's work *Critias*, the gods divided up the earth, with Atlantis being Poseidon's portion.[2802]

Tyre city was the postdiluvian "strong city," and a rich empire of commerce and trade.[2803] Likewise, Babylon city in the end times will be the "mighty city" of commerce and trade in the seventh beast empire.[2804] The future prophetic Babylon city of the end-time empire can be discerned through the merchant and commerce aspects of Tyre, while the mystery religion aspect reflects Babel city and Nebuchadnezzar's Babylon city, and the bloodthirsty nature of end-time Babylon reflects Assyria's Nineveh city. Isaiah employed Tyre and Babylon; Jeremiah allegorized Babylon; Zephaniah and Nahum utilized Nineveh for end-time Babylon.[2805]

The dual prophecy of Ezekiel 26 foretelling Nebuchadnezzar's destruction of Tyre also provides end-time details that did not occur during the Babylonian destruction: "And they shall take a lamentation for thee, and say to thee, How art thou destroyed, that was inhabited of seafaring men, the renowned city"—a city and ruling class that will be taken down to the pit of old time, set low in the desolate places of old, not to be inhabited until God sets glory in the land of the living.[2806] Tyre rose back to prominence in the Persian, Greek, and Roman empires.

> Rev 18:11 And the merchants of the earth.. ..

> Rev 18:18 And cried when they saw the smoke of her burning, saying, What city is like unto this great city!

> Rev 18:19 And they cast dust on their heads, and cried, weeping and wailing, saying, Alas, alas, that great city, wherein were made rich all that had ships in the sea by reason of her costliness! for in one hour is she made desolate.

Knowing Tyre and its king were penned into prophetic allegory helps explicate the Ezekiel 28 dual prophecy where King Tyrus was portrayed as an archetypical

---

[2801] Wayne, *Genesis 6 Conspiracy*, 128, citing *Encyclopedia Americana*, Vol. 3, 577: Berosus; Greer, *Atlantis*, 13, 21; Sitchin, *The Lost Book of Enki*, introduction, 4.13, 15; 21.14.

[2802] Greer, *Atlantis*, 11, quoting Timaeus 24d, 25d.

[2803] Josh 19:29; 2 Sam 24:7; Ezek 27:1–36; Zech 9:2–3.

[2804] Mighty city: Rev 18:9–19.

[2805] Isa 13:19–22; 14:4; 21:9; 23:1–18; 47:1–15; 48:19–22; Jer 51:1–64; Nah 1:10–15; 2:1–13; 3:1–19; Zeph 2:13–15.

[2806] Ezek 26:6, 15–20.

antichrist figure like Nimrod, the Assyrian, and the king of Babylon. Tyrus in this prophecy is described as a demigod offspring of the gods, granted the divine right to rule by the Baalim of Mount Hermon's assembly. In typical antichrist narcissism, Tyrus declares himself to be God, reigning from the seat of God just as Satan/ *Heylel* attempted as recorded in Isaiah 14:12–14. Tyrus of Ezekiel 28 was a special prince/*nagiyd* of civil, military, and religious institutions,[2807] an antichrist figure. Tyrus was tallied as part of the Terrible Ones,[2808] and a mighty/gibborim[2809] like the kings of Ezekiel 32.[2810] King Hiram in David and Solomon's time descended from the Tyrus dynastic bloodline of Terrible Ones.

> Ezek 28:2 Son of man, say unto the prince of Tyrus, Thus saith the Lord God; Because thine heart is lifted up, and thou hast said, I am a God, I sit in the seat of God, in the midst of the seas; yet thou art a man, and not God, though thou set thine heart as the heart of God.

When Solomon grew old, his heart turned from God and toward the Baalim pantheon of gods via King Hiram of Tyre and the many foreign wives Solomon married:

> 1 Kings 11:4 For it came to pass, when Solomon was old, that his wives turned away his heart after other gods.. ..

> 1 Kings 11:5 For Solomon went after Ashtoreth the goddess of the Zidonians, and after Milcom the abomination of the Ammonites.

God had appeared twice to Solomon,[2811] yet Solomon allowed himself to be led astray. For doing so, God proclaimed the northern tribes would later split away, leaving only Judah, Benjamin, and some Levites governed by the Davidic bloodline.[2812] God then raised up an adversary against Solomon, the patronymically named King Hadad (Adar and Adad according to Josephus) of Edom. Hadad descended from the "king's seed in Edom"[2813] the roy-el Horim bloodline. Accordingly, Solomon's nemesis rose up out of David's Aramaean campaign against Hadadezer. After the Edomites were defeated in Salt Valley, Joab's men slew every male in Edom, but Hadad, a boy at that time, fled to Egypt with the aid of his

---

[2807] H5057—*nagiyd, naw-gheed'*: a commander of civil military or religious; captain; chief; excellent thing; chief; leader; noble; prince; chief ruler.

[2808] Ezek 28:7–9.

[2809] Ezek 32:12, 21, 27.

[2810] Isa 14:4–7, 15–21; 25:3–5; Ezek 26:17; 28:7–8.

[2811] 1 Kings 9:1–9; 2 Chron 7:11–12.

[2812] 1 Kings 11:1–13. Josephus, *Ant.*, Book 8, 7:6.

[2813] 1 Kings 11:14. Josephus, *Ant.*, Book 7, 5:2, note 11; Book 8, 8:7.

father's servants.[2814] Pharaoh found favor in Hadad, so much so that Pharaoh provided the sister of his wife in marriage for Hadad[2815] that beget a new pure-blood elvin/fairy/pharaonic dynasty in exile. Hadad's wife bore a son named Gunubath, who was raised in Pharaoh's royal court with Pharaoh's children.[2816]

One deduces the favor Pharoah found in Hadad was based upon a kin dynastic bloodline from the Aboriginal dukes/*allowphiym* of Seir. Hadad, Hadar, Hadadezer, and Behadad according to *Ellicott's Commentary* were titles for the Edomite and Syrian kings from the royal family of the Horim of Genesis 36, and a Syriac title of genealogical descent from the sun god cognate to the Pharaoh title and royal bloodline.[2817] Josephus noted that in the days of David, ten generations of kings reigned in Syria with the Hadad title of their royal bloodline.[2818] Hadad of Solomon's generation was viewed as the "last scion of his royal house"[2819] in Edom. This often overlooked narrative reflects the respect Hadad's bloodline maintained throughout the ancient world.

After news reached Egypt that David and his chief general Joab had died, Hadad returned to Edom to oppose Solomon and to renew the Amalekite, Edomite, Rephaim blood oath against Israel. Hadad, though, was unable to muster a successful rebellion against Solomon's numerous garrisons throughout Edom.[2820]

God raised yet another adversary against Solomon from Syria, Rezon son of Eliadah. Rezon escaped David's war against Hadadezer of Zobah. Rezon/*Rzown*, meaning prince, derives from *razan*, defined as heavy, weighty, and a prince. Rezon was a Horim/Hivvim-descended bloodline relative of Hadadezer. According to Josephus, Hadad fled to Rezon and renewed the ancient alliance with the Syrians.[2821] After Hadadezer's defeat, Rezon collected the remnant of Hadadezer's defeated army, then captured Damascus, and reigned there as Solomon's nemesis for the remainder of Solomon's life.[2822] After Solomon's death, Rehoboam was crowned king, but Jeroboam rebelled splitting away the northern tribes, not to be united until the end times.[2823]

[2814] 2 Sam 8:12–14, 1 Kings 11:15–17; 1 Chron 8:11–13; Ps 60:1, 8, 9. Josephus, *Ant.*, Book 8, 7:6.

[2815] 1 Kings 11:18–19.

[2816] 1 Kings 11:18–22.

[2817] Ellicott, *Old Testament Commentary*, Vol. 3, 54, note 14: Hadad the Edomite, 1 Kings 11.

[2818] Josephus, *Ant.*, Book 7, 5:2, citing Nicolaus/Nicolens of Damascus's fourth book of his histories.

[2819] Ellicott, *Old Testament Commentary*, Vol. 3, 54, note 14: Hadad the Edomite, 1 Kings 11.

[2820] Josephus, *Ant.*, Book 8, 7:6.

[2821] Ibid.

[2822] 1 Kings 11:23–25. H7331—*Rzown, rez-one*: prince; son of Eliadah, a Syrian, who led a kingdom at Damascus in the time of David and Solomon; H7336—*razan, raw-zan*: to be weighty; honorable; a prince; ruler; judicious; commanding.

[2823] 2 Kings 12:1–33; 2 Chron 21:1–19.

The bloodline dynasties of Edomites continued to reign after Solomon's death and well into the reign of the monarchy of Israel and Judah. Accordingly, the Hadad title resurfaced in Israelite history in the reign of King Baasha of Judah and King Asa of Israel. Benhadad of Damascus and Syria came to Asa's aid against Baasha of Judah.[2824] Benhadad, meaning the son of Hadad and king of Hadad/Baal, was the bloodline descendant of Rezon of Damascus and of Hadadezer of Zobah via Tabrimon, son of Hezion of Damascus.[2825]

Later, during Israel's King Ahab reign circa 870–850 BC, another Benhadad of Syria, son of Hazael of Damascus, attacked Israel with thirty-two kings armed with many horsemen and chariots.[2826] Hazael previously held the Damascus kingship title Hadad as part of the ten succeeding Hadad kings.[2827] Benhadad descended from the originating Hadad of Damascus David battled; Josephus stated that the Hadad of King Ahab's reign was the third most powerful Hadad king of the ten-king dynasty, bent on avenging his forefather.[2828] Nevertheless, Ahab defeated Benhadad and his impressive alliance in a great slaughter. One year later, Benhadad returned with another great army to avenge his loss, but suffered another punishing blow.[2829]

The prophet Elisha traveled to Damascus to meet with a sickly King Benhadad. Benhadad instructed Hazael, the king's son, to inquire whether Benhahad would live or die. Benhadad died and was succeeded by Hazael.[2830] Ahab's son Joram battled this Hazael of Syria after Ahab died.[2831] Inscribed on the Black Obelisk of Shalmaneser II (c. 860–825 BC), a Haza'ilu/Hazael of Damascus was recorded as having fought two battles against Joram.[2832] Also, in the reign of King Joram (c. 850–841 BC), Edom rebelled against King Jehoram of Judah and once more established a southern Edomite king. King Joram of Israel battled the Edomites at Zair, seemingly for Judah, and defeated the rebellious Edomites. Nonetheless, the Edomites remained in rebellion against Judah thereafter.[2833]

Hazael of Syria was succeeded by yet another Benhadad in the reigns of Jehoahaz of Israel (c. 814–799 BC) and Jehoash of Judah (c. 827–800 BC), when another series of wars were fought and Israel was overcome by the Syrian kings,

---

[2824] 2 Kings 15:16–22; 2 Chron 16:1–7.

[2825] 2 Kings 15:18. H2383—*Chezyown, khez-yone'*: vision; a Syrian king, father of Tabrimon and grandfather of Ben-hadad; identical with 'Rezon' the contemporary of Solomon. Ellicott, *Old Testament Commentary*, Vol. 3, 55, note 23: Rezon son of Eliadah, 1 Kings 11.

[2826] 1 Kings 19:15–17; 20:1–21; 2 Chron 20:5–6.

[2827] Josephus, *Ant.*, Book 7, 5:2; Book 8, 14:1.

[2828] Ibid., Book 7, 5:2.

[2829] 1 Kings 20:22–43.

[2830] 2 Kings 8:1–15.

[2831] 2 Kings 8:28–29.

[2832] Ellicott, *Old Testament Commentary*, Vol. 3, 132, note 15: Hazael, 2 Kings 8.

[2833] 2 Kings 8:16–22.

until the Syrians were finally defeated again.[2834] Edom and their kings remained free from Judean rule for centuries, which eventually produced Herod and his plot to kill the Messiah while Jesus was still a baby.[2835]

> 2 Kings 8:22 Yet Edom revolted from under the hand of Judah unto this day.

The fact that the Edomite/Amalekite Elvin/*Alluwph* bloodline survived until the time of Jesus and beyond, as well as the people of Edom, explicates why Edom was assigned end-time prophecies. In fact, many of the nations Israel warred with are reserved for judgment in the last year of this age. The prophecies of Amos during the reigns of Uzziah of Judah, and Jeroboam son of Joash of Israel, and Jeremiah's prophecies in the time of Nebuchadnezzar, foretold the coming end-time destruction of Damascus with the sending of "fire into the house of Hazael, which will devour the palaces of Benhadad" for their transgressions against Israel. Edom of the south, too, will be punished with fire for its transgressions against Israel: destroyed by fire.[2836] Tyre, Ammon, Moab, and the Philistines are other nations reserved for judgment.[2837]

Ergo, the oppression neighboring nations levied against Israel and Judah, the transgenerational wars past fought, and the spurious offspring of fallen angels, is the larger requisite context to better discern end-time prophetic allegory and chronology. The ongoing war by fallen angels and their offspring, the rebellious ones against all who follow God: those in "heaven," and those on earth makes sense of New Testament warnings that we fight against the "visible and invisible," and "against principalities, against powers, against the rulers of darkness, of this world, against spiritual wickedness in high places." As such, the saints are instructed to "take unto you the whole armor of God, that ye may be able to withstand in the evil day."[2838]

[2834] 2 Kings 8:28–29; 10:32; 12:17–18; 13:3–25; 2 Chron 22.
[2835] Matt 2:13–21.
[2836] Jer 49:27; Amos 1:4, 11, 12.
[2837] Amos 1:6–10, 13–15; 2:1–2.
[2838] Col 1:16; Rom 8:38–39; Eph 6:12–13.

Section VI
Prehistory, History, and Prophecy

2 Pet 3:3 Knowing this first, that there shall come in the last days scoffers, walking after their own lusts,

2 Pet 3:4 And saying, Where is the promise of his coming? for since the fathers fell asleep, all things continue as they were from the beginning of the creation.

2 Pet 3:5 For this they willingly are ignorant of, that by the word of God the heavens were of old, and the earth standing out of the water and in the water:

2 Pet 3:6 Whereby the world that then was, being overflowed with water, perished:

2 Pet 3:7 But the heavens and the earth, which are now, by the same word are kept in store, reserved unto fire against the day of judgment and perdition of ungodly men.

CHAPTER 58

PHARAOH AND BEAST EMPIRES

Matt 24:15 When ye therefore shall see the abomination of desolation, spoken of by Daniel the prophet, stand in the holy place, (whoso readeth, let him understand:)

Matt 24:16 Then let them which be in Judaea flee into the mountains. ..

Bridging New Testament prophecy with Old Testament prophecy and prehistory begins with the chronological events Jesus set down in the books of Matthew, Mark and Luke.[2839] Within his end-time template, Jesus set down a clear prophetic chronological marker for all to "understand": the abomination in the temple "spoken by Daniel the prophet."[2840]

Daniel set the timing for the abomination in the end times at the midpoint of the last week of seven years of the seventy weeks, set aside to finish transgression, end sin, make reconciliation for iniquity, bring in everlasting righteousness, anoint the Most Holy, and to seal up prophecy and vision.[2841] Discerning of a day

---

[2839] Matt 24:3–24, Mark 13:5–13, Luke 17:20–37; 21:8–38.
[2840] Dan 9:27; 11:32–36; 12:11–13, Matt 24:15–20, Mark 13:14–18; Luke 21:20–24; 2 Thess 2:4; Rev 13:4–18.
[2841] Dan 9:24, 27.

as a prophetic year and Jesus' reference to the abomination in the temple in His template are essential to determine the sequential order of end-time events.

The entire last week of years occurs after "the people [Romans] of the prince that shall come shall destroy the city [Jerusalem] and the sanctuary [second temple]" in the end/*qets*, meaning the end times.[2842] Further, Jesus was clear that the signs and events He outlined were told in a chronological order, utilizing the Greek word *tot'eh* meaning then, at that time, or when as in Matthew 24:16: "Then let them which be in Judaea flee into the mountains"; this is used throughout Jesus' end-time oration.[2843]

If one assembles passages and prophetic allegory from the book of Revelation and Daniel's chapters 2, 7, 8, 9, 11, and 12 around Jesus' chronological events and overarching signs, the fog begins to lift from the Revelation prophecy. One can then slide all other prophecies from both testaments into that template. Revelation and Daniel's prophetic allegory intersects with and explicates the dual prophecies of Isaiah 13, 14, 22, 25, and 34, Jeremiah 50–51, and Ezekiel 26, 28, 29, 31, and 32 with respect to Babylon, Satan, Antichrist, antichrist-like figures, beast empires, and the Terrible Ones. Moreover, one distills from the dual prophecies important prehistorical context and defining allegory for end-time prophetic events and players, as well as fundamental Holy Covenant prophecies assigned to the epoch of the prophets. Through dual prophecies, one begins to grasp the supernatural symmetry embedded into prophecy throughout the Bible that "the thing that hath been, it is that which shall be. .. and there is no new thing under the sun."[2844]

As such, the Ezekiel 32 dual prophecy is steeped in prehistory, describing events and figures past. It is a prophecy for Ezekiel's era, and it provides prophetic details for the end-time resolution to the angelic rebellion and creation of giants. Ezekiel's lament expands upon prophetic allegory deployed in Isaiah 13–14, and 22, Jeremiah 50–51, Ezekiel 28–29, Daniel 8, and other prophecies employing similar prophetic allegorical and prophetic markers assigned to important players and events past and future. Similar prophetic allegory and markers connect New Testament prophecy to Old Testament prophecy, even though the English translation comes from Greek and Hebrew respectively.

Pharaoh was the central figure in the Ezekiel 32 dual prophecy. Egypt was the first beast empire, followed by Assyria. In the Ezekiel 32 dual prophecy, the king of Babylon's romp through the known world was foretold, whereby he would subdue the bloodline kingdoms of the known world, while establishing Nebuchadnezzar as an archetypical antichrist figure as depicted in Isaiah 14. Likewise, Pharaoh was described as a young lion of nations, and a whale of the seas (Gentile

---

[2842] Dan 9:26–27. H7093—*qets, kates*: the end, as in the end times, the end of time, or the end of space.
[2843] G5119—*tot'-eh*: the when, as in at the time and then: then; at that time; when; transliterated: tote. Matt 24:9, 10, 14, 16, 21, 23, 30, 40; Mark 13:14, 21, 26, 27; Luke 21:10, 20, 21, 27.
[2844] Eccl 1:9.

nations) who thrashes in the troubled waters of nations, trampling/fouling its rivers/branches. Fouledst/*raphas*[2845] is not directly rooted to *rapha*/giant(s), but it is part the same series of words, suggesting an ancient connection to the Terrible Ones. Further, *raphas* is cognate with the Aramaic format *rphac* meaning to stamp/trample, employed to describe the fourth and "terrible" beast empire of Rome (Dan 7:7, 19).[2846] Egypt was the first Rephaim kingdom to rise to a beast empire status with the ancient branch/daughter of the original Babel religion; later came Assyria, Babylon, and as will the end-time seventh beast empire.[2847] Knowing this context explicates why Pharaoh and the "king of Babylon" and the "Assyrian"[2848] were cast as antichrist figures in prophetic allegory, who held the staff of the wicked and scepter of royals.

The Pharaoh prophesied in the Ezekiel 29 and 32 was Necho. He was defeated by Babylon at Carchemish along the Euphrates River,[2849] but many details in these prophecies chronicled are at odds with what occurred in Pharaoh Necho's reign—details akin to the "king of Babylon" and "Assyrian" in other dual prophecies. Thus, Pharaoh in Ezekiel 32:2 is described allegorically "as a whale in the seas." Whale/*tanniyn* means dragon, serpent, sea monster, dinosaur, or whale, which derives from *tan* meaning elongated monster preternaturally formed: a sea serpent or dragon.[2850] The narrative and its prophetic allegory strongly suggest a sea serpent or dragon creature which would reflect a better translation than whale and correlate with biblically documented sea monsters like Leviathan, and or supernatural beings like fallen angels like Satan and seraphim. In this light, then, Ezekiel 29 in its prophetic allegory described Pharaoh as the great dragon/*tanniym* of the rivers,[2851] defining and connecting Pharaoh in prophetic allegory to Antichrist, Satan, and the four beast empires that rise out of the sea in Daniel 7.[2852] However, the four great beasts/*cheyva'* and five empires were not dragon or Leviathan-like beasts,[2853] even though they came from the sea of *goyim*/nations.

The prophetic allegory, though, comes together in Revelation 13, when the fifth empire rises from the fourth as the ten-horned empire from the sea. The multiheaded end-time empire is depicted as a Hydra dragon of the nations/sea in Revelation 13:1–2 and is analogous to both the multiheaded Leviathan sea

---

[2845] Ezek 32:1–2. H7515—*raphas, raw-fas'*; to trample; roil water; foul; be fouled; stamp; tread.

[2846] H7512—*rphac, ref-as'*; Aramaic: stamp; tread; trample.

[2847] Rev 17:3–10.

[2848] Isa 14, 29.

[2849] 2 Chron 35:20.

[2850] H8577—*tanniyn, tan-neen'*; or *tanniym*: a sea-serpent; dragon; serpent; whale; dinosaur; H8565—*tan*: to elongate; a monster as preternaturally formed as a sea serpent; dragon; dinosaur: the plesiosaurus.

[2851] Ezek 29:3.

[2852] Dan 7:2–8, 17–25.

[2853] H2423—*cheyva', khay-vaw'*: an animal; beast: beast; animal.

serpent/dragon and with Satan, who is also called a dragon.[2854] Pharaoh then, in Ezekiel 29 and 32, is analogous with the sea serpent, dragon, or Leviathan as both similes imply.

> Ezek 29:3 Speak, and say, Thus saith the Lord GOD; Behold, I am against thee, Pharaoh king of Egypt, the great dragon that lieth in the midst of his rivers, which hath said.

The future ten-horned end-time empire of Revelation 13 will extend out of the former fourth-beast empire of Daniel 7 (and Daniel 2), strutting ten crowns upon the ten horns as well as flaunting personas of other beast empires past, represented by seven heads with seven blasphemous names/crowns:[2855] Egypt, Assyria, Babylon, Persia, Greece, Rome, and the coming revived Roman empire. The end-time beast will be already present before the midpoint of the last years as depicted in Revelation 12, when Israel flees to the wilderness at the time of the abomination; a beast empire described as the Great Red/*poorhros'* Dragon, as in fiery red, will sport seven heads, ten horns, and seven crowns upon the seven heads.[2856] The scarlet-colored (reddish orange) seven-headed, ten-horned beast empire with seven crowns and seven blasphemous names on the seven heads is depicted once more in Revelation 17 as the multiheaded beast ridden by the woman, the universal mystery religion of Babylon.[2857]

The seven heads of the multiheaded beast represent both seven mountains the woman sits on and the seven (antichrist-like) kings of the seven empires, just as the beast/Antichrist will be the king of the eighth empire. The seven mountains represent the religious mountain or high place/seat of the mystical religions from each of the beast empires, the daughters of Babel. Babylon derives biblically from Babel, where Nimrod imposed his mystical religion upon the Noahites. Babylon was the allegorical name used for Rome city that was established around their seven holy mountains, known in the time of John of Patmos and before, as the high seat of polytheism.[2858] At the time of the Roman empire, "five are fallen, one is, and the other is not yet come,"[2859] but when the seventh beast empire comes, it will reign for a short time (three and a half years).

[2854] Leviathan: Ps 74:14; Isa 27:1. Dragon Rev 12:3, 4, 7, 9, 13, 16, 17; 16:13; 19:20, 20:1–3.
[2855] Rev 12:3; 13:3–5, 12.
[2856] Rev 12:3, 6, 13, 17. Red: G4450—*poor-hros*: fire-like as in flame-colored red; burning; fiery trial.
[2857] Rev 17:3.
[2858] Rev 17:9–10. G897—*bab-oo-lone*: origin Hebrew Babel: confusion; Babylon City, the capital of Chaldea/Babylon; the territory of Babylonia; allegorically Rome, the seat of idolatry and the enemy of Christianity.
[2859] Rev 17:9.

In Greek mythology, the Hydra was a female multiheaded sea dragon, the offspring of the gods Echidna and Typhon, whose central head was immortal.[2860] In Sumerian mythology Tiamat was the goddess of chaos, the waters of creation, the mother of gods, and a goddess of the sea described as a dragon with a tail.[2861] Tiamat was further depicted as a dragon with feet, legs, a tail, and wings on the Babylon Cylinder in her battle with Bel (Baal), the god who slew Tiamat.[2862] Biblically, the female Leviathan/dragon was slain by God in prehistory. God will also destroy the male in the end times,[2863] which may also be prophetic allegory regarding Satan and his dragon/Leviathan empires.

The dragon was depicted in mythology as protected with armor-like scales and "terrible" fighting powers that included fire-breathing to reap destruction. The Greeks and Romans termed their standard-bearers *Draconarius* because they carried the dragon as their ensign. The formidable Greek Hydra Dragon's seven ferocious heads possessed the ability to heal or grow back those heads.[2864] In medieval alchemy (Rosicrucianism) the dragon was an emblem drafted by chemists and apothecaries that was prominently displayed on their drug-pots.[2865] Azazel was the leader of the antediluvian seraphim Watchers whom polytheist adepts memorialized as the Khem of Mendes of Alchemy and Rosicrucianism, the Goat of Mendes, and the angel of Capricorn. "Khem" in alchemy is an Egyptian word for black and the source word for alchemy.[2866]

Azazel and other fallen angels are the strong/*'el* ones of the abyss prison recorded in Ezekiel 32, versus the mighty/*gibbowr* kings, both who speak to Pharaoh "out of the midst of hell with them that help him: they are gone down."[2867] The strong ones are the former angels, "the chief ones of the earth," imprisoned with their "dead" kings of nations recorded in Isaiah 14.[2868] Chief ones/*'attuwd* means hairy he-goat(s) and figuratively leaders of people[2869] that conjures up images of satyrs, devil gods, and Duke Seir of the Horim in Edom. The chief ones

---

[2860] *Encyclopedia Americana,* Vol. 14, 539: Hydra; Rose, *Giants, Monsters & Dragons,* 183: Hydra.

[2861] Smith, *The Chaldean Account of Genesis,* 44, The Babylon Legend of the Creation, Tablet 1 lines 1-9; 60,63, 64, 6th fragment K3364, lines 2–8.

[2862] Ibid., 70, 72, 6th fragment K3364, lines 17–47.

[2863] Ps 74:14; Isa 27:1.

[2864] *Encyclopedia Americana,* Vol. 9, 294: Dragon; Vol. 14, 539: Hydra; Rose, *Giants, Monsters & Dragons,* 183: Hydra

[2865] Ibid., Vol. 9, 294: Dragon.

[2866] Wayne, *Genesis 6 Conspiracy,* 685–686, citing Gardner, *Lost Secrets,* 88; Gardner, *Grail Kings,* 219; Gardner, *Realm of the Ring Lords,* 133; Collins, *Ashes of Angels,* 27.

[2867] Ezek 32:21. H410—*'el*; H1368—*gibbowr*.

[2868] Isa 14:9.

[2869] H6260—*'attuwd,* at-tood': or *attud,* at-tood': full grown he-goats/rams and figuratively leaders of the people: goats; rams; chief ones.

are the degraded impassioned angels sent to the abyss and "raised up from their thrones all the kings of the nations."[2870]

The strong/*el* he-goat/*`attuwd* is the transitional allegory that connects fallen Watchers like the scapegoat/*`aza'zel* to the degraded devil goat gods, the satyrs/*sa`iyr*, hairy/*sa* and Watchers/*`Iyr*[2871] documented in Isaiah 13:21 and 34:14; and the devils/*sa`iyr* of Leviticus 17:7 and 2 Chronicles 11:15. Satyrs are as the fallen dragons/*tanniym* of Isaiah 13:22 and 34:13. As such, Azazel may very well be the destroyer, Abaddon/Apollyon that leads the degraded Watchers out of the abyss in the first three and a half years of the last seven (Rev 9:7–12).

Ergo, the *tanniym* allegory of Ezekiel 32 penned to describe Pharaoh ought to be understood as the dragon/*tanniym* of Ezekiel 29, because Egypt was the first postdiluvian beast empire, the first of the seven heads of the end-time dragon empire sponsored by Satan. Pharaoh then was understood in ancient Israel as a Rephaim antichrist-like figure leading one of the Houses of Dragon, and one of the Terrible Ones. Knowing this makes sense of whom Pharaoh is speaking to in the Ezekiel 32 dual prophecy, and that the prophecy foretold Pharaoh's destruction and slaughter[2872] along with the nations of the Middle East by king Nebuchadnezzar—"the terrible of nations." Pharaoh's destruction was an ancient illustration and foreshadowing to the greater end-time destruction of Babylon and Antichrist when the stars, sun, and moon will be covered with a cloud and not provide light.[2873] The hearts of many nations will be "vexed," and kings of nations will be terrified and afraid. The swords of the mighty/*gibbowr* will fall, and the "pomp of Egypt and all the multitude shall be destroyed."[2874]

[2870] H3678—*kicce', kis-say'*: covered as in a throne; canopied seat; stool; throne; seat of honor; seat or throne of royal dignity, authority, and power.

[2871] H5799—*`aza'zel*: goat of departure or the scapegoat; entire removal; scapegoat; the goat sacrificed for the sins of the people; H5795—*'ez, aze*: goat; kid; female goat; H8163—*sa`iyr*; shaggy: a he-goat; a faun; devil; goat; hairy, kid; rough satyr; H5894—*`iyr, eer*; a watcher angel.

[2872] Ezek 32:3–5; 39:3–7; Joel 2:20; 3:15; Rev 14:20; 19:17–18.

[2873] Isa 13:10; Ezek 32:3–15; Joel 2:20; 3:15; Matt 24:29; Rev 6:12; 9:12; 16:10.

[2874] Ezek 32:3–16.

CHAPTER 59

TYRUS AND SHEBNA

Ezek 28:2 Son of man, say unto the prince of Tyrus, Thus saith the Lord GOD; Because thine heart is lifted up, and thou hast said, I am a God, I sit in the seat of God, in the midst of the seas; yet thou art a man, and not God, though thou set thine heart as the heart of God.

"Pomp" is a word used in Ezekiel 32:12 and 30:19, describing Pharaoh's antichrist-like attributes and reflecting the same pomp attributed to Satan/*Heylel's* fall depicted Isaiah 14:11. Pomp/*ga'own* is defined as majestic, pride, and the arrogance of the nations fostered by their gods, religions,[2875] rituals, and demigod kings.

Ga'own, applied to describe Egypt's pomp, was translated as "excellency" and "arrogancy" with Babylon.[2876] Like Satan/*Heylel's* prophesied fall to the grave, antichrist figures like the Assyrian king and the king of Babylon/*Helel* fall to the grave in Isaiah 14's dual prophecy in like manner of Tyrus in Ezekiel 28.[2877] Pomp conveys the overreach, splendor, arrogance, and pride of the Babel religion, the "terrible" Nephilim/Rephaim empires, and antichrist-like figures past and will be

---

[2875] H1347—*ga' own, gaw-ohn'*: arrogancy; excellency; majesty; pomp; pride; proud; swelling; arrogance of nations and their religions.
[2876] Isa 13:11, 19; Ezek 32:12.
[2877] Isa 14:11–19, 25; Ezek 28:8–10, 17.

reflected in the end-time seventh empire, Babylon, and Antichrist.[2878] Tyrus, *Helel*, Pharaoh, and the Assyrian and Rephaim kings listed in Ezekiel 32 were cast down to the abyss prison for their arrogance and crimes—as Satan will be in the end times.[2879]

Dual prophecies further make sense of Isaiah 22 with respect to Eliakim son of Hilkiah, and Shebna who drew breath during king Hezekiah's reign over Judah circa 715–686 BC, and in the generation when the Assyrian empire temporarily bent the world to its will, demolished Israel, and exiled the northern kingdom's remnant. In Isaiah 22 a sepulchre (burial tomb) was readied by Shebna, a scribe of a very high position in Hezekiah's court. Eliakim was the master of Hezekiah's household and the temple.[2880] Contrarywise, I find it odd that God would clothe this Eliakim with the robe of the one whom the grave is being prepared for; that God would strengthen this Eliakim with God's girdle (sash of high priest); and commit God's government into this Eliakim's hand as the father of Jerusalem's inhabitants in the day God calls "my servant Eliakim, son of Hilkiah."[2881]

The Isaiah 22 dual prophecy employed people of Hezekiah's court as prophetic allegory for Jesus' end-time visitations, and for His crucifixion and entombment. Thus, God will anoint and proclaim[2882] His Servant Eliakim to reign over His government, an edict reserved for Jesus/Joshua.[2883] Eliakim/*'Elyaqiym'* is defined as "God raises up" or "sets up," from *'El*/God and iakim/*quwm* meaning to establish, confirm, strengthen, and raise up,[2884] and prophetic for Jesus' crucifixion, time in the grave, resurrection, and return to reign. Moreover, God's government will be inherited by Eliakim, the son of the high priest Hilkiah,[2885] understood again as prophetic allegory. Adding to the prophetic allegory is Hilkiah/*Chilqiyah's* name, compounded from *cheleq* and *Yahh* meaning "my portion is Jah," the short form of Jehovah/Yahweh/*Yhovah*.[2886] The prophetic allegory of Hilkiah, father of Elia-

---

[2878] Isa 13:11, 19; Jer 51:6–8, 13, 18, 37; Ezek 28:2; Dan 7:20, 25: 8:10, 11, 25; 11:36–39; Rev 13:5–10; 17:3–6; 18:16.
[2879] Sides of abyss: Isa 14:15. Satan cast into the abyss: Rev 20:1–3.
[2880] Isa 22:15–24. Eliakim: 2 Kings 18:18, 26, 37; 19:32; 23:34; 2 Chron 36:34; Heb 12:41; Isa 20:20; 36:3, 11, 22; 37:2. H471—*'Elyaqiym', el-yaw-keem'*: God of raising; God sets up; son of Hilkiah, master of Hezekiah's household. Shebna: 2 Kings 18:18, 26, 37; Isa 22:15; 36:11, 22; 37:2. H7644—*Shebna', sheb-naw'*: to grow; growth; vigor. *Strong's Cyclopaedia*, Vol. 4, 255: Hilkiah.
[2881] Isa 22:20.
[2882] Isa 20–25. H7121—*qara', kaw-raw'*: call out and address by name; cry out; proclaim; renowned; preach; read aloud; to summon; invite; commission; appoint.
[2883] Zech 3:1–10.
[2884] H471—*'Elyaqiym', el-yaw-keem'*; from 410 and 6965: God of raising or God sets up; H6965—*quwm, koom*: rise; set up; establish; stir up, strengthen; succeed; arise; rise; become powerful.
[2885] Isa 22:20. *Strong's Cyclopaedia*, Vol. 4, 255 Hilkiah.
[2886] H2518—*Chilqiyah, khil-kee-yaw'*; from *cheleq* and *Yahh*: portion of Jah: my portion is Jehovah; father of Eliakim; high priest.

kim the high priest, foreshadows *Yhovah* of the *Elohiym* in His future Melchizedek high priest status, while Hilkiah allegorically represents Elohiym/*El* whose Son, the Word, later became flesh and was anointed by God. The prophetic allegory becomes crystal-clear in verse 22 where Eliakim will be given the keys to the house of David (Hezekiah in the prophecy's period), whereby anything Jesus opens or closes none shall undo.[2887]

> Isa 22;22 And the key of the house of David will I lay upon his shoulder; so he shall open, and none shall shut; and he shall shut, and none shall open.
>
> Isa 22:23 And I will fasten him as a nail in a sure place; and he shall be for a glorious throne to his father's house.
>
> Isa 22:24 And they shall hang upon him all the glory of his father's house.

Just as the book of Zechariah describes a high priest prefiguration of Jesus, Joshua/*Yhowshuwa* who replaces Satan as high priest, so Isaiah 22 discusses a mystery figure, Shebna, who is a prophetic allegory for Satan. Shebna ordered a sepulchre hewed for himself from a rock on high, but Shebna was carried away in a mighty captivity by Assyria.[2888] The language is very much like the end-time capture of Satan, his imprisonment in the abyss, and his destruction at the end of the millennium.[2889] Shebna's sepulchre/*qeber* was a burying tomb/grave hewed/*chatsab*[2890] out of stone on high, and a "graveth habitation" that can mean grave, temple, or dwelling place in a rock/*cela`* or a stone stronghold.[2891] The prophetic allegory conveys that Satan hewed a great temple or fortress, perhaps the "House of Judgment," the "Archeion," where Satan will be pulled from and sent to the abyss prison. God drove Shebna in the time of the Assyrian Apocalypse from his "station" and "state," then pulled him down.[2892] "Station" is defined as a garrison,

---

[2887] Rev 3:7.
[2888] Zech 3:1–10. Isa 22:16–17.
[2889] Rev 20:1–3, 7–10.
[2890] H6913—*qeber, keh'-ber*: a sepulchre; a burying place; grave; tomb; H2672—*chatsab, khaw-tsab'*: to cut or carve wood or stone; to hew; split; square; quarry; engrave; made by mason.
[2891] Graveth: H2710—*chaqaq, khaw-kak'*: to hack; engrave; cut into stone or metal; inscribe; a grave; a lawgiver; governor; appoint; decree. Habitation: H4908—*mishkan, mish-kawn'*: a residence; a grave; the temple; and specifically, the tabernacle dwelling place or tent; a habitation, a dwelling; habitation; Rock: H5553—*cela`, seh'-lah*: be lofty; a craggy rock; a rock/stone fortress; stones; a cliff, a rock.
[2892] Isa 22:16–19.

an outpost, or a standing-place; "state" means an office, state, or service; and "pull down" means to overthrow, destroy, break into pieces, pluck down, and ruin.[2893]

Moreover, Shebna, the ruler of the "rock,"[2894] is reflective of Satan/*Helyel* and like the king of Babylon/*Helel's* fall to the pit prison in *Sh'owl* (14:13–20), as well as Tyrus' fall to the pit prison in Ezekiel 28:5–19. Tyrus/*Tsor* also means rock,[2895] just as both Satan and Shebna are/were rulers of the rock, all who did widespread traffic of merchandise and iniquities. Ezekiel's prophecies portrayed king Tyrus as an archetypical antichrist figure like Nimrod, the Assyrian, and the king of Babylon. Accordingly, Tyrus was classified as one of Terrible Ones,[2896] a beast king, even though he was not king over one the seven prophetic beast empires.

Both the Ezekiel 28–29 kings of prophecies were set in the same period as the Pharaoh of Ezekiel 30–32. Both Ezekiel 28 and 29 engaged similar prophetic allegory to that of the king of Babylon/*Helel* and the Assyrian king in Isaiah 14. The king-of-Tyrus prophecies was set among the romp of the terrible of nations, Nebuchadnezzar against the Terrible Ones of Ezekiel's era, the Rephaim kings of Ezekiel 32, which included the beast economic empire of Tyre/Tyrus, and Egypt. Antichrist will do the same to Egypt, Babylon, and end-time Tyre.[2897]

As such, Tyrus was selected for Ezekiel 28 as a prophetic antichrist-like figure for his pomp/arrogance in the spirit of *Heylel*/Satan and the end-time Antichrist. Tyrus' economic and commerce empire is understood in part as prophetic allegory for the end-time Babylon religion and then Antichrist's eighth empire. Just as Tyre was a worldwide trading and commercial organization, so will Babylon be, followed by Antichrist's worldwide economic and trading system with the mark of the beast system. Additionally, Tyrus too wished to raise his majestic and opulent throne to heaven as Satan and *Helel* attempted in Isaiah 14. Tyrus was yet another *Helel*-like king of Babylon, just as Antichrist will attempt to raise his throne to heaven.[2898]

> Isa 23:8 Who hath taken this counsel against Tyre, the crowning city, whose merchants are princes, whose traffickers are the honorable of the earth?

[2893] Isa 22:19–25. Station: H4673—*matstsab, mats-tsawb'*: an office; a military post; garrison; or station; outpost; State: H4612—*ma'amad, mah-am-awd'*: attendance; office; place; state; function; service; H2040—*harac, haw-ras'*: to pull down; pull apart into in pieces; break; destroy; beat down; overthrow; pluck down; throw down; G5184—*too'-ros*; of Hebrew origin H6865 *Tsor*: Tyre; a rock; a Phoenician city, an ancient flourishing city in commerce.

[2894] Isa 22:16.

[2895] Job 2:2; Ezek 28:5–19. H6865—*Tsor, tsore*; or *Tsowr, tsore*; a rock; Tyre or Tyrus.

[2896] Isa 14:4–7, 15–21; 25:3–5; Ezek 26:17; 28:7–8.

[2897] Jer 51:1–64; Ezek 29:18; Dan 11:43; Rev 17:13–17; 18:1–24.

[2898] Dan 8:10–11.

In the Ezekiel 31 dual prophecy, the great "cedar tree of Lebanon with fair branches" was the so-called Assyrian in Eden,[2899] where the Assyrian, the "terrible of nations" (Nebuchadnezzar) cuts down Pharaoh and his multitudes.[2900] Ezekiel 31 connected the Assyrian and king of Babylon/*Helel* of Isaiah 14 to Nebuchadnezzar in its allegory, as well as linking Tyrus's destruction in the same beast campaign during Ezekiel's generation; note that Babylon was founded by the Assyrians.[2901] Cedar and oak trees were utilized in Ezekiel 27:3–6, reflecting Tyrus/Tyre's mighty navy and his pride, wealth, and beauty; likewise, Amos 2:9 connected Amorites to cedars and oaks of Bashan in a simile for their size, strength, and pomp.

> Ezek 27:3 And say unto Tyrus, O thou that art situate at the entry of the sea, which art a merchant of the people. .. thou hast said, I am of perfect beauty.

> Ezek 27:4 Thy borders are in the midst of the seas, thy builders have perfected thy beauty.

> Ezek 27:5. .. they have taken cedars from Lebanon to make masts for thee.

> Ezek 27:6 Of the oaks of Bashan have they made thine oars.

Tyre was described in Isaiah 23 as the "daughter of Tarshish" and the "virgin daughter of Zidon," reflecting an end-time like Babylon in its commerce, religion, and destruction.[2902] "Daughters of famous nations"[2903] is prophetic allegory often overlooked that contains important context. Women, daughters, and prostitutes in scriptural allegory often represent polytheist religions like Egypt's Heliopolis and her priests. Thus, the daughters/mysticism are the same "daughters of famous nations" of Ezekiel 32 and their bloodline priests cast down "with them that go down into the pit," the "nether"[2904] parts of the earth. The mother is the woman of Revelation 17, Babylon/Babel/Chaldea, from which her daughters spread first to Egypt and then to the world, to sit as the queens of kingdoms atop the beast empires past and future.[2905]

[2899] Ezek 31.3, 9, 18.
[2900] Ezek 31:11–18.
[2901] Isa 23:13.
[2902] Isa 23:10–12.
[2903] Ezek 32:18.
[2904] Ezek 32:18: H8482—*tachtiy, takh-tee*: lowermost; the depth; a pit: lowest; lower parts.
[2905] Ps 137:8; Isa 47:2, 5, 6, 8; Jer 50:42; 51:53; Ezek 23:36–45; Hos 2:13; Zec 2:7; 5:7; Mal 2:11; Rev 17:7, 9, 15, 16, 18; 18:3, 4, 7, 9, 23, 24.

> Isa 47:1 Come down, and sit in the dust, O virgin daughter of Babylon, sit on the ground: there is no throne, O daughter of the Chaldeans: for thou shalt no more be called tender and delicate.. ..

> Isa 47:5 Sit thou silent, and get thee into darkness, O daughter of the Chaldeans: for thou shalt no more be called, The lady of kingdoms.. ..

> Isa 47:7 And thou saidst, I shall be a lady for ever.

> Zech 2:7 Deliver thyself, O Zion, that dwellest with the daughter of Babylon.

The pomp of Egypt and Tyrus was akin to Satan and *Helel* king of Babylon's fall in Isaiah 14:11. Further, pomp appropriately describes the daughters of Babel/Babylon throughout history and will again in the end times with Babylon's splendor, arrogance, hubris, and majesty. Babylon will fall like Satan in the end times. The coming end-time Babylon religion will be the mother of harlots who rides and reigns the Hydra beast from the sea as lady of kingdoms and beast empires past and future, the daughter of Chaldeans, the daughter of Babylon, and the daughters of the nations/*goyim*.[2906]

> Rev 17:4 And the woman was arrayed in purple and scarlet color, and decked with gold and precious stones and pearls, having a golden cup in her hand full of abominations and filthiness of her fornication.

[2906] Rev 17:2, 5, 15, 18.

CHAPTER 60

THE MYSTERIOUS TREES OF EDEN

Ezek 31:3 Behold, the Assyrian was a Cedar in Lebanon with fair branches.. ..

Ezek 31:8 The cedars in the garden of God could not hide him: the fir trees were not like his boughs, and the chestnut trees were not like his branches; nor any tree in the garden of God was like unto him in his beauty.

Beast empire religions past and future were and will be oath-bound theocracies devoted to the destruction of Adamites, to prevent them from being raised up like angels. Just as the Invisible Ones swore oaths atop Mount Hermon to create giants, their spurious visible offspring continue in that accursed oath-based theology as their *raison d'etre.*[2907]

One ought to be suspicious of any organization, government, religion, or institution that demands sworn oaths. Christians are instructed not to swear oaths, that one will be held accountable to God if they do. Christians are instructed to simply let your word be your word.[2908] Israel was required to swear an oath to uphold the Holy Covenant and were held accountable for their failure to uphold the oath via the curses of the covenant that plague them to this day, and for a little

---

[2907] Eph 6:12; Col 1:16.
[2908] Lev 6:3–5; Num 20:2; Deut 6:13; 23:21; Ps 23:3–4; Zech 5:3–4; Matt 5:33–37; 23:16–22; James 5:12.

longer. Oaths are demanded by those who reign over this world in veneration of their serpentine godfathers. One might anticipate that the coming Babylon religion, its sponsored ten-king end-time empire, followed by the Antichrist with his religion, will demand oaths of allegiance, with the latter punctuated by the mark of the beast and the beast system.

The Naphalim that swore oaths went to the abyss prison both before and after the flood. As such, the abyss/pit in prophecy is a prophetic marker and allegory for discernment, where one can bridge the New Testament Greek to the Old Testament Hebrew. The daughters of famous nations (Ezek 32:18) were cast down to the "pit." The allegory indicates that the daughters were of the Rephaim priest and priestess class and the queens of heaven (mother goddesses) of the beast religion, sent to the pit prison along with the Terrible Ones. They were cast down to the "nether parts of the earth, with them that go down into the pit." The "pit" is an Old Testament phrase for the prison, the bottomless pit/abyss in the New Testament, located within the underworld, known as Hades in Greek and *Sh'owl* in Hebrew. The pit prison was created for fallen angels and the worst of the demons who will be released in the first three and a half years of the last seven.[2909] Both the strong/*el* imprisoned fallen angels and the mighty/*gibbowr* speak to Pharaoh in the Ezekiel 32 prophecy from "the midst of hell"/*Sh'owl*, from the abyss; the Terrible Ones were slain with the sword from the earth, likely by decapitation.[2910] The terrible branches of the Rephaim and Nephilim were imprisoned in the sides of the bottomless pit with the fallen angels jailed in the inner part of the shaft.

> Isa 14:15. .. yet thou shalt be brought down to hell, to the sides of the pit.

> Ezek 32:23 Whose graves are set in the sides of the pit, and her company is round about her grave: all of them slain, fallen by the sword, which caused terror in the land of the living.

The Terrible Ones in Ezekiel 32 were sent to the abyss for causing "terror in the land of the living" both before and after the flood. They were sent to prison because of the wickedness and iniquity they levied against humankind.[2911] The Terrible Ones, and/or their descendants, will do so again with the "beginning of sorrows" of the Fig Tree generation leading up to the last seven years. The Fig Tree generation will emulate the days of Noah before the flood, immediately after

---

[2909] Ezek 32:18; 1 Pet 3:19; 2 Pet 2:4; Jude 1:6; Rev 9:2. H8482—*tachtiy, takh-tee*: lowermost; the depths; a pit; nether or lower parts; H953—*bowr, bore*: a pit hole; a cistern; prison; dungeon; fountain; well; H7585—*sh'owl, sheh-ole*: or *shol, sheh-ole*: Hades; world of the dead; a subterranean place including its inmates; grave; hell; pit; the underworld; a place the wicked and punishment; the place of exile.

[2910] H410—*el*; H1368—*gibbowr*.

[2911] Isa 13:11; Ezek 28: 6, 7; 32:12, 18, 20, 21, 25.

the flood, and during the days of Lot and Sodom.[2912] Knowing this this begins to make sense of the two great end-time wars recorded in the Old Testament led by "mighty men,"[2913] descendants of the giants, disembodied demon spirits, or travelers/passengers. The "mighty" Terrible Ones who reigned in Ezekiel's period[2914] later joined those who spoke from the pit prison. These Terrible Ones will be released from the pit prison in the first half of last seven years, along with the fallen angels that bring about the war of the 200-million-man army.[2915]

Before their eternal punishment the Terrible Ones past and future will greet Satan when he is sent to the abyss. Satan, at that time, will be viewed as a dragon/*tanniym* and Leviathan of Isaiah 27:1. The kings of the nations in Isaiah 14:9 will be stirred from the "dead"/rapha', the spirits of the Rephaim.[2916]

> Isa 14:9 Hell from beneath is moved for thee to meet thee at thy coming: it stirreth up the dead for thee, even all the chief ones of the earth; it hath raised up from their thrones all the kings of the nations.
>
> Isa 14:10 All they shall speak and say unto thee, Art thou also become weak as we? art thou become like unto us?
>
> Isa 14:11 Thy pomp is brought down to the grave, and the noise of thy viols: the worm is spread under thee, and the worms cover thee.

With all this as context, one can then begin to discern the cryptic prophecy in Ezekiel 31 where Pharaoh and his multitude was asked, "Whom art thou like in thy greatness?" In response, Pharaoh was instructed: to behold the "Assyrian cedar" whose fair/beautiful branches possessed a shadowing shroud and was of high stature. Oddly though, Assyria at this time was sliding into decline while Nebuchadnezzar's beast Babylonian empire was rising. Pharaoh Necho was compared to the Assyrian, and then as the Assyrian connects to the end-time Antichrist. Further, the Assyrian cedar tree was the greatest tree in Eden[2917] and as such, before the flood. Asshur/Assyria was not in Eden before the flood. In the Genesis Eden account, the only trees named in Eden were the "tree of life" and the "tree of the knowledge of good and evil." One deduces then Ezekiel 31 is a dual prophecy because Pharaoh Necho's prophecy also has end-time implications along with its embedded prehistory details and allegories.

Lebanese and Mount Hermon cedars were the giant trees of the Middle East, growing to a girth of forty to fifty feet, and a height up to one hundred feet.'[2918]

[2912] Matt 24:6–8, 32–44; Mark 13:5–8, 28–31; Luke 17:26–27; 21:8–11.

[2913] Ezek 39:11, 14, 15, 18, 20; 32:12, 21, 27; Joel 2:7; 3:9, 11.

[2914] Ezek 32:12.

[2915] Rev 9:1–21.

[2916] H7496—*rapha'*.

[2917] Ezek 31:2, 3, 8, 9, 18.

[2918] *Nelson's*, 1002–1003: plants of the Bible.

The oak tree too was a giant-like tree growing a massive trunk,[2919] and renowned for growing in Bashan/Mount Hermon.[2920] In Amos 2:9 the Amorite's size, strength, and pomp were compared allegorically within a grammatical simile of giant cedar and oak associated with Mount Hermon, and the creation of Nephilim and Rephaim. Oak and cedar trees were used to carve idols.[2921] The great oak tree, Bile, was renowned by the Tuatha De Danann tribe of D'Anu,[2922] and Ditanu. The Tuatha De Danann were further renowned as the "Fair Folk" and the "Fairy People,"[2923] and akin to the fair branches of the Assyrian tree. Cedar and oak trees were employed in Ezekiel 27:3–6, reflecting Tyrus' mighty and powerful navy, as well as his pride, wealth and beauty in like manner as the trees of Ezekiel 31.

> Ezek 31.3 Behold, the Assyrian was a cedar in Lebanon with fair branches, and with a shadowing shroud, and of an high stature; and his top was among the thick boughs.

Pharaoh Necho represented the bloodlines of the Rephaim Pharaonic dynasty and an antichrist-like figure of the first postdiluvian beast empire in the book of Ezekiel, and as such was compared to the Assyrian second beast empire and antichrist-like figures with other trees in Eden. The branches of the Assyrian cedar tree in Eden were "fair," so much so that all the trees in Eden envied the cedar's fair branches. Fair/*yapheh* appears thirty-seven times in the Old Testament and means beautiful as in bright and handsome, generally used in relationship with fair white or fair skin, just as the various Rephaim/Horim/Indo-Aryan branches were fair/pale-skinned and were renowned as the Shining Ones of the Albi-gens.[2924] Fair is a constitutive occult allegory for fairy queens and princes of the Elvin bloodline of giants and mystical religions. Similarly, cedars and oaks of Lebanon, Hermon, and Bashan were the same allegories employed for blond, fair-skinned Amorites in Amos 2:9, and in Isaiah 2's "Day of the Lord" prophecy against the proud and lofty, just as Nephilim and Rephaim were proud and lofty. Further, Isaiah 14 employed cedar trees for Lucifer/*Heylel*'s pride and rebellion, the Assyrian, and the king of Babylon/*Helel*.[2925]

Moreover, the Assyrian cedar of "fair branches, and with a shadowing shroud, and of an high stature" is reminiscent of allegories describing Satan/*Heylel*. Shroud and shadowing combine to mean a forest canopy that shadows or covers what is

---

[2919] *Nelson's*, 1007: plants of the Bible.

[2920] Deut 4:47; Josh 12; 1 Chron 5:23.

[2921] Isa 44:14; Ezek 27:5.

[2922] Wayne, *Genesis 6 Conspiracy*, 123; 664, 668, citing Peter Beresford Ellis, *The Celts* (London: Robinson, 2003), branches.

[2923] Gardner, *Ring Lords*, 30–31, 58; Evan-Wentz, *Fairy Faith*, 22, 27, 53, 59, 62.

[2924] Ezek 31:3, 9. H3303—*yapheh, yaw-feh'*: beautiful; bright; fairest; fair; handsome; Gardner, *Ring Lords*, 24, 30, 31, 34, 35, 58, 62, 64–75, 268.

[2925] Isa 2:12, 13; 14:8, 12, 13, 25.

below; these trees were of "high stature" and "thick boughs."[2926] The Ezekiel 31 prophecy, with its reference to Eden and covering imagery, additionally described the covering of the wings of Eden's cherub, Satan, in Ezekiel 28.[2927] Satan's world-wide cherubic winged canopy cast the shadow where the nations dwell under-neath, and kin allegory to "the face of the covering cast over all people, and the vail that is spread over all nations," employed in the book of Isaiah regarding Satan.[2928] Additionally, the phraseology in Ezekiel 31 is consistent with Tyrus and Satan's description in Ezekiel 28: as beautiful/*yophiy* and bright/*yiph`ah* as in shin-ing, and as in beauty and splendor of the anointed cherub of Eden.[2929]

The Assyrian tree in the actual Eden garden was Satan, the greatest of the trees/angels that were also there by implication and as noted in Ezekiel 28.[2930] The cedar tree (Satan), corrupted by his pride, beauty, and high stature, tried to raise his throne up to heaven like the world tree of polytheism,[2931] and by implication as did the Assyrian, *Helel*, and all antichrist-like figures. Among the branches of the cedar tree of Eden, "fowls of heaven made their nests in his boughs," another allegory this time for the winged Naphalim and/or cherubim who rebelled with Satan. Under the shade, the covering and protection of the cedar/Satan all the great/*rab* nations, the beast empires dwelled[2932] in the Naphalim/Nephilim World Order. However, "The branch of the Terrible Ones shall be brought low"[2933] in the end times—consistent prophetic allegory for the branches/bloodlines that reign on the earth for Satan and council of gods. Accordingly, and as an end-time foreshad-owing, Pharaoh and his multitude was "brought down to the nether parts of the earth" like the trees of Eden and like the slain branches.[2934]

> Ezek 31:6 All the fowls of heaven made their nests in his boughs, and under his branches did all the beasts of the field bring forth their young, and under his shadow dwelt all great nations.. .. Ezek 31:13 Upon his ruin shall all the fowls of the heaven remain, and all the beasts of the field shall be upon his branches.

[2926] Ezek 31:3. H6751—*tsalal, tsaw-lal'*: hovering over; to shade; be dark; shadowing; H2793—*choresh, kho'-resh*: a forest; wood; wooded height.

[2927] Ezek 28:13–16.

[2928] Isa 25:6–8; Ezek 31:6.

[2929] Exod 25:20; 37:9; 1 Kings 8:7; 1 Chron 28:18; Ezek 28:7, 14, 16, 17. H3308—*yophiy, yof-ee'*; beauty: beauty; H3314—*yiph ` ah, yif-aw'*; splendor; beauty; brightness: splendour; brightness; shining.

[2930] Ezek 31:8, 9, 18.

[2931] Ezek 31:7–10.

[2932] Ezek 31:6; Amos 1:5. H5775—*`owph, ofe*: a bird; as covered with feathers; a covering with wings; flying; flying creatures; H1040—*Beyth ` Eden, bayth ay'-den*: house of pleasure or delight; a synonym for Eden.

[2933] Isa 25:5.

[2934] Ezek 31:18.

Pharaoh was delivered into the "mighty one of the heathens," Nebuchadnezzar, the "terrible of nations," where he was slain and brought down to the nether parts of the earth,[2935] the pit/*bowr*, as were the Assyrian and other Terrible Ones past and future. Pharaoh and the Assyrian were "cut off," *karath,* meaning to destroy, kill, cut down with a sword or decapitation.[2936]

Hell and grave derive from *Sh'owl* as in Isaiah 14:9–15, while the pit/*bowr* is in *Sh'owl;* the spirits of the "dead"/*rapha'* are the kings of the nations in the abyss prison,[2937] the Terrible Ones cut off/*karath* in Isaiah 14. They "lie in glory, every one in his own house" (Isa 14:18). Lie/*shakab* means cast down; lie down as in rest, sleep, or death; and deceased. Thus, Ezekiel 31 spoke of Pharaoh's glory/*kabowd*: copious glorious, splendor, rich, reputation, and reverence, which derives from *kabad* meaning weight, weighty, heavy, make heavy, glorious and of reputation to the Eden trees. Thus, the king's and Pharaoh's greatness/*godel*—pride, insolence, stoutness, and greatness[2938]—further describes tall, stout, and fair-skinned giants.

Thus, the kings of Ezekiel 31 and their multitudes slain by the "terrible of nations," Nebuchadnezzar were brought down to a place described in Isaiah 14 as "the house of the prisoners," with house/*bayith* defined as a house, a home, a prison, a dungeon, or a family and its descendants.[2939]

> Isa 14:17 That made the world as a wilderness, and destroyed the cities thereof; that opened not the house of his prisoners?
>
> Isa 14:18 All the kings of the nations, even all of them, lie in glory, every one in his own house.

The Rephaim kings were placed in their sarcophagi with their riches, but their demon *rapha'* spirits did not sleep. They were cast down to their reserved dungeon among their terrible ancestors to await their familial descendants, and as the abominable branches cast out of their graves/*qeber*: sepulchre/tomb.[2940]

[2935] Ezek 31:11, 12, 14.
[2936] Ezek 31:18. H3519—*kabowd, kaw-bode'; kabod, kaw-bode';* weight in the sense of splendor; glorious glory; honorable: honor; honorable; gloriously; splendor; reputation; H3772—*karath.*
[2937] Job 26:5; Ps 88:10; Prov 21:16; Isa 14:9; 26:14, 19. H7496—*rapha', raw-faw';* a ghost of the dead or deceased: dead; deceased; ghosts of the dead; shades; spirits.
[2938] Ezek 31:18. H3519—*kabowd, kaw-bode'; kabod, kaw-bode';* from 3513: weight in the sense of splendor; glorious; glory; honorable; reputation; H3513—*kabad, kaw-bad':* to be heavy; to make weighty; glory; great, heavy; noble; H3772—*karath, kaw-rath';* H1433—*godel, go-del':* magnitude; greatness as in stoutness: stout.
[2939] Isa 14:18. H7901—*shakab, shaw-kab':* to lie down or rest; allegory to lay with a lover sexually; lie down as in death; decease; cast down; to lie down to sleep; take rest; H3519—*kabowd, kaw-bode';* H3513—*kabad, kaw-bad;* H1004—*bayith:* a house; a family; a court; a daughter; dungeon; prison; temple; organized body of descendants.
[2940] Isa 14:19. H6913—*qeber, keh'-ber;* a sepulcher, as in a burying place.

THE TERRIBLE ONES

Isa 25:5 Thou shalt bring down the noise of strangers, as the heat in a dry place; even the heat with the shadow of a cloud: the branch of the terrible ones shall be brought low.

"Asshur" is the root word and lineage for the Rephaim hybrid Assyrian of Isaiah 14:25, symbolic in prophetic allegory for end-time antichrist in this prophecy.

Pharaoh was compared to the Assyrian cedar in Eden for his greatness and pomp, as were other nations, and as branches of Satan's World Order (Ezek 31:1–18). Pharaoh spoke with the slain kings of nations cut off by the sword (likely beheaded), kings "which caused terror in the land of the living."[2941] Asshur/ *'Ashshuwr* and all his company were listed first. Company/*qahal* is defined as an evil assembly and/or evil multitudes. Asshur, a son of Shem, was the eponymous name for the Assyrian people that left Shinar and Nimrod to establish Nineveh, as well as Rehoboth, Calah, and Resen,[2942] seed cities for the second beast empire. In the same spirit as Nimrod, the daughters of Asshur produced hybrid humans via intermarriage with Mesopotamian Rephaim, such as Arioch, Gilgamesh, and Sargon.

> Accad was believed founded, but more than likely inherited, by Sargon the Great around the twenty-third to the twenty-fourth century B.C., when his men overran the Sumerian homeland. Sargon was the first to conquer and then turn the alliance of Mesopotamian cities

---

[2941] Ezek 32:21, 23.
[2942] Gen 10:11, 12, 22. Asshur: H804—*'Ashshuwr*; H6951—*qahal, kaw-hawl'*: assembly; company; congregation; multitude; convocation; assembly for evil counsel, war, or invasion.

into an empire, winning thirty-four battles and pushing into Awan of Elam and Mari in the north. Sargon maintained representatives of all the old ruling families (Nephilim) at his court, honoring their "exalted" lineages.[2943]

Sargon was a grand king with a preternatural mythos, whom many kings later claimed as their progenitor.[2944] Sargon's Akkadian and/or Anunnaki tribes from the mountains of the north defeated Lugalzaggesi of Uruk.[2945] Sargon became a patronymic king title for Assyrian kings such as Sargon I of Assyria (c. 1850 BC) and Sargon II (c. 722 BC), with the latter reigning at the time of or just before the Israelite exile, between Shalmaneser and Sennacherib.[2946]

Asshur, Pharaoh, and the kings of Ezekiel 32 imprisoned into the sides of the abyss will play a prophetic role in the end times, as will other Nephilim and Rephaim locked in the abyss prison. As one example, the Assyrian/Asshur will be laid waste in the end times, just as Babylon did to Assyria in Ezekiel's time. The Assyrian Antichrist and his land will be destroyed for invading the Covenant Land in the aftermath of the Gog war,[2947] where Antichrist will tread on the land for three and a half years. Assyria's end-time destruction includes the "land of Nimrod," the first king/*Helel* of Babel/Babylon. The end-time Assyrian destruction will occur at a time when the awakened lost tribes of Israel held in worldwide concentration camps will be set free by "breaker," their king and Lord/*Yehovah* to lead them in the great Second Exodus.[2948] At that time the Assyrian will be crushed in the mountains of the Covenant Land.[2949]

Mic 5:5 And this man shall be the peace, when the Assyrian shall come into our land: and when he shall tread in our palaces, then shall we raise against him seven shepherds, and eight principal men.

Mic 5:6 And they shall waste the land of Assyria with the sword, and the land of Nimrod in the entrances thereof: thus shall he deliver us from the Assyrian, when he cometh into our land, and when he treadeth within our borders.

[2943] Wayne, *Genesis 6 Conspiracy*, 204, citing *Nelson's*, 1130: Sargon; and Bauer, *History of the World*, 98–101; Evans, *Dragons: Myth and Legend*, 51–52.
[2944] *Nelson's*, 1130: Sargon; Bauer, *History of the World*, 95–97.
[2945] Bauer, *History of the World*, 97–98, citing *The Sargon Legend*, Segment B in electronic text corpus of Sumerian Literature, and Kramer, *The Sumerians*, 324; Rohl, *Lost Testament*, 41-page note.
[2946] *Nelson's*, 1130: Sargon; *Strong's Cyclopaedia*, Vol. 9, 357: Sargon.
[2947] Dan 11:22–35; Luke 21:20–24.
[2948] Isa 61:1–11; Mic 2:2–23; Luke 4:17–20.
[2949] Isa 14:25; Dan 11:45; Mic 2:12–13; 5:6–9; Rev 19:15–21.

Mic 5:7 And the remnant of Jacob shall be in the midst of many people as a dew.

Elam was the second king described in the pit cells. His multitudes also were slain, then sent to the nether reaches of the earth, for the "terror" they reaped while on earth. These disembodied spirits carry their shame to their prison, for the might they misused while on earth.[2950]

Elam/`Eylam was the second-born son of Shem, just before Asshur. Elamites dwelled in a province of Babylon,[2951] as did Chedorlaomer, king of Elam, one of the giant kings in the war of giants.[2952] Elamites/Owlam occupied the cities of Susa and Awan, a people that intermixed with offshoot (likely Kadmonim) Aryans of the Indus valley, Persian Aryans, and Amorites to form the Persian and Mede peoples that were subdued by the Rephaim king Sargon the Great.[2953] The Babylonian historian Berosus stated that Elamites/Aryans from the Indus valley were the bloodline source of the Mede dynasties that eventually succeeded as the Persian/ Mede (beast) dynasty from Nebuchadnezzar's Babylon (beast) empire.[2954] In Ezekiel's era, Elam was conquered by Nebuchadnezzar, treated like rivals and outcasts, and then scattered by Babylon. The Elamites regrouped shortly thereafter, and were listed among the Medes and their kings when they overthrew Babylon. Elamite posterity then merged with another people to become the Persians,[2955] a people led by the Aryan kings.

Like Asshur, modern Elam will meet with end-time destruction, and become a nation the lost tribes of the Israelite northern kingdom exodus from.[2956] Isaiah 22's dual prophecy concerning Assyria's attack on Jerusalem, prophesying Satan's end-time imprisonment into the abyss, foretold a day when Elam will be trodden down. Elam faced destruction in Nebuchadnezzar's time and will again face destruction in the end times, in the time of "trouble," "Jacob's trouble": the time of the Second Exodus.[2957] One deduces Elam and Asshur will be included in the great end-time Persian alliance that will partake in the counterfeit Armageddon war that occurs before the midpoint of the last seven years,[2958] the war Antichrist rides to power on as the counterfeit messiah.

[2950] Ezek 32:24.
[2951] Gen 10:22; Jer 49:38–39; Dan 8:2. H5867—`Eylam, ay-lawm`; Josephus, Ant. 1:6:4.
[2952] Gen 14:1, 9.
[2953] Bauer, History of the World, 88, 89, 104. Rohl, Lost Testament, 118–119. H5867—`Eylam, ay-lawm`; Josephus, Ant. 1:6:4.
[2954] Smith, The Chaldean Account of Genesis, 144–145.
[2955] Isa 21:2; Jer 25:25; 49:36; Acts 2:9.
[2956] Isa 11:11; Jer 49:34–39.
[2957] Isa 22:5–6; Jer 30:7; Dan 12:1.
[2958] Ezek 38:5; Joel 1–2; Rev 9:15–19.

Meshech and Tubal were tallied next in Ezekiel 32 as part of the Terrible Ones. They too were slain as kings of terror of powerful nations, kings accompanied by their multitudes that Babylon destroyed. Oddly though, Meshech, Tubal and perhaps their multitudes were not delivered to the pit prison to be with their brethren, the mighty/*gibbowr* warriors of old, even though "they were the terror of the mighty in the land of the living."[2959] It follows that something more is attributed to Meshech and Tubal. Know that Meshech and Tubal were words or names from foreign origins, even though both were listed sons of Japheth in the table of nations. Meshech established a nation that settled in the north; it is generally associated in Scripture with Tubal, Magog, and Moschi, according to *Strong's Dictionary*. The latter was a nation that dwelled in the land bordering Armenia and Colchis. Tubal was in eastern Asia Minor.[2960]

What is curious regarding Meshech and Tubal is that these kings and nations were connected to Gog and Magog in the end-time counterfeit Armageddon war, although Gog does not surface in the table of nations. "Son of man, set thy face against Gog, the land of Magog, the chief prince of Meshech and Tubal, and prophesy against him."[2961] Gog, like Meshech and Tubal, is a foreign word adopted into Hebrew as a prophetic antichrist figure of the end times. Gog was a patronymic name/title for a race, the giant Gyges kings of Greece, northwest Assyria, and Asia Minor.[2962] In the Greek tradition both Gog and Magog were patriarchal giants from Scythia;[2963] Gog is the name the Septuagint translates for Agag. Gog was a dynastic name for giant kings of Magog, Meschech, Tubal, and Moschi nations in ancient times, and will be again in the end times.

Meshech, according to historians, was a barbarous people whose branch tribe, the Moschi, dwelled between the Black and Caspian seas as allies of Tubal, the Tibarini.[2964] The Moschi were an early, powerful alliance after the flood that warred often with Assyrians that recorded them as the Muschai and Tybarenians on inscriptions, and as the Mashaoash by Egyptians.[2965] During the early postdiluvian years, the Meshech confederacy served their Scythian overlords from the Gog and Magog nations. Meshech/Moschi's name evolved into the Muskovs,

---

[2959] Ezek 32:26–28.

[2960] Gen 10:2; 1 Chron 1:5; Ezek 27:13; 32:26; 38:2, 3; 39:1. H4902—*Meshek, meh'-shek*: drawing out; a son of Japheth and his people descended that settled in the north; a nation associated with Tubal, Magog and Moschi, a people on the borders of Colchis and Armenia; H8422—*Tuwbal, too-bal'*; or *Tubal, too-bal'*: you will be brought; a son of Japheth and his people who settled a in east Asia Minor. *Strong's Cyclopaedia*, Vol. 6, 126: Meshech.

[2961] Ezek 39:1–3.

[2962] *Encyclopedia Americana*, Vol. 13, 7: Gog. H1463—*Gowg; gohg*; of foreign derivation.

[2963] Rose, *Giants, Monsters & Dragons*, 245: Gog.

[2964] *Strong's Cyclopaedia*, Vol. 6, 126: Meshech, citing Herodotus, 3:94, 7:78; Bochart, *Phaleg*, 3:12; Strabo, 11:344, 378, 478; Pliny 7:11.

[2965] Ibid., Vol. 6, 127.

from which the Russian/Rus nation derived from. Russians patrial-named their royal city Moscow, after Meshech.[2966] Moreover, Josephus recognized Meshech/ Moshoch as the Mosocheni (Moschi) and as the Cappadocians.[2967]

Magog, meaning land of Gog, derives from (Aryan) Sanskrit: *mah* meaning great, and a Persian/Aryan word meaning mountain (likely *gog* that also means mountain in *Strong's Dictionary*[2968]), and Sanskrit *maha* meaning land[2969] forming the land of a great mountain, or the land of the great Gog. Magog was located the mountains between Cappadocia and Media and was considered as a Scythian or Tartar tribe, and biblically grouped with Gomer, the Cimmerians, the Madia/ Medes, Javan, Meshech, and Tiras in the table of nations.[2970] Josephus noted the Greeks classified the Magogites founded by Magog as Scythians. Josephus further classified Madia as the Medes; that Gomer was the Galatians; that the Javan was Ionia from whom the Greeks derived; that Tubal/Thobel were the Iberians who originally dwelled between Euxine and the Caspian Sea; and that Tiras/Thiras were the Thir-asians called the Thracians by the Greeks.[2971] Further, *Strong's Cyclopaedia* classified the Magogites as Aryan Scythians related to the Aryan Medes, and as northern tribes that dwelled in the Caucasus Mountains between Euxine and he Caspian Sea. Magogites, according to Jerome, migrated to India, and were a people renowned as a "terror to Middle Asia." It follows that Scythians, Tartars, Indians, and Aryans by implication, were classified as cognate or very closely related peoples.[2972]

Tubal was alternatively recorded as the Tibareni, and the Tuplai in Assyrian inscriptions, and were grouped with the Moschi. According to Herodotus, the Tubal/ Tibareni formed the nineth satrapy of the Persian empire, as well as an army of Xerxes commanded by Ariomardus, the son of Darius (D'arius).[2973] The Tubalites were regarded as Scythians and Aryans, who migrated across the Mediterranean, to India, and to the Caucasus Mountains.[2974] One muses as to the patronymic connection of Tubal with Tubal-Cain.

Further, in occult circles Tubal was claimed as a patriarchal and founding giant for Iberian Celts in Spain, who migrated from Scythia. The genealogical connection was documented by an Italian monk, Annius of Viterbo (c. AD

[2966] Ibid., Vol. 6, 127, citing Rawlinson's Herodotus, 4:22.
[2967] Josephus, *Ant.*, Book 1: 6:1.
[2968] H1463—*Gowg*: mountain.
[2969] *Strong's Cyclopaedia*, Vol. 5, 653: Magog
[2970] Gen 10:2; 1 Chron 1:5. H4031—*Magowg, maw-gogue*: land of Gog; a son of Japheth; a barbarous northern region between Cappadocia and Media. *Strong's Cyclopaedia*, Vol. 5, 653: Magog; Vol. 10, 571: Tubal.
[2971] Josephus, *Ant.*, Book 1: 6:1.
[2972] *Strong's Cyclopaedia*, Vol. 5, 653: Magog.
[2973] Ibid., Vol. 10, 571: Tubal, citing Rawlinson's Herodotus 1:535, 3:94, 7:78.
[2974] Ibid., Vol. 10, 571: Tubal, citing Rawlinson's Herodotus 1:535.

1432–1502).[2975] Annius created a genealogy of giants from Japheth he claimed was Iapetus, claiming Noah, Ham and Shem were also giants. Annius claimed Japetus/Japheth/Iapetus was an important giant patriarch of nations.[2976] Accordingly, Iapetus' progeny like Magog, Tubal, Meshech, Madai, Tira, Gomer, and Javan would be giants as well. In this occult history, the Japhethian bloodline was connected to the giant Scythes, son of Hercules and half-woman and half-snake (goddess); Hercules was the son of Zeus.[2977] Hercules spawned several lines of dynastic kings, the Heraclides, of which one branch reigned in Lydia and was succeeded by the Gyges dynasties also connected with Gog.[2978] What seems more likely is that the Japhethites intermarried with giants and accepted their names, or were changed to names of giants in Scripture for dwelling among giants.

Tiras only appears twice in the Bible (Gen 10:2; 1 Chron 1:5) and is a word foreign in origin. Josephus accredited Tiras/Thiras as the patriarchal founder of the Thracians.[2979] Thrace was regarded in ancient history as the northern region of Macedon that overlapped into parts of Scythia.[2980] Thracians worshipped the (war) god Mars/Ares, Bacchus (a satyr goat god), and Diana (a mother goddess, and goddess of the fairies and Tuatha De Danann).[2981] Thracians in some parts of Greek mythology were the offspring of Thrax, son of the war god Ares; Ares also spawned Romulus and Remus of Roman mythology.[2982] Herodotus listed a Thracian city named "Tyrodiza."[2983] One contemplates whether Tiras was patronymic for king Tyrus in Ezekiel 28–29 and patrial for Tyre, and whether Tiras was assigned in the same name tradition as Magog.

One further contemplates if Tubal and Meshech's separation or delay of punishment is related to the end-time Gog-Magog war and the war of Revelation 20. Certainly, of the greater Gog alliance, only Gog, Magog, Meshech, and Tubal, and the army with them, have been reserved for utter destruction on the mountains of Israel in the end-time Gog war, along with fire sent to destroy Magog.[2984] Satan, Gog, and Magog will be finally defeated in Revelation, when Satan will then be sent to the Lake of Fire after the second Gog-Magog war.[2985]

[2975] Rose, *Giants, Monsters & Dragons*, 367: Tubal.

[2976] Ibid., 167: Ham; 194: Japheth, Japetus, and Japetus Junior.

[2977] Wayne, *Genesis 6 Conspiracy*, 606, citing Howard Reid, *Arthur, the Dragon King* (London: Headline Book Publishing, 2001, 119; *Encyclopedia Americana*, Vol. 14, 121–123: Hercules.

[2978] Herodotus, *Histories*, Book 1, 6–14; *Encyclopedia Americana*, Vol.13, 7: Gog and Magog.

[2979] Josephus, *Ant.*, Book 1, 6:1.

[2980] *Encyclopedia Americana*, Vol. 26, 591: Thrace.

[2981] Herodotus, *Histories*, Book 5:1–28.

[2982] Parks, *Encyclopedia of World Mythology*, 96: Ares.

[2983] Herodotus, *Histories*, Book 7:26.

[2984] Ezek 39:1, 3, 5.

[2985] Isa 22:16–19; Rev 20:1–15.

Rev 20:8 And shall go out to deceive the nations which are in the four-quarters of the earth, Gog and Magog, to gather them together to battle: the number of whom is as the sand of the sea.

Ezekiel 32:29 moved onto the Terrible Ones of Edom and their hybrid Horim kings with their might/*gbuwrah*, who were sent down to the pit. "Might" in this case is translated from the female plural format of gibborim.[2986] The female format of gibborim is used sixty-two times in the Old Testament for might, strength, power, mighty, force, and mastery. One deduces that many of the dukes of Edom and Seir before Ezekiel's era were sent to the pit prison.

Gbuwrah is also the Hebrew word translated as "might" of the Sidonians in Ezekiel 32:30. The princes of the north and the Sidonians were the next nations of terror listed. The Terrible Ones of Sidon included Tyre/Tyrus/Tiras by implication. Sidonians were "ashamed" because of their might/*gbuwrah*; they were slain and sent to bear that shame with others in the pit prison. One ponders whether "the princes of the north" refers to other peoples that migrated to the north of Sidon, to Asia Minor along with Magog, nations like Gomer and his son Togarmah. Gomer and Tiras were brothers of Magog and Meshech and sons of Japheth.[2987] What we do know is that Gog, Magog, Meshech, Tubal, Persia, Gomer, and Togarmah were tallied as nations of terror in the end-time Gog war and were nations of terror in ancient times.[2988]

In the same spirit, Pharaoh in Ezekiel 29 and 32, like the other Rephaim-descended kings destroyed by Nebuchadnezzar for causing terror, was apportioned intriguing parallel punishment, and similar prophetic allegory when set alongside the Gog war in Ezekiel 38–39. God set hooks into Pharaoh's jaw, then dragged him out to the open fields at Carchemish, where Pharaoh was defeated by Babylon. In the same way, Gog will be dragged out for slaughter with hooks set into his jaw in the end-time war.[2989] Moreover, Pharaoh Necho's army was slaughtered in the northern mountains of Israel, then devoured by beasts and birds in a great feast. Likewise, the mighty ones of Gog will be devoured in a similar feast.

End-time Egypt will be destroyed at the hands of Antichrist, and then Antichrist, the Assyrian, will be slaughtered on the mountains of Israel in the Armageddon feast.[2990] And in this line of thought and imagery, the Assyrian/Antichrist will be broken, the cockatrice/serpent from the serpent root (Gen 3:15; 6:1–4), who will produce as his fruit the fiery flying serpent. The fiery flying serpent is a seraphim, a rebellious Watcher, and an ancient dragon that will give Antichrist his power and who the world will worship.[2991]

[2986] Ezek 32:29. H1369—*gbuwrah*.

[2987] Gen 10:2–4; 1 Chron 1:5–6; Ezek 32:30; 39:1–3, 5–6.

[2988] Ezek 38:2–7.

[2989] Ezek 29:4, 19; 38:3–4; 39:2–5.

[2990] Isa 14:25; Dan 11:42–45; Rev 16:12–16; 19:20.

[2991] Dan 11:30–38; 2 Thess 2:1–12; Rev 12:1–18; 13:1–18; 17:7–18; 18:1–24.

CHAPTER 62

THE GREAT AND MIGHTY MEN OF THE END TIMES

Rev 6:15 And the kings of the earth, and the great men, and the rich men, and the chief captains, and the mighty men, and every bondman, and every free man, hid themselves in the dens and in the rocks of the mountains.

Because the New Testament was penned in Greek instead of Hebrew, we inherited a filtered transmission for key contextual Hebrew words like gibborim and Rephaim in the Old Testament. We can connect the references to prehistory and prophetic narratives each testament speaks to, but with constrained contextual certainty as it connects to the Fig Tree generation.

Indeed, the New Testament relies on the Old Testament for its history, context, and prophecies to define many prophecies and allegories in the New Testament. As such, prophetic accuracy requires one to bridge the same events and prophecies written down in Greek to the older Hebrew prophecies and to Hebraic understanding. Further, one is required recognize Jesus was Jewish, His disciples were Jewish, and that Jesus was the Alpha-Omega who spoke to the elect of Judah, Israel, and Christians that followed; therefore, we must assemble all Scripture—and by implication, all prophecy—around what Jesus said, not vice versa.

Gibborim, meaning "mighty ones" or "giant" in Hebrew, was penned to describe Nephilim, but *gibbowriym* can mean a warrior, a tyrant, a champion, strong, valiant, upright, a chief, etc.[2992] Gibborim was often penned to describe the chiefs and leaders as a variant title for dynastic kings descending from Rephaim giants like the kings of Ai, Gibeon, Persia, Medes, and the terrible kings listed in the abyss/pit prison in Ezekiel 32. Gibborim included the mighty/*gibbowr* princes of the earth prophesied in the end-time Gog war that will include Gog, Magog, Meschech, Tubal, Persia, Cush/Ethiopia, Libya, Gomer, and Togarmah. [2993]

From a New Testament prophetic perspective, one is guided to seek similar Greek words that might infer that gibborim, Terrible Ones, and Rephaim indeed are the end-time princes, kings, and great men as translated in English New Testaments. "'Great' men of the earth" in Revelation 18:23 derives from *megistan'es* meaning grandees, magnates, great men, lords, nobles, and chief, as derived from *meg'istos* meaning greatest and exceedingly great.[2994] *Megistan'es* was a Greek title for a tribal leader or chief, meaning a great and powerful man and the grandees of a kingdom. Grandees' etymology derives from Latin *grandis,* meaning big,[2995] but seems to be Greek in origin based on *Strong's Dictionary's megistan'es* and its Greek designation. Grand/Grandee was understood as impressive in size and appearance, majestic, noble, magnificent, revered, chief, loftiness and grand, as in old, pedigree, and genealogical.[2996] The etymology of "grand" descends from Middle English *grant* meaning large and big, from Old French grant/grand for large and tall, and from Latin *grandis* meaning big, great, mighty, powerful, and weighty. *Webster's* additionally defines "grand" as chief, highest rank, exalted, and magnificent.[2997]

The etymology of "mega" derives from Greek *megas,* translated also as "great" in the New Testament 149 times,[2998] and derives from Indo-European *meg,* meaning great, large, vast, big, tall, mighty, powerful, and important.[2999] "Great" is defined by *Webster's* as large, larger, huge, chief, weighty, rank, and a direct descendant as in great-grandfather and bloodline. Its English etymology tracks through Old English *great* meaning big, tall, stout, massive, and from West German, Old Saxon, and

---

[2992] Gen 6:4; Job 16:14. H1368—*gibbowr.*

[2993] Gen 10:8–9, Josh 8:2–3, 10:1–2; Ezek 32:12, 21, 27; 38:1-8; 39:1, 18, 20; Dan 11:1–4.

[2994] Rev 6:15, 18; G3175—*meg-is-tan'-es*; plural from 3176: grandees; great men; lords; magnates; nobles; chief men; transliterated: megistanes. G3176—*meg'-is-tos*: greatest; very great; exceeding great; transliterated: megistos.

[2995] https://everipedia.org/wiki/lang_en/megistane; https://www.etymonline.com/word/grand.

[2996] *Webster's,* 176: grand. https://www.etymonline.com/word/great.

[2997] https://www.etymonline.com/word/grand; *Webster's,* 176: grand.

[2998] Including: Rev 1:10; 2:22; 6:4, 12, 17; 7:14; 8:8, 10; 9:2, 14; 11:8, 11, 12, 13, 15, 17, 18, 19; 12:1, 3, 9, 12, 14; 13:2, 5, 13, 16; 14:2, 8, 19; 15:1, 3; 16:1, 9, 12, 14, 17, 18, 19; 16:21; 17:1, 5, 6, 18; 18:1, 2, 10, 16, 18, 19, 21; 19:1, 2, 5, 17, 18; 20:1; 21:11, 12.

[2999] https://www.etymonline.com/word/mega; *Webster's,* 252: mega.

Dutch as *grauta*, *grot*, and *groot* respectively.[3000] Ergo, we might discern *megistan'es* as kin to Old Testament giant kings, the mighty ones and "men of renown."

Moreover, Mark's gospel translated *megistan'es* for Herod's lords, as distinct from his chiefs and captains.[3001] Herod traced his Edomite pedigree back to the *alluwphs*/dukes of Edom, Horim, and Hadad dynasties. *Megistan'es* was translated for "great men" of the earth who dominate the merchant trade through Babylon. Merchants will be the oligarchical bloodline nobility in the last years.

> Rev 18:23. .. for thy merchants were the great men of the earth; for by thy sorceries were all nations deceived.
>
> Rev 18:24 And in her Babylon was found the blood of prophets, and of saints, and of all that were slain upon the earth.

Accordingly, Revelation 6:15 classified the end-time "kings of the earth" as cognate to "the great men, and the rich men, and the chief captains," indicating a gibborim relationship. Revelation 6 detailed the different groupings of the great men/*megistan'es* that included bloodline kings, military warrior bloodlines, and the wealthy noble elite bloodlines holding sway over government, commerce, and the armies throughout the world. Further, the great men and kings are cognate to the mighty men/*doonatos'* meaning powerful and strong, also recorded in Revelation 6:15.[3002] *Doonatos'* derives from *doo'namahee* meaning capable, strong, and powerful, as does *doo'namis*, a word that angelic powers is translated from,[3003] denoting a relationship with fallen angels.

The New Testament phrases "great men," "chiefs," and "mighty men" are not unimpeachably definitive and direct derivatives like Nephilim or Rephaim offspring descended from Daniel 2's metallic dynasties, but it does seem likely that Revelation is connecting the kings in the same spirit as one connects Revelation 13 and 17's ten-king end-time beast empire to the prophetic beast empires set down in Daniel 2, 7, 8, and 11. Certainly, the mighty men/*doonatos'* in Revelation 6:15 are eerily similar to the text describing the antediluvian giants: "mighty men" and "men of renown/*shem*/*shemayim*,"[3004] the Nephilim kings, warriors, and oligarchic nobles.

One further notes mighty/*doo'namis* angels recorded in 2 Thessalonians 1:7 and the mighty/*iskhooros'* angels of Revelation 10:1 and 18:21. Accordingly, mighty men/*iskhooros'* surfaces again in the Armageddon war with the kings and

---

[3000] *Webster's*, 177: great.
[3001] Mark 6:21.
[3002] Mighty: Luke 1:49; 24:19; Acts 7:22; 18:24; 1 Cor 1:26; 2 Cor 10:4, Rev 6:15. Strong: Rom 15:1; 2 Cor 12:10; 13:9. G1415—*doo-nat-os'*: powerful; mighty man; power; strong; transliterated: dunatos.
[3003] G1415—*doonatos'*; G1411—*doo'namis*; G1410—*doo'namahee*.
[3004] Gen 6:4.

the captains, indicating a closely knotted organizational structure throughout the end times.[3005] Mighty men/*iskhooros'*, as it is translated into English in Revelation 19, is understood in Greek as mighty, powerful, strong man, and violent, reflecting a relationship with the Mighties of the rebellious Naphalim.

Fittingly, the mighty/*iskhooros'*/*doonatos'* and great/*megistan'es* men, and the kings/*basilyooce'* of Revelation 6, 18, and 19, are the *roi-el*/*royal* descendants, Rex Deus from the pantheon of rebellious gods/angels.[3006] By implication, the future ten end-time beast kings and Antichrist beast king will be dynastic kings from the great "mighty men which were of old," and the famous/*'addiyr*, mighty/*'atsuwm*, and great/*rab* kings like Og and Sihon of Bashan.[3007]

> Rev 19:18 That ye may eat the flesh of kings, and the flesh of captains, and the flesh of mighty men.

The dynastic bloodline kings and mighty men of Revelation descend from Daniel's metallic dynasties that formed the great/*rab*/*saggiy'* giant/Rephaim statue of empires. The ten-toed/king end-time empire of iron and clay empire will extend out of the Rephaim's iron legs.[3008] The end-time empire of the giants, with ten toes extending out of two feet, may represent two dominate kinds of bloodlines and/or geopolitical alliances comprising five leaders from each. It follows that the Daniel 2 prophecy incorporated the "iron and clay" allegory. We understand iron as a forged metal of iron, limestone, coke, and air, representing commingled bloodlines (of Rome) that extended out of the first three beast empires descended from Rephaim ancestors. Similarly, Greece was the bronze empire, commingled tin with and copper, whereas silver and gold were pure metals of Persia and Babylon, representing the bloodline purity of the first two empires. The commingled iron Rephaim bloodlines will mix with a nonmetal: a lower quality material, "clay" in the end-time empire. In this line of thinking, recall that "man" was formed from "dust of the ground," and that man/*'adam* is defined as a red/ruddy human, humankind, a lower degree of man, and which derives from another *'adam* meaning flush, rosy, red, and ruddy [3009] cognate to another *'adam* meaning the first

---

[3005] Rev 16:14; 19:18.

[3006] Mighty Men: G2478—*is-khoo-ros'*. King: G935—*bas-il-yooce'*: a sovereign; king; transliterated: basileus.

[3007] Ps 135:10–12; 136:18–21.

[3008] Dan 2:31–33, 37–43.

[3009] Gen 2:7. Man: H120—*'adam, aw-dawm'*; from 119: ruddy/red; human being; species of mankind: a low man; H119—*'adam, aw-dam'*: to show blood in the face; flush; rosy; be dyed or made red/ruddy; reddened; H121—*'Adam, aw-dawm'*; the same as 120: red.

human. Further, ground/*'adamah* means soil, red soil, and red earth in Genesis 2:7, and derives from the source word *'adam*.[3010]

Ergo, one deduces that the red soil/clay humans are a lower stock of being, or severely diluted Rephaim bloodlines that will form half of the end-time hegemony with the iron-descended Rephaim from the four metallic empires. Thus men/*enash* in Daniel 2:43 is understood as a mortal weak man or mankind.[3011] This is consistent with the prophetic allegory for "miry clay" in Daniel 2:43. Miry/*tyn* is defined as mud or clay with clay/*chacaph* defined as potsherd (an archaeological pottery fragment unearthed).[3012] Red clay and red earth was the preferred material utilized in ancient pottery craft. However, iron does mix with clay to form a lasting or strong empire. It will be broken into "pieces"[3013] in last seven years.

> Dan 2:43 And whereas thou sawest iron mixed with miry clay, they shall mingle themselves with the seed of men: but they shall not cleave one to another, even as iron is not mixed with clay.

> Dan 2:44 And in the days of these kings shall the God of heaven set up a kingdom, which shall never be destroyed: and the kingdom shall not be left to other people, but it shall break in pieces and consume all these kingdoms, and it shall stand for ever.

The diluted royal bloodlines from the four Rephaim beast empires will mingle their seed with the frail, feeble, inferior red clay, end-time descendants of Adam and Noah. This discernment is confirmed when juxtaposed with themselves/*hava'* in "mingle themselves," and cleave/*hava* in Daniel 2:43 that is defined as to come to pass; arise; to be; mingle and cleave.[3014] Both derive from *'arab* as does "mixed" in "mixed with clay" in Daniel 2:43 that is defined as mingle oneself with, join together, and commingle, while seed/*zra* is defined as posterity and offspring.[3015] The end-time dynastic kings will "mingle themselves with the seed of men." This

---

[3010] Ground: H127—*'adamah, ad-aw-maw'*: soil from its redness; country; earth; ground; husbandman; tilled ground; land; H125—*'adamdam, ad-am-dawm'*: reddish: reddish; red earth.
[3011] H606—*enash*; Aramaic *en-ash'* corresponds to 582: a man; human being; mankind; H582—*'enowsh, en-oshe'*; from 605: a mortal man: husbands; merchantmen; man; mankind; H605—*'anash, aw-nash'*: frail; feeble; desperate; incurably sick; woeful. H605—*'anash*.
[3012] Miry: H2917—*tiyn, teen*; Aramaic word corresponding to 2916 clay: miry; clay; H2916—*tiyt, teet*: sticky; dirt swept away; mud; clay; mire; H2635—*chacaph, khas-af'*: a clod as in clay; potsherd. *Webster's*, 313: Potsherd: pottery fragment unearthed of archaeological value or relic.
[3013] Dan 2:43–44.
[3014] (Mingle) themselves: H1934—*hava', hav-aw'*; Aramaic or *havah* and *havaw*: to exist; to be; become; came to pass; time, times; come into being; cleave; mingle one's self.
[3015] Seed: H2234—*zra', zer-ah'*; Aramaic: posterity; seed; offspring. Cleave: H1934—*hava'*. Mix: H6151—*'arab, ar-ab'*: to comingle; mingle oneself, mix; join. Cleave: H1934—*hava', hav-aw'*.

is the seed God destroys in the end-time documented in Psalm 21:10: pure and commingled.

Daniel's ten end-time mighty kings are royals that descend from the great/*saggiy'* giant, an image that was exceedingly bright/*ziyv* like a Rephaim Shining One. The prophetic allegory is clear, but there is yet one more prophetic allegory that pulls all these allegories together. The shining giant statue's appearance was terrible/*dchal*, Aramaic for terrible,[3016] as in the Terrible Ones and their branches that continued throughout history and will continue until Armageddon.[3017] At least five kings, or one foot, will not be human because the Rephaim metallic empire kings mingle themselves with the seed of men physically, through demonic possession, or both. Kings/*melek*, the iron,[3018] will mingle themselves with humans/clay in the end-time.[3019]

> Dan 2:31 Thou, O king, sawest, and behold a great image. This great image, whose brightness was excellent, stood before thee; and the form thereof was terrible.

The spurious Rephaim royal bloodline concept is consistent with New Testament terms like princes/*ar'khone* and its present participle, *ar'kho,* meaning kings, nobles, chiefs, and rulers.[3020] *Ar'khone* is translated as the "'prince' of the power of the air" and "the 'prince' of this world," whom the Naphalim, demons, and Rephaim kings report to via the council of the gods.[3021] The ancient kings in Sumer and elsewhere held titles as Watchers on earth in the tradition of their godfathers, which affirms a connection between the kings in the New Testament with Rephaim kings who both invoke their divine right to rule: "they that are great" and the great ones/*meg'as* defined as large, loud, mighty, and exceedingly great,

---

[3016] Dan 2:31. Great: H7690—*saggiy', sag-ghee*; Aramaic: large in size, or number; exceedingly great. Brightness: H2122—*ziyv, zeev*; Aramaic: brightness; splendour; countenance. Terrible: H1763—*dchal, deh-khal'*; Aramaic: to slink as in to fear; dreadful; terrible: fear; dreadful; terrible.
[3017] Isa 25:3–12.
[3018] Dan 2:44. H4430—*melek*: a king; a royal.
[3019] Gen 2:7. H121—*'Adam, aw-dawm'*: Adam the name of the first man; red; H126—*'Admah, ad-maw'*; red earth; city in the Siddim valley. H127—*'adamah, ad-aw-maw'*; soil from its general redness: earth; ground; country; husbandman; husbandry.
[3020] G758: Rulers: Luke 23:13, 35; 24:20; John 7:26, 48; 12:42; Acts 3:17; 4:5, 8; 13:26, 27; 14:5; 16:19; Rom 13:3. Prince: Matt 9:34; 12:24; Mark 3:22; John 12:31; 14:30; 16:11; Eph 2:2; Rev 1:5. Ruler: Matt 9:18; Luke 8:41; 18:18; John 3:1; Acts 7:27, 35; 23:5. Chief: Luke 11:15; 14:1; John 12:42. Princes: Matt 20:25; 1 Cor 2:6, 8. Ruler's: Matt 9:23. Princes: G758—*ar'-khone;* present participle of 757; G757—*ar'-kho*. Mark 10:42; Rom 15:12.
[3021] John 12:31; 14:30; Eph 2:2.

which is part a series of words that include *meg'istos* and *megistan'es*, with the latter translated as "great men" in Revelation 6:15.[3022]

The New Testament kings, the great ones and mighty princes, intersect with additional Old Testament end-time prophecies like the Gog war of "the latter days" (end-time), but before the Second Exodus led by Jesus,[3023] and before the abomination and Revelation 12's war in heaven. Gog's army and alliance will be led by the mighty men/*gibbowr* and princes/*nasiy'* of the earth.[3024] The "princes of the earth," the "mighty men," and the "men of war" of the Gog alliance will be slaughtered in the counterfeit Armageddon, as the "fatlings of Bashan" of Mount Hermon, and in like manner as Jesus will slay the "kings of the earth, captains, and mighty men" at the Armageddon battle.[3025] The "fatlings of Bashan" imagery paints the princes and mighty men of the ten-king end-time empire as dynastic descendants (Rephaim bulls)) of the Baalim of Mount Hermon and Ugarit.

Accordingly, the Gog war is the Joel 1–2 war that will feature the mighty men/*gibbowriym* featured in Joel 2:1–7: "They will run like mighty men; they shall climb the wall like men of war." The Joel 1–2 war begins with the blowing of the trumpet, the sixth trumpet[3026] that announces the great war documented in Revelation 9:16–19. The northern army will be great/*rab* and strong/*'atsuwm*, both words associated with gibborim, Rephaim kings, and their ancient armies.[3027] It follows that the northern Gog army will be bolstered with mighty/*gibbowr* and strong/*'atsuwm* warriors described as a locust army in Joel 1–2, and akin to the locust/*gowyim* army from the east led by a king/Gog who comes to destroy Israel.[3028] Locust/*'arbeh*, palmerworm/*gazam*, and cankerworm/*yekeq* are varieties of grasshoppers and was an allegory for ancient Rephaim-led armies like the Midian, Amaleqim, sons of the east/Kadmonim.[3029]

[3022] Great: Matt 20:25, Mark 10:42. Great ones: Mark 10:42; Acts 8:10. G3173—*meg'-as*; compare to 3176 and 3187: great; mighty; loud; great as in mass and weight; large; spacious as measured in height, length, or width; great in number, rank, scale, or deeds; transliterated megas; G3175—*meg-is-tan'-es*; G3176—*meg'-is-tos*.

[3023] Ezek 37:15-28; 38:8; 39:23–29; Dan 7:8, 20; Mic 2:11–13; 5:5–15. G1136—*gogue*; of Hebrew origin H1463 *Gowg*: a symbolic name for a future Antichrist; mountain; king of the land of Magog from the north.

[3024] Ezek 39: 18, 20. Mighty: H1368—*gibbowr*. Princes: H5387—*nasiy'*.

[3025] Ezek 39:18–20; Rev 19:18–21.

[3026] Joel 2:1, 15; Rev 9:14.

[3027] Joel 2:2, 20.

[3028] Amos 7:1. The Septuagint translates "the king of locusts" as "King Gog." H1471—*gowy*.

[3029] Joel 1:4; 2:25; Judg 6:3, 5; 7:12. H697—*'arbeh, ar-beh'*: locust; grasshopper; locust swarm; H1501—*gazam, gaw-zawm'*; devour as in a kind of locust; a palmerworm; locusts; H3218—*yekeq, yeh'-lek*: to lick up; or devourer; a young locust: cankerworm or caterpillar.

Joel 1:4 That which the palmerworm hath left hath the locust eaten; and that which the locust hath left hath the cankerworm eaten; and that which the cankerworm hath left hath the caterpiller eaten.

The locust army also describes mounted scorpion-like chimera troops that will be distinct from the creatures led by Abaddon/Apollyon out of the pit prison in Revelation 9. The two hundred-million-man mounted army will be the locust described in Joel 1–2, mounted on chimera horses.[3030] The riders, the mighty men of war, will be distinct from the chimera creatures. The mounted warriors' armor will feature multicolored breastplates of fire, jacinth (red and black), and brimstone. The chimera creatures will sport lionlike faces that breathe out fire, smoke, and sulfur. The tail will be snakelike, inflicting injury[3031] akin to scorpions. The locust army appears to be highly advanced biological weapons developed for war, perhaps akin to the unicorn chimera beasts that Nephilim rode into war upon before the flood.

The mounted chimera locust army will gather, after the abyss prison is opened in Revelation 9, and likely assembled by the demons and fallen angels to be released, akin to but distinct from the Armageddon gathering in Revelation 16 and 19. The locust-mounted chimera army will be destroyed before Antichrist, who will take credit for winning to begin his rise to power.[3032]

Revelation 9	Joel 1–2
Locust-numbered army of 200,000,000	Locust army; largest ever past or future
Army rides horses	Appearance of horsemen and chariots
Lion-headed horses	Teeth (and likely face) of a lion
Power of horses from mouths breathing fire	Horses/chariots destroy with fire
Tails were like serpents with heads	No description of horse tails
Human heads on riders not described further	Faces cause terror
Riders/horses wear fire/brimstone breastplates	Rider/horse not wounded by the sword
A third of the heavens darkened	Sun, moon, and stars do not shine

---

[3030] *Encyclopedia Americana,* Vol. 6, 513: chimera: body front a lion, middle body a goat, and serpent/dragon tail, and fire-breathing; https://www.merriam-webster.com/dictionary/chimera.
[3031] Rev 9:17–19.
[3032] Ezek 38:21–22; 39:3–5; Dan 11:22–23.

Mighty men/gibborim surface again in the Joel 3 prophecy of the Armageddon battle, in the time of the gathering of all nations to the valley of Jehoshaphat when God is pleading/*shaphat*,[3033] meaning judging scattered Israel (at the time of Second Exodus). The timing of the Joel 3 war comes after God "brings again the captivity of Judah and Jerusalem," when Antichrist moves his armies into Jerusalem.[3034] This war will be the time of proclaiming to Gentiles to prepare for war, to wake up the mighty men/gibborim, all the men of war, to beat "plowshares into swords, and. .. pruninghooks into spears" when even the weak will say they are strong/*gibbowr*, and the time when all the heathen/goyim and the mighty ones/gibborim will come down for the harvest,[3035] Armageddon. This will be the war that follows three and a half years after the fall of Babylon and their mighty men/gibborim. The Joel 3 war includes the mighty men/*gibbowrim* of Teman and Esau punished in "the great "day of the Lord," when the mighty man/*gibbowr* will cry bitterly.[3036]

One might wish to prepare for physical bloodline descendants of Rephaim, perhaps new giants, or those who somehow survived, disembodied demon spirits, and fallen angels in the end times. The Bible consistently nudges Christians to be mindful of those underwriting the coming Naphalim/Nephilim World Order. We will once again see giants' seditious influence imposed on the destiny of Adamites with apocalyptic consequences, this time by fire.

Matt 24:37 But as the days of Noe were, so shall also the coming of the Son of man be.

[3033] Ezek 37:1–28; Dan 12:1–3; Joel 3:2: time of resurrection, judgement, trouble, and exodus. H8199—*shaphat, shaw-fat'*: judge; pronounce sentence; vindicate or punish; govern; litigate; advent for final judgment; avenge.
[3034] Dan 11:29–32; Joel 3:1; Luke 21:20–21.
[3035] Joel 3:9–16.
[3036] Jer 51:30, 56, 57; Joel 3:9; Obadiah 1:9; Zeph 1:14.

CHAPTER 63

THE FIRST WOE: SCORPION CREATURES

Rev 9:1 And the fifth angel sounded, and I saw a star fall from heaven unto the earth: and to him was given the key of the bottomless pit.

Rev 9:2 And he opened the bottomless pit; and there arose a smoke out of the pit, as the smoke of a great furnace; and the sun and the air were darkened by reason of the smoke of the pit.

Rev 9:3 And there came out of the smoke locusts upon the earth: and unto them was given power, as the scorpions of the earth have power.

The scorpion creatures that scurry out of the abyss prison in Revelation 9 precede the two hundred-million-man locust war. The scorpion monsters are interrelated yet distinct from the locust army. The scorpion-like monsters are the first of three dreadful woes in the days/years of the seven trumpets;[3037] the two-hundred-million-locust war is not the second woe.

[3037] Rev 8:13; 9:12; 11:4; 12:12.

The scorpion monsters, also called locusts,[3038] will be released before the mid-point of the last seven years. Unlocking the abyss prison with a key infers the release of the impassioned fallen angels, likely by a loyal angel but perhaps by a fallen, not imprisoned angel, and/or perhaps Azazel or Satan. The abyss prison release may be connected to the Gog war via the prophetic allegory embedded into the Gog war. One might anticipate that demon spirits will also be released and will be provided dwelling places for their spirits, an *oiketerion*.[3039] The release may explain how illicit angelic technology is developed or completed to produce chimera-like war creatures in Revelation 9. One deduces knowledge is already being developed with the aid of demons and fallen angels not sent to the abyss prison in preparation. The locust war of Joel 1–2, Ezekiel 38–39, and Revelation 9:13–21 seemingly emanates from the first woe with the scorpion-like monster release.

Scorpion monsters will be "given power, as the scorpions of the earth have power,"[3040] as in authority over mankind and government, a potentate, strength, and or as in the degraded angelic order of powers.[3041] The scorpion monsters are an angelic locust army by the inference of the prophetic allegory, a rebellious army/host, *tsaba' and sabahowth*[3042] of destroyers led by Abaddon/Apollyon, the destroyer angel. However, the scorpion-like monsters are commanded not to hurt the vegetation of earth, unlike the locust army that follows and destroys a third of the earth's vegetation. The scorpion-like angelic monsters will sting like scorpions and torment those who do not have God's seal on their foreheads for five months.[3043]

"Scorpion" is translated in the New Testament from *skorpee'os:* as a lobster-like (or crablike) creature with a venomous sting in its tail.[3044] *Skorpee'os'* source word *skopos'* means a watch, sentry, and scout,[3045] as in Watcher angel. Scorpio in Greek and Roman mythology was a god of war and god of Hades/Tartarus in the underworld/Sheol. Ialdabaoth was "cast down into Tartarus by Sophia,"[3046] just as Azazel, leader of the rebellious host in First Enoch, is the leader of abyss Watchers, whom Scripture entitled Abaddon in Hebrew and Apollyon in

---

[3038] Rev 9:3, 7.

[3039] G3613—*oy-kay-tay'-ree-on.*

[3040] Rev 9:3.

[3041] G1849—*ex-oo-see'-ah.*

[3042] G4519—*sab-ah-owth'*; of Hebrew origin 6635 *tsaba'*: armies; Sabaoth; as in; a military epithet of God; transliterated: sabaoth.

[3043] Rev 8:8–12; 9:4–6, 18.

[3044] G4651—*skor-pee'-os*: a scorpion with poisonous stinger in its tail; sting; transliterated: skorpios.

[3045] G4649—*skop-os'*; a watch as in a sentry; scout; those who watch; a mark.

[3046] Robinson, *The Nag Hammadi Library,* 168: *Hypostasis of the Archons,* 95:10.

Greek.[3047] Those stung by the scorpion-like tails will seek death for five months but will not find it.[3048]

The locust army of scorpion Watchers will appear like horses prepared for war. They will wear crowns of gold reflecting their ancient authority, have faces of humans with women's hair, possess teeth like a lion, have wings that thunder like chariots rushing into battle, and will have tails with stingers like scorpions.[3049] These beasts are led by Abaddon/Apollyon as their king. In my way of reckoning this mercurial prophecy, the scorpion-like beasts with human faces will be either degraded Watcher angels or some form of angelic destroyers within the rebellious hierarchy, akin to the earthly Philistine spoilers.

In the Sumerian zodiac, Scorpio derives from Akrabu, meaning scorpion-man. In the Old Testament, scorpion is translated into English from `aqrab and akrawb' and is additionally translated in its plural format Akrabbim/Aqqrabiym, the Scorpion Ones.[3050] Moreover, scorpion-men or creatures were recorded as Aqrabuamelu in Babylonian, Assyrian, and Akkadian mythology, and alternatively known as Girtiblili/Girtablulu. The Girtablulu are thought by some researchers to be a compounded word: gir-tab meaning scorpion, and lu-ulu, which means untamed man.[3051] Tiamat, the serpentine parent goddess, created the first generation of parent gods. She also created the scorpion gods for battle.[3052] Scorpion gods were documented in several myths including the *Enuma Elish,* the Babylonian version of the *Epic of Gilgamesh, The Legends of Izdubar,* and were depicted on several Assyrian reliefs and intaglios. Tiamat created the scorpion gods to oppress the offspring gods, and to avenge Apsu, and for plotting to kill the other parent gods. Scorpion gods possessed cruel weapons no god could resist:

> Tiamat made weighty her handiwork,
> Evil she wrought against the gods her children.
> To avenge Apsu, Tiamat planned evil.. ..
> All that Tiamat had plotted he repeated unto him,
> Saying, "Tiamat our mother hath conceived a hatred for us,

[3047] Enoch 54:5; Rev 9:11.

[3048] Rev 9:4, 5, 6, 10.

[3049] Rev 9:7—10.

[3050] *Sumerian Dictionary,* 2: Scorpio. Scorpion: Deut 8:15; 1 Kings 12:11, 14; 2 Chron 10:11, 14; Ezek 2:6. H6137—`aqrab, ak-rawb': a scorpion; a scourge; knotted whip. Akrabbim: Num 34:4; Josh 15:4; Judg 1:36. H4610—*Ma`aleh ` Aqrabbiym, mah-al-ay` ak-rabbeem';* from 4608 and plural of 6137: steep ascent of scorpions; a pass on Palestine's border.

[3051] Nadine Nys, *Girtablullu and Co.: A New Function of the Scorpion-Man in the Ancient Near East* (Bible Lands e-Review 2016/S1, University of Ghent and University of Leuven), 1, citing F.A.M. Wiggermann, ed., *Mesopotamian Protective Sprits: The Ritual Texts* (Groningen: Styx, 1992), 44.

[3052] Rose, *Giants, Monsters & Dragons,* 143: Girtiblili; 160: Tiamat; Guiley, *Demons & Demonology,* 227: scorpion people; Smith, *Chaldean Account of Genesis,* 44.

With all her force she rageth, full of wrath.

All the gods have turned to her,

With those, whom ye created, they go at her side.

They are banded together and at the side of Tiamat they advance;

They are furious, they devise mischief without resting night and day.

They prepare for battle, fuming and raging;

They have joined their forces and are making war…

…Hath made in addition weapons invincible; she hath spawned monster–serpents,

Sharp of tooth, and merciless of fang.

With poison, instead of blood, she hath filled their bodies.

Fierce monster–vipers she hath clothed with terror,

With splendor she hath decked them; she hath made them of lofty stature.

Whoever beholdeth them is overcome by terror,

Their bodies rear up and none can withstand their attack.

She hath set up vipers, and dragons, and the monster Lahamu,

And hurricanes and raging hounds, and scorpion–men,

And mighty tempests, and fish–men and rams;

They bear cruel weapons, without fear of the fight.

Her commands are mighty; none can resist them;

After this fashion, huge of stature, hath she made eleven monsters.[3053]

The Aqrabuamelu/Girtablilu were described in the *Legends of Izdubar* as boasting "crowns like the lattice of heaven," "burning with terribleness," "their appearance was like death," and that they appeared as half-men and half-scorpions with large scorpion tails.[3054] Chimera-like scorpion gods were depicted on the *Assyrian Cylinder Seal* and the *Babylonian Cylinder Seal*[3055] with large elongated human heads covered by conical caps, Gilgamesh-like beards, sporting wings on a horselike body whereby the large scorpion tail curves up and away from the body, thick lionlike legs, and large avian or talon-like feet. The scorpion gods guarded the rising and the setting of the sun (and/or the gates of the sun

[3053] L. W. King, trans., *The Enuma Elish: The Epic of Creation* (Blackmask Online, 2001, www.blackmask.com), Tablet 2 lines 1–32.
[3054] Smith, *The Chaldean Account of Genesis*, 200, 213, The Legends of Izdubar, Tablet 8, Col. II lines 6–7.
[3055] Ibid., 214; Nys, *Girtablullu and Co.*, 5.

god Shamash), guarded the Gate of Hades, and were beings that sent fear and terror into Izdubar:[3056]

1. Of the country hearing him.. ..
2. To the mountains of Mas in his course.. ..
3. who each day guard the rising sun.
4. Their crown was at the lattice of heaven,
5. under hell their feet were placed.
6. The scorpion-man guarded the gate,
7. burning with terribleness, their appearance was like death,
8. the might of his fear shook the forests.
9. At the rising of the sun and the setting of the sun, they guarded the sun.
10. Izdubar saw them and fear and terror came into his face.
11. Summoning his resolution he approached before them.
12. The scorpion-man of his female asked:
13. Who comes to us with the affliction of god on his body
14. To the scorpion-man his female answered:
15. The work of god is laid upon the man,
16. The scorpion-man of the hero asked.. ..

In the *Chaldean Account of Genesis*, Smith translated the *Tablet of the Seven Wicked Spirits*: "the scorpion gods possessed a fiery sting that rained out from their tails,"[3057] while on the *Tablet of Enuma Elish* and the *Mesopotamian Cylinder Seal* scorpion gods were depicted with the same scorpion physique described in the above accounts, but additionally with large wraparound eyes and heads covered with large hats, shooting powerful arrows of destruction.[3058] Other recollections added the scorpion gods donned a crown of horns that denoted their divinity, as well as sporting a "snake-headed penis,"[3059] while some depictions displayed them with some form of armor-like ribbing on the torso.[3060] *The Epic of Gilgamesh* described the scorpion gods in the Mashu mountains of Lebanon as "terrifying," "whose look is death," and "whose frightful splendor overwhelms mountains."

[3056] Smith, *Chaldean Account of Genesis*, 200, The Legends of Izdubar, Tablet 8, Col. II, lines 3–11; 15:260; Heidel, *The Gilgamesh Epic*, 7, 8, 21, Tablet 9, Col. II lines 1–9, 65.
[3057] Smith, *Chaldean Account of Genesis*, Col. I, line 7.
[3058] Nys, *Girtablullu and Co.*, 6.
[3059] Guilley, *Encyclopedia of Demons & Demonology*, 227: scorpion-people; Nys, *Girtablullu and Co.*, 5.
[3060] Nys, *Girtagllullo and Co.*, 5.

The scorpion gods terrified "a demigod like Gilgamesh" who then became gloomy, dismayed, fearful, and prostrated before them.[3061]

The Aqrabuamelu were the guardians for Shamash's temple, his mountain, the gate to Hades, "whose peak r[each] the banks of heaven, whose breast reaches down into the underworld, The scorpion-men keep watch at its gate."[3062] The Gate of Hades is located at the foot of Mount Hermon, in the Cedar Forest, and reigned over by King Humbaba of the Gilgamesh/Izdubar epics. Aqrabuamelu were Watchers in the *Epic of Gilgamesh* for the gates of Shamash at Mount Mashu and the entrance to the land of darkness, the underworld. Scorpion creatures opened and closed the doors for Shamash as he traveled from the underworld each day and returning at night.[3063] As such, the Aqrabuamelu were connected to the Naphalim of Sheowl where the pit prison is located, and the same beings depicted in Revelation 9:7–11.

One deduces that Gilgamesh/Izdubar's postdiluvian encounter with the scorpion monsters occurs before the offspring gods like Baal were sent to the abyss. Two incursions of giants and scorpion creature creation, one before the flood and one after, may explain why similar but distinct differences appear among scorpion creatures depicted on reliefs,[3064] although one of the three said types cited was a man-faced anunnaki/cherub and not a scorpion monster. Hence two slightly different depictions may indicate two incursions or two creatures. Perhaps, scorpion creatures are degraded warrior Watchers, the Cherubim, and akin to degraded seraphim, satyr goat-gods. One muses of the cherubim/kerubim are the Kerubuamelu/Aqrabuamelu. Kerubs were renowned in the ancient world as protectors wielding flaming swords, commissioned to guard the gates into Eden with a flaming sword(s),[3065] and depicted as guarding palace and temple entrances in the Middle East,[3066] just as cherubim Watchers encircled God's throne.

Tiamat was a parent creator goddess of the gods, as was Sophia, Gaia, and others before the flood. Izdubar/Gilgamesh were postdiluvian giants. One resolves the polytheist conundrum by reckoning two incursions of giants, that the postdiluvian Gilgamesh inherited the hero title and stories in the epics because there was also an antediluvian Gilgamesh. Gilgamesh in the Enochian *Book of Giants* mentioned the panic-stricken accounts of giants regarding the imminent flood catastrophe.[3067] It follows that offspring mother goddesses also

---

[3061] Heidel, *Gilgamesh Epic*, 8, 11, 66, citing Tablet 9, Col. II, lines 1–22.

[3062] Heidel, *Gilgamesh Epic*, 65, Tablet 9, Col. II, lines 4–6.

[3063] Ibid., 66–67, Tablet 9, Col. IV, lines 33–50.

[3064] Nys, *Girtablullu and Co.*, 1–5.

[3065] *Strong's Cyclopaedia*, Vol. 2, 232: Cherubim. Gen 3:25.

[3066] *Unger's Bible Dictionary*, 222: Cherub.

[3067] Lumpkin, *Book of Giants*, 21, 66, 4Q531 fragment 1, 4Q530 Col. II.

succeeded antediluvian goddesses like Tiamat, just as the offspring goddess Isis was associated with scorpions, and that Isis was renowned as a scorpion goddess who employed seven scorpion creatures to protect her: Tefen, Mastetef, Petet, Tjetet, Matet, Mesetet, and Befen.[3068] Moreover, Egyptians recorded Ankit as a name of a monstrous scorpion, and Anu-ab the scorpion that stung and killed the god Horus.[3069] As such, postdiluvian degraded cherubim were also sent to the abyss along with Baal and Isis.

According to Aztec legend such scorpion gods were called Tzitzimime/ Tzitzimtl, as recorded in the *Aztec Codex,* the *Codex Magliabechiano, the Codex Tudela,* and the *Codex Borgia.*[3070] These scorpion gods were the offspring of the parent goddess, Citlalinicue. The Tzitzimime possessed arms and tails of scorpions.[3071] They were further described with large round eyes, sporting long disheveled black hair on skeletal heads, human faces, sharp talons on the hands and feet, and a scorpion tail and a snakehead tail (noting the *Codex Tudela* shows fire or poison being emitted from the tail as well as ribbed chest armor).[3072] The Tzitzimime, meaning "dangerous beings," ate humans, and were classified as preternatural gods/stars once regarded as fallen ones (Naphalim) after they were cast out/fell from heaven for their desecration and sacrilege against other gods.[3073] Aztec scorpion gods were an order of degraded fallen angels akin to the degraded satyr Watchers, and were likely degraded cherubim.

Humans that encountered the sting of these scorpion gods found their bodies quaked, their limbs withered and twisted, and foam spewed from their mouths akin to an epilepsy fit, but far more severe.[3074] Revelation 9:6 comes to mind: "And in those days shall men seek death, and shall not find it; and shall desire to die, and death shall flee from them."

[3068] E. A. Wallis Budge, *An Egyptian Hieroglyphic Dictionary* (London: John Murray, 1920), Vol. 1, 81: As tfa-uh meaning "Isis is the Scorpion-goddess, Rec. 24, 160; 179: uha-t Mettenich stele 73, seven scorpions of Isis: 216, 218, 253, 268, 328.

[3069] Budge, *An Egyptian Hieroglyphic Dictionary,* Vol. 1, 125: Ankhit Tuat IV; 115: Anu-ab, Mett. Stele 189.

[3070] Cecelia F. Klein, *The Devil and the Skirt: An Iconographical Inquiry into the Prehispanic Nature of the Tzitzimime,* (Cambridge: Cambridge University Press, 2000), 39, 40; fig, 1a *Codex Magliabechiano* (after Nuttall 1978: folio 76r); fig 1b *Codex Tudela* (after Tudela de la Orden 1980: folio 46.

[3071] Guilley, *The Encyclopedia of Demons & Demonology,* 259: Tzitzimime.

[3072] Klein, *Devil and the Skirt,* 17, fig. 1b, ig 14.

[3073] Guilley, *The Encyclopedia of Demons & Demonology,* 258: Tzitzimime; Klein, *The Devil and the Skirt,* 18, 20, 22.

[3074] Ibid., 28, citing Sahagun 1950–1982, 1:19, 71, 72, 4:81; Ortiz de Montellano, 1990, 132, 152, 159, 161.

Revelation 9	Aqrabualmelu Ancient Accounts
Crowns on their heads	Conical crowns/caps with horns
Long hair like women	Long hair and beards
Faces of men	Faces of men
Teeth like lions	Not depicted
Shape of the locusts were horselike	Horselike torsos
Breastplates of iron for battle	Ribbed-like armor
Large thundering wings	Large wings
Tails and stingers like scorpions	Scorpion tails with stingers raining venom

Rev 9:12 One woe is past.. ..

THE SECOND AND THIRD WOES

CHAPTER 64

Rev 9:11 And they had a king over them, which is the angel of the bottomless pit, whose name in the Hebrew tongue is Abaddon, but in the Greek tongue hath his name Apollyon.

Rev 9:12 One woe is past; there come two woes more hereafter.

Abaddon/Apollyon is the title provided in Scripture for the fallen angelic king of the scorpion creatures that will scurry out of the abyss to commit more appalling crimes against humanity. Just as Abaddon/Apollyon will bring the first woe with him, it follows that the notorious Naphalim would be associated with the second and third woes.

Scripture foretold three woes will plague humanity in the days of the seven trumpet blasts that precede the wrath bowls tallied in Revelation 16. In the biblical context, a woe is defined as a "primary exclamation of grief expressed, as in woe or alas."[3075] In Jesus' end-time chronology oration to His disciples, Jesus referred to a time of woe "in the days" of and events that bring about the abomination, and the events that happen thereafter.[3076] Jesus orated the end-time events in a linear sequence of events marked with Jesus' reference to Daniel's account of the abomination to identify the midpoint of the last seven years, [3077] and to distinguish

---

[3075] G3759—*oo-ah'ee*; a primary exclamation of grief; as in woe and alas.
[3076] Matt 24:19; Mark 13:17; Luke 21:23.
[3077] Dan 9:27.

between the two tribulations/afflictions.[3078] I believe Jesus purposefully selected exacting words to record the linear sequence, words that included the Greek word *tot'eh* meaning then, when, and at that time, translated in Jesus' oration as "then."[3079]

Jesus's woe marker in conjunction with Revelation 8–9 indicate the three woes dominate a period before and after the abomination beginning just before the Gog war. Accordingly, the three woes will occur after the fourth trumpet and through the "voices of the trumpet of the three angels, which are yet to sound."[3080] And thus, "in the days of the voice of the seventh angel, when he shall begin to sound, the mystery of God should be finished, as he hath declared to his servants the prophets."[3081]

The second woe occurs at the end of the three and a half-year commission of the two witnesses that begins at the start of the last seven years and ends at the time of the abomination. The two witnesses prophesy against Babylon and against the ten-king world government. Most of the world's population will hate the two prophets for catastrophes they will prophesy—the catastrophes contained within the seal and trumpet judgments. The two witnesses will prophesy in the first 1,260 days of their commission (prophesy utilizes thirty-day months: forty-two months), and at the three and a half-year point Jerusalem will be trampled by Antichrist and the Gentiles, which will figuratively be called Sodom and Egypt thereafter.[3082] The two witnesses will be slain when their commission is finished by "the beast that ascendeth out of the bottomless pit," by Abaddon/Apollyon and in the time of the sixth trumpet.[3083] Both the first and the second woes occur because the abyss prison will opened to release Abaddon/Apollyon.

> Rev 11:14 The second woe is past; and, behold, the third woe cometh quickly.
>
> Rev 11:15 And the seventh angel sounded; and there were great voices in heaven, saying, The kingdoms of this world are become the kingdoms of our Lord, and of his Christ.

One deduces that the third woe may also be connected to the release of Abaddon/*abaddohn'* is a Greek transliterated word derived from Hebrew, *'abaddown* meaning a destroying angel, the fallen prince angel of the pit

---

Matt 24:9, 21, 29; Mark 13:19, 24.
[3079] G5119—*tot'-eh*: the when; as in: then; at the time; at that time. Then: Matt 24:9, 10, 14, 16, 21, 23, 30, 40; Mark 13:14, 21, 26, 27, 28; Luke 21:10, 20, 21, 27.
[3080] Rev 8:13.
[3081] Dan 11:28–35; Matt 24:31; Luke 21:20; 1 Cor 15:52; 1Thess 4:16; Rev 10:7; 11:15.
[3082] Rev 11:2.
[3083] Rev 9:11–13; 11:1–15.

prison.[3084] In Greek the king of the abyss was entitled Apollyon/*apolloo'ohn*, also defined as the "destroyer" angel akin to Satan, but a princely fallen angel in the bottomless pit,[3085] noting Satan does not go to the pit prison until after Armageddon. Abaddon/Apollyon, the destroyer, is a Naphalim from the antediluvian epoch, and one of the Satans classified as the destroyers of the antediluvian world in the book of Enoch.[3086]

The third woe is not clearly spelled out in Revelation, but two passages in the days of the seventh trumpet to rise as contenders as part of the same traumatic sequence of events when Antichrist comes to power. The first woe contender is recorded in Revelation 12 after Satan and his angels lose the war in heaven. Satan and all his angels will then be cast down to earth at the midpoint of the last seven years: "Woe to the inhabiters of the earth and of the sea! for the devil is come down unto you, having great wrath, because he knoweth that he hath but a short time."[3087]

Satan and Antichrist will then vent their wrath on Judah fleeing Jerusalem, the awakened lost tribes of Israel, Judah around the world, and the "remnant" of all those who keep the commandments of God and uphold the testimony of Jesus.[3088] "Remnant" indicates that the rapture occurs at about the same time, but just before the mark implementation, thus saving Christians from the "trial" and the "wrath of God" reserved for the last year for the latter.[3089] Satan and his angels will vent their fury on all who remain that will be loyal to God and Jesus. Antichrist will parade humankind into slaughter under the curses of the wrath bowls that culminate at Armageddon. One might anticipate Satan will play a very visible role in the last three and a half years as part of the tripart axis of evil of Satan as the counterfeit of God, the female Tiamat and/or Sophia-like goddess as the counterfeit Holy Spirit, and Antichrist as the counterfeit messiah promising a counterfeit millennium. At this time of the third woe Antichrist will usurp power, assisted by Abaddon/Apollyon:

> Rev 17:8 The beast that thou sawest was, and is not; and shall ascend out of the bottomless pit, and go into perdition: and they that dwell on the earth shall wonder, whose names were not written in the book

---

[3084] G3—*ab-ad-dohn'*: a destroying angel; angel-prince of the bottomless pit; transliterated: Abaddon. H11—*'abaddown*, ab-ad-done'; as in a perishing/death and Hades: destruction; place of destruction; ruin.
[3085] G623—*ap-ol-loo'-ohn*: a destroyer as in a satan; angel of the bottomless pit; transliterated Apolluon.
[3086] Enoch 40:3; 65:6, 69: chapter heading.
[3087] Rev 12:7–12.
[3088] Rev 12:13–17.
[3089] Rom 5:9; 1 Thess 1:10; 5:9, Rev 3:10; 16:1–21.

of life from the foundation of the world, when they behold the beast that was, and is not, and yet.

Babylon's destruction is the second candidate for the third woe. "Alas, alas that great city" is used three times in Revelation's destruction of Babylon.[3090] Alas derives from *ooah'e*, as does woe.[3091] Babylon's destruction utilizes two woes three times in Revelation 18; it is first documented in Revelation 14 immediately after the commission of the 144,000 firstfruits, after the angel preaches the final gospel to the world when the hour of judgment is about to come. Babylon's destruction comes just before the mark is decreed by the false prophet, and after the saints are instructed to come out of Babylon in preparation for rapture, but before the great harvest in the year of the Lord's wrath in Revelation 14's last three- and one-half year summary.[3092] It and occurs at the end of the days of seventh trumpet, early in the last three and a half years before the wrath bowls.

Babylon's destruction comes about because the ten kings give their power to Antichrist.[3093] It intersects with Abaddon/Apollyon's release from the abyss and with Antichrist taking power, and thus a possible nexus for the third woe. Antichrist comes to power after the first two woes, in that time Satan will be cast to the earth with his woe, at the time of Babylon's destruction woes declared six times. Both events seem to merge to become the third woe: Antichrist's reign in the last three and a half years.

Antichrist's beast empire that "was, and is not," yet is still to come "is of"/*ek*, as in from or out of the ancient seven beast empires and kings, which will be the eighth beast empire. Antichrist will be the little that horn grows among the ten kings, and a king that will go to perdition.[3094] Perditon/*apo'lia* means destruction, perishing, destroying, and eternal punishment in the Lake of Fire,[3095] just as Abaddon and Apollyon mean destruction and destroyer. Knowing this makes sense that Antichrist was labeled as the "son of perdition; who opposeth and exalteth himself above all that is called God, or that is worshipped; so that he as God sitteth in the temple of God, shewing himself that he is God."[3096] Perdition/*apo'lia* derives from *apol'loomee*: destroy or give over to the Lake of Fire,[3097] which is directly connected to Apollyon/*Apolloo'ohn* as the participle *apol'loomee*.[3098] *Apol'loomee* is the source

---

[3090] Rev 18:10, 16, 19.

[3091] G3759—*oo-ah'ee*; a primary exclamation of grief; woe; alas.

[3092] Rev 13:11–18; 14:6–20; 18:4.

[3093] Rev 17:16.

[3094] Dan 7:8, 24, 25; Rev 17:8, 11. G1537—*ek; ex*: denoting origin; from, out of; away from.

[3095] G684—*ap-o'-li-a*: destruction; waste; perish; pernicious; destroying; utter destruction; eternal misery in hell.

[3096] 2 Thess 2:3–4.

[3097] G622—*ap-ol'-loo-mee*: to destroy; perish; lose; be lost; ruin; death; eternal misery in hell.

[3098] G623—*ap-ol-loo'-ohn*.

word for *apollonee'ah*/Apollo the sun god, but Apollo is a distinct god from the destroyer, Apollyon.[3099]

> Rev 17:11 And the beast that was, and is not, even he is the eighth, and is of the seven, and goeth into perdition.

"The son of perdition" title was also used for Judas for his evil betrayal of Jesus so that "scripture might be fulfilled"[3100] when Judas permitted Satan to enter him to complete the betrayal of Jesus.[3101] One ponders whether this is the same kind of event that occurs with Antichrist. In occult religions, avatar-capable gods like Vishnu or Shiva (the destroyer god) commandeered humans as their avatara. Sharabha/Narashima, a lion demigod was an avatara of Shiva, just as Buddha was an avatara of Vishnu, noting Antichrist is often referenced as the new or future Buddha. The avatara receives wisdom and power from the avatar,[3102] and is understood as an incarnation in the same way the new-age christ-consciousness unity with the gods is known as an incarnation, and C. S. Lewis' lion Aslan was an incarnation of Jesus. Antichrist might be an avatara "whose coming is after the working of Satan with all power and signs and lying wonders," and "they worshipped the dragon which gave power unto the beast: and they worshipped the beast, saying, Who is like unto the beast?"[3103] Accordingly, Antichrist's power will come from Satan and Satan's sponsored dragon/beast empires,[3104] but Antichrist will additionally have a relationship with Apollyon. Antichrist will honor a god his postdiluvian fathers did not honor: a "god of forces," a god of war. This sounds eerily like Azazel in *First Enoch,* the leader of the Watchers sent to the abyss prison.[3105]

> Dan 11:37 Neither shall he regard the God of his fathers, nor the desire of women, nor regard any god: for he shall magnify himself above all.
>
> Dan 11:38 But in his estate shall he honor the god of forces: and a god whom his fathers knew not shall he honor with gold, and silver.

Forces/*ma'owz*, used throughout Daniel 11, means forces, fortress, strong, stronghold, etc. *Ma'owz's* source word is *'azaz,* of similar meaning but

[3099] G624—*ap-ol-lo-nee'-ah*: deity of the sun; Apollon; belonging to Apollo; transliterated: Apollonia; G625—*ap-ol-loce'*: given by Apollo; transliterated Apollos.
[3100] John 17:12.
[3101] Luke 22:3; John 13:27.
[3102] Wayne, *Genesis 6 Conspiracy*, 296; 351, citing Beirlein, *Parallel Myths*, 246.
[3103] 2 Thess 2:9; Rev 13:4.
[3104] 1 Thess 5:3; Rev 12:2–4; 13:1–2.
[3105] Enoch 10:3; 13:1; 54:1.

including "impudent" as in bold or presumptuous.[3106] Antichrist will not honor the gods/ *'elohiym* of his fathers but will honor the god/ *'elowahh* of forces,[3107] Azazel, the seraphim was degraded to a nature goat god, as were Pan, Aigepan, Faunus, Innus, Bacchus, Baphomet, Cernunnos, and Cern.

Pan's parents are unconfirmed in Greek mythology.[3108] Pan, Innus, and Faunas originated in Arcadia[3109] as gods of shepherds.[3110] Cyclopean offspring were regarded in Greek mythology as uncivilized shepherds, Hyksos kings were renowned as shepherd kings; both donned dark shaggy hair akin to satyrs and Duke Seir. In 423 BC Greek playwright Euripides penned a "satyr" comical play titled *Cyclops*.[3111] One might muse if there is an ancient connection to cyclopean giants and goat gods and shaggy dark-haired giants. Satire/satyr is a literary composition where wickedness or folly is "censured" and held up to "reprobation," to challenge to those in power who appear in the world not as themselves."[3112] Greek satyr plays were the source for present word "satire."[3113] Azazel was the antediluvian destroyer, one of the degraded devil gods discussed in Leviticus 17 and 2 Chronicles 11, and the satyr gods of Isaiah 13 and 34.

Azazel, according to the book of Enoch, spoiled the antediluvian world with his works and illicit knowledge of weapons and the art of warcraft. He was the "spoiler" and the "destroyer" god of earth. "And Azazel taught men to make swords, and knives, and shields, and breastplates, and made known to them the metals of the earth and the art of working them." "And the whole earth has been corrupted through the works of that were taught by Azazel: to him ascribe all sin."[3114] Azazel was ascribed all sin of the antediluvian world as the scapegoat, the second goat sacrificed on the Day of Atonement.[3115] Scapegoat is defined as someone blamed and/or punished for the wrongdoings of another or for others.[3116] Biblically, scapegoat/ `aza'zel* is understood as a "complete sending away" into "solitude" and "rendered for an utter removal."[3117]

[3106] Dan 11:7, 10, 19, 29, 31, 38. H4581—*ma`owz, maw-oze*; from 5810; H5810—`*azaz*.
[3107] God of his fathers: H430—*'elohiym*. God of forces and god his fathers knew not; H433—*'elowahh*.
[3108] *Encyclopedia Americana*, Vol. 21, 223:
[3109] Ibid., 223: Pan; Pausanias, *Description of Greece*, Vol. VIII, Arcadia, 103.
[3110] *Encyclopedia Americana*, Vol. 21, 223; Pausanias, *Description of Greece*, Vol. VIII, Arcadia, 125; *U.X.L. Encyclopedia of World Mythology*, Vol. 1, 807: Pan.
[3111] *Encyclopedia Americana*, Vol. 5, 363: Cyclops.
[3112] Ibid., Vol. 24, 313: satire.
[3113] Rose, *Giants, Monsters, & Dragons*, 322: satyr.
[3114] Enoch 8:1; 9:6; 10:8.
[3115] Lev 16:9–10.
[3116] *Webster's*, 359: scapegoat.
[3117] *Unger's*, 129: Azazel.

Azazel was the destroyer and spoiler god of the antediluvian world. He led the Naphalim for Satan according to the book of Enoch. Azazel "committed fornication, and they were led astray, and became corrupt in their ways." "The whole earth has been corrupted through the works that were taught by Azazel: to him ascribe all sin"; "Ye have wrought great destruction on the earth."[3118] Antediluvian crimes included sins against the earth where all flesh was corrupted (Gen 6:12), including vegetation and animals.

Sin/*chatta'ah* is defined as an offense, habitual offenses, and punishment associated with the sin.[3119] Corrupt/*shachath* means ruin, spoil, spoiler, destroy, decay, pervert, etc. Corrupt and destroy, as penned in the flood narrative, both derive from *shachath* for the sins committed and the punishment thereof[3120] by the flood, and the imprisonment of Watchers. Sins begat by the fallen angels went beyond the violence that could alternatively been translated as unrighteousness, injustice, or cruelty,[3121] all of which applied to the sinful corruptions. The sins, measured by the level of corruption described, included corruption of the vegetation genome, animal DNA, and human DNA, of which Nephilim creation and their violence was just one of many angelic atrocities, sins atoned for on the Day of Atonement with the sacrifice of the scapegoat/Azazel.[3122]

Enoch 10:1 Bind Azazel hand and foot, and cast him into the darkness: and make an opening in the desert, which is in Dudael, and cast him therein.. ..

Enoch 10:8 And the whole earth has been corrupted through the works that were taught by Azazel: to him ascribe all sin.

Enoch 54:4–6. .. "For whom are these chains being prepared?" And he said to me: "These are being prepared for the hosts of Azazel, so that they may take and cast them into the abyss of complete condemnation, and they shall cover their jaws with rough stones as the Lord of Spirits commanded. And Michael, and Gabriel, and Raphael, and Phanuel shall take hold of them on that great day, and cast them on that day into the burning furnace, that the Lord of Spirits may take vengeance on them for their unrighteousness in becoming subject to Satan and leading astray those who dwell on the earth."

[3118] Enoch 8:2; 10:8; 12:4.

[3119] H2403—*chatta'ah, khat-taw-aw'*: an offence; habitual offences; sinfulness and its penalty: sin offering; punishment; sinner; guilt.

[3120] Gen 6:7, 11, 12, 13, 17; 7:4; 9:15. H7843—*Shachath*.

[3121] H2555 —*chamac, khaw-mawce'*; violence; cruelty, unrighteousness, injustice.

[3122] Lev 16:9, 10, 26.

Adding to Enochian references recognizing Azazel as the leader of the fallen angels sent to the abyss prison, the book of Enoch references the mighty kings of the end times as well as Azazel, his associates, his armies, and his demons:

> Enoch 55:3. .. Ye mighty kings who dwell on the earth, ye shall have to behold Mine Elect, how he sits on the throne of glory and judges Azazel and all his associates, and all his hosts in the name of Spirits.

> Enoch 10:12–13 And their sons have slain one another, and they have seen the destruction of their beloved ones, bind them fast for seventy generations in the valleys of the earth, till the day of their judgment and of their consummation, till the judgment that is for ever and ever is consummated. In those days they shall be led off to the abyss fire: to the torment and the prison in which they shall be confined for ever.

Knowing Azazel is the destroyer and spoiler fallen angel of the abyss who returns in the last seven years makes sense of Jeremiah 51's dual prophecy. A destroying wind will blow against Babylon in the end times, after the Revelation 9 counterfeit Armageddon war. The details of the destruction of the Babylonian beast empire of Jeremiah's period and the end-time religion was embedded into this prophecy, with the latter providing context to Antichrist's usurping of power. The "destroying wind" is methodology for Babylon's destruction caused by some form of weapon of mass destruction. Or, wind/*ruwach* could be translated as spirit, in this case an evil angelic spirit. As such, the narrative indicates a spirit/*ruwach* angel when coupled with destroying/*shachath*: a spoiling, destroying angel raised against end-time Babylon.

> Jer 51:1 Thus saith the LORD; Behold, I will raise up against Babylon, and against them that dwell in the midst of them that rise up against me, a destroying wind.

The Jeremiah 51 "spoilers" "come unto her from the north," and her princes/*sar* and mighty men/*gibbowr*, will be laid into a perpetual sleep.[3123] The spoilers/*shadad* means to oppress, lay waste, and violently destroy,[3124] and indeed they destroy Babylon in verses 54–55, whereby "destroyed" derives from 'abad meaning to blot out, make vanish, destroy, perish, and to die.[3125] 'Abad is the source word for Abaddon/'Abaddown, noting 'Abaddown takes its meaning in part from 'Abad/

[3123] Jer 51:48, 53, 56, 57.
[3124] H7703—*shadad, shaw-dad'*: burly; powerful; to ravage; a destroyer; oppress; spoiler; lay waste; destruction.
[3125] H6—*'abad.*

Hades.[3126] *'Abaddown* is utilized three times in the book of Job and one time in Proverbs for destruction in association with hell/*Sh'owl*.[3127]

When *'abad/'abaddown* is combined with spoiler/*shacath/shadad*, Babylon's destruction intersects with the Azazel spirit/angel as the king of the abyss host through as the "destroyer," "spoiler," and "god of forces" that Antichrist will honor. It follows that Antichrist will work intimately with Azazel/Abaddon/Apollyon to enforce his empire, and to destroy Babylon, permitting him to usurp absolute control over the world. Antichrist will destroy Babylon before the wrath bowls, and after the ten kings hand their power over to Antichrist to destroy Babylon, at the midpoint of the last seven years or shortly thereafter (Rev 17:16–18).

> 2 Pet 2:4 For if God spared not the angels that sinned, but cast them down to hell, and delivered them into chains of darkness, to be reserved unto judgment.

[3126] H11—*'abaddown.*
[3127] Job 26:6; 28:22; 31:12; Prov 15:11. H6585—*sh'owl.*

CHAPTER 65

THE KING OF JERUSALEM TITLE

2 Thess 2:3 Let no man deceive you by any means: for that day shall not come, except there come a falling away first, and that man of sin be revealed, the son of perdition;

2 Thess 2:4 Who opposeth and exalteth himself above all that is called God, or that is worshipped; so that he as God sitteth in the temple of God, shewing himself that he is God.

Knowing that the son of perdition will exalt himself above God in the Jerusalem temple injects the notion that Antichrist's pedigree will allege to have demigod bloodlines. Anticipate that the Antichrist will usurp all of Jesus' titles including "first being by interpretation King of righteousness, and after that also King of Salem, which is, king of peace."[3128]

The titles Antichrist will arrogate include "King of Kings, and Lord of Lords," "Wonderful, Counselor, The mighty God, The everlasting Father, The Prince of Peace," and "Melchizedek king of Salem."[3129] As outrageous and unimaginable as this sounds from a Christian perspective, most of the world will accept the delusion, including many Christians: "For there shall arise false Christs, and false prophets, and shall shew great signs and wonders; insomuch that, if it were pos-

---

[3128] Heb 7:2.
[3129] Respectively, Rev 17:14; 19:16; 1 Tim 6:15; Isa 9:6; Gen 14:18.

sible, they shall deceive the very elect. Behold, I have told you before."[3130] Know then that Antichrist will receive a fatal head wound that somehow will heal to fake a resurrection. This deception begins worship of the beast. Worshippers will ask who is like him and who can make war with him, because he receives his power from Satan.[3131]

Similarly, the original Rephaim kings of Jerusalem after the flood like Adonizedek, entitled the "King of Jerusalem," was aligned with the kings of Hebron/Kriatharba. Adonizedek's name means lord of righteousness.[3132] Jerusalem was a city prized by Rephaim after the flood, perhaps prized from before the flood,[3133] and will be the epicenter city of end-time prophecy. The city the Judeans recaptured in 1967 is perhaps the prophetic marker beginning the Fig Tree generation; one might anticipate spurious forces setting down a transgenerational plot to claim Jerusalem as their own. One might further anticipate Antichrist will stake his King of Jerusalem claim and his "divine right to rule" when he will be crowned in the temple: the abomination.

The "divine right to rule" is and was asserted by royals bestowed upon them by their "deity" as the chosen demigod representatives of that "deity," and "accordingly they are not responsible to their subjects for their method of governing, nor to any other human court of appeal"; that "all power and government was vested in the king who 'could do no wrong,'" begat at the ceremonial consecrations of their crowning rituals.[3134] The deity they worship is not necessarily the God of the Bible. The royal's occult ceremonial rituals include sworn oaths to and in the spirit of their godfathers. The "divine right to rule" and "little god" doctrines was a constitutive right and belief fervently asserted by the Unicorn Dynasty, the Stuart kings, and intensely so with King James I,[3135] patron king for the KJV Bible.

One might anticipate a royal bloodline and heraldry like the ennobled house of Stuart, which boasted the unification of Rex Deus bloodlines from the Merovingians, the Dalriada dynasties of Tara in Ireland, the Celtic Camelot dynasty of Wales, Norse bloodlines from Rollo via the de Bruce and Saint Claire houses, David and Saul's bloodlines, as well as alleged bloodlines from Jesus and Mary Magdalene via the Celtic and Merovingian dynasties. The Stuart bloodline, the heraldic "House of Unicorn," commingled with so many Rex Deus bloodlines that they were regarded as the most ennobled bloodline of their era.[3136] "Scion" is

---

[3130] Matt 24:24–25; cf. Mark 13:22–23.

[3131] 2 Thess 2:9; Rev 13:2, 3, 4, 12.

[3132] Josh 10:1, 3, 5, 23; 12:10. H139—'Adoniy-Tsedeq, ad-o"-nee-tseh'-dek.

[3133] Ezra 4:15. H5957—`alam, aw-lam'.

[3134] Encyclopedia Americana, Vol. 9, 2-1: Divine Right.

[3135] Ibid., Vol. 9, 2-1: Divine Right. Lomas, Invisible College, 82; Wayne, Genesis 6 Conspiracy, 477, citing Baigent and Leigh, Elixir, and the Stone, 226.

[3136] Wayne, Genesis 6 Conspiracy, 473–477, citing Gardner, Lost Secrets, 21, 216; Gardner, Bloodline, 315; Gardner, Realm, 44; Knight and Lomas, Uriel's Machine, 461. Deut 33:17.

an occult allegory identifying original Rephaim bloodline branches grafted with other Rephaim bloodlines that originated from the Baalim of Mount Sirion/Sion/Hermon council of gods. Moreover "scion" is a classic occult double entendre stemming from Old French, *Sion*, was deployed in preparation for Antichrist's pedigree and King of Jerusalem title.[3137]

Thus, the Stuart coat of arms prominently displays a unicorn as does the British coat of arms, while the Hanover coat of arms displays dual unicorns. One might anticipate then that a scion boasting unicorn heraldry will deploy the unicorn references inserted into the KJV to support his pedigree as false credentials for his Messiah claim. "Unicorn" was unexplainably substituted for *r'em*/wild bull nine times in the KJV. Unicorn/*R'em* is the young bull of Sirion/Mount Hermon conjuring up images of the bull cult of Baal worship.[3138] The young unicorn's horn will be "exalted" and "anointed," just as Antichrist is described as a little horn in the book of Daniel. The people of the world will be "pushed together" by the horn of the unicorn. The strength of the unicorn will eat up the nations and his enemies, "break their bones, and pierce them through with his arrows" as a king higher than Agag (Gog in the Septuagint),[3139] pronounced "Agawg."[3140] One might anticipate Gog will return as one of the many end-time wannabe antichrist figures. One notes Gog is equivalent to a mountain—likely Hermon.[3141]

> *Septuagint* Num 24:7 There shall come a man out of his seed, and he shall rule over many nations; and the kingdom of Gog shall be exalted, and his kingdom shall be increased.

> *Septuagint* Num 24:8 God led him out of Egypt; he has as it were the glory of a unicorn: he shall consume the nations of his enemies, and he shall drain their marrow, and with his darts he shall shoot through the enemy.

Moreover, horn/*qeren* figuratively means power, a mountain, a place in Bashan, and a single horn,[3142] thought to be the mountain in Bashan captured by Israel (Isa 5:1). As such, Gog will be one of the ten horns/*qeren* of the end-time empire descended Mount Hermon gods, and akin to Antichrist's strength: "emi-

---

[3137] Webster's, 360, scion. Etymology-onlin.com/scion.

[3138] Ps 29:6

[3139] Num 24:6–9; Deut 33:17; Ps 92:10. Little horn: Dan 7:8, 24, 25; 8:9, 10, 11, 23, 24, 25.

[3140] H90—*'Agag, ag-ag'*; or *Agag, Ag-awg'*.

[3141] G1136—*gogue*; of Hebrew origin H1463: a future Antichrist; equivalent with a mountain; the king of the land; H1463—*Gowg, gohg*: a northern nation; mountain; the prophetic prince of Rosh, Meshech and Tubal, and Magog.

[3142] H7162—*qeren*; from 7161: a horn: horn; a musical instrument; animal's horn; H7161—*qeren*: an animal's horn; cornet; elephant's tooth; a peak of a mountain; a hill; power; horn of strength; a flask; a place in Bashan.

nent, summit, and or horn" as in *qeren*.[3143] Anticipate that the fruitful hill and the vineyard of Israel in Isaiah 5:1 and Numbers 24:7, respectively, will be among many Scripture manipulations Antichrist counterfeits his resumé with as the spurious son of perdition.

> Isa 5:1. .. My well beloved hath a vineyard in a very fruitful hill.. ..
>
> Isa 5:7 For the vineyard of the LORD of hosts is the house of Israel.

One ought not to be surprised that the author of the "Daemonologie, In Forme of a Dialogue, Divided into Three Books" was titled the "Mighty Prince King James," who asserted his "divine right to rule" doctrine bestowed in him by his divine inheritance from the Baalim council of the gods. Knowing King James' self-entitlement as the "Mighty"/*Gibbowr* "Prince" helps explicate why unicorn was substituted for wild bull/*r'em* in his patronized KJV. The "Mighty Prince James" of the Stuart dynasty boasted a unicorn and a lion to frame their coat of arms. Knowing this makes sense as to why Rosicrucian editor Francis Bacon and his likely masonic translators connected lions, unicorns, and Mount Hermon, noting the lion represents a fallen angelic lion-god like Nergal and the unicorn is in part an allegory for a cherub Watcher. Translators deviously connected Israel with the unicorn and lion and as "he couched" instead of "they" (Israel) in "as a great lion" in Numbers 24:8–9 to represent King James' heraldic genealogies, and/or one of his posterities. Agag, lion, and unicorn were cleverly associated in Numbers 24:7–8 and elsewhere.

> Song 4:8. .. look from the top of Amana, from the top of Shenir and Hermon, from the lions' dens, from the mountains of the leopards.
>
> Ps 29:6 He maketh them also to skip like a calf; Lebanon and Sirion like a young unicorn.
>
> Ps 22:21 Save me from the lion's mouth: for thou hast heard me from the horns of the unicorns.

KJV unicorn markers were inserted into Moses' end-time blessings to Israel's twelve tribes, and specifically to Joseph's sons Manasseh and Ephraim, as recorded in Genesis and Deuteronomy. Ephraim was prophesied to become great in the latter years, greater than Manasseh who would be great after Ephraim. Ephraim would hold the gates, cities, and ports of their enemies, and become a community or multitude of nations.[3144] Gate/*shaar* means opening, door, gate, a city, or a

---

[3143] Num 24:8, strength: H8443—*tow`aphah, to-aw-faw'*: strength; eminence, lofty horns, summit as in eminence of towering horns, peaks.
[3144] Gen 22:17; 26:60; 48:4–20; 49:22–26; Deut 33:17.

port[3145] such as Gibraltar, Singapore, Hong Kong, Falkland Islands, etc. The Stuart and Hanover dynasties of England in some circles are thought of as the branch from Israel and Ephraim, the multitude[3146] of people/nations that manifested as the British Commonwealth. Thus, England and its king, the horn, along with his commonwealth of nations would "gore" their enemies around the earth like wild bulls/*r'em* and in the occult overlay: like unicorn kings.

> Deut 33:17. .. and his horns are like the horns of unicorns: with them he shall push the people together to the ends of the earth: and they are the ten thousands of Ephraim, and they are the thousands of Manasseh.

As such, the contrived unicorn marker merges with the horns of Daniel 7's ten-king end-time empire, which brings the single-horned Antichrist beast to power. In the book of Daniel, the single-horned king becomes manufactured prophetic allegory for Antichrist's bloodlines. Antichrist will build upon Satan's counterfeits with reimagined scriptural interpretations, definitions, allegories, prophecies, and revisionist history to deceive humankind and the elect.[3147] For example, "fruitful" of the "hill" (Mount Hermon) in Isaiah 5:1 derives jointly from two words: *ben* meaning son(s), children, branch, bloodline house, and member of an order; and from *shemen* meaning olive oil, oil, and anointing oil.[3148] Anticipate that Isaiah 5:1, 16, 19 and 24 will be reimagined, stating the "Beloved One" and the "Holy One" of Israel will be the anointed Antichrist, the branch/bloodline and horn/son of Bashan/Mount Hermon. Antichrist's royal demigod pedigree will be offered with alleged Israelite pedigree providing credibility to the counterfeit messiah coming to save the world.

> Ps 2:1 Why do the heathen rage, and the people imagine a vain thing?
>
> Ps 2:2 The kings of the earth set themselves, and the rulers take counsel together, against the LORD, and against his anointed.

The little horn will speak great things in a domineering character, from great power, and is further depicted in Daniel 7 as "more stout"[3149] than the other ten

---

[3145] H8179—*sha`ar, shah'-ar*: an opening; a door; gate; city; port.
[3146] Gen 48:4. H6951—*qahal, kaw-hawl'*: an assembly; company; congregation; multitude; organized body.
[3147] Matt 24:24.
[3148] H1121—ben; H8081—*shemen, sheh'-men*: olive; anointing oil; oiled; fat; fruitful land or valleys.
[3149] Dan 7:8, 20; 11:36; Rev 13:1, 2, 4, 5, 6, 7. Great things: H7260—*rabrab, rab-rab'*; Aramaic from 7229: huge in size; domineering in character; great; power; captain; chief. Stout: H7229—*rab, rab*: captain; chief; great, lord; master; stout.

horns, just as the giants were arrogant, hubris, and stout. Anticipate that spurious forces will manipulate the "eyes" "in this horn" as an allegory for the three eyes of Antichrist. The horn in occult allegory is the third eye that communicates with the Invisible Ones, the ascended masters of the Great White Brotherhood, and is the third eye that will communicate and receive power from Satan and/or Azazel.

> Dan 7:20 And of the ten horns that were in his head, and of the other which came up, and before whom three fell; even of that horn that had eyes, and a mouth that spake very great things, whose look was more stout than his fellows.

Anticipate that Mount Hermon's alternate name, Mount Sion/*Siy'on* (the French transliteration of Zion) will be speciously reimagined as Jerusalem's holy mountain; Zion of Jerusalem derives from *Tsiyown*. The polytheist interpretative approach to their scripture will be deployed by gnostic moles within Christianity to activate doctrinal mines buried in the KJV reserved for the end times. Anticipate a renewed gambit to assert the Septuagint's authority as an older surviving Old Testament manuscript, to spark a renaissance of Mount Hermon as the sacred mountain with a reimagined history and importance. One might anticipate that these progressive doctrinal pillars, along with the de-deification of Jesus and the denouncing of Paul as a heretic, will permeate the coming Babel-like universal religion, the ten-horned end-time and single-horned Antichrist empire—all of whom will honor and obey the Baalim council of Mount Hermon.

> Deut 4:48 From Aroer, which is by the bank of the river Arnon, even unto Mount Sion, which is Hermon.

Mount Sion/Hermon's base has been host to some of the most celebrated occultic sacred sites and temples of antiquity, which includes the "Rock of the Gods" where a large cave, the "Gate of Hades" of Baal is located. Adjacent to the gateway to the underworld is the white-domed temple dedicated to the goat god Pan/Azazel. The white house of Pan, and other ancient temples built there are the polytheist Priories of Sion of old. Royal Masonic founders of modern secret societies commandeered Jerusalem's Zion/*Tsiyown* identity to speciously shroud their polytheist beliefs, loyalty, and agenda within a clever occult double entendre. The Sion/*Siy'on* legominism, and "arty" "green language"[3150] is a protective veneer concealing the

---

[3150] Wayne, *Genesis 6 Conspiracy*, 70–71. Legominism is the occult practice of concealing truth within superficial text or symbols like those in Holy Grail literature and the obscure symbols in Freemasonry; 331–332, citing Greer, *Atlantis*, 36, 54, 55, 238: Greek Legomenon the original source word for Latin, *occultis*, as coined by G. I. Gurdjieff; Booth, *Secret History of the World*, 176.

royal masonic core that established modern western secret societies with Templars, and were royal masons who crowned their King of Jerusalem in a small priory on the rock of Mount Zion. "Once the Christian Crusaders retook Jerusalem, an unanticipated new order, sponsored by Mason/Rex Deus organizations was unaccountably ordained by papal bull. This order was, of course, the Knights Templar, which originally consisted of nine founding members from European aristocracy, although Rex Deus records indicate there were eleven. The original nine were not the impoverished monk's revisionist history would have us believe. All nine, or eleven, derived from important, royal Flemish and French families."[3151]

The founding Order of the Knights of the Temple of Sion included "Hugh de Payen, Geoffrey de St. Omer, Payen de Montifier, Archambaud de St.-Amand, Andre de Montbard, Gondemare, Rosal, Geoffrey Bisol, Godfrey de Bouillon, Fulk of Anjou, and Hugh of Champagne." Hugh de Payen married into the powerful Sinclair/St. Clair family, with Marie St. Clair who was the ancestor of second grandmaster of the Priory of Sion that began in AD 1188, after the fall of Jerusalem. Hugh de Payen's battle partner was Henri St. Claire, one of the unnamed original founders of the royal order of masons who held royal knight titles. Henri St. Claire later "became the first Earl of Roslin and founder of the St. Claire line which built Roslin Chapel (now known as Rosslyn) and became the legendary Grand Master Mason of Scotland";[3152] his posterity founded freemasonry after the fall of the Knights Templar.[3153]

The Templar Order at the adept level worshipped a head or a skull of a goat god named Baphomet, a fallen angel of Celtic and Galatian tradition (Scythian). Baphomet was "rendered as the Head or Source of Wisdom," whom the Templars entitled *agios ischyros Baphomet* (Holy Strong Baphomet),[3154] and like the mighty/*iskhooros'* angels in the book of Revelation.[3155] Some indicate the head of Baphomet had three faces,[3156] noting Azazel is renowned in polytheism as the Watcher goat god who provided knowledge to the antediluvians. In the occult tradition Baphomet is translated as "Bapho Mitra or Father Mithras also identified as Samael the Dragon, the Head Dragon and/or PenDragon."[3157] Mithras

---

[3151] Wayne, *Genesis 6 Conspiracy,* 405–406, citing Addison and Childress, *Knights Templar,* 2.

[3152] Knight, *Uriel's Machine,* 458.

[3153] Wayne, *Genesis 6 Conspiracy,* 424, citing Sora, *The Lost Treasure of the Knights Templar,* 112–117, 179; Keith Laidler, *The Head of God,* (London: Weidenfeld & Nicolson, 1998), 3, 4, 28, 110, 180–181.

[3154] De Vere, *The Dragon Legacy,* 221; Philippe L. De Coster, *Knighthoods OSFAR+C and Poor Knights of Christ* (Ghent: Skull Press Publications 2008), 7, 141, 143, 145.

[3155] G2478—*iskhooros'.* Rev 10:1; 18:21.

[3156] Charles G. Addison, The *History of the Knights Templars, the Temple Church, and the Temple* (London: Longman, Brown, Green, and Longmans, 1842; e-book #38593, Project Gutenberg, 2012), 218, from the apostolic bull detailing the charges against the Templars.

[3157] De Vere, *The Dragon Legacy,* 221; Laidler, *The Head of God,* 181.

was the god of Mithraism of Rome that originated in Zoroastrianism, the religion of the Indo-Aryans.[3158] The "sacred head" the Templars worshipped was hairy and bearded,[3159] reminiscent of shaggy, hairy, satyr goat gods. When asked by an inquisitor "What was the face like?" Templar Fra Raoul responded: "It seemed to me it was the face of a demon, a maufe (an evil spirit). Every time I saw it I was filled with such terror, I could hardly look, trembling in all my members."[3160]

> Baphomet has Angel Wings (Swan feathers) and a torch between his horns. Its right arm is raised with the index finger extended. On the forearm is written the word Coagula. The finger points to the new moon. Its left arm points down and to the side and the index and little finger are extended in the form of the horns the goat.. .. On its forehead there is displayed a pentagram with the single point upper most. In the simpler form, the goat's head traces the figure of the inverted pentagram and thus it is to be understood that one pentagram equals the other. Therefore, if the single point pentagram represents the Goddess, then she and the goat are one, as is represented by the combining of male and female sexual attributes in one symbol. Such a thorough union of the two sexes negates the individuality of both. ... Its legs are the legs of Pan. Its head is the head of Khem, which conjoined to the serpent or Dragon's torso represents Leviathan. ... Entwined around the Phallus of Baphomet are the serpents of the type represented on the caduceus of Hermes. .. . The Phallus as staff or Tree of Life is the Planta-genista in one sense, in being capped by an egg, is the symbol of potential which qualifies the image. Conclusion: Baphomet is a type of Chem-Zoroaster who is the Quinotaur associated with Meroveus[3161] [patriarch of the Merovingian dynasty].[3162]

One might want to anticipate that rival numerous numinous antichrists will arise.[3163] Scioned bloodlines worldwide will present themselves in hubris gambits to become Antichrist through political intrigue, wars, and rumors of wars, which includes those royals who have secretly claimed their authority from Mount Hermon/Sion, and the King of Jerusalem title for almost a millennium via Rephaim and Israelite bloodlines.

[3158] Wayne, *Genesis 6 Conspiracy*, 683, citing Bauer, *History of the World*, 264–265; 491, citing Hancock and Bauval, Talisman 21; Laidler, *The Head of God*, 198–199; De Vere, Nicholas, *The Dragon Legacy*, 221.
[3159] Laidler, *The Head of God*, 180–181.
[3160] Ibid., 182.
[3161] De Vere, *The Dragon Legacy*, 221–222.
[3162] Wayne, *Genesis 6 Conspiracy*, 462, citing Gardner, Realm, 17—18.
[3163] Matt 24:25; Mark 13:22; 1 John 2:18; 4:3.

THE ELVIN HOUSES OF VERE, ANJOU, AND PLANTAGENET

CHAPTER 66

1 Tim 1.4 Neither give heed to fables and endless genealogies, which minister questions, rather than godly edifying which is in faith: so do.

One should anticipate rival European bloodlines in addition to the Stuart and Hanover Antichrist ambitions, such as bloodlines connected to founding Templars and their Priory at Mount Zion. Understanding Rex Deus Templar gambits during the Crusades is important to discerning the context and sedition that will come in the days of the trumpet when Antichrist is coronated.

One should not be surprised to learn that gnostics work tirelessly to hide and reimagine history. Accordingly, they zealously dismiss the Priory of Sion organization as a conspiratorial fairy tale, and will do so until the last ten years or so. As such, I wrote this in *The Genesis 6 Conspiracy*: "One must note for the record, though, to date, no so-called bona fide, historical evidence has surfaced to support the suspicion that the Priory of Sion ever existed, but this so-called lack of evidence seems to be misdirection to me by powerful Rex Deus families."[3164]

[3164] Wayne, *Genesis 6 Conspiracy*, 406.

Michael Baigent, Richard Leigh, and Henry Lincoln penned a controversial investigative book into the alleged bloodlines of Jesus and Mary Magdalene in the 1980s. In this occult work, the authors quoted from the *Dossier Secrets* of the ultra-secret Prieure de Sion organization and from Rene Grousset's three-volume tome on the Crusades, a work quoted often by historians. According to Baigent, Leigh, and Lincoln, the *Dossier Secrets* referred to "Baudouin I, younger brother of Godfrey de Bouillon, Duke of Lorraine, and conqueror of the Holy Land. On Godfrey's death, Baudouin accepted the crown offered him and thereby became the first official King of Jerusalem." Grousset documented that there existed through Baudouin I [Baldwin I] a "'royal tradition.' And because it was 'founded upon the rock of Sion,' this tradition was 'equal' to the reigning dynasties in Europe," and that the Prieure de Sion was at that time known as the "Ordre de Sion."[3165]

If true, Grousset's research, knowingly or unknowingly, captured the trans-generational and classic gnostic double entendre tactic to conflate Mount Hermon/Sion, Rephaim bloodlines, the "Rock of the Gods," and the Mount Sion temple(s), with a priory close to the Templar headquarters in Jerusalem/Zion and the Rock of Zion of King David.

Historian and author Jean Markale accounted the Brotherhood of the Red Cross was a fusion of the Essenes, the Johanites/Nazorenes, and Godfrey de Boullion's group the Priory of Sion. Markale further noted that the Priory of Sion established the Knights Templar as its own private and subversive military arm, under a veil of legitimacy and integrity, through an official Catholic-sponsored organization, which became fully accepted and integrated into mainstream Christianity. The Knights Templar then, according to Markale, became an exoteric creation of an esoteric order employed as a militia organization, subject in all respects to the Priory of Sion.[3166] Further, in the book published in 1842, *The Templars in Bohemia*, historian Prokop Chocholousek wrote that under the leadership of Hugh de Payen the original nine (or eleven) knights established themselves as the "Knights of Sion" and the "Ordre de Sion" as the secret order of royals behind the Knights Templar.[3167] As such, Templars were the junior order.

Because the existence to the Priory of Sion was judged a hoax by the puppet-like mainstream media and establishment, an inquiry into Baigent, Leigh, and Lincoln's sources is warranted to establish their veracity. Grousset often quoted William of Tyre as his source for his details on the kings of Jerusalem, so I will

---

[3165] Michael Baigent, Richard Leigh, and Henry Lincoln, *The Holy Blood and the Holy Grail* (London: Arrow Books Limited, 1996), 111–112, citing Renee Grousset, *Histoire Des Croisades et du Royaume Franc de Jerusalem*, 3 vols, 1934–36, XIV, quoting William of Tyre: *History of Deeds Done beyond The Sea*, XIV.

[3166] Wayne, *Genesis 6 Conspiracy*, 408, citing Jean Markale, The *Templar Treasures at Gisors*, 66–71.

[3167] Baigent, Leigh, and Lincoln, *The Holy Blood and the Holy Grail*, 494–495, citing P. Chocholousek, *Templariv Chechach*, Prague, 1842, 5–12.

quote directly from *A History of Deeds Done beyond the Sea,* as well as other sources whose documentation dates to the same period, and other historians.

Jerusalem was captured July 15, 1099 by de Bouillon and his crusader army, chiefly drawn from modern Belgium, Luxemburg, northern France, and the lower Rhine region, all of which were included within the duchy of Lower Lorraine, reigned over in part by de Bouillon. The crusade began as "'the pious and glorious enterprise' of rescuing the Holy Sepulchre of Christ from the foul abominations of the heathen." The Church of the Holy Sepulchre, originally named the Church of the Resurrection, was built by the Edict of Emperor Constantine to envelop the believed sacred monument site discovered by Empress Helena, mother of Constantine.[3168]

"Godfrey was among the first to take up the cross, together with his two brothers Eustache and Baldwin, which is generally thought to be the Patriarchal Double Cross of Jerusalem, known also as the Jerusalem Cross."[3169] The originating "nine noble knights formed a holy brotherhood in arms and entered into a solemn compact. .. in the holy church of the Resurrection in the presence of the patriarch of Jerusalem."[3170] De Bouillon and the originating founders of the Knights Templar established a patriarchate,[3171] defined as an office of religious jurisdiction with a residence of a church patriarch that included a community of related families under the authority of a patriarch.[3172] The newly established Latin patriarchs resided at the king's court in Jerusalem and oversaw the four provinces of the Latin Kingdom of Heaven, whereby Bethlehem, Ascalon, and Hebron fell under the jurisdiction of the Jerusalem patriarch.[3173]

Masonic historians note de Bouillon's distinguished pedigree was sustained through "'secret preservers' within the House of Lorraine." These secret backers" established themselves in the abbey on Mount Zion that later became renowned as the infamous Priory of Sion. This mysterious senior group of royals later officially established the junior Knights Templar Order led by Hugh de Payen in 1118.[3174] In the "Craft," the Priory of Sion is alternatively known as the "Prior de

---

[3168] Addison, *History of the Knights Templar, the Temple Church, and the Temple,* 1–3; *Catholic Encyclopedia,* Vol. 8, 362: Jerusalem.

[3169] *Catholic Encyclopedia,* Vol. 9, 362–363: Lorraine.

[3170] Addison, *History of the Knights Templar, the Temple Church, and the Temple,* 5.

[3171] *Catholic Encyclopedia,* Vol. 8, 368: Jerusalem; Russell Maloney, "History of the Cross of Lorraine," *The New Yorker,* September 9, 1944, 17.

[3172] *Webster's,* 291: patriarch; *Encyclopedia Americana,* Vol. 21, 402: patriarchs.

[3173] *Catholic Encyclopedia,* Vol. 8, 368: Jerusalem: Four provinces: centered at Caesara, Nazareth, Petra, and Tyre.

[3174] Herbert Dorsey, *The Secret History of The New World Order* (Parker, CO: Outskirts Press, 2014), Kindle version, 300.

Scion,"[3175] the secret backers who were the council of barons that elected the kings of Jerusalem.

De Bouillon then was unanimously elected July 22, 1099, by this council of barons, as the Lord of Jerusalem, the "supreme leader of the realm" and "Defender of the Holy Sepulchre," even though Raymond, count of Toulouse, was widely favored by many of the crusaders. The Holy Sepulchre and order thereof became the chief Christian institution during the kingdom of Jerusalem. As understood in feudal times, greater barons were great lords who were "tenets-in-chief of the Crown" who held the lands and crown of the king in "capite,"[3176] and akin to the philistine lords. De Bouillon was referred to as a "prince" and a "duke" but reigned only one year before dying.[3177]

De Bouillon declined the title as King of Jerusalem and its royal crown/diadem, even though his successors accepted the crown and pomp to establish the kingdom of Jerusalem.[3178] De Bouillon did accept the balance of the authority that came with the titles, whereby succeeding kings of Jerusalem venerated de Bouillon as their patriarch to the dynasty. De Bouillon's subjects adored him as the "best of kings";[3179] so much so that de Bouillon was coronated with the "crown of fairy thorns"[3180] that represented Duke Godfrey's alleged Elvin bloodline from the Merovingians, the dukes of Edom, and Jesus. De Bouillon was giant-like: "tall of stature, not extremely so, but still taller than the average man"; "strong beyond compare, with solidly built limbs and stalwart [stout][3181] chest"; "his features were pleasing, his beard and hair of medium blond."[3182]

De Bouillon's brothers included Baldwin count of Edessa and Eustace; Eustace's daughter Matilda married King Stephen of England (c. 1135–1154).[3183] De Bouillon's mother Ida received an oracle about her three sons foretelling "three great princes, the first of whom will be a duke, the second a king, and the third a count," noting the third, William/Eustace remained in Lorraine. Duke Godfrey was succeeded by his brother King Baldwin, and William/Eustace succeeded the

[3175] Ibid., 308, 374.

[3176] *Webster's*, 32: baron; *Encyclopedia Americana*, Vol. 3, 272: baron.

[3177] William of Tyre, *A History of Deeds Done beyond the Sea*, trans. Emily Atwater Babcock and A.C. Krey (New York: Columbia University Press, 1943), Vol. 1, 116, 2:1, note 2; 378, 9:2; 385, 9:5, note 14, 388, 9:6; *Catholic Encyclopedia*, Vol. 8, 361–362. H.J. A. Sire, *The Knights of Malta* (New Haven, CT: Yale University Press, 1996), 15.

[3178] William of Tyre, *History of Deeds*, Vol. 1, 393 9:9; *Catholic Encyclopedia*, Vol. 8, 361–362: Jerusalem; Sire, *Knights of Malta*, 15.

[3179] William of Tyre, *History of Deeds*, Vol. 1, 392, 9:9.

[3180] De Vere, *The Dragon Legacy*, 3, 32.

[3181] *Webster's*, 394: stalwart.

[3182] William of Tyre, *History of Deeds*, Vol. 1, 387, 9:6.

[3183] Ibid., Vol. 1, 386, 9:5, and note 17.

throne in Lorraine as count[3184] of the royal line. Previously, de Bouillon was the duke of Lotharingia that boasted an "illustrious" genealogy descended from the original Frankish kings. His father, Lord Eustace II the Elder, was count of Boulogne in Reims. De Bouillon's mother Ida of Lower Lorraine was of "high lineage, distinguished among the noble matrons" and of "exalted rank," as the sister of the "excellent Godfrey, duke of Lorraine who succeeded to the duchy."[3185]

Godfrey de Bouillon held Anjou bloodlines from the kings of Lorraine, via the Vere bloodline.[3186] The house of Vere had previously left Anjou and the Comite of Anjou circa AD 800. The house of Vere was one of the branches of the Angevin dynasties but was not the senior branch; it was a junior branch that extended out of the first of three houses of Anjou. The Vere coat of arms contained a field of red and gold symbolizing the phoenix, superimposed by a white star that symbolized ascending to the throne of the world. When supported by two dragons, the coat of arms becomes the official seal of the house.[3187] Red and gold colors accompanied the coat of arms of the Merovingians, Plantagenet, Spencer, Mandeville, and the Jacobite house of Scotland.[3188]

Godfrey de Vere de Bouillon was further ennobled with royal bloodlines that descended from an ancient bloodline, from the "Ancient Royal Doctrine" as an Elvin king.[3189] The house of de Vere traces their royal ancestry back to the Merovingians and allegedly includes the Davidic bloodline scioned into the Tuatha De Danann royalty, the tribes of d' Anu,[3190] which in part is patronymic in the first syllable of the Anjou. Rex Deus (kings of god) believe Benjamite bloodlines grafted into the Merovingian bloodlines, and that de Bouillon, Anjou, and de Payen of Lorraine claimed descent from via Dagobert.[3191] Merovingians also claimed Davidic bloodlines via intermarriage with Celtic grail dynasties of Wales, when Eurgen married the Merovingian Aminadab.[3192]

The Merovingian kings in this heraldic tradition were the priestly and kingly bloodline descended from the Arya, Sidhe, and Scythian giants,[3193] the ancient grail bloodline that was later grafted into various Israelite bloodlines. "The Priory of Sion insists the Holy Grail is not a cup or a chalice but rather an alle-

[3184] Ibid., Vol. 1, 386–88, 9:5–7; 387, note 19.
[3185] Ibid., Vol. 1, 116, 2:1, note 1; 386, 9:5–7, note 17.
[3186] De Vere, *The Dragon Legacy*, 15, 112, 120, 121.
[3187] Ibid., 3, 16.
[3188] Ibid., 3–4.
[3189] Ibid., 32, 121.
[3190] Ibid., 21, 340.
[3191] Baigent, Leigh, Lincoln, *The Holy Blood and the Holy Grail*. 282–284, 365. Laidler, *Head of God*, 137; Peter Blake and Paul S. Blezar, *The Arcadian Cipher* (London: Pan Books, 2001), 131.
[3192] Laurence Gardner, *Bloodline of the Holy Grail* (Rockport, MA: Element Books Inc., 1996), 147, 164, 236.
[3193] De Vere, *The Dragon Legacy*, 84.

gory encrypted with Rex Deus secrets, a Legominism." Most lay people naively believe the "Grail" was the chalice containing Jesus' blood collected by Joseph of Arimathea at the crucifixion, whereas in gnosticism Joseph collected the Messianic bloodline from the cross. However, in Rex Deus tradition, the pure form of grail is San Greal, meaning "royal bloodline," and to others, Sang Real, again meaning "royal blood." According to Rex Deus genealogist Laurence Gardner, the "Grail" always secretly represented the royal bloodline, the Messianic Sang Real of Judah, and not the chalice we are all familiar with. The Priory of Sion further insisted that Holy Grail and Arthurian tales encrypted the genealogy to the royal bloodline of Mary Magdalene and Jesus, descending through the Merovingian dynasty.[3194] Grail literature was patronized by Rex Deus houses and the Knights Templar, and that the Holy Grail, the Sangreal bloodline, housed the secrets to the Kings of God dynasty.

The "Grail Code" observed by grail kings like the Knights of the Round Table, the Knights Templar, and the Elvin royals maintained a "behavioral manifestation" "devoted to a 'particular form of consciousness,'" a divine essence attuned to a specific organization working toward a common good and agenda. This harmonious consciousness participation required a "Hive Mind—a collective consciousness—or at least a heightened capacity toward sensitivity and the anticipation of the needs of all within the genome.. .. Without the 'Hive Mind' (symbolized in the Dragon Dynasty by the Merovingian Bee, the Phoenician 'House of the Gods' and the hexagonal figure of the Tree of Life of the Kabala) the Grail Code is a meaningless set of unattainable social aspirations." "The Grail Code" was applicable only to grail blood produced by a specific genome.[3195] The ten end-time kings will have "one mind"/*gno'-may*, one cognition: to give their power and strength to the beast in the end times.[3196]

The badge of the bee was the heraldic imagery of the Merovingians. "Bees live as equal entities in hives under the rule of one Sovereign who is chosen and created from their number, by the administration of "Royal Jelly" (Dergflaith) by and from the body of the previous Queen. In this respect the clans of the Danann, the Elvin King Tribes of the Western-Aryans, once replicated in their social structure the organization of the hive. Furthermore, the hexagonal construction of the bee's incubation chamber, their place of origin or birth, is repeated in the hexagonal shape of the Kabalistic Tree of Life (the Planta-Genista, the family tree of Origen)."[3197]

[3194] Wayne, *Genesis 6 Conspiracy*, 444, citing Wallace-Murphy, Hopkins, and Simmons, *Rex Deus*, 27; Brown, *Da Vinci Code*, 162, 219, 250; Gardner, *Lost Secrets*, 213.

[3195] De Vere, *The Dragon Legacy*, 47–49.

[3196] Rev 17:13. G1106—*gno'-may*: cognition; opinion; resolve; judgment; mind; will; transliterated: gnome.

[3197] Ibid., 149.

Wolfram von Eshenbach cryptically affirmed the Knights Templar were grail guardians from a hermetic, secret society complete with reticent rituals, initiation, and an agenda to attain world domination.[3198] This was an odd assertion because the Templars were not yet established as an official order in the days of King Arthur. Eshenbach's affirmation reflected an ancient red/rosy cross order was reestablished by de Bouillon, which elucidates why imagery of Templars overflow among the Knights of the Round Table literature. In fact, Gardner wrote that the Templars were successors to the Knights of the Round Table, as reincarnated Sangreal Order of grail guardians protecting the grail treasure and secrets.[3199] Templars in "Royal Masonic" history originated with the first and second Jerusalem temples built by the "Royal Arch Masons," and an order resurrected as the Order of the Red Cross by Constantine.[3200]

Today, Jerusalem is recognized as positioned between Mount Zion to the west and Mount Moriah to the east, but in the Old Testament Mount Zion was the eastern mountain, by the Hinnom valley between where God's "foundations are in his holy mountains."[3201] The east mount was the Old Testament location for the first temple. Thus, on the west mountain of Zion in the time of the Crusades, and adjacent to the Tower of David, a small church popularly called "Sion" was located, as understood by contemporary mountain locations.[3202] Sion is the French transliteration for Zion and the occult double entendre for Mount Hermon.

Mackey wrote that the "Higher Order" established the Knights of the Temple (of Mary) in Zion at the priory at Zion in AD 1118 as the genesis for modern "Western Masonry." The Knights Templar were renowned as the "Order of The Temple in Zion."[3203] Baldwin I assigned housing for the Knights Templar Order of Sion at Baldwin I's palace located near the former temple on Mount Moriah.[3204] The Templars did not have a temple of their own at first, but the "D'jame al Asca" and various buildings around it became the property of the kings of Jerusalem, denominated by William of Tyre as "'the palace,' or royal house to the south of the Temple of the Lord, vulgarly called the *Temple of Solomon*" on Mount Moriah.[3205]

The Notre Dame du Mont Sion on the contemporary Mount Moriah location was destroyed in AD 1291 after the Templars lost control of Jerusalem. Thus, the early order established in AD 1090 by Godfrey established the council of greater baron kings of Jerusalem, which in turn elected the Jerusalem kings who

---

[3198] Wayne, *Genesis 6 Conspiracy*, 462, citing Markale, *Treasure at Gisors*, 253.

[3199] Gardner, *Lost Secrets*, 214.

[3200] Knight and Lomas, *Book of Hiram*, 417–427; De Vere, *The Dragon Legacy*, 79.

[3201] Ps 87:1–2. Cunelife, *The Holy Land: An Oxford Archaeological Guide*, 115: Mount Sion.

[3202] William of Tyre, *History of Deeds*, Vol. 1, 343, 8:3.

[3203] Mackey, *History of Freemasonry*, 249–252.

[3204] Ibid., 229.

[3205] Addison, *History of the Knights Templar*, 10.

was the secret order of higher degreed royal masons, and the true power behind both the Templars and Jerusalem kings, known as the Order of the Priory of Sion of Mary. Godfrey de Bouillon's original order was alternatively named the "Vere Order of Anjou," ennobled royal "Guardians of the Royal Secret," the "Secret of Secrets."[3206] King Baldwin de Vere de Bouillon, at his succession in AD 1100, established "the original 'Hierarchical Rule'" of the Templars.[3207]

Baldwin II, at his succession in 1118, sponsored the founding of the lower orders, which included the Knights of the Temple, the Knights Templar. Baldwin II appointed a new name to the newly restructured order: The Knights of the Temple of Solomon.[3208] Hugh de Payen, Fulk Anjou, and Godfrey St. Omer were among these founders, whereby de Payen became the first grandmaster. Some historians note, though, that Fulk Anjou became a member in 1120.[3209] De Payen was viewed as one of the "two most valiant soldiers of the cross, who fought with great credit and renown at the siege of Jerusalem."[3210] In 1128, St. Bernard, de Payen's son-in-law and nephew of an original Templar, Andre de Montbard, carried the debate in Rome to establish the Templar Order with a papal bull. Thereafter, Templars donned a white garb with a red cross.[3211]

When the Temple Order increased in numbers, de Payen established subpriors, whereby the superior order within the country was entitled the Grand Prior, and later the Master of the Temple.[3212] Prior and priory were terms synonymous for temples and rank within the Templar Order. Upon de Payen's return to Jerusalem from Rome, he and the ruling grandmasters were received with great distinction by King Baldwin II, the clergy, and the barons of the kingdom of Jerusalem. A grand council was assembled, where war measures were undertaken and extended into the Christian territories under de Payen's authority[3213] until he died in 1136. He was succeeded by Lord Robert, the Burgundian, son-in-law of Anselm, Archbishop of Canterbury.[3214]

At the time of Jerusalem's capture, the small and humble church called Sion was positioned close to Mount Sion/Zion. The priory was deemed as too small. Godfrey de Bouillon and his dynastically intentioned regime ordered a church of

---

[3206] Gardner, *Shadow of Solomon*, 113; De Coster, *Knighthoods OSFAR+C and Poor Knights of Christ*, 3, 7; De Vere, *The Dragon Legacy*, 79.

[3207] De Vere, *The Dragon Legacy*, 270.

[3208] Ibid., 79.

[3209] William of Tyre, *History of Deeds*, Vol. 1, 524–526, 12:7; vol. 2, 40, 13:2; Addison, *History of the Knights Templar*, 11–12.

[3210] Addison, *History of the Knights Templar*, 11.

[3211] William of Tyre, *History of Deeds*, Vol. 1, 524–526, 12:7, notes 22 and 23; Addison, *History of the Knights Templar*, 11–12; Wayne, *Genesis 6 Conspiracy*, 436, citing Markale, *Treasures at Gisors*, 112–117; Paul Naudon, *The Secret History of Freemasonry* (Rochester, VT: Inner Traditions, 2005), 63.

[3212] Addison, *History of the Knights Templars*, 27.

[3213] Ibid., 36.

[3214] Ibid., 37.

"massive and lofty construction" to be built to enclose the older and smaller Priory of Sion within it.[3215] The church of Mount Sion was the home to the archdeacon of Jerusalem, who received revenues from the "Temple of the Lord on Mount Moriah and the place of Calvary."[3216] The leader of the Sion church was referred to as the "prior of Mt. Sion."[3217] Charles Addison wrote, "There is, moreover, at Jerusalem another temple of immense spaciousness and extent, from which the brethren of the knighthood of the Temple derive their name Templars, which is called the Temple of Solomon, perhaps to distinguish it from the one above described [the palace known as the D'jame al Acsa on Mount Moriah], which is the Temple of the Lord."[3218] Thus, the original small church called Sion was located within the city walls, the stronghold and/or fortress of Jerusalem. Jerusalem from the times of Emperor Constantine forward became widely known as Sion (city) among Christians, and was popularly used to identify both Jerusalem and Mount Zion.

The Benedictine Abbey of St. Mary was founded in 1050 in Latin Jerusalem, by the monks of St. Mary who accompanied the merchants from Amalfi. The Abbey of St. Mary, in tradition, was the site and home of Mary and where the angel announced the birth of St. John.[3219] Christians named their first church in Jerusalem, the center from which their bishops ruled, the Coenaculum and/or Cenacle renowned as the church of Sion, which was believed to be the house of Mary and the location of the Last Supper.[3220] The church of Sion of St. Mary was renowned as the "Holiest and Glorious Sion, mother of all churches."[3221] Crusaders then built a new church over the Coenaculum/Cenacle,[3222] commissioned by Godfrey de Bouillon: the Abbey Notre Dame de Sion of Mary located on the "rock of Zion," the mountain/foundation of Zion and the stronghold of Zion.

De Bouillon additionally established, for his loyal "train of monks," the monastery of St. Mary in the valley of Jehoshaphat and Bethlehem, where it became one of the wealthiest monasteries in the Holy Land, and where Baldwin I became the first abbot and archbishop of Caesarea. This second priory of Mary was the l'Abbaye de Notre Dame that stood until 1291.[3223] Tradition after de Bouillon's reign indicates Jerusalem kings first were elected at the Priory on Sion and officially confirmed and consecrated at the l'Abbaye de Notre Dame in Bethlehem, Jesus' birthplace.

De Bouillon was buried at the Holy Sepulchre at Golgotha in July of 1100, where additional places were reserved for Godfrey's succeeding kings of

---

[3215] William of Tyre, *History of Deeds*, Vol. 1, 343–344, 8:24; 382, 9:2.

[3216] Ibid., Vol. 1, 425, 10:7,

[3217] Ibid., Vol. 1, 536, 12:13.

[3218] Addison, *History of the Knights Templars,* 10.

[3219] Sire, *Knights of Malta,* 12.

[3220] *Catholic Encyclopedia,* Vol. 8 355–356: Jerusalem.

[3221] Ibid., Vol. 8, 355: Jerusalem, citing Intercession in "St. James Liturgy," Ea. Brightmen, 54.

[3222] Ibid., Vol. 8, 355: Jerusalem.

[3223] William of Tyre, *History of Deeds*, Vol. 1, 392, 9:9, and note 24.

Jerusalem.[3224] The council of greater barons elected Baldwin I in Jerusalem at the Priory of Sion.[3225] Baldwin I was later anointed by Patriarch Daimbert of the church of Sion with the "royal diadem" of the King of Jerusalem on December 25, 1101, at l'Abbaye de Notre Dame in Bethlehem.[3226] Baldwin I also succeeded as archbishop of the Sion city, and archbishop to the group of monks who established the "monastery of St. Mary of the Valley of Jehoshaphat for Godfrey."[3227]

Biblically, a diadem translates from *tsaniyph* meaning a turban, hood, or mitre, as well as from *tsphiyrah* meaning a crown, coronet, a wreath (crown), and/ or a chaplet (wreath or garland for the head). *Tsphiyrah* was also oddly translated as "morning" in the KJV.[3228] One might allegorically manipulate the diadem of kings of Jerusalem as the kings of the morning, akin to *Heylel/Helel* son of the morning;[3229] an archetypical title for the antichrist figure.

Baldwin I died in 1118 in a war waged against the caliphate of Egypt.[3230] The greater barons chose Baldwin de Bourg of Edessa to succeed. Baldwin II reigned until 1131. He had previously traveled with Godfrey to the Holy Land in the first crusade.[3231] Baldwin II's daughter Melisende married Fulk V the Count of Anjou, who fathered Geoffrey Plantagenet.[3232] Baldwin II was a cousin to Godfrey and was additionally "surnamed Aculeuss," meaning a sharp horn,[3233] yet another connection with the occult unicorn dynastic allegory. Baldwin II was described as Rephaim-like, of "tall stature, striking appearance, and pleasing features.. .. His thin blond hair was streaked with white. .. his beard, though thin, reached to his breast; his complexion was vivid and ruddy."[3234]

Baldwin de Bourg was Anjou, Plantagenet, and perhaps the latter's patriarch. The Plantagenets were regarded as the younger familial cousins to the second house of Anjou, and of Elvin pedigree.[3235] Matriarchally, the Plantagenets derived from two

---

[3224] Ibid., Vol. 1, 413, 9:23, note 53; *Catholic Encyclopedia,* Vol. 8, 362: Jerusalem.

[3225] *Catholic Encyclopedia,* Vol. 8, 362: Jerusalem.

[3226] William of Tyre, *History of Deeds,* Vol. 1, 427–428, 10:9; *Catholic Encyclopedia,* Vol. 8, 362: Jerusalem.

[3227] William of Tyre, *History of Deeds,* Vol. 1, 437–438, 10:16, note 16, citing Gilbert de Nogent Guiberti gesta dei per Francos, R.H.C.O,c., IV, 183, 251.

[3228] H6797—*tsaniyph, tsaw-neef'*: headdress as in cloth wrapped around; diadem; turban; hood; mitre. Job 29:14; Isa 3:23; 62:3; Zech 3:5. H6843—*tsphiyrah, tsef-ee-raw'*: a crown encircling the head; a turn of affairs; diadem; wreath; coronet; plait; chaplet; morning. Morning: Ezek 7:7, 10. Diadem: Isa 28:5.

[3229] Isa 14:12.

[3230] *Catholic Encyclopedia,* Vol. 8, 362: Jerusalem.

[3231] Ibid., Vol. 8, 362: Jerusalem.

[3232] Ibid.

[3233] William of Tyre, *History of Deeds,* Vol. 1, 518, 12:2, note 1; *Catholic Encyclopedia,* Vol. 8, 362: Jerusalem.

[3234] William of Tyre, *History of Deeds,* Vol. 1, 521–522, 12:3.

[3235] De Vere, *The Dragon Legacy,* 16, 120, 121.

Anjou bloodlines, "Melusine daughter of King Elinos of Albany, and Melisende, the daughter of Baldwin de Bourg of Jerusalem."[3236] The Plantagenet mythos indicates their name derived from "Planta-Anu" and/or "planta-genista" meaning the "plant of generations," "the Tree of Life."[3237] The Plantagenets received ennobled bloodlines from the senior house of Anjou Elvin bloodlines, via Melusine; her senior heir was Maelo de Vere. The Plantagenet name descended from Melusine's younger sister Plantanu and a junior branch of the Imperial and Royal House of Vere.

Baldwin II was crowned King of Jerusalem in his succession authorized by the Order of Sion's greater barons,[3238] through the "ancient law of hereditary succession" as Godfrey and Baldwin I's kin.[3239] Baldwin I and II's priory coronations were an occult Antichrist ritual foreshadow, which overlayed Mount Hermon/Sion spiritual centers, temples of Baal and Pan imagery onto Mount Zion/Sion of Jerusalem. The counterfeit Jerusalem king title begat end-time preparation and the seditious gambit that will be fulfilled when Jerusalem becomes the "New-Sodom" City of Light on a hill/mountain. The future Dragon/Elvin Antichrist will likely claim the Jerusalem title "owed" as his right of inheritance," in the "Kingdom of Heaven on Earth" at the abomination.

Oddly though, Count Eustace/William, Godfrey's second brother (in Lorraine at that time), was not elected King of Jerusalem as the first selection, which should have been the norm under the "law of hereditary succession." Eustace/William acquiesced to Baldwin I's chosen successor due to the need to have a king quickly crowned, and to lead against the many foes of the Kingdom of Heaven. Urgent circumstances can intervene and be recognized against "accepted hereditary succession" in rare occasions, as was the case at this time.[3240] Thus, Baldwin II from Edessa was elected king because "the count of Edessa is present," and he was a "kinsman of the king, energetic, valiant, in battle, and estimable in every respect.. .. He was solemnly anointed and consecrated according to custom April 12, 1118. The royal insignia of the diadem was then bestowed upon him."[3241] Later Baldwin II was ritually anointed in the l'Abbaye de Notre Dame in Bethlehem as were his predecessors, on December 25, 1118.[3242]

Knowing the accounts detailed by William of Tyre makes sense of other historical references. Enroute to the crusade, Godfrey de Bouillon, along with Hugh the Great (de Payen), passed the winter at Apulia along the border of Calabria,[3243]

[3236] Ibid., 120.
[3237] De Vere, *The Dragon Legacy,* 120.
[3238] *Catholic Encyclopedia,* Vol. 8, 362: Jerusalem.
[3239] William of Tyre, *History of Deeds,* Vol. 1, 518, 12:3.
[3240] Ibid., Vol. 1, 519–521, 12:3, note 7.
[3241] Ibid., Vol. 1, 520–521, 12:3.
[3242] Ibid., Vol. 1, 535, 12:12.
[3243] Ibid., Vol. 1, 149, 2:22.

home of Calabrian Benedictine monks.[3244] There, Godfrey met with the monks to revive the ancient Order of Sion, and to plot the establishment of the Templar Order. Calabrian monks were initiated into Pythagorean philosophy (Gnosticism). Thereafter, a conclave of Calabrian monks arrived in Jerusalem around 1090,[3245] which makes sense of William of Tyre referencing Calabrian monks among Godfrey's conquering armies.[3246] Godfrey founded the novel Templar Order of Sion with a small group of bloodline princes and Benedictine monks after capturing Jerusalem. The novel order was first known as Priory of Sion, so named in a small priory after taking Jerusalem in 1099.[3247]

Albert Mackey's *History of Freemasonry* documented de Bouillon headquartered the Order of Sion in Jerusalem at the Abbey Notre Dame de Sion. In 1118, de Payen's junior order was centered close to the temple site. Both the older and the younger Temple Orders reflected the names of their establishment location, the Order/Priory of Sion, and the Knights of the Temple of Solomon respectfully. In 1118, nobles of the knightly rank of "Templar" from the Priory of Sion, swore vows for the new junior order when Hugh de Payen was elected the first grandmaster with the Fulk V of Anjou at his side.[3248] The ceremony was overseen by Baldwin II, who assigned the Templar Order residence within the royal palace near the site of the former second temple, where the head of the order was located until the fall of Jerusalem.[3249] The novel junior order reported to the senior Priory of Sion until 1188, when the Priory of Sion split away with the "Cutting of the Elm" ritual at Gisor Castle, because the junior order had betrayed their mission set out by de Payen to protect Jerusalem, after the loss of Jerusalem to Saladin in 1187.[3250]

Hugh de Payen was a royal Payen of the Lorraine region, a vassal lord to Hugh of Champagne. However, de Payen's royal bloodlines were worthy enough to marry Catherine (or Marie) St. Claire from of the Normandy Rollo bloodline.[3251] De Payen of Templar fame was related to St. Bernard's family, the Montbard family by marriage. St. Bernard was in service to the Count of Champagne. St. Bernard's uncle Andre de Montbard was one of the founding nine knights of the order and a vassal to Hugh, the Count of Champagne, who was a large donor

---

[3244] *Catholic Encyclopedia*, Vol. 12, 332.

[3245] Wayne, *Genesis 6 Conspiracy*, 407, citing Brown, *Secret Societies*, 70, 102.

[3246] William of Tyre, *History of Deeds*, Vol. 1, 380, 9:2.

[3247] Wayne, *Genesis 6 Conspiracy*, 480, citing Sora, *Lost Treasures of the Knights*, 12.

[3248] William of Tyre, *History of Deeds*, Vol. 1, 524–526, 12:7; Vol. 2, 40, 13:26, note 57; Sire, *The Knights of Malta*, 18.

[3249] Mackey, *History of Freemasonry*, 227.

[3250] Wayne, *Genesis 6 Conspiracy*, 408, 412, citing Markale, *Treasure at Gisors*, 69, 76, 97.

[3251] Wayne, *Genesis 6 Conspiracy*, 480, citing Knight and Lomas, *The Second Messiah*, 97, 276–277; Sora, *Lost Treasure of the Knights Templar*, 96, 177–178; Baigent, Leigh, and Lincoln, *Holy Blood and the Holy Grail*, 86, 442, citing Henri de Lenoncourt.

to Clairvaux and the Benedictines.[3252] It was at the Council of Troyes where the Templar Order became a Cistercian order, under St. Bernard's authority. From 1128 forward, St. Bernard was the "Patron" and "Protector" of the Templar Order to whom Templars from that point on then swore an oath of obedience. St. Bernard mandated that the Templar Order was to be obedient to Mary Magdalene, whereby they consecrated all the Notre Dame cathedrals to her.[3253]

History corroborates Baigent, Leigh, and Lincoln's assertion that Godfrey de Boullion and Hugh de Payen were of royal Lorraine bloodlines; that de Bouillon formed the Order of the Temple of Sion; that de Bouillon begat a royal dynasty based on the royal tradition of hereditary right claiming the title as the King of Jerusalem; that the Jerusalem regents owed their succession to the greater baron Order of Sion originally formed from among the eleven founding novel Knights Templar; and that Godfrey and the first kings were crowned in the small priory on Mount Sion.

[3252] Wayne, *Genesis 6 Conspiracy,* 435, citing Markale, Treasure at Gisors, 114, 129.
[3253] Ibid., 435-436, citing Markale, *Treasure at Gisors,* 86, 114–117, 120; Naudon, *The Secret History of Freemasonry,* 63, 92; Gardner, *Shadow,* 105–108, 110, 281.

THE DRAGON KINGDOM OF HEAVEN

Matt 8:11 And I say unto you, That many shall come from the east and west, and shall sit down with Abraham, and Isaac, and Jacob, in the Kingdom of Heaven.

Matt 8:12 But the children of the kingdom shall be cast out into outer darkness: there shall be weeping and gnashing of teeth.

Knowing the Anjou pedigrees that make claim to the Jerusalem king title, and the Anjou Templar relationship, reveals some of the main European Antichrist contenders that will rise.

Anjou became a province in France in the seventh or eighth century AD. Anjou's capital city, Angers, was positioned on the Maine River, a tributary of the Loire River.[3254] The Angevin province was the source name accepted by its ruling French family, who established the dukes of Angiers and the first house of Anjou in the ninth century AD with Fulk I Anjou, circa 888–938.[3255] The royal houses of Vere, likely from the royal Latin Verus and/or royal Pictish Vere families,

---

[3254] *Encyclopedia Americana*, Vol. 1, 714: Anjou.
[3255] Ibid.

was begat by King Vere of Anjou de Vere (c. 659–704) and his Dragon Queen Melusine (685–714).[3256] The House of Vere begat the senior house of Anjou, the junior Plantagenet from the Anjou regions of Lorraine, and the Anjou house of Naples, Sicily, Aragon, Hungary, and Cypress.[3257] The Anjou were descendants of Royal Scythians, Fairies, the Shining Ones, Elvens, Tuatha De Danann, and the lords Anu,[3258] noting the mythos defines *d'anjou* as born of Anu.[3259] The Anjou were part of the Gentry, "a most noble tribe, a race of luminous beings. .. the shining belonging to this world."[3260] Gentry, as it applies to the fairy Elvin bloodline in occult royal circles, derives from Latin *gens* understood as "of the blood" and bloodline and perhaps a word play on a Genealogical Tree. The "Fairy Gens" is the fairy blood and of the Dragon bloodline, members of a specific genetic strain,[3261] the Albi-gens. Elvin is understood as the Noble White Elves of the fairy kind akin to the larger/giant, white elves depicted in the Lord of the Rings, and the Fairy Sidhe of the Tuatha De Danann. Elven/Fairy in royal masonic and occult allegory represents the matriarchal bloodline, while Dragon represents the patriarchal bloodline.[3262]

The Anjou were at one time the most powerful house of Dragon in continental Europe. Fulk V Anjou (c. 1092–1143) warred with England's Henry I (1112–1119). Fulk V's son Geoffrey IV Plantagenet succeeded Fulk V as count and married Matilda, daughter of Henry I that produced Henry II king of England. Henry II reigned from 1151 with the Count of Anjou title in 1151, which begat the second Angevin house of Anjou.[3263] Geoffrey IV had three sons: Henry II of England, Geoffrey surnamed Plantagenet, and William Long Sword.[3264] The third house of Anjou was established when the Anjou became kings of Naples and Sicily in the thirteenth century with the accompanying titular King of Jerusalem. Descendants of the Latin third house of Anjou became kings in France, Aragon, and Hungary.[3265]

The pure Dragon/Fairy gene is rare, and mostly found among the Royal Dragon/Scythian families. The Royal Scythians, the Tuatha De Danann, were the original Fair Folk, a superior race of renowned beauty. Only the "fairest" of their realms were selected as fairy queens and dragon kings. Kings and queens were selected for "tall stature, the palest of complexion, redness and red-gold of their

---

[3256] Gardner, Realm, 58, 324–325, 355–364.

[3257] *Encyclopedia Americana*, Vol. 1, 714: Anjou.

[3258] Gardner, *Realm*, 58, 324–325, 355–364; De Vere, *The Dragon Legacy*, 12–127, 340.

[3259] Gardner, *Realm*, 55–58, 324–325, 355–364; http://www.houseofvere.com/ver.htm.

[3260] Wayne, *Genesis 6 Conspiracy*, 667, citing Evans-Wentz, *The Fairy Faith*, 22, 27, 53, 59, 62.

[3261] De Vere, *The Dragon Legacy*, 115, 120.

[3262] Wayne, *Genesis 6 Conspiracy*, 578, citing Rose, *Giants, Monsters, and Dragons*, 102–104; Gardner, *Grail Kings*, 171, 200, 312; Gardner, *Realm of the Ring Lords*, 3.

[3263] *Encyclopedia Americana*, Vol. 1, 714: Anjou.

[3264] William of Tyre, *History of Deeds*, Vol. 2, 49, 14:1.

[3265] *Encyclopedia Americana*, Vol. 1, 714: Anjou.

hair, green/hazel eyes, and their 'framing faces',"[3266] and second for blond hair and blue-eye traits. The European ancient Elvin genes trail back through the Mitanni dynasty, the Royal Scythians, the Tuatha De Danann, and Horim for more than eighty generations, wherein the demigod, dragon, fairy genes maintained their unique blood and bloodlines. Those of the pure Fairy/Dragon gene believe they do not require, nor need adhere to human laws or authority, because they are transcendent, integrated, and intelligent beings: "Overlords unto themselves— the members of a separate race—a "Royal Priesthood, a Peculiar People, and a Holy Nation."[3267]

The Fairy/Dragon gene is alternatively known as the "Gene of Isis," deriving from the Greek word *genes* meaning born of a kind: those born from the mother goddess Isis, and thus the gene of fallen angels.[3268] The Fairy/Isis gene likely the produces Rh-negative blood, which is absent of the "D antigen," and a gene that produces four Rh- negative blood types inexplicably added at some point in time to the four Rh-positive blood types. The compound word antigen, in its first syllable, derives from "anti" from Greek, Latin, and French *anti*, meaning against, opposed, and/or opposite. Antigen's second syllable "gen," meaning "something produced," derives from French *gene* and Greek *genes* meaning "born of" and "produced by," which derives from the same source as *genos* meaning "birth" and *genea* meaning "race and family," from the Indo-European root, *gene* to "give birth and beget," with derivatives referring to "procreation and familial and tribal groups."[3269] Rh-negative blood is most common among the royal families.

Fairy gene and Rh-negative blood is cognate to the Rosicrucian and Nazi "Vril" theology. Vril in Polytheist Aryan theology is the belief in a mysterious potency held within certain bloodlines that will engender a future race of superior beings.[3270] Rosicrucian esoteric theology was the furtive source for Nazi occult-ism, Nazi Aryanism, and Vril ideology, according to Baigent and Leigh.[3271] As such, the Anjou gentry was the Albi-gens from *Albi/albus,* Old French and Latin meaning white, shining one, bright, pale-skinned, fair, and hoar(y), whereby gens derives from Latin for race, tribe, and in royal circles, the "Elvin blood."[3272] The compounded Albi-gens formed the Cathar word "Albigensian."[3273] Gnostic Cathar and Albigensian religions were centered in France, in a region reigned over by the

---

[3266] De Vere, *The Dragon Legacy,* 1, 32, 109.

[3267] Ibid., 36–37.

[3268] Gardner, *Grail Kings,* 219.

[3269] https://www.etymonline.com/word/antigen.

[3270] Greer, *The Element Encyclopedia,* 341: Vril.

[3271] Michael Baigent and Richard Leigh, *Secret Germany: Stauffenberg and the Mystical Crusade against Hitler* (London: Arrow Books, 2006), 315–322.

[3272] https://www.etymonline.com/search?q=albi; https://etymologeek.com/ron/albi/90876344; De Vere, *The Dragon Legacy,* 120; *Websters*: Hoar; Dictionary.com: hoary.

[3273] De Vere, *The Dragon Legacy,* 120; Gardner, *Realm,* 315.

Merovingian kings, home of the French Knights Templar, and the furtive religion of the Merovingians and Templars.[3274]

Ergo, the "illustrious" Fulk V "the magnificent" of Anjou, son of Fulk IV Rechin, the Count of Touraine and Anjou,[3275] succeeded Baldwin II as the King of Jerusalem in 1141. Fulk V Anjou was described as "ruddy man like David." Fulk V had previously married Melisende, the eldest daughter of Baldwin II, with the expectation of succeeding Baldwin II.[3276] Further, "Foulques V d'Anjou" was from the lineage of the Lusignan kings of Cyprus.[3277] Baldwin II was anxious to arrange marriage for his daughter to ensure a bloodline succession. At the advice of the nobles, the greater barons, Fulk V was sent for. The marriage took place within a few days of his arrival. Baldwin II died August 21, 1141, and thereafter on September 14 Fulk V and Melisende were crowned and consecrated according to custom and hereditary right.[3278] The ruddy-skinned Fulk V was a "powerful prince according to the flesh," and an "experienced warrior."[3279] Fulk died November 10–11, 1142, 1143, or 1144, depending on the historian.[3280]

Among Fulk V's daughters was Sibylla, who married first William Clito, son of Robert of Normandy, the brother of Henry I. The marriage was annulled because of "consanguinity" (immediate bloodline kinship). Sibylla later married Thiery, the count of Flanders.[3281] Fulk V additionally produced two sons, Baldwin III and Amaury. Baldwin III succeeded Fulk V at age thirteen, and in the beginning reigned jointly with his mother. Baldwin III reigned beginning in 1144.[3282] Sibylla, half sister of Baldwin III by their father, arrived in the Holy Land with her husband Thierry the count of Flanders at the time Baldwin III was in his early adulthood. There was wide concern in matters of succession "among the princes of the realm" because Baldwin III had yet to marry.[3283] Baldwin III bestowed the city of Askalon to Amaury on August 12, 1153 or 1154 after its capture.[3284] Baldwin III was believed to have been poisoned while visiting in Antioch and died while traveling in Beirut, on February 10, 1162, without children.[3285]

[3274] Wayne, *Genesis 6 Conspiracy*, 412, citing Addison and Childress, *The Knights Templar*, 10–15.

[3275] William of Tyre, *History of Deeds*, Vol. 2, 49, 14:1; *Encyclopedia Britannica*, https://www.britannica.com/biography/Fulk.

[3276] Ibid., Vol. 2, 38, 13:24; 47, 14:1; *Catholic Encyclopedia*, Vol. 8, 362.

[3277] Gardner, *Realm of the Ring Lords*, 365.

[3278] William of Tyre, *History of Deeds*, Vol. 2, 50–51, 14:2.

[3279] Ibid., Vol. 2, 47, 14:1; *Catholic Encyclopedia*, Vol. 8, 362.

[3280] Ibid., Vol. 2, 134–135, 15:27 and note 31; Vol. 2, 139, 16:3.

[3281] Ibid., Vol. 2, 49, 14:1.

[3282] Ibid., Vol. 2, 136–137, 16, note 31.

[3283] Ibid., Vol. 2, 264, 18:264.

[3284] Ibid., Vol. 2, 233–234, 17:30, note 58.

[3285] Ibid., Vol. 2, 293, 18:34.

Baldwin III's brother Amaury I, count of Jaffa and Askalon was elected king through "hereditary right." He reigned from 1162–1174.[3286] Amaury I, during Baldwin III's reign married Agnes, the daughter of the count of Edessa that produced two children, Baldwin and Sibylla. During the crowning, Amaury was forced to annul this marriage because it was deemed by the barons that the marriage violated the royal guidelines of marrying "within the fourth degree of blood kinship." Agnes thereafter married Hugh d'Ibelin.[3287] Amaury I wedded "Princess Maria, who had previously received the gift of royal unction and consecration was daughter of John Cromenus the protosebastos."[3288] Amaury I died July 11, 1173, or 1174, depending on the historian.[3289]

Baldwin IV, son of Amaury I and Agnes of Edessa, was the king portrayed in the 2005 movie *Kingdom of Heaven*, likely named to foreshadow Antichrist's future declaration to the "Kingdom of Heaven" on earth in Jerusalem as its king. Baldwin IV was a pupil of William of Tyre and was afflicted with leprosy. He reigned from 1174–1185.[3290] The thirteen-year-old Baldwin IV was crowned according to custom through hereditary right as elected by the order of barons; his sister Sibylla was then brought to Jerusalem.[3291] In the third year of Baldwin IV's reign, William the Younger, marquis of Montferrat, surnamed Long Sword, arrived at the invitation of the barons and the king. William married Sibylla forty days later, but William died five months later from illness, which left Sibylla pregnant with the future Baldwin V. The marriage was arranged one year previous, when Baldwin and the baron council swore a solemn oath to alleviate succession concerns due Baldwin's leprosy affliction.[3292] William's burial in Jerusalem was presided over by William Archbishop of Tyre with great magnificence that reflected the tragedy of the chosen successor.[3293] Later, Balian d'Ibelin, brother of Baldwin of Ramlah, married Queen Maria, widow of King Amaury, with Baldwin IV's consent.[3294] In the movie *Kingdom of Heaven*, Balian was portrayed as a blacksmith and as the illegitimate son of a Templar named Godfrey d'Ibelin, who knighted Balian just before his death.

Raymond count of Tripoli and Bohemond prince of Antioch, kinsmen of Baldwin IV, journeyed to Jerusalem, which alarmed Baldwin IV. At that time, Baldwin IV's widowed sister Sibylla, mother to future king Baldwin V, had yet to

---

[3286] *Catholic Encyclopedia*, Vol. 8, 362: Jerusalem; William of Tyre, *History of Deeds*, Vol. 2, 296–297, 19:1.

[3287] William of Tyre, *A History of Deeds*, Vol. 2, 300–301, 19:4.

[3288] Ibid., Vol. 2, 244, 20:1.

[3289] Ibid., Vol. 2, 395–396, 20:31, note 63; Sire, *The Knights of Malta,* 24.

[3290] Ibid., Vol. 2, 397, 21:1; *Catholic Encyclopedia*, Vol. 8, 362.

[3291] Ibid., Vol. 2, 398–399, 21:1–2.

[3292] Ibid., Vol. 2, 415–416, 21:12–13; *Catholic Encyclopedia*, Vol. 8, 362.

[3293] Ibid., Vol. 2, 416, note 24, 21:13.

[3294] Ibid., Vol. 2, 425, 21:18.

marry again. Baldwin IV then "hastened the nuptials of his sister" to marry Guy Lusignan, son of Hugh the Brown, king of Cypress.[3295]

In addition to his leprosy, Baldwin IV was struck with a severe fever that took his life, and died without marrying and without sons in 1185.[3296] Before his death, Baldwin summoned his nobles, Sibylla, and Guy Lusignan to appoint Guy the "regent of the realm," which begat a transgenerational rivalry to the Jerusalem king title.[3297] Baldwin IV quickly became unhappy with Guy's competency and moved jointly with his mother and the barons to reverse his decision. Baldwin IV and the baron council then opted to crown the young Baldwin V with the royal unction,[3298] naming his cousin Raymond of Tripoli to the regency.[3299] Guy Lusignan pushed back against Baldwin V's succession, but the barons at first opted to appoint Raymond as the guardian for Baldwin V.[3300] Baldwin V died from poisoning in 1186.[3301] Then, Raymond of Tripoli was duped into traveling from Jerusalem, whereby the crown was conferred to Guy Lusignan through a coup sponsored by Renaud de Chatillon and Girard Ridfort, the grandmaster of the Templars.[3302] Renaud de Chatillon then forced the barons to reelect Guy Lusignan and Sibylla as king and queen of Jerusalem. Guy Lusignan began his reign in 1186.[3303] Previous to the coup, Renaud de Chatillon married Constance, the widow of Raymond of Antioch, in 1153.[3304]

The Kingdom of Heaven fell to Saladin in 1187, where Lusignan was captured. He traded Askalon to Saladin in return for his release, and then led a failed crusade in 1188. In 1190, Sibylla died. The greater barons determined Lusignan incompetent and temporarily transferred the regency to Raymond, count of Tripoli.[3305] However, Sibylla's sister Isabella, wife of Conrad Count Montferrat, disputed the kingship transfer. Richard the Lionheart of England arbitrated the kingship dispute, whereby he awarded the title on July 28, 1191 to Guy Lusignan but that Conrad Count of Montferrat would be the successor thereafter. Conrad was assassinated in April 1192. Guy Lusignan reigned until 1192 before resigning. He died in 1194 in Cyprus.[3306]

[3295] Ibid., Vol. 2, 446, 22:1. *Catholic Encyclopedia* Vol. 8, 362: Jerusalem.
[3296] *Catholic Encyclopedia,* Vol. 8, 362.
[3297] William of Tyre, *History of Deeds*, Vol. 2, 492, 22:25; *Catholic Encyclopedia,* Vol. 8, 362.
[3298] William of Tyre, *History of Deeds*, Vol. 2, 502–503, 22:29.
[3299] Sire, *The Knights of Malta*, 10.
[3300] William of Tyre, *History of Deeds*, Vol. 2, 507–509, 23:1.
[3301] *Catholic Encyclopedia,* Vol. 8, 362.
[3302] Sire, *Knights of Malta*, 10.
[3303] *Catholic Encyclopedia,* Vol. 8, 362.
[3304] William of Tyre, *History of Deeds*, Vol. 2, 235, 18:1, note 1.
[3305] *Catholic Encyclopedia,* Vol. 8, 362.
[3306] Ibid.

Guy Lusignan's widow Sibylla had previously named Henry I the Count of Champagne as the Jerusalem king successor. Henry I was then elected by the greater barons. Henry I reigned from 1194–1197. Sibylla's sister Isabella married a fourth husband, Amaury of Lusignan, king of Cyprus, brother of Guy Lusignan. Amaury held the Jerusalem kingship title from 1197–1205.[3307]

Amaury of Lusignan's successor was his daughter Melisende. She married Bohemonde IV, the prince of Antioch (Sicilian kings), but the greater barons opted to elect Mary, daughter of Isabella and Conrad Count of Montferrat, instead. Thereafter the barons requested the king of France provide a husband for Mary. Phillip Augustus II of France selected John of Brienne to accept the Jerusalem kingship title. John of Brienne hesitated at first but accepted the title from 1210–1225. After losing a crusade in 1218, John of Brienne gave his daughter Isabella/Yolande in marriage to Emperor Frederick II.[3308] Frederick II then usurped the Jerusalem regency through intrigue[3309] in 1243 through his son Conrad, but the barons support renounced Conrad's rights and declared the regency return to its rightful heirs.

Alix of Champagne, queen of Cyprus and daughter of Henry I, then accepted the Jerusalem regency based on her genealogical descendancy and nearest relative of Isabella of Brienne.[3310] Alix Champagne died in 1244, when her son Henry Lusignan King of Cyprus assumed the regency until his death in 1257. King Hugh IV Lusignan of Cyprus assumed the title as Hugh II even though the succession was disputed by Conradin, the grandson of Frederick II. Hugh II died in 1267, which set off another succession dispute by d'Ibelin the regent of Jerusalem in 1276. In 1277, Mary of Antioch sold her rights to the Jerusalem kingship to Charles I Anjou King of Naples,[3311] who was crowned by Pope Clement IV in 1266. Charles I Anjou descended in part from the Capetian dynasty, then gained the "King of Jerusalem" title.[3312] His son Charles II the Lame of Anjou married Maria of Hungary in 1270, the daughter of Stephen V and mother of Charles Martel d'Anjou, whereby the house of Anjou-Sicily then reigned over the kingdom of Hungary, Croatia, Provence, Poland, and held rights to Jerusalem.[3313]

The above additional realms added to the Sicilian Anjou came about after the death of Andrew/Andreas III (1290–1300), the last of the Arpadian House and dynastic Hungarian kings. A succession dispute erupted between Rudolf of the Hapsburg dynasty and by King Charles Martel of Naples; but Charles Robert,

---

[3307] *Catholic Encyclopedia*, Vol. 8, 362, 364.

[3308] Ibid., Vol. 8, 362.

[3309] Ibid., Vol. 8, 362–363.

[3310] Ibid.

[3311] Ibid., Vol. 8, 363–364.

[3312] Ibid.

[3313] *Encyclopedia Americana,* Vol. 19, 695; *Catholic Encyclopedia*, Vol. 7, 550.

nephew of Naples' King Charles, was elected with the support of the Vatican. However, Charles Robert maintained his father's claim to the Naples kingship.[3314] Arpad was the first of the Hungarian dynastic kings that began in 907, a king and people who traced their ancestors back to the Scythian horsemen overlords from before 1000 BC. [3315]

King Stephen, Duke of Geza, succeeded the Hungarian throne circa 997. He petitioned Pope Sylvester II (999–1003) for "the royal dignity and the confirmation of his ecclesiastical acts and ordinances.. .. Sylvester acceded to Stephen's request, sent him a royal crown, and confirmed his ecclesiastical regulations. .. and also received the title of Apostolic King and Apostolic Legate, the right to have a legate's cross [a double cross] carried before him, and other privileges, but modern investigation has shown the Bull of the Pope Sylvester bestowing these honors is a forgery of the seventeenth century."[3316] However, under Bela III the legate Double Cross of de Boullion and Jerusalem became official royal Hungarian heraldry in the late twelfth century.[3317] Accordingly, the taciturn Double Cross reunited with the Anjou King of Jerusalem title and claims.

In 1397, Sigismund of Luxemburg, German Emperor and King of Bohemia became king of Hungary, reigning until 1437.[3318] Sigismund was a descendant from the Lusignan "Dragon Kings of Draconis." Members of this court donned "the insignia of the dragon incurved into a circle, with a red cross—the very emblem of the original Rosi Crucis, which had identified the Grail succession from before 3000 BC."[3319] After Sigismund's death, succession disputes and the Turkish wars[3320] saw the King of Jerusalem title and Double Cross pass to the Anjou of Lorraine.

Good King Rene d'Anjou, born in 1408, held an impressive array of titles including Count of Provence, Count of Piedmont, Count of Guise, Duke of Anjou, Duke of Calabria, Duke of Lorraine, king of Hungary, king of Naples and Sicily, and the King of Jerusalem.[3321] As part of his Hungarian kingship rights, Rene I's inherited "Double Cross of Anjou" thereafter became renowned as the

---

[3314] Ibid., Vol. 14, 507; *Catholic Encyclopedia*, Vol. 7, 550; Gardner, *Bloodline of the Holy Grail*, 129, citing The Revd Pere Lacordaire, *St. Mary Magdalene,* Thomas Richardson, Derby, 1880, chs. 106–8.

[3315] *Catholic Encyclopedia*, Vol. 7, 549; *Encyclopedia Americana*, Vol. 14, 506.

[3316] *Catholic Encyclopedia*, Vol. 14, 506.

[3317] Ibid., Vol. 7, 550.

[3318] *Encyclopedia Americana*, Vol. 14, 508; *Catholic Encyclopedia*, Vol. 7, 551.

[3319] Gardner, *The Grail Kings*, 313; C. W. Leadbeater, The *Hidden Life in Freemasonry* (1926; UK: Global Grey, e-book, Kindle edition, 2015), 164:772.

[3320] *Catholic Encyclopedia*, Vol. 7, 551.

[3321] Baigent, Leigh, Lincoln, *Holy Blood and Holy Grail*, 138–139.

Double Cross of Lorraine in 1437,[3322] when Rene I of the second house of Anjou became Duke of Upper Lorraine (German Lothringen), after his father-in-law Charles II died. Rene I of Lorraine was the first ruler to merge the Duchy of Lorraine with the house of Bar. He married Isabelle Lorraine, Charles II's daughter. Rene I was the grandfather of the Rene II, son of Iolande de Bar, who accompanied Joan of Arc; both donned the Double Cross of Lorraine in battle. Rene I's coat of arms "boasted" the Duchy of Anjou and claimed the kingdoms of Hungary, Sicily/Naples, Jerusalem, and Aragon.[3323] Rene I and his descendants maintained their claims to the Naples throne even after Rene lost the battle and the throne to Alphonso V of Aragon in 1443.[3324]

The Lorraine/Lotharingen/Lothringen region was established with the Treaty of Verdun in 843 during the division of Charlemagne's empire. Lorraine was reigned over at that time by King Lothair I and II, from which the Lorraine name derives. The region was separated into Lower and Upper Lorraine in 945. After Gozelo II's death, Lower Lorraine was conferred to Godfrey the Bearded (1065–1069) and then was reigned over by his son Godfrey the Hunchback, who adopted Godfrey de Bouillon. Godfrey de Bouillon previously had been "enfeoffed" a duchy by the German King Henry IV. After de Bouillon's death in Jerusalem in 1100, Henry V bequeathed the duchy to Godfrey count of Brabant. Thereafter, the Lower Lorraine became known as Brabant; but in 1404, the duchy was united with Burgundy.[3325] Thus, in 1431 Isabella, daughter of Charles I, succeeded to the throne of Lorraine with her husband Rene I of Anjou and Bar that was succeeded by Rene II (1473–1508). Rene II received from his maternal inheritance Lorraine, Bar, Pont-a-Mousson, and Guise, with his paternal inheritance Vaudemont, Joinville, Aumale, Mayenne, Elbaeuf, and the Anjou rights or pretensions to Naples and Italy.[3326] Rene II donned the Cross of Lorraine on his victory banners as well as on his coins.[3327]

Ergo, through Mary of Antioch, two rival branches of the Anjou claimed rights to the King of Jerusalem title, in addition to the related rival Lusignan house of Cyprus.[3328] One of the claims remained with the Anjou of Naples, while the second claim was maintained by the dukes of Lorraine via the Hungarian succession of kings, which was passed on to the Hapsburg dynasty via Maria Theresa's marriage to Francois de Lorraine. *The Catholic Encyclopedia* describes the legacy of the

---

[3322] Ibid., 447; William Monter, *A Bewitched Duchy: Lorraine and its Dukes 1477–1736* (Geneva: Libraire Droz S.A., 2007), 23.
[3323] Monter, A *Bewitched Duchy*, 23, note 6; Michel Parisse, *Histoire de la Lorraine*, Vol. 3 (Nancy: Presses Universitaires de Nancy, 1990), 218, 233.
[3324] *Encyclopedia Americana*, Vol. 19, 695–696.
[3325] *Catholic Encyclopedia*, Vol. 9, 363: Lorraine. *Encyclopedia Americana*, Vol. 17, 628.
[3326] Ibid., Vol. 9, 363.
[3327] Monter, A *Bewitched Duchy*, 23.
[3328] *Catholic Encyclopedia*, Vol. 8, 365.

Jerusalem regency as "a curious path of history."[3329] However, the rival Lusignan kings of Cyprus, and the Anjou kings of Italy until 1946, continued to stake their claims through the Antioch Sicilian bloodline. The King of Jerusalem title was held by the Lusignan/Amaury bloodline until 1485 when Charlotte, daughter of John III of Cyprus, married Louis of Savoy, and ceded her claim of the Jerusalem title to Charles Savoy, her Italian nephew.[3330] The Anjou House of Savoy kings reigned in Italy until 1946, but still claim rights to the King of Jerusalem title.

The Hapsburg-Lorraine King of Jerusalem title claim passed onto King Juan Carlos Bourbon of Spain, which included the Lorraine claim to the Naples throne, and then to his son King Felipe IV who now holds the title. One should note the Hapsburgs also currently maintain a rival claim via Karl von Hapsburg son of Otto, the last crown prince of the Austrian-Hungarian Empire.

The double-headed cross was the symbol of ancient Aryan kingship, donned by Godfrey de Bouillon of Lorraine in his coat of arms, and then by the Templars.[3331] The ancient cross was authorized by the patriarch of Jerusalem before Templars accepted the "Maltese-style" cross in 1128 from St. Bernard. Further, the double-headed eagle was featured in the Austrian-Hungarian coat of arms that also dates to Sumerian Indo-Aryan kings and their Anunnaki gods. The ancient Double Cross staff and glyph was a symbol of rule for Shining Ones, giants, and a taciturn emblem memorializing an angelic spawned race who received wisdom and the [alleged] secrets of immortality maintained through their polytheist religions[3332] from their godfathers.

The arms double crossing the pole on the Cross of Lorraine represents the "scion" of many giant bloodlines with Jesus' bloodline. The Double Cross is "a seal/signet of the "royal secret," and the doctrine of the "Forgotten Ones," the "Shining Ones"—ancient gods and their offspring.[3333] In royal masonic symbolism the Double Cross is described as a "long line with two crossed bars upon it, has for uncounted thousands of years been the special sign of the Supreme Being."[3334] And, "If one draws lines joining each of the two ends. .. we get the double axe, the double-headed battle-ax."[3335] The double-headed axe was the favorite weapon of giant kings, as wielded in *Gargantua and Pantagruel: Five Books of the Lives, Heroic Deeds and Sayings* by the giant king Pantagruel against three hundred other giants.[3336] Archaeological discoveries on Crete found double axe symbolism associ-

---

[3329] Ibid., Vol. 8, 364.

[3330] Ibid.

[3331] Maloney, "History of the Cross of Lorraine," 17; *Catholic Encyclopedia*, Vol. 9, 362–363.

[3332] Gardner, *Lost Secrets*, 28–36; Mackey, *History of Freemasonry*, 118, 130, 146; De Vere, *The Dragon Legacy*, 66.

[3333] Gardner, *The Shadow of Solomon*, 113; De Vere, *The Dragon Legacy*, 79, 112.

[3334] Leadbeater, The *Hidden Life in Freemasonry*, 47:244, referencing Figure 8: 242.

[3335] Ibid., 48:247, referencing 47:242 figure 8b, c, and d.

[3336] Rabelais, *Gargantua and Pantagruel*, Book 2: XXXIX.

ated with their gods; and in the palace of Minos at Knossos, the double axe was called the Labrys, "the symbol of the Supreme."[3337]

The Templars formally recognized, in Article 4 of the *Roncelin Document,* a seditious secret that only "Consoled Brothers" knew, the royal adepts and grand-masters, which remains hidden from the children of the "New Babylon" (as in end-time Babylon). The purpose to the inner Templar Order as was not to protect Christian pilgrims, but rather to conquer the world and establish a "United King-dom" of the world (Kingdom of Heaven) for the grand monarch to reign over, a bloodline King of Jerusalem descendant,[3338] which sounds eerily similar to King James I's United Kingdom, yet another rival house seeking the King of Jerusalem title. Gisors Castle (place of the Cutting of the Elm), on a street called the Grande Monarque, the grand monarch of Rex Deus bloodlines, is the place occultists believe the grand monarch will make his grand appearance before unifying the brotherhood of all men.[3339] These beliefs remain alive and well from the European perspective in the contemporary "Genesis 6 Conspiracy."

[3337] Leadbeater, The *Hidden Life in Freemasonry,* 49:248, referencing illustrations at the dig by Sir Arthur Evans.
[3338] Gardner, *Lost Secrets,* 233.
[3339] Markale, *Treasure at Gisors,* 46, 253–268.

THE NEW TEMPLARS

CHAPTER 68

Col 2:18 Let no man beguile you of your reward in a voluntary humility and worshipping of angels, intruding into those things which he hath not seen, vainly puffed up by his fleshly mind.

To better discern end-time events, one requires a basic understanding to the organizational and hierarchal structure of the spurious posterities within their royal masonic secret societies. The Knights Templar Order was the first of the modern secret societies bent on bringing about a "United Kingdom" of world government and a universal religion, the "New Babylon."[3340]

Comprehending the fall of the Templar Order is important to comprehending the Naphalim World Order that Templar genitive organizations are plotting to bring about Antichrist. After the fall of Jerusalem in 1187, the senior Priory of Sion order held their junior Templar Order responsible for betraying the sacred Templar oath to protect Jerusalem, as set down by Hugh de Payen.[3341] The junior Templar Order reported to the senior Priory of Sion until 1188 when the Priory of Sion split away with the "Cutting of the Elm" ritual at Gisors Castle in 1188.[3342] The "Cutting of the Elm" in occult history marked the separation of the senior Rosy Cross order from the junior Red Cross Order of the Templars.

Templar operations halted on Friday, October 13, 1307, when French King Phillip the Fair and the Roman church seized Templar assets and arrested the

---

[3340] Gardner, *Lost Secrets,* 233.
[3341] Wayne, *Genesis 6 Conspiracy,* 412, citing Markale, *Treasure at Gisors,* 69, 76, 97.
[3342] Ibid., 408, 412, citing Markale, *Treasure at Gisors,* 69, 76, 97.

Templars in Paris.[3343] Templar adept Pierre d'Aumont escaped with eighteen ships from La Rochelle in Brittany to Mull of Kintyre, Scotland, at the orders of grandmaster Jacque Molay, who had previously arranged to safeguard much of the Templar treasure and records before the Templar demise.[3344] D'Aumont led a group of seven adepts: Gaston de la Pierre Phoebus, Guidon de Montanor, Gentili da Foligno, Henri de Montfort, Luis de Gromoard, Pierre Yorrick de Rivault, and Cesar Minvielle, as well as fifteen other Templars who were welcomed in Scotland by their Templar brethren. On June 24, 1313, d'Aumont was elected by the assembly at Mull to grandmaster, and officially established the new Templar church independent of Rome, complete with abbots and bishops but no Pope.[3345] In 1316, and under the protection of King Philip V, four Templars initiated to the "Secret of Secrets" (the Royal Secret of the Priory of Sion) met with newly elected Pope John XXII of Avignon in November 17 of the same year, and a plan was made to begin a new "Rule" of the (Templar) order to be thereafter known as the "Friars of Rosy Cross."[3346]

On January 5, 1317, in Avignon Pope John XXII awarded the "Rule of the Order" to the Higher Friars of the Rosy Cross on the condition the new order would be governed by thirty-three members of a holy college from the Roman church, led by the Pope's nephew. However, the Templars poisoned the college leader on the 6th, whereby they replaced him with Templar Knight Enguerard de Ners and a new college of thirty-three made up of pure-blood polytheist royals. The new French faction of the Rosy Cross order escaped Avignon to Monfort Sur Argens Commandery, and then determined to set a destiny apart from the Pope. Pope John XXII then issued, in 1317, the Papal *Extravagantes Decretal: Spondent Pariter* (both guarantee) forbidding the practice of alchemy, one of the primary studies and practices of Rosicrucian order.[3347]

Robert the Bruce, king of Scotland, thereafter instituted the Rosy Cross order for the Templar adepts in 1323.[3348] Accordingly, the new Holy College of thirty-three became official in 1333 as the "Invisible Ones" in honor of demons and fallen angels; the Invisible College of thirty-three that created the Rosicrucian order.[3349] "The Council of Thirty-Three" oversee to this day through the lower "Committee of Three Hundred" and the lower Rosicrucian orders—thus, a senior order and two junior orders. The Rosicrucian order were known within the Craft as the

---

[3343] Addison, *History of the Knights Templar*, 203; Ian Gittins, *Unlocking the Masonic Code Secrets of the Solomon Key* (London: Collins, 2007), 85.

[3344] Mackey, *History of Freemasonry*, 260; De Coster, *Poor Knights of Christ*, 3.

[3345] De Coster, *Poor Knights of Christ*, 3; Markale, *Treasure at Gisors*, 264; Gardner, *Lost Secrets*, 233.

[3346] De Coster, *Poor Knights of Christ*, 3–4.

[3347] Ibid., 5.

[3348] Gardner, *Lost Secrets*, 233.

[3349] De Coster, *Poor Knights of Christ*, 4–5.

"New Templars and Templists."[3350] The senior Invisible Templar Order set out to preserve their mystical, ancient knowledge in new institutions, while concealing their presence; organizations they created[3351] like the Royal College, known also as the Invisible College. The founders of the Rosicrucian order are regarded in occult organizations as "an inner world group" of great adepts holding power and wisdom that essentially makes them demigods compared to mundane humans, the secretive "College of Invisibles," and the obscure force behind the modern junior Rosicrucian order.[3352]

With the failed gambit to restart the Templar Order within the Roman church in 1317, Royal Masons of the Rosi Crucis rebuilt and decentralized many facets of the Templars' power and influence so as not to be so easily taken down again. As such, Rosicrucianism began before its fabled founding in 1378 by Christian Rosencreutz,[3353] as details above indicate regarding the senior Priory of Sion order. However, 1378 was the beginning to lower orders begat by Rex Deus kings, their Royal Masonic orders, and the refugee Templar adepts begat with the establishment of Ordo Draconis in Hungary. The Dragon Court of Luxemburg, from which Sigismund king of Hungary descended from, donned the insignia of a dragon incurved into a circle around a red cross, which was the same emblem adopted by the Rosicrucian order.[3354] Sigismund inherited this legacy through the throne of Hungary in 1397,[3355] as a descendant of the Lusignan "Dragon Kings of Draconis,"[3356] and through his Scythian and Pict ancestry via the Angevin Royal House, the Imperial Dukes of Angiers.[3357] The ancient Aboriginal bloodline descended thorough the "Dragon Kings of Anu," the Tuatha De Danann (Picts) from the "Egyptian Dragon Dynasty of Sobek," and the Anjou lineage-derived house of Merovingians.[3358] Accordingly In 1411, Sigismund was crowned Holy Roman Emperor,[3359] antichrist title in addition to the King of Jerusalem title.

The Dragon Court was officially established in 1408 as the Ordo Draconis with twenty-three kin Rex Deus sovereigns, and registered in Budapest.[3360] The Inner Court, the secret and senior *Sarkeny Rend,* acted as the repository for ancient knowledge and secrets,[3361] which was likely the seeds for the Committee of Three

---

[3350] Ibid., 5.

[3351] Ibid.

[3352] Wayne, *The Genesis 6 Conspiracy,* 544, citing Browne, *Secret Societies,* 95.

[3353] Mackey, *History of Freemasonry,* 331.

[3354] *Encyclopedia Americana,* Vol. 14, 508; *Catholic Encyclopedia,* Vol. 7, 551.

[3355] Gardner, *Realm of the Ring Lords,* xvii, 242; De Vere, *The Dragon Legacy,* 16.

[3356] Gardner, *Grail Kings,* 313; Leadbeater, The *Hidden Life in Freemasonry,* 164:772.

[3357] De Vere, *The Dragon Legacy,* 15.

[3358] Ibid., 16.

[3359] Gardner, *Realm of the Ring* Lords, xvii, 242

[3360] Ibid.; De Vere, *The Dragon Legacy,* 15–16.

[3361] Gardner, *Grail Kings,* 316.

Hundred order. "The family officers" of the Inner Court were/are Vere grandmasters of Britain and Europe, who venerate the Egyptian Ankh as the Albigensian Cross.[3362] Ordo Draconis was established to regain the thrones of Europe and to advance the Pursuits of Thoth.[3363] The Rosicrucian junior order over time became a conduit organization between the newly founded orders below the Rosicrucian order, and the higher royal masonic orders. The upper orders separated into the ascending orders Committee of Three Hundred, the Council of Thirty-Three, and the Thirteen European Families at the apex.

Henry Collins Agrippa founded the Guild of Mages, in 1510. Members studied the forbidden aspects of seven sacred sciences as masters of alchemy and magic. The Guild of Mages, according to Michael Mair's (1568–1622) manuscript, gave birth to the Brothers of the Gold Cross fraternity in Germany in 1570, and is thought widely to be the root organization for the junior Rosicrucian order.[3364] Hence, this was the nascence to age of the Rosicrucian Manifestos and Rosicrucian enlightenment. It follows then that the Rosicrucian organization was fabled to have been founded by Father Christian Rosencreutz.[3365] According to Masonic historians, Rosencreutz was a mythos created to hide the order's true origins, created by Johan Valentin Andrea as an arcane patriarch for the Rosicrucian syncretic movement and their vision to establish a perfect utopian society based on science, mystical faith, and reason.[3366] Rosencreutz's mythos noted he studied all forms of mysticism under knowledgeable adepts during his numinous tour through the Middle and Near East. Valentin wrote two infamous books, *Fama Fraternities* and *Discovery* of the *Fraternity of the Most Noble Order of the Rosy Cross,* published posthumously in 1614 and 1615 in Germany and renowned as the Rosicrucian manifestos. *In The Chymical Wedding of Christian Rosenkreu*tz by Andrea, Rosenkreutz declared he was a "Brother of the Red-Rosy Cross" and an acceptable respected guest, as he journeyed through the royal portals on his arcane quest.[3367] The mythos noted that when Rosencreutz returned to Germany from his mystical tour, he formed a small fraternity of four members that then grew to eight, all of whom later set out to the four winds of the earth to reform and transform the world.[3368]

Christian Rosencreutz's tomb was allegedly found in 1604, ten years before the publishing of *Fama Fraternities*. It follows that the Abbot of Adesberg, Johan Valentin Andrea, likely became the founder for the Rosicrucian visible and junior

[3362] De Vere, *The Dragon Legacy,* 16–17.
[3363] Gardner, *Realm of the Ring Lords,* 242.
[3364] Naudon, *Secret History of Freemasonry,* 242–243.
[3365] Mackey, *History of Freemasonry,* 331.
[3366] Gittins, *Unlocking the Masonic Code Secrets of the Solomon Key,* 100.
[3367] Andrea, *The Chymical Wedding of Christian Rosenkreutz, 1690,* 12.
[3368] Wayne, *Genesis 6 Conspiracy,* 541, citing Hancock and Bauval, *Talisman,* 258–261. Booth, *Secret History,* 306.

order. In 1616, Andrea published another Rosicrucian work titled *The Chemical Wedding of Christian Rosenkreutz*.[3369] In 1623, Rosicrucianism made its public appearance as the College of the Brothers of the Rose Cross, claiming to possess the perfect knowledge of the Most High. This new brotherhood was formed with thirty-three mysterious members at the core, known as the Invisible Ones. The lower Rosicrucian order has actively worked through literary and entertainment associations to promote their obscure beliefs, history, and genealogies in plain sight, while preparing the masses for the coming end-time universal religion and the royal masonic world government, the United Kingdom, and the New Atlantis. Rosicrucian Francis Bacon's Spear Shaker Society and Knights of the Helmut societies manufactured the new Babel language for the KJV, and penned Shakespearean literature works are two examples of their influence. One should not be surprised that Priory of Sion grandmasters and its kin members of the other Inner Circle of royals played key roles in establishing the new hierarchy of decentralized secret societies to replace the Knights Templar. One might also note the rise of the junior Rosicrucian order with grandmasters like Flamel in 1398 and later Andrea in 1637 from the arts and sciences.

Jean Gisors (1188–1220)	Marie de Saint Claire (1220–1266)
Guillaume De Gisors (1266–1307)	Edouard de Bar (1307–1336)
Jeanne De Bar (1336–1351)	Jean De Saint Claire (1352–1366)
Blance D' Evereaux (1366–1398)	Nicolas Flamel (1398–1418)
Rene D'Anjou (1418–1480)	Iolande De Bar (1480–1483)
Sandro Botticelli (1483–1510)	Leonardo Da Vinci (1510–1519)
Connetable De Bourbon (1519-1527)	Ferdinand De Gonzaque (1527–1575)
Louis De Nevers (1575–1595)	Robert Fludd (1595–1637)
J. Valentin Andrea (1637–1654)	Robert Boyle (1654–1691)
Isaac Newton (1691–1727)	Charles Radclyffe (1727–1746)
Charles De Lorraine (1746–1780)	Maximillian De Lorraine (1780–1801)
Charles Nodier (1801–1844)	Victor Hugo (1844–1885)
Claude Debussy (1885–1918)	Jean Cocteau (1918–1963)

Freemasonry was founded immediately after the Templar adepts escaped to Scotland in 1307. The Sinclair clan were patron guardians to the refugee Templar organization, noting freemasonry still honors its Templar heritage in titles like the

---

[3369] Ibid.; Naudon, *Secret History of Freemasonry,* 240; Gittins, *Unlocking the Masonic Code Secrets of the Solomon Key,* 100.

Knights Templar or KTs. William Sinclair founded freemasonry. His name was transliterated from St. Claire, as a descendant of Henry de Saint Claire, the knight who accompanied de Payen in the First Crusade; Marie de Saint Claire married Hugh de Payen. Another Marie de Saint Claire was the second Priory of Sion grandmaster after Jean Gisors, after the Cutting of the Elm at Gisors Castle in 1188.[3370]

The Illuminati began in the 1500s in Rome, led by enlightened mathematicians and astronomers who opposed Roman church dogma. One deduces Botticelli and Da Vinci, as Priory grandmasters, played an important role in the novel Illuminati. Galileo is believed to have formed the first "think tank" of enlightened ones, the "Illuminati." The Roman church arrested Galileo and ruthlessly hunted the Roman Illuminati, whereby the group fled Italy to resurface among the Bavarian elite, which included freemasons and the Rothschild (Bauer) and Bilderberger families. The Bavarian Illuminati later merged with the Freemason order, populating the lower adept degrees. Freemasonry focused on the military and politics, while the Illuminati focused on world government, the destruction of Christianity, and bringing about their universal religion.[3371]

The Rothschild family, formerly the Bauer family, was funded circa 1700 to replace the banking arm outside the Roman church, and in part the former Templar banking juggernaut,[3372] and as a front to launder the hidden wealth of the "Princes of Masonry." The banking system reports to the pure-blood family representatives in the Committee of Three Hundred who direct the IMF, World Bank, and the World Economic Association.

In 1662 a charter issued by Charles II Stuart of England founded the Invisible College known outwardly as the Royal Society, led by the Gresham 12 consisting of Freemason adepts and Rosicrucians. The society was modeled after the spirit of Rosicrucian Francis Bacon and his expressed ideas for a New Atlantis,[3373] based on an antediluvian world empire made up of ten Nephilim kings and Enochian mysticism. The Royal Society was created to preserve and perpetuate the occult's inherited knowledge, the gnosis of the ages, and to advance the experimental philosophy of Francis Bacon.[3374] The Royal Society influenced education outside the Roman church with their theology/philosophy and their genitive organizations. The Royal Society reports to the Rosicrucian order.

[3370] Lomas, *Invisible College*, 182, 274; Sora, *Lost Treasure*, 96, 77, 112–119, 179; Baigent, Leigh, and Lincoln, *Holy Blood and Holy Grail*, 443–445.

[3371] Wayne, *Genesis 6 Conspiracy* 520–521, citing Gary H. Kah, *En Route to Global Occupation* (Lafayette, LA: Huntington House, 1996), 24; Demond Wilson, *The New Age Millennium*, 21, 86, 91; Marrs, *Rise of the Fourth Reich*, 13; Brown, *Angels and Demons*, 39–42, 47, 199.

[3372] Wayne, *Genesis 6 Conspiracy* 520–521, citing Kah, *Enroute to Global Occupation*, 14; Marrs, *Rule by Secrecy*, 58.

[3373] Lomas, *Invisible College*, 23, 208, 212, 245; Mackey, *History of Freemasonry*, 229, 310.

[3374] Wayne, *Genesis 6 Conspiracy*, 438, citing Wallace-Murphy and Hopkins, *Rosslyn*, 126; Mackey, *History of Freemasonry*, 301, 304.

THE THELEMIC TREE

CHAPTER 69

Deut 16:21 Thou shalt not plant thee a grove of any trees near unto the altar of the LORD thy God, which thou shalt make thee.

Deut 16:22 Neither shalt thou set thee up any image; which the LORD thy God hateth.

Trees, like the World Tree and Tree of Life, are important allegories in the occult. The World Tree is a mediator, unifier, and separator of the World Parents, Father Sky and Mother Earth.[3375] Because trees can live for centuries, their extraordinary lifespan represents in part the immortality of the gods and the immortal spirit given to the original Nephilim,[3376] and Rephaim.

Dragons are regarded as protectors of the World Tree in a similar way that cherubim protected Eden. Atlanteans honored the Tree of Life under which sacred and secret rituals were performed, akin to Anunnaki in Sumerian reliefs performing rituals around what many think was a Tree of Life. Atlanteans named this tree the Dragon Tree, which they tapped for its healing qualities.[3377] Biblically, trees like the oak and cedar were connected to Mount Hermon, Nephilim, Rephaim, and polytheism,[3378] and groves were commonly connected to idolatry and nature

---

[3375] Wayne, *Genesis 6 Conspiracy*, 122, citing Leeming and Leeming, *A Dictionary of Creation Myths*, 287.
[3376] Ibid., citing David E. Jones, *An Instinct for Dragons*, 121–128.
[3377] Joseph, *Destruction of Atlantis*, 28–29.
[3378] Isa 2:14; 44:14–17; Ezek 6:13; 27:6; Hos 4:3; Amos 2:9.

worship of gods.[3379] Moreover the ash and elm trees were associated with poly-theism, and grove derives from `Asherah, `Ashtoreth, Astarte, and Ishtar.[3380] One contemplates the connection between Asherah, groves, and the ash tree, noting the "ah" is a female plural format in Hebrew.

Ash/`Oren was a wood used to carve idols, and a tree associated with the oak also used to make idols. The ash tree appears only once in the KJV (Isa 44:14), and is translated as cedar, pine, fir, or laurel tree in other English translations. The ash tree appears with the cedar and oak, but not in association with groves or idols.[3381] Similarly, elm trees appear only once in the KJV, in association with oak trees, mountains, and idolatry. Elm/'elah, the feminine format of 'ayil, was translated eleven other times in the KJV as an oak tree, and translated one time from 'ayil, the source word for trees in Ezekiel 31:14's giant trees of Eden. Elm/'elah is also defined as a terebinth tree, and a strong tree, just as 'ayil is defined as anything strong, a chief, a mighty tree, and a mighty man. Elon/'Eylown, the Hittite father-in-law of Esau, also derives from `'ayil and means mighty.[3382]

One deduces that the elms/'elah in Hosea 4:13 could have or should have been translated as "oak tree," and more likely a mighty terebinth tree, but the KJV translators without explanation chose the elm. The elm, French orme, is sacred in Gnosticism, as venerated in the Sages of Light sect of Ormus. Templars administered high justice in Paris under a great and legendary elm tree. The occult Cutting of the Elm ritual at Gisors Castle represented a significant event that separated the Knights Templar from the Priory of Sion organization, and perhaps something more like a genealogical split.[3383] The Family Tree, the Genealogical Tree, or Phylogenetic Tree is generally depicted as a giant umbrella tree, an elm tree that likely came about as an arcane merging of Isaiah 11:1's stem/trunk[3384] or tree of Jesse, "And there shall come forth a rod out of the stem of Jesse, and a

---

[3379] Exod 34:13–15; Deut 7:5; 12:2–3; 16:21–22; Judg 3:7; 6:26–30; 1 Kings 14:23; 15:15; 16:33; 2 Kings 17:10, 16; 18:4; 23:4–16; 2 Chron 14:3; 15:16; 17:6; 33:3, 19; 34:3–7; Isa 17:8; 26:9; Jer 17:2; Mic 5:14.

[3380] H842—'asherah, ash-ay-raw': Asherah or Astarte a Phoenician and Canaanite goddess; consort of Baal; an image of Asherah; groves for idol worship; sacred trees or poles set up near an altar; same as 6253; H6253—`Ashtoreth, ash-to'reth: Phoenician goddess of love, fertility, and war; Ashtoreth; Ishtar.

[3381] Isa 44:14. H766—'oren, o'-ren; the ash tree; fir tree; cedar tree; Strong's Cyclopaedia, Vol. 1, 456–457: Ash. Cedar: ESV, ISV. Laurel: Berean, NASB, CSB, HCSB, GNT, MSB. Pine: NKJV, Sept., CEV. Fir: NASB 1997 and 1977, LSB, Amplified, ERV ASV.

[3382] Elm: Hos 4:13. H424—'elah, ay-law'; feminine of 352; an oak; strong tree; elm; oak; teil-tree; terebinth tree; valley where David killed Goliath. Oak 11 times, elm 1 time. H352—'ayil, ah'-yil; strength; anything strong; specifically, a chief; an oak; strong tree; mighty man; mighty tree; terebinth tree. Oaks: Isa 1:29. Eden Trees. Ezek 31:14. H356—'Eylown, ay-lone'; Elon, cognate with terebinth and mighty; Esau's Hittite father-in-law.

[3383] Naudon, Secret History of Freemasonry, 105–107; Markale, Treasures at Gisors, 40, 66, 68, 69, 71.

[3384] H1503—geza', geh'-zah: the trunk or stump of a tree; stem; stock.

Branch shall grow from his roots" with Giovanni Boccaccio's family tree of gods in *On the Genealogy of the Gods of the Gentiles* (c. 1360) funded by King Hugh IV Lusignan king of Cyprus, Hugh II King of Jerusalem.[3385]

The Family Tree is an allegory for the occult Tree of Life and the tree often depicted as the World Tree. The Family, Genealogical and World Trees are represented as deciduous trees symbolizing reincarnation because they shed their leaves but return to life, while evergreen trees represent immortality because most never lose their needles.[3386] Accordingly, the hierarchy of secret societies and genitive organizations is represented with the evergreen tree. Royal masonic orders dwell at the apex functioning like Invisible Ones through their lower trunk organizations. Imagine the western secret society hierarchy like a giant cedar tree with a tall, straight trunk/stem consisting of several central secret societies, all with branches angled down from their trunk positions. Place the Thirteen European Families' trunk secret society at the treetop. Immediately below is the trunk Council of Thirty-Three (families), then the Committee of Three Hundred, the Rosicrucian order, the Illuminati, and the Freemason order at the bottom of the trunk organizations. Just as the World and Phylogeny Trees receive their life, genealogy, authority, and alleged reincarnation from the roots extending into the earth, so does the secret society evergreen tree receive its power and authority from within the earth, from realm of Hades and underworld gods.

Knowing the Thelemic world trees connect heaven and earth, father sky and mother earth, and that the descendants of giants' power is authorized and nourished from Hades, the occult home of the gods brings full understanding into Amos 2:9:

> Amos 2:9 Yet destroyed I the Amorite before them, whose height was like the height of the cedars, and he was strong as the oaks; yet I destroyed his fruit from above, and his roots from beneath.

Royal masonic orders populate the branches for the three highest trunk organizations with orders like the Order of the Golden Fleece, and the Knights of the Seraphim, Knights of St. John, Ordo Draconis and their genitive lower royal masonic orders. Each trunk organization has many branches begat with lead branch organization that has a descending hierarchy of organizations that branch out and down from the lead. Branch organizations have a descending hierarchy that report up the branch organizations to the lead organization, extending out of the central trunk organization. Hence each branch is led by organizations like the

---

[3385] *Encyclopedia Americana*, Vol. 4, 140–141.
[3386] Wayne, *Genesis 6 Conspiracy*, 122, citing Flemming, *Heroes of the Dawn*, 34, and Jones, *An Instinct for Dragons*, 90.

Royal Society, the Rothschild banking organization, the Bilderbergers, the Club of Rome report, and the World Economic Forum, branching out from the Committee of Three Hundred in this example. The Skull of Bones and Bohemian Grove are branches extending out of the Illuminati.

The premise for the contemporary secret society organizational structure was penned into writings by medieval writers, like the junior Rosicrucian order founder, as the Thelemic organization as it is known among the Princes of Masonry. The Thelemic Tree organizational structure was revealed in the writings of the Rosicrucian, Francois Rabelais. Rabelais and his writings are renowned in the occult for his cryptic green language (legominism), along with other famous writers utilizing the same cryptic literary craft, such as Wagner, Bach, Shakespeare, and C. S. Lewis.[3387] Abbey Francois Rabelais (1494–1553) was one of five famous writers whose literary craft accelerated the formation of secret societies after the fall the Templars. The other four were Thomas More (1477–1535), Abbey John Valentin Andrea (1586–1654), Robert Fludd (1574–1637), and Francis Bacon (1560–1626).[3388] Rabelais' work presented the "constitution of a society of free men," while his book *Gargantua and Pantagruel* is a collection of encoded stories regarding rampaging giants that teems with the green language concealing occult secrets.[3389]

In chapters 52–58, Rabelais' religious order, centered at the Abbey of Theleme, was built by the giant Gargantua.[3390] Initiate lives at the abbey's order were spent not in studying laws, statutes, or rules, but spent according to their own free will and pleasure. The only rule was "Do What Thou wilt, [like little gods] because they desire what they are denied [by the laws God in the Bible]," viewed as "that bond of servitude wherein they are so tyrannously enslaved; for it is agreeable with the nature of man to long after things forbidden and to desire what is denied us." Initiates were taught knowledge to help discipline their desires.[3391]

Rabelais framed polytheistic dualism with Satan as the equal of God who are matched in games that play out in perpetuity: "I can conceive no other meaning in it but a description of a set at tennis in dark and obscure terms. The suborners of men are the makers of matches, which are commonly friends. After the two chases are made, he that was in the upper end of the tennis-court goeth out, and the other cometh in.. .. The globe terrestrial is the tennis-ball. After playing, when the game is done, they refresh themselves before a clear fire, and change their

[3387] Booth, *Secret History of the World*, 52, 53, 88, 176.
[3388] Naudon, *Secret History of Freemasonry*, 239–241.
[3389] Ibid., 52, 53, 88, 176, 239–241; Booth, *Secret History of the World*, 287.
[3390] Rabelais, *Gargantua and Pantagruel*, Book 1: LII.
[3391] Ibid., Book 1: LVII.

shirts; and very willingly they make all good cheer, but most merrily those that have gained."[3392]

Gargantua was the son of the giant Grangousier. "Gargantua at the age of four hundred fourscore forty and four years begat his son Pantagruel, upon his wife named Badebec, daughter to the king of the Amaurots in Utopia, who died in childbirth," because the beastly baby was too large to deliver.[3393] Rabelais provided Gargantua's genealogy back to antediluvian giants beginning with the giant Chalbroth. Gargantua's phylogeny tree included Hurtali, a king who survived the flood by hanging onto Noah's ark (akin to gnostic accounts of King Og or Tubal-Cain). Gargantua begat Nimbroth, possibly Rabelais' accounting for Nimrod. The genealogy then branches into Greek-like or Indo-Aryan-like names like Atlas, Titius, Eryon, Aegeon, and Porus, with the latter a giant who fought Alexander the Great.[3394] Before the flood, "three medlars" from the stars arrived. They were fair and beautiful to behold to the eye, as well as delicious to eat (understood in Gnosticism for sex, as in Eve eating from the fruit of Eden's tree being understood as sex with Satan). Thus, "many women ate of the fruit of the gods that produced offspring that grew in length of body, and of those came the Giants, and of them Pantagruel. And the first was Chalbroth."[3395]

Thus, the Thelemic doctrine and the hierarchy that extended the inner being of certain humans is that of the gods,[3396] from the counterfeit spirit received by giants from the fallen angels. The Thelemic Tree is populated at the apex by the inner adept beings, by the pure bloods of the royal dynasties. The word *thelema* is English for a Greek word meaning will, from the verb *thelo,* adopted by secret societies from Rabelais' writings,[3397] and also drafted from the New Testament. The word *thel'aymah* transliterated as thelema surfaces sixty-two times as will, and one time each for desire (Eph 2:3) and pleasure (Rev 4:11);[3398] both should have been translated as "will." Both of the latter translations for *thel'aymah* seemingly were translated by Baconian-sponsored translators to insert the occult doctrine of "their own free will and pleasure."[3399]

Matt 6:10 Thy kingdom come. Thy will be done in earth, as it is in heaven.

[3392] Ibid. Book 1: LVIII.

[3393] Ibid., Book 2: II.

[3394] Ibid., Book 2: I.

[3395] Ibid.

[3396] *Encyclopedia Britannica*: Thelema, https://www.britannica.com/topic/Thelema.

[3397] Ibid.

[3398] G2307—*thel'-ay-mah*; a determination; a command; a choice; a desire; a pleasure.

[3399] Rabelais, *Gargantua and Pantagruel*, Book 1: LVII.

> Rev 4:11 Thou art worthy, O Lord, to receive glory and honor and power: for thou hast created all things, and for thy pleasure they are and were created.

Polytheists then draft Matthew 6:10, Luke 11:2 and all other scriptural references as God's will into their dogma as: the will of the gods' kingdom to come (reigned over by Antichrist) and the will of the gods will be done in earth, as it is done in heaven, as in above so below. Hades is regarded as heaven where roots to the Thelemic Tree extend out of with its power. It follows that Rabelais' allegoric Theleme order is the spiritual life sap flowing through the Thelemic Tree trunk and to all the branches for the plethora of secret societies planning to impose Bacon's Utopian New Atlantis, devoted to Our Lady of Babylon, goddess of pleasure, and the will of the gods.

Babalon (Babylon) is the goddess of pleasure in the Rosicrucian Ordo Templi Orientis, in gnostic groups in general,[3400] and part of the allegory to the Babylon goddess that rides the seven empires of the end times. The work of the Babalon goddess is the secret to the Holy Grail held in the hand of "our Lady the Scarlet Woman, Babalon the Mother of Abominations, the bride of chaos, that rideth our Lord the Beast.. .. In the outstretched hand of Babalon, is the Cup of Abominations. This cup is the Holy Grail. It represents the potential for divintity, and infinity, that lies within the flesh; the Secret of the Holy Grail is the Mystery of the Divinity."[3401]

[3400] https://www.britannica.com/topic/Thelema; *A Very Basic Guide to Devotional Work with the Goddess Babalon* (Temple of Our Lady of yhe Abyss, n.d.), https://files.elfsightcdn.com/4696283d-2afb-47e0-b743-2f3b0c4da019/7f3a661e-323f-4498-ae57-d3367fce5b2b.pdf), 4.

[3401] *A Very Basic Guide,* 5.

CHAPTER 70

THE JESUITS

Isa 19:11 Surely the princes of Zoan are fools, the counsel of the wise counselors of Pharaoh is become brutish: how say ye unto Pharaoh, I am the son of the wise, the son of ancient kings?

Isa 19:12 Where are they? where are thy wise men? and let them tell thee now, and let them know what the LORD of hosts hath purposed upon Egypt.

Many believe Jesuits begat freemasonry and other secret societies, and that all secret societies report to the Jesuit Order. Jesuits have been, are, and will play a major role in bringing about the end times, but the order is not the puppeteer for the transgenerational and transmillennial conspiracy.

The Jesuit founding conspired to ascension to power within the Roman church, and their pivotal end-time role is a discernment important to understanding prophetic fulfillment. Ignatius of Loyola's Jesuit Order conception post-dated the Rosicrucian order, the incarnated junior organization for the senior Priory Sion order that split from their junior Templar Order in 1188 for losing Jerusalem.[3402] In short, the Jesuit Order was the gambit by Rex Deus bloodlines to replace the fallen Knights Templar within the Roman church.

Ignatius/Inigo of Loyola (1491–1556) was born from Basque nobility at Loyola Castle in Spain. The Basque nobility rank was *"parientes maires,"*[3403] roughly

---

[3402] Markale, *Templar Treasure*, 69, 76, 97; Baigent, Leigh, and Lincoln, *Holy Blood and Holy Grail*, 441; Greer, *Element Encyclopedia*, 368.

[3403] *Catholic Encyclopedia*, Vol. 7, 639; John Hungerfore, *Saint Ignatius of Loyola: Imitator of Christ 1494 to 1555* (New York: P. J. Kenedy & Sons, 1922), 4; Severin Leitner, "The Spirituality of

translated from Spanish as older and perhaps bigger relatives. Ignatius possessed ancient royal bloodlines recognized by the nobility class at that time. Ignatius' heraldic coat of arms included seven bend gules (seven red diagonal bands) for Onaz, argent (silver or white), a pot (likely for battles past) and chain sable (black chain symbolizes a reward or captivity in past battles) set between two gray wolves (noble and courageous in battle and representing the patriarch god like Anubis or Nibhaz).[3404]

Ignatius was injured in battle in 1521 after undertaking a military career in 1517. While recovering, he received an apparition of Mary that begat his conversion and commission at the Feast of Our Lady's Assumption.[3405] He saw "Our Lady" and the infant Jesus and received an overwhelming "initiation" described as an "intense consolation."[3406] This initiation is very odd to me because "The Secret Rule of the Order of the Templars made a distinction between the regular [lower] members and the Consoled Brothers [the Adepts], who were the Keepers of the Message. The Secret Rule of the Order was set down in *The Book of Baptism of Fire and the Secrets Set Down by the Master Roncelin*. Consoled Brothers were gnostic Cathar Perfecti, meaning those who have received the Consolamentum. Consoled Brothers were the 'Pure Ones' who were in contact with the divine, ready to rejoin the kingdom of light from where they were driven during the revolt of the [fallen] angels; only the Consoled Brothers knew the Secret Rule of the Order."[3407] Once Ignatius' health was restored, he pilgrimaged to the closest "shrine of Our Lady" to thank his "Queen for his conversion," where he received more stirring "consolations." Thereafter, Ignatius called Mary "the Immaculate Queen of the Universe."[3408] Everything about Ignatius' first visions were steeped in gnostic language, dogma, and with Templar connections, specifically his consoled initiation as a purebred royal into the Perfecti.

Ignatius, in March of 1522, journeyed to "Our Lady at Montserrat" sanctuary "like a knight of chivalry" to become the soldier taking up arms for Christ,[3409] Templar-like. In Catholicism, a "regular order of knighthood means a brotherhood or confraternity which combines with the insignia of knighthood, the privileges of a

---

Peter Faber," *Review of Ignatian Spirituality*, 1970–2011, 109: 2; Donald Attwater, *The Penguin Dictionary of Saints*, second edition updated by Catherine Rachel John (Wrights Lane, UK: Penguin Books, 1983), 174.

[3404] *Catholic Encyclopedia*, Vol. 7, 639; John Pollen, *Saint Ignatius of Loyola* (New York: P. J. Kenedy & Sons, 1922), 4.

[3405] Ibid., Vol. 7, 639–640; *Our Lady of Fatima Crusader Bulletin*, salvemariaregina.info, Vol. 41, Issue No. 113, St. Ignatius of Loyola, Knight of Mary quoting his biography.

[3406] Pollen, *Saint Ignatius of Loyola*, 8; *Our Lady of Fatima Crusader Bulletin*, St. Ignatius Of Loyola biography.

[3407] Wayne, *Genesis 6 Conspiracy*, 427; Markale, *The Templar Treasure*, 166, 167, 185, 187, 220.

[3408] *Our Lady of Fatima Crusader Bulletin*, Vol. 41, No. 113, St. Ignatius of Loyola biography.

[3409] Ibid.

monk."[3410] However, as Tertullian stated: "Christianity and the profession of arms were incompatible" and "was condemned as heretical." But in the age of crusade chivalry, religion and the profession of arms were reconciled or perhaps rationalized. A "new understanding" rested on a vow that a dignified soldier elevated the "chevalier to monk status" with a "special blessing for the monk-knight: Benedictio Novus Militis."[3411] The knight required the confirmation of the Pope for their clergy status, and the authorization of a prince,[3412] all of which Ignatius obtained.

Ignatius spent three days at Montserrat sanctuary during the Feast of Annunciation, in self-examination and meditation before the "altar of the Blessed Mother of God," before embarking on his commission.[3413] Mary's intercessions with Ignatius were common, estimated at twenty to forty, and were accredited his ascetic and mystical indoctrination to prepare Ignatius for his commission. At Montserrat, Mary chose Ignatius to be her soldier to rebuild the Christian church under her instructions,[3414] the Templar New Babylon. Ignatius devoted three days of communication with the Mary apparition at Our Lady at Montserrat in Catalunya/Catalonia where Santa Maria is venerated. Ignatius then traveled to eleven other churches dedicated to the "Mother of God," acting as the "holy knight of Mary."[3415]

By 1150 Templars had assembled considerable holdings throughout the Iberian Peninsula and established castles at Montserrat, an important region of gnostics, Templar, and Essene settlements, along with Catalunya in southern France.[3416] Columbus' lead ship, the *Santa Maria*, flew the Templar flag. None of this is coincidental. Templars, gnostics, and many royal bloodlines venerated Our Lady/Notre Dame as Mary Magdalene, whom they allege was the wife of Jesus and Sophia's representative on earth, cognate with ancient queens of heaven like Isis.[3417]

Templars were students of the Benedictine monks, who taught the Templars building skills and kept very close ties with Templars. Templars reorganized the mason guilds in the twelfth century as patrons for the trade guilds, which were wholly independent of the Roman church. The reorganized masons became known as the Children of Solomon, instructed by St. Bernard's Cistercian order in the knowledge of Solomon. This Jerusalem-based knowledge, art gothique, built the Notre Dame gothic cathedrals.[3418] From 1128 forward, St. Bernard, patron and protector of the Templar Order, mandated Templars to be obedient to Mary

---

[3410] *Catholic Encyclopedia*, Vol. 10, 304–307.
[3411] Ibid., Vol. 3, 691–692.
[3412] Ibid., Vol. 10, 304–307.
[3413] Pollen, *Saint Ignatius of Loyola*, 9.
[3414] *Our Lady of Fatima Crusader Bulletin*, Vol. 41, No. 113, St. Ignatius of Loyola biography.
[3415] Ibid.
[3416] Addison, *History of the Knights Templar*, 10.
[3417] Jer 6:9; 44:17, 18, 19. Knight and Lomas, *Uriel's Machine*, 371; Gardner, *Lost Secrets*, 210.
[3418] Naudon, *Secret History of Freemasonry*, 34–35, 51, 61; Knight and Lomas, *Book of Hiram*, 52, 336; Booth, *Secret History*, 259; Gardner, *Lost Secrets*, 22, 221–223.

Magdalene and her teachings. Templar masons consecrate all the Notre Dame cathedrals to Mary Magdalene.[3419]

> The Mary apparitions of Lourdes; Fatima; Medjugorje; the countless minor Mary apparitions, and Joan of Arc's Mary apparitions preached a common doctrine connected to a Revelation prophecy. Mary apparitions tout Mary (Babylon) to be the queen of kingdoms, the queen of all the people of the earth, and the bringer of peace (through the Covenant of Death). Mary apparitions trumpet a variety of expressions espousing the same theme: "I am the Queen of Peace. I am the Mother of God, I am the Mother of All People on Earth," just as she was described by the prophets Isaiah and John. She is also described regularly as "Our Lady" and "Our Lady of Peace." She preaches a doctrine of peace and cooperation and uniting under one true religion. And she says that if the world does not repent, it will destroy itself from the face of the earth: "You cannot imagine what is going to happen, nor what the Eternal Father will send to the earth. That is why you must be converted! Renounce everything. Do penance.. .. Persevere and help me convert the world."[3420]

The worship of Mary as the mother of God began in 431 at the Council of Ephesus. Unfortunately, the tradition incorporated emulated the worship of Isis, and included rituals that originated in Babylon.[3421]

> Isa 47:5 Sit thou silent, and get thee into darkness, O daughter of the Chaldeans: for thou shalt no more be called, The lady of kingdoms.

After the Montserrat vision, Ignatius set out in his new life as a "knight" would do (with oaths and dedication), which led him to Manresa for ten months and more Mary intercessions. Manresa was the place where Ignatius received his calling.[3422] He meditated in a cave that became renowned as the "Shrine of Manresa," receiving numerous favors/experiences from the Mary apparition.[3423] At one point, Ignatius was in a meditation- induced trance for eight days and nights; he entered

---

[3419] Gardner, *Shadow of Solomon,* 105–108, 281.
[3420] Wayne, *Genesis 6 Conspiracy,* 355, 356, citing Isa 28:19–25; 30:1; Dan 9:27; Hos 6:7; Amos 8:14; Rev 17; 18; Janet T. Connell, *The Visions of the Children: The Apparitions of the Blessed Mother at Medjugorje* (New York: St. Martin's Press, 1992), 4, 173.
[3421] Dorsey, *Secret History of The New World Order,* 171, citing Alexander Hislop, *The Two Babylons.*
[3422] Pollen, *Saint Ignatius of Loyola,* 10–11.
[3423] *Our Lady of Fatima Crusader Bulletin,* Vol. 41, No. 113, St. Ignatius of Loyola biography; Pollen, *Saint Ignatius of Loyola,* 10.

the cave a "spiritual tyro" and left a "master," complete with the "Spiritual Exercises" doctrine and instructions first published in 1548.[3424] At the Monastery of the Little Hours, Ignatius was taken in vision by Mary to a place beyond the earth to see the Holy Trinity. "Such was the Ascetic and Mystical training which the Blessed Virgin Mary gave to her soldier before sending him into the world in order, not unlike Francis Assisi, to rebuild the church of Christ."[3425]

After Manresa, and at the mystically significant age of thirty-three, Ignatius decided to become educated[3426] in the degrees of the seven liberal arts (the seven sacred sciences that begat mysticism and secret societies[3427]) a period lasting eleven years beginning in Spain and finishing in Paris with his theology degree and his MA degree in 1535.[3428] Ignatius combined this education with his Mary indoctrination to establish, guide, and interpret Scripture with the gnostic interpretive approach.

Ignatius met important individuals during his formal education who would play pivotal roles in the founding of the Jesuit Order. Jesuits began in 1534 principally from three young men with several objectives—Peter Faber, Francis Xavier, and Ignatius of Loyola—and murky silent backers. Faber's family included close relationships and membership into "Carthusian Priors,"[3429] "the Order of Bruno" established in 1084 that was closely related to the Cistercians, and the Calabrian Monks of the Pythagoras mystery schools.[3430] Calabrian monks were the gnostic order that partnered with Godfrey de Bouillon, de Payen, Fulk Anjou, and Cistercian orders to establish and support the Knights Templar.

Francis Xavier, like Ignatius, was a Basque from Navarre-Aragon, born in the Royal Xavier Castle of Navarre. Xavier/Xabier/Javier means "bright" and/or a "new house," reflecting the town of his birth and his nobility. His mother Dona Maria de Azpilcueta Aznarez was heiress to two noble Navarre families.[3431] Xavier received a law degree at the Bologna University, with Master of Arts and Aristotle Philosophy degrees from the University of Paris.[3432] The Basque mythos states they descended from the Atlantean race, and that their superior royal bloodline originates in prehistory from the gods: Homo-Atlantis. This mythos states Basques seeded postflood Egyptian, Sumerian, and Scythia, as supported by many researchers. Some

[3424] Pollen, *Saint Ignatius of Loyola,* 10–11; Attwater, *The Penguin Dictionary of Saints,* 174.
[3425] *Our Lady of Fatima Crusader Bulletin,* Vol. 41, No. 113, St. Ignatius of Loyola biography.
[3426] *Catholic Encyclopedia,* Vol. 7, 639–640.
[3427] Wayne, *Genesis 6 Conspiracy,* 58–64.
[3428] Pollen, *Saint Ignatius of Loyola,* 13.
[3429] Leitner, "Spirituality of Peter Faber," 2.
[3430] *Catholic Encyclopedia,* Vol. 3, 388–392; Vol 2, 13–14; Les Moines Chartreux, "Histoire," https://chartreux.org/moines/histoire.
[3431] *Catholic Encyclopedia,* Vol. 6, 235; James Brodrick, *Saint Francis Xavier (1506–1552)* (London: Burns, Oates & Washbourne Ltd, 1952), 16; Attwater, *Dictionary of Saints,* 139.
[3432] *Catholic Encyclopedia,* Vol. 11, 767.

historians connect Basques to the Scythian/Aryan ethnic group that migrated up the Danube as far as Finland, and to the Scythian Tartars that migrated into Hungry, Ukraine, Russia, and Mongolia.[3433] Basques were the first settlers of Spain and southern France after the flood. They spoke a language unknown to the rest of the European peoples. Basques do not possess ethnic similarities to the "Noachites" but do indicate physical and linguistic kinship with the Mongols.[3434]

Faber too was a noble who finished his education at the University of Paris (the College Saint-Barbe, receiving a Master of Arts degree), where he became a roommate and lifelong friends with Francis Xavier and Ignatius.[3435] The three founders of the Jesuits were all from significant ancient royal bloodlines, regularly participated in dubious gnostic and mystical rituals, and were dedicated to restructuring the Roman church in their preferred gnostic image.

Faber's biography and diary "Memoriale" included accounts of his regular communication with angels, described oddly as with spirits of both good and evil; his guardian angel was his closest ally. Faber believed he had received enlightenment and clarity in his consciousness, to surround himself with "protecting angels and spirits."[3436] In prayer, Faber addressed these spiritual entities he described as angels, guardian angels, saints, holy souls, the Trinity, and the incarnate Jesus. These entities were his "all-present protectors."[3437] Faber, by the descriptions of these entities, seems to have been regularly communicating with fallen angels and demons in a similar manner to the Mary apparition Ignatius communicated with.

In Paris, Faber was known as Master Faber. His studies trained him in the knowledge of logic and philosophy. Christian humanism, medieval scholasticism, and popular devotion shaped his spiritualism[3438] as it shaped Ignatius and Xavier. Philosophy, the love of wisdom, derives from Greek *phileo*, "to love," and from *sophia*, "wisdom," which endeavors to develop a consistent worldview and way of life based on a peculiar zeal in the arts, sciences, or any branch of knowledge (seven sacred sciences). Philosophy is concluded by elites to be superior to the sciences; it is their arbiter dedicated to harmonizing and uniting the sciences.[3439] Sophia is the mother goddess of wisdom in gnosticism, the Queen of Heaven. Thus, the Jesuit spirituality and the Bible was viewed through the lens of mysticism and allegorical

---

[3433] Alexander Winchell, *Preadamites: The Existence of Men before Adam* (Chicago: S. C. Griggs and Company, 1888), 64, 377–380.

[3434] Winchell, *Preadamites*, 149–150.

[3435] *Catholic Encyclopedia*, Vol. 11, 767; Joseph N. Tylenda, *Jesuit Saints and Martyrs*, 2nd edition (Chicago: Loyola Press, 1998).

[3436] Leitner, "Spirituality of Peter Faber," 10–11.

[3437] Ibid., 18.

[3438] Ibid., 2.

[3439] *Unger's*, 1005: Philosophy; *Nelson's*, 988–989: Philosophy; *Encyclopedia Americana*, 710, Vol. 21, 771.

interpretation. All the initiates of the Jesuit Order were commissioned to imitate Jesus,[3440] in the gnostic sense to serve as little gods on the path to godhood.

> Col 2:8 Beware lest any man spoil you through philosophy and vain deceit, after the tradition of men, after the rudiments of the world, and not after Christ.

The new ascetic Jesuit Order was bound into a brotherhood of oaths, initiations, and rituals in 1534 at Montmarte, where the fledgling order swore vows to "poverty and chastity": *magna animorum Laetitia et exultione*.[3441] The Society of Jesus began in 1534 when six young men were initiated into the Society, in Paris, with goals of "converting hearts and the minds" to their beliefs.[3442]

In 1537 the Jesuits arrived in Rome where, they adopted the name *La Compagnia di Gesu*, the Company/Army of Jesus as understood in the military sense. Pope Paul III issued a papal bull on September 27, 1540, the *Regimmi Miltantis Ecclesia* that appointed Ignatius the "General of the order."[3443] A 1540 papal bull, *Soceata*/Society, was dubiously misdrafted instead of *Compagnia* that thereafter became their official name.[3444] In fact, the original Society of Jesus was a military order established in 1450 by Pius II to fight the Turks, and to aid in spreading the Christian faith worldwide. Ignatius' new Society of Jesus accepted the same commission as the first order.[3445]

The Jesuit Order was created in the spirit of the Knights Templar to change the Roman church from within, and to bring about the New Babylon. The Jesuit Order's constitution demanded a leader for life, a general, and for all initiates of the army to take oaths of loyalty to the Roman church with the intention to completely overhaul it with the Mary cult. Thus the Society of Jesus was consecrated under the patronage of "Madonna Della Strada," a title for Mary in the Church of the Gesu in Rome, the mother church of the Jesuits, at the instruction of Ignatius shortly before his death.[3446]

Rene d'Anjou (1418–1480) was the grandfather of the Rene d'Anjou who accompanied Joan of Arc.[3447] As such, there are direct connections between the Templars, the King of Jerusalem title, the bloodline Aragon of Spain, the Mary

---

[3440] *Catholic Encyclopedia,* Vol. 14, 81–82.

[3441] Pollen, *Saint Ignatius of Loyola,* 17, 44.

[3442] Regina, *Our Lady of Fatima Crusader Bulletin,* Vol. 41, Issue No. 113, St. Ignatius of Loyola, quoting his biography.

[3443] *Catholic Encyclopedia,* Vol. 14, 81–82; Pollen, *Saint Ignatius of Loyola,* 23.

[3444] Pollen, *Saint Ignatius of Loyola,* 22–23.

[3445] *Catholic Encyclopedia,* Vol. 14, 81–82.

[3446] Gregory Waldrop, "The Dramatic Restoration of the 'Madonna della Strada," *America: The Jesuit Review,* December 21, 2009, https://www.americamagazine.org/issue/720/art/object-devotion.

[3447] Baigent, Leigh, and Lincoln, *Holy Blood and Holy Grail,* 447–448.

apparitions of Ignatius, the Jesuit knight order, their gnostic religions, and their agendas for world government and the New Babylon.

The Jesuit Order expanded quickly between 1541 and 1556 in Europe and around the New World from Canada to Brazil, to Africa and India through the Christian colonization,[3448] where Jesuits advanced the Roman church's agenda as well their own. Jesuits expanded their influence into Roman church education with authority granted to the Jesuit Order by Paul III in 1540, which sanctioned the establishment of Jesuit colleges, universities, and schools, and the authority to educate priests[3449] with their mystical lens, the seven sacred sciences, philosophy, and their proposed New World Order under one religion. Ergo, masonic sources state Jesuits from the beginning adopted the Egyptian model to interpret religion and Scripture: through the "Pursuits of Thoth."[3450] The Jesuit Order adopted initiation vows and rituals from the Egyptian religions and/or hermeticism, to unite their priesthood in like manner as the College of Memphis.[3451] The approach in 1559 was outlined in *Ratio atque Institutio Studiorum Societatis Iesu* (Official Plan of Studies for the Society of Jesus), based in Aristotelian philosophy.

In 1534 at Montmarte, Ignatius established a "squadron of sincere and more effective followers, complete with vows, oaths, and initiations,"[3452] devoted to the Jesuits' lofty agenda. The loyalty oath sworn to by Jesuits thereafter, the *obligatio ad peccandum,* meaning obligation under sin, can be understood as obligation up to the point of sin or an "obligation to sin" when required to carry out the instruction or to protect the order with the highest pressure possible.[3453] The oath uses classic gnostic double entendre tactics to hide their beliefs and agenda in plain sight.

In 1534 the order began to live as ascetic Jesuits, akin to Essenes and their Heliopolis-based cult. In 1538, the Jesuit Order was established as a "Teaching Order" by Pope Paul III, and in 1539 began to carry out projects for the Pope,[3454] all the while gaining more influence. In 1540 Paul III granted the Society of Jesus a "Roman College" with authority to establish Jesuit seminaries to teach upcoming priests. In 1543 the *Injunctum Nobis* bull (enjoined upon us) removed the previous restriction in *Regimini Militantis Ecclesiai* limiting Jesuit membership to sixty members.[3455] Between 1541 and 1550, a new constitution for the Jesuit Order was

---

[3448] Pollen, *Saint Ignatius of Loyola,* 27–41; *Catholic Encyclopedia,* Vol. 14, 81–82.

[3449] Ibid., 41–42; *Catholic Encyclopedia,* Vol. 14, 81-82.

[3450] Mackey, *History of Freemasonry,* 290.

[3451] Ibid.

[3452] Pollen, *Saint Ignatius of Loyola,* 44.

[3453] Ibid., 46.

[3454] Ibid., 42.

[3455] *Catholic Encyclopedia,* Vol. 14, 81–82.

worked on, completed, and enshrined with a papal bull by Pope Julius III in 1550, the *Exposit Debition*; the final touches were added after Ignatius' death in 1556.[3456]

According to masonry, Jesuits strove to be confessors and counselors of kings, to control education, to ultimately to control every government's policy.[3457] Some of highest-degree Rosicrucian rituals contain similarities to Jesuit rituals, because both source their religious originates in Egyptian and Greek mysticism.[3458] Freemasonry and Rosicrucianism were only connected to Jesuits as founders who assigned Jesuits a separate agenda within the larger schema,[3459] an order that reports up to the royal masonic societies. Knowing this makes sense that the Templar Montesa Order led by Francis Borgia funded and then usurped control of the Jesuit Order to ensure the Jesuits became the New Templars within the Catholic Church.

The Jesuit branch order reports to royals in the senior Rosicrucian order, through the Italian Black Nobility of the Committee of Three Hundred or possibly the Council of Thirty-Three. The junior Rosicrucian trunk order reports to higher senior order of the Committee of 300. The Council of Thirty-Three, the Invisible Ones, reports to the European Thirteen Families. The Thirteen European Families seemingly send representatives to senior Thirteen Families throughout the world.

[3456] Pollen, *Saint Ignatius of Loyola*, 44–45; *Catholic Encyclopedia*, Vol. 14, 81–82.
[3457] Mackey, *History of Freemasonry*, 287, 292.
[3458] Ibid.
[3459] Ibid.

FRANCIS BORGIA AND THE MONTESA ORDER

Rev 18:3 For all nations have drunk of the wine of the wrath of her fornication, and the kings of the earth have committed fornication with her, and the merchants of the earth are waxed rich through the abundance of her delicacies.

Francis Borgia/Borja met Ignatius of Loyola when Ignatius was arrested and imprisoned by Inquisition servants in 1529, whereby Borgia secured Ignatius' release.[3460] In time, Borgia recognized the "potential in the extreme military devotion being preached by Ignatius of Loyola."[3461] Borgia was involved with the Jesuit Order from that point on.

During the early years of the Jesuit movement Borgia, the third Duke of Gandia, funded Ignatius' fledgling order, providing life to Ignatius' radical dream.[3462] Ignatius "zealously begged" for Borgia's funding for some time before Borgia

---

[3460] *Catholic Encyclopedia*, Vol. 6, 213–217; Leitner, "Spirituality of Peter Faber," 7; Dorsey, *Secret History of The New World Order,* 475.

[3461] Dorsey, *Secret History of The New World Order,* 475.

[3462] *Catholic Encyclopedia*, Vol. 6, 213–217; Pollen, *Saint Ignatius of Loyola,* 29.

acquiesced.[3463] Borgia later became a Jesuit, the general of the order, and then a saint, fondly remembered as a "founding father in the full sense."[3464] None of the above details regarding Borgia appear to be coincidental.

Francis Borgia was the son of Juan Borgia and the royal princess Juana of Aragon. Francis' great-grandfather was Pope Alexander VI, Rodrigo Borgia, who reigned from 1492–1503.[3465] Another Borgia became noteworthy as Pope as well: Alfonso de Borgia, Pope Calixtus/Callistus III, who established the family's influence in Italy. Calixtus III became Pope in 1455 and was a kinsman of the Italian Caesar Borgia clan.[3466] The Aragonese Borgia were a branch of the Italian Black Nobility Borgia that traced their bloodlines back to Augustus and Julius Caesar via the "gens Julia" of Julius; to the spurious Rephaim, Romulus and Remus; and their parents Mars/Ares and Silvia/Rehea the granddaughter of King Numitor of Alba. Rodrigo Borgia/Pope Alexander VI produced eight sons, one named Pedro Luis who acquired land in the kingdom of Valencia via his hereditary right as the Duchy of Gandia.[3467] Francis Borgia's matriarchal grandfather was the King of Aragon.[3468]

Knowing Borgia's bloodlines explains how he gained influence in 1527 in the court of King Charles V (1516–1558). Charles was a descendant of the house of Hapsburg who received through hereditary right: "so many lands that the sun never set on his dominions." Charles was the son of Philip I, Duke of Burgundy, the son of Maximilian Hapsburg. Charles' mother was Joanna, daughter of Ferdinand I of and Isabella of Aragon.[3469] Charles was elected the Holy Roman Emperor in 1519, succeeding his grandfather Maximilian I Hapsburg. In 1516 when Ferdinand King of Aragon and Spain died, Charles V was named successor even though Juana/Joanna of Aragon was still living. Charles assumed the title king of Castille (1517) and moved to Spain shortly thereafter.[3470] Charles controlled the clergy in his empire by transferring benefices' property to further the ministry and the right of receiving/collecting revenue.[3471] The Hapsburg connection to Spanish kingships explains how the King of Jerusalem title later passed to Juan Carlos Bourbon.

Francis Borgia rose quickly in the Spanish royal court. He became a favorite of Charles, whereby Borgia was appointed Viceroy of Catalonia in 1539. In 1543 Borgia became Duke of Gandia after his father died. During this time, Francis

---

[3463] Pollen, *Saint Ignatius of Loyola,* 42.

[3464] Ibid.

[3465] *Catholic Encyclopedia*, Vol. 6, 213–217.

[3466] "Borgia Family," *Encyclopedia Britannica,* https://www.britannica.com/topic/Borgia-family; *Catholic Encyclopedia* Vol. 3, 183, 187–188; Vol. 6, 213–217; Sire, *Knights of Malta* 128, 149.

[3467] *Catholic Encyclopedia*, Vol. 6, 213–217; *Encyclopedia Americana,* Vol. 23, 664, 676–677.

[3468] *Encyclopedia Americana*, Vol. 13, 664.

[3469] *Catholic Encyclopedia*, Vol. 3, 625–629; *Encyclopedia Americana*, Vol. 6, 319–320.

[3470] *Encyclopedia Americana*, Vol. 11, 122.

[3471] *Catholic Encyclopedia*, Vol. 6, 213–217; Vol. 2, 173–174; *Encyclopedia Americana*, Vol. 6, 319–320; Vol. 21, 743.

Borgia continued to fund Ignatius. In 1546 Borgia invited the Jesuit Order to Gandia to initiate Borgia as the Jesuit "Protector" and "disciple."[3472] In 1550, Borgia left the king's court to be with Ignatius with Charles' full blessing. The Duchy of Gandia then passed on to Borgia's eldest son. In 1554, Borgia was ordained a priest of the Jesuit Order, whereby Ignatius then appointed Borgia the "Commissary General" of the Jesuits and accredited him thereafter with popularizing the Jesuit Order in many countries. In 1565, Francis Borgia became the third "Vicar General" while still reporting to the Spanish court. With *Solicitudo Omniun Ecclesiarum* Borgia added to the rules of the Jesuit Order in 1567 and became a favorite of four popes: Julius III, Pius IV, Pius V, and Gregory VIII.[3473]

As such, Jesuit Father Francis Borgia announced in 1558 his joint funding for Spanish Jesuits with Philip II, successor to Charles V, and that the Jesuits were to aid in the Inquisition and persecution of Protestants.[3474] Borgia then traveled back to Seville Spain to listen in person to a priest named Constantino, whose sermons made him a celebrity in Spain. Borgia ordered Father Juan Suarez, rector of the Jesuits in Salamanca, to leave for Seville to establish a house of Jesuits to investigate Constantino (the hidden Lutheran) as part of the Inquisition against Protestants.[3475]

Adding to the Spanish intrigue, after the Templar suppression in 1307, "two remnants remained after the fourteenth century, the Order of Christ in Portugal and the Order of Montesa in Spain. In the twelfth century Portugal borrowed their rule through Templar support and founded the Portuguese Order of Aviz. Almost at the same time, there arose in Castille the Order of Calatrava."[3476] Ferdinand V of Spain/Ferdinand II of Aragon inherited military orders as their grandmaster: the Calatrava, Alcantara, and Santiago orders.[3477] Understanding military orders were connected to the Templars and Francis Borgia reveals the Jesuit evolution into the New Templars dedicated to bringing about the New Babylon, because chivalric knight orders were all modeled after the Knights Templar organization.[3478] King Philip II, son of Charles V,[3479] held a festival on October 8, 1559, where the last grandmaster of the "military order of Montesa attended, Don Pedro Luis de Borja, who succeeded his father Francis Borgia after Francis joined the Jesuit Order circa 1555."[3480] Knowing Francis Borgia was the grandmaster of

---

[3472] *Catholic Encyclopedia,* Vol. 6, 213–217; Attwater, *Penguin Dictionary of Saints,* 141.

[3473] *Catholic Encyclopedia,* Vol. 6, 213–217.

[3474] Don Adolfo de Castro, *The Spanish Protestants, and Their Persecution by King Phillp II; A Historical Work,* trans. Thomas Parker (London: Charles Gilpin, 1851; Internet Archive, 2007), 85–86, citing a quote from the signed letter from Borja to Pedro de Ribadeneyra.

[3475] Ibid., 221–222.

[3476] *Catholic Encyclopedia,* Vol 10, 305; Vol. 11, 534.

[3477] *Encyclopedia Americana,* Vol. 11, 122.

[3478] Ibid.

[3479] *Encyclopedia Americana,* Vol. 21, 743.

[3480] De Castro, *The Spanish Protestants,* 110–111.

the Montesa Order that succeeded the Templar Order, before he joined the Jesuit Order, reveals how closely Borgia worked with Holy Roman Emperor Charles V and his son Philip II. The Montesa Order, after Don Pedro Luis de Borja, merged into the Jesuit Order as the New Templars, whereby Montesa Order assets were reunited with the Spanish crown,[3481] events most historians mysteriously ignore.

Hence, the gambit of creating the Jesuit Order by the senior Rosicrucian order to reestablish Templars within the Roman church, included assigning a more limited scope of objectives within the greater schema than what the first Templars held. Knowing this explicates why Francis Borgia, royal aide to Charles V of Spain, became the patron for Ignatius' order in 1527—because the king of Spain controlled the Royal Montesa knight order since its inception in 1317 to safeguard Templar assets.[3482] Now, Holy Roman Emperor Charles V, from a bloodline branch of the Austrian Hapsburgs and Castilian Trastamara, revitalized Charlemagne's vision of a "universal monarchy." Charles V oversaw American exploration,[3483] whereby Jesuits once fully established were placed at the forefront of colonization. Charles' predecessor King Ferdinand was granted a series of Vatican bulls in 1493 to explore the New World by Pope Alexander VI, Rodrigo Borgia, which explicates why Charles welcomed Francis Borgia into his court. Alexander VI issued *Inter Caetera* and *Didum Siquidem* that divided the New World land discovered between Spain and Portugal, and *Piis Fidelium* that authorized Spanish kings to be "sovereigns of a New World." Both bulls led to the Treaty of Tordesillas and established faculties to appoint missionaries.[3484]

Even though the Aragonese Templar Order was pronounced innocent of the crimes committed by Templars in other locations, and despite the protest launched by King James II of Spain and Valencia in 1312, Pope Clement V's bull of 1312 of punishment applied to the Aragon Templar Order as well.[3485] However, in 1317, King James II was granted by Pope John XXII authority over the Templar possessions.[3486] James II established a military order to take charge of the Templar assets, an order that did not differ in any way from the Templar Order. Thereafter, the Montesa Order was commissioned to defend Spain from the Islamic Moors and pirates.[3487] Thus, the Montesa Order was founded in 1317 in the reign of Pope John XXII to replace the Templar Order in Spain, but the agreement was "in

---

[3481] *Encyclopedia Americana,* Vol. 19, 402; *Catholic Encyclopedia,* Vol. 11, 534.

[3482] *Catholic Encyclopedia,* Vol. 6, 213–217; Vol. 9, 305; Vol. 11, 534.

[3483] David Armitage, *The Idealogical Origins of the British Empire* (Cambridge: Cambridge University Press, 2000), 2; *Catholic Encyclopedia,* Vol. 6, 213–217.

[3484] Ibid., Vol. 11, 455; *Encyclopedia Americana,* Vol. 11, 122.

[3485] *Catholic Encyclopedia,* Vol. 10, 305; Vol. 11, 534; *Encyclopedia Americana,* Vol. 19, 402.

[3486] *Catholic Encyclopedia,* Vol. 11, 534; *Encyclopedia Americana,* Vol. 19, 402.

[3487] *Catholic Encyclopedia,* Vol. 11, 534.

a certain sense of continuation" of the Templar Order.[3488] The Montesa Order derived its name from St. George and its principal stronghold, the castle of Montesa. Pope John XXII further ordered the new Montesa Order in Spain/Catalan to absorb the Cistercian/Calatrava order of Aragon established by Pope Alexander III in 1164. The Montesa Order was then dedicated to "Our Lady,"[3489] yet another link with the Mary cult of the Jesuits. The year 1317 was the same year of the failed plan to begin a new "rule" of the order Templars within the Catholic Church that were to be known as the "Friars of Rosy Cross."[3490]

Important context for all these kingly gambits surfaces when one learns that King Alphonso I of Aragon had previously, and enthusiastically accepted the Templar Order into their lands from the time of their Catholic inception in 1128 at the Council of Troyes. Templars set up headquarters in Tomo, Portugal in 1160.[3491] Alphonso's Knights of Calatrav "sprang out of the Order of the Temple" as Portuguese Templars.[3492] In 1179, the papal *Manifestis Probatum* issued by Pope Alexander III established Alphonso I as the first king of Portugal (Port of the Grail).[3493] In 1309, King Denis/Diniz of the Bourgogne dynasty placed Portuguese Templar assets under his control. He then created the Order of Christ known also as *Christi Militia* in 1317 for refugee Templar knights. King Denis was son of Alfonso III by his second wife Beatrice of Castile, and grandson of king Alfonso X of Castile, who married Elizabeth of Aragon.[3494] Denis/Deniz received a papal bull in 1319, *Ad Ea Ex Quibus* (to carry out), through Pope John XXII, whereby the new knight order accepted some of the Knights of Calatrava, where both were under Cistercian control. Pope John XXII issued another bull in 1323 that authorized King Denis to turn over the suppressed Templar estates to the Order of Christ, an order flush with former Templars.[3495] The result was a "continuation of the former Templar Order"[3496] again through Aragonese influence. Denis' agreement with John XXII for the Order of Christ in 1317 was the same year as the establishment of the Spanish Montesa Order by King James II of Spain, which took control of all Spanish Templar assets as "the continuation" of the Templar Order.[3497] Both maneuvers completed the kings'

[3488] Ibid.; "Military Order of Montesa," nobility.org, August 12, 2013, http://www.nobility.org/2013/08/12/military-order-of-montesa.

[3489] Ibid.

[3490] Coster, *Knighthoods*, 3–4.

[3491] William Moseley Brown, Simeon B. Chase, and Paul Tice, *Highlights of Templar History: Includes the Knights Templar Constitution* (Whitefish, MT: Kessinger Publishing, 2003). 48.

[3492] *Catholic Encyclopedia*, Vol. 3, 698.

[3493] Ibid., Vol. 11, 534; "Military Order of Montesa."

[3494] Ibid., Vol. 3, 698; Vol. 12, 301.

[3495] Ibid., Vol. 3, 698; Vol. 12, 301.

[3496] Ibid., Vol. 3, 698; Vol. 10, 305; Vol. 12, 301.

[3497] Ibid., Vol. 11, 534.

gambit, awaiting opportunity to reestablish the Templars in the Roman church—which presented itself two hundred years later with Francis Borja.

The strategic maneuvering for Templar assets began with Clement V's bull *Ad Providam* (to emerge) in 1312, which granted rights of seized Templar property to the Knights of St. John Hospitallers. The Montesa Order officially succeeded the older Calatrava order, whose knights became new Montesa recruits.[3498] In Aragon, the Order of Our Lady of Ransom, founded in 1218, was included among the Templar-modeled orders absorbed by the newly founded Montesa Order after the suppression of the Templar Order.[3499] Moreover, Templars by 1150 assembled considerable holdings in the Iberian Peninsula and established castles in Montserrat, a location where the gnostic Essenes/Rex Deus settled, and a key location on the road to Ignatius founding the Jesuit Order.[3500] Accordingly, in 1319 King Henry Trastamara of Castile received the Templar lands in Castille claimed by the Knights of St. John, in return for providing the Knights of St. John commanderies in Aragon. King Henry then acceded control of the former Templar Lands to the Calatrava/Montesa Order.[3501] Fifteen grandmasters reigned over the Montesa Order until 1587, with Francis Borgia and his son being the last two grandmasters, whereafter the assets were reunited with the crown by Philip II.[3502]

The Montesa Order dedicated their order to "Our Lady" at the Montesa Castle under gnostic Cistercian oversight,[3503] just as the Templars, Knights of St. John were, and just as Jesuits worshipped Mary and had the same organizational structure and religion of Templars, and were led by royals. Knowing Jesuit leaders were royals and gnostics, and that they were the new Templar soldiers burrowed into Catholicism to completely restructure the Roman church, makes sense that they accepted the Templar schema to bring about the New Babylon. Articles 4 and 18 of "Secret Rule of the Order" (Templar Order) in *The Book of Baptism of Fire and the Secrets Set Down by the Master Roncelin* stated that only Templar adepts understood that the "New Babylon" was the true Templar agenda.[3504] The original Secret Rule still exists in two copies: one in the Vatican and the other in Hamburg, preserved by Br. Mathieu de Tramlay until 1205, by Robert de Samfort, proxy of the Temple in England (1240), and then by the Master Roncelin de Fos.[3505]

[3498] Ibid.
[3499] Ibid. Vol. 10, 305.
[3500] Addison, *History of the Knights Templar,* 10.
[3501] Sire, *Knights of Malta,* 43.
[3502] *Catholic Encyclopedia,* Vol. 11, 534; "Military Order of Montesa".
[3503] Ibid.
[3504] De Coster, *Knighthoods,* 7, Art. 18; Markale, *Templar Treasure,* 185–188.
[3505] De Coster, *Knighthoods,* 5.

Rev 17:5. .. MYSTERY, BABYLON THE GREAT, THE MOTHER
OF HARLOTS AND ABOMINATIONS OF THE EARTH.

The diabolical New Babylon schema required the reestablishment of the Templar banking system within the Roman church. Controlling banking is a constitutive tactic and elemental institution required for control of the world. Templars established the first international banking network and were the financiers for most of the thrones of Europe.[3506] Templars facilitated fund transfers between Europe and the Holy Land. They were the greatest money institution ever created, developing exchange notes, the check, and creative forms of credit.[3507]

Outside the Roman church, the originally surnamed Bauer family, later surnamed Rothschild, was established by royal masonic organizations and families to control banking.[3508] The house of Rothschild became the mask for Templar banking outside of Switzerland, independent of the Roman church. Rothschild banks funded the Rex Deus agenda outside of the Roman church's influence. The Rothschilds grew rich by funding European wars and utilizing that debt to manipulate malcontent monarchs for their greater agenda. The Rothschilds indebted all the royal houses of Europe to them, including the famous Hapsburg dynasty.[3509]

Just as Templars donned the Red Cross for their emblem, their sister Order of St. John, the Hospitallers donned the white cross.[3510] Likewise in 1307, Clement V issued the bull *Pastoralis Praeemin*entiae (Pastor Preeminence) to confiscate all Templar assets, which set off a scramble across Europe to gain control of Templar wealth. Many Templar adepts fled to other knight orders including the Knights of St. John for protection, smuggling with them most of the French assets. In 1308, Clement V issued *Faciens Misericordiam* (granting forgiveness) to prosecute Templars for blasphemy. He abolished the Templar Order in 1312 with the bull *Vox in Excelso* (a voice from on high), which set off a series of historical events and intrigue, some discussed thus far in this chapter. Just as some French Templar wealth sailed off to Scotland, the larger balance was smuggled to Switzerland for safekeeping among the Knights of St. John, out of the reach of the French king and the Pope. The Templar smuggling gambit became the genesis for Swiss banking, with the Swiss white cross national flag reflecting the Knights of St. John's white cross. The Knights of St. John appeared Christian but were established by royal masons and Cistercian gnostics (c. 1040), modeled after the Knights Templar.[3511]

[3506] Gardner, *Lost Secrets*, 222.
[3507] Markale, *Templar Treasure*, 125, 145.
[3508] Wayne, *Genesis 6 Conspiracy,* 503–510.
[3509] Ibid.
[3510] Markale, *Templar Treasure*, 76, 97.
[3511] *Catholic Encyclopedia*, Vol. 10, 305.

In fact, de Boullion in 1099 provided the Hospitallers with their first endowment in the newly formed feudal state, which prompted many kings and nobles to follow suit, which made the Hospitallers rich and powerful.[3512] By 1113, the Hospitaller organization in Jerusalem, led by Brother Gerard, grew to the point where it required a corporate establishment and was ordained by Pope Paschall II's bull *Pie Postulatio Voluntatis*, and was served by Benedictine/Cistercian monks of the Abbey of St. Mary.[3513] The "white cross of peace on a blood-red field of war" was adopted as the Hospitaller symbol in the time of the wars against Saladin,[3514] and later by the Swiss.

Swiss mercenaries employed abroad returned to Switzerland with large sums of money, which in part became the seed money for the genesis of the Swiss banks and banking system. "To this day, what gives Swiss banks their special distinction is not their corporate inventiveness, which is on the level of the Marble Savings Account, of Rutland, Vermont, but their fortress like security, which is emphasized by the Swiss army. Often, a high-ranking officer in the Swiss bank will be a high-ranking officer in the army." In the foyer of the Federal Assembly in Bern stand four sculptures of mercenaries, honoring the original founders of Swiss banking.[3515] The hidden, anonymous founders were mercenary Knights of St. John and Templars.

In 1180, Kuno von Buchsee of the Knights of St. John Order, after returning from fighting in the Crusades, donated his assets to Hospitallers in the Bern-Mittelland region.[3516] In 1187, the German Knights of St. John priory was appointed to govern the new Swiss outposts, with Bubikon becoming the chief commandery in 1192,[3517] confirmed later that year by Pope Celestine III's order. Thereafter this Swiss region was converted into a Hospitaller/Knights of St. John commandery and was gifted additional lands by neighboring nobles.[3518] The Swiss commandery later became a haven for fleeing Templars, and their wealth in 1307.

In 1315, Duke Leopold of Habsburg attacked several hundred Swiss with his two-thousand-knight and nine-thousand-foot-soldier army. He was met with unexpected and unaccounted-for military prowess, and the new Swiss "Halberd" weapon mounted on a long pole to bring down cavalry. Leopold lost almost two thousand warriors that day.[3519] The famous Swiss mercenaries were called as such to disguise the abolished Templars, who exchanged the wealth they smuggled and loyalty for haven among the Hospitallers, which also in part transformed the Swiss

---

[3512] Sire, *Knights of Malta,* 3.
[3513] Ibid., 4.
[3514] Ibid., 20.
[3515] John McPhee, *La Place de la Concorde Suisse* (New York: Farrar, Straus, Giroux, 1983), 56.
[3516] *Grundlagenbericht: Zum Fusionsentscheid der Gemeinden Diemerswil und Muchenbuchsee* (2021), 6, http://www.diemerswil.ch/media/Grundlagenbericht.pdf.
[3517] Sire, *Knights of Malta,* 191, 193.
[3518] *Grundlagenbericht,* 6.
[3519] McPhee, *La Place de la Concorde Suisse,* 48, 49.

into a banking juggernaut and a formidable military state. Swiss mercenaries, Switzers, became Pontifical Swiss Guard at the Vatican and famous warriors recorded in *Hamlet* as guards for the king.[3520] Switzers donned the white cross because they could not don the red cross for obvious reasons.[3521]

The Knights of St. John are governed by an elected prince of royal bloodlines; it is an order that venerates Mary under the title of "Our Lady of Mount Philermo(s)," known as "Marian spirituality." Hospitallers attributed their success against the Ottoman siege of Malta in 1565 to Mary's intercession, and observe her feast on September 8.[3522] In 1523, the Hospitallers were defeated in Rhodes by Suleiman the Magnificent, the year Ignatius began his Jesuit mission.

As King of Aragon, Charles V of Spain inherited the hereditary right and Anjou claim to throne of Naples, a "papal fief," which dragged Charles into Italian and Vatican politics. This led to the papal and Italian wars between 1521–1529.[3523] In 1527, the war caused the Vatican Bank of Rome to collapse, when Charles invaded Rome, defeating the Swiss Guard;[3524] Switzer leadership was likely in on the plan. Francis Borja was directed by Charles to manage Vatican banking, with plans to move it to Switzerland. In 1528, Borja began his sponsorship for Ignatius' Jesuit Order. Borja later joined, with Charles' blessing.[3525]

In 1529, the holdout Italian states and Clement VII sued for peace with Charles, whereby the subsequent *Intra Arcana* (inside secret or mystery) granted authority of the Americas to Charles, whereby science and Christianity later spread throughout the colonies under his institutions.[3526] Knowing this make sense of Pope Paul III's 1542 papal bull that established the Jesuit Order, *Regimini militantis Ecclesiae* (the Government of the Church Militia), authorizing Jesuits to lead the education within the Roman church and then to establish Catholicism and education throughout the colonies, which set in motion the plan to usurp Vatican banking via Borja and the Montesa Order. In 1543, Paul III issued *Injunctum Nobis,* which repealed a clause in the 1542 bull that limited the numbers in the Jesuit Order. In 1550 Pope Julius III issued the final approval for the Jesuit Order with *Exposit Debitum* (duty demands). In 1551, Borja joined the Jesuit Order.[3527] In 1565, Borja became the third "Father General," renowned as the "Second Founder."

[3520] William Shakespeare, *Hamlet,* Act 4, Scene 5.

[3521] McPhee, *La Place de la Concorde Suisse,* 49.

[3522] "The Icon of Our Lady of Philermos," Sovereign Order of Malta, https://www.orderofmalta.int/sovereign-order-of-malta/the-icon-of-our-lady-of-philermos.

[3523] *Catholic Encyclopedia,* Vol. 6, 213–217; *Encyclopedia Americana,* Vol. 6, 319–320.

[3524] Ibid.

[3525] *Catholic Encyclopedia,* Vol.6, 213–217.

[3526] Ibid.

[3527] Ibid.; Attwater, *Penguin Dictionary of Saints,* 141.

In 1572, Pope Gregory XIII granted Borja's Jesuit Order the rights to Vatican "banking and commerce" and New World commerce, which Borja moved to Switzerland in 1572 and where Templar wealth also moved.[3528] Thus, Vatican and Templar/Hospitaller banking was positioned to partake in royal masonic agendas. Jesuits controlled New World commerce, knowledge, education, and historical records in the Americas under Charles' authority. In 1584 Pope Gregory III issued *Ascendente Domino* (Ascending Domino) to confirm the Jesuit constitution and the privileges already granted to it by popes Paul III, Julius III, Paul IV, and Pius V.

In 1587, King Phillip II, son of Charles V and grandmaster of the Order of the Golden Fleece of the scioned Bourbon/Hapsburg royal bloodlines united the Montesa Order into the Bourbon royal orders.[3529] The Order of the Golden Fleece is a recognized Catholic order of Austria and Spain, even though it is regarded as a secular order. The order was founded by Duke Philip the Good of Bruges, Belgium, and was approved by Pope Eugene IV in 1433. The hereditary right from the house of Burgundy to rule the Order of the Golden Fleece has been disputed since the 1700s,[3530] and continues today between the Bourbon family of Felipe VI of Spain and the Austrian Hapsburg-Lorraine family led by Karl von Hapsburg. The Golden Fleece order has a mythos suggesting it is the most historic and prestigious chivalric order in the world, and thought to include knights such as Queen Elizabeth II (and now King Charles III), Emperor Akihito of Japan, and other ennobled royals from around the world, while the Austrian order boasts another impressive list of royals past and present. Golden Fleece imagery descends from Jason and the Golden Fleece of the gods in Greek history, woven on looms of the gods into the clothing to maintain the immortality of their flesh.

Pope Clement XIII, pressured by European nobility and the demands of Charles III Bourbon of Spain, agreed to suppress Jesuit criminality in Portugal and France in 1768. By 1769 Charles III— who continued to threaten the Pope along with ambassadors from Naples, France, and Spain— forced Clement XIII to disband the Jesuit Order throughout the world. However, Clement III died mysteriously the day before the bull was to be issued.[3531] In 1769, The Rothschild family were appointed guardians for Vatican treasury and banking,[3532] to arrest control from rogue Jesuits. Accordingly, Charles III Bourbon insisted that the incoming Pope must disband the Jesuit Order and continued to press Pope Clement XIV until Charles III succeeded. In 1773 Clement XIV suppressed the Jesuits with *Dominus Redemptor Noster* (our master and redeemer).[3533] After enjoying the

---

[3528] Dorsey, *Secret History of the New World Order*, 527.

[3529] *Catholic Encyclopedia,* Vol. 10, 305, 534.

[3530] Ibid., Vol. 10, 305.

[3531] Ibid., Vol. 4, 32–34; Dorsey, *Secret History of the New World Order*, 575.

[3532] Dorsey, *Secret History of the New World Order*, 684.

[3533] *Catholic Encyclopedia,* Vol. 4, 34–38.

favor of popes and kings for more than two hundred years, overwhelmingly hostility erupted from most of the international nobility, whereby Jesuit missions, colleges, and churches were suddenly seized or destroyed. Jesuits were banished and denounced by the Pope in a gambit akin to the Templar suppression. Some attributed the Jesuit demise to tyrannical "absolutism" imposed by the Bourbon family that began with at the same time the Golden Fleece order split into two factions. However, Jesuits found some protection from the royals in Prussia, Russia, and Austria, where Jesuits were permitted to continue as a teaching organization.[3534]

By 1773, Jesuits were again internationally powerful, akin to the power and influence Templars once wielded; and like the Templars, the Jesuits went rogue. Jesuits no longer submitted to senior Rosicrucian or royal bloodline oversight. They challenged the powerful Bourbon Spanish royal family, their agenda, and control of worldwide banking, likely with support of the then-rival Austrian/Hapsburg Golden Fleece order. Pope Clement XIV disbanded the Jesuit Order under the ruse of Jesuit criminal activity, political insurrection, and treason to ensure that the Jesuits did not interfere with the bloodline agenda.[3535] Clement XIV also died mysteriously in 1774.[3536]

During the French Revolution and Napoleonic Wars, both Pius VI (1798–1800) and Pius VII (1809–1814) were held captive in France. Pope Pius VII resolved during his captivity to reestablish the Jesuit Order, as a full chivalric knight order. In 1814 Pius VII, with *Solicitudo Omnium Ecclesiarum* (care of all the churches), r-established the Society of Jesus. *Sollicitudo Omnium Ecclesiarum* did not replace all the power and authority of previous Jesuit glory days but relegated them to work within the church and to missionary commissions.[3537] However, in 1884, Pope Leo XIII issued *Domiter Inter Alia* (among other things we lament), which nullified the 1773 *Dominus Redemptor Noster* bull and reinstated all previous Jesuit privileges and authority.[3538] In 1870, the "Papal Black Nobility" became famous for backing Pope Pius IX against the House of Savoy/Anjou attempt to seize control of the Vatican.[3539] Popes were confined in the Vatican until the 1929 "Lateran Treaty," when Black Nobility were provided dual citizenship in Italy and the Vatican.[3540]

[3534] Ibid, Vol. 14, 81–82.

[3535] Ibid., Vol. 14, 81–112; Dorsey, *Secret History of the New World Order*, 567.

[3536] Dorsey, *Secret History of the New World Order*, 582; *Catholic Encyclopedia*, Vol 4., 34–37; Vol. 14, 82–112.

[3537] *Catholic Encyclopedia*, Vol. 14, 81–82.

[3538] Ibid., Vol. 14, 81–82; *Encyclopedia Americana*, Vol. 26, 517.

[3539] Ibid., Vol. 12, 135–137.

[3540] Ravi Madanayake, *Black Nobility Terror: Oligarch Elitism* (University of Colorado thesis, 2019), 4.

The senior Italian Black Nobility includes the Pacelli, Borgia, Orsini, Borghese, Masimo, Colonna, Conti families and more.[3541] The Black Nobility of Venice trace their bloodlines back through Emperor Justinian,[3542] while other Italian families trace their bloodlines back to Augustus and Julius Caesar. The junior Italian Black Nobility traces its roots back to the ancient trading empires of Babylon, Persia, Greece, and Phoenicia that later settled in Venice beginning in 1063 and the first Crusades.[3543] They surfaced with Genoan/Venetian dynastic families that controlled the trade rights to the Middle East, whereby they supported crusaders with their navy and military,[3544] bringing them into a relationship with royal knight orders like the Templars. The junior Black Nobility were bankers before the Templars and thought to be the expertise that helped create Templar banking.[3545] The junior Black Nobility is represented in the upper Rosicrucian order, while the senior orders populate the Committee of Three Hundred,[3546] with some in the Council of Thirty-Three and the Thirteen Families.

[3541] Ibid., 5.

[3542] John Coleman, *Conspirators' Hierarchy: The Story of the Committee Of 300,* fourth edition (Las Vegas: World Int. Review, 2010), 126.

[3543] Coleman, *Conspirators' Hierarchy,* 11; Madanayake, *Black Nobility Terror,* 6.

[3544] Coleman, *Conspirators' Hierarchy,* 5, 36. Madanayake, *Black Nobility Terror,* 6.

[3545] Coleman, *Conspirators' Hierarchy,* 17, 79, 80, 117.

[3546] Ibid., 1, 5, 86.

CHAPTER 72

OUR LADY/NOTRE DAME: MARY

Nah 3:3. .. and there is a multitude of slain, and a great number of carcasses; and there is no end of their corpses; they stumble upon their corpses:

Nah 3:4 Because of the multitude of the whoredoms of the well favored harlot, the mistress of witchcrafts, that selleth nations through her whoredoms, and families through her witchcrafts.

Mary apparitions have a long and revered history within the Catholic Church and will begin to levy more influence in the Fig Tree generation, and into the last days. These apparitions have an inexplicable relationship with the doctrines of gnostics, Jesuits, and the polytheist organizations united in a schema to bring about the New Babylon.

As previously mentioned, Mary worship as the mother of God began in 431 at the Council of Ephesus, which incorporated into Mary veneration rituals and imageries that emulated Isis worship, ancient Babylonian rituals, and attributed Mary the "functions of divinity." From that time forward, Mary was a proclaimed a virgin *ante partum, in partu, post partum* (before giving birth, while giving birth,

THE GENESIS 6 CONSPIRACY PART II

and after giving birth), which was confirmed as dogma in 649 at the Lateran Council, and again in 675 at the Tolentino Council.[3547]

Shortly after Ignatius of Loyola received his Mary apparition, another appeared in Guadalupe, Mexico, to Juan Diego, ten years after Cortez defeated the Aztec empire. Juan encountered a "young girl, radiant in the golden mist, who identified herself as the ever-virgin Holy Mary, mother of the True God."[3548] The Marian Guadalupe apparition is part of the Black Madonna mythos of "dark colored, ancient Greek Madonnas" renowned as "miraculous." Mexicans dubbed Mary "La Morena, the dark-complexioned woman" because of her brownish flesh tones.[3549] The Guadalupe apparition thereafter led to millions of Central and South American conversions to the Catholic faith, led by the Jesuit Order.

The golden rays and crescent moon surrounding the Guadalupe apparition are "motifs taken from Revelation 12:1, which many believe represent the Virgin." Other imagery in Guadalupe motifs are forty-six stars, golden fleur-de-lis, and an angel at the feet of Mary[3550]—symbols of fallen angels prostrating to Sophia, noting the flower motif is Anjou and Plantagenet. In gnosticism, Sophia created the Twelve Archons. Guadalupe apparition imagery is identical to a Spanish painting by Bonanat Zaortiza, *The Virgin of Mercy*, displayed in the Museo de Arte de Cataluna in Barcelona dated a hundred years after the Guadalupe apparition.[3551]

In 1814 Pope Pius VII, with *Solicitudo Omnium Ecclesiarum*, reestablished the Society of Jesus. In 1830 Catherine Laboure, a person who claimed to have a "personal angel," received a Mary apparition in Paris. In 1846, two children in the French Alps, Melanie and Maxim Mathieu, encountered a brilliant light that enveloped a woman claiming she was the Virgin Mary. The early nineteenth-century apparitions (and reestablished Jesuit Order) bolstered the Mary movement within the Catholic Church, demanding a proclamation of "Mary's Immaculate Conception."[3552]

Pius IX, a devout believer in the "Blessed Virgin," issued letters in 1849 soliciting views on Immaculate Conception.[3553] In 1854 Pius IX "proclaimed the Immaculate Conception of the Blessed Virgin as a church dogma in the *Ineffabilis*

[3547] Dorsey, *Secret History of the New World Order,* 171, citing Alexander Hislop, *The Two Babylons;* Joe Nickell, *Looking for a Miracle: Weeping Icons, Stigmata, Visions & Healing Cures* (Amherst, NY: Prometheus Books, 1998), 31, citing Marcello Craveri, The Life of Jesus, trans. Charles Lamm Markham (New York: Grove Press, 1967), 27, 28.

[3548] Nickell, *Looking for a Miracle,* 29, 30.

[3549] Ibid., 32, citing Anna Brownell Jameson, *Legends of the Madonna as Represented in Fine Arts* (London: Longman's, Green, 1902) xxxiv; Smith, *The Image of Guadalupe,* 61.

[3550] Ibid., 32.

[3551] Ibid., 132, citing Philip Serna Callahan, *The Tilma Under Infra-Red Radiation,* 18, 22.

[3552] Ibid, 170–172.

[3553] *Catholic Encyclopedia,* Vol. 12, 135–137: Pope Pius IX.

Deus (indescribable God)."[3554] With a stroke of the pen "Mary was preserved exempt from the stain of all original sin at the moment of her animation, and sanctifying grace was given to her before sin could have taken effect in her soul"; thus, sin "was never in her soul" as the "new Eve who was to be the mother of the new Adam."[3555] In 1858, eighteen Mary apparitions of Our Lady of Lourdes manifested in southern France, as witnessed by fourteen-year-old Bernadette Soubirous.[3556] After Bernadette was pressed by officials to ask the apparition's name, the spirit responded to Bernadette with nothing but a "cryptic smile." On the fourth asking, the apparition said, "Que soy era *Immaculada Councepiou* (I am the Immaculate Conception)," speaking in perfect Occitan dialect.[3557] Lourdes is located in the Occitanic region of Catalunya, Basque, Aragon, and Rennes Le Château—home of the Templars, Cathars, Albigensian, Essenes, Alain, Merovingians, and Mary Magdalene.[3558]

Further, Lourdes was occupied with people who spoke the Bigourdian/Bergundian dialect of French, who worshipped a goddess of water, the cognate goddess of their Ligurian neighbors, Marja Gambustas that was known in short form as Morgana, "the personification of an all-powerful spirit that protected grottos and replenished the land's springs." Morgana was the transliterated Roman Greek goddess Diana[3559] of the Tuatha De Danaan. Two-thousand-year-old Diana temples populated Occitan just west of Lourdes.[3560] Bigourdians believed mountain springs were the "elixir of Mother Earth" from "the 'immaculate' womb of Mother Earth" that supplied miraculous healing powers.[3561] Gnostics refer to the Lourdes apparition as the "Sibylline woman."[3562]

The Lourdes apparition was described by Bernadette as a beautiful lady, "lovelier than I have ever seen."[3563] The Lourdes apparition was described in many ways, but the consensus describes Mary as wearing a white veil, a blue dress, a golden rose on each foot, holding a rosary of pearls [of wisdom], and associated with caves and grottos of polytheist mother goddesses. "I saw a lady dressed in white, wearing a

---

[3554] Ibid., Vol. 7, 674–680; Vol. 12, 135–137; Charles River Editors, *The Sanctuary of Our Lady of Lourdes: The History and the Legacy of the Catholic Church's Haven of Miracles* (Ann Arbor, MI: Charles Rivers Editors, Kindle version, 2018), 42.

[3555] *Catholic Encyclopedia*, Vol. 7, 674–680.

[3556] Ibid., Vol. 9, 389–392.

[3557] Charles River Editors, *The Sanctuary of Our Lady of Lourdes*, 33.

[3558] Baigent, Leigh, and Lincoln, *Holy Blood and Holy Grail*, 452, 454; Charles River Editors, *The Sanctuary of Our Lady of Lourdes*, 15.

[3559] G735—*ar'-tem-is*: Greek goddess Diana borrowed by the Asiatics; complete light: flow restrained. Acts 19:24–36.

[3560] Charles River Editors, *Sanctuary of Our Lady of Lourdes*, 9–10.

[3561] Ibid., 11.

[3562] Ibid., 27.

[3563] *Catholic Encyclopedia*, Vol. 9, 389–392.

white dress, a blue girdle and a yellow rose on each foot, the same color as the chain of her rosary; the beads of the rosary were white.. .. From the niche, or rather the dark alcove behind it, came a dazzling light. .. a beautiful young woman, bathed in a halo of light instantly brightened the interior of the pitch-black cave, emerged from the grotto. A glittering cloud of gold carried the arresting figure, dressed in a porcelain-white robe cinched by a broad blue sash, and a matching veil, to recess the upper-right corner of the cave. As soon as the woman stepped off the cloud and onto the niche, bushes of white eglantine and golden roses sprouted around the cranny and by her bare feet."[3564]

In 1862, Pope Pius IX authorized the veneration of Mary of Lourdes. He granted through the bishop of the diocese the permission and justification "in believing in the apparition," as essentially a "canonical coronation" to the apparition image, and then granted status to build the Basilica of Our Lady of the Rosary (Notre Dame du Rosaire de Lourdes). After the basilica was built, it "was consecrated, and the statue was solemnly crowned."[3565]

In 1880, Pope Leo XIII issued *Dolemus Inter Alia* (among other things, we lament), which annulled *Dominus Ac Redemptor Noster* that suppressed the Jesuit Order in 1773, fully reinstating all previous Jesuit privileges and authority. Pope Leo XIII granted Our Lady Montserrat (the location of Ignatius' apparition) minor basilica status in 1881.[3566] Our Lady of Monserrat was depicted in the Black Madonna tradition, elevated to the patron of Catalonia, and canonically crowned by Pope Leo XIII in 1881.[3567] The art designation for the above style of pose is called "Throne of Wisdom" (Sophia), where Mary is depicted with a very elongated face holding an orb in her right hand.

In 1917, "Our Lady" appeared at the Cova da Iria in Fatima, Portugal six times before three children, bringing three prophecies. Portugal, the port of the grail nation, was sponsored by Templars, just as the Lourdes and Montserrat apparitions appeared in important gnostic and Basque/Scythian locations. The Fatima Marian apparition was described as "more brilliant than the sun and radiated a light more intense than a crystal glass filled with sparkling water, when the rays of the burning sunshine through it (*Fourth Memoir*)." She claimed she was an angel from heaven, the "angel of peace," and the guardian angel of Portugal. She told

[3564] Fr. Paolo O. Pirlo, *Our Lady of Lourdes: My First Book of Saints, Sons of Holy Mary Immaculate* (Paranaque City, Philippines: Quality Catholic Publications, 1997), 49–50; Dianne Thomas, *The Grotto of Our Lady of Lourdes* (Durham, UK: White Lyon Films, 2022, Kindle version); Charles River Editors, *Sanctuary of Our Lady of Lourdes*, 27.
[3565] *Catholic Encyclopedia*, Vol. 9, 389–392; Vol. 12, 135–137.
[3566] Ibid., Vol.9, 169-172; "Catholic Church News," *The New York Times*, August 27, 1886.
[3567] Dorothea and Wolfgang Koch, "The Mystery of Montserrat: A Sacred Mountain of Christianity," *Catholic Exchange*, November 12, 2021, mhttps://catholicexchange.com/the-mystery-of-montserrat-a-sacred-mountain-of-christianity.

them on the first vision to "Pray the Rosary every day, in order to obtain peace for the world and the end of the war."[3568]

The first Fatima vision described beings burning in the earth as the ultimate consequence of human sin. The second vision predicted WWI would end, but a worse war would follow. The third vision, a prediction seemingly about Russia for the end of the twentieth century and/or the end times, has been kept secret to this day. The prophecy was sealed in letter on January 3, 1944 and sent to the Pope in 1957.[3569] In 1946, Pope Pius XII granted "canonical coronation" for the Fatima image and Chapel of the Apparitions. In 1950 Pius XII added to the "Immaculate Conception" doctrine of Mary of Pope Pius IX, with the dogma of the "Assumption of Mary" via a papal bull, *Munificentissimus Deus* (the most bountiful God).[3570] Pius XII utilized the authority papal infallibility from *Pastor Aetermus* (the eternal shepherd) instituted in 1871 by Pope Pius IX,[3571] whereby Pius XII proclaimed that Mary had already ascended to heaven in bodily form:

> [Mary] having completed the course of her earthly life, was assumed body and soul into heavenly glory.. .. And so it is that the bodies of even the just are corrupted after death, and only on the last day will they be joined, each to its own glorious soul. Now God has willed that the Blessed Virgin Mary should be exempted from this general rule. She, by an entirely unique privilege, completely overcame sin by her Immaculate Conception, and as a result she was not subject to the law of remaining in the corruption of the grave, and she did not have to wait until the end of time for the redemption of her body.[3572]

"The Assumption" and its feast day, first extended to the entire Catholic dominion by Pius IX, became an official feast day celebrated every August 15 as incorporated by Pius XII in 1950 in *Munificentissimus Deus*.[3573] The feast celebrates

[3568] Jimmy Akin, "Getting Fatima Right," *Catholic Answers*, May 8, 2019, https://www.catholic.com/magazine/print-edition/getting-fatima-right.
[3569] Ibid.
[3570] *Catholic Encyclopedia*, Vol. 1, 7; Vol. 7, 674–680; Nickell, *Looking for a Miracle*, 169, citing Allan Schreck, *Catholic and Christian: An Explanation of Commonly Misunderstood Beliefs*, 173–181.
[3571] *Catholic Encyclopedia*, Vol. 6, 23–32; Vol. 12, 135–137; "Pius XII," *Encyclopedia Britannica*, https://www.britannica.com/biography/Pius-XII.
[3572] Ibid., Vol. 1, 7; Vol. 6, 23–32; Vol. 7, 674–680; Pope Pius XII, "*Munificentissimus Deus*— Defining the Dogma of the Assumption," pars. 4–6, November 1, 1950; Nickell, *Looking for a Miracle*, 169.
[3573] *Catholic Encyclopedia*, Vol. 1, 7; Vol. 6, 23–32; Vol. 7, 674–680; Vol. 12, 135–137.

Mary's physical body ascending to heaven, even though the manner, date, and the certainty of where Mary died is unknown.[3574]

The Society of Jesus was consecrated in the "way of Our Lady" under her saintly patronage as "Madonna Della Strada" (a title for Santa Maria) in the Church of the Gesu in Rome, mother church of the Jesuits, and at the instruction of Ignatius shortly before his death.[3575] One might anticipate that the Mary cult will swallow Catholicism via the Jesuit Order, and then charge to consume much of Christianity before merging with polytheist religions. Lourdes, Fatima, Medjugorje, countless minor Mary apparitions, along with Joan of Arc, the Knights of St. John, and Ignatius' apparitions preach a common doctrine connected to end-time Revelation prophecy. The Mary cult foretells the coming of Babylon and the woman who will sit on many waters, who rides the beast of empires past and future. Medjugorje apparitions tout the Mary apparition to be the queen of kingdoms and the people: the bringer of peace,[3576] the Covenant of Death.[3577]

> Rev 17:1 I will shew unto thee the judgment of the great whore that sitteth upon many waters:
>
> Rev 17:2 With whom the kings of the earth have committed fornication, and the inhabitants of the earth have been made drunk with the wine of her fornication.

In 2010 the Vatican formed a new commission to investigate the Medjugorje Mary apparitions, led by Cardinal Camillo Ruini, retired Vicar General of Rome. In 2013, Jesuit Pope Francis replaced Benedict XVI. In 2014 Cardinal Ruini's commission submitted findings to the "Congregation for the Doctrine of Faith," whereby Pope Francis venerated Medjugorje and linked them to Fatima and other apparitions. In 2017, Ruini's commission released its findings and recommended that the first seven days of the apparitions be approved, and that Medjugorje be transformed into a pontifical sanctuary. Later in 2017, Medjugorje's papal envoy Archbishop Henryk Hoser said, "every indication is that the apparitions will be approved, even as early as this year." In 2018 Archbishop Hoser moved to Medjugorje as apostolic visitor for the parish of St. James, placing Medjugorje under Vatican control.[3578] In his homily, Archbishop Hoser said, "Let us now ask

[3574] Ibid., Vol. 1, 7; Vol. 6, 23–32; Vol. 7, 674–680.
[3575] Ibid., Vol. 14, 87; Waldrop, "The Dramatic Restoration of the 'Madonna della Strada.'"
[3576] Janet T. Connell, *The Visions of the Children: The Apparitions of the Blessed Mother at Medjugorje* (New York: St. Martin's Press, 1992) 4. Isa 28:15–18; Dan 9:27.
[3577] Isa 28:15–18; Dan 9:27.
[3578] Ann Vucic, "The Church's Response to Medjugorje Apparitions—Updated Time Line," Church News, August 17, 2018, https://www.tektonministries.org/timeline-of-churchs-response-to-medjugorje-2.

the fundamental question: Why do so many people come to Medjugorje every year? The clear answer is this: they come to meet someone, to meet God, to meet Christ, to meet his mother. And then to discover the path that leads to the joy of living in the house of the Father and of the Mother; and ultimately to discover the Marian way as the more certain and sure one."[3579]

A methodical, transgenerational schema was executed to introduce the New Babylon with a god-and-goddess pantheon through Marian apparitions and gnostic moles burrowed into the Roman church. One might anticipate the Roman church will venerate Medjugorje's visionaries—Mary's false prophets who make the way for the New Babylon.

> Matt 24:11 And many false prophets shall rise, and shall deceive many.

The Medjugorje apparition is addressed as "Our Lady" and "Our Lady of Peace." She preaches a doctrine of peace united under one "true religion," and that if the world does not repent, we will destroy ourselves from the face of the earth: "You cannot imagine what is going to happen, nor what the Eternal Father will send to the earth. That is why you must be converted! Renounce everything. Do penance.. .. Persevere and help me convert the world."[3580] The Mary dogma is the doctrine of Nimrod (and Semiramis of Babel). [3581] "The Blessed Mother tells the visionaries: "I am the Queen of Peace. I am the Mother of God. I am the Mother of All People on Earth."[3582] The Mary apparition is the mother goddess who chose Ignatius to build the New Babylon.

The six Medjugorje visionaries say: "Mary will crush the head of Satan (Genesis 3:15).. .. If all the people of the earth live out the Fatima peace plan, which the visionaries have outlined, all people would live in peace and abundance."[3583] Anticipate that the Mary will be trumpeted worldwide as the sign in Revelation 12:1–3: the woman wearing a crown of twelve stars clothed with the sun, with the moon under her feet: "They say she appears standing on a cloud wearing a gray dress, a white veil, and a crown of twelve stars." "The visionaries at Medjugorje unhesitatingly refer to her as a great and mysterious sign, and a woman possessed of inordinate beauty. This lady and queen comes in such light, they say, that she seems to be actually clothed with the sun. She has a crown of twelve stars, and she stands on a cloud, as she is described in Apocalypse 12:1."[3584]

[3579] Ibid.
[3580] Connell, *Visions of the Children*, 173.
[3581] Gen 11:1–4.
[3582] Connell, *Visions of the Children*, 4.
[3583] Ibid., 34–35.
[3584] Ibid., 73, 121.

Gnostic doctrine describes Sophia as surrounded by the sun, moon, and stars.[3585] In Gnosticism Sophia is the polytheist Holy Spirit equivalent who came to Mary to bring about the polytheist dragon messiah. In gnostic allegory, the sun/light that clothes the Mary apparitions are Osiris (Satan); the moon is Isis (Sophia); and Horus is the baby antichrist at Isis' feet forming the masonic trinity. The twelve stars/angels/archons (created by Sophia) are also the twelve aeons of zodiac or universe.[3586] Signs and astrology are core doctrines to spurious religions and false prophets who will craftily manipulate end-time Scripture and signs to deceive people to convert. Thus, the Medjugorje apparition stated, "Be converted! It will be too late when the sign comes. Beforehand, several warnings will be given to the world. Have people hurry to be converted.. .. Hurry to be converted. Do not wait for the great sign. For unbelievers, it will be too late to be converted."[3587]

> Rev 12:1 And there appeared a great wonder in heaven; a woman clothed with the sun, and the moon under her feet, and upon her head a crown of twelve stars:
>
> Rev 12:2 And she being with child cried, travailing in birth, and pained to be delivered.

Jacov, one of the six visionaries initiated at Medjugorje, stated, "When the permanent sign comes people will come here from all over the world in even larger numbers. Many more will believe.. .. The Blessed Mother said that there will be some who will not believe even after the permanent sign comes.. .. It [the sign] will be something that has never been on the earth before."[3588]

Mirjana, another of the six visionaries, said, "The first two secrets will be warnings to the world—events that will occur before a visible sign is given to humanity. This will happen in my lifetime. Ten days before the first and second secret I will notify Father Patar Ljubicic. He will pray and fast for seven days, and then he will announce these to the world.. .. I know the day and the date."[3589] The visionaries indicate there are a total of ten secrets/predictions. As per Mirjana, "The first secret will break the power of Satan."[3590] And per Vicka, "The Blessed Mother has promised to leave a permanent sign on Apparition Hill. This is the third secret."[3591]

[3585] Gardner, *Lost Secrets*, 210.

[3586] *Pistis Sophia*, Book II (London: John M. Watkins, 1921), 122–123, 145–146; Bentley Layton, trans., *The Gnostic Scriptures: Ancient Wisdom for the New Age*, 25, 36; Willis Barnstone, *The Other Bible* (New York: Harper & Row, 1980), 53.

[3587] Connell, *Visions of the Children*, 172.

[3588] Ibid., 96.

[3589] Ibid., 60–61.

[3590] Ibid., 60–61.

[3591] Ibid., 115.

One might anticipate the feminization of the Holy Spirit to begin to take root in in Protestantism in preparation to convert non-catholics to the coming woman of Babylon deception.

Babylon understood as Rome city dates to at least Tertullian's time in his work, *Adversus Marcionem* (c. 207–208), a conclusion later adopted by Jerome and Augustine. "Babylon also in our [St.] John is a figure of the city of Rome, as being like [Babylon] great and proud in royal power, and warring down the saints of God."[3592] Tertullian, Irenaeus, and Augustine understood Babylon to be prophetic allegory for end-time Rome and religion. Eusebius wrote in *Church History* (2.15.2) circa fourth century, citing Papias (60–130), that Peter was in Rome when he wrote 1 Peter, saying he was in Babylon. Peter wrote letters in Rome from before AD 68, letters which included Peter's Babylon allegory.[3593] It follows that John of Patmos was provided prophetic allegory well known among the Jewish people and early Christians to describe the end-time throne of idolatry. As such, the comparison of Rome to Babylon was documented in the Apocrypha book of 2 Esdras 15:46, with the end-time destruction of Babylon. Moreover, the Essene Dead Sea Scrolls utilized Babylon as a Pesher code for Rome and its leader in CD 1:5–1 (*Damascus Document/Cairo Damascus*), to avoid persecution.[3594]

[3592] Tertullian, *Adversus Marcionem*, Book III, chapter 13, https://www.newadvent.org/fathers/03123.htm.

[3593] 1 Pet 5:13.

[3594] Dead Sea scroll fragment CD1:5–1 discusses Nebuchadnezzar's 390-year wrath period. The king of Babylon is decoded in Qumran tradition, from Essene Pesher, to be of the length of the Roman occupation of Judea, which they derived from 390 days/years recorded in Ezekiel 4:5.

CHAPTER 73

ROGUE JESUITS

Rev 17:16 And the ten horns which thou sawest upon the beast, these shall hate the whore, and shall make her desolate and naked, and shall eat her flesh, and burn her with fire.. ..

Rev 17:18 And the woman which thou sawest is that great city, which reigneth over the kings of the earth.

Jesuit operatives sponsored by the Italian Black Nobility continue to be active and effective in the larger network of global secret societies.[3595] Anticipate that the Jesuits will once more go rogue, temporarily upending the world order and agenda set in place by Rex Deus kings, before the end-time kings plot to destroy the New Babylon.

The rogue Jesuit gambit may already be afoot, furtively calculating when to supersede the current New World Order schema, which the pure-blood secret society orders have thus far failed to bring about. The Club of Rome was formed to speed up the process for world government, but this Rex Deus gambit has also stalled.

With this in mind, know that in 1968 at the Accademia Dei Lincei of Rome, "The Club of Rome" was founded in part and sponsored by David Rockefeller,[3596] and by extension the Rothschild banking dynasty, whom the Rockefeller's report to as part of the Rothschild stable of agents.[3597] The Club of Rome though was and is populated at the senior level by the Venetian and Genoa Black Nobility, the

---

[3595] Coleman, *Conspirators' Hierarchy*, 16, 27, 35, 111, 185.
[3596] Greer, *Encyclopedia of Secret Societies*, 128–129.
[3597] Jim Marrs, *Rule by Secrecy* (New York: HarperCollins, 2000), 59–62; Kah, *En Route to Global Occupation*, 14–15, 116.

larger European Black Nobility, and the London Nobility.[3598] The Club of Rome has less than one hundred members; all are CFR members[3599] guided by senior Rosicrucian pure bloods from the Committee of Three Hundred.[3600]

This secret society claims to hold the keys to world peace and global prosperity through world government,[3601] boasting they understand the "problematique":[3602] "It is this generalized meta-problem (or meta-system of problems) which we have called and shall continue to call the 'problematique' that inheres in our situation."[3603] The secret society selected and contracted experts in its branches of working ranks: new-science scientists, globalists, environmentalists, future planners, and internationalists "of every stripe."[3604] This organization's objective is to oversee regionalization and then unification of the world, which it has deviously divided into ten political and economic regions.[3605] Thus in 1973, the Club of Rome commissioned a contrived report on anticipated apocalyptic problems, submitting resolution models for peak oil, population explosion, and global-warming disasters[3606] through world government solutions.

In 1968, Jesuits morphed their activities around the world into social work, ecumenism, human rights, and politics, which corresponded with the creation of the Club of Rome gambit. Jesuit ecumenism promotes global Christian unity and exportation of "religious liberation" ideology designed to undermine conservative Christianity. "Liberation theology" was conceived by higher royal masonic organizations and was assigned to the Jesuit Order. Thereafter Jesuit liberation theologists were assigned to work in various Committee of Three Hundred organizations including the Club of Rome.[3607] It follows that in 1968, Jesuit Superior General Father Pedro Arrupe refocused Jesuits with "a preferential option for the poor," opening the door to liberation theology.[3608] Liberation theology derived from social masonry, as a synthesis of Christian and Marxist theology focused on social concern for the poor through political liberation for the oppressed.[3609] The Fabian Society developed social masonry in the 1800s and first launched against the Russian Czars in the form of communism.[3610]

[3598] Coleman, *Conspirators' Hierarchy,* 1, 5, 11.

[3599] Kah, *En Route to Global Occupation,* 40.

[3600] Greer, *Encyclopedia of Secret Societies,* 128–129; Coleman, *Conspirators' Hierarchy,* 2, 4, 5, 7.

[3601] Kah, *En Route to Global Occupation,* 40; Coleman, *Conspirators' Hierarchy,* 10.

[3602] Kah, *En Route to Global Occupation,* 40.

[3603] The Club of Rome, "The Predicament of Mankind: The Quest for Structured Response to Growing World-Wide Complexities and Uncertainties," 1970.

[3604] Coleman, *Conspirators' Hierarchy,* 10.

[3605] Kah, *En Route to Global Occupation,* 40.

[3606] Greer, *Encyclopedia of Secret Societies,* 128–129.

[3607] Coleman, *Conspirators' Hierarchy,* 16, 111.

[3608] "Jesuit," *Encyclopedia Britannica,* https://www.britannica.com/topic/Jesuits.

[3609] Coleman, *Conspirators' Hierarchy,* 203, citing Chris Cook, *Dictionary of Historical Terms,* second edition.

[3610] Wayne, *Genesis 6 Conspiracy,* 523–524, citing Epperson, *Masonry: Conspiracy against Christianity,* 297; Marrs, *Rise of the Fourth Reich,* 8–9; Booth, *The Secret History of the World,* 393.

Liberation theology teaches biblical doctrine through the gnostic interpretative approach and through the lens of the poor, and by implication through Jesuit socialistic politics, liberation/revolution, and the philosophy of the seven sacred sciences. Before the Jesuit Francis became Pope, he "accepted the premise of liberation theology, especially the poor.. .. The option for the poor comes from the first centuries of Christianity. It's the Gospel itself. If you were to read one of the sermons of the first fathers of the Church, from the second or third centuries, about how you should treat the poor, you'd say it was Maoist or Trotskyist."[3611] In 2014, Pope Francis met with Arturo Paoli, an Italian priest and recognized liberation theologian, in a meeting that signaled "reconciliation" between the Vatican and the liberationists.[3612] In 2019 at the World Youth Day held in Panama, Francis discussed changing attitudes toward liberation theology with a group of thirty Central American Jesuits: "Today we old people laugh about how worried we were about liberation theology. What was missing then was communication to the outside about how things really were."[3613]

Francis utilizes liberation theology as one of his tactics to usher in the New Babylon by partnering with left-wing progressive global socialism and their guiding parent secret societies. Francis does this through the ruse of Ignatius of Loyola's 1534 founding vows of poverty, chastity, and obedience for the order. Social masonry, Gnosticism, green theology, and Marian apparitions dominates contemporary Jesuit policy, underpinning their globalist agenda. During a visit to South America, Pope Francis appealed to the world by linking climate change to greed and financial interests referencing Mother Earth/Isis/Mary: "Let us say no to an economy of exclusion and inequality, where money rules. .. economy kills. That economy excludes. That economy destroys Mother Earth."[3614]

The Jesuit oath for initiates include Mary (of the apparitions), John the Baptist (whom gnostics believe was a gnostic and who the Knights of St. John are named after), Ignatius of Loyola, the matrix of God, and the ideological dynamite that Jesuits have the power and authority to overthrow governments:

> Now, in the presence of Almighty God, the Blessed Virgin Mary, the blessed Michael the Archangel, the blessed St. John the Baptist, the

---

[3611] John L. Allen, Jr., "Hard Questions about Francis in Argentina and a Lesson from Chile," *National Catholic Reporter*, April 12, 2013, https://www.ncronline.org/blogs/all-things-catholic/hard-questions-about-francis-argentina-and-lesson-chile.

[3612] John L. Allen, Jr., "Truisms in Catholic Life and a Rundown of Rome News," *National Catholic Reporter*, January 24, 2014, https://www.173.ncronline.org/blogs/all-things-catholic/truisms-catholic-life-and-rundown-rome-news.

[3613] Pope Francis, "'Put Your Lives at Stake': Pope Francis in Dialogue with the Jesuits of Central America," *La Civiltà Catolica*, February 14, 2019, https://laciviltacattolica.com/put-your-lives-at-stake.

[3614] Anna Matranga, "Pope Francis Apologizes for Church's 'Sins' against Indigenous Peoples," CBS News, July 10, 2015, https://www.cbsnews.com/news/pope-francis-apologizes-for-catholic-churchs-sins-against-indigenous-peoples.

holy Apostles St. Peter and St. Paul and all the saints and sacred hosts of heaven, and to you, my ghostly father, the Superior General of the Society of Jesus, founded by St. Ignatius Loyola in the Pontificate of Paul the Third, and continued to the present, do by the womb of the virgin, the matrix of God, and the rod of Jesus Christ, declare and swear, that his holiness the Pope is Christ's Vice-regent and is the true and only head of the Catholic or Universal Church throughout the earth; and that by virtue of the keys of binding and loosing, given to his Holiness by my Savior, Jesus Christ, he hath power to depose heretical kings, princes, states, commonwealths and governments.[3615]

The oath goes onto state that the Jesuits will make relentless war against all those who will not swear allegiance to the Catholic/universal religion (the New Babylon), to exterminate them from the face of the earth. This includes liberals, progressives, and any who will not swear an oath to the coming universal religion, a precursor to the mark of the beast and its oath. The universal church will turn against liberal and progressive elites as well as Christians when they seize control:

I furthermore promise and declare that I will, when opportunity present, make and wage relentless war, secretly or openly, against all heretics, Protestants and Liberals, as I am directed to do, to extirpate and exterminate them from the face of the whole earth; and that I will spare neither age, sex or condition; and that I will hang, waste, boil, flay, strangle and bury alive these infamous heretics, rip up the stomachs and wombs of their women and crush their infants' heads against the walls, in order to annihilate forever their execrable race. That when the same cannot be done openly, I will secretly use the poisoned cup, the strangulating cord, the steel of the poniard or the leaden bullet, regardless of the honor, rank, dignity, or authority.[3616]

Francis says the current world order and its leaders make all the wrong decisions, while calling the NWO: a "New World political authority" and "states."[3617]

[3615] Brooky R. Stockton, *A Family under God: A Biblical Resource for God's Law Order in the Christian Home* (Tijeras, NM: Nike Insights, 2015) 137, citing Carlos Didler, *Subterranean Rome* (New York, 1843); The Jesuit Oath of Induction recorded in the Congressional Record (House Bill 1523, Contested election case of Eugene C. Bonniwell against Thos. S. Butler, Feb 15, 1913, 3215–3216).

[3616] Didler, *Subterranean Rome.*

[3617] Sarah Pulliam Bailey, "10 Key Excerpts from Pope Francis's Encyclical on the Environment," *The Washington Post*, June 18, 2015, https://www.washingtonpost.com/news/acts-of-faith/wp/2015/06/18/10-key-excerpts-from-pope-franciss-encyclical-on-the-environment/?noredirect=on&utm_term=.57d196490c0a.

To this end, Francis calculates and plots how to unite Christians into one church, while preparing to include polytheism under his umbrella religion via the coming Mary cult and doctrinal change:

> He [Francis] seeks to unify all religions, even including nonbelievers, on important global topics. For example, in November 2012 he brought leaders of the Jewish, Muslim, Evangelical, and Orthodox Christian faiths together to pray for a peaceful solution to the Middle East crisis. He has a positive relationship with the Eastern Orthodox Churches; he has friendly meetings with Evangelical Protestants in Argentina; and he has long been recognized as a friend of the Jewish and Islamic communities.[3618]

As such, a Catholic document, "Human Fraternity for World Peace and Living Together," "instructs all persons who have faith in God to unite to advance the awareness of the great divine grace that makes all human beings' brothers and sisters." "The pluralism and the diversity of religions, color, sex, race and language are willed by God. .." and "Therefore, the fact that people are forced to adhere to a certain religion or culture must be rejected."[3619]

Even though the Catholic Church is not a member of the World Council of Churches, it has worked closely with the council for more than forty years, sending observers to all major WCC conferences. The "Pontifical Council for Promoting Christian Unity" nominates twelve members to the WCC's "Faith and Order Commission" as full members. The Catholic Church is a member of other ecumenical bodies such as the National Council of Churches in Australia and the National Council of Christian Churches in Brazil. Knowing this makes sense of what Pope Francis said in 2018 at the World Council of Churches meeting: "The Lord asks us for unity; our world, torn apart by all too many divisions that affect the most vulnerable, begs for unity." On the plane home Francis told reporters that this "was a journey to unity" and "a desire for unity."[3620]

Addressing the WCC, Francis referenced Mark 16:15: "Our lack of unity is in fact not only openly contrary to the will of Christ but is also a scandal to the world and harms the most holy of causes: the preaching of the Gospel to every

---

[3618] "Argentine Jews Praise Pope Francis for Interfaith Dialogue," Fox News, December 7, 2015, https://www.foxnews.com/world/argentine-jews-praise-pope-francis-for-interfaith-dialogue.

[3619] Mary Rezac, "Pope Signs Declaration Saying God 'Wills' Religious Pluralism. What Does This Mean?" *Catholic Herald*, February 5, 2019, https://catholicherald.co.uk/news/2019/02/05/pope-signs-declaration-saying-god-wills-religions-pluralism-what-does-this-mean.

[3620] Ibid.

creature."[3621] Pope Francis often speaks employing a double entendre, while communicating his hidden, true meaning, and in this case "creatures." Creature/ *ktis'is* can be translated creature, creation, being, and creating.[3622] "Creature" in Mark 16 is an odd translation by the KJV translators, particularly when set alongside Matthew 28's parallel account, nations/*eth'nos* meaning a multitude, tribes, races, Gentiles, or nations.[3623] The Vatican recognizes there must be alien life forms, as testified to by the high-ranking Vatican representative for alien life forms and UFOs, Monsignor Corrado Balducci.[3624] The Vatican is preparing to initiate aliens into Babylon, Nephilim, Rephaim, and other Naphalim-created creatures.

Another example of Pope Francis's double-speak occurred in Boston with the "failure of the cross" speech, signaling that the resurrection will eventually be relegated to an allegory, known in gnostic literature as an eucatastrophe: "We must not be afraid to contemplate the cross as a moment of defeat, of failure. When Paul reflects on the mystery of Jesus Christ, he says some powerful things. He tells us that Jesus emptied himself, annihilated himself, was made sin to the end and took all our sins upon himself, all the sins of the world: he was a 'rag,' a condemned man. Paul was not afraid to show this defeat and even this can enlighten our moments of darkness, our moments of defeat."[3625]

What Francis and his Marian cult will preach will not be the true gospel of Jesus Christ but the gospel of end-time world umbrella religion: Babylon. In 2017, Francis replaced Cardinal Gerhard Ludwig Mueller, head of "Congregation for the Doctrine of the Faith" (who was perpetually at odds with Francis' doctrinal changes), with Jesuit Archbishop Luis Francisco Ladaria Ferrer.[3626] Rogue Jesuits have complete control over Catholicism. Anticipate that they will release the Marian cult when the current globalists fail, drag the world into war, and cause cataclysmic sorrows.[3627]

[3621] Gerard O'Connell, "Pope Francis Calls for Concrete Action to Promote Christian Unity, *America: The Jesuit Review*, June 21, 2018, https://www.americamagazine.org/faith/2018/06/21/pope-francis-calls-concrete-action-promote-christian-unity.

[3622] Creature: G2937—*ktis'-is*: building; creation; creature; individual things; beings; ordinance; transliterated: ktisis.

[3623] Matt 28:19. G1484—*eth'-nos*: a race; tribe; foreigner; non-Jewish person; Gentile; heathen; a nation; a people; Gentile Christians; transliterated: ethnos.

[3624] Zecharia Sitchin, *Journeys to the Mythical Past* (Rochester, VT: Bear & Company, 2007), 136–143.

[3625] Alessandro Di Bussulo, "Pope at Mass: The Cross Teaches Us Not to Fear Defeat," *Vatican News*, https://www.vaticannews.va/en/pope-francis/mass-casa-santa-marta/2018-09/pope-francis-mass-santa-marta.html.

[3626] Philip Pullella, "Pope Shakes Up Vatican by Replacing Conservative Doctrinal Chief," Reuters, July 1, 2017, https://www.reuters.com/article/us-pope-mueller/pope-shakes-up-vatican-by-replacing-conservative-doctrinal-chief-idUSKBN19M3GH.

[3627] Matt 24:6–8.

Section VII:
The Fig Tree Generation

Matt 24:32 Now learn a parable of the fig tree; When his branch is yet tender, and putteth forth leaves, ye know that summer is nigh:

Matt 24:33 So likewise ye, when ye shall see all these things, know that it is near, even at the doors.

Matt 24:34 Verily I say unto you, This generation shall not pass, till all these things be fulfilled. Matt 24:35 Heaven and earth shall pass away, but my words shall not pass away.

BABYLON

Isa 47:1 Come down, and sit in the dust, O virgin daughter of Babylon, sit on the ground, there is no throne O daughter of the Chaldeans for thou shalt no more be called tender and delicate.

Knowing the conspiratorial context to how the descendants of giants plan to bring about the end-time in the Fig Tree Generation is key to unlocking allegories embedded in Revelation's Babylon.

End-time Babylon will be an opulent shining city, a universal religion, a rich corporate enterprise, a ruthless geopolitical organization, and an advanced technological beast empire. Many limit their understanding to just one or two of the faces of end-time Babylon, but to fully comprehend the terror that is coming in the Fig Tree Generation, one must discern each Babylonian facade of and how those facets intersect and interact. Comprehending Old Testament details referencing ancient polytheist religions are additional keys to unlocking Revelation's obscure allegories. Old Testament prophecies are a Rosetta stone for Revelation's prophetic allegory, which decodes the meanings captured within specific words describing Babylon.

"The prophetic Babylon city was defined through three ill-famed examples from antiquity. Revelation allegorized this future city as Babylon; Isaiah employed Tyre and Babylon; Jeremiah allegorized Babylon; Zephaniah and Nahum utilized Nineveh."[3628] Each of the cities describe important traits for end-time Babylon. Nineveh and Babylon were royal cities of the Assyrian and Babylon beast empires, just as Babylon city will be for the end-time seventh beast empire that rises phoe-

---

[3628] Wayne, *Genesis 6 Conspiracy*, 315. Isa 47:7–9; 47:1; Jer 51; Nah 1:10–15; 2:1–13; 3:1–19; Zeph 2:13–15.

nix-like from the ashes of the sixth Roman beast empire. Babel, Babylon, and Tyre portray the opulence of end-time Babylon.[3629] Tyre was the famous home of global traders in the ancient postdiluvian world that reflected the worldwide economic and commerce powerhouse end-time Babylon city will become. Nineveh, the ancient city of blood and torture, represents the persecution and genocide Babylon will inflict on the saints in the latter Fig Tree Generation, and all who resist Babylon's forced worship.[3630] One should anticipate Babylon's persecution will increase intensity/sorrows while still in the womb, a sharp increase when it is born, and exponentially increase in the last ten years.[3631]

Building on the notion that Babylon was prophetic allegory for Rome, Babylon/*Baboolone'* in the book of Revelation derived from Nimrod's Babel city, tower, and mystery religion imposed on the Noahites. Babylon/Babel was the ancient capital city of the Chaldeans, meaning tyranny; it was understood as the most corrupt seat/throne of polytheism and the enemy of Christianity; and was the Babylonian city of the beast Babylon empire of Nebuchadnezzar, its territory, and its mystery religion.[3632] Babylon will be the home of worldwide tyranny, a hideous and terrifying beast to all who oppose the great end-time religion.

> Rev 17:18 And the woman which thou sawest is that great city, which reigneth over the kings of the earth.

> Rev 18:24 And in her was found the blood of prophets, and of saints, and of all that were slain upon the earth.

Just as Babel was a city, Babylon was a city, and Rome was a city, future Babylon will be centered in a great city whose organizational tentacles will reach into all the nations of the world. End-time Babylon is called a city nine times in the book of Revelation: 14:8; 17:18; 18:2, 10, 16, 18 (2 times), 19, and 21. It will be a city where religious, political, and commercial organizations are centered. End-time Babylon city will endeavor to reach into heaven, as did Nimrod's Babel city.

> Gen 11:4 And they said, Go to, let us build us a city and a tower, whose top may reach unto heaven.

End-time Babylon will reflect the original Babel syndrome: its Babel religion, government, and tyranny, which held universal sway over all the Noahites

---

[3629] Isa 13:9; Rev 17:4; 18:3, 7.

[3630] Rev 17:5; 18:24.

[3631] Matt 24:8–11; Rev 2:10; 6:9–11; 7:9–17; 18:24.

[3632] G897—*bab-oo-lone'*; of Hebrew origin H894: capital of Chaldea; literal figurative for tyranny; confusion; city of the Babylonian kings; territory of Babylonia; an allegory for Rome as the most corrupt seat/throne of idolatry and the enemy of Christianity; transliterated: Babulon; H894—*Babel, baw-bel'*: confusion; Babylon, including Babylonia and the Babylonian empire.

when Nimrod usurped power as an antichrist archetype. Babel was the prehistoric postdiluvian epicenter for the mystery religions disseminated by its daughters (of Babylon) to all the beast empires and kingdoms throughout the world and throughout the generations. Babel's genitive daughter religions made the way for other postdiluvian antichrist-like figures such as Nebuchadnezzar. End-time Babylon's opulence (Rev 17:4) will be on full display, just as opulence was on display in Babel and Babylon. Thus, Nebuchadnezzar of Babylon was depicted in prophetic allegory as the royal-like lion and the head of gold in the beast and metallic empire prophecies of Daniel. Nebuchadnezzar's opulent Babylon city boasted the hanging gardens, gigantic blue walls, and blue towers.[3633]

> Ps 137:8 O daughter of Babylon, who art to be destroyed. ..

Rome was the tyrannical Roman beast empire and city where a succeeding daughter of Babel was seated in the spirit of Babel. It follows that John's vision requires "wisdom" to discern that Babylon was an allegory for Rome as the seat/throne of idolatry and the enemy of Christianity of that time,[3634] and that Babylon will once more sit on the seven ancient mountains/hills of Rome in the end times: "And here is the mind which hath wisdom. The seven heads are seven mountains, on which the woman sitteth" (Rev 17:9). One further deduces that the "wisdom" John encourages his readers to seek included discerning Babylon's allegory for the "Great Mother of Harlots."

> Rev 17:4 And the woman was arrayed in purple and scarlet color, and decked with gold and precious stones and pearls, having a golden cup in her hand full of abominations and filthiness of her fornication:
>
> Rev 17:5 And upon her forehead was a name written, MYSTERY, BABYLON THE GREAT, THE MOTHER OF HARLOTS AND ABOMINATIONS OF THE EARTH.

Great/*Meg'as* in "Babylon the Great" is defined as splendid on a grand scale, in the external appearance, size, and age, something high in rank and authority with the hubris to overreach the providence of their created being.[3635] End-time Babylon will be akin to the beast empires past led by Rephaim descendants that worshipped the Naphalim. Babylon's woman, the mother goddess, and her religion will arrive on a grand scale, hubris, and glamour beyond description. One might

---

[3633] Jer 51:7, 53; Dan 2:37; 4:30; 7:4.

[3634] G897—*bab-oo-lone'*: allegory for Rome as the most corrupt seat/throne of idolatry and enemy of Christianity.

[3635] G3173—*meg'-as*: big; exceedingly' great or greatest; high/lofty; splendid on a grand scale of external appearance; large; loud; mighty; strong; great in age; great in eminence; proud; arrogant; derogatory to God, a being or something thing that oversteps its providence of creation; transliterated: megas.

anticipate that fallen angels will accompany the "woman," bringing the ancient religion, knowledge, and technology from antediluvian Enochian mysticism.

Revelation 17 described Babylon six times as a woman/*goonay*,[3636] meaning a betrothed woman as in the mother goddess partner to the male god of the pantheon. Betrothed, by implication, indicates a virgin, as with the Mary the apparition, and as Babylon is depicted as the (future) widow at the time of her destruction.[3637] In this line of thinking, Babylon is reminiscent of Zechariah 5:9, where Babylon will be stirred up to sit as the queen of empires, oddly by two female beings with the wind/*ruwach* in their wings—angels who take a feminine form. Zechariah 5's two women have wings like storks/*chaciydah*: female storks (*ah* is the female plural suffix), a word meaning feathered, deriving from *chaciyd* meaning holy one, godly, faithful.[3638]

Zechariah's vision opens with a giant flying scroll described by an accompanying angel. The scroll represents a curse that will go throughout the entire earth for those who steal and swear oaths falsely in God's name. The ephah/basket will be set down in the women's home in Shinar.[3639] The two female angels will set the woman in place to go forth throughout the earth, in a house/*bayith* (a polytheist temple and a dark place) between heaven and earth.[3640] Shinar (Babel/Babylon) indicates the woman is the mother goddess of the Babylon religion.

Further, the scroll appears to be the same prophetic imagery as the scrolls Jesus will unseal to release the curses and catastrophes penned therein (Rev 5:1–14; 6:1–17). Ephah/*'eyphah*, as used in Zechariah, 5 is sometimes translated into English as "basket." Accordingly, the curse that will envelop the world is an ephah that extends from the woman of Babylon/Shinar as she sits on her throne between the ephah/scales. An ephah in antiquity was alternately a measure of a quantity, often established with scales.[3641] Scales are reminiscent of the imagery of the black horse in Revelation's third seal. The scroll's prophetic imagery and the ephah/scales in Zechariah 5 and Revelation 5–6 indicate that both prophecies speak to the same event: Babylon's rise just before the start of the last seven years (Dan 9:27).

> Zech 5:5 Then the angel that talked with me went forth...
>
> Zech 5:6 And I said, What is it? And he said, This is an ephah that goeth forth. He said moreover, This is their resemblance through all the earth.

[3636] G1135—*goo-nay*; a woman; specifically, a wife: a betrothed woman; by implication in many cases a virgin; a widow; transliterated: gune. Rev 17:3, 4, 6, 7, 9, 18.

[3637] Isa 47:1, 7–15; Rev 18:7.

[3638] H2624—*chaciydah, khas-ee-daw*; feminine of 2623: stork; feather; feathers; feathered; H2623—*chaciyd, khaw-seed*: religiously pious; a saint; godly; holy one; faithful one.

[3639] Zech 5:1, 2, 3, 4, 11.

[3640] H1004—*bayith, bah'-yith*: a house; court; daughter; door; dungeon; family; prison; temple; family; a prison Sheol, a place of darkness.

[3641] H374—*'eyphah, ay-faw*: an ephah or measure for grain; a measure in general; dry measure of quantity equal to three seahs, ten omers; liquid measure of nine imperial gallons or forty liters; rabbinical writings are one-half this amount.

Zech 5:7 And, behold, there was lifted up a talent of lead: and this is a woman that sitteth in the midst of the ephah.

Zech 5:8 And he said, This is wickedness.

Zech 5:9 Then lifted I up mine eyes, and looked, and, behold, there came out two women, and the wind was in their wings; for they had wings like the wings of a stork: and they lifted up the ephah between the earth and the heaven.

Zech 5:10 Then said I to the angel that talked with me, Whither do these bear the ephah?

Zech 5:11 And he said unto me, To build it an house in the land of Shinar: and it shall be established, and set there upon her own base.

Revelation 17's woman of Babylon is referenced as "her" seven times, suggesting a goddess. "Her" derives from *owtos'*, a reflexive pronoun indicating a baffling wind blowing backward,[3642] or rebelling. *Outos'* derives from *ahayr'*, meaning breathe, breath, or air,[3643] likely indicating that "her/she" who rides the beast empires is not human. And as we have covered, wind/*ruwach* in the Old Testament means wind or breath, and as well the spirit of a human, an angel, or the Holy Spirit. I find it tantalizing that *ahayr'* in this application may be a transliteration or double entendre of the Hebrew female suffix *ah* and `*iyr* that could be understood as a powerful or female Watcher. Certainly, the texts of Zechariah 5 and Revelation 17 seem to indicate a powerful goddess/`*elowahh* in Hebrew, and Greek *the-hah*[3644] who sits on the seat/throne of Mystery Babylon past and future. It follows that the four riders in Zechariah 6 and Revelation 6 referred as he/him/ *owtos'* might be understood as powerful Watchers.

Great/*Meg'as* mother goddess of ancient pantheons like "the Great goddess Diana"[3645] and their mystical religions is expressed in Revelation as "Mystery, Babylon the Great, the Mother of Harlots and Abominations of the Earth" (Rev 17:5). Mother/*may'tare* means mother as in the source and the motherland.[3646] Latin *magna* means great and is the Greek equivalent of *meg'as*, reflected in the Roman goddess appellation for Cybele of Rome in the time of John of Patmos as the Magna Mater/*May'tare*, just as other Queens of Heaven like Isis, Rhea, Inanna, Ashteroth, and Sophia held the "mother of the gods" title. Magna Mater sky goddesses were renowned in antiquity as the "queens of heaven," as recorded on the

---

[3642] G846—*ow-tos'*: the idea of a baffling wind blowing backwards; reflexive pronoun self: him; her, himself, herself, themselves, itself, he; she, it.

[3643] G109—*ah-ayr'*: to breathe; air; "naturally circumambient"; blow air; the atmospheric region; transliterated: aer.

[3644] G2229 —*the-hah*: a female god; goddess.

[3645] Acts 19:24–37.

[3646] G3384—*may'-tare*: a mother; motherland; figuratively the source of something; transliterated: meter.

Venus Tablet of Ammisaduqa, where Venus was celebrated as the "Bright Queen of Heaven,"[3647] and as Diana the Great was understood as "complete light."[3648]

Inanna's name included a few Sumerian words: *In* meaning the; *Nin* meaning woman or lady; and An/Anu: sky, heaven, or heavenly one that forms—the lady of heaven or the female heavenly one. In the Sumerian epic *Descent of Inanna* she stated, "I am Inanna, Queen of Heaven."[3649] Inanna/Semiramis, Queen of Heaven reigned from the third millennium BC in Chaldea/Babylon and was implemented or reinstated by Nimrod at Babel, which continued into Israel's time.[3650]

> Jer 7:18. .. and the women knead their dough, to make cakes to the queen of heaven, and to pour out drink offerings unto other gods.

Knowing the Queen of Heaven was the ancient worldwide great mother goddess makes sense of Revelation's allegorical description introducing the woman of Babylon as the "great whore who sits on many waters."[3651] Whore/*por'nay* is defined as prostitute, a harlot, and figuratively an "idolator of Babylon i.e., Rome the chief seat of idolatry"[3652] on the seven hills of Rome. *Por'nay* derives from *por'nos*: a fornicator and whoremonger.[3653] The "great whore," Babylon, fornicates with the kings of the earth, which includes the ten kings of the end-time seventh beast empire. Fornication/*porni'ah* means illicit sexual behavior of any form, and figuratively Rome the seat of idolatry,[3654] indicating the end-time Babylon mother religion will sit on the scarlet beast of empires as the scarlet dressed queen enthroned in Rome.

> Rev 17:2 With whom the kings of the earth have committed fornication, and the inhabitants of the earth have been made drunk with the wine of her fornication.

> Rev 17:16 And the ten horns which thou sawest upon the beast, these shall hate the whore.

[3647] Enuma Anu Enilil Tablet, Venus Tablet of Ammisaduqa, Tablet 63. Jer 7:18; 44:17, 18, 19, 25.
[3648] G735—*ar'temis*: Diana; "complete light": "flow restrained."
[3649] *Sumerian Dictionary*, 6, 18: Conjunctions: the/ Ina; Lady: Nin; 3, Anu: heaven; 16, An: heaven, Anu: heavenly one. Diane Wolkstein and Samuel Noah Kramer, *Inanna, Queen of Heaven and Earth: Her Stories and Hymns from Sumer* (New York: Harper Collins, 1983), 54–55.
[3650] Also, Jer 44:17, 18, 19, 25.
[3651] Rev 17:1, 15, 16.
[3652] G4204 —*por'-nay*: figurative for idolater; harlot; whore; idolatress of Babylon, i.e., Rome, the chief seat of idolatry; transliterated: porne.
[3653] G4205—*por'-nos*: a male prostitute; a debauchee libertine; fornicator; a man who indulges in unlawful sexual intercourse; transliterated: pornos.
[3654] G4202—*por-ni'-ah*: harlotry; adultery; incest; illicit sexual intercourse of any form; fornication; idolatry and defilement of idolatry through eating sacrifices offered to idols; transliterated: porneia. Rev 17:1–2, 16.

Revelation entitled Babylon the "Mother of Harlots and Abominations,"[3655] the ancient source and goddess for polytheist rituals and religions both before and after the flood. "Harlots" also derives from *por'nay*. Abomination/*abdel'oogmah* means detestable as in a special kind of idolatry,[3656] which is distributed in a golden cup/grail to drink in true occult tradition.

> Rev 17:4 And the woman. .. having a golden cup in her hand full of abominations and filthiness of her fornication.

Cup/*potay'reeon* is a drinking vessel and figurative for lot or fate. Similarly, Jeremiah 51:7 described the Babylon-like golden cup/*kowc* of lots or potions, and an unclean owl,[3657] reminiscent of occult owl imagery associated with queens of heaven and mother goddesses like Lilith. Unclean owls conjure up images of satyrs, dragons, and screech owls such as those of Isaiah 34:13–14; owl/*liyliyth* means night owl, a female night demon, and a goddess[3658] renowned in the occult as a former queen of heaven, mother goddess degraded to Queen of Demons, and the original "scarlet woman."[3659] Babylon is the feminine cupbearer of the scarlet beast of empires, whose kings willingly and willfully drank the wine of Babylon's fornications from the golden grail of fate that intoxicated her subservient kings that made them mad—the blood wine that leads to Antichrist.

> Jer 51:7 Babylon hath been a golden cup. .. that made all the earth drunken: the nations have drunken of her wine; therefore the nations are mad.

> Rev 17:2 With whom the kings of the earth have committed fornication, and the inhabitants of the earth have been made drunk with the wine of her fornication.

Ezekiel 23's allegory of two daughters of one mother defines the prophetic mother of the harlot's mysterious imagery: Aholah named for Samaria, and Aholibah for Jerusalem, referenced Israel and Judah's backslides into polytheism's mother religion. The allegorical language penned in Ezekiel 23 described the worship of polytheism's pantheon of gods as identical to Revelation 17's religious

[3655] Rev 17:4–5.
[3656] G946—*bdel'-oog-mah*: a detestation in aspecial kind of idolatry; abomination; transliterated: bdelugma.
[3657] G4221—*pot-ay'-ree-on*: drinking-vessel; a cupful; figuratively, a lot or fate; a divine appointment; transliterated: poterion; H3563—*kowc, koce*: a cup as a container; a lot as in a potion; an unclean bird; owl.
[3658] H3917—*liyliyth, lee-leeth'*: a night spectre: screech owl; name of a female goddess remembered as a night demon; nocturnal animal inhabiting desolate places like and owl.
[3659] Davidson, *Dictionary of Angels*, 174–175; Gilley, *Encyclopedia of Demons*, 146–147; *Encyclopedia of World Mythology*, 646–648.

allegories for Babylon's abomination, adultery, whoredoms, harlots, the women goddess, and the cup of desolation making the people drunk.

> Ezek 23:2 Son of man, there were two women, the daughters of one mother:
>
> Ezek 23:4. .. Thus were their names; Samaria is Aholah, and Jerusalem Aholibah.
>
> Ezek 23:33 Thou shalt be filled with drunkenness and sorrow, with the cup of astonishment and desolation, with the cup of thy sister Samaria.
>
> Ezek 23:36. .. wilt thou judge Aholah and Aholibah? yea, declare unto them their abominations;
>
> Ezek 23:37 That they have committed adultery, and blood is in their hands, and with their idols have they committed adultery.. ..
>
> Ezek 23:43 Then said I unto her that was old in adulteries, Will they now commit whoredoms with her, and she with them?
>
> Ezek 23:44 Yet they went in unto her, as they go in unto a woman that playeth the harlot.

The woman's name in Revelation is "Mystery Babylon." Mystery/*Moostay'reeon* means a secret, mystery, hidden knowledge, and the silence imposed by initiation oaths in polytheist religions:[3660] mysticism. Ancient Babel/Enochian mysticism will be the mother religion reestablished in the end times, a worldwide religion that will be forced upon the people of the Terminal Generation with the same temerity as hubris beast kings did in the past. The Queen of Babylon will be seated on "many waters": the Gentile Sea of nations.[3661] The Queen of Empires will sponsor Daniel 9:27's seven-year "covenant with death."[3662] Anticipate Babylon will select the negotiator, the one who then will begin his rise to Antichrist. The "covenant with death" will make the way for Antichrist's eighth beast empire. Babylon will be a universal religion: a kingmaker, the most powerful geopolitical and economic organization on the planet at that time, powered by her religious populace.

> Rev 17:1. .. I will shew unto thee the judgment of the great whore that sitteth upon many waters.. ..
>
> Rev 17:15. .. The waters which thou sawest, where the whore sitteth, are peoples, and multitudes, and nations, and tongues.

[3660] G3466—*moos-tay'-ree-on*: a secret; a mystery through the idea of silence imposed by initiation into religious rites; hidden thing(s); mysteries as in religious secrets confided only to the initiated, and not to ordinary mortals.
[3661] Dan 7:2, 3; Rev 13:1.
[3662] Isa 28:15, 18.

CHAPTER 75

THE SEVEN HILLS OF BABYLON

Rev 17:9 And here is the mind which hath wisdom. The seven heads are seven mountains, on which the woman sitteth.

When the Babylon queen of kingdoms ascends to power with the support of apocalyptic false prophets predicting contrived catastrophes, she will reign from her ancient throne of idolatry. Babylon will reign late in the Fig Tree Generation, from the seven ancient mountains or hills. Mountain/*or'os* can be translated as a mountain(s) or hill rising from a plain.[3663]

The ancient cities Rome and Constantinople emerge as the most plausible suspects for end-time Babylon city. Both are religious centers for a major religion, both were capitols within the east and west divisions of the former Roman empire, and both have seven ancient hills. Constantinople is the home to the Temple of Sophia, the gnostic Queen of Heaven. Rome, though, was acknowledged as the senior and original Roman capital where their beast emperors reigned from. Rome hosts the Pantheon, the temple of all gods. No other ancient seven-hilled city possesses the mythos of Rome, or its equally renowned seven hills mythos.

Archaeological excavations indicate Etruscan habitations from before the eighth century BC were established at Palatine Hill, in the Alban hills near the Tiber River, which the ancients called the *Rumo*. Some time later the Sabines and

---

[3663] G3735—*or'-os*: a mountain; hill; a mount; transliterated: oros. Matt 5:14; Luke 4:29; Rev 17:9.

Latins settled on the Quirinal and Esquiline hills. Between the Palatine and Quirinal hills rose Capitoline Hill, the ancient home of a sacred grove of trees where ancients worshipped the god Jupiter in his famous temple. The Latin, Sabine, and Etruscan settlements on three hills merged sometime before 509 BC. In the reigns of the seven renowned kings, the city expanded to encompass all seven hills; thereafter known as the Septimontium,[3664] which Romulus and Remus originally established in 753 BC: Palatine, Aventine, Caelian, Capitoline, Esquiline, Quirinal, and Viminal.[3665] After the fourth century BC, walls were built around the Septimontium to create the nucleus for Rome city. Thereafter the Septimontium Festival celebrated the enclosing of the wall of Rome around the famous seven hills.[3666]

The worship of Jupiter and his temple on Capitoline Hill (*Templum Jovis Capitolini*) dates to the Aboriginal settlements,[3667] likely to just after the flood by giants, and perhaps before the flood. The seven-mountain mythos is an occult standard in polytheism akin to the seven wandering stars of the pantheon recorded in most polytheist religions, and just as ancient Rome had seven major gods: Saturn, Jupiter, Sol, Diana, Mercury, Venus, and Mars.

Rome's genesis began when King Numitor Silvia went to Latium. He was a descendant from the Trojan King Aeneas, a son of Venus. Numitor's granddaughter was Rhea Silvia. Aeneas was succeeded by his son Julus/Ascanius, the patriarch of the gens Julia/Julus, and ancestor of Rhea Silvia,[3668] to whom many of the Italian Black Nobility trace their genealogy back. Rhea Sylvia was consecrated as vestal virgin (dedicated to the virgin goddess Vesta) after Numitor's brother Amulius usurped the crown. Thereafter, the Roman god Mars raped Rhea, produced two sons, Romulus and Remus (Rephaim). Rhea was cast into prison while her twin sons were cast into the Tiber River. Romulus and Remus were saved by a she-wolf (a goddess).[3669] At this time, the Lupercalia celebration on Palatine Hill was already an annual polytheist festival, suggesting an older lost history. The festival was imported from the Arcadians, a festival dedicated to the god Lycaean Pan (the satyr degraded goat-god and former Watcher), whom the Romans called Inuus.[3670] Later, Rome's founding twins argued over which of the hills should be the center for their new city; Romulus preferred Palatine, while Remus preferred Aventine.[3671]

[3664] *Catholic Encyclopedia*, Vol. 13, 167; *Encyclopedia Americana*, Vol. 23, 664; *Strong's Cyclopedia*, Vol. 9, 109.

[3665] *Encyclopedia Americana*, Vol. 23, 664; Titus Livius, ed. Ernest Rhys, trans. Robert Canon, *The History of Rome* (London: J.M. Dent & Sons Ltd., 1905), Book 1, 1:4.

[3666] *Strong's Cyclopaedia*, Vol. 9, 109–110, 538.

[3667] *Encyclopedia Americana*, Vol. 13, 660.

[3668] *Encyclopedia Americana*, Vol. 13, 664; *Strong's Cyclopaedia*, Vol. 9, 109.

[3669] Livius, *History of Rome*, Book 1, 1:3–4; *Encyclopedia Americana*, Vol. 13, 664.

[3670] Livius, *History of Rome*, 1:5; *Encyclopedia Americana*, Vol. 13, 664.

[3671] Livius, *History of Rome*, 1:7; *Encyclopedia Americana*, Vol. 13, 664.

Vatican Hill was not included within the ancient walls of Rome. By AD 848–852 and Pope Leo IV, the Vatican lands were encircled within Rome's expanded outer walls.[3672] The Vatican is located west of the Tiber River on Vaticum Hill, named after the Etruscan town Vatica/Vaticum in Ager Vaticanus.[3673] Vaticum Hill/*Mons Vaticanus* was a local Etruscan god's home, and a place known for polytheist prophecy.[3674] Vatica/Vatika was an Etruscan and Hindu goddess. Vatican/*Vaticanus* derives from the Latin/Etruscan word *vatic/vatik* meaning "oracular," which in turn derives from Latin/Etruscan *vates*, meaning a seer or a prophet. The second word of the compounded Vaticanus, *canus*, in Latin means old, wise, white, gray, and hoary,[3675] terms associated with Scythian, Rephaim, and Horim tribes. The center for Catholicism is situated on an ancient Etruscan settlement, the Vatica/Vaticum hill.

Vaticum Hill was the home of a Cybele temple, and temples consecrated to Apollo and Mars—ruins from which the first St. Peter's Church was built from in AD 324.[3676] The Cybele temple was a Phrygian temple consecrated to the mother goddess Cybele/Sibylline from before 600 BC.[3677] Vaticum Hill was a "necropolis" worship site from prehistory, which later was rededicated to the goddess Cybele in 204 BC with a new temple during the Second Punic War, when Hannibal of Carthage was plundering the countryside. This Phrygian temple became a branch temple from the main Phrygian Palatine Hill temple. Cybele was typically depicted sitting on her seat/throne at Palatine Hill as "Mother of The Gods," the seat/throne of Mystery Babylon past and future.

At the time of Hannibal's violent romp through Italy's countryside (204–205 BC), strange omens appeared in and around Rome city, including "showers of stones which had fallen during the year."[3678] Sibylline books at *Mons Vaticanus* were inspected with respect to the strange omens and Hannibal's plundering. Oracular writings were found that indicated Rome would win a "grand victory over the foreign invader," and that the invader would be driven out, if the "Mater Idaea" was brought to Rome. Romans in the past, from before the Gaul invasion of 390 BC, consulted the Sibylline oracular writings for guidance when pestilence, inexplicable omens, and invasions occured. The Sibylline books became

---

[3672] *Catholic Encyclopedia*, Vol. 15, 276; *Strong's Cyclopaedia*, Vol. 9, 538.

[3673] *Catholic Encyclopedia*, Vol. 15, 276.

[3674] *Strong's Cyclopaedia*, Vol. 10, 729; Sergio Delli, *Le Strade di Roma* (Rome: Newton & Compton, 1990), 947.

[3675] http://www.latin-dictionary.net/definition/7942/canus-cana-canum.

[3676] Milton S, Terry, trans. *The Sibylline Oracles* (New York: Eaton & Mains, 1899), 3; *Strong's Cyclopaedia*, Vol. 9, 110; https://www.merriam-webster.com/dictionary/vatic; https://etymologeek.com/lat/Vaticanus; https://wordsmith.org/board/ubbthreads.php?ubb=showflat&Number=141737.

[3677] Terry, *The Sibylline Oracles*, 3.

[3678] Livius, *History of Rome*, Book 1; Book 29, 29:10.

so important that two custodians were assigned to care for the writings, and later, ten keepers.[3679] The Romans, in the desperation caused by Hannibal, turned their thoughts to transporting the goddess idol to Rome.[3680] Roman dignitaries traveled to Delphi and Pergamum to convene with a King Attalus, whereby the king directed the Roman dignitaries to Phrygia. There, Attalus gifted the Romans the sacred stone renowned as the "Mother of the Gods," bidding the Romans to transport it to Rome. The sacred image of the goddess was taken to the Temple of the Victory on Palatine Hill.[3681] Palatine Hill then became the home for the Temple of Venus and the Temple of the Magna Mater.[3682]

Cybele was the most honored goddess of the Phrygian empire in Greece from before of the first millennium BC. Cybele was the precursor to Rhea and was the "Mother Goddess" or "Mater" of Phrygia. According to Greek historian Pausanias, Sibyl/Cybele was the "first Herophile," a goddess among the most ancient postdiluvian gods and goddesses. Cybele was honored at Delphi with a great stone, perhaps a figurine or a stone from heaven. She was the daughter of Zeus and Lamia (daughter of Poseidon); in Hebrew mysticism, a Lamia was a title for Lilith. Cybele was the first goddess to chant oracles, followed later by other oracles. Cybele was entitled Idaea, goddess of the nearby forest called Idas.[3683]

The Phrygian empire was recorded in the Assyrian annals during Tiglath-Pileser's reign circa 1116–1098 BC. The Phrygian empire rose from the Anatolian plateau of Asia Minor after the demise of the Hittite empire in the mid-twelfth century BC and was heavily influenced by the Hittite culture.[3684] The Hittites of southeast Anatolia worshipped the goddess Kubaba, linked to the Kybebe, Kybele, and Cybele goddesses of similar appearance, dress, and headdress.[3685]

The branch Palatine/Phrygian temple on Vaticanus Hill, and the temple inside the ancient city of Rome on Palatine Hill, were renowned in the Roman empire's mythos, well before John of Patmos penned the Revelation vision circa AD 95–96. Adding to John's generational context, Rome minted the *Dea Roma* coin in AD 71, with Emperor Vespasian on one side and a Roman goddess wielding a sword while enthroned on seven hills on the flip side, to assert Vespasian had descended from the Roman goddess Venus, or perhaps that Vespasian was honoring the (daughter of Babylon) religion and its mother goddess Cybele. Amor

---

[3679] Ibid., Book 1; Book 3, 3:10; Book 5, 5:13; Book 6, 6:42, 6:65; Book 7, 7:27–28; Book 22, 22:9.

[3680] Ibid., Book 1; Book 29, 29:10.

[3681] Ibid., 29:11–14.

[3682] Ibid., Book 1, 29:37

[3683] Pausanias, *The Description of Greece*, Book 10, 239, 240; Gardner, *Realm of the Ring Lords*, 226–227.

[3684] Hannah Sisk, "Mother Goddess, Male World, Myriad Social Classes: The Cult of Cybele's Impact on Phrygian Culture" (ARCH 0351, Brown University, 2009), 2, 4.

[3685] Ibid., 5.

was the Roman male god of love, the son of Venus; Amor is an anagram of Roma (Rome) spelled backward. John's "wisdom" guidance indicated Christians were aware of the Palatine Hill and Cybele history.[3686]

Vespasian, subsequent Roman emperors, and powerful bloodline families of Rome were familiar with Sibylline Oracles regarding Rome's future. The Cybele/ Sibylline prophecies were well documented in Roman historical records penned by Livius, Pausanius, Plutarch, and Greek historians.[3687] Accordingly, Babylon was equated with Rome in the Sibylline prophecies.[3688]

> Return of Nero. For Hellas, thrice-wretched, shall the poets make lament, when the great and god-like king of great Rome breaks through the ridge of the Isthmus: he whom Zeus himself, they say, begot. This king, terrible and shameless, shall flee from Babylon, hated by every mortal and by all good.. ..[3689]

> The downfall of "Babylon"—Rome. But when after the fourth year a great star shines, which shall of itself destroy the whole earth and from heaven a great star shall fall on the dread ocean and burn up the deep sea, with Babylon itself and the land of Italy, by reason of which many of the Hebrews perished.. ..

> .. . because thou didst seek after enchantments, adultery was in thy midst, with unlawful intercourse with boys, thou woman-hearted city, unrighteous, evil, and wretched beyond all. Woe to thee, thou city of the Latin land, all unclean.. ..[3690]

> Vipers, thou shalt sit a widow on thy hills, and the river Tiber shall bewail thee, his consort, with thy murderous heart and ungodly mind… But thou saidst: "I am alone, and none shall despoil me." Yet now shall God who lives for ever destroy both thee and thine, and no sign of thee shall be left anymore in the land, nor of the old time when the Great God brought thee to honor. Abide thou alone, thou lawless city: wrapt in burning fire, inhabit thou in Hades the gloomy house of the lawless.[3691]

[3686] Rev 17:9.
[3687] Terry, *The Sibylline Oracles*, 4: Preface.
[3688] H. N. Bates, teans., *The Sibylline Oracles, Books III–V* (London: Society for Promoting Christian Knowledge, 1918), Book V, 99:143; 100:155–178.
[3689] Ibid., *Books III–V,* Book V, 99:137–154.
[3690] Ibid., *Books III–V,* Book V, 100:155–178.
[3691] Ibid., *Books III–V,* Book V, 101:170

Rev 17:16 And the ten horns which thou sawest upon the beast, these shall hate the whore, and shall make her desolate and naked, and shall eat her flesh, and burn her with fire.

An infiltrated and corrupted Catholic religion—and the Jesuit and Templar New Babylon idolizing Mary in the mother goddess tradition—may be the initial entrance, renaissance, and epicenter for the scarlet dressed woman/goddess riding the scarlet beast of empires. If so, we should anticipate the world religious center will be transferred to Rome's seven hills, and specifically to Palatine or Capitoline Hill, with Vaticanus Hill submitting as the Catholic branch in the universal and umbrella religion.

CHAPTER 76

BABYLON'S BEAST SYSTEM

Rev 17:3 So he carried me away in the spirit into the wilderness: and I saw a woman sit upon a scarlet-colored beast, full of names of blasphemy, having seven heads and ten horns . . .

Rev 17:7 And the angel said unto me, Wherefore didst thou marvel I will tell thee the mystery of the woman, and of the beast that carrieth her, which hath the seven heads and ten horns.

End-time Babylon will become a worldwide organization that will reach beyond religion. Babylon will control global politics and commerce, all the while growing opulent through its enterprises. End-time Babylon's grip will squeeze its "great riches,"[3692] tribute, from every person and organization in the world, through its imposed, enforced, and futuristic commercial beast system.

Babylon, through its geopolitical alliance of ten kings, will merge technologies currently being developed: artificial intelligence, quantum computing, digital cryptocurrency, a quantum-capable digital medical and messaging technology for disease prevention and long life, sophisticated gene and DNA altering and replication technology, along with advanced pharmaceuticals, nanotechnology, and blockchain-merged surveillance technology for digital passports merged with medical history, social credit history, digital currency—all of which will funnel

---

[3692] Rev 18:17.

through implant technology. In short, Babylon will create the platform that Anti-christ will inherit at the midpoint of the last seven years: "And he causeth all, both small and great, rich and poor, free and bond, to receive a mark in their right hand, or in their foreheads: And that no man might buy or sell, save he that had the mark, or the name of the beast, or the number of his name."[3693] Anticipate Babylon will grow rich through this beast system through an imposed tribute or progressive tax on all commercial transactions worldwide[3694]—a tax to prevent the apocalypse and fund the promised utopia.

The ten kings will fornicate with Babylon's worldwide religion,[3695] impos-ing and enforcing the spurious religion and her beast system. The ten kings will do the bidding of Babylon, ensuring the end-time bloodline oligarchs cooperate, and all who do so will grow rich. The oligarchs and their corporations will be "the merchants" that "grew rich by her"[3696] beast system. The "merchants are the great men of the earth."[3697] Anticipate a scenario where contrived catastrophes akin to pestilences and wars provide opportunities for corporations to amass great wealth and severely diminish small businesses. The bloodline elite and their families will grow in wealth: "And the kings of the earth, who have committed fornication and lived deliciously with her. ..". Delicious/*strayneeah'o* is defined as to live in luxury, and to be wanton,[3698] like Babylon.

Some end-time oligarchs and royals will grow rich from Babylon's beast health-care system: "thy merchants were the great men of the earth; for by thy sorceries were all nations deceived."[3699] Sorcery/*farmaki'ah,* transliterated *as pharmakeia,* and rooted in *farmakyoos'/pharmakeus,* is defined as pharmaceutical medications, a spell giving potions issued by a pharmacist or druggist, concoctions used in idola-try, a poisoner, magical arts, and sorcery. *Farmakos'/*sorcerer also derives from *far-makyoos'.*[3700] Knowing sorceries is communicating pharmaceuticals, legal or illegal, indicates that the great men of the earth will include the pharmaceutical oligarchs and leaders of commercial, professional, and research medical organizations that

---

[3693] Rev 13:16–17.
[3694] *The Protocols of the Learned Elders of Zion,* 10:12; 20:7.
[3695] Rev 17:2; 18:3, 9.
[3696] Rev 18:3, 15.
[3697] Rev 18:23.
[3698] G4763—*stray-nee-ah'-o*: live deliciously; to be wanton; to live luxuriously; excessive strength; eager desire; transliterated: streniao.
[3699] Rev 18:23.
[3700] G5331—*far-mak-i'-ah*; from 5332: medication; pharmacy; magic; sorcery; witchcraft; administering of drugs; poisoning; magical arts used in idolatry; seductions of idolatry; transliterated: pharmakeia; G5332—*far-mak-yoos'*; a drug; spell-giving potion: a druggist; pharmacist; poisoner; magician; sorcerer; transliterated: pharmakeus; G5333—*far-mak-os'*; the same as 5332: sorcerer; transliterated: pharmakos. Rev 9:21; 18:23; 21:8; 22:13.

will forcibly medicate the population in exchange for participation in the Babylon beast system.

One might anticipate that the worldwide healthcare systems will be the delivery system for the *farmaki'ah* to pacify the masses in worship, for travel, and to help cope with the contrived catastrophes of the sorrows/birth pangs reserved for the Fig Tree Generation: wars, rumors of wars, famine, pestilence, and earthquakes. Anticipate as well as that the *farmaki'ah* miracle cures will play an important role for the many contrived pestilences that will plague our generation. The *farmaki'ah* will evolve into implants in preparation for the mark of the beast implementation at the midpoint of the last seven years. One might also anticipate that because of the scourge of pestilence, famine, wars, and other contrived catastrophes, people will demand the most efficient delivery systems, which will come in the form of very technologically advanced implants with the potential to link into a worldwide geomancy matrix and interdimensional beast system.

Knowing that *farmaki'ah* will be one of the necessary control levers for Babylon's beast system, and for the ten-king beast empire, illuminates another cryptic passage recorded in Revelation 9. After the seal catastrophes, five trumpet disasters, followed by the sixth trumpet when the abyss is opened just before the midpoint of the last seven years, when catastrophes will destroy twenty-five percent and then thirty-three percent of the population respectively, medically pacified people will still cling to their pharmaceuticals from Babylon's occultic, alchemic sorceries. Such will be the addiction, dependency, and dominance of Babylon and her *farmaki'ah*.

> Rev 9:23 Neither repented they of their murders, nor of their sorceries, nor of their fornication, nor of their thefts.

The seventh empire's ten beast kings will grow jealous of Babylon's power and wealth until intense hatred overwhelms the ten. One deduces the hatred will include Babylon's covenant agreement that will protect Israel and their rights to sacrifice on a wing of the Jerusalem temple. The protection guarantee will likely be backed by some of the western five kings in the time of the Ezekiel 38–39, Joel 1–2, and Revelation 9 war, started by some eastern kings described in Daniel 11:22. As a result, a great and overwhelming army/armies will be swept away before Antichrist. The hatred of the ten kings will drive them to conspire with Antichrist to destroy Babylon, just after the midpoint of the last seven years, which will introduce in the reign of Antichrist. Babylon will be destroyed by fire in one day and left for only "the habitation of devils [demons], and the hold of every foul spirit, and a cage of every unclean and hateful bird."[3701]

[3701] Rev 17:16; 18:2, 8, 9, 18.

Isaiah 13's dual prophecy provides details and context that meshes perfectly with Babylon's end-time destruction: "And Babylon, the glory of kingdoms, the beauty of the Chaldees' excellency, shall be as when God overthrew Sodom and Gomorrah. It shall never be inhabited, neither shall it be dwelled in from generation to generation" (Isa 13:19–20). Pangs and sorrows of pain, as with a "women that travaileth," will lead to Babylon's destruction as a sign for the coming of the "day of the LORD. .. with wrath and fierce anger" (Isa 13:8–9). This begins the great tribulation of the last three-and-a-half years, not seen since the beginning of the world. [3702]

Such will be the utter destruction of Babylon by Antichrist, the ten kings, and the angels that escape from the abyss (Rev 9) shortly before. Just as Revelation described Babylon's destruction as a place thereafter for demons, foul spirits, and unclean and hateful birds, with the latter seemingly an allegory for fallen angels, Isaiah 13:21–22 detailed these creatures as wild beasts, doleful creatures, owls, satyrs, and dragons—fallen angels or demons.

Revelation 17's prophetic allegory and destruction for the end-time mystery religion and its goddess meshes perfectly with the prophecy in Isaiah 47:

> O daughter of the Chaldeans: for thou shalt no more be called, The lady of kingdoms.. .. And thou saidst, I shall be a lady for ever: so that thou didst not lay these things to thy heart. .. thou that art given to pleasures, that dwellest carelessly, that sayest in thine heart, I am, and none else beside me; I shall not sit as a widow, neither shall I know the loss of children. .. wisdom and thy knowledge, it hath perverted thee; and thou hast said in thine heart, I am, and none else beside me. [3703]

> But these [two things] shall come to thee in a moment in one day, the loss of children, and widowhood: they shall come upon thee in their perfection for the multitude of thy sorceries, and for the great abundance of thine enchantments.. .. Stand now with thine enchantments, and with the multitude of thy sorceries, wherein thou hast labored from thy youth; if so be thou shalt be able to profit, if so be thou mayest prevail. Thou art wearied in the multitude of thy counsels. Let now the astrologers, the stargazers, the monthly prognosticators, stand up, and save thee from these things that shall come upon thee.[3704]

Further connecting Revelation 17–18 to Isaiah 47 are the Hebrew words utilized in the Isaiah chapter. Enchantments/*cheber* is defined as a spell, magician, and a society or company of magicians/charmers. Sorceries/*kesheph* means

---

[3702] Matt 24:7, 8, 21; Mark 13:19; Luke 21:11.
[3703] Isa 47:5, 7, 8, 10.
[3704] Isa 47:9, 12, 13, 14.

magic, sorcery, and witchcraft derived from *kashaph*, meaning whispering a spell, enchant, sorcerer and sorceress, which is also the source word for *kashshaoh*, a magician or sorcerer. Astrologers/*habar* and stargazers/*chozeh* are "horoscopists," "seers," and "prophets."[3705] The sorceries/*kesheph* series of words mesh perfectly with Revelation 17's sorceries/*farmaki'ah*, as does the timing of both prophecies: after the abomination and start to Antichrist's reign that leads to desolation and Armageddon. Knowing that Isaiah 47 is Revelation 17's companion prophecy, one should not be surprised that Babylon's destruction was described identically.

> Isa 47:9 But these two things shall come to thee in a moment in one day, the loss of children, and widowhood: they shall come upon thee in their perfection for the multitude of thy sorceries, and for the great abundance of thine enchantments.

> Isa 47:11 Therefore shall evil come upon thee; thou shalt not know from whence it riseth: and mischief shall fall upon thee; thou shalt not be able to put it off: and desolation shall come upon thee suddenly, which thou shalt not know.

> Isa 47:14 The fire shall burn them; they shall not deliver themselves from the power of the flame: there shall not be a coal to warm at, nor fire to sit before it.

> Rev 18:8 Therefore shall her plagues come in one day, death, and mourning, and famine; and she shall be utterly burned with fire: for strong is the Lord God who judgeth her.

Babylon's sudden destruction was further detailed in the Jeremiah 51 dual prophecy. The Antichrist will destroy/*schachath* the earth in the last three-and-a-half years of this age. He will be the destroying wind/spirit/*ruwach* as well as Babylon's destroyer/*abad*, who is intimately connected to the one who comes up out of the abyss, Abaddon/Apollyon, also meaning destroyer.[3706]

> Jer 51:1 Thus saith the LORD; Behold, I will raise up against Babylon, and against them that dwell in the midst of them that rise up against me, a destroying wind...

[3705] H2267—*cheber, kheh'-ber*: a society; a company; a spell; charmer; magician; enchantment; H3785—*kesheph, keh'-shef*; from 3784: magic; sorcery; witchcraft; H3784—*kashaph, kaw-shaf'*: whisper a spell; enchant; practise magic; sorcerer/sorceress; witchcraft; H3786—*kashshaph, kash-shawf'*; from 3784: a magician; sorcerer; H1895—*habar, haw-bar'*: "horoscopists"; astrologer; H2374—*chozeh, kho-zeh'*: a beholder in vision; seer; prophets.
[3706] Jer 51:1, 11, 25, 55; Rev 9:11; 17:8, 11. H11—'*abaddown*; from 6; H6—'*abad*; G623—*ap-ol-loo'-ohn*.

The "destroying wind" could be understood literally or figuratively, but likely should be understood as both, with the literal describing the methodology of Babylon's destruction, caused by some form of weapon of mass destruction—perhaps nuclear. Further, wind/*ruwach* can refer to an evil angelic spirit, as in fallen angel, just as angels are spirit beings. The narrative and context in Jeremiah 51 indicates a spirit, an angel, when coupled with destroying/*shachath*. A spoiling, destroying spirit will be raised up against end-time Babylon: The "spoilers shall come upon her from the north." Babylon's princes, captains, rulers, and mighty men/ *gibbowriym* will be put into a perpetual sleep.[3707] The spoilers/*shadad*, meaning to oppress and lay waste, will violently destroy/*'abad* Babylon.[3708] Accordingly, when *'abad/'abaddown* is combined with spoiler/*shacath*, Babylon's destruction intersects with Azazel as the leader of the host of the abyss via his "destroyer" and "spoiler" credentials, and as the god of forces Antichrist will honor.[3709] Antichrist will work intimately with Azazel/Abaddon/Apollyon to establish his empire, and to destroy Babylon before the wrath bowls are poured out, and after the ten kings hand their power over to Antichrist at the midpoint of the last seven years, or shortly thereafter.[3710] Knowing this explicates the cryptic prophesies in Revelation 17:

> Rev 17:8 The beast that thou sawest was, and is not; and shall ascend out of the bottomless pit, and go into perdition: and they that dwell on the earth shall wonder, whose names were not written in the book of life from the foundation of the world, when they behold the beast that was, and is not, and yet is.

> Rev 17:11 And the beast that was, and is not, even he is the eighth, and is of the seven, and goeth into perdition.

[3707] Jer 51:48, 53, 56, 57.
[3708] H7703—*shadad, shaw-dad'*: to be burly; powerful; to ravage; a destroyer; oppress; spoiler; lay waste; destroyer. Jer 54–55. H6—*'abad*.
[3709] Dan 11:37–38; Rev 9:11.
[3710] Rev 17:16–18.

CHAPTER 77

THE FOUR HORSEMEN OF THE APOCALYPSE

Rev 5:9 And they sung a new song, saying, Thou art worthy to take the book, and to open the seals thereof: for thou wast slain, and hast redeemed us to God by thy blood out of every kindred, and tongue, and people, and nation.

Anticipate that Revelation's prophecies will be manipulated and reimagined in unprecedented ways in the end times to deceive and delude, first by Babylon and then by Antichrist. If one does not consider Babylon's rise to power throughout the Fig Tree Generation and within that context, one loses important pieces of end-time chronology, opening the door to deceptions.

Anticipate that the interpretive approach to Scripture and end-time prophecy by polytheist forces will deviously create delusions with designs to move up the end-time timetable, to confuse Christians, and to deceive the world into accepting the Ezekiel 38–39, Joel 1–2, and Revelation 9 war as Armageddon. Specious forces will present a fallacious god in a counterfeit religion, false prophets, several dragon messiahs, disingenuous knowledge and signs, and contrived disasters. "And for this cause God shall send them strong delusion, that they should believe a lie: That they all might be damned who believed not the truth, but had pleasure in righteousness."[3711] To achieve this delusion, nemesis groups will steadily increase efforts to diabolically restructure event chronology, in part by conflating Revelation events and dismissing inconvenient Scripture.

Because the book of Revelation burgeons with numerous obscure allegories and a multitude of prophesied events, people become confounded and open to creative interpretations, even though the reimagined interpretations contradict Scripture. Comprehending the book of Revelation requires one to place prophecy around what Jesus said, defining prophetic allegory from within Scripture, and including all relevant passages to ensure there are no conflicts in event chronology. The events and calamities that will occur after each of the seven seals Jesus opens will unfold in perfect harmony and sequence with what Jesus said in Matthew 24, Mark 13, Luke 17 and 21, as one would/should expect. "The Revelation of Jesus Christ, which God gave unto him, to shew unto his servants things which must shortly come to pass; and he sent and signified it by his angel unto his servant John."[3712]

John of Patmos was provided a revelation/*apokal'oopsis* vision by Jesus' angel.[3713] John was commissioned to bear witness to "the testimony of Jesus Christ, and of all things that he saw. .. the things which are, and the things which shall be hereafter," which was the "testimony" "of the word of God" whose "testimony is the spirit of prophecy."[3714] As such, the Revelation prophecy was addressed to the seven churches that "are," regarding events "seen. .. hereafter" in vision. Jerusalem had been destroyed well before John's vision. Hence, the events John saw beginning in Revelation 5 up to Revelation 14:7 were ordained to unfold in the three-and-a-half years that include the abomination events (Rev 13:4–18), even though many say the abomination occurred before Jerusalem's destruction in AD 70. Accordingly, the first three-and-a-half years includes Antichrist's rise among the horns of the end-time empire (Dan 7:8, 20) from the signing of the covenant (Dan 9:27), as well the major events of his rise to power (Dan 11:21–31).

John was stated again to be "in the Spirit on the Lord's day" for the visions he received.[3715] John was still "in the Spirit" of his vision when a door was opened in heaven, and heard a voice saying "Come up hither, and I will shew thee things which must be hereafter."[3716] John's body was not transformed into a new body to live forever, as will happen in rapture;[3717] John died some time later and will be

---

[3711] 2 Thess 2:11–12

[3712] Rev 1:1.

[3713] G602—ap-ok-al'-oop-sis; from 601: disclosure of truth; manifestation, appearance; be revealed, revelation; Transliterated: apokalupsis.

[3714] Rev 1:1–2, 19; 19:10, 13.

[3715] Rev 1:10.

[3716] Rev 4:1.

[3717] 1 Cor 15:50–53.

part of the resurrection of the firstfruits.[3718] John was "immediately" "in the spirit" when he saw God's throne room in heaven,[3719] and was later in the spirit for the testimony of prophecy (Rev 19:10). Spirit/*pnyoo'mah* is cognate to the Hebrew spirit/*ruwach* that included the "prophetic spirit" as part of *ruwach's* many meanings, the "inspiring state of prophecy."[3720] Accordingly, John was not physically in heaven but in the Spirit to receive and bear witness to the vision, a vision akin to Ezekiel and Daniel's visions.

John's vision revealed four riders and their horses that will enter the end-time prophetic stage after Jesus unseals the first four of seven seals,[3721] to begin the denouement of this age:

> Rev 6:1 And I saw when the Lamb opened one of the seals, and I heard, as it were the noise of thunder, one of the four beasts saying, Come and see.

> Rev 6:2 And I saw, and behold a white horse: and he that sat on him had a bow; and a crown was given unto him: and he went forth conquering, and to conquer.

Jesus will likely open the seals just before Daniel 9:27's covenant is confirmed, beginning the last seven years. The beginning of the seven-year covenant holds important prophetic information that helps to explain details regarding the riders and how their afflictions and/or tribulations intersect with the birth sorrows Jesus prophesied: wars, earthquakes, pestilence, and famine.[3722] The riders will appear before the covenant negotiations as an extension of the calamities caused by the increasing sorrow intensity. People will believe they can no longer stay the status quo course—that a drastic correction will be required lest they destroy themselves from the face of the earth. The worst of the coming contrived cataclysms will be predicted by Babylon's false prophets. Knowing this makes sense of Revelation 2:10's impoverished prophetic Smyrna church that will be tried in tribulation for ten days. Understood with Daniel 9:27's week or seven prophetic days/years, the ten days/years of tribulation will begin three years before, when Babylon rises to power through her false prophets.

[3718] 1 Cor 15:20–23.

[3719] Rev 4:2.

[3720] G4151—*pnyoo'-mah;* G4152—*pnyoo-mat-ik-os';* from 4151: of the Divine Spirit; of God the Holy Spirit; one who is filled with the Spirit of God; G7307—*ruwach*: prophetic spirit; "inspiring ecstatic state of prophecy."

[3721] Rev 6:1–8.

[3722] Matt 24:6–8.

One should not be surprised that Daniel's end-time prophetic allegory, prophecies, and visions mesh perfectly with Jesus' end-time "Revelation"[3723] made known to John of Patmos, and with Jesus' oration in Matthew 24, Mark 13, and Luke 17 and 21. One should expect this to be so. Accordingly, Jesus established an important prophetic chronology marker, referencing the abomination as the midpoint of the last seven years, ending the first three-and-a-half-year tribulation of saints that begins the great tribulation of the world and the time of Jacob's trouble. Martyred saints depicted in Revelation 7 will come out of the three-and-a-half-year tribulation/affliction Jesus speaks of in Matthew 24.[3724] Daniel 12:1 marked the time when Michael stands, after the abomination when Judea flees Jerusalem, also recorded in Revelation 12's war in heaven when Michael fights Satan.

> Matt 24:15 When ye therefore shall see the abomination of desolation, spoken of by Daniel the prophet, stand in the holy place, (whoso readeth, let him understand:).

In this line of thinking, Revelation 2's ten days/years of tribulation is yet another prophetic chronology marker, connecting Revelation 2, 6, and the entire Revelation prophecy to Daniel and his prophetic allegories and chronology. If so, there will be an additional three-year tribulation/persecution period of the saints before the last seven years when Babylon comes to power, but less severe than in the first three-and-a-half or last three-and-a-half years. The three-year tribulation assigned to the impoverished prophetic Smyrna church will work in harmony and concurrently with the seals, trumpets, and wrath bowls, and progress in intensity like the birth pangs. The three persecutions appear to be part of catastrophes of each of the seals (25 percent), trumpets (33 percent), and the wrath bowls (100 percent). As such, Revelation 6's seal catastrophe culmination will be preceded by the first three-year tribulation before the last seven years begins. Christians might want to anticipate ever-rising levels of persecution, fomented by the rise of Babylon and her false prophets. Then comes the tribulation of the saints after the covenant signing, followed by the great tribulation of those who refuse the mark of the beast, and refuse to worship Antichrist and Satan. I would counsel Christians to not confuse to persecution during the early birth pangs, or Babylon's persecution as it rises to power, with the two more severe tribulations of the last seven years.

> Rev 2:10 Fear none of those things which thou shalt suffer: behold, the devil shall cast some of you into prison, that ye may be tried; and

---

[3723] Dan 4:5–11; 7:1–15; 8:1–27; 9:21–27; Rev 1:1.
[3724] Jer 30:7; Dan 12:1; Matt 24:9, 15–20, 21; Rev 7:9–14.

ye shall have tribulation ten days: be thou faithful unto death, and I will give thee a crown of life.

The first of four riders of Revelation 6 gallops onto the world's stage mounted upon a white horse. The rider emerges displaying a "bow. .. and a crown was given unto him: and he went forth conquering, and to conquer."[3725] The bow, crown, and rider will be unleashed to go forth through the earth, to establish Babylon's subservient ten-king empire established with Daniel 9:27's covenant signing, which begins the week of years to end sin, reconcile iniquity, bring in everlasting righteousness, to anoint the Holy One of Israel, and to seal up vision and prophecy.[3726]

The first rider's bow and crown allegories hold important information. Bow/ *tox'on* was penned once in the New Testament, in Revelation 6:2. *Tox'on* does not mean a weapon of war, as most would understand a bow in this application. Rather *tox'on* is defined as the simplest of fabrics. *Tox'on* derives from *tik'to*, meaning to bring forth, bear fruit, and the travail of a women giving birth.[3727] The first rider also emerges with a crown/*stef'anos*. *Stef'anos* means an honorary wreath of righteousness, a garland presented to victors in contests like the ancient Greek Olympics, a mark/crown/wreath of royalty and bloodlines from the gods; and a crown/wreath of righteousness awarded to the servants of God.[3728]

The definitions of "bow" and "crown" directs one to search out history and prehistory for context, as the imagery was understood by John. The idioms are reminiscent of Greek white-robed gods and their reigning Nephilim and Rephaim spurious offspring, who proudly donned the laurel wreath of Apollo, created from Daphne after she morphed into a laurel tree: "When on the point of being overtaken by him, she prayed to her mother, Ge, who opened the earth and received her, and in order to console Apollo she created the evergreen laurel tree" (Ovid *Metamorphosis* 1:452). "And the crown of laurel was given to the victors in the Pythian games, for no other reason I think (that according to the prevalent report) Apollo was enamored of Daphne the daughter of Ladon." Daphne in Greek tradition means laurel,[3729] the laurel/Daphne of the mountain/*oros,* known in Greek known as *laurel nobilis* (noble or royal), an aromatic evergreen tree. Laurel is the source word for Lorraine of the Austrian Hapsburg and French Lorraine dynasties of the Anjou, de Bouillon, and de Payen.

[3725] Rev 6:2.
[3726] Dan 9:24.
[3727] G5115—*tox'-on*; from 5088: a bow of the simplest fabric; a bow; transliterated: toxon; G5088—*tik'-to*; a strengthened form of *tek'-o*: produce from seed, as a mother; a plant; the earth; bear; be born; bring forth; be delivered; be in travail; a woman giving birth; transliterated: tikto.
[3728] G4735—*stef'-an-os*; to twine or wreathe; a badge; wreath of royalty; a prized wreath awarded in public games; a crown; a wreath of righteousness; transliterated: stephanos.
[3729] Pausanias, *The Description of Greece*, book 10, 231, and note 2.

The historical context for the definitions of bow and crown indicates that one should anticipate that the universal religion and its sponsored ten kings will deploy imagery from prehistory to establish their mythos, gods, religion, and bloodline pedigree from a time when gods and giants walked among humans. One might anticipate ancient robes and the wreath crown iconology represents the birth of a Babylon-supported end-time beast empire negotiated by a Rephaim royal blood-lined candidate that unites a world devastated by wars and catastrophes. One deduces Antichrist will don the white robe of the gods when he is crowned at the abomination with a laurel wreath crown, counterfeiting Jesus' crown/*stef'anos* of thorns/*ak'anthah*.[3730]

Anticipate as well that the covenant of death will likely be venerated as with a flying laurel wreath banner akin to the stylized wreath logo the United Nations and WHO organizations currently don today in their emblems, surrounding a flattened globe image overlaid onto a sun disc and/or ley lines of the earth. Both organizations are part of the Fig Tree Generation organizations preparing for the birth of Babylon. One might further anticipate that Babylon's false prophets and counterfeit saints will wear white robes.[3731]

> Rev 6:2 And I saw, and behold a white horse: and he that sat on him had a bow; and a crown was given unto him: and he went forth con-quering, and to conquer.

The four rider(s), described as "he" and "him," derive(s) from *owtos'/autos*, a reflexive pronoun for a baffling wind, from *ahayr'* meaning breath, or air,[3732] akin to the feminine pronouns attributed to the Babylon woman. As such, the rider of the white horse does not seem to be human. Moreover, the Revelation 6 riders and horses are connected to the four horse-drawn chariots prophesied in Zechariah 6, an end-time prophecy that culminates with the return of the Branch/Jesus, who will build the "temple of the Lord" for the millennium.[3733]

Zechariah's prophesied horse-drawn chariots imply a rider by implication and application, defined by the angel as "the four spirits of the heavens that go forth from standing before the Lord to all the earth" (Zech 6:5). The spirits/*ruwach* dwelling in heaven and from the throne room are angels.[3734] The four spirits/angels

---

[3730] Matt 27:29; Mark 15:17; John 19:5. G173—*ak'anthah*: thorn; bramble; brier, thorny plant; transliterated ankantha.

[3731] Rev 6:11; 7:1–13.

[3732] G846—*ow-tos'*: a baffling backward wind; the reflexive pronoun for self; himself; herself; themselves; itself; he; she; G109—*ah-ayr'*; to breathe unconsciously; respire; to blow air; air; wind.

[3733] Zech 6:12.

[3734] H7307—*ruwach*. H8064—*shamayim*.

of the heavens that stand before God are the prophetic four winds of prophecy and heaven. The four chariot riders of Zechariah 6 come forth to fulfill prophecy in a spirit connected to conquering and war.[3735] One contemplates whether the four winds are the four archangels documented in First Enoch: Michael, Gabriel, Raphael, and Phanuel/Uriel.[3736] One also ponders the connections to the four winds at the time of Jesus' sign for rapture.[3737]

> Enoch 40:8–9. .. "Who are these four presences which I have seen and whose words I have heard and written down?" And he said to me: "This first is Michael, the merciful and long-suffering: and the second, who is set over all the diseases and all the wounds of the children of men, is Raphael: and the third, who is set over all the powers, is Gabriel: and the fourth, who is set over the repentance unto hope of those who inherit eternal life, is named Phanuel." And these are the four angels of the Lord of Spirits and the four voices I heard in those days.

Each of the four riders from Zechariah and Revelation go throughout the earth to permit what must take place in prophecy. The last three Revelation riders bring forth the consequences from the white horseman that permits conquering/war, directly connected to the ten kings and empires prophesied to rise in Daniel 2, 7, 8 and Revelation 13 and 17. Moreover, Daniel 7's prophecy of beast empires rose from the sea and were stirred up by the "four winds of heaven" (v. 2). Consistent language and prophetic allegory are keys that unlock prophetic allegory and prophetic chronology, if we heed the prophetic markers. Hence, the four riders of Revelation 6 will stir up the seventh empire from the sea in the end times that begins to reign after Babylon sponsors the covenant to begin the last seven years.

> Rev 13:1 And I stood upon the sand of the sea, and saw a beast rise up out of the sea, having seven heads and ten horns, and upon his horns ten crowns, and upon his heads the name of blasphemy.

The same prophetic allegory was penned in Daniel 8 for Alexander's empire that was later broken into four parts led by the "notable ones."[3738] The four kings

---

[3735] Zec 6:5; Rev 6:1–8.
[3736] Enoch 40:1–9; 53:6; 71:8, 9, 12. *Smith's:* "Ra'phael (the divine healer). According to Jewish tradition, the four angels which stood round the throne of God-Michael, Uriel, Gabriel, Raphael."
[3737] Matt 24:31.
[3738] H2380—*chazuwth, khaw-zooth'*: a look; striking appearance; revelation; compact; agreement; notable one; vision; oracle of a prophet.

agreed to rule the empire in four parts after Alexander's death. The four notable ones rose toward the "four winds of heaven."[3739] Winds/*ruwach* surfaces with the four winds of empires in Daniel 7–8, Zechariah 6, and Revelation 6. Daniel 8 works as a companion prophecy with Daniel 7 for defining Revelation 13 and 17's seven horned kings and empires, with Rome and revived Rome extending out of the five Greek empires as it pertains to Daniel 8. Antichrist, as suggested in Daniel 8, rises out of the Greek and Roman empires; Rome was part of and succeeded the Greek empire.

> Dan 8:8 Therefore the he goat waxed very great: and when he was strong, the great horn was broken; and for it came up four notable ones toward the four winds of heaven.

In Zechariah 6, the white horses go to the north, the cognate Revelation 6 rider of conquering and conquest. The red horse was not provided a direction in Zechariah, but in Revelation the red horse follows the white horse to bring war throughout the world. The black horse of Zechariah goes to the north as well; Revelation's black horse comes with scales (famine). Zechariah's "grisled" and "bay" horses (spotted on an indistinct background) go to the south and are the Revelation pale horse that brings death.[3740] The seal judgments bring the increased intensity of the contrived birth pangs of war, rumors of war, famine, pestilence, and earthquakes to 25 percent destruction of the people and the earth.

> Rev 6:4 And there went out another horse that was red: and power was given to him that sat thereon to take peace from the earth, and that they should kill one another: and there was given unto him a great sword.. ..
>
> Rev 6:8 And I looked, and behold a pale horse: and his name that sat on him was Death, and Hell followed with him. And power was given unto them over the fourth part of the earth, to kill with sword, and with hunger, and with death, and with the beasts of the earth.

The Zechariah 6 prophecy follows the Zechariah 5 prophecy when wickedness will be placed in Shinar/Babylon as an ephah/ *'eyphah*: a measure in general, or a measure of grain representing an economic system. Zechariah 5 describes this economic system as a house of thieves, liars, and a curse that envelops the entire earth.[3741] The coming corrupt ephah economic system of Zechariah 5:6 will be

---

[3739] Dan 8:8–9.
[3740] Zech 6:6–8; Rev 6:1–8.
[3741] Zech 5:4. H374—*'eyphah*.

a "curse that goeth forth over the face of the whole earth" and a "resemblance through all the earth."[3742] Curse/*'alah* is an imprecation or oath of cursing, while resemblance/`*ayin* can mean an eye, knowledge, mental or spiritual faculties, affliction, or conceit.[3743] The prophetic allegory seems to be indicating an all-seeing-eye spiritual and global police state that will require oaths of allegiance to Babylon and the fallen Watchers of Mount Hermon, a hi-tech beast system skewed to pamper the rich and noble elite while starving the poor. Micah 6 defines this "abominable" economic system as the "treasures of wickedness in the house of the wicked," utilizing the Hebrew word *'eyphah,* translated as scant measures. The treasures of wickedness will be gained through "wicked balances and deceitful weights."[3744] The abominable measures and balances of Micah 6 and Zechariah 5 produce treasures for the house of thieves of Zechariah 5:3–4,[3745] which seemingly reflect Revelation 6:5's black-horseman balances.

The balances/*dzoogos* of Revelation 6:5 means to join by a yoke as in servitude, obligation, slavery, controlling humans, a mosaic law, and scales,[3746] describing Babylon's oppressive economic system. One might anticipate that a Jesuit or Essene ascetic diet set to law will be imposed by the Babylonian religion, but not on the elite. Babylon will impose an economic system designed to burden and/or enslave most through the corrupted and wicked distribution of food. The elite will grow rich on the backs of serving and slave classes, as they did in prehistory.

Babylon's coming tribulation(s) is further explained by the "hand" that grasps the balances. Hand/*khire* means "the hand hollowed to hold the balances," figuratively, holding power[3747] through the balances. Measure/*khoy'nix,* meaning a dry measure, was enough food for one human for a day[3748] that will be dispensed for a penny/*daynar'eeon* in the ephah system of Micah 6 and Zechariah 5. A *daynar'eeon* was a Roman silver coin valued at a day's labor,[3749] as defined in Matthew 20:2–13. Knowing this brings context to Revelation 17–18, whereby Babylon's economic system is enforced by the ten kings. As such, the wine and oil of Revelation 6:6 will

---

[3742] Zech 5:3, 6.
[3743] H423—*'alah, aw-law':* an imprecation; curse, cursing, execration, oath, swearing; oath of covenant; H5869—`*ayin, ah'-yin;* an eye; an affliction; conceit; an eye showing mental and spiritual faculties; knowledge.
[3744] Mic 6:10–11.
[3745] Zech 5:3–4.
[3746] G2218—*dzoo-gos':* a coupling; servitude to a law or obligation; mosaic law; the beam of the balance connected to scales; pair of balances; yoke; a burden; bondage; slavery; imposed troublesome laws; controlling the destinies of humans; transliterated: zugos.
[3747] G5495—*khire:* the idea of hollowness for grasping; the hand as means or instrument; grasping; a hand symbolizing might and power of God or a god; transliterated: cheir.
[3748] G5518—*khoy'-nix:* a dry measure containing four cotylae or two setarri that is less than one liter; the amount to support a human for one day; transliterated: choinix.
[3749] G1220—*day-nar'-ee-on;* of Latin origin: a denarius or ten asses; pence, a penny-worth; a Roman silver coin that was at that time the average pay for a day's wages; transliterated: denarion.

be reserved for the opulent kings, nobility, and merchant oligarchs.[3750] The woman of Babylon's economic system in Revelation 17–18 is reflected in Zechariah 5:6–8 with the woman and wickedness that sits between the ephah, and the balances in Revelation 6:5.

> Rev 6:5. .. I heard the third beast say, Come and see. And I beheld, and lo a black horse; and he that sat on him had a pair of balances in his hand.
>
> Rev 6:6 And I heard a voice in the midst of the four beasts say, A measure of wheat for a penny, and three measures of barley for a penny; and see thou hurt not the oil and the wine.
>
> Matt 20:2 And when he had agreed with the laborers for a penny a day.

After riders permit havoc throughout the earth, the sixth seal will bring a great earthquake along with the great wars, famine, and pestilence. The destruction will be so intense that the kings, military men, and rich will hide themselves in caves and dens prepared in rocks, mountains, and will say, "the day of his wrath is come; and who shall be able to stand?"[3751] And yet, the trumpet and wrath bowls with stronger disasters will still come.

Revelation 6:9–11 helps sets the timetable for the seal opening and the calamities released by the four riders. The martyred saints shown before God's throne are those who testified for God and were slain. They are part of the firstfruits in the resurrection sequence: "every man in his own order: Christ the firstfruits; afterward they that are Christ's at his coming."[3752] The firstfruits are told to wait a little longer for "brethren, that should be killed as they were, should be fulfilled" (Rev 6:11). The firstfruits likely include the twenty-four elders shown in Revelation 5–6, who will be instructed to wait for those saints yet to be martyred in the tribulation/affliction of the first three-and-a-half years. Firstfruits include the 144,000 and the commission and martyrdom of the two witnesses that will be completed as the seventh trumpet blows in Revelation 11:1, to begin the days of the last trumpet that overlap a little into the last three-and-a-half years.[3753]

> Rev 10:7 But in the days of the voice of the seventh angel, when he shall begin to sound, the mystery of God should be finished, as he hath declared to his servants the prophets.

[3750] Rev 18:3.
[3751] Rev 6:12–17.
[3752] 1 Cor 15:23.
[3753] Rev 7:1–17; 11:1–14; 14:5

> Rev 11:15 And the seventh angel sounded; and there were great voices in heaven, saying, The kingdoms of this world are become the kingdoms of our Lord, and of his Christ; and he shall reign for ever and ever.

The slain firstfruits of Revelation 6 are depicted in the fifth seal after the four horses of the first four seals, and are the martyred saints "slain for the Word of God, and for the testimony which they held"[3754] up to the beginning of the last seven years; they include saints slain in the three years of tribulation preceding the last seven years. The first rider represents the lead-up to and establishment of the end-time empire sponsored by Babylon. The three other horses represent the consequences thereof that convince the inhabitants of the earth to bind together in a worldwide covenant and a New Babel, led by the woman of Babylon and her false prophets.

Accordingly, Revelation 7:1 marks the start to last seven years after the seals are opened, and when the 144,000 (Rev 7:1–8; 14:1–5) and the two witnesses (Rev 11:1) begin their three-and-a-half year mission to preach the gospel to the world, awaken lost Israel, and to stand firmly against Babylon and the seventh beast empire. The two witnesses and the 144,000 will be hated for their prophecies and revelations. The first three-and-a-half years conclude at the abomination, and martyrdom of the two witnesses and the 144,000 firstfruits (Rev 11:3–13; 14:5). The two witnesses' prophetic calamities begin with the four winds that stop blowing.

> Rev 7:1 And after these things I saw four angels standing on the four corners of the earth, holding the four winds of the earth, that the wind should not blow on the earth, nor on the sea, nor on any tree.

> Rev 11:6 These have power to shut heaven, that it rain not in the days of their prophecy: and have power over waters to turn them to blood, and to smite the earth with all plagues, as often as they will.

The discombobulation of the first three-and-a-half years reach an apex with Antichrist's gambit to seize power after a counterfeit Armageddon war prophesied in Revelation 9. The four spirits sent from God are likely the angels who unlock fallen angels chained at the Euphrates near the end of the seventh trumpet blast and the end of the first three-and-a-half years. The chained ones are fallen angels released at the same time the abyss is opened.

[3754] Rev 6:9.

Rev 9:14 Saying to the sixth angel which had the trumpet, Loose the four angels which are bound in the great river Euphrates.

Rev 9:15 And the four angels were loosed, which were prepared for an hour, and a day, and a month, and a year, for to slay the third part of men.

Rev 9:16 And the number of the army of the horsemen were two hundred thousand thousand: and I heard the number of them.

CHAPTER 78

THE TRIBULATION OF THE SAINTS

Rev 2:9 I know thy works, and tribulation, and poverty, (but thou art rich) and I know the blasphemy of them which say they are Jews, and are not, but are the synagogue of Satan.

Much confusion exists around the sequential unfolding of end-time events. Many conflate end-time tribulations with the wrath of God, and the seal, trumpets, and wrath bowls as the same. Some say the tribulation will last seven years; others say three-and-a-half years; some say there is not a defined tribulation period. Discerning the distinction between the wrath and tribulation concepts is another important key to sequencing end-time chronology. Tribulation was, is, and will be a burden required by the saints to endure at the hands of those who rule this world until Armageddon. God's wrath is a specific set of judgments, in a specific time frame, reserved for those who do not choose Jesus and God. The wrath of God begins with the wrath bowls late in the last three-and-a-half years, a distinct trial and judgment that God and Jesus promise to save us from—but not from tribulation.

Wrath is more severe than tribulation and is sourced from God. The pouring-out of God's wrath, indignation, anger, and vengeance extends out the apex of the great tribulation of the last three-and-a-half years, after the abomination, not before. The wrath of God is reserved for the last year of the final week of years, "to make reconciliation for iniquity, and to bring in everlasting righteousness."[3755] God's wrath bowls will be poured out on those who accept the mark of the beast and those who worship Antichrist and Satan.

Conversely, the tribulation of the saints is the persecution by the rulers of this world against those who accept Jesus as their Redeemer and God Most High, until the time of the abomination. The tribulation of the world, versus the saints, envelops part the resurrection sequence, as well as collects all the saints from both the old and new Holy Covenants as the bride of Jesus, in preparation for the "marriage supper of the Lamb."[3756] Jesus instructed that we should expect tribulation, but to have faith that He has overcome this world. Moreover, the book of Acts recorded "that we must through much tribulation enter the kingdom of God."[3757] Hence, we need to distinguish tribulation applications outside of end-time prophecy from tribulation events before the opening of the seal judgments in Revelation 6, as well from tribulation events in the first three-and-a-half years of the last seven, and the great tribulation of the last three-and-a-half years.

Knowing this make sense that New Testament gospel writers penned separate Greek words to distinguish tribulation the saints will go through from the wrath of God against those who reject God in the last year. "Tribulation" surfaces twenty-one times in the New Testament KJV, deriving from Greek *thlip'sis*, defined as afflicted, anguish, burden, persecution, oppression, and trouble.[3758] *Thlip'sis* is recorded forty-five times and was translated eighteen times as affliction, afflictions, and afflicted; three times as trouble; and one time each for anguish, burden, and persecution. Unfortunately, the KJV translators' choices are not always clear or consistent, which has added confusion to discerning end-time chronology.

Paul, in Romans 8, added that tribulation included persecution, famine, peril, and the sword, to be sheep for slaughter levied upon the saints by rulers of this world in his time, and in the time to come. But Paul also noted that tribulations are not able to separate us from Jesus. Tribulation horrors listed by Paul are the same as the end-time sorrows prophesied for the Fig Tree Generation, so one ponders why so many conclude that Christians will not partake in end-time tribulation.

> Rom 8:35 Who shall separate us from the love of Christ? shall tribulation, or distress, or persecution, or famine, or nakedness, or peril, or sword?
>
> Rom 8:36 As it is written, For thy sake we are killed all the day long; we are accounted as sheep for the slaughter.

[3755] Dan 9:24.
[3756] Rev 19:7–9.
[3757] John 16:33; Acts 14:22.
[3758] G2347—thlip'-sis: pressure; afflicted; affliction; anguish; burdened; persecution: tribulation; trouble; oppression. Transliterated: thlipsis.

Additionally, 2 Thessalonians 1 states God will repay those in the end-time who levy tribulation against Christians, and after Jesus is "revealed from heaven with his mighty angels," "immediately after the tribulation of those days," after the abomination, and then will take "vengeance" on the oppressors at Armageddon,[3759] those souls of evil who do evil to both Israel and to Gentiles (Christians), described in Romans 2. The inference is that Christians will indeed suffer tribulation in the end times—indeed, not only Christians but Judah and Israel in a heightened manner. But justice against the persecutors of all the saints, at the end of the great tribulation, will come with the "wrath" of God in the last year.

> Rom 2:5 But after thy hardness and impenitent heart treasurest up unto thyself wrath against the day of wrath and revelation of the righteous judgment of God;
>
> Rom 2:6 Who will render to every man according to his deeds:
>
> Rom 2:7 To them who by patient continuance in well doing seek for glory and honor and immortality, eternal life:
>
> Rom 2:8 But unto them that are contentious, and do not obey the truth, but obey unrighteousness, indignation and wrath,
>
> Rom 2:9 Tribulation and anguish, upon every soul of man that doeth evil, of the Jew first, and also of the Gentile.

Romans 2:8 grouped indignation/*thoomos'* with wrath/*orgay'*; both Greek words are also translated in the New Testament as "wrath," just as wrath/*orgay'* applies to events Jesus describes as the "days of vengeance" in the last three-and-a-half years in the book of Luke.[3760] The "desolation thereof" of the last three-and-a-half years begins when Antichrist's armies surround Jerusalem, bringing about the "abomination that causes desolation spoken by Daniel the prophet," when much of Judah will flee Jerusalem.[3761] The days/years of vengeance/*ekdik'aysis* (Luke 21:22) will bring the "great distress" and then wrath/*orgay'* (justifiable abhorrence, indignation, anger, or vengeance) on earth as the extension thereof of "those days" of the great tribulation (Matt 24:21).[3762] The book of Luke described the "great tribulation" not seen since the beginning of the world as events that leads to wrath.

[3759] 2 Thess 1:6–9; Matt 24:29–31, 15–20; Mark 13:24–27, 13–20, respectively.

[3760] Luke 21:22–23.

[3761] Luke 21:20–21; Matt 24:15; Mark 13:14; Dan 11:31, respectively.

[3762] Vengeance: G1557—*ek-dik'-ay-sis*: vindication; retribution; revenge; punishment; transliterated: ekdikesis; G3709—*or-gay'*: violent passion; justifiable abhorrence; punishment; anger; indignation; vengeance; wrath; transliterated: orge.

Luke 21.22 For these be the days of vengeance, that all things which are written may be fulfilled.

Luke 21.23 But woe unto them that are with child, and to them that give suck, in those days! for there shall be great distress in the land, and wrath upon this people.

Matt 24.21 For then shall be great tribulation, such as was not since the beginning of the world to this time, no, nor ever shall be.

Mark 13.19 For in those days shall be affliction, such as was not from the beginning of the creation which God created unto this time, neither shall be.

Wrath/*orgay'* (Luke 21:23) is the same group of wrath/*orgay'* events penned in 1 Thessalonians 1:10 and 5:9 that Jesus will save us from, and the wrath that God has not appointed us to suffer—but this does not preclude the saints from suffering affliction/*thlip'sis*[3763] before the abomination, the years leading up to the signing of the seven-year covenant in Daniel 9:27, and perhaps a short time after the abomination. The wrath of God is reserved for the last three-and-a-half years toward the end of "great tribulation" in the time/day/year when "the wrath of God cometh on the children of disobedience."[3764] The wrath/*orgay'* of God appears thirty-six times in the New Testament, penned to specifically reference the year of the Lord's wrath bowls culminating with Armageddon. *Orgay'* is also translated as God's indignation in Revelation 14:10; vengeance in Romans 3:5; and anger in Mark 3:5, Ephesians 4:31, and Colossians 3:8.[3765]

"Wrath" is alternately translated into English in the New Testament from *thoomos'*, meaning fierceness, indignation, anger, wroth, and wrath. It is penned "wrath" in the end-time sequence of events leading to Armageddon in Revelation 12:12; 14:8, 9, 19; 15:1, 7; 16:1; 18:3, and drafted as "fierceness" in Revelation 16:19 and 19:15.[3766]

Orgay' and *thoomos'* are grouped together as indignation/*orgay'* and wrath/*thoomos'* in Revelation 14:10, in relationship to the pouring-out of the cup of

---

[3763] Matt 24.9–14.
[3764] Col 3:6. Disbelief: G543—*ap-i'-thi-ah*: obstinate; rebellious; disobedience; opposition to the divine will; unbelief; transliterated: apeitheia.
[3765] G3709—*orgay'*. Wrath, 31: Luke 3:7; 21:23; John 3:36; Rom 2:5, 8; 4:15; 5:9; 9:22; 12:19; 13:4–5; Eph 2:3; Col 3:6; 1 Thess 1:10; 2:16; 5:9; 1 Tim 2:8; Heb 3:11; 4:3; James 1:19-20; Rev 16:19; 19:15. Anger, 3: Mark 3:5; Eph 4:31; Col 3:8. Indignation, 1: Rev 14:10. Vengeance, 1: Rom 3:5.
[3766] G2372—*thoo-mos'*: fierceness; indignation; wrath; wroth; anger; to become incensed; to provoke to anger; transliterated: thumos. Wrath: Acts 19:28; Gal 5:20; Eph 4:31; Col 3:8; Heb 11:27; Rev 12:12; 14:8, 10, 19; 15:1, 7; 16:1; 18:3. Fierceness: Rev 16:19; 19:15. Indignation: Rom 2:8. Wraths: 2 Cor 12:20.

God's wrath. Fierceness is translated from *thoomos'*, and wrath is translated from *orgay'* in the Revelation 16:19 passage, depicting the time of the pouring-out of the seventh bowl at Armageddon. Additionally, *thoomos'* is translated as fierceness, and *orgay'* is translated as wrath in Revelation 19:15, connecting both to the same set of events in the last three-and-a-half years; *thlip'sis* does not appear in those passages.

> Rev 14:10 The same shall drink of the wine of the wrath of God, which is poured out without mixture into the cup of his indignation; and he shall be tormented with fire and brimstone in the presence of the holy angels, and in the presence of the Lamb.

> Rev 16:19 And the great city was divided into three parts, and the cities of the nations fell: and great Babylon came in remembrance before God, to give unto her the cup of the wine of the fierceness of his wrath.

> Rev 19:15 And out of his mouth goeth a sharp sword, that with it he should smite the nations: and he shall rule them with a rod of iron: and he treadeth the winepress of the fierceness and wrath of Almighty God.

Thus tribulation/affliction/*thlip'sis* of the saints is not the punishment of the wicked in the wrath, but a testing for Christians to pass. Nor is the tribulation of the saints the great temptation, because God will keep us "from the hour of temptation, which shall come upon all the world, to try them that dwell upon the earth" (Rev 3:10), which occurs after the abomination with the forced implementation of the mark of the beast. Temptation/*pirasmos'* is a test sent by God to prove one's faith, tribulation.[3767] Conversely, the temptation of Antichrist is to convict the unbelievers, not the true believers; thus God will spare the truly faithful from this temptation. As such, saints of weaker faith will have to earn their reward through the fire of the great tribulation, by refusing the mark of the beast. Remember, after the abomination, "there shall arise false Christs, and false prophets, and shall shew great signs and wonders; insomuch that, if it were possible, they shall deceive the very elect" (Matt 24:24).[3768] God will spare the saints from the Antichrist temptation, but not the tribulation temptations of Babylon.

> James 1:12 Blessed is the man that endureth temptation: for when he is tried, he shall receive the crown of life, which the Lord hath promised to them that love him.

[3767] G3986—*pi-ras-mos'*: temptation; try; trial; proving; adversity, affliction, trouble sent by God to test or prove one's character or faith; transliterated: peirasmos.
[3768] Dan 12:1–3, 10–13; Rev 13:15–18; 14:12; 20:4.

The Old Testament references to the "wrath of God" mesh perfectly with New Testament wrath references, revealing the same sequential order of end-time events. Wrath in the Old Testament is translated utilizing four Hebrew words: *qetseph*, *chemah*, *'aph*, and *`ebrah*, for words like indignation, fury, furious, anger, angry, and rage in end-time applications.[3769] In like manner, Old Testament prophecies testify God's wrath is part of a series of events in the last three-and-a-half years that culminates with the year of the Lord's vengeance after the Year of the Lord's Favor.[3770]

[3769] H7110—*qetseph, keh'-tsef*: rage; strife; foam; indignation; sore; wrath; God's anger. Wrath: Num 1:53; 16:46; 18:5; Josh 22:20; 1 Chron 19:2; 27:24; 2 Chron 19:10; 24:18; 29:8; 32:25–26; Esth 1:18; Ps 38:1; 102:10; Eccl 5:17; Isa 54:8; Jer 10:10; 21:5; 32:37; 50:13; Zech 7:12. Indignation: Deut 29:28; 2 Kings 3:27; Isa 34:2.

H2534—*chemah, khay-maw'*: furious; indignation; rage; wrath. Fury: Gen 27:44; Lev 26:28; Isa 27:4; 34:2; 42:25; 51:13, 17, 20, 22; 59:18; 63:3, 5, 6; 66:15; Jer 4:4; 6:11; 7:20; 10:25; 21:5, 12; 23:19; 25:15; 30:23; 32:31, 37; 33:5; 36:7; 42:18; 44:6; Lam 2:4; 4:11; Ezek 5:13, 15; 6:12; 7:8; 8:18; 9:8; 13:13; 14:19; 16:38, 42; 19:12; 20:8, 13, 21, 33, 34; 21:17; 22:20, 22; 24:8; 30:13, 14, 15; 36:6; 38:18; Dan 8:6; 9:16; 11:44; Mic 5:15; Nah 1:6; Zech 8:2. Wrath: Num 25:11; Deut 29:23, 28; 2 Sam 11:20; 2 Kings 22:13, 17; 2 Chron 12:7; 34:21, 25; 36:16; Esth 2:1; 3:5; 7:7, 10; Job 19:29; 21:20; 36:18; Ps 37:8; 59:13; 76:10; 78:38; 88:7; 89:46; 90:7; 106:23; Prov 15:1; 16:14; 19:19; 21:14; 27:4; Jer 18:20; Ezek 13:15. Poison: Deut 32:24, 33; Ps 58:4; 140:3. Furious: Prov 22:24; 29:22; Ezek 5:15; 25:17; Nah 1:2. Displeasure: Deut 9:19; Ps 38:1. Hot: Deut 9:19; Ps 38:1. Rage: 2 Kings 5:12; Prov 6:34. Anger: Esth 1:12. Furiously: Ezek 23:25. Heat: Ezek 3:14. Indignation: Esth 5:9. Wrathful: Prov 15:18.

H639 —*'aph, af*: ire: anger. Anger: Gen 27:45; 30:2; 44:18; 49:6–7; Exod 4:14; 11:8; 32:19, 22; Num 11:1, 10; 12:9; 22:22, 27; 24:10; 25:3, 4; 32:10; Deut 6:13, 14, 15; 7:4; 9:19; 13:17; 29:20, 23, 24, 27, 28; 31:17; 32:22; Josh 7:1, 26; 23:16; Judg 2:14, 20; 3:8; 6:39; 9:30; 10:7; 14:19; 1 Sam 11:6; 17:28; 20:30, 34; 2 Sam 6:7; 12:5; 24:1; 2 Kings 13:3; 23:26; 24:20; 1 Chron 13:10; 2 Chron 25:10, 15; Neh 9:17; Job 9:5, 13; 18:4; 21:17; 35:15; Ps 6:1; 7:6; 27:9; 30:5; 37:8; 56:7; 69:24; 74:1; 77:9; 78:21, 38, 49, 50; 85:3, 5; 90:7, 11; 145:8; Prov 15:1, 18; 16:32; 19:11; 21:14; 27:4; Isa 5:25; 7:4; 9:12, 17, 21; 10:4, 5, 25; 12:1; 13:3, 9, 13; 14:6; 30:27, 30; 42:25; 48:9; 63:3, 6; 66:15; Jer 2:35; 4:8, 26; 7:20; 10:24; 15:13, 14; 17:4; 18:23; 21:5; 23:20; 25:37, 38; 30:24; 32:31, 37; 33:5; 36:7; 42:18; 44:6; 49:37; 51:45; 52:3; Lam 1:12; 2:1, 3, 6, 21, 22; 3:43, 66; 4:11; Ezek 5:13, 15; 7:3, 8; 13:13; 20:8, 21; 22:20; 25:14; 35:11; 43:8; Dan 9:16; 11:20; Hos 8:5; 11:9; 13:11; 14:4; Joel 2:13; Amos 1:11; Jonah 3:9; 4:2; Mic 5:15; 7:18; Nah 1:3, 6; Hab 3:8; 3:12; Zeph 2:2, 3; 3:8; Zech 10:3. Wrath: Gen 39:19; Exod 22:24; 32:10, 11, 12; Num 11:33; Deut 11:17; 1 Sam 28:18; 2 Kings 23:26; 2 Chron 12:12; 28:11, 13; 29:10; 30:8; Ezra 8:22; 10:14; Job 14:13; 16:9; 19:11; 20:23, 28; 32:2, 3, 5; 36:13; 40:11; 42:7; Ps 2:5, 12; 21:9; 55:3; 78:31; 95:11; 106:40; 110:5; 124:3; 138:7; Prov 14:29; 24:18; 29:8; 30:33. Face, 19: Gen 3:19; 19:1; 24:47; 48:12; Num 22:31; 1 Sam 20:41; 24:8; 25:41; 28:14; 2 Sam 14:4, 33; 18:28; 24:20; 1 Kings 1:23, 31; 1 Chron 21:21; 2 Chron 20:18; Isa 49:23; Ezek 38:18. Angry: Ps 76:7; Prov 14:17; 22:24; 29:22.

H5678—*`ebrah, eb-raw'*: anger; rage; wrath; fury. Wrath: Gen 49:7; Job 21:30; Ps 78:49; 85:3; 90:9, 11; Prov 11:4, 23; 14:35; 21:24; Isa 9:19; 10:6; 13:9, 13; 16:6; 48:29, 30; Lam 2:2; 3:1; Ezek 7:19; 21:31; 22:21, 31; 38:19; Amos 1:10, 11; Hab 3:8; Zeph 1:15, 18. Rage: Job 40:11; Ps 7:6. Anger, 1: Prov 22:8.

[3770] Dan 11:31–45; Isa 34:8; 61:2, 63:4.

Old and New Testament end-time prophecies mesh chronologically with Jesus' template and with Daniel's. Accordingly, Daniel revealed that after Messiah was cut off, a prince would come to destroy Jerusalem. This event was fulfilled in AD 70 by Tiberius Julius Alexander. Daniel then prophesied immediately before detailing the last seven years, "and the end thereof shall be with a flood, and unto the end of the war desolations are determined" (Dan 9:26). The end/*qets* in this application means the end of time,[3771] as in the fulfillment of the seventieth week. Hence, the end times are described in the last seven years in Daniel 9:27, wherein the last three-and-a-half years will come like "a flood": quick and with extreme calamities and wars described in Daniel 11:22–30. Thus, the flood begins with "the arms of a flood," an overwhelming army that will be destroyed just before Antichrist marches his armies to Jerusalem to set up the abomination, which begets the great tribulation.

Daniel 9:26 said in contemporary parlance and congruent with the narrative: after Jerusalem was destroyed in AD 70, wars would continue to the end-time, the last seven years when wars, desolations, destruction, and horrors that have been permitted will occur in increasing intensity and scope until all that was decreed will be fulfilled. We know from Daniel 9:26-27 that seven years, the last of seventy weeks of years to complete visions and prophecy and to "anoint the most Holy,"[3772] has been reserved for the end times, a period Jesus described in two distinct parts before and after the abomination, while referencing the prophet Daniel for understanding that divided the last seven years with the abomination.

Now, factor in that 1 Thessalonians 1:10 and 5:9 clearly state that the saints are not appointed to, nor will be delivered to, suffer end-time wrath. God's wrath does not begin with the negotiated seven-year covenant, but after the abomination when Antichrist comes to power and is officially revealed to begin the great tribulation culminating with the wrath bowls poured out. Thus, God's wrath comes after Revelation 15, after the Year of the Lord's Favor[3773] and in the day/year of the Lord's wrath.[3774] God and Jesus promised we would not suffer wrath but would suffer tribulation in the Fig Tree Generation and into the last seven years; those who are not raptured and do not take the mark of the beast will suffer tribulation by Antichrist.

> Rev 2:10 Fear none of those things which thou shalt suffer: behold, the devil shall cast some of you into prison, that ye may be tried; and ye shall have tribulation ten days: be thou faithful unto death, and I will give thee a crown of life.

[3771] H7093—*qets, kates*: end; at the end of time; end of space.
[3772] Dan 9:24.
[3773] Isa 61:1–3; Luke 4:18–20; 2 Thess 2:4.
[3774] Ps 75:6; Isa 2:12–13; 13:6; 34:8; Nahum 1:6; Zech 14:1–21; Zeph 1:17–18, 2:1–15; Rev 16:2–17.

Jesus instructed that Christian tribulation/affliction/persecution of the saints begins before the abomination, and in the verse immediately following the sorrows as an extension of the sorrows. Affliction/*thlip'sis* [3775] in Matthew 24:9 is the same Greek word that "tribulation" is translated into English from in Matthew 24:21 and 29. One is puzzled as to why KJV translators translated *thlip'sis* as "afflictions" in Matthew 24:9; some English translations translated *thlip'sis* as "persecuted," while others like the New King James Version translated as "tribulation."[3776] Mark and Luke added details to the affliction/tribulation regarding Matthew 24:9, stating that followers of Christ will be delivered to councils and be beaten, flogged, imprisoned, and slain for Jesus' sake.[3777]

Matt 24:9 Then shall they deliver you up to be afflicted, and shall kill you: and ye shall be hated of all nations for my name's sake.

What is fascinating about Mark and Luke's details is that Jesus decreed He would ensure that the Spirit of wisdom will testify through persecuted Christians, for the veracity of who Jesus is with their lives,[3778] before Jesus returns. Mark 13:11 confirms the wisdom that will be spoken by Christ-followers will derive from the Holy Spirit.[3779] Thus, whether the restrainer of 2 Thessalonians 2 is the Holy Spirit or Michael, both will be present in the first three-and-a-half years, and until Antichrist is crowned at the abomination. As such, Michael permits beast empires to rise while on earth but fights to prevent Antichrist from coming to power before the ordained time.[3780]

Moreover, "tribulation" and "affliction," without explanation, were used interchangeably by KJV translators for the same set of events. To underline the consistently inconsistent nature of KJV translators, in 1 Thessalonians 3:3–4 affliction/*thlip'sis* and tribulation/*thlip'sis* were translated in the same narrative, describing the same sufferings Christian are appointed to suffer.

1 Thess 3:3 That no man should be moved by these afflictions: for yourselves know that we are appointed thereunto.

1 Thess 3:4 For verily, when we were with you, we told you before that we should suffer tribulation; even as it came to pass, and ye know.

[3775] G2347—*thlip'-sis*.
[3776] Persecuted: NIV, NLT, Berean, CSB. Tribulation: NKJV, NASB, ESV, ASV, Amplified.
[3777] Mark 13:9; Luke 21:12.
[3778] Mark 13:11; Luke 21:23–15.
[3779] See also Acts 6:3; 1 Cor 2:4; 12:8, 9, 10.
[3780] 2 Thess 2:4, 6, 7, 8, 9.

The same flip-flop translation of *thlip'sis* occurs in Mark 13:19 and Matthew 24:21 for the same event: the great tribulation of the world in the last three-and-a-half years. Mark 13 was translated as affliction/*thlip'sis* for this event, whereas Matthew 24 was translated as tribulation/*thlip'sis*.

> Matt 24:21 For then shall be great tribulation, such as was not since the beginning of the world to this time, no, nor ever shall be.

> Mark 13:19 For in those days shall be affliction, such as was not from the beginning of the creation which God created unto this time, neither shall be.

Many Christians in the affliction/tribulation of the saints will be offended/*skandalid'zo*, meaning scandalized, seduced, entrapped, and caused to fall away.[3781] Christians will hate each other because of what will take place: Babylon will seduce many Christians away from God, and in so doing will cause many Christians to betray each other before the abomination. I would encourage one to compare 2 Thessalonians 2:1–4 regarding Jesus' return, the falling away, and the gathering to what Jesus stated in Matthew 24:9–31, to bring event chronology into focus. Paul referenced Jesus and cited the events that will occur before Jesus gathers His people to Him.

> 2 Thess 2:1 Now we beseech you, brethren, by the coming of our Lord Jesus Christ, and by our gathering together unto him,

> 2 Thess 2:2 That ye be not soon shaken in mind, or be troubled, neither by spirit, nor by word, nor by letter as from us, as that the day of Christ is at hand.

> 2 Thess 2:3 Let no man deceive you by any means: for that day shall not come, except there come a falling away first, and that man of sin be revealed, the son of perdition;

> 2 Thess 2:4 Who opposeth and exalteth himself above all that is called God, or that is worshipped; so that he as God sitteth in the temple of God, shewing himself that he is God.

Falling away/*apostasee'ah* means apostasy, defection, and rebellion[3782] by many Christians and its leaders. The offended/*skandalid'zo*, those who fall away or sin

---

[3781] Matt 24:10. G4624—*skan-dal-id'-zo*: scandalize; to entrap, trip up; stumble; entice to sin, apostasy; offend; cause to fall away; transliterated: skandalizo.
[3782] G646—*ap-os-tas--ah*: defection from truth; apostasy; falling away; forsake; transliterated: apostasia.

in Matthew 24:10 before Jesus' coming in Matthew 24:29–31, will participate in a time of terror when a reorganized Christianity will be folded into the universal religion—Babylon. Moreover, gathering/*epeesoonagogay'* of 2 Thessalonians 2:1 is defined as a complete collection, assembly together, and gathering of Christians into one place.[3783] "The gathering," the rapture, is included in a summary of events leading up to Jesus' days of visitation[3784] after the abomination in 2 Thessalonians 2:1–17.

The beginning of sorrows in the Fig Tree Generation leads to Babylon's rise, her false prophets, and then falling away because the contrived wars, famine, pestilence, and earthquakes. Catastrophes will open the portal for false prophets, offering false hope to step forward, in a world of lukewarm Christians led by church leaders who do not teach prehistory and prophecy— a world well prepared for deception by false prophets, and for the de-deification of Jesus and the discarding of Paul's teachings. Mass defections from the faith will isolate those who stay loyal to Jesus as subhumans not worthy to enter the promised utopia. Christians and family members will betray each other on an unimaginable scale, serving up the true saints for genocide.[3785] Iniquity will abound. Love will grow cold in the dystopian rise, and then the reign of terror imposed by Babylon, her the false prophets, and the seventh empire. Once in power, Babylon will sponsor the "covenant of death"[3786] to begin the last seven years. The covenant signing will occur just before Jesus opens the seals that begins the first three-and-a-half years, triggering the 144,000 evangelists from twelve Israelite tribes to preach the gospel and awaken lost Israel, along with the two witnesses, followed by the angel to preach the gospel to the world.[3787]

This makes sense of Revelation 2, 3, 6, and 7 with respect to the firstfruits of the resurrection sequence detailed in 1 Corinthians 15:23–24, which will include the twenty-four elders. More firstfruit saints will be raised at the beginning or just before the commencement of the last seven years, immediately after opening of the fifth seal. These firstfruits will be told to wait a little longer for firstfruit saints to be martyred by Babylon in the tribulation of the saints of the first half of the last seven years, and perhaps a little longer.[3788] Babylon will become drunk with the blood of the saints past and future.[3789]

[3783] G1997—*ep-ee-soon-ag-o-gay'*: a complete collection; specially, a Christian meeting for worship; assembling; gathering together; transliterated: episunagoge.

[3784] Hos 9:7.

[3785] Matt 24:10–13; Mark 11:14; Luke 21:12–19; Rev 7:9–14.

[3786] Isa 28:18; Dan 9:27.

[3787] Matt 24:14; Mark 13:10; Rev 7:1–8; 11:1–14; 14:1–5, 6–7.

[3788] Rev 6:11; 7:14.

[3789] Rev 17:6; 18:24.

CHAPTER 79

THE GREAT TRIBULATION

Matt 24:21 For then shall be great tribulation, such as was not since the beginning of the world to this time, no, nor ever shall be.

The Revelation 7:9–17, Mark 13:9–13, Luke 21:12–19, and Matthew 24:9–14 tribulation will be waged by Babylon against saints who testify and are martyred for Jesus as firstfruits. The "great tribulation" and "affliction" in the book of Mark was translated from the same word, *thlip'sis,* for the same account will be waged by Antichrist and the false prophet.

The great tribulation, "such as was not since the beginning of the world to this time," will be greater in intensity and scope than the tribulation against the firstfruit saints. Just as the birth pangs get stronger with catastrophes, so will the tribulation after the abomination. Chronologically, Antichrist destroys Babylon after the abomination,[3790] and then persecutes Judah: "And the dragon was wroth with the woman, and went to make war with the remnant of her seed, which keep the commandments of God, and have the testimony of Jesus Christ."[3791] Thereafter, the false prophet implements the mark the beast system and the forced worship of Antichrist and Satan.[3792]

[3790] Rev 12:17; 17:6, 16.
[3791] Matt 24:15–20; Mark 13:14–19; Luke 21:20–24; Rev 12:12–17.
[3792] Rev 13:4–10, 11–18; 14:9, 11; 16:2; 19:20; 20:4.

The great tribulation of the last three-and-a-half years will be so terrible that Jesus declared that unless the days were shortened no life would be saved. The reign of Antichrist will begin with great signs, wonders, and false Christs and prophets when even the elect would be deceived (Matt 24:21–29). Then, "immediately after the tribulation those days," the day(s)/year(s) of abomination and Antichrist coming to power, Jesus will return.[3793] "Those days" include immediately after the skies will darken in the days of the fourth and fifth trumpet blasts, and after the days of the three woes.[3794] Jesus further marked that the timing of His coming occurs immediately after the powers/*doo'namis* of the heavens are shaken. Powers/*doo'namis* are the angels recorded in 1 Peter 3:22, and authorities in Ephesians 1:21, the mighty ones.[3795] The powers of the heavens that will be shaken are the angels in heaven during the angelic war described in Revelation 12, when Judea flees to the wilderness because of the abomination in the days of the seventh trumpet. This is the time when the rebellious angelic host will be cast down to the earth.

Antichrist will drag some of God's starry host down to the earth, and will trample on those angels when Antichrist magnifies "himself even to the prince of the host, and by him the daily sacrifice was taken away, and the place of his sanctuary was cast down. And an host was given him against the daily sacrifice by reason of transgression, and it cast down the truth to the ground; and it practiced, and prospered."[3796] Antichrist will turn defeat to his advantage on earth, claiming indeed he does make war successfully against God, witnessed by his captured angelic "powers."

Jesus will return first after the gospel is preached by the 144,000, two witnesses, and the angel of Revelation 14:6 "to them that dwell on the earth, and to every nation, and kindred, and tongue, and people," and as "a witness unto all nations; and then shall the end come" (Matt 24:14; Mark 13:10). With the timing well marked by Jesus in His template, He will return with His sign and on the clouds of heaven for all to see for rapture, resurrections, Second Exodus, and then for Armageddon in "one of the days of the Son of man" and in the "days of his visitation."[3797]

> Matt 24:30 And then shall appear the sign of the Son of man in heaven: and then shall all the tribes of the earth mourn, and they shall see the Son of man coming in the clouds of heaven with power and great glory.

[3793] Immediately: G2112—*yoo-theh'-oce*: directly; at once; as soon as; forthwith; immediately; shortly; straightway; a straight course; transliterated: eutheos. Those: G1565—*ek-i'-nos*: that one; this; those; transliterated: ekeinos.

[3794] Rev 8:12, 13; 9:2.

[3795] Mark 13:24, 26; Luke 21:27; 1 Pet 3:22. G1411—*doo'-nam-is*.

[3796] Dan 8:10–11; Rev 12:6, 7–9.

[3797] Luke 17:22, 26; Hos 9:7, respectively.

Knowing the return chronology makes sense of what Jesus and Paul stated: "but he that shall endure until the end shall be saved" (Matt 24:13), and "But every man in his own order: Christ the firstfruits; afterward they that are Christ's at his coming. Then cometh the end, when he shall have delivered up the kingdom to God, even the Father; when he shall have put down all rule and all authority and power" (1 Cor 15:23–24). Knowing the resurrection sequence of the firstfruits include the saints that will be martyred for their testimony and triumphed through the blood of the Lamb,[3798] and the 144,000,[3799] explains the firstfruits seen in the vision before the throne in Revelation 12 just after the war in heaven, when Judea flees Jerusalem and will be protected for 1,260 days, three-and-a-half prophetic years.[3800]

> Rev 12:11 And they overcame him by the blood of the Lamb, and by the word of their testimony; and they loved not their lives unto the death.

The great tribulation/*thlip'sis* after the abomination meshes perfectly with Old Testament prophecy, when Michael stands up to fight for the people of Israel and Judah "in time of trouble, such as never was since there was a nation even to that same time: and at that time thy people shall be delivered, every one that shall be found written in the book."[3801] Michael will stand at the midpoint of the last seven years in the time of trouble/*tsarah*, the time of Jacob's trouble/*tsarah*, a time so terrible none is like it, but Jacob will be saved out of that time. *Tsarah* is defined as distress, adversity, affliction, anguish, tribulation, and trouble,[3802] and is the Hebrew equivalent to *thlip'sis*. The time of Jacob's trouble/tribulation in the "great tribulation" after the abomination will unfold in the days/years of Jesus' return when "The days of visitation are come, the days of recompence are come; Israel shall know it" (Hos 9:7).

Old Testament end-time prophecies for Israel and Judah unfold in a parallel track with church end-time prophecy in the first three-and-a-half years, and will begin to merge into one track with the return of Jesus in the last three-and-a-half years, in the Year of the Lord's Favor and then the supper of the Lamb. Accordingly, Daniel's seventieth week will "finish the transgression, and to make an end of sins, and to make reconciliation for iniquity, and to bring in everlasting righteousness, and to seal up the vision and prophecy, and to anoint the most

---

[3798] Matt 24:9–10; Mark 13:9–13; Luke 21:11–19; Rev 6:10–11; 7:14.
[3799] Rev 14:1–7.
[3800] Rev 12:6–9.
[3801] Dan 12.1.
[3802] Jer 30:7; Dan 12:1. H6869—*tsarah, tsaw-raw'*; adversary; adversity; affliction, anguish; distress; tribulation; trouble.

Holy."[3803] Transgression/*pesha`* means revolt, rebellion, sin, trespass, and God's forgiveness of those transgressions.[3804] Israel's reconciliation will begin with the awakening of the lost tribes in the first three-and-a-half years, followed by the Judean flight from Jerusalem: "When ye therefore shall see the abomination of desolation, spoken of by Daniel the prophet, stand in the holy place, (whoso readeth, let him understand:). Then let them which be in Judaea flee into the mountains"; and "For then shall be great tribulation, such as was not since the beginning of the world to this time, no, nor ever shall be."[3805]

The midpoint of the last three-and-a-half years is also the time when Jesus will keep His saints from "the hour of temptation, which shall come upon all the world, to try them that dwell upon the earth."[3806] Keep/*tayreh'o* is defined as to guard, watch over, preserve, and reserve[3807] the chosen saints from the "hour of temptation" in Revelation 3:10. One wants to be careful with the application for the meaning here not to overreach. Temptation/*pirasmos'* is defined as adversity, time of trial, and testing of character and fidelity, enticement to sin, and temptation to rebel against God.[3808] Thus, God has promised to keep the faithful saints from the temptation to rebel against God and side with Antichrist in the last three-and-a-half years, and thus be saved from the wrath in the last year,[3809] but not spared tribulation. Israel, Judah, and saints not raptured will endure the great tribulation, but not the wrath of God.

"Hour of temptation" in Revelation 3:10 can mean a literal hour, a day, a time, or a season.[3810] Hour/*Ho'rah* is the same term used in Revelation 17:12 when the ten beast kings conspire with Antichrist to bring him to power, and to destroy Babylon. *Ho'rah* is the same term penned to describe the time of Babylon's destruction, and the same hour the two witnesses will be resurrected to heaven after their three-and-a-half-year commission, at the time of the second woe, and just before the seventh trumpet (Rev 11:12–14). Moreover, hour/*ho'rah* is the same word in Revelation 14:7 to announce "the hour of his judgment has come," immediately after the angel preaches the gospel to the world for the last time in verse 6, followed by Babylon's destruction in verse 9. Biblical prophecy and allegory support other prophecies with similar terms and allegory utilization, which additionally links

---

[3803] Dan 9:24, 27.
[3804] H6588—*pesha`, peh'-shah*: a revolt; rebellion; sin; transgression; trespass; punishment for transgression; God's forgiveness; offering for transgression.
[3805] Matt 24:15–16, 21.
[3806] Rev 2:22; 3:10.
[3807] G5083—*tay-reh'-o*; a watch; to guard from loss or injury; keeping the eye upon; preserve; reserved from; keeper; keep; transliterated: tereo.
[3808] G3986—*pi-ras-mos'*: adversity; temptation; trial; test; affliction; trouble; transliterated: peirasmos.
[3809] 1 Thess 1:10; 5:9–10.
[3810] G5610—*ho'-rah*: an hour; a day; instant; season; short time; transliterated: hora.

Old and New Testament prophecy as chronology markers like trumpet blasts. It follows that the hour of testing many Christians will be saved/kept from occurs in the same season that Antichrist will usurp power, the hour of the abomination, Babylon's destruction, and the mark of the beast, which will introduce the great tribulation of the world leading to the wrath bowls in the last year.

> Rev 17:12 And the ten horns which thou sawest are ten kings, which have received no kingdom as yet; but receive powers as kings one hour with the beast.

> Rev 18:10 Standing afar off for the fear of her torment, saying, Alas, alas, that great city Babylon, that mighty city! for in one hour is thy judgment come.

After the falling away and abomination occurs, the gathering happens (2 Thess 2:3) when Jesus comes for rapture; then for Second Exodus before the wrath bowls in the last year; then for Armageddon in the days of His visitation. Jesus decreed, and Paul underscored, that Christians ought not to be fooled or deceived for any reason by signs from Babylon, its false prophets, or the Naphalim World Order.[3811] Jesus' clear and irrefutable "sign" of His coming will be seen around the world, as lightning coming from the east and west, shortly after the abomination.[3812]

[3811] Matt 24:24–26; Mark 13:21–23; Luke 21:8; 2 Thess 2:1–5.
[3812] Matt 24:27; Mark 13:26; Luke 17:24; 2 Thess 2:4–5.

CHAPTER 80

THE ELECT IN THE TIME OF JACOB'S TROUBLE

Jer 30:7 Alas! for that day is great, so that none is like it: it is even the time of Jacob's trouble; but he shall be saved out of it.

Because many antichrists will come to deceive many, Antichrist's revealing is identified by his official crowning and abomination rituals in the temple,[3813] to eliminate deception. All unfinished prophecy designated for Israel and Judah will be completed in the last three-and-a-half years, including their reconciliation to God and their Messiah when Jesus returns (Dan 9:24).

Antichrist's crowning and abomination acts begin the great tribulation, the time of Jacob's trouble punctuated by Judah's flight from Jerusalem, and Antichrist and Satan's war waged against Judah, Israel, and all who hold to the testimony of Jesus.[3814] Jesus, Daniel, and Jeremiah prophesied a time of trouble/tribulation for Judah and Israel that will begin when the birth-pang catastrophes approach full intensity, in a time the world has not seen since creation. Knowing this makes

---

[3813] Matt 24:15–20, 23–25; Mark 13:14, 21–22; Luke 21:20; 2 Thess 2:3–6; 1 John 2:18; 4:3; Rev 13:5–18.
[3814] Jer 30:7; Dan 9:27; 11:29–31; 12:1-13; Mark 13:14, 21–22; Luke 21:20; 2 Thess 2:4; Rev 13:4–7.

sense that Jeremiah connected birthing sorrows with Jacob's trouble and the great tribulation and restoration before God's fury/wrath in the "latter days."[3815]

Israel's lost tribes will awaken, likely at the preaching of the 144,000 in the first three-and-a-half years as part the Holy Covenant reconciliation preparation. One contemplates whether the 144,000 relate to God's sanctified firstborn discussed in Exodus 13:2 and Numbers 3:13, perhaps reserved from ancient times to complete their holy mission, to be sacrificed as firstfruits, and in like manner of reservation, martyrdom, and resurrection as the two witnesses. Accordingly, Judah and lost Israel are represented as the "twelve stars" and "the woman, and the remnant of her seed" (Rev 12:1, 17) that the dragon and Antichrist endeavor to wipe from the face of the earth. At the nascence to the last three-and-a-half years, Israel and Judah will recognize Jesus as their Messiah and Redeemer. They will refuse to accept the mark of the beast, will not worship Antichrist, and will not worship Satan.

Jesus will lead the Second Exodus of Judah and Israel in the "days of his visitations" and "recompence," from around the world.[3816] Israel will join with those of Judah who will flee from Jerusalem to the wilderness at the time of the abomination, and as marked in Revelation 12. It follows that an exodus prophetic allegory would be embedded into Revelation 12 to identify the Second Exodus event and wonder. And indeed, there is: the "wings of the eagle" that invigorated the first exodus will electrify the Second Exodus.

> Exod 19:4 Ye have seen what I did unto the Egyptians, and how I bare you on eagles' wings, and brought you unto myself.

> Rev 12:14 And to the woman were given two wings of a great eagle, that she might fly into the wilderness, into her place, where she is nourished for a time, and times, and half a time, from the face of the serpent.

In the time of Jacob's trouble, all faces that have not believed in God and Jesus will turn pale. After fleeing Judah is saved, the larger exodus event will begin, another resurrection will occur, and the judgment of Israel and Judah will bring them back into Holy Covenant. Israel and Judah's resurrection is foreshadowed by David's resurrection in the time of exodus and trouble.

> Jer 30:6. .. wherefore do I see every man with his hands on his loins, as a woman in travail, and all faces are turned into paleness?

> Jer 30:7 Alas! for that day is great, so that none is like it: it is even the time of Jacob's trouble; but he shall be saved out of it.

[3815] Jer 30:6–7, 17–24.
[3816] Jer 30:9–22; 31:1–40; Hos 9:5.

Jer 30:8 For it shall come to pass in that day, saith the LORD of hosts, that I will break his yoke from off thy neck, and will burst thy bonds, and strangers shall no more serve themselves of him:

Jer 30:9 But they shall serve the LORD their God, and David their king, whom I will raise up unto them.

Jer 30:10 Therefore fear thou not, O my servant Jacob, saith the LORD; neither be dismayed, O Israel: for, lo, I will save thee from afar, and thy seed from the land of their captivity; and Jacob shall return, and shall be in rest, and be quiet.

Michael stands up in the time of Jacob's trouble after the abomination, when Daniel's people, those whose names are in the book of life, will be delivered to fulfill God's Holy Covenant promises. Daniel 12's prophetic reference to those who sleep in the dust of the earth is not a reference to Christians of 1 Thessalonians 4:16–18, but to another resurrection for Israel and Judah.

Dan 12:1 ... and at that time thy people shall be delivered, every one that shall be found written in the book.

Dan 12:2 And many of them that sleep in the dust of the earth shall awake, some to everlasting life, and some to shame and everlasting contempt.

Daniel 12's resurrection, and Jeremiah 30's raising of David references Ezekiel's 37's prophecy of "dry bones," when King David is raised up, resurrected. Ezekiel 37 is a wonder prophecy for most, and begins to make sense when one recognizes it triangulates with Jeremiah 30 and Daniel 12 via David and by Jacob's trouble, as well as with numerous Old Testament Second Exodus prophecies. Daniel 12 and Jeremiah 30 connect the timing of the trouble to the last three-and-a-half years. Jeremiah 30 introduced the resurrection of David to be king of a united Israel again, and is part of the firstfruits resurrection or a distinct resurrection reserved for Israel. Ezekiel 37 connects the resurrection of Israel to Daniel 12 and the resurrection to judgment or everlasting life. Ezekiel 37 further connected Israel's resurrection to the Second Exodus, the reunification of Israel and Judah as "one stick," under David who will be their king.[3817] Some of resurrected Judah and Israel will receive everlasting life; others will receive everlasting contempt and shame. Christian saints, Judah, and Israel will not endure the wrath bowls. However, many Christians not raptured will require baptismal fire,

---

[3817] Ezek 37:1–28.

as will awakened lost Israel and visible Judah, who will have to endure patiently through much of the great tribulation.[3818]

> Ezek 37:9 Then said he unto me, Prophesy unto the wind, prophesy, son of man, and say to the wind, Thus saith the Lord God; Come from the four winds, O breath, and breathe upon these slain, that they may live
>
> Ezek 37:10 So I prophesied as he commanded me, and the breath came into them, and they lived, and stood up upon their feet, an exceeding great army.
>
> Ezek 37:11 Then he said unto me, Son of man, these bones are the whole house of Israel: behold, they say, Our bones are dried, and our hope is lost.. ..
>
> Ezek 37:12. .. Behold, O my people, I will open your graves, and cause you to come up out of your graves, and bring you into the land of Israel.
>
> Ezek 37:13 And ye shall know that I am the LORD, when I have opened your graves, O my people, and brought you up out of your graves,
>
> Ezek 37:14 And shall put my spirit in you, and ye shall live, and I shall place you in your own land.

The Second Exodus will be led by the Word, Jesus, Israel's Messiah, along with King David, and perhaps "seven shepherds and eight principal men" that might include Elijah. Jesus will lead the Second Exodus as the "breaker," and David will pass before them with "Lord on the head of them," in the time of the Assyrian/Antichrist's reign, after he invades Jerusalem and the Covenant Land.[3819] Jesus, as the Lord/*Yhovah* of the *Elohiym*, "saves" and "leads" and "breaks" Israel's yoke in the time of the Second Exodus.[3820] "The breaker" Lord/*Yhovah* will preach deliverance and liberty to the captives. Jesus will break open the prisons where Israel will be imprisoned, in the Year of the Lord's Favor, when He proclaims the coming "day [year] of vengeance" that will follow, the year of wrath.[3821]

Second Exodus was promised to Israel and Judah and then bound into the Holy Covenant shortly after the first Exodus (Deut 30). God remembers His Holy Covenant forever. God promised not only to disperse His people if they did not uphold the Holy Covenant as part of the curses of the covenant, but to gather His people back to Him in the end times. The Redeemer Jesus will call lost Israel "by

---

[3818] Rev 14:12–13.
[3819] Mic 2:12–13; 5:5–7.
[3820] Jer 30:3, 5, 7, 8, 9, 10, 18; Ezek 37:9, 19, 21, 28; Mic 2:13; 5:4.
[3821] Isa 61:1–3; Mic 2:13; Luke 4:17–19.

thy name" and gather them back to God after Babylon is destroyed.[3822] God will gather lost Israel after they awaken and return to their God in the end times—after Jesus' sign when all Israel and Judah accept Jesus as their Messiah.

> Deut 30:1. .. when all these things are come upon thee, the blessing and the curse, which I have set before thee, and thou shalt call them to mind among all the nations, whither the LORD thy God hath driven thee,

> Deut 30:2 And shalt return unto the LORD thy God, and shalt obey his voice according to all that I command thee this day, thou and thy children, with all thine heart, and with all thy soul;

> Deut 30:3 That then the LORD thy God will turn thy captivity, and have compassion upon thee, and will return and gather thee from all the nations, whither the LORD thy God hath scattered thee.

> Isa 43.1 But now thus saith the LORD that created thee, O Jacob, and he that formed thee, O Israel, Fear not: for I have redeemed thee, I have called thee by thy name; thou art mine.

After the abomination, after the powers of the heavens will be shaken, and "immediately after the tribulation of those days. .. then [tot'eh] shall appear the sign of the Son of man in heaven: and then shall all the tribes of the earth mourn, and they shall see the Son of man coming in the clouds of heaven with power and great glory."[3823] Know that in the Old Testament, Jesus' sign is described as an ensign/ *nec* that appears in the time of the trumpet and exodus, but before the day/year of the Lord's harvest of the end times.[3824] *Nec* is the "ensign of the people, to it shall the Gentiles seek" from the root of Jesse who will "set his hand again the second time to recover the remnant of his people, which shall be left. .. and he shall set up an ensign for the nations, and shall assemble them the outcasts of Israel, and gather together the dispersed of Judah from the four corners of the earth."[3825]

Nec is also translated as "standard" in the book of Isaiah: the "standard to the people" at the time of the Second Exodus when all Israel will be called "the holy people, the redeemed of the Lord."[3826] One deduces from Isaiah 11, 18, 49 and 62 that Jesus' ensign/standard/sign will be on display at the time of rapture, exodus, and Armageddon for all to see in the days of Jesus' visitations. Further, a banner/ *nec*, a sign, will be raised at the time of the destruction of Babylon, when all are

---

[3822] Isa 41:1–28; 43:1.
[3823] Matt 24:29–30.
[3824] Isa 18:1–7. H5251—*nec, nace*: a signal; banner; ensign; standard; sign.
[3825] Isa 11:10–12.
[3826] Isa 49:22–23; 62:10–11

asked to come out of Babylon, indicating the timing of Jesus' first visitation shortly before the fall of Babylon,[3827] and just before the temptation trial of the mark.

Awakened Israel, and then Judah dwelling worldwide, like the Christian saints will be persecuted and locked away in concentration camps by Babylon. From these internment camps, Israelites will look upon Jesus' sign, ensign, standard, and banner with hope and faith their Messiah will come for them. One deduces from Old Testament and New Testament prophecies that both Israel and Judah will accept Jesus as their Redeemer at the time of His sign and rapture.[3828] Then, Israel and Judah will prepare for exodus and reconciliation from around the world, which will come in the Year of the Lord's Favor, followed by the day/year of vengeance and Armageddon.

> Isa 61:1. .. the LORD hath anointed me to preach good tidings unto the meek; he hath sent me to bind up the brokenhearted, to proclaim liberty to the captives, and the opening of the prison to them that are bound;
>
> Isa 61:2 To proclaim the acceptable year of the LORD, and the day of vengeance of our God; to comfort all that mourn.. ..
>
> Isa 61:9 And their seed shall be known among the Gentiles, and their offspring among the people: all that see them shall acknowledge them, that they are the seed which the LORD hath blessed.

Jesus' unmistakable sign for rapture will be a discernible sign for Judah to recognize Jesus as the one they pierced at the crucifixion, and a sign for awakened Israel. Jesus' sign will seemingly include, among discernible signs for Israel, His crucifixion wounds for all the earthly tribes to see and mourn over.[3829] As such, Jesus will defend Judah and Israel at a time when Jesus is seen over them, when "his arrow shall go forth as lightning, and the LORD God will blow the trumpet" (Zech 9:14), a scene reminiscent of Jesus' sign at the last trumpet.[3830] Arrow/*chets* can also be translated as a wound as in Job 34:6,[3831] and is reflective of Revelation 1:7: "Behold, he cometh with clouds; and every eye shall see him, and they also which pierced him: and all kindreds of the earth shall wail because of him. Even so, Amen." Understanding Zechariah 9:14–16 as Jesus' sign appears to makes sense when set alongside the mourning that will come with Jesus' sign in Matthew 24:27–31, Mark 13:26, and Luke 17:24: "as the lightning cometh out of the east, and shineth even unto the west" (Matt 24:27). The mourning will include the house of David/Judah mourning as for their only son, the one they pierced.

[3827] Isa 13:1–3; Jer 51:45; Rev 4–5.
[3828] Rom 11:1–32; Heb 8:8–13.
[3829] Matt 24:30; Mark 13:27; Rev 1:7.
[3830] Matt 24:27–31; 1 Cor 15:52.
[3831] H2671—*chets, khayts*: a piercer; an arrow; a wound; the shaft of a spear.

Zech 12:10. .. I will pour upon the house of David, and upon the inhabitants of Jerusalem, the spirit of grace and of supplications: and they shall look upon me whom they have pierced, and they shall mourn for him.. ..

Zech 12:11 In that day shall there be a great mourning in Jerusalem, as the mourning of Hadadrimmon in the valley of Megiddon.

Zech 12:12 And the land shall mourn, every family apart; the family of the house of David.

Jesus will return on the clouds of heaven. He will send His angels at the sound of a great trumpet (seventh trumpet) to gather "his elect from the four winds, from one end of heaven to the other."[3832] Some believe, though, the elect saved at this time references only Israel and Judah, the chosen people of God, and not the church saints. However, elect/*eklektos'* is defined as the chosen of God, the best of humankind, and Christians who believe in salvation through Jesus.[3833] Paul testified to and spoke to Gentile Christians, the elect, whom he endured for so they might obtain Jesus' salvation. Paul spoke to Gentile Christians as the "chosen" of Jesus, in the same way John prophesied in Revelation 17:14: "that all that are with him [the Lamb], are called, and chosen, and faithful." Christians are referred to as the elect/*eklektos'* and the chosen/*eklektos'* twenty-three times in the New Testament, and nineteen times outside of Jesus' oration in Matthew 24 and Mark 13.[3834] Jesus instructed disciples, apostles, Paul, and future Christian elect, to teach Jesus' Gospel to all nations.[3835] Jesus, as the Alpha-Omega (Rev 22:13), spoke to the disciples, to visible Judah, and to lost Israel as the chosen people of the Holy Covenant.

2 Tim 2:10 Therefore I endure all things for the elect's sakes, that they may also obtain the salvation which is in Christ Jesus with eternal glory.

"Chosen" was penned in Old Testament Hebrew to describe Israel and Judah as a special people. Chosen/*bachar* surfaces in Deuteronomy 7:6 and 14:2 for all the tribes of Israel, a word meaning selected; elected, appointed, and choicest, while special/*cgullah* is defined as a peculiar treasure and valued property,[3836] the

---

[3832] Matt 24:31; Mark 13:27; 1 Cor 15:52; 1 Thess 4:16; Rev 10:7; 11:15–19.

[3833] G1588—*ek-lek-tos'*: select; chosen; elect; chosen by God; salvation through Christ; appointed by God; best of its kind; transliterated: eklektos.

[3834] G1588—*eklektos*. Elect: Matt 24:24, 31; Mark 13:22, 27; Luke 18:7; Rom 8:33; Col 3:12; 1 Tim 5:21; Titus 1:1; 1 Pet 1:2; 2:6; 2 John 1:1, 13. Chosen: Matt 20:16; 22:14; Luke 23:35; Rom 16:13; 1 Pet 2:4, 9; Rev 17:14. Elect's: Matt 24:22; Mark 13:20; 2 Tim 2:10.

[3835] Matt 28:12-18; Mark 16:15.

[3836] H977—*bachar, baw-khar't*: to select; appoint; choose; choice; excellent; join; acceptable; H5459—*cgullah, seg-ool-law'*: jewel, a peculiar treasure, proper good, special: peculiar treasure; possession; property; valued property.

people of God, but a people not yet saved by their Redeemer Jesus, which will occur in the end times.

> Deut 7:6 For thou art an holy people unto the LORD thy God: the LORD thy God hath chosen thee to be a special people unto himself, above all people that are upon the face of the earth.

Thus, "chosen" as penned in the New Testament for Christians is cognate to the chosen and special people of Israel and Judah in the Old Testament. Knowing this makes perfect sense when compared with the book of Romans: Israel is not "cast away"; "the firstfruit" and "the root be holy so are the branches"; "all Israel shall be saved: as it is written, There shall come out of Sion the Deliverer, and shall turn away ungodliness from Jacob: For this is my covenant unto them, when I shall take away their sins."[3837] Jesus' sign will begin Israel and Judah's reconciliation and restoration through accepting Jesus as their Messiah, who will bring them back into the covenant as part of Jesus' chosen ones: chosen ones for the bride's supper (Rev 12:6).[3838] Israel too is referenced as the bride in the Old Testament.[3839]

> Isa 61:10. .. for he hath clothed me with the garments of salvation, he hath covered me with the robe of righteousness, as a bridegroom decketh himself with ornaments, and as a bride adorneth herself with her jewels.
>
> Hos 2:16 And it shall be at that day, saith the LORD, that thou shalt call me Ishi [husband[3840]]; and shalt call me no more Baali.

[3837] Rom 11:1–36.
[3838] Rev 12:6; 19:7–10.
[3839] Isa 54:5; Jer 3:1, 6–8; Ezek 16:8–32; Hos 2:19; Rom 7:23k 9:25.
[3840] H376—'iysh, eesh.

ANTICHRIST: THE BEAST OF EMPIRES

Rev 17:11 And the beast that was, and is not, even he is the eighth, and is of the seven, and goeth into perdition.

Antichrist will be a creature deriving in part from prehistory, beast kings, and beast empires, a creature past prophesied to somehow reappear in the end times. Antichrist/*Antee'khristos* in Greek is defined as the opponent or adversary of the Messiah Jesus, and cognate to `*eyphah* in Hebrew, meaning darkness.[3841] The first word in the compound word anti-Christ derives from *antee'*, a word transliterated as *anti* meaning in place of, against, or before. Ante/*anti* is a prefix recruited to denote contrast, substitution, opposite, or requital, while *khristos'* means anointed and an epithet for the son of God.[3842] Antichrist is generally understood as the adversary of Christ or a substituted Christ, the prism one is guided to view scriptural references of Antichrist through, and perhaps in part from the word

---

[3841] G500—*an-tee'-khris-tos*; an opponent of the Messiah; antichrist; adversary of Jesus; synonymous with H5890. H5890—`*eyphah, ay-faw'*: obscurity; darkness.

[3842] G473—*an-tee'*: opposite; as in instead of; in place of; against; to denote contrast; substitution; requital; transliterated: anti; G5547—*khris-tos'*: the Messiah; an epithet of Jesus; anointed and consecrated son of God; transliterated: Christos.

"before." My assertion is supported within Antichrist's cognate term, false Christs/ *psyoodokh'ristos* (transliterated as *pseudochristos*) meaning a "spurious Messiah."[3843] I find the definition of "spurious" eye-popping: not genuine, counterfeit, and of illegitimate birth (like the Rephaim and Nephilim). One might deduce Antichrist will possess a pedigree back to giants of the "before time."[3844]

Accordingly, some suggest that *anti* derives from Latin *ante* meaning before, as in antediluvian,[3845] as in before the flood, before Jesus, and as an alternate understanding deriving from Greek *antee'*. However, the Latin *ante* does not directly connect back to the older Greek *antee'/anti* etymologically, although the words do indicate a kinship through the Greek definition of before/*ante'*; *ante'* is additionally defined as against. As such, some bend the "before" understanding as a wedge issue to sow doubt with Christians, to redefine Antichrist as a being that became Christ first, and thus the true (dragon) messiah setting up the end-time deception. Accordingly, the dragon messiah will also come before Jesus and will counterfeit everything about Jesus. The Latin *antechrist* spelling was first enlisted in older French circa AD 1228 in a poem "*Tornoiement de l'Antechrist*," by a French monk who translated it as such into modern French (Huon de Mery from Gerrmaine-des-Pres, near Paris). Nostradamus opted to utilize the modern French spelling, *antechrist*, in his writings regarding three antichrist figures, versus the older French spelling of the original manuscript: *Li Tournoiemenz Anticrist*. Thus, Antichrist ought to be understood as a false, substitute, and adversary messiah first, and understood in part as before, but not as the Antichrist will be (falsely) presented as the first and original Messiah.

Antichrist(s) are spurious counterfeit spirit(s) created by fallen angels: "And every spirit that confesseth not that Jesus Christ is come in the flesh is not of God: and this is that spirit of antichrist, whereof ye have heard that it should come; and even now already is it in the world." (1 John 4:3). Of/*ek* in "not of God" is defined as the point of origin.[3846] It follows that if the spirit of antichrist does not originate with God, then those spirits are demonic, disembodied spurious offspring of fallen angels that were in the world at the time of John and before. Antichrist spirits are liars that deny Jesus is the Christ and deny both the Father and the Son, demonic spirits that remain at work until the true Antichrist is revealed with his crowning in the temple.[3847] The antichrist spirit is not fallen angelic spirit but one should anticipate that the avatara Antichrist will have a fallen angelic avatar supplying his powers, perhaps a demonic avatar. It follows that Antichrist will in part will be from "before," as with the incarnation into Antichrist of the spirit of the Anti-

---

[3843] Matt 24:24; Mark 13:22. G5580—*psyoo-dokh'-ris-tos*: a spurious Messiah; false Christ; one who falsely makes claim to be the Messiah; transliterated: pseudochristo;. synonymous with H5890.
[3844] Deut 2:12; Josh 11:10.
[3845] *Webster's*, 16: ante.
[3846] G1537—*ek*: denoting origin as in out of, from, by, away from.
[3847] 2 Thess 2:4, 7–8; 1 John 2:22.

christ, perhaps a Nimrod or antediluvian giant, and an incarnation of an angelic avatar spirit known as the *christo*/christ consciousness in polytheism.

Antichrist will be a spiritual chimera beast, a creature who denies the Father and Son in his ignorance, arrogance, temerity, and hubris. Fallen angels utilize humans, Nephilim, Rephaim, and disembodied demonic spirits of the latter two to slander loyal angels, God, Jesus, and the Holy Spirit, because fallen angels know the power of God Most High. The psalmist says, "So foolish was I, and ignorant: I was as a beast before thee."[3848] A spiritual beast is ignorant before God, incapable of appreciating the knowledge, power, goodness, and love of the Alpha-Omega, too callous to learn from God. Spiritual beasts are banned from heaven. They "despise dominion, and speak evil of dignities.. .. But these speak evil of those things which they know not: but what they know naturally, as brute beasts, in those things they corrupt themselves." Knowing the spirit of antichrist attributes makes sense of why Antichrist will possess the temerity to "magnify himself above every god and shall speak marvelous things against the God of gods, and shall prosper till the indignation be accomplished: for that that is determined shall be done" (Dan 11:36).

Antichrist will be "more stout" than the ten kings. He will speak "great things. .. great words against the most High." Antichrist will try "to change the times and laws"; will speak great blasphemies against God and all those who dwell in heaven; and will make war "with the saints. .. for a time, times, and the dividing of a time" (three-and-a-half years).[3849] Antichrist will magnify himself as "the prince of the host"; will deny the Father and the Son; and will trample on truth and Jerusalem during the rebellion/transgression that causes desolation[3850] in the great tribulation.

The false prophet, the counterfeit Elijah, will exercise all the power of Antichrist and on behalf of Antichrist. The false prophet will speak like a dragon/ *drak'own*,[3851] like a Satan on behalf of Antichrist, Satan, the host of fallen angels, and for the religion and government of Antichrist. Accordingly, the dragon is described as the beast of empires and Satan in Revelation 12, 13, and 17.

The false prophet will create a technologically advanced wonder, an image/ *ikone'* (a likeness or statue)[3852] of Antichrist that will speak, think, and have the power to enforce the worship of Antichrist. The image will have the power and capability to slay those who refuse to worship Antichrist, and will control transactions of every kind and method through the imposed mark of the beast.[3853] One deduces the mark will be the Babylon-like, highly sophisticated, technological, and comprehensive implant system delivering digital portals to deliver perpetual

---

[3848] Ps 73:22; Jude 1:8, 9, 10.
[3849] Dan 7:8, 20, 21, 25; Rev 13:4–10.
[3850] Dan 8:10, 11, 12; 9:26–27; 11:36, 12:7; 2 Thess 2:4; 1 John 2:22; Rev 11:2.
[3851] Rev 13:15. G1404—*drak'-own*.
[3852] G1504—*i-kone'*: a likeness; a statue; a profile; a representation; an image; transliterated: eikon.
[3853] Rev 13:15–18.

healthcare (pharmaceuticals, vaccines, and all kinds of bots and supplements), access to the global commerce system, communication systems; and will impose a twenty-four hour surveillance and social credit system through AI, quantum computing, digital currency, and all kinds of digital, genetic, and subatomic scientific technology currently being developed and readied for implementation. Babylon will put the beast system in place for Antichrist to usurp and advance.

The false prophet will give life/*pnyoo'mah* to the image that will become a sentient-like being. The image will be an *oykaytay'reeon*, technologically created as a dwelling place[3854] for demonic spirit(s) that control artificial intelligence and technology. The image will be a talking idol: "And he had power to give life unto the image of the beast, that the image of the beast should both speak, and cause that as many as would not worship the image of the beast should be killed."[3855] Talking idols are reminiscent of mysterious Old Testament passages like Zechariah 10:2: "For the idols have spoken vanity, and the diviners have seen a lie, and have told false dreams; they comfort in vain." These idols were unique: they spoke vanity/*'aven* as in iniquity, mischief, lies, and manifested false dreams to the diviners/*qacam* meaning soothsayers or false prophets. Most idols do not speak, and derive from *gilluwl* and `*eliyl*.[3856] The idols/images described in Zechariah 10 were consulted for advice and prophesied for those who possessed them, as Nebuchadnezzar did:

> Ezek 21:21 For the king of Babylon stood at the parting of the way, at the head of the two ways, to use divination: he made his arrows bright, he consulted with images, he looked in the liver.

Talking idols housed spirits who advised their servants, the wizards and necromancers that God forbid Israel to consult (Lev 20:6; Deut 18:11). Talking idols (Ezek 21:21; Zech 10:2) were *traphiym* spirits translated in the KJV as teraphim/idols.[3857] Teraphim were images stolen by Rachel, a wife of Jacob, from her father Laban, when they fled the land of the east. *Traphiym* were distinct idols of a god, more than just family heirlooms; they talked.[3858] *Traphiym,* according to *Strong's Cyclopaedia,* has a matching Hebrew female plural format *teraphoth* that was akin to Greek goddesses like Cybele who consulted idols for oracular purposes.[3859]

[3854] G4151—*pnyoo'-mah*; G3613—*oy-kay-tay'-ree-on.* 2 Cor 5:2; Jude 6.

[3855] Rev 13:15–18.

[3856] H205—*'aven, aw-ven':* vanity; wickedness; an idol; affliction; evil; false; iniquity, mischief; wickedness; H7080—*qacam, kaw-sam':* determine by lot or magical scroll; to divine; a diviner; a soothsayer; false prophets; H457—*'eliyl, el-eel':* specifically, an idol of false gods; H1544—*gilluwl, ghil-lool'; gillul, ghil-lool':* an idol; idols; image.

[3857] Judg 17:5; 18:14, 17, 18, 20; Hos 3:4.

[3858] H8655—*traphiym, ter-aw-feme':* teraphim; a family idol; idol; images used for idolatry.

[3859] *Strong's Cyclopaedia,* Vol. 10, 280: teraphim

Traphiym is further rooted in the Hebrew word *rapha'*,[3860] the root word for Rephaim and evil spirits, noting Israel at times sacrificed to devils/*shed* and/or demons.[3861] Some biblical scholars derive the male singular format of *Traph* from Syriac *Araph*,[3862] the name Josephus identified with Goliath's father. It follows that familiar spirits/*owb* are connected to images/*traphiym* idols in 2 Kings 23:24 and to idolatry/*traphiym* in 1 Samuel 15:23.[3863]

The end times are destined to experience the return of the teraphim, multiple demons in multiple idols first with Babylon and its the false prophets, and then with Antichrist, the false prophet, and the image of the beast. Antichrist's teraphim idol will "cause that as many as would not worship the image of the beast should be killed" (Rev 13:15). Those who receive the mark, who worship Antichrist and worship Satan, will be judged for their actions, sentenced to torment day and night with fire and brimstone in the lake of fire for ever and ever.[3864] The lake of fire is the place of the second death after the judgment,[3865] and the place where some will be tormented forever: those who take the mark, Antichrist, false prophet, fallen angels, and Terrible Ones/demons.[3866] Accepting the mark of the beast will be cognate to crimes committed by fallen angels and demons that crosses the threshold of forgiveness.

> Matt 12:31 Wherefore I say unto you, All manner of sin and blasphemy shall be forgiven unto men: but the blasphemy against the Holy Ghost shall not be forgiven unto men.
>
> Matt 12:32 And whosoever speaketh a word against the Son of man, it shall be forgiven him: but whosoever speaketh against the Holy Ghost, it shall not be forgiven him, neither in this world, neither in the world to come.

The sacrifice of the Lamb of God covers all sins and blasphemies, except for those who blaspheme or speak against the Holy Spirit. Blasphemy is defined as vilifying, speaking evil against, slandering, railing against, and in so doing being abusive and injurious.[3867] One might look at this kind of blasphemy as reimagining the Holy Spirit to be an angel manifested in the physical world as a wife

---

[3860] H7495—*rapha'*.

[3861] Deut 32:17; Ps 106:37. H7700—*shed, shade*; a doemon; devil; demon.

[3862] *Strong's Cyclopaedia*, Vol. 10, 280: teraphim.

[3863] H178—*'owb, obe*: a mumbler; a necromancer; familiar spirit; one who evokes the dead ghost or spirit.

[3864] Rev 13:4, 8, 13–16; 14:9; 16:2; 19:20; 20:4.

[3865] Rev 20:13–15.

[3866] Matt 13:41–42; 25:41, 46; Mark 9:43, 45; Rev 14:10; 19:20; 20:10, 14; 21:8.

[3867] G988—*blas-fay-me'-ah*: vilification especially against God; blasphemy; evil speaking; railing against; slander; injurious; impious; transliterated: blasphemia; G989—*blas'-fay-mos*: scurrilous; calumnious; a special impious against God; blasphemer; railing; speaking evil; slanderous; abusive; transliterated: blasphemos.

or consort of another angel, as in polytheism's mother goddess concept with Ashtaroth/*'Asharowth* of the Baalim as one example. The mother/fertility goddess creates life through physical sexual reproduction with her partner god or humans to produce offspring gods, demigods, and all kinds of creatures with counterfeit spirits documented in prehistory; all of which is slanderous and injurious to the Spirit of God, who provides life at God's command. The Holy Spirit is not a wifely partner of God but God's life-sustaining Spirit, working in partnership with the Word of God to create at God's command.

Oaths/*'owth/oth*[3868] meaning mark, sign, omen, and warning that was sworn by Watchers to create demigod giants both before and after the flood passed on their immortal spirit as counterfeit spirits, which was a violation against the laws of creation and the Holy Spirit. Naphalim Watchers, their technology, and their demigods corrupted/*shacath* the antediluvian world's plant genomes and DNA of land animals. The Naphalim world was an initiated order of oaths, rituals, and blasphemies against the Holy Spirit, sins not forgivable and punishable by perpetual torture in the lake of fire. Demigod giants railed against the Holy Spirit in their rituals and blasphemies, while they raised up their fallen mother goddesses to substitute for the Holy Spirit. One deduces that those who accept the mark of the beast, through oath-based worship of Antichrist and Satan, will accept into them the counterfeit wisdom/*sofee'ah*/Sophia[3869] mother goddess spirit as the divine essence, the Atman, and the *christo* consciousness.

> Rev 13:5 And there was given unto him a mouth speaking great things and blasphemies; and power was given unto him to continue forty and two months.

> Rev 13:6 And he opened his mouth in blasphemy against God, to blaspheme his name, and his tabernacle, and them that dwell in heaven.

In polytheism the Atman derives from ancient Hindu theology for a term in the *Rigveda* identifying a "universal self," the "inmost self," or an essence akin to a breath that is linked to the Brahman in the Upanishads and Bhagavad Gita.[3870] The Atman/Brahman in Hinduism is the nebulous "unborn being/non-being" that neither the gods nor demons know of its manifestation, and that the Atman dwells in all gods like Vishnu, Siva, Indra, Nagas, Maruts, and Krishna as its creator.[3871] Thus the Brahma is the Hindu triad with Brahman as the creator, Vishnu

---

[3868] H226 —'owth;oth: sign, omen; mark; warning; miracle; banner; token; standard.

[3869] G4678 —sofee'ah: wisdom.

[3870] *Encyclopedia Americana*, Vol. 2, 507b; *The Bhagavad Gita,* trans. Swami Nikkhilananda (New York: Haddon Craftsman, 1944), 239–242, 10:8–15; 288, 13:7–12.

[3871] *Bhagavad Gita*, 242–249, 10:12–32.

as the preserver of life, and the Shiva the destroyer.[3872] The Atman is alternatively known as the supreme self, divine consciousness, divine light, divine, knowledge, and divine bliss that can dwell in your body.[3873] The Atman is invisible and can be absorbed into the body, but is not affected or intermixed with the body. The Atman is the existence of all knowledge in all dimensions by which its invisible fire consumes all sin, makes one perfect, and permits one to attain supreme peace as one with the divine essence of the universe. One attains immortality and the final stage of evolution through the fire of the knowledge of the divine essence, the Atman.[3874] The invisible and unmeasurable Atman and its knowledge merges with measurable particles at the quantum level, sending its knowledge instantaneously through all dimensions through quantum entanglement, which can be tapped into as the "lamp of wisdom" via meditation and yoga.[3875]

The mark/*khar'agmah* of the beast will be a conduit to create the New Man concept, a new kind of demigod status with hive-mind capacity. The mark implant will be a wonder-technology for a multidimensional nexus to the entire beast system. It will promise all kinds of miracle-like healthcare, therapeutics, and pharmaceuticals, and will offer immortality in the physical world with unlimited knowledge through the Atman. Anticipate that the healthcare delivery system through the mark implant will change genes, DNA, and the elemental building blocks of life.

Mark/*khar'agmah* was defined in antiquity as "a scratch or etching as in a stamp or badge of servitude," a branded mark of ownership, and a graven sculptured figure of idolatry.[3876] "Graven" is translated from *charash*, understood as writing etched into a table and on hearts. It follows that the mark will embed a legally binding title of ownership and blasphemy upon the hearts and within DNA, genes, and blood types through changes made therein by the spirit of the divine essence, administered by Antichrist's teraphim. *Charash* can also mean hold, secrecy, conceal, and remain silent about.[3877] One might anticipate that the mark

---

[3872] *Encyclopedia Americana*, Vol. 4, 393.

[3873] *Bhagavad Gita*, 136-137, 4:23–25; 163–167, 6:7–18; 287–289, 13:7–12.

[3874] Ibid., 125–133, 4:6, 10, 19, 23, 25, 30, 31, 38, 145, notes; 241, 10:11; 242, 10:12–14; 288, 13:12.

[3875] Ibid., 241, 10:11.

[3876] G5480—*khar'-ag-mah*: a scratch or etching as in stamp or badge of servitude; an imprinted or branded mark; a sculptured figure as in graven or mark of idolatry; transliterated: charagma.

[3877] H2790—*charash, khaw-rash'*: plough; scratch; engrave with the use of tools; to fabricate any material; figuratively to devise in a bad sense; secrecy; conceal; remain silent; peace; hold. Peace: Held: Gen 24:21; 34:5; Num 30:7, 11, 14; 1 Sam 10:27; 25:36; 2 Kings 18:36; Neh 5:8; Esth 7:4; Isa 36:21. Silence: Ps 32:3, 22; 50:3, 21; Isa 41:1. Tongue: Esth 7:4; Job 6:24; 13:19; Hab 1:13. Devise: Prov 3:29; 14:22. Deviseth: Prov 6:14, 18. Holdest: Esth 4:14; Hab 1:13. Holdeth: Prov 11:12; 17:28. Kept: Ps 32:3; 50:21. Conceal: Job 41:12. Graven: Jer 17:1. Imagine: Prov 12:20. Left: Jer 38:27. Quiet: Judg 16:2. Rest: Zeph 3:17. Secretly: 1 Sam 23:9. Speak: 2 Sam 19:10. Speaking: Jer 38:27.

will include an oath/'*owth*, as is required in all polytheist religions and introduced by fallen angels on Mount Hermon—an oath of loyalty to Antichrist and Satan, and opposing and denying the Holy Spirit, Jesus, and God. Thus, God will hold people accountable to a blasphemy against the Holy Spirit sworn to in polytheist oaths. *Charash* can mean peace as well, as utilized twenty-six times in the Old Testament, all of which is reminiscent of Antichrist's peace and safety promises.[3878]

> Exod 32:16 And the tables were the work of God, and the writing was the writing of God, graven upon the tables.
>
> Jer 17:1 The sin of Judah is written with a pen of iron, and with the point of a diamond: it is graven upon the table of their heart, and upon the horns of your altars.

"Graven" is additionally translated in the Old Testament from *pecel*, as it was penned for graven images, carved or manufactured idols; idol/ *'eliyl* is an image of a false god and its divination.[3879] Graven/*pecel* as a manufactured idol is important as it relates to the mark definition of a graven or sculptured idol and image of Antichrist. Further, graven/*khar'agmah* is utilized in the book of Acts to describe gold, silver, and stone idols, as graven idols made by humans.[3880] The Antichrist image might be a holographic projection produced by fallen angelic technology, an advanced conduit for the beast technology implant scratched or embedded into the hand or forehead with written AI and quantum bit programming and daemon algorithms.

> Lev 26:1 Ye shall make you no idols nor graven image, neither rear you up a standing image, neither shall ye set up any image of stone in your land, to bow down unto it.

Antichrist will be a spiritual beast: "the man of sin. .. who opposeth and exalteth himself above all that is called God, or that is worshipped; so that he as God sitteth in the temple of God, shewing himself that he is God."[3881] Scripture identifies Antichrist as the beast:[3882] "that thou sawest was, and is not; and shall ascend out of the bottomless pit, and go into perdition: and they that dwell on

---

[3878] Dan 11:21; 1 Thess 5:3.
[3879] H6459—*pecel, peh'-sel*: an idol; carved graven image; graven. Graven: Exod 20:4; Lev 26:1; Deut 4:16, 23, 25; 5:8; 27:15; Judg 17:3, 4; 18:14, 17, 20, 30, 31; 2 Kings 21:7; Ps 97:7; Isa 40:19, 20; 42:17; 44:9, 10, 15, 17; 45:20; 48:5; Jer 10:14; 51:17; Nah 1:14; Hab 2:18. Carved: Judg 18:18, 2 Chron 33:7. Image: Jer 10:14; 51:17. H457—*'eliyl*.
[3880] Acts 17:29.
[3881] 2 Thess 2:3–4.
[3882] Rev 13:3, 4, 12, 14, 15; 17:8, 11, 12, 16, 17; 19:19; 20:4, 10.

ANTICHRIST: THE BEAST OF EMPIRES

the earth shall wonder, whose names were not written in the book of life from the foundation of the world, when they behold the beast that was, and is not, and yet is.. .. The beast that was, and is not, even he is the eighth, and is of the seven, and goeth into perdition."[3883] Antichrist is the eighth empire and a beast king, as were his predecessor antichrist, beastlike figures: "These great beasts, which are four, are four kings, which shall arise out of the earth.. .. And there are seven kings: five are fallen, and one is, and the other is not yet come."[3884]

Somehow, Antichrist will rise out of the abyss prison. Perhaps this occurs when Antichrist receives a mortal head wound but lives, counterfeiting Christ's resurrection. This event will take place after the abyss prion is opened, just before the midpoint of the last seven years, when Antichrist usurps power.[3885] One might anticipate that the dragon messiah will manipulate a specific verse in the book of John to build on his mythos and counterfeit resurrection. Anticipate then that Antichrist will claim to be one raised up as Moses lifted the serpent (fiery serpent/ seraphim).[3886] Anticipate that Antichrist will then promise godhood in the physical world to the inhabitants of the earth, delivered through the mark of the beast and the image of the beast, and its highly advanced technology supplying perpetual healing, akin to the raised seraphim/dragon in the time of the first Exodus, and the new body promised Christians in the resurrection.[3887]

> John 3:14 And as Moses lifted up the serpent in the wilderness, even so must the Son of man be lifted up:
>
> John 3:15 That whosoever believeth in him should not perish, but have eternal life.

The Antichrist beast will rise out of the sea, both the abyss and the abyss/sea of nations, just as the seven beast empires past and future rise out of the sea.[3888] Michael will sit down late in the first three-and-a-half years, to permit the coming of Antichrist. The beast empires of the last days are the hydra red dragon monster of Revelation 12, 13, and 17.[3889]

> Rev 13:1 And I stood upon the sand of the sea, and saw a beast rise up out of the sea, having seven heads and ten horns, and upon his horns ten crowns, and upon his heads the name of blasphemy.

[3883] Rev 13:1, 2, 17; 17:8, 11.
[3884] Dan 4:17; Rev 17:10.
[3885] Dan 9:27; 11:31–39; 2 Thess 2:4; Rev 13:3, 4–18; 9:1–12.
[3886] Num 21:7–9. Fiery Serpent: H8314—*saraph*: Num 21:6, 8; Isa 6:1–4.
[3887] 2 Cor 5:1–10; Eph 4:22–24; Phil 3:21.
[3888] Dan 7:2–8, 17–25.
[3889] Rev 12:3, 13:1–4, 17:7–14.

Antichrist will receive his power from the dragon, the ten kings of the beast empire, Satan, and/or perhaps Azazel/Apollyon/Abaddon as the son of perdition/ *apo'lia*.[3890] Judas too is called a son of perdition in John 17:12 as someone Satan entered to betray Jesus,[3891] and thus a prophetic allegory for an adversary of Jesus. One deduces that the son of perdition refers to a counterfeit demon spirit and/or fallen angelic spirit, one that comes out of the abyss. On the angelic side one might select Azazel as the destroyer god of war before the flood, but because the beast spirit lurks and is from the seven beast empires, one may also wish to anticipate a past antichrist candidate: perhaps Nimrod of Babel, or Nebuchadnezzar of Babylon who created an image of himself to worship, an image of gold ninety to one hundred five feet tall and nine to ten and a half feet wide.[3892] Perhaps Antichrist will be a beast king like Alexander the Great, as Antichrist seems to be directly connected to Alexander in Daniel 8.[3893] Alexander is the rough goat in the vision, noting rough derives from Hebrew *sa`iyr*/satyr, a degraded goat-god like Azazel.

Dan 8:21 And the rough goat is the king of Grecia: and the great horn that is between his eyes is the first king.

[3890] 2 Thess 2:3, 9; Rev 12:3, 4, 9, 17; 13:2, 4, 5; 17:8, 11, 12, 16, 17.
[3891] Luke 22:3; John 13:27.
[3892] Dan 1:1.
[3893] Gen 10:8–9; Dan 8:21, 23–25.

CHAPTER 82

ANTICHRIST'S REIGN OF TERROR

Rev 13:5 And there was given unto him a mouth speaking great things and blasphemies; and power was given unto him to continue forty and two months.

Antichrist will usurp power after taking credit for saving the world from the counterfeit Armageddon war of Ezekiel 38–39, Joel 1–2, and Revelation 9. His reign of terror will continue until the ordained time concludes, and when the desolation poured out on Antichrist ends at Armageddon.[3894]

Whatever pedigree Antichrist struts out to stake his claim as the dragon messiah, anticipate that the house of Dragon gens will be trace back to degraded hairy (*sa*) Watchers (`*iyr*) and their spurious offspring that deny Jesus as the Son, Word of God, Messiah, and Redeemer, as the Antichrist who "opposes and exalteth himself" against God and Jesus.[3895] Antichrist will be a seed from the "terrible of nations," a Terrible One/`*Ariytim* described in Ezekiel's dual prophecy that states: "Wilt thou yet say before him that slayeth thee, I am God? but thou shalt be a man, and no God, in the hand of him that slayeth thee" (Ezek 28:9). Antichrist will be the apex of the Terrible Ones' narcissism, arrogance, and pride, the "haughtiness of the terrible" that will be laid low in the end times.[3896] Antichrist will be the Ter-

---

[3894] Dan 9:27; 11:31; 12:11; Rev 16:1–21.
[3895] 2 Thess 2:4.
[3896] Isa 13:11; 29:20.

rible One, of the "terrible ones" destroyed upon a mountain among a "multitude of all the nations" when Jesus removes the "covering cast" and the "vail that is spread over all nations" at Armageddon.[3897]

Antichrist will flaunt the imagery of the metallic empires of giants: the gold of Babylon reflecting its opulence, arrogance, and temerity with the desecration of the temple; the silver of Persia representing military armor, expertise, and the laurel bar of bravery in battle; the bronze of Greece reflecting the speed of Alexander's conquest and the shining seraphim raised up on a pole to cure the world; and the iron of Rome depicting its strength, ruthlessness, and viciousness who will trample all who oppose the empire (Dan 2). Moreover, Antichrist's empire will reflect the beast empires of Daniel 7 with the regalia and royal pedigree of the lion beast of Babylon. The Persia bear will be represented in the ancient world's understanding where bear gods dispensed punishment for disrespectful or rebellious behavior, and as Persia clenched three ribs in its mouth (Egypt, Assyria, Babylon), so will Antichrist overthrow three kings.[3898] Antichrist will viciously and quickly seize his empire reflecting the leopard empire of Greece, while the Roman beast empire will be reflected as a diverse and changed[3899] empire that will trample all the earth under its feet. As such, the Antichrist and his empire will rise as an eleventh horn from the seventh empire of ten horns as the eighth empire.

Antichrist's reign after his crowning will transition quickly into tyranny to wage the "great tribulation," even while speciously promising a millennium of "peace and safety," instead bringing "sudden destruction" that "cometh upon on them as travail upon a woman with child, they shall not escape" (1 Thess 5:3). It follows then that 1 Thessalonians 5:1–2 includes the contextual end-time chronology for the sudden destruction: "the day of the Lord so cometh as a thief in the night," first for rapture as a thief, and then Armageddon as a thief at the sixth wrath bowl.[3900] Knowing Jesus comes for rapture like a thief in the night during Antichrist's reign, but before the wrath bowls are poured in the day/year of the Lord's wrath when Jesus again comes like a thief, explains "For God hath not appointed us to wrath [sudden destruction], but to obtain salvation by our Lord Jesus Christ, Who died for us, that, whether we wake or sleep, we should live together with him" (1 Thess 5:9–10), and "to wait for his Son from heaven, whom he raised from the dead, even Jesus, which delivered us from the wrath to come."[3901]

Jesus will save us not only from the year of the wrath bowls, the day/year of the Lord, but will also "keep us from the hour of temptation, which shall come upon all the world, to try them that dwell upon the earth," the "hour" when the ten kings give their power to Antichrist, when all gather for war against the Lamb

---

[3897] Isa 29:5, 6, 7, 20; 25:3–10.
[3898] Dan 7:8, 20.
[3899] H8133—*shna', shen-aw'*: alter, change, be diverse; transformed.
[3900] Matt 24:43–44; Mark 13:2–37; Luke 12:39–40; Rev 3:3; 16:15.
[3901] 1 Thess 1:10.

at Armageddon.[3902] This temptation/*pirasmos'* is a time of testing and fiery trial, which the saints will be saved from. This is the time when Michael stands, which begins the time of trouble, testing, purification, and exodus for Israel. Purification/ *tsaraph* is defined as smelting, refining, a test by fire for people not raptured.[3903]

> Dan 12:10 Many shall be purified, and made white, and tried; but the wicked shall do wickedly: and none of the wicked shall understand; but the wise shall understand.

The above chronology makes sense of the events detailed in Daniel 11. After the overwhelming Gog army is swept away before Antichrist, along with a prince of the covenant[3904] from among the ten kings' seventh empire, Antichrist will launch his meteoric rise to power through a league with the ten kings in a hive-like mind, to overthrow Babylon and share power under Antichrist. Daniel 11 and Revelation 17 indicate a period of perhaps a year or so after the Gog war destruction, until the midpoint of the last seven years. In this hour, Antichrist will act deceitfully, fraudulently with a small group of people, the ten bloodline kings of the world empire. They will plot, speak, and act with treachery, craft, and "subtilty,"[3905] akin to the serpent with Eve in Eden. The league/*chabar* will utilize magic spells, fascination, and the charm of the rising pendragon messiah to mesmerize the global population, supported by the power of Satan with "signs and lying wonders."[3906] Babylon will have false prophets, but Antichrist will have *the* false prophet, the counterfeit Elijah who will appear to be a lamb but will speak like a dragon (seraphim or a Satan). The false prophet will perform counterfeit miracles that include bringing fire down from the heavens at will, miracles that deceive the masses so that they will accept the delusion, accept the mark, and then worship Antichrist—miracles that will include a counterfeit resurrection from a mortal head wound.[3907]

When the richest empires, likely three western empires, begin to feel secure, Antichrist will invade them and distribute their wealth to the poorer empires and their nations.[3908] Antichrist will plot the overthrow of fortresses for "a time," a year after the Gog war before he is crowned in Jerusalem.[3909] The year of plotting the overthrow of kings will include a large battle against a king from the ten-king end-time empire,

---

[3902] Rev 3:10; 17:12–14.
[3903] Dan 12:1–13; Rev 12:1-18. H6884—*tsaraph, tsaw-raf'*: to fuse metal as in refine; purge; purify; smelt; test.
[3904] Ezek 38:18–23; 39:1–20; Dan 9:27; 11:22; Joel 1:6–20; 2:1–11; Rev 9:15-21.
[3905] H4820—*mirmah, meer-maw'*: deceiving; fraud: craft; deceitfully; guile, subtilty.
[3906] Dan 11:22–23. H2266—*chabar, khaw-bar'*: magic spells; fascination; charm; couple together; a fellowship; join; league; unite; an alliance. 2 Thess 2:9.
[3907] Rev 13:3–15.
[3908] Dan 7:8, 20; 11:22–23.
[3909] Dan 11:24.

"the king of the south," another possible antichrist wannabe who will march to war with a great/*gadowl* and mighty/*atsuwm* army but will not stand/*`amad*: endure. Supporters of Antichrist's alliance, along with traitors within the king of the south's inner circle, "they that feed of the portion of his meat," will plot, and will "forecast devices" that will cause the great southern army to be "overflowed" as in swept away, "destroyed," and "slain."[3910] After the battle, Antichrist and the king (perhaps a new one) of the south will become allies, because together they do "mischief" thereafter. Mischief derives dually from *mera`*: a confidential friend, wickedness, and evil, and *ra`*: evil, distress, and affliction. Each will lie/*ka'ah*[3911] likely to each other and the people of the world that they can change the times, will begin a new age, and that Antichrist's millennium has come, but the "end shall be at the time appointed."[3912]

After defeating the king of the south, Antichrist will return to his land with the riches plundered from the southern war, to continue his exploits. His heart will be bent against the Holy Covenant, awakened Israel, Judah in Jerusalem and around the world, and all who hold to the testimony of Jesus. Antichrist will then return to the south, seemingly to cancel his alliance with the king of the south, but this time the ships of Chittam/*Kittiy* meaning bruisers, Cyprus, or coastlands from the west step up to oppose Antichrist. Antichrist will become grieved, disheartened[3913] at the western opposition (likely North America or an alliance of America and many of the British Commonwealth nations). Antichrist will turn away from the southern march to vent his fury against the Holy Covenant.[3914]

Thus, Antichrist will turn to march against the Covenant Land at the "appointed time." He will "have intelligence with them that forsake the holy covenant." This is the time of the abomination.[3915] Intelligence/*biyn* is defined as cunning and discernment to instruct or teach.[3916] People will wonder after Antichrist as to his origins (the one who once was and now is again from the abyss), his counterfeit resurrection, his intellect, his stoutness as in physical strength, his audacious and skillful oratory, the counterfeit Armageddon he takes credit for winning, his avant-garde warcraft skill, his specious discernment of Scripture, his "lying won-

---

[3910] Dan 11:25–26. H5975—`amad, aw-mad`: to stand; remain standing; abide; appoint; arise; cease; confirm; continue; dwell; be employed; endure; establish; leave; make; be present. Overflow: H7857—*shataph, shaw-taf`*: drown overflow; overwhelm' rinse; wash away; conquered. Devices: H4284—*machashabah, makh-ash-aw-baw`*: a contrivance; a machine; intention; plan; a plot; cunning work; curious work; purpose.

[3911] Dan 11:27. H4827—*mera`, may-rah`*: wickedness; do mischief; confidential friend; H7451— *ra`, rah`*: bad; evil; adversity; affliction; calamity; distress.

[3912] Dan 11:27.

[3913] H3512—*ka'ah, kaw-aw`*: to deject; be grieved, make sad; disheartened; be cowed.

[3914] Dan 11:28–29. H3794—*Kittiy, kit-tee`*: patrial Cyprus, Kittite or Cypriote; an islander in general; Greeks or Romans in the west; bruisers.

[3915] Dan 11:30–31.

[3916] H995—*biyn, bene*: separate mentally; distinguish; understand; consider; cunning; diligently; direct; discern; eloquent; inform; instruct; have intelligence; know; mark; perceive; teach.

ders," the power and signs he receives from Satan, the miracles and signs performed for Antichrist by the false prophet, and the promises of godhood in his counterfeit millennium or new age. The blasphemous and great words Antichrist will speak, and his alleged power to change the times and the laws will be so convincing, spoken with such skill, and supported by such mysterious and unimaginable miracles by the false prophet, that the impossible delusion will be made real for the time of testing and great tribulation: "that they should believe a lie: That they all might be damned who believed not the truth, but had pleasure in unrighteousness."[3917]

> Dan 7:25 And he shall speak great words against the most High, and shall wear out the saints of the most High, and think to change times and laws: and they shall be given into his hand until a time and times and the dividing of time.

> Matt 24:24 For there shall arise false Christs, and false prophets, and shall shew great signs and wonders; insomuch that, if it were possible, they shall deceive the very elect.

Antichrist's arms/*zrowa`*, his armed military forces, will rise to pollute/*chalal* the temple from its strength. *Chalal* is the same Hebrew word translated that Nimrod "began" to be a mighty one, and understood as to break your word or vow, dissolve or to open a wedge, pollute, violate, and defile ritually and sexually.[3918] The inference intended with "pollute" as it pertains to Antichrist's gambit seems to indicate something will change spiritually and/or physically with Antichrist that is akin to what led Nimrod away from following God and/or to become a *gibbowr*/ mighty one. Perhaps Antichrist's metamorphosis physically and spiritually begins with his mortal head wound, his healing, and counterfeit resurrection as an avatara of the avatar Satan or Azazel, and/or possessed by a demon spirit from a Nephilim, Rephaim, or perhaps Nimrod's spirit. Further, Daniel 7 stated Antichrist will be diverse/*shna'* from the ten kings, meaning altered, transformed, and changed.[3919]

Acordingly, one may wish to keep in mind *rapha*/healing is the root word for *rapha*/demon and *rapha*/giant. Antichrist is described as stout/*rab*, as Rephaim were described.[3920] Antichrist will be very strong/`*atsam* and mighty/`*atsam* as in bone-crushing strong, utilized to describe Rephaim of the mighty seven nations.[3921] Strong/`*az* along with `*azaz*/stout was used to describe the Terrible Ones.[3922] As such, Antichrist will do unspeakable evil against the Holy Covenant.

[3917] 2 Thess 2:11–12.
[3918] H2490—*chalal.*
[3919] H8133—*shna', shen-aw'*: alter; change; be diverse; be changed; transformed.
[3920] Dan 7:20.
[3921] Dan 8:8, 24; 11:23.
[3922] Isa 25:3–4.

He will reward flatteries and promises/*chalaqqah*[3923] to those who violate the Holy Covenant or act against those who uphold the Holy Covenant. Those of Judah and awakened Israel who understand will instruct many, even though they will be persecuted, imprisoned, and slain for days/years before the Second Exodus.[3924]

Antichrist, after crowning himself in the Jerusalem temple, will magnify himself above every god and the God Most High. He will be successful until the time of indignation/anger/wrath.[3925] Although Antichrist will claim himself to be God, he will secretly in his estate (private quarters) "honor the god of forces," likely Satan and/or Azazel.[3926] The god(s) Antichrist will worship is described in the Daniel 11 prophecy as a foreign god, *neckar 'elowahh*. Foreign/*Neckar* means from another country, region, or heathendom,[3927] with the latter reflecting a people or race that does not acknowledge the God of the Bible. The term foreign god(s) seems to be referencing gods not worshipped or known before, and which will be kept secret even in the last three-and-a-half years. Further, although it is also used to describe God fifty-two times in the Bible, mostly in the book of Job (forty times), the four Daniel applications of god/*'elowahh* describe a god other than the most High God,[3928] *'elowahh* is the feminine format.[3929] One ponders not only if Satan is worshipped in secret but perhaps Satan's partner goddess/Leviathan who was slain in prehistory.

Antichrist's reign will be a reign of terror: persecution, genocide, corruption, forced worship, and wickedness of every kind. Antichrist will make war against Christians not raptured, Judah, the awakened tribes of Israel, and all those who refuse accept the beast mark or to worship Antichrist and Satan. These are the times/years when "patience and faith" is required of the saints.[3930] During Antichrist's reign of terror, he will strike against the mightiest strongholds and/or countries, promoting those who acknowledge Antichrist as rulers and redistributing the land for gain and money. Antichrist's temerity and terror will largely go unchecked for the first two-and-a-half years. However, at the time/*'eth* of the end/*qets* events will begin to swing against Antichrist when the king of the south and the king of the north storm out like a flood against Antichrist. Antichrist will engage these two kings/empires and invade many lands.[3931] This will begin the Year of the Lord and His wrath.

[3923] H2514—*chalaqqah, khal-ak-kaw'*: flattery; smoothness; fine promises.

[3924] Dan 11:3–35; Rev 12:13–17. H7919—*sakal, saw-kal'*: intelligent; understand; have good success; consider; prudent; wise; have insight.

[3925] H2195—*za'am, zah'-am*: froth at the mouth; fury, especially of God's displeasure with sin; anger; indignation; rage.

[3926] Dan 11:36–38. H3653—*ken, kane*: a stand as in pedestal or station: base; estate; office; place; pedestal; foot.

[3927] H5236—*nekar, nay-kawr'*: foreign, a foreigner, or heathendom: alien; strange; foreign.

[3928] H433—*'elowahh*.

[3929] Dan 11:37, 38, 39: *'elowahh* four times.

[3930] Dan 7:21; 2 Thess 1:4; Rev 12:17; 13:7, 10, 16; 14:12.

[3931] Dan 11:40. H6256—*'eth*: season; time; year as in Dan 12:7 and Rev 12:14. H7093—*qets*: end time.

THE YEAR OF
THE LORD'S WRATH

CHAPTER 83

Isa 34:8 For it is the day of the LORD's vengeance, and the year of recompences for the controversy of Zion.

Discerning end-time chronology requires one to distinguish between the seven years of the end/*qets*, and the appointed/*mow`ed*/*mowged* time for specific events in the last three-and-a-half years. The words end/*qets* and the appointed/*mow`ed*/*mowged* were grouped together in the Old Testament prophecy to denote the solemn assembly that closes out this age.

Qets is translated fifty-three times as "end" in the Old Testament, and fifteen times specifically identifying the last seven years as defined in Daniel 9:26–27.[3932] *Mow`ed*/*mowged* was penned 147 times, and translated twenty times as "appointed."[3933] End/*qets* and appointed/*mow`ed* were grouped together five times to identify important Antichrist events in the last three-and-a-half years when Antichrist comes to power at the abomination, and the rise of the kings of the south and north that begins the Year of the Lord's wrath, culminating with Armageddon.[3934]

Armageddon—*har*/mount *mowged*/*mow`ed*, the Semitic and vowelless Hebrew H-R-M-G-D—was to be understood in the "Hebrew tongue," not the

---

[3932] End (time): Dan 8:17, 19; 9:26; 11:6, 27, 35, 40, 45; 12:4, 6, 9, 13; Hab 2:3.

[3933] Appointed: Dan 8:19; 11:27, 29, 35, 40; Hab 2:3.

[3934] Dan 8:17, 19; 11:27, 35; Hab 2:3.

Greek translation.[3935] H-R-M is the Semitic root word for Hermon, Satan's mountain of mountains alternatively called Mount Sion, and Satan's earthly counterfeit mount of the assembly/*mow`ed/mowged*. Knowing that Jesus instructed the saints to mark and discern the abomination as prophesied by Daniel in his prophecies, as well as John's instructions to discern Armageddon in the Hebrew tongue, leads one back to Daniel 11's last three-and-a-half years, to the appointed/*mow`ed/mowged* end/qets time/*`eth* (an appointed year) that likely should be understood as culminating at the assembly at Satan's mountain for the Armageddon discernment, and Antichrist's appointed destruction. One might further assign a dual meaning to H-R-M-G-D as the Hermon assembly.

Accordingly, "time, times" in Daniel 12:7 is translated into English from *mow`ed/mowged* and not from *`eth;* "time, times, and half (a time)" is generally understood as three-and-a-half years. *Mow`ed/mowged* is further translated as the time for the yearly Feast of Leavened Bread in Exodus 34:18 in "the time/ *mow`ed/mowged* of the month of Abib, for in the month of Abib thou camest out of Egypt," which likely should have been translated as "appointed congregation" or "annual appointed assembly." Similarly, the "appointed assembly" likely is a better translation than "time" in 1 Samuel 9:24, when Samuel feasted with Saul at the time God selected Saul for kingship. *Mow`ed/mowged* is additionally translated as "appointed" twenty times, "feasts" nineteen times, and "congregation" 147 times.[3936] One deduces a time was a yearly period set between appointed holy feasts, just as *`eth* is a time/year. Similarly, Armageddon will be a solemn *charam/ cherem* mountain assembly/*mow`ed/mowged* and or "solemn feast" in Hebrew for the feast of birds and animals, as Revelation 19:17 depicts the feast in Greek "gathered. .. into a place called in the Hebrew tongue Armageddon" (Rev 16:16).[3937]

In the appointed time/year for the accursed utter destruction culminating at the place of the solemn assembly of Armageddon, the kings of the north and south will launch the Year of the Lord's wrath bowls. By this time, Jesus will have already come for the rapture and Second Exodus as part of "the days of the Son of man," when

---

[3935] Rev 16:16.
[3936] Congregation: Exod 27:21; 28:43; 29:4, 10, 11, 30, 32, 42, 44; 30:16, 18, 20, 26, 36; 33:7; 35:21; 38:8, 30; 39:32, 40; 40:2, 6, 7, 12, 22, 24, 26, 29, 30, 32, 34, 35; Lev 1:1, 3, 5; 3:2, 8, 13; 4:4, 5, 7, 14; 4:16, 18; 6:16, 26, 30; 8:3, 4, 31, 33, 35; 9:5, 23; 10:7, 9; 12:6; 14:11, 23; 15:14, 29; 16:7, 16, 17; 17:4, 5, 6, 9; 19:21; 24:3; Num 2:1, 2, 17; 3:7, 8, 25, 38; 4:16; 6:10, 13, 18; 7:5, 89; 8:9, 15, 19, 22, 24, 26; 10:3; 11:16; 12:4; 14:10; 16:2, 18, 19, 42, 50; 18:4, 6, 21, 23, 31; 19:4; 25:6; 27:2; 31:54; Deut 31:14, 30; Josh 18:1; 19:51; 1 Sam 2:22; 1 Kings 8:4; 1 Chron 6:32; 9:21; 23:32; 2 Chron 1:3, 6, 13; 5:5; Ps 75:2; Isa 14:13. Appointed: Exod 23:13, 14, 15; Num 9:2, 3, 7; Josh 8:13, 14; Judg 20:38; 1 Sam 13:11; 20:35; 2 Sam 24:15; Job 30:23; Isa 1:14; Jer 8:7; 6:17; Dan 8:19; 11:27, 29, 35; Hab 2:3. Feasts: Lev 23:2, 4, 37, 44; Num 15:3; 29:39; 1 Chron 23:31; 2 Chron 2:4; 8:13; 31:3; Ezra 3:5; Neh 10:33; Lam 1:4; 2:6; Ezek 36:38; 46:9; Hos 2:11; Zech 8:19.
[3937] Rev 19:17–18. Solemn assembly: Lev 23:36; Num 29:35; Deut 16:8; 2 Kings 10:20; 2 Chron 7:9; Neh 8:18; Joel 1:14; 2:16; Amos 5:21; Zeph 3:18. Solemn feast: Num 15:3; Deut 16:15; 2 Chron 2:4; 8:13; Ps 81:3; Lam 1:4; 2:6, 7, 8; Ezek 36:38; 46:10; Hos 2:12; 12:10; Nah 1:55; Mal 2:3.

"the days of visitation come, the days of recompence are come."[3938] The Second Exodus will be fulfilled during the Year of the Lord's Favor,[3939] which will be followed by the year of recompense and vengeance when Jesus will tread "the winepress alone; and of the people there was none with me: for I will tread them in mine anger, and trample them in my fury; and their blood shall be sprinkled upon my garments, and I will stain all my raiment. For the day of vengeance is in mine heart, and the year of my redeemed is come."[3940] The year of the Lord's wrath, anger, fury, vengeance, and indignation will be poured out over Antichrist's entire world empire:

> Ps 75:8–10 For in the hand of the LORD there is a cup, and the wine is red; it is full of mixture; and he poureth out of the same: but the dregs thereof, all the wicked of the earth shall wring them out, and drink them. But I will declare for ever; I will sing praises to the God of Jacob. All the horns of the wicked also will I cut off; but the horns of the righteous shall be exalted.

> Nah 1:6 Who can stand before his indignation? and who can abide in the fierceness of his anger? his fury is poured out like fire, and the rocks are thrown down by him.

> Zeph 1:17–18. .. And their blood shall be poured out as dust, and their flesh as the dung. Neither their silver nor their gold shall be able to deliver them in the day of the LORD's wrath; but the whole land shall be devoured by the fire of his jealousy: for he shall make even a speedy riddance of all them that dwell in the land.

The appointed end-time wrath poured out in the year of the wrath will be a larger dose than the prophecy of Jeremiah in the days of Nebuchadnezzar. Exploits of beast kingdoms past reflect lesser portions of the beast empire conquest, religious reach, persecution, war, and wrath destruction. Old Testament foreshadowing in these accounts provide discernment for the prophetic allegory poured out in the full portion in the Year of the Lord's wrath.

> Jer 25:15 For thus saith the LORD God of Israel unto me; Take the wine cup of this fury at my hand, and cause all the nations, to whom I send thee, to drink it.

> Jer 25:16 And they shall drink, and be moved, and be mad, because of the sword that I will send among them.

[3938] Hos 9:7; Luke 17:22, 26.
[3939] Isa 61:1–8; Luke 4:18.
[3940] Isa 34:8; 63:3–4.

Jer 25:17 Then took I the cup at the LORD's hand, and made all the nations to drink, unto whom the LORD had sent me:

Jer 25:18 To wit, Jerusalem, and the cities of Judah, and the kings thereof, and the princes thereof, to make them a desolation, an astonishment, an hissing, and a curse; as it is this day.

Ergo, one might anticipate that at the appointed time when the kings of the north and south kick off the last year with their campaigns will manifest many of the first bowl wraths. The first bowl poured out will begin the last year, just before the kings of the north and south revolt against Antichrist.

Hab 2:3 For the vision is yet for an appointed time, but at the end it shall speak, and not lie: though it tarry, wait for it; because it will surely come, it will not tarry.

Rev 16:1 And I heard a great voice out of the temple saying to the seven angels, Go your ways, and pour out the vials of the wrath of God upon the earth.

The first bowl causes "noisome and grievous sores" upon those who will take the mark to worship Antichrist.[3941] Noisome/*kos'ak* is generally understood as evil, injurious, and of a bad nature, while harmful and grievous/*ponayros'* is understood as evil, diseased, morally culpable, anguish, pain, trouble; and "the evil" (*ponayros'*) of Satan (Matt 6:13). The sore/*hel'kos* is defined as a wound, likely a sore that discharges pus.[3942] The sore/wound will be a calamity attached directly to Antichrist worship,[3943] the rituals performed to and through his image, and interaction with the mark implant. Both the mark and the rituals of worship imply some form of physical and spiritual incompatibility and a crime against God, Jesus, the Holy Spirit, and the laws of creation that produces a painful state of toil, and distinguishing new marks of evil identifying them as Satan's doomed ones. One deduces the people and kings who swear oaths of allegiance to Antichrist and accept the mark of the beast will rec-

---

[3941] Rev 16:2

[3942] Noisome: G2556—*k-os'ak*: worthless; depraved; injurious; bad; of a bad nature; troublesome; destructive; baneful; evil; harm; ill; noisome; wicked; transliterated: kakos. Grievous: G4190—*pon-ay-ros'*; a derivative of 4192: hurtful as in evil; calamitous; diseased; morally culpable; derelict, vicious; malice; the devil, wicked; hardship; painful; a bad nature. The word is used in the nominative case in Matthew 6:13, usually denoting a title in Greek. Hence Christ is saying, deliver us from "the Evil," and is probably referring to Satan; transliterated: poneros; G4192—*pon'-os*: toil in anguish; pain; trouble; transliterated: pono. Sore: G1668—*hel'-kos*: an ulcer; a sore; a wound; a wound producing a discharge of pus; transliterated: helkos.

[3943] G4352—*pros-koo-neh'-o*: meaning to kiss, like a dog licking his master's hand; to prostrate oneself in homage and worship; transliterated: proskuneo.

ognize the plague as coming from God, and the implications that will soon follow. It follows that many will hold Antichrist accountable for their marked destruction soon to come. The kings of the north and south will revolt against Antichrist at this appointed time, because of wrath sores from the first bowl.[3944]

The kings of the north and south will push/*nagach*, meaning to gore or wage war against Antichrist with many chariots, horsemen, and ships.[3945] Antichrist then begins his destructive romp through many countries that will begin the same kind of destruction as the wars and catastrophes of the birth pangs, seals, and trumpets;[3946] however, this dose will be full-strength. As such, the second wrath bowl will be poured over the sea, killing everything therein; the third wrath bowl will be poured over all the rivers and fountains, producing tainted drinking water. The people of Antichrist's eighth world empire will be forced to drink contaminated water in the last year.[3947]

The same pattern of full-strength sorrows continues in the fourth and fifth wrath bowls poured out over the sun, so that the sun will scorch those who worship Antichrist. The response of the marked will not be to repent but to blaspheme God and those in heaven, as spiritual beasts do. The sun and stars will then go dark from the clouds of destruction rising around the earth from the wars thereof, so much so that Antichrist's global empire will be in darkness. The marked will gnaw their tongues in pain because of the sores of the mark and burns from the sun.[3948]

The sixth wrath bowl will trigger the Euphrates River to dry up;[3949] its dams will have been released or destroyed at the midpoint of the last seven years, in a gambit by Antichrist and Satan to destroy fleeing Judah after witnessing the abomination: "And the serpent cast out of his mouth water as a flood after the woman, that he might cause her to be carried away of the flood." "In the day that the great trumpet is blown" "The LORD shall beat off from the channel of the river [Euphrates] unto the stream of Egypt, and ye shall be gathered one by one, O ye children of Israel." "And your covenant with death shall be disannulled, and your agreement with hell shall not stand; when the overflowing scourge shall pass through, then ye shall be trodden down by it."[3950]

The scorching sun of the fourth wrath bowl will dry up the shallowed waters of the Euphrates. As a result, a way will be prepared for armies to pass over and to gather the mountain of assembly.[3951] The Kadmonim/*Qadmoniym* and KKK giant

---

[3944] Dan 11:40.

[3945] Dan 11:40–41. H5055—*nagach, naw-gakh'*: to but with the horns; gore, thrust at; push; wage war against.

[3946] Dan 11:41–43.

[3947] Rev 16:3–7.

[3948] Rev 16:8–11.

[3949] Rev 16:12.

[3950] Isa 27:1–10, 12–13; 28:13–21; Rev 12:15–16.

[3951] G2090—*het-oy-mad'-zo*: to prepare; provide; make ready; necessary preparations; from the oriental custom of sending on before kings on their journeys persons to level the roads and make them passable.

bloodline "kings of the east"[3952] will then begin their march at the appointed time when the world prepares for total war. To ensure all the kings of the global empire and their armies gather, the sixth wrath bowl commissions unclean/demonic spirits and devils[3953] from the mouths of the false prophet, Antichrist, and the dragon/Satan to perform miracles/*saymi'on*: signs and wonders before the end-time kings and the whole world, to persuade them to gather for the "great day of God Almighty."[3954] Demons from the mouth/*stom'a* could alternatively be translated as a commanded by each of the three, noting the devil/Satan/*deeab'olos* is the prince and leader of the demons, and that Antichrist and the false prophet will receive power and authority from the dragon/Satan.[3955] It follows that each will have authority to command demons to go forth to perform signs and wonders.

Tidings, news, and/or reports from the east/*mizrach* and the north/*tsaphown* will trouble/*bahal* Antichrist. *Bahal* is defined by such words as vex, alarm, frighten, and terrify.[3956] One understands that Antichrist will be concerned with the eastern alliance, and other end-time kings joining with the king of the north to march against Antichrist, but the "kings of the east" (*hay'leeos*) is seemingly not what terrifies Antichrist.[3957] Remember, Antichrist will be the lord of war and destruction on the earth: "Who will be able to make war with him?" (Rev 13:4).

What terrifies Antichrist will be the coming of Jesus for the battle and vengeance at Armageddon. When the kings of the east and all the kings of the earth assemble for war, this will be the appointed time the book of Revelation prophecies state Jesus will come again like a "thief" (Rev 16:15) as part of his days/years of visitation.[3958] Knowing this elucidates Antichrist's terror, manifested by the tidings from the north/*tsaphown*. *Tsaphown* is defined as hidden, a place of unknown, a place of gloom, and figuratively the north, a word derived from *tsaphan* meaning hidden ones.[3959] Jesus and His sudden appearance of his hidden army of "sanctified

---

[3952] Gen 15:15; Rev 16:12. H6935—*Qadmoniy*.

[3953] Rev 16:13–14. Unclean: G169—*ak-ath'-ar-tos*: impure as in ceremonially lewd, demonic; and foul; transliterated: akathartos. Devils: G1142—*dah'ee-mown*; a daemon or supernatural spirit of an evil nature; a devil; and inferior deity; an evil spirit; transliterated: daimon.

[3954] Rev 16:14. G4592—*say-mi'-on*: supernatural: miracle, sign, token or wonder; transliterated: semeion.

[3955] Rev 12:9; 13:2, 4, 11, 12. G4750—*stom'-a*; the mouth as if a gash in the face; by implication language; figurative an opening and the front or edge of a weapon; face; the thoughts and orders of a man uttered by his mouth; transliterated: stoma.

[3956] Dan 11:44. H926—*bahal, baw-hal'*: to tremble inwardly; suddenly alarm or agitate; frighten; vex; disturb; terrify; dismay; make haste.

[3957] Dan 11:44; Rev 16:8. H4217—*mizrach, miz-rawkh'*; from 2224: place of sunrise; the east; eastward. G2246—*hay'-lee-os*: the sun; by implication light; the light of day; rays of the sun; the east. Transliterated: helios.

[3958] Hos 9:5–7; Luke 17:20.

[3959] H6828—*tsaphown, tsaw-fone'*; or *tsaphon, tsaw-fone'*; from 6845: hidden, dark; used only of the north as a place of gloom and unknown; northward; H6845—*tsaphan, tsaw-fan'*: to hide; treasure up; hidden ones; to hoard; reserve; store up.

ones," and those who "rejoice in my highness" who suddenly appear to "battle" the "nations gathered,"[3960] will be what terrifies Antichrist. Jesus is the One from the north, and the One from the rising of the sun/*shemesh*, the east,[3961] who will come to tread on the princes at Armageddon:

> Isa 41:25 I have raised up one from the north, and he shall come: from the rising of the sun shall he call upon my name: and he shall come upon princes as upon morter, and as the potter treadeth clay.

> Isa 41:26 Who hath declared from the beginning, that we may know? and beforetime, that we may say, He is righteous?

At this appointed time, all the sins committed against Israel and Judah in the past and future, including Israel's kin nations, will be avenged by *Yhovah* during the events leading up to and including Armageddon.[3962] Edom, Moab, and Ammon, peoples Israel was commanded not to war with in the Covenant Land conquest in the days of Moses, will escape Antichrist's wrath when he wages war against the king of the south (Dan 11:41), but they will not escape God's wrath, "For it is the day of the LORD's vengeance, and the year of recompences for the controversy of Zion."[3963]

Jesus' sword of heaven will come against Idumeans, to the descendants of Esau/Edom, a people reserved for God's end-time judgment, utter destruction, for Israel's sake.[3964] Jesus' sword will be soaked in blood against the Idumeans at the sacrifice and slaughter in Bozrah.[3965] Edom's utter destruction comes just before Armageddon when "the indignation of the LORD is upon all nations, and his fury upon all their armies: he hath utterly destroyed them, he hath delivered them to the slaughter. Their slain also shall be cast out, and their stink shall come up out of their carcasses, and the mountains shall be melted with their blood."[3966] Jesus will utterly destroy/*charam* the mighty/*gibbowr* of Teman and the wise of Edom by the mount of Esau (Mount Seir),[3967] for the violence of Amalekite and Edomite kingdoms past, especially in the days of Israel and Judah's "calamity" and "distress" of the end times. Edom will be punished by Jesus for three to four reasons: because Edom "pursued his brother with the sword"; "cast off all pity" for Israel and Judah; because "his anger did tear perpetually"; and because "he kept his wrath

---

[3960] Isa 13:3–4; Rev 19:14–15.
[3961] H8121—*shemesh, sheh'-mesh*: to be brilliant; the sun; by implication, the east; figuratively, a ray; east; eastward; sunrise; battlements and shields glittering.
[3962] Isa 34:7–9.
[3963] Isa 34:8.
[3964] Isa 34:5–6; Mic 2:12. H2764—*cherem*; from 2763—*charam*.
[3965] Isa 34:7.
[3966] Isa 34:1–2.
[3967] Gen 36:33; 1 Chron 1:44.

for ever."[3968] Therefore, "Edom shall be a desolate wilderness, for violence against the children of Judah, because they have shed innocent blood in their land"; "the people against whom the Lord has indignation for ever."[3969]

The final events of God's wrath begin with Edom, a sight that will further terrify Antichrist and perhaps the tidings from north and east reported to Antichrist, who is in the south at this time. Jesus will come out of Edom and Bozrah after He treads the winepress that will stain his white garments red with the blood of the Edomites, to begin the day of vengeance. Edom's destruction will occur after *Yhovah's* year of favor and redemption, in just cause for Israel's affliction/*tsarah* during the time of Jacob's trouble.[3970]

> Isa 63:1 Who is this that cometh from Edom, with dyed garments from Bozrah? this that is glorious in his apparel, traveling in the greatness of his strength? I that speak in righteousness, mighty to save.
>
> Isa 63:2 Wherefore art thou red in thine apparel, and thy garments like him that treadeth in the winefat?
>
> Isa 63:3 I have trodden the winepress alone; and of the people there was none with me: for I will tread them in mine anger and trample them in my fury; and their blood shall be sprinkled upon my garments, and I will stain all my raiment.

Moab and Ammon are part of the of the divine retribution against the kin nations for their crimes against Israel and Judah past and future. Like Edom, fire will be sent to Moab for the same "three transgressions. .. and for four."[3971] Moab will be destroyed like Sodom and Gomorrah with fire and brimstone, to become a "perpetual desolation," a place of thorny weeds and salt pits.[3972] Moab will be utterly destroyed as part of the resolution to the Terrible Ones at Armageddon, on a mountain with a slaughter/feast of "fat things" when Jesus will destroy the covering and veil that shadows the world.[3973] Moab in part was the land of Sihon; Heshbon and Jahaz were the places where Israel defeated Sihon, and were referenced in the destruction of Moab by Nebuchadnezzar that may well be a dual prophecy for end-time Moab.[3974] Ammon will be destroyed for the same reasons with fire, and left desolate like Sodom and Gomorrah.[3975]

[3968] Joel 3:19; Amos 1:11.
[3969] Isa 11:14; Ezek 35:15; 36:5; Joel 3:19; Amos 1:6; 9:12; Oba 1:8–16; Mal 1:4.
[3970] Isa 63:6–8.
[3971] Isa 11:14; Amos 2:1–3.
[3972] Zeph 2:9.
[3973] Isa 25:6–10.
[3974] Num 21:23–28; Deut 2:32–37; Isa 15:1–9.
[3975] Isa 11:14; Amos 1:13–15; Zeph 2:9.

CHAPTER 84

ARMAGEDDON

Rev 16:16 And he gathered them together into a place called in the Hebrew tongue Armageddon.

Reports from the north and the east will so terrify Antichrist that he will retreat from the south where he plundered the Egyptians, Libyans, and Ethiopians (Africa).[3976] Antichrist will then begin a death-and-destruction march toward the north and east with "great fury," a burning rage to "destroy," exterminate and annihilate.[3977] Antichrist will "utterly make away many," *charam*: utterly destroy ritually.[3978] Antichrist will establish his tabernacles/encampment and his royal pavilion tent, his palace-tent, between the sea (Mediterranean) and the "glorious holy mountain," Mount Hermon of the Baalim assembly of the gods, and Satan's holy mountain.

At this time, the Philistines will be punished for the same "three and four reasons" as Moab, Ammon, and Edom were utterly destroyed.[3979] The Philistines appear to be part of those whom Antichrist will "make away with many."[3980] One might conclude Edom in the south, Ammon, and Moab might be part of Antichrist's last romp of fury, but it seems more likely that Jesus will execute judgment

---

[3976] Dan 11:44.

[3977] Dan 11:43–44; Zeph 2:12. Fury: H2534—*chemah, khay-maw'*: burning anger; poison from its fever; hot displeasure, furious; burning rage; wrath.

[3978] Destroy: H8045—*shamad*: to desolate; destroy; annihilate; exterminate. Make away: H2763—*charam*.

[3979] Isa 11:14; Amos 1:3–8; Zeph 2:14.

[3980] Dan 11:44.

THE GENESIS 6 CONSPIRACY PART II

on Israel's kin nations as He moves north to Mount Hermon on the east of the Jordan River, through Ammon and Moab, and as indicated by the Isaiah 63:1–4 prophecy stating that Jesus will begin treading the winepress in Edom. In this line of thinking, Antichrist will march up the Mediterranean coast through Gaza and then Tyre, destroying each [3981] on his way to his holy mountain, Sion. Thus, Jesus will complete the judgment of the Syrian Edomites and Moabites just before the Armageddon battle. Knowing this elucidates that the Syrian/Edomite destruction and the Moabite destruction was included among the destruction of the Terrible Ones on the mountain, likely Hermon.

> Isa 25:5 Thou shalt bring down the noise of strangers, as the heat in a dry place; even the heat with the shadow of a cloud: the branch of the Terrible Ones shall be brought low.
>
> Isa 25:6 And in this mountain shall the LORD of hosts make unto all people a feast of fat things, a feast of wines on the lees, of fat things full of marrow, of wines on the lees well refined.
>
> Isa 25:7 And he will destroy in this mountain the face of the covering cast over all people, and the vail that is spread over all nations.
>
> Isa 25:9 And it shall be said in that day, Lo, this is our God; we have waited for him, and he will save us: this is the LORD; we have waited for him, we will be glad and rejoice in his salvation.
>
> Isa 25:10 For in this mountain shall the hand of the LORD rest, and Moab shall be trodden down under him, even as straw is trodden down for the dunghill.

Knowing Antichrist's route explicates why Antichrist "shall plant the tabernacles of his palace between the seas in the glorious holy mountain; yet he shall come to his end, and none shall help him" (Dan 11:45). Antichrist's tabernacles (tents) of his palace (pavilion or palace-tent) from where he will command his forces will be centered between the seas (Mediterranean, Black, Caspian, and Dead Seas) and the glorious mountain.[3982] Glorious/*tsibiy* is defined as splendor, beautiful, prominence, and conspicuous like a gazelle and roebuck,[3983] of which both animals boast prominent and conspicuous horns. Additionally, *tsibiy* derives from *tsabah* meaning to swell, amass, fight, and "specifically array an army." Both

---

[3981] Amos 1:6–10. Ellicott, *Old Testament Commentary*, Vol. 5, 399, note 42.

[3982] Tabernacle: H168—*'ohel, o'-hel*: a tent; a covering; a dwelling place; home; tabernacle. Palace: H643—*'appeden, ap-peh'-den*: a pavilion; palace-tent; palace. Sea: H3220—*yam, yawm*: a sea; a large body of water; specifically, the Mediterranean Sea.

[3983] Glorious: H6643—*tsbiy, tseb-ee'*; prominence; conspicuousness; splendor; beautiful; glorious; a gazelle; roebuck.

Hebrew words are part of a series of words that includes *tsaba'*, used translate the host: an army, or an army of angels.[3984] *Tsibiy* and its associated words indicate Hermon is the mountain where the Armageddon armies assemble. Further, *tsibiy* is reminiscent of horn/*qeren* alternatively translated as a mountain, power, and a place in Bashan. Antichrist is the little horn granted authority and the divine right to rule from Satan's council of Naphalim of Mount Hermon and its peaks, the Hermonim.[3985]

The mountain Antichrist will encamp at will be the holy mountain/*qodesh har*, a sacred place, a consecrated place, a hallowed place, and a sanctuary; *qodesh* derives from *qadash*, which can be translated defile and tabooed.[3986] The "glorious holy mountain" prophesied in Daniel 11 is not Mount Zion in Jerusalem, but the mountain of the council/congregation of the gods, the mountain of the assembly and gathering,[3987] the mountain where of the harem-anathema oath was sworn to obliterate humankind by creating spurious Nephilim offspring, Mount Hermon.

The book of Revelation instructs that the place where the armies of the world will be gathered/*soonag'o*: assembled or convened by demons is to be understood "in the Hebrew tongue"; gathered/*soonag'o* is similar language in Daniel 11:45 for the place Antichrist's armies will encamp: the "glorious holy mountain" and the place of gathering/assembly for the Revelation armies.[3988] As such, Armageddon, Mount/*Har* Megiddon/*Mgiddown*, as generally understood in the original Hebrew and Semitic H-R-M-G-D, is not and cannot be a valley, as in the "valley of Megiddon" (Megiddo) recorded in Zechariah 12:11, because the timing marked for that passage by Jesus' sign occurs at midpoint of the last seven years in verse 10:

> Zech 12:10 And I will pour upon the house of David, and upon the inhabitants of Jerusalem, the spirit of grace and of supplications: and they shall look upon me whom they have pierced, and they shall mourn for him, as one mourneth for his only son, and shall be in bitterness for him, as one that is in bitterness for his firstborn.

[3984] H6638—*tsabah, tsaw-baw'*: to amass; swell; and specifically, to array an army against to fight; H6635—*tsaba'*.

[3985] H7161—*qeren*. Ps 42:6.

[3986] Dan 11:45. Holy: H6944—*qodesh, ko'-desh*; from 6942: a sacred place or thing; consecrated thing or place; dedicated thing or place; hallowed thing or place; holiness; sanctuary. H6942—*qadash, kaw-dash'*: pronounce; consecrate; appoint; clean or hallowed; defile; tabooed. Mountain: H2022—*har, har*.

[3987] Ps 82:1–8. Congregation: H5712—*'edah*: a stated assemblage; specifically, a concourse; a family or crowd; assembly; company; congregation; a gathering; multitude; swarm.

[3988] Rev 16:14, 16. G4863—*soon-ag'-o*: to lead together; collect; convene; convoking; to entertain; assemble; come together; gather; lead into, resort; take in. Transliterated: sunago.

Perhaps one could associate Megiddo metaphorically for the battle of Har Mowged/Mow`ed because *Mgiddown* is defined as a rendezvous point, a place of crowds, and a valley close to Jerusalem.[3989] Even though Armageddon's definition in *Strong's Dictionary* indicates it could be defined as hill/mount or city of Megiddo, it is never referenced in Hebrew as a hill or mountain, *har*,[3990] and there is not a Mount Megiddo.

On the other hand, Joshua awarded Megiddo city to the tribe of Manasseh, located west of the Jordan River and in the Jezreel valley, in the north and west of the Covenant Land.[3991] One ponders then, whether the great numbers of the Armageddon armies might spill over into the valley of Jezreel that Megiddo city was located in; Manasseh's inheritance included lands east of the Jordan that included Bashan of Mount Hermon.[3992] As such, one might assert John was communicating in part and allegorically through Zechariah's prophecy, knowing Greek translation complications, and that the last battle will be fought at the foot of a mountain of the assembly of Baal and the Baalim who reigned from Mount Hermon. In this allegorical context the valley of Megiddo would be understood as the valley of Jezreel where Megiddo city was located, which could hold more meaning in juxtaposition with Hadadrimmon in the Zechariah prophecy. Both Megiddo and Hadadrimmon can be defined as meeting places and/or assemblies; Hadadrimmon is named after two Syrian gods of the Baalim: Hadad and Rimmom.[3993]

> Zech 12:11 In that day shall there be a great mourning in Jerusalem, as the mourning of Hadadrimmon in the valley of Megiddon.

Megiddon/Megiddo derives from *gadad*, meaning assembling of troops or crowds, and to attack and invade.[3994] *Gadad* is equivalent to *guwd*, meaning to invade and attack, while *gad* in Baalgad, located west of the Jordan River in the

---

[3989] Valley of Megiddo: 2 Chron 35:22. H4023—*Mgiddown, meg-id-done'*; Zech 12, or *Mgiddow, meg-id-do'*: rendezvous; a place of crowds; a Canaanite city; a place close to Mount Carmel, Nazareth, and Jerusalem; Megiddo.

[3990] G717—*ar-mag-ed-dohn'*.

[3991] Megiddo (city): Josh 12:21; 17:11; 1 Chron 7:29; 2 Kings 4:12; Valley of Jezreel: Josh 17:16; Judg 6:33; Hos 1:5.

[3992] Num 32:33; Josh 13:29–31; 17:11; 22:7.

[3993] H191—*Hadadrimmown, had-ad-rim-mone'*: rendezvous; a place of crowds; a place in the valley of Megiddo in Palestine where a national lamentation was held for the death of King Josiah; named after two Syrian gods. Megiddo: Josh 12:21; 17:11; Judg 1:27; 5:19; 1 Kings 4:12; 9:15; 2 Kings 9:27; 23:29–30; 1 Chron 7:29; 2 Chron 35:22. H7417—*Rimmown, rim-mone'; Rimmon, rimmone'*; or *Rimmownow*: pomegranite; a Syrian storm deity.

[3994] H1413—*gadad, gaw-dad'*: to crowd; also, to gash as if by pressing into; assemble or gather crowds or troop; cut oneself; attack; invade.

Lebanon valley under Mount Hermon, means troops and fortune.[3995] The valley including Megiddo and the Lebanon valley are seemingly connected to the valley of Jehoshaphat as prophetic allegory for the Armageddon armies that will overflow the lands under Mount Hermon toward the Mediterranean coast.

> Josh 11:17 Even from the mount Halak, that goeth up to Seir, even unto Baalgad in the valley of Lebanon under Mount Hermon: and all their kings he took, and smote them, and slew them.

> Josh 12:7 And these are the kings of the country which Joshua and the children of Israel smote on this side Jordan on the west, from Baalgad in the valley of Lebanon.

Joel and Zephaniah also prophesied about Armageddon:

> Joel 3:9–14 Proclaim ye this among the Gentiles; Prepare war, wake up the mighty men, let all the men of war draw near; let them come up: Beat your plowshares into swords, and your pruninghooks into spears: let the weak say, I am strong. Assemble yourselves, and come, all ye heathen, and gather yourselves together round about: thither cause thy mighty ones to come down, O LORD. Let the heathen be wakened, and come up to the valley of Jehoshaphat: for there will I sit to judge all the heathen round about. Put ye in the sickle, for the harvest is ripe: come, get you down; for the press is full, the fats overflow; for their wickedness is great. Multitudes, multitudes in the valley of decision: for the day of the LORD is near in the valley of decision. The sun and the moon shall be darkened, and the stars shall withdraw their shining.

> Zeph 3:8 Therefore wait ye upon me, saith the LORD, until the day that I rise up to the prey: for my determination is to gather the nations, that I may assemble the kingdoms, to pour upon them mine indignation, even all my fierce anger: for all the earth shall be devoured with the fire of my jealousy.

Joel foretold a time when the world will receive a proclamation/*qara'*, a reading aloud to invite or summons by name[3996] for the Gentile nations to prepare

---

[3995] H1464—*guwd, goode*: to crowd upon as in attack; invade; overcome; H1409—*gad, gawd*; from 1464; fortune; troop; transliterated: gad; H1171—*Ba`al Gad, bah'-al gawd*; from 1168 and 1409: Baal of Fortune; Baal-Gad; a city in Syria noted for Baal-worship, located at the most northwestern point to which Joshua's victories extended.

[3996] Proclaim: H7121—*qara', kaw-raw'*: to call out; address by name; read aloud; summon; invite; call for; proclaim.

for war, whereby prepare/*qadesh* means to consecrate or sanctify war with due religious and ritual rites. Joel's proclamation instructs to wake the mighty men/ gibborrim[3997] to come up, reflecting the demons that will come out of the mouths of the false prophet, Antichrist, and Satan to summon and gather the kings of the whole world to Armageddon.[3998] Joel prophesied the world will be summoned to assemble/`uwsh, to hasten, lend help, or aid in their gathering that includes the gathering of the mighty ones/gibborim[3999] to come to the valley of Jehoshaphat for the treading of the winepress.

Many connect the valley of Jehoshaphat to the Kidron Valley below the Mount of Olives because of the great earthquake prophesied in Zechariah 14:4 and Revelation 16:19, when Jesus will stand on the Mount of Olives east of Jerusalem. The earthquake will split the mountain into two, going from east to the west, sending its rubble northward and southward and creating a great valley dividing Jerusalem into three parts—an earthquake that will destroy cities worldwide. Although this earthquake occurs at the time of Armageddon, and all nations will be gathered against Jerusalem at that time,[4000] the Zechariah and Revelation valley does not appear to be the valley of decision of Jehoshaphat. Remember, nations will fight against Antichrist and his capitol until Jesus appears at the Armageddon battle, and that the Armageddon armies will not be slain by an earthquake. The Armageddon armies will gather to the mountain of assembly not to the Mount of Olives. Moreover, the valley of Jehoshaphat[4001] may not be a valley as such.

Neither the Bible nor Josephus identified such a valley. Perhaps then, Jehoshaphat ought not to be understood as the actual name of a valley. Perhaps we should understand the location by the Hebrew meaning for Jehoshaphat, and as many ancient translators rendered the Joel translation, as the plain/valley of judgment.[4002] Jehoshaphat/ *Yhowshaphat* derives from *Yhovah* and *shaphat* meaning *Yhovah*/Jesus' judgment, and the valley of decision/*charuwts* meaning decision and place of a sharp threshing instrument.[4003] It follows then that if Mount Hermon is

---

[3997] Prepare for war: Jer 6:4; 12:3; 22:7; 51:27, 28; Mic 3:5. Prepare: H6942—*qadash*. Ellicott, *Old Testament Commentary*, Vol. 5, 444, Joel 3:9, note 9. Mighty men: H1368—*gibbowr*.

[3998] Rev 16:13–16.

[3999] Assemble: H5789—`uwsh, oosh; to hasten; assemble; to help; lend aid. Gather: H6908— *qabats, kaw-bats*: to grasp as in collect; assemble; gather; heap, resort; take up.

[4000] Zech 14:2.

[4001] Joel 3:12.

[4002] *Strong's Cyclopaedia*, Vol. 4, 807-808.

[4003] H3092—*Yhowshaphat, yeh-ho-shaw-fawt*'; from 3068 and 8199: Jehovah-judged; a valley near Jerusalem; the place of ultimate judgment; maybe the deep ravine which separates Jerusalem from the Mount of Olives through which the Kidron flowed; H3068—*Yhovah*; H8199—*shaphat, shaw-fat*': to judge, pronounce sentence for or against; vindicate; punish; avenge; condemn; execute judgment; rule. Valley of decision: H2742—*charuwts, khaw-roots*': a trench, a threshing-sledge having sharp teeth; a sharp, threshing instrument; wall; decision.

the mountain of assembly for the gathered armies, the valley of Mount Hermon would be the valley of decision and judgment. The valley below Mount Hermon is the valley of Lebanon toward the west of Mount Hermon with Baalgad as the northwestern edge, as viewed from Jerusalem.

Even though Mountain Hermon will be the focal point for the Armageddon armies to gather below, one deduces the multitude of troops would spill over into other valleys nearby and perhaps as far as the Megiddo valley of Jezreel and beyond. Knowing this makes sense of Isaiah's prophecies:

> Isa 13:4–5 The noise of a multitude in the mountains, like as of a great people; a tumultuous noise of the kingdoms of nations gathered together: the LORD of hosts mustereth the host of the battle. They come from a far country, from the end of heaven, even the LORD, and the weapons of his indignation, to destroy the whole land.

> Isa 34:2–4 Come near, ye nations, to hear; and hearken, ye people: let the earth hear, and all that is therein; the world, and all things that come forth of it. For the indignation of the LORD is upon all nations, and his fury upon all their armies: he hath utterly destroyed them, he hath delivered them to the slaughter. Their slain also shall be cast out, and their stink shall come up out of their carcasses, and the mountains shall be melted with their blood. And all the host of heaven shall be dissolved, and the heavens shall be rolled together as a scroll: and all their host shall fall down, as the leaf falleth off from the vine, and as a falling fig from the fig tree.[4004]

The day and year of the Lord will be a time of wrath, the denouement to the great tribulation of the last three-and-a-half years, and the resolution to the angelic rebellion. The prophet Zephaniah recorded that the day and year of the Lord's wrath will be a time of distress, desolation, darkness, and fire against the world—a day and time when the mighty men/gibborim will "cry," roar "bitterly" as in a roar of anger and/or a harlot's end.[4005] The "day," perhaps year of darkness leading up to Armageddon, is reminiscent of the fourth wrath bowl where the sun begins to scar the worshippers of Antichrist and Satan, and the time the worshippers of evil will blaspheme God. Then the fifth bowl will cause the beast's kingdom to be full of darkness, where the Satan worshippers continue to blaspheme God, followed by the sixth wrath bowl that gathers armies to Armageddon. [4006]

[4004] Isa 13:4–5; 34:2–4.
[4005] Zeph 1:8–15. H6873—*tsarach, tsaw-rakh'*: a shrill; to whoop; cry; roar; H4751—*mar, mar*: bitter; angry; chafed; discontented; as in a harlot's end or end of wickedness.
[4006] Rev 16:10–16.

Thus, the day of the Armageddon battle will be neither light nor dark, no distinction from day or night.[4007] On that day, Jesus will create an earthquake beginning in Jerusalem at the Mount of Olives that will destroy fortresses and the cities worldwide, an earthquake from the seventh bowl not seen since "men were upon the earth" that will lead into hail from heaven[4008] and the other calamities Jesus will deliver Himself. Jesus will strike the nations with a plague, causing men to walk blind on the day of slaughter. Their eyes will "consume away" in their sockets, as in melt, dissolve, or rot away, as will their tongues and all the beasts of war; people worldwide will turn to kill each other just before their blood will be poured out like dust.[4009]

The day of the Lord battle begins after Jesus comes out of Edom and Bozrah with blood-soaked clothes, and after the earthquake in Jerusalem: "The LORD also shall roar out of Zion, and utter his voice from Jerusalem; and the heavens and the earth shall shake: but the LORD will be the hope of his people, and the strength of the children of Israel" (Joel 3:16). Jesus will then levy God's fury, slaughtering the world's armies—a time when the host of heaven fall to the earth, the unicorns come down, and all the streams, dust, and land will be turned into burning pitch and brimstone.[4010] Jesus will ride onto the battlefield upon "a white horse; and he that sat upon him was called Faithful and True, and in righteousness he doth judge and make war" (Rev 19:11). He will ride onto the battlefield with eyes blazing like fire, wearing many crowns on which His name will be written on it that no one knows, dressed in robes dipped/dyed in blood (from Edom and Bozrah) followed by the armies (host and saints) from heaven riding on white horses wearing fine white clothes.[4011] "And he hath on his vesture and on his thigh a name written, KING OF KINGS, AND LORD OF LORDS" (Rev 19:16), of whom "These shall make war with the Lamb, and the Lamb shall overcome them: for he is Lord of lords, and King of kings: and they that are with him are called, and chosen, and faithful."[4012]

"And out of his [Jesus] mouth goeth a sharp sword" (Rev 19:15) made by the God Most High for his servant Israel/*Yisra'el*, meaning "will rule as God" in whom God will be glorified: Jesus who will raise up and restore Israel, as the Redeemer of Israel and light for the Gentiles.[4013] Jesus' "sharp sword" is the "sharp" double-edged sword of Jesus recorded in Revelation 2:12. The "Word of God," the double-edged sword, is sharper than any other two-edged sword, which is able to

---

[4007] Joel 3:15; Amos 5:18; Zech 14:6–7.

[4008] Zeph 1:16; Zech 14:4–5; Rev 16:19–20.

[4009] Zeph 1:17; Zech 14:12, 13, 15. H4743—*maqaq, maw-kak'*: to melt; flow; rot; dwindle; vanish; consume away, dissolve; pine away.

[4010] Isa 34:1–7; Zeph 1:1–2; Zech 14:1–2; Mal 4:1.

[4011] Rev 1:16; 7:9; 19:11, 12–14.

[4012] Rev 17:14; cf. 1 Tim 6:15.

[4013] Isa 63:1–7. H3478—*Yisra'el, yis-raw-ale'*; he will rule as God; a symbolical name of Jacob; Jacob's posterity, Israel.

pierce and separate soul and spirit.[4014] Jesus is the Word of God that God speaks through, will then "smite the nations and he shall rule them with a rod of iron" (Rev 19:15), and "he shall smite the earth with the rod of his mouth and the breath of his lips shall he slay the wicked."[4015] Jesus will "break them with a rod of iron, and dash them in pieces like a potter's vessel," and "as vessels of a potter shall they be broken to shivers."[4016] "And there fell upon men a great hail out of heaven, every stone about the weight of a talent: and men blasphemed God because of the plague of the hail; for the plague thereof was exceeding great" (Rev 16:21).

"And he [Jesus] treadeth the winepress of the fierceness and wrath of Almighty God" (Rev 19:15), treading "the winepress alone; and of the people there was none with me; for I will tread them in my anger, and trample them in my fury; and their blood shall be sprinkled upon my garments, and I will stain my remnant."[4017] "And the angel thrust in his sickle into the earth, and gathered the vine of the earth, and cast it into the great winepress of the wrath of God. And the winepress was trodden without the city, and blood came out of the winepress, even unto the horse bridles, by the space of a thousand and six hundred furlongs." "Put ye in the sickle, for the harvest is ripe: come, get you down; for the press is full, the fats overflow; for their wickedness is great. Multitudes, multitudes in the valley of decision: for the day of the LORD is near in the valley of decision."[4018] "For the indignation of the LORD is upon all nations, and his fury upon all their armies: he hath utterly destroyed them, he hath delivered them to the slaughter. Their slain also shall be cast out, and their stink shall come up out of their carcasses, and the mountains shall be melted with their blood."[4019]

> Rev 19:17 And I saw an angel standing in the sun; and he cried with a loud voice, saying to all the fowls that fly in the midst of heaven, Come and gather yourselves together unto the supper of the great God;
>
> Rev 19:18 That ye may eat the flesh of kings, and the flesh of captains, and the flesh of mighty men, and the flesh of horses, and of them that sit on them, and the flesh of all men, both free and bond, both small and great.

God has appointed a sacrifice on the day of the Lord and bid/*qadas*, reserved for "his guests" the kings and princes, for all that are clothed in strange/*nokriy*

[4014] John 1:1–14; Heb 4:12.
[4015] Isa 11:4.
[4016] Ps 2:9; Rev 2:27; 12:5.
[4017] Isa 63:3.
[4018] Joel 3:13; Rev 14:15–20; see Isa 18:4–7.
[4019] Isa 34:2–3.

apparel when the earth is devoured by fire.[4020] One deduces the end-time kings, princes, and roy-el nobility will dress oddly in some ritualistic manner that reflects their hubris, religious beliefs, and loyalties. "For afore the harvest, when the bud is perfect, and the sour grape is ripening in the flower, he shall both cut off the sprigs with pruning hooks, and take away and cut down the branches. They shall be left together unto the fowls of the mountains, and to the beasts of the earth: and the fowls shall summer upon them, and all the beasts of the earth shall winter upon them. In that time shall the present be brought unto the LORD of hosts of a people scattered and peeled, and from a people terrible from their beginning hitherto; a nation meted out and trodden under foot, whose land the rivers have spoiled, to the place of the name of the LORD of hosts, the mount Zion." [4021]

The appointed sacrifice on the mountains and valleys of the Covenant Land will express God's and Jesus' indignation for the spurious offspring and their terrible deeds, whereby birds will "eat the flesh of kings, and the flesh of captains, and the flesh of mighty men, and the flesh of horses, and of them that sit on them, and the flesh of all men, both free and bond, both small and great." (Rev 19:17–18). The Armageddon sacrifice or feast/*mow`ed* will bring down the "lees," the dregs, and the "noise of strangers as the heat in a dry place," the "branch of the Terrible Ones," "in this mountain" where and when Jesus makes "unto all people a feast of wines on the lees, of fat things full of marrow, of wines on the lees well refined."[4022] "Thine hand shall find out all thine enemies: thy right hand shall find out those that hate thee. Thou shalt make them as a fiery oven in the time of thine anger: the LORD shall swallow them up in his wrath, and the fire shall devour them. Their fruit shalt thou destroy from the earth, and their seed from among the children of men. For they intended evil against thee: they imagined a mischievous device, which they are not able to perform."[4023]

Jesus "will break the Assyrian in my land, and upon my mountains tread him under foot: then shall his yoke depart from off them, and his burden depart from off their shoulders."[4024] After the slaughter of the Armageddon battle, "the beast was taken, and with him the false prophet that wrought miracles before him, with which he deceived them that had received the mark of the beast, and them that worshipped his image. These both were cast alive into a lake of fire burning with brimstone" (Rev 19:20).

However, one might translate "cast alive" in Revelation 19:20 a little differently. "Alive" derives from *dzah'o* and is translated as such fifteen times in the New

---

[4020] Zeph 1:7–18; Mal 4:1. H6942—*qadash*. Mountain: Strange: H5237—*nokriy, nok-ree*: strange, foreign; adulterous; different; alien; outlandish, unknown; unfamiliar.
[4021] Isa 18:4–7.
[4022] Isa 25:5–6. Lees: H8105—*shemer, sheh'-mer*: something preserved as in the settlings of wine dregs; dregs.
[4023] Ps 21: 8–11.
[4024] Isa 14:25.

Testament, but is translated 129 times as to live, living, liveth, lived, quick, lively, livest, life, or lifetime.[4025] The alternative translation to "cast alive" into the lake of fire might very well be "cast to live" in the lake of fire forever, noting Adamites were appointed to die once and after this the judgment.[4026] Moreover, no one will survive the double-edged sword levied at the Armageddon battle by Jesus, and thus the Assyrian/Antichrist will be broken and tread underfoot in the battle. Thus, Antichrist will be slain in a similar manner as was Asshur, the Assyrian Terrible One,[4027] with a stroke of the sword to Antichrist's neck to ensure he does not recover as in Revelation 13:3, and then thrown directly into the lake of fire to burn alive forever.

One further ponders whether the sword is designed to decapitate all the mighty ones/gibborrim, Nephilim, Rephaim, and all who accepted the mark, to prevent what the implant might try to do to heal the wound. "And the remnant were slain with the sword of him that sat upon the horse, which sword proceeded out of his mouth: and all the fowls were filled with their flesh" (Rev 19:21). Further, Jesus' slaying Antichrist with a sharp sword aligns with Isaiah 14:5–6: "The LORD hath broken the staff of the wicked, and the sceptre of the rulers. He who smote the people in wrath with a continual stroke, he that ruled the nations in anger, is persecuted, and none hindereth."

Knowing Antichrist (and the false prophet) will suffer a first death of a Rephaim beast at Armageddon makes sense of other mysterious details recorded in Isaiah 14 and Ezekiel 28:

> Isa 14:19 But thou art cast out of thy grave like an abominable branch, and as the raiment of those that are slain, thrust through with a sword, that go down to the stones of the pit; as a carcass trodden under feet.

[4025] G2198—*dzah'-o*; a primary verb: to live; lifetime; live a lifetime; endless life; to pass through life in the manner of living; quick'; transliterated: zao; 144 times. Live: 55: Matt 4:4; 9:18; Mark 5:23; Luke 4:4; 10:28; 20:38; John 5:25; 6:51, 57, 58; 11:25; 14:19; Acts 17:28; 22:22; 25:24; 28:4; Rom 1:17; 6:2; 8:12–13; 10:5; 14:8, 11; 1 Cor 9:14; 2 Cor 4:11; 5:15; 6:9; 13:4; Gal 2:14, 19, 20; 3:11, 12; 5:25; Phil 1:21–22; 1 Thess 3:8; 5:10; 2 Tim 3:12; Titus 2:12; Heb 10:38; 12:9; James 4:15; 1 Pet 2:24; 4:6; 1 John 4:9; Rev 13:14. Living, 34: Matt 16:16; 22:32; 26:63; Mark 12:27; Luke 15:13; 20:38; 24:5; John 4:10–11; 6:51, 57, 69; 7:38; Acts 14:15; Rom 9:26; 12:1; 14:9; 1 Cor 15:45; 2 Cor 3:3; 6:16; Col 2:20; 1 Thess 1:9; 1 Tim 3:15; 4:10; 6:17; Heb 3:12; 9:14; 10:20, 31; 12:22; 1 Pet 2:4; Rev 7:2, 17; 16:3. Liveth 25: John 4:50, 51, 53; 11:26; Rom 6:10; 7:1, 2, 3; 14:7; 1 Cor 7:39; 2 Cor 13:4; Gal 2:20; 1 Tim 5:6; Heb 7:8, 25; 9:17; 1 Pet 1:23; Rev 1:18; 4:9, 10; 5:14; 15:6, 7. Alive 15: Matt 27:63; Mark 16:11; Luke 24:23; Acts 1:3; 9:41; 20:12; 25:19; Rom 6:11, 13; 7:9; 1 Thess 4:15, 17; Rev 1:18; 2:8; 19:20. Lived 4: Luke 2:36; Acts 26:5; Col 3:7; Rev 20:4. Quick 4: Acts 10:42; 2 Tim 4:1; Heb 4:12; 1 Pet 4:5. Lively 3: Acts 7:38; 1 Pet 1:3; 2:5. Livest 2: Gal 2:14; Rev 3:1. Life 1: 2 Cor 1:8. Lifetime 1: Heb 2:15.

[4026] Heb 9:27.

[4027] Ezek 32:22.

Isa 14:20 Thou shalt not be joined with them in burial, because thou hast destroyed thy land, and slain thy people: the seed of evildoers shall never be renowned.

Ezek 28:7 Behold, therefore I will bring strangers upon thee, the terrible of the nations: and they shall draw their swords against the beauty of thy wisdom, and they shall defile thy brightness.

Ezek 28:8 They shall bring thee down to the pit, and thou shalt die the deaths of them that are slain in the midst of the seas.

Ezek 28:.9 Wilt thou yet say before him that slayeth thee, I am God? but thou shalt be a man, and no God, in the hand of him that slayeth thee.

Ezek 28:18 Thou hast defiled thy sanctuaries by the multitude of thine iniquities, by the iniquity of thy traffick; therefore will I bring forth a fire from the midst of thee, it shall devour thee, and I will bring thee to ashes upon the earth in the sight of all them that behold thee.

Ezek 28:19 All they that know thee among the people shall be astonished at thee: thou shalt be a terror, and never shalt thou be any more.

Not only does Jesus judge the spurious offspring of fallen angels, but He will assemble the fallen angels for humankind to judge them for their crimes against humanity.[4028] Fallen angels will then be cast into the lake of fire, the place of punishment "prepared for the devil and his angels,"[4029] the demonic spirits of false prophet, Antichrist, all Terrible Ones, those with the mark, and those who worship Antichrist and Satan.[4030]

Satan, though, will be sent first to the pit prison, and then sent to the lake of fire at the denouement of the millennium, and afterward he will be released from the abyss prison for a very short time. After a thousand years of righteous rule by Jesus, many of humankind will be led by Satan into another failed rebellion from God and Jesus[4031]—demonstrating that whether angel or human, some will always rebel unless God writes His laws on our hearts.[4032]

Rev 20:10 And the devil that deceived them was cast into the lake of fire and brimstone, where the beast and the false prophet are, and shall be tormented day and night for ever and ever.

[4028] 1 Cor 6:1–4.
[4029] Matt 25:41; 2 Pet 2:4; Jude 1:6.
[4030] Rev 13:17; 14:10; 15:2.
[4031] Rev 19:1–9.
[4032] Jer 31:33; Ezek 11:19; 36.26; Heb 8:10; 10:16; 2 Cor 3:3.

BIBLIOGRAPHY

Bibles

The Access Bible, New Revised Standard Version with the Apocrypha. New York: Oxford University Press, 1999.

The Bible Study Suite with the Authorized King James Version (Red Letter), Hebrew/ Greek Dictionaries and Concordance, Easton's and Smith's Bible Dictionaries. Packard Technologies, Kindle edition, 2010.

The Hebrew Hebrew-Greek-& English Bible: The Holy Scripture of the Old & New Testaments in the Original Languages with English Translation. Westminster Leningrad Codex Hebrew, Tischendorf 8th Edition Greek, 1917 Jewish Publication Society OT, Lexham English Bible English NT. Kindle edition, 2014.

The Holy Bible, New International Version, NIV, Copyright 1973, 1978, 1984 by Biblica, Inc. Used by permission of Zondervan. www.zondervan.com.

Septuagint, Complete Greek and English edition, Delphi Classics: Ancient Classic Series. 2016, Kindle edition.

Barker, Kenneth, general editor. Burdick, Arnold, John Stek, Walter Wessel, and Ronald Youngblood, associate editors. *The NIV Study Bible.* Grand Rapids, MI: Zondervan, 1985.

Brenton, Sir Lancelot C. L., translator. *The English Translation of the Septuagint Bible, Contemporary English Version.* 1851, Kindle edition.

Strong, James. *KJV Bible with Comprehensive Strong's Dictionary.* Best Books Kindle edition, 2015.

Dictionaries and Encyclopedias

The American Universal Encyclopedia: A Complete Library of Knowledge, A Reprint of the Edinburgh and London Edition of Chambers Encyclopedia. New York: S. W. Green's Sons Publishers, 1882.

The Catholic Encyclopedia. Eds. Charles G. Herberman, Edward A. Pace, Conde A. Pallen, Thomas J. Shahan, and John Wynne. New York: Robert Appleton Company, 1907.

Dictionary.com. Copyright © 2018 Dictionary.com, LLC.

The Encyclopedia Americana. Montreal, Toronto, Vancouver, Winnipeg: Americana Corporation of Canada Ltd., 1956.

The Jewish Encyclopedia: A Descriptive Record of the History, Religion, Literature, and Customs of the Jewish People from the Earliest Times to the Present Day. New York and London: Funk and Wagnalls, 1903.

The Sumerian Dictionary. Ebook pdf, https://www.magicgatebg.com/Books/INDEXII/Sumerian_Dictionary.pdf.

Webster's New Compact Format Dictionary. New York: Essential Publications, 1986.

Easton, Matthew George, *Easton's Dictionary and World English Bible.* Norway, TruthBeTold Ministry, 2017.

Ellicott, Charles John. *An Old Testament Commentary for English Readers.* London, Paris, and New York: Cassell, Petter & Galpin & Co, 1882.

M'Clintock, John, and James Strong. *Strong's Cyclopaedia of Biblical, Theological, and Ecclesiastical Literature.* New York: Harper & Brothers, 1867.

Mills, Watson E., and Roger Aubrey Bullard. *Mercer Dictionary of the Bible.* Macon, GA: Mercer University Press, 1990.

Parks, Rebeca, ed. *Encyclopedia of World Mythology.* Farmington Hills, MI: Gale, Cengage Learning, 2009.

Peter, Ed, and Tara Hogan. *Sumerian Cuneiform English Dictionary.* Mug Sar Dictionary: e-book pdf, https://ia800903.us.archive.org/25/items/SumerianCuneiformEnglishDictionary12013CT26i14PDF/Sumerian%20Cuneiform%20English%20Dictionary%2012013CT%2026i14%20PDF.pdf#page51.

Unger, Merrill F., and R. K. Harrison. *The New Unger's Bible Dictionary.* Chicago: Moody Bible Institute, 1988.

Youngblood, R. F., F. F. Bruce, and R. K. Harrison. *Nelson's New Illustrated Bible Dictionary.* Oxford: Nelson Publishers, 1995.

Older and Ancient Books

Addison, Charles G. The *History of the Knights Templars, the Temple Church, and the Temple.* London: Longman, Brown, Green, and Longmans, 1842.

Andreae, Johann Valentin. *The Chymical Wedding of Christian Rosenkreutz, 1690.* Adobe Acrobat edition prepared by Benjamin Rowe, October 2000.

William of Tyre. *A History of Deeds Done beyond the Sea.* Trans. Emily A. Babcock and A. C. Krey. New York: Columbia University Press, 1943.

Barnstone, Willis. *The Other Bible.* New York: HarperCollins, 1984.

Bates, H. N., translator, *The Sibylline Oracles, Books III–V.* London: Society for Promoting Christian Knowledge, 1918.

Billington, Clyde E. "Goliath and the Exodus Giants: How Tall Were They?" *Journal of the Evangelical Theological Society*, JSTOR 50.3 (2007).

Boughton, Willis. *History of Ancient Peoples.* New York: Knickerbocker Press, 1897.

Budge, Wallis, E. A. *An Egyptian Hieroglyphic Dictionary.* London: John Murray, 1920.

Charles, R. H., trans. *The Book of Enoch.* Originally published 1917; Web edition created and published by Global Grey, 2013, Kindle edition.

Charles, R. H., trans. *The Book of Jubilees. From the Apocrypha and Pseudepigrapha of the Old Testament.* Oxford: Oxford Press, 1913. Kindle edition.

Cooper, William Rickets. *An Archaic Dictionary, Biographical, Historical, And Mythological: From the Egyptian, Assyrian, and Etruscan Monuments And Papyri.* Samuel Bagster And Sons, London UK, 1876.

"Demmon." *The Lost Book of King Og: The Only Written Words of the Rephaim.* Independently published, 2017.

George, Andrew R. "The Gilgames Epic at Ugarit." *Aula Orientalis*, 25:2 (2007). https://eprints.soas.ac.uk/5654z.

Ginzberg, Louis. *Legends of the Bible.* Old Saybrook, CT: Jewish Publication Society of America, 1956.

Heidel, Alexander. *The Gilgamesh Epic and Old Testament Parallels.* Chicago: University of Chicago Press, 1949. E-Book Edition by Misty and Lewis Gruber.

Johnson, Ian, translator. Homer. *The Odyssey.* Revised edition. Nanaimo, BC: Vancouver Island University, 2019.

King, L. W., trans. *The Enuma Elish: The Epic of Creation.* Blackmask Online, 2001. www.blackmask.com.

Layton, Bentley. *The Gnostic Scriptures: Ancient Wisdom for the New Age.* New York: Doubleday, 1995.

Mackey, Albert. *The History of Freemasonry.* New York, NY: Gramercy Books, A Division of Random House Value Publishing, Inc., 1996.

McCrindle, J. W., *Ancient India as Described by Ktesiast the Knidian: A Translation of His "Indika."* Calcutta: Thacker Spink & Co., 1881.

Nikkhilananda, Swami, trans. *The Bhagavad Gita.* New York: Haddon Craftsman, 1944.

Parker, John, trans. Dionysius. *The Works of Dionysius the Areopagite.* London: John Parker and Co., 1897; Grand Rapids, MI: Christian Classics Ethereal Library, 2004, ccel.org/ccel/dionysius/works.html.

Plutarch. *Selected Lives, The Parallel Lives of the Noble Grecians and Romans.* Franklin Center, PA: The Heirloom Library of H. R. Koehn of the Franklin Library, 1982, from the Dryden Translation of 1676.

Pliny the Elder, *Natural Histories*, AD 77, Book VIII.

Pope, Alexander, trans. *The Iliad of Homer*, 1899; www.gutenberg.org/licensw, 2006.

Rawlinson, George, trans. Herodotus. *The Histories.* Moscow, ID: Romans Road Media, 2013.

Recinos, Adrian, Delia Goetz, and Sylvanus G. Morley. *Popol Vuh, The Ancient Book of the Ancient Quiche Maya.* Norman, OK: University of Oklahoma Press, 1950.

Robinson, James M. *The Nag Hammadi Library.* New York: HarperCollins Publishers, 1990.

Rhys, Ernest, ed. Titus Livius. *The History of Rome.* Trans. Canon Roberts. London: J. M. Dent & Sons Ltd., 1905.

Sayce, Archibald Henry. *The Races of the Old Testament.* Second edition. Oxford: Religious Tract Society, 1893.

Sergent, Ichabod, trans. *The Book of Lamech of Cain: and Leviathan.* Independently published, Kindle edition, 2019.

Shilleto, Arthur Richard, trans. Pausanias. *The Description of Greece.* London: George Bell and Sons, 1886.

Terry, Milton S., trans. *The Sibylline Oracles.* New York: Eaton & Mains, 1899.

Urquhart, Sir Thomas, and Anthony Peter Martteux, trans. Rabelais, Francois. *Gargantua and Pantagruel: Five Books of the Lives, Heroic Deeds and Sayings of Gargantua and His Son Pantagruel.* Derby, UK: Moray Press, 1894; Kindle edition, 2004.

Whiston, William, with commentary by Paul L. Maier. *The New Complete Works of Josephus*. Grand Rapids, MI: Kregel Publications, A Division of Kregel, Inc.,, 1999.

Wyatt, N. *Religious Texts from Ugarit*. Second edition. New York: Continuum International Publishing Group, 2006.

Other Documents and Sources

"A Very Basic Guide to Devotional Work with the Goddess Babalon." Temple of Our Lady of the Abyss, n.d. https://files.elfsightcdn.com/4696283d-2afb-47e0-b743-2f3b0c4da019/7f3a661e-323f-4498-ae57-d3367fce5b2b.pdf.

Antiguo Oriente, Volume 13, Social Sciences UCA Ed. Buenos Aires: Libreria Elcosteño, 2015.

De Coster, Phlippe L. Knighthoods OSFAR+C and Poor Knights of Christ. E-book, Ghent, Belgium: Skull Press Publications, 2008–2013.

Elitzur, Yoel. "The Meaning of Gilgal." *Revue Biblique* 126, Issue 3 (2019).

Finkelstein, Israel. *Journals for the Study of the Old Testament*. London: Continuum Publishing Group, 2002.

Grundlagenbericht: Zum Fusionsentscheid der Gemeinden Diemerswil und Muchenbuchsee. 2021.

Klein, Cecelia, F. *The Devil and the Skirt: An Iconographical Inquiry into the Prehispanic Nature of the Tzitzimime*. Cambridge: Cambridge University Press, 2000.

Leitner, Severin. "The Spirituality of Peter Faber." *Review of Ignatian Spirituality*, Number 109.

Madanayake, Ravi, *Black Nobility Terror: Oligarch Elitism*. Thesis, University of Colorado, 2019.

Moran, William L., trans. *The Armana Letters*. Baltimore: Johns Hopkins University Press, 1992.

Nougayroll, Jean, Emmanuel Laroche, and Charles Virollaud. *Ugaritica V: New Texts of the Accadians, Horites, and Ugarites from the Archives Ugarit's Private Library*. Stony Brook, NY: Stony Brook University Press, 1968.

Nys, Nadine. *Girtablullu and Co: A New Function of the Scorpion-Man in the Ancient Near East*. University of Ghent and University of Leuven, 2016.

Our Lady of Fatima Crusader Bulletin, salvemariaregina.info.

Sire, H. J. A. *The Knights of Malta*. New Haven, CT: Yale University Press, 1996.

Sisk, Hannah. *Mother Goddess, Male World, Myriad Social Classes: The Cult of Cybele's Impact on Phrygian Culture*. Brown University, ARCH 0351, 2009.

Woodhead, Daniel E. *As the Days of Noah Were, So Also Shall the Coming of the Son of Man Be*. Scofield Seminary, 2014.

Books

Attwater, Donald. *The Penguin Dictionary of Saints*. Second edition, updated by Catherine Rachel John. Wrights Lane, UK: Penguin Books, 1983.

Baigent, Michael, and Richard Leigh. *Secret Germany: Stauffenberg and the Mystical Crusade against Hitler*. London: Arrow Books, 2006.

Bane, Theresa. *The Encyclopedia of Giants and Humanoids in Myth, Legend, and Folklore*. Jefferson, NC: McFarland and Company, 2016.

Barber, Richard. *Myths and Legends of the British Isles*. New York: The Boydell Press, 2004.

Bauer, Susan Wise. *The History of the Ancient World from the Earliest Accounts to the Fall of Rome*. New York: W. W. Norton & Company, 2007.

Benner, Jeff A. *Learn to Read Hebrew: Volume 2*. College Station, TX: Virtual-bookworm.com Publishing Inc., 2011.

Benz, Frank L. *Personal Names in the Phoenician and Punic Inscriptions*. Rome: Bible Institute Press, 1972.

Berlitz, Charles. *The Mystery of Atlantis*. New York: Norton Publications, 1969.

Bierlein, J. F. *Parallel Myths*. Toronto, ON: Ballantine Publishing Group, 1994.

Cahill, Thomas. *The Gifts of the Jews*. Toronto, ON: Anchor Books, 1999.

Charles River Editors. *The Sanctuary of Our Lady of Lourdes: The History and the Legacy of the Catholic Church's Haven of Miracles*. Kindle edition, 2018.

Coleman, Dr. John. *Conspirators' Hierarchy: The Story of the Committee of 300*. Fourth edition. Las Vegas: World Int. Review, 2010.

Collins, Andrew. *From the Ashes of Angels*. Toronto, ON: Penguin Group, 1997.

Connell, Janet T. *The Visions of the Children: The Apparitions of the Blessed Mother at Medjugorje*. New York: St. Martin's Press, 1992.

Cooper, Diana. *The Wonder of Unicorns: Ascending with the Higher Angelic Realms*. Rochester, VT: Inner Traditions, 2008.

Cunelife, Barry. The *Holy Land: An Oxford Archaeological Guide from Earliest Times to 1700*. Fifth edition. New York: Oxford University Press, 2008.

Davison, Gustav. *A Dictionary of Angels including the Fallen Angels*. New York: The Free Press, 1971.

De Castro, Don Adolfo. *The Spanish Protestants, and Their Persecution by King Phillp II: A Historical Work*. Trans. Thomas Parker. London: Charles Gilpin, 1851; digitalized by the Internet Archive, 2007.

De Vere, Nicholas. *The Dragon Legacy: The Secret History of an Ancient Bloodline*. San Diego: The Book Tree, 2004.

Donnelly, Ignatius. *Atlantis: The Antediluvian World*. New York: Dover Publications, 1976.

Dorsey, Herbert. *The Secret History of The New World Order*. Parker, CO: Outskirts Press, 2014. Kindle edition.

Elitzur, Yoel. *Places in the Parasha: Biblical Geography and Its Meaning*. Trans. Daniel Landam, New Milford, CT: Maggid Books, 2020.

Friar, Stephen. *A New Dictionary of Heraldry*. New York: Harmony Books, 1987.

Gardner, Laurence. *Genesis of the Grail Kings*. London: Bantam Press, 2000.

Gardner, Laurence. *Realm of the Ring Lords*. Gloucester, MA: Fair Winds Press, 2003.

Gittins, Ian. *Unlocking the Masonic Code: Secrets of the Solomon Key*. London: Collins, 2007.

Greer, John Michael. *The Element Encyclopedia of Secret Societies*. London: Harper Element, 2006.

Greer, John Michael. *Atlantis: Ancient Legacy, Hidden Prophecy*. Woodbury, MN: Llewellyn Publications, 2007.

Guiley, Rosemary Ellen. *The Encyclopedia of Demons and Demonology*. New York: Facts on File, 2009

Guiley, Rosemary Ellen. *The Encyclopedia of Angels*. Second edition. New York: Facts on File, 2003.

Hall, Manly P. *The Secret Teachings of All Ages*. New York: Jeremy P. Tarcher, 2003. Original publication 1928.

Hancock, Graham, and Robert Bauval. *Talisman: Sacred Cities, Sacred Faith*. Toronto, ON: Doubleday Canada, 2004.

Hutter, Manfred. *The Luwians: Handbook of Oriental Studies—Section One: The Near Middle East*. Ed. H. Craig Melchert. Leiden: Konninklyke Brill LV, 2003.

Joseph, Frank. *The Destruction of Atlantis*. Rochester, VT: Bear and Co., 2002.

Kent, Roland G. *Old Persian: Grammer, Text, Lexicon*. New Haven, CT: American Oriental Society, 1950.

Khan, Geoffrey, *The Tiberian Pronunciation of Biblical Hebrew*. Cambridge: Open Book Publishers, 2020.

Knight, Christopher, and Richard Lomas. *The Hiram Key*. London: Arrow Books Ltd., 1997.

Knight, Christopher, and Richard Lomas. *The Book of Hiram*. London: Century, 2003.

Knight, Christopher, and Richard Lomas. *Uriel's Machine: The Ancient Origins of Science*. London: Arrow Books Ltd., 2000.

Laidler, Keith. *The Head of God*. London: Weidenfeld & Nicolson, 1998.

Leadbeater, C. W. *The Hidden Life in Freemasonry*, 1926. UK: Global Grey, Kindle edition, 2015.

Lomas, Robert. *The Invisible College*. London: Headline Book Publishing, 2002.

Mackillop, James. *Dictionary of Celtic Mythology*. New York: Oxford University Press, 1998.

Monter, William. *A Bewitched Duchy: Lorraine and Its Dukes 1477–1736*. Geneve, France: Libraire Droz S.A., 2007.

Marshall, Peter. *The Philosopher's Stone: A Quest for the Secrets of Alchemy*. London: Pan Books, 2002.

Myers, E. A. *The Ituraeans and the Roman Near East: Reassessing the Sources*. Cambridge: Cambridge University Press, 2010.

Murphy-O'Connor, Jerome. *The Holy Land: An Oxford Archaeological Guide from Earliest Times to 1700*. New York: Oxford University Press Inc, 2008. Kindle edition.

Naudon, Paul. *The Secret History of Freemasonry*. Rochester, VT: Inner Traditions, 2005.

Nickell, Joe. *Looking for a Miracle: Weeping Icons, Stigmata, Visions & Healing Cures*. Amherst, NY: Prometheus Books, 1993. Kindle edition.

Pinsky, Robert. *The Life of David*. New York: Schocken Books, 2005.

Pirlo, Paolo O. *Our Lady of Lourdes: My First Book of Saints*. Paranaque City, Philippines: Sons of Holy Mary Immaculate—Quality Catholic Publications, 1997.

Pollen, John Hungergore. *Saint Ignatius of Loyola: Imitator of Christ 1494 to 1555*. New York: P. J. Kennedy & Sons, 1922.

Porter, J. R. *The New Illustrated Companion to the Bible*. London: Prospero Books, 2003.

Roberts, J. M. *History of the World*. New York: Oxford University Press Inc., 1993.

Rohl, David. *Legend: The Genesis of Civilization*. London: Century Random House UK Ltd., 1998.

Rohl, David. *The Lost Testament: From Eden to Exile: The Five-Thousand-Year History of the People of the Bible*. London: Century Random House UK Ltd., 2002.

Rose, Carol. *Giants, Monsters, and Dragons: An Encyclopedia of Folklore, Legend, and Myth*. New York: W. W. Norton & Company, 2001.

Seward, Demond. *Jerusalem's Traitor: Josephus, Masada, and the Fall of Judea*. Cambridge, MA: DeCapo Press, 2009.

Silberman, Neil Asher, and Israel Finkelstein. *David and Solomon*. New York: Free Press, 2006.

Sitchin, Zecharia. *The Lost Book of Enki*. Rochester, VT: Bear and Company, 2004.

Stepien, Marek. *From the History of State System in Mesopotamia—The Kingdom of the Third Dynasty of Ur*. Rektora Uniwersytetu Warszawskiego I Dyrecje Insytutu Historycznego, Akme, Strudia Historica, 2009.

Stockton, Brooky, R. *A Family under God: A Biblical Resource for God's Law Order in the Christian Home*. Tijeras, NM: Nike Insights, 2015.

Thomas, Dianne. *The Grotto of Our Lady of Lourdes*. Durham. UK: White Lyon Films Ltd., 2022. Kindle edition.

Wayne, Gary. *The Genesis 6 Conspiracy: How Secret Societies and the Descendants of Giants Plan to Enslave Humankind*. Sisters, OR: Deep River Books, 2014.

Wilson, Demond. *The New Age Millennium: An Expose of Symbols, Slogans and Hidden Agendas*. Forestville, MD: Demond Wilson Enterprises Inc./CSE Books, 1998.

Winchell, Alexander. *Preadamites: The Existence of Men before Adam*. Chicago: S. C. Griggs and Company, 1888.

Yildirim, Dr. Kemal. *The Ancient Amorites (Amurro) of Mesopotamia*. Saarbrucken, Germany: Lambert Academic Publishing, 2017.

PRAISE FOR GARY WAYNE'S
THE GENESIS 6 CONSPIRACY

How Secret Societies and the Descendants
of Giants Plan to Enslave Humankind

"Gary Wayne's book is definitely required reading. Much of history has been stifled and/or hidden. This book meticulously examines the information we do have and builds a thorough foundation of truth. Today's church system is sadly lacking in teaching its members real Biblical truth. The Bible is after all a historical document. I highly recommend this book as I believe the world will be facing [Nephilim] again. And we are not prepared for the next incursion."

—Jeanine A.

"Gary Wayne has done something that no other author has dared to do: exhaustively research and compile arcane Christian esoterica into one compendium. This is truly a staggering work. . . . Gary Wayne is brave enough to leave no stone unturned in his Arthurian quest for the holy grail of Truth that has been buried by the powers that be for centuries. This book is worth every penny."

—Jonathan A. Goss

With more than a thousand 5-star reviews,
this book is NOT to be missed.

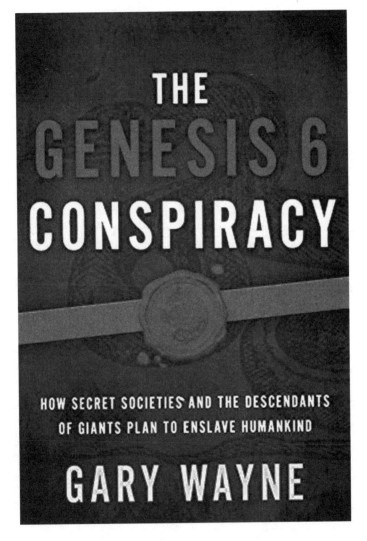

Over and over again, readers are calling it:

"Genius" "Brilliant" "Thought-provoking" "Essential"